FOURTH EDITION

INTRODUCTION TO PSYCHOLOGY

Clifford T. Morgan
University of Texas, Austin
Richard A. King
University of North Carolina at Chapel Hill

McGraw-Hill Book Company
New York
St. Louis
San Francisco
Düsseldorf
Johannesburg
Kuala Lumpur
London
Mexico
Montreal
New Delhi
Panama
Rio de Janeiro
Singapore
Sydney
Toronto

Introduction to Psychology

Library of Congress Catalog Card Number 71-139560
07-043085-3
1 2 3 4 5 6 7 8 9 0 V H V H 7 9 8 7 6 5 4 3 2 1

This book was set in Helvetica by Black Dot, Inc., and printed by Von Hoffman Press, Inc. The designers were J + M Condon; the drawings were done by J + M Condon, Inc., and Donald and Ann Crews. The editors were John Hendry, Robert Weber, and Mary Barnett. John F. Harte supervised production.

Special acknowledgments and credits begin on page 715.

CONTENTS

PREFACE

The aim in this fourth edition, which is essentially the same as that in the previous three editions, is twofold: to provide a broad coverage of the more important and representative areas of psychology that concern psychologists in the latter part of the twentieth century, and to deal in some depth with each topic selected.

Many decisions about what to include and what to exclude have been difficult. One guide has been an idea of what a student should know when he takes a second course in psychology. Further, most of the students in an introductory course will not major in psychology, and we have tried to include information that students can apply to their fields of interest and to their lives. We hope we have succeeded in presenting a well-rounded, factual, and nontrivial picture of psychology for any student who is getting his first serious introduction to the subject.

Instructors, as well as students, approach the introductory course from different points of view. Instructors have different tastes and habits in presenting their courses, and they must adapt to the time available for the course as well as to the needs of their students.

To meet these differing needs of students and instructors, the book has been organized flexibly. It provides the instructor with considerable freedom in planning both the material he will cover and the way in which he will cover it. Suggestions in "To the Instructor" include outlines for two different course approaches: a life-oriented course and a science-oriented course. These outlines are merely examples, and can be adapted by instructors in a variety of ways. The chapters themselves have been written to accommodate either approach, and cross references have been provided to explain terms and concepts as they appear. The chapters are in a sequence intended for a comprehensive course. Learning and motivation are stressed early, the more applied aspects of psychology later. The chapters on the biological bases of behavior are last because they draw on the concepts developed in the first part of the text. Finally, the glossary at the end of the book aids in using the text however the course is organized.

Many people have contributed to this edition. A number of reviewers gave detailed criticism and advice on how to revise the chapters, and we thank them. We also with to thank the many instructors and students who used earlier editions and criticized them constructively for us. We are especially grateful to the staff of the McGraw-Hill Book Company, and in particular to John Hendry, Basic Book Editor, and Robert Weber, Editing Supervisor. Credit to the many individuals and publishers who kindly permitted the use of their material is given on the pages where the material appears and in the References and Acknowledgments.

Clifford T. Morgan
Richard A. King

This book has been written and organized with the expectation that instructors may want to omit chapters and to assign material in an order different from that of the book. Each instructor must make his selection in the light of the time available to him and the needs of his students. In the hope of simplifying this task, we offer here two possible alternative arrangements.

Life-oriented course

The Science of Psychology (Chapter 1)

Behavioral Inheritance (Chapter 2)

Principles of Learning (Chapter 3)

Human Learning, Remembering, and Forgetting (Chapter 4)

Thinking and Language (Chapter 5)

Motivation (Chapter 6)

Arousal, Emotion, and Conflict (Chapter 7)

Psychological Testing (Chapter 10)

Personality (Chapter 11)

Behavior Disorders (Chapter 12)

Therapy for Behavior Disorders (Chapter 13)

Social Influences on Behavior (Chapter 14)

Attitudes and Beliefs (Chapter 15)

Organizational Psychology (Chapter 16)

Science-oriented course

The Science of Psychology (Chapter 1)

Behavioral Inheritance (Chapter 2)

Principles of Learning (Chapter 3)

Human Learning, Remembering, and Forgetting (Chapter 4)

Thinking and Language (Chapter 5)

Motivation (Chapter 6)

Arousal, Emotion, and Conflict (Chapter 7)

Perception (Chapter 8)

Psychological Measurement and Statistics (Chapter 9)

Psychological Testing (Chapter 10)

Personality (Chapter 11)

The Nervous System (Chapter 17)

Sensory processes (Chapter 18)

Brain and Behavior (Chapter 19)

TO THE STUDENT

You may take it for granted that psychology deals with many of the problems of everyday life and thus with many things that you have already experienced; therefore you are in a position to derive some personal benefits from the study of psychology. In a formal college course, however, it is not possible for the instructor to relate everything that you experience to everything that is taught. Hence, to get the most from the course, you should try to make many of these applications yourself. You should continually ask yourself "How does this apply to my experience?" and "How can I put to use what I am learning?" If you do this, you will profit much more from the course than if you simply learn by rote what is assigned.

Here are some suggestions for the reading of each chapter. You might begin by reading the summary. Obviously it does not cover everything that is in the chapter, but it does hit the high spots. After reading the summary, skim the headings before settling down to a careful reading. In the few minutes that it takes to do this, you can add a few details and get the overall organization in mind.

Many students try to read textbooks the way they read novels; they sit passively, running their eyes over the words and hoping that some information will sink in. But textbooks are packed with facts and explanations. To assimilate them, you must work actively at the task. Read every sentence carefully; be sure you understand what it says. Reread paragraphs and sections that you have difficulty with; to fully understand what follows, usually you must understand what went before.

Many students fail to grasp the subject they are studying because they do not give sufficient attention to illustrations and tables. In this book, the illustrations and tables are fully as important as the corresponding discussions in the text. When you encounter a reference to one of them, you should turn to it promptly and study it carefully. In some cases, we have used illustrations to teach something that is not included in the text. At appropriate points in your reading, usually before going on to a new heading, you should scan the illustrations to make certain you have examined them and gleaned all you could from them.

Every technical subject uses terms whose definitions must be learned, and psychology is no exception. Ordinarily a definition is given in the text whenever a new term is introduced. Since chapters will not always be assigned in the order of their arrangement in the book, a glossary is included in the back of the book. You should be especially cautious not to neglect a definition just because the term is already familiar to you. Do not, for example, pass over words like "attitude," "personality," "intelligence," and "motive" because these are words that you use in everyday speech. In psychology these and other common terms often have specialized meanings that differ from those commonly employed. Make sure you know the *psychological* definitions of all terms.

Science is produced by scientists, and it is common practice in science to ascribe particular experiments and ideas to the scientists who have contributed them. Sometimes this practice is annoying and distracting; so we have tried not to use too many names. But to give credit where credit is due, we have put the names of the experimenters in parentheses where particular studies or ideas are cited. These names refer to the reference section at the back of the book; use it if you want to learn more about the topic under discussion.

This edition has three appendixes. Appendix 1 is for those students who might be interested in psychology as a professional career. Appendix 2 explains how to find more information about topics in psychology. Appendix 3 provides some basic formulas and calculations used in psychological measurement and statistics; it supplements Chapter 9.

There is also a *Study Guide* that you may purchase and use as an aid in study and review. This guide contains exercises that not only make the study of psychology more interesting but also permit you to assess for yourself how well you have mastered the material.

The ignorant man marvels at the exceptional; the wise man marvels at the common; the greatest wonder of all is the regularity of nature.

G. D. Boardman

Most of us want to know why people do what they do. We feel, probably correctly, that we might be a little happier if we understood the causes of our own behavior; we feel that we might be more successful in dealing with others if we knew more about their behavior. But what a difficult job this is, and what diverse answers have been given to questions about behavior over the history of human thought!

Beginning the Study of Psychology

The urge to understand ourselves and others better is both a help and a hindrance in undertaking the study of psychology. It helps because it motivates, and motivation is an extremely important factor in learning. It helps, too, because the subject is intrinsically interesting for both student and teacher.

But ready-made interest in psychology can also be a hindrance, in that it leads some students to think they know more about psychology than they really do, just because they have always enjoyed observing people. Such observations are sometimes trivial, superficial, or simply wrong. Hence as you study this book you should be prepared to find that although many of your observations are correct, some of them do not stand up under analysis. One job of a psychology course is to provide a framework within which you can make a beginning toward accurately understanding your behavior and that of others. But it is only a beginning; the knack of applying principles to specific cases is not easily won.

This text's approach We have already said that there are many approaches to the study of behavior. In this book we have chosen one approach from the many. First, the very object of study—behavior—is the result of selection by the authors; this bias is discussed further in the next section on the definition of psychology. Second, we have chosen to rely on observation as a source of knowledge, rather than on intuition or the voice of authority. Our model, or idea, of what psychology should be like is taken from the biological sciences. Finally, we view behavior as a natural event; we think of behavior as subject to study in the same way that sciences study any natural event. The implication of this view is that we believe behavior is *determined* by factors which we can isolate and analyze. Of course, many factors determine a bit of behavior. The first part of the text is a discussion of some of the major determiners and principles of behavior.

This is, then, an objective, science-oriented textbook which seeks to identify and explain the factors that determine behavior. But the student should not be repelled by these cold-seeming words. He may feel that we are not concerned about human beings, about their problems, or about their feelings. But a curious paradox exists: the more objective knowledge that we obtain about behavior, the more we understand the "whys" of behavior, the more we understand what it means to be a human being. The result of such detached analysis is often a sort of scientific humanism.

Definition of psychology Now let us see specifically what psychology is. If you ask a psychologist to define his subject, he will probably give you the generally accepted definition: *Psychology is the science of human and animal behavior.* Upon hearing this definition, the person untrained in psychology is likely to be surprised at three of the important words: *science, animal,* and *behavior.* "Is psychology really a science?" he may ask. Why "behavior" rather than "mind" or "thoughts" or "feelings"? And why "animal" behavior? What has animal behavior to do with psychology?

Let us consider separately each of these three words, beginning first with science. A *science* is a body of systematized knowledge. Such knowledge is gathered by carefully observing and measuring events—sometimes, but not necessarily, in experiments set up by the scientist to produce the events he is studying. The things and events observed are systematized in various ways, but mainly by classifying them into categories and establishing general laws or principles that describe and predict them as accurately as possible. Science may be distinguished from art in that *art* is a skill or knack for doing something which is acquired by study, practice, and special experience.

Psychology, by these definitions, is both an art and a science. The division of psychology into art and science makes the whole field anything but coherent (Koch, 1969); for instance, the chasm between sensitivity training groups (art) and the physiological study of the brain processes controlling behavior (science) is very wide and probably not bridgeable. But art, being a skill which develops through special experience, is difficult to learn from books and classroom study. Moreover, artistry in psychology, as in medicine or engineering, is perhaps best developed after mastering the subject matter of the underlying science. The psychological arts, as we see them displayed in psychotherapy, politics, diplomacy, salesmanship, and other fields, are as yet rather ineffective in solving some of our most serious human problems.

And what about the record of psychology as science? We wish we had more scientific knowledge of human behavior. As it is, in some areas we must rely upon primitive observations and shrewd guesses; in other areas, the scientific work which has been done leaves much to be desired with regard to control and generality. But the efforts of many research workers over the last century have provided a body of knowledge and of scientific principles which, it seems to us, is the best foundation for developing an understanding of behavior. It is for all these reasons that we stress *science* in our definition of psychology in this book.

PSYCHOLOGISTS STUDY ANIMAL BEHAVIOR

Figure 1.1 *Rat in a Skinner box. The equipment in the background is for recording and programming the experiment. (Photo by Eliot Elisofon. Life Magazine, © 1958 by Time, Inc.)*

We come now to the word *behavior.* Behavior, rather than mind or thoughts or feelings, is the subject of psychology as we define it, because it alone can be observed, recorded, and studied. No one ever saw, heard, or touched a mind, but one can see and hear behavior. One can see and measure what a person does, or hear and record what a person says—which is vocal behavior. Anything else must be inferred. We do, indeed, infer that mental processes take place and that people think and feel, but for systematic knowledge of psychological events we are limited to the observation of behavior.

Now, finally, the word *animal.* Science does not arbitrarily limit itself to any one realm of events or to that knowledge which has immediate practical value. In fact, nearly everyone—even our most pragmatic politicians and businessmen—has now learned that pursuing knowledge for its own sake ultimately has great practical value. And animal behavior can be as fascinating a study as human behavior, if not more so. Therefore, just as the zoologist studies the form and function of all members of the animal kingdom, the psychologist systematically observes animal as well as human behavior. Animal behavior is, then, a legitimate area of study in its own right (see Figure 1.1).

But there is another, equally important reason for studying animal behavior. Many similarities exist between animal and human behavior. In fact, animals, either naturally or after they have been taught in the laboratory, display in more rudimentary forms some of the kinds of behavior which people display. Thus a study of animal behavior is a great aid in understanding human behavior. We are able to do many important experiments with animals that we cannot do with people, because human beings cannot be treated like guinea pigs.

Animal experiments, however, require careful interpretation if their results are to be applied to human beings. Many behavioral differences exist between man and other animals. Men are not rats or monkeys; rats and monkeys are not men. We cannot be confident that the details of animal behavior will be applicable to human behavior. Yet often the basic principles developed and refined in studies of other animals can be generalized to man.

The behavioral sciences Although behavior is the subject of psychology, it is by no means the exclusive property of psychology. Several other disciplines make the study of human and animal behavior their business. These include psychiatry, anthropology, sociology, economics, political science, and history. Taken together, these have recently come to be called the *behavioral sciences.* Each of them focuses upon certain aspects of behavior, although differences among them are not always clear-cut.

Sociology and social anthropology are concerned with the behavior of groups of people. Specialists in these fields study the cultures and social structures of various societies or groups living together. The sociologist typically deals with modern, literate cultures, such as our own; the anthropologist, with more primitive cultures. Each science has devised its own methods and acquired its own fund of information. At the present time, however, the lines between them are becoming fainter as they pool their knowledge and apply each other's methods.

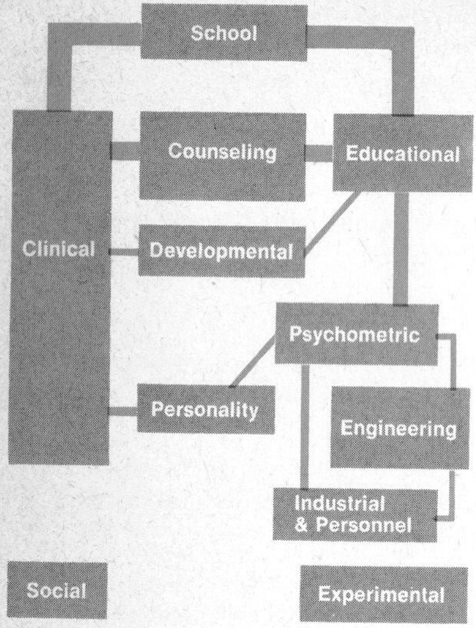

PSYCHOLOGISTS WORK IN MANY AREAS

Figure 1.2 *The subfields of psychology and the relationships between them. The size of each rectangle suggests the relative number of psychologists who work in that subfield; the thickness of the lines connecting the rectangles gives a rough indication of the relationships between subfields. (Modified from Lockman, 1964.)*

History, of course, is a behavioral science because it attempts to reconstruct and understand the events—mostly events of human behavior—that make history. Economics and political science deal, respectively, with economic and political behavior, which are simply the aspects of human behavior one sees institutionalized in trade and government. To a certain extent, both subjects are historical sciences because they make use of records of past events.

The *natural sciences,* such as physics, chemistry, and biology, are not, of course, behavioral sciences; yet scientists in these disciplines sometimes have occasion to study behavior. Some of our most useful knowledge about human perception, for example, has come from physicists and biological scientists who ventured to measure human reactions to different kinds of physical stimuli. Anatomists and physiologists, who are primarily concerned with structures and functions of the body, have also contributed greatly to our knowledge of behavior by studying physiological factors related to behavior. Zoologists have long been interested in the behavior as well as the classification of animals, and a special branch of zoology—ethology—is concerned with animal behavior. Zoologists have contributed much to our understanding of animal and, by extension, human behavior.

It has become increasingly difficult to set boundary lines between the sciences which study behavior. No such boundaries really exist in practice; scientists of different labels work side by side on the study of behavior. For instance, it is impossible to distinguish certain types of sociologists from certain types of psychologists by the work they do or the methods they employ. The same statement might be made about certain types of psychologists and physiologists. Psychology, as a behavioral science, is very diverse; it is a meeting ground for the natural sciences, such as physics and biology, and the behavioral sciences, such as sociology, economics, and political science.

The Subfields of Psychology

Another way to define psychology is to describe what psychologists actually do. An exhaustive description of the whole field cannot be attempted here, because the activities of psychologists are varied indeed. But we can enumerate and describe the major categories, or subfields, of work within psychology, and perhaps this will bring us closer to an understanding of the field as a whole.

The growth of professional psychology has been rapid in the last 30 years; the American Psychological Association—the psychologist's professional organization—now has about 30,000 members. The distribution of this group among the major subfields of psychology is shown in Table 1.1, which also lists the major job activities of psychologists.

The 11 major subfields of psychology and the relations between them are shown in Figure 1.2. The size of the rectangles indicates the relative number of psychologists in each of the subfields; the strength of the relationships between subfields is suggested by the thickness of the lines between the rectangles. For instance, a close relationship exists between psychometric psychology (measurement and testing) and industrial and educational psychology. Conversely, the experimental

Table 1.1 *The major subfields of psychology and primary jobs of psychologists.*

Source: Based on Cates, 1970.

		Percentage of total
Subfield:	Clinical	29
	Experimental	10
	Counseling	10
	Educational	10
	Industrial & personnel	7
	School	9
	Social	3
	Developmental	3
	Personality	2
	Psychometric	2
	Engineering	2
	Miscellaneous	11
Primary activity:	Teaching	23
	Clinical practice	15
	Administration	19
	Basic research	7
	Psychological testing	10
	Counseling practice	6
	Applied research	5
	Industrial consulting	2
	Clinical research	2
	Miscellaneous	10

and social psychologists seem to have little to do with the other subfields. In the descriptions which follow, an attempt is made to characterize each of these subfields.

Clinical psychology At the present time, clinical psychology is the largest field of specialization in psychology; it employs about 29 percent of all psychologists (Cates, 1970; Lockman, 1964). When the number of individuals in clinical psychology is added to the number in counseling psychology, which is closely related, the percentage swells to about 40 percent of the entire profession.

In order to understand better what clinical psychology is, we should first distinguish among three kinds of specialists who do clinical work: psychiatrists, psychoanalysts, and clinical psychologists.

Both *psychiatrists* and *psychoanalysts* hold an M.D. degree (although there are a few nonmedical psychoanalysts). Usually, they have been trained in medicine and then have had specialized training in the diagnosis and treatment of deviant behavior. Such training consists largely of work in psychiatric wards and hospitals and usually does not include any substantial amount of work in psychology. The psychoanalyst is actually a psychiatrist, but he differs from other psychiatrists in that he subscribes to the general theory of personality and treatment of disorders put forth by Sigmund Freud and his followers.

The *clinical psychologist,* on the other hand, takes his basic training in psychology rather than in medicine. After that, usually in the last 2 or

3 years of postgraduate training, he goes on to specialize in psychological diagnosis, psychotherapy, and research into the causes and alleviation of disturbed behavior. His training in diagnosis emphasizes the administration, scoring, and interpretation of psychological tests. His training in *psychotherapy,* like that of the psychiatrist and psychoanalyst, includes training in psychoanalytic techniques and other interview methods of helping patients solve their emotional problems. The term psychotherapy refers to psychological methods of treating behavior disorders and maladjustment, as distinguished from shock therapy, drug therapy, and other medical methods of treatment.

The classification and treatment of mental illness have long been the responsibility of the psychiatrist. He began, however, to enlist the aid of psychologists in his work when he found that intelligence tests helped him estimate what he could accomplish by psychiatric care and treatment. He came to rely on psychologists even more when they developed tests for the assessment of personality. Today he regularly looks to them for aid in *personality diagnosis.* From their tests and professional opinions, as well as from his own interviews and knowledge of case histories, he arrives at a diagnosis and strategy of treatment for mental illness.

For some psychiatrists, aid in diagnosis is all that is expected or accepted from the psychologist. In other cases, the psychologist may also assist in psychotherapy. Certainly most clinical psychologists of recent vintage are trained and equipped to participate in therapeutic work. In many hospitals, especially those of the Veterans' Administration and other public agencies, the need for psychotherapists is unusually great. In such institutions, clinical psychologists frequently undertake considerable psychotherapy. This is less often the case in private practice and private hospitals; here the matter rests with the preferences of the psychiatrist in charge. It should be pointed out, however, that many psychologists, working both in hospitals and in private practice, are currently conducting psychotherapy on their own responsibility. In such cases, they refer their patients to a physician if any physical complications are present that require medical care.

Although considerable progress has been made in the diagnosis and treatment of mental disorders, we still have a long way to go before we can feel that the problems are reasonably well in hand. There is a pressing need for research in this area, as everyone concerned will agree. Since the psychiatrist is trained primarily for *practice* and not for research, whereas the psychologist is typically trained in *research* and its methods, the psychologist has assumed an increasingly responsible role in the field of psychiatric research.

In recent years, the idea has been gaining acceptance that psychiatric diagnosis and care should be in the hands of a psychiatric team consisting of a *psychiatrist,* a *psychologist,* and a *social worker.* In such a team, the psychiatrist has final responsibility for the care of the patient. The psychologist assumes leadership in research and assists in diagnosis and therapy. The social worker provides information about the family and background of the patient. Social workers may also work with family members in order to enlist their aid in the therapy and rehabilitation of the patient.

TESTING MAY GIVE VALUABLE INFORMATION

Figure 1.3 *Clinical and counseling psychologists use tests of various kinds in measuring abilities and diagnosing personality problems. (New York University Testing and Advisement Center.)*

Community mental health centers are another recent development in which clinical psychologists are much involved. There are local centers to which people with problems come for help, including psychotherapy. Many of them are tax-supported, and they provide much-needed facilities for psychotherapy in lower-income areas. By being available during the earlier stages of behavior deterioration, such centers may also prevent minor disturbances from becoming serious ones.

Counseling The work of the counseling and guidance psychologist is somewhat different from that of clinical psychologists. He works with individuals having less serious problems than those requiring the services of a psychiatric team. He counsels individuals with emotional or personal problems who need some expert guidance. Thus he may serve as a screen to separate those who need no more than wise counseling from those who need intensive psychiatric attention.

The counseling and guidance psychologist also helps individuals with vocational and academic problems. Working in schools, in industry, in colleges, and indeed in private practice, he administers tests of intelligence, aptitudes, interests, and personality and gives such guidance as is needed (see Figure 1.3). Often this is a matter of informing parents of the abilities and limitations of their children, or of helping a student improve his study habits, or of advising him about a vocational choice, or of helping a person work out a minor personal problem. The counseling psychologist may also engage in psychotherapy. When he does, he must always be on the alert for severe emotional problems that should be referred to a psychiatrist or clinical psychologist for a final judgment.

The employment of counseling psychologists has increased substantially in recent years. Many colleges and universities have established psychological clinics or counseling centers. Some of the larger industrial and manufacturing concerns have formal counseling programs to give aid in solving personal problems. Many schools, particularly high schools, employ counselors whose chief duty is to help students with their vocational and personal problems.

Experimental psychology Many psychologists (about 10 percent) are not primarily engaged in work which has a direct application to practical problems. Instead, they are interested in experimental psychology, the aim of which is the understanding of the fundamental causes of behavior. *Sensation and perception, learning and memory, motivation,* and the *physiological basis of behavior* are the primary problems of experimental psychology. In other words, the experimental psychologist would like to know how we are able to experience our environment and the variables which determine our interpretation of it; he would like to know how behavior is modified and how these modifications are retained; he would like to know what urges us on and gives direction to our behavior; and he would like to know the ways in which the nervous system functions to produce behavioral results. Much of this text is devoted to a consideration of the knowledge which experimental psychologists have obtained about these fundamental problems.

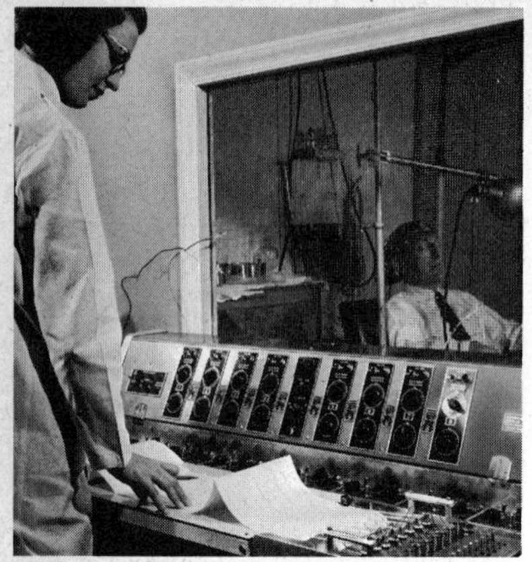

THE PHYSIOLOGICAL PSYCHOLOGIST STUDIES THE RELATIONSHIP OF BRAIN TO BEHAVIOR

Figure 1.4 *An electroencephalogram (EEG) is being recorded so that the gross electrical activity of the brain can be studied. (Richard Saunders, Scope Associates, Inc.)*

The experimental psychologist is especially fond of controlled experiments. In order to achieve the required degree of control, it is often necessary to use animal subjects. Another reason for the use of animal subjects is that we can often understand a process better if we can trace its development from simpler to more complex animals. Comparing the behavior of one species with another and tracing the development of processes is the job of the *comparative psychologist. Physiological psychology* (or *biopsychology,* as it is sometimes called), the investigation of the physiological basis of behavior, is another specially named subdivision of experimental psychology (see Figure 1.4).

Experimental methods are not unique to experimental psychology; many psychologists who would not be called experimental psychologists use experimental methods. For instance, social and personality psychologists may use experimental designs. Thus *experimental psychology is distinguished as much by its problems as by its methods.*

Industrial, personnel, and engineering psychology Some years ago, business and industry made relatively little use of scientific psychology. Recently, though, the situation has been changing. As Table 1.1 shows, an appreciable percentage of psychologists are now employed in business and industry.

The first applications of psychology to industrial problems were in the use of intelligence and aptitude tests. Today many of the larger business firms have well-established programs of selection and placement that make substantial use of psychological tests. They are also finding other applications of psychology to problems of training, to supervision of personnel, to improving communications, to counseling employees, and to alleviating industrial strife. Psychologists are seldom in managerial positions which would enable them to deal directly with these problems, but they are called upon as consultants. Moreover, an increasing number of businessmen are getting some training in business and industrial psychology.

Firms of industrial psychologists are also growing in number and prestige. They are usually incorporated and sell their services to many different concerns. For one business, they may set up a selection program; for another, they may make recommendations concerning its training program; for another, they may examine the problems of supervision and human relations within the company; and for still another, they may survey consumer attitudes toward products or the effectiveness of the company's advertising. Utilizing the services of nonstaff psychologists seems to appeal to many businesses as being more efficient than employing psychologists on a permanent basis. It has advantages for the psychologists, too, allowing them to become familiar with similar problems in different enterprises and conserving their time for the solution of practical problems rather than enmeshing them in routine nonpsychological duties that are likely to be involved in regular employment. At any rate, the separate firm of psychologists is becoming an established way of putting psychology to work in industry.

World War II opened up another application of psychology to industry, sometimes called *human engineering* or *engineering psychology.* It concerns the *design of equipment* and the tasks of the individuals who

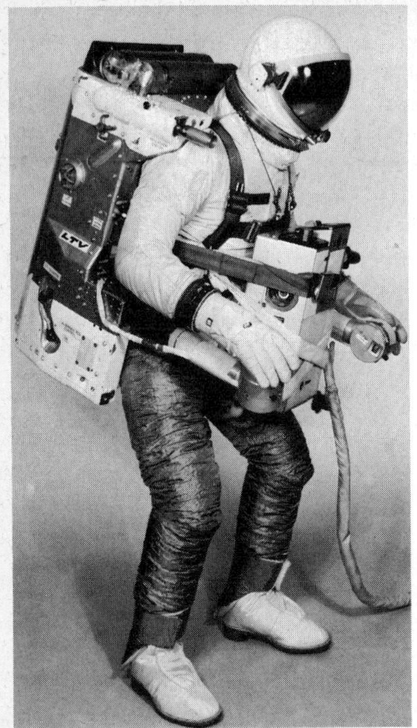

Figure 1.5 *A personal "extravehicular life-support system" developed for the United States space program. It includes a space suit (in itself a very complex engineering problem), an air supply, and a jet propulsion system (the backpack). The design of such complicated systems often involves engineering psychology. (NASA.)*

operate the equipment. To such design problems psychologists brought their knowledge of perception, of learning, and of experimental methods of measuring human performance under various conditions. Thus they became involved in the design of gun controls, airplane cockpits, and other devices which had to work efficiently often under conditions which severely taxed both the equipment and its human operators. Since then, psychologists engaged in human engineering have helped design an ever-widening range of products—stoves, refrigerators, cranes, printing presses, computer controls, and spacecraft interiors, to name just a few (see Figure 1.5).

School and educational psychology Counseling psychologists who are involved in the testing and guidance of individual students are usually called *school psychologists.* Testing provides information which can be useful in the diagnosis and disposition of behavior difficulties. A large part of the job of the school psychologist consists of working with students who need some sort of special attention. For instance, the school psychologist may recommend, after a study of the case, that a student with reading difficulties be assigned to a remedial-reading class; students with mild adjustment problems may be counseled by the school psychologist. In some colleges and universities, school psychologists are employed to evaluate and administer the tests used in the selection of new students. Some school psychologists may do a great deal of vocational counseling, but most of this work is done by *school counselors* who have specialized in testing and counseling courses in a department of education. In practice, the difference between school psychologists and school counselors is often not clear.

Educational psychology may include school psychology, but educational psychologists as such are usually involved with more general, less immediate problems than the majority of school psychologists or school counselors. Educational psychologists are especially concerned with increasing the efficiency of learning in school through the application of psychological knowledge about learning and motivation.

Social psychology We all belong to many different kinds of groups—our family, an informal friendship clique, our social class, to mention a few. The groups we belong to affect our behavior and shape our attitudes about many things. Social psychologists devote themselves to the study of the effects of group membership upon individual behavior. Social psychology merges into sociology, but a distinction can be made between the two disciplines: the primary interest of the social psychologist is the ways in which individual behavior is influenced by group membership; the sociologist is much more concerned with the group as such—its structure and formal characteristics. In his quest for information concerning group effects on individual behavior, the social psychologist uses various methods of study, experimental and otherwise.

Social psychologists have developed and perfected techniques that have found important practical application, such as attitude measurement and opinion surveys of political and social issues. For instance, these techniques have provided much information about the reasons for ghetto riots and the effects of segregation and racial prejudice.

Developmental psychology Developmental psychologists study and describe behavioral changes which accompany changes in age. Since behavior and abilities change most rapidly during the first few years of life, *child psychology* is often used as a synonym for much of developmental psychology. Behavioral changes with age at the other end of life, old age, are also much studied by this subfield. Developmental psychology has both research and applied aspects. For instance, a great deal of research has been done on the development of thinking in children. Are progressive and systematic changes taking place in the nature of thought as a child grows older? On the applied side, developmental psychologists may work with disturbed children. The kinds of deviant behavior found in adults are often different from those found in children, and the clinical psychologist must use quite different methods to treat them.

Personality psychology The interests of personality psychologists and clinical psychologists overlap to a great degree. Both are primarily interested in the individual case. Beyond this, there are differences in emphasis. Clinical psychologists typically apply knowledge to the amelioration of deviant behavior; personality psychologists are largely concerned with understanding the nondeviant, or normal, individual case.

A wide range of techniques and strategies is used by the personality psychologist in his study of individuals' personality traits and behavior. He may, for instance, make carefully recorded observations in naturalistic settings, use interviews, or give psychological tests.

The personality psychologist may also do experiments aimed at developing general principles which can be applied to the understanding of the behavior of normal individuals. Such experiments may be carried out under controlled conditions in the laboratory or in naturalistic settings.

The ways in which a personality psychologist seeks information are largely determined by the particular *personality theory* he holds. Personality theories are general statements about the factors which determine individual behavior. For instance, Freudian, or psychoanalytic, personality theory states that many manifestations of behavior are expressions of unconscious motives; stimulus-response (S-R) theories stress learning as the prime determiner of individual behavior. The Freudian personality theorist often uses the free-association interview technique in his quest for information; the stimulus-response theorist usually employs controlled experimentation. Whatever his theory or methodology, the personality theorist attempts to describe and to understand the causes of the behavior of an individual.

Psychometric psychology Tests and other devices for measuring human abilities are the province of the psychometrician. He is concerned with the development of new tests, research on the usefulness and stability of tests, and the development of statistical techniques. Psychometricians supply some of the tools used by psychologists in the applied fields of school, counseling, industrial, and clinical psychology. Those who are primarily responsible for giving and scoring tests are sometimes called *psychometrists* rather than psychometricians.

Psychology as Science

We have said that psychology is both an art and a science, but we have elected to stress its scientific aspects. In support of this emphasis, we shall briefly discuss the scientific characteristics of psychology, its uses of scientific methods, and its employment of theory as a scientific tool.

Scientific characteristics of psychology Psychology as a science is first of all *empirical*. That is to say, data are gathered by experiment and observation; psychology as a science does not rely on intuition, opinion, or belief. The psychologist does experiments or makes observations which other psychologists can repeat; he obtains data, often making quantitative measurements, that others can verify. This approach is to be distinguished from one which forms opinions on the basis of untested experience, or which argues from premises that cannot be tested.

Not that scientists do not have opinions or do not occasionally argue with one another. Indeed, they often disagree on the interpretation of results. Scientists must also reason by inference: for example, since $A=B$ and $B=C$, they infer that $A=C$. If the scientist had only his opinions and inferences, however, he would have no science. What makes his science secure as science are the unarguable facts, the observations which he has made and which others can check, and the instances of $A=B$ and $B=C$ with which no knowledgeable person can argue. Also of crucial importance is his ability to do *research* and through it to establish new observations. Without research his science would become static. He would not be able, as he now is, to erase gradually the areas of ignorance and conflicting opinion. Through research, psychology already has acquired a wealth of facts and is continuing to amass additional ones. In a later section of this chapter, we consider in more detail what psychological research means.

Psychology as a science is also *systematic*. Observations and experiments, though essential to science, are by themselves of little use. They can be selected to suit one's purpose, or acquired without any purpose at all and jumbled into a disorderly, meaningless pile. What is important in science is that observations "make some sense"; they must be capable of being summarized economically by a limited number of principles. The principles may be merely a system of classification, such as we find in zoology, or they may be rather precise laws stating the order or relationship among the phenomena observed, such as we meet, for example, in physics. In any case, we attempt in science to systematize our observations in an orderly and economical way.

The effort to develop a science follows a circular path from observations to principles and back again to observations. The first part of the circle has been called *induction*. We make observations wherever we can, without too much rhyme or reason to them, and then, after careful analysis, we attempt to formulate tentative principles that we think pretty well summarize our observations. Next we trace the part of the circle called *deduction*. We reason that, if our inductive analysis is correct, we should be able to predict observations not yet made. We then set out to collect new observations according to some plan that will test the adequacy of our tentative summarizing principles. Sometimes our tentative principles prove to be wholly or partly wrong; at other times they are correct. If our analysis is wrong, we analyze our results again and test this new deduction. Even if the analysis is correct, our work is not finished. Either we will wish to analyze at a more fundamental level, or the confirmed deduction will suggest other analyses. It is a truism that every confirmed deduction shows up the need for further analysis and research. There are no "final" answers in science. But by systematically following the path from observations to principles to observations, we are continually formulating, modifying, and extending principles to accord with observations.

Another distinguishing feature of science is *measurement*. We rank highest among the sciences the one that has developed the most precise measurements. For that reason, physics is usually credited with being the most "scientific" of the sciences because its measurements are so precise. Actually, measurement is not always essential to science. In a field such as zoology, for example, the important principles may consist of a systematic classification of the members of the animal kingdom. Such a classification is not measurement in the strict sense of the word. In psychology, too, we learn classifications of different kinds of behavior. However, most of our problems are questions of "more than" or "less than."

Psychologists would like to know, for example, whether children of highly intelligent parents are brighter than those of less intelligent parents. To answer a question such as this, we need measurements that tell us *how intelligent* both parents and children are. Since most psychological problems are quite complex, it has not been easy to devise methods of measurement for studying them. Later in the book we summarize the methods that have been developed. Although we usually do not delve into the details of such measurements, almost every discussion in this book is rooted in the measurement of behavior.

Careful *definition* of terms is essential to clear thinking in science. This is especially true in psychology, where we would like to give precise definitions to terms which are used imprecisely in everyday language. For example, can we find some way to give such words as *intelligence, memory, motivation, learning, attention,* and *emotion* definitions that will convey the same meaning from one psychologist to the next? Can we find a way to make sure that psychologist X knows what psychologist Y is referring to when he is using the concept of "intelligence"? The trick in science, and in psychology, is to define concepts by relating them to something observable.

One way of making sure that we are defining concepts in terms of observables is to use *operational definitions* (Bridgman, 1927). When we define a concept operationally, we define it in terms of measurable and observable operations. For example, the concept of length is defined in terms of observable measuring operations—How many times was the ruler put down when measuring a table? In psychology, such concepts as intelligence may be defined in terms of the observable operations performed to measure them; intelligence might be operationally defined as a score on a certain test. With a definition of this sort, many of the vague and emotional meanings of the concept of intelligence are lost. For purposes of scientific communication, this is exactly what is wanted; what is lost in richness is gained in precision. We are now sure that psychologist X and psychologist Y are talking about the same thing when they refer to intelligence; they are talking about a score on a test.

Although it is not related to measuring operations, we have already used another operational definition when defining psychology. We can observe the professional behavior of those who call themselves psychologists. An operational definition of psychology simply consists of a description of the professional behavior of these people. Similarly, memory, motivation, learning, and attention may be described operationally, that is, in terms of observables.

Methods of psychology How can we find out about behavior systematically and scientifically? There are many ways of making observations in psychology. The *experimental methods* are used to investigate behavior which can be brought into the laboratory and studied under controlled conditions. The method of *systematic observation* is used to study behavior in situations which cannot be controlled or manipulated by the observer. When using this method, the psychologist observes and analyzes "nature's experiments." Finally, by intensive study of the problems and behaviors of an individual person, it is possible both to understand the individual and to arrive at some general principles of behavior. This method of studying the problems and behaviors of a single person is termed the *clinical method.* We shall now examine each of these methods of investigation in a little more detail.

EXPERIMENTAL METHODS The essence of the experimental methods is simple. The experimenter (1) changes or varies something, (2) keeps other conditions constant, and (3) looks for an effect of the change or variation upon the system he has under observation. Since psychology is the science of *behavior,* the experimenter looks for an effect of the changes he has made upon behavior. Simple enough, but let us examine experimental methods in greater detail.

First of all, the experimental methods involve *variables.* A variable, as the word implies, is something which varies. Ideally, it is a condition which can be measured and which varies quantitatively. In Figure 1.6, for example, one variable is the amount of light required to make an object just visible to an observer. The amount of light can be varied in standard light units. In many cases, however, a variable may be merely the presence or absence of a condition. Suppose that we wish to do an experiment to determine the effects of a tranquilizing drug on memory span as measured by the number of digits which can be repeated after hearing a list of them spoken once. Here we might simply compare the performance of groups of subjects with and without tranquilizers. In this example, the tranquilizer is a variable because one group of subjects gets it while the other does not.

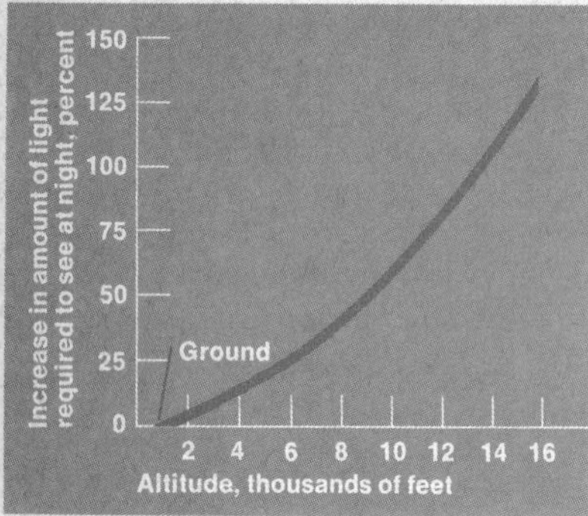

DEPENDENT VARIABLES ARE PLOTTED ON THE VERTICAL AXIS; INDEPENDENT VARIABLES ON THE HORIZONTAL AXIS

Figure 1.6 *In plotting the results of experiments in psychology, the horizontal axis (abscissa) represents the independent variable—in this case, altitude; the vertical axis (ordinate) represents the dependent variable—in this case, the percentage of increase in the amount of light required to see at night. (After Millikan, 1948.)*

Variables may be either independent or dependent. An *independent variable* is a condition set by or selected by the experimenter—a stimulus presented, a drug administered, or so many feet of altitude. The *dependent variable* is the subject's behavior or report—his response to a stimulus, his score on an intelligence test, or his report of seeing or not seeing a light. The dependent variable is called dependent because its value depends, or may depend, on the value of the independent variable, the one independently set by the experimenter.

In every experiment we must have at least one independent variable and one dependent variable. In the preceding example, the tranquilizer was an independent variable because we could vary its amount—in this case, all or none—independently of other factors in the experiment. Memory span, on the other hand, was a dependent variable because we were interested in whether or not variations in memory span would depend upon the tranquilizer.

In some experiments, we may have more than one dependent variable. In the tranquilizer experiment, for example, we could have had more dependent variables by measuring other things besides memory span—speed of reaction, perhaps.

When the results of an experiment are presented in a graph, it is customary to let the horizontal axis (also called the *abscissa* or *x* axis) represent the independent variable and the vertical axis (also called the *ordinate* or *y* axis) the dependent variable. Figure 1.6, for example, shows the results of an experiment on the effects of high altitude (lack of oxygen) on visual sensitivity. The experimenter simulated altitude by varying the amount of oxygen in a sealed chamber. Altitude, or oxygen, then, was the independent variable; it is plotted on the abscissa, or horizontal axis. The subjects were tested at different altitudes for the amount of light necessary to see a standard test object. This light, expressed as a percentage of increase in the amount of light required at ground level, is the dependent variable and is plotted on the ordinate, or vertical axis of the graph. Thus the convention for plotting graphs permits us to identify at a glance the independent and dependent variables.

Another very important characteristic of the experimental methods is *control.* In an experiment, it is important that only the variables be allowed to change. Factors other than the independent variable which might possibly affect the dependent variable must be held in check. It would do no good to study the effects of varying an independent variable while other factors, unknown to the experimenter, varied also. In an experiment we must *control* variables or conditions which will give misleading results. Two main strategies are used to control extraneous variables. One strategy employs *control groups;* in the other, each *subject serves as his own control.*

Suppose that we decide to use the control-group method in the experiment on the effects of tranquilizers on memory span. Ideally, we wish to have a control group composed of subjects *matched* with those of the experimental group in every relevant way except one—the experimental subjects receive the tranquilizer while the control subjects do not. If the two groups are alike in every respect except the independent variable, we can then say with some confidence that differences in the dependent variable of memory span are due to the tranquilizer.

What are some of the factors which might affect the results and which must be controlled? Obviously we would want the subjects in the control and experimental groups to be equal in memory span before the experiment. To make certain of this, we would probably give all the subjects a preliminary memory-span test and assign them to the control and experimental groups so that individual differences in memory span were equalized in the two groups. Variables such as intelligence, sex of the subject, and so forth, which do not seem to be so immediately relevant, might also be controlled by matching the subjects.

In drug experiments of this kind, another not-so-obvious variable should also be controlled. The subjects might be influenced by the knowledge that they have been given a tranquilizer; they might try to act as they *think* they should under the effect of a tranquilizer. To control this possibility, the control subjects would be given inactive pills, called *placebos,* which appear identical to the tranquilizer pills. Subjects therefore would not know whether they were in the experimental or control group. The technique of not letting subjects know which group they are in is called the *single-blind technique.*

At this point, you will probably feel that things have been well controlled. There is, however, another difficulty. The experimenter knows, when he gives the memory-span test, which subjects are in the experimental and control groups. How can this affect the results? After all, experimenters are supposed to be honest—the unforgivable sin in science is the falsification of results. However, a substantial number of experiments indicate that the experimenter, in good faith, can affect the outcomes of experiments unconsciously and in subtle ways (Rosenthal, 1964). These outcomes tend to be influenced in the direction desired by the experimenter. Human subjects presumably pick up subtle guiding cues from him.

The obvious way to control for this effect is to keep the experimenter in the dark about which subjects are in which group. A person who never has any contact with the subjects may assist the experimenter by assigning code numbers to them. The experimenter who does not know the code can then run tests on the subjects without knowing whether they are in the experimental or control groups. This technique of disguising group membership from both the subjects and the experimenter is known as the *double-blind technique.*

Perhaps better control can be achieved more easily when *each subject serves as his own control.* One of the few well-controlled studies of the effects of marijuana on psychological performance will serve as our example (Weil et al., 1968).

The experimenters tested the behavior of subjects *before* and *after* smoking marijuana. Two groups of subjects were employed—naïve, or inexperienced, users, and experienced users. The experimenters then compared the *difference* between the subjects' "before" and "after" behavior on certain tasks, one of which was the digit-symbol substitution test shown in Figure 1.7. With this sort of before-and-after technique, there is no need to control the initial behavior (in this case, before-smoking performance) and certain other variables; they do not change during the course of the experiment because the same subject is used throughout.

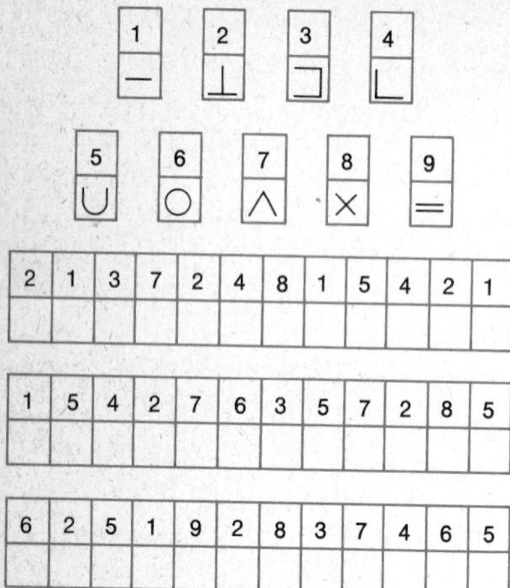

IN SOME EXPERIMENTS THE SUBJECT SERVES AS HIS OWN CONTROL

Figure 1.7 *A portion of the digit-symbol substitution test used in the experiment on the effects of marijuana on behavior. Subjects were allowed 90 seconds to fill in as many blanks as possible with the appropriate code symbols from the key. Their performance on this task is shown in Table 1.2 (Weil et al., 1968, from* Psychopharmacologia, *1964.)*

The subjects' performance scores are shown in Table 1.2. Note that, on the average, large doses produced greater deterioration in performance for naïve subjects—a *dose-response* curve was obtained. Only high doses were given to the chronic users; surprisingly, their performance was on the average slightly better 15 minutes after smoking and again 90 minutes after smoking. Although double-blind procedure was used—the experimenters did not know which subjects received placebos—it was often impossible to disguise the marijuana so that the subject did not know he was getting a dose. In an ideal experiment of this sort, a complete double-blind procedure would be used.

Unfortunately, the use of the before-and-after technique in which each subject is his own control sometimes introduces another problem: Practice effects may obscure the results. For instance, the marijuana experiment also included a test of eye-hand coordination, which was run several times on the same subject. As more and more trials were run, the subjects' eye-hand coordination improved—apparently from practice. Such practice effects made it impossible to assess the effects of marijuana on the test. When practice effects are minimal, or when they can be controlled, this before-and-after, or baseline, method probably affords the best control of subject differences and extraneous variables.

A powerful variant of the method of using baselines occurs when subjects are given training until a stable and reliable level of performance—the baseline—is reached (Sidman, 1960). Then the experimental variables are introduced and departures from this stable baseline are noted.

It is literally true that an experiment is no better than its controls. The careful student will be critical of the controls in an experiment. He will look for uncontrolled variables which might make the results of an experiment inconclusive. It is a mark of scientific sophistication to be able to spot defects in experimental controls. As you go on into the original literature in psychology or other experimental sciences, you should develop this skill.

Repetition is another important aspect of experimental methods. We can repeat an experiment. In elementary chemistry, for example, we can demonstrate that water is made up of oxygen and hydrogen simply by burning hydrogen (that is, combining it with oxygen) and collecting the water that results. Anyone with the proper equipment can do this experiment, and it has been done repeatedly. In psychology, we can demonstrate that recitation is an aid to study by having two groups study something, one with recitation and one without, and later measuring differences in memory. If such an experiment is performed under the proper conditions, it will show that material studied with recitation is remembered better. This experiment has been performed many times.

The advantages of repetition are obvious. If we are able to repeat an observation over and over again under controlled conditions, we can be sure of it beyond all reasonable doubt. Then, too, the same experiment can be performed by different people. A scientist in England and one in the United States can do the experiment, and though widely separated in time or place, they can agree on the same observations. Agreement between different observers is an important advantage.

Table 1.2 *Performance on the digit-symbol substitution test after smoking marijuana.*

Note: Scores are the average increase or decrease over the baseline in number of correct substitutions on the digit-symbol test.
Source: Based on Weil et al., 1968.

Dose	Naïve subjects, after smoking		Chronic users, after smoking	
	15 min.	90 min.	15 min.	90 min.
Placebo (no drug)	+0.9	+0.4	—	—
Low dose	−1.2	−2.6	—	—
High dose	−5.1	−3.9	+0.25	+2.8

Indeed, it is this kind of "check-up-ability"—as one distinguished scientist, J. B. Conant, has called it—that is essential to science. Finally, the repeatability of an experiment makes it convenient. We can do it at will, without waiting for the next opportunity to make a casual observation. This convenience lets us create such opportunities at our pleasure; it saves a lot of time that otherwise would be wasted waiting for the right observation.

The experimental method also has *limitations.* In many ways the experiment is the best method the scientist has, and he uses it whenever he can. It is such a good method that scientists often neglect to point out its disadvantages, but knowing them is of some value in appreciating the data it yields.

Perhaps the most obvious shortcoming is that *it cannot always be used.* Physicists, chemists, and other natural scientists do not often face this difficulty, because the lights, sounds, and chemicals that they work with never object to their experiments. People and animals are not so docile; they are not always willing to cooperate. It is hardly possible, for example, to experiment with what makes a happy marriage—for obvious reasons. We dare not experiment with many things in psychology.

A second limitation of the experiment is that *it is artificially arranged by the scientist.* In an attempt to uncover important variables, the psychologist must select particular ones. To do this, he must often be something of a detective and act on hunches or suspicions. In selecting his variables, he may be fortunate enough to pick those which are significant; but he may have bad luck and do an experiment that actually means nothing. Worse yet, he may have an experiment that seems to mean something it really does not mean. Indeed, the scientist and psychologist must continually guard against false conclusions that come from limited and somewhat artificial experiments. No matter how careful scientists are, they make mistakes.

A final limitation of the experiment is that *it sometimes interferes with the very thing it attempts to examine.* Physicists long ago discovered, in the field of quantum mechanics, that their experiments sometimes interfered with the behavior of small particles so that their measurements of this behavior were in error. Psychologists have even more trouble on this account.

Consider, for example, the attempt of the psychologist to find out how people tire when they are exposed to loud noises for a long time. He brings people into the laboratory and subjects them to loud noises (the independent variable). Then he measures their performance with all

Table 1.3 *Results of adjective self-ratings by men and women: Personality traits on which there was a marked difference. An example of the method of systematic observation.*

Source: Based on data from Bennett and Cohen, 1959.

More characteristic of women	More characteristic of men
Social empathy (sympathetic understanding of others)	Social coarseness
Social warmth	Social iniquity
Social unselfishness	Overt aggressiveness
Social morality	Personal maturity
Social honesty	Technological feelings
Negligence	
Imprecision	
Impetuousness	
Personal fear	
Personal weakness	
Happiness	
Euphoria	
Covert (hidden) hostility	
Democratic feelings	
Domestic feelings	

sorts of tests (the dependent variables) only to find—he thinks—no fatigue. It turns out that when people know they are in an experiment they are highly motivated to perform well and will not show the fatigue they might exhibit under normal circumstances. Or, to take another example, if a psychologist brings subjects into an experiment in which they know that their personalities are being studied, they are usually not their normal selves, but may show quite unusual aspects of their personality. Hence the possibility that people or animals may not behave in an experiment as they normally do is something we have to consider seriously in psychological experiments.

SYSTEMATIC OBSERVATION What alternatives to the experimental methods do we have? One alternative has no generally accepted name, but we shall call it the *method of systematic observation*. Others call it the survey method. Whatever the name, it is similar to the experimental method in that variables are measured, but it is different in that one cannot willfully manipulate the independent variable—nature has already done this. The researcher simply makes the most systematic study he can of conditions as he finds them.

Many studies of the differences in behavior between groups of people—sometimes called *differential psychology*—must be conducted by the method of systematic observation. The groups are there and the behavioral differences may be studied and described. As a further step, we may try to discover the origins of the group differences that we observe. For example, consider the differences in self-concepts of men and women (Bennett and Cohen, 1959).

Large groups of men and women, ranging in age from 15 to 64, were asked to pick adjectives from a long list which they considered most and least characteristic of themselves. (This is a variety of the so-called *adjective-checklist* technique of self-rating.) The experimenters then grouped the adjectives so that related adjectives were formed into clusters. For instance, the adjectives *loving, affec-*

THE METHOD OF SYSTEMATIC OBSERVATION, LIKE THE EXPERIMENTAL METHOD, YIELDS SCIENTIFIC RESULTS

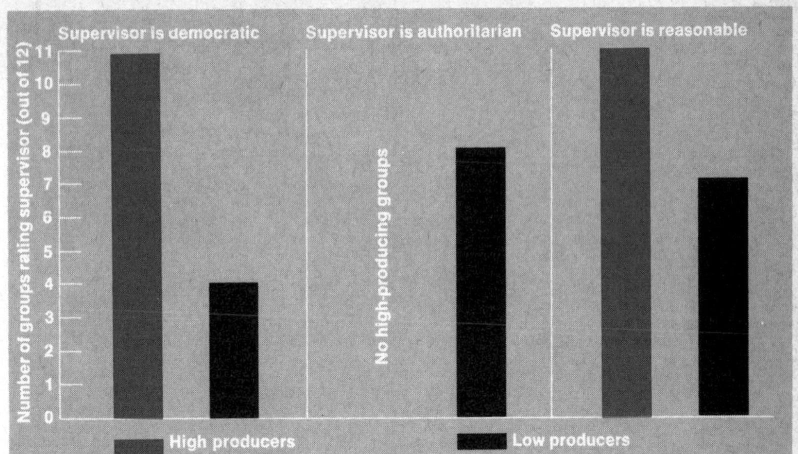

Figure 1.8 *In this example of systematic observation, most high-producing groups in the office of a large insurance company regarded their supervisors as democratic and reasonable; several of the low-producing groups considered their supervisors authoritarian. (Based on data from Katz et al., 1950.)*

tionate, and *tender* were grouped together in the cluster called "social warmth." In this way a group of personality traits was formed. Some of the differences between men and women on these traits are shown in Table 1.3.

In attempting to explain the differences indicated by the table, we might speculate that women have learned to regard themselves in one way, men in another. As we shall see in Chapter 14, a great deal of pressure is put on children to learn the attitudes and behaviors, or roles, appropriate to their sex. Such pressure is part of the process of *socialization*—learning the appropriate behaviors and attitudes and roles by boys and girls is called *sex typing;* girls learn to think and act like women, boys like men. The different self-perceptions listed in Table 1.3 are probably the result of this particular differential learning process.

Another example of the method of systematic observation comes from an industrial situation (Katz et al., 1950).

A large insurance company found that like many companies, it had some groups of clerical workers which were producing a relatively large amount of work, while other groups were low producers. It wanted to know whether the leadership of the groups had anything to do with productivity. It selected 12 high-producing groups and 12 low-producing groups, matched well for number of workers in the groups, for the ages of the workers, and for the kind of work done. This matching was necessary in order to "control" such variables. The members of the groups were interviewed about their opinions of their supervisors. Did they consider the supervisor to be democratic or authoritarian? Did they consider him reasonable?

The results are summarized in Figure 1.8. Of the 12 high-producing groups, 11 thought their supervisor was both democratic and reasonable, while none considered him authoritarian. Several of the low-producing groups, on the other hand, regarded their supervisor as authoritarian rather than democratic and reasonable. From such results, it could be concluded that the personality of the leader, as perceived by his subordinates, was clearly related to the group's production.

Systematic observation methods are applicable to a large number of problems—the study of public opinion and the factors affecting it, the effects of advertising on consumer purchases, factors involved in success in college, and even such basic questions as the role of heredity and environment in the development of intelligence, to name just a few examples. Today these methods of systematic observation are contributing much to the science of psychology, particularly to our knowledge of personality, social processes, and industrial problems.

CLINICAL METHODS Clinical methods ordinarily are used only when people come to psychologists with problems. Little Alice is doing badly in school, and her parents bring her to the psychologist to find out why. Little Basil is throwing temper tantrums, not eating his meals, crying all night, and generally making life miserable for his parents. Chumly, an otherwise fine young boy in high school, is caught stealing nickels from the Sunday school collection plate. Or young Mr. Squabble, married for 5 years, comes in worried because he and his wife just cannot get along. Such examples could go on endlessly. All are people with problems who come to the clinical psychologist for help.

Not all clinical problems require thorough study. When they do, the psychologist usually begins by getting a detailed account of the person's past history and his family relations, commonly from interviews with the person and his associates. Very often he may have a specially trained social worker study the person's social background and environment.

Then the psychologist will use tests of various kinds that have been developed through previous research. He may use intelligence tests, reading tests, interest tests, tests of emotional maturity and personality, or any of a large number he has at his command. From these and the biographical information, he will try to make a diagnosis of the problem —and then he will take steps to try to remedy it. The tests, the diagnosis, and the remedy will vary with the individual cases. We shall study later in more detail some of the problems dealt with by clinical psychologists.

We are concerned here with the clinical method as a tool in science. As a method, it combines features of clinical observation, experiment, and systematic observation. Working with individual cases, the clinician may *observe* some factor he considers to be important. By observation of cases, for example, Sigmund Freud discovered that dreams often reflect strong desires people have but are unconscious of. In general, however, clinical observation does not provide much scientific information. It is usually too subjective, casual, uncontrolled, and lacking in precise measurement. What appear to be cause and effect in one case may not be in another. Even in a single case it is extremely difficult to sort out the significant causal factors with certainty. Probably the greatest value of clinical observation is that it suggests fruitful ideas which may be investigated more rigorously by experimental and systematic observation methods.

Theory in scientific psychology Having reviewed methods of collecting observations in psychology, we should complete the picture by indicating the role of theory in psychology.

To the layman the word "theory" sometimes has an unsavory connotation. It may mean simply somebody's unsupported and unfounded notion of how things ought to be done. Or it may mean a set of principles obtained from books or highly artificial situations that do not work out very well in practice. Even in science, we have had some theories that turned out to be wrong or misleading.

Theory, nevertheless, is an important part of science. In fact, it is one of the chief objectives, for science makes its greatest advances when it arrives at theories which neatly summarize many observations and predict accurately what can be expected to happen in new situations. Theory in science serves three important functions.

It serves, first, as a sort of *scientific shorthand*. A theory can summarize and generalize a lot of observations. In physics, for example, the law of gravitation is a very simple way of summarizing a host of observations about apples, stones, and feathers falling to the ground and about planets and spacecraft moving in their orbits. Instead of spelling out a great array of physical observations, the law of gravitation very neatly and briefly encompasses them all. In psychology, we have developed a principle—the principle of reinforcement—that the behavior of people and animals is strengthened or weakened by the use of reward or punishment. This, in a sense, is a theory that may not be entirely correct, but it is useful because it summarizes the essence of literally hundreds of experiments about learning. Hence a theory, to the extent that it states laws or principles, is a useful shorthand way of summarizing observations.

Theory is also a *predictor*. It lets us tell in advance—given certain conditions—what will happen. And the ultimate object of all science is to predict. If science were just a collection of observations, and if one could never predict from one set of observations to another, there would be little point in science. It would do us little good to find out something, because it would never apply to any other situation. A well-developed theory is like a model house or a road map. A map, for example, depicts many of the features of a geographical area, but not all of them. Its main purpose is to tell us how we may travel in the area. Similarly, a theory lays out for us in advance many of the important features of an area of knowledge. A good map must be reasonably accurate, but it cannot tell us everything about an area. Likewise, to be useful, a theory must represent fairly well the observations it encompasses, but it need not be perfectly accurate or predict every possible detail.

Another important use for theory, even if a theory is inaccurate or wrong, is to *guide* us in collecting further observations in research. It was a theory about the nature of the atom that led atomic scientists to the experiments resulting in the atomic bomb. It was a theory—namely, that reinforcement is important in learning—which led to many experiments whose results eventually changed our methods of education. In these and many other cases, theories have been guides for research, and they have been the basis on which scientists decided how to take their next steps in making observations. When a theory is wrong or inadequate, the discrepancy is soon discovered in the course of the experiments and we modify the theory. When it is correct or largely correct, we keep it and use it as a guide for other experiments that add further details to our knowledge.

Origins of Psychology

A description of the field of psychology is one aim of this chapter. Toward that end, we can take another tack—the historical approach. An understanding of the origins of psychology should help us to appreciate psychology as a discipline and science. Two general trends—one concerned with the questions asked, the other with methods—deserve our attention.

Trend in problems Man has been curious about himself ever since he has been able to think abstractly. We have changed the wording, but since the beginning we have wrestled with such questions as: How do we experience the world around us? What is the relationship, if any, between our experience of the world and the working of our body? Can we measure experience and behavior? Under what conditions do we learn things? What are the roles of environment and heredity, or nurture and nature, in producing behavior? Why do people differ so much in temperament and behavior? Why do some people have severe behavior problems? None of these questions has been completely answered, but progress has been made. One very broad generalization about the approach to these problems is that the major emphasis in psychology has shifted from the study of mental, that is, inner, processes and experience to external, or observable, behavior. This is why we defined psychology as the science of *behavior.* Let us hasten to point out that this shift is only one of emphasis. Early psychologists were relatively more concerned with attempts to measure and understand the mind, while later psychologists are generally more concerned with attempts to measure and understand behavior.

Trend in methods The history of psychology has been characterized by an increasing use of the empirical method: the reliance on observation as the way of answering questions. Most psychologists prefer to depend upon verifiable observations rather than upon intuition or fiat from prestigious authorities. This trend has almost invariably met resistance from groups who feel that their beliefs might be upset or their accepted authorities challenged by new observations or by principles based on them. Historically, resistance to the empirical method was first shattered in settling questions about the physical world; hence physics and chemistry were first established as sciences. It took longer to overcome opposition to probing the world of living things and thus to put biology, psychology, and the social sciences on an empirical basis. Even today a hue and cry is raised when psychological data that run counter to established attitudes are brought forth. Nevertheless, psychology continues to prosper as an empirical science.

Before the dawn of modern science, observation and the interpretation of data were the business of the *philosopher.* Beginning with the ancient Greeks, philosophers learned a great deal about the world around them, attempted to arrange their learning in an orderly way, and speculated on its meaning. Thus philosophy became the parent of our modern departments of knowledge. As philosophers increased their knowledge, they developed specialities within the field of philosophy. Natural philosophy dealt with areas now included under physics, chem-

INFLUENTIAL FIGURES IN THE DEVELOPMENT OF PSYCHOLOGY

Figure 1.9 *Wilhelm Wundt, William James, Sigmund Freud, Ivan P. Pavlov, Max Wertheimer, J. B. Watson, and B. F. Skinner. (Bettmann Archive, Free Lance Photography, Bettmann Archive, Bettmann Archive, United Press International, Underwood & Underwood, Boris of Boston.)*

istry, and the natural sciences; mental philosophy was concerned with what is now the field of psychology; and moral philosophy considered many of the social problems now encompassed by the social sciences. Thus philosophy is the parent of our modern sciences, both natural and social. This fact is still reflected in the awarding of the Ph.D. (doctor of philosophy) degree to postgraduate students in such diverse subjects as chemistry, psychology, and economics.

Sooner or later, the new sciences, like most children, had to leave the fold. What gave tremendous impetus to the movement, however, was the discovery of a new method, the *experimental* method. As we have seen, the method of systematic observation limits the scientist to observing the events and things that nature has provided for him, and observing them, moreover, under nature's conditions. The experimental method, on the other hand, enables the scientist to make those events happen which he needs to observe in order to develop a science, and to do this under conditions of his own choosing.

Physicists and chemists were the first to discover and exploit the experimental method. With the aid of this method, they formulated many of the principles of physics and chemistry still taught today. In time, physicists and physiologists began to experiment on some of the problems encompassed in psychology, such as color vision, hearing, and brain functions, which we shall study later. As these problems yielded to the experimental method, it became more and more evident that psychology, like the other sciences, could forge ahead only by developing experimental methods suited to its own unique problems.

In 1860, Gustav Fechner (1801–1887) published a book, *Elemente der Psychophysik,* which is taken by some to mark the beginning of experimental psychology. This book was concerned with the measurement of sensory experience. In 1879, Wilhelm Wundt (1832–1920) founded the first laboratory of psychology at the University of Leipzig in Germany. Perhaps the first laboratory actually came before that, because William James at Harvard was known to be doing experiments too. In any event, experimental laboratories of psychology mushroomed as the movement got under way. In the United States, the first formal laboratory was set up at Johns Hopkins University in 1883. Within a few more years, laboratories had been established at most major universities in the country.

A science, like a child, must have time to mature. It takes thousands and thousands of experiments, performed with different methods and under different conditions, to establish a healthy body of scientific observations and principles. In the meantime, especially when observations are scarce and new methods are developing, there is likely to be a period of "isms" characterized by different points of view which are often espoused with considerable zeal. Psychology went through such a period during which different schools of thought occupied the limelight. As psychology has matured, it has become much more eclectic —there has been a good deal of selection of what seems best from all the schools. (This, for instance, is an eclectic textbook.) Because these schools are important in the history of psychology, we shall discuss some of the most outstanding. Several of the leaders of these schools of thought are pictured in Figure 1.9.

Structuralism The first school, or "ism," owes its character to the ideas prevalent during the time in which experimental psychology got under way. The physical scientists of that day could claim great success, not only for their experimental method, but also for their atomic theory of matter. This theory, or set of principles, stated that all complex substances could be analyzed into component elements, much as elementary physics or chemistry is explained today.

It was only natural that the first experimental psychologists should follow this example, and they did. They started searching for *mental elements* into which, they hoped, all mental contents could be analyzed. The element, they thought, must be a *sensation,* such as red, cold, sweet, or putrid. To search for these elements and the rules for combining them, they used a special kind of experimental method called *introspection* (Boring, 1953). A subject was trained to report as objectively as possible what he experienced in connection with a certain stimulus, disregarding the meanings he had come to associate with the particular stimulus. He might, for example, be presented with a colored light, a tone, or an odor and asked to describe it as minutely as possible. It was hoped that in this way the mental content of an experience would be reconstructed from elementary sensations.

Many valuable observations were collected in this way, and some aspects of the method are still being used. The approach, however, proved too narrow, for it was limited to reports of what a person experienced. Moreover, it gradually became apparent that mind cannot be thought of as a structure made up of elementary sensations (Wertheimer, 1923). Hence structuralism gave way to other approaches to the study of psychological events.

Functionalism One of these new approaches, much influenced by the Darwinian theory of evolution, came to be known as functionalism. Two of its most influential proponents were William James (1842–1910) and John Dewey (1859–1952). James's textbook, *The Principles of Psychology* (James, 1890), is a classic statement of the functionalist point of view. Functionalists were interested in the fact that behavior and mental processes are adaptive—they enable an individual to adjust to a changing environment. Thus they sought to study the adaptive *functions* of behavior and mental processes, not merely their structure.

To study functions, the functionalists extended experimental methods to include not only the method of introspection but also the *observation of behavior*—what a person does. Instead of limiting themselves to the description and analysis of sensory experience and of mental content, they emphasized the total activity of the individual—how he learns, how he forgets. So functionalism had two chief characteristics: the study of the total behavior and experience of an individual, and an interest in the adaptive functions served by the things an individual does.

Behaviorism Functionalism tended to put the emphasis on the observation of behavior, but it still accepted the introspection of mental processes as a legitimate method. Another now famous psychologist, John B. Watson (1878–1958), went a step further. Beginning about 1912, Watson rejected the introspective method completely and insisted that psychological experiments be restricted to the study of behavior (Watson, 1925). This position characterized the school known as behaviorism.

Behaviorism had three other important characteristics. One was an emphasis on conditioned reflexes as the elements—the building blocks—of behavior. Behaviorism, in fact, was very much like the structuralism it rejected in that it viewed complex processes as built up out of more elementary ones. Its elementary building block, however, was the conditioned reflex rather than the sensation. We must leave the detailed explanation of the conditioned reflex to Chapter 3, but we can describe it loosely as a relatively simple learned response to a stimulus. Watson felt that man's complex behavior was made up almost entirely of sets of conditioned reflexes.

Another closely related characteristic of behaviorism was its emphasis on learned, rather than unlearned, behavior. It denied the existence of instinct or of inborn tendencies. To Watson, almost all that a man becomes is a matter of the conditioning of reflexes. One of his most famous statements, in fact, was that he could take almost any infant and through proper training make him into a beggar, a lawyer, or any other kind of person he desired.

Behaviorism, finally, was characterized by an emphasis on animal behavior. It held that there is no important difference between man and animals and that we can learn much about man by the study of animals. This emphasis, in the hands of Watson and his students, led to an enormous amount of animal experimentation, which continues to the present day and has helped significantly in the solution of many psychological problems.

These characteristics of behaviorism have left their mark on modern psychology. Although behaviorism often went to extremes, it made an important underlying point that the data of psychology, like those of any science, must be out in the open for all to see. In other words, the observations of psychology must be public observations which others can repeat and check. Behaviorism thus had a lot to do historically with gaining acceptance for the current definition of psychology used throughout this book.

The behaviorist school has left its mark on psychology in still another way. Several newer, neobehaviorist schools have sprung from the original stem. These schools, which were especially prominent in psychology during the late 1930s and the 1940s, were characterized by attempts to develop general theories of behavior—usually from a few animal experiments. Supporters of the rival theories of Tolman (1932), Hull (1943), and Guthrie (1952) often engaged in rather acrimonious debate and attempted to set up "crucial experiments" to show that the predictions from their theory were correct and those from other theories were wrong. Some useful data were obtained from these experiments, but the idea of doing crucial experiments turned out to be a delusion. The major fault was that the predictions did not follow uniquely from the theories—you could predict almost any result by proper combinations of the theoretical terms. Since this flirtation with general theories, behaviorists have turned toward small-scale theories from which unique predictions can be made. Behaviorism, and psychology in general, has also turned

GESTALT PSYCHOLOGY EMPHASIZES THE PERCEPTION OF ORGANIZED CONFIGURATIONS

Figure 1.10 *The dots are perceived, not as so many isolated elements, but as a square and a triangle on a line.*

toward the collection of "theoretically neutral data" (Koch, 1951). Some present-day behaviorist groups have a definite bias against explicit theory (Skinner, 1961).

Gestalt psychology While behaviorism was displacing introspectionism in the United States, another school of thought, starting about 1912, was gaining ground in Germany. This was gestalt psychology, founded by Max Wertheimer (1880–1943) and his colleagues K. Koffka and W. Köhler (Wertheimer, 1912; Koffka, 1935; Köhler, 1947). *Gestalt* is a German word having no exact translation, but meaning something like *form, organization, or configuration*.

Gestalt psychology, like structuralism before it, was greatly influenced by concepts developing in physics. Coming along some thirty years later, however, the new concepts were now field concepts of such things as the pattern of lines making up a magnetic field. For that reason, gestalt psychologists, and particularly their modern descendants, are sometimes called *field theorists.*

Gestalt psychologists were characterized, first of all, by an opposition to "atomism." They felt that both structuralism and behaviorism had taken the wrong path in looking for elements such as sensations or conditioned reflexes. Our experiences and our behavior, they held, are not compounded from simple elements. Rather they are patterns, or organizations, somewhat analogous to a magnetic field, in which events in one part of the field are influenced by events in another part. A gray piece of paper, for example, is gray only in relation to its background or to something with which it is compared. On a black background, it appears light; against a white background, it appears dark. A series of dots in any orderly arrangement is perceived as a pattern. When, for instance, you view the dots in Figure 1.10, you do not perceive merely isolated dots. Rather, you see a square and a triangle sitting on a line. The dots are somehow *organized* in perception so that they are seen as a configuration. It will be possible to explain and illustrate the concept of organization better when we come to the subject of perception, but the point made by gestalt psychologists is that the patterns or forms of our experience cannot be explained by compounding elements. As some were fond of saying: "The whole is more than the sum of its parts."

Gestalt psychology was also characterized by the use of a method called *phenomenology*. This is like the structuralists' introspection, with one important difference. The structuralists believed in *trained* introspection for the purpose of dissecting the supposed elements of experience. The gestaltists, on the other hand, believed in naïve introspection. That is to say, they wanted to study what something looked like to an observer. Put another way, they held that the raw phenomena of experience as reported without elaboration or analysis were legitimate observations. Thus phenomenology is a kind of method of natural observation applied to human perceptions.

Devotion to the phenomenological method led early gestalt psychologists to emphasize the study of human experience and perception, but they were also empirical scientists who studied a wide range of problems. They have, for example, made important contributions to our understanding of learning, thought, and problem solving, which we shall take up at the appropriate time.

Psychoanalysis Psychoanalysis is not a major school of psychology, for it originated outside the laboratory in medical practice. It has had an effect on psychology, however, particularly in recent years. Moreover, it is so often confused with psychology that its nature and role need to be explained.

Psychoanalysis was founded and developed during the years 1885 to 1939 by Sigmund Freud (1856–1939). Freud, a Viennese psychiatrist, frequently found himself unable to handle the problems with which his patients confronted him within the diagnostic tenets current at the time. Psychiatry was then characterized by an elaborate system of classifying mental disorders. But this system mainly pigeonholed people without providing very convincing explanations of the causes of the disorders or offering very effective methods of treatment.

Freud concerned himself with problems both of understanding and of treatment. Being a physician, he made little use of the techniques and concepts of scientific psychology. He was also limited, so to speak, to the method of natural observation, that is, to studying whatever he could observe in the course of treating his patients. But he was a keen observer. He developed hypotheses as he went along and tried to test them in his interviewing and treatment of patients. In this sense, he was empirical and something of an experimentalist, even though he could not really experiment in a systematic way. Being a prolific writer, he had a wide influence on the thinking of psychiatrists and psychologists, on modern literature, and even on the general public.

Out of his experience, Freud developed a method of treatment and a theory of personality. The word *psychoanalysis* primarily refers to the treatment method. The emphasis of this treatment is on *free association* —the patient freely associates, or thinks and says whatever comes to mind. The psychoanalyst makes much use of these free associations in analyzing the causes of the patient's difficulty. The theory of personality is known as the Freudian, or psychoanalytic, theory. This theory is elaborate, stressing the role of motives, often hidden and repressed from both the individual and society.

Freud's theory of personality, rather than his method of treatment, is of greater interest to psychology (Dollard and Miller, 1950). The theory contains many unverified assertions, but it has nevertheless been valuable, for it has been a stimulus to further systematic research. In some cases research has given support to Freud's notions, while in others it has not. Psychologists therefore do not subscribe fully to the theory. They merely regard it as a deductive guide in planning research on the nature of personality.

Psychologists tend to take the same attitude toward other theories of personality which have grown up in the psychoanalytic tradition. The famous split of 1911–1912 between Freud and his adherents Alfred Adler and Carl Jung gave rise to two rival psychoanalytic schools. Jung's school is sometimes called the "analytical school," while Adler's school is sometimes called "individual psychology." The history of the psychoanalytic movement is further complicated by the changing theoretical views held by Freud himself and by the many neo-Freudian theories developed by others in more recent times. We shall describe some of the neo-Freudian theories when we discuss personality theories in Chapter 11.

All the schools, or "isms," described here have been important in the development of modern psychology. Each emphasized a different aspect of psychology or a different method of observation. None was completely right or wrong. All had some beneficial effect on the development of the science of psychology.

Today these major schools have largely disappeared. Few psychologists, if any, identify themselves completely with one school. Some lean more toward one than another, but this bias is very evident only in matters close to the frontiers of psychology where one finds alternative theories about the explanations of events. This is as it should be, for it leads people to do different kinds of experiments. Thus theoretical differences among psychologists do exist, and there are many unsolved problems in psychology, just as in physics and biology. We shall not stress the theoretical differences or the unsolved problems, though we shall sometimes mention them. Instead we shall focus on the basic, well-established facts and principles of modern scientific psychology.

Synopsis and summary

You may wonder why we have spent so much time describing the science of psychology. One reason is simply that most people have a hazy notion of what psychology actually is and what psychologists do. By defining, by describing some of the subfields of psychology, and by providing a capsule history of the field, we have tried to make you aware of psychology as it actually is and not as the Sunday supplements picture it.

Another reason has to do with the word *science.* Most of us are not used to thinking of behavior as something which can be described and understood by using the tools of science. Yet it is possible to build up a structure of reliable knowledge about behavior through the use of scientific method. The things that we do, think, and experience have their causes, and these may be sought on many levels—from the physiological to the sociological.

That we may come to understand the causes of behavior has tremendous implications. It is also grounds for sober reflection. As we begin to understand more about behavior, the ability of people armed with psychological knowledge to predict and control the behavior of others will grow. The ethics of the use of this power is a potentially serious problem. That such a problem looms in the future is a tribute to the power of the scientific method. Because it is such a powerful tool, this text emphasizes scientific, rather than intuitive, data.

1. Although the beginning course in psychology offers much that has practical value, the student should expect to acquire from it only the rudiments, not profound knowledge or skill.
2. Psychology, the science of human and animal behavior, covers a wide range of problems. Not only does it deal with people and understanding them; it also deals with the problems of social groups, learning and perceiving, intelligence and abilities, working efficiently, and many others.
3. Psychology is one of the behavioral sciences. These disciplines include certain aspects of history, economics, sociology, political science, anthropology, and other social sciences. Psychology also draws on such natural sciences as physiology and physics in its attempt to explain behavior.
4. Psychology, for the first few years after its establishment as a scientific subject, was mainly a pure academic science. It began to have practical applications during World War I. Now it is growing at a very fast rate.
5. Psychologists do many things, and psychology has many subfields. Clinical psychology is the largest single subfield. It deals with research, diagnosis, and the therapy of deviant behavior. Other large subfields within psychology are counseling, experimental psychology, industrial and personnel psychology, school and educational psychology, social psychology, psychometric psychology, developmental psychology, and personality psychology.
6. Psychology as a science is (*a*) empirical, (*b*) systematic, (*c*) dependent upon measurement, and (*d*)

careful about using operational definitions of terms.

7. The experimental method has been a cornerstone in the emergence of modern psychology. The essence of this method is that an independent variable is changed under controlled conditions and an effect on a dependent variable is sought. Control is often achieved by using special control groups or by arranging it so that subjects can serve as their own controls.

8. The experimental method cannot be used in every case. When it cannot, scientific information can be obtained through the method of systematic observation. The clinical method is a special method in which information is obtained by an intensive study of an individual—usually one with a behavioral problem.

9. Theory is essential in scientific psychology, as in every science. It serves as (*a*) a scientific shorthand, (*b*) a predictor of facts, and (*c*) a guide to further research.

10. For many years, psychological research was guided by different schools of thought; structuralism, behaviorism, gestalt psychology, functionalism, and psychoanalysis. These schools, however, have tended to dissolve as more and more factual information has accumulated.

Related topics in the text

Appendix 1 Careers in Psychology The training of a psychologist in graduate school is described here. You will find discussions of the qualifications for graduate study in psychology and of the specialized training necessary in several of the subfields of psychology.

Appendix 2 How to Look It Up General suggestions for further reading are given at the end of each chapter. But you may wish to know more about a specific topic; if so, this appendix will give you valuable hints about sources of information in the library. Of course, your instructor will probably be able to steer you to sources of information on specific topics.

Chapter 9 Psychological Measurement and Statistics Techniques for ordering and describing data are outlined in Chapter 9. The correlation coefficient, a measure of the degree of relationship between two sets of data, and tests of statistical significance are also described.

Suggestions for further reading

American Psychological Association. *A career in psychology.* APA, 1970. (Paperback.)
A description of the major activities of psychologists and the training needed for psychology as a career. Available at a nominal charge from the American Psychological Association, 1200 Seventeenth St., N.W., Washington, D.C. 20036.

Bachrach, A.J. *Psychological research: An introduction.* (2d ed.) New York: Random House, 1965. (Paperback.)
An interesting and informal account of experimental methods in psychology.

Baker, R.A. (Ed.) *Psychology in the wry.* New York: Van Nostrand Reinhold, 1963. (Paperback.)
A collection of amusing, satirical articles in which psychologists make fun of their own pomposity and other shortcomings.

Boring, E.G. *A history of experimental psychology.* (2d ed.) New York: Appleton Century Crofts, 1950.
An authoritative and well-written history of experimental psychology that is a standard work in its field.

Guilford, J.P. (Ed.) *Fields of psychology.* (3d ed.) New York: Van Nostrand Reinhold, 1966.
A textbook of psychology organized in terms of the various content and professional subfields of the discipline.

Kimble, G.A., and Garmezy, N. *Principles of general psychology.* (3d ed.) New York: Ronald, 1968.
Chapter 1 of this text contains a fine summary of psychology as an objective science.

King, R.A. (Ed.) *Readings for an introduction to psychology.* (3d ed.) New York: McGraw-Hill, 1971. (Paperback.)
A book of readings designed to accompany this text.

Psychology Today
A magazine containing popularly written articles on psychological topics; very much "with it."

Sidman, M. *Tactics of scientific research: Evaluating experimental data in psychology.* New York: Basic Books, 1960. (Paperback available.)
An account of one very fruitful strategy of doing research in experimental psychology.

Webb, W.B. (Ed.) *The profession of psychology.* New York: Holt, 1962.
Descriptions of their jobs by psychologists engaged in several of the most prominent subfields of psychology.

Woodworth, R.S., and Sheehan, M.R. *Contemporary schools of psychology.* (3d ed.) New York: Ronald, 1964.
A summary of the various schools of psychology, their historical origins, and their important contributions to psychological theory.

PART ONE

BASIC PRINCIPLES OF BEHAVIOR

Why men behave like apes,
and vice versa.
E. A. Hooton

We may think we are only a little lower than the angels, but we must not forget that we are a species of animal. *Homo sapiens* is our name. We have a family tree spanning the millions of years that life has been evolving on this planet. We are remarkable creatures with bodily structures and psychological capacities which have come into being through evolutionary pressures over the millennia. Roughly speaking, bodily structures and behaviors which lead to better adjustment of animals to their environments tend to be the ones which persist. Under the pressures of evolution, behavior patterns have developed which are as much a part of our species nature as our structure and physiology. Understanding such *species-specific* behavior helps clarify the problem of explaining behavior

One aspect, then, of our animal nature that we wish to examine is our *human species heritage*. Within this evolutionary species heritage, variations among individuals exist that are inherited. *Hereditary variations*, within the limits set by our species nature, are another aspect of our nature. We might call these variations a person's *individual genetic constitution*. We know that people vary in behavior because of differences in their individual genetic constitutions. Hence our species heritage and different individual genetic constitutions partially determine our behavior. Another way of putting this is to say that people may behave differently from chimpanzees because of differences in species heritage; people may behave differently from other people because of differences in individual genetic constitutions.

Evolution and Behavior

Behavior helps animals, including man, adjust to an ever-changing environment. Lower animals have innate behavior patterns developed through the pressures of evolutionary forces. The patterns that favored survival have persisted; those which were less adaptive have disappeared.

When talking about human behavior, people often use the term *instinct* to refer to what is assumed to be an innate pattern of behavior. They say that a mother instinctively cares for her young, that a man has an instinct to fight, or that a father instinctively leaps into the water to save his drowning child. Such uses of the term, unfortunately, are loose, unscientific, and incorrect. They tend to confuse behavior that is impulsive or automatic with behavior that is inherited (in other words, unlearned). Such uses of the term instinct also imply that calling a pattern of behavior an "instinct" explains the behavior. But all that has been done is to give the behavior a name, or a label; no analysis has really been made. Perhaps the behavior is not innate at all; perhaps it is learned.

Such an explanation by labeling is termed *reifying*. In the history of psychology, reifying has been especially prevalent when people have claimed that instinct is a basis of human and animal behavior. Because of problems such as these, instinct was long a controversial word among psychologists. Some, like John B. Watson, the founder of behaviorism, denounced the word because they did not believe that any human behavior, except simple reflexes, is inborn or unlearned. Others defended instinct because they were convinced that innate behavior does exist. Today, although there is difference of opinion about instinct in psychology (see Lehrman, 1953; Beach and Jaynes, 1954; Lorenz, 1965), studies made by the zoologists known as *ethologists* have provided convincing evidence of innate behavior patterns in lower animals. In addition, the controversy over the word instinct has died down, partly because we define and use the term more precisely now. Generally, we shy away from the label *instinct,* and use the terms *innate* and *instinctive* only when we are sure they are appropriate.

Types of innate behavior patterns *Taxes* are innate tendencies to orient the body toward certain stimuli; the circling of a moth around a light is a taxis. *Reflexes* are also innately organized responses to certain stimuli. Although they may involve many parts of the body, as in the startle reflex to a sudden intense stimulus, they are typically much more limited in scope than taxes. Reflexes also differ from taxes in that they do not necessarily involve orientation toward the stimulus which elicits them. In fact, one important class of reflexes is the group of withdrawal reflexes in which the response is to move away from the eliciting stimulus.

Instinctive behavior often involves quite a complex organization of movements. Sometimes the term *fixed action pattern,* or FAP, is used as a synonym for certain types of instinctive behavior. To qualify as an innate fixed action pattern, or *instinct,* a behavioral pattern must satisfy several conditions:

1. It should be generally characteristic of a species. In other words, one must have good evidence that the behavior is genetically determined, or that it is the product of evolutionary development. It should also be found, perhaps somewhat modified, in closely related species of animals.

2. The behavior should appear full-blown, or completely organized, without any previous training or practice at the first appropriate time it occurs. This is a test of its being innate rather than learned. But recent work has shown that great care should be exercised in the definition of exactly what it is that is instinctive. As we shall see later in this chapter (see page 57), analysis of many examples of "instinct" indicates that learning plays a role in many of them.

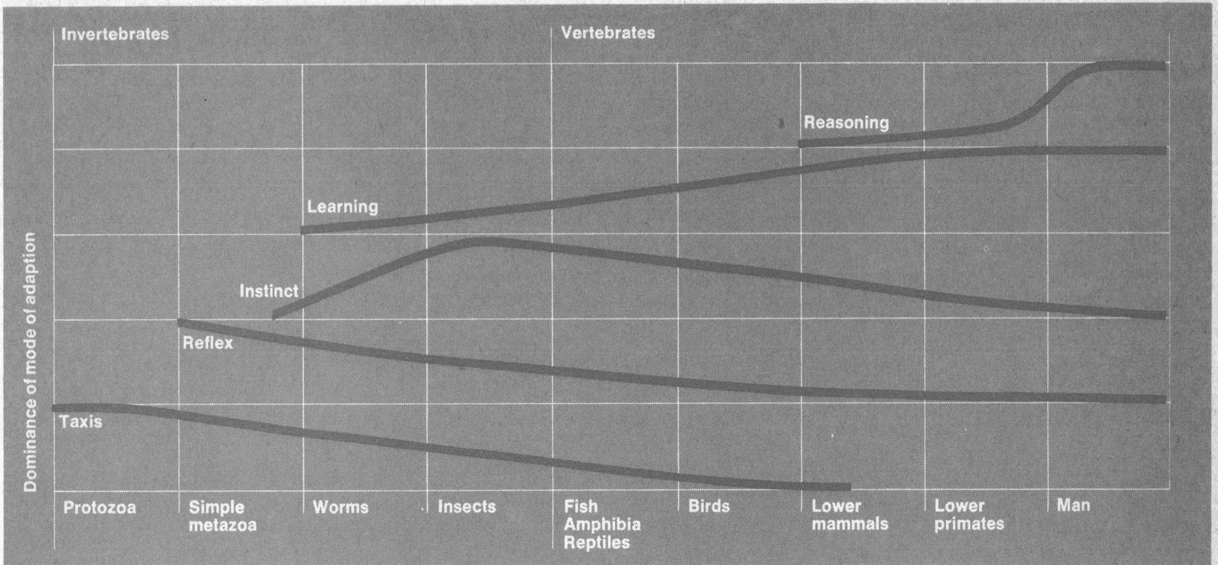

THE DECLINE OF INSTINCT AND THE GROWTH OF REASON

Figure 2.1 *The relative amounts of various classes of behavior in the phylogenetic series. The terms* instinct, reflex, *and* taxis *are defined in this chapter.* Learning *refers to a change of behavior as a result of experience (see Chapter 3);* reasoning *here refers to the use of symbolic representations of the world to solve problems (see Chapter 5). The relative amount of each behavior is shown by the height of each curve within its own block. For instance, man has no taxis behavior, reflexes and instincts are relatively unimportant, and learning and reasoning are important. (After Dethier and Stellar, 1970.)*

3. The behavior should be constant in form, or *topography.* Every time it occurs it should be essentially the same.

4. The behavior should continue for some time in the absence of the stimulus conditions which evoke, or elicit, it. In other words, it may be triggered by some stimulus, but it is not controlled by that stimulus. Some ethologists have claimed that instinctive behavior patterns are triggered by certain stimuli called *innate releasing stimuli.* These investigators believe that the nervous systems of many lower animals are organized in such a way that an instinctive pattern of behavior will occur when the releasing stimulus triggers the nervous system. They argue that the organized pattern is held in check, or inhibited, until the releasing stimulus removes the inhibition; then the pattern within the nervous system can express itself in an organized pattern of behavior. Such a pattern of behavior is the fixed action pattern. In lower animals, some aspects of sexual behavior, social behavior, aggressive behavior, prey-catching behavior, and the orientation of the young toward their parents have been shown by fairly convincing experiments to be instinctive—but see page 57. This last requirement, that instinctive behavior persist in the absence of the stimuli which evoke it, distinguishes such behavior from taxes and reflexes, since neither the taxis nor the reflex persists for any appreciable time after the stimulus has been removed.

Using this definition of "instinctive," we find that instinctive behaviors are not so common in higher animals as we might have thought. Figure 2.1 shows the relative amounts of several types of behavior in the *phylogenetic* animal series—the progression from lowest to highest forms of animal life. In lower animals examples of instinctive behavior abound.

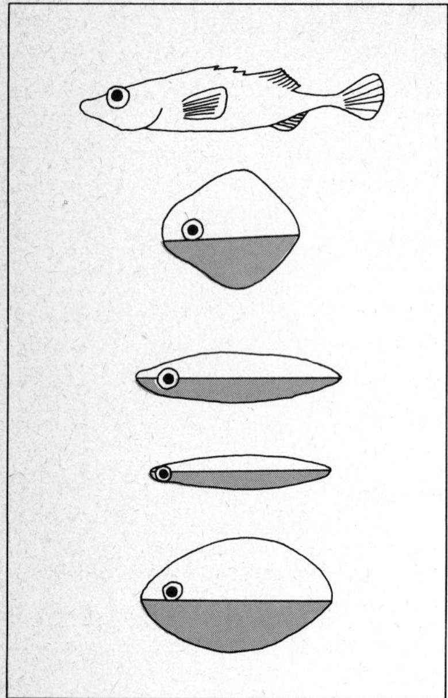

WHAT MAKES A MALE STICKLEBACK MAD?

Figure 2.2 *Models of the male stickleback fish used in an experiment to isolate the stimulus which triggers fighting behavior in the male of that species. The top model, accurate except for its lack of a red belly, was not attacked by the male fish. The other three models, much less accurate but with red bellies, were fiercely attacked. The stimulus, a red belly, is said to be an innate releasing mechanism: it triggers instinctive behavior. (From Tinbergen, 1951.)*

For instance, the fighting behavior of the male stickleback fish seems to be instinctive and triggered by the innate releasing stimulus of the red coloration of the belly of other males (Tinbergen, 1951):

To test the hypothesis that the red belly is the releasing stimulus, a number of models were prepared. The model at the top of Figure 2.2, an accurate model of a stickleback in all respects except its lack of a red belly, did not elicit fighting behavior. The other three models, even though quite different from the shape of a stickleback, did trigger fighting attacks. The common thing about these three models is that the bellies were painted red.

Another interesting example of behavior which is probably instinctive, but which has not been rigorously tested to rule out the possibility of learning, concerns the expression of emotion in social situations by wolves and dogs. The argument that this behavior is instinctive is an indirect one: it says that because the same emotional expressions can be seen in both wolves and dogs, clearly the behaviors have persisted after thousands of years of domestication. Figure 2.3 shows some examples of these patterns of emotional expression.

To say that instinctive behavior is inherited or that it is the result of evolutionary development is not to say that it is necessarily present at birth. Actually, it may appear at various times in the life cycle up to sexual maturity or even later. The body takes time to develop and mature along lines laid down by the genes. Patterns of behavior that depend on growth and maturation can be, and are, inherited even though they may not be present at birth. Furthermore, instinctive behavior patterns seen early in life may drop out so that they are not present during later stages of maturation. We shall discuss the role of maturation in more detail shortly.

We have seen that instinctive patterns of behavior are common in lower animals. When it comes to human beings, we cannot say with certainty that any instinctive patterns exist, with the possible exception of a few that mature without practice (walking, for instance). Man seems to have become such a malleable creature, so able to learn to adapt to his world, that instinctive behavior is not a prominent human characteristic.

The evolutionary heritage Although innate fixed action patterns are not a prominent characteristic of human behavior, man's evolutionary heritage does express itself in his behavior in a more general way. We are a species with a particular evolutionary history behind us, and this history has resulted in the development of particular structures and a particular type of nervous system that set limits on, and provide potentialities for, our behavior.

The limits are perhaps obvious. For instance, we perceive, or experience, the world in certain ways. What we see, what we feel, what we taste and smell, are determined by the fact that we have particular organs for receiving stimuli, called *receptors,* which are sensitive only to certain types of energy. We have a particular brain structure which allows us to make use of information from the receptors only in certain ways. Much is going on around us that we miss because we have neither the re-

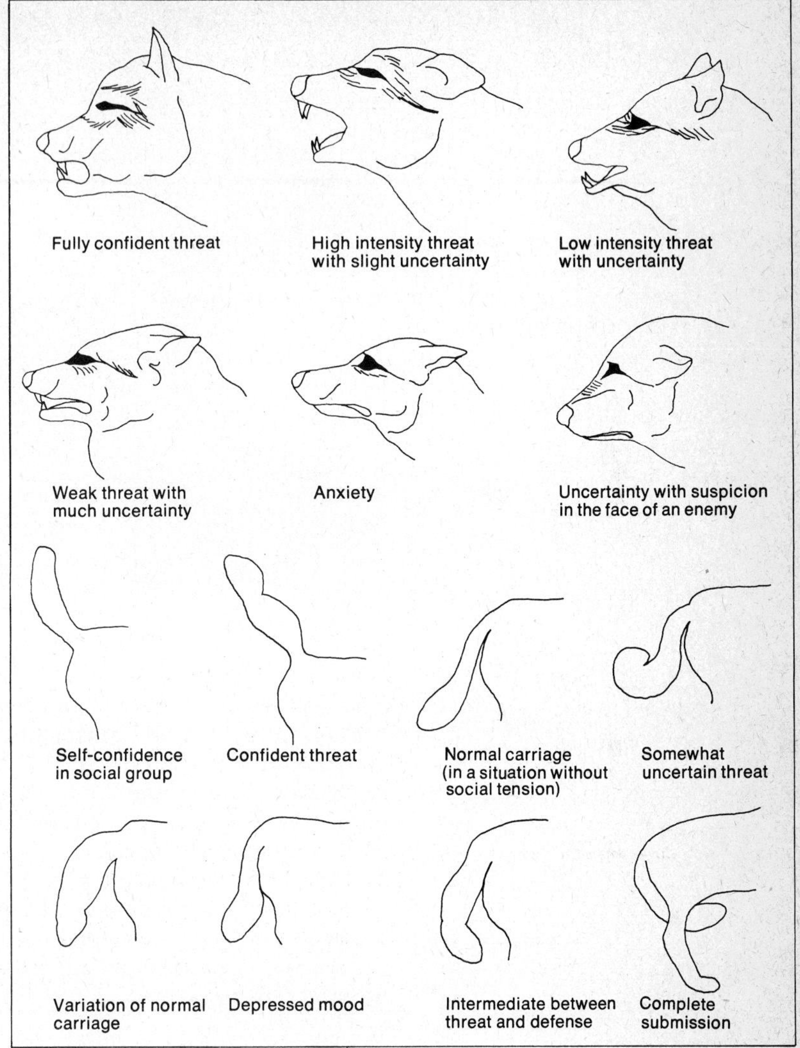

Figure 2.3 *The expression of emotion in wolves. Such patterns of behavior in social situations appear to be innate, since they are still seen in the domesticated dog. (From Thorpe, 1963; after Schenkel, 1948.)*

ceptors nor the brain structures necessary for its perception. We can hardly imagine the world of our experience if this one set of limitations—our perceptual systems—were different.

But owing to our evolutionary history, we also have exceptional potentialities for behavior. For instance, we are the species best able to represent the world in symbolic terms. We do it in speech for the most part. We are probably able to utilize symbols so well because our brains are uniquely organized for it (see Chapter 19). Not only do certain areas of man's brain make it possible to achieve fine, coordinated movements of the tongue, lips, and vocal apparatus, but elaboration of other areas of the brain probably enables him to use speech symbols in representing the world to himself in thought.

Our ability to represent the world in sounds may be unique to man.

RECENT EVIDENCE INDICATES THAT THE ABILITY TO SYMBOLIZE IS NOT LIMITED TO MAN

Figure 2.4 *The chimp Washoe, here shown with one of her mentors, giving the sign, or gesture, for "drink." After 22 months of training, Washoe had mastered 30 such gestures and was able to use them in simple combinations. It should be noted that the chimp learned to use these gestures symbolically—to stand for concepts including things and relations. It was not simply a matter of her imitating a model when she was shown the gesture; if she gestured only when the model gestured, there would be no reason to suppose that the chimp was symbolizing at all. (Courtesy of R. A. Gardner and B. T. Gardner.)*

Early experiments with chimpanzees showed that they could learn and use only a few words. For instance, a childless couple took a new-born chimpanzee into their home and reared it as they would a child (Hayes and Hayes, 1951). Their idea was that an ape might learn to talk like a human baby if given all the love and attention possible. Yet after almost 3 years, although the chimpanzee would occasionally use the words *mama, papa,* and *cup* meaningfully, it had not developed its linguistic skills beyond that. But more recently, in an experiment now in progress, it has been found that the capacity of the chimpanzee to use meaningful symbols is far greater than researchers had previously thought (Gardner and Gardner, 1969):

Perhaps the failures in previous attempts to teach language to chimpanzees were due to the fact that the chimpanzee's vocal apparatus is less well developed than man's. But chimpanzees are adept at hand manipulations; perhaps chimpanzees could learn a gestural language. The American Sign Language (the deaf sign language used in North America) provided the symbols.

A young female chimpanzee is being taught to communicate using this sign language. After 22 months of training, it made more than 30 appropriate gestures. For instance, it symbolized *flower* by taking the tip of the index finger and touching one nostril. This is somewhat different from the correct American Sign Language form, but the chimpanzee used it consistently when it wished to communicate something about a flower. If it wished to communicate something about a cat, it used the American Sign Language symbol for cat which represents the cat's whiskers. To make this sign, the thumb and index finger grasp the hair near the side of the mouth and then are drawn outward away from the mouth.

The chimpanzee did not use such symbols only to stand for specific objects; rather, it seemed to use them for whole classes of objects. Thus the symbols were truly concepts (see Chapter 5). For instance, the chimpanzee gave the symbol for *flower* not only for real flowers but also for pictures of them. The animal also combined symbols: For example, it gave the symbols for *open* and *flower* when it wished to be let into a flower garden through a locked gate. It used the symbols for *listen* and *dog* when it heard an unseen dog barking.

The training used in this experiment is similar to that given human infants (see Figure 2.4). Perhaps the most common way infants learn symbols is through imitation learning—a variety of perceptual learning (see Chapter 3). For instance, the American Sign Language symbol for toothbrush, a movement of the index finger across the front teeth, was given by the experimenters while the animal was having its teeth brushed. In time the chimpanzee learned to imitate this response and to use it for toothbrushes. The experimenters have arranged the animal's life into a routine pattern in which the appropriate symbols are given over and over again during the daily round.

Another training technique used with the chimpanzee is operant conditioning (see Chapter 3). Operant conditioning works on the following principle: If a reward is given after some behavior occurs, the particular behavior which is rewarded becomes more likely to occur again. Chimpanzees, at least young ones, like to be tickled, and tickling can serve as a reward. Use of the symbol for "more" was established by operant conditioning in this way: The experimenter gave the sign for "more" while playing with the chimpanzee and tickling it. If the animal imitated this sign, it was rewarded by further tickling, which served to strengthen the "more" response. As a result of being rewarded, the "more" symbol was learned and transferred to other situations. Such transfer, of course, shows that the chimpanzee was using the "more" response as an abstract symbol.

This experiment is still underway, and we shall have to wait to see the eventual level of linguistic skill reached by the chimpanzee. But it seems safe to say now that chimpanzees possess, to some extent, the ability to represent objects and events in the world symbolically. We men are not alone in our potentiality for symbolizing, although our evolutionary heritage probably makes us better at it.

Many other potentialities are given by capacities for function built into the human brain through evolution. To the degree that human aggressiveness is controlled by brain structures and functions, we have an aggressive heritage. Studies of the human brain have shown that stimulation of a certain part of the region known as the *limbic system* (see Chapter 17) with small electric currents can lead to aggressive, emotional outbursts. Tumors in this region can also produce aggressive behavior. On the other hand, electrical stimulation of other portions of the limbic system has an inhibiting effect upon aggressive behavior. Thus our potentiality for aggression and other sorts of emotional behavior is to some extent a part of our evolutionary heritage. As a matter of fact, most of the psychological functions which have a direct basis in the functioning of the brain—hunger, thirst, sexual behavior, emotion, memory capacity, learning capacity, and so on—may be considered parts of our evolutionary heritage (see Chapters 17 and 19).

Maturation of behavior We have seen that human behavior is not characterized by fixed action patterns. Instead, certain potentialities for behavior are given by the particular type of brain we have as part of our species heritage. Many behaviors and potentialities which depend upon the central nervous system (that is, upon the brain and spinal cord),

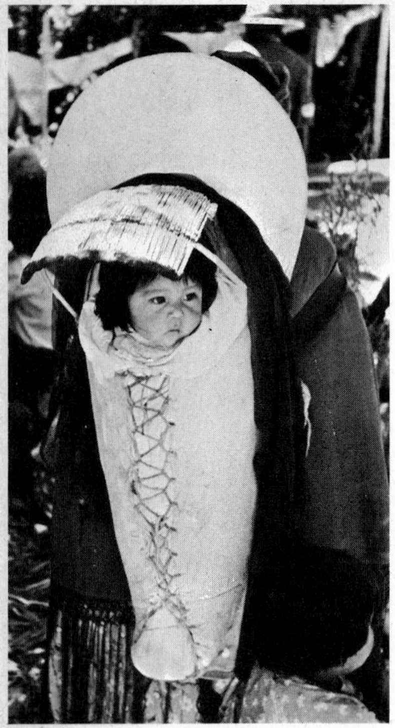

Figure 2.5 *A Shoshone Indian baby is carried firmly bound in a cradle board, protected by a sunshade. The infant goes wherever the mother goes, and the cradle is hung on a bush while the mother gathers berries or digs roots. The practice of baby bundling, which is common in some Indian and Eskimo groups, restricts the baby's opportunity to practice reaching, sitting, creeping, and walking. Yet the child develops these abilities at the same ages that unbound children do—which proves that maturation, not learning, is involved. Such basic motor activities are a part of our species heritage. (Courtesy of E. Adamson Hoebel.)*

and which are not learned, develop as the nervous system grows after birth. We are not finished at birth; rapid growth of the nervous system and connections within the nervous system take place in the first few years of life. The fulfillment of our species heritage must await the completion of this growth. Such growth is called *maturation;* behaviors and potentialities which depend upon it are said to have *matured.* As maturation occurs, new behaviors become possible, and the sequence of appearance of these behaviors is quite regular.

Motor maturation, or the growth of the ability to use limb muscles, can be illustrated by the sequence of stages involved in the maturation of walking. Note that we "mature to walk"; we do not "learn to walk," as is commonly said. The evidence that walking is a pattern which matures without practice comes from many sources. One study has taken advantage of the practice of the Hopi Indians in restricting the behavior of their babies during infancy (Dennis, 1940):

The Hopis bind their infants tightly to a board so that the infants cannot move for most of the day. (Other groups, such as the Shoshone, also do this; see Figure 2.5.) Usually the infant is unbound for only an hour or two a day while he is cleaned. Hence he does not get the same opportunity to practice sitting, creeping, and walking that normal unbound infants do. Yet the bound children develop the ability to sit, creep, and walk just as rapidly as children who are never bound. It seems, then, that it takes little or no practice for a human child to develop these capacities.

The following experiment employed the method of *co-twin control* to study the role of maturation in the development of motor skills (Gesell and Thompson, 1929):

Two girls who were identical twins, and who thus had identical heredity and the same maturational schedules, were the subjects. One girl, twin T, was trained in special activities such as climbing, while the other twin, C, was given no opportunity to practice these activities. After 6 weeks, twin T progressed from not being able to climb stairs at all to making five stairs in 26 seconds. At this point, control twin C was allowed to try the stairs. On her first attempt and without prior practice, she climbed all five stairs in 45 seconds. With only 2 weeks of training, twin C could make the stairs in 10 seconds. The same results were found in other types of basic activity.

From evidence of this kind, we can draw the conclusion that maturation, not learning, is responsible for the development of such basic behavior patterns as walking and climbing in human children. Maturation of these activities is part of our species heritage.

We can accurately chart the pattern of maturation in walking. The infant lifts his head before he sits up, he sits before he crawls, and he crawls before he walks. Actually, there are many little—and, to the parent, absorbing details in this development. These details fit into an orderly sequence; they make a *pattern* which is almost the same in every human infant. The pattern is uniform because it is the result of maturation of the response mechanisms which are, in turn, part of our evolutionary heritage.

SOME BABIES ARE SLOW, SOME FAST, BUT MOTOR SKILLS APPEAR IN A DEFINITE ORDER

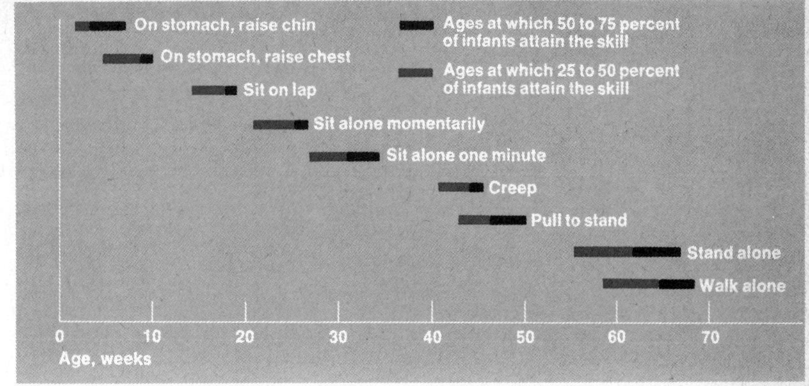

Figure 2.6 Norms for the development of some important motor skills in the human infant. (Based on data from Shirley, 1931.)

Although the *sequence* of changes is orderly, the exact age at which a particular behavior appears varies somewhat from child to child. Figure 2.6 shows both the sequence and the range of ages at which some important milestones of motor maturation are reached. The mark near the center of each bar indicates the average, or median, age at which the skill is attained; the median age is the age at which one-half of a typical population of infants attains the skill. The leftmost edge of each bar is the age at which the fastest quarter of infants attain the skill; the right edge is the age at which three-quarters acquire it. Note that the fastest quarter and the slowest quarter of infants lie outside the range of the bars. Consider now the skill of standing alone. The median age at which children stand alone is about 62 weeks, but one-quarter of the children can stand alone at 56 weeks, and another quarter have not reached this stage of development by 66 weeks. The full range of ages at which this skill is attained, of course, is considerably greater.

Many other abilities mature. The ability to perceive the world matures; the ability to grasp objects (called *prehension*) matures and goes through a sequence of orderly maturational steps. The ability to use language also seems to mature; presumably, connections must be made within the brain and biochemical changes must take place there before speech areas can function. Again there is an orderly sequence of changes; some of the major milestones in speech and motor development are compared in Table 2.1. Thus at age 2 most children can run and walk up and down stairs with one foot forward; at the same age they usually have a vocabulary of about 50 words, and two-word phrases are common. (It is interesting to compare this language development of the human at age 2 with that of a slightly older chimpanzee, an animal with a different species heritage—see the previous section.)

Readiness for learning Maturation governs not only specific behaviors but also certain readinesses, or potentialities. Some things, obviously, are never acquired by maturation alone; they must be learned. A person does not acquire the ability to read or to do arithmetic by maturation alone; he has to learn to do it. But maturation plays an essential role even in such skills; what matures is the readiness, or potentiality, for

Age (years)	Some motor milestones	Some speech milestones
1	Stands; walks when held by one hand	Syllabic reduplication (repeats syllables over and over); signs of understanding some words; applies some sounds regularly to signify persons or objects—that is, says his first words
1.5	Prehension and release fully developed; gait propulsive; creeps downstairs backward	Repertoire of 3 to 50 words not joined in phrases; trains of sounds and intonation patterns resembling discourse; good progress in understanding
2	Runs (with falls); walks stairs with one foot forward only	More than 50 words; two-word phrases most common; more interest in verbal communication; no more babbling
2.5	Jumps with both feet; stands on one foot for 1 second; builds tower of six cubes	Every day new words; utterances of three and more words; seems to understand almost everything said to him; still many grammatical deviations
3	Tiptoes 3 yards; walks stairs with alternating feet; jumps 1 yard	Vocabulary of some 1,000 words; about 80 percent intelligibility; grammar of utterances close approximation to colloquial adult; syntactic mistakes fewer in variety, systematic, predictable
4.5	Jumps over rope; hops on one foot; walks on line	Language well established; grammatical anomalies restricted either to unusual constructions or to the more literate aspects of discourse

Table 2.1 *Motor and speech development compared.*

Source: After Lenneberg, 1969.

learning them. Until the readiness appears in the schedule of maturation, there is no point in attempting to learn them.

The following case dramatically illustrates this point (Davis, 1947):

A deaf-mute mother hid her infant daughter from practically all outside contact until she was more than 6 years old. The child was thus deprived of almost all opportunity to learn spoken language. When neighbors discovered the child at 6, she could not speak; she uttered only incomprehensible sounds. In 2 months of training, however, she learned many words. By that time too, she started putting sentences together as fast as a child normally does at 3 years of age. Of course, she had to learn the vocabulary of English and the rules of constructing sentences, but her progress was rapid. Her case demonstrates that the capacity or readiness for learning language is something that matures without practice, even though learning is required to develop skill.

There are many kinds of readiness. Generally, each appears at a characteristic age. Readiness for learning speech typically matures in a child's second year, that for learning to read at about 6 years. In each case, the readiness appears rather abruptly, usually over the course of a few weeks. When it comes, the child's progress in learning takes a spurt. Before he is ready, he learns slowly, and training is almost useless. When he is ready, he learns rapidly if he has the opportunity to learn. From observations such as these we infer that a characteristic time arrives for the maturation of an ability or readiness.

All children, however, do not mature at the same rate. Some mature slowly, others rapidly. In general, if one ability matures slowly, others

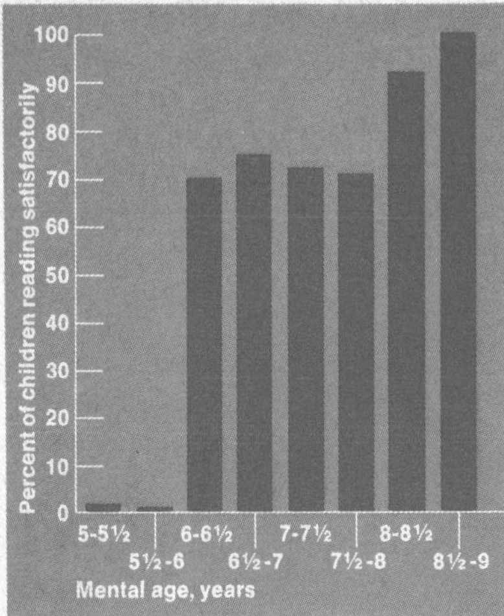

AT MENTAL AGE 6, BUT NOT MUCH BEFORE, A CHILD IS READY TO LEARN TO READ

Figure 2.7 *Reading readiness and mental age. The number of children making satisfactory progress in learning to read jumps rapidly between the mental ages of 6 and 6½ years. (Morphett and Washburn, 1931. By permission of The University of Chicago Press.)*

will too, though this is not always so. A child's overall rate of maturation of abilities is something that can be measured. It is, in fact, just what intelligence tests for children do measure. Most children's intelligence tests sample several of a child's abilities and supply an overall score called a *mental age* (MA). The MA is arrived at by comparing the child's score with that of average children at various age levels. If, for example, a child's overall ability is the same as that of the average 6-year-old, he is given an MA of 6, regardless of what his *chronological age* (CA) happens to be. Thus the MA is the measure of an individual's general level of maturation of abilities. The IQ is simply MA/CA multiplied by 100 (see Chapter 10).

The point that each readiness comes to maturity fairly abruptly can be demonstrated by using the MA to match children on their maturational level and then comparing them on some skill, such as reading (Morphett and Washburn, 1931):

One hundred and forty-one children were given an intelligence test when they entered the first grade. The test furnished an MA for each child. About halfway through the year, without knowing the test results, teachers rated each child on his progress in learning to read, giving him either a "satisfactory" or an "unsatisfactory." Figure 2.7 shows that the percentage of children making satisfactory progress in reading rises sharply from zero to about 70 percent during the 6 months between an MA of 6 years and an MA of 6½ years. We would not have seen this jump, however, if the CA of the children had been used, for they were all about 6 years old, and slight differences among them in CA were inconsequential.

The practical implication of studies such as these is that we must wait until an ability or readiness is mature before attempting to teach skills that depend on readiness. Our common practice in the United States of programming the education of children on the basis of CA does not recognize this point. Children 6 years old vary in general readiness, that is, in MA. For instance, some of them may have MAs of 4½ or 5; others may have MAs of 8 or 9. The child of low MA cannot profit from training until he is considerably older, chronologically, than the child of very high MA. Since the time to start training in reading is at a mental age of 6 to 6½, the common practice of admitting children to school at a CA of 6 is all right for average children, but not for duller and brighter ones.

Thus our species heritage determines when certain behaviors and potentialities will mature during the first few years of life. Except for a few basic patterns of behavior such as walking, our species heritage does not give us fixed action patterns. At most it provides certain potentialities and readinesses for learning. Later in the chapter we shall see how our species heritage and environmental forces interact to shape our patterns of behavior.

Individual Genetic Constitution

Our species heritage, as we have seen, sets broad limits on behavior. But within the limits and framework established by our evolutionary species heritage, each of us inherits somewhat different tendencies for behavior.

These inherited individual differences may be called our *individual genetic constitutions,* the study of which forms a large part of the field of *behavior genetics.*

In the history of thought about human nature, many observations have been made on the pedigrees of famous men. For example, the Bach family contained an extraordinary number of eminent musicians. Perhaps such musicianship could be traced to differences in individual genetic constitution; perhaps the brain areas controlling coordination of the fingers were well developed in this family. But unfortunately such pedigree studies are somewhat ambiguous because we cannot be sure of the role played by the environment, or *nurture,* in the development of the behaviors under study.

One way to show that individual traits are genetic is by differential breeding for the behavior. To begin to establish a behavioral trait of a certain species as genetic, we might breed together those individuals with a high degree of the trait under study; we would also breed together individuals with a low degree of the trait. We would keep the environmental conditions constant and test the offspring of the two groups through successive generations. If we obtained a clear separation of behavior on the trait in this *differential breeding* experiment, we would begin to believe that the trait under study has a genetic component (look ahead to Figure 2.11).

Our study of behavior genetics will be aided by knowing a few basic genetic concepts, which are discussed next. Then we shall explore the inheritance of intelligence, the inheritance of emotionality, and the inheritance of schizophrenia.

Mechanisms of heredity Human individual differences begin at conception. There is no behavior until about 8 weeks after conception, 7 months before birth, but behavior is greatly affected by the genetic potential received at conception. At conception, two *germ cells,* one a *sperm cell* from the father and the other an *egg cell,* or *ovum,* from the mother, unite to form a new individual, at this stage called a *zygote.* Each of the two germ cells, sperm and ovum, which unite to form the zygote, consists of a dark nucleus surrounded by a light watery substance, the *cytoplasm.* The whole cell, nucleus and cytoplasm, is enclosed in a membrane. When the two cells form a zygote, they merge their parts into a single cell of the same general structure. The part of the zygote that interests us here is the nucleus, for it contains the genetic material that transmits hereditary characteristics from the parents to the new individual.

CHROMOSOMES The genetic material consists of *chromosomes* and *genes.* The genes are the real genetic units, but they are carried on chromosomes.

The term *chromosome* means colored body, and it is so called because it stains darkly when treated with special dyes. It can then be seen under the microscope as a twisted string of odd-sized and odd-shaped beads in the nucleus of the cell. Chromosomes are visible in most of the cells of the body. But only the chromosomes in the sperm, egg, and zygote have anything to do with inheritance. The merger of the

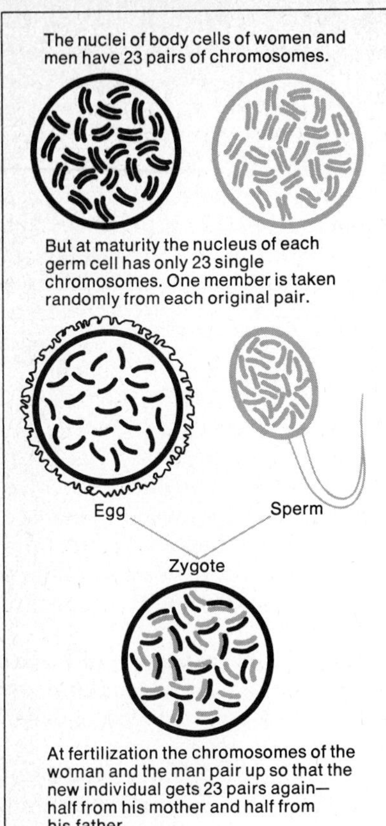

A NEW INDIVIDUAL IS FORMED BY THE UNION OF THE MOTHER'S EGG AND THE FATHER'S SPERM

Figure 2.8 *The mechanism of transmission of chromosomes from parents to offspring.*

chromosomes of the egg cell and the sperm cell, when they form the zygote, is the only genetic link between an individual and his parents.

Each species of animal has a characteristic number of chromosomes per cell. In the case of man, the number is 46. The chromosomes occur in pairs: thus human chromosomes are arranged in 23 pairs (see Figure 2.8). The egg and sperm cells, however, pass through a stage in their production when the pairs of chromosomes split apart, leaving only one of each pair—a set of 23 single chromosomes—for each germ cell. The two single sets from the sperm and egg combine to make new pairs when the sperm and egg unite. Therefore, as Figure 2.8 shows, we find 23 pairs of chromsomes in the zygote.

GENES Genes are carried on the chromosomes, and for our purposes they may be thought of as the units of heredity. They are complex chemical packets, very probably parts of the large *deoxyribonucleic acid* (DNA) molecules found in the nuclei of cells. Because of their composition and chainlike construction, DNA molecules can carry the code both for their own reproduction and for the ultimate production of substances, called enzymes, which control the formation of proteins within a cell.

The modern concept of a gene is that it is "a functional area required for the formation of an enzyme" (Bonner, 1961). By controlling enzymes and thus the production of proteins within a cell, and by somehow influencing the interaction of cells with each other, genes are able to determine the kind of tissues formed to make the various organs and the structure of the body. That is to say, they direct the course of the body's development. This is the basic mechanism of inheritance, for it is in this way that genes duplicate in the new individual the characteristics present (whether visible or not) in his ancestors.

Genes always work in pairs, one member of which comes from the mother and the other from the father. A pair of genes working together directs the development of some particular characteristic of the body or of behavior. Sometimes two genes in a pair are identical even though they come from different parents. Then there is no doubt about the characteristic they will produce. If, for example, each gene of a pair is so constituted that it will produce blue eyes, the new individual will certainly have blue eyes; or if both genes are "brown-eyed," the individual will surely have brown eyes.

Often two genes of a pair are not identical, but govern the same characteristic in slightly different ways. In other words, slightly different genes may be present at the corresponding places on the chromosomes from the mother and father. The different kinds of genes which may be present at a place on a chromosome are called *alleles.* Many alleles may be present at one location. For instance, there are three alleles which determine human A, B, AB, and O blood types. Usually one gene is dominant over the others, and the outcome that we observe depends upon which gene is dominant and which genes are recessive. A *dominant gene* is one whose characteristic will show up when paired with another gene; it produces the observable characteristic—the *phenotype.* A *recessive gene,* conversely, is one whose characteristic will not be observable when it is paired with a dominant gene. As Figure 2.9 demon-

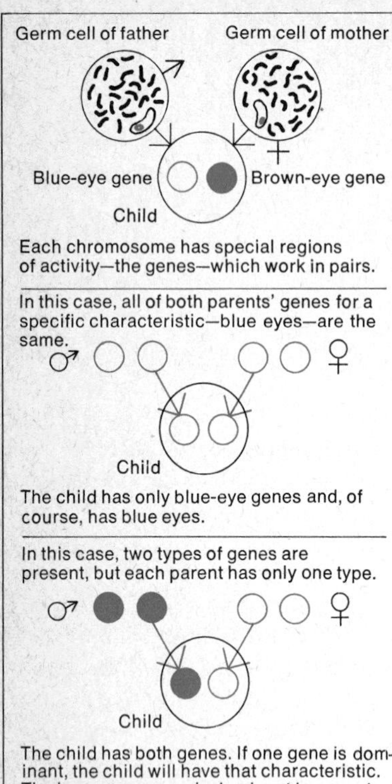

INHERITANCE OF EYE COLOR: DOMINANCE AND RECESSIVENESS

Figure 2.9 *The inheritance of brown and blue eyes. Brown is the dominant gene; if both brown-eye and blue-eye genes are present in the child, he will have brown eyes.*

strates, brown eyes are a dominant characteristic, and blue eyes are a recessive one.

The actual genetic constitution of an individual—the *genotype*—may contain the recessive gene, but its effect is not expressed. The only way we can tell that the recessive gene is there is by knowing that one parent possessed the recessive characteristic, or by observing that some of the offspring of the person have the recessive characteristic. The offspring can have the recessive characteristic only when both of the genes governing a particular trait are recessive. This can happen only when both mother and father have the recessive genes which, by chance, may pair to determine a certain characteristic. Table 2.2 lists common characteristics that may be either dominant or recessive.

MULTIPLE DETERMINATION Traits that are determined by a single pair of genes, such as the traits given in Table 2.2, nicely illustrate the basic principles of genetics. In general, these simply determined traits depend on the presence or absence of some one thing in a tissue or organ of the body. Eye color, for example, is a matter of pigmentation of the iris. The pigmented iris is brown, the unpigmented appears blue. Color blindness is probably caused by lack of a photosensitive substance in the eye. Something as complex as a particular kind of mental retardation can sometimes even be traced to a single pair of genes. In such cases the individual lacks a single substance in the brain necessary for its normal functioning. Hence traits that are determined by single pairs of genes depend on the presence or absence of some one thing in the body that affects the structure or appearance of an organ.

Many traits, obviously, depend on more than one thing. For example, athletic ability, intelligence, temperament, and susceptibility to some mental illnesses, or behavior disorders, have a hereditary basis, although they are not entirely determined by heredity. Insofar as they are, they are determined by many pairs of genes, not just one. In some cases of multiple determination, usually where a small number of genes is involved in establishing a characteristic, geneticists have been able to work out the rules of inheritance. In most cases of multiple determination, however, this has been impossible, just because the situation has proved too complicated. Without knowing the rules, it is nevertheless possible to conclude from well-designed studies of inbreeding and crossbreeding that a particular trait is an instance of multiple determination. A little later we shall discuss some studies of the hereditary bases of intelligence, emotionality, and behavior disorders.

FAMILY INHERITANCE Each species of animal, man included, has its set of chromosomes and genes that determine the particular characteristics of the species. Within a species, the combination of genes an individual receives is a matter of chance. First, it is chance that determines which member of a pair of genes goes into a sperm or egg when the pairs of chromosomes are divided into single sets. Consequently, no two sperm or egg cells are alike, for each receives a random set of genes. Second, it is purely by chance that a particular sperm fuses with a particular egg to form a zygote. Since the number of genes is very large, the

***Table* 2.2** *Some dominant and recessive characteristics.*

Source: Modified from Krech et al., 1969.

Dominant	Recessive
Brown eyes	Blue eyes
Dark or brunette hair	Light, blond, or red hair
Curly hair	Straight hair
Normal hair	Baldness
Normal color vision	Color blindness
Normal sight	Night blindness
Normal hearing	Congenital deafness
Normal coloring	Albinism (lack of pigment)
Immunity to poison ivy	Susceptibility to poison ivy
Normal blood	Hemophilia (lack of blood clotting)

number of possible combinations of genes is astronomical. There is an extremely small chance that any two individuals can have exactly the same genetic makeup. We therefore expect individuals to differ widely in their heredity and thus in their traits.

Individuals of the same family, however, can be expected to have similar genes and traits. Each parent contributes half of his genes to his child, and the child in turn contributes half of his genes to his children. Although each half is unique, it often happens that some of the genes of a brother and sister are identical. So too are some of the genes of parent and child. Thus it is to be expected that brothers and sisters will resemble each other, and their parents as well, in some traits. A child may also resemble a grandparent, but to a lesser degree, for a child on the average receives only a quarter (one-half of one-half) of the genes of a particular grandparent.

In only one case can two or more individuals have absolutely identical heredities. This is the case of *identical twins* (or identical triplets, identical quadruplets, and so on). Identical twins develop from the same zygote. If a zygote divides into two cells, each separately goes on to form a new individual. Since each cell has the same genes as the zygote, the heredity of the two individuals will be identical. Developing as they do from a single zygote, identical twins are sometimes known as *monozygotic* (MZ) twins. Since sex is determined genetically, monozygotic twins will always be of the same sex; they will also be identical in many other respects (see Figure 2.10).

Not all twins, however, are identical. Most twins are fraternal twins—twins that develop from two separate eggs of the mother and hence begin as two zygotes formed independently by the union of two different sperms with two different ova. Fraternal twins, often called *dizygotic* (DZ) twins, are no more alike genetically than ordinary brothers and sisters *(siblings)* born at different times. Fraternal twins may or may not be the same sex. Hence when twins are not the same sex, they are fraternal, not identical. The only unique thing about fraternal twins is that they are born at the same time and thus have more similar environments, both before and after birth, than brothers or sisters born separately.

Twins are extremely useful in the study of the relative contributions of heredity and environment to behavior. Since identical twins have identi-

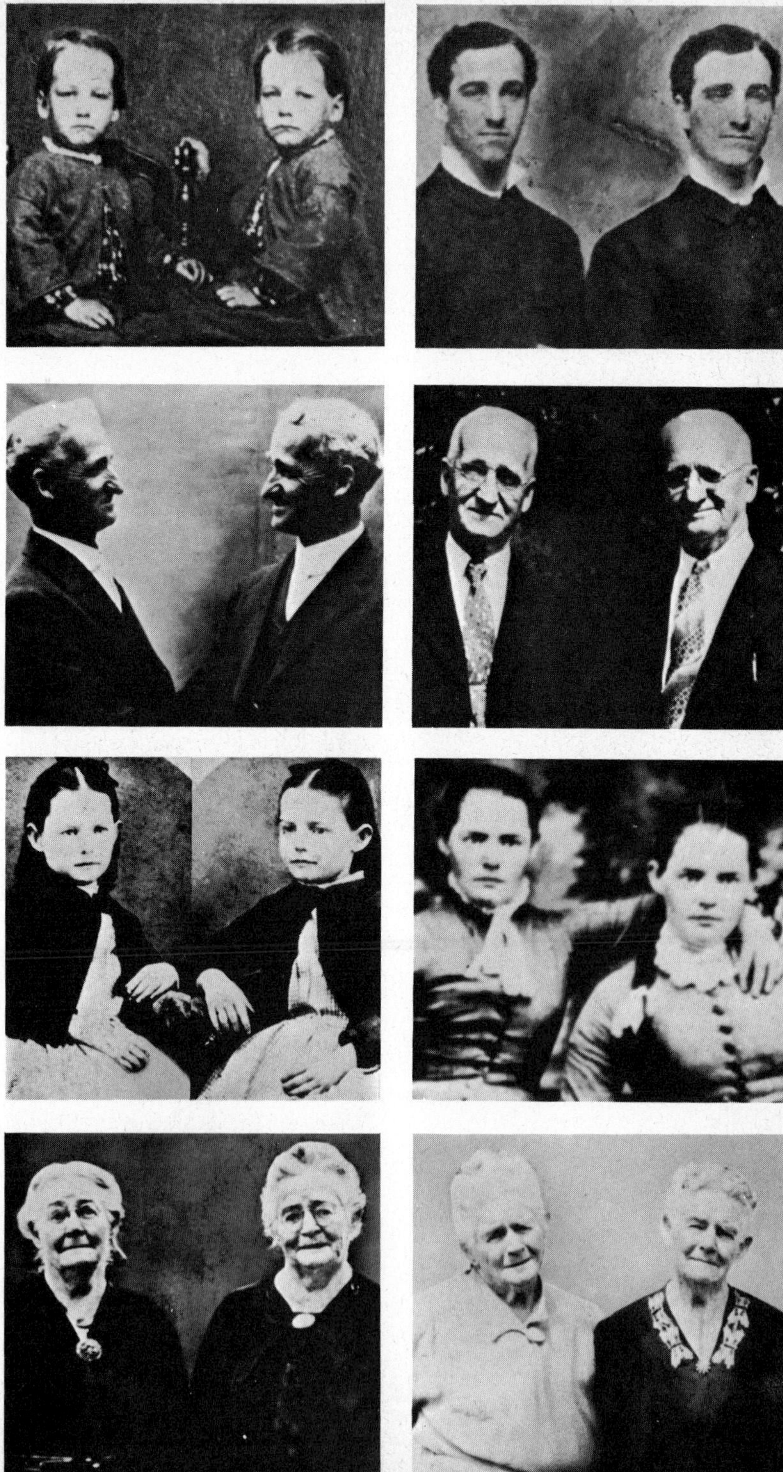

Figure 2.10 *Identical twins have the same heredity. The hereditary potentialities bequeathed at birth persist throughout life. (From Kallmann and Jarvik, 1959. By permission of L. F. Jarvik, J. E. Birren, and The University of Chicago Press.)*

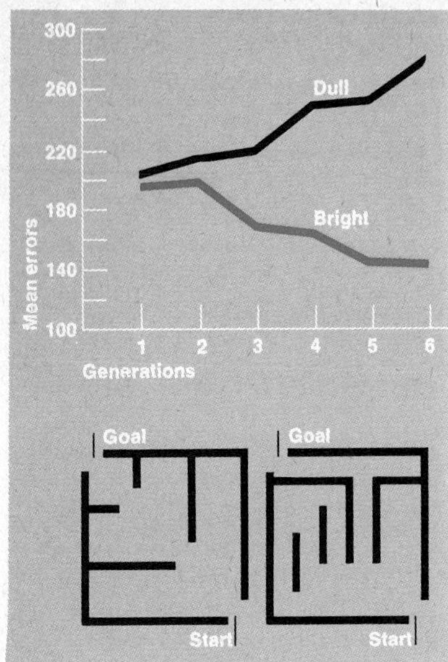

RATS CAN BE BRED FOR "DULLNESS" AND "BRIGHTNESS"

Figure 2.11 *Results of selective breeding for rat "intelligence." The performance of several generations of "dull" and "bright" rats in a Hebb-Williams maze, where a rat must find its way around a set of barriers to reach a food box. A series of problems with the barriers in different positions is presented. (Two sample problems are shown at bottom.) The total number of errors a rat makes is the measure of its maze-learning ability, or "intelligence." (Based on Thompson, 1954; Rabinovitch and Rosvold, 1951.)*

cal heredities, any differences between them must be explained on the basis of different environments. But since fraternal twins are no more alike genetically than ordinary siblings, differences between fraternal twins could be attributed to genetics only if their environments were identical—a situation which cannot be achieved.

The inheritance of intelligence Intelligence is a difficult concept to define. When we are discussing lower animals, it may not even be an appropriate term; perhaps in such cases we should speak of an aptitude for adjustment to various environmental situations. In man, intelligence is a general term covering a person's aptitude in a wide range of tasks involving vocabulary, numbers, problem solving, spatial relationships, and so on. It is measured by standardized tests which usually evaluate several aptitudes, with emphasis on verbal skills (see Chapter 10). A score on an intelligence test can be converted into an *intelligence quotient*, or *IQ*, which indicates the individual's relative standing in the population. Since such an intelligence quotient reflects several aptitudes, not just one, and since each of these in itself is fairly complex, we should expect to find that the inheritance of intelligence in both animals and humans is determined by many genes. And this seems to be the case.

LOWER ANIMAL STUDIES Even though it is difficult to define intelligence in animals, a number of differential rearing studies have developed strains of animals differing in learning, or problem-solving, ability. For instance, Tryon (1940) started with a group of rats and selectively bred the best maze learners with the best maze learners and the worst with the worst. As breeding of this sort continued, a clear separation of "maze bright" and "maze dull" rats was found. The following experiment illustrates a selective breeding experiment in which the problem-solving task is probably somewhat more difficult than a simple maze (Thompson, 1954):

The apparatus used was a Hebb-Williams maze, a kind of "intelligence test" for rats. It consists simply of a square enclosure with a starting box in one corner and a food box in the opposite corner. The hungry rat must find its way from the start box to the food box. But the problem is complicated by putting a series of barriers between the starting box and the food box so that the animal must make detours to reach the food box. The number of errors made in a series of problems is the measure of "intelligence" in the Hebb-Williams maze.

Selective breeding was done in an attempt to develop individuals which made few errors—"bright" rats—and those which made many errors—"dull" rats. By breeding dulls with dulls and brights with brights for six generations, a pronounced separation of strain behaviors in this maze was obtained (see Figure 2.11). Such a finding is partial evidence for the genetic basis of an adaptive ability and a kind of "rat intelligence."

But it is difficult to specify the actual genetic basis of this adaptive ability in terms of the genes and chromosomes involved. Perhaps the ability is too complexly controlled to permit such an analysis; then too, perhaps the rat is too complex an animal for genetic studies of the chro-

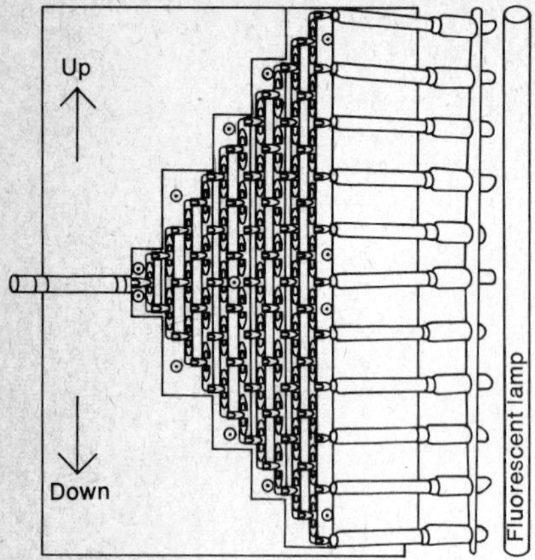

UP OR DOWN? THE FRUIT FLY INHERITS THE ANSWER

Figure 2.12 *A maze used to study the genetic basis of geotaxis (the instinctive tendency to move either with or against the force of gravity) in fruit flies. Flies put into the tube at left are lured through the vertically oriented maze by a light at the other end. Those with a strong positive geotaxis move downward and collect in the lowermost tube at right; those with strong negative geotaxis collect in the topmost tube at right. Those with weaker geotactic tendencies find their way into one of the middle tubes. By selectively breeding the flies which moved upward or downward through the maze, the experimenter eventually produced two distinct fruit fly strains—one with strong positive and one with strong negative geotaxis. (After Hirsch, 1959.)*

mosomal control of the behavior being studied. In order to study the actual genetic mechanisms of behavior, simpler tasks and simpler animals have been used (Hirsch and Erlenmeyer-Kimling, 1962):

The animals used in this experiment were fruit flies, the standard animal for chromosome analysis because of its genetic simplicity and its ability to breed rapidly. The behavior studied was *geotaxis*—the instinctive tendency of animals to go against or with gravitational forces. Negative geotaxis, going against the force of gravity, and positive geotaxis, going with the pull of gravity, were measured in a special apparatus shown in Figure 2.12 (Hirsch, 1959). The flies were put in the single tube at the left and, after making a series of choices, arrived at one of the final collecting tubes at the right. The flies flew through the maze because another taxis, *phototaxis,* was at work—they were attracted toward a fluorescent light at the end of the maze. Cones at the choice points prevented retracing. It was a relatively easy matter to make accurate counts of the number of flies entering the final eleven collection tubes. As might be expected, more flies entered the middle collection tubes, but some found their way to the uppermost and some to the lowermost tubes. Those arriving at the uppermost tubes were displaying strong negative geotaxis, while those arriving at the lowermost tubes were showing strong positive geotaxis. Two populations of fruit flies, those with positive and negative geotactic tendencies, were established through many generations of selective breeding. When these populations were compared with each other and with the unselected population, it was found that changes in three chromosomes accounted for a large part of the differences in geotactic behavior.

THE GENETICS OF HUMAN INTELLIGENCE Since differential breeding is impossible in the case of human beings, we must study human genetics by making use of naturally occurring family relationships. A natural family—parents and children who are related by blood—offers us the opportunity to compare individuals who differ in inheritance by various degrees and who have relatively similar environments. To make such a comparison, we use a statistical index called a *correlation coefficient,* which expresses the degree to which pairs of individuals obtain similar scores on certain tests. A correlation of 1.00 indicates perfect agreement (tests, however, are never perfectly reliable, so we never obtain correlations of 1.00). A correlation of 0.00 indicates no relationship; scores are randomly distributed. In between, various degrees of correlation are possible (see Chapter 9).

The bars in Figure 2.13, which represent data from many studies, show average, or median, correlations between pairs of individuals. One set of bars depicts pairs reared together; the other, pairs reared apart. Both demonstrate that IQ correlations vary as a function of degree of closeness of family relationship; the correlations are highest for the closest hereditary relationship—MZ twins—and lowest for unrelated people. But similarity of environment also plays a role; IQ correlations are always higher for the people reared together. Thus measured IQ is a function of both nature, or heredity, and nurture, or environment; we shall have more to say about this shortly.

Similar data, shown in Table 2.3, also indicate that both nature and nurture play a role in the determination of IQ. The highest correlation of

Table 2.3 *Correlations of intelligence scores (IQs) and heights for pairs of individuals with different degrees of relationship.*

Heredity	Relationships	Correlation of intelligence	Correlation of height	Environments
Same	Identical twins*	.88	.93	Very similar
Similar	Fraternal twins (same sex)*	.63	.64	Very similar
	Siblings † ‡	.51–.53	.54–.60	Similar
	Parents and children‡	.49	.51	Similar
Somewhat similar	Grandparents and grandchild‡	.34	.32	Slightly similar
	Uncles (aunts) and nephews (nieces)‡	.35	.29	Slightly similar
Slightly similar	Cousins	.29	.24	Slightly similar

*Newman et al., 1937.
†McNemar, 1942.
‡Burt and Howard, 1956.

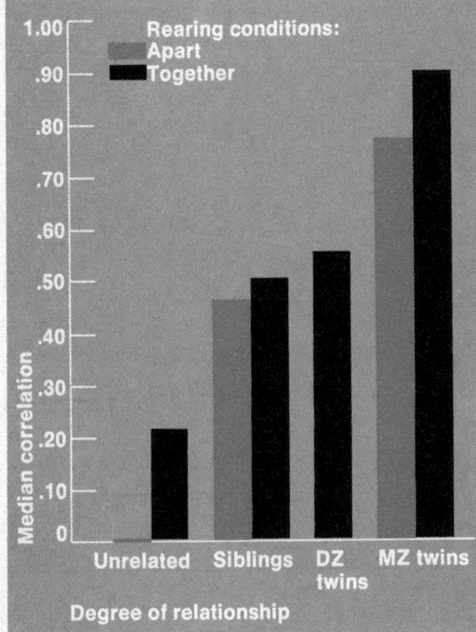

GENETICS, ENVIRONMENT, AND INTELLIGENCE

Figure 2.13 *Median IQ correlations of pairs of individuals with several degrees of relationship. The correlations were obtained from many studies in which family members were brought up apart or together; both rearing conditions are shown for all but the DZ twins. (Too few studies have been made of DZ twins reared apart.) Note that in both conditions, IQ correlations increase with increasing degree of genetic similarity. (Based on Erlenmeyer-Kimling and Jarvik, 1963.)*

.88 is obtained between identical twins, who have the same heredity and very similar environments. The correlation drops to .63 for fraternal twins of the same sex, who have about the same environmental similarity as identical twins but less similarity in heredity. This difference between identical and fraternal twins indicates that heredity is a factor in IQ. The correlation drops again from fraternal twins to siblings, who have about the same degree of hereditary similarity as fraternal twins, but less similarity in their environments. This difference between fraternal twins and siblings indicates that environment is a factor in IQ. Sibling pairs and parent-child pairs have, on the average, about the same degree of hereditary similarity and fairly similar environments. As one might expect, the correlation coefficients for these two kinds of pairs are about the same, although they are slightly lower for the parent-child pairs. There is another drop in correlation for grandparent-grandchild and uncle-nephew pairs, and still another for pairs of cousins.

Note that the correlations for height are about the same as those for intelligence. Height correlations tend to run a little higher than IQ correlations for closely related individuals and a little lower for remotely related ones. But the fact that the two sets of correlations closely parallel each other makes us believe that heredity plays about as important a part in the physical characteristic of height as it does in intelligence.

From studies of this kind, we see that when heredity changes, leaving environment relatively constant, the correlation of intelligence test scores between groups of relatives drops. Hence heredity is a factor in intelligence. On the other hand, when the degree of hereditary similarity remains constant and the similarity of environment changes, the correlations also go down. Hence environment is also a factor. Unfortunately, we cannot tell from such data which is the more important factor, if indeed either is; we can tell only that both are involved.

Table 2.4 *Comparison of IQs of identical twins reared apart.*

Source: Based on Newman et al., 1937.

Number of twin pairs	Educational advantage	Age at separation (in months)	Average difference in IQ between twins	Superiority in IQ points of twins with greater advantages
6	Very unequal (5.1 on 10-point scale)	15	15.2	15.2
7	Somewhat unequal (2.4 on 10-point scale)	9	5.4	4.6
6	Relatively similar (1.6 on 10-point scale)	24	4.5	1.0

To evaluate the relative roles of heredity and environment in intelligence, we must refer to another kind of study, one that is more difficult to do. Such a study seeks to compare the intelligence of identical twins reared apart in different environments. Heredity is thereby held constant while environment varies. In one study, 19 sets of twins were tested (Newman et al., 1937):

Most of the twins had been separated at less than 2 years of age, although one pair parted as late as 6. The intelligence of each set of twins was tested later, at ages varying from 11 to 59, but twins in each pair were tested at the same age. To obtain a measure of the different environments of each twin, judges independently rated their educational advantages on a scale of 1 to 10. From such ratings, the sets of twins could be divided into three general groups: those with very dissimilar environments, those with very similar environments, and those in between (see Table 2.4). Twins with nearly similar environments differed hardly at all in intelligence. But those who had very dissimilar environments differed by sizable amounts—on the average, 15 points. Those in between differed by about 5 points, which is not a particularly significant difference.

We may therefore conclude that a relatively poor environment handicaps a person's intelligence quotient. It is interesting, however, that the correlation between the IQs of identical twins reared apart was .77. This is somewhat poorer than the .88 shown in Table 2.3 for identical twins reared together, but it is still better than that for fraternal twins and siblings reared together. Thus again we find that both heredity and environment are important in intelligence. This interesting and complex relationship between heredity and environment, or nature and nurture, is discussed in the last section of the chapter.

Inheritance of emotional responsivity It seems fairly obvious that emotionality has some hereditary basis. For instance, marked differences in savageness occur among wild and domesticated animals. Gray rats, wolves, and lions are savagely emotional, whereas their domesticated counterparts—white rats, dogs, and cats—are relatively less prone to fierce emotional outbursts. It is true, of course, that wild animals can be tamed to some degree if the process is started early enough. But they seldom, if ever, become as placid as the commonly domesticated animals. Even when they are raised entirely in human company, many species of wild animals, such as the chimpanzee, are still potentially dangerous by the time they reach adulthood. Conversely, if normally tame animals, such as the cat and dog, are allowed to grow up away from human beings, they become relatively wild. But they are still more tamable than animals whose ancestors have always been wild.

The case for emotional inheritance does not rest on such uncontrolled observation, however. Hereditary factors in emotion have been studied experimentally. Some years ago, savageness and tameness were compared in the wild gray rat and the laboratory white rat (Stone, 1932):

The white rat, gently handled in the first few months of life, easily becomes tame enough to pose no threat to the experimenter. But the wild gray rat, although it improves somewhat with taming procedures, always remains a tense, emotional animal, ready to attack and bite at the least provocation. When the two are crossbred, some of the young inherit the relatively tame disposition of the white parent, others the savageness of the gray parent. Savageness, moreover, is linked to hair color—but to the tan pigment factor rather than to gray. The hair of the wild rat appears to be gray because it is a mixture of two colors: a light tan, and a brown so dark that it is practically black. These two pigment factors are separable genetically. In the crossing of white and wild gray rats, if the young inherit the tan pigment, they will be savage; if they inherit the black pigment or no pigment at all (white hair color), they will be tame. Thus it has been possible to develop a strain of black rats which are almost as tame or tamable as the white rat and which are now frequently used in laboratories. But no such strain of tan rats has been developed.

In another experiment, rats selected from various laboratory colonies were tested in an *open-field situation* and crossbred (Hall, 1938).

The "open-field" is a large compartment that usually elicits fear, as evidenced by copious urination and defecation, when rats are first placed in it. The amount of such emotional behavior in 145 rats was objectively measured in a 2-minute test given each day for a number of days. On succeeding days, the rats habituated to the situation and showed less and less fear.

Of the original 145 rats, 7 of the most emotional females were mated with 7 of the most emotional males. Similarly, 7 of the least emotional males were mated with 7 unemotional females. This kind of inbreeding was continued for several generations. The results were striking even in the first generation. The offspring of emotional animals were considerably more emotional than those of unemotional animals. In fact, the scores of the emotional group were seven times those of the other group.

Such experiments leave no doubt that savageness and fear in the rat are largely determined by heredity. This conclusion has been confirmed in other animals, particularly in the dog (Scott, 1958). Unfortunately, the problem has not been studied extensively in human beings. There is one experiment, however, that has some bearing on the question (Jost and Sontag, 1944):

Children between 6 and 12 years of age were studied over a 3-year period. Various bodily states known to be associated with emotion were measured, including skin resistance, pulse and respiration rates, and salivation. Although the measurements were not of emotionality itself, presumably these bodily states are part of emotional expression. Pairs of identical twins, pairs of siblings, and pairs of unrelated children were used. The idea was to see whether the twins, with identical heredity, were more alike than siblings or unrelated children in bodily states associated with emotion. Correlation coefficients were used to express the degree of similarity in bodily reactions between pairs of twins, pairs of siblings, and pairs of unrelated children. (Remember that the highest possible correlation coefficient is 1.00; the lowest possible, 0.00. Relatively high correlation coefficients indicate that there is a great deal of similarity between members of a pair; low correlation coefficients indicate little similarity.) When the correlations of the scores on the different measures were combined, the results over the three years of the study were:

	Year 1	Year 2	Year 3
Identical twins	.434	.470	.489
Siblings	.255	.406	.288
Unrelated	.164	.017	.080

The correlations are not high, probably because measures of bodily states vary considerably from time to time. But the correlations between identical twins are consistently higher than those for siblings, which in turn are higher than those for unrelated individuals. On the whole, these relationships indicate that heredity has a role in the bodily states concerned in emotion.

All indications are that emotionality is at least in part an inherited characteristic in both human beings and animals. More research on the inheritance of emotionality in human beings is sorely needed, however, in order to determine in what degree it is inherited, in what learned.

Inheritance of behavior disorders Good evidence exists for the inheritance of tendencies for certain types of behavioral, or emotional, disorders. The manic-depressive psychosis, for instance, is a behavior disorder characterized by very wide swings of mood from depression to elation; it has been shown to have a hereditary basis (Kallmann, 1951). But the behavior disorder most studied with regard to inheritance is schizophrenia (Rosenthal and Kety, 1968).

Schizophrenia, contrary to popular belief, is not a "split personality" in the Jekyll-Hyde sense. Instead, it is a serious behavioral or emotional disorder characterized by the following symptoms: confused, bizarre, and rigid patterns of thought; inappropriate emotional responses; deficiency in the ability to feel pleasure and displeasure; and suspiciousness of other people (see Chapter 12). Not all these symptoms are invariably present in a particular person suffering from schizophrenia. Other symptoms may also appear in some patients. Some schizophrenics

Table 2.5 *The incidence of schizophrenia and related disorders in pairs of monozygotic twins. The findings summarized here provide strong evidence that both schizophrenia itself and related behavioral problems are inherited.*

Source: Based on Heston, 1970.

Investigator	MZ twin pairs	Schizophrenia	Other significant abnormality	Normal, or mild abnormality
Essen-Möller	9	0	8	1
Slater	37	18	11	8
Tienari	16	1	12	3
Kringlen	45	14	17	14
Inouye	53	20	29	4
Gottesman and Shields	24	10	8	6
Kallmann	174	103	62	9
Totals	358	166 (46.4%)	147 (41.1%)	45 (12.6%)

may have *hallucinations*—sensory experiences for which no appropriate stimulation of the receptors exists—and *delusions*—bizarre ideas which usually center around thoughts of persecution or of grandeur.

Is the tendency for this and related behavior disorders inherited? Table 2.5 gives some of the data on the incidence of schizophrenia and related disorders in MZ twins. If one member of the MZ twin pair develops schizophrenia, in 46 percent of the cases the other one develops it also; in about 41 percent of the cases the other twin develops a severe behavioral problem. Thus in only about 13 percent of the cases is the MZ twin of a schizophrenic free from a diagnosed psychiatric disorder. Other statistics on DZ twin pairs and pairs of siblings show agreement with respect to schizophrenia in about 12 percent of the cases (Slater, 1968)—a figure far higher than the 1 percent incidence of schizophrenia in the population as a whole. From such data it may be argued that both heredity and environment play a role in the origin of schizophrenia. But the difference between the percentages of agreement in DZ and MZ twins is strong evidence for a genetic basis of the tendency toward schizophrenia. So is the high occurrence of related disorders in the MZ twin brothers or sisters of schizophrenics.

Nature and Nurture

We have seen that we have a species heritage and individual genetic constitutions which contribute to behavior. These make up our "animal nature." But it is obvious that influences from the environment, or *nurture,* also contribute a great deal to behavior. We have already touched on the joint contribution of nature and nurture to measured IQ; we shall discuss environmental factors in the origins of schizophrenia in Chapter 12; and in Chapter 3 we shall focus on learning as one of the principal agents through which the environment exerts its influence. But now we want to say more about the joint contributions of nature and nurture.

The relative contributions of nature and nurture, or heredity and environment, in the determination of particular behaviors have long been the subject of much debate. Part of the difficulty has arisen because the problem has been cast in terms of nature *versus* nurture or heredity *versus* environment. The "versus" gets into the discussion because people often argue for one against the other, taking either the view that a man's hereditary nature pretty much determines the kind of person he can be, or the contrary view that men are more or less equal in heredity and that the environment in which they are nurtured determines what they become. But such arguments are really futile, for actually both heredity *and* environment, or nature *and* nurture, jointly fashion a person's abilities, skills, and psychological characteristics. The problem is not to choose between them but rather to recognize the contributions made by each in determining particular behaviors.

Inheritance seems to set the broad limits—the potentialities—for behavior. Nurture, or the environment, seems to determine whether the potentialities will be realized. For instance, a person may have the genetic potentiality to be tall, but this potentiality may fail to be expressed because of factors in the environment, such as malnutrition early in life. Another way of saying this, with our previous discussion of hereditary mechanisms in mind, is that such a person has the *genotype*—potentiality—for being tall, but that the *phenotype*—the thing which is actually observed—is the result of the joint action of nature (the genotype) and nurture (malnutrition, in this case).

Interaction of nature and nurture While we might think of nature—the genotype in this case—as contributing potentialities for behavior, we should not think that it sets fixed genetic limits for behavior. Such fixed limits do not exist, because the genotype must always act through the environment to produce the observed behavior—the phenotype. In other words, genotypes can be expressed in many different phenotypes; a range of outcomes is possible from a single genotype. The genotype puts flexible boundaries on this range. It does not, in higher animals, set limits or specify particular behaviors. The behavior of an individual, then, always depends upon the *interaction* of his genotype with his particular environment; it does not depend simply upon his genotype. One implication of this interaction is that it is not really meaningful to ask about the relative contributions of heredity and environment in a particular person. The behavior of the individual as we observe it—the phenotype—is for each person the result of a set of interactions unique to him. We can only unravel the contributions of nature and nurture and their interaction by studying groups, or populations, of people or animals. The range of reactions possible from a single genotype should also make us skeptical of statements attributing differences between groups—in measured IQ, for example—to a simple genetic difference.

Studies of the contributions of nature and nurture to behavior We have already considered some differential breeding studies on the contribution of nature to behavior. We have also discussed studies of human families that attempt to evaluate the roles of nature and nurture in behavior. There are several other strategies that have been used to attack this complicated problem. One strategy is the *epigenetic* approach to the study of the development of behavior (Kuo, 1967). This approach focuses on the *interaction* of nature and nurture. Other strategies attempt to make a rough evaluation of nature and nurture in the development of behavior by manipulating the early environment in some way.

THE EPIGENETIC APPROACH In the epigenetic approach to the study of nature-nurture interactions, the intertwining of the two elements is seen clearly. For instance, some behaviors of young animals are genetically controlled and are instinctive, but the environment (nurture) plays a role in shaping these behaviors until the final form of the behavior is no longer a simple matter of the expression of a genotype. Then this newly shaped behavior modifies other behaviors as they emerge. So the sequence goes something like this: Genetically controlled behavior is modified and shaped by the environment; this newly shaped behavior then interacts with other genetically controlled behaviors to modify them and be modified by them; and so on. The essence of the epigenetic approach is that there is a continual interplay between genetically controlled behaviors and the environment during the course of development. The outcome of this interplay is the phenotype—the observed behavior. This approach should remind us again that the genetic contribution to behavior is that of a potential interacting with environmental influences.

The following example will make this idea a little clearer (Hailman, 1969):

This study concerned the accuracy of the pecking behavior of laughing gull chicks—a common seagull of Eastern North America. The hungry chicks peck at the red bill of adults and stimulate them to regurgitate food in this way. To test accuracy of pecking, schematic models of the gull head were drawn on cards and records were made of the number of hits made by the chicks on the red bill drawn on the cards. On the first day after hatching, about 33 percent of the pecks were hits; on the fourth day, about 80 percent were hits.

It seems, then, that genetics provides the basis for pecking—the machinery and the motivation—but experience in the environment, and perhaps the reward of getting fed (see page 76), is necessary to perfect the genetically given potentiality. As the chick grows, pecking is incorporated into new and more complex behavior, and still more new behaviors emerge that interact with the earlier behaviors to modify them. So the epigenetic mix, or mosaic, of nature and nurture unfolds. As we indicated earlier in the chapter, such an analysis indicates that, even in lower animals, instincts are not usually simple expressions of genetic potentials; behavior is a complex mix of the unlearned and learned, or of nature and nurture. But this is just restating our conclusion about the genotype and environment in different terms.

IMPOVERISHMENT OR ENRICHMENT OF THE ENVIRONMENT So-called "impoverishment" or "enrichment" studies give us a rough indication of the hereditary or environmental components in the development of behavior. In these studies a developing animal is raised in an environment that is impoverished or enriched in some way. If impoverishment or enrichment makes little difference in the later behavior of the animal, the behavior under study is considered to have a large genetic component. If, on the other hand, the later behavior is affected by the environment during development, a contribution of nurture is considered to have been shown. Here is one example of an impoverishment, or deprivation, study (Harlow, 1962):

As part of a series of studies exploring the effect of early isolation on emotional and social behavior, baby monkeys were raised under several different conditions. Control animals were raised with their mothers and allowed to play with other small monkeys. Experimental monkeys were raised under several different types of isolation conditions. Baby monkeys of one group were taken from their mothers soon after birth and raised alone in cages which allowed them to see and hear, but not play with, other baby monkeys. Other experimental monkeys were raised under conditions of true solitary confinement and not allowed to see or hear other monkeys.

The social, emotional, and sexual behavior of the experimental monkeys from both groups was markedly abnormal. For instance, although sexual motivation was apparently normally strong, the experimental monkeys tended to be inept and ignorant of the rules of monkey "courtship." So inept were they that very few of the isolated female monkeys became pregnant. In fact, these monkeys could not be used for laboratory breeding stock. The isolated monkeys tended not to develop stable social hierarchies or "pecking orders"; nor did they play so vigorously and maturely as the control animals when tested in a special monkey "playroom." The totally isolated monkeys also tended to be submissive and fearful in threatening situations.

The *crucial period* for the development of social skills in the monkey seems to be during the first year, but after the first 3 months of life. Isolation during the first 90 days seemed to produce little effect on social and emotional behavior. It was also found that only a few minutes of social experience each day would prevent the consequences of social isolation. After a monkey had been raised in isolation, however, social experience did little to make behavior more normal.

The major conclusion to be drawn from this experiment is that early nurture contributes much to the development of monkey social-sexual behavior. Such behavior is not established by the genes; input from the environment is required for its development. But we might have expected this result, because we have already seen that instinctive behavior, which is genetically controlled, is practically lacking in man and the higher primates. On the other hand, we have also seen that certain general abilities, such as intelligence, have a large genetic component; we would not expect such abilities to suffer much permanent loss from deprivation, and other impoverishment experiments bear this out (Harlow and Griffin, 1965).

The experiment also illustrates the concept of the *critical period.* The critical-period idea is that the environment will have its greatest effect at a certain time in the life history of the developing organism. Impoverishment of the environment during the first 3 months of life had no effect on monkeys' social-sexual behavior; the critical period for this effect came in the subsequent 9 months. Critical periods for the influence of the environment have been noted in many other studies.

The interpretation of this experiment with monkeys seems fairly straightforward. But questions have arisen about the interpretations of such monkey experiments and of similar experiments with dogs; this is one of the reasons why deprivation experiments are not considered ideal for assessing the contributions of nature and nurture to behavior. The following experiment was one of the early studies of dogs in an impoverished environment (Thompson and Melzack, 1956):

Puppies were raised singly in closed pens that admitted light from the top but denied them any experience with the outside world or with each other. As controls, littermates of these puppies were raised as pets. These conditions were maintained for the first 6 to 9 months of life, at which time the isolated puppies were taken out of their pens and treated like the controls. Differences between the two groups were observed and recorded.

The pups reared in isolation were markedly different. They were naïve and immature in many respects. Strange objects, such as an umbrella or a balloon, readily excited them, whereas the control pups showed little interest in the objects. The isolated pups ran around randomly and generally were more excitable than the controls. In tests of learning to solve specific problems, the isolated pups were greatly inferior to the controls. Even after several years, there were observable differences between the groups. Such specific learning deficiencies may have been related to the increased emotionality of the isolated puppies.

There is no doubt that behavior is altered by deprivation, but in many of these studies it is not clear that nurture is necessary for the actual *development* of behavior in the animals. Deprivation may have effects on behavior not because it interferes with development, but because it works in other ways. One alternative explanation is that the capacity for the behavior exists genetically but that deprivation causes the genetic capacity to deteriorate. Another interpretation is that the animals in the deprived condition have not learned to habituate to the overwhelming array of stimuli in the normal environment. These animals may be emotionally overwhelmed by sudden exposure to so much stimulation at the end of the deprivation period (Fuller, 1967).

Human cases of extreme environmental impoverishment, such as might be seen in certain foundling homes or orphanages, have also been studied. As you might expect, the results are somewhat ambiguous, and control groups are often lacking. Most of the studies have been concerned with measured IQ, and most have found IQ deficits during the period of early deprivation. Yet most have also found that the intellectual deficits are not permanent (Skeels and Dye, 1939). Such a result supports our belief that the genetic contribution to measured intelligence is great. When children are removed from the restricted environment, they tend to catch up; although there are exceptions, dramatic increases of 20 to 30 IQ points are possible.

The animal studies on environmental enrichment are even more difficult to interpret than those on deprivation. About all we can say is that early environmental enrichment often has an enhancing effect on problem-solving ability (King, 1958). But the effects are usually obtained only when the enriched-environmental animals are compared with impoverished-environmental animals. The difficulty with this comparison is that the difference may be due to the impoverishment, not to the enrichment. We cannot reach firm conclusions about nature and nurture from these studies.

Human studies of environmental enrichment are among the most interesting and controversial of all. As yet they do not throw much light on the nature-nurture issue, but they have significant implications for social policy. Can early environmental enrichment of children from impoverished families actually increase their measured intelligence? Controversy over this question centers on the effect of special enrichment programs, such as the ambitious, federally funded Project Headstart, designed to prepare impoverished children for school (Jensen, 1969; Kagan, 1969). Most of the IQ gains from such programs have been modest, ranging from about 1 to 10 IQ points. This is what might be expected if the environment of impoverished people, while not what it should be, is still rich enough for children to go a long way toward their genetic potential. IQ differences in this case would be due to differences in genetics. But of course, this interpretation may not be the correct one: on the other side it can be argued that the gains were small because the enrichment of the environment was too little and too late. In general, this is what the controversy is about. However, such controversies are probably futile because of the range of reactions that can come from a particular genotype (see page 56).

Fortunately for social policy, IQ is probably not so important as more specific abilities—such as motivation, attention span, verbal skill, and number ability—for success in school and life. Relatively large gains have been obtained by enrichment programs focusing on the development of special skills which are needed in school (Bereiter and Engelmann, 1968).

Synopsis and summary

We have tried to set the stage here for Chapter 3 on Principles of Learning. We have discussed the contribution of nature, in combination and interaction with nurture, as a determiner of behavior. We turn next to the role of learning in the determination of behavior.

It may be safe to conclude that our animal nature—our species heritage and our individual genetic constitution—does not by itself determine specific behaviors, except for those which are almost completely due to maturation, or growth. Fixed action patterns and instincts seem almost nonexistent in humans. Our species heritage and genetic constitution appear to provide us with potentialities for behavior, but the actual behavior that is observed depends on the interaction of nature with nurture.

1. We have a species heritage from evolution; we also inherit individual potentialities for behavior.
2. Taxes, reflexes, and instinctive patterns are innate types of behavior seen mainly in the lower animals. Instinctive patterns consist of behaviors that are (*a*) characteristic of the species, (*b*) unlearned, (*c*) constant in form, and (*d*) persistent in the absence of the stimulus which elicits them.
3. Our evolutionary heritage does not express itself in fixed action patterns; rather, it unfolds in *potentialities* for behavior.
4. In addition to its role in behavioral potentialities, our species heritage is expressed in the maturation of certain behaviors and in the maturation of readiness for learning.
5. The field concerned with inherited individual differences in behavior tendencies is called behavior genetics.
6. Chromosomes, genes, dominance, and family inheritance are concepts basic to the understanding of behavior genetics.
7. Examples of genetic potentialities are the inheritance of intelligence in humans and lower animals, the inheritance of emotional respon-

sivity, and the inheritance of certain behavior disorders, such as schizophrenia.
8. The relationship of nature and nurture is complex. The observed behavior, or phenotype, is a result of the interaction of nature and nurture.
9. Studies analyzing the development of behaviors (the epigenetic approach) and studies in which the environment is impoverished or enriched are ways of investigating the contributions of nature and nurture to behavior.

Related topics in the text

Chapter 3 Principles of Learning The environment has its major effect through the mechanism of learning. The major types of learning are discussed in this chapter.

Chapter 6 Motivation Physiological motives—hunger, thirst, and sex, for example—depend in part upon innate mechanisms.

Chapter 13 Therapy for Behavior Disorders Schizophrenia is discussed in terms of its symptoms and causes.

Chapters 17 and 19 in Part Five, Biology of Behavior Brain mechanisms, some of them innate, are described in these chapters.

Suggestions for further reading

Birney, R. C., and Teevan, R. C. (Eds.) *Instinct.* New York: Van Nostrand Reinhold, 1961. (Paperback.)
An interesting collection of papers on innate factors in behavior.

Bonner, D. M. *Heredity.* Englewood Cliffs, N.J.: Prentice-Hall, 1961. (Paperback.)
Genetics from the point of view of modern molecular biology.

Dethier, V. G., and Stellar, E. *Animal behavior: Its evolutionary and neurological basis.* (3d ed.) Englewood Cliffs, N.J.: Prentice-Hall, 1970. (Paperback.)
A short but authoritative book on animal behavior which discusses the role of the nervous system in controlling behavior.

Fuller, J. L., and Thompson, W. R. *Behavior genetics.* New York: Wiley, 1960.
The genetic bases of behavioral characteristics, such as intelligence, personality, temperament, and behavior disorders, are lucidly discussed.

Hirsch, J. *Behavior-genetic analysis.* New York: McGraw-Hill, 1967.
Genetic aspects of psychological characteristics in man and animals are considered.

Klopfer, P. A., and Hailman, J. P. *An introduction to animal behavior: Ethology's first century.* Englewood Cliffs, N.J.: Prentice-Hall, 1967.
Animal behavior described from an ethological viewpoint.

Munn, N. L. *Evolution and the growth of human behavior.* Boston: Houghton Mifflin, 1955.
A comprehensive text on psychological development which includes chapters on the evolutionary aspects of animal behavior.

Mussen, P. H., Conger, J. J. and Kagan, J. *Child development and personality.* (3d ed.) New York: Harper & Row, 1968.
A textbook on child development that stresses the role of learning and socialization.

Stern, C. *Principles of human genetics.* (2d ed.) San Francisco: Freeman, 1960.
Genetic principles are applied to human physical and behavioral traits. An authoritative, well-written text.

Thorpe, W. H. *Learning and instinct in animals.* (2d ed.) London: Methuen, 1963.
A source book on animal behavior. Relatively easy to read and full of interesting examples of innate behavior in lower animals.

Tinbergen, N. *The study of instinct.* Oxford: Clarendon Press, 1951.
One of the classic books on animal behavior. Introduces many of the historic experiments and concepts of ethology.

Habits are at first cobwebs,
then cables.
Spanish proverb

I grow old learning something
new every day.
Solon

Learning is a key process—some would say *the* key process—in human behavior; it pervades everything we do and think. In one way or another, it influences the language we speak, our customs, our attitudes and beliefs, our goals, our personality traits, both adaptive and maladaptive, and even our perceptions. In this chapter we cover the fundamental principles of learning in order to be in a better position to understand how learning plays its role.

Importance of learning Consider the changes that take place in a child's behavior during his first few years of life. During this period he is molded, or socialized, to become a functioning member of his society. To be able to do this in any culture, he must learn a staggering number of things. These include learning appropriate ways of interacting with people, learning appropriate ways of eating and eliminating waste, learning to avoid potentially dangerous situations, learning to think somewhat logically and realistically, learning the values and customs of his group, learning to perceive the world as others perceive it, and learning the many distinctive responses and adjustments that make him different from other people. It is a wonder that he ever learns *all* these things. The fact that he does testifies to the remarkable plasticity of human behavior and the human nervous system.

This plasticity seems to extend throughout the animal kingdom. Although it is still uncertain whether unicellular organisms can learn (Katz and Deterline, 1958), such lowly organisms as the flatworm possess a rudimentary learning capacity (Warren, 1965), and learning has repeatedly been demonstrated in vertebrates from fishes to man. The number and kinds of things that can be learned increase markedly in the higher mammals, and man is distinguished by his enormously greater capacity.

Definition of learning *Learning* may be defined as any relatively permanent change in behavior which occurs as a result of experience or practice. This definition, it should be noted, has three important elements: (1) Learning is a *change in behavior,* for better or worse. (2) It is a change that takes place through *experience or practice;* changes due to growth, maturation, or injury are not to be considered as learned. (3) The change, to merit the term learning, must be *relatively permanent,* that is, it must last for a fairly long time. This rules out change due to motivation, fatigue, adaptation, or the sensitivity of the organism.

This last point leads to an important distinction to be made between learning and *performance.* Many factors, both learned and unlearned, affect performance. At the same time, how an organism performs is all that we can measure or study. Hence we must infer, by appropriate control or knowledge of the conditions affecting performance, when performance has been changed through learning and when it has been changed by other factors. Moreover, unlearned and learned factors interact in complex ways. For example, many kinds of behavior, even learned behavior, depend on motivation. A rat that has learned a maze does not perform well unless it is hungry or motivated in some way. In this case, learning is not manifested in performance until it is brought out through motivation. When studying learning processes, psychologists must be very careful to remember the various factors that affect performance.

Kinds of learning What we learn can be named or classified in dozens of ways, from the general to the specific. Here, for guidance through the main sections of this and the following chapter, we make some general distinctions. One is between stimulus (perceptual) learning and response learning. If we are learning something about a stimulus, it is *perceptual learning.* If we learn to make a particular response or group of responses, it is *response learning.* As a practical matter, all the learning that we measure is response learning; but by manipulating stimuli in the course of observing responses, we can infer when stimulus learning has taken place.

Limiting ourselves for the moment to response learning, we can distinguish between single- and multiple-response learning. In single-response learning, one particular response is associated with a specific stimulus or stimulus situation. When that is the case, we speak of conditioning. Conditioning, therefore, is a restricted form of learning in which a single response is acquired. This single-response learning can be subdivided further into *classical conditioning, operant conditioning,* and *aversive conditioning.* These three kinds of conditioning will be the subject of three of the major sections of the chapter. Through studying them, we can illustrate the basic principles that govern learning. First, however, let us consider the major factors encountered in any kind of learning.

Factors in Learning

There are a great many phenomena of learning. All have technical names, and the conditions under which they occur are in many cases rather complicated. The student can easily become lost in a profusion of terms if he has no framework in which to put them. Many of the phenomena, however, involve the same or similar factors combined in slightly different ways. By first considering the factors that are common to many learning phenomena, it will be easier to understand the phenomena when they are described in detail.

Arousal and motivation The most fundamental condition for learning to take place is that the organism be in a reasonably high state of arousal.

Although it has been claimed that some learning can take place during sleep, such learning is so minimal as to be debatable. Certainly for learning to proceed efficiently, a subject must be wide awake and alert to the environment.

We can go further and say that in most learning situations the organism is not merely aroused, it is motivated in some way. Actually, a wide-awake organism is easily motivated by environmental stimuli. Lights, sounds, odors, etc., bring out exploratory reactions in animals and people and cause them to notice (learn) features of the environment. But in the case of animal learning, the motivation is usually more specific. It consists of being hungry, thirsty, or deprived in some other way. Or it may involve punishment provided by the experimenter. In few if any instances does much observable learning take place in the absence of motivation.

Motivation is important in at least three ways. First, it is a condition for eliciting behavior. For example, an organism that is not hungry does not salivate in the presence of food as much as a hungry organism does. Hence if we wish to condition salivation, we must make the subject hungry. Or in a more complex case, if a rat is to learn a maze, it must at least walk through it. Rats will do this merely to explore, but they are more active when they are hungry.

Second, motivation is necessary for reinforcement, which in turn, as we shall see, is an essential condition of learning. For the moment, let us think of reinforcements as rewards or punishments. A punishment is its own motivation, but a reward must be appropriate to the motive. Food, not water, for example, is the appropriate reward for a *hungry* rat, and water is the appropriate reward for a *thirsty* rat. Thus by motivating a subject, we make some relevant object a reinforcement.

Motivation is also important in a third and related way: it controls the *variability* of behavior. When learning a new habit, a motivated organism will run through an extensive repertory of responses, one of which may be "correct." For example, suppose a mother is interested in teaching her child, who is a little thirsty, to say "milk" when a glass of milk is shown to him. One way of doing this is to show the child a glass of milk while saying "milk" at the same time. If the child says "milk," he will be given a sip as reinforcement. If he is motivated, the child will quickly run through many behaviors; he may grab for the glass; he may cry; he may shake his head; he may stick his tongue out at his mother; or he may imitate and say "milk"—the "correct" response. If he is not motivated, this repertory of responses will be less likely to occur. The same point applies to certain nonphysiological motives. Curiosity and exploratory drives bring the individual into wider contact with his environment and thus increase the possibilities of performing the correct response.

We may say in summary that motivation is important because (1) it brings out appropriate behaviors to be learned, (2) it permits reinforcement to occur, and (3) it increases the variability of behavior, thus raising the probability that a correct response will occur.

Association One factor that is common to most situations in which learning takes place is *association*. The term association as used here means some connection in time and place between two events. The

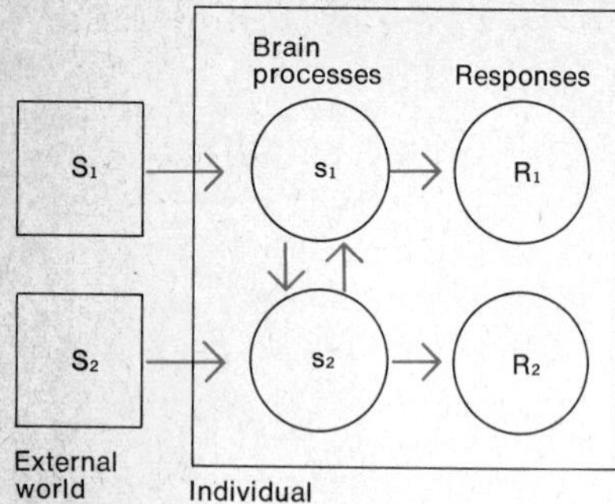

IN LEARNING WE MAY ASSOCIATE A STIMULUS WITH ANOTHER STIMULUS OR WITH A RESPONSE

Figure 3.1 *Schematic diagram of the associations formed in sensory-sensory (S-S) and stimulus-response (S-R) learning. Events in the external world are represented within the individual by sensory brain processes which can be thought of as being connected in the course of S-S association. Similarly, external events, and the sensory nervous processes aroused by them, can be associated with responses to form S-R connections.*

connection usually first exists in the physical world. For example, fires and many other things that light up are hot. Hence the physical events of light and heat are often connected, or *associated,* with one another. Lightning and thunder usually occur in close sequence, so the light and sound may be connected. These connections in the physical world provide opportunities for an organism to form associations from experiencing two events simultaneously or in close succession.

The formation of such associations is a function of the brain. The process involved has not yet been discovered, but it is almost certainly not a simple connection like that formed when two wires are joined (Lashley, 1950). For purposes of discussion, it may be assumed that the process in the brain representing one event becomes associated with the process representing the other event. This means that once an association has been formed, the initiation of one process tends to arouse the second process in the absence of any physical event which ordinarily sets off the second process. Stated symbolically, if S_1 and S_2 are two events in the physical world, and s_1 and s_2 are the corresponding processes in the brain, the occurrence of S_1 and S_2 together will tend to form an association between processes in the brain, so that s_1 can now arouse s_2 or s_2 arouse s_1 (see Figure 3.1).

SENSORY ASSOCIATIONS The view that learning involves an association between processes in the brain representing stimulus events experienced by a person was formulated by English philosophers during the eighteenth and nineteenth centuries. The conception was called *associationism,* and those who subscribed to it were *associationists.* They regarded the experience s_1 aroused by the external event S_1 as a *sensation,* and the process s_1 aroused by S_2 in the absence of S_1 as an *idea.* An idea in this sense has also been called an *image.* Within this framework, the associationists then attempted to formulate laws stating the conditions under which ideas were learned by association. In other words, they inquired into how s_1 comes to be aroused by S_2 in the absence of S_1.

Late in the nineteenth century, when experimental work on learning got under way, the language of associationism was revamped because rigorous experimentalists felt they could not experiment with "ideas" or "images." Although the inference that the processes aroused in sensory association are often ideas or images is probably correct, it was all too easy to lapse into loose, untestable speculation about the properties of ideas. For this reason, psychologists stopped talking about the association of ideas and began referring simply to association, sensory association, or to S-S association, meaning association between two stimuli (Spence, 1951).

STIMULUS-RESPONSE ASSOCIATIONS Another kind of association, an S-R or stimulus-response association, is more easily studied. In this case the learner associates a stimulus event with a response. For instance, when you learn a foreign-language vocabulary you are forming S-R associations; the foreign word is a stimulus for your English response, or vice versa. When driving a car we are almost continuously engaged in making learned responses to stimuli: the traffic light turns red and we stop; it turns green and we start; we speed up to pass another car; and so on through the whole range of near-automatic responses (see Figure 3.1).

The example of driving a car illustrates another point about S-R connections: the stimulus may come from the response itself. When we move, the movement causes stimulation to arise in the receptors of our muscles and joints—these are called *kinesthetic* receptors. This stimulation, although little of it ever reaches consciousness, is fed back into the nervous system and can, through learning, form a connection with the next response. This response, like the one before it, feeds back information that can connect with the next response, and so on. In this way, a *chain* of associations between *response-produced stimuli* and responses is formed. Such a chain can be very long and complex.

Some skilled acts, but not all, are chains of the sort just described. Consider the shifting of gears in automobiles equipped with a manual gearshift. We first step on the clutch, and this provides response-produced stimuli which are associated with the response of pushing the gearshift. This in turn provides a cue for letting up on the clutch. On the other hand, some complex acts, particularly those requiring very rapid sequences, are certainly not chained in this way (Lashley, 1951). A skilled musician, in playing an arpeggio, makes responses far faster than information from the responses can be fed back into the nervous system. Thus in this instance, a previous response cannot provide the stimulation for the next one. Rather, the chaining must take place entirely in the nervous system. Nevertheless, the concept of the chaining of response-produced stimuli and responses is important in understanding certain learned sequences of behavior.

S-R associations lend themselves nicely to objective observation, and for this reason they have received the greatest attention in psychological experiments. S-S associations can be studied only in roundabout ways and therefore have been relatively neglected. Indeed, some psychologists have attempted to explain all association as S-R association, and this is one of the points on which theorists still disagree. An increasing body of evidence, however, shows that both kinds of associations can be formed.

CONTIGUITY The concept of association implies contiguity. That is to say, for two physical events to be connected, and hence for the corresponding processes in the brain to become associated, the events must occur at approximately the same time and place. They must be contiguous, or paired, events. For this reason, contiguity has long been stated as a basic law governing the formation of associations.

What must be contiguous varies with different learning situations. In simple conditioning, as we shall see, it is the contiguity of two stimuli that is essential for learning. In this case, we speak of the pairing of stimuli. In other somewhat more complex learning situations, it is the contiguity of a response and a reward or punishment that is important for learning. For example, we give a dog a bit of food when he performs a trick, or we slap a child's hand when he reaches for a lighted cigarette. In every case, it is the pairing of events—making them contiguous—that is essential in learning.

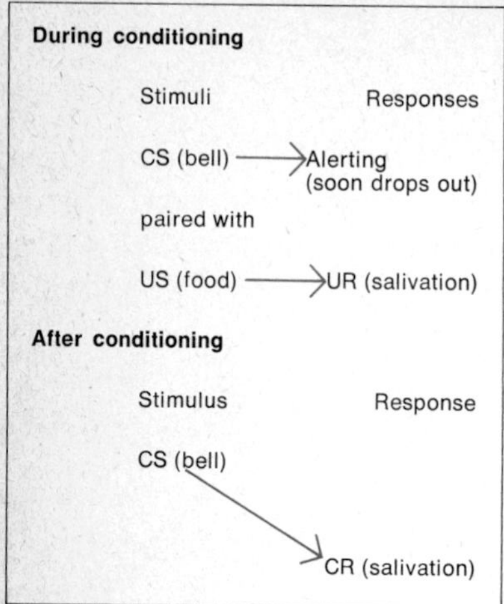

CS + US = CR

Figure 3.2 *Schematic diagram of the classical conditioning process. During conditioning, a neutral stimulus (bell), called the conditioned stimulus (CS), is paired a number of times with an unconditioned stimulus (US)—food—which evokes an unconditioned response (UR)—salivation. As a result of continued pairing, the conditioned stimulus comes to produce salivation, which is now called the conditioned response (CR), in the absence of the unconditioned stimulus (US).*

INTERFERENCE Still another aspect of forming associations deserves emphasis—the possibility of interference among associations. One stimulus may become associated with two different stimuli or with two different responses. If the two associations with the single stimulus are incompatible, one tends to block or interfere with the other.

The learning of two languages at the same time is an example. Children who are reared in bilingual homes are slower in language development than those who learn only one language at home. A child learns a good deal of language by associating a word (R) with some stimulus (S). He learns to associate "hot" with the sight of the fire on the stove or a lighted match. But if he must learn to associate *heiss* (German for "hot") or *chaud* (French for "hot") at the same time, he has two different associations (R_1 and R_2) for the same visual stimulus (S). He cannot say them both at the same time. Hence one association interferes with the other and neither association is built up so rapidly as it might be. The principle of mutual interference of associations is a general one which accounts for several of the phenomena of learning and forgetting.

Reinforcement Another important term, one the psychologist repeatedly uses when talking about learning, is *reinforcement.* This term has two meanings, depending on the kind of learning situation he is talking about. In simple conditioning, it merely refers to the second stimulus of the pair being presented. Why the reinforcement is the second rather than the first will become clear later in the chapter. However, here we are concerned with the other meaning of reinforcement. This corresponds to what we commonly call reward or punishment. Examples of the many things which can serve as reinforcement are food for a hungry animal or human being, certain "pleasing" tastes (Pfaffmann, 1964), praise for a child, a "Well done!" from the boss, or escape from punishment.

Reinforcement is of such obvious importance in learning that it was long ago dignified as the *law of effect* (Thorndike, 1911). This law states that an act which has a satisfying effect—for instance, satisfaction of a drive, escape from punishment, or relief from fear—will be learned, but an act which has an unpleasant effect—such as frustration of a motive, punishment, or fear—will not be learned. It is relatively easy to observe that reinforcement does indeed strengthen certain kinds of associations. The simple fact that reinforcement works to strengthen associations has been called the *empirical law of effect* (Hall, 1966).

In contrast to the empirical law of effect is a so-called *theoretical law of effect* (Kimble, 1961). This refers to the hypothetical mechanism through which reinforcement acts to strengthen associations. There are several theories about this mechanism, which we shall discuss later in the section "Theories of Learning." In any case, whatever the mechanism, reinforcement helps strengthen associations in response learning. Whether it is necessary for acquiring *all* associations is a question that will be considered in the section dealing with perceptual learning.

We have discussed three basic factors in learning: motivation, association, and reinforcement. The next and principal part of this chapter treats four basic kinds of learning situations: classical conditioning, operant conditioning, aversive conditioning, and perceptual learning. A final section considers some theoretical aspects of learning. For the

PAVLOV CONDITIONED DOGS TO SALIVATE WHEN THEY HEARD A BELL

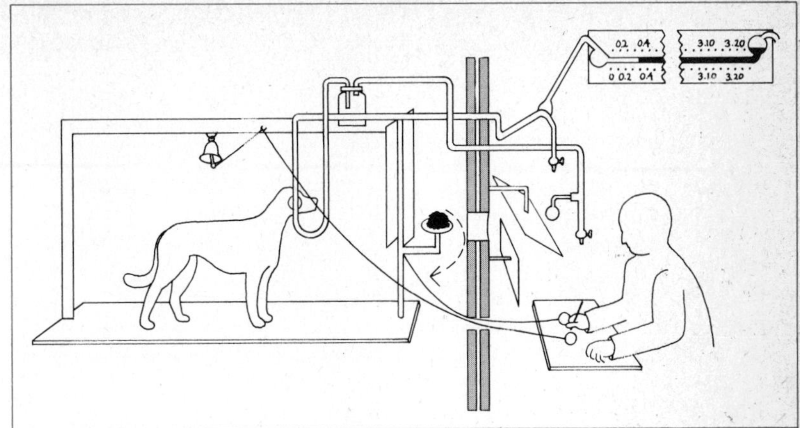

Figure 3.3 *Pavlov's apparatus for studying the conditioned salivary response. The amount of saliva is measured by means of a tube attached to a cup placed over one of the salivary glands. The apparatus is in a soundproof room with a one-way vision screen between the experimenter and the dog. The experimenter can sound the bell (CS) and present food (US) by remote control. (After Pavlov, 1928.)*

most part, the experiments described and the illustrations employed refer to animal learning. We have good reason to believe, however, that the *principles* derived from animal learning experiments apply well to human learning. In Chapter 4, we will focus on human learning.

Classical Conditioning

Classical conditioning gets its name from the fact that it is the kind of learning originally studied in the "classical" experiments of Ivan P. Pavlov (1849–1936). Beginning in the late 1890s, this famous Russian physiologist introduced the concept of conditioning and established many of its basic principles (Pavlov, 1927, 1960). Much of present-day Russian psychology is based on the conditioned response and theories of its significance in human and animal behavior. Although classical conditioning is sometimes called *respondent conditioning,* the term classical is used here.

Salivary conditioning To present a picture of the phenomena of classical conditioning, which is summarized in Figure 3.2, we shall describe a number of experiments, starting with a typical Pavlovian experiment. But first it is necessary to state some definitions. The essential operation in classical conditioning is a *pairing* of two stimuli. One, initially neutral in that it elicits only a general alerting, not a specific response, is called the *conditioned stimulus* (CS); the other, which consistently elicits a specific response, is called the *unconditioned stimulus* (US). The response elicited by the unconditioned stimulus is the *unconditioned response* (UR). As a result of the pairing of the conditioned stimulus (CS) with the unconditioned stimulus (US), the previously neutral conditioned stimulus comes to elicit the response. Then it is called the *conditioned response* (CR). With these terms in mind, we can now describe a typical experiment in classical conditioning.

Pavlov devised an operation and an apparatus for measuring the flow of saliva (see Figure 3.3). The apparatus consisted in part of a tube running from a cup

THE UPS AND DOWNS OF CLASSICAL CONDITIONING

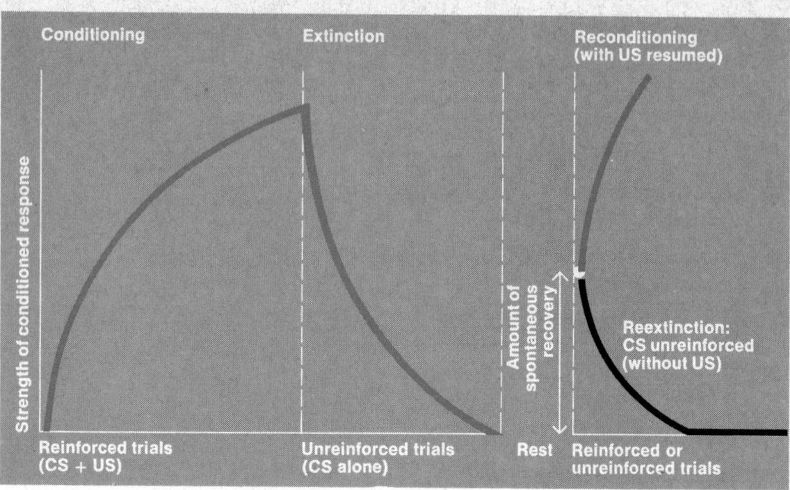

Figure 3.4 *Schematic diagram of the course of conditioning, extinction, reconditioning, and reextinction. Spontaneous recovery after a rest period is shown by the vertical arrow. (After McGeoch and Irion, 1952; adapted from Gregory A. Kimble and Norman Garmezy,* Principles of General Psychology, *3d ed. Copyright © 1968, The Ronald Press Company, New York.)*

attached to a dog's cheek. This cup was arranged in such a way that it collected drops of saliva flowing from the parotid salivary gland which had been displaced to the outside of the cheek. The saliva replaced air in the tube from the cup, and this in turn displaced a colored fluid in a calibrated instrument which looked somewhat like a thermometer and from which small changes could be read. The animal was placed in a soundproof room equipped with a one-way vision screen through which it could be seen. By remote control, Pavlov could swing a food pan out within the dog's reach or, alternatively, puff some powdered food into its mouth through a special apparatus. He could also present the dog with several other kinds of stimuli, including the sounds of a bell, buzzer, or metronome.

In a typical experiment, Pavlov trained the dog by sounding a bell (the CS), immediately afterward presenting food (the US), and then measuring the amount of saliva secreted (the UR). After pairing the sound of the bell with food a few times, the effects of the training were tested by measuring the amount of saliva which flowed when the bell was presented alone without food. Pavlov resumed the paired presentation of bell and food a few more times and then tested with the bell alone. He found that as training proceeded, the amount of saliva secreted in response to the bell alone (the CR) gradually increased. This increase over test trials could be plotted as a learning curve.

In Figure 3.4 the left-hand curve is a conditioning curve typical of an experiment in salivary conditioning. It is drawn without specifying the number of trials or the amount of saliva, although these measurements would be plotted on a graph representing an actual experiment. This curve, also called an *acquisition curve,* shows that the strength of the response on test trials gradually increases with more and more pairings of CS and US. Note that the curve gradually flattens; that is, each increase due to a trial is less than the preceding one. In other words, the curve is negatively accelerated; that is, it is a curve of "diminishing returns."

Flexion conditioning Another famous Russian, the neurologist and anatomist Bekhterev (1857–1927), pioneered the school of "reflexology"

IN SOME CONDITIONING EXPERIMENTS, THE CR MAY ANTICIPATE THE UR

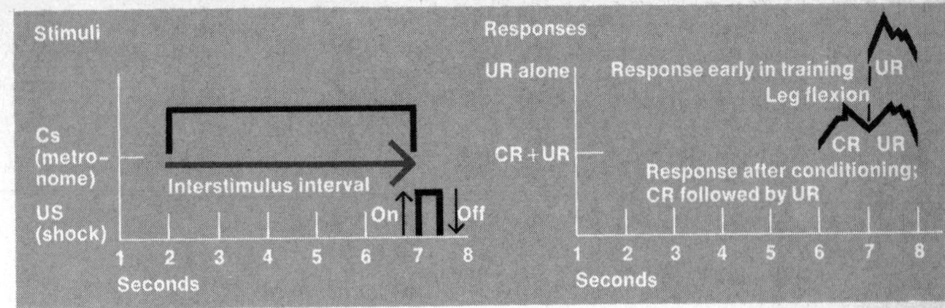

Figure 3.5 *Time relationships between the CS and US, and between the unconditioned and conditioned responses (UR and CR). The experiment employs unavoidable shock to the leg of a sheep as the US. The interstimulus interval is the time between the onset of the CS and the onset of the US. This diagram shows an anticipatory CR. (Modified from Liddell et al., 1934.)*

and another type of classical-conditioning experiment (Bekhterev, 1932). The principal difference between Pavlov's and Bekhterev's experiments is in the unconditioned stimulus and its response. Instead of food, Bekhterev used shock to the forelimb or hindlimb as his US; this produces an unconditioned response of arm or leg flexion. Other details of these experiments are as follows:

The subjects may be human or animal. In the case of animals, the shock (US) is usually applied to the bottom of a foot. In the case of human subjects, it may be delivered to either a foot or hand. To take just one case, let us assume that a human subject is used and the shock is applied to the hand.

Shocking the back of the hand causes a rapid and brisk bending or flexion of the hand. This is the unconditioned response. Just before the shock is delivered, however, another kind of stimulation (CS)—a tone, for instance—can be presented. After several pairings of the tone followed by shock, that is, pairings of the conditioned and unconditioned stimuli, the subject promptly flexes his hand when the tone is presented. This flexion response to a previously neutral stimulus is the *conditioned response* in this type of experiment.

An acquisition curve similar to that for the Pavlovian experiment can be plotted. In this situation, however, the measure on the ordinate (vertical axis) is not the strength of the conditioned response; it usually is the percentage of times that a conditioned response is given to the conditioned stimulus. For instance, the percentage of conditioned responses on each block of 10 trials may be plotted.

Two important features of this type of experiment should be noted. One is that the subject cannot escape the shock. He always receives it following the presentation of the conditioned stimulus. In this respect, it is like the Pavlovian experiment in which food always follows the CS; it is unlike experiments discussed later in this chapter in which the subject can escape or avoid shock. A second feature, and one in which it is unlike the Pavlovian experiment, is that no test trials are employed. In salivary conditioning, test trials consist of presenting the CS without the US to see whether salivation occurs with the CS alone. In Bekhterev's experiment, this is unnecessary because the conditioned response anticipates, that is, occurs prior to, the presentation of the shock (see Figure 3.5). For this reason, CRs in such an experiment are sometimes called "anticipatory" CRs. These are a distinct advantage, for they permit the experimenter to assess the progress of conditioning trial by trial rather than to check it only on interspersed test trials.

Contiguity in conditioning Several points can be made concerning the pairing operation, that is, the contiguity of CS and US, in classical conditioning. One concerns reinforcement. In classical conditioning, the conditioned stimulus is said to be "reinforced" by the unconditioned stimulus. Hence, the operation of pairing itself is the reinforcement in classical conditioning. This is the other meaning of reinforcement we alluded to in the earlier discussion of reinforcement and the law of effect.

Another point is that there is an *interstimulus interval* in the pairing that is optimal for conditioning to take place. The interstimulus interval is the time between the onset of the CS and the onset of the US. The pairing of CS and US may be such that they occur simultaneously, but it is more usual for the US to follow the CS by a definite interval. This produces better conditioning and also permits the use of "anticipatory" responses. The optimal interstimulus interval varies with the situation and the kind of response employed as the UR, but in general, relatively short interstimulus intervals, about 1/2 second, are optimal for the development of classically conditioned responses (Kimble, 1967).

Extinction and spontaneous recovery So far, the discussion has concerned the *acquisition* of a conditioned response. If, after a conditioned response has been acquired, the procedure is changed so that only the CS is repeatedly presented without being followed by the US, another phenomenon is encountered. This is the *extinction* of the conditioned response—a gradual weakening of the strength of the response (salivation, in Pavlov's experiment), or a decrease in the frequency of responses (flexion, in Bekhterev's experiment). Extinction may be illustrated as follows:

In another of Pavlov's experiments, a conditioned dog was placed in the apparatus in the usual way. The bell was presented without food, just as had been done in the test trials of the conditioning procedure. In this case, however, the bell was never accompanied by food. On trial after trial, the dog heard only the bell and never saw or received food. The amount of saliva was measured in the usual way. As the procedure was continued, the amount of saliva that was secreted when the bell was presented gradually diminished until it reached a level little different from its level at the beginning of the experiment (see the middle curve, labeled "extinction," in Figure 3.4).

If one stopped experimenting at this point, he might conclude that the extinction procedure had simply erased what had been learned in the conditioning procedure. But this is not true. Rather, extinction is a process of learning to *inhibit* the response acquired in conditioning. It is a new learning superimposed on the old without really destroying the original conditioned response. This conclusion can be reached in two ways.

First, it can be concluded from a phenomenon known as *spontaneous recovery*. A conditioned response which has been extinguished may spontaneously recover some of the strength lost in extinction during an interval of rest following extinction (see the curve, lower right, in Figure 3.4). If, for example, a dog whose conditioned response has been extinguished is brought back into the experimental situation and the

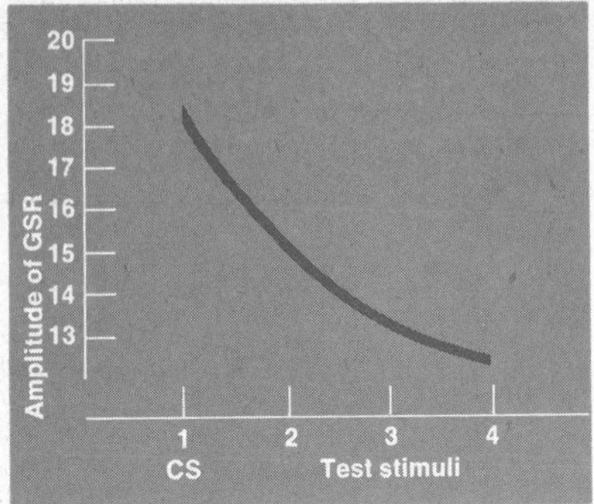

WE TEND TO RESPOND TO STIMULI THAT RESEMBLE THOSE WE HAVE BEEN CONDITIONED TO

Figure 3.6 *Generalization of a conditioned galvanic skin response. Stimulus 1 (CS) was the tone to which the GSR was originally conditioned. Stimuli 2, 3, and 4 were tones of increasingly different frequency. Note that there is less generalization as the difference between the CS and the other tones increases. (After Hovland, 1937.)*

presentation of the bell is resumed, the amount of salivation is considerably greater than it was at the end of the previous series of extinction trials. This increase shows that even after extinction, some degree of association remains between the bell and salivation. The conditioning has not been entirely lost.

Secondly, *reconditioning* is more rapid than original conditioning. In this case, the procedure is to reinstate the reinforcement, or pairing, of the US and CS given in the original conditioning. When Pavlov did this, he obtained the general results shown in Figure 3.4, upper right: The reconditioning following extinction occurred more rapidly than the first conditioning. Indeed, an experimenter can condition, extinguish, condition, and extinguish, and up to a certain point, the animal conditions a little faster each time and extinguishes a little more rapidly than the time before. Thus the original conditioning is not erased by extinction; instead, learning both to respond and not to respond is taking place. The animal is learning *when* to do one or the other.

Stimulus generalization Pavlov discovered very early that if he conditioned an animal to salivate at the sound of a bell, it would also salivate at the sound of a buzzer or the beat of a metronome, though to a lesser degree. Thus the animal tended to *generalize* the conditioned response to stimuli that were different from, but somewhat similar to, the one to which it was specifically conditioned.

The example of stimulus generalization we shall use here comes from a study of the galvanic skin response (GSR) in man (Hovland, 1937). The galvanic skin response is usually measured as a decrease in the resistance of the skin to the flow of a minute electrical current. The mechanisms responsible for it are quite complex. Such decreased resistance of the skin is characteristic of alertness and aroused emotional states, and it is one of the responses measured by the lie detector or polygraph. For our present purposes, it is enough to state that the GSR can be manipulated in the laboratory and can be used as an unconditioned response to the unconditioned stimulus of a strong, painful shock. The following experiment shows stimulus generalization in connection with GSR conditioning (Hovland, 1937):

An electric shock was the unconditioned stimulus for the GSR. The experimenter began by conditioning the subject's GSR to the sound of a pure tone of a particular frequency. This was done by presenting the shock and tone (the CS) simultaneously, or nearly so. After the GSR had been conditioned to the tone, Hovland measured the strength of the conditioned GSR given to tones that were of frequencies different from the original tone (the conditioned stimulus). Figure 3.6 indicates the results of this experiment. As we would expect, the tone, or CS, used in the original conditioning evoked the largest GSRs; tones similar in frequency to the CS evoked the next-largest GSRs; tones furthest in frequency from the original CS evoked the weakest responses. Thus a rough rule of thumb can be formulated: *The greater the similarity between stimuli, the greater the generalization between them.*

Many responses and characteristics of people seem to be acquired through the processes of conditioning and generalization illustrated in the experiment with the GSR. There the shock served as an unconditioned stimulus eliciting pain in the subject, and the conditioned stimulus elicited a fear of pain. This simple experiment serves as a model for the development of people's irrational fears (see Figure 3.18). Such fears or phobias are irrational because they are acquired through accidental conditioning to some stimulus, then generalized to situations that otherwise would not be frightening.

Primary and secondary reinforcement We have said that reinforcement in classical conditioning is the pairing of the US and CS. At this point, such a statement must be qualified. The pairing of the US and CS is really *primary reinforcement,* for other kinds of reinforcement are possible. A second kind is called, logically enough, *secondary reinforcement.* In secondary reinforcement some neutral stimulus is paired with the CS after the CS has acquired the ability to elicit the US. Conditioning will occur in this case; that is, the new CS, which we may call CS_2 will come to elicit the US through being paired with the CS_1. Pavlov called this kind of learning *higher-order conditioning.* It may be illustrated by another Pavlovian experiment:

In the first stage of the experiment, a dog was conditioned in the usual way to salivate to the sound of a metronome. After the dog was well conditioned, the second "higher-order" stage was begun. A card with a black square on it was thrust into the dog's view just before the metronome was sounded. No food was given during this second stage. In effect, then, the card was being paired with the sound of the metronome. After several pairings of the card and metronome, the dog started to salivate when the card with the black square on it was presented. Thus, although the card was never paired with food, it nevertheless came to elicit salivation.

The higher-order stage of this experiment is not really different from any classical conditioning if we remember that an unconditioned stimulus was defined as one which consistently elicits a reflexlike response. In this experiment, as a result of conditioning in the first stage, the salivation is conditioned to the sound of the metronome—that is, the metronome now consistently elicits the response of salivation. In the second higher-order stage, the card with the black square is the conditioned stimulus, while the metronome, which consistently elicits the response, acts as an unconditioned stimulus.

At first glance, one might think that higher-order conditioning would have no limits; one might pair the second CS with a third, a third with a fourth, and so on. In fact, however, there is a limit, and it is usually at the point of second-order conditioning. The reason is that while the second-order CS is being paired with the first-order CS, the latter is being extinguished because it is being presented without pairing with the primary reinforcement. A way around such extinction, up to a point, is to intersperse trials in which the primary CS and US are re-paired. By doing this and pairing another stimulus with the card, Pavlov was able (although with great difficulty) to carry higher-order conditioning one more stage—to a third-order stimulus. Second-order conditioning, however, is relatively easy, and undoubtedly occurs often in everyday learning situations. Therefore the concept of second-order conditioning and its companion, *secondary reinforcement,* is an important one.

Significance of classical conditioning We have dwelt on salivary and flexion responses because psychologists used them to uncover some of the basic principles of conditioning. These particular responses, however, have little significance in the human being's everyday learning. Undoubtedly they are more important in the conditioning of emotional responses. Later under the section "Aversive Conditioning" we shall discuss experiments on such responses. In the meantime, let us point out briefly some examples of the real-life significance of classical conditioned responses.

Many of our subjective feelings, from violent emotions to subtle nuances of mood, are probably conditioned responses. A face, a scene, or a voice may be the conditioned stimulus for an emotional response. No wonder we are not always able to identify the origins of such emotional responses. Generalization, higher-order conditioning, and the fact that we learned many of these responses before we could talk and label them, all make it difficult to trace such feelings back to their conditioned beginnings. According to some, much of what is called the "unconscious" consists of just such unknown conditionings (Dollard and Miller, 1950). At least, this is one way of looking at it.

Although the origins of conditioned emotional responses often remain obscure, it is sometimes possible to discover their roots in ourselves and others. In the following quotation, the author describes the development and elimination of a conditioned fear response in a young boy. He also describes the origins of some of his own conditioned emotional responses. Perhaps you can discover such responses and some of their origins in your own experience.

Before and after tonsillectomy a boy was given examination and treatment by a white-coated, shiny-instrument-wielding physician. For a year and more thereafter he was terrorized by the very sight of a barber wearing his white coat and manipulating his nickeled clippers and scissors. . . . This fear reaction was eventually overcome by a barber who set a bowl of goldfish near the child, directing his highly interested attention to them, and saying "fish," meanwhile working upon the boy's hair unobtrusively and casually. . . . Later the child, upon hearing the word "fish" or "haircut" or "Dayton's" (the barber's shop) spoken aloud would smile, and with a hand describe circular gestures accompanied by rising and falling vocal inflection (mimetic of the swimming of the goldfish).

A college student relates that once he greatly enjoyed Chopin's Marche Funebre, but that ever since he heard it played in a certain naval hospital whenever the body of an unfortunate sailor was being removed for burial, he has been unable to react to it with anything but extreme depression. . . . And who does not still react with a touch of dread to the mere words "Lidice" or "Dachau" or "March of Death" or "Iwo Jima"? . . . The writer acknowledges a strangely warm, almost affectionate liking for pink willow-pattern dinnerware, which he can trace back to childhood lunches eaten from a pink plate. . . . In good contrast is the case of Arnold Bennett, who once wrote of a sudden dejection that came upon him whenever he saw anything pink; eventually he was able to trace it to the pink-colored almshouses of the English countryside. (Modified slightly from Dashiell, 1949, page 433.)

Perhaps many of the symbols we use are the result of conditioning. A *symbol* is simply something which stands for something else. One theory of symbol formation traces these steps (Allport, 1924): A child is shown a doll and an adult says the word "doll." The child imitates the sound he hears and says "doll." In this example, the sight of the doll is the CS, the saying of "doll" by the adult is the US, and the imitative response by the child is the UR. According to simple classical conditioning, the child will soon come to say "doll" when he sees that object, or a similar one, because of the pairing of sight of the doll with the saying of the word. Saying "doll" when shown a doll is thus a conditioned response. Perhaps classical conditioning plays a part in giving us the tools of thought—words. However, operant conditioning, to which we now turn, undoubtedly plays a part also.

Operant Conditioning

Operant conditioning can be distinguished from classical conditioning in the following ways:

1. Classically conditioned responses are *elicited* responses, but those learned in operant conditioning are *emitted* responses. The elicited responses of classical conditioning are relatively fixed, reflexlike responses such as salivation or limb flexion, but the emitted responses of operant conditioning are variable responses—such as running, walking, pecking, or pushing—which before learning are unrelated to the US. These acts "operate" on the environment and for that reason are termed *operant behavior.*
2. In classical conditioning, the CS is a specified stimulus, such as the sounding of a bell, *presented* intermittently by the experimenter for a brief period in association with the US. In operant conditioning, on the other hand, the CS is a *situation*—for example, a box with a lever in it—that is present throughout the learning period. The organism is free to "operate" at any time.
3. In classical conditioning, the US is paired with the CS no matter what the subject does; there is no contingency of reinforcement in such conditioning. In operant conditioning, however, the reinforcement is *contingent* upon what the subject does. For this reason, operant conditioning is sometimes called *instrumental conditioning* (or learning), because what the subject does is instrumental in securing reinforcement.
4. Whereas in classical conditioning the reinforcement is the pairing of the CS and US, in operant conditioning the reinforcement is usually (but not always) a stimulus, such as food or water, that satisfies a drive. Or it may be anything in which the subject is interested, such as an object to play with or look at. Reinforcement in operant conditioning can also be escape from or avoidance of a painful situation, such as shock.

REINFORCEMENT MAKES PRESSING THE BAR A HIGHLY PROBABLE RESPONSE

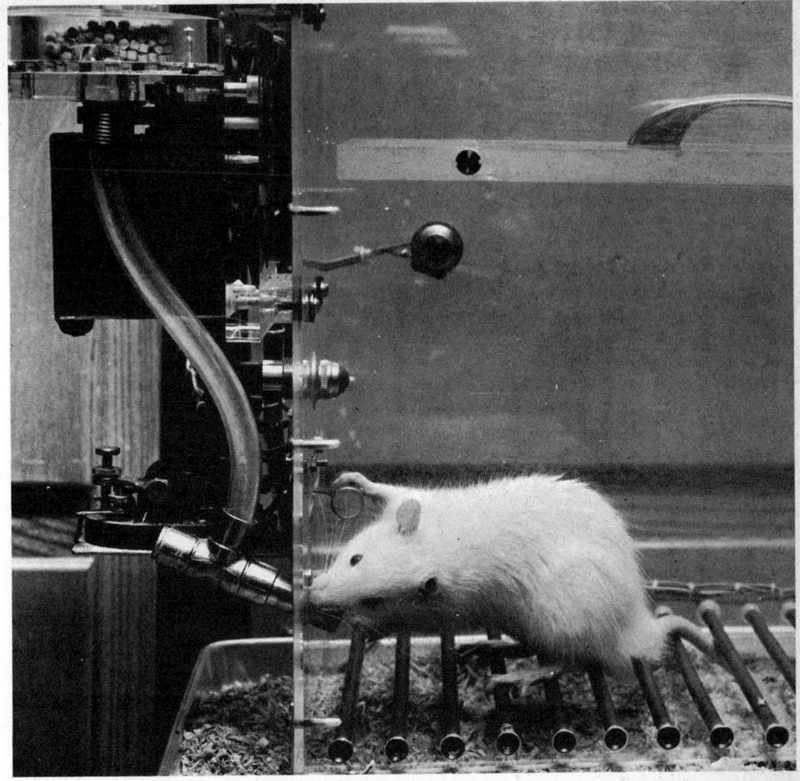

Figure 3.7 *A rat in a Skinner box, or (more recently) standard operant chamber. When the rat pushes the bar, a pellet is delivered from the feeder. The delivery of the pellet constitutes the* reinforcement *in this Skinner box. The box can also be arranged so that not every response produces a pellet* (partial reinforcement). *(Pfizer, Inc.)*

In this case we speak of aversive conditioning. More generally, reinforcement in operant conditioning is *any stimulus or situation which strengthens the response that precedes it.*

After an example, which should make things clearer, we shall return to these differences between classical and operant conditioning.

The apparatus for this demonstration is a simple box with a lever at one end. The lever is a switch which may operate a food-delivery or water-delivery mechanism. Alternatively, the lever may be wired so that it turns off a shock given to a rat through the grid floor of the box. In other words, reinforcement is contingent upon operation of the lever. Such a box, called a *Skinner box* (or, more recently, a standard operant chamber, was first used by B. F. Skinner to study operant conditioning.

Suppose a hungry rat is placed in this box (see Figure 3.7). After an initial period of inactivity, the rat, being hungry, begins to explore the box and eventually presses the lever. A pellet of food is released; that is, reinforcement is contingent upon the lever press. After eating, the animal continues exploring, stopping to wash itself from time to time. After a while it presses the lever again, and again a pellet is released; then it presses the lever a third time. After the fourth press, the rat presses the lever rapidly, and operant behavior is in full swing.

THE LEARNER "DRAWS" A RECORD OF HIS RESPONSES WITH A CUMULATIVE RECORDER

Figure 3.8 *A cumulative recorder. Each response causes the pen to move, or step, a very small distance to the left as we view the recorder in the photograph. As responses accumulate, the pen moves gradually to the left. Time is represented by the moving paper; as the paper moves at a constant rate under the pen, the learner traces a cumulative record of his responses. The rate of response is shown by the slope of the response lines on the paper; the response curves on this record indicate high rates of response where the line has a steep slope and pauses in responding where the line flattens out. The short tick marks indicate when reinforcement was given. After the pen reaches the right edge of the paper, it is reset to the left, and the record continues. The record is thus a continuous one; it is broken up simply to keep it within the bounds of the paper. (Ralph Gerbrands Co.)*

Each depression of the lever is recorded on a device called a *cumulative recorder.* On such a recorder, each response causes a pen to make a very small movement on a piece of paper which moves at a constant speed (see Figure 3.8). Thus a cumulative and continuous record of responses is plotted against time, and the rat "draws" a record of his responses with this device. The slope of the curve is the measure of response rate: High rates of response give steep slopes, while low rates of response result in shallow slopes. When no responses are being emitted, the line drawn on the cumulative recorder has no slope. In the demonstration we have been describing, the rate of response was very low initially—the first response occurring after 15 minutes, and the second about 35 minutes later. After about 30 more minutes, the response rate increased and the slope on the cumulative recorder increased correspondingly (see Figure 3.9).

This simple demonstration illustrates the basic features of operant conditioning. Although a rat was the subject in that instance, much human learning is also the result of reinforcement for particular responses. The learner, first of all, is motivated toward some goal, and he engages in general exploratory activity. In the course of such activity, he happens to make (emit) a response which is instrumental in achieving the appropriate goal. This response becomes more probable and becomes the learned response.

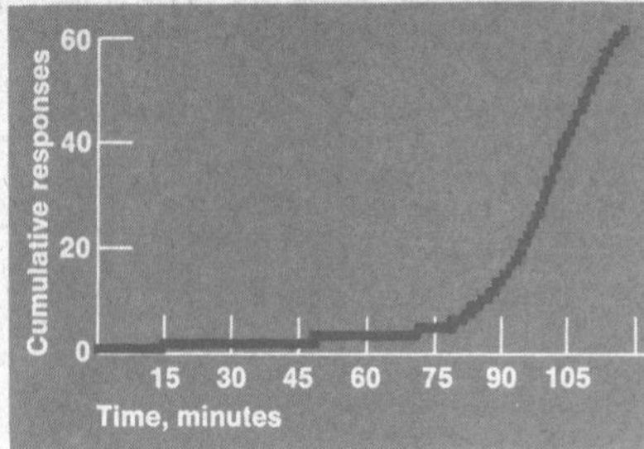

LOW RATES OF RESPONSE PRODUCE SHALLOW SLOPES; HIGH RATES PRODUCE STEEP SLOPES

Figure 3.9 *A record of responses from a rat in the demonstration Skinner Box. Note that this is a cumulative graph; the number of responses made in any period are added to the number made in the preceding period. The rat did not make its first response until about 15 minutes after being placed in the box; it did not make its second response until about 35 minutes later. The effect of food reinforcement becomes strong after about 80 minutes: the rate of response then is high and fairly steady. When this record was made, every response was reinforced.*

Operant conditioning does not require elaborate apparatus; it goes on around us all the time. Its essential feature is that reinforcement follows a response. Experiments have shown that we can change the verbal responses of other people by judicious use of reinforcement. One experimenter reinforced subjects by saying "hm-mmm" when they said plural nouns (Greenspoon, 1955). A large increase in the number of plural nouns occurred as a result of this reinforcement. In another experiment, subjects were reinforced for expressing attitudes toward a particular topic—the Harvard University philosophy of general education—during an interview over the telephone (Hildum and Brown, 1956). In one condition, with "good" as the reinforcer, the subjects who were reinforced for endorsing general education shifted toward a more favorable attitude, whereas those reinforced for anti- opinions shifted toward a less favorable attitude. Apparently attitudes as well as particular responses (giving plural nouns, for example) can be learned through the use of reinforcement.

Shaping We have seen that one of the differences between operant and classical conditioning is the freedom of the learner to emit responses. This makes it possible, in operant conditioning, to *shape* behavior through the appropriate use of reinforcement. For instance, instead of waiting for the first response to be emitted by the rat in the demonstration, the experimenter would probably shape behavior through reinforcement. First, the hungry rat would have been allowed to habituate to the Skinner box. Next, the animal would be given pellets from the food magazine until it ate promptly, that is, it would be "magazine trained." Finally, shaping of the pressing response would begin. Whenever the rat wandered into the front part of the box near the bar, the experimenter would press a switch releasing a food pellet, thus reinforcing this behavior. The rat would then be required to get a little closer to the desired response of pressing the lever. Perhaps it would be reinforced for putting its paws on the bar, and then for only actually pressing the bar. A skillful experimenter can shape such behavior with a very few reinforcements in a relatively short time. Note that the essential thing about shaping is that the learner is led to the final response through learning a chain of simpler responses leading to the final response. In other words, the learner comes to approximate the final response through a series of successive steps. The technique of shaping is sometimes called the method of *successive approximations.*

It should be obvious that the principle of shaping is a general one, applying to human instrumental conditioning as well as to lower animals. As an example, let us take a report of shaping the behavior of a seriously disturbed child (Wolf et al., 1964):

In addition to numerous other difficulties, this boy was practically blind after a series of operations for cataracts when he was two years old. It was extremely important for him to wear glasses, and this behavior was shaped by successive approximations to the desired final response of continuously wearing the glasses. The child was placed in a room where several empty glasses frames were lying around. Whenever he picked up one of these, he was reinforced with small pieces of candy or fruit. Soon he touched the frames quite often, but it was extremely

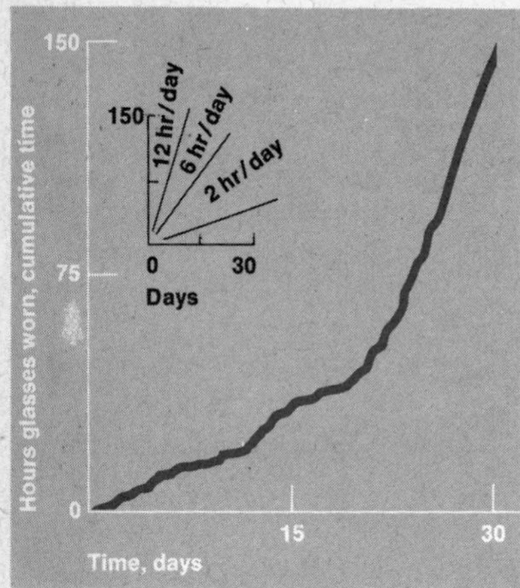

OPERANT CONDITIONING IS NOT RESTRICTED TO ANIMALS

Figure 3.10 *A cumulative response curve for the behavior of glasses wearing in a disturbed child. This response was shaped. Note that the final rate of response is quite high—approximating 12 hours per day. The inset graph shows the slopes which correspond to three rates of response—2 hours per day, 6 hours per day, and 12 hours per day. This sort of key often appears in cumulative response curves. (After Wolf et al., 1964.)*

difficult to shape the next step in the chain, putting the glasses on in the proper way. The therapists arranged to use more powerful reinforcers by making bites of lunch contingent upon having the glasses closer and closer to the proper wearing position. In a very short time, with this more powerful reinforcer, it was possible to shape both the behavior of putting on the glasses and the behavior of looking through them after they had been put on properly. The boy was soon wearing his glasses for 12 hours each day. A cumulative response curve for this behavior is shown in Figure 3.10. Although the curve does not show the frequency of a discrete event such as lever pressing, it may be interpreted in the same way as any cumulative response curve. Note that the slope of the curve becomes steeper and finally stabilizes with a steep slope.

Probably we all can think of responses which are shaped—if not deliberately shaped—in the process of child rearing. Many attitudes and beliefs, customs, learned goals, and certain aspects of the use of language, for example, can result from such shaping by means of reinforcement.

Extinction In operant conditioning, just as in classical conditioning, it is possible to remove, or *extinguish,* a learned response *by withholding reinforcement.* If, for example, a rat in a Skinner box no longer gets food when it presses the lever, its rate of responding gradually slows down until the animal makes no more responses than it did before it was trained. When the number of responses is no greater than it was before any training, the behavior is said to be *extinguished.* A sample cumulative extinction curve resulting from the withholding of reinforcement is shown in Figure 3.11.

Primary and secondary reinforcement By definition, a reinforcing stimulus or event of some sort is necessary in operant conditioning. In such conditioning, we have seen, anything that strengthens a response may be considered a reinforcer.

As in classical conditioning, we can make a distinction between primary and secondary reinforcement. A *primary reinforcement* is reinforcement by a stimulus, or reinforcer, that is effective for the untrained subject. In classical conditioning, however, the primary reinforcer *elicits* the natural response (such as salivation), while in operant conditioning it *shapes* the response by causing the subject to do, ever more frequently, whatever leads to primary reinforcement.

As for secondary reinforcement, the meanings of the term in classical and operant conditioning are comparable. The pairing of a second stimulus with the primary reinforcement over a series of trials results in the second stimulus acquiring the ability to call forth the response attached to the primary reinforcement. At this point it becomes a *secondary reinforcer.* As in classical conditioning, there is a limit imposed by extinction on the order of pairing that can be effective. For most purposes, the limit is at secondary reinforcement; third- and fourth-order stimuli acquire little reinforcing effect.

Secondary reinforcement in operant conditioning can be illustrated by the following example (Fox & King, 1961):

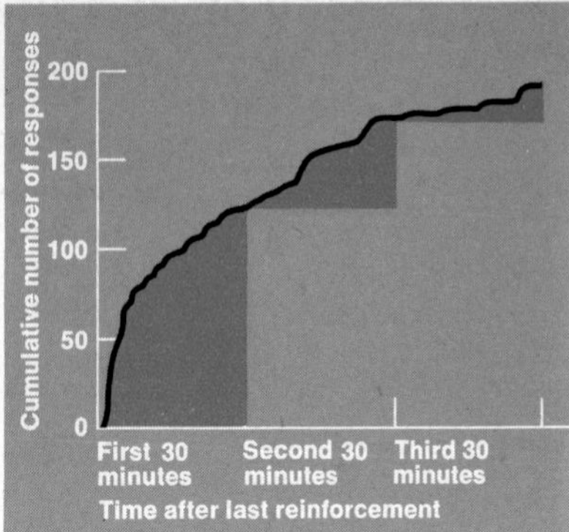

WITHOUT REINFORCEMENT, OPERANT RESPONSES GRADUALLY EXTINGUISH

Figure 3.11 *An extinction curve for a rat in a Skinner box. When no food is given for presses of the lever, the rate of pressing gradually slows down. The dark areas indicate the relative numbers of responses added in each 30-minute interval. (After Skinner, 1938.)*

The sound of a buzzer in itself is not reinforcing to a rat. If, however, the buzzer is paired with a *primary reinforcer*, it will acquire the ability to reinforce. The experiment begins by sounding a buzzer every time a rat is given a sip of sugar water. Then the rat is put in a Skinner box and allowed to learn, for the first time, to press the lever. Instead of reinforcing the rat with sugar water, however, the experimenters reinforce it with the buzzer that had been paired with sipping sugar water. The buzzer now works very well as a *secondary* reinforcer to increase the rate of lever pressing.

In addition to serving as reinforcement for the learning of *new* responses, secondary reinforcers can also act to *maintain* behavior when no primary reinforcement is forthcoming after a response. This is shown in the following experiment (Bugelski, 1938):

Rats were trained to press a bar in a Skinner box with a click accompanying the presentation of primary reinforcement. After the animals had learned the response, two groups were formed. Neither group received primary reinforcement for bar presses, but in one group bar presses were followed by the click. In the other group, no stimulus followed bar presses. The results showed that responding was maintained far longer in the "click group" than in the "'nonclick group."

As always, these examples merely illustrate a principle which seems important in human behavior. The instance of a child learning to behave in the way demanded by his culture, that is, becoming socialized, comes to mind. Parents rarely use primary reinforcers, except for escape from punishment, to shape behavior. Instead, secondary reinforcers, such as praise, encouragement, and threat of punishment, are used to shape new learning and to maintain learned behavior. In this case, the words used have become secondary reinforcers because they were paired in the past with primary reward or punishment.

Partial reinforcement So far we have been discussing the case in which every response is reinforced. A situation that is far more common in everyday life, and that can easily be studied in the laboratory, is one in which only a certain proportion of the responses are reinforced. In other words, *partial* instead of *continuous reinforcement* is involved.

Partial reinforcement is ordinarily administered according to some plan or schedule—at least, it is in experiments on partial reinforcement. For that reason the term *schedule of reinforcement* is sometimes used more or less synonymously with the term partial reinforcement. The schedule may consist of reinforcing, say, every fourth response; in that case, it is a *ratio schedule.* Or it may be a schedule of reinforcing once every minute, provided that the subject makes a response in the interval; in this case, it is an *interval schedule.* More complicated arrangements are possible, and some of these will be described. At the extremes, we have situations in which either all or no responses are reinforced. The first of these is *continuous reinforcement (crf)*; the second, *extinction (ext).* But both are instances of a schedule of reinforcement.

As a general rule, where comparisons of partial and continuous schedules of reinforcement have been made, learning is found to be slower

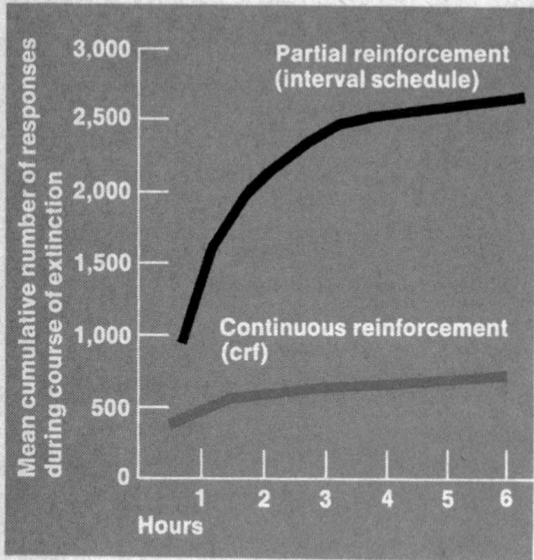

PARTIAL REINFORCEMENT OF OPERANT RESPONSES RESULTS IN HIGH RESISTANCE TO EXTINCTION

Figure 3.12 *Resistance to extinction after 100 percent and partial reinforcement. Responding is much more resistant to extinction after partial reinforcement: almost five times more responses were made after the partial schedule. (Modified from Jenkins et al., 1950.)*

under partial schedules, especially in classical conditioning (Reynolds, 1958). However, after comparable degrees of learning have been reached, subjects who learned under partial schedules usually maintain behavior far longer in the absence of any reinforcement. A more technical way of stating this is that there is greater resistance to extinction after most schedules of partial reinforcement. An illustration of the very great differences in resistance to extinction of partial and continuously reinforced responses is given in Figure 3.12. This greater resistance to extinction after partial schedules is one reason why, in everyday life, human beings and animals tend to persist in responding long after reinforcement has ceased. Although some responses may be maintained by secondary reinforcement, others, learned early in life, may persist merely because they were strongly learned during the course of many partially reinforced trials. Parents and others simply are not, and cannot be, consistent in meting out reinforcements.

Partial reinforcement schedules can be arranged in several ways (Ferster and Skinner, 1957). The delivery of reinforcement may be made contingent upon the *number*, *rate*, or *pattern* of responses. Delivery of reinforcement may also depend upon *time*, without regard to the number, rate, or pattern of response.

The *fixed-ratio schedule* (FR) is an example of a partial schedule in which the number of responses determines when reinforcement occurs. A certain number of responses must be made before a reinforcement is produced: that is, there is a fixed ratio of nonreinforced responses to reinforced responses. For example, every third (ratio of 3:1), fourth (4:1), or hundredth (100:1) response might be reinforced. Under the FR schedule, the rate of response tends to be quite high and relatively steady, as indicated in Figure 3.13*a*.

The *fixed-interval schedule* (FI) is one in which reinforcement is given after a fixed interval of time. No reinforcements are forthcoming, no matter how many responses are made, until a certain interval of time has gone by. Behavior under this schedule tends to vary in rate during the interval. Immediately after a reinforcement the rate is low, but it increases steadily during the interval until the next reinforcement is given. In a cumulative record, this tends to produce a "scalloped" record, as in Figure 3.13*b* which shows typical behavior under a fixed-interval schedule.

Schedules can also be made variable, for example, *variable-ratio* (VR) and *variable-interval schedules* (VI) can be set up. In the *variable-ratio schedule*, subjects are paid off after a variable number of responses. For instance, reinforcement might come once after two responses, again after ten responses, again after six responses, and so on after different numbers of responses. A variable-ratio schedule can be specified in terms of the *average number* of responses needed for reinforcement. Under *variable-interval schedules*, the individual is reinforced first after one interval of time, then after another interval, and so on, the schedule being specified by the *average interval*. Both of these variable schedules produce especially great resistance to extinction and steady rates of responding. (See Figure 3.13*c* and *d* for examples of behavior under variable-interval and variable-ratio schedules.) The

FIXED-RATIO, FIXED-INTERVAL, VARIABLE-INTERVAL, AND VARIABLE-RATIO CUMULATIVE RECORDS

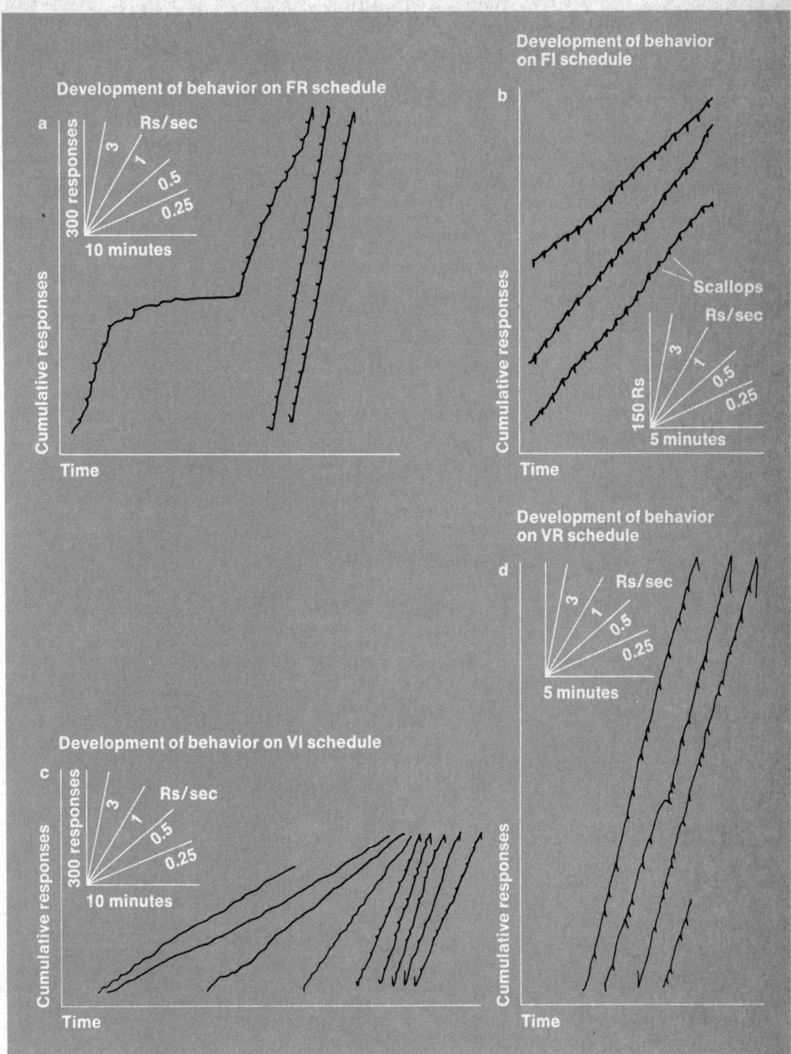

Figure 3.13 *Characteristic cumulative response records for four partial schedules of reinforcement in which pigeons pecked at keys. Note two things about these records: First, the horizontal or vertical slashes on the response curves show when reinforcements were given. Second, although the record for each schedule is in several sections, the response curves are really continuous: the long, continuous response records have been cut and displaced on the paper to save space.*
(a) *The development of characteristic responding on a* fixed-ratio *schedule of partial reinforcement. The rate of response increases to a steady rate of about 3 responses per second.*
(b) *The development of characteristic responding on a* fixed-interval *schedule of reinforcement. Note the "scallops" in the final portion of the record.*
(c) *The development of characteristic responding on a* variable-interval *schedule of reinforcement. Note that the reinforcement marks come at variable intervals. Note also the high, steady rate of response—especially in the 5th to 8th segments.*
(d) *The high, steady rate of responding characteristic of* variable-ratio *schedules of reinforcement. (Modified from Ferster and Skinner, 1957.)*

four schedule arrangements given in Figure 3.13 are only samples from a multitude of possible schedule types (see Ferster and Skinner, 1957).

Rough parallels may be found between these reinforcement schedules and some everyday situations. Fixed ratios of reinforcement are somewhat like being paid for piecework—except that such payment is usually not made after a certain number of pieces but at the end of a pay period. In that case, payment is really on a combination of fixed-ratio and fixed-interval schedules. The latter, taken alone, is like being paid on a fixed salary (except that most employers will not permit an employee to make only a few "responses" near the time of the paycheck). The variable-interval schedule is precisely how one is paid in such gambling situations as slot machines; these pay at quite unpredictable intervals.

EVEN PIGEONS MUST WORK TO EAT

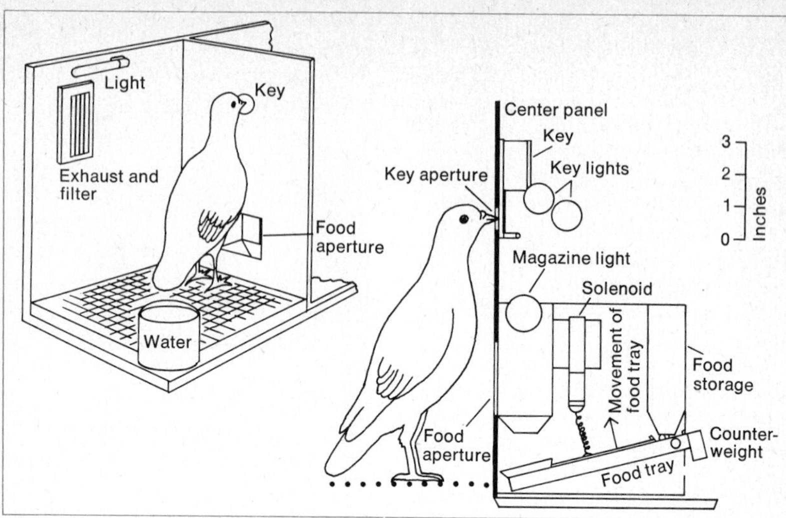

Figure 3.14 *Left, a Skinner box for pigeons. Key pecking is the response which is reinforced. Reinforcement (food) is given when the food dipper comes up to the floor of the box where the pigeon can reach it. Right, a side view of the front part of the Skinner box for pigeons. Note the key and food tray especially. The key is a translucent panel which can be illuminated by the key lights. (Modified from Ferster and Skinner, 1957.)*

Stimulus generalization We have already seen that a response classically conditioned to a particular CS will also be made to other stimuli which are similar in some way to that CS. In operant conditioning, stimulus generalization also takes place. The response in operant conditioning is made in a particular stimulus situation—in a Skinner box with a certain type of light, for example. If the stimulus situation is changed, the response still occurs, but at a lower rate than in the original stimulus situation. The rate will further depend upon the degree of similarity between the original training situation and the changed stimulus situation. The following experiment will illustrate stimulus generalization in operant conditioning (Olson and King, 1962):

Instead of rats, pigeons, another standby in studies of operant learning, were used. A pigeon was required to learn to peck a translucent key, which was a switch mounted on the wall of a Skinner box for pigeons (shown in Figure 3.14). In the original learning, a moderately bright light illuminated the key. After the operant pecking response to this stimulus had been well learned and the rate of response was high and steady, the animals were tested with six other light intensities on the key. These test stimuli were spaced in steps of equal intensity from low to high. In the graph of Figure 3.15, the original stimulus is called 8; the more intense stimuli are 2, 4, and 6; and the less intense stimuli are 10, 12, and 14. The graph shows that there is a tendency to respond to these new stimuli, and that this tendency depends upon the degree of separation between the original and test stimuli.

Discrimination learning In a sense, discrimination is the opposite of stimulus generalization. In stimulus generalization the response spreads to similar stimuli, whereas in *discrimination learning* the response comes to be made to one stimulus, but not to others. The method of achieving discrimination is simply to reinforce responses to one stimu-

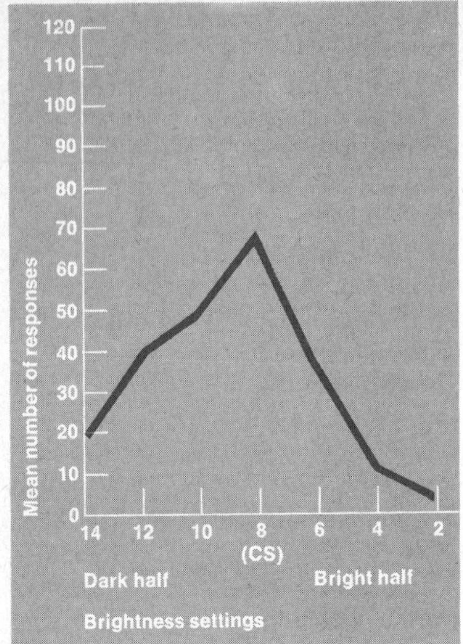

RESPONDING FALLS OFF AS STIMULI BECOME MORE DIFFERENT FROM THE ORIGINAL

Figure 3.15 *A generalization gradient for operant learning. Note that the greatest number of responses were made to the original stimulus—somewhat loosely called the CS in this graph. As the stimuli became more and more different from the original stimulus, the number of responses diminished. This happened with both the brighter and dimmer stimuli. (Modified from Olson and King, 1962.)*

lus, called the *positive stimulus*, or S^D, and not to reinforce—that is, to extinguish—responses to all other stimuli, called the *negative stimuli*, or S^Δ. The following experiment illustrates discrimination learning in a pigeon Skinner box (Hanson, 1959):

The bird was reinforced only for responses when the translucent key was illuminated by a light which appeared yellow-green to human observers. The pigeon received reinforcements during the intervals of yellow-green illumination on a variable-interval schedule; this was done to ensure a rather high and steady rate of response. If another light, say a red one, illuminated the key, the pigeon received no reinforcement. Under these conditions the pigeon learned to peck during the yellow-green, but not the red, periods. After a discrimination has been learned in a situation of this kind, the change in behavior when the stimuli are shifted is dramatic—almost like turning a faucet on or off. The ability of a stimulus to control behavior (the turning on and off of responses, in this case) is sometimes referred to as the *stimulus control of behavior.*

Discrimination is not simply a laboratory curiosity. When, for example, a child first learns to associate words with objects, he tends to generalize. All animals are "bow-wow," all men are "dada," and anything he can eat is a "cookie." When he finds that some animals do not bark or let him pet them, that all men do not react like "dada," or that some things do not taste at all like cookies—when he finds, in other words, that some objects are not reinforcing—his generalized responses to them extinguish. Thus through differential reinforcement and extinction he comes to discriminate properly. In fact, we might suggest that skill in almost anything is largely a matter of the extent to which behavior is under stimulus control. The expert discriminates differences in stimuli, responding to some and not to others that the novice may not even notice.

Autonomic conditioning Before concluding this section on operant conditioning, we shall turn to one of the more dramatic developments in recent research on conditioning. This is the operant conditioning of such autonomic responses as heart rate, vasodilation (dilation of blood vessels), and intestinal contractions. (The autonomic nervous system is described in detail in Chapter 7.)

It has long been known that autonomic responses can be *classically* conditioned. Salivation, in fact, is an autonomic response, and it conditioned well in Pavlov's classical research on conditioning. It was not known, however, that these responses could serve as *operants*—meaning that they could be made to occur or not, depending on whether they were rewarded in some way. The fact that they can has been convincingly demonstrated in the last few years (Miller, 1969). Of the many experiments done, let us take one example.

Rats were implanted with electrodes in an area of the brain where electrical stimulation is rewarding. (This area was known from other research in which rats that had electrodes implanted there would press a bar repeatedly to obtain brief electric shocks; see Chapter 17.) At the same time, they were equipped with devices for measuring heart rate and intestinal contraction. The heartbeat varies somewhat in rate from time to time, and intestinal contractions occur intermittently, just as a rat's ambulatory behavior varies in a Skinner box. The experimenter, watching his instruments, could look for times when the heart sped up or slowed down and then could present a rewarding stimulation to the brain. Or he could present the same reward for the occurrence or nonoccurrence of intestinal contractions.

Altogether, there were four groups of rats. One group was rewarded for a fast heartbeat, another for a slow heartbeat, a third for intestinal contractions, and a fourth for intestinal relaxation. Records were, of course, kept of heart rate and intestinal contractions for the period preceding the reward. Otherwise the experiment was conducted in the same way as a learning experiment with bar pressing.

The results are given in Figure 3.16. On the left are the intestinal contraction scores of the four groups, showing that the group rewarded for intestinal contractions learned to "contract," while those rewarded for intestinal relaxation learned to "relax." The left-hand graph also demonstrates that the groups rewarded for a change in heart rate showed little systematic change in the intestinal contraction score. In the right-hand graph are the results for the heart-rate groups. Those rewarded for a fast heartbeat learned to quicken the beat, and those rewarded for a slow heartbeat learned to slow the heart, while neither group learned anything about intestinal contractions.

This experiment shows that what we have thought of as involuntary responses can in fact be voluntary, in the sense that they can be learned as instrumental operants if reward is made contingent upon them. Many other kinds of responses have been learned in this way: increases or decreases of urine formation, which are accomplished through changes in blood flow to the kidney; contractions of the stomach; changes in blood pressure that are independent of heart rate; and even changes in brain waves. In one interesting experiment showing that such learning can be quite discriminating, rats learned to dilate the blood vessels of one ear when rewarded for doing so, but not to dilate vessels in the other ear, since such changes were unrewarded (Di Cara and Miller, 1968). Unbelievable? But true!

These experiments are still too new for us to evaluate their practical significance in animals and human beings. We have no idea how much learning of autonomic responses goes on in everyday life, although some of the feats of Yoga seem to be of this kind. Perhaps such learning accounts for some of the ills we have come to call psychosomatic. Perhaps it can be used in a therapeutic way to combat such disorders as high blood pressure or kidney disease. Only time and further research will tell.

Aversive Conditioning

In the preceding sections on classical and operant conditioning, we have dealt almost exclusively with *positive reinforcement,* that is, with reinforcers which satisfy drives such as hunger and thirst. An exception was the description of Bekhterev's experiment on flexion conditioning. Now we turn to learning that involves *negative reinforcement*—something that is painful, uncomfortable, or fearful. In learning with such a

AUTONOMIC RESPONSES CAN BECOME CONDITIONED OPERANTS

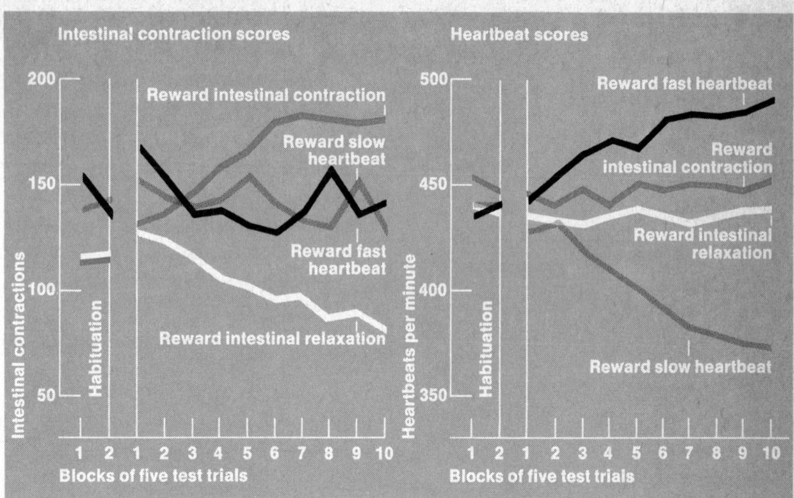

Figure 3.16 *Both intestinal contractions and heart rate were measured for all animals (rats in this case). Four groups were used, and the scores on each measure constitute the curves in each graph. On the left, two groups were rewarded for changes in intestinal contractions, one for an increase and the other for a decrease. On the right, two were rewarded for changes in heartbeat, one for an increase and the other for a decrease. In each case, the reinforced responses were learned, but the unreinforced responses were not. (From Miller and Banuazizi, 1968.)*

reinforcer, a mixture of classical and operant conditioning usually takes place in two stages, although the Bekhterev experiment is an example of simple classical conditioning.

Aversive conditioning situations can be classified into three basic categories: emotional conditioning, escape conditioning, and avoidance conditioning. The third category of avoidance conditioning can be further divided into active and passive avoidance conditioning. Let us see what the general differences are between these conditioning situations; then we can consider them one by one.

Suppose, as is usually the case, that the aversive stimulus is a mild shock, and our conditioning procedure is to pair a signal such as a buzzer with the shock. We can arrange the conditioning situation in three ways that differ in what the animal is permitted to do.

1. The subject may be permitted neither to escape nor to avoid the shock. The buzzer and shock come on together, and the animal can do nothing but take the shock. If, after some trials of this procedure, the subject is tested with the buzzer alone, it will show evidence of *emotional conditioning*. In the case of a rat, it squeals, jumps around, defecates, and urinates—all responses that normally occur to the shock alone. This reaction to the buzzer is known as a *conditioned emotional response.*

2. The subject is not permitted to avoid the shock, but it can escape after the onset of shock. We arrange two compartments, in either of which the rat can be shocked. In this case we omit the buzzer and simply shock the animal from time to time on whatever side it happens to be. As soon as the shock comes on, the subject shows the usual emotional response that includes some jumping around. In the course of running or jumping, the animal gets into the other compartment where there is no shock. Thus by making the specific response of running to the other compartment, the animal *escapes* from the shock. With repeated trials, the response is shaped, and the subject comes to make the response

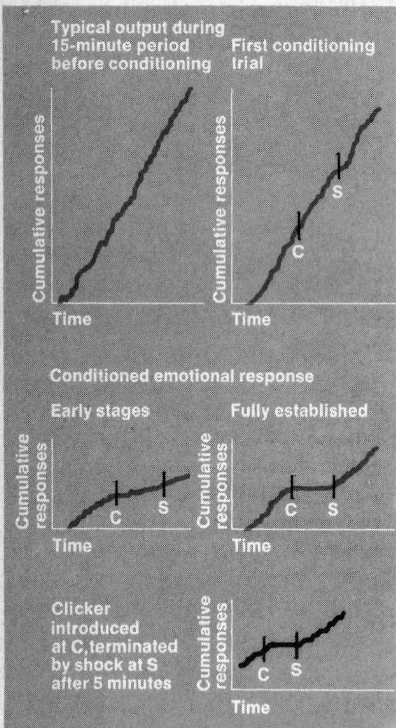

THE CONDITIONED EMOTIONAL RESPONSE (CER) IS SHOWN BY A "PLATEAU" ON THE CUMULATIVE CURVE

Figure 3.17 *Development of a conditioned emotional response in which rats inhibit bar pressing in a Skinner box. The lines in the graphs are cumulative response records.* C *on the graph lines marks the point at which the clicker is introduced;* S *marks the point, in separate conditioning trials, at which the clicker is terminated and an electric shock is administered. The development of the conditioned emotional response is shown by the flat spots, or "plateaus," which grow more prominent between* C *and* S *as the conditioning trials proceed. (Modified from Hunt and Brady, 1951.)*

very rapidly as soon as the shock is applied. This learning is *escape conditioning*.

3. The animal can avoid the shock altogether. We have two compartments as in escape conditioning, but we add a warning signal by sounding a buzzer a few seconds before the shock is applied. By responding to the warning signal and getting to the other compartment before the shock comes on, the animal learns to avoid shock. This learning is therefore called avoidance conditioning.

a. Avoidance conditioning, as we indicated, can be of two kinds. The type just described is *active avoidance,* because the animal makes a specific response that actively avoids the shock.

b. The avoidance situation can be modified, however, to require a passive avoidance response. Food can be placed at one end of the compartment and left until the animal has learned to go there when it is hungry. But shock can then be applied to the same compartment whenever the animal ventures into it. This situation is one of *passive avoidance,* for the animal must learn *not* to go into the shocked compartment.

Conditioned emotional response In its simplest form the first kind of conditioning, emotional conditioning, is difficult to measure objectively. Pairing a buzzer and a shock causes the animal to make a variety of conditioned emotional responses to the buzzer, all of which signify fear. But how does one measure fear or count emotional responses? A way has been devised. It combines the emotional, or fear, conditioning with an operant response such as bar pressing. The following is a typical experiment of this kind (Hunt and Brady, 1951):

Rats first learned to press a bar in a Skinner box for water reinforcement. The reinforcement was given on a variable-interval schedule, and a high and steady rate of response, which could serve as a baseline, was established. Next the rats were given "fear trials," which consisted of the presentation of a short clicking sound and a mildly painful electric shock when the clicking sound was turned off. In a sense, the clicking sound served as a cue for the coming electric shock. As more and more fear trials were given, the conditioned emotional response of crouching and failing to press the bar increased in strength. The development of the conditioned emotional response is shown by the flat places, or plateaus, in the steady curve of responding (see Figure 3.17).

Animal experiments are important because of the variables which can be investigated and the control which can be exercised, but experiments on the conditioning of fear can sometimes also be done with human beings. The way in which we may learn to fear certain things is illustrated in this description of a famous experiment with an infant named Albert (Watson and Rayner, 1920).

Albert was an 11-month-old boy who displayed no fear of animals. When shown a rabbit (see Figure 3.18), he expressed delight and made no effort to get away. Later, however, he was shown a white rat, and at the same time heard a loud and sudden noise. This natural stimulus for fear had the expected effect; he shrank back. The procedure was repeated several times on different occasions. He was

A BABY LEARNS FEAR OF AN OBJECT BY ASSOCIATING IT WITH AN EVENT HE IS AFRAID OF; THEN HE GENERALIZES THE FEAR TO SIMILAR OBJECTS

Figure 3.18 *Conditioning and generalization of fear in the infant. Upper left, before conditioning, the child approaches a white rabbit without fear. Upper right, a loud noise, which startles and scares the infant, is paired with the presentation of a white rat. Lower left, the child, after conditioning, appears to be afraid of the rabbit. Lower right, he is afraid of other white furry objects. (After Watson and Rayner, 1920.)*

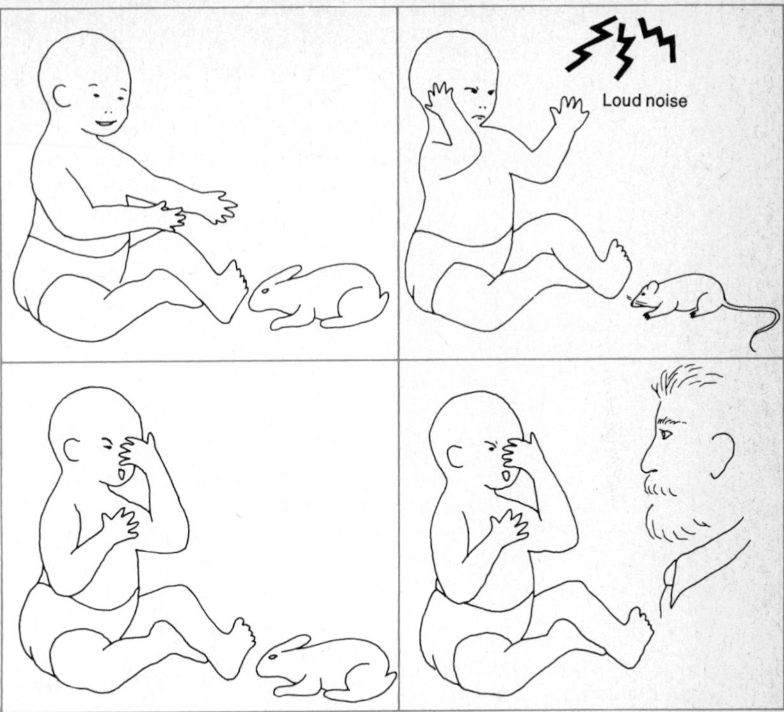

then presented with the white rabbit which formerly had caused no fear. Now, however, he was frightened by the sight of the rabbit and attempted to get away from it. He was then tested with a number of other white furry objects, including a white beard on a man. All these provoked fear.

This experiment demonstrates two points. One is the *conditioning* of fear. Any stimulus regularly present when a fear response is made can itself become a stimulus for fear. The other is the phenomenon of *generalization*. The fear that is learned is not necessarily restricted to the conditioning stimulus, but generalizes to similar objects—in this case to all white furry objects. Both conditioning and generalization are important factors in building up our repertory of fears.

Escape conditioning and active avoidance conditioning From the distinctions made above, the reader might expect to consider escape conditioning separately from avoidance conditioning. That is not necessary, however, because the learning of an active avoidance requires that an escape response first be learned. Hence in the course of one experiment, we can see the conditioning of both escape and active avoidance (Solomon and Wynne, 1953):

A dog was placed in a compartment which was divided into two halves by a low fence—one that the dog could easily jump over. The floor was an electric grill through which shock could be administered. In each training trial a buzzer was

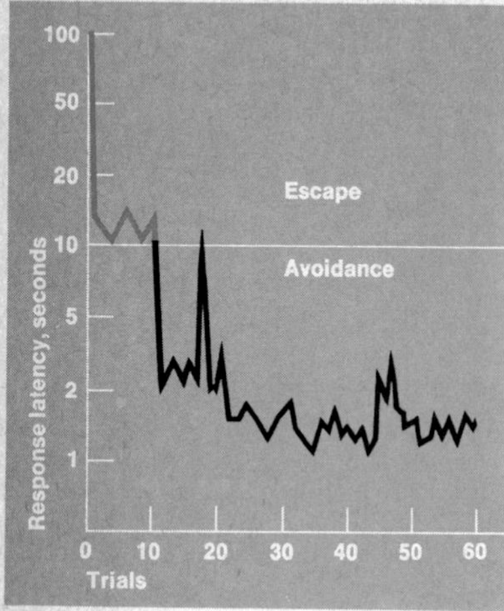

LEARNING TO AVOID PUNISHMENT TAKES PLACE RATHER ABRUPTLY AFTER A PERIOD OF LEARNING TO ESCAPE PUNISHMENT

Figure 3.19 *Acquisition of an avoidance response to a buzzer. Note the fairly sudden transition from escape to avoidance. Note, too, that the time scale is not linear—the times on the vertical axis, or ordinate, are plotted on a logarithmic scale. (Modified from Solomon and Wynne, 1953.)*

turned on, and this was followed in 10 seconds by a shock on the side of the compartment where the dog was. The dog was supposed to jump over the fence to the other side of the compartment at some time within this 10-second interval. If he did, the buzzer was turned off and no shock was given; if he did not, he got a shock which was continued until he jumped over the fence. Since the jumping is instrumental in escaping from shock or in avoiding shock, it may be said to be a response of the same kind as lever pressing.

A curve for this kind of learning is shown in Figure 3.19, where the time to make a response after the onset of the buzzer—the *latency* of response—is plotted for each trial. If the latency was more than 10 seconds, the response might be classed as an escape response, because the shock had come on and the dog was escaping from it. If the latency was less than 10 seconds, the response might be called an avoidance response, because the dog jumped the fence *before* the shock came on and thus avoided it. As can be seen in Figure 3.19, the dog in this experiment went for a number of trials without making any avoidance responses. Then relatively suddenly the dog began to learn to avoid, and within a few more trials he was avoiding quite consistently.

What is happening in the course of this avoidance conditioning can be analyzed as follows (Solomon, 1964): First, an emotional fear response to the buzzer is being classically conditioned. This association builds up in the early trials; when the buzzer is turned on, the dog alerts, squirms, yelps, and shows various other signs of fear. Second, while fear conditioning is going on, the animal simply learns to *escape* from shock as rapidly as possible; escape learning is taking place. In Figure 3.19 this learning is shown by a drop in the curve to a point just above the line representing correct avoidance responses. Third, the animal makes a response or two before the shock comes on, and the buzzer is turned off; now avoidance conditioning is building up. The cessation of the buzzer after these correct, or preshock, responses is reinforcing because the conditioned stimulus for fear—the buzzer—is turned off. Thus the reinforcement for the avoidance response is fear reduction, and this is sufficient to maintain the response.

Passive avoidance conditioning The experiment just described is one in active avoidance, for the animal learns *what to do,* and this learning does not conflict with any other habit or motive. In *passive avoidance* experiments, on the other hand, we teach the organism *what not to do.* In the simplest case, a passive avoidance response is in conflict with some habit built on a physiological drive. For example, suppose that we train a rat to run down an alley for food. After the rat has learned this behavior, we electrify a section of the alley between the start box and the food. After a number of trials, the rat learns to avoid shock by not leaving the start box. Learning this passive avoidance conflicts with the habit, strongly motivated, to run the alley for food.

There are several kinds of passive avoidance, but for our purposes here we will distinguish only two. The kind just illustrated is passive avoidance of an *operant* response previously learned through positive reinforcement. What the subject must avoid is doing something he has previously *learned* to do. A second kind is avoidance of a *consummatory response,* such as eating or drinking. We may electrify a food dish so that when the animal goes to eat, it receives a shock. If the shock is sufficiently strong, the animal will soon learn not to eat.

Passive avoidance conditioned by negative reinforcement may be coupled with operant conditioning that is produced by positive reinforcement. For example, a Skinner box may be so arranged that it has two levers under two glass panels. The task is to learn a light-dark discrimination in which light is "correct" and dark is "incorrect." When one panel is lighted, pushing the bar beneath it delivers a pellet of food; but if the bar is pushed under the dark panel, shock is delivered through the bar. Here passive avoidance is learned for the incorrect stimulus along with operant bar pressing for the correct stimulus. This arrangement is frequently used in experiments on discrimination learning in animals and human subjects, for it commonly results in more rapid learning than experiments based on either positive or negative reinforcement alone.

Extinction and suppression We have seen that in classical and operant conditioning, an extinction procedure regularly produces extinction of responses. If reinforcement by the US is withdrawn, the conditioned response gradually extinguishes. This is not always the case, however, in avoidance conditioning. Whether extinction occurs and how rapidly it occurs depend on the kind of avoidance involved and other features of the situation.

First note an important difference in extinction between avoidance conditioning with negative reinforcement and operant conditioning with positive reinforcement. In the extinction of habits learned with positive reinforcement, the subject knows, so to speak, when the positive reinforcement is no longer being presented. If a rat has learned to push the bar in the Skinner box for food, it receives no food when the schedule is changed to an extinction procedure. Thus, in responding, the subject learns that no reinforcement is present. This is not the case in avoidance behavior. If an animal has been trained to avoid a shock by shuttling from one end of a box to another when a buzzer sounds, it has no way of knowing that the shock is no longer there so long as it performs the learned habit. This is an important factor in extinction, or lack of extinction, of avoidance behavior.

First let us consider active avoidance. In some experiments, like the one described above, dogs have been known to jump at the sound of a buzzer for *thousands* of trials after the shock has been turned off completely. Some dogs appear never to extinguish. Such a result undoubtedly varies somewhat from one strain to another, from one species to another, and with experimental procedures; but resistance to extinction, when an intense, painful event is to be avoided, is very great.

A combination of reasons helps to explain this very great resistance to extinction. One is that fear responses are slow to extinguish even under the best of conditions for extinction training. However, these conditions are not met in avoidance conditioning. In making avoidance responses, the learner leaves the original fear-producing situation—a signal paired with shock—*before* receiving shock. As we pointed out above, he has no chance to experience the pairing of *no* shock with the fear-producing stimulus, which is the condition required for extinction training of fear.

MILD PUNISHMENT MAY SUPPRESS A RESPONSE TEMPORARILY RATHER THAN ELIMINATE IT

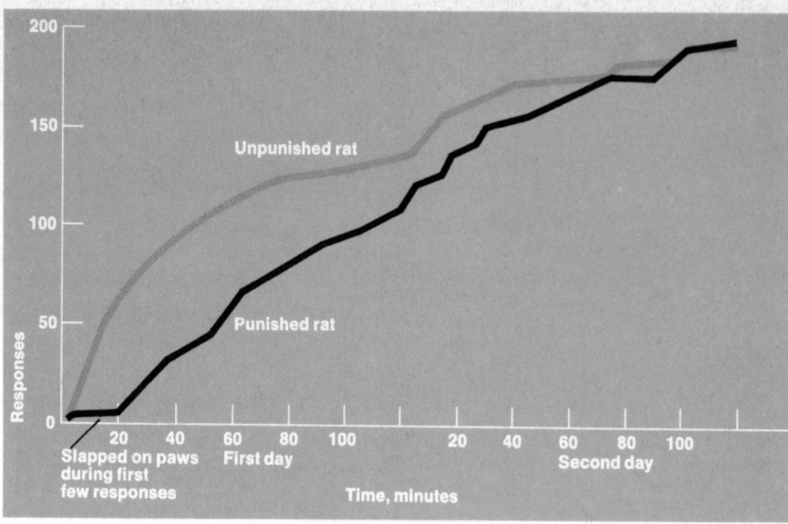

Figure 3.20 *The effect of punishment on extinction. Punishment at first depresses the extinction curve, but in the long run the punished rat makes as many responses as the unpunished animal. (After Skinner, 1938.)*

Finally, the operant part of the avoidance response is being reinforced by fear reduction throughout the period when no shock is being given. Hence, on the one hand, conditioned fear is not extinguished because the avoidance response prevents the possibility of extinction training, and on the other hand, the avoidance response is reinforced by the reduction of fear.

This resistance to extinction is reminiscent of avoidance behavior in human beings. A person who once learned to avoid snakes or mice frequently goes on avoiding them all his life. So it is too with the avoidance of water, high places, airplanes, and many other things. People do not easily get over habits of avoiding things. Getting rid of *unwanted* avoidance behavior (some of which is very useful) can be quite a problem.

Now let us consider a case of passive avoidance. In this one, the subject is punished for responses previously learned through positive reinforcement (Skinner, 1938).

Two rats were trained in the usual way in a Skinner box by reinforcing them with pellets of food for pressing the lever. Then they were placed on an extinction schedule. One of the rats, however, was slapped on the paws for the *first few responses* made during extinction. This was done by a device connected to the lever. The responses of the other rat, a control rat, were extinguished in the usual way.

The results of the experiment are given in Figure 3.20. The two curves in this figure are extinction curves obtained from the two rats after an equal amount of conditioning. The initial effect of the punishment, slapping, was to reduce the rate of responding. At least for a time, the punished rat responded much more slowly after the slapping than did the unpunished rat. Curiously enough, in this experiment the punished rat later responded at a fairly high rate even after the unpunished rat had slowed down (that is, the punished rat's curve develops a generally steeper slope after the initial flattening). The important thing to notice, however, is that in the end the two rats made just about the same total number of extinction responses.

In this case, passive avoidance consisted only of a temporary suppression of the lever-pressing habit, and in the long run had no effect on the habit. But note the conditions: The punishment was a mild one, and it was not administered often enough to build up fear to the point of completely suppressing the habit. It was like slapping a child's hand slightly now and then for getting into the cookie jar. Both forms of punishment are effective only temporarily. On the other hand, by giving a strong punishment *every* time the rat pushes the lever, it is possible to suppress all lever-pressing behavior completely and permanently.

Punishment As the reader may see by now, avoidance conditioning is relevant to questions of the value of punishment in changing habits. In everyday life, punishment is widely used in an attempt to prevent or eliminate undesirable behavior. Parents introduce it in various ways in bringing up their children; society uses it to prevent crime. And often the punishment proves ineffective; witness the steadily increasing crime rate in most United States cities.

What do we know about the effective use of punishment to teach avoidance behavior? There is much that we do not yet understand. But there is also much that we do, having learned it through hundreds of experiments with both animals and human subjects. As we proceed with our examination of punishment we should keep in mind the distinctions already made between active and passive avoidance. And in the case of passive avoidance (which will be the most important kind), we should remember the differences between avoidance of learned responses and avoidance of consummatory behavior.

Active avoidance is easily taught to animals, as our example of the dog in the shuttle box showed. In theory, it could as easily be taught to children, but in practice there are few situations in life requiring active avoidance learning, that is, learning *what to do* to avoid punishment. An infantryman learning to take cover at the sound of a shot and schoolchildren learning a firedrill are examples of active avoidance. These, however, are sophisticated responses built on prior learning, and there are few such cases in civilized society. In general, our society has arranged things so that active avoidance responses are not required.

On the other hand, a great deal of our learning from cradle to grave consists of passive avoidance responses—*what not to do.* We learn not to play with fire, not to steal, not to exceed the speed limit, and so on endlessly. The Ten Commandments, for example, consist entirely of "Thou shalt nots." Parents and society attempt to teach "don'ts" through reward and punishment, and often through punishment alone. But the use of punishment to teach such avoidance behavior effectively is a tricky matter.

INTENSITY The most important factor in the effectiveness of punishment seems to be its intensity. If punishment is quite strong, the behavior being punished will usually be entirely and permanently suppressed. A child burnt by a fire usually learns permanently not to put his finger in the fire. And if all punishment of unwanted behavior could be this strong, parents would have little difficulty in teaching their children the appropriate avoidances. But such strong punishment (say, a bad whipping) is likely to cause physical harm, which is an undesired effect. Hence we tend to scale down the punishment to something weaker. And here we begin to encounter trouble, for mild punishments tend to be ineffective. A common result of mild punishment is a temporary, but not permanent, suppression of behavior. This was illustrated by the experiment in which the rat in the Skinner box was given a few slaps for pushing the bar. The punishment temporarily suppressed bar pressing, but after a while the pressing was resumed, and in the long run, punishment had no effect at all.

CONSISTENCY Another factor in the effectiveness of punishment is, of course, the consistency with which it is administered. A mild punishment that only temporarily suppresses behavior can be effective for a long time if it is administered often. The experiment involving slapping of the rat in the Skinner box has been repeated using regularly administered punishment, with the result that bar-pressing behavior is completely suppressed (Church, 1963). Carried over to human behavior, this principle means that if punishments are to be effective, especially if they are mild, they should be consistently applied. Otherwise their effects are likely to be short-lived.

PROXIMITY The *proximity* of punishment in time and space to the behavior being punished is also important. The principle of contiguity applies here, as it does in most learning. Other things being equal, punishment is most effective when it is administered right at the point when the unwanted behavior occurs. The farther removed it is from that behavior, the less effective it will be. Well-intentioned parents who do not want to punish a child when they are angry often violate this principle by delaying the punishment.

STRENGTH OF RESPONSE Also significant is the "strength" of the punished response. Put another way, how badly a person wants to do something determines how effective or ineffective punishment may be in teaching him not to do it. This strength of response in turn depends on several things; for example, on whether or not the response has become an ingrained habit, and on whether or not the response is otherwise rewarded. Consider the behavior of a habitual robber: if not quickly caught and punished, robbery is a highly rewarding behavior. By the simple act of taking it from someone else, a robber obtains more money more quickly than does a man making an "honest living." If he succeeds in robbery a good many times without being caught, the habit becomes very strong. The fact that he will be punished—or in fact is punished, even with long imprisonment—frequently is ineffective in breaking the habit. And in part, this is why well-established criminal behavior is so hard to break with any amount of punishment short of life imprisonment. Also frequently involved is lack of an alternative route to reward—for example, lack of a regular job.

ADAPTATION Another factor in the effectiveness of punishment is *adaptation* to punishment. People adapt to pain and punishment, especially if it is mild. What at first may serve to suppress a behavior temporarily may through adaptation begin to have little or no effect. Children have been known to persist in punished behavior, even though the punishment is consistently administered, simply because they come to regard the punishment as "not so bad." They suffer it because it is more than offset by the reward obtained from the forbidden behavior.

REWARDED ALTERNATIVES If there is a suitable alternative route to a reward, even a mild punishment can be extremely effective. When a hungry rat is punished for taking one route that it has learned to a goal box, it quickly stops using that route if another, even somewhat longer, route is made available (Solomon, 1964). A child who has been caught and punished for stealing may continue doing it so long as there is no other way to get money. On the other hand, if he is offered the alternative of working to earn money, even though it is a harder route, he may stop stealing.

CONSUMMATORY RESPONSES Finally, the effectiveness of punishment also depends on whether the act being punished is a learned operant response or a consummatory response that satisfies a need. Offhand, one might think that consummatory responses such as eating and drinking, since they are innate, would withstand punishment better than operant responses. This is not the case, however (Solomon, 1964). A rat who receives an electric shock at its food tray quickly learns to avoid the tray no matter how hungry it is. It may even starve itself to death without venturing back to see if the shock is still there. The reason for this, we believe, is that shocking a consummatory response makes shock and the response more highly contiguous, and thus more closely associated, than is usually the case in shocking operants.

If punishment of one consummatory response is combined with reward of an alternative consummatory response, the effectiveness of shock is even more dramatic. If puppies, for example, are given a swat with a newspaper when they start to eat horsemeat, but they are allowed to eat pellets without punishment, they quickly learn to eat only pellets and to shun horsemeat. The learned aversion is so strong that they starve to death if presented only with horsemeat. We do not go to such extremes in training children, but a good general principle is to couple punishment of unwanted behavior with reward for approved behavior. In punishing a child, a parent should not stop with the punishment and leave him on his own, but should try to provide him immediately with an opportunity to do something for which he can be rewarded.

CUE FUNCTIONS OF PUNISHMENT In sophisticated organisms, a large repertory of alternative responses has already been acquired before a punishment is administered, so that it is not necessary for the subject to *learn* a new or alternative response through punishment. In such cases punishment, especially if it is mild, merely serves as a cue for selecting the correct response from the repertory. The punishment, or

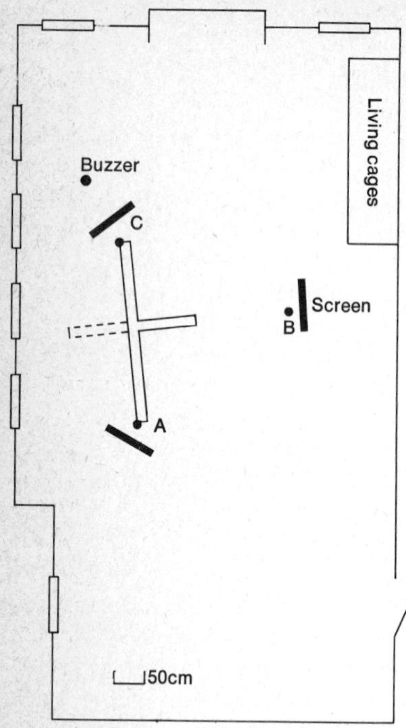

ANIMALS CAN LEARN THE PLACE AT WHICH AN EVENT OCCURS WITHOUT LEARNING A SPECIFIC RESPONSE

Figure 3.21 *The experimental room in Gleitman's study of place learning. Screens were set up directly behind points marked* A, B, *and* C. *Vertical stripes were painted on the screen at* A; *horizontal stripes were on the screen at* B; *the panel at* C *was unpainted. In addition, a buzzer was located behind* C, *and the animal could always see the windows and other objects in the room. The tracks ran between* A *and* B, A *and* C, *or* B *and* C. *They are not shown in this figure. Two positions of the T maze for testing choices between* A *and* C *are shown. (After Gleitman, 1955.)*

some sign that punishment is coming, merely tells the individual what is "right" and "wrong." It tells him how he is doing.

Many of the little punishments used in society serve as such cues. A low grade in an hour examination is a kind of punishment that tells a student where he stands in his mastery of the subject. Critical remarks made about a person's clothes or behavior may induce him to change his ways. In fact, all words of reproof come to have cue functions, since reproof or "wrong" stands for potential punishment. So long as the person has something else he can do when he runs into a punishment cue, he can quickly learn to do the "right" thing.

CONCLUSIONS ABOUT PUNISHMENT Active avoidance—learning *what to do*—is easily taught to animals and children. But as a practical matter, passive avoidance—learning *what not to do*—is of greater interest. The effectiveness of punishment in teaching passive avoidance depends on several factors: (1) The more intense the punishment, the more effective it is. Mild punishments, other things being equal, tend to suppress unwanted behavior only temporarily. (2) The more consistently punishment is administered, even if it is mild, the more effective it will be. (3) The closer punishment occurs in time and space to the behavior being punished, the more effective it will be. (4) The stronger the undesirable habit, the less effective punishment will be. (5) Organisms adapt to punishment, especially mild punishment, and this weakens its effectiveness. (6) Punishment, even when mild, can be extremely effective if it is coupled with a rewarded alternative. As a practical matter, this is the best way to use punishment. (7) Punishment of consummatory behavior, such as eating, can be quite effective, causing the organism to avoid the punished goal permanently. (8) In educated organisms, such as school children and human adults, mild punishment often is extremely effective because it serves as a cue for choosing already learned alternatives that are "right."

Perceptual Learning

In the preceding sections dealing with classical conditioning, operant conditioning, and aversive conditioning, the emphasis has been on the learning of *responses.* In each case, the learner acquires a response to a situation—an S-R association is formed—which he did not make in that situation prior to learning. In addition to responses, however, changes can and do occur in the way a learner perceives his world. We shall see what these changes are, but for the moment let us simply say that the learner comes to know something about the stimulus situation that he did not know before. Such changes in perception are called *perceptual learning,* which involve the formation of stimulus-stimulus, or S-S, associations. There are several ways of telling when such learning has taken place. We shall consider a few examples.

Place learning One kind of perceptual learning is learning the place at which some event occurs, and the routes to and from the place. This is like learning where the post office is, or learning any set of spatial

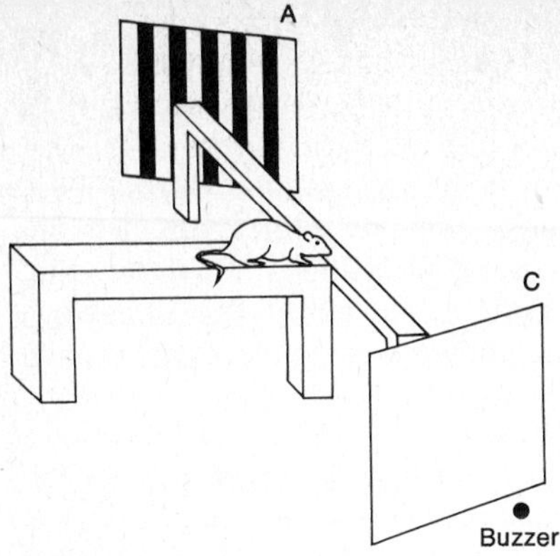

Figure 3.22 *A rat on an elevated T maze similar to that used in Gleitman's study of place (S-S) learning. Panels* A *and* C *(see Figure 3.21) are shown. This animal has been drawn in the car from* A *to* C *and is now being tested for* A *or* C *choices.*

relationships. It is called *place learning* and can be illustrated by the following experiment (Gleitman, 1955):

The basic purpose of the experiment was to give rats two contiguous experiences, without requiring them or permitting them to form any stimulus-response association, and then to determine by further tests whether the two stimulus situations had become associated. In this case, one stimulus situation was a shock and the other consisted of the places in the apparatus at which the shock was turned on and off. In order to eliminate the possibility of the animals forming any stimulus-response associations, they were carried through the apparatus in small Plexiglas cars.

Figure 3.21 gives the experimental arrangement. As it shows, there were three possible tracks, *A* to *B*, *B* to *C*, or *A* to *C*, over which the rat could be carried. The ends of the track were marked by distinctively painted panels and a buzzer (the stimuli). Each animal was drawn over one of the tracks 18 times. The shock was turned on as soon as the animal had been placed in the car and was turned off at the end of the ride, which took about 20 seconds. If S-S associations were formed during the course of this experience, the rat should associate the stimuli at the beginning of the ride with the beginning of shock and the stimuli at the end of the ride with relief from shock.

To determine whether such associations had been formed, it was necessary to have a test situation in which the rat could make a choice between the two stimulus situations, that is, the beginning and end of the track. To provide such a situation, the track was removed from the apparatus, and a T maze was put in its place with the crossbar of the T lying where the track had been (see Figures 3.21 and 3.22). Now the rat was placed in the stem of the T and observed to see which way it turned. Of a total of 35 animals tested in this way, 26 turned in the shock-off direction at the end of the track, while only 9 turned in the shock-on direction at the starting point. This result showed that S-S associations had been formed in the absence of any stimulus-response associations by the rat during the training trials.

Changed-response experiments Another way of demonstrating the formation of S-S associations is the so-called *changed response* experiment. The rationale of the changed-response experiment is as follows: A task is learned with one set of responses, and then something is done so that these original responses can no longer be utilized; different responses must be used. If the subject can show that he can solve the problem with the different responses, the original learning probably did not consist of S-R associations. If S-R associations formed the basis of the original learning, great disruption should take place when the subject is forced to change to other responses which had never been associated with the stimuli of the learning situation. In most changed-response experiments, very little disruption takes place when the responses are changed. This is what might be expected if S-S associations had been formed, that is, if cognitive maps had been built up and the subject knew about the situation and could use alternative responses to reach the goal.

You can easily try an informal changed-response experiment. Most of us are not ambidextrous; we learn to write with one hand or the other.

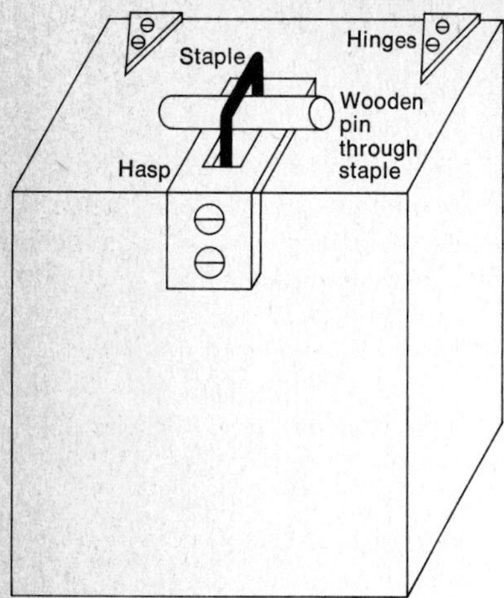

Figure 3.23 *Diagram of a box like the hasp box used by Lashley in his changed-response experiments in learning. The monkey had to open the box to reach the food.*

Try writing your name with a pencil held in your nonpreferred hand. The result will be shaky, but it will resemble, in general form at least, what you do with the preferred hand. Even when the responses are nothing alike, the result is roughly the same, as the following experiment shows. Rats were first trained to swim through a maze (Macfarlane, 1930). Then the water was covered by a floor and the rats were required to run through the maze. Swimming transferred to running with almost no errors; the rats made no more errors after the switch than before. Karl Lashley, (1890–1958) performed several of these changed-response experiments (Lashley, 1924).

In one experiment, monkeys were first trained to open boxes to get food. Rather precise sequences of response were required to open the boxes. One of them, the hasp box, was secured by an ordinary gate hasp and staple with a wooden pin through the staple (see Figure 3.23). The monkey needed to pull the wooden pin, lift the hasp, and then hold up the lid of the box before it could reach the food. After this sequence of responses had been well learned, the experimenters removed an area of each monkey's cerebral cortex (and probably some underlying fibers) which regulates movement of the hand and arm muscles. This operation at first made the hand and arm spastically, or "stiffly," paralyzed. But with time, there was gradual and almost complete recovery of motor function, although some residual spasticity and weakness often remained. This residual paralysis forced the monkeys to solve the problem with different hand and arm movements after the operation. But even though different movements were now employed, the animals retained the learned sequence of steps needed to solve the problem.

The case of one monkey was especially clear. This animal was right-handed before the operation. As a result of the operation, paralysis was more pronounced in the right hand than in the left hand. Postoperatively, the much-weakened right hand was used at first, but when this proved ineffective the monkey switched to the left hand. Performance transferred from the right to the left hand, even though completely different sets of muscles were being used.

The monkeys apparently had not learned a chain of stimulus-response connections, but had learned the *relationship* between the hasp, the pin, and the opening of the box. To put this in human terms for a minute, the monkeys had simply learned "what led to what," or "how to open the box."

In studies on the sequence of responses necessary for maze learning, Lashley reached conclusions similar to those we have just considered.

Observations on the behavior of animals with pronounced motor disturbances following spinal or cerebellar injuries emphasize the relative unimportance of the movement system. Animals which have learned the maze before the development of the motor inco-ordinations continue to traverse it, although the manner of progression may be almost completely altered. One drags himself through with his forepaws; another falls at every step but gets through by a series of lunges; a third rolls over completely in making each turn, yet manages to avoid rolling into a cul-de-sac and makes an errorless run. . . . If the customary sequence of movements employed in reaching the food is rendered impossible, another set, not previously used in the habit, and constituting an entirely different motor pattern, may be directly and efficiently substituted without any random activity. (Lashley, 1929, pages 136–137.)

Latent learning The experiments just described make it clear that S-S associations can be formed and that such S-S associations may include the learning of spatial relationships or cognitive maps. Now we turn to another question that has been given considerable experimental study. This is the question of whether any need reduction, or more generally, any reinforcement, is necessary in perceptual learning. The experiment in which rats were carried through an apparatus in a car does not appear to involve need reduction, but other experiments are directed more specifically to the question. They are called *latent-learning* experiments. In general, these experiments permit subjects, usually rats, to explore an apparatus when they are fully fed and unmotivated, at least physiologically. Later they are tested to see whether they have learned anything during the exploration. One such experiment is as follows (Seward, 1949):

After 6 days of adaptation in a straight-alley maze, rats were allowed to explore a T maze with distinctive compartments (end boxes) at the ends of the crossarm. On the test day, each animal *was allowed to explore the T maze* for 3 minutes and then was kept for approximately 25 minutes in a remote detention box. Next each rat was taken from the detention box, put into one of the distinctive end boxes, and allowed to eat for approximately 1 minute. Immediately after eating, each rat was placed in the starting box at the base of the stem of the T and allowed to choose between the empty goal boxes. Food odors were controlled by having food outside both goal boxes. Of the 32 rats, 28 (87.5 percent) went to the end box in which they had been fed. One control experiment, in which no exploration was allowed before feeding in the end box, indicated that prior exploration of the T maze was necessary for this result: 27 of the 55 rats (49 percent) chose the end box in which they had been fed in this control experiment. This is very close to the chance expectation—50 percent. Other control experiments strengthened the case for latent learning and learning without reinforcement.

One interpretation of these results is simply that the animals were making S-S associations, that is, building cognitive maps, while they were exploring the T maze. When food was introduced, the latent S-S associations were put to use and most of the animals were able to find their way to the end box in which they had been fed. This latent learning did not seem to depend upon any obvious need- or drive-stimulus reduction reinforcement. Thus the experiment seems to be a relatively clear demonstration of S-S learning without reinforcement.

Spontaneous discrimination Sometimes it is possible to tell that perceptual learning has taken place without using rewarded tests like those given in the previous experiment. To do this requires some subtle measure of the effect of different stimuli on the organism's behavior. The following experiment is an example (Thompson and Solomon, 1954):

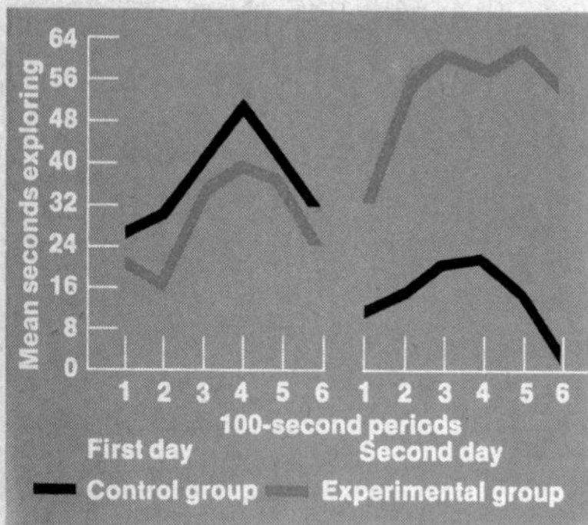

RATS LEARN DIFFERENCES IN THEIR ENVIRONMENT WITHOUT OBVIOUS REWARD

Figure 3.24 *Spontaneous discrimination of patterns. On the first day of this experiment, both groups of rats were presented with a striped stimulus. On the second day, the experimental group was presented with a triangular stimulus, and the control group was again presented with the striped stimulus. As the graphs indicate, rats spent more time looking at a new stimulus than at one they were used to. (Thompson and Solomon, 1954.)*

Forty-eight rats were divided into an experimental group and a control group. Each rat was kept in a separate cage, which was so constructed that the experimenter could attach a box to it. On the wall of the box was a stimulus card. Two cards were used: one showed a set of black and white stripes, the other an isosceles triangle. A box with one of these cards was attached to a cage, and the experimenter clocked the amount of time the rat looked at the card in a 100-second period. Six such periods were allowed on one day, and six more on another day. For the control group, only the striped card was presented. The experimental group, however, looked at the striped card on the first day and the triangle on the second.

The results are shown in Figure 3.24. The amount of time the rats spent looking at the cards increased during the first 400 seconds, possibly because they had to become habituated to the strange stimulus. After that, their looking time declined. When the same stimulus was presented to the control group on the second day, the rats spent very little time looking at it. Their curiosity had been "satisfied." But the experimental rats spent considerably more time looking at the new triangular stimulus. Obviously, they knew the difference. They must have formed a discrimination between the stimuli; otherwise one group would not have differed so much from the other in "looking time."

Spontaneous discriminations of this sort are probably the prerequisite for associating a particular response with a stimulus, that is, for learning what to react to in a stimulus situation. If we did not notice differences in the world around us, we could not learn to respond appropriately to them. The learning of discriminations in the absence of any clear-cut reward thus plays an important part in learning to make particular responses to cues.

Insight Experiments in which the solution to a problem appears to come by a sudden insight have been cited as showing perceptual learning. In a typical insight experiment, a problem is posed and a period follows during which no apparent progress is made. Suddenly the solution comes. A learning curve of insight learning would show no evidence of learning followed *suddenly* by evidence of almost complete learning. Another characteristic of insight learning is that it generalizes widely to similar problems.

Many experiments performed on chimpanzees seem to show insight. One of the simplest requires the animal to reach for food with a stick when it cannot be reached by hand. The following quotation describes such an experiment on a chimpanzee named Nueva:

Nueva was tested three days after her arrival. . . . She had not yet made the acquaintance of the other animals but remained isolated in a cage. A little stick is introduced into her cage; she scrapes the ground with it, pushes the banana skins together into a heap, and then carelessly drops the stick at a distance of about three-quarters of a metre from the bars. Ten minutes later, fruit is placed outside the cage beyond her reach. She grasps at it, vainly of course, and then begins the characteristic complaint of the chimpanzee: she thrusts both lips—especially the lower—forward, for a couple of inches, gazes imploringly at the observer, utters whimpering sounds, and finally flings herself on to the ground on her back—a gesture most eloquent of despair, which may be observed on other occasions as well. Thus, between lamentations and entreaties, some time passes, until—about seven minutes after the fruit has been exhibited to her—she suddenly casts a look at the stick, ceases her moaning, seizes the stick, stretches it out of the cage, and succeeds, though somewhat clumsily, in drawing the bananas within arm's length. Moreover, Nueva at once put the end of her stick behind and beyond the objective, holding it in this test, as in later experiments, in her left hand by preference. (Modified slightly from Köhler, 1925, pages 32–33.)

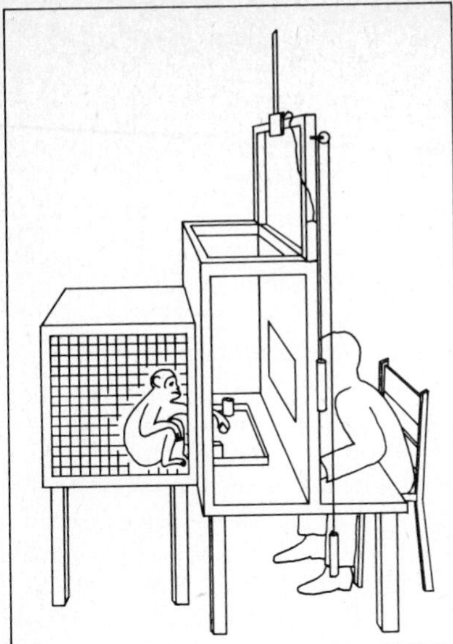

Figure 3.25 *The Wisconsin General Test Apparatus (WGTA). (After Harlow, 1949.)*

The crucial part of this description is the *sudden* look at the stick and the subsequent correct use of the stick—that is, insightful behavior—without any trial-and-error fumbling.

Learning sets What accounts for the sudden solution that is the hallmark of insight learning? It may be sudden perceptual reorganization, or it may depend upon previous learning. We usually see such sudden solutions in organisms that have had considerable opportunity—and capacity—for previous learning. How may insight learning depend on what has already been learned? The period before the sudden solution might simply be the time necessary to remember and reconstruct past learning. According to this point of view, insight learning is nothing more than the carry-over, or *transfer,* of previously learned habits, with some rearrangement, to a new situation.

That transfer from previous problems to a new problem can result in sudden solutions has been shown in a series of experiments by Harlow (1949). Whereas the usual experiment stops after one problem, or at most two or three, the same subjects here continued to new ones, finally completing as many as 344. Some of the later problems were similar to earlier ones, but others required the subject to *reverse* his response to the same cues—a type of learning called *discrimination-reversal learning.* The apparatus used in these two-choice (correct versus incorrect) discrimination problems, the Wisconsin General Test Apparatus (WGTA), is shown in Figure 3.25.

What did the subjects learn here? Only a specific problem? Or did they learn something that transferred to the next problem and then the next? The answer is given in Figure 3.26, which is based on discrimination-reversal learning. The percentage of correct responses on the *second* trial of each problem is the dependent variable. The first trial acts as an "instruction" to the subject, telling him that the problem has been changed. What he learns on the first new trial is measured by his performance on the *second* trial. If he has learned nothing, his *second* trial score will be chance—in this case, 50 percent correct. If he has learned to transfer from previous problems, the second-trial score should approach perfection—100 percent correct. The first "instruction" trial tells the subject who has learned to transfer from previous problems to stick with a correct solution, but to switch to the other alternative if the choice on the first problem is incorrect. The sophisticated subject has learned a rule: If correct, stick with the same response; if incorrect, switch to the other response.

In the reversal problems used to obtain the results of Figure 3.26, the subjects were given a few trials (6 to 11) on a problem. Then the problem

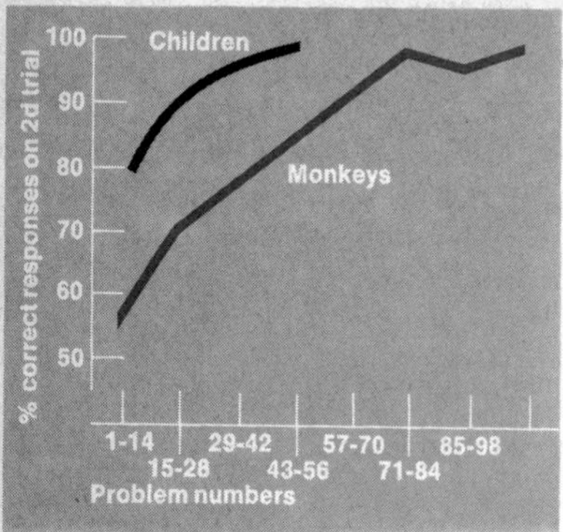

WE LEARN TO LEARN BY REPEATEDLY LEARNING PROBLEMS THAT ARE DIFFERENT BUT OF THE SAME GENERAL KIND

Figure 3.26 *The curves show learning-to-learn of visual discriminations by children and monkeys. Note that these are not the usual type of learning curve; percentage correct on the* second trial *of a problem set is plotted against problems. (Modified from Harlow, 1949.)*

was reversed so that the correct alternative was incorrect for the next group of 6 to 11 trials. Next the correct alternative was reversed again, and so forth through approximately 98 problems.

In Figure 3.26, results are presented from such a series of reversal problems for both monkeys and children. Note that the monkeys initially performed at a chance level. But they gradually improved until in later problems they approached very near perfection on the *second* trials of each group of problems. The children started at a higher performance level, indicating greater initial sophistication with this type of problem, but the trend was the same.

From these results we may conclude that (1) the amount by which a subject can profit from a single experience can, through learning, increase from nothing to a great amount; (2) interproblem improvement is a transfer effect from one problem to another. This transfer process is called *learning set,* or sometimes, *learning to learn.* Since performance in later problems reached near perfection—that is, there was one-trial learning or complete transfer—it is clear that sudden solutions were regularly made on problems near the end of the series. If we did not know the past history of these subjects, their performance would be truly astonishing. In most insight experiments, the past reinforcement history of the subjects is not known, and they may be transferring from previously reinforced learning. There is much evidence that sudden solutions—the indicators of insight learning—grow out of specific conditioning and learning. In short, in learning to learn, we may learn to produce insights.

Theories of Learning

As we indicated in Chapter 1, psychologists, like other scientists, are continually formulating and testing theories to account for various data in their field. No data have received more theoretical attention than those related to learning. Almost from the beginning of learning research, theories have been put forward to help explain what goes on in the learning process. In recent years these efforts have intensified, and learning theory is now an important part of the subject of learning. The beginning student ought to be aware of the general form of these theories and the trends they are taking.

Theoretical approaches Two general approaches to learning theory can be recognized. The distinction between them most often made by writers on the subject is one between *continuity* and *noncontinuity* theories (Deese and Hulse, 1968; Hall, 1966). These can also be called *association* and *field* theories, respectively. Using both sets of terms helps to clarify what is meant.

Continuity, or association, theory had its origins in Pavlovian conditioning but has been extended to cover other kinds of conditioning and perceptual learning. Applied to response learning, this theory says simply that the fundamental process in learning is the *gradual* formation of an associative bond between a stimulus and a response, or between two or more stimuli. As we shall see below, it recognizes the special role of reinforcement in strengthening this association, but the basic learning process is viewed as the strengthening that gradually occurs.

Noncontinuity, or field, theory had its origins in gestalt psychology, particularly in experiments on insight and perceptual learning. To field theorists, the term association implies a mechanical formation of connections that they believe does not occur. Rather, they view learning as basically an *abrupt* or *sudden* change in the perception of the world, or field. Sometimes they use the term *perceptual reorganization.* Even in response learning, they say, the important event is a change in the way relations among stimuli are perceived. They claim that such a change occurs abruptly instead of gradually, and that this is the link in learning a response.

In physics and other fields there are sometimes theories that conflict with each other, yet hold their own because each is better at explaining a particular set of data than the other. The same is true here. Association theory does better in accounting for conditioning and relatively simple habit formation. Field theory is better at explaining fairly sophisticated learning, which is often based on prior association learning, as in the insight experiments.

Mathematical models As we noted in Chapter 1, each science attempts to express its knowledge of its field in general laws or principles. When these principles are *not* known precisely, they are expressed in words as in the statement that reinforcement strengthens the responses that are reinforced. When, however, the exact relationship between variables (say, between reinforcement and response strength) is known, the principle can be stated in mathematical terms—that is, in equations. When a series of principles is expressed in a set of equations covering various relationships among variables, the set forms a *mathematical model.* Such a model, or series of models, is the goal of science, for it provides the ultimate in precision. Psychology, like some of the "softer" sciences, has not generally achieved this goal. But it has done so in certain areas, one of which is learning (Atkinson et al., 1965).

The equations in mathematical models are developed by identifying certain variables that can be measured and by assuming that they have a certain mathematical relationship to each other—for example, that one can be multiplied or divided by the other. In psychology, it is the associationists who have done the most with mathematical models, for the building of an association from trial to trial yields learning curves that can be described by equations. The perceptual reorganization assumed by the field theorists, on the other hand, implies certain sudden perceptions that are not so predictable. Below we shall present an example of an elementary mathematical model of learning.

Association theory Association theory, we have said, is one of two general theoretical approaches to learning. More specifically, the kind of theory that applies mathematical models to animal learning has several names. One is *neobehavioristic theory,* because it follows in the footsteps of behaviorism, using conditioning as its basic process. Yet it also makes allowance for other factors in learning, such as motivation.

Sometimes it is called *Hull-Spence theory* (Logan, 1959) after its founder, Clark L. Hull (1943, 1951), who first outlined the theory in its mathematical form, and a younger colleague of Hull's, Kenneth W. Spence. In recent years Spence has refined the theory considerably and given it more rigid experimental tests.

The Hull-Spence learning theory, like most learning theories, regards learned responses as *probabilistic.* This means that though we cannot predict in the course of learning whether a response will be made on any particular trial, we can assign a probability that it will. Such a probability or tendency is what we try to predict with our learning model.

In Hull-Spence theory, the probability of a response is the product of two general factors: (1) drive, motivation, or other features of the learning situation, and (2) habit strength, that is, the degree of association which has been built up (or extinguished) in previous trials. Expressed in a simple equation, the Hull theory is

$$E \text{ (tendency to respond)} = D \text{ (drive)} \times H \text{ (habit strength)} \qquad (1)$$

This equation says that on any particular trial in a learning or extinction situation, the tendency to respond is a product of motivational level and habit strength.

Motivational or drive level can be measured in such terms as hours of deprivation. A rat that has learned a response which is rewarded by food will be more likely to perform the response if it is 22 hours hungry than if it is only 3 hours hungry. Habit strength, however, is not so directly measured. To predict habit strength, Hull assumed that the number of reinforced trials previously experienced was the important factor. He framed a *law of habit formation* and expressed it as follows:

$$H = 1 - 10^{-aN} \qquad (2)$$

In this equation, N is the number of reinforced trials, and a is a parameter giving the rate at which learning proceeds. The equation says, basically, that habit strength increases with number of reinforcements, but that the increase becomes less and less as learning becomes more perfect (reaches 1). Said in a different way, learning follows a negatively accelerated curve—a law of diminishing returns.

This is one of the first and simplest mathematical models of learning. To illustrate it, we will follow Hull's analysis of an experiment performed by another psychologist (Perin, 1942).

Hungry rats were placed in a bar-pressing situation. Different rats were given a varying number of reinforcements, from as few as 5 to as many as 95. Later they were placed back in the box and subjected to an extinction procedure, and the number of responses made during extinction was recorded. In this phase of the experiment some of the rats were only 3 hours hungry, while others were 22 hours hungry. By statistical procedures in common use among psychologists, estimates of the value of D and of a in equations 1 and 2 were made. The value of D (or drive level) at 22 hours turned out to be 66; that for 3 hours, 25. The rate of learning a was estimated to be .02.

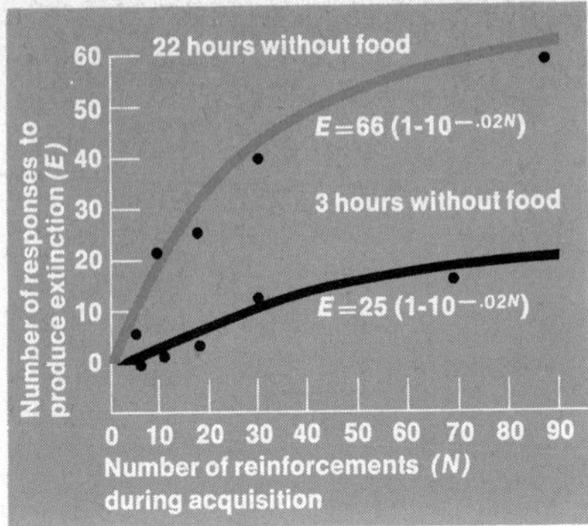

A MATHEMATICAL MODEL CAN PREDICT BEHAVIOR

Figure 3.27 *Hull's mathematical analysis of Perin's data Each dot represents the actual behavior of a group of rats in a bar-pressing experiment. The number of reinforcements—food as reward for bar pressing—given each group during the acquisition phase is indicated on the horizontal axis, or abscissa; the number of bar-pressing responses actually made during the extinction phase is shown on the vertical axis, or ordinate.*

The lower set of dots represents the behavior of rats which were 3 hours hungry during the extinction phase, and the upper set of dots those which were 22 hours hungry. The curves were calculated by applying the equation in Hull's model to Perin's experimental data.

As the figure indicates, the fit of the mathematical model to the experimental data is a good one. In this case, the mathematical analysis was done after the experiment was performed, but Hull's model could have predicted it. The model has, in fact, been used predictively in similar experiments. (Analysis by Hull, 1951; data from Perin, 1942.)

With these values, the equation for tendency to respond (equation 1) could be solved, giving the curves in Figure 3.27. There the dots show the number of responses made during extinction, and the curves are the numbers predicted by the mathematical model. The fit—the correspondence between the curve and the experimentally derived numbers—is a good one. The model, then, fits the data in this experiment.

Thus mathematical learning theorists, like other builders and users of mathematical models, employ models to predict outcomes of experiments. By testing their models in this fashion and modifying them as needed, they are gradually developing models of increasing sophistication which cover all sorts of learning situations.

Theories of reinforcement In the model above, it was assumed that *reinforcement* strengthens a habit. This is sufficient for a learning model, or at least for most of them, but it bypasses the interesting and important question of what reinforcement really is. The question has long puzzled psychologists and is not entirely solved today. In an attempt to find an answer, different theories of reinforcement have been proposed.

The *need reduction* theory holds that the satisfaction of bodily needs (for instance, hunger and thirst) is the crucial factor in learning associations (Hull, 1943). The term "reward" is sometimes used instead of reinforcement when the need reduction theory is discussed. Another form of this theory, and one that attempts to make more explicit the term need reduction, is the *drive-stimulus reduction* theory (Miller, 1961). According to it, reinforcement is due to a reduction in the intensity of stimulation arising from need states. For example, the reduction of hunger pangs or the pain from an electric shock would be reinforcing. Experiments designed to test the theory sometimes show the importance of drive-stimulus reduction, but this phenomenon is by no means the complete explanation of reinforcement.

In the *terminal-response* theory, a reinforcer is regarded as an event that takes the learner out of the learning situation (Guthrie, 1952). Consequently the last-made stimulus-response association is the one that is preserved, because it is not followed by other associations that might interfere with it. The theory thus emphasizes lack of further interference after the terminal, rewarded response is made.

A third theory, the *stimulus* theory, holds that some stimuli are inherently reinforcing—sweet tastes, for example (Guttman, 1953). Novel stimuli also seem to be reinforcing in some circumstances because they satisfy "curiosity," (Butler, 1954). For instance, a monkey will learn to make a response which permits him to look out of a closed cage; even a mere look at the experimenter may be reinforcing (see Chapter 6). Of course, to assess whether a stimulus is inherently reinforcing, we must first rule out the possibility that it has become a secondary reinforcer through learning, and some examples can be criticized on this basis. There is, nevertheless, good evidence that at least some stimuli are unlearned reinforcers (Pfaffmann, 1964).

A fourth theory is called the *response* theory (Premack, 1965). It states that if a weak response occurring at a low rate is followed by a stronger response occurring at a high rate, the weak response tends to be strengthened. Learning to press a bar to receive food or drink is a weak response that is reinforced because it is followed by the strong response of eating or drinking.

Since each of these theories of reinforcement seems to be supported by certain kinds of experiments, none of them can be completely ruled out. For the present, we find some merit in all of them, but we do not yet have a satisfactory general theory of reinforcement. This is one of the problems that continue to challenge the experimental and theoretical psychologist.

Synopsis and summary

We have emphasized three basic processes through which the learning of a single response may come about. These are classical conditioning, operant conditioning, and perceptual learning. Aversive conditioning, although we discussed it in detail, is not listed as one of the three because it occurs in two stages, consisting of classical and operant conditioning. Rather than attempt to bring all learning under one process, as was done in the heyday of learning theory, we have emphasized that it occurs by different processes. Much of our knowledge about these has come from experiments with lower animals. The exact results cannot be applied to human beings; rather, the *processes* uncovered by animal research can be applied in understanding human learning. We have attempted to show when, and in what areas, classical conditioning, operant conditioning, and perceptual learning are important in human life.

1. Learning is any relatively permanent change in behavior occurring as a result of experience or practice.
2. Certain factors are common to many situations in which learning takes place. These include the following: arousal and motivation, association between stimuli or between stimuli and responses, and reinforcement.
3. In classical conditioning, a neutral conditioned stimulus (say, a bell) is paired with an unconditioned stimulus (say, food) that evokes an unconditioned response (salivation). After repeated pairings of the two stimuli, the conditioned stimulus will elicit a response similar to the unconditioned response. This elicited response is called the conditioned response (CR).
4. The phenomena of extinction, spontaneous recovery, stimulus generalization, and second-order conditioning are typical of classical conditioning. Extinction—the weakening of the conditioned response—is obtained by presenting the conditioned stimulus (CS) without pairing it with the unconditioned stimulus (US). In spontaneous recovery, a conditioned response (CR) that has been extinguished recovers (spontaneously) some of the strength lost in extinction after an interval of rest. Stimulus generalization is the tendency to give conditioned responses to stimuli which are similar to the conditioned stimulus (CS). In second-order conditioning, the conditioned response of a first conditioning is paired with a new neutral stimulus. As a result, this new neutral stimulus will call forth the conditioned response (CR).
5. In operant conditioning, the CS is a situation—for example, a box with a lever in it—that is present throughout learning. The organism is free to "operate" on it at any time. The reinforcement, however, is contingent on what the subject does. For this reason, operant conditioning is sometimes called instrumental conditioning (or learning), because what the subject does is instrumental in securing reinforcement.
6. In operant conditioning, a primary reinforcer is simply one which is effective without prior training; a secondary reinforcer is one which becomes effective after it has been paired with a primary reinforcer. Both primary and secondary reinforcers may be given on every trial (continuous reinforcement) or on a certain proportion of trials (partial reinforcement). Schedules of partial reinforcement of operant behavior include the fixed-ratio, fixed-interval, variable-interval, and variable-ratio schedules.
7. Aversive conditioning includes escape conditioning, active avoidance conditioning, and passive avoidance conditioning. In escape conditioning, the organism learns to escape from a noxious situation after experiencing it. This usually precedes avoidance conditioning. In active avoidance conditioning, the organism learns *what to do,* usually in response to a signal, to avoid punishment. In passive avoidance, the animal learns *what not to do* to avoid punishment. Passive avoidance conditioning is common in everyday life.
8. The effectiveness of punishment in passive avoidance conditioning depends upon a number of factors: intensity, consistency, and proximity of punishment to the behavior being punished; the strength of the punished response; adaptation to punishment; whether or not there are rewarded alternatives to the punished behavior; and whether it is an operant or a consummatory response being

punished. In general, an ideal combination of conditions is required to make punishment highly effective.

9. Perceptual learning refers to cases in which we learn something about a stimulus situation that we did not know before. One view of perceptual learning is that it consists of the association of stimuli (S-S learning). An alternative point of view is that perceptual learning is the reorganization of the perceptual field under the influence of an obstructed need.

10. Place learning, or learning the routes to and from a place at which some event occurs, changed-response experiments, and the spontaneous formation of discriminations all show that perceptual learning of the S-S type occurs.

11. Some insight experiments seem to give evidence supporting the view that perceptual learning consists of reorganization of the perceptual field. The past experience of the learner, however, must be known before we can be sure of it. The way in which past experience can produce results mimicking those of true insight learning is shown by experiments on learning sets, that is, learning to learn.

12. The phenomena of learning have been the subject of considerable theory. Two general theoretical approaches have prevailed; association theory, which views learning as the formation of associations, and field theory, which claims that learning consists of a reorganization of the perceptual field.

13. The association approach has been extensively developed in the form of mathematical models that state in equations what can be expected to happen in various learning and extinction situations. These models emphasize the variables of motivation (drive level) and reinforcement.

14. There are several theories of reinforcement, each having some merit: need reduction theory, terminal-response theory, stimulus theory, and response theory.

Related topics in the text

Chapter 5 Thinking and Language Insight learning is related to problem solving. A discussion of problem solving is given in this chapter dealing with thinking and language.

Chapter 8 Perception Perceptual learning consists of learning to associate stimuli. Although some perception is definitely innate (unlearned), much of it is altered by previous perceptual learning.

Chapter 11 Personality Learning is a key concept in the development of personality traits. The application of learning principles to the origin of personality traits in childhood is discussed in this chapter.

Chapter 19 Brain and Behavior What has been learned about the physiological basis of learning is covered in this chapter. This knowledge has been greatly expanded in recent years, but clarifying the role of the nervous system is one of the most challenging areas of psychology today.

Suggestions for further reading

Birney, R. G., and Teevan, R. C. (Eds.) *Reinforcement.* New York: Van Nostrand Reinhold, 1961. (Paperback.)
A book of readings giving different points of view on learning. Various theories of reinforcement are represented by selected papers.

Deese, J., and Hulse, S. H. *The psychology of learning.* (3d. ed.) New York: McGraw-Hill, 1967.
An introductory textbook on animal and human learning.

Hall, J. F. *The psychology of learning.* Philadelphia: Lippincott, 1966.
A fairly comprehensive textbook with an emphasis on motivational factors in learning.

Hilgard, E. R., and Bower, G. H. *Theories of learning.* (3d ed.) New York: Appleton Century Crofts, 1966.
A scholarly but readable summary and evaluation of the major theories of learning.

Hill, W. F. *Learning: A survey of psychological interpretations.* San Francisco: Chandler, 1963. (Paperback.)
Some of the major psychological theories of learning are discussed.

Holland, J. G., and Skinner, B. F. *The analysis of behavior: A program for self-instruction.* New York: McGraw-Hill, 1961. (Paperback.)
By working through this programmed textbook, the student can achieve a thorough grounding in the terminology and techniques of operant conditioning.

Honig, W. K. *Operant behavior.* New York: Appleton Century Crofts, 1966.
A textbook covering the principles of operant behavior and conditioning.

Kimble, G. A. *Hilgard and Marquis' conditioning and learning.* New York: Appleton Century Crofts, 1961.
A complete revision of one of the standard texts on classical and instrumental (operant) conditioning. Thoroughly covers significant experiments in various kinds of conditioning as well as the major theoretical issues in learning.

King, R. A. (Ed.) *Readings for an introduction to psychology.* (3d ed.) New York: McGraw-Hill, 1971. (Paperback.)
A book of readings designed to accompany this text.

Pavlov, I. P. *Conditioned reflexes.* New York: Dover, 1960. A reprint of Pavlov, I. P. *Conditioned reflexes.* (Trans. by G. V. Anrep) London: Oxford, 1927.
A description of Pavlov's classical experiments on conditioning. Not a difficult book to read after the fundamentals in this chapter have been mastered.

The stream of thought flows on; but most of its segments fall into the bottomless abyss of oblivion. Of some, no memory survives the instant of their passage. Of others, it is confined to a few moments, hours, or days. Others, again, leave vestiges which are indestructible, and by means of which they may be recalled as long as life endures. Can we explain these differences?
William James

This chapter stresses learning that is characteristically human—especially the learning of verbal materials—but it builds upon the facts and principles developed in the last chapter. There we covered three basic types of learning—classical conditioning, operant conditioning, and perceptual learning—and certain principles such as reinforcement. Although the examples were mostly from animal learning, the points made are also applicable to human learning. For example, the learning of verbal associations has been regarded as a special form of classical conditioning (Hull et al., 1940), and much of human verbal learning falls into the category of operant conditioning. In the early stages of human development, reinforcement for operant learning is similar to operant reinforcement for animals in that it may consist of the satisfaction of some bodily need. But as the human matures, reinforcement often becomes a "self-reward"—the pleasing knowledge that "I got it right this time." We shall also see that perceptual learning, the third type of learning discussed in Chapter 3, is important in human learning.

Types of Human Learning

The number of ways in which human learning situations can be constructed, or can occur naturally in the growth of a child, are almost infinite. Merely the situations devised for human learning experiments are too numerous to count. To organize this profusion into a manageable scheme, learning psychologists have proposed various systems of classification (Melton, 1964). The one used here divides human learning into six general categories: (1) conditioning, (2) motor learning, (3) discrimination learning, (4) verbal learning, (5) problem solving, and (6) concept learning.

Conditioning Conditioning experiments similar to those performed on animals are possible with people as subjects. Using the classical Pavlovian sequence of pairing a conditioned stimulus (CS) with an unconditioned stimulus (US), we can condition a number of responses such as the knee jerk, forefinger flexion, and eyelid closure. The response that has been most thoroughly studied, eyelid conditioning, is demonstrated in the following experiment (Hartman et al., 1960).

A subject is seated in a chair with a holder for positioning his head and eyes. Near one of his eyes is a tube through which puffs of air can be directed onto the

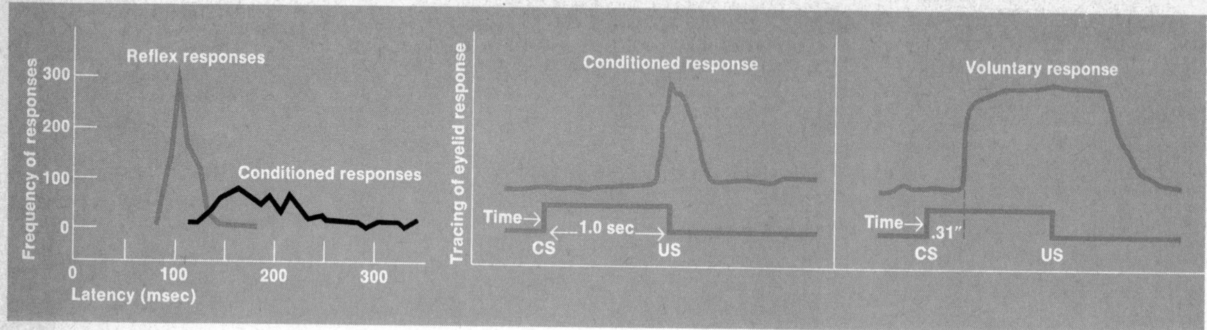

THE HUMAN EYEBLINK CAN BE CLASSICALLY CONDITIONED

Figure 4.1 *Left-hand graph shows distribution of latencies (times in milliseconds following CS) of the eyelid response to a flash of light. Reflex responses occur to strong flashes (Hilgard, 1931). Right-hand graphs show difference in form between the conditioned response and a voluntary response (Kimble, 1964). The conditioned response occurs about 1 second following the CS, the voluntary response about 1/3 (0.31) of a second afterward.*

cornea of the eyeball. This serves as the US and causes a reflex closing of the eyelid to occur about 0.1 second later (in other words, the response has a *latency* of 0.1 second). For a CS, a flash of light is used that comes on about 2 seconds before the US. By some method, either photographic or electrical, the eyeblink is recorded on a time scale showing its relation to the CS and US. The experiment proceeds in Pavlovian fashion, giving paired presentations of CS and US. As the trials are repeated, one can see the development of eyelid conditioning.

The typical conditioned response is a rapid, partial contraction of the eyelid following the light stimulus by about 1 second, thus occurring somewhat before the air puff (US) is delivered. This is an anticipatory response much like the flexion response discussed in Chapter 3. However, in place of this response, subjects sometimes respond in a different pattern, with an eyelid contraction made about 0.3 second after the CS and lasting somewhat longer than the other response (see Figure 4.1). Some individuals give a lot of these responses, while others give them relatively infrequently. Because the response occurs so quickly and lasts so long, and because subjects report that they are more aware of giving this response than the other, it has been called the *voluntary response* (Kimble, 1964).

This experiment shows that classical conditioning occurs in human as well as in animal subjects. Other experiments prove that such conditioning has other properties of classical conditioning, including extinction, spontaneous recovery, and stimulus generalization.

As we have seen, the experiment described above also demonstrates that another kind of response, called the voluntary response, sometimes develops. Whether it does or not depends on individual differences in subjects and on the instructions given them. Some people are just plain voluntary responders; others will make voluntary responses if they are instructed to do so and will not if they are told to refrain. These so-called voluntary responses should not, however, be dismissed as mere intrusions in classical conditioning. Rather, they can be regarded as operant or instrumental responses to the stimulus situation (Kimble, 1964), much like bar pressing in the Skinner box. In this case, they serve to protect the subject's eye from the ensuing air puff. Hence the words voluntary and instrumental are equally applicable here, which gives us an inkling of what "voluntary" means. The important point is that in experiments like these we can demonstrate both classical and operant conditioning in human beings.

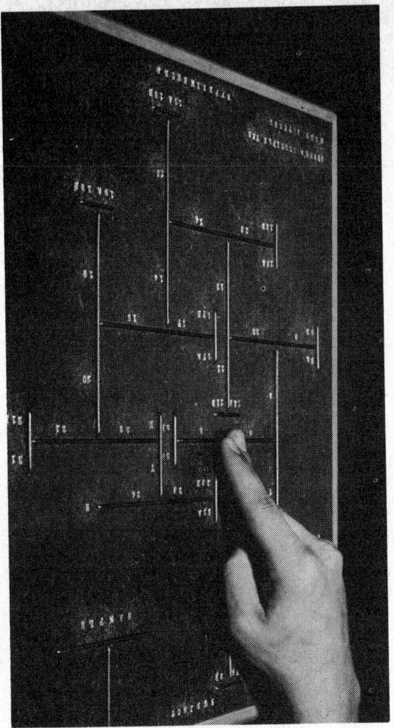

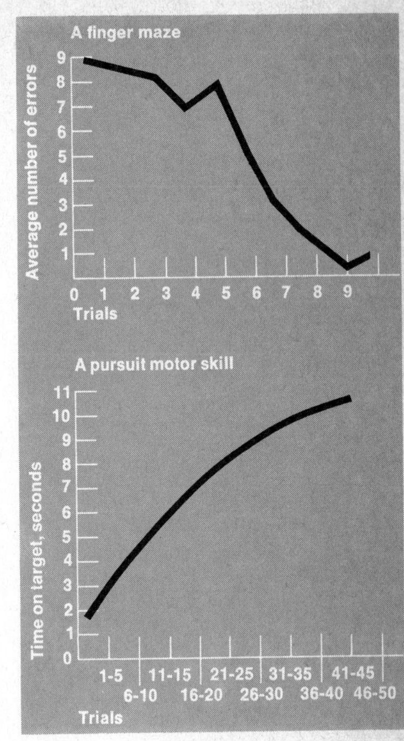

MANY METHODS AND DEVICES ARE USED TO STUDY HUMAN LEARNING

Figure 4.2 *Two devices for studying human learning. At left, a finger maze (see upper curve in Figure 4.3); at right, a rotary pursuitmeter (see lower curve in Figure 4.3).*

NUMBER OF ERRORS OR TIME ON TARGET MAY BE USED TO MEASURE MOTOR LEARNING

Figure 4.3 *Two examples of motor learning curves. The upper curve shows errors in learning a finger maze; the lower curve, time on target in learning a pursuit motor skill.*

Motor learning Another kind of operant learning readily seen in humans is the learning of motor skills—variously called psychomotor learning, motor learning, or skill learning. This includes all kinds of things people learn to *do:* eating with fork and spoon, talking, handwriting, typewriting, driving a car, etc. Since these skills are acquired at home, school, and in everyday life, the psychologist cannot very well study their acquisition in any controlled, quantitative way. Instead, he must resort to tasks that are not normally in a person's repertoire. Two—maze learning and rotary pursuit learning—are illustrated in Figure 4.2. Many others, including the learning of telegraphy, have also been used. Such skills, although not so simple as bar pressing and not strictly shaped by the contiguity of reward and response, are nevertheless complex varieties of operant (instrumental) behavior.

The measurement of motor learning is somewhat more complicated than counting the number of bar presses or the quantity of emitted responses. In general, measuring the acquisition of a skill involves scoring the accuracy of response. Such scoring can be of two types, which we shall illustrate by our two examples of maze learning and rotary pursuit learning.

In maze learning, the elimination of errors serves as the scoring system for tracing the course of learning. The upper curve in Figure 4.3, for example, shows the improving performance of college students working on a finger maze. Their task was to learn to find their way from one end of the maze to the other by following the "true path." An alternative way to measure elimination of errors in motor learning is to record the time required for the task. In the case of the maze, it could be the time to complete a trial (not shown); this obviously becomes shorter as fewer errors are made.

In rotary pursuit tracking, time on target serves as a measure. The lower curve in Figure 4.3 graphs the percentage of time a learner is able to keep a small metal stylus in contact with a moving disk. A subject working on this problem can be seen in Figure 4.2. The apparatus, which is used in studies of motor learning, is known as the rotary pursuitmeter or pursuit rotor. The curve shows that as learning proceeds, the learner is able to keep the stylus on the target an increasing percentage of the time.

Discrimination learning We have just seen that parallels can be drawn between animal and human learning of classically conditioned responses and of operant motor responses. A further parallel can be found in discrimination learning. It has been observed that animals in experiments and children in daily life learn discriminations in the same way.

The human infant undergoes considerable training that is comparable to the training of animals in discrimination situations (see page 84). The general characteristic of these situations is that two stimuli occur, either simultaneously or successively, and one or the other is frequently rewarded or punished. In this way the infant, before he can talk and perhaps walk, will learn to distinguish between mother and strangers, milk and solid food, a cold gas stove or one with a burning flame, a dog and a doll, and so on. We can see that in each case some reward or punishment accompanies a particular object, and in this way various objects are discriminated. In fact, we have good reason to believe that these discriminations must be acquired before the child can begin to learn language, that is, before he can attach verbal labels to differences in stimuli. Unfortunately, as in the case of many motor skills, such learning occurs in the natural environment, so that we are unable to study it systematically under laboratory conditions. As we see it going on, however, it appears to proceed according to principles that have been worked out in animal research.

As in the case of motor skills, the psychologist can construct situations that are not familiar to the human subject in order to study systematically certain aspects of discrimination learning in human beings. Three such situations will be described: (1) probability learning, (2) incidental learning, and (3) reversal learning.

PROBABILITY LEARNING Some years ago, it was pointed out that the everyday learning of discriminations is *probabilistic* (see Brunswik, 1956). With this term, we imply that both the stimuli to be discriminated and the reinforcements attached to them vary from occasion to occasion. On the stimulus side, for example, we seldom see objects from exactly the same angle, or from the same distance. Hence an object that is closer is *probably* larger, but not always; one that has a certain shape is *probably* a man, not a woman. On the side of reinforcement, where there is smoke, there is *probably* fire; something white in a glass is *probably* milk; the sound of an engine *probably* means an approaching automo-

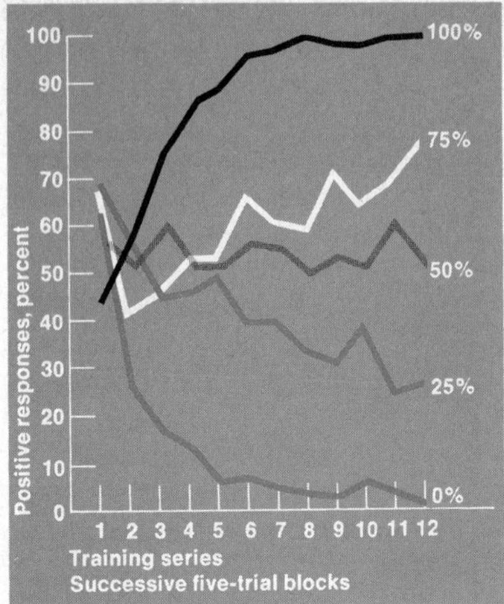

HUMAN SUBJECTS TEND TO MATCH PROBABILITIES IN THEIR GUESSING

Figure 4.4 *Probability matching. Subjects are asked to guess whether a second light will appear following a first light. For one group, the second light follows 100 percent of the time, for another 75 percent, and so on. All groups start out guessing at about the 50 percent (chance) level, but as training proceeds, each group begins to guess about the same percentage as the actual percentage that does occur. This tendency to match the probability of guessing with the probability of occurrence is called probability matching. (After Grant et al., 1951.)*

bile. Learning discriminations of this sort is a probabilistic matter and for that reason has been called probability learning.

How does human learning in such probabilistic situations proceed? There are several ways of arranging experiments to answer this question. One is as follows:

In a typical experimental situation, a subject is presented with a panel which has two lights and a button. By pressing the button, he predicts whether the second light will come on after the first one does. If he thinks the light will come on, he presses the button; if not, he does nothing (or perhaps presses a second button so that the experimenter will know when he has made a choice). The experimenter, of course, has arranged things ahead of time so that the second light comes on after the first according to some set pattern, or with some particular probability. . . . [Human] beings apparently learn to make predictions according to the probability that the to-be-predicted event will occur.

You can see this effect in Figure [4.4], which reports some data from an experiment of Grant, Hake, and Hornseth (1951). They arranged things so that the second light would come on at random for different groups 100, 75, 50, 25, and 0 percent of the time. All groups started out by predicting at a chance level; that is, they all guessed that the second light would come on about 50 percent of the time. As training progressed, however, the groups diverged, and the subjects in each group eventually wound up predicting that the second light would come on just about as often as it did, in fact, come on. (Deese and Hulse, 1967, p. 167.)

This phenomenon of the probability of a response matching the probability of the event is known as *probability matching.* It is virtually unique to human beings. Lower animals almost always choose an *optimum strategy* in which they select 100 percent of the time the event that in fact occurs 75 percent of the time and in this way register 75 percent hits. In probability matching, on the other hand, the person who chooses the event 75 percent of the time obtains considerably fewer hits (75 percent × 75 percent + 25 percent × 25 percent = 62.5 percent).

Why one strategy is chosen over the others is not entirely clear. However, an important difference between animal experiments and human experiments such as the light-prediction study described above is in the type of reinforcement used regularly in animal experiments, where correct guesses are usually rewarded and incorrect ones punished. If one does the same thing with human subjects—that is, gives punishment as well as reward—they shift to an optimum strategy rather than probability matching (Estes, 1964). But even in some rewarded situations, such as gambling, human subjects probability-match. For example, if one has made a choice several times in a row and has been wrong each time, he becomes more certain that he will be correct the next time (an instance, incidentally, of the "gambler's fallacy"). In any case, it seems to be the general rule that in probabilistic discrimination situations, human beings tend to match rather than to adopt optimum strategies.

INCIDENTAL LEARNING Typical discrimination situations encountered by people, unlike those in animal experiments, tend not only to be probabilistic but to involve *multiple cues.* That is, the stimulus has more than one aspect which might be discriminated. "Mother," for example, is different from other people in having a certain size, color of hair, voice quality, etc. If a person drives repeatedly from one place to another in a city, he can use as cues not only the distance in blocks and the pattern of left versus right turns, but also such objects as traffic lights, gas stations, and other unique features at points along the route. In other words, discrimination learning is not just between black and white, or left and right, but entails many cues that can be discriminated. What happens in situations like this?

To answer the question, we need to distinguish between *incidental* and *intentional* learning (Postman, 1964). In human discrimination learning, intentional learning is the discrimination of cues intended by the subject. In this case, what the person intends to learn is determined by his prior experience, by directions others give him, or by instructions from an experimenter. Incidental learning is any discrimination formed that is other than the one intended. The difference can be illustrated by the following closely related experiments:

Subjects were given a series of geometric forms to memorize (Bahrick, 1954). The forms were different colors, but nothing was said of that by the experimenter. Hence the intended cues were the forms of the figures, and the incidental cues were the colors of the forms. When the subjects were tested for their retention of the forms and of the colors, they remembered the forms better, but they also did fairly well on the colors. Thus considerable incidental learning took place.

Notice that in this experiment the incidental cues were intrinsic to the intentional ones. One being embedded in the other, the subject could hardly miss noticing both. What happens when the incidental cues are extrinsic to the intentional ones? Another experiment explored this question (Mechanic, 1962):

Pairs of three-letter syllables were presented, one above the other, to three groups of subjects. All three groups were asked to learn only the pair below. However, one group was asked to pronounce both members of the pair, not just the one they were to learn. Another group was asked to cancel certain letters in each syllable without pronouncing the syllables.

The results were as follows: All subjects learned the "intentional" syllables better than the "incidental" ones. Those who were not required to do anything with the incidental cues learned very little about them, but those who were required to pronounce both syllables remembered the incidental syllables fairly well. The subjects who were required only to cross out letters in the syllables fell in between in their retention of the incidental syllables.

What these experiments and others like them teach us is that incidental and intentional discrimination learning are *not* fundamentally different. Simply intending to learn something does not make learning it easier; it is what the person does that makes the difference. If he looks at and *responds* to different stimuli equally often, he will, other things being equal, learn something about incidental as well as intentional cues. Nevertheless, the distinction is of some importance: it indicates that in learning discriminations with multiple cues, we will learn primarily those that we intend to learn, because these are the only ones we *respond* to.

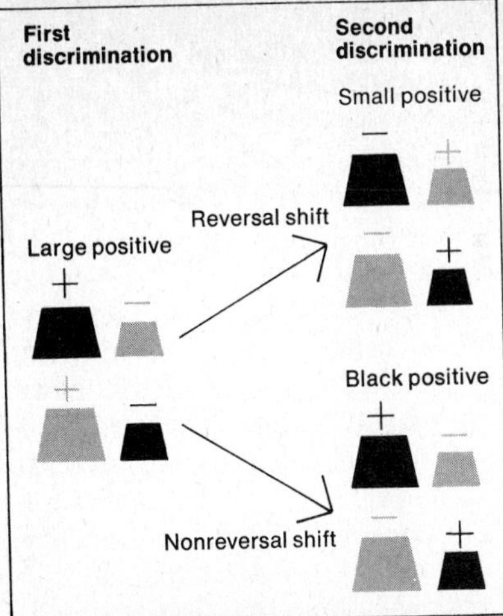

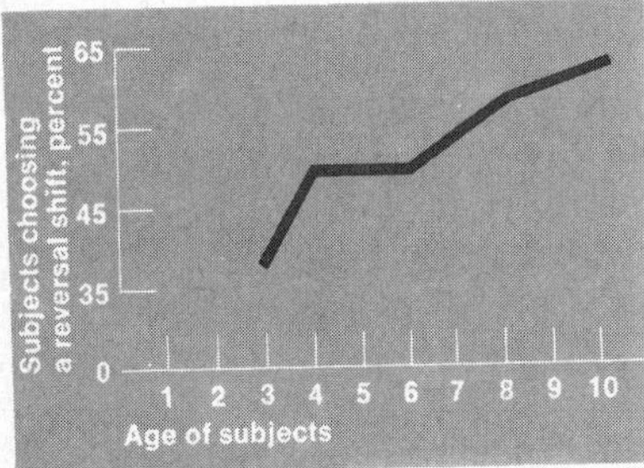

REVERSAL SHIFTS BECOME EASIER FOR CHILDREN AS THEY GROW OLDER

Figure 4.5 *Reversal and nonreversal shifts. In each case, subjects first learn the discrimination on the left in which size is relevant and* brightness *is irrelevant. In a reversal shift, the same cues are still relevant or irrelevant, but* small *is now correct in contrast to* large. *In a nonreversal shift,* brightness *becomes relevant and* size *irrelevant.*
When children are given a preference in the second discrimination (see curve), young ones choose to make the nonreversal shift, but older ones choose the reversal shift. (Kendler and Kendler, 1962.)

REVERSAL LEARNING Another experimental arrangement for studying discrimination learning has some interesting implications for the development of learning abilities in animals and children. This arrangement is similar to incidental learning in that there is more than one cue for discrimination. After one discrimination has been acquired, however, the subject is shifted to a task which may be the reverse of the first, or he may be asked to perform the same task but with a shift in the cues utilized. One such experiment is as follows (Kendler and Kendler, 1962):

The stimuli employed in the first learning of a discrimination are illustrated in Figure 4.5. Each stimulus is a pair of black and white pyramids, but the two pairs differ in size, and the larger pair is the correct one. After this discrimination is learned, a shift is made in one of two ways: In simple reversal shift, the small pair is made positive and the large pair negative. Size is still the relevant variable, but which size is correct is reversed. In nonreversal shift, the same pairs of stimuli are employed, but now brightness is the relevant cue; the black stimuli, rather than the large, are correct.

The results one gets on these shifts depend on the subjects used. With rats and young children, the reversal shift is difficult, and the nonreversal shift is relatively easy. These subjects can more easily shift the dimension they discriminate than they can reverse the discrimination on which they have been trained. On the other hand, older children and college students shift more easily in the opposite way. They learn to reverse more quickly than they learn to shift the dimension used as a cue. Further, if children of different ages are permitted to make a choice after original learning between a reversal shift and a nonreversal shift, their tendency to pick the reversal shift increases until it becomes the dominant one at about age 6 (Figure 4.5).

What is different about rats and young children on the one hand and older children on the other to account for results like these? We have good reason to believe that the important difference is in *verbal* capacity. By the time a child is 6, he can verbalize the size discrimination by saying "Large is correct," and when the reversal shift is made, he can verbalize the shift as "Small is correct." Since the brightness variable is incidental in the first discrimination, it is easier to verbalize the shift from large to small than to learn the new label "black" when the nonreversal shift is made. This use of words as an intervening link in making a discrimination is known as *mediation*—a concept that will become important to us later on. The process of mediation need not be verbal, and it certainly does not have to be consciously formulated. It may be an image or any other association aroused internally to act as a cue. Nevertheless, mediation of some kind starts to become an important variable in sophisticated organisms that have been through a lot of learning, including verbal learning.

Verbal learning As we have indicated, many of the elementary forms of learning that take place in children elude experimental study because they occur in everyday life. This kind of learning is best studied experimentally in animals. But it is clear that once the groundwork has been laid, the most significant kinds of learning for human beings involve

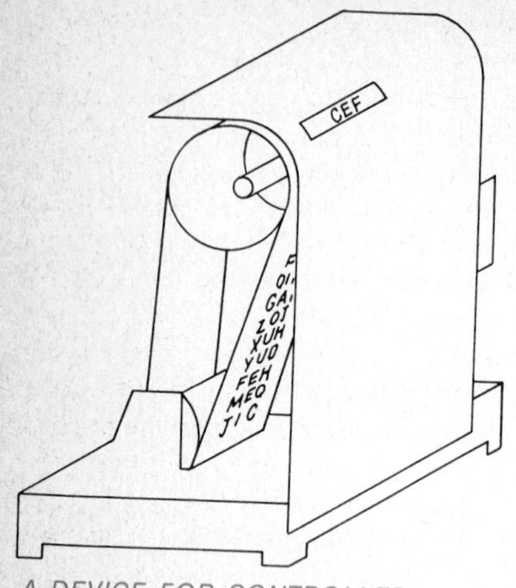

A DEVICE FOR CONTROLLED PRESENTATION OF STIMULI

Figure 4.6 *A diagram of Gerbrands's memory drum, an apparatus for the study of verbal learning. The list shown in the drum is arranged for learning by the serial-anticipation method. (Modified from Ralph Gerbrands.)*

X
CEF
DAX
VUQ
SIJ
QAP
GAH
ZOJ
XUH
YUD
FEH
MEQ
JIC

Figure 4.7 *A list of CVC nonsense syllables of low association value arranged for serial-anticipation learning. The x at the beginning of the list is the cue for the anticipation of the first syllable in the list; thereafter each syllable serves as the cue for the anticipation of the next one. (Syllables taken from Glaze, 1928.)*

words—verbal learning. Virtually all the learning taking place in formal education is verbal learning, and even most informal learning in older children and adults occurs by the verbal route. For that reason, the great majority of experimental studies of human learning focus on verbal learning. And verbal learning, we shall see, is an important link between elementary nonverbal learning processes on the one hand, and language and thought on the other.

The way in which verbal associations are formed has been the subject of considerable experimental study. Various experiments employ different materials and different methods of presentation. The material used may vary from highly meaningful stories to almost meaningless *nonsense syllables.* Nonsense syllables usually consist of three-letter combinations in either of two forms: (1) The CVC type begins and ends with a consonant, having a vowel in the middle; *zeb, cor, muv,* and *dib* are examples. (2) The consonant trigram consists of three consonants; *zqj* and *xfg* are examples. Nonsense syllables are used because their association value can be evaluated more easily than that of words (Underwood and Schulz, 1960).

Nonsense materials, or indeed more meaningful words or phrases, may be learned by different methods. Three of the most common are *serial-anticipation, paired-associate,* and *free* learning.

SERIAL ANTICIPATION In this method of studying verbal learning, a list of the syllables to be learned is constructed (see Ebbinghaus, 1885). The words are presented one at a time for a standard time interval—usually 2 seconds—in the window of a device called, somewhat inappropriately, a *memory drum* (see Figure 4.6). The first time the list is presented (see Figure 4.7), the subject has no chance of knowing what successive syllables are correct. But beginning with the second run, he is asked to *anticipate* the syllable that follows the one he is looking at in the window. If the list consisted of *cef, dax, vuq, sij,* and so on, he would first be shown *cef* and expected to say *dax.* Two seconds later, *dax* would appear in the window, telling the subject whether or not he was correct and also giving him the cue for anticipating *vuq.* This would go on until the end of the list; then the list would be repeated until he reached a certain *criterion of learning*—for example, getting all syllables correct on one run through the list.

PAIRED-ASSOCIATE LEARNING In this method, *pairs* of nonsense syllables, words, numbers, or other symbols are shown to the subject. He must learn to associate the first member of a pair, the stimulus (S) member, with the second, or response (R) member. In other words, he must learn a series of S-R associations; given the stimulus member, he must be able to respond with the response member. (In the serial-anticipation method described above, each item except the first and last is both a response and a stimulus.) This kind of learning is similar to the learning of a foreign-language vocabulary list in which the stimuli are the words of one language and the responses are words of another language.

Paired-associate learning experiments often utilize a memory drum. The tape for the drum is usually prepared so that the stimulus term of the

Stimulus (S)	Response (R)
QEW	
QEW – ZAJ	
KEZ	
KEZ – FUH	
QOS	
QOS – MIF	
XAJ	
XAJ – NUX	
GUX	
GUX – PIW	
WUJ	
WUJ – BOF	
DAQ	
DAQ – ZUY	
CEJ	
CEJ – KOJ	

Figure 4.8 *Nonsense syllables arranged for paired-associate learning. The stimulus member of each pair is presented first, and the task is to learn the response which goes with each stimulus. Thus when* qew *appears, the correct response is* zaj. *After the stimulus item has appeared, the stimulus-response (S-R) pair appears. Presentation of the S-R pair confirms correct associations and serves as a learning trial after incorrect responses.*

stimulus-response pair precedes the paired stimulus and response members (see Figure 4.8). The subject must learn to give the response that goes with the stimulus term when it is shown alone in the window. After a short interval, the drum advances to the stimulus-response pair and the subject sees whether or not he has made a correct response. If it was not correct, the presentation of the stimulus-response pair gives him a chance to learn the association. Then the drum moves to the stimulus term of the next S-R pair, and the process is repeated until the end of the list. In order to prevent the learner from simply memorizing the order of the correct responses, the order of the items is changed from trial to trial. In practice, therefore, several lists containing the same stimulus-response pairs in different orders are used in an experiment.

FREE LEARNING Serial-anticipation and paired-associate experiments are the classical methods of studying verbal learning. They are designed to illuminate the process of forming simple associations, stripped more or less of acquired meaning, between verbal stimuli and responses. In recent years, however, psychologists have become more interested in the ways people learn meaningful material. For this purpose the free-learning method has been increasingly employed (Underwood, 1964*a*). In free learning, a subject is presented, either visually or orally, with a series of words and is later asked to reproduce them in any order he can. Because the subject reports without being given the stimuli, the disadvantage of this method is that the experimenter cannot identify the stimuli involved in the recall. The advantage is that it permits us to study the way in which the learned responses are *organized*. Examples will be given a little later on.

Problem solving and concept learning Up to this point we have discussed four types of human learning: (1) conditioning, (2) motor learning, (3) discrimination learning, and (4) verbal learning. The remaining two, (5) problem solving and (6) concept learning, or attainment, are treated at length in the next chapter. We will examine them briefly here.

A problem is any situation in which an organism can discover some relationship in its environment by some sort of manipulation. A Skinner box and similar apparatuses may be called problem boxes; in such a box, for example, the subject by trial and error may discover that pushing a bar will lead to food. In this instance problem solving is no more than operant conditioning, because only responses without thought processes are involved. Human beings do occasionally solve problems or puzzles in the same way, but in general they make use of prior verbal learning. Most problems can be stated in words, and then by verbal reasoning (which is a kind of thinking, as discussed on page 171) and at times also by some trial-and-error activity, a solution can be attempted. That is why human problem solving comes under the heading of thinking.

A similar analysis is applicable to concept learning. Learning a concept is learning to react to some common property in a group of objects. A concept learning task can be, and has been, set up for animals to solve. For example, triangles can be constructed in different ways—by lines, groups of dots, solid figures—and in different orientations, and a rat can be taught to choose any object having the characteristic of "triangularity" (Fields, 1932). In this case, learning a concept amounts to stimulus generalization (see page 84) in a discrimination learning situation. Again, however, human concept learning is usually not accomplished in this way. Instead, verbal labels are attached to the common properties of objects, so that concept learning becomes a variety of verbal learning. In fact, almost all the words people learn are labels for concepts: house, wood, fruit, girl, man, school, etc. In each case the word applies to a common property of objects that can vary in all sorts of ways—there are tall girls, short girls, young girls, and so on. Once a person has learned these concepts, he can manipulate them in language and thinking. Indeed, they become the tools of thinking, and that is why we find it appropriate to consider concept learning later in connection with thinking.

Factors in Human Learning

Things to be learned can be learned rapidly, slowly, or not at all, depending on a number of factors governing learning. The educator is interested in such factors because they determine how efficiently education can proceed. Psychologists are interested in them for what they contribute to an understanding of the learning process. The principal factors affecting the rate of human learning can be divided into three main groups: (1) those lying within the individual, (2) the methods used in learning, and (3) the meaningfulness of the material to be learned.

Individual factors Individuals differ in all sorts of ways, many of which have little to do with learning ability. Those that do influence learning fall into five main categories: intelligence, chronological age, motivation, previous learning, and anxiety.

INTELLIGENCE Intelligence, in the sense of an IQ score on an intelligence test, is, as might be expected, positively related to learning. Generally, people with higher IQs learn new material more rapidly. However, learning is not always related to intelligence (Woodrow, 1946). One implication of this is that intelligence cannot be defined solely in terms of learning ability.

CHRONOLOGICAL AGE All kinds of learning ability, and particularly verbal learning, depend in part upon chronological age (Thorndike et al., 1928). From approximately age 5, when the first accurate measurements on verbal learning are possible, verbal learning ability steadily increases until approximately 17 to 20. Thereafter verbal learning ability remains fairly constant, dropping only slightly, until approximately 50 years of age. Beyond 50 there is a fairly sharp drop in the ability to learn new material. Data of this sort have been used in the construction of intelligence tests for adults.

MOTIVATION Motivation, the learner's "desire to learn," is important; we learn more efficiently when we are trying to learn. For instance, although we handle 1-dollar and 5-dollar bills almost every day, most of

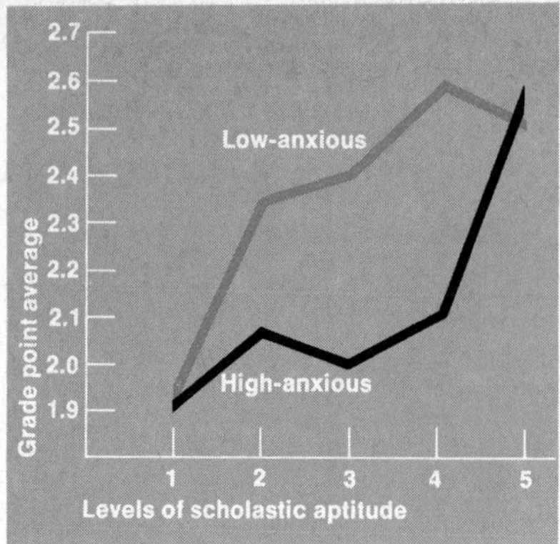

FOR MOST STUDENTS, ANXIETY IS A HINDRANCE TO LEARNING

Figure 4.9 *Grade point averages for college students of different aptitudes scoring high or low on a test of anxiety. For those very low or very high in scholastic aptitude, anxiety made no difference. But among students of average aptitude, the high-anxious students did considerably worse than the low-anxious ones. (Spielberger, 1962.)*

us cannot describe the pictures on the backs of these bills. Incidental learning, as we have seen, is possible; but only under special laboratory conditions does the degree of incidental learning approach that of intentional learning (Postman, 1964). For efficient learning, the individual must intend to learn.

PREVIOUS LEARNING Another important individual variable is learning sophistication: How much does the person bring with him from previous learning? In other words, the amount of transfer from previous learning will partially determine the rate of learning here and now. Both positive and negative transfer effects are possible, as we shall see. Has the individual "learned how to learn"—one kind of positive transfer—or has he learned habits which interfere with new learning—negative transfer? The factor of relevant previous learning is so important that we later devote a major section to it ("Transfer of Training," pages 129–133).

ANXIETY The last individual factor in learning is anxiety. Most of us carry a certain amount of anxiety, which tends to mount in preparing for and taking examinations, but some of us are generally more anxious than others. With appropriate tests, we can score people on an anxiety scale of high to low anxiety. We may ask how an individual's anxiety level bears on his learning ability. This question has received a great deal of attention in recent research.

The answer depends on the learning task. For simple eyelid conditioning, anxiety is a good thing; high-anxious subjects condition more rapidly than low-anxious subjects (Spence, 1964). For many simple tasks, such as discrimination learning, anxiety level makes little or no difference. But in more complicated tasks such as school learning, anxiety is a hindrance. This has been demonstrated in a number of experiments; perhaps the most dramatic is a study of academic success (Spielberger, 1962):

Two groups of college students were chosen, one with high-anxiety scores and the other with low scores. Each group was further subdivided by their scores on a scholastic aptitude test, subgroup 1 being the lowest and 5 the highest in scholastic aptitude. Then their grade point averages were correlated with their aptitude levels. The result is seen in Figure 4.9. As one would expect, there was high correlation between aptitude and grade point average. At the extremes of aptitude, anxiety level made no difference. With low aptitude, the high-anxiety student did about as poorly as the low-anxiety one; if their aptitudes were very high, the two did equally well. In between, however, the two groups differed markedly. The low-anxiety subjects performed much better in college than the high-anxiety ones did.

A study of this sort, of course, does not reveal exactly what the relationship is between anxiety and learning. High anxiety may mean that the student cannot keep his mind on his studies; or it may mean that he is so anxious about nonacademic matters that he fails to study as much as he should; or it may mean that he is hampered in his performance in a test situation. In any case, there is a strong general relationship between anxiety level and such measures of learning as grade point average.

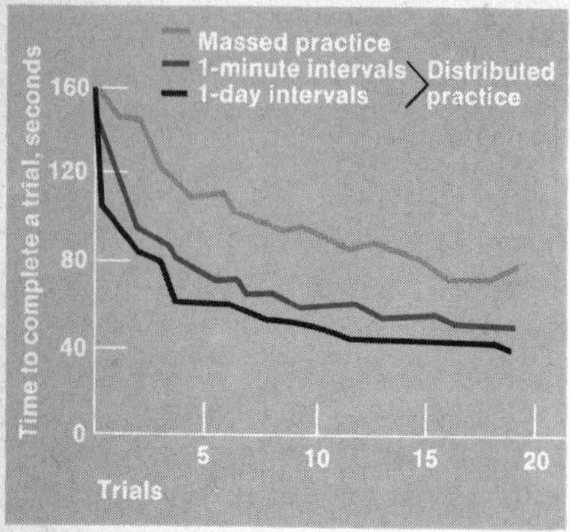

LEARNING IS USUALLY FASTER UNDER CONDITIONS OF DISTRIBUTED PRACTICE

Figure 4.10 *The effect of massed and distributed practice on motor learning—in this case, a mirror-drawing task. (Modified from Lorge, 1930.)*

Methods of learning Because a knowledge of the most efficient methods for learning is useful to the educator, they have been subjected to an enormous amount of research. This section summarizes that knowledge.

DISTRIBUTION OF PRACTICE One of the most important factors determining how rapidly a person learns is the rate at which he practices the task. For a wide variety of situations, short periods of practice interspersed with periods of rest permit more efficient learning than does continuous, or massed, practice (Hall, 1966). This statement is true for motor habits, such as learning to use a typewriter. It is also true for many, though not all, verbal habits, such as learning a list of paired associates. One important exception is tasks that involve problem solving or inductive thinking. Even so, the rule of facilitation of learning by the distribution of practice is one of the most general in human learning. To illustrate this point, we shall take up motor learning and verbal learning separately.

Figure 4.10 illustrates the effect of distributed practice upon *motor learning*—in this case a mirror-drawing task (Lorge, 1930).

The subject's task was to trace a complex pattern with a pencil, viewing the pattern and his pencil in a mirror that reversed the apparent direction of movement. Thus everything the subject did appeared to be reversed. One group learned the task with massed practice; as soon as they completed one tracing of the pattern, they began another. Another group was allowed 1 minute of rest between trials. A third group did only one trial a day and therefore had 24 hours of rest between trials. Notice the large and consistent difference between the learning curve for massed practice and those for distributed practice. Even an interval of 1 minute between trials gave considerably better results than massed practice.

For most motor tasks, the difference between massed and distributed practice is usually not so great as it was in this experiment. Also in most situations there is some optimal way to intersperse practice and rest to obtain the most rapid learning. Three features can be varied: (1) the length of the practice period, (2) the length of the rest period, and (3) the location of the rest periods in the course of learning.

Practice periods for most tasks should, in general, be short. For within limits, the longer they are, the more they tend toward continuous practice and thus slow the rate of learning (Kimble and Bilodeau, 1949). On the other hand, practice periods should not be so short as to break up the task into artificial or meaningless units.

In general, the longer the rest, the more effective a given amount of practice. However, very long rest periods, say 24 hours, do not make learning much more rapid (Lorge, 1930). In other words, the optimal length of a rest period is probably quite short—a matter of minutes—for most tasks, and increasing it beyond a relatively brief optimal time will not materially increase the rate of learning.

No clear-cut recommendations can be made about the location of rest periods, because experiments with different kinds of tasks give different results (Hall, 1966). The best general summary we can provide concerning distribution of practice is this: It is much more important to

Table 4.1 *Average number of trials required to reach successive criteria of learning under massed and distributed practice.*

Source: Modified from Hovland, 1938.

	Criteria of learning (syllables correct)					
	2	4	6	8	10	12
Massed condition	1.55	3.04	5.27	7.20	10.38	14.89
Distributed condition	1.48	2.83	4.41	6.47	8.73	11.18

have short practice periods interspersed with frequent short rest periods than to have only one or two long rest periods and one or two long practice periods.

The facilitation of learning produced by distribution of practice has applications both to college study and to work in business or industry. Although learning a task and working at a task that we can already do well are not comparable in every respect, the facts about distribution of practice apply to the distribution of periods of rest and work in vocational situations as well.

Distribution of practice usually, but not always, facilitates *verbal learning.* For instance, a faster rate of learning was obtained under conditions of distributed practice when lists of 12 nonsense syllables were learned by the serial-anticipation method (Hovland, 1938).

In this experiment the trials—complete runs through the 12 nonsense syllables—followed each other either with a 6-second pause (massed condition) or with a 126-second interval (distributed condition). As shown in Table 4.1, learning was faster in the distributed condition. In order to reach a criterion of 12 correct anticipations, an average of 11.18 trials was required under the distributed condition; 14.89 trials were required under the massed condition. The number of errors was smaller in the distributed condition, especially errors in the middle of the list.

The facilitating effect of distributed practice is usually not nearly so great for verbal learning as it is for motor learning. In fact, an analysis of variables producing the distributed-practice effect shows that distributed practice sometimes retards or has no effect on verbal learning (Underwood, 1961). Although the reasons are not fully understood, three factors help explain the results. One, which is important in motor learning, is a kind of fatigue—not muscle fatigue but a work-induced inhibition—that accumulates during practice. Rest periods allow recovery from this inhibition and thus greatly facilitate learning. In verbal learning, on the other hand, work inhibition is not so significant. Here the other two factors come into prominence: One is interference among verbal responses; if this is high because the responses involved are similar (page 131), distribution of practice is helpful. The last factor is organization of material (page 125); if the material is meaningful and coordinated, it is learned better under the massed condition. From this exception to the distributed-practice effect, we can learn the lesson that even so simple a bit of behavior as paired-associate learning is not easily understood.

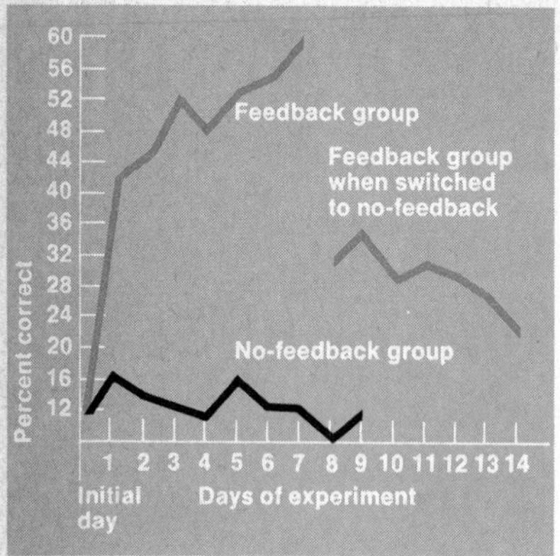

KNOWLEDGE OF RESULTS AIDS LEARNING; WITHOUT IT THERE MAY BE NO LEARNING AT ALL

Figure 4.11 *Effects of knowledge of results on learning. Blindfolded subjects had the task of drawing a line the same length as a piece of wood they could feel with their hands. After the first day, in which no knowledge of results was given, the feedback group was told whether or not it was correct, that is, within ±0.20 inch of the exact length. The no-feedback group continued with no knowledge of results. On the eighth day, the feedback group was switched to no feedback, with the results shown. The feedback group was at all times superior to the no-feedback group. Since the latter group was showing no improvement, it was stopped after the ninth day. (Modified from Baker and Young, 1960.)*

KNOWLEDGE OF RESULTS Another important factor in motor and verbal learning is *knowledge of results* (Bilodeau, 1966). Ideally, a person should know on each trial exactly how well he has done. If he is shooting at targets, he should know after each shot just how close he came to the target and in what direction he was off. If he is learning golf, he should be able to see exactly where his ball goes. When it is not possible to supply this kind of information, the next best thing is to give him knowledge of "hit or miss," that is, to notify him whether he was correct or incorrect. This is not so helpful as information about the extent and direction of an error, but it does provide some guidance.

An experiment (Baker and Young, 1960) which repeats an old experiment (Thorndike, 1932) with some modifications illustrates the value of knowledge of results in learning a simple skill. For convenience in describing the experiment, let us speak of knowledge of results as "feedback" of information.

The task was to reproduce as accurately as possible the length of a 4-inch piece of wood. The subjects were blindfolded throughout the experiment and never saw the piece of wood. They could, however, feel it with their hands whenever they wanted to. To reproduce its length, they inserted a pencil in a slot running from left to right and drew a line on graph paper. They were scored as correct when the line drawn was within ±0.20 inch of 4 inches. Each subject drew 200 lines a day in blocks of 20 at a time; about a half-minute of rest was given between each block.

Two groups of subjects participated. Both groups began with a pretraining day in which they drew 200 lines and received no knowledge of the results. This was to allow the experimenters to find out whether the subjects were roughly equal at the outset. On the average, subjects were accurate about 12 percent of the time. Then one group, the feedback group, had 7 days during which the subjects were told whether they were right or wrong, that is, within ±0.20 inch of the correct length; but they were not told the direction of their errors. The other group, the no-feedback group, was run for 9 days with no knowledge of results. At the end of its 7 days of knowledge of results, the feedback group was switched over to no feedback for 7 days.

The outcome of the experiment is shown in Figure 4.11. The curves are somewhat bumpy because the number of subjects (12) was small, but they nevertheless show clear-cut differences. The no-feedback group made no consistent progress throughout the experiment. At the end, it was performing accurately on about 12 percent of the trials. The feedback group, on the other hand, improved rather steadily while receiving knowledge of results, finally reaching about 60 percent accuracy. As soon as the feedback was stopped, however, the group's accuracy dropped abruptly to about 30 percent. Still the feedback group performed better than the no-feedback group.

The experiment shows that learning is aided by knowledge of results—indeed, knowledge of results in some kinds of learning (gunnery, for example) is essential. It also shows that, even if one has to perform without feedback, he is better off if he has had feedback during the learning process.

It is also important that knowledge of results be timely. If a gunner fires a group of shots without seeing, after each shot, the hole that he has made in a target, he will not progress so rapidly as he will if he does immediately see (or know) the result of each shot. (On U.S. Army and Marine Corps rifle ranges, for instance, a target observer gives each trainee immediate feedback after each shot on how he scored—or missed.) The reason is probably obvious; the learner needs to associate what he is doing correctly or incorrectly on each trial with the outcome of the trial. He can do this best if he immediately learns the details of the outcome. Otherwise all he knows is that he has generally been missing the mark.

Knowledge of results also aids learning by being an incentive. A person who knows how he is doing is much more interested in learning than one who is not. Especially on tedious tasks where he is likely to get bored, supplying him with some kind of record of his accomplishment helps to maintain his interest. Thus knowledge of results aids learning by improving motivation for learning.

READING VERSUS RECITATION Many other variations in methods of practice affect the rate of learning. One that is particularly interesting for the student concerns the difference between reading and active recitation in the memorizing of verbal material (Morgan and Deese, 1969). By itself, reading is vastly inferior to reading plus active recitation. In other words, if you only read something without reciting what you have read, learning is much less effective than when you read and also actively recite it, either aloud or subvocally. As a matter of fact, if as much as 80 percent of study time is spent in active recitation, the result is better learning than when all the time is spent reading (Gates, 1917). This is particularly true for disconnected material, such as a foreign-language vocabulary, but it also applies to highly organized, meaningful material.

We cannot make such clear statements about other modes of practice. For example, we cannot say unequivocally that it is better to learn by reading than by listening. Many investigators have done experiments on this problem, with no clear-cut results. The answer probably lies in differences between individuals. Some people may learn better by ear, others by eye.

WHOLE VERSUS PART LEARNING One of the questions facing the student, the actor, or anyone who must memorize a large amount of material is whether to study it as a whole or to learn it in parts. In memorizing a poem or a part in a play, should one go over the whole thing several times, or take one part at a time and memorize it piecemeal? In studying a vocabulary list in a foreign language, should one keep going through the whole vocabulary list, or take it in small groups? Should one master the sections of a chapter one at a time, or work through the whole chapter several times?

The issue of *whole versus part learning* has been extensively studied. Some of the early experiments on memorizing poetry seemed to indicate that the whole method was superior to the part method. Later studies have not been so clear-cut (Deese and Hulse, 1967). Each method has its advantages and disadvantages (McGeoch and Irion, 1952).

Part methods are advantageous when a part is easily separable from a

Figure 4.12 *Elementary school pupils using learning programs. Top, teaching machines; bottom, computer-aided instruction. (Hella Hammid, from Grolier Incorporated; Monkmeyer.)*

whole, as putting and driving are in golf. Furthermore, when the whole is so large that one cannot go through it without running into the disadvantages of massed practice, as in rehearsing a long part in a play, the part method is preferable. The part method also has the advantage of maintaining more interest, because it gives knowledge of results and a sense of achievement more quickly. The part method, on the other hand, has the disadvantage that one must do considerably more memorizing to link the parts together after they have been learned individually. A person is also likely to mix up the parts or get them in the wrong order.

The whole method tends to be more effective under the following conditions: when the learner is intelligent enough to learn things quickly; when practice can be distributed over a number of sessions; and when the material is so meaningful that it easily hangs together. In general, the whole method of learning is more effective than one might expect, especially for meaningful material that is not too long. And though we cannot positively say that either method is always better or even usually better, the whole method is probably slightly better than the part method for most learning situations.

In the practical situation faced by the student, the best recommendation is to follow a flexible plan that combines both methods. The student should probably start with the whole method, watching out for difficult parts that need particular effort, then shift to the part method, and finally go back to the whole method again. In studying a chapter in a textbook, for example, he should read it over once, then study its individual parts carefully, and finally read it over again as a whole.

PROGRAMMED LEARNING We have now covered a number of methods that make a difference in the way people learn. Knowing them, our problem is to design learning situations so that these methods are combined efficiently. Our traditional tools—teachers and textbooks—do not always provide or require of the learner the most effective methods of learning. To supplement these tools and to put into practice our knowledge of the best ways to learn, learning programs of one kind or another have been developed (Taber et al., 1965). Such programs can be recorded in either textbook or machine form. In book form, they are usually called *programmed texts*. In machine form, they can be incorporated in a machine, called a *teaching machine*, specifically designed for teaching certain subjects. Or they can be put into a general-purpose computer along with many other kinds of programs, in which case we speak of *computer-aided instruction* (see Figure 4.12).

Learning programs, however they are presented, usually consist of a series of questions or problems to be answered by the learner. After giving each answer, the student finds out whether he has been right or wrong. He goes through the problems in a prearranged order that has been carefully worked out to provide the most efficient sequence, particularly one in which each response builds on preceding responses.

Programs of this sort capitalize on some of the factors we have described as being important in learning. For one thing, they give the learner something to respond to and thus encourage him to be an *active participant* in learning. This provides motivation that might otherwise be lacking, and it requires active recitation. The basic principle here is that if you give someone a puzzle, or merely ask him a question, he will usually rise to the occasion—he will respond. If, as soon as he has answered one question or completed one task, you give him another, he will respond again. If the problems you put are reasonable and interesting and are problems he knows he ought to be doing, he will tend to keep working for a long period of time—usually much longer than he will keep his attention focused on a textbook or a lecture. Unfortunately, not all programmed texts and machines have been designed so that their material is interesting and motivating. But a properly designed learning program puts questions or problems to a student in such a way that he is stimulated to make responses.

A second feature of programmed learning methods is that they permit the student to *proceed at his own pace*. Lectures certainly do not do this, for they require the same amount of time and attention from everybody. They are too slow for the fast learner and too fast for the slow learner. This is also true of recitation techniques. Learning programs, on the other hand, can be given to students individually, and each student can work away at the program as rapidly or as slowly as his abilities and work habits permit.

A third feature of most learning programs is that the *steps* in learning are made reasonably *small*. From what is known of animal and human learning, as well as from teaching experience, it may be concluded that almost every student can progress in small steps, while relatively few are capable of large ones. Small steps ensure that what a person has learned he has learned well, and that he is really ready to take the next steps. Small steps also ensure that relatively few wrong responses—responses which may impede the shaping of the final product—are made. With textbooks and lectures, the steps taken are frequently too large because there is not space or time to spell out every little step.

Finally, a fourth principle is that both teaching machines and programmed textbooks provide *immediate knowledge of results* (reinforcement). The learner receives immediate information about the correctness of his responses.

Meaningfulness of material The kind of material to be learned makes a considerable difference in the rate at which it can be mastered. As we shall see, *meaningfulness* is a key factor in ease of learning. Before we examine the qualities which make a piece of material meaningful, we shall touch upon two methods by which psychologists analyze the difficulty of tasks to be learned.

Some tasks are hard, others easy. One of the two general methods for studying what makes them hard or easy is to present two tasks in succession and see how the learning of the first one affects learning of the second. When we do this we say we are studying transfer of training, because we are measuring transfer, either positive or negative, of one bit of learning to another. This effect on difficulty of a learning task turns out to be complicated, but it is known in considerable detail, and it is the subject of the next section entitled "Transfer of Training."

A second way of studying the ease or difficulty of learning different tasks is to vary the features of the tasks and determine how each feature contributes to ease of learning. This kind of research has been done with both motor and verbal learning. Because most school learning is verbal learning and because we know the most about it, we shall restrict ourselves here to verbal learning.

A number of features of verbal material affect the rate at which it can be learned. *Pronounceability* is one; syllables or words that are easily pronounced are learned more readily than those that are difficult to pronounce. *Discriminability,* or perceptual distinctiveness, is another. Suppose, for example, that you are presented with the following list to learn: *gub, kev, 406, dac, rul, hof.* The number stands out, and you will probably learn it more readily than any of the nonsense syllables (Postman and Phillips, 1954). Doubtless you can think of other examples. In fact, if you consider the things you remember best in your personal experiences or even in your formal college studies, many of them will be the experiences that were most different, or in some way stood out most, from the experiences that went before or followed them. Such "standing out" is what we mean by discriminability.

The factor that is by far the most important in verbal learning, however, is meaningfulness, a term which refers to the associations evoked by items to be learned. These associations can vary in their number and in the way they are related to each other in categories and hierarchies, as the following descriptions show.

NUMBER OF ASSOCIATIONS If items to be learned are considered one at a time and not in relation to each other, each has a degree of meaningfulness that can be measured and expressed as an association value, or index. In the case of learning lists of words or nonsense syllables by the method of serial anticipation, meaningfulness can be measured by counting the number of associations which subjects can give to the word or nonsense syllable (Noble, 1952*a*). The greater the number of associations, the greater the meaningfulness. And in general, the greater the meaningfulness, the faster the rate of learning. Both points are illustrated by the following experiments (Noble, 1952*a*, 1952*b*):

A long list of two-syllable words was constructed. Some were ordinary English words; others were nonsense words, or "paralogs." An index of meaning was obtained for each word by counting the average number of associations given by a group of subjects to each word in a 60-second period. Indices ranged from a low of 0.99 associations for the nonsense paralog *gojey* to 9.61 associations for the word *kitchen.* (Incidentally, in measuring meaning this way, it turned out that some English words had lower indices of meaning than some nonsense words. The nonsense word *rompin,* for example, had a higher index than the real, but rare, English words *icon, matrix,* and *bodkin.*) On the basis of these indices, three lists of words were selected. One list had an average index of meaning of 1.28, a second had an index of 4.42, and the third an index of 7.85.

Subjects were then compared on their rate of learning the lists by the method of serial anticipation. The list with the low index of meaning took almost three times as many trials to learn as the list with the high index. The list with the intermediate index was between the extremes.

It is notable that all the words in these lists were two-syllable words and that the number of words in each list was the same. The only signi-

List 1 (low)	List 2 (high)
apple	Bob
football	rabbi
emerald	cow
trout	rumba
copper	Bill
theft	priest
hat	horse
table	foxtrot
cruiser	Joe
trumpet	bishop
doctor	dog
head	tango
wide	John
blue	minister
gasoline	cat
cotton	waltz

Table 4.2 *Examples of word lists used in Underwood's experiment on learning items low and high in conceptual similarity.*

Source: Modified from Underwood, 1964*a*.

ficant difference between the three sets was meaningfulness as measured by the number of associations given to them. Meaningfulness made one list easy to learn, another list relatively difficult, and a third list very difficult. These results on meaningfulness show that it is easier to learn things which are associated with earlier established sets of associations—a phenomenon similar to the positive-transfer effect which we discuss later. Retention of meaningful material is also better than that of meaningless material.

CONCEPTUAL CATEGORIES The method just described gives the meaningfulness of individual items in a list to be learned. The meaningfulness of the list, however, is not simply the sum total of these association values. The items of the list have different degrees and kinds of association with each other. The meaningfulness generated by such relations among items is called *organization* (Mandler, 1967), and this organization contributes much to ease of learning the list.

Two general kinds of organization can be distinguished: conceptual and hierarchical. The two can operate separately or in combination. First we shall consider conceptual organization, then a combination of conceptual and hierarchical, and finally a nonconceptual, but associative, hierarchy.

A *conceptual category* is a class that includes a number of members (see pages 117 and 155). If learning material is selected and arranged so that it falls into a limited number of such categories, learning is greatly speeded as the following example demonstrates (Underwood, 1964*a*):

Four lists of 16 words each were read to subjects at the rate of one every 5 seconds, during which period the experimenter spoke the word twice. Two of the lists contained words with little similarity among them; two had words with high inter-item similarity. An example of each kind of list is given in Table 4.2. In the high-similarity list, items in each block of four were presented in random order, not in the order shown in the table. The subjects were not told anything about the kinds of words they would hear; they were simply instructed to remember as many items as they could and write them down later in any order.

The mean number of items recalled was 11.18 for list 1 and 14.57 for list 2—a sizable difference in favor of the high-similarity list. Similar results were obtained on the other pair of lists. Moreover, 38 percent of the subjects had perfect recall for the high-similarity lists, while only 3 percent had perfect scores on the low-similarity lists. Another interesting result was that in recalling the words from list 2, most subjects recalled them category by category: they wrote down, say, "Bob," "Bill," "Joe," "John," then "cow," "horse," "dog," "cat," and so on. This was evidence that they were organizing the items into clusters of similar meaning.

This idea of *clustering* can serve as a basic concept in understanding verbal learning (Bousfield, 1961). If there is some way of grouping items in lists and if subjects are left to their own devices, as they are in a free-learning and -recall experiment (page 117), they will form some set of categories that will aid them in learning. Such clustering may take the form of conceptual categories as illustrated above, or of hierarchies as discussed below; it depends on how the items relate to each other.

CONCEPTUAL HIERARCHIES Organizing items into similar conceptual categories is one step in tapping the meaningfulness that may be inherent in a list. But concepts may in turn be grouped into categories at a higher level, making *conceptual hierarchies* of three or four (sometimes more) levels starting with concrete instances and ascending to general concepts. When the material to be learned can be organized in such a hierarchy by the learner, as it could in the following experiment, the meaningfulness generated by the combination of concept and hierarchy is a powerful aid to learning (Bower et al., 1969).

Two groups of subjects were presented with a total of 112 words to be learned using a free-recall procedure. The 112 words were arranged in "trees" of approximately 28 words on four cards, one card per tree (Figure 4.13, top). The subjects were permitted to look at each card for a time calculated at 2 seconds per word. The four cards containing the 112 words constituted one trial, and a total of four trials were run. At the end of each trial, the subjects repeated orally all the words they could remember.

The difference in the treatment of the two groups was that one had the words presented in conceptual hierarchies like the top drawing in Figure 4.13; this was the "blocked" group. The other group saw the same words, but they were arranged randomly on the trees of the four cards so that words having obvious conceptual relations were not adjacent; this was the "random" group. The only difference between the two groups was the blocked versus random arrangement of the items.

The results were striking: The blocked group recalled 73 words after the first trial and 106 after the second, and it had perfect scores of 112 on the third and fourth trials. The random group, in contrast, managed only 21 correct responses after the first trial, 39 after the second, 53 after the third, and 70 after the fourth. Thus learning was about three times as fast for the blocked group as for the random group on the first two trials. Even after the fourth trial, the random group's progress was slow.

ASSOCIATIVE HIERARCHIES Conceptual hierarchies like the one at the top of Figure 4.13 provide the most meaningfulness possible in an organization of words, for they capitalize on all three sources of meaningfulness: associative, conceptual, and hierarchical. Other intermediate organizations are possible. In one of these, the learner makes use of the meaningfulness of individual words and arranges them into *associative hierarchies* without ordering them conceptually. An example taken from the same study as above is given in the bottom drawing of Figure 4.13.

This arrangement, like the conceptual hierarchy, has been compared with random arrangements in experiments using blocked and random groups. As one might predict from the lesser meaningfulness of the associative hierarchy, the blocked group did not learn it as quickly as blocked subjects learned the conceptual hierarchy. After four trials with only 44 words, the blocked group still could not recall the associative hierarchy perfectly. It did considerably better, however, than the random group.

To summarize, the meaningfulness of material is derived from the

WORDS ARRANGED IN HIERARCHIES ARE LEARNED RAPIDLY

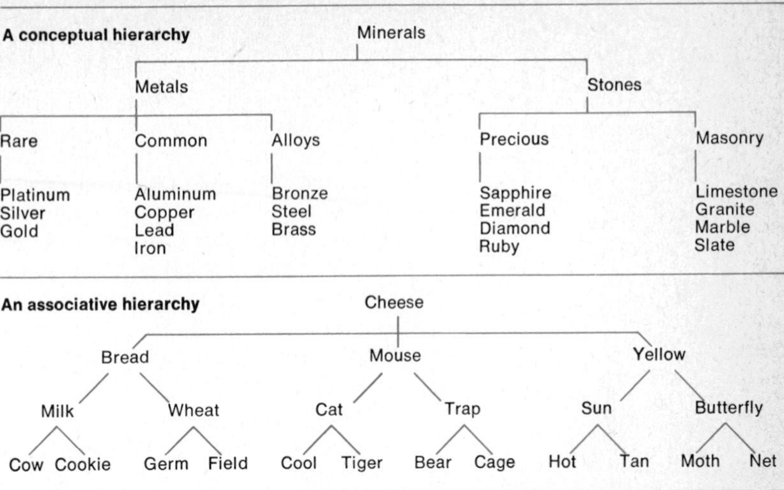

Figure 4.13 *Examples of word "trees" arranged in hierarchies. Top, a conceptual hierarchy for "minerals." Bottom, an associative hierarchy for "cheese." (Modified from Bower et al., 1969.)*

associative value of its individual items and from the conceptual and hierarchical relations among them. Ease of learning varies enormously depending on degree of meaningfulness.

Transfer of Training

One of the most important problems in the psychology of learning is that of the *transfer of training.* The fact that you are engaged in a program of academic study indicates society's implicit faith in transfer of training, namely, that what you learn in school will be useful later.

Principles of transfer Two fundamentally different types of transfer of training need to be understood clearly. Suppose I have learned that in order to keep the attention of my class in introductory psychology, I must tell a joke every 10 minutes or so. This seems to be a reasonably successful device; so I try it in my class in personality psychology, and it works there too. This is an example of *positive transfer.* What I have learned to do in one situation applies equally well in another situation. Suppose, however, that I try to carry it one step further and use the technique in a talk that I give at the faculty club. Here I discover that my jokes fall flat and the technique fails miserably. This is an example of *negative transfer.* What worked in one situation is not applicable to another situation.

Therefore, positive transfer occurs when something previously learned benefits performance or learning in a new situation. Negative transfer occurs when something previously learned hinders performance or learning in a new situation.

This informal exposition of transfer can be made more rigorous by experimentation; we can investigate some of the conditions which determine whether transfer will be positive or negative. Since the term transfer refers to the effect of previous learning upon subsequent learning, the following type of experimental design is appropriate (modified from McGeoch and Irion, 1952):

Experimental group:	Learn task 1	Learn task 2
Control group:	Rest	Learn task 2

If there has been positive transfer from task 1 to task 2, the experimental group will do better, by taking fewer trials to learn to a criterion, than the control group in learning task 2; if there has been negative transfer from task 1 to task 2, the experimental group will not do so well as the control group in learning task 2.

Similarity of stimuli and responses One of the most important variables determining whether transfer will be positive or negative is the degree of similarity of the stimuli and responses in the two tasks. Paired-associate learning has been used to investigate this variable (Bruce, 1933).

The paired-associate lists for the two tasks were made up of stimulus-response pairs of nonsense syllables. Several different types of paired-associate lists were prepared (see Table 4.3). In one experimental condition, the stimuli were different in the lists of tasks 1 and 2, but the responses were identical; in a second pair of lists, the stimuli were identical but the responses were dissimilar; in other lists, either the stimuli or the responses in task 2 were similar to those in task 1. Other control lists were used in the experiment, but these were most important.

The results of this famous experiment are summarized in the right-hand column of Table 4.3. They are typical of many experiments done since (Martin, 1965). Some of the major points concerning stimulus-response similarity and transfer that come out of these experiments can be summarized as follows:

1. Learning to make identical responses to new stimuli results in *positive transfer* (conditions 1 and 3 of the Bruce experiment).
2. Learning to make new (dissimilar, opposite, or antagonistic) responses to similar or identical stimuli results in *negative transfer* (condition 2 of the Bruce experiment).
3. The amount of transfer, regardless of whether it is positive or negative, is a function of stimulus similarity. The greater the stimulus similarity between tasks 1 and 2, the greater the amount of transfer.
4. Whether transfer is positive or negative is largely dependent upon response similarity.

SIMILARITY OF STIMULI We have seen that very strong positive transfer results when the stimuli are similar and the responses are identical (condition 3 of the Bruce experiment). Positive transfer increases with increasing similarity of the stimuli in previous and subsequent learning. This same fact was expressed in different terms in Chapter 3 under the heading "Stimulus Generalization." In that case, a galvanic skin response (GSR) conditioned to a tone of one frequency was also evoked when tones of similar frequency were presented. The strength of the response

Experimental condition	Relation of S-R items in the two tasks	Task 1		Task 2		Direction of transfer
		Stimulus	Response	Stimulus	Response	
1	Stimuli dissimilar—responses identical	LAN	QIP	FIS	QIP	Slightly positive
2	Stimuli identical—responses dissimilar	REQ	KIV	REQ	ZAM	Negative
3	Stimuli similar—responses identical	BES	YOR	BEF	YOR	Very strongly positive
4	Stimuli identical—responses similar	TEC	ZOX	TEC	ZOP	Slightly positive

Table 4.3 *Sample stimulus-response items from the Bruce experiment on transfer.*

Source: Modified from Bruce, 1933.

varied with the closeness of the test frequency to the original training frequency. Such stimulus generalization is a case of positive transfer. In verbal learning, but probably not in stimulus generalization, there is some positive transfer even when the stimuli are dissimilar but the response is the same (condition 1 of the Bruce experiment).

Let us cite two further examples. After a person has learned to drive one make and model of car, he usually has little difficulty in transferring what he has learned to another car. Instruments on the new dashboard may be arranged somewhat differently, the windshield may be a little higher or larger, and many minor features of the two cars may be different. In general, however, the stimulus situations presented by the two cars are similar; hence positive transfer is high. In learning languages, if a person has studied Greek, his progress in Latin is faster; if he has studied Latin, his learning of French is made easier; and Latin is also helpful in mastering Italian or Spanish. In each case, the two languages have many similarities, and similar stimulus situations produce positive transfer of training.

SIMILARITY OF RESPONSES Positive transfer may increase with increasing similarity of responses in the original and new situations (condition 4 of the Bruce experiment). However, two responses may be so dissimilar that they are opposites, or near opposites. In that case, the result is negative transfer (condition 2 of the Bruce experiment). Again in the example of driving two cars, positive transfer from one to the other usually occurs not only because the stimulus situations are similar, but also because nearly identical responses are required. In both cases, the driver uses his right foot to brake the car, his right foot to accelerate it, and his left foot to operate the clutch, if there is a clutch. To take another example, if a person has learned to play tennis, he finds it easier to learn ping-pong or badminton because similar responses and skills are involved in all three games.

In some cases, opposite responses are required in two situations, with resulting negative transfer. If a person is used to steering a sled and then tries to learn to pilot a plane, he will have difficulty because extending a right foot makes a sled go to the left and a plane to the right. Many people have trouble learning to steer a boat with a tiller because it requires that one push the tiller to the left in order to make the boat turn right, and this seems unnatural.

Negative transfer can be a matter of life and death when a pilot changes from one type of airplane he has flown for a long time to a plane with rather different controls. In the new plane he may have to do exactly the opposite of what he has been accustomed to. Airplane accidents are occasionally caused in this way (Chapanis et al., 1949). In one incident, a pilot who was undershooting the field in attempting to land tried to correct his approach by pulling back on the throttle and pushed the stick forward. This was the reverse of what he should have done, and the plane nosed into the ground. Afterward—he was fortunate enough to survive to tell the tale—he explained that he was accustomed to flying planes in which the throttle was operated with the right hand and the stick with the left hand. In this plane the positions of the controls were different, so that he used his left hand on the throttle and his right hand on the stick. In an emergency he had reverted to his old habits, with almost fatal consequences. In recent years, airplane controls have become more standardized in an effort to avert such disasters.

In summary, we can say that similarity of stimuli and of responses accounts for positive transfer. A dissimilarity of responses, in which opposite or competing responses are required, accounts for negative transfer. It should be noted that virtually all learning in human beings involves transfer.

TRANSFER OF TRAINING IN FORMAL EDUCATION The whole of our formal educational program assumes that a certain degree of positive transfer takes place between what is learned in school and what is needed in daily life. It is not surprising, therefore, that psychological studies of transfer of training have had a profound influence upon contemporary education.

Most authorities agree on the existence of direct transfer of the sort which we have been discussing—the so-called "transfer of elements." But a more general theory of transfer—*formal-discipline* theory—has been questioned. At one time the notion was fairly widespread that only a limited number of mental faculties needed to be trained, and that once these had been trained they could be used in a great variety of situations. Thus schoolboys used to study Greek, Latin, Euclid, and Aristotle, not so much because of their intrinsic value but because these studies were supposed to train the mind. At one time, too, there was widespread belief in the notion that one could train schoolchildren to be neat in their appearance and in the care of their belongings by teaching them to be neat in their arithmetic and spelling papers. This general notion has been called the *mental-faculty* theory of transfer or, on occasion, the formal-discipline theory. It has been almost completely abandoned today, largely because experimental studies on transfer of training have not supported it.

Some years ago, educational psychologists studied the transfer of Latin grammar to English grammar, of Euclidean geometry to the ability

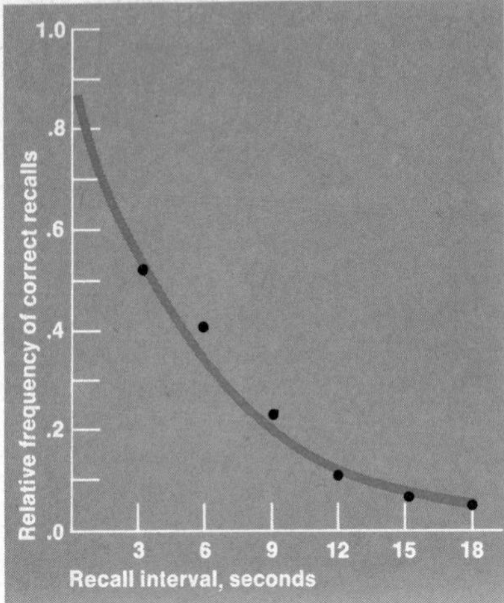

SHORT-TERM STORAGE OF INFORMATION IS VERY LIMITED

Figure 4.14 *A short-term forgetting (retention) curve. Note that the frequency of correct responses has dropped to practically zero after 18 seconds. (From Peterson and Peterson, 1959.)*

to solve reasoning problems, and of classical physics to the ability to understand the mechanical problems of daily life (Stroud, 1940). The results were discouraging. In nearly every case some positive transfer occurred, but it was disappointingly small. Educators have gradually relinquished the notion that one can instill a general ability through sheer exercise of a particular faculty or habit.

In modern times, educators have been concerned not with "mental discipline," but with producing the greatest amount of positive transfer of elements from school subjects to everyday life. Part of the technique for accomplishing this is to make school problems as realistic as possible. Hence the modern arithmetic book attempts to cast its problems in a form that makes them like the real-life experience of the child. At the higher levels of education, positive transfer can best be increased by making it clear to the learner that what he is learning can be transferred to other situations. Even the old subjects which were of special delight to the adherents of formal discipline can be made useful by bringing this point home. A study of Euclidean geometry *can* aid a student in improving his ability to reason if he has a good and patient teacher with a flair for pointing out the elements that can be transferred from the formal subject to our daily experiences.

Remembering and Forgetting

One of the most interesting problems to the student of learning is that of retention. How much of what we learn do we retain? Why do we forget? Why do we find it difficult to remember certain common things? What produces the distortions of memory that are the familiar experience of everyone?

Remembering and forgetting are but opposite sides of the same coin (look ahead to Figure 4.15, and note the vertical scales at either end). What we have forgotten is simply the difference between what we have learned and what we have retained. We can measure directly only what has been retained, of course, but sometimes, especially when we are concerned with theories of why we forget, our emphasis is upon forgetting rather than upon remembering.

Short-term memory The phrase *short-term,* or immediate, *memory* refers to the temporary storage of information for a few seconds. In *long-term memory,* material is stored for hours, days, years, or a lifetime. An interesting experiment illustrates the great amount of forgetting which can take place in a very short time after a single exposure to a stimulus (Peterson and Peterson, 1959).

The subject heard the experimenter say a consonant trigram followed by a number, for example, CHJ 506. When he heard the number, the subject was instructed to count backward from it by threes until he was given a signal. The counting was done to prevent rehearsal by the subject. At the signal, the subject attempted to recall the syllable. The intervals between presentation and the signal for recall were 3, 6, 9, 12, 15, or 18 *seconds;* the frequency of correct recalls for each of these intervals is shown in Figure 4.14. Perhaps the most interesting thing about this figure is the surprising amount of forgetting after 18 seconds: The syllable is almost completely out of storage by that time. (No wonder it sometimes seems as if we cannot learn anything!) Further analysis has shown that such rapid forgetting does not occur on the first few trials; it is only after several trials that the effect becomes prominent. This points to interference by previous activity—called proactive interference—as being important in the experiment.

The limited storage capacity of short-term memory is also shown by the fact that the memory span for a single repetition is about seven items long (Miller, 1956*b*). Without regrouping or reorganizing the information as we receive it, most of us cannot retain more than about seven items, for example, digits, after one exposure to them. However, most of us have learned to recode the information into "chunks." The trick is to recode the information as we receive it. Seven-digit telephone numbers, for example, come close to the span of immediate memory. Some of us have trouble remembering them because we are not good at recoding them. It helps, however, if we "chunk" the number by grouping the first three and last four digits separately. In addition, where the digits vary little in a given area, we can recode by noting the difference between the first three and, say, our own number, then concentrate on the last four digits. From the standpoint of human memory, it was a mistake to replace the first two letters with digits, for the combination of letters and digits permitted much easier "chunking."

Besides being limited in capacity, short-term memory is highly susceptible to disruption, a fact which has received much study (Broadbent, 1958). Most of us have had the experience of being interrupted in the middle of dialing a telephone number and winding up with a wrong number or an incomplete one. The amount of disruption of short-term memory by another competing demand for attention depends upon the amount of information being held in short-term storage (Brown, 1958). With only a little information in short-term memory, as in a telephone number, a considerable amount of interfering activity is needed; with much information in short-term memory, a little interference will be effective in disrupting memory.

Two hypotheses have been proposed to account for the effects of disruptive tasks on short-term memory. These have been described as follows:

One might think of a trace which fades as fast as it is established and requires to be strengthened at intervals by rehearsal; or one might think of the stored information as passing round a recurrent circuit which periodically runs through a channel used in the perception of fresh information. (Broadbent and Heron, 1962, page 190.)

According to the first of these hypotheses, interruption would interfere with the telephone dialing because there was no time for rehearsal when the interruption occurred immediately after a response. According to the second hypothesis, the memory of the last number dialed would be disrupted as it passed through the part of the circuit which was processing the new incoming, interfering information.

To summarize, a single exposure to stimuli in human verbal learning does not usually produce long-term retention. Exceptions to this rule include exposures to particularly vivid or threatening stimuli. But in general, a considerable amount of exposure to the material and many learning trials are usually required to obtain long-term retention.

Measuring long-term retention Of the several ways of measuring long-term retention, we shall describe three: *recall, recognition,* and *savings.*

RECALL The method of recall is especially suitable for studying the retention of verbal material, such as a poem or a section of a textbook. In the recall method, the subject must reproduce, with a minimum of cues, something that has been learned in the past. Of the different methods, recall yields the smallest amount of measurable retention because it is always harder to recall something "cold" than it is to relearn or to recognize something. The essay examination, for example, utilizes the recall method of measuring retention.

RECOGNITION A second method, the method of recognition, is most frequently used in objective examinations consisting of multiple-choice questions. The subject must simply recognize whether or not he has been exposed to the information before. The amount of retention measured is inflated by a factor of chance, however, and for this reason the recognition method is the least useful for experimental purposes.

SAVINGS The method most frequently chosen by psychologists for experimental studies of retention is the method of savings. The subject learns again a task that he learned some time before. The measure of retention is the *difference* in time or number of trials required for original mastery and for the second learning—the savings from the first learning. Suppose, for example, that it took 20 repetitions to learn to repeat a certain poem without making any errors; after a period of a month it took only 10 repetitions to relearn the poem. The savings would be 50 percent. Such a method has the advantage of being very sensitive and, at the same time, reliable. Furthermore, it can show negative values. For example, suppose that for some reason it took 30 trials to relearn the poem; this would represent a negative savings of 50 percent. A general formula for computing a percentage savings score is

$$\frac{\text{Number of trials (or time) to learn originally } \textit{minus} \text{ number of trials (or time) to relearn}}{\text{Number of trials (or time) to learn originally}} \times 100$$

The concept of savings is not new; it is simply an application of positive and negative transfer to the measurement of retention.

Another important point about the savings method is that it may show retention long after the other methods have ceased to indicate that there is anything retained. A dramatic story illustrates this point (Burtt, 1941).

THE LARGEST AMOUNT OF FORGETTING TAKES PLACE RIGHT AFTER LEARNING

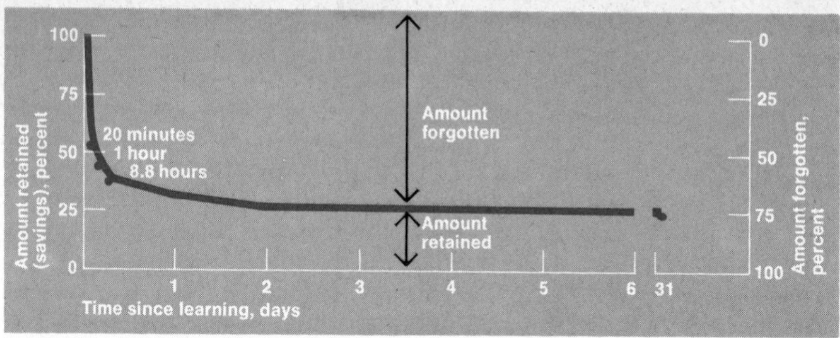

Figure 4.15 *A long-term forgetting (retention) curve. (Data from Ebbinghaus, 1885.)*

Some years ago a psychologist undertook to read his son passages in Greek from Sophocles's *Oedipus Tyrannus.* This may not be such a remarkable thing for a professor to do, except that the son was only 15 months old. Each day for three months the professor read the same three selections of 20 lines each to the boy. When the boy was 8 years old, he was required to learn these selections by rote plus some others of equal difficulty with which he had had no experience. It took the boy an average of 435 repetitions per selection to master the new selections; only 317 repetitions, on the average, were required to master the three old selections. Thus even in infancy, exposure to complex nonsense material—since that is surely what it was to the subject of this experiment—results in savings at a later date.

Here is the moral: Don't be too upset about the precipitous decline in *recall* of the material that you learn in school; you will probably find considerable *savings* whenever you have an opportunity to use that material again or need to relearn it.

Retention curves for long-term memory How much of what we learn stays with us after a period of time? Of course the answer depends upon the method used to measure retention: savings produces the longest-lasting retention; recall generally gives less evidence of retention; and the recognition method gives the largest retention score immediately after learning. The first attempt to answer this question was made by the German psychologist Ebbinghaus (1885). Using the method of savings with himself as a subject, Ebbinghaus did many experiments on memory. In a typical experiment, he memorized a list of nonsense syllables such as *zeb, bep, cex, rab,* and so on; he waited for varying periods, 20 minutes to 31 days; then he relearned the same syllables. In this way he was able to measure retention by the savings method for different intervals between original learning and relearning.

Ebbinghaus's results are shown in Figure 4.15. The savings are great for short intervals, but they decline rapidly during the first day after original learning. Thereafter the decline is much less abrupt. This kind of curve is *negatively accelerated*—it changes more rapidly at the beginning than at the end. Such a negatively accelerated curve of retention is the rule; practically all retention curves have this general shape.

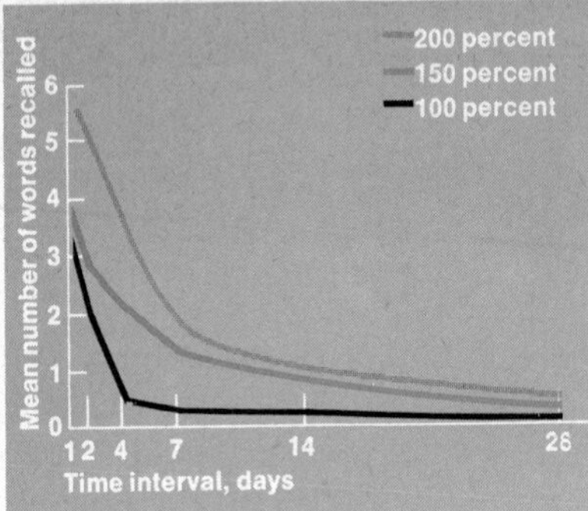

OVERLEARNING AIDS RETENTION

Figure 4.16 *Retention curves after different amounts of practice. The curve marked 100 percent means that learning proceeded to a criterion of one perfect repetition; 150 percent means that half again as many trials were given as were needed to reach criterion; 200 percent means that twice as many trials were given as were needed to reach criterion. (Data from Krueger, 1929; figure from Hovland, 1951.)*

In some studies of verbal and motor learning, however, the retention curve does not drop during the first few minutes after learning. In fact, early in the retention period the subject may do better than he did at the end of learning (Ward, 1937). This improvement in retention over that at the end of learning is called *reminiscence*.

Amount retained Among the many variables which may influence amount of retention, some of the most significant seem to be (1) *meaningfulness of the material which was learned,* (2) *degree to which the original material was learned,* (3) *amount of interference.*

MEANINGFULNESS AND LONG-TERM RETENTION Many investigators have contrasted the retention of meaningful material with that of nonsense material (Kingsley and Garry, 1957). Educational psychologists, for example, have studied the ability of students to remember material learned in school after periods of rest away from formal education. In general, they have observed a negatively accelerated curve similar to that in Figure 4.15. But the curve usually does not fall so fast or so far as the curve for nonsense syllables, which shows that meaningful material is more likely to be retained. Such studies make quite clear the relative difficulty of remembering simple isolated facts and the relative ease of retaining meaningful and organized material. This ties in with what we found earlier—that it is much easier to learn sense than nonsense. Here we see that it is also easier to retain sense than nonsense. Actually, one is the consequence of the other; the reason we do not remember nonsense or difficult material is that we never learned it very well in the first place (Underwood, 1964*b*).

DEGREE OF LEARNING AND LONG-TERM RETENTION As we might expect, more complete mastery of the original material leads to better memory of the material. This is illustrated by the following experiment (Krueger, 1929):

Subjects learned lists of single-syllable nouns to three different degrees: 100 percent learning, 150 percent learning, and 200 percent learning. The 100 percent learning means that the materials were learned to a criterion of a single correct repetition. In the 150 percent learning, subjects practiced for half again as many trials as were needed in the original learning; in the 200 percent condition, twice as many trials were given—in other words, the materials were *overlearned.* Memory for the nouns was tested by both the savings and recall methods after varying numbers of days—1 to 28. The results are shown in Figure 4.16. They indicate that the amount of retention depended upon the amount of overlearning: greater amounts of overlearning led to better retention. The results also show that a moderate amount of overlearning was effective in promoting retention—the difference between the 100 percent and the 150 percent groups was great. This difference was especially pronounced at relatively long intervals after the original learning. Notice also that the difference between the 150 percent and 200 percent groups was less, after long intervals, than that between the 150 percent and 100 percent groups. This suggests that some overlearning is very effective, but that a great deal of overlearning may not do much more—a point of diminishing returns

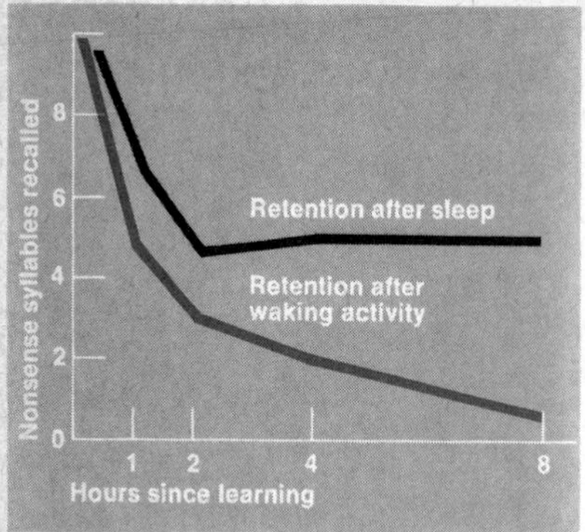

MEMORY IS BETTER PRESERVED DURING PERIODS OF LOW MENTAL ACTIVITY

Figure 4.17 *The effect of waking activity and sleep on memory. Sleep is the best case of low-interference activity. (Modified from Jenkins and Dallenbach, 1924.)*

is reached. Thus for good retention there is probably an optimum degree of overlearning which depends upon the type of material and how well it needs to be retained.

INTERFERENCE EFFECTS We have already seen that short-term memory can be disrupted by interfering activity. This is true also of long-term memory. One kind of interference in long-term memory is caused by subsequent or *interpolated activity* and is sometimes called *retroactive inhibition,* because the interpolated activity interferes with something learned before. Another kind of interference is referred to as *proactive inhibition.* In this, an antecedent activity interferes with ability to remember materials that come after the activity.

To illustrate retroactive and proactive interference, suppose that you go to a large party where you are introduced to many new people. By the time the evening is over, you will probably have forgotten, or at least mixed up, the names of many people whom you met. The retention of names heard early in the evening will be interfered with because you heard so many names later; this is retroactive inhibition. On the other hand, you probably also experienced difficulty in remembering the names of those to whom you were introduced later in the evening, for it is more and more difficult to remember names as you are introduced to more and more people. Here a previous or antecedent activity interferes with the memory of the subsequent one—an instance of proactive inhibition.

The interfering effect of interpolated activity, or retroactive inhibition, is often studied in experiments which use the following design (McGeoch and Irion, 1952):

Control condition:	Learn 1	Rest	Measure retention of 1
Experimental condition:	Learn 1	Learn 2	Measure retention of 1

If retroactive interference has occurred, a comparison of the retention curves for the control and experimental conditions will show less retention in the experimental condition. The important thing about this design is that *interfering interpolated activity* occurs in one condition, but not in the other. As an extreme example, suppose that in the control condition, sleep followed the learning of 1, whereas in the experimental condition, normal waking activity (which involves some amount of learning of various kinds) followed the learning of 1. If interfering interpolated activity is really a variable in retention, we would expect to find much greater retention when sleep followed the initial learning. Such an experiment with just these results has been done (Jenkins and Dallenbach, 1924):

Two subjects learned lists of 10 nonsense syllables just before going to bed in the laboratory. At various times after going to sleep (1, 2, 4, and 8 hours), they were awakened and retention was tested by the recall method. Then the same subjects learned similar lists, and retention was tested after 1, 2, 4, and 8 hours of

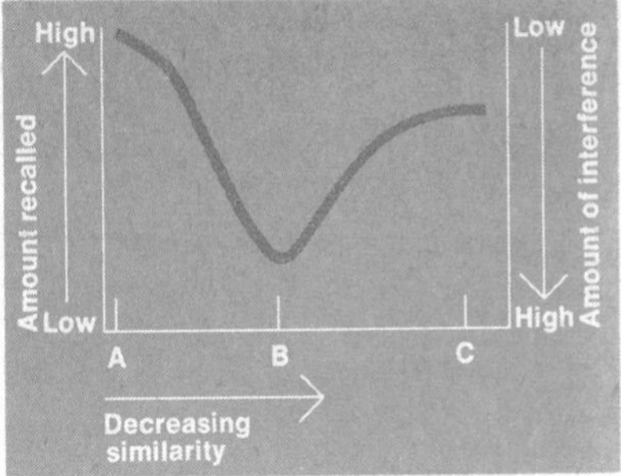

THE AMOUNT OF RETROACTIVE INTERFERENCE DEPENDS UPON SIMILARITY

Figure 4.18 *The Skaggs-Robinson hypothesis concerning the effect of stimulus similarity on amount recalled and retroactive interference. The degree of similarity between the original and later tasks is shown on the abscissa. As this similarity decreases from A (high similarity) to B (intermediate similarity), the amount of interference increases and amount recalled decreases; as this similarity decreases still farther from B (intermediate similarity) to C (dissimilarity), interference decreases and amount recalled increases. (Modified from Robinson, 1927.)*

normal daily waking activity. The curves shown in Figure 4.17 illustrate that retention was much greater after sleep than after daily waking activity.

If we may reverse the beast-to-man line of reasoning customary in psychology to a man-to-beast one, similar differences have been found when cockroaches were used as subjects (Minami and Dallenbach, 1946). Flattering, is it not?

The interfering effects of antecedent activity, or proactive inhibition, are often studied by using the following experimental design (modified from McGeoch and Irion, 1952):

Control condition:	Rest	Learn 2	Measure of retention of 2
Experimental condition:	Learn 1	Learn 2	Measure of retention of 2

If proactive interference has occurred, subjects in the experimental group will retain less than those in the control group.

SIMILARITY AND INTERFERENCE Sleep, as was noted above, represents a minimum of interpolated activity. In the waking state, various kinds of interpolated activity are possible, and the kind of activity determines the degree of interference with retention. More specifically, the *similarity* of interpolated material and original material is important, but the relationship is not simple.

An early and relatively simple statement of the relationship is known as the Skaggs-Robinson hypothesis (Skaggs, 1925; Robinson, 1927). This states (1) that when the interpolated and original material are quite similar, interference will be minimal; (2) that when the two materials are very dissimilar, interference will be small, but greater than when they are very similar; and (3) that an intermediate degree of similarity causes the greatest interference. In the first case, interference is minimal because learning the interpolated material is like having more learning trials on the original material. In the second case, because there is little similarity, there is little transfer, either positive or negative. But in the third case, when there is an intermediate degree of similarity, the subject has a greater tendency to confuse what was learned in the interpolated period with what was learned originally. Figure 4.18 is a diagram of the predictions to be made from the Skaggs-Robinson hypothesis. Experimental support for this hypothesis has been mixed; some experiments support it; some do not. It serves, however, as a first approximation to the actual state of affairs.

So far in this discussion of similarity we have been talking about retroactive inhibition, or interference from interpolated activity. However, interpolated activity certainly does not seem sufficient to account for the amount of forgetting that is recorded in experimental situations. A substantial amount of it must be caused by proactive interference (Underwood, 1957).

Suppose that a person learns a single list of nonsense syllables and is tested for recall 24 hours later. Usually he has forgotten about 65 percent of the list by then (see Figure 4.15). This is a great deal of forgetting to be explained by subsequent interpolated activity outside the laboratory,

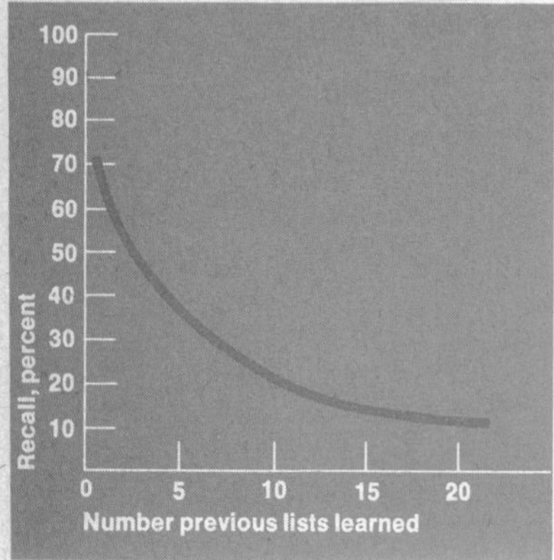

PRIOR LEARNING CAN INTERFERE WITH LATER LEARNING AND RECALL

Figure 4.19 *Recall depends upon the number of lists learned prior to the list which is under test. This curve is a summary of the results obtained by many experimenters over many years. (Modified from Underwood, 1957.)*

especially when extralaboratory activities are likely to be quite dissimilar to the laboratory-learned lists (see Skaggs-Robinson hypothesis). Instead, it seems possible that the subject's prior experience with words and syllables may have a proactive interfering effect on retention of the list learned.

This hypothesis has been tested in the laboratory by having subjects learn more than one list. In fact, in most laboratory experiments, the subject learns not just one list but many in the course of the experiment. So it is possible to make an analysis of a number of experiments in which subjects have learned two or more lists (Underwood, 1957). Such an analysis shows that retention after 24 hours is very much a function of the number of lists learned prior to the one under test (see Figure 4.19). In addition, when no prior lists have been learned, retention is much better than when they have. Retention, then, depends very much on the existence of prior learning that interferes proactively with material learned. Extrapolating this general result to learning outside the laboratory, we can conclude that prior learning, and particularly strongly ingrained habits, are sources of interference in the retention of verbal materials.

PRACTICAL IMPLICATIONS Students often ask how well they will remember what they learn in college some years later. How good is truly long-term retention? Unfortunately, the answer is that without practice it is disappointingly small. Interference, as we have emphasized, will take its toll in a few months following a course, and without further review will push retention down to some small fraction of what it was on the day of the final examination.

But the picture is not as bleak as it may seem, and things can be done to improve it. In the first place, the measures we have emphasized are those of *recall;* we have seen that retention as measured by *recognition* and *savings* is always much better. Hence though a person's long-term recall may be poor, he will still be able to *recognize* terms, concepts, etc., at times when they are useful. Moreover, if he has occasion to relearn the forgotten material, he can do it in a fraction of the time. (If anyone really wants to remember what he has learned, he should regularly review his books and notes.) Graduate students, lawyers, and doctors find that relearning is fairly rapid when they must take comprehensive examinations covering many years of training. And of course, it helps considerably to learn things well in the first place, by spacing of practice, by overlearning, and by frequent review.

Qualitative changes in remembering In the preceding discussion we were concerned with the *amount* of material remembered or forgotten after original learning. In some kinds of learning, there is also a qualitative change in the person's memory of the material.

You may have played the game of Gossip. A group of people arrange themselves in some order. The first person tells a story to the second, the second passes it on from memory to the third, and so on. The last version is compared with the original narrative. The results are usually astonishing and sometimes amusing. The "message" undergoes many changes. It is usually shortened and very much distorted in meaning.

SMALL DISTORTIONS ACCUMULATE TO PRODUCE A CHANGE IN KIND

Figure 4.20 *Marked changes are evident in the successive reproductions of a figure. The original drawing was seen by one subject, who was asked to reproduce it. A second subject looked at this reproduction and then copied it from memory. The same procedure was repeated throughout the series. Note how the distortions of memory change the figure from the conventionalized Egyptian symbol for the owl to a picture of a cat. (Modified from Bartlett, 1932.)*

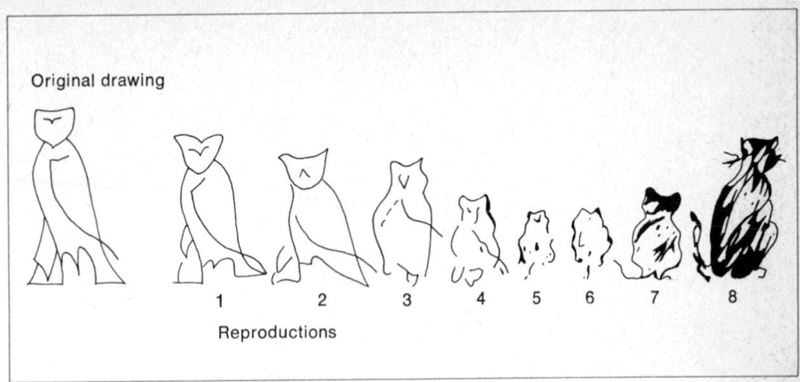

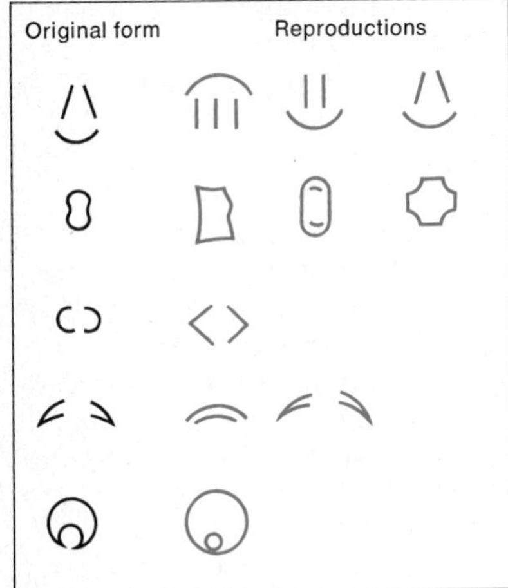

PERCEPTIONS ARE DISTORTED AND SIMPLIFIED IN MEMORY

Figure 4.21 *Changes in memory for forms. The forms in the left-hand column were presented to subjects; when later asked to recall the forms, the subjects reproduced the versions shown in color at the right. Note the distortions. (Modified from Gibson, 1929.)*

This simple game serves as a useful model of certain kinds of social communication. Similar results have been found for visual memory (see Figure 4.20).

Gossip is also interesting because the changes in the narrative as it passes from one player to another parallel the changes in memory which can take place within one individual. If we ask a person to reproduce something after various intervals, we see that his memory of the thing undergoes similar losses and distortions. A British psychologist has studied these qualitative changes very closely (Bartlett, 1932). He finds that in verbal narrative, details are forgotten; the story loses much of its richness and becomes a threadbare structure. Certain phrases and words become stereotyped and appear in each repetition.

Similar changes occur in memory for perceptual objects. If subjects are shown visual forms and are later asked to reproduce them, retention often suffers from a loss of detail. Further, the forms tend to become more general, more symmetrical, or "normalized," and more similar to familiar objects, or "assimilated" (see Figure 4.21).

The next question is, why do such qualitative changes occur in some kinds of remembering during the period following learning? One of the most important changes seems to take place at the time of the original perception. It has been shown, for instance, that a verbal label given to a visually perceived form may influence memory in a marked way (Carmichael et al., 1932):

Each subject was presented with several rather ambiguous stimulus figures and one of two lists of words. Some subjects, for instance, were shown an ambiguous figure in conjunction with the word *bottle;* other subjects were shown the same figure but were at the same time presented with the word *stirrup* from the other word list. Sometime later, the subjects were asked to draw the figures they had seen (this time they were not presented with words). A sample of the results is shown in Figure 4.22. The subjects' drawings from memory of the ambiguous figures were usually much less ambiguous than those figures really were: If a figure had originally been presented with the word *bottle* the drawings tended to look like bottles; if the figure had been presented with the word *stirrup*, the drawings looked more like stirrups.

SOMETIMES WE REMEMBER THE LABEL RATHER THAN THE OBJECT OR EVENT ITSELF

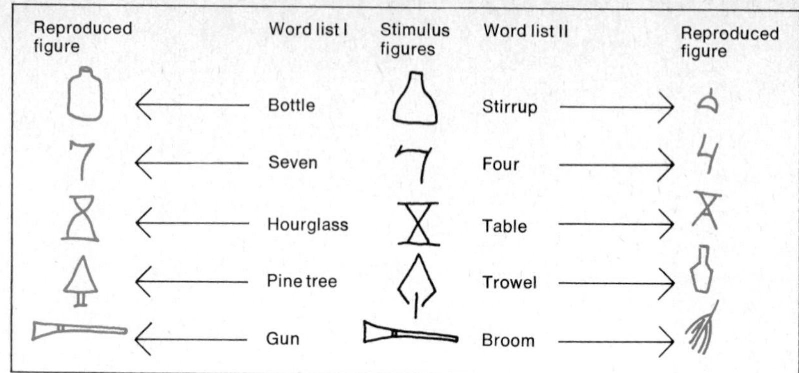

Figure 4.22 *In this experiment, subjects were shown the stimulus figures in the middle column and at the same time were presented with the label in one of the word lists. Later the subjects were asked to reproduce the figures they had seen. Typical reproduced figures for subjects given the labels in word list I are shown at the left; for subjects given words from word list II, the reproduced figures are shown on the right. (Modified from Carmichael et al., 1932.)*

This experiment indicates that a great deal of forgetting may be due to the use of words to condense complex perceptions. We tend to remember the words, or labels, and not what has actually been experienced.

Another reason for qualitative changes in retention is that the person may not perceive the original material accurately. Consequently the first time he reproduces the figure or story, the original error in perception will be there. In the next reproduction, he may remember what he reproduced the first time, and the error will persist. Furthermore, he may even make an error in the perception of his reproduction. Thus it is possible for another error, which can become cumulative, to get started with each reproduction. These repeated errors in perception should be more than enough to produce qualitative memory changes, and should satisfactorily account for such seemingly remarkable transformations as those found in the game of Gossip, for instance.

Theories of Learning, Memory, and Forgetting

This chapter's survey of human learning, remembering, and forgetting shows that we know many facts about learning; indeed, we possess an enormous welter of facts. As Chapter 1 noted, however, facts are not enough. If we want to advance beyond mere cataloging of observations and simple findings, we must try to encompass the facts with a limited set of theoretical principles. We must construct theories and then test them against already known facts as well as against new facts obtained in experiments designed to test the theories. Let us see what we have in the way of theory in the area of human learning.

As a matter of fact, we have a profusion of theories—almost too many to count. In mathematical learning theory alone (that is, theory developed to the point of a quantitative model), we could list a dozen or so. Most of the theories, however, are "mini" theories; they are concerned with phenomena encountered in using one particular learning method. If we try to group such theories into general classes, we settle on the two groups mentioned in the last chapter: *continuity* and *noncontinuity* theories. These are considered below under association theory and organization theory, respectively. Their mathematical forms are then discussed under incremental versus one-trial theories. Finally, in the last two sections we consider the promising theories of memory and of forgetting.

Association theory In human learning as in animal learning, the oldest and generally the strongest of learning theories is *association theory*. This assumes, as discussed in Chapter 3, that stimuli and responses which are contiguous in time and space become associated. The theory in its simplest form does pretty well in accounting for conditioning and simple nonverbal learning. But when it is applied to verbal learning, which will be our chief concern here, it needs elaboration. This has been done in what is called the two-stage theory of verbal learning (Underwood and Schulz, 1960).

According to two-stage theory, the first stage in verbal learning is the acquisition of responses. When presented with the pair of nonsense syllables *zak-xof*, the subject learns *xof* as a response without necessarily remembering that it is associated with *zak*. Evidence for this comes from many paired-associate studies which tabulate the kinds of errors made by subjects early in the learning of a list. The interesting point about such errors is that the wrong responses made are virtually always items appearing somewhere in the list; few, if any, responses not on the list are made before they are correctly associated with the appropriate stimulus words.

As learning of a list proceeds, one can see second-stage learning, that is, the association of responses with stimuli. The subject gradually acquires more and more correct associations of the responses learned in the first one or two trials until he has learned the list perfectly.

Organization theory The two-stage association theory accounts well for the learning of material low in meaning, such as strange words or nonsense syllables. With more meaningful material, however, something more is required: there must be some kind of *encoding* in terms of previously learned associations. These associations may be of two general kinds: second-order habits, or concepts.

To illustrate a second-order habit, suppose one of the response items in paired-associate learning is *gdo* (Underwood, 1964*a*). In previously learning words, the subject has built up letter associations as they occur in words, and his reaction to *gdo* will not be the mechanical matter that it would be, say, to *xof*. Instead, he will usually turn these letters into something like *god* or *dog* and then remember that the *g* or the *d* is out of place. Thus he encodes the response in terms of habits already acquired. In so doing, he makes the response easier to learn, for encodable responses like *gdo* are learned much more rapidly than others.

To illustrate encoding in terms of concepts, let us turn back to Table 4.2 (page 127). Here, list 2 gives four words for each of four concepts (a man's name, a religious leader, an animal, and a dance). We saw that this list was more easily learned and remembered than list 1, which contains random words not ordered according to concept. Even in list 1, however, some encoding goes on. In learning English words, such as *apple, football, emerald,* and *trout,* the person does not just learn the words; he learns that one is a fruit, the other something used in a sport, another a jewel, and the last a fish. Moreover, he can often tell you that

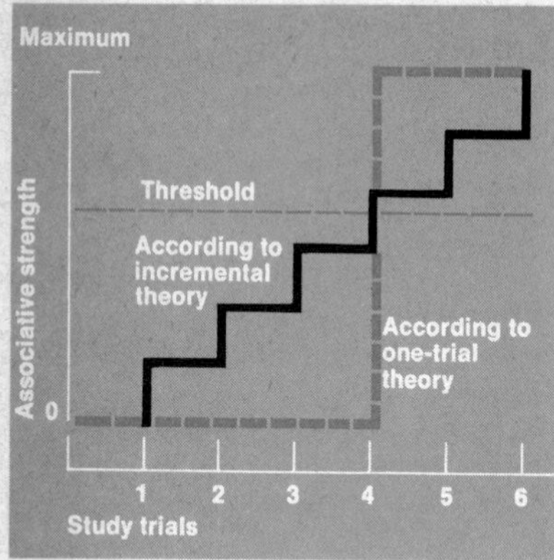

ARE ASSOCIATIONS FORMED GRADUALLY, OR ARE THEY ALL-OR-NONE?

Figure 4.23 *The difference between the incremental and one-trial theories of verbal learning. The learning of a single paired associate,* zak-xof, *is shown.*
According to the incremental theory, the association between zak *and* xof *is strengthened a little on each trial. Eventually, by the fourth trial in this example, the association becomes strong enough to exceed the threshold of response, and the subject makes the correct response.*
But according to one-trial theory, the strength of the zak-xof *association increases from zero to full strength on a single trial: the fourth one. (Modified from Underwood and Keppel, 1962.)*

"It was some kind of fruit" even when he cannot remember the exact response. And when he makes an error, it is frequently a response of the same general class. To take an everyday example, suppose you are having difficulty recalling a name. You are very likely to be able to give certain characteristics of the name, such as that it is a two-syllable English word which begins with G or rhymes with ball. Thus you have encoded the name in terms of your concepts of names.

Phenomena such as these point to *organization* in learning rather than to mere association (Mandler, 1967). Newly acquired responses fit into existing hierarchies or categories of response previously learned. Such organization is a distinctive feature of meaningful learning. Theorists who stress this feature are not necessarily at odds with association theory, for association theory can be stretched to fit it; but they are interested in studying the characteristics of such organization more than the history of associations leading up to it.

Incremental versus one-trial theories The two theoretical approaches just described are forms of *continuity* and *noncontinuity* theories introduced in Chapter 3. According to continuity theory, associations are built up in increments accruing from trial to trial. According to noncontinuity theory, each association is really a reorganization of memory that takes place completely in one trial or not at all. This distinction has led to opposing theories of learning, one called *incremental theory* and the other *one-trial theory*.

The following example illustrates the difference between one-trial and incremental theories as applied to verbal learning (Underwood and Keppel, 1962):

Suppose a subject is presented with a list of paired associates, one member of which is *zak-xof*. The first time through, of course, he cannot get it correct because he has never seen it before, but on the next trial—the first test trial—he might. However, let us assume that on the first test trial he does not get this pair correct; that is, when presented with *zak* alone he does not respond with *xof*. On the second and third test trials he still does not get it correct, but on the fourth test trial he says *xof* when he sees *zak*.

(The *one-trial theory* says that the subject did not learn anything about this particular paired associate until the fourth trial, but that thereafter, except for some forgetting, he will always respond correctly to the stimulus term *zak*.) The dashed line of Figure 4.23 shows the period of no learning and the quantal jump in associative strength predicted by one-trial learning theory.

One form of the *incremental theory* (especially Hull, 1943, 1951, 1952) says that the association of *zak* with *xof* is strengthened a little bit on each trial, but that the correct response will not be made until associative strength has exceeded a certain value—the *threshold value*, shown by the thin dashed line in Figure 4.23. The solid line suggests the increments of associative strength which the incremental theory predicts will be added on each trial. The threshold has been drawn so that the associative strength predicted by incremental theory is crossed on the fourth trial. When associative strength for an item has crossed the threshold, there is a high probability that it will remain above the threshold and be correct on succeeding trials.

In showing how the one-trial and incremental theories can be formulated to predict the same behavior, this example illustrates why it is often difficult to make crucial tests of theories. The experiments that have been devised to test these two theories sometimes favor one and sometimes the other. We can make some sense out of the diverse findings, however, if we assume that one theory applies in some learning situations and the other in other situations. In general, the incremental theory fits simple conditioning and nonsense learning, and the one-trial theory applies best to the learning of meaningful or organized material. In a few mixed situations, the evidence seems to indicate that some responses are learned in one trial while others are learned incrementally.

Memory-store theory Another way of constructing a learning theory so that it can account for both one-trial and incremental learning as well as for some other phenomena of learning has been proposed by two mathematical psychologists (Atkinson and Shiffrin, 1968). In particular, their theory attempts to explain the difference in short-term and long-term memory discussed earlier in the chapter. It is called the *memory-store theory.*

In this theory, the learning mechanism is regarded as a memory system consisting of three components: a sensory register, a short-term store, and a long-term store. Take a telephone number as an example: When you locate a number in a telephone directory, the information enters your sensory register—it is perceived, at least momentarily. But how easy it is to lose it there! You close the book, start to dial, and realize that you haven't remembered; the number has not entered the short-term store. For it to enter this store, according to memory-store theory, a little rehearsal is required. You must make an effort to remember, usually with some subvocal repetition of the number. Once the number is in the short-term store, you can dial it and complete your call. At this point, the number can be "lost" so that it never enters the long-term store. We saw earlier that short-term memory suffers when other distracting activities immediately follow; memory-store theory holds that such distractions prevent short-term memories from entering the long-term store. For information to be transferred from the short- to the long-term store, you usually must rehearse the information several times until you are sure you have "memorized" it.

A key notion in this theory is *rehearsal.* In verbal learning, rehearsal is usually a vocal or subvocal repetition of a response, but in the simplest case it is merely keeping the response in mind—not letting other information in—long enough to deposit a permanent memory trace. Looking at learning in this way, one can see that getting a memory into the sensory register can be considered a one-trial, all-or-none matter, but holding it in the long-term store can be an incremental matter of the degree to which it is rehearsed.

Forgetting: Interference versus decay This leads us, finally, to a closer look at the question of forgetting. Short-term forgetting can be simply a matter of not getting the information into the long-term store. This failure in turn can be a result of insufficient rehearsal caused by interference from other incoming information or from other responses.

But assume that the information is processed into the long-term store so that it is thoroughly learned; yet some days later, we no longer remember it. Such forgetting is commonplace. How do we account for it?

Two theories have been proposed to deal with this phenomenon. One, the *decay theory,* holds that a *memory fades* with the mere passage of time. This is sometimes called the "leaky bucket hypothesis" (G. A. Miller, 1956*a*). The other theory is that things thoroughly learned—things that have entered the long-term store—are forgotten because new learning interferes with or displaces them. This is the *interference theory* (Underwood, 1957).

It is impossible to conduct a crucial test of these theories because we cannot arrange life so that it is free from interference, even in the laboratory. Other activities, some of them similar to what the person has learned, usually intervene between original learning and any test of retention. The closest we can come to an interference-free situation is one in which the subject is asleep between learning and the test. In this case, as we have seen, retention is at its best. Also, from the various experiments on retroactive inhibition and interpolated activity between learning and retention tests, it appears that much if not all of forgetting can be explained by interference. Hence, although we cannot say that it is the only factor in forgetting, we feel certain that it is the principal factor.

Synopsis and summary

We have discussed some of what is known about human learning, remembering, and forgetting. Certain variables affecting human learning and some of the reasons for forgetting have been fairly well determined. We now know that distribution of practice, knowledge of results, recitation, and meaningfulness of the material will usually increase the rate of learning. And the influence of prior learning on present learning, an influence called transfer of training, is an exceedingly important factor in human learning. We have also seen that the degree to which the material was learned and the amount of interference with the original material are the most important variables controlling the rate of forgetting.

1. Six categories of human learning can be distinguished: (*a*) conditioning, (*b*) motor learning, (*c*) discrimination learning, (*d*) verbal learning, (*e*) problem solving, and (*f*) concept learning. The first three obey principles similar to those seen in classical and operant conditioning and perceptual learning in animals. Problem solving and concept learning are considered briefly in this chapter, but they are more fully treated in Chapter 5 because they involve thinking. Most of this chapter is about verbal learning.

2. Classical conditioning—for example, of the eyeblink—occurs in human as well as animal subjects, but it is sometimes complicated by "voluntary" responses. Motor learning is operant learning in which a skill is acquired. It is measured either by elimination of errors or by increases in accuracy.

3. Three kinds of discrimination learning were described. (*a*) In probability learning, one stimulus is correct a certain proportion of the time. People generally learn to match the proportion of their responses with the probability of being correct. (*b*) In incidental learning, the subject discriminates features of stimuli other than those he intentionally learns. In most situations little incidental learning takes place. (*c*) In reversal learning, a person first learns a discrimination with one stimulus correct. The situation is then switched so that the second stimulus becomes the correct one. For rats and young children this reversal is difficult to learn, but for older children and adults it is relatively easy because they can verbalize the switch.

4. Experimental studies of human learning often use nonsense syllables and the serial-anticipation or paired-associate learning methods. In the serial-anticipation method, the subject learns a list in which preceding items serve as cues for responding with the succeeding items; in the paired-associate method, the subject learns a list of S-R associations. A third method, free learning and recall, permits a subject to learn responses in any order they happen to occur.

5. Individual differences in intelligence, age, motivation, previous learning, and anxiety level affect the rate of learning.

6. Of the many variables that affect rate of learning, three of the most

important are (*a*) distribution of practice over time, (*b*) provision for knowledge of results, and (*c*) time spent in recitation and reading or merely reading alone. Programmed textbooks and teaching machines incorporate these principles.

7. The characteristics of the material to be learned are important in determining the ease of learning. Material that is highly meaningful and highly organized is more easily learned than material low in meaning or nonsense material.

8. Transfer of training refers to the effect of learning one task on the subsequent learning of another. Transfer may be either positive or negative, and the amount and kind of transfer depend upon the similarities of responses and stimuli in the original and subsequent tasks.

9. In formal education, school subjects that have little in common have little or no transfer value. Except for learning to learn, the degree of transfer from one school subject to another depends upon elements which the two subjects have in common.

10. Two memory processes, short-term and long-term, have been distinguished. Short-term memory is limited in capacity and highly susceptible to disruption as compared with long-term memory.

11. The three basic methods of measuring retention are recall, recognition, and savings. Of these, recall is the least sensitive, and savings (in relearning of the same material) the most sensitive measure of retention. Even when there is little retention as measured by recall, there may be considerable retention as measured by the time required to relearn (savings). Whether measured by recall, recognition, or savings, the retention curve is usually negatively accelerated.

12. Variables which influence the amount retained in long-term memory are (*a*) meaningfulness of the material, (*b*) degree of learning of the material, and (*c*) interference with the learned material. Greater meaningfulness and overlearning enhance retention. Interference is especially important in producing forgetting. The interference can be produced by previously learned material (referred to as proactive inhibition) or by material learned subsequent to the original learning (referred to as interference due to interpolated activity, or retroactive inhibition). The amount of interference is a function of the similarities between the interfering material and test material.

13. Qualitative changes take place in the process of forgetting, particularly in recall of stories or pictures. Some of the details are smoothed out or lost; others are accentuated. Most of these changes are explained by verbal labeling or perceptual distortion at the time of the original event.

14. Two general theories attempt to account for the major phenomena of human learning: (*a*) association or continuity theory, and (*b*) organization or noncontinuity theory. They lead, respectively, to incremental and one-trial theories of how learning takes place. One-trial, noncontinuity theory probably applies best to learning highly meaningful and organized material; incremental, continuity theory best describes what occurs in nonsense learning.

15. Memory-store theory assumes that we have a sensory register, a short-term store, and a long-term store; information can be lost at either of the first two stages so that it does not get into the next one.

16. Of two theories of forgetting, the decay theory and the interference theory, the interference theory is favored, because in experimental research most forgetting is caused by interfering learning or activity.

Related topics in the text

Chapter 3 Principles of Learning
General principles and types of learning are described in this chapter.

Chapter 5 Thinking and Language
The solving of problems and the learning of concepts are discussed in this chapter because they are types of learning that require thinking.

Chapter 19 Brain and Behavior
The roles of certain parts of the brain in learning are described.

Suggestions for further reading

Adams, J. A. *Human memory.* New York: McGraw-Hill, 1967.
A summary of the facts and theories about human memory.

Bilodeau, E. A. (Ed.) *Acquisition of skill.* New York: Academic, 1966.
A summary and critique of the field of motor learning.

Deese, J., and Hulse, S. H. *The psychology of learning. (3d ed.)* New York: McGraw-Hill, 1967.
A short textbook on learning.

Hall, J. F. *The psychology of learning.* Philadelphia: Lippincott, 1966.
A comprehensive textbook of animal and human learning.

Hilgard, E. R., and Bower, G.H. *Theories of learning. (3d ed.)* New York: Appleton Century Crofts, 1966.
A survey and analysis of various theories of learning.

King, R. A. (Ed.) *Readings for an introduction to psychology.* (3d ed.) New York: McGraw-Hill, 1971.
A book of readings designed to accompany this text.

Melton, A. W. (Ed.) *Categories of human learning.* New York: Academic, 1964.
A symposium on the types of human learning and their interrelationships.

Morgan, C. T., and Deese, J. *How to study.* (2d ed.) New York: McGraw-Hill, 1969.
An application of learning principles to techniques of study.

Stephens, J. M. *The psychology of classroom learning.* New York: Holt, 1965.
An application of learning principles to school learning.

Man began to think in order that he might eat, now he has evolved to the point where he eats in order that he may think.
W. P. Montague

Out of chaos the imagination frames a thing of beauty.
J. L. Lowes

A well-known sign in certain business offices commands us to THINK. What is the sign telling us to do? As we shall see, it is telling us to make use of the great human ability to represent the world to ourselves in symbols. Symbolic representation of the world, whether simple or complex, is the keystone of any definition of the thinking process.

The Thinking Process

Thinking involves symbols. A symbol is a stimulus used to stand for, or represent, something else. Many words in languages—nouns, for example—are symbols; the word *house* is a symbol because it stands for the object house.

The symbolic activity of thinking can be very simple or very complex. In its simplest form, it means little more than "remember" or "recall." Suppose that we see a road sign saying, "Think—speed kills." Used this way, "think" merely tells us to remember, or to reactivate, a previously made symbolic connection between fast driving and fatal accidents. Similarly, if someone asks you to recall the name of the founder of the Southern Christian Leadership Conference and to think about some of the things he did, you are being asked only to recall associations you have once learned. The process of recall under these circumstances involves only a small amount of symbolic representation. But at the other extreme, the word "think" may refer to such highly rigorous and reflective activity as a scientist undertakes when he attempts to solve a complex problem. He may spend hours or days juggling mathematical formulas, drawing diagrams, or merely imagining various ways in which the problem might be solved.

Whether thinking is simple or complex, it always seems to involve one thing: a *symbolic mediating process*. When we think, something links past learning with our present responses. Mediating processes fill in the gaps between the stimulus situation and the responses we make to it. When we are solving problems, these processes substitute for things we might otherwise do overtly in a trial-and-error manner.

Suppose that you have a jigsaw puzzle to put together. The hard way to work out the puzzle would be to try fitting every piece to every other piece. This would be solving the puzzle by plain trial and error. If there were many pieces in the puzzle, the process would take an interminable time and millions of trial-and-error fittings. You will probably have to do some of this, but only to choose between two or three possibilities that are very close to the correct one. Mostly you will think. The steps in your thinking will represent what you might otherwise do by trial and error. You will often think of putting the pieces together in a certain way without actually doing it. You will try putting them together in your head, and decide whether they will or will not go together before trying with your hands. Thus by thinking, you will do much more economically and quickly what you might do by trying all the pieces in all their possible places.

Your thinking represents, symbolizes, or takes the place of observable behavior and the physical rearrangement of stimuli. The thinking process is a mediating process. To say so is to indicate how the thinking process functions—it connects. But this does not tell us what thinking is. What goes on inside a person when he thinks? What is the thinking process?

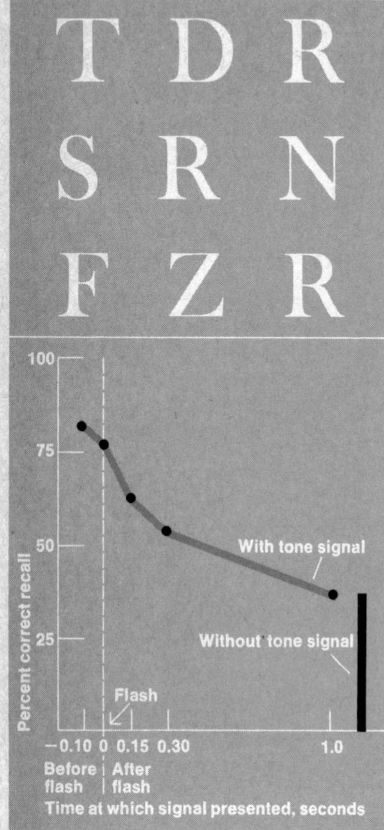

Figure 5.1 *An experiment on iconic imagery. Top, a 3 × 3 block of letters used in the experiment; bottom, the results of the experiment. First, the 3 × 3 letter block was flashed for 50 milliseconds (at the point where the dashed line intersects the time scale). Subjects could recall very few of the letters about a second after the flash (degree of recall is indicated by height of black bar at right). Next, various tone signals, each indicating that a particular row of letters in the 3 × 3 block would be the "recall target," were given at various time intervals before and after the letter block was flashed. Recall of the letters was markedly greater with the tone signals than without them, as the graph curve shows. (After Sperling, 1960.)*

Trace processes Perhaps the simplest kind of thinking, or symbolic-mediating process, is a memory trace that lasts some period of time and can serve in place of a stimulus cue in the solution of simple problems. Symbolic trace processes of this sort have been much studied, and the evidence indicates that both long-term and short-term memory traces exist (see Chapter 4). Some of the most interesting experiments have investigated the short-term, or *iconic,* traces (Neisser, 1967). Here is an experiment on short-term images (Sperling, 1960):

A device for the brief presentation of visual information—a *tachistoscope*—was used by Sperling to show groups of letters (in 3 × 3 blocks) such as those in Figure 5.1. The exposure time was 50 milliseconds (50 thousandths of a second)—a very brief flash indeed. Under these conditions, subjects could recall only a few of the letters a little over a second after the flash (see Figure 5.1, bar at right).

But when the experiment was done in a slightly different way, recall was much better. Subjects were instructed that a tone presented *after* the flash was the signal for recall of one of the three rows of letters. A high tone was the signal for the top row, a middle tone for the middle row, and a low tone for the bottom row. When a tone signal was given 150 or 300 milliseconds *after* the flash of the letters, recall for the critical, or target, row was markedly greater than when no signal had been given (see Figure 5.1).

This finding was interpreted as indicating the persistence of a visual trace; in other words, an image which could be "scanned" was in the nervous system for a brief period of time. The subjects reported such fleeting images. According to this type of interpretation, the signal after the flash directed the subjects to scan a portion of the decaying image. If the time between the flash and the signal to scan was short, recall was better than with no signal because, at short intervals, the image was still present to be scanned.

Another interesting discovery in this experiment was that recall for a critical row was also quite good if the signal was given just *before* the flash (see Figure 5.1). This finding can be interpreted as showing that the "before" signal, by indicating what row the subject should concentrate on, enabled him to scan that portion of the image of the flash containing the required information.

Images in thought Longer-lasting memory traces, sometimes called images, are also involved in the symbolic representation of the world

Figure 5.2 *A picture for a test of eidetic imagery. (G. W. Allport.)*

necessary for thinking. Perhaps the extreme in the ability to imagine the world is experienced by those few people who have *eidetic imagery.* Some people, most often young children, have "photographic memories" for things they have seen—they have almost perfect images of visual material (Haber, 1969). To test yourself, look at the picture in Figure 5.2. *Do not read further until you have inspected the picture for 35 seconds.*

Now, without looking at the picture, can you spell the German word in it? In one experiment, 3 out of 30 English schoolchildren, unfamiliar with German, could spell the word forward and backward; 7 spelled it with only two mistakes. They, and other "eidetikers," often hesitate a moment before recall. During this time they seem to "project" their image on a "mental screen," to inspect it, and then to read it as if it were actually there. Some people can recall a page of print so accurately that they can repeat any word or line on demand, shifting to different parts of the page as requested.

Most people do not have eidetic imagery, but they usually report that they have images. Hence, even though we cannot observe another person's images objectively, we believe that they exist. In some individuals, visual images apparently predominate. Auditory imagery occurs frequently, and even odors and tastes are said to be imagined by some individuals. Images of muscular sensations, of pain, hunger, and other organic sensations are relatively rare. And there are some people who report an almost total lack of all imagery.

So far as human thinking is concerned, the question about images is not whether they exist, but what function they have in thinking. Are they the mediating process in thinking? This issue was once hotly debated; some answered with a resounding "yes," others with a vehement "no." To answer the question scientifically, psychologists have conducted rigorous experiments on the role of images in thinking.

The simplest kind of experiment is to ask a person to report on his experiences. One can instruct him, for example, to recall his breakfast table and describe what kind of images he has. Most people will give a fairly detailed description, thus proving that they have images. This kind of experiment, however, tells us only what images, and relatively how many, a person may have; it tells us little about the mediating function of images in thinking.

Another kind of experiment requires the subject to solve some manipulative problem, such as tracing his way blindfolded through a maze with his finger or a pencil (Davis, 1932, 1933). After he has done this, he is quizzed about his imagery. Many people in such an experiment report truly functional visual imagery; they solve the maze by building up a "mental map" of it as they go along. Consequently they can draw the maze afterward, sometimes including the blind alleys as well as the true path. Other persons solve the maze by a purely verbal method; they count or name correct turns but do not "see" the maze as a whole in their mind's eye.

Imageless thought Experiments of the sort just described indicate that images may promote learning and that they may at times have a mediating function in thinking. But there are other kinds of experiments on the role of images in thinking. One of these, the "thought experiment," was first carried out about 1900. A group of psychologists in Würzburg, Germany, who were much interested in understanding thought and consciousness, performed it many times. They gave their subject a rather simple intellectual problem, such as "Name a fruit," and then asked him to describe the images he had in arriving at the answer.

The Würzburg psychologists were surprised to discover that very few images were uncovered in this way. Moreover, images did not seem to be necessary to solve this kind of problem. If the problem was to name a fruit, the subject could often say "apple" immediately, yet be unable to detect any image of a fruit or apple. Apparently the thinking involved in making the appropriate response did not necessarily involve any images. Hence the possibility of *imageless thought* was conceived, a notion which was quite controversial at that time.

Two products of the imageless-thought hypothesis have proved to be significant. One is the discovery that many of the important events in thinking may not be conscious. We cannot catch and inspect an idea or a thought as we can a bird or a butterfly. This suggests that an idea is more like a process than an object. The other product of the hypothesis is that thought often seems to be governed by a *set* that is formed before the thought occurs. A set is a readiness to think or respond in a predetermined way. If you are given a stimulus word, a thought seems to run off automatically, just as if you had already done your thinking before you start! And what the thought is depends on the set. If you see, for example,

$$\begin{array}{l} 6 \\ \underline{4} \end{array}$$

you can give a quick answer, but whether it is 2, 10, or 24 depends on whether you are set to subtract, add, or multiply. Of course, with the appropriate instructions, any one of these sets could have been established. Set, as a theoretical concept, has become a most important term in the psychologist's vocabulary. We cannot observe it objectively; yet in order to explain thinking, we must assume that it exists. (We shall discuss set in more detail later in the chapter.)

Having gotten this far but no further, the early experimental psychologists faced a predicament. They conceived of psychology as the science of conscious experience (see page 22); yet they had established the fact that thinking could take place with no conscious content. The "higher mental processes" had eluded their search. To be sure, images did sometimes accompany thoughts, but the important thing was that images were not essential to thought. The introspective method (see page 24) had come up against a blank wall, for a person cannot very well introspect if he has nothing to introspect about.

We can conclude, then, that images may sometimes be the mediating processes of thinking, but since thinking can go on without them, other kinds of mediating processes must also exist.

Implicit responses in thought When this conclusion had been reached by the early psychologists, it occurred to those with a behavioristic bent that some of the content of thinking might consist of small muscle movements.

Perhaps, they suggested, *implicit muscle responses,* not seen by the naked eye but large enough to send back impulses to the nervous system, were essential elements in the flow of thinking. This hypothesis was set forth some 50 years ago by John B. Watson as the explanation of thought.

Two steps are necessary to test the hypothesis. One is to confirm or deny the existence of implicit muscle responses during thinking. The second step is to demonstrate that such implicit responses serve as symbols or cues in the flow of thinking. This is difficult to prove, but it is a more reasonable possibility than might at first appear.

The idea that implicit muscle responses are a part of thinking is made plausible by the relationship between thinking and learning. Thinking begins in learning, and a good deal of learning, as we have seen, is acquired by doing. We can suppose that learned responses become smaller and smaller as they are practiced, and that thinking consists of these movements reduced from the larger movements of original learning.

Some early experiments did indicate that such implicit movements occur when a person is thinking (Jacobsen, 1932; Max, 1937). But other evidence suggests that muscle movements are not usually the symbolic mediating responses of thought. For instance, thought was not impaired in certain heroic experiments in which the subject's muscles were paralyzed by the drug curare (Smith et al., 1947; Solomon and Turner, 1962). The conclusion seems to be that, although muscle movements may accompany thought, they are not the essence of it.

Language in thought Language is one of the major tools of thought. The words of language, or the units of meaning, can be combined into a stupendous number of sentences to represent the relationships between objects and events in the world around us. It has been estimated that there are roughly 100,000,000,000,000,000,000 possible sentences in English that are 20 words long (Miller, 1965). Such an inexhaustible supply of possible sentences provides a tool of great richness for the symbolic representation of the world.

Another important characteristic of language as a tool of thought is that it is structured by certain formal rules. By this we mean that by following the rules we can generate or comprehend any of the 100 quintillion sentences mentioned above. The study of languages as systems of rules is the job of *linguistics.* Linguists concerned with the rules of language sounds are *phoneticians;* those who study the meanings of words are *semanticists;* and the linguists known as *grammarians* study the rules for combining words into meaningful sentences. Within psychology, the field of *psycholinguistics* applies principles developed in linguistics to try and understand the ways people use language.

Psycholinguists are mainly concerned with the ways in which people generate language and comprehend it. But to some extent a description of the formal rules of language may give us ideas about the processes involved in using language as a tool of thought. If these formal rules specify certain ways in which the world can be symbolized, then they are, to some extent, also the rules of thought. We adults can symbolize very complex relationships, but our thinking may be more limited than we realize by language rules. The role of these rules in limiting thought is perhaps best studied in the early stages of language development, when it is relatively primitive (Braine, 1963):

As a result of extensive study of the speech of young children about 2 years of age, some of the first simple grammatical rules for the construction of sentences have been specified. At this age, children form two-word sentences without auxiliary verbs (*do, have, will*), articles (*the, a*), determiners (*this, that*), quantifiers (*some, any*), and most pronouns. The grammar of two-word sentences at this age is thought to consist of a class of *pivot* words and *open* words. The pivot class is a rather small group of words with which other words may appear. A pivot word for a particular child might be *bye-bye.* He then uses *bye-bye* with other words such as *daddy, car, mommy,* and *house* to compose the sentences "Bye-bye daddy," "Bye-bye house," and so on. The pivot word tends to have a relatively stable position in the sentence; in this case *bye-bye* was used in the initial position. Since the other position in the two-word sentence can be filled by any number of other words, these words are termed open. Open words can occur either as single-word utterances or with pivot words. But if a child is using a word as a pivot, it rarely occurs alone or with other pivots. Psychologists have speculated that the initial division into pivot and open classes later grades into the more familiar adult classification of nouns, verbs, and adjectives. But at the two-word stage, we cannot say that a child is using his pivot and open words in adult ways.

A child in the primitive two-word stage obviously has neither the words nor the grammatical rules to symbolize the world in the sophisticated fashion of an adult. Adult abstract thinking is a matter of an adequate vocabulary and an ability to use the formal grammatical rules in an intuitively correct fashion. Since abstract thinking depends so heavily on language, perhaps this is the reason why intelligence tests are so heavily weighted with subtests of language abilities (see Chapter 10).

Concept Attainment

Words and the rules for the formation of sentences, as we have just seen, are important aspects of language. Words and images, the symbolic mediators in thought, may refer to something specific or to something general. Something specific might be "the house I lived in as a boy." Something general might be "house" (any house), or "red," "government," "goodness," or the like. The general symbolic mediators are termed *concepts.* The accuracy and adequacy of our concepts are important considerations in our ability to use thought productively in the solution of problems.

Concept attainment is the process of isolating a common property, or properties, of objects or events. The common properties thus isolated are known as *concepts.* By "common property" we mean some feature that is the same in several otherwise different situations. It may be "redness," "triangularity," "meticulousness," or any of thousands of possible characteristics of things, situations, or people.

CONCEPT FORMATION CAN BE STUDIED EXPERIMENTALLY

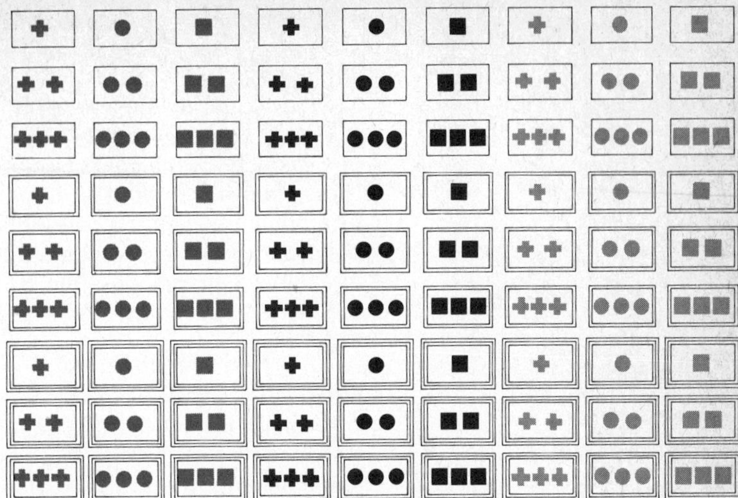

Figure 5.3 *Cards used in a study of concept formation. Note that they differ in four ways: in the number of figures, in the color of the figures, in the shape of the figures, and in the number of borders. (After Bruner et al., 1956.)*

Concepts enable us to divide things into classes. With a concept of redness, we can sort objects into the classes of "red" and "not red." With a concept of fruit, we can classify things into "fruit" and "not fruit." The common property forms the concept and is the basis for making such classifications.

Since the number of common properties is practically unlimited, there is almost no end to the number of classes or of concepts that can be formed. Classes of classes exist, and classes of classes of classes. There can be a concept for any level of grouping. In the class of "dwelling unit" are the subclasses houses, apartments, and caves. In the class of "house" are the subclasses mansions and cottages. Cottages include red ones and white ones. Houses and caves can be big or little, if grouped according to the property of size. And so on and on as far as we wish to go.

Types of concepts The term concept, we have seen, refers to properties which objects and events have in common. If only one set of common properties defines the concept, we may call it a "simple" concept. In Figure 5.3, for example, any card with a circle on it would be a simple concept; these cards have only one common property—circle. But most concepts are "complex," because several common characteristics enter into their definition (Bruner et al., 1956).

CONJUNCTIVE CONCEPTS This type of concept is defined by the joint presence of several characteristics. For instance, among the cards in Figure 5.3, which were used in an experimental study of concept formation, all the cards with three green squares comprise a conjunctive concept. The joint presence of three of something, greenness, and squareness defines the concept in this case. Such conjunctive concepts seem to be fairly easy for people to achieve.

DISJUNCTIVE CONCEPTS A member of a disjunctive concept class contains at least one element from a larger group of elements. For example, suppose we take three green squares as our group of elements. Any card in Figure 5.3 which has three of anything, *or* contains something green, *or* contains squares, has one element from the larger group and is a member of the concept class. A strike in baseball is an example of a disjunctive concept (Bruner et al., 1956). A strike is a missed swing, *or* a pitch at which the batter does not swing but which passes over the plate between the shoulders and knees, *or* a foul ball if there are not already two strikes, *or* a foul bunt if there are already two strikes on the batter. Disjunctive concepts seem to be relatively difficult for people to attain.

RELATIONAL CONCEPTS This type of concept is defined in terms of relationships between the elements in a situation. In Figure 5.3, for instance, all the cards with more borders than figures exemplify one such relational concept. Thus a relational concept does not depend upon the absolute properties of objects or elements; instead, relational concepts are defined in terms of constant relationships between the elements.

Words and concepts In principle, one does not have to know words or a language in order to have a concept. Indeed, many of our concepts are formed without the benefit of words and are poorly expressed with words. The only requirement for concept attainment is that some property of objects be correctly discriminated. For example, by giving rats extensive training with all sorts of triangles, it has been possible to teach them the concept of triangularity. When trained, they avoid jumping to nontriangles but will jump to almost any kind of triangle, despite differences in detail among the triangles. In this case, the rats signify their attainment of the concept of triangularity by their discrimination in jumping (Fields, 1932).

In practice, however, words are very important in concept attainment. Language, in fact, is so closely linked to human concept attainment that the definition of a concept is almost synonymous with the definition of a word (Osgood et al., 1957). This is because most words are used as labels to refer to some common property of objects. (The exception is *proper* nouns.) To appreciate this, just select any set of words you want and ask yourself what they mean, or how they are defined. Take "red." Red is not the name of any one thing, but rather the name for anything having the property of "redness," regardless of its other characteristics. Hence red is the name for a concept, for it arouses in you the concept of redness. Take "wagon," "house," "school," "tree," or any other common noun. In each case, the concept aroused is the property that many different objects have in common.

Abstraction In attaining word concepts, we learn either simultaneously or successively to do two things. One is to discriminate the property, or properties, that several objects have in common. This is called *abstraction.* The other is to assign a particular *word label* to the abstracted property or properties. When the label is consistently applied to the property or properties abstracted, the concept has been learned. Let us

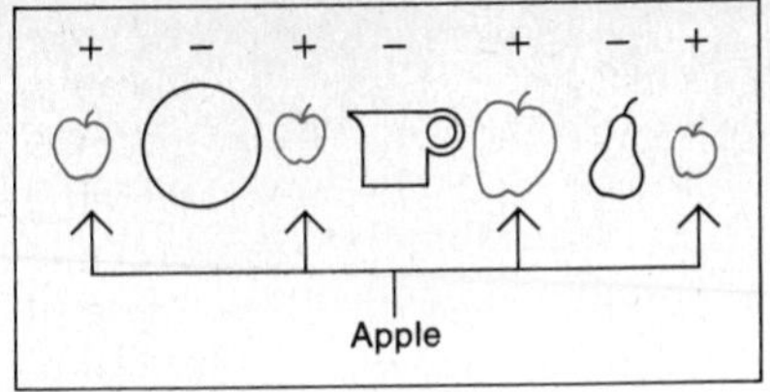

EARLY CONCEPTS ARE LEARNED THROUGH DISCRIMINATION AND GENERALIZATION

Figure 5.4 *Concept attainment. A child hears the word "apple" when he sees some objects, but not others. And he is rewarded if he says "apple" when he sees some objects, but not others. In this way, he generalizes the concept of apple and distinguishes it from other concepts. (After Johnson, 1948.)*

illustrate by taking a case of conjunctive concept attainment in children.

First is the process little Charlie goes through in learning the names of things (see Figure 5.4). Suppose that whenever an apple is offered to Charlie, someone says "apple." People say nothing at all or something else whenever they offer him a ball, a cup, or a triangular block. This gives Charlie a chance to associate "apple" with the fruit of that name. In addition, he may be aided by being given an apple whenever he says "apple." The apples he associates with "apple" in this way will vary somewhat in size and shape, but they will all be more or less round, they will be edible, and they will have stems.

Having learned this, Charlie will have the conjunctive concept of apple. But it might not be the concept of apple as we use that concept. In fact, it might turn out to be our conjunctive concept of "fruit," for which he uses "apple," meaning any fruit roughly of apple size that he can eat. This is because his concept of apple is any "round, juicy object I can eat." These are the common properties of apples, but they are also the common properties of many fruits. He will have generalized too much, but quite justifiably. In fact, he will be exhibiting the phenomenon of stimulus generalization which we have previously encountered (Chapter 3). Such generalization to similar objects, of course, is exactly what is required for concept attainment. But to learn the right concept of "apple," he will need more training in distinguishing the properties of apples from those of pears, plums, and other fruits. In due course, he will certainly get it.

Concept attainment will proceed as rapidly as Charlie can learn to discriminate the differences between objects and at the same time abstract their similarities, thereby forming classes of objects. It will also depend on the *naming responses* available to him. Without appropriate words to label the classes, he will lack the means of responding to them. If appropriate words are available, he can attach a word meaning to each class. Thus in concept attainment, discrimination and abstraction go hand in hand with the naming of classes.

Consider people's concepts of color. Human beings can discriminate several thousand colors, and we have names for dozens of them. In practice, however, we use only a small number of the color concepts that are possible. A young child is usually taught names for red, green, yellow, and blue, but seldom is he taught crimson, magenta, scarlet, or shocking pink. To him, "red" is first just a name for one property of his red wagon, but he comes to use it for a class of colors of similar properties and hence to use it as a concept. The end points of the class may not be certain; he may wonder whether to call an orange-red "red," "yellow," or "orange," or he may hesitate with purple. Yet the middle points are instantly labeled red, and the class is named for its most frequent elements. On the other hand, lacking names for purple or magenta, he may not build up these color concepts until the time when he has learned the words.

Methods of learning concepts Much of our education, both formal and informal, consists of learning concepts. Partly for this reason, concept attainment has been studied extensively. One of the questions frequently asked about it is, How do people learn concepts? That is, what methods do they use? Several methods can be distinguished.

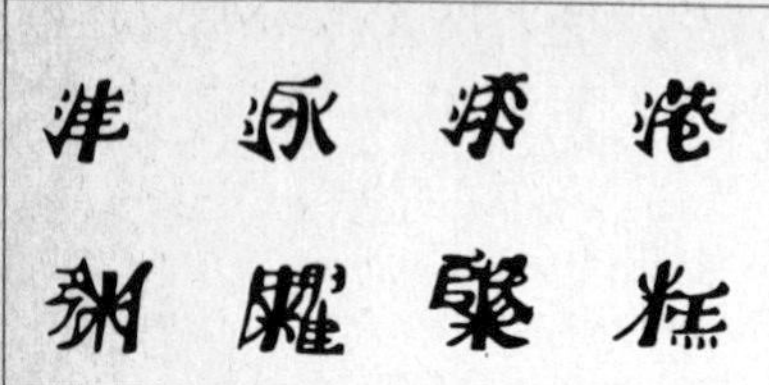

Figure 5.5 *Characters used in a study of concept formation by discriminative learning. (After Hull, 1920.)*

DISCRIMINATIVE LEARNING One of the ways of learning concepts, especially simple and conjunctive ones, is the way Charlie learned "apple" and "fruit." The person has the problem of attaching word labels to objects, and in the course of learning to do this abstracts some common properties of objects. A classic experiment illustrating this route to simple concept attainment used Chinese characters as "nonsense" material (Hull, 1920):

College students were presented with one card at a time from a pack of 12. On each card was a different Chinese character. As a card was shown, the experimenter said a nonsense word, like *oo, yer,* or *li.* The first time through the pack, the subject merely repeated the nonsense word after the experimenter. Next, the cards were shuffled and again exposed serially. This time, and on succeeding runs through the pack, the subject attempted to anticipate the correct word. When wrong, he was corrected. Runs were made through the pack until the subject had learned the correct "name" for each Chinese character.

Next a second pack of 12 cards with Chinese characters was presented. The subject was instructed to use the same 12 names he had learned with the first pack, and to start guessing on the first run through the pack. He continued calling until this pack was learned. The same procedure was again followed with four more packs of 12 cards, all containing different characters.

Unknown to the subject, the same name was always used when a particular part, or "radical," appeared in the character. Although all characters were different, one part of the "oo" character was the same, and a character containing this common property was in each deck. The same was true of each character given a particular name. The two rows of characters in Figure 5.5 illustrate this. Those in the first row were given the same name, but each character appeared in a different deck. Similarly, each character in the second row was assigned the same name, and each appeared in a different deck.

The learning of a concept in this experiment was measured by the number of incorrect responses made on the first trial of the runs through the 12-card packs. The maximum number of errors, of course, is 12. The average numbers of errors made by the subjects were:

Pack number	2	3	4	5	6
Errors on first run through pack	8.7	7.6	6.3	5.5	5.0

Note that the subjects were learning to abstract and label correctly some of the common parts of the characters. The task was so complex, however, that they were, on the average, far from perfect. See if you can pick out the common part or radical in the characters of each row in Figure 5.5.

The learning in this experiment is probably analogous to the process young children go through in learning simple and conjunctive concepts, except that it was purposely made complex enough to be difficult for college students.

CONTEXT A second way to learn concepts, especially simple and conjunctive ones, is through context. If we do not know the meaning of a word, but see or hear it used in different contexts, we usually develop a fairly accurate idea of its meaning. The following example is taken from an experiment on conjunctive concept attainment (Werner and Kaplan, 1950). See if you can tell what a "corplum" is:

A corplum may be used for support.
Corplums may be used to close off an open place.
A corplum may be long or short, thick or thin, strong or weak.
A wet corplum does not burn.
You can make a corplum smooth with sandpaper.
The painter used a corplum to mix his paints.

These sentences were presented to subjects one at a time, after which the subjects were asked what "corplum" meant and why they thought so.

You will undoubtedly discover the concept of corplum from the statements made about it. You will find that it expresses the same concept as another word you already know. However, if you did not know the word but were familiar with the properties of corplums, you would still be able to define a corplum. In fact, you would be able to write several more sentences about the properties of corplums.

DEFINITION A third way of learning new concepts is by definition. In fact, most of the concepts you attain in the later stages of your education are learned in this way. You have learned many concepts in this book by having them defined for you. Of course, you also use a dictionary for this purpose. In any case, you learn the concept by having it described in other words. Most 6-year-old children, for example, have never seen a zebra, but they have a concept of zebra (Osgood et al., 1957). They have seen pictures of it and been told that it is an animal that has stripes, that looks and runs like a horse, is about the same size as a horse, and is usually found wild. This gives them a fairly accurate concept of zebra.

Factors affecting concept attainment It is of practical, as well as academic, value to know what helps or hinders concept attainment, for we would like to improve our methods of teaching concepts to people. We know that a good many factors make a difference. Here are a few of them.

TRANSFER One factor, which is also important in other learning, is transfer (see Chapter 4). When a person already knows a concept similar to the one being learned, he can learn it rapidly. This is positive transfer. But similarity can be tricky; it can also produce negative transfer. If a new concept appears to be similar to a known concept, but is also quite different in some important respect, the person may have trouble understanding it. Here, to capitalize on transfer, the teacher must point out both the similarities and the differences.

DISTINCTIVENESS A second factor in concept attainment is the degree to which common elements are isolated, grouped, or otherwise made conspicuous. For want of a better term, we shall call this *distinctiveness.* Anything that is done to make the common property of the concept stand out aids concept attainment; whatever obscures it or embeds it in irrelevant details retards concept attainment.

In the experiment on Chinese characters cited above, for instance, the students were very slow to learn the "concepts" because the common element was embedded in complex characters, and the characters were presented in jumbled order. If all the characters with the same common property had been grouped together, as they are in Figure 5.5, concept attainment would have been much easier.

OTHER FACTORS Three other factors help to determine the effectiveness of concept attainment (Johnson, 1955). One is *ability to manipulate materials.* If a person is allowed to rearrange, redraw, or reorganize the materials containing common properties, he is more likely to learn or discover the appropriate concepts. Another is the *instruction* or *general purpose* a person has. If he is told to try to discover a common element, that is, to search for the concept, he does better than if he is not given such a general purpose. Finally, a person usually learns faster if he has *all the relevant information available at the same time* instead of being given only a piece at a time.

Meaning of concepts Concept learning is like other kinds of learning: the concept can be learned well or poorly, accurately or inaccurately. The concept one person learns may or may not be the same concept another person learns. In fact, it is apparent from everyday conversations with people that they often have very different concepts of the same thing. This is especially true in abstract realms such as politics or religion.

A distinction is sometimes made between denotative and connotative meanings of concepts. The *denotative meaning* of a concept is its socially accepted definition; the *connotative meaning* is its emotional and evaluative meaning—its "goodness" or "badness," for instance. Differences in the connotative meanings of concepts are an important source of misunderstanding and failure of communication among people. What, for instance, does "liberal" mean to you? The measurement of connotative meanings of concepts is a significant problem in psychology.

Individual differences in learning concepts and their meanings raise the question of how we can measure the meaning of a concept. How can we tell how well a concept has been learned? How can we measure differences among people in what they understand the meaning of concepts to be? These questions have answers, though the answers vary with the purpose of the question and with the types of concepts. In general, four methods of measuring the meanings of concepts can be distinguished. The first two are most useful with the denotative meanings of concepts we attempt to teach in school, where there is some standard for deciding whether or not a concept is correct. The last two are most useful with connotative meanings of concepts that have no such standard; they are of interest in studying personality and social processes.

FREE RESPONSE The simplest and most straightforward way of finding out what a concept means to a person is to ask him to *say* what it means. This is the free-response method. The results depend on the instructions given and upon the concepts tested.

A child's concept of "dog" can be tested by asking him to describe a dog. His description can be scored "accurate," "too general," "abstract," "concrete," "irrelevant," and so forth, with a fair degree of interscorer agreement. In fact, items of this kind are used on intelligence tests and scored with good reliability. When the description avoids irrelevancies and includes only the generally accepted meaning, we call it a *definition*. The description may also be pictorial, as when a child is asked to draw a triangle or a college student is asked to draw a neuron. The descriptions are influenced, of course, by the subject's skill in verbal and pictorial techniques as well as by his mastery of the concept.

DISCRIMINATION The free-response method obviously is subjective, and it is often difficult to score reliably. A more objective method makes use of a set of discriminations. A person is shown a variety of objects, or pictures of people or things, and asked to indicate whether each one is or is not an instance of the concept. Alternatively, he may simply be asked to classify objects according to specified common properties. Such a test can yield an objective score, in terms of right and wrong answers, of the accuracy of a person's concept.

The two methods, free response and discrimination, do not always give the same results. People frequently can provide a dictionary or verbal definition of a concept, but make mistakes in choosing instances of the concept. Conversely, people may be able to identify the common (or uncommon) characteristic in a group of objects and still not be able to give a correct verbal statement of the concept. In the experiment on Chinese characters, for example, some students learned to use the correct names for characters without being able to point out the common characteristic they named.

Disagreement in results of the two methods is not puzzling. If a person has learned concepts by context or by definition in terms of other concepts, he is more likely to do well with the free-response method. On the other hand, a person who has acquired concepts by simple learning through experience with instances of the concept will probably do better on the discrimination method. This is one of the reasons why strictly formal education, limited to books, can turn out students who do not understand "practical" concepts. And it is one reason why schools attempt to supplement verbal instruction with laboratories and other more concrete methods of teaching concepts.

WORD ASSOCIATION Another technique for testing the meaning of concepts is particularly suited to studying an individual's idiosyncratic concepts. With the word-association method, we can find out whether his concepts are substantially different from most people's. The person is given a word and asked to reply with the first association that comes to mind. Normally he will respond with a word that is in the same class of concepts as the stimulus word. If he replies with something not usually related to the stimulus word, it is an indication that his personal concepts are, in some respects, different from those of people in general.

SEMANTIC DIFFERENTIAL A more sophisticated method of measuring the connotative meaning of concepts is called the semantic differential

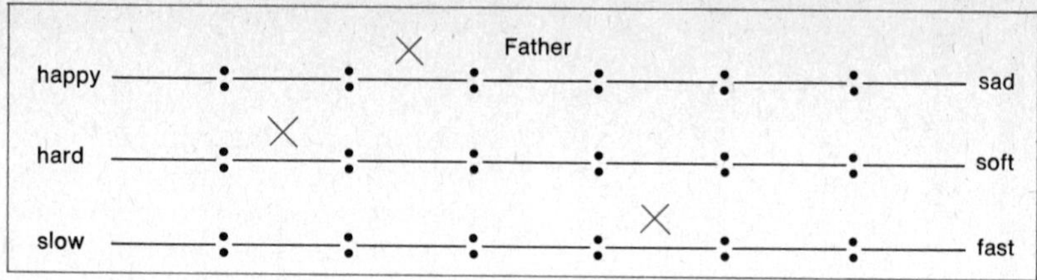

Active

child
engine
Tornado
Rage **Flea**
Anger
War
Scalding
leadership
puppies
birth
happy
progress
Mosquito
sweeping
brother
patriot
brave
Steal
Criminal
Mad
sex
eating
car
America
Thief
Devil
light
cop
mother
Danger
bright
courage
God
Nasty
Trouble
kitchen boat
money justice
sister
eat income
church
Sin
Frightful
heal
see
Pain
family
brilliant
Abortion
song
me
memory
farm
Bible
Crooked
Feverish
dawn
piano
complete
Divorce
woman
pretty
bath
gleaming clean
health faith
Bad
lady
Putrid
sunlight
baby
graceful
Fraud
charming
color
nice
holy
Discomfort
food
Neurotic
beautiful
art
coal
Grief
sky
Rancid
constant
fragrant
sweet
Stench
bodice
rose
barn
Starving
Heartless
root
Weak
Strong
jelly
refined
lake
house
dough
stars
blue
Leper
flower
comfort
Sunday
trees
rose
garment
peace
Late
flowers
stem
Slime
Sickness
bed
Inferior
butter
Deformed
silk
Gloomy
smooth
moon
Indifferent
cushion
sleep
Stagnant
chair
mild
Dreary
relaxed
calm
table
Lagging
statue
Lazy

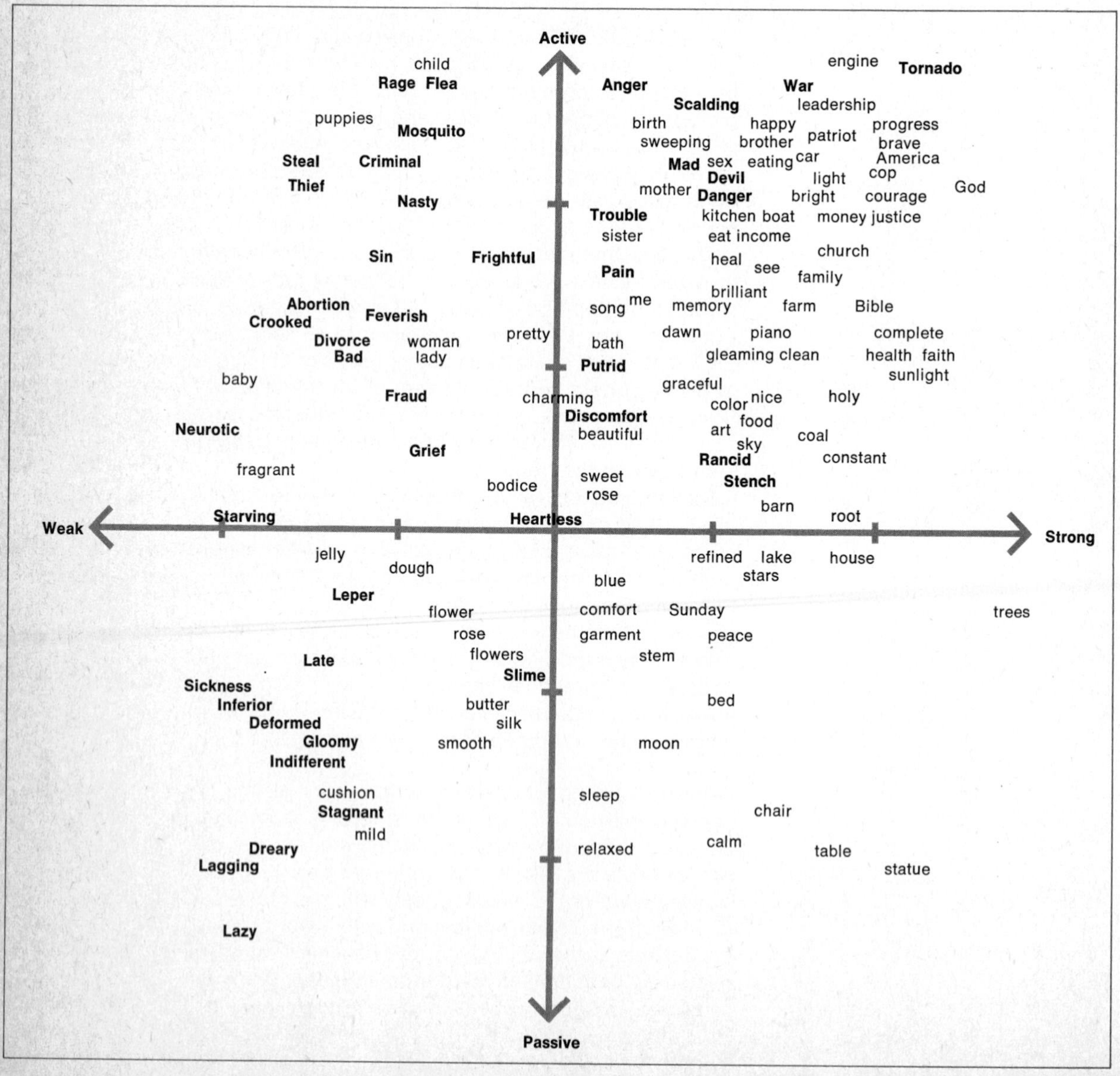

Passive

THE SEMANTIC DIFFERENTIAL MEASURES THE CONNOTATIVE MEANING OF A CONCEPT

Figure 5.6 *Some scales from a semantic differential. A person rates a concept, in this case "father," on 20 to 50 bipolar scales, three of which are illustrated. (After Osgood et al., 1957.)*

CONCEPTS MAY BE LOCATED IN "MEANING SPACE"

Figure 5.7 *Concepts placed with respect to three factors derived from the semantic differential. The three factors are activity (active-passive), potency (weak-strong), and evaluation (good-bad). The position of the concept with respect to the axes locates it on the activity and potency dimensions. The evaluative factor is represented by the way the words are printed: "Good" concepts are in light type; "bad" concepts in dark type. For instance,* **Anger** *is rated as strongly active, slightly strong, and "bad." (From Carroll, 1964. Based on data from Jenkins et al., 1958.)*

(Osgood et al., 1957). So far, it has been applied primarily as a research tool, but it has many possible uses. Its basic purpose is to analyze concepts in terms of a limited number of dimensions of meaning and to compare these dimensions in various groups of people, including different national and language groups. It can also be used in attitude measurement, in mass communication, and in personality measurement.

To obtain a semantic differential, two things are required: a concept, and two or more scales. The concept can be a word such as "father," "sin," "symphony," "Russian," or "America." Each scale consists of two polar words, such as "happy-sad," "hard-soft," "slow-fast." When presented to a subject, a scale has seven spaces between the words at each end (see Figure 5.6). The subject is asked to place every concept at some position on each scale. The concept being judged might be "father," for example. If the seven positions from left to right on the scale are given numbers 1 to 7, the subject might judge "father" as a 3 on the happy-sad scale, 2 on the hard-soft scale, 5 on the slow-fast scale, and so forth. The subject does the same thing for "father" on the remainder of the scales, which may number anywhere from 20 to 50. Then he repeats the procedure with the other concepts.

The result of scaling concepts in this way is a semantic differential for each concept. The differential gives the meaning of the concept by showing its positions on the scales. If we desire, we can draw a profile for each concept that shows its position on each scale. Then we can compare profiles for different concepts. To the extent that one profile corresponds to another, the connotative meaning of those two concepts is similar. To the extent that they differ, their connotative meanings are different.

The semantic differential has also been used in other ways. It has served as a method of analyzing the whole system of concepts used by individuals in a culture. But in obtaining the average result from large groups of people, the meaning of "meaning" becomes distorted. Consider the differences in connotative meaning of the word "army"; a pacifist would scale it one way, a graduate of West Point another (Carroll, 1964). Thus the "meaning" of a concept in a complex culture cannot be made completely clear.

In any case, factor analysis has been utilized to analyze the scales for many concepts. Such analysis reveals that the scales can be grouped into three classes, or factors, which have been designated *evaluation, potency,* and *activity.* Scales which measure goodness and badness, fairness and unfairness, or other similar characteristics make up the evaluation factor. Scales which measure strength and weakness, heaviness or lightness, or characteristics of this sort make up the potency factor. And scales which measure speed, activity and passivity, or the like, make up the activity factor.

Thus the many scales can be condensed into three "superscales," evaluation, potency, and activity, which appear to be the major dimensions of connotative meaning for a great number of our concepts. An interesting way to depict the connotative meaning of many different words is shown in Figure 5.7.

RESEARCH USE OF THE SEMANTIC DIFFERENTIAL We have seen that denotative concepts are learned. The semantic differential has been used to show that connotative meanings can also be learned (Staats and Staats, 1957):

One experiment combined elements of classical conditioning (see Chapter 3) and paired-associate learning (see Chapter 4). Six nonsense syllables were used, and each was paired with several words. Two of the nonsense syllables, *yof* and *xeh*, were crucial: *yof* was always paired with words having a pleasant connotation (*healthy, gift,* and so on); *xeh* was always paired with words having an unpleasant connotation (*sad, fear,* and so on). Most of the subjects did not detect this arrangement because of the other nonsense syllables and words which disguised the crucial relationships. Data from those who did detect it were not used.

In terms of classical conditioning, the nonsense syllable can be considered a conditioned stimulus; the pleasant or unpleasant word can be considered the unconditioned stimulus which elicits an unconditioned mediating response—a pleasant or unpleasant meaning. The pleasant and unpleasant meanings are common to all the words which follow *yof* or *xeh.* Is the appropriate connotative meaning attached to the nonsense syllables? The answer seems to be "yes." Changes in the appropriate direction do occur in the semantic differential—the nonsense syllable *yof* was evaluated more positively than *xeh.*

Uses of concepts Concepts are ways of classifying the diversity of elements in the world around us. As such, they are convenient tools in problem solving and logical reasoning. Whether or not a problem will be solved is, in part, a matter of the appropriateness of the concepts brought to bear on it:

Among the factors that may determine whether an individual will solve a problem are the following:

1. The individual's repertory of relevant concepts.
2. The concepts evoked in the individual by the structure of the problem.
3. The individual's skill in manipulating the concepts evoked, his strategy of solution, his flexibility in changing his mode of attack, and his ability to perceive the relevance of a concept. (Carroll, 1964, page 85.)

Solution of Problems

Thinking consists of mediating processes, many of which are words, images, and concepts. But this statement does not say what starts thinking, what guides it, or what brings it to a stop. A river is more than water. It springs up somewhere, it changes course, it flows sometimes swiftly and sometimes slowly, and eventually it ends in the ocean. Thinking too has beginnings, courses, and ends. What explains them?

Motivation For one thing, thinking is usually motivated. As one of the leading investigators in this area has said, thinking involves "the desire, the craving to face the true issue . . . , to go from an unclear, inadequate relation to a clear, transparent, direct confrontation" (Wertheimer, 1959).

Table 5.1 *Practice and test problems used by Luchins. The five practice problems require a roundabout method of solution; the test problem can be solved easily. But most subjects who acquired a set by solving the practice problems used the long method of solving the test problem; they were blind to the easy method.*

Source: Luchins, 1954.

Problem number	Given the following empty jars as measures			Obtain this amount of water
	A	B	C	
1. Practice	21	127	3	100
2. Practice	14	163	25	99
3. Practice	18	43	10	5
4. Practice	9	42	6	21
5. Practice	20	59	4	31
6. Test	23	49	3	20

Thus he stresses the *directedness* of thought processes. Instead of just "happening" by association, each stage in thinking is controlled by motives.

On the basis of all we now know, we ought to differentiate at least two kinds of motives in thinking: (1) A motive that evokes the problem-solving behavior; for instance, such motives may be love, greed, curiosity, or ambition. (2) A motive induced by the problem itself to complete or anticipate its solution. The former gets thinking started; the latter carries it through to solution.

In order to account for the thought processes of great thinkers, such as scientists, artists, writers, and inventors, we might have to postulate a third kind of motivation: a lifelong interest in creative production or in solving challenging problems.

Habit and set Thinking is also guided, and often impeded, by habit and set. Practice in solving problems one way tends to "set" us to solve a new problem in the same way, provided that the new problem situation contains stimuli similar to those in the practiced problems. This is the secret of many trick jokes and puzzles. In one trick, for example, you spell words and ask a person how he pronounces them. You use names beginning with Mac, like MacDonald, MacTavish. Then you slip in "machinery" and see if he pronounces it "MacHinery." With the set for names, he may fall into your trap.

Set may be produced by immediately preceding experiences, by long-established practices, or by instructions which revive old habits (see "Transfer of Training," Chapter 4). It biases the thinker at the start of his problem, directing him away from certain families of responses and toward others. It acts as an implied assumption. Like transfer of training, it can be either positive or negative in its effects. If it is helpful, we say, "How clever I am!"; if a hindrance, we say, "How blind I was!".

One investigator did a systematic experiment on habitual set, using the problems in Table 5.1. The first five problems require a roundabout solution; the sixth is very simple (Luchins, 1954):

In the sixth problem, the subject is required to say how he would measure 20 quarts of water when he has only three jars holding 23, 49, and 3 quarts, respectively. Subjects solve it the easy way by filling the 3-quart jar from the 23-quart jar, provided they have no interfering set. However, if they have just worked out the previous problems by a longer method—that is, by filling the middle jar, from

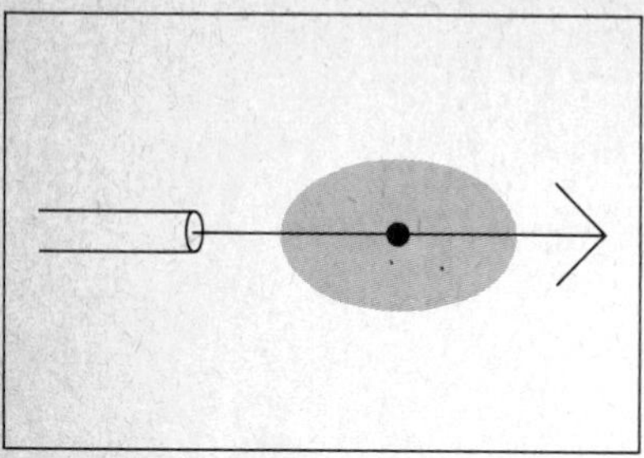

Figure 5.8 A schematic diagram of the "tumor" problem. How can the tissue-destroying rays be used to kill the tumor without killing the healthy tissue around it? (Duncker, 1945.)

it filling the jar to the right twice and the jar to the left once, leaving the required amount in the center jar—they commonly use the long method and do not notice the short one. Amazingly, 75 percent of a college group were blind to the easy method after having practiced the long method for only five trials.

The frequency of habitual, blind solutions is reduced by (1) warning the subject "Don't be blind! Look sharp, now!" just before the critical trial, (2) reducing the number of practice trials, and (3) separating the practice and critical trials by several days or weeks. However, comparative data show that habit strength and set, as indicated by number of practice trials, can be much stronger factors than any warning against them.

A special variety of the effect of set is *functional fixedness.* We may be so accustomed to using particular objects in particular ways that we cannot see new ways of using them when new ways are needed. The following experiment shows this effect (Adamson, 1952):

One of the problems was to find a way of mounting three candles on a *vertical* screen. The subjects were provided with the candles, three small pasteboard boxes, five thumbtacks, and five matches. The problem is not a difficult one; the solution is simply to stick the candles on the boxes with melted wax and then to use the thumbtacks to attach the boxes to the screen.

Boxes, of course, are usually containers and not platforms. Fixation on this function was established for an experimental group of subjects by placing the tacks, candles, and matches in the three boxes before giving them to the subjects. No attempt was made to establish functional fixedness in the subjects of the control group; the three empty boxes, together with the other materials, were simply placed on the table.

Members of the experimental group had difficulty with this problem: only 12 out of 29 (41 percent) solved it in the allotted time of 20 minutes. On the other hand, 24 out of 28 (86 percent) of the people in the control group solved the problem. Similar results were obtained with other problems.

These results provide strong evidence for functional fixedness as a particular kind of set which hinders problem solving. One advantage of temporarily quitting a problem which cannot be solved is that you may come back to it with a fresh approach—that is, functional fixedness may be broken.

Processes in problem solving To sum up, thinking begins with some kind of felt need which cannot be immediately met, a problem, and a motive to solve the problem. It is guided—either helped or hindered—by some set or determining tendency, such as previously learned habits. Now when we ask about the processes through which the problem gets solved, we can distinguish among mechanical processes, solution through understanding, and insightful solutions.

MECHANICAL SOLUTIONS In attempting to solve a puzzle, you sometimes —but not very often—stumble on the right answer. By trying first one way, then another, you finally hit on the one that works. In the process, you have probably made many "stupid" errors which show that you do

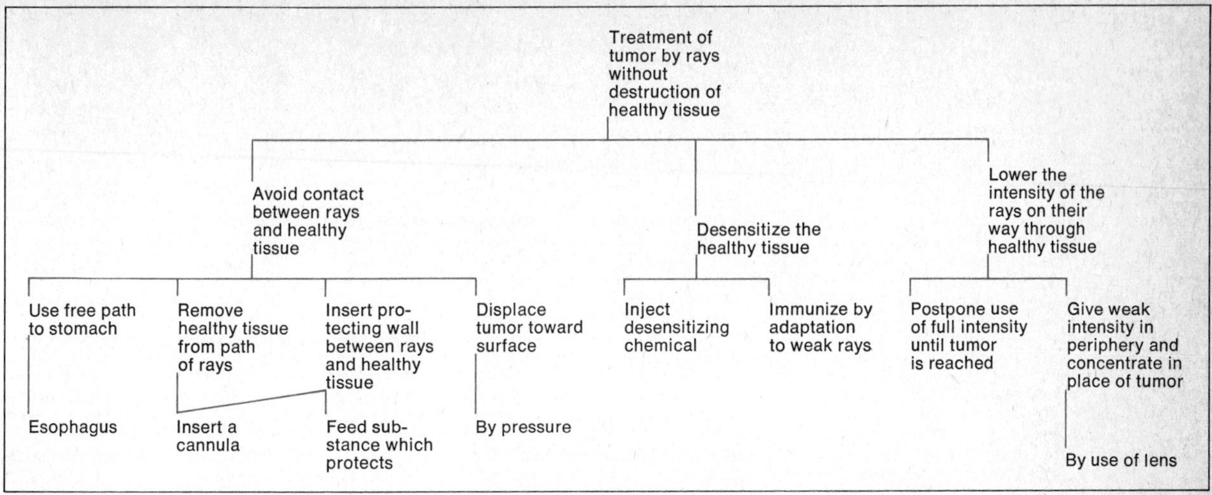

THE "TREE" OF SOLUTIONS TO A PROBLEM

Figure 5.9 *General, functional, and specific solutions given by one subject to the "tumor" problem. General solutions are on the second line from the top, functional solutions on the third line, and specific solutions on the bottom line. The solution shown at right happens to be the most practical in this particular case. (Duncker, 1945.)*

not understand the problem. This trial-and-error method, as it might be called, is, of course, not very productive or efficient.

A second kind of mechanical solution may come by rote. If you are given a column of figures to add, you immediately start thinking according to rules which you have learned, and in due time you come up with the answer. Or if you are asked to spell a word or give the directions for going from one place to another, you do a minimum of thinking and a lot of just plain sequential remembering in order to give the answer. You merely reproduce what you have already learned. To understand this way of solving problems, almost all we need to know is how the solutions were learned in the first place.

SOLVING PROBLEMS BY UNDERSTANDING Problems would hardly be problems if we could solve them so automatically. Many problems are solved by working from general principles back to specific means by which the end can be achieved. We may start with a general understanding of what constitutes a solution of the problem and gradually work out a functional solution—the means by which a general solution can be realized (Duncker, 1945; Wertheimer, 1959). The following example illustrates the search for functional solutions (Duncker, 1945):

College students were presented with this problem: "Given a human being with an inoperable stomach tumor, and rays which destroy organic tissue at sufficiently high intensity, by what procedure can one free him of the tumor by these rays and at the same time avoid destroying the healthy tissue that surrounds it?" The problem is diagramed in Figure 5.8; general and functional solutions given aloud by one subject are shown in Figure 5.9. The general solutions are on the second line from the top; functional solutions are on the third line. The subject, guided by understanding of the goal, worked from general to functional solutions.

At first, subjects often seek impractical functional solutions. For instance, "use a free path to the stomach" is a functional solution because it shows that the subject understands that the problem necessitates getting the rays to the stomach without hitting healthy tissue on the way. It is an impractical solution, however. Gradually, the subject approximates functional solutions which are more practical, and finally he hits one that works. In the case of this problem, a good practical solution might be to cross weak rays at the site of the tumor. Each of the individual rays would be too weak to damage tissue, but the sum of several rays on the tumor would kill it.

This example shows that when subjects think out loud, it is often possible to trace the steps involved in reaching practical specific functional solutions.

SOLVING PROBLEMS BY LOGICAL REASONING In the understanding process that we have just considered, the steps in the solution process do not necessarily follow formal logic; rather, they proceed by trial and error from an understanding of what would constitute a functional solution. Sometimes, however, the solution to problems comes by following a sequence of logical steps in the formal thinking process called *reasoning.* (Logical reasoning, both as it is involved in problem solving and as it is influenced by psychological processes, is given more extensive treatment later.)

INSIGHTFUL SOLUTIONS Sometimes the solution to a problem, instead of involving understanding processes or formal logic, just seems to come suddenly, and the subject or experimenter cannot account for it. In such a case, insight has occurred out of mechanical processes or the search for functional solutions, but it represents a completely new experience to the thinker. "Aha! I have it" is a characteristic outburst when suddenly he grasps the solution to a baffling problem. He has produced a novel solution—novel to him, at least—through thinking. If the solution is truly novel, he has invented or created something that he can pass on to other members of society for them to use in their "rote-thinking" processes (see the following section, Creative Thinking). We have already studied some examples of insight and how they may be explained by previous learning (see Learning Sets, Chapter 3). Let us now look more closely at insight in human thinking. The following story is perhaps the classic example of insight:

King Hiero had recently succeeded to the throne of Syracuse and decided to place a golden crown in a temple as a thank offering to the gods. So he made a contract at a fixed price, and weighed out the gold for the contractor at the royal scales. At the appointed time the contractor delivered his handiwork beautifully made, and the king was delighted. At the scales it was seen that the contractor had kept the original weight of the gold. Later a charge was made that gold had been removed and an equivalent weight of silver substituted.

Hiero was furious at being fooled, and, not being able to find any way of detecting the theft, asked Archimedes to put his thought to the matter.

While Archimedes was bearing the problem in his mind, he happened to get into a bath and noticed that when he got into the tub exactly the same amount of water flowed over the side as the volume of his body that was under water. Perceiving that this gave him a clue to the problem, he promptly leapt from the tub in a rush of joy and ran home naked, shouting loudly to all the world that he had found the solution. As he ran, he called again and again in Greek, "Eureka, Eureka . . . I have found it, I have found it." (Humphrey, 1948, page 115. As translated from Vitruvius.)

Incidentally, the contractor cheated. The silver in the crown, having a larger volume than an equal weight of gold, made the crown displace more water than it would have if it had been solid gold.

As we shall see more clearly in the next section, insight seems to be the result of much combination and recombination of mediating processes going on beneath the level of consciousness (Campbell, 1960). From reports of creative workers—the mathematician Poincaré (1913), for example—it seems that concentrated conscious thinking about a problem may sometimes get one into a symbolic blind alley. When this has happened, insight often comes later, while the person is not consciously thinking about the problem and is actively engaged in doing something else. However, insights do not suddenly appear out of nowhere—they blossom in fields which have been thoroughly prepared by study of the various aspects of the problem. Insights may also be incorrect—they require testing to see if they really do represent the solution.

Creative thinking The creative thinker, whether artist, scientist, or inventor, is trying to achieve something new. He may be trying to solve a particular mathematical problem, or trying to express an idea in novel ways, or trying to achieve new and pleasing combinations of forms, colors, or word sounds.

Creative thinking in the arts has been the subject of much comment. The ideas often seem to "bubble up" in a seemingly spontaneous manner. This sort of thinking is similar to insight, and it seems likely that the ideas rise to consciousness after much unconscious rearrangement of symbols. Here is the poet A. E. Housman's account of his own creative thinking:

Having drunk a pint of beer at luncheon—beer is a sedative to the brain, and my afternoons are the least intellectual portion of my life—I would go out for a walk of two or three hours. As I went along, thinking of nothing in particular, only looking at things around me and following the progress of the seasons, there would flow into my mind, with sudden and unaccountable emotion, sometimes a line or two of verse, sometimes whole stanzas at once, accompanied, not preceded, by a vague notion of the poem which they were destined to form part of. . . .

When I got home I wrote them down, leaving gaps, and hoping that further inspiration might be forthcoming another day. Sometimes it was, if I took walks in a receptive and expectant frame of mind; but sometimes the poem had to be taken in hand and completed by the brain, which was apt to be a matter of trouble and anxiety, involving trial and disappointment, and sometimes ending in failure. (Housman, 1933, pages 48–49.)

In addition to such autobiographical and impressionistic accounts of creative thinking, a great deal of controlled research is being done on creativity. For instance, attempts have been made to obtain objective measures of it (Torrance, 1962). Using such tests, it has been found that creativity is not necessarily highly related to conventional measures of intelligence—that is, to intelligence test scores (Getzels and Jackson, 1962). It seems to be a dimension of intellect not tapped by conventional intelligence testing. Other studies have been made of the stages of creative thinking and the personality traits of creative people. Basically, however, we know little about the cause of creativity.

STAGES IN CREATIVE THINKING The steps involved in the thinking of outstanding creative thinkers have been studied through interviews, questionnaires, and introspection (Wallas, 1926). Though each of these persons has his own way of thinking, and this depends somewhat on the kind of problems to be solved, their thinking seems to have a recurring pattern. It tends to proceed in five stages: (1) preparation, (2) incubation, (3) illumination, (4) evaluation, and (5) revision.

In stage 1, *preparation,* the thinker formulates his problem and collects the facts and materials he considers necessary for its solution. Very frequently he finds that he cannot solve the problem, even after hours or days of concentrated effort. Often he deliberately or involuntarily turns away from the problem; he is then in stage 2, *incubation.* During this period, some of the ideas that were interfering with the solution of the problem tend to fade. On the other hand, things he experiences or learns in the meantime may provide the clue to the solution. During incubation, the unconscious processes may be at work. In stage 3, *illumination,* the thinker often has an "Aha!" insight experience. An idea for the solution may suddenly dawn on him. Next, in stage 4, *evaluation,* he determines whether the apparent solution is in fact the correct one. Frequently it turns out to be wrong, and the thinker is back where he started. In other cases it is the right idea, but it needs some modification or requires the solution of other relatively minor problems. Thus stage 5, *revision,* is reached.

This description of the mental processes of the creative thinker is far from satisfactory. One day, through research, we should be able to understand the pattern better. This description does, however, provide a general picture of the steps that are frequently involved in the solution of problems by talented and creative people.

PERSONALITY TRAITS OF CREATIVE THINKERS Is there anything special about creative persons, in addition to their creativity? Do they share common personality characteristics? Some evidence, obtained from objective and projective personality tests (see Chapter 10), indicates that they do:

---

1. Original persons prefer complexity and some degree of apparent imbalance in phenomena.
2. Original persons are more complex psychodynamically and have greater personal scope.
3. Original persons are more independent in their judgments.
4. Original persons are more self-assertive and dominant.
5. Original persons reject suppression as a mechanism for the control of impulse. This would imply that they forbid themselves fewer thoughts, that they

dislike to police themselves or others, that they are disposed to entertain impulses and ideas that are commonly taboo. (Slightly modified from Barron, 1963, pages 208–209.)

A knowledge of these important differentiating traits may enable us someday to find the antecedent conditions in early life which give rise to them and to the predisposition toward creative thinking. We can hope that research will uncover some of the characteristics of family life which produce creative thinkers.

Logical reasoning We have just seen that solutions to problems can be obtained in many ways, and logical reasoning is one of these ways. Now we wish to discuss logical reasoning more fully. Perhaps you are accustomed to use the words *reasoning* and *thinking* as though they mean the same thing; we commonly do it in everyday talk. But there are many instances of thinking that do not involve reasoning. Dreams, for example, can be considered a type of thought, and the illogical patterns of dreams are well known (see Chapter 13).

What, then, is reasoning? A little boy was on the right track when he answered, "Putting two and two together." Reasoning certainly is not just any kind of thinking. It involves solving a problem by *following rules* which govern the putting of two or more elements of past experience together to make something new.

VERBAL REASONING Most human reasoning makes use of symbols—especially verbal symbols. Since we use words so extensively to communicate our thoughts to others, we get in the habit of depending on words for thinking. Yet word meanings often are vague or ambiguous, and we can be led astray by them. Also, when we reason with verbal symbols alone, we may find it impossible to test whether our conclusion is correct, for we often lack the opportunity to compare the verbal conclusion with actuality.

To help us, society develops standards or norms for checking the results of our reasoning. People have come to believe that certain statements are "reasonable" while others are not. When a person makes an "unreasonable" statement, people tell him so immediately and discourage him from further foolish talk. The trouble with culturally defined standards of reasonableness is that what is reasonable to one group may be completely unreasonable to another. "It stands to reason that . . . ," a white college debater argues; but he completely forgets that the conclusion may not be obvious to, say, a Black or a Chinese opponent.

To make the standards for reasoning as precise as possible, philosophers and mathematicians, over the centuries, have given us rules for reasoning. The systematic organization of these rules is called logic, and it prescribes what kinds of implications statements can have and what kinds of conclusions can be drawn from them. Any reasoning that does not conform to these rules is dubbed "illogical" or "fallacious." Since so much in human affairs hangs on the question of how logical we are in our thinking, we should study some of the psychological factors involved in the logical and illogical thinking of human beings.

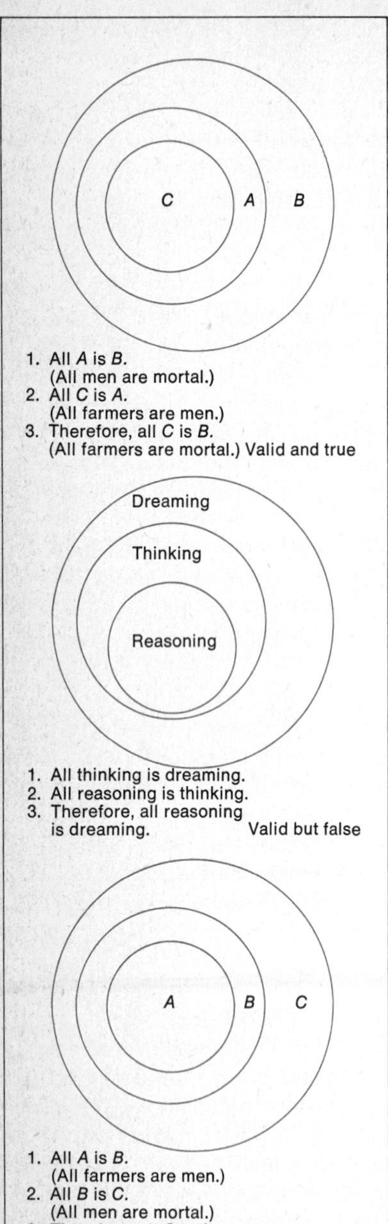

SIMPLE DIAGRAMS SOMETIMES AID LOGICAL THINKING

Figure 5.10 *Circles (sometimes called Euler's circles or Venn diagrams) for the representation of simple logic problems.*

LOGICAL THINKING Suppose one conducts a test of reasoning in children and asks them this question: "If all 6-year-olds are in school, and if Johnny is 6, then where is Johnny?" The psychologist should not be surprised if the answer is, "I hate school," "He's home sick with a cold," though the logician would be! To the psychologist, the child's answer is "reasonable" because it is a simple association with a stimulus, without regard to logical rules. This is what people learn long before they learn to reason, let alone reason by the formal rules of logic.

As children grow older they learn to respond according to certain instructions and rules, and to keep their associative responses within certain bounds. Suppose I test a high school student: I instruct him that whenever I say a word, I want him to respond with a word that is a class name for objects of the same kind. Now I give him the word *table.* He will give me back *furniture* or some comparable word. But he will not say *chair,* because that would violate the rule that his response must name a class that includes *table.* He has learned to follow a rule.

Now for a more complex case. In college, the student may learn syllogisms, one form of which is:

1. All *A* is *B.*
   (All men are mortal.)
2. All *C* is *A.*
   (All farmers are men.)
3. Therefore, all *C* is *B.*
   (All farmers are mortal.)

This syllogism (see Figure 5.10, top) follows one of the rules of logic and the student can learn it, perhaps by rote. But he will immediately encounter difficulty in applying the rule to his thinking about situations in daily life, because emotional factors intrude into the reasoning process, because it is difficult to know whether the premises are true or false, and because of the relative complexity of even the most simple syllogisms. For instance, the form of the syllogism above *looks* suspiciously like the following:

1. All *A* is *B.*
   (All farmers are men.)
2. All *B* is *C.*
   (All men are mortal.)
3. Therefore, all *C* is *A.*
   (All mortals are farmers.)

The conclusion is unsound because it does not follow from 1 and 2 (see Figure 5.10, bottom). These are very difficult verbal discriminations even in symbol form. They become harder when put in word form. Many of the statements made in politics, business, and everyday life seem to belong in valid syllogisms when the syllogisms are really fallacious. A political candidate, for example, may say:

Inflation leads to high taxes.
High taxes lead to tax scandals.
So let's cut taxes!

and we may respond with, "I want lower taxes. Say, he makes good sense!"

ILLOGICAL THINKING One of the reasons why it is hard to think logically, then, is that it is difficult to tell verbal reasoning which follows the rules of logic from that which does not. Besides, there are plenty of other reasons why we have trouble always being logical: Our ordinary conversation is not made from a logical mold—and how dull it would be if if were!—but rather from the interplay of personal and motivational factors. We have learned to use language to sell a magazine subscription, to persuade a reluctant parent, to hail a cab, or to stimulate a mood. Seldom do we use words in order to "think straight." Furthermore, we may have received excessive training in logical confusion. For example, a grown-up says to a child, "Give me one good reason why you disobeyed me!" The frightened child cannot do so; he lies or rationalizes until the adult is satisfied with his answer.

Then too, life itself has a way of confronting us with illogical coincidences, such as the thunderstorm on the only day we play hooky from school. Here an *animistic* fallacy—that our truancy *caused* the thunderstorm—is fostered by nature and often exploited by a moralistic parent. Society's encouragement of such fallacious reasoning is religiously systematic in some cultures and is widespread in our own, especially where cause-and-effect relationships are concerned. Not only can it lead to a wrong theory of thunderstorms; it can also lead to wrong habits of reasoning which interfere with the practice of logic.

DISTORTIONS IN REASONING Ordinarily, then, we have a strong tendency to respond to "logic" stimuli with free associative responses, even when we may be trying our best to be logical. And such responses tend to distort our reasoning. Some circumstances are more likely than others to evoke free associations and thus distortions in reasoning. Since logical thinking is important to all of us, let us look at some common distortions.

One factor is the *complexity* of the stimulus situation. If a logical fallacy is presented to people in a complicated way or along with a mass of complex facts and statements, they are less likely to detect it.

A related source of distortion in reasoning is the language in which premises are expressed. An important factor in such distortion is what has been called the *atmosphere effect* (Sells, 1936). This refers to the impression that a statement may make on a person, predisposing him to give a yes or no answer quite apart from the logical implications of the statement. If, for example, the premises of the syllogism are presented in the affirmative, "All *p*'s are *q*'s, and all *q*'s are *t*'s," people tend to reject any negative conclusions containing "no" or "are not." When the premises are split, however, that is, when one is stated affirmatively and the other negatively, they tend to accept negative conclusions. Such atmosphere effects are apparently common; college students, at least, are amazingly subject to them.

Another important factor is what we might call the *opinion effect* on reasoning. As might be expected, numerous experiments have shown that emotion-producing material and words which evoke strong *pre-*

judices, beliefs, or *opinions* may effectively prevent discriminative, logical deductions. In other words, prejudices, beliefs, and opinions about the statements in the formal syllogism can interfere with the correct use of the formal logical rules of reasoning.

The opposite often occurs too: The logic may be sound, but the conclusion may be incorrect because it is based upon a false, or counterfactual, set of premises. Here is an example:

1. All thinking is dreaming.
2. All reasoning is thinking.
3. Therefore, all reasoning is dreaming.

The conclusion is false, since the basic premise is false, but the deduction from the premises is logically valid (see Figure 5.10, middle).

We conclude, then, that while logic is a powerful tool in the solution of problems, it does not guarantee correct solutions. On the one hand, prejudice, belief, and opinion may conquer logic when both contend in the same man. The causes are psychological; they lie in the learning history of the individual. In other words, we are all primarily "psychological," not logical, even when we "reason." On the other hand, accurate logical reasoning cannot guarantee correct problem solutions based on false premises.

Development of Language and Thought

Complex processes such as thinking and language are sometimes better understood by studying their development. *Developmental psychologists* study the evolution of these processes from their earlier, simpler beginnings. Many developmental psychologists are child psychologists, because it is in childhood that development occurs most rapidly. The earlier and simpler processes are relatively easy to understand, and by tracing them and their changes we can often see how the final complex process came to be.

In this chapter we have stressed the idea that language is the main tool of thought—that language forms thought, so to speak. Language development and thought development, according to this view, are directly related. Other psychologists maintain that thought can exist independently of language and that thought, action, and language are all processes a person uses to adapt to his environment. In other words, language is an outgrowth, not a cause, of some more general basic thought capacity—or as it is sometimes called, *cognitive* capacity. In order to reflect these two points of view, we shall discuss language development and thought development separately.

Language development The course of the development of language is one of differentiation (see Table 5.2). The infant begins his vocal life with the birth cry, and for the first month of life his vocalizations are restricted to generalized undifferentiated crying and perhaps some grunting noises. Late in the first month, or during the second month, children appear to use different cries for various states of discomfort, hunger, and pain. About the third month, spontaneous babbling sounds

Table 5.2 *The development of language in the infant, based on the results of eight major studies of infant development. The numbers represent the range of average ages obtained in the different studies.*

Source: Modified from McCarthy, 1946.

Language behavior	Average age, months after birth
Cries, grunts, and makes other respirant sounds	0
Makes different sounds for discomfort, hunger, and pain	1
Makes vowel sounds like *ah, uh, ay*	1–2
Looks toward sound of human voice	2–4
Babbles and coos	3–4
Talks to himself, using sounds like *ma, mu, do, na*	4–6
Makes sounds of pleasure and displeasure	5–6
"Sounds off" when he hears a familiar voice	6–7
Puts sounds together and repeats them over and over like *mamama-mama, boŏboo, dadada*	6–9
Imitates sounds made by others	9–10
Understands gestures (can wave bye-bye and often can say it)	9–12
Understands and responds to simple commands ("Hold the spoon," "Look at the doll baby")	11–15
Imitates syllables and simple words (the first word?)	11–15
Says two different words	12
Says three to five different words	13–18
Understands and responds to the "don'ts" ("Don't touch that," "Don't spit it out")	16–20
Names one object or picture in book (cup, ball, doggy, baby, etc.)	17–24
Combines words into phrases ("Go out," "Give me milk," "Where ball?")	18–24
Identifies three to five familiar objects or pictures	24
Uses phrases and simple sentences	23–24

emerge. At first they consist mainly of gurgling, but soon coos and perhaps gutteral noises and vowel-like sounds are heard. From the initial babbling sounds, more and more varied sounds are differentiated, and these tend to be repeated over and over again. Babbling is apparently a pleasurable process for the infant.

The babbling period is usually regarded as a time when the infant practices the use of his maturing vocal muscles. The use of the vocal apparatus also plays a role in directing its development. The child feels the muscle movements at the same time that he hears the sound; such feedback leads to better control of the muscles involved in speech. In this way the child develops the smoothness and coordination necessary for even the simplest speech.

Two phenomena which appear between 6 and 10 months are very important in the development of speech. The first is repetitive syllabification, or the repetition of the same sound over and over (*ma-ma-ma-ma-ma,* for instance). The second is the beginning of imitation. In both processes the child learns to modify his vocal responses in response to external stimuli. In repetitive responding he changes the sound very slightly on each repetition, thus getting a feel for the range of sounds he can control. In imitation he learns to pattern his own vocal responses after the adult speech around him. Imitation follows the sounds and facial movements of the adult model. Imitation in this early stage must be an important process in aiding the child to acquire the intonation and pronunciation patterns of his native language.

In the period from about 1 year to 18 months, the child succeeds in differentiating his "first word" from vocal behavior which at birth was undifferentiated crying and occasional grunts. This is a remarkable feat, of which parents are justifiably proud. But it is only a beginning; the first word is also undifferentiated. That is, a child may use the word *mama* in several contexts to mean "Mama, come here," "That's mama," "Where's mama?" and so on. He has yet to substitute more differentiated two- and three-word utterances for single-word undifferentiated ones. It is when he begins to combine words into utterances of two or more words that he is commonly considered to be using "language." At this point, study of the development of *grammar* can begin; now we can examine the rules used to combine words into meaningful sentences.

STAGES IN THE DEVELOPMENT OF GRAMMAR Grammars are rules for putting words together into sentences that have meaning for others. One of the most impressive things about language is that we can construct and understand new sentences—meaningful strings of words—never before encountered. It is as if we play a game in constructing and decoding sentences in which there are certain grammatical rules. If the rules are followed, the meaning of the sentence will be clear; if not, the sentence will be ambiguous and will not have the intended meaning. The rules seem to be intuitive, and we are usually not aware of their existence; but we have learned them early in life and act as if they are there. One of the great contributions of linguistics is the analysis of languages in order to find the rules for construction and decoding of sentences (Chomsky, 1965).

The period of language development after the first words are attained—the time between 1 and 5 years of age—is the initial period of grammatical acquisition. This period has been divided into three stages (Brown et al., 1970). The study of grammatical development and the division of the developmental process into stages is a huge task, involving the collection of a large sample of children's speech, which is then sifted carefully to uncover the rules. For instance, a child is not credited with having a rule for plural endings unless he uses the rule with more than one word on one occasion. Such detailed analysis has so far been carried out for only three children, named Adam, Eve, and Sarah. Adam and Eve are children of graduate students, and Sarah is the daughter of working-class parents. The three stages we shall describe from analysis of the language of these children should not be taken as norms of grammatical development. Instead, they provide a rough picture of the development of language within the frame of reference of psycholinguistics.

Stage 1 This stage begins at about 18 months, when children first string words together consistently. One of the main grammatical rules of stage 1—the pivot word–open word rule—was described earlier in this chapter. Another characteristic is that the child's language tends to be "telegraphic": the sentences he produces resemble the telegrams adults write when they wish to save words. His sentences include the

WUG /-IZ/, WUG /-S/, OR WUG /-Z/

Figure 5.11 *An imaginary animal used in a study of the formation of plural words by children. Most—91 percent—pluralized this word correctly. (From Berko, 1958.)*

important, information-filled words and leave out the connecting words, those that can easily be guessed from context. The child might say, "See truck." Here he has left out the pronoun *I* and the article *the*, but the meaning is fairly clear. The words that are omitted are the "little" words, or the *functors*, which serve a grammatical function rather than carry specific meaning.

But it would not be correct to think that such telegraphic sentences are merely shortened, incomplete versions of adult sentences. The following are some utterances of the children Adam and Eve that are not likely to be imitations of adult speech: "Two foot"; "A bags"; "A this truck"; "You naughty are." The structure of these sentences differs from that of any sentence a child is likely to hear an adult speak. Even at this early grammatical stage, children are *creating* sentences and sentence structures of their own. They just do not yet have the proper grammatical rules.

Stage 2 The average length of utterances at the beginning of this stage, which seems to occur in the period between 22 and 32 months, is about 2.5 words. Now many pronouns and some articles and modifiers have appeared in children's speech. Some of the nouns and verbs have inflections, and occasional prepositional phrases occur. Still there are no auxiliary verbs, indefinite pronouns, clauses, or phrases embedded within sentences.

Stage 3 The average length of sentences at the beginning of this stage is about 3.5 words. The age at which children reach stage 3 varies greatly—it is somewhere between 25 and 38 months. The child's sentences now contain a wide variety of auxiliary verbs used in many contexts. Practically all the noun and verb inflections are present, and complex sentences with embedded phrases are emerging. Thus by about 3 years of age, the child's grammar is very much like adult grammar; it has most of the adult rules. Of course, a 3-year-old has a relatively limited vocabulary, and his sentences are still not so complex as those of an adult.

Even though most of the grammatical rules are present at the end of age 3, some rules are relatively slow to develop and have not fully emerged by age 5 or 6. Among them are the rules concerning word form and pronunciation (Berko, 1958):

To test the ability of kindergarten and first-grade children to use the plural endings (the /-iz, -s, -z/ sounds) correctly, the experimenter presented pictures of imaginary animals. One example is shown in Figure 5.11. The experimenter said, "This is a wug." Then the child was shown a picture of two such animals and the experimenter said, "Now there is another one. There are two of them. There are two ______." The experimenter hoped to elicit the plural word *wugs*, which is formed with the /-z/ sound according to English rules of pluralization. Nonsense syllables and nonsense animals were used to rule out the possibility that children had simply memorized a plural word from hearing adults say it. The experimenter wanted to test the ability of children to use the rule system *productively* by seeing if they could apply it to construct the plural of a new "word." Most of the children (91 percent) were able to pluralize *wug* correctly. With other new "words," a majority (79 to 91 percent) used the /-z/ and/-s/ sounds productively. But less than half of the children (28 to 36 percent) were able to use the /-iz/ sound correctly with new "words." Their mastery of the grammatical rule was incomplete.

Overgeneralization of grammatical rules is also characteristic of children's grammar at this stage of development. In English, most verbs take the regular past-tense endings /-d, -t, -ed/. But some verbs have irregular past-tense forms (*go-went, come-came, do-did*). These irregular, or strong, verbs form a relatively small group but are used with great frequency, so that the child has to learn them first by rote memory before he acquires the rule. Later, when he learns the regular past-tense rule, he *overgeneralizes* the rule and applies it to the irregular forms that he has already learned saying ("goed," "comed," "doed"). These forms are strong evidence that the child is actually using a grammatical rule, because he almost certainly never heard such language from his parents. In the experiment described above, adults and children were asked the past tense of the nonsense verb *gling.* Many of the adults chose either *glang* or *glung;* but most of the children said *glinged,* applying their regular past-tense rule (Berko, 1958).

SEMANTIC DEVELOPMENT The meaning of sentences and words is the concern of *semantics.* Some combinations of words meet all the grammatical requirements of well-formed sentences, but they still do not seem to be correct. Such a sentence might be "The rock was sorry." We do not usually attribute human emotions to inanimate objects. Thus another set of rules is needed to tell us when a word may or may not be used. Linguists suppose that each word in a person's vocabulary is stored in a "dictionary" or "lexicon" along with a set of "markers" which determine when and how that word may be used. The markers of *sorry,* for instance, would prohibit its use with inanimate objects.

We have just seen that grammatical development is quite advanced by the age of 5—a remarkable achievement. But semantic development lags behind. The sentence "The rock was sorry" seems strange to adults, but young children may not find it odd. Children's semantic systems and markers are more flexible than those of adults; for instance, children do not make as many distinctions as adults concerning which verbs can go with which nouns. To some extent, children's fantasy stories are based on this lack of semantic differentiation.

Besides the use of anomalous sentences by children, there is other evidence that semantic development is slower than grammatical development. Psychologists have long used word-association tests to try to measure what people mean by the words they use (see page 161). In such a test, a person is given a word and asked to respond with the first other word that comes to mind. Adults normally reply with a word that is the same part of speech as the stimulus word; such a response is called *paradigmatic.* For instance, to the word *black* an adult would probably say *white;* to the word *horse* he would be likely to say *cow.* But young children are much more likely than adults to give an association that is another part of speech; such a response is called *syntagmatic.* For example, a child might respond to *black* with *night,* to *horse* with *ride.* Thus systems of semantic markers seem different for children and adults.

It is difficult to say when semantic development is complete. Just as a person adds to his vocabulary throughout adulthood, it seems that he continues to add semantic markers, or rules, to items in his lexicon for many years after his syntactic development is complete.

PROCESSES IN LANGUAGE DEVELOPMENT We now have some idea that language development, after its initial stages, consists of closer and closer approximation to the grammatical and semantic rules of adult speech. But *how* does a child acquire language? What sorts of processes are involved in the development of language and the rules governing it? This is one of the questions that has generated much controversy in psycholinguistic circles. Some psychologists have proposed that much of our language ability is innate, or inborn (Lenneberg, 1967). Others have stressed the role of learning, especially classical and operant conditioning, in the acquisition of language (see Chapter 3).

Classical conditioning has been proposed as a model to account for two aspects of the learning of language: the association of seemingly arbitrary sounds with meanings, and the very young child's imitation of adult speech.

It has often been said that language is an arbitrary system of social communication. This conclusion is reached from the observation that no necessary relationship usually exists between the characteristics of an object and the sound that represents it. Just why the word *shoe* means a leather garment worn on the foot is not easily answered. Classical conditioning may help to provide an explanation for the arbitrary connection of certain sounds with particular objects and events. Just as in Pavlov's famous experiments, an arbitrary signal—a bell, for example—came to elicit salivation when it was paired with food (see Chapter 3), so an arbitrary signal like the word *milk* can come to signal the presentation of a bottle of warm milk. A child should not have much trouble associating the sound of the word, or the arbitrary signal, with milk.

Classical conditioning can also be used to account for the beginning of imitation (Mowrer, 1960). According to this point of view, a child learns to imitate because he cannot distinguish between the sounds he makes and the sounds made by his parents. For instance, when his mother bathes or feeds him, she makes characteristic sounds which become associated with the pleasurable sensations produced by being bathed or fed. The child learns that these sounds are associated with happy states, and he tends to make the sounds himself. He will try in his vocalizations to copy those of the parent as much as possible, because it was these sounds that were paired with the comforting situation in the first place. When he reproduces parental sounds fairly well, we say he is *imitating.*

When a child has begun to imitate sounds, it is relatively easy to teach him the names of things. The parent makes the sound that is the name of the object; this sound serves as an unconditioned stimulus (US) that evokes imitation, or an unconditioned response (UR), from the child. If the object is present at the same time, it will serve as a conditioned stimulus (CS). This is a simple classical conditioning situation in which the sight of the object being named, the CS, is paired with the adult's vocalization, which serves as a US to elicit the child's imitative response

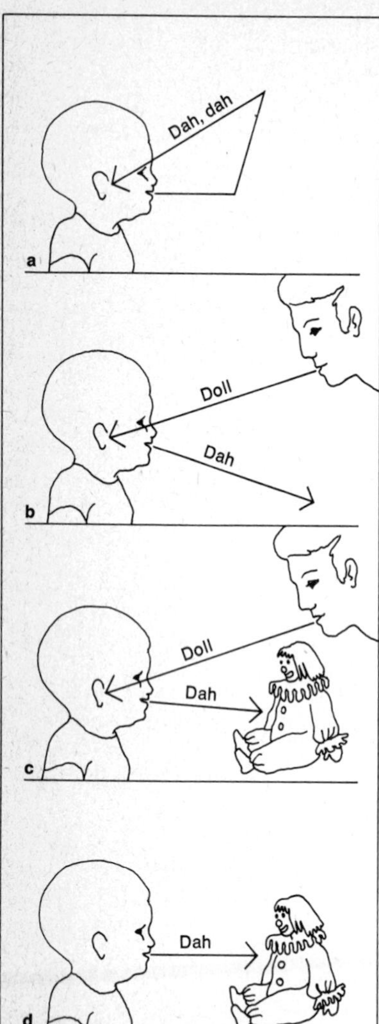

A CHILD LEARNS IN STAGES TO ASSOCIATE A SOUND WITH AN OBJECT

Figure 5.12 *Associating a sound with an object.*
(a) *Uttering the sound is associated with hearing it.*
(b) *An adult makes a similar sound which the child imitates.*
(c) *The sound is often accompanied by the object to which it refers.*
(d) *Sight of the object by itself is finally sufficient to elicit the sound. (After Allport, 1924.)*

as the UR. Soon, as a result of the pairing of the two stimuli, the child will give the response to the sight of the object; this learned response is, of course, a conditioned response, or CR (see Figure 5.12). Such a process might be involved in learning to give names to, or label, objects in the environment. We can speculate that this conditioning process becomes very efficient and in time takes place with only a few pairings of object and word.

Operant conditioning has also been proposed as a mechanism in language learning. The basic idea of operant conditioning is that responses which produce reinforcement become stronger (see Chapter 3). In other words, the contingencies of reinforcement shape all behavior, including language behavior. For example, a child may be taught to say "cookie" by a shaping process. Responses that are emitted by the child which sound like the desired response are reinforced by giving him a cookie. The response of saying "cookie" is gradually shaped because, later in learning, approximations of the correct response are not reinforced; only the correct response, "cookie," is reinforced. Since parents readily respond to cries and verbal behavior with attention and comforting, a great deal of verbal behavior may be reinforced and shaped in this way. If nothing else, the *amount* of a child's verbal behavior may be influenced by operant conditioning (Rheingold, et al., 1959).

While some aspects of language learning may be based on the giving and witholding of reinforcements, the operant conditioning account of language acquisition has been criticized because it seems artificial. In reality, parents do not wait for their children to emit reinforceable vocal responses, nor do they set up carefully consistent reinforcement contingencies. In addition, there is so much material to master in learning the grammar of language and the semantic rules that it would be almost too much to expect parents to reinforce, deliberately or not, only grammatically and semantically correct utterances.

Some psychologists feel that neither classical nor operant conditioning is sufficient to account for children's very rapid learning of the complicated sets of grammatical and semantic rules that comprise language. These psychologists propose that human beings are endowed with a species-specific ability (see Chapter 2), or potentiality, to grasp the rules of grammar and to organize the lexicon meaningfully. According to these *nativists*, as they are called, specific words may be learned, but human beings are endowed with a "prewired" system that makes possible their rapid learning of the rules of the language game. Research continues in an effort to give an adequate account of the processes by which language is attained.

Development of thought Adaptation to the environment involves both thought and action. In a series of studies over the years, the psychologist Jean Piaget has sought to describe the stages in the development of thought during the first few years of life.

A key idea in Piaget's view of intellectual development is the *schema*. Schemas are organized patterns of thought and action that are used in the attempt to adapt to the world. They recur over and over, but they are not fixed and rigid. On the stimulus, or intake, side, schemas are constantly being modified by the process known as *assimilation*, in which new information and new discoveries about the world are incorporated into existing schemas. Children often distort information about the world so that it will fit with, or can be assimilated into, existing schemas. We shall consider some examples of distortion in the earlier stages of intellectual development. On the output side, schemas are modified in the process of being used to adapt to the world. The use of schemas in the adaptation process is termed *accommodation* by Piaget.

Certain types of schemas are characteristic of the various stages of development described by Piaget and his collaborators. The first schemas in life are concerned with the coordination of the sensory and motor, or movement, systems; these schemas are important in the stage of *sensorimotor* operations (birth to age 2). In later stages, language and thought become possible, and children use *representational* schemas in which the world is symbolized in thought. These later stages are the stage of *preconceptual thought* (ages 2 to 4), the stage of *intuitive thought* (ages 4 to 7), the stage of *concrete operations* (ages 7 to 11), and the stage of *formal operations* (beginning about age 11). This list of stages, somewhat simplified, is taken from Mussen (1963). The ages, of course, are only rough indicators of the periods when each stage predominates.

SENSORIMOTOR OPERATIONS Early in this period the infant does not differentiate himself from the environment and simply uses the reflex equipment which he has at birth or shortly after. As he grows, he progresses through substages, and finally, at about 18 months, begins to be able to use thought and imagination to solve problems. The invention of new ways of dealing with the environment is one characteristic of this final period of the sensorimotor stage; another characteristic is the beginning of foresight—the ability to evaluate the consequences of future actions. Only the bare beginnings of foresight are present at this age.

PRECONCEPTUAL THOUGHT In the stage of preconceptual thought, objects begin to stand for other things—representational thought begins. For instance, toy wooden blocks can stand for building bricks, and toy bulldozers may be treated as the real thing. This stage has its beginnings in the first uses of imagination and invention at the end of the sensorimotor period, and it ends in the stage of intuitive thought.

INTUITIVE THOUGHT During the stage of intuitive thought, the child begins to group objects and events into classes, but the grouping is based upon some dominant and outstanding perceptual characteristic of the situation. In this stage he is not able to make general statements; his thought is tied to immediate perceptual characteristics. Experiments on *conservation* illustrate the type of thought (Piaget, 1952):

Suppose that a child is shown a glass of water which is half full. Then the water is poured into a tall, thin cylinder while he watches. The level of the water in the cylinder rises much higher than it did in the glass, but the amount has not changed. A child in the stage of intuitive thought would probably say, when asked, that there was more water in the tall, thin cylinder. His judgment seems based on the outstanding perceptual characteristic of this situation—the height of the water. In other words, the child does not appreciate that the amount of water has been "conserved" in spite of appearance.

Experiments on the conservation of number also illustrate thought at this stage of intellectual development. Suppose a child is presented with a row of identical pennies on a table. If the experimenter puts down just as many pennies directly opposite the original row, the child will usually reply, when asked, that the number of pennies is the same in the two rows. A simple manipulation will change this judgment of the child. If the experimenter puts the same number of pennies down in the second row, but with greater spacing between them so that the row looks longer, the child usually will reply that there are more pennies in the second row. Here again, the dominant perceptual characteristic of the situation, the length of the row, determines the response of the child.

Two other characteristics of the intuitive stage of thought are (1) egocentrism and (2) the emphasis on successive states of a situation, rather than the transformations by which one state grades into another. *Egocentrism* refers to the inability of the child to take the point of view of another person; he has difficulty describing how a situation would look to someone else. Emphasis on states rather than transformations means that the child in the intuitive stage does not have a grasp of the fact that a situation can change gradually and grade into a new one; he emphasizes the beginning and end states.

CONCRETE OPERATIONS In the next stage, the stage of *concrete operations,* the child becomes less egocentric, begins to be able to deal with transformations rather than end states, and is able to group objects and events on the basis of several concrete observations. He is still bound to concrete situations, but he is not bound to single outstanding perceptual characteristics as he was previously. Children in this stage are able to think about many different concrete instances of events relating to the problems they are now trying to solve. They are able to bring this thought to bear on the concrete problem at hand. Conservation is present at this stage because children are able to *reverse* concrete operations. In the water-pouring example, they can see that the same amount of water would still be in the two vessels if the operations were reversed and the water were poured from the tall cylinder into the glass. Note that this last example is still a concrete situation. Abstract thought is not involved, for this is the hallmark of the next, and final, stage.

FORMAL OPERATIONS In the stage of *formal operations,* children begin to use formal verbal rules of thought and logic; they begin to formulate and test hypotheses. They can think abstractly, and they can generalize, using abstract concepts, from one situation to another.

Intellectual development as described in these stages involves both physical maturation and learning. Some of the early development in the sensorimotor stage depends mainly upon physical maturation. The later stages seem to depend more upon learning, and they are not so regular as our account implies. One of the criticisms of Piaget's description is that it may give too inflexible a picture of intellectual development. This account of Piaget's description is only a brief outline; his complete description of intellectual development covers many more facets of childhood thinking.

Synopsis and summary

Thinking and using language, the two awesome achievements of man, are very closely linked. The symbols of language are the major mediating responses used in thinking in general and in such specific types of thought as concept formation, problem solving, creative thinking, and reasoning. When the symbols of language and thought stand for properties common to more than one object or event, they form the concepts which are essential to the solution of problems. Problem solving consists of manipulating the symbols of language and thought in an attempt to reach a particular goal. Creative thinking is also loosely goal-directed, but the rearrangement of symbols is more difficult to follow than in problem solving. Perhaps this is because the symbols in creative thinking are not usually entirely language symbols; imagery is important. Also, the rearrangement of symbols in creative thinking may be largely unconscious.

1. Thinking involves the use of symbols and may be called a symbolic mediating process. In other words, when we think, we use symbols that represent objects and events in the world to link present responses with past experience.
2. The symbolic processes in thinking may be traces, images, implicit responses, or language. Of these, language is probably the most important in most types of thought.
3. The field of psycholinguistics analyzes the ways in which people use language; the study of the role of language in thought is one concern of psycholinguistics.
4. General, as opposed to specific, mediating processes are known as concepts. Concept attainment is the process of isolating a common property, or properties, of objects or events. Concepts are important because their adequacy is related to success in problem solving.
5. Concepts may be of several sorts: simple, conjunctive, disjunctive, or relational.
6. Children initially learn concepts by learning to discriminate both the differences and the common properties of objects and events. At the same time that they learn these discriminations, they are learning the word labels which are applied to the common properties.
7. After the first concepts are learned, additional concepts are often acquired by (*a*) deriving meanings from the contexts in which words are used, and (*b*) learning definitions of concepts in terms of other words.
8. Among the factors that affect the ease with which concepts are learned are: (*a*) transfer from other concepts, (*b*) distinctiveness of the common elements, (*c*) opportunity to manipulate the materials, (*d*) type of instructions given, and (*e*) simultaneous presentation of relevant information.
9. The meaning of a concept can be measured in different ways: (*a*) by free response, which is similar to giving a word definition of it, (*b*) by discrimination and classification of words and objects, (*c*) by word associations, and (*d*) by the semantic differential.
10. The semantic differential, which is obtained by rating the concept on several scales, gives a measure of the connotative meaning, or the emotional and evaluative meaning, of concepts. The denotative meaning of a concept—its socially accepted definition—is usually measured by the free-response, or definition, method.

11. Thinking is often directed; it solves or attempts to solve problems. Such problem solving requires motivation, and especially a goal toward which thinking is directed. Thinking is also aided or impeded by habits and by sets. One type of set that is an impediment to problem solving is called functional fixedness.
12. Problems can be solved by a number of processes. Among these are mechanical processes, understanding processes, and insight.
13. Creative thinking is frequently characterized by five stages between perception of a problem and attainment of a solution: (*a*) preparation, (*b*) incubation, (*c*) illumination, (*d*) evaluation, and (*e*) revision. In addition, creative thinking probably involves unconscious rearrangement of symbols.
14. Reasoning involves thinking in which the thought elements are combined according to well-defined rules. Such rules are the rules of logic. But logical rules are seldom followed in everyday reasoning because (*a*) it is very difficult to discriminate logical from fallacious lines of reasoning, (*b*) our past experiences often predispose us to illogical reasoning, and (*c*) such factors as the atmosphere effect and prejudice can easily distort reasoning.
15. The complex processes in language and thought can be approached by the study of their development from simpler forms.
16. Language development is at first a matter of differentiation from the sounds of early infancy. Initial babbling is followed by repetition of the same sound and by imitation. By the time a child is 12 to 18 months old, he has differentiated his first word out of the noise.
17. After children begin to use words, grammar develops. Grammars are the rules for putting words together into sentences. Three main stages in the development of grammar have been outlined. Much of grammatical development is complete by age 5 or 6.
18. Semantics is concerned with the meaning of sentences and words. The ability to construct semantically correct sentences develops more slowly than the ability to construct grammatically correct ones.
19. Classical conditioning may be an important process in language learning because (*a*) it may be the basis for the attachment of word sounds to objects, and (*b*) it may account for the development of imitation.
20. Operant conditioning may also be a mechanism that shapes language behavior in that verbal responses which produce reinforcement become stronger.
21. Some psychologists feel that neither classical nor operant conditioning can do justice to children's rapid learning of the very complex sets of grammatical and semantic rules. These nativists propose that man is endowed with a species-specific ability for language learning.
22. According to Piaget, thought develops in children through a number of stages, each characterized by certain dominant schemas. A schema is an organized pattern of thought and action that recurs over and over.
23. The major developmental stages in which certain schemas are dominant are called (*a*) the stage of sensorimotor operations, (*b*) the stage of preconceptual thought, (*c*) the stage of intuitive thought, (*d*) the stage of concrete operations, and (*e*) the stage of formal operations.

Related topics in the text

Chapter 2 Behavioral Inheritance
Motor development and language development are compared and the concept of human species potentials for behavior and language is introduced.

Chapter 3 Principles of Learning
The principles of classical and operant conditioning discussed in Chapter 3 may be important in understanding the processes involved in learning language.

Chapter 4 Human Learning, Remembering, and Forgetting. Problem solving and concept formation are considered as complex forms of learning.

Chapter 19 Brain and Behavior The speech areas of the human brain are described.

Suggestions for further reading

Beard, R. M. *An outline of Piaget's developmental psychology for students and teachers.* New York: Basic Books, 1969.
A short, concise presentation of the basic ideas developed by Piaget.

Brown, R. *Words and things.* New York: Free Press, 1958.
An engrossing account of the role of language in psychology.

Carroll, J. B. *Language and thought.* Englewood Cliffs, N.J.: Prentice-Hall, 1964. (Paperback.)
An introduction to thinking which stresses language as the symbolic system most important in thought.

Deese, J. *Psycholinguistics.* Boston: Allyn and Bacon, 1970 (Paperback.)
A concise account of the modern contributions of psycholinguistics.

Duncan, C. P. (Ed.) *Thinking: Current experimental studies.* Philadelphia: Lippincott, 1967. (Paperback.)
A representative set of current articles covering such fields as problem solving, set, originality of thinking, and concept learning.

Ghiselin, B. (Ed.) *The creative process: A symposium.* New York: Mentor, 1955. (Paperback.)
Selections from creative artists and scientists who talk about their own creative processes.

Ray, W. S. *The experimental psychology of original thinking.* New York: Macmillan, 1967. (Paperback.)
A text and a set of readings on problem solving.

Reeves, J. W. *Thinking about thinking.* New York: Braziller, 1965.
Various approaches to the subject of thought from Locke to Freud to modern psychology.

Thomas, R. *The psychology of thinking.* Baltimore: Penguin, 1959. (Paperback.)
An elementary textbook which covers many of the important problems in the psychology of thinking.

Wertheimer, M. *Productive thinking.* (rev. ed.) New York: Harper, 1959.
A revised edition of a classic theoretical analysis of thinking; also contains many ideas about ways of solving problems.

To understand human behavior better, to gain insight into and to explain the actions of people (including one's self), the student turns to psychology and, especially, to the study of motivation. Practical considerations also lead to this study. We desire to understand, to influence, and to control our own behavior and that of others.

P. T. Young

One man wants to be a doctor. Another strives for power in the political world. Here is a person who is ravenously hungry and, at the moment, wants nothing more than to eat. A girl is lonely; she wants friends. A man has just committed murder, and we say that his motive was revenge. These are just a few examples of the motives that play so large a part in human behavior. They run the gamut from basic wants, such as hunger and sex, to complicated long-term motives, such as political ambition or the desire to get married. We never see these wants directly, but we know they exist from the way we feel, from what people do and say, and from the common observation that people seem to work for things. In other words, we infer that a motive exists from behavior—what people and animals do.

The fact that motives must be inferred, rather than directly observed, makes them difficult to investigate and to understand. As one psychologist has put it, "Motivational concepts are devised to account for or deal with the most subtle, complex, and difficult to isolate of all psychological processes" (Appley, 1970). *For this reason, we must settle for something less than perfect clarity in our analysis of motivation.*

The Nature of Motivation

Several hundred words in our everyday vocabulary refer to people's motives: for example, *wants, striving, desire, need, motive, goal, aspiration, drive, wish, aim, ambition, hunger, thirst, love,* and *revenge.* Each has its own connotation and is used in a certain context. Some can be defined with reasonable precision, but on the whole the problem of terminology is difficult. The student should pay special attention to the way terms are defined and used in this chapter.

The motivational cycle *Motivation* is a general term. It refers to states within the organism, to behavior, and to the goals toward which behavior is directed. In other words, motivation has three aspects: (1) a motivating state within the organism, (2) behavior aroused and directed by this state, and (3) a goal toward which the behavior is directed. When the goal is achieved, the state that caused the behavior subsides, thus ending a cycle until the state is aroused again in some way (see Figure 6.1). Motivation, therefore, is a cycle of these three stages.

The first stage, the motivating state, has various names, depending on the psychologist doing the naming, on certain subtle distinctions that

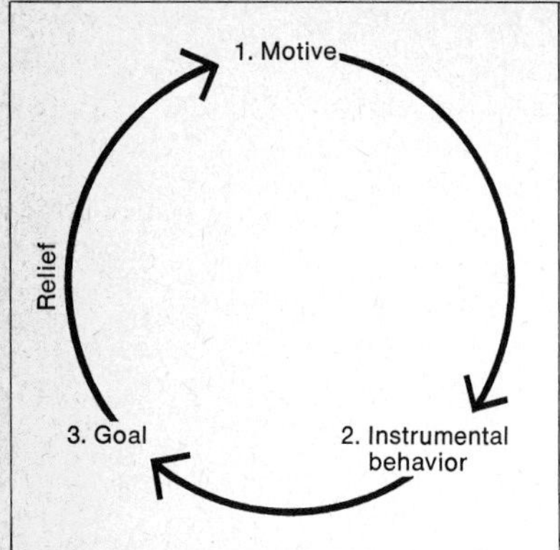

MOTIVATION IS CYCLIC

Figure 6.1 *The motivational cycle.*

can be made, and on whether one is talking about animal or human motivation. *Drive* is most often used for this state in animal motivation, particularly when we are sure the motivation has a physiological basis. Drive is regarded as impelling an animal to action. *Need* is more frequently applied to the motivating state in man, particularly in social motivation. *Motive* is a general term covering both drive and need, and this is the word we will use at first. But later, in discussing human motivation, we will refer to need and use it interchangeably with motive.

The second stage of the motivational cycle is the behavior that is instigated by the motive. This (operant) behavior is usually instrumental, sooner or later, in reducing the motive. Hunger, for example, motivates an individual to explore for food. His exploratory behavior is instrumental in satisfying or reducing the motive, but it is only a means toward the goal of satisfaction.

The third stage of the motivational cycle is the reduction or satisfaction of the motive. This is ordinarily achieved by reaching some *goal.* In thirst, for example, lack of water in the body is a need (first stage) motivating the individual. This need arouses exploratory behavior (second stage) to find water. The goal of drinking water when it is found (third stage) satisfies the thirst and terminates the motivational cycle until the need for water builds up again.

Goals, naturally, depend on the motive that is active. If a person is motivated by hunger, his goal is food; if he is motivated by sex drive, his goal is sexual satisfaction; if he needs affection or companionship, his goal may be marriage, joining a club, or going to the local poolroom. These goals are *positive goals*—goals the individual approaches or attempts to reach. *Negative goals* are those which the person tries to escape from or avoid, such as dangerous or unpleasant situations.

For the basic physiological motives, goals are relatively fixed and unchangeable. If one is thirsty, for example, water is about the only goal that will do, although there are many forms in which the water may be consumed. If one is hungry, nothing but food will do. For more complex motives, however, any of several alternative goals may do. One may satisfy a need for recognition, for example, by becoming a pillar of the church, rising to eminence in politics, or becoming the best golf player in town. So, although goals must be appropriate to one's motives, the study of goals is itself a complex aspect of the study of motivation.

The three stages in motivation are illustrated strikingly by this incident which occurred in a hospital (Wilkins and Richter, 1940).

A 3-year-old boy was admitted for observation because he showed certain abnormalities of physical development. After 7 days on the regular hospital diet, the boy suddenly died. Autopsy showed that the child's adrenal glands, which are located on the top of the kidneys, were abnormal. Normally the secretions of the adrenal glands keep the salt in the body from flowing out in the urine. But in this abnormal case, the boy had lost salt faster than he could replace it on the standard hospital diet. It seemed clear that the boy died of a salt deficiency.

After the boy's death, his parents reported that he had never eaten properly. Unlike most children, he hated anything sweet, but seemed to crave salty things. He eagerly licked the salt off bacon and crackers, and although he would not eat them, he would always ask for more. One day when he was about eighteen months old, he got the salt shaker off the table and began to eat the salt voraciously. From then on, whenever he came into the kitchen, he would point to the cupboard where the salt shaker was kept and scream until someone let him have the salt. By this time his parents had discovered that he would eat fairly well if they put three or four times the normal amount of salt on his food and, in addition, let him eat about a teaspoonful of plain table salt a day.

This unfortunate case illustrates well the stages of motivation as they apply to physiological motives: (1) the boy's body had a physiological need for salt; (2) this need brought about several kinds of instrumental behavior, including attempts to get the salt shaker from the table and the cupboard; (3) the goal was salt, and once he got it his need was relieved and the craving temporarily disappeared.

All motivation, of course, does not have an immediate physiological basis, and many needs, especially complex social needs, can go unsatisfied without resulting in death. Nevertheless, these three stages form the typical pattern of both simple and complex motivated behavior.

Classification of motives Attempts to classify motives have produced several different schemes, each of which has merit but also poses certain problems. One dichotomy employed for a long time was between primary, unlearned, physiological motives on the one hand, and secondary, learned, social motives on the other. The trouble with this has turned out to be that the corresponding pairs in the dichotomy are not opposites. Although all physiological motives are unlearned, not all social motives are learned. Also, some motives that are unlearned are neither physiological nor social. Besides that, psychologists are uncertain about whether some motives are learned or unlearned—and about how they are learned if they are learned. Hence this approach to classification has gradually been abandoned.

To avoid some of the dilemmas of a dichotomous grouping, this chapter will use a threefold classification, with a major section devoted to each. The first type is *physiological motives,* which are known to be primary and unlearned. The second is *unlearned general motives:* motives that we now can be sure are unlearned, or largely so, yet are not physiologically aroused. And the third consists of *social motives,* which are for the most part learned. Because the question of how they are learned is an important one, a section on the *learning of motives* precedes the discussion of social motives.

Physiological Motives

Physiological motives, which stem from physiological changes within the body, may be instigated by one or more of the following: (1) external stimuli, (2) tissue needs, (3) hormonal substances in the blood. In most instances we know a great deal about the physiological basis of the motive. This information is covered in Chapter 19 on the physiological basis of behavior; the discussion here will focus on the behavior associated with the motive. Some of the major physiological motives are hunger, thirst, sex, maternal motives, and pain, fear, and anger. They are among the mechanisms by which the body preserves *homeostasis.*

Homeostasis Homeostasis is the tendency of the body to maintain a balance among internal physiological conditions (Cannon, 1932). Such a balance is essential for the individual's survival. Body temperature must not get too high or too low. Blood pressure must not rise or fall beyond certain limits. The blood must not be too acidic or alkaline; it must not contain too much carbon dioxide; it must not become too concentrated; it must have a certain amount of sugar in it. If these limits are exceeded, the individual becomes sick and may die.

Physiologists have discovered that many homeostatic mechanisms are involved in keeping conditions within normal limits. Consider, for example, the control of body temperature. Normal body temperature in man is 98.6°F. The temperature usually stays near that point because the body can cool or heat itself. If a person's body temperature gets too high, he perspires and the resultant evaporation of liquid cools the body. If his temperature threatens to fall, he shivers and steps up his metabolism. Shivering burns the body's fuels faster and thus generates extra heat. In addition, many animals can insulate themselves against heat loss by fluffing their fur and creating a dead-air space around their skin. (All that is left of this mechanism in human beings is the goose pimples we get when we are too cold.)

Physiological mechanisms take care of many of the problems of maintaining a homeostatic balance, but the body also makes use of *regulatory behavior* (Richter, 1943)—behavior that has the effect of regulating internal physiological conditions. Such regulatory behavior is instrumental in satisfying physiological motives. When the body becomes depleted of water or food, for example, it cannot maintain a balance by calling on its physiological mechanisms. Rather, it must obtain more water and food from the outside. It does this through motivating the behavior that normally succeeds in procuring more water and food; after that, the homeostatic balance is restored. The important point, then, is that physiological motives are part of a more general physiological mechanism for maintaining homeostatic balance within the body. Now let us consider some of the principal physiological motives.

Hunger The body is always using up materials in growth, in the repair of tissues, and in the storage of reserve supplies. Indeed, every function of our bodies from heartbeat to thinking requires energy, and this energy must ultimately come from the metabolism of food. Thus a tissue need for food is created, and this generates the hunger motive.

GENERAL HUNGER When people need food, they usually report that they are hungry. For some, hunger means a feeling of strong contractions in the stomach, and it used to be thought that these contractions were the source of the hunger motive (Cannon, 1934). It was later shown, however, that contractions are not regularly associated with hunger, and in fact are more likely to occur after eating than before (Davis et al, 1959). Moreover, there are cases in which people still report hunger after their entire stomachs have be removed (Wangensteen and Carlson, 1931). Some people report a feeling of weakness and lightheadedness when they are hungry. The surest indication of hunger in an animal or person, however, is that he "wants something to eat."

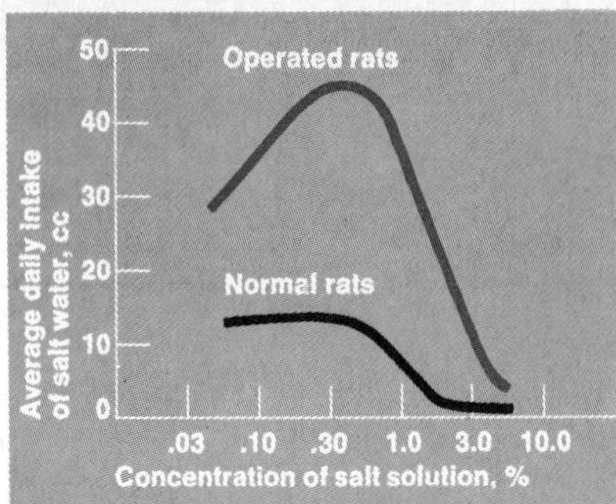

PREFERENCE FOR SALT DEPENDS UPON THE AMOUNT OF SALT RETAINED IN THE BODY

Figure 6.2 *Salt preferences of normal rats and of rats after removal of the adrenal glands. The operated animals drank much larger quantities of salt solution until the salt concentration offered them became quite high. Plain water was available at all times. (After Bare, 1949.)*

Probably the physiological source of the hunger motive is some product of metabolism circulating in the blood, but we have not found out what it is. We do know that eating behavior is controlled, in part, by two centers in the brain (Chapter 19). One, an eating center, causes the organism to search for food and to eat when it is available; the other, a satiety center, responds to food in the mouth or stomach by inhibiting further eating.

Hunger, incidentally, is not entirely controlled internally. People (and animals) will eat when they have had "enough to eat." The smell or sight of good food can entice a person to eat who otherwise would not say that he is hungry. Or the taste of food may have the same effect; after a taste of peanuts, for example, we may want more. This is an illustration of the *stimulus* factor in motivation, which plays a role even in motives with a strong physiological basis.

SPECIFIC FOOD NEEDS Besides this response to appetizing tastes and odors, people and animals have preferences and aversions for particular kinds of food, not just food in general. These preferences and aversions sometimes reflect specific bodily needs, as in the case of the boy who craved salt. The same sort of need can be created experimentally in rats by surgical removal of the adrenal glands. The operation causes rats to lose salt constantly, so that they must eat extra amounts of it if they are to live. This they do by drinking large quantities of salt water (see Figure 6.2).

Aversions are also seen in eating behavior. One is the result of eating a particular kind of food (Young, 1944). If an animal's need for protein is satisfied, it avoids protein, although it may still be hungry and highly motivated to eat a fat or carbohydrate (sugar). Aversions also develop for diets that are deficient in needed substances (Rozin, 1967), and such aversions appear to be learned. For example, rats that are maintained on a diet deficient in thiamine (vitamin B_1) acquire an aversion for the diet. When given the opportunity, they avidly eat novel diets even if the new diets do not contain thiamine. Such aversions help the organism to find a balanced diet.

Thirst Water is just as necessary for survival as food. It is an important item in the body's use of food, and it is constantly being lost through the lungs, skin, and kidneys. What is it about the need for water that makes us thirsty and therefore motivated to drink water?

Forty years ago physiologists gave the same kind of answer they did to the question about hunger (Cannon, 1934): they thought dryness of the throat provided the basis for thirst. While it is true that people sometimes drink because their mouths are dry, it has now been proved in many ways that a dry mouth cannot be the sole factor in thirst. One striking proof comes from experiments with dogs (Adolph, 1941).

By careful surgery, the esophagus—the tube from the throat to the stomach—of each dog in these experiments was brought out through the skin of the neck. Then it was opened in such a way that everything the dog drank ran out of the upper part of the opening. The dog could be kept alive by putting food and water directly into the stomach through the lower part of the opening. When the dog was offered

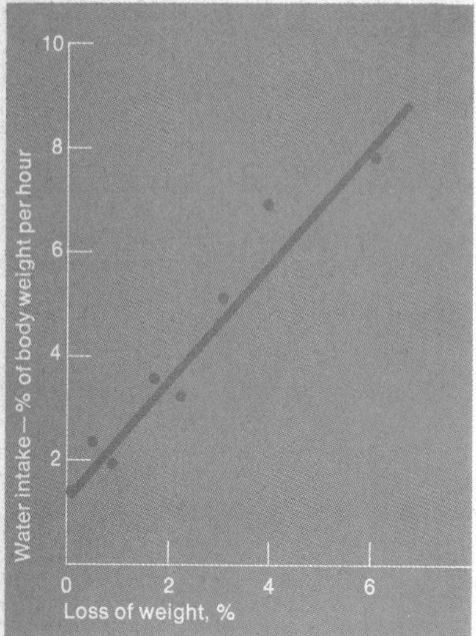

WATER INTAKE IS PROPORTIONAL TO LACK OF WATER IN THE BODY

Figure 6.3 *Sham drinking and water deficit. Dogs were operated on so that they could drink water without any of it getting into their stomachs. The amount of water they lapped up in a standard experimental period was directly proportional to the amount they lost from their bodies through water deprivation. (After Adolph, 1941.)*

water, it drank just about what it needed—as judged by the amount of water lost through deprivation (see Figure 6.3)—and then stopped, even though none of the water got into its body. Of course, after a while it drank again and kept repeating the process until water was put into its stomach. One important point is that the dog had some way of metering the water as it passed through the mouth, and it continued to drink an amount proportional to the water loss even though the mouth and throat were moistened by the first drinks.

The next step in the experiment was to put enough water directly into the dog's stomach to satisfy its biological needs and then let it drink. When the dog was offered water right after its stomach was filled, it again drank just about the amount it needed. But if it had to wait 15 to 30 minutes after its stomach was loaded, then it did not drink at all. So a second important point is that after water had been in the stomach for a short time, thirst was satisfied.

What happens to make thirst go away when water is put directly into the stomach? The evidence seems to point in this direction: Lack of water makes all the cells in the body give up water. Some cells in the hypothalamus, a region of the brain, are especially sensitive to loss of water. Through their connections with other parts of the brain, they can regulate thirst according to the relative amount of water in the body (see Chapter 19).

But this physiological cause of thirst is not the only mechanism involved. Thirst, like hunger, is another case of a physiological motive that is not entirely physiological. A *psychogenic* drinking, that is, excessive drinking with a psychological cause, can be seen in animals placed on certain reinforcement schedules (Falk, 1967). If food-deprived rats are put in a Skinner box and rewarded intermittently with small amounts of food, they develop a pattern of excessive drinking in between food reinforcements, taking in more water than is required for homeostasis. The causes of this psychogenic drinking are still being studied, but it illustrates that even the most physiological of motives can be modified through learning.

Sex We classify sexual motivation as physiological because (1) it is characteristic of all higher animal species, (2) it culminates in a physiological event (orgasm), and (3) its mainspring in animals, if not in man, is hormonal. Even so, in higher animals habits as well as hormones play a role.

SEX HORMONES The testis of the male and the ovary of the female secrete hormones that are responsible for the development of the secondary sex characteristics of the body as well as for much of the sexual behavior of the two sexes. When the sex glands mature at puberty, the masculine and feminine body forms, hair distribution, vocal characteristics, and adult sex organs also develop. At the same time, in animals as well as in human beings, interest in the opposite sex typically develops in a sharp spurt. If the sex glands fail to develop properly or are removed in experimental animals, very few of the typical sex characteristics will show up in the individual.

Among lower animals, such as the rat, the sex hormones are more crucial than among the higher animals, such as chimpanzees and men

(Beach, 1965). The spayed female rat will never mate again unless given hormones artificially. The male may continue to mate for a short while after castration, but he then becomes incapable of sexual motivation unless it is restored with sex hormones. The same operations on human beings do not have such clear effects. In some cases among both sexes, removal of the sex glands makes sexual motivation disappear. But in equal numbers of cases, sexual motivation is unaffected by castration or ovariectomy. The picture is further complicated by the fact that men and women who are sexually impotent or frigid may still have perfectly normal supplies of sex hormones. The information we have on monkeys and chimpanzees also indicates that the higher animals really do not depend crucially on sex hormones. The males in these species can be castrated without noticeable effect on sexual motivation. And it is clear that female monkeys and chimpanzees show sexual motivation at times when their hormonal supply is very low. This is not true among the lower female animals.

So for all animals, the sex hormones are important in the development of physical sexual characteristics and sexual motivation. In sexual behavior, however, hormones are much more important among the lower animals than the higher.

HABITS AND SEXUAL MOTIVATION While the sex hormones play a relatively smaller role in the sexual behavior of higher animals, *habit* and *experience* play a larger one (Beach, 1947). This can be illustrated by comparing the rat and the monkey. Rats raised in isolation mate normally the first time they are tested. The male rat may be inhibited by emotional situations, but the female resists all except the most severe disturbances.

In monkeys and chimpanzees, the story is quite different (Yerkes, 1943; Harlow, 1962). The male has to learn to mate, usually being taught by an experienced female. The female chimpanzee, on the other hand, learns to use sexual behavior for nonsexual purposes. For example, she will often win out against a much larger male in competition for food by presenting herself sexually to the male and then making off with the food as he focuses his attention on her.

Habit, then, is much more important in the sexual behavior of man and the higher animals than it is among the lower animals. Habit can cause sexuality to persist even when sex hormones are absent. And, of course, habit frequently determines the way in which human beings express their sexual motivation and the kinds of sexual outlets they prefer.

Maternal motive In lower animals such as the rat, maternal behavior is an unlearned pattern of instinctive behavior that is characteristic of the species (but see the caution on page 34). Maternal behavior is motivated behavior arising, like sex behavior, from a physiological motive. Indeed, instinctive behavior is characteristically motivated behavior (see Figure 6.4).

The maternal motive has its basis in a combination of hormones secreted during pregnancy and shortly afterward. One of the most important of these hormones is *prolactin*, a product of the pituitary gland. Secretion of prolactin is stimulated by the presence of a fetus in the uterus. Prolactin in turn stimulates the mammary glands, which supply milk for

Figure 6.4 *Maternal behavior. A white-footed mouse hovers over her young of only a few hours. (Tom McHugh, Photo Researchers, Inc.)*

nursing the young; but it is also important in maternal behavior in lower animals. When it is injected into a virgin female rat that has been given the young of another rat, the injected rat will accept the young and care for them in much the same way that the natural mother would (Lehrman, 1961).

Even though maternal behavior has a hormonal basis, like other physiological motives it is modified by psychological factors (Campbell and Misanin, 1969). Animals such as hamsters and rats show considerably more maternal behavior after they have had experience with young than before. Even animals not under the influence of maternal hormones, such as nonpregnant females, will display typical maternal behavior patterns after they have been exposed to young for a couple of weeks. Hence hormones tend to ensure maternal behavior in the natural mother, but this behavior can also develop through experience.

In the last statement we used the term develop rather than learn, because the emergence of such behavior does not involve conditioning or reinforcement in the sense usually associated with true learning (see Chapter 3). As such, experience with young may very well bring out unlearned motives, and the experience may be an adjunct to, or substitute for, hormonal arousal of the motive.

Maternal behavior in animals, then, is under the control of both hormones and experience with young. What can be said about the maternal motive in the human female? No scientific analysis of this motive has so far proved possible. We can only make inferences from animals and from casual observations of human mothers. Maternal motives are virtually universal in the human race, which would tend to indicate that they have a physiological basis; but exceptions do exist. Occasionally there are mothers who display no desire to keep and take care of their infants. (This is also true in animals.) On the other hand, mothers of illegitimate babies given up for adoption frequently want desperately to get their babies back, despite the social stigma and other drawbacks. Then too, maternal behavior is a social norm in most human cultures (see Chapter 14), so that social pressures for appropriate maternal behavior also exist. All things considered, we may guess that human maternal motives have a physiological basis in hormones and in experience with young, as they do in animals, but that they are also bolstered by social learning and pressures.

Pain, fear, and anger Pain is a sensation; but it also can be a powerful motive. It is classified as a physiological motive because various physiological reactions accompany it—increases in blood pressure, heart rate, and rate of breathing. Sense organs for pain, which are probably free nerve endings, are widely distributed throughout the skin, blood vessels, and internal organs (see Chapter 18). These sense organs are usually stimulated by some injury to the tissues of the body. The individual then strives to remove the injurious stimulus. If that cannot be done, or if it does not help, he looks for some way to relieve the pain.

The body is equipped with certain automatic mechanisms for avoiding pain. A sudden pain in a limb, for example, makes a person *reflexly* withdraw his limb from the source of stimulation. He does not have to think about it; he just withdraws, immediately and quickly. Sometimes when the source of pain is deep within the body, there is no way to withdraw from the source of injury. In such cases, the individual tries many techniques to reduce the pain. Modern pain-killing drugs are, of course, the most effective technique. But they can fail, and often they are not available. Then the individual may writhe, tear at his flesh, lie down, try to sleep, try not to move, or try to distract himself. Since none of these actions is very helpful, the individual may become preoccupied with his pain and endlessly continue his efforts to reduce it. Such pain constitutes a powerful motive that channels tremendous efforts toward the one goal of relief.

Fear and anger are motivated reactions with physiological as well as behavioral components. In each species of animal there are certain unlearned stimuli for these reactions (see Chapter 7). In almost all animals including man, a strange object, sound, or movement serves as a stimulus for fear; so does loss of bodily support. Other fear-provoking stimuli vary from one species to another. There are also certain species-specific stimuli for eliciting anger (see Figure 2.2). Besides these, general causes of anger in animals and people are pain and frustration. Pinching a dog's tail is a good way to get it to bite you; frustrating it by taking away its bone is another. Almost any kind of frustration angers a child, as you can see when he loses a toy or cannot do what he wants to do.

More complicated, and also more important in human behavior, are learned fears and hostilities. These will be considered later in the chapter.

Unlearned General Motives

If we look at the everyday behavior of adults, children, and animals, we can hardly escape the conclusion that relatively little of it is directly

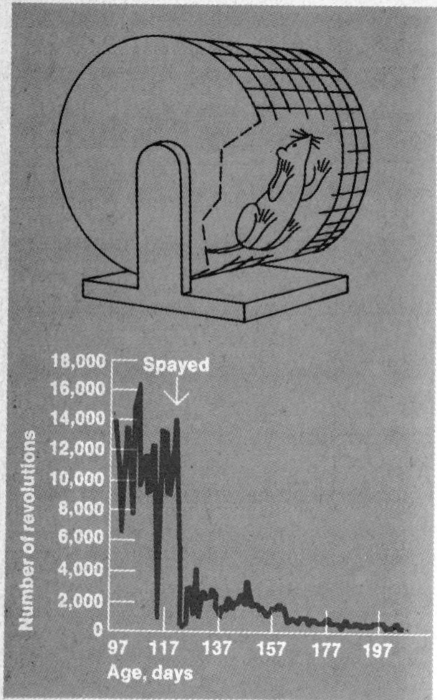

FEMALE RATS IN SEXUAL HEAT ARE USUALLY VERY ACTIVE

Figure 6.5 *Activity and sexual motivation measured in a running wheel. The normal female rat shows peaks of activity when in sexual heat, which occurs about every fourth day. After the sex glands are removed by spaying, activity drops to a low level. (Richter, 1927.)*

motivated by physiological motives. True, people say they work to provide food and shelter for themselves, which may be a way of saying they are working to satisfy physiological motives. Yet a great deal that they do cannot be explained at all on this basis.

Think of the amount of time people spend just looking at things—at newspapers, books, television, plays, sports, canyons, mountains, and "points of interest." Think of the amount of activity that goes into playing games, skiing, boating, hiking, hunting, and touring. Most of this looking and moving about is not connected in any obvious way with physiological motives. Neither is the play of kittens, nor the romping and whooping of children.

Despite the lack of any obvious physiological basis for such motives, some psychologists have tried to find a connection. In some cases they have succeeded, as we shall see. Increasing evidence, however, points to the existence of some basic unlearned motives which are not physiological in the sense we have used. As yet, no satisfactory term for these motives has been coined, so we are calling them "general motives," just to have a name for them. They include motives for activity, for perceiving the world, for exploring and manipulating things, for physical or social contact with other people and things; they also include some aspects of the fear motive.

Activity The motive for bodily activity is generally characteristic of all species. Both human beings and animals spend a good deal of time moving about for no apparent reason except that it satisfies this motive. Appearances, however, may be deceiving, for activity sometimes can be explained by the presence of a physiological motive.

Generally, whenever an animal (or human being) is hungry, thirsty, or in physiological need, it becomes more active—an animal will run, pace, sniff, or explore its environment. Such changes in activity accompanying a physiological motive have been studied extensively (Cofer and Appley, 1964).

One technique is to put an animal in a wheel so constructed that it revolves when the animal walks. A counter mounted on the side of the wheel counts the number of revolutions made in any particular period. Figure 6.5 shows the record of running activity of a female rat during, between, and after periods of high sexual need (heat). At the peak of heat, the rat ran hundreds or even thousands of revolutions a day, but between periods of heat, activity greatly diminished. The sex glands were removed by spaying when the rat was about 122 days old, and the sex cycle was thus abolished. Thereafter, activity was permanently reduced to a low level.

Similar records have been obtained for other motives, such as thirst and hunger. So long as the organism remains in good health, activity increases with the presence of a physiological motive.

Activity may also have its origin in sensory stimulation (Hall, 1956). Lights, horns, or any other strong stimulus will generally rouse an organism and make it more active. Sometimes this is because the stimulation is annoying or disturbing. On the other hand, the stimulation does not need to be disturbing; its very novelty may arouse the organism's interest or curiosity. Such curiosity is itself a motive.

But is activity as such a motive, even with no physiological or sensory stimulation behind it? The evidence shows that it is. One fact supporting this conclusion is that activity can be pent up by deprivation (Hill, 1956).

Rats were confined in small cages where they had enough room to stand up or lie down, but not enough to walk around. One group was confined for 5 hours, another for 24 hours, and a third for 46½ hours. A control group was not confined at all. After confinement, the experimental animals were placed in running wheels, and their activity was measured for a period of an hour and a half. The amount of activity measured in this time varied with the duration of the confinement. Rats confined for the longest time were the most active; the control group was least active.

A second kind of evidence supporting the existence of an activity motive is that activity itself can act as a reinforcer for learning a habit (Kagan and Berkun, 1954).

Rats, two at a time, an experimental subject and a control, were placed in running wheels and studied simultaneously. Each rat was provided with a lever which it could freely press throughout the period of observation. The control animal's lever, when pressed, did nothing but provide a record of lever pressing. The experimental animal's lever, on the other hand, released the brakes on both wheels so that both animals could run. By pushing the lever, the experimental animal released these brakes for 30 seconds. At the end of the 30-second period, the brakes were reapplied until the experimental animal again pushed its lever.

With this experimental design, both animals had the same opportunity for running in their respective wheels. For the experimental animal, however, the opportunity to run could be a reinforcement for its lever pressing. Was it? The experimental animal pushed the lever significantly more—in some cases two or three times more—than the control animal. It appears, then, that running in the wheel was itself a reinforcement which satisfied an activity motive.

Curiosity Some years ago it was found that a bright light has motivating properties for a rat in a box. If things were so arranged that the rat could turn off a light shining overhead by pushing a lever, the animal quickly learned to push it. It was thought, therefore, that light was somehow annoying to the rat—perhaps fear-producing. However, it has since been shown that animals—in this case mice, but we have no reason to believe it makes a difference—can just as easily be trained to turn a light *on* (Kish, 1955). In fact, they can be taught to push a lever to produce almost any kind of novel stimulation, such as clicks of a switch or movement of a platform. Sometimes a period of habituation is required—a period in which the subjects get used to the situation, possibly to get over their fear—but after that, the novel stimulation is reinforcing. The important point here is that novel stimulation is motivating; pushing a lever to obtain such stimulation is merely one means of demonstrating this motivation.

This interest in novel stimulation has been called a *curiosity motive.* It has been demonstrated in a variety of experiments with animals as well as in casual observations of children and adults. Rats will explore new

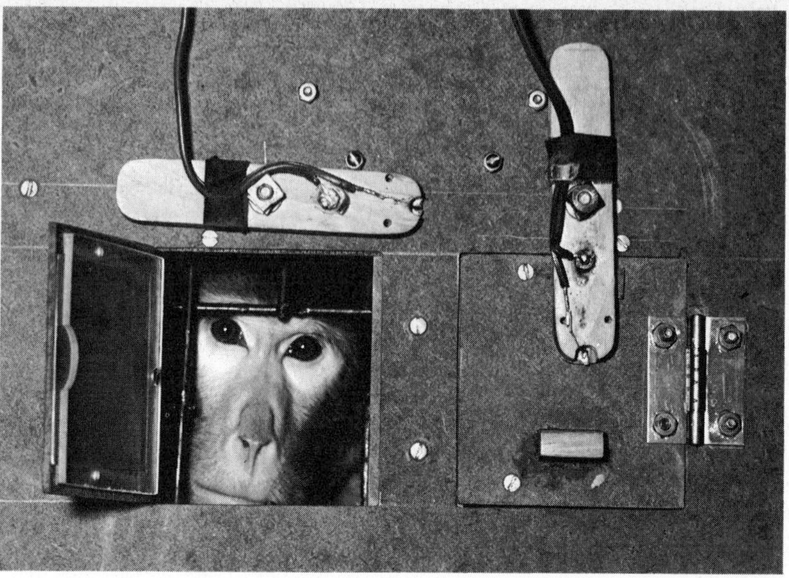

Figure 6.6 *Monkey peeping out of the apparatus used to measure curiosity motivation. If it pushed the correct door, the monkey was reinforced by being allowed to look outside for a few seconds. The reinforced response increased in frequency, while the unreinforced response declined. (H. F. Harlow, Primate Laboratory, University of Wisconsin, 1953.)*

mazes or areas in which they are placed, as well as strange objects in their environment. Dogs, monkeys, and children often approach and examine things around them. In natural situations, they are able both to sense and to manipulate things. In experiments, however, sensing and manipulation can be studied separately. The motive to experience the sensory environment is called the curiosity motive; the motive to *do* things with objects is termed the *manipulative motive,* which will be discussed in another section. The following experiment illustrates the curiosity motive (Butler, 1953, 1954):

Monkeys were confined in a closed box that had two small doors on one side (see Figure 6.6). Because of the way monkeys bounce around in boxes, a monkey would frequently strike each door by accident. Each door had a visual stimulus mounted on it. If the monkey happened to push the one marked with stimulus 1, the door opened, and the animal could look outside for a few seconds. If it pushed the door with stimulus 2, nothing happened. Thus the only reward for learning to discriminate between the two stimuli was the privilege of looking out the door that would open when pushed.

The monkeys readily learned the discrimination, thus demonstrating that they were motivated by the opportunity to look. Once an animal learned to push the correct door, the number of pushes made in a given period became a measure of its curiosity motive. This varied with what the monkey could look at. If there was an "interesting" scene on the outside, such as another monkey or a moving toy train, it opened the correct door often. It did not respond so frequently when all it could see outside was an empty room.

A curiosity motive, like other motives, can be satisfied. Interest in a novel object or situation tends to diminish, in time, as the following experiment demonstrates (Welker, 1956):

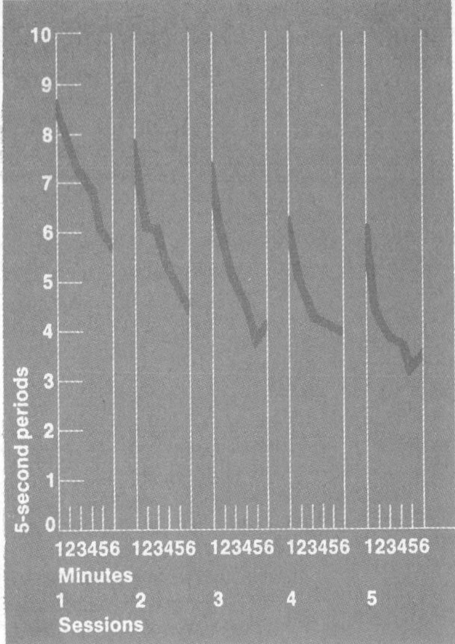

CHIMPANZEES LIKE TO PLAY WITH NOVEL OBJECTS, BUT SOON LOSE INTEREST IN THEM

Figure 6.7 *Curiosity drive in chimpanzees. The number of 5-second periods out of 6 minutes each day during which a chimpanzee made some response to a set of objects. Interest was always highest at the beginning of each session. (Welker, 1956.)*

Chimpanzees were presented successively with different novel objects, such as pieces of wood with different shapes, sticks that could be moved, lights that could be switched on and off, a chain, and so on. The number of times each chimp manipulated the object or made other observable responses to it was recorded for successive 5-second periods. Each set of objects was presented for one period of 6 minutes each day. When the experiment was over, the number of 5-second periods in which the chimp made some response to each set of objects was counted. It was clear that interest was highest at the beginning of the period and waned steadily during the succeeding minutes (see Figure 6.7). When the object was presented again the next day, interest was rearoused, though not quite so much as on the preceding day. Then it gradually waned again.

Curiosity, of course, can be observed in infants and children as well as in monkeys and chimpanzees. When we give a baby a new toy he is deeply interested at first, but in time the novelty wears off. Such reactions can now be studied systematically in infants too young to "play" with toys by recording where they look when presented with various stimuli (Caron and Caron, 1968). The important variable seems to be complexity. When shown simple patterns, like squares or circles, infants look at them, then quickly habituate. They examine more complex figures, including human faces, for a longer period. Thus curiosity can be seen even in the first few months of human life.

Evidence indicates that the curiosity motive is unlearned. It appears early in human infants and is seen in naïve animals, and in neither case are there grounds for believing that it has been learned. True, curiosity is an adaptive motive, for it can lead to the discovery of objects that will satisfy other motives. Yet in the experiments with it, the subjects have been fully supplied with all the physiological essentials: there has been no opportunity for curiosity to be reinforced and thus to become a learned motive.

Manipulative motives It is difficult if not impossible to separate what is done in exploring a novel situation from what is experienced in it. That is to say, we have not yet determined whether the motive involved in manipulating the environment is different from the motive which leads the organism to look at or experience it. So it is not possible to say whether there is a manipulative motive distinct from a curiosity motive. We do have experiments, however, which show that a need to manipulate objects is strong enough to motivate learning. Here is an example (Harlow and McClearn, 1954):

Three monkeys were given seven problems to learn. In each problem two screw eyes were placed on a board in front of the monkey. One of the eyes could be removed from the board; the other could not. The question was whether the monkeys would learn to pick the removable one of the pair, using color as a cue. The two screws were always different colors. For example, in the first problem a red screw was removable and a green one was not. The monkey was scored correct when he unscrewed the red eye without attempting to unscrew the green; then another problem with screws of two other colors was presented. Removal of the screw eye was the only reinforcement the monkey got. The monkeys learned to make the discrimination reasonably well, thereby demonstrating that this simple discrimination could be learned without any motivation or reinforcement except the manipulation of the screw eyes.

This is one of many experiments that show the existence of a motive or motives variously called curiosity motive, exploratory or manipulatory motive. The experiments have been done on animals because an experimenter can know the conditions under which animals have been raised and can precisely control the conditions of experimentation. From such studies we can be reasonably sure that the comparable motives we have all casually observed in human beings are unlearned and have considerable importance in the motivation of behavior.

Sensory stimulation Closely related to the curiosity and manipulative motives is a need for sensory stimulation. Indeed, it may be that a need to experience changing stimulation, or stimulus variation, is the basic motive, while these others are just two expressions of it. At any rate, it is possible to demonstrate the need for sensory stimulation experimentally in human adults (Bexton et al., 1954).

The subjects were college students, who were paid $20 a day to lie on a comfortable bed 24 hours a day except for the time required to eat and go to the toilet. Each bed was in a small, lighted cubicle, which was quiet except for the hum of an exhaust fan. The subjects wore translucent goggles which permitted them to see light but not objects. They also wore gloves over their hands and cuffs over their forearms to reduce manual manipulation and manual experience. In short, everything was arranged to keep sensory stimulation and activity to a minimum.

This might seem to be an easy way to make money; but most of the subjects soon found the situation so intolerable that they refused to continue after two or three days. They began to have hallucinations, some of which were merely bizarre patterns, while others were much like dreams. They became disoriented in time and space, and the disorientation lasted for some time after they had left the cubicle. They lost their ability to think clearly: they made poor scores on problems given them to solve, and they were unable to concentrate on anything for very long. In brief, they began to resemble people suffering from mental disorders, and they wanted nothing more than to get out of the situation.

This was the first major experiment in sensory deprivation. Many similar studies have since measured all sorts of related factors (Zubek, 1969). One of the important variables turns out to be the personality of the subject; some people can tolerate sensory isolation much better than others (Petrie, 1967). The results, however, leave no doubt that people need the stimulus changes normally experienced in everyday living.

Affectional motive We would all agree that love is a powerful motive in human affairs. People's love is extended in many directions—to their parents, their brothers and sisters, their wives and husbands, their children, their friends, their pets. People love to such a degree that almost every story, play, or magazine article portraying the things people do or work for has love as a major or minor theme.

What is this thing called love? Where members of the opposite sex are concerned, it often has a large sexual component. Leaving this aside, however, love or affection for others is still a motive of considerable importance. And the question is, What is the affectional drive? How does it originate? Is it innate or learned? Toward what is it directed?

ORIGIN OF AFFECTIONAL MOTIVE As in the case of other motives not rooted in physiological needs or hormones, the affectional motive may develop from one or both of these sources: It may be an unlearned motive that, given the opportunity, emerges in the normal course of maturation. And it may be learned through experience with people, because people are instrumental in satisfying physiological motives for food, drink, and so forth. These two alternatives do not need to be mutually exclusive, just as maturation and learning are not mutually exclusive. It is possible that the affectional motive is unlearned, but that the particular objects of affection are largely learned. Indeed, so far as we know now, this is the correct view. To see how we arrive at this conclusion, let us consider the scientific evidence.

It would be logical to study the origin of the affectional motive by observing its development in humans from birth onward. As in the study of many similar problems, however, we do not have sufficient opportunity to control human experience. In addition, the human infant is so slow to develop its motor abilities that it is not capable of giving us measurable responses to various situations at an early age. As one investigator put it, "By the time the human infant's motor responses can be precisely measured, the antecedent determining conditions cannot be defined, having been lost in a jumble and jungle of confounded variables" (Harlow, 1958).

For these reasons, we turn again to animal subjects. The baby monkey is suitable not only because it resembles the human infant in its form and response to other members of its species, but because its motor capabilities develop quite early. Within 2 to 10 days after birth it moves around on its own and manipulates objects, so that we can measure what it does and does not respond to. The baby monkey can be suckled on the bottle, and thus can be brought up without any contact with other monkeys or with human beings. One series of experiments on the development of affectional motivation in baby monkeys made use of mother surrogates (Harlow, 1958):

The monkeys were raised singly in cages designed to provide a comfortable environment and to take adequate care of bodily needs. In one experiment, each cage was equipped with two mother surrogates. One mother surrogate was a cylindrical wire-mesh tube with a block of wood at the head (see Figure 6.8). This was called the "wire mother." The other "was made from a block of wood, covered with sponge rubber, and sheathed in tan cotton terry cloth." This was called the "cloth mother," and it resembled a real mother much more than the wire mother did. Behind each mother was a light bulb that provided radiant heat for the infant.

Either "mother" could be outfitted with a nursing bottle placed in the center of its "breast." For one group of monkeys the bottles were placed on the cloth mothers, for another group on the wire mothers. Figure 6.9 shows the amount of

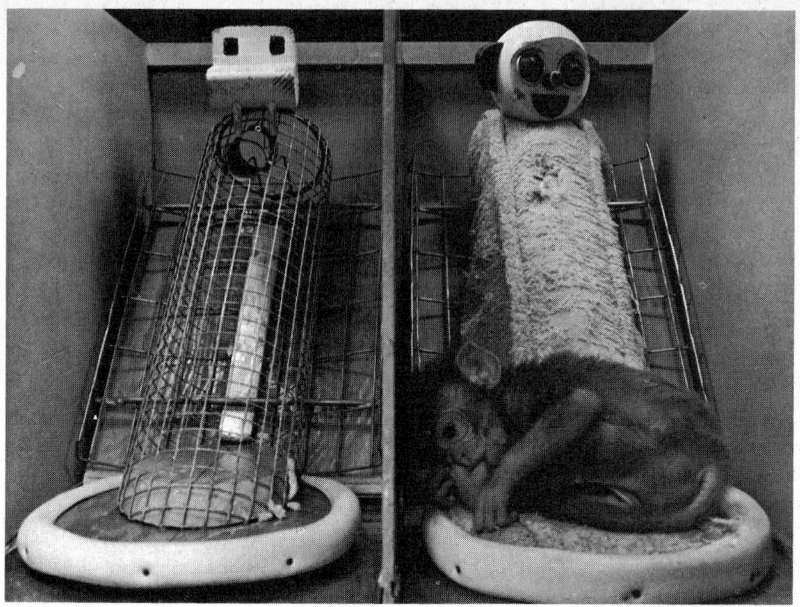

Figure 6.8 Mother surrogates made of wire and of cloth used in experiments on the affectional motive in monkeys. At right, a baby monkey huddles against a cloth surrogate mother on which it is not fed; at far right, the baby monkey maintains contact with the cloth surrogate mother while feeding from the wire mother's bottle. (H. F. Harlow, Primate Laboratory, University of Wisconsin.)

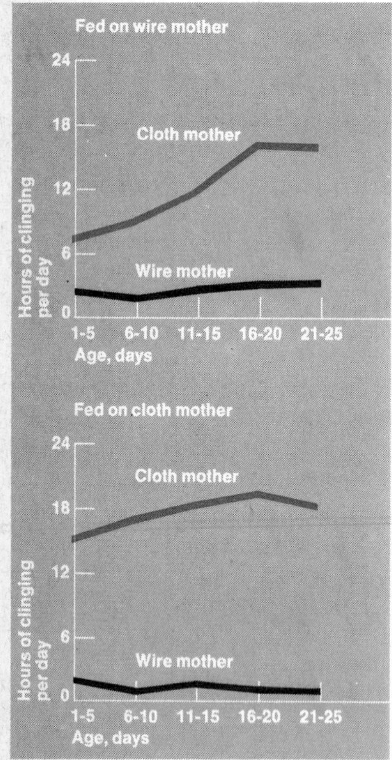

BABY MONKEYS PREFER CLOTH MOTHERS TO WIRE MOTHERS, REGARDLESS OF WHICH "FEEDS" THEM

Figure 6.9 Whether they are fed on cloth or wire mothers, infant monkeys prefer to cling to cloth mothers. (After Harlow, 1958.)

time spent with each mother. As might be expected, monkeys nursing on cloth mothers spent most of their time with the cloth mother and very little time with the wire mother. Those nursing on wire mothers spent *relatively* more time with the wire mother than did the first group, but from the very beginning they spent *more* time with the cloth mother than they did with the wire mother. And as the experiment progressed, monkeys nursing on wire mothers spent more and more time with the cloth mother. Hence babies in both groups showed a strong preference for the cloth mother surrogate.

This experiment brings out two interesting points. The first is that the monkeys seemed to possess a motive to have contact with, or to be near, a mother. This was beyond any physiological drive for food and water, for they spent 15 hours or more a day with a "mother" when only an hour or so was sufficient for feeding. The second point is that the choice of a mother was not associated with feeding. If the affectional motive for a mother were learned through feeding, one would expect those nursing on wire mothers to prefer the wire mother; yet they spent more time with the cloth mother. Apparently, there was an unlearned tendency to seek "contact comfort" with something resembling a natural mother.

FEAR, CURIOSITY, AND AFFECTION Other experiments tell us how fear, curiosity, and affectional motives may conflict with one another (Harlow, 1958).

In a series of tests on the monkeys raised with mother surrogates, an infant monkey was placed in an open-field situation, a room 6 feet square, with a 6-foot ceiling, designed to evoke both fear and exploratory drives (see Figure 6.10). The room contained a number of strange objects that usually elicit exploration and

Figure 6.10 *Open-field situation for studying fear and exploratory drives in infant monkeys. In the absence of the mother surrogate, the monkey huddles in a corner crying because it is afraid of the strange objects in the situation. (H. F. Harlow, Primate Laboratory, University of Wisconsin.)*

manipulation in the baby monkey. The size of the room and the strangeness of the objects could also be expected to make the animal somewhat fearful. In some tests there was a mother surrogate in the room; in others there was not.

The presence or absence of a "mother" made a great difference. In her presence, indices of emotionality, based on vocalization, crouching, rocking, and sucking, were cut in half. The infant also came to use the mother as a base of operations. It would cling to or manipulate the mother, then venture out to explore the room and the objects, then return to the mother. The mother was a haven of safety that helped to allay fear in the strange situation, thus freeing the infant from a conflict between fear and curiosity drives.

This experiment illustrates the interplay of affectional, fear, and exploratory motives. In a novel situation, fear and curiosity are in conflict. When fear is the stronger motive, it reduces curiosity and exploration. Conversely, if fear is somehow reduced, curiosity can take over and dominate behavior. Fear may be reduced by habituation, or becoming accustomed to the fear-provoking situation. It may be reduced, too, by the presence of an affectional object, which seems to provide a "feeling of security" that speeds the habituation of fear and permits curiosity to prevail. Such an object thus provides support for the satisfaction of curiosity motives.

This conclusion, derived from experiments, fits in well with casual observation. Kittens venture out from their mother to play, but they usually remain in her vicinity and return to her periodically. The human infant, after being with its mother for a while, plays happily nearby, but returns frequently to tug at her skirt. Left alone, especially in a strange situation, the infant is likely to stop playing and become afraid.

In summary, present evidence supports the following conclusions about the affectional motive. It makes its appearance relatively early in the life of an infant. It is not learned; rather, it appears in the normal course of maturation. It is not necessarily associated with feeding or with the satisfaction of physiological needs. It is a motive to have contact with, or to be near, some object that provides "contact comfort." How much the object must resemble another individual we do not know; perhaps it need only be soft and warm. The affectional object allays fear in strange situations, providing a "feeling of security" and thereby supporting the curiosity motive.

Competence We conclude this discussion of unlearned general motives with some observations about babies and growing children. Anyone who has had much experience with young children can confirm these comments without recourse to formal experiments.

If we watch a baby who has matured to the point of creeping and is about "ready" to stand, we can notice the enormous effort he puts into getting himself to a standing position. Holding on to the railing of, say, a playpen, after many tries, he finally pulls himself up to a standing position. At this point, he is very likely to let out a shriek of delight, burst into laughter, and otherwise express his joy at this accomplishment. And he doesn't do it necessarily for an audience: the same thing will happen when he doesn't know he is being watched. Obviously, the baby had a very strong urge "to stand," and doing it was quite a satisfaction.

The same thing can be observed at earlier and later stages of development. Once he is able to creep, he spends a lot of time at it with obvious enjoyment. Or later, when he can walk, he displays an almost compulsive desire to keep at it, again thoroughly liking it and being frustrated if for some reason he is prevented from doing it. (Dember and Jenkins, 1970.)

Such observations lead to the general conclusion that organisms are strongly motivated to exercise their potentialities; they want to do what they can do. This kind of motivation has been called an *effectance* motive, or a motive for *competence* (White, 1961). It seems clear that competence motivation is unlearned—a point we should keep in mind when we consider social motives such as the needs for achievement and power. These needs undoubtedly receive some social reinforcement; for example, when parents praise or reward various accomplishments. But they have an important unlearned component of competence motivation and do not require a complicated explanation. To some writers (White, 1961), the motivation for competence subsumes various other motives, such as curiosity and manipulation. These may indeed be expressions of the more general competence motive. Classification, however, is less important than understanding that such motives are unlearned and are not derived through reinforcement from physiological motives.

Learned Motives

There appears to be a world of difference between the motives of a monkey and those of a man, or between those of a child and those of an adult. The motives we have been discussing, such as hunger, thirst, curiosity, and affection, are all present in the human adult, but he has others as well: he is motivated by such things as power, status, achievement, and social approval. What is the difference between the unlearned motives that emerge through normal maturation and the motives that prevail in the conduct of human affairs? Some part of the difference is surely due to learning, but how much learning takes place, and how is it accomplished?

Psychologists used to assume that only the innate motives are physiological, and that complex human motives must be derived from physiological motives through learning. They then proceeded to design experiments in which motives might be learned. In some cases, as we shall see, they were successful, but in others they were not. In the meantime, they discovered that some motives (those discussed in the previous section) are unlearned, yet resemble the so-called complex motives developed through learning. Thus scientific views of how complex human motives arise have been changing.

To understand how motives can be learned, we must first distinguish between primary and secondary goals and between positive and negative ones. A *primary* goal is the goal of an unlearned motive; it is anything satisfying the motives we have discussed so far—for example, food, water, objects to manipulate, sensory stimulation and avoidance of pain. The latter is a *negative* goal, while goals like food and sensory stimulation are *positive* ones. If we are to have learned motives, we need

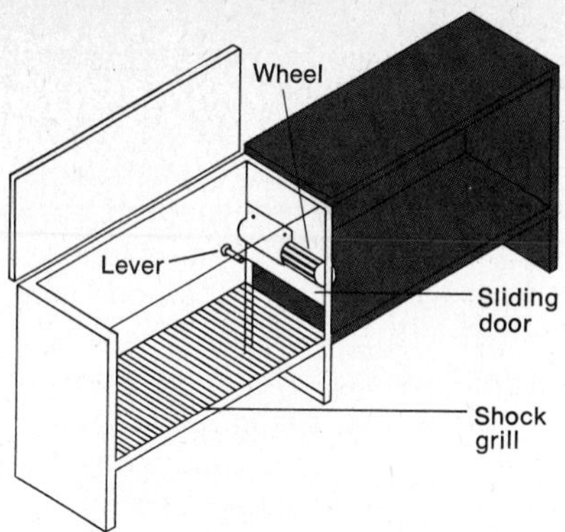

AN ACQUIRED FEAR OF A WHITE BOX MOTIVATES LEARNING TO ESCAPE INTO A BLACK BOX

Figure 6.11 *Apparatus for studying acquired fears in rats. Electric shock can be delivered through the grill in the floor of the white box. (After Miller, 1948a.)*

to establish learned or *secondary* goals. A secondary positive goal, for example, might be money; a secondary negative goal could be avoidance of failure. In each of these examples a new goal that is different from the unlearned one has been acquired, and we infer that a motive to attain this goal has been learned. Hence the crucial step in learning motives is acquiring secondary goals. As we shall see, evidence that this does happen is stronger for negative than for positive goals.

Secondary negative goals As Chapter 3 explained, there are several kinds of learning. One is called *classical conditioning.* Three elements are involved in the conditioning process: an unconditioned response, an unconditioned stimulus, and a conditioned stimulus. The unconditioned response is ordinarily an unlearned response to the unconditioned stimulus. The conditioned stimulus is some stimulus that has little or no effect on the individual prior to conditioning. During conditioning, however, it is paired, that is, presented along with, the unconditioned stimulus. When the two stimuli are presented together—it may be once or dozens of times—the conditioned stimulus acquires the ability to elicit a response that is much like the unconditioned response.

The conditioning process can be illustrated by the conditioning of a fear response (see Chapter 3). An electrical shock which is slightly painful produces an unlearned fear response in both man and animals. The shock serves as an unconditioned stimulus for the unconditioned response: fear, in this case. By pairing the shock with some otherwise harmless stimulus—a bell, a light, or even the sight of a box—we can soon obtain a conditioned fear response to the previously innocuous stimulus, as shown by the following experiment (Miller, 1948*a*):

White rats, one at a time, were placed in a white box separated from a black box by a door (see Figure 6.11). In the floor of the white compartment was a grill through which shock could be applied. First, each rat was placed in the white box for a 60-second period, during which no stimulus was applied. Then, for a period of 60 seconds, brief shocks were given every 5 seconds. At the end of this period, the door between the compartments was opened, and the shock was turned on steadily. By running into the black box, the rat could escape the shock. This sequence was repeated on 10 different occasions; *after that, the shock was not used again.*

On five subsequent occasions, rats were placed in the white box with the door open. As one might expect, fear conditioning to the white box was strong enough to motivate them to run immediately to the black box. Following these five trials, the door was closed, but it could be opened if the rat turned a wheel just over the door. In trying to escape, rats turned the wheel accidentally and thus discovered the means of escape. This general procedure was repeated for 16 trials. During the course of the trials, the rats learned to turn the wheel more and more promptly. After they had learned the wheel-turning response well, the wheel was adjusted so that it no longer opened the door. Instead, a lever could be depressed to open the door. The rats quickly learned this response too.

Here the white box became a secondary negative goal through simple fear conditioning accomplished by associating shock with the white box. This learned fear of the white box then served as motivation for

A CHIMP CAN LEARN THE VALUE OF "MONEY"

Figure 6.12 *A chimpanzee using tokens (secondary positive goals) to obtain food (primary positive goal). The animal has learned to place poker chips in the machine to get fruit. Chimps in this experiment would "work" to obtain chips, and would hoard them when they could not spend them immediately. (Yerkes Laboratories of Primate Biology, Inc., Henry W. Nissen, photographer.)*

learning other habits such as wheel turning or bar pressing—any response linked to escaping from the secondary negative goal.

The process illustrated in the experiment is typical of human motivation. Most of the things we now fear as adults we did not fear as infants. We learned to fear them by a conditioning process. These learned fears, in many cases, serve as secondary negative goals motivating us to learn new habits to escape or avoid the situations giving rise to learned fears.

Secondary positive goals As with secondary negative goals, the crucial step in the learning of secondary *positive* goals is in pairing some previously neutral situation with a primary goal—in this case a positive one. To test whether the pairing has created a secondary goal powerful enough to motivate further learning, we must find out whether the organism will learn to do something to obtain the secondary goal. An experiment to demonstrate this kind of goal learning was done many years ago (Wolfe, 1936).

Chimpanzees were taught how to get a grape or a raisin by putting a poker chip in a small vending machine, called a Chimpomat (see Figure 6.12). The experimenter simply showed a hungry chimpanzee how to insert the chip into the slot of the Chimpomat and collect his reward at the bottom. The animals learned this operation very quickly. What is more important for our purposes is that after this initial learning, the chimpanzees clearly came to *value* the chips if they could be traded in for food treats. In one part of the study, the experimenter had the chimpanzees pull a heavily weighted box into their cages in order to get a poker chip hidden in it. As a matter of fact, the chimpanzees would pull in the weighted boxes to get chips even when they could not spend them immediately. They simply hoarded large numbers of chips and waited patiently for the chance to spend their hoard.

Later, the experimenter complicated the lives of the chimpanzees even more by teaching them to use a red chip to obtain food, a blue one for water, and a white one to get out of their cages and run around. The chimpanzees worked hardest for the particular chip that would satisfy their dominant need at the moment.

The parallel between the poker chips and money is obvious, since the chimpanzees were working for poker chips in almost the same way people work for money. Money, indeed, is a secondary goal which we learn to value because it can be used to satisfy simple motives—at first for candy, a bottle of pop, or admission to the movies, and later for other things which themselves are learned as secondary goals. The principle, however, is not limited to money. Almost any thing or situation that is consistently associated with the satisfaction of primary motives will be learned as a secondary goal.

Convergence of goals On closer examination, the learning of secondary positive goals has its limitations. These goals are not sufficient to explain complex motives such as the need to achieve, or a desire to amass a fortune.

One of the reasons is that secondary goals, like any operant behavior, readily extinguish when primary reinforcement no longer accompanies them. Psychologists who have done experiments with animals and children report that secondary positive goals do not continue to be goals very long unless they are backed up by the satisfaction of primary motives. If we do not pay off a chimpanzee's poker chips with food at regular intervals, the animal soon loses interest in working for poker chips. We are familiar with similar cases in human affairs. People who work for money merely to eat do not work much more than is necessary to eat. (We see this frequently in young people without family obligations, who may have few goals other than their immediate bodily comforts.) The point is that a secondary goal does not become a permanent goal in itself merely because it is reinforced for a time with some physiological goal. Something else is required.

Two additional factors enter into the equation: permanent secondary goals may include both the negative goal of fear, and a *number* of positive motives, not just one. Fear will be discussed in the next section. Regarding positive motives, we should note that more than one kind of motivation may be linked, at one time or another, to a secondary goal. Even a rat pushing a bar in a Skinner box satisfies a manipulation motive as well as the hunger motive. The same is true of the chimpanzee operating the Chimpomat. In human affairs, working to make money entails not only satisfactions that money can buy but also activity motives, curiosity motives, and competence motives. Hence several motives can converge, so to speak, on one secondary goal. This explains why some people work to amass fortunes long after their physical needs are met.

Take the case of the penniless boy who becomes a millionaire. He starts out with a bundle of motives, both physiological and general. To stave off hunger he begins working, and money becomes a secondary goal. In his work he finds some satisfaction for his activity motive, and since the work provides all sorts of novel situations, including some challenging problems, it helps satisfy his curiosity motive. The work brings him in close relationship with men who become his friends, and thus it satisfies an affectional motive. Other motives may also be involved. After he has made his million, he is still motivated to work because it satisfies nonphysiological motives other than the need for food and shelter. Out of habit, he may keep saying to himself that he is still motivated to make money; he may be unaware of his true motives. This points to the complex nature of human motivation.

Generalization of fear Negative goals may also be involved in the case of the poor boy who becomes a millionaire. In fact, the learning of negative goals probably explains more about complex human motivation than the learning of positive ones. Fear conditioning has three properties that make it important. First, unlike operant conditioning for positive goals, it does not easily extinguish (this was discussed in Chapter 3 on learning). Consequently learned, or secondary, negative goals last longer without reinforcement than secondary positive goals.

The second property of learned, or conditioned, fear is that it easily generalizes—another topic dealt with in Chapter 3 (see Figure 3.18). *Generalization* is a tendency to respond in the same manner to all situations that are in some degree similar. This definition is a bit circular, because in practice we are forced to infer that situations are similar when they are responded to in the same way. But take the example of the rat that is conditioned to fear a white box. If, as a result of the conditioning, the rat now displays fear when placed in a gray box, or a larger box, or a box of a different shape, we say that generalization has taken place. The rat is giving the same fear response to situations that are somewhat similar, though they are not the same.

The process of generalization accounts for some of the things observed in complex motivated behavior. A person who is highly motivated to please people, whether they are teachers, strangers on a bus, or anybody else, may merely be generalizing from his experience with his father, who was difficult to please and who regularly resorted to punishment when he was displeased. Everyone can think of examples from his own experience.

The third important property of conditioned fear is that it can become attached to the frustration of other motives. This can be demonstrated in animals and recognized in humans in the ordinary circumstances of life. A child punished by being made to go without supper learns to fear loss of a meal. A person without money who has experienced real hunger fears the situation in which it occurs, so that he can learn to fear being without money. An intense desire to make money, often seen in those who have been poor, may represent an unextinguished fear of poverty more than it does the positive goal of making money to satisfy wants. This fear of frustration is sometimes called a *safety need* (page 546), a need to feel certain that other motives, particularly the strong physiological ones, will be satisfied. Thus a safety, or security, motive is powered by fear.

Owing to these properties of learned fear, it is not surprising that fear is a substantial component of many human motives. How important it is varies with the motive and with the individual's history of fear conditioning. In several motives discussed in the next section, fear is a significant factor even though it is blended with secondary positive goals.

Social Motives

Having studied the physiological and general motives, and the ways in which positive and negative goals can be learned, we are ready to consider complex human motives. Since these always involve other people in some way, they are called social motives. They are frequently referred to as *needs* by research workers in the field, so we will use that term interchangeably with motive.

Psychologists have been searching for, but have not yet found, a definite classification of social motives. All sorts of lists can be made for different purposes, but we have no assurance that any of them is the "right" one in the sense that it is a comprehensive listing of independent motives. (See page 369 for such a list.)

Part of the problem is ignorance. In the case of most proposed motives, we have not yet found ways to measure, then analyze, their source and operation. In a few instances, as we shall see, this has been done, and we have a fairly clear picture of how the motive is acquired and how it is expressed. The other part of the problem which makes classifying social motives difficult is that motives and goals are interconnected in too many ways. Two individuals with the same apparent goal may be satisfying quite different motives; those with a similar motive may satisfy it by pursuing different goals.

Consequently we cannot attempt to classify human social motives; instead, we shall consider a limited number about which we know the most. These will provide some understanding of the way social motives function in people.

Measurement of motives In order to learn much about anything, one must be able to measure it (page 289). Motivation is no exception and is especially difficult to measure in human beings. Work on this problem has taken three general paths: (1) projective tests, (2) inventories or scales, and (3) situational observations.

PROJECTIVE TECHNIQUES Projective methods of measuring personality are discussed in detail in Chapter 10. Used as personality tests, they emphasize detection of dominant needs or motives. Hence they have been chosen as a promising means of studying human motives.

The principal projective test used in the study of motivation is the Thematic Apperception Test (TAT). Described on page 359, it consists of 20 ambiguous pictures about which the subject is asked to make up a story. In each case the story is scored according to the number of themes in it that reflect certain needs. When the TAT is used as a personality test, all the pictures are presented in turn to the subject, and 20 or so different needs are scored for relative strength.

For instance, one picture shows a boy seated at a desk with a book open in front of him. The subject is shown this picture and asked to describe what is happening, what led up to the situation depicted, what the people in the picture are thinking, and what will happen in the future. Here are stories told about the picture by two individuals (spelling and grammar have not been corrected).

Person 1

1. This brings to mind T. Edison who is dreaming of possible inventions rather than turning to his studies. A poor student, Edison is probably worried about his future.
2. Probably he is doing poorly in school or is thinking of his girl or perhaps he is being reprimanded by the teacher for inferior work.
3. I think he is dreaming of some childhood invention that he would much rather be working on than studying the boring subjects of grammar school.
4. He is destined to become one of the greatest of American inventors devoting his entire life to things such as the light bulb, phonograph.

Person 2

1. The boy in a classroom who is day dreaming about something.
2. He is recalling a previously experienced incident that struck his mind to be more appealing than being in the classroom.
3. He is thinking about the experience and is now imagining himself in the situation. He hopes to be there.

4. He will probably get called on by the instructor to recite and will be embarrassed. (Smith and Feld, 1958, pages 698–699.)

These stories, together with others told by the same two people about other cards, were scored for achievement imagery according to a standard system. Which of the stories here shows greater achievement imagery?

When the TAT is employed to measure only one motive—say, achievement—two changes are made in the way it is administered. First, only pictures especially relevant to that motive are presented, which generally means that only 4 or 5 are used out of the total 20. Secondly, a special scoring system is devised to measure effects of experimental manipulation of the need. In one study of achievement need, male subjects in a relaxed condition were shown achievement pictures, and their stories were scored. On another occasion, seven tests were first given to make the same subjects "achievement-oriented." All the tests involved a measure of performance: they included anagrams, scrambled-word tests, pencil-and-paper motor tests, and a test of "creative imagination." Then the subjects were presented again with the relevant TAT cards, and their stories were recorded. Thus two sets of stories were obtained: one told when the men were in a relaxed state, and the other when they were achievement-oriented (McClelland et al., 1953).

In this case the scoring system for measuring achievement motivation was developed by comparing the two sets of stories and giving weight only to the themes that distinguished between the relaxed and achievement-oriented states. Hence only those themes that appeared because of the *induced* achievement need were regarded as measuring this motive. The same general method has been used to set up a scoring system for other needs, such as needs for affiliation, aggression, and power.

INVENTORIES Personality inventories (page 355) have also been adapted for the study of particular motives. These inventories consist of questions to answer true or false, or sometimes of alternative statements to choose among. The Edwards Personal Preference Record scores socially desirable responses and hence is relevant to the motive for social approval. Since fear and anxiety enter into many of the social motives, certain tests of anxiety have also been used. Taylor's Manifest Anxiety Test seems to be a good measure of general anxiety level, while the Mandler-Sarason Test Anxiety Questionnaire measures anxiety in taking achievement tests. Other inventories too have been adapted or invented for research in the area.

Unfortunately, measures of motivation obtained with inventories seldom correlate highly with those derived from projective tests. They have been helpful, however, in research on the social motives (Cofer and Appley, 1964).

SITUATIONAL TESTS A third way to measure human motives is to create situations in which a person's actions indicate his dominant motives or show whether they have changed in strength. For example, the affiliation need can be measured by giving the subject a choice between waiting in a room by himself or waiting in a room with other people. A child's aggressiveness can be measured by letting him play with dolls and observing the number of times he does something aggressive or destructive with them. Or aggression might be studied by insulting somebody to see what angry things he says in reply. Situational tests like these have sometimes been illuminating in research on human motives.

Now let us examine studies in several areas of social motivation: achievement, affiliation, status, aggression, and cognitive dissonance.

Achievement need The achievement need has been studied more than any other social motive (McClelland et al., 1953; Atkinson and Feather, 1966). It is regarded as a motive for success in performing tasks, and it is almost always measured by the TAT, scored as described above. By giving a person a few selected achievement-related pictures and noting the themes in the stories he tells, we arrive at a score for the strength of his general achievement need. This score can be used like any other, such as an IQ, to make comparisons between various groups or to divide people into high achievement need and low achievement need groups for further analysis.

PERFORMANCE Once a measure of achievement need was available, investigators immediately wanted to find out whether achievement motivation affects actual achievement—that is, performance in school or on experimental tasks. In the many such studies which have been published, correlations on the whole are good. People high in achievement need generally do better on tasks than those who are low. In one study, for example, the two groups were tested on scrambled-word puzzles (Lowell, 1952).

College students scoring high and low in achievement need were given a scrambled-words test consisting of a booklet of ten pages, each of which contained 24 sets of scrambled letters from which words could be made. Subjects were permitted 2 minutes per page to rearrange the 24 sets of letters into words.

The high- and low-scoring subjects started the test at about the same level of performance. But the high group soon speeded up, so that on the last two pages they were unscrambling 50 percent more words than the low scorers. In this case the high scorers *learned* to improve their performance, while the low scorers did not.

Analysis of the two groups on other measures revealed that high-scoring subjects had somewhat higher scholastic aptitude scores—that is, they were brighter than low-scoring subjects. But when a statistical correction was made for this difference, the correlation between scrambled-word output and achievement need was lowered only from .48 to .44 (see page 301). This indicates that most of the difference seen in performance on the scrambled-word test was probably due to achievement need, not intelligence.

The exact way in which subjects high in achievement need excel those who are low in it varies from task to task. In some instances they do better at the outset, presumably because their high need has developed knowledge or skills that make them more proficient at the task. In some cases, as in the experiment above, they learn faster; in others, they accomplish more in less time. Whatever the form of their superior achievement, they do in general excel at tasks that are difficult enough to discriminate different levels of performance (Cofer and Appley, 1964).

Other performance measures besides experimental tasks are also related to achievement need. It has a correlation of about .40 with intelligence and aptitude scores, probably for two reasons. First, motivation to achieve has some effect on intelligence scores over a period of several years. Second, intelligence itself probably affects achievement need: the brighter a person is, the more he can be challenged by difficult tasks. Correlations of achievement need with college grades are erratic; sometimes they are significant, sometimes not. Correlations with grades are more consistently significant in high school than in college, probably because the range of both achievement need scores and levels of achievement is greater in high school than in college (Applezweig et al., 1956).

FEAR OF FAILURE When results in various achievement need studies (particularly studies of risk taking, described in the next section) did not always come out as anticipated, research workers began to suspect that fear of failure plays a role in achievement motivation. The difference in performance between subjects scoring high and low in achievement need was usually clear enough, but those in the middle sometimes performed more like low scorers than would be expected. So psychologists decided to take a look at this variable.

In examining the TAT stories from which the original scoring was devised, they detected certain negatively toned themes, especially in the middle-scoring subjects, that might indicate fear of failure. Because these themes were achievement-related, they had originally been lumped with positive themes representing hope for success. The experimenters now reanalyzed their data and revised the scoring system to yield two scores, one for hope of success and the other for fear of failure (Moulton, 1958). The first measured a *positive* motive for achievement, the second a *negative* fear of failure. The original achievement need score had been a mixture of the two.

Knowing of the two components, investigators could look for other ways of measuring them. One inventory that we mentioned earlier, the Mandler-Sarason Test Anxiety Questionnaire, has proved to be a good measure of fear of failure. It is frequently employed with the TAT method to yield separate measures of each motive.

RISK-TAKING BEHAVIOR Undertaking a task of some difficulty involves both a challenge for achievement and a risk of failure. This is as true of attempting a college education as it is of smaller projects. How do differences in achievement need on the one hand, and fear of failure on the other, affect the risks people are willing to take? This question is easily attacked experimentally, because many games present the opportunity for balancing risk and the chance of success. Subjects in the following study, for example, had to choose how much risk they would accept for how much possibility of achievement (Atkinson and Litwin, 1960).

DIFFERENCES IN ACHIEVEMENT NEED AND IN FEAR OF FAILURE AFFECT THE RISKS PEOPLE ARE WILLING TO TAKE

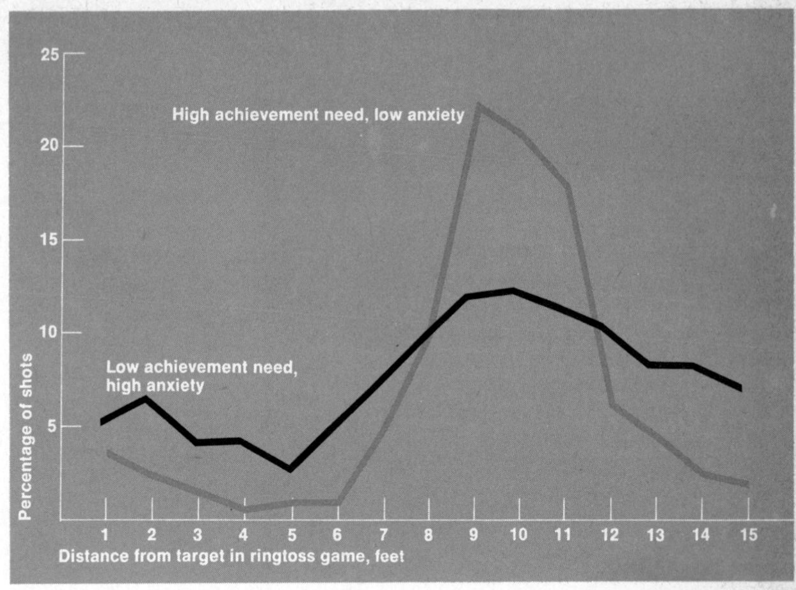

Figure 6.13 *Percentage of shots taken by each player in a ringtoss game. The group that was high in achievement need and low in test anxiety tended to shoot from intermediate distances, mostly 7 to 12 feet. Thus they balanced their chances of success with the risks of failure. The group that was low in achievement need and high in test anxiety distributed choices of distance more evenly. Other groups, not shown here, representing the high-high and low-low combinations of achievement need and anxiety were also more evenly distributed than the high-low group. (Modified from Atkinson and Litwin, 1960.)*

Male college students played a ringtoss game in which a ring is thrown onto a peg from some distance. They were permitted to choose their own distance within a range of 1 to 15 feet. Achievement motivation was induced by having them compete under the instruction, "See how good you are at this." Naturally, a student who could ring the peg at 15 feet was better than one who could ring it at a closer distance, but his risk of failure was also greater. The question was what distance each would choose to shoot from.

Subjects were tested separately for achievement need (with the TAT) and for fear of failure (with the Test Anxiety Questionnaire). Four groups making up each combination of high and low achievement need and high and low test anxiety were compared. The results for the two extreme groups (high-low and low-high) are shown in Figure 6.13. Note that those scoring high on need for achievement and low on fear of failure overwhelmingly chose intermediate risks, mostly in the 7- to 12-foot range. This distance represents a compromise between the chance of success and the risk of failure. By contrast, subjects who scored low on achievement motivation and high on test anxiety distributed their choices more evenly among shorter and longer distances.

THEORY OF RISK TAKING A precise theory of achievement motivation has been developed to account for the two curves shown in Figure 6.13 (Atkinson and Feather, 1966). It can be expressed in mathematical form, but we will present it in words. Considering for the moment only achievement need, not fear of failure, the person high in achievement need chooses intermediate risks for two reasons. First, accomplishing easy tasks that anyone can do does not give him a feeling of achievement; second, difficult tasks with "long odds" of success yield so few successes that these do not satisfy the achievement need either. Only in the middle

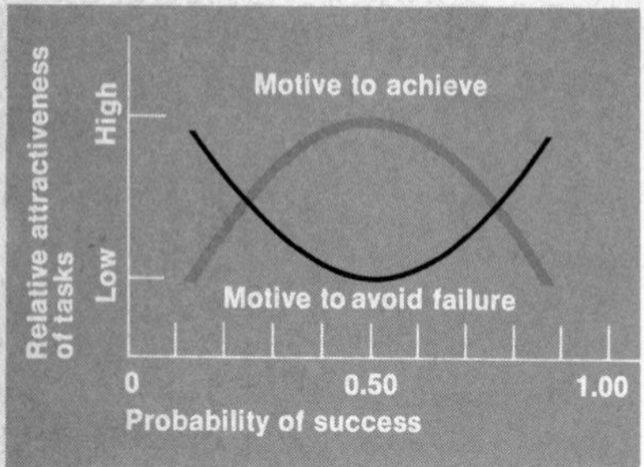

TASKS OF MODERATE DIFFICULTY ARE MOST ATTRACTIVE TO PERSONS WITH HIGH ACHIEVEMENT NEED AND LEAST ATTRACTIVE TO THOSE WITH HIGH FEAR OF FAILURE

Figure 6.14 *A strong motive to achieve makes tasks with moderate probability of success more attractive than very easy tasks (no challenge) or very hard ones (too little chance for achievement). But a strong motive to avoid failure leads to avoidance of the middle range of difficulty, because this is where the person can be compared with high achievers. The motive to achieve is the dominant motive; the motive to avoid failure modifies but does not replace it. (Adapted from Atkinson and Feather, 1966.)*

range of difficulty is there both a reasonable chance of success and enough challenge to provide some feeling of achievement. This idea is depicted in Figure 6.14 by the colored curve, which indicates that the motive to achieve makes tasks with moderate probability of success (abscissa) more attractive (ordinate) than tasks of either low or high probability of success. This is the theoretical curve that corresponds to Figure 6.13's highly peaked curve obtained for a group with high achievement motivation and low fear of failure.

But as the black curve shows in Figure 6.14, the motive to avoid failure produces a curve of attractiveness for tasks of different difficulty which is just opposite to that for achievement motivation. If a person who fears failure chooses difficult tasks with low probability of success, he will do about as badly as anyone else. Thus failure on such a task is not really failure compared with the performance of other people. He can also minimize fear of failure by choosing easy tasks on which the chances of success are high. It is the middle range of difficulties that he tends to avoid, because this is the zone where comparisons with high achievers can be drawn. To fail on a task for which the chances of comparative achievement are greatest is indeed failure.

We can assume further that fear of failure is always *mixed* with some need for achievement. Even those scoring *relatively* low in achievement need in our society, particularly those at the college level, have considerable achievement motivation. Thus the dominant tendency in choosing risks would be that given by the colored curve for "motive to achieve" in Figure 6.14. The motive to avoid failure would simply modify this dominant tendency by spreading out the sharply peaked curve for achievement motivation. This is what we see in the curve for low-high subjects in Figure 6.13.

SOURCE OF ACHIEVEMENT MOTIVATION How does achievement motivation, high or low, develop in the normal adult? A substantial amount of research available on this question suggests the tentative answer that achievement motivation grows out of independence training in childhood. Independence training consists of parental demands for the child to do such things as standing up for one's rights, knowing one's way around town, going out to play, and trying things for oneself.

One source of evidence on this point comes from cross-cultural studies. We can evaluate the relative importance of achievement need in various societies or ethnic groups and correlate this with child-rearing practices (McClelland et al., 1955). The folk tales of several North American Indian tribes, for example, were analyzed to obtain a score on achievement need for each tribe. Patterns of child rearing were then studied to determine how much emphasis each tribe placed on early and severe independence training. It was found that the two measures correlated. Another ethnic study focused on religious groups with different achievement need scores. In this study Catholics had lower scores on the average than either Protestants or Jews did, and surveys of parents showed that Protestants and Jews expected their children to acquire certain elements of independence training earlier than Catholic parents did.

More direct evidence comes from studies of parents of individuals high and low in achievement need (McClelland et al., 1953). In one experiment it was found that an overall rating of the *severity* of upbringing (the amount of independence expected of the child), which was derived from evaluations by subjects, agreed moderately with their achievement need scores. In another study, college students who saw their parents as distant, unfriendly, or severe had higher achievement need scores than students who saw their parents as close, loving, and helpful. An interviewer who rated the mothers of 29 eight-year-old boys on independence training found that these ratings correlated with the children's achievement need scores (Winterbottom, 1958). The number of demands made by the mothers was not so important as how *early* they were made.

The link between independence training and achievement need is not too hard to see. Independence itself is a kind of achievement. Through exhortation, reward, praise, and probably some punishment, parents can teach children habits of mastering challenging tasks.

Affiliation need By and large, human beings are gregarious. Most of their waking hours are spent with other people—parents, family, friends, neighbors, club members, and so on. Modern society, of course, throws people together in work, entertainment, and living; but it does not cause these affiliative tendencies. People in primitive societies are also gregarious. And almost all human beings seek the company of others even when there is no particular pressure to do so.

Students of human motivation consider affiliation to be a need that can vary in strength like other needs. Using methods similar to those for scoring achievement need on the TAT, they have developed keys for rating people on the affiliation motive according to their responses to TAT pictures. Beyond that, little has been done with the TAT to analyze either the source or the operation of affiliation need. Some interesting work, however, has been done with situational tests in which the simple measure of affiliation need is whether a person chooses to be with other people or wishes to remain by himself. The following study used this technique and linked affiliation to fear (Schachter, 1959).

Two groups of girls, none of whom knew each other, served as subjects. When they came to the experimental room, they were met by a man calling himself Dr. Gregor Zilstein, who was surrounded with an impressive array of equipment. The doctor gave a brief lecture on the importance of electric shock in research, and then told one group of girls (called the high-anxiety group) that they would receive painful, but not harmful, shock. He told the other group (called the low-anxiety group) that they would receive mild tickling shock. He explained that there would be a short delay before the experiment began, and that they could either wait alone or wait in a nearby classroom with other girls. First, however, he asked them to answer a questionnaire measuring their anxiety about shock and registering their preference for waiting alone or with other girls. The girls were then offered the choice of leaving (without credit) or of remaining for the experiment. After each had given her decision—and before the promised delay—the experiment ended, with Dr. Zilstein explaining its purpose.

These were the results: About a third of the girls in the high-anxiety group refused to continue the experiment, but none in the other did. This seemed to indicate that high anxiety had in fact been created in one group and not in the other. As for the measure of affiliation need, 20 of the 32 girls in the high-anxiety group chose to wait with other girls, whereas only 10 of the 30 girls in the low-anxiety group did. Thus anxiety level made a significant difference in their choice.

The interpretation of the experiment is obvious: anxiety is an important factor in the affiliation motive. Other experiments along the same line confirm this relationship. Whether it is the only factor is not known at the present; all we can say is that anxiety increases the tendency to affiliate. It may be that when anxiety is felt in a situation where the company of other people is available, the anxiety has become a learned cue for seeking companionship.

Approval motive Another social motive that has received considerable study is the need for the social approval of others (Crowne and Marlowe, 1964). Almost any personality test, whether the TAT or pencil-and-paper tests, reveals a person's desire, weak or strong, to behave in ways that are socially acceptable. A number of scales measure this need, but one developed specifically for extensive research on the approval motive is the Marlowe-Crowne Social Desirability Scale.

When ratings on this scale are correlated with the results of other tests and with behavior in experimental situations, a picture of the approval-dependent person emerges. He is more favorable than most toward tasks set by others, even when the tasks are dull. He is more socially conforming, and more susceptible to persuasion. He tends to give more conventional associations in a word-association task, and he is more cautious in risk-taking situations. He is, finally, more likely to seek affiliation than the person scoring lower on social desirability. To sum up, the person with a high need for social approval depends on such approval for a feeling of self-esteem. Thus the approval motive stands between an affiliation motive on one side and a need for status on the other.

Status The motive for status or power is a need that has been recognized in the TAT system of scoring. But these power need scores have been used mainly in clinical counseling; little has been done with them in research. In lieu of solid research findings, we must fall back on more general observations.

Most people are motivated to achieve some status among their fellowmen. At its minimum, this motive consists of a need to be thought well of, to have a respectable standing among the people one knows, and not to be considered inferior. At its maximum, it can be a desire to achieve the highest possible status in one's community, in one's profession, or in some other frame of reference. In the middle ranges, this motive is a desire to recognize just where one stands in the status system, to know who is up and who is down, and to behave accordingly. Status systems vary from one group to another. A person's particular status motives depend not only on his own personality, but also on the group he happens to be in.

Status motives may take several different forms. One is the desire to achieve a *rank* in the hierarchy of the group. Efforts to attain such a rank can be observed not only among members of the rigidly stratified military profession but also in most human groups. It has also been observed in groups of animals living together (Schjelderup-Ebbe, 1935). Common barnyard hens, for example, quickly establish a "pecking order" among themselves. The most dominant hen pecks most of the other hens. The least dominant hen, on the other hand, is pecked by all other hens but has no pecking rights of her own. In between, in relatively fixed rank, are hens which can peck those below them but not those above.

Such a pattern of pecking and ranking is almost universal in human relationships. We see it in groups of children playing together, in the sizes and furnishings of businessmen's offices, in the seating of guests at a formal luncheon, and in numerous details of everyday life.

Other closely related examples of status motives are those for prestige and for power. The need for *prestige* is the need to feel better than other persons with whom one compares oneself. In daily life there are many ways in which prestige is sought and achieved. Children of 5 or 6 may consider a pair of roller skates, a new dress, or a cowboy suit a symbol of prestige. A little later, athletic skill becomes a way of achieving prestige. Among adults such symbols as dress, money, automobiles, and homes are regarded as ways of feeling better than the other fellow.

The need for *power* is similar to, but not quite the same thing as, the need for prestige. Some people shun or ignore prestige, yet aspire to power over their fellowmen. Think, for example, of the businessman who quietly and inconspicuously builds up an industrial empire; or consider the professional politician who holds no public office but "pulls the strings" that move the officeholder. Such individuals display a desire for status, but in a different way from those who aspire to achieve prestige.

Each group, community, and society, whether primitive or modern, has its own status system. How such a system arises and what function it serves are discussed in Chapter 14. So far as the individual is concerned, status is a secondary goal that stands for the satisfaction of many primary motives. Persons of a particular status can expect to make a certain amount of money, live in a certain style, and be treated in certain ways. Thus status more or less guarantees that an individual may be able to satisfy other motives. It also frees a person from the fear that he might lose some of the satisfactions that go with his status.

Aggression The tendency to fight or aggress can be measured by any of the three general methods used for the other social motives—that is, by projective tests, personality inventories, and situational tests. Systems for scoring aggression have been worked out for the TAT (Lindzey and Kalnins, 1958) and for another projective test, the Rorschach (Buss, 1961). Inventories have also been constructed with such items as "If somebody hits me first, I let him have it," and "I never get mad enough to throw things" (Buss, 1961). Aggression in children can be measured by putting them in a doll-play situation. From such measures employed in systematic research, a certain amount has been learned about the sources of aggression.

Because man always finds himself at war somewhere, and because violence and aggression are common problems in many societies, it is often asserted that aggression is instinctive. Psychologists find no basis for this claim—at least, not in its blunt form. True, animals vary greatly in aggressiveness, from relative tameness to extreme savageness (page 52), and these differences have a hereditary basis. People also have measurable temperamental differences in aggressiveness. Nonetheless, there is no evidence that aggression is a motive, like hunger or sex, which demands satisfaction. Rather, research has demonstrated that it is a reaction or response to certain kinds of situations (Cofer and Appley, 1964; Berkowitz, 1968).

First, aggression is a response to *frustration,* such as the thwarting of efforts or the loss of goal objects. This conclusion emerged from extensive experiments with children, and at one time psychologists felt that frustration was the only source of aggression (Dollard et al., 1939). We now know that there are others as well, but that frustration is one circumstance which sometimes, though not always, provokes aggression (Appley, 1962). If you take a toy away from a child or a bone away from a dog, you will probably elicit an aggressive response. If you have a frustrating day, you will tend to become more irritable, and more likely to "fly off the handle."

Second, aggression is often a reaction to *injury, insults,* or *threats.* A dog or cat quickly becomes angry if we pinch its tail. In human experiments, the most dependable way to elicit aggression is by insults or attack (Buss, 1961).

Third, aggression is a reaction to *deprivation.* Animals do most of their fighting over or about food. In the ecology of the jungle, the only way meat-eating animals survive is by killing to obtain food. Thus aggression is a means of satisfying primary drives; in other words, it is reinforced as an instrumental response. The same is true of much human aggression: warring Indians, as well as the plundering Vikings and the Romans, fought mainly to get things they wanted. Many crimes of violence today are committed for the same reason.

These three general types of situations that arouse aggression are frequent in daily life. For one reason or another, we have all had hundreds of occasions to be angry. The question, then, is whether we develop a need for aggression as a result of these experiences. The answer is probably no. Rather, through learning we may develop overly aggressive responses to various stimuli. Aggression, like fear, is easily conditioned, and conditioned stimuli generalize (page 73). If a child has come to hate his father, he may, through generalization, react with hostility to all authority figures. Frustrating situations may generalize in a similar way. Moreover, if aggression has proved an effective means of getting what one wants, it may become a habitual way of reacting to satisfy other motives.

There is one sense in which aggression may serve as a short-term need (Buss, 1961). Aggression in our society is frequently punished, so that it cannot always be expressed. We dare not aggress against some people and in some situations. In these circumstances, hostility can simmer and linger on, and we may develop a need for *catharsis.* Blowing off at somebody or something, even if it is not at the "correct" object, seems to vent the aggression. However, this is not the same thing as a continuing or recurrent need for aggression.

Cognitive dissonance A kind of human motivation which is usually, but not always, social is known as discrepancy, or more commonly *dissonance,* motivation. The idea is that the perception of a discrepancy is motivating, and that we attempt to reduce the discrepancy somehow. The most dramatic illustration of dissonance as a motive is the strange behavior of a religious cult that had predicted the end of the world (Festinger et al., 1956).

The members of the cult believed that on a certain hour of a particular day, God would begin to destroy the world with earthquakes and floods. A few of the faithful, however, would be picked up and saved by flying saucers. The cult gathered to wait for the event. As the hour approached and passed, nothing happened. They checked their watches in disbelief, became distraught, and then fell despondent for several hours. They were experiencing the dissonance of the contradiction between what they had predicted and what had (or had not) happened.

Several hours later, the leader of the group (a woman) rose and excitedly announced that she had found the explanation. God had told her that He had saved the world because of what the group had done; their action had spread faith around the world. The group's behavior changed drastically. They started singing, called in the wire services, and announced the good news. By constructing an "explanation," they had eliminated the dissonance of contradiction between their beliefs and the failure of the world to end.

Many experiments have been done to test the dissonance motive, and it holds up fairly well (Brehm and Cohen, 1962). In fact, cognitive dissonance is an important concept in understanding attitude change. For that reason, it will be discussed further, and in more detail, in Chapter 15.

Synopsis and summary

Perhaps you noticed the many references to other chapters in this chapter on motivation, and perhaps you realized that it is because motivation is a central concept in psychology. Motives develop through maturation, so we need to know something about the principles of growth and maturation. Motives are learned, so we need to know about learning and some of the phenomena of learning. Motives and emotions are closely related because emotional states are motivating—they energize behavior and direct it toward or away from situations.

Motives are extremely important in personality. In the first place, the strengths and kinds of motives differ from person to person. The description of these differences comprises a large part of the characterization of personality. In the second place, motives conflict with each other and so produce frustration, and the reactions of an individual to frustration —his defenses, for example—are an important part of the description of personality.

Motives are learned in a cultural setting, and different cultural groups stress different motives. So an appreciation of cultural differences is important in the study of motivation. Some motives are the result of activity in specific parts of the central nervous system—the hypothalamus, for example—so knowledge of the anatomy and physiology of the central nervous system is necessary for understanding some physiological motives.

It should be apparent that an introductory textbook like this could be organized around the topic of motivation. References to motivation occur again and again throughout the book. We have simply introduced some basic points about motivation in this chapter.

1. Motivation can be represented as a cycle consisting of three parts: (*a*) a motive that arouses (*b*) instrumental behavior, which leads in turn to (*c*) a goal that satisfies the motive. (Sometimes the term need is used in place of motive.)
2. Motives can be divided into those with a physiological basis, general unlearned motives, and social motives.
3. Physiological processes within the body tend to maintain a balance called homeostasis. When this balance is disturbed, the resulting physiological need arouses regulatory behavior (such as seeking food, water, or a mate), which eventually restores the balance.
4. Motives such as hunger and thirst appear to depend upon chemical conditions in the body. Food preferences result partly from body needs. Aversions develop when an organism is satiated with one kind of food, or when it is given foods deficient in important essentials. These aversions cause the organism to prefer novel foods and in this way to obtain a balanced diet.
5. In lower animals, sexual motives depend on sex hormones. But in human beings, learning is very important, and these motives can exist in the absence of hormones. Eating and drinking are also affected by learning.
6. General bodily activity increases when a motive, such as hunger or sex, is present. Activity is also a motive in its own right. It is satisfied by opportunities for exercise, and it serves as the basis for learning new responses.
7. Interest in novel stimulation has been called the curiosity motive. Closely related to it is a need for sensory stimulation and stimulus change. A manipulative motive may be aroused by the opportunity to manipulate objects. Both curiosity and manipulation may serve as motivation for learning new responses.
8. An affectional motive for "contact comfort" with a motherlike object appears to be unlearned. Its satisfaction can alleviate fear and support the motive of curiosity.
9. The need to exercise one's potentialities—to do what one can do and to experience what can be experienced—encompasses the general motives. It has been called an effectance or competence motive.
10. Secondary goals are learned goals. Secondary *negative* goals (fears) can be learned through classical conditioning and serve to motivate avoidance learning in many new situations. Such secondary negative goals extinguish slowly. Secondary *positive* goals, such as money, can be acquired by connecting them with the reinforcement of other motives. Such goals rapidly extinguish unless they are repeatedly reinforced.
11. Motivation in human beings often involves a convergence of goals. Several motives may be satisfied by the same goal, and vice versa
12. Social motives can be measured by projective techniques, by inventories, or by situational tests. Of these, projective tests have been used most in research on social motivation.
13. The social motive most thoroughly studied is achievement need. The strength of this need correlates with intelligence, with academic performance, and with performance on various tests.
14. Need for achievement is opposed by fear of failure. In risk-taking situations, persons high in achievement need prefer intermediate risks in which the chances of success and failure are about equal. Persons high in fear of failure, however, frequently choose very easy or very difficult tasks.
15. Need for achievement seems to be the result of early independence training. Children who are expected to do things on their own at an early age develop a strong need for achievement.
16. Need for affiliation is linked to fear, for persons often seek the company of others when they are afraid. A need for social approval is reflected in conforming behavior; it represents a dependency on others for one's self-esteem. A family of motives revolving around dominance, power, status, and prestige can be recognized.
17. Aggression is not an inborn motive but rather a reaction to frustrating circumstances or to situations in which the organism is threatened or insulted. It also can be reinforced by the satisfaction of other motives.
18. A dissonance or discrepancy between two perceived facts can be motivating. When faced with such dissonances, a person attempts in some way to reduce the discrepancy.

Related topics in the text

Chapter 3 Principles of Learning The principles of classical and operant conditioning are especially important in the learning of motives.

Chapter 7 Arousal, Emotion, and Conflict Since emotions can serve as motives, this is a logical chapter to read next.

Chapter 11 Personality Many theories of personality—Freudian theory, for example—are basically motivational theories.

Chapters 17 and 19 in Part Five, Biology of Behavior The roles of the internal environment and the nervous system in motivation are detailed.

Suggestions for further reading

Atkinson, J. W. *An introduction to motivation.* New York: Van Nostrand Reinhold, 1964. *A scholarly analysis of motivation emphasizing the theory of human motivation.*

Atkinson, J. W., and Feather, N. T. (Eds.) *A theory of achievement motivation.* New York: Wiley, 1966. *The application of a theoretical model to many phenomena of achievement motivation.*

Berkowitz, L. (Ed.) *Roots of aggression.* New York: Atherton, 1968. *A symposium summarizing studies on the sources of aggression.*

Berlyne, D. E. *Conflict, arousal, and curiosity.* New York: McGraw-Hill, 1960. *A compendium and systematic treatment of curiosity and exploration in motives.*

Bindra, D. *Motivation: A systematic reinterpretation.* New York: Ronald, 1960. *A textbook on motivation and theoretical analysis of the problems of motivation.*

Cofer, C. N., and Appley, M. H. *Motivation: Theory and research.* New York: Wiley, 1964. *A thorough summary of experiments in motivation from many areas of psychology.*

Crowne, D. P., and Marlowe, D. *The approval motive: Studies in evaluative dependence.* New York: Wiley, 1964. *An account of a series of studies showing differences between people high and low in need for social approval.*

Ford, C. S., and Beach, F. A. *Patterns of sexual behavior.* New York: Hoeber-Harper, 1951. (Paperback available.) *A good account of sexual motives and practices in animals and in different human societies.*

Fuller, J. L. *Motivation: A biological perspective.* New York: Random House, 1962. (Paperback.) *An easily read account of motivation, with special emphasis on the physiological motives.*

Jones, M. R. (Ed.) *Nebraska symposium on motivation.* Lincoln, Nebr.: University of Nebraska Press, 1953 to present. (Later editions by David Levine and W. J. Arnold.) (Paperbacks.) *Papers delivered at the Nebraska Symposium on Motivation have been collected into volumes each year since 1953. The papers cover most topics in the field of motivation—from physiological motivation to motivation in human personality.*

Morgan, C. T. *Physiological psychology.* (3d ed.) New York: McGraw-Hill, 1965. Chaps. 12, 13, 14. *A textbook summary of the physiological factors in motivation.*

Murray, E. J. *Motivation and emotion.* Englewood Cliffs, N.J.: Prentice-Hall, 1964. (Paperback.) *An elementary textbook on motivation which covers most of the important aspects of the subject.*

Rethlingshafer, D. *Motivation as related to personality.* New York: McGraw-Hill, 1963. *A summary of the experimental work on motivation.*

Young, P. T. *Motivation and emotion: A survey of the determinants of human and animal activity.* New York: Wiley, 1961. *A textbook covering various aspects of the topic of motivation.*

Emotion is both organizing
(making behavior more effective)
and disorganizing; it is both
energizing and debilitating.
D. O. Hebb

We civilized members of Western culture like to think of ourselves as rational beings who go about satisfying our motives in an intelligent way. To a certain extent we do that, but we are also emotional beings—more emotional than we often realize. Indeed, most of the affairs of everyday life are tinged with feeling and emotion. Joy and sorrow, excitement and disappointment, love and fear, hope and dismay—all these and many more are feelings we experience in the course of a day or week.

Without such feelings, life would be pretty dreary. Our feelings add color and spice to living; they are the sauce without which life would be dull fare. We anticipate with pleasure our parties and dates, we remember with a warm glow the satisfaction we got from giving a good speech, and we even recall with amusement the bitter disappointments of childhood. On the other hand, when our emotions are too intense and too easily aroused, they can get us into a good deal of trouble. They can warp our judgment, turn friends into enemies, and make us as miserable as if we were sick with fever.

Just what is emotion? It is many things at once. It is a state of behavioral arousal, varying from deep sleep to intense activity. It is also a physiological (or bodily) state that can be measured by physical means of several kinds. At the same time, it is an experience (something we feel) and an expression (exhibited by our posture and facial expression). Finally, as we saw in the last chapter, it is a motivating force determining what we strive for or try to avoid. In this chapter we shall study these different aspects of emotion. At the end, we shall extend some of the points made in earlier chapters on learning and motivation in order to see how emotion arises from frustration and conflict.

Sleep and Arousal

Physiologically the central dimension of emotion is a sleep-arousal dimension. Our most intense emotions occur only when we are highly aroused. At this end of the scale, the relationship between emotion and arousal is a two-way affair. Intense emotions cause a high level of arousal, or excitement, but a state of high arousal also makes it more likely that we will react to situations with intense emotions. When emotions cause arousal, they can prevent the relaxation necessary for sleep (an anxious person, for example, has trouble sleeping). For sleep, at the other end of the scale, is a state in which emotions are at their lowest ebb.

THE PUPILS ENLARGE WHEN A PERSON IS AROUSED BY AN INTERESTING PICTURE

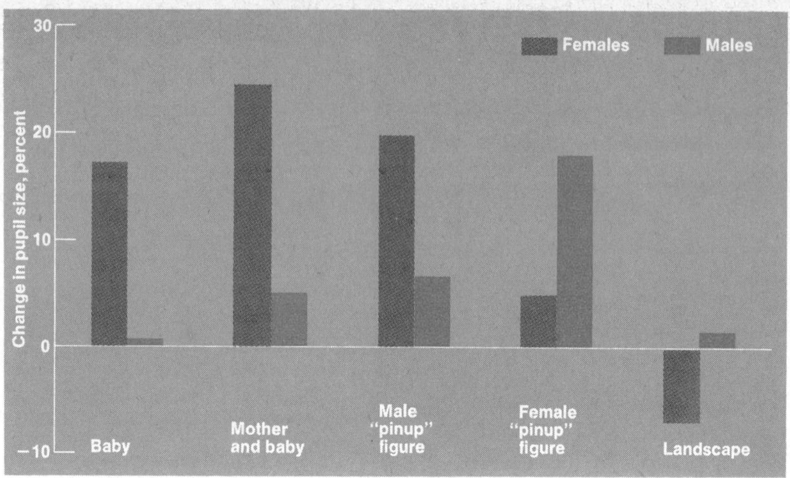

Figure 7.1 *Pupillary reactions in females and males to five pictures. Pictures most interesting to females (baby, mother and baby, and a male "pinup" figure) caused a sizable enlargement of the pupil, while the picture most interesting to males (a female "pinup" figure) evoked a similar reaction in them. (From Hess, 1965,* Scientific American.*)*

Stages in sleep and arousal We all know from our own experience that sleep varies in depth from drowsiness, a twilight zone between sleep and waking, to sound sleep from which it is difficult to arouse a person. For many years, the ease or difficulty of waking a person with some stimulus such as a sound was used as a measure of depth of sleep. More recently, however, we have learned that the *electroencephalogram* (EEG), which is a record of "brain waves," provides a good index of the state of sleep. This also has the advantage that it can be used without waking or disturbing the sleeping person. Hence the EEG has become our standard measure of depth of sleep. In addition, it can distinguish between states of arousal in awake persons, as we shall see later.

SLEEP Changes in the EEG with different stages of sleep are described in detail in Chapter 17. To summarize them briefly, the shifts occurring in the brain waves between the waking state and deep sleep are basically changes from one frequency to another. In the awake but relaxed person, the dominant frequency is 10 cycles per second—the alpha rhythm. In deep sleep, the frequency slows to 1 to 3 cycles per second—the delta rhythm. In between, we see mixtures of fast and slow waves.

There is an interesting exception to these general statements. It is *paradoxical* sleep. In this state, the person is in deep sleep by some standards, such as the difficulty of shaking him awake or waking him with a loud noise. Yet according to the EEG he is in light sleep—his brain waves show the typical faster waves that are characteristic of light sleep and waking. This stage is also known as REM sleep, because it is accompanied by rapid eye movements (REMs) not seen in the other stages of sleep (Chapter 17). REM sleep is the stage in which the most dreaming occurs. If a person is awakened when REMs are observed and when his EEG shows a mixture of fast and slow waves, the chances are very great that he will report dreaming. Apparently in this stage the brain is active, as it is in waking, but it is somehow cut off from the outside world.

AROUSAL The EEG also tells us something, at least in a crude way, about the state of arousal of a waking person. As mentioned above, the awake but relaxed subject typically has an EEG pattern in which the 10-per-second alpha rhythm is prominent. But if he is aroused in almost any way—startled by a loud sound, presented with a visual stimulus, given a problem to solve, or required to put his attention to a stimulus or task—this EEG pattern gives way to an *activation* pattern. Such a pattern consists of fast, irregular waves; the regular activity of the relaxed state is blocked out. Hence we can tell from the EEG alone whether a person is relaxed or alerted.

To make somewhat finer distinctions between states of arousal, a number of other measures can be used: heart rate, blood pressure, breathing rate, skin conductance, or pupil size. (These will be discussed in more detail later, when we consider bodily states in emotion.) Two out of this list provide good measures of state of arousal in the awake person. One is skin conductance. If a small amount of electricity—it is so small that a person cannot feel it—is passed across an area of the skin (usually the palm of the hand), the resistance to the flow decreases (conductance increases) as a person becomes more alert and aroused. Another good measure of arousal is changes in pupil size, as illustrated by the following experiment (Hess and Polt, 1960):

Male and female subjects were individually shown a series of pictures, most of which had been chosen to interest one sex more than the other. The set included pictures of a baby, a mother and a baby, a male "pinup" figure, a female "pinup" figure, and a (more neutral) landscape picture. While the subjects viewed the pictures, pupil size was measured photographically with a camera that snapped pictures at intervals of two per second. Similar measurements were made during a control period just before the pictures were shown, so that the changes in pupil size which were caused by the pictures could be determined.

Sample results are given in Figure 7.1. Three of the pictures (a baby, mother and baby, and a male "pinup" figure) caused a sizable dilation of the pupils in female subjects, while the two others caused little dilation, or even constriction. (The fact that uninteresting or unpleasant pictures can evoke constriction has been confirmed in other experiments.) In contrast, the pupils of male subjects widened in viewing female "pinups" but showed less change for other pictures. The differences obtained here are just what one would expect from the respective interest, or arousal, values of the pictures for the two sexes.

The physiological basis for this result is known, as we shall see later. The point here is that alerting or arousal reactions are expressed in pupillary enlargement. This occurs with all sorts of "interesting" stimuli (Hess, 1968). In homosexuals, the pupils widen more in response to homosexual than to heterosexual pictures. People show pupil dilation when given a task to solve, when looking at other people with large pupils (see Figure 7.2), and when presented with almost any stimulus that can be considered interesting or arousing. Pupil responses can even be used to measure the interest value of an advertisement.

ORIENTING REACTION Another indication of arousal in both humans and animals is the *orienting reaction,* which has been studied a great

Figure 7.2 *Which photograph do men like better? The pictures are identical except that the girl's pupils were retouched to make them larger in the one at left and smaller in the one at right. In an experiment on attitudes and pupil size which employed similar photos, most of the male subjects responded much more strongly to the photo with the larger pupils. Some said one picture was "prettier" or "softer" than the other, but none noticed the differences in pupil size. (Hess, 1965,* Scientific American; *Camera Clix.)*

deal by Russian investigators. This, as the term implies, is an organism's orientation to a new stimulus or to a stimulus change. The orientation consists of tensing muscles and of changing the position of the body and the head in order to maximize the effectiveness of the stimulus. The exact nature of the orienting reaction depends on the stimulus, the species of organism, its age, its present state of arousal, and other factors. A cat seeing the slightest movement of something readies itself to pounce on whatever it is. A dog hearing the faintest sound of another dog perks up its ears, stands at attention, and makes ready to defend its territory. An infant turns his head and eyes toward any novel stimulus, such as a toy or strange face.

The orienting reaction stands at the intersection of several concepts already discussed in this and earlier chapters. First of all, it is a *reflex* response to novelty. What is novel depends on both unlearned tendencies and previous learning, but the response itself is basically unlearned. Secondly, it is linked to *attention;* in fact, one might say that it is a form of attention in which the organism focuses on novelty. Thirdly, it is a link with curiosity motivation; it is a reaction of "What is it?" that readies the organism for exploration of any further changes in stimulus conditions. Finally, it is an indication of arousal that primes the organism to respond more speedily and more vigorously to whatever follows. In this sense, the orienting reaction is an increased motivation to respond to conditions in the environment.

Arousal and motivation We have already said that arousal is a central dimension of emotion, for whatever the emotion, its intensity is proportional to the level of arousal. Let us extend this statement to say that arousal is a basic dimension of motivation. Various motives have different goals—food, water, exploration, etc.—but they have in common an arousal of the organism. The more intense the motive, the higher the level of arousal.

This common dimension of various motives is important in many theories of behavior, although the names and the meaning given to it vary with the theorist and the kinds of behavior he wishes to explain. In one major learning theory (see page 104), general level of arousal is called drive level and is considered one of the two general factors determining the probability or intensity of a response (the other is habit strength). In this theory the particular drive or motive operating is a matter of detail; the important dimension of motivation is the drive or arousal level. In many theories of emotion, arousal level is regarded as the common dimension of emotion (Cofer and Appley, 1964.) As we shall see later, the level of arousal is the common dimension in the classification of emotional expression. And in theories of human motivation, it is the arousal level (of, say, an achievement motive) that is used as a measure of the strength of the motive (McClelland et al., 1953). Thus arousal level is often regarded as the central aspect of motivation, whether it be emotional motivation, physiological motivation, or any other kind.

Arousal and performance How is arousal, or general drive level, related to performance? You might think offhand that the more aroused a person is, the better he can perform various tasks; and this is generally true. Many years ago, psychologists found that increasing a subject's tension level by having him squeeze something very hard aided his performance on such tasks as memorizing, adding columns of figures, and naming letters (Bills, 1927). In animal studies too it has been found, as would be predicted from Hull-Spence learning theory (page 104), that increased arousal produced by severe deprivation of motives improves performance in learning situations. In general we can say that for animals and human beings, increasing arousal is accompanied by improved performance in all sorts of tasks, from learning a maze to solving complex mental problems.

However, there is an important exception: very intense emotion may *impair* performance, as illustrated by the following anecdote (adapted from Schlosberg, 1954):

A sleeping man is near the zero level of arousal. His brain is relatively inactive, his muscles relaxed, and the sympathetic part of his nervous system (discussed in the next section) is functioning at a low level. In this state, he does not respond to most stimuli. But now the alarm clock rings, waking him up and thus markedly raising his level of arousal. His muscles become active, his eyes open to visual stimuli, and his movements in bed or about the room all evoke the feedback of sensory impulses, which further increase his level of arousal.

Within an hour the subject has aroused to the point of functioning efficiently. He is alert and doing well at the things he has to do. Now, however, he looks for a book he cannot find. This frustration further arouses him to the point of being slightly irritated. He continues to hunt for the book without success. As the search goes on, he becomes more and more angry and thus even more highly aroused, eventually working himself into a "blind rage." In his present state he wouldn't be able to find the book even if it were under his nose.

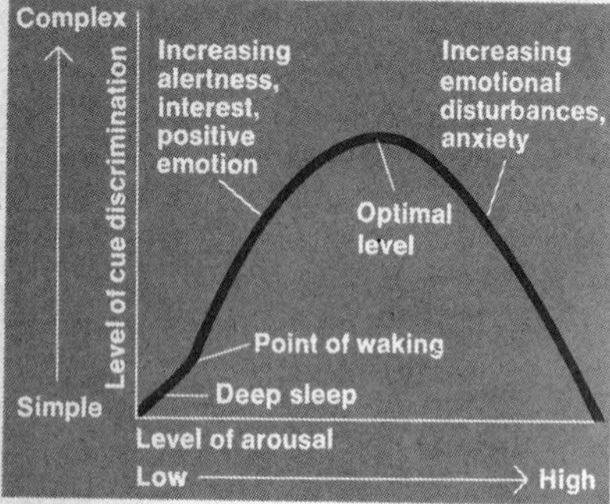

BEYOND AN OPTIMAL LEVEL, EMOTIONAL AROUSAL IMPAIRS PERFORMANCE IN MOST TASKS

Figure 7.3 *The inverted U-shaped relationship between efficiency of functioning and level of emotional arousal. Up to a certain level of arousal, the ability to respond correctly to cues—that is, to perform well—improves. Beyond that level, further arousal increasingly hampers performance. This relationship is usually found in all but the simplest tasks that require undiscriminating cue responses. (Modified from Hebb, 1955.)*

This general point has been amply confirmed in research, but it must be refined to be correctly understood. It is not true of simple tasks requiring stereotyped, undiscriminated responses: an angry man can lift as much weight or run as fast as, if not faster than, a mildly annoyed one. It is when a person must discriminate among cues, or do appropriate things at different times, that intense emotion impairs performance. Formally stated, the principle is that performance is an inverted U-shaped function of level of arousal when cues must be discriminated. As represented in Figure 7.3, ability to respond correctly to cues is low, but not entirely lacking, in the low-arousal state of sleep. The ability increases with rising arousal up to an optimal level. Thereafter, as the person becomes more intensely disturbed (aroused), his performance declines. The epigraph at the beginning of this chapter expresses the same point in another way: "Emotion is both organizing (making behavior more effective) and disorganizing; it is both energizing and debilitating" (Hebb, 1966).

A practical example was given in Chapter 4 on human learning. There we saw that students who had a very high level of anxiety usually did not do as well in their college studies as students with low anxiety. The general principle for tasks of any great difficulty is that a certain amount of emotional motivation is good, but too much of it impairs performance.

Physiological Changes in Emotion

As the nervous system increases its activity from states of deep sleep to those of intense emotion, certain definite physiological changes occur. Everyone has noticed some of them at times when he has been excited, terrified, or enraged, but he was probably not aware of all of them. These changes can be studied in two general ways: (1) by asking people who have experienced intense emotion what they felt; (2) by making direct physiological measurements of the changes. One example of the first method was a survey of individuals who had suffered intense fear (Shaffer, 1947):

The study used about 4,000 airmen who flew in combat in World War II. As can be seen in Table 7.1, they were asked to say whether they "often" or "sometimes" experienced certain symptoms while flying combat missions. A wide variety of bodily changes was included in the list of symptoms: pounding heart, tense muscles, dry mouth, "cold sweat," need to urinate, and nausea.

Direct physiological measurements, the second and more objective method of studying bodily changes in emotion, reveal an even wider variety of changes, as we shall see.

Table 7.1 *Percent of men reporting various bodily symptoms of fear in combat flying. Over 4,000 fliers in World War II were included in this survey.*

Source: After Shaffer, 1947.

Symptom	Often	Sometimes	Total
Pounding heart and rapid pulse	30	56	86
Muscles very tense	30	53	83
Easily irritated, angry, or "sore"	22	58	80
Dryness of the throat or mouth	30	50	80
"Nervous perspiration" or "cold sweat"	26	53	79
"Butterflies" in the stomach	23	53	76
Sense of unreality, that this couldn't be happening	20	49	69
Need to urinate very frequently	25	40	65
Trembling	11	53	64
Confused or rattled	3	50	53
Weak or faint	4	37	41
After mission, not being able to remember details of what happened	5	34	39
Sick to the stomach	5	33	38
Not being able to concentrate	3	32	35

Autonomic changes From physiological studies we know that many of the bodily changes which occur in emotion are initiated by a part of the nervous system called the *autonomic system* (see Figure 7.4). They are therefore called autonomic changes.

The autonomic system consists of many nerves leading from the brain and spinal cord out to the smooth muscles of the various organs of the body (see Chapter 17), to the heart, certain glands, and to the blood vessels serving both the interior and exterior of the body. The autonomic system has two parts which often, but not always, work in opposition to each other. One part, the *sympathetic system*, increases the heart rate and blood pressure and distributes blood to the exterior muscles. It is this part which is activated when we become emotional—or at least, when we become fearful or angry. The other part of the system, called the *parasympathetic system,* tends to be active when we are calm and relaxed. It does many things that, taken together, build up and conserve the body's stores of energy. For example, it decreases the heart rate, reduces the blood pressure, and diverts blood to the digestive tract.

This is an oversimplified account of the functions of the two systems. The parasympathetic system can, in certain instances, be active in emotion. Indeed, it usually increases in activity whenever the sympathetic system does.

When the sympathetic part of the autonomic system steps up its discharges, as it does in some emotional states, it produces several symptoms that are worth noting. One set concerns the circulation of the blood. In fear, for instance, the blood vessels serving the stomach, intestines, and interior of the body tend to contract, while those serving the exterior muscles of the trunk and limbs tend to become larger. In this way, blood is diverted from digestive functions to muscular functions, and the body is prepared for action that may involve great muscular activity. At the same time, nervous impulses to the heart make it beat harder and faster,

THE AUTONOMIC NERVOUS SYSTEM, ESPECIALLY ITS SYMPATHETIC DIVISION, BECOMES MORE ACTIVE IN EXCITEMENT, FEAR, AND ANGER

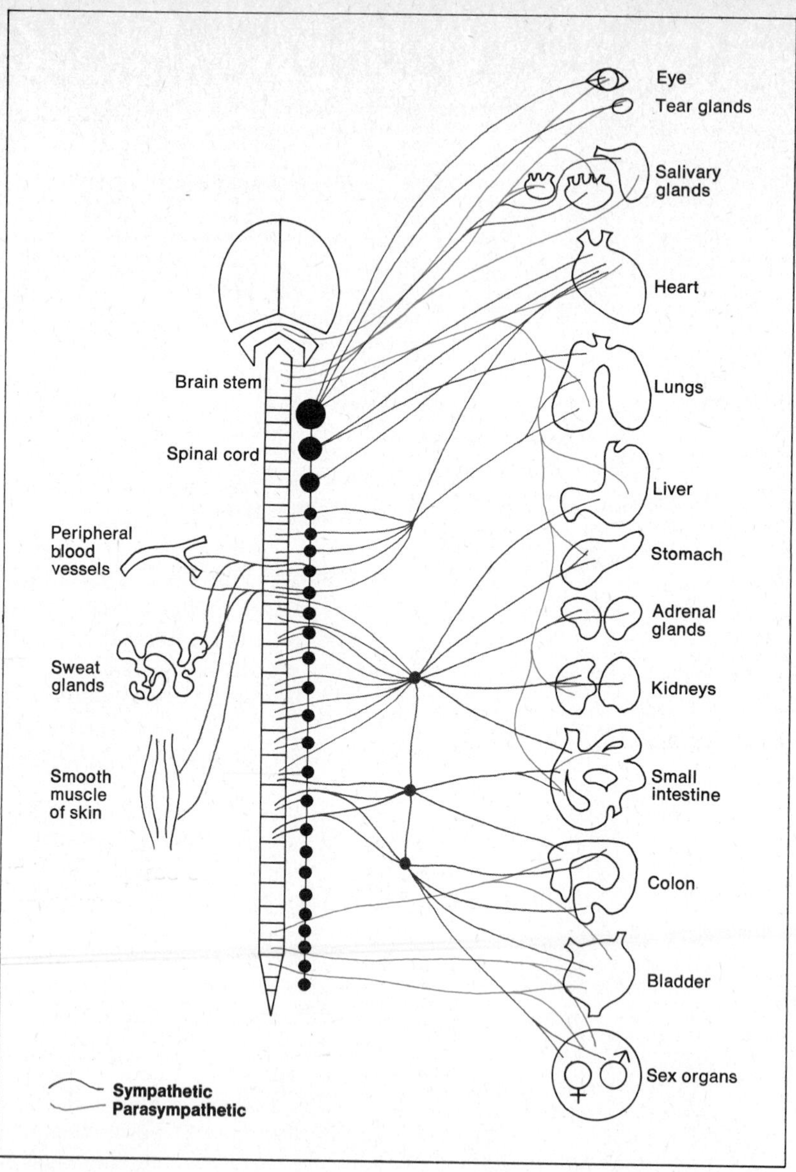

Figure 7.4 *Schematic diagram of the autonomic nervous system. The autonomic nervous system consists of nerves and ganglia, or collections of nerve cells, that serve blood vessels, glands, and other internal organs of the body. It has two main divisions: the parasympathetic system, shown in color, and the sympathetic system, shown in gray. The peripheral blood vessels, sweat glands, and smooth muscles of the skin are served by many parts of the sympathetic system besides those shown.*

the blood pressure goes up, and the pulse rate is quickened. Thus more blood is pumped through the circulatory system to the muscles.

Besides these changes in circulation, the sympathetic system produces several other bodily changes in fear. Perhaps you have noticed some of them yourself. One is a change in the size of the pupil of the eye, which is ordinarily regulated by the amount of light entering the eye. In fear (and arousal, as we saw above), the pupil becomes larger. Perhaps you have seen this if you have observed a fearful cat or person. Another change is a drying of the mouth. This occurs because the sympathetic system stops the secretion from the salivary glands, which ordinarily keeps the mouth moist. Still another is the change in the movements of the stomach and intestines. As can be seen in x-ray pictures, contractions of the stomach and intestines are stopped or reversed in strong emotion.

Another response of the sympathetic system in emotion is the discharge of the hormones *epinephrine* (adrenaline) and *norepinephrine* (noradrenaline). Nerve impulses in the sympathetic system which reach the adrenal glands, located on top of the kidneys, cause the secretion of these hormones. From this point, the hormones go into the blood and circulate around the body. Epinephrine affects many structures of the body. In the liver, it helps mobilize sugar into the blood and thus makes more energy available to the brain and muscles. Epinephrine also stimulates the heart to beat harder. (Surgeons use epinephrine to stimulate heart action when the heart has weakened or stopped.) In the skeletal muscles, epinephrine helps mobilize sugar resources so that the muscles can use them more rapidly. Thus epinephrine duplicates and strengthens many of the actions of the sympathetic system on various internal organs. The major effect of norepinephrine is to constrict peripheral blood vessels and thus raise blood pressure.

One other bodily change in emotion has been used extensively by psychologists in experiments on learning and personality—the change in the galvanic skin response (GSR), or skin conductance. A GSR shows up as a change in the resistance of the skin when a very small electrical current is passed through the skin. In emotional states, the GSR is a decrease in the resistance of the skin to the passage of electrical current.

Patterns of autonomic change In most experiments dealing with physiological changes in emotion the particular emotion studied has been fear, for it can be easily elicited by electric shock in the laboratory. But are there different patterns of physiological change in different emotional states?

In general, the answer is no. From time to time, however, investigators have reported very subtle differences between emotional states. Some remain to be verified, but one has been duplicated frequently. This is the phenomenon called *directional fractionation* (Lacey, 1967). In it, heart rate goes in a direction opposite to other changes such as skin conductance (GSR). Normally in sympathetic arousal they both increase, but in directional fractionation, they do not:

A task commonly used to elicit directional fractionation is one in which people are required to detect and note colors and patterns flashed before them. They are instructed to remember these stimuli for later recall. While watching the colors and patterns, subjects show deceleration (slowing) of heart rate while their skin conductance increases.

In another task, people are asked to listen to tape-recorded thoughts made by an actor portraying a man dying of injuries. Again their heart rate decelerates while skin conductance increases.

The common feature in these tasks and in others which induce directional fractionation is that the subject, although alert or aroused, is intent merely on listening and taking in external stimuli. If, on the other hand, he must actively react in some way—physically, or even with mental activity, such as solving arithmetic problems—the usual sympathetic pattern of increased heart rate and increased skin conductance occurs.

Although such differences in the pattern of autonomic change can be demonstrated, it seems unlikely that most variations in mood, arousal, or emotion are accompanied by differences in bodily states which can be detected by the person experiencing the emotion. If so, research to date has not revealed them. Also, the pattern in emotion varies markedly from individual to individual. Each person shows similar patterns of autonomic response to a wide variety of stressing situations (Lacey, 1967).

Theories of emotion Although the relationship between bodily states and emotions is not clear, various theories have been proposed concerning its nature.

JAMES-LANGE THEORY This theory proposes the following sequence of events in emotional states. First, we perceive the situation which will produce the emotion; next, we react to this situation; and finally, we notice our reaction. The perception of the reaction is the basis of emotional experience. Note that the emotional experience occurs *after* the bodily change: the bodily states (internal changes or overt movements) precede the emotion which is felt. As William James has succinctly put it: "We feel sorry because we cry, angry because we strike, afraid because we tremble" (James, 1890).

EMERGENCY THEORY In contrast to the James-Lange theory, the emergency theory holds that the bodily states in emotion are simultaneous with emotional feeling (Cannon, 1927, 1929). They do not cause the felt emotion—the emotional feeling and the felt emotion occur together. This theory states that sensory input initiated by the emotion-producing external situation triggers nerve cells in certain lower parts of the brain. Activity from these areas of the brain is then fed in two directions: to the cerebral cortex, where the activity of the lower brain centers is received and felt as emotion; and to the body structures, where the changes characteristic of emotion occur. Thus in the emergency theory the physiological states are the bodily expression of the activity of the lower brain centers. They prepare the person or animal for emergency reactions—"flight" or "fight." Some of the lower centers of the brain which are important in emotion are discussed in Chapters 17 and 19.

COGNITIVE THEORY This theory, which has some affinities with the James-Lange theory, states that the emotion which we feel is our interpretation of the stirred-up bodily states (Schachter and Singer, 1962). The basic idea is that the bodily state of emotional arousal is much the same for many different emotions, and that even when there are physiological differences, they cannot be sensed. This means that the autonomic changes described above are ambiguous, and any number of emotional feelings might be felt from very similar bodily states. We then interpret and label—or have cognitions about—the physiological state; we experience the emotion which seems appropriate to the situation in which we find ourselves. The sequence of events in the production of emotional feeling, according to this theory, is (1) perception of the emotion-producing situation, (2) a stirred-up bodily state which is ambiguous, and (3) interpretation and labeling of the bodily state so that it fits the perceived situation.

Imagine a man walking alone down a dark alley; a figure with a gun suddenly appears. The perception-cognition "figure-with-a-gun" in some fashion initiates a state of physiological arousal; this state of arousal is interpreted in terms of knowledge about dark alleys and guns and the state of arousal is labeled "fear." Similarly a student who unexpectedly learns that he has made Phi Beta Kappa may experience a state of arousal which he will label "joy." (Schachter and Singer, 1962, page 380.)

This theory has led to some interesting experiments. Suppose that a physiological state could be induced by drugs and that the situation could be changed to elicit different interpretations of the same physiological state from different subjects. They would then have different thoughts—cognitions—about the same physiological state, and their emotional feelings should be different if the theory is correct. This sort of experiment is done informally every day with a common drug—ethyl alcohol or, to be plainer, booze. The emotional feeling of a person who has had a few drinks varies markedly with the situation in which he finds himself. Presumably the physiological state is about the same, but the interpretation can be very different. If he is at a gay party, he may feel elated; if he is in a gloomy bar, he may feel depressed. A similar phenomenon has been noted with some of the experimental drugs which affect mood. Lysergic acid (LSD-25), for instance, produces different moods in the same individual. These may range from euphoria to fear and hostility. One important determiner of the differences in mood is the situation in which the drug is taken (see Chapter 19).

More precise evidence for the cognitive theory comes from controlled experiments such as this one (Schachter and Singer, 1962):

Male college students were the subjects, and the experimenters attempted to induce a state of physiological arousal by giving injections of epinephrine (adrenaline). The subjects were told, however, that they were receiving a vitamin compound.

In one part of the experiment, the subjects were not given any information about the effects which the injection would have; they were left free to interpret the mild state of physiological arousal as best they could. The next part of the experiment consisted of putting the subjects into two different situations: one designed to be happy, the other designed to be perceived as a situation which might give rise to anger. These situations were produced by a confederate of the experimenter, who put on two different acts. In the happy situation, he skylarked and fooled around according to a definite script. In the angry situation, he and the subject were given a questionnaire with many personal questions on it, and the confederate showed increasing irritation—again following a script—with the experiment and the experimenters as he answered the questions.

Thus subjects had the same states of physiological arousal, but they were exposed to situations about which they might be expected to have different cognitions. The main question was whether they would have different emotional feelings. These feelings were measured by having the subjects fill out rating scales of their moods.

The results showed that subjects who were not informed about the reason for their state of physiological arousal tended to feel the emotion and behave in ways appropriate to the situation in which they were placed. Subjects who had been informed that the injection would produce physiological effects interpreted the bodily state as due to the injection and did not tend to experience emotions appropriate to the perceived situation.

The cognitive theory of emotions seems, then, to be supported by both informal and experimental evidence. At least, it provides a way of accounting for the many emotional moods which may accompany very similar physiological states.

The "lie detector" The public hears a good deal about a "lie detector" that sometimes can be used to detect a person's guilt in a crime. This device makes use of several of the autonomic changes we have just described. Although there are several versions of the lie detector, it almost always measures blood pressure, respiration, and GSR. The use of such measurements to detect lying rests on the assumption that autonomic changes are not under voluntary control—that a person can lie and hide the overt expression of emotion, but cannot control the autonomic changes which accompany fear and anxiety.

In a lie-detection test, the subject is presented with words and questions carefully chosen to arouse emotion if he is guilty of lying, but to leave him unmoved if he is not. He is usually asked a series of questions while a record is made of his physiological responses. Some of the questions are "neutral"; they are routine items such as, What is your name? Where do you work? Where did you go to school? and so on. Others are "critical"; they concern the crime the person may have committed. The critical questions are designed to evoke fear of detection or feelings of guilt about the crime. After the questions have been asked, the examiner compares the record for neutral questions with that for critical ones. If he finds that emotional responses are distinctly higher for the critical ones than for the neutral ones, he has reason to feel that the person is guilty. If there is no systematic difference, he concludes that the person is innocent.

A skilled operator who has specialized in lie detection must frame the questions, administer the test, and interpret the records if the results are to have any validity. Even so, such a test often fails to reach a conclusion. Some individuals are so emotional about being investigated for a crime that they show very strong reactions to many of the neutral questions. On the other hand, some individuals, particularly hardened criminals, may be so unafraid generally that their autonomic changes are no greater for critical questions than for neutral ones. Consequently, the lie detector does not always detect the lie.

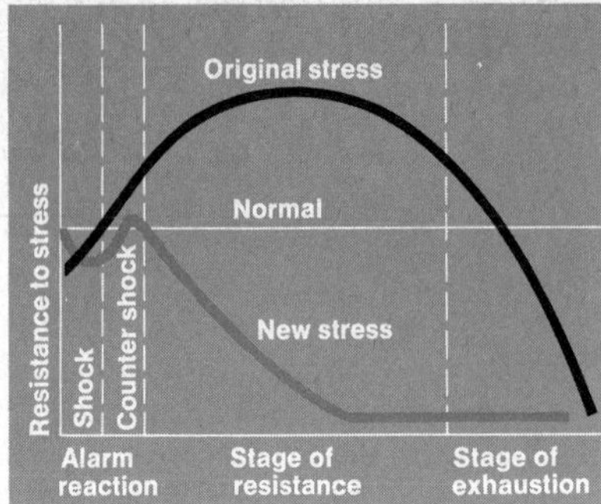

A PERSON DEVELOPS SOME RESISTANCE TO A CONTINUED STRESS: AT THE SAME TIME, HE HAS LESS RESISTANCE TO A NEW STRESS

Figure 7.5 *The general-adaptation syndrome. Responses to stress are divided into three stages: the alarm reaction, resistance, and exhaustion. If the stress is severe enough and prolonged enough, the individual does not recover in the resistance stage, but enters an exhaustion stage which may terminate in death. The black line represents resistance to a continuous original stress; the colored line, resistance to a new stress imposed in different stages of the adaptation syndrome. (After Selye, 1950.)*

Psychosomatic reactions The bodily changes that take place in anger and fear mobilize the body's energy and strength to deal with an emergency—the fear- or anger-producing situation. As we have seen, emotion has frequently been called an emergency reaction of the body (Cannon, 1929). Stepped-up circulation makes energy available to the brain and muscles faster than it otherwise would be. Slowing of digestion and shunting of blood to the muscles do the same thing. In brief, each bodily change in some way makes it possible for the organism to react more quickly, exert more strength, run faster, or fight harder in emotional emergencies.

If, on the other hand, a person is plagued with chronic anxiety or hostility that smolders on day after day and month after month, the accompanying autonomic changes also go on without any letup, and the effects are not desirable ones. In time the high heart rate and blood pressure, the increased secretion of hormones, and the alteration of digestive function can bring about actual damage to tissues and organs of the body. Or if the chronic autonomic effects do not themselves cause harm, they can make the individual more susceptible to infection or less able to recover from any diseases he may contract. In this way, chronic tension and anxiety bring about disorders of the body. These disorders are called psychosomatic—"psycho" meaning mind, and "soma" meaning body—because they are induced by psychological stresses.

It has been demonstrated that many disorders have a psychosomatic basis in some people: peptic ulcers, high blood pressure, asthma, dermatitis, obesity, and others. Ulcers have been produced experimentally in rats, dogs, and monkeys that are subjected to a regimen in which they suffer chronic fear (Brady, 1958).

Although we have convincing proof that anxiety and chronic fear can induce such disorders as ulcers, we cannot conclude that all ulcers are psychosomatic. Indeed, ulcers and the other diseases mentioned above occur in people who are not under any obvious psychological stress. There are factors besides chronic anxiety that can produce them. For this reason, it is often difficult to determine whether a disease is wholly or partly psychosomatic. In a great many cases, probably a combination of causes exists, and the psychological stress only aggravates a disorder or predisposes a person to it. Emotional stress, nonetheless, is the precipitating cause of a great many physical complaints.

General-adaptation syndrome Some of the bodily changes that take place in emotion also occur under other kinds of stress: overwork, prolonged exposure to cold or heat, severe burns or pain, or the ravages of disease. Therefore we call any condition that makes the body mobilize its resources and burn more energy than it normally does a *stress.*

Three stages appear to occur in the body's reaction to stress (see Figure 7.5). Taken together, they are called the *general-adaptation syndrome.* The first stage, the *alarm reaction,* consists of the typical bodily changes in emotion that we have reviewed. If the stress continues for some time, however, a person (or animal) enters a second stage called *resistance to stress.* In this stage, he recovers from his first burst of emotion and tries to endure the situation as best he can. Such endurance, however, puts considerable strain on his resources. He may eventually reach a third stage, the stage of *exhaustion.* When he arrives at this point, he has exhausted his internal resources for dealing with continued stress. We do not see the third stage too frequently in emotional stresses, but in cases of exposure to severe heat or cold, the person may finally weaken and die.

The first stages of the adaptation syndrome represent an attempt by the body to protect the organism from stress. Unfortunately, however, an individual often pays a great price for this adaptation. This point is indicated in Figure 7.5 by the curve labeled "New stress," which represents a decreasing ability to defend against new stresses—infection, exposure, excessive fatigue—while the person shows increased resistance to the original stress, say, emotional tension. As a result, the person may develop such diseases as hypertension, rheumatism, arthritis, ulcers, allergies, and many related physical disorders. These disorders are seldom caused by psychological stress alone; yet the stress may be crucial. It may aggravate ordinary physical causes of disorder to produce a disease that would not otherwise occur.

The particular diseases, whether behavioral or physical, that develop in reaction to stress depend upon the person's weak spots and upon the kind of stress he suffers. In any case, they are apparently caused by changes in bodily metabolism that are produced by stress. There are many such changes, but they are not yet fully understood. The most general one is a reaction of the *adrenal gland,* the organ that seems to respond most promptly and most vigorously to stress.

Two substances secreted by the adrenal gland are especially important. One is epinephrine, which as we have seen, mimics the action of the sympathetic nervous system by increasing the heart rate and blood pressure and by making sugar available to the brain and muscles. The second is *cortin,* which contains many hormones that control sodium, water, and other chemicals in the internal environment. One of the components of cortin is *cortisone.* Cortisone and the *adrenocorticotropic hormone* (ACTH) have both received wide publicity as remedies for rheumatism, arthritis, and similar disorders. ACTH stimulates the adrenal gland to secrete cortin and hence cortisone.

To understand how these facts relate to the general-adaptation syndrome of reaction to stress, refer again to Figure 7.5. Note that in the second stage of the adaptation syndrome, resistance to continued stress is increased. This means that *too much* adrenal secretion is being produced. In this stage, therefore, such diseases as hypertension (high blood pressure) and heart disease are prevalent. In fact, the symptoms of these diseases can be duplicated in animals by injecting an excess of adrenal hormones. On the other hand, in the later stages of adaptation to prolonged stress, the person's resources become exhausted. This is accompanied by—and in part, caused by—an exhaustion of adrenal hormones. Then diseases like rheumatism and arthritis can result. Such drugs as ACTH, which gives added stimulation to the adrenal gland, and cortisone, which takes the place of insufficient adrenal hormone, have helped in the treatment of these diseases. The drugs compensate for the exhaustion of adrenal activity that is a result of prolonged stress.

Tranquilizing drugs Other kinds of drugs are required for the treatment of extreme states of anxiety and emotional upset. For many years, only general sedatives—that is, sleeping pills—were available. If an individual was greatly upset and needed calming down, he was given a sedative just as if he were tense and anxious and could not go to sleep. Sedatives will calm a person, but they often incapacitate him temporarily. They act generally on the nervous system to slow it down instead of specifically calming the bodily states in emotion.

However, medical research has now developed drugs that are relatively specific for emotional behavior. A number of them are available, and each has somewhat different effects. In general, they act selectively on the parts of the nervous system concerned in emotion. They are "emotional sedatives" rather than general sedatives. They make the person tranquil without making him sleepy or greatly reducing his ability to function. Hence they are called *tranquilizers* or *tranquilizing drugs* (see Chapters 13 and 19).

By acting on the nervous system, tranquilizers can save wear and tear on the body. They reduce heart rate, blood pressure, muscular tension, and other autonomic states in emotion. Thus they make the individual more comfortable and mitigate his feelings of misery. Usually, however, they do not rid him of his fears or the causes of anxiety. In fact, persons taking tranquilizing drugs generally report that they still worry; the tranquilizer merely keeps them from feeling so bad.

The tranquilizers available today have their limitations. In the first place, they do not cure anything. They provide temporary relief which often makes it possible for the physician to proceed with other forms of treatment. Second, some individuals seem resistant to the tranquilizing effects of the drugs. Finally, they may have undesirable side effects. Especially when used for a long period, they can induce muscular tremor, high blood pressure, and other harmful conditions. People must therefore be cautious in using these drugs; they should be taken only under proper medical supervision.

Emotional Expression

When a person is very angry, or very much afraid, or very joyful, we usually can recognize what his emotion is by the way he behaves. But which patterns of behavior distinguish one emotion from another? And how accurate are we in telling one emotion from another?

In examining these questions, we shall first consider a fundamental and universal pattern of emotional response: the *startle pattern*. *Facial and vocal expression* are also ways of expressing emotion; so are *postures and gestures.* But as we shall see, it is difficult to judge emotional expression correctly unless we also know the situation that gave rise to the emotion.

The startle response Perhaps the most primitive of all emotional patterns is the startle response. At least, in careful studies of many individuals, it has been found that this response is more consistent among most people than any other emotional pattern. You can easily observe

Figure 7.6 *Differences in emotional expression. These people are watching the same event, but what varieties of emotion are being expressed? (Charles Harbutt, Magnum.)*

the response by tiptoeing up to a person who is deep in thought and suddenly yelling "boo," or by clapping your hands loudly when he does not expect it. The reaction you get is what psychologists call the *startle pattern* (Landis and Hunt, 1939).

The whole response takes place very rapidly, in a consistent pattern. The first part of the reaction is a rapid closing of the eyes. The mouth widens in a suggestion of a grin. Then the head and neck are thrust forward, often with the chin tilting up, and the muscles of the neck stand out. The uniformity of this emotional reaction from one person to another makes us believe that it is an inborn response which is modified very little by learning and experience. And the startle response is one of the very few emotional reactions of which this is true.

Facial and vocal expression Emotional patterns other than the startle pattern differ from person to person and culture to culture. Each individual develops somewhat unique ways of expressing emotion. Figure 7.6, for example, shows some people at a political rally. The objective situation is roughly the same for all of them; yet notice the great differences in their facial expression. When you look at each face separately, it is difficult to say what emotion is being expressed.

If emotions are classified into two general groups, those which seem pleasant and those which seem unpleasant, we can observe some consistent differences in the expression of most people's mouths. In general, the mouth turns down in the unpleasant emotions, up in the pleasant ones. The same is true of the eyes; they slant up in mirth, and droop in sadness. Leonardo da Vinci stated this as a principle to be used in depicting emotional expression.

In order to study facial patterns, psychologists have presented pictures of faces reflecting various spontaneously aroused emotions and have asked people to judge what the emotions were. In this kind of experi-

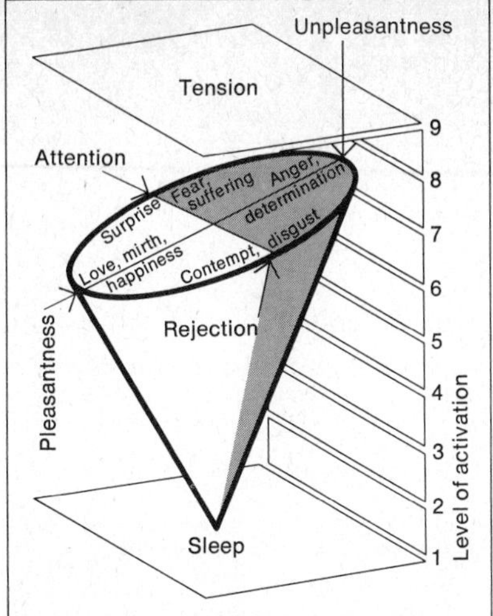

EMOTIONAL EXPRESSION CAN BE JUDGED FAIRLY ACCURATELY ON THREE DIMENSIONS: SLEEP-TENSION, ATTENTION-REJECTION, AND PLEASANTNESS-UNPLEASANTNESS

Figure 7.7 *A solid representing three dimensions of facial expression in emotion. The top surface is sloped to show that unpleasant emotions, such as anger and fear, can reach higher levels of activation than the more pleasant emotions. (After Schlosberg, 1954.)*

ment, where the judges see only the face, they agree fairly well upon whether the emotion is pleasant or unpleasant, but not upon which emotion it is. In general, the same result is obtained for expressions posed by professional actors.

Some work on this problem indicates that three dimensions of emotional expression can be judged with reasonable reliability (Engen et al., 1957, 1958). As shown in Figure 7.7, these are *pleasantness-unpleasantness, attention-rejection,* and *sleep-tension.* The first dimension, as its name implies, is the degree to which a facial expression represents feelings of pleasantness or unpleasantness. On the second dimension, attention-rejection, attention is characterized by wide-open eyes and often by flared nostrils and open mouth, as if to bring the sense organs to bear on the object. In rejection, the eyes, lips, and nostrils are tightly shut, as if to keep out stimulation. The third dimension, sleep-tension, is another name for the dimension of sleep-arousal discussed earlier. It refers to the level of tenseness or excitement portrayed. At one extreme is the relaxation of sleep; at the other is the expression of extreme emotional arousal.

People ordinarily express a good deal of emotion with their voices. Screams denote fear or surprise; groans, pain or unhappiness; sobs, sorrow; and laughter, enjoyment. A tremor or break in the voice may denote deep sorrow; a loud, sharp, high-pitched voice usually expresses anger. Vocal expressions and facial expressions are helpful cues in distinguishing one emotion from another.

Posture and gestures Emotions are expressed by posture and gestures as well as by the face and voice. In fear, a person flees or is "rooted to the spot." In anger, he usually makes aggressive gestures and may even clench his fists and move to attack. In sorrow, a person tends to slump with face downward, and in joy, he holds his head high and his chest out. Such signs of emotion are taken for granted in this society.

But how consistently is emotion actually expressed in this way? As in facial expressions, individuals differ widely. When judges have only the expressions of the hands and forearms to observe, they agree fairly well for highly conventional expressions, such as worship, but agreement becomes more difficult for the less conventional gestures. If they are permitted to see both the facial expression and the gesture, their agreement improves considerably, though it is still far from perfect (Kline and Johannsen, 1935).

Studies of emotional expression in different societies show that it is largely learned. Indeed, a "language of emotion" seems to characterize each culture. The Chinese may express surprise by sticking out their tongues, disappointment by clapping their hands, and happiness by scratching their ears and cheeks. In our society, sticking out our tongue is more likely to be a sign of defiance, clapping hands a sign of happiness, and scratching our ears a sign of worry.

Knowing the situation Thus any single aspect of emotional expression —facial, vocal, postural, or gestural—is not a very reliable sign of the type of emotion involved, for these components of expression are not uniform from one person to the next. When judges are given all of them together, they agree much better than when they consider the components singly. Even so, they make a fair number of mistakes and may confuse such different emotions as anger and fear.

In order to judge emotional expression most accurately, we need to see not only the pattern of expression, but the situation in which the emotion occurs. When both the situation and the expression are known, judges are far more reliable in naming the emotion (Klineberg, 1954). Since all of us know fairly well what our own emotions are in various situations, we know what the other person's are likely to be. So it is by situation, more than by expression, that we are able to distinguish different emotions. The kinds of situations that tend to evoke emotion will now be described.

Emotional Situations

As discussed earlier, all the various shades of mood and emotion can be fitted somewhere into the three dimensions of pleasantness-unpleasantness, attention-rejection, and sleep-tension shown in Figure 7.7. In this section we shall use another system of classification that divides emotions into three primary types: pleasure, fear, and anger. Pleasure, of course, is virtually a synonym for pleasantness, while fear and anger lie on the unpleasant end of the pleasantness-unpleasantness scale.

Pleasure Of the many different things that give us pleasure, all are covered by one general principle: Pleasure is a reaction to the satisfaction of a motive or the achievement of a goal. This principle applies to both unlearned or primary motives, including curiosity and exploration, and learned or secondary motives, those concerned with social approval, status, and so on.

DEVELOPMENT Early in life, the child shows signs of pleasure when he is physically comfortable. If an infant is well fed, dry, and warm, and if there are no pins sticking in him, he is usually relaxed, smiling, and cooing. By the second or third month, he shows signs of pleasure when he sees a human face or hears a friendly voice. Still later he expresses pleasure when he exercises a new skill, such as reaching out and shaking a rattle, or when somebody plays peekaboo with him. In general, as children develop, they find pleasure in situations that are novel but not frightening, that keep them entertained, and that offer them some success in what they try to do.

Smiling and laughing are specific expressions of pleasure that occur, just as fear and anger do, in different situations at different ages (Washburn, 1929). Apparently the nervous system of the infant must mature somewhat before he can smile, for smiling does not begin until he is about 2 months old. After that, for a time, smiling is a response to being tickled or stroked. Then it begins to occur when there is an interesting noise or some unusual movement—as when parents wave their arms, dance, stand on their heads, or pull toys around the floor to entertain him.

As the affectional drive matures, the child takes pleasure in having physical contact with adults—clinging to them, riding piggyback, climbing all over them, and so on. When curiosity and exploratory motives develop, he takes pleasure in pulling things apart, playing with toys, and exploring. By the time adolescence arrives, and many secondary goals have been established, the boy or girl derives pleasure from social activities of various sorts and from achievement in athletics or school classes.

HUMOR AND LAUGHTER In adults, smiling and laughter occur in an increasing variety of situations. These appear to fall into two general categories. One is a situation in which a person can express his superiority, hostility, sexuality, or other usually unacceptable behavior in a socially acceptable manner. Children laugh when they see a playmate in a silly or sorry predicament, or when they manage to annoy someone by teasing him. Thus they express superiority or hostility without the risk of being punished for it. Some adults laugh at "dirty" stories, thereby expressing sexual preoccupations that are otherwise socially unacceptable. The second type of situation in which laughter occurs involves incongruity. A person laughs when there is some contrast or incongruity between what a situation is perceived to be and what it is supposed to be.

Funny stories usually have elements of the first situation—an expression of superiority, hostility, or sexuality. But they rely primarily on the development of an incongruity. The good storyteller manages to build up an expectation of one thing, but in his punch line he delivers a surprise. Something happens that we did not expect. This provides the incongruity. The more intense the initial expectation, and the quicker the switch to a different outcome, the better the joke. The surprise, however, must be reasonable; it must be something that could be the outcome of the story had we not been led to expect something else. Thus the incongruity must make sense. Something that is just different or completely implausible usually falls flat.

Fear As in the case of pleasure, the situations that produce fear change in the course of development from infancy to adulthood. In the infant and young child, unlearned fears are caused primarily by strange situations that are sudden or unexpected. A loud noise, for example, does not necessarily elicit fear, but one that comes suddenly usually does. Similarly, strange objects, like stuffed animals or false faces, produce fear mainly when they appear unexpectedly. Thus the natural stimulus for fear is a strange situation encountered suddenly and unexpectedly.

As children grow older, they may be afraid of imaginary creatures, of being left alone, of the dark, and of potential bodily harm—in other words, of threats. Some of the situations that produce fear at different ages are compared in Figure 7.8. Late in childhood, children become especially fearful of social humiliation and ridicule—social threats—and are much less bothered by the noises and strange things that scared them in infancy.

When the individual reaches adolescence and early adulthood, social situations take on increased importance as sources of fear (Wake, 1950). In early adolescence (between 11 and 16 years of age), he may still fear animals and potential injury or threats, but social fears are more promi-

BABIES ARE MOST FEARFUL OF NOISES AND STRANGE THINGS; OLDER CHILDREN, OF ANIMALS AND THREATS OF HARM

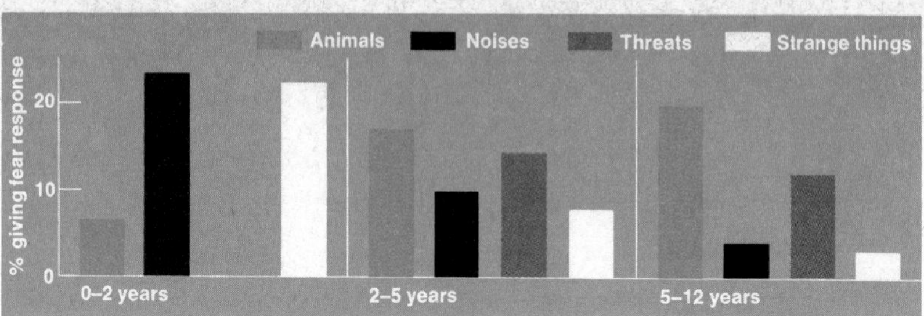

Figure 7.8 *Situations evoking fear in infants and children. Groups of youngsters were exposed to four different classes of stimuli: (1) animals, (2) noises, or things that made noises, (3) threats of illness, injury, or death, and (4) strange things or people. The bar graphs show the percentage of each group giving a fear response to the four classes of stimuli. (After Jersild et al., 1933.)*

nent. These include fears of being left out of a group, of making a *faux pas*, of being ridiculed, or of talking to certain people. In early adulthood (18 to 24 years), social fears become even more important, at least among university students.

Several factors are involved in the development of fear behavior. One, of course, is the conditioning of fear (see page 88), but others are important too. In order to learn fear, a child need not be conditioned; he can acquire fear symbolically through the example of his parents or through their stories. This can happen whenever his memory and imagination are developed to the point where he is able to imagine the fearful things his parents tell him about.

Figure 7.9 *Threat of punishment is often used to motivate behavior. (Jeffrey Norton.)*

Another factor is the child's developing perception of the world. A very young baby is not too discriminating; he cannot tell one face from another or one animal from another. If he is used to one face or one animal, another will not appear strange. As he learns and matures, however, he comes to discriminate one face from another and becomes aware of the fact that a face is connected with a head. At that point, the face of a stranger or a disembodied face is something unexpected, and he shows fear of it. Hence the fear emerges only when the perception of what is familiar and what is strange makes it possible. This conclusion is supported by studies of fear in chimpanzees:

> Some of the chimpanzees of the Yerkes colony might have a paroxysm of terror at being shown a model of a human or chimpanzee head detached from the body; young infants showed no fear, increasing excitement was evident in the older (half-grown) animals, and those adults that were not frankly terrified were still considerably excited. These individual differences among adults, and the difference of response at different ages, are quite like the human differences in attitude toward snakes, the frequency and strength of fear increasing with age. . . . The increase fits in with the conception that many fears depend on some degree of perceptual development. (Modified from Hebb, 1949, page 243.)

As we saw in Chapter 6, fear is easily acquired through conditioning, and each person's fears may be different in some respect from those of others. Someone who has had a fall from a height may go through life fearing high places. A child who was once lost and terrified in a crowd of people may, even as an adult, fear crowds. If at some time a child is locked up in a dark closet, he may afterwards be afraid to stay in a

Table 7.2 *Sources of annoyance. 659 individuals of both sexes, ranging from 10 to 90 years of age, were asked to indicate the things that annoyed them.*

Source: After Cason, 1930.

Class of annoyance	Different annoyances, %
Human behavior (Most common: a person blowing his nose without a handkerchief; a person coughing in one's face; a person cheating in a game; a woman spitting in public; the odor of dirty feet; a child's being treated harshly)	59.0
Things and activities not connected with people (other than clothes)	18.8
Clothes and manner of dress	12.4
Physical characteristics of people that could be altered	5.3
Physical characteristics of people that are unalterable	4.4

room with all the doors closed. If fears such as these are very strong, they are called *phobias* (see page 408).

Parents and society, of course, deliberately use fear of punishment to enforce their demands and teach approved ways of behaving. The punishment may be something painful, such as a whipping. But most often it is frustration of other motives—loss of money, such as through fines (see Figure 7.9); loss of freedom, or imprisonment, which frustrates a number of motives; or loss of social approval, status, and related social goals.

Anger and hostility The situations that make children and adults angry have one thing in common: interference with goal-directed activity. Frustration of any want or ongoing activity is likely to provoke anger. Restraining a person or requiring him to do things he does not want to do may provoke anger at any age.

What varies with age is the kinds of things people do and do not want to do. We are thus led back again to the development of unlearned and learned motives. In infants, simple restraint, which frustrates activity and exploratory motives, is a common cause of anger. In children, frequent provocations include being required to sit on a toilet seat, having things taken away, having the face washed, being left alone, losing the attention of an adult, and failing to accomplish something that is being attempted. In older children and adolescents, the causes of anger shift, as we might expect, from physical constraints and frustrations to social frustrations and disappointments. Sarcasm, bossiness, shunning, or thwarting of social ambitions become frequent occasions for anger.

Social frustrations are also common causes of anger in adults. Most adults have learned to contain their anger, however, so that we seldom observe outright displays of it. More frequent are the mild feelings of anger that we call annoyance. One psychologist studied common annoyances and irritations by asking people to list them (Cason, 1930).

From the replies of over 600 people, ranging in age from 10 to 90, he listed almost 18,000 annoyances. When duplications were eliminated, the number was reduced to about 2,600. Tabulating these into various categories, he found that more than half the common annoyances are things that other people do, such as blowing their noses without handkerchiefs, coughing in one's face, smelling dirty, or treating others unkindly (see Table 7.2). Almost all these annoyances are socially disapproved behaviors or things that we just do not want other people to do Only a small minority of common annoyances have to do with *things*—for example, a late bus or train—but even these were mostly frustrations of a motive.

The particular way of expressing anger changes with age. Among preschool children, anger is more likely to take the form of temper tantrums, surliness, bullying, and fighting. Among adolescents and adults, these expressions become more subtle, indirect, and verbal; they include sarcasm, swearing, gossiping, and plotting. This change in the mode of expression of anger is obviously brought about by social pressures.

Parents and society try in various ways to suppress angry behavior. Children are usually punished for outbursts of anger. In adults, even the slightest display of anger may be frowned upon as socially disapproved behavior. So, both by failing to reinforce anger and by punishing its expression, society attempts to teach us not to get angry.

This raises an interesting problem. The punishment of anger is itself frustrating and hence anger-provoking. First, inability to express anger—to blow off steam—is frustrating because it prevents achievement of one's goal, namely, to attack or destroy whatever is doing the frustrating. Second, since any sort of punishment can be frustrating, the threat of punishment can be anger-provoking. Therefore society in its effort to suppress anger actually provokes it. The result is not so much to teach people not to be angry as it is to teach them not to express anger. Anger smolders inside instead of coming out into the open.

Anger can be conditioned and generalized in the same way as fear. We get angry at whatever keeps us from achieving our ends, and if the same thing often frustrates us, we acquire a conditioned hostility toward the obstacle and other things similar to it. A harsh father, for example, who frequently makes his son angry by restricting the son's activities, may become such a stimulus for anger that the boy feels generally hostile to all superiors if he generalizes to them the feelings he has toward his father. Such conditioned hostility is fairly common among older children and adults.

Attitudes The tendency to react emotionally to people and things formerly associated with emotional behavior helps to account for our preferences and aversions. We prefer the kinds of things which formerly gave us pleasure, and we are averse to those which made us fearful or angry. The same explanation applies to our attitudes. An *attitude* is a tendency to respond positively (favorably) or negatively (unfavorably) to certain persons, objects, or situations. In other words, it is a tendency to react emotionally in one direction or another. Whichever it is depends on our previously conditioned emotional reactions to certain kinds of people or things and the subsequent generalization to similar people or things.

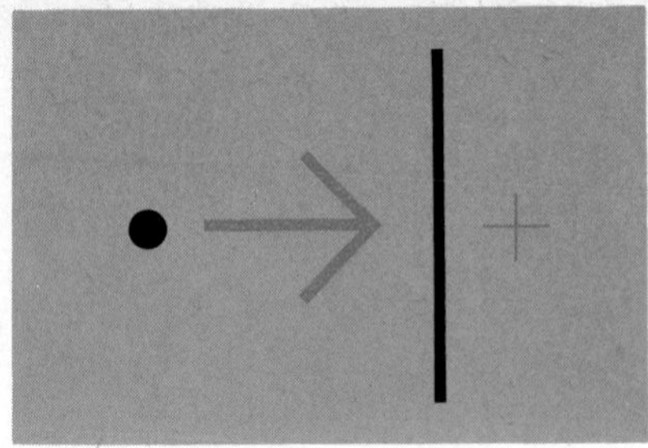

A PERSON ATTRACTED TO A POSITIVE GOAL MAY BE FRUSTRATED BY A BARRIER

Figure 7.10 *Frustration by environmental and personal obstacles. A barrier (vertical line) stands between the individual (dot) and the goal (+) that attracts him. The barrier may be another person or object in the environment, or it may be something such as the individual's own lack of ability or skill.*

Attitudes are discussed at length in Chapter 15. Here we want to point out that they are emotionally toned tendencies formed through conditioning and generalization.

Anxiety, Frustration, and Conflict

So far, we have used the term *fear* but have avoided the word *anxiety.* The dividing line between the two is not sharp, but it can be drawn. Fear, like anger, is a reaction to a specific object or situation; the person knows what he is afraid of or angered at. Anxiety, on the other hand, is a general state of apprehension or uneasiness in which the object of the fear or anger is unclear. Anxiety is usually less intense but more persistent than fear or anger, although some individuals suffer brief or prolonged attacks of anxiety that are agonizingly severe.

Anxiety, fear, and anger are intertwined. Mild anger, called hostility, usually arouses anxiety because the expression of anger, or hostile behavior, has in the past often been punished (see the earlier section, Anger and Hostility). Hence feelings of hostility arouse vague fears of punishment, and thus anxiety. Anxiety also occurs through the generalization of fear (page 89) from one situation in which fear was learned to other similar situations. But the situation most frequently giving rise to anxiety is one of *frustration of motives.* This relationship comes about in two ways: First, as we have seen, frustration tends to provoke aggression, or hostility, which in turn engenders anxiety from *fear of punishment.* Secondly, frustration arouses *fear of failure* to obtain the satisfaction of motives (positive goals) or to obtain relief from unpleasant situations (negative goals). Because of this close connection between frustration and anxiety, psychologists have done intensive research on the sources of frustration.

Sources of frustration Generally speaking, frustration may be classified by sources into environmental, personal, and conflict frustration.

ENVIRONMENTAL FRUSTRATION By making it difficult or impossible for a person to attain his goal, *environmental obstacles* frustrate the satisfaction of motives. An obstacle may be something physical, such as a locked door or lack of money. Or it may be established by people—parents, teachers, or policemen—who prevent us from achieving our goals. In general, environmental obstacles are the most important sources of frustration for children; what usually prevents children from doing the thing they want to do is some restraint or obstacle imposed by their parents or teachers.

A frustration can be schematized by a diagram such as that in Figure 7.10. The box denotes the total *environment* of the person, the dot stands for the *person,* and the vertical line represents the *thwarting* of the motive. In such diagrams goals are depicted by either a + or a − sign, called a *valence.* A plus sign indicates a goal to which the person is attracted; a minus sign, a goal which repels him—punishment, threat, or something he fears or has learned to avoid. The arrow is used to indicate the direction of motivating forces acting on an individual. This

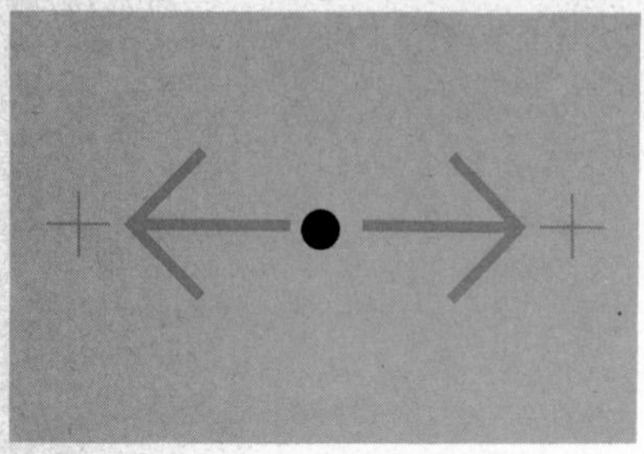

FRUSTRATION MAY BE CAUSED BY CONFLICTING ATTRACTIONS TO TWO GOALS

Figure 7.11 *Approach-approach conflict. The individual is attracted at the same time by two goals that are incompatible.*

particular method of depicting frustrating situations was devised by Lewin (1935) and helps us visualize the sources and effects of frustration.

PERSONAL FRUSTRATION As children grow up and move toward adulthood, *unattainable goals* become increasingly more important as sources of frustration and anxiety. These are largely learned goals that cannot be achieved because they are out of reach of the person's abilities. A child may learn to aspire to high academic achievement, but lack the ability to make better than a mediocre record. He may want to join the school band, play on the football team, be admitted to a certain club, or take the lead in a play, but he may be frustrated because he does not have the necessary talents. The trouble is that an individual may learn goals—levels of aspiration—that are too high for his level of performance. In this case the frustration shown as the vertical line in Figure 7.10 represents a barrier within the person himself.

CONFLICT FRUSTRATION The adult, as well as the child, has his share of environmental obstacles and unattainable goals, but his most important source of frustration is likely to be *motivational conflict*—a conflict of motives. In expressing anger, for example, a person is usually caught in such a conflict. On the one hand, he would like to vent his rage; on the other, he fears the social disapproval that would result if he did. The anger motive is thus in conflict with the motive for social approval. In Western societies, sexual motivation is often in conflict with society's standards of approved sexual behavior.

Types of conflict Of the three general sources of frustration described above, the one that causes the most persistent and deep-seated frustrations in many individuals is motive conflict. This kind of frustration is usually the most important in determining a person's anxieties, or "hang-ups." On analysis, it seems that such frustration can arise from three major kinds of conflict, which have been called approach-approach, avoidance-avoidance, and approach-avoidance.

APPROACH-APPROACH CONFLICT As the name implies, approach-approach conflict occurs between two positive goals—goals that are equally attractive at the same time (see Figure 7.11). For instance, a physiological conflict arises when a person is hungry and sleepy at the same time. In the social context, a conflict may arise when one wants to go to both a political rally and a swimming party which are scheduled for the same night. The proverbial donkey is supposed to have starved to death because he stood halfway between two piles of hay and could not decide which to choose. Actually, neither donkeys nor people often "starve themselves to death" merely because they are in conflict between two positive goals. Such a conflict is usually resolved by satisfying first one goal, then the other—for example, eating and then going to bed if a person is both hungry and sleepy—or by choosing one of the goals and giving up the other. Thus approach-approach conflicts do not generate much anxiety.

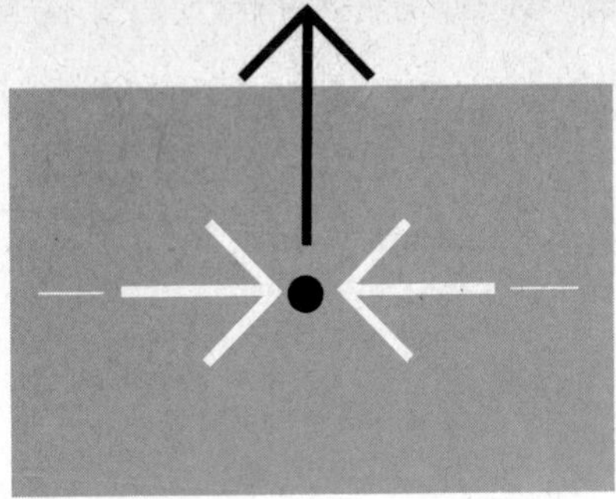

FRUSTRATION MAY BE CAUSED BY TWO OR MORE NEGATIVE GOALS

Figure 7.12 *Avoidance-avoidance conflict. The individual is caught between two threats, fears, or situations that repel him. In addition to the negative goals shown, there are usually other barriers or negative goals in the periphery of the situation to prevent the individual from "leaving the field" (black arrow) in order to escape conflict.*

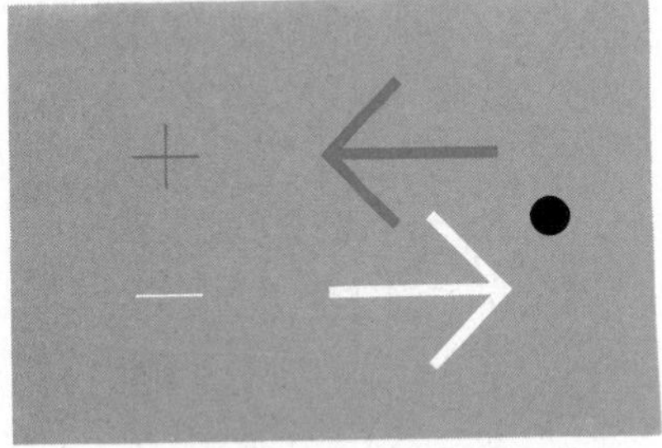

FRUSTRATION MAY BE CAUSED BY A SITUATION THAT IS BOTH ATTRACTIVE AND REPULSIVE

Figure 7.13 *Approach-avoidance conflict. The individual is attracted to a positive goal, but this goal also has a fear or threat (negative goal) associated with it. Such a conflict is difficult to resolve and tends to evoke a good deal of anxiety.*

AVOIDANCE-AVOIDANCE CONFLICT A second type of conflict, avoidance-avoidance, involves two negative goals (see Figure 7.12), a fairly common experience. A child must do his arithmetic or get a spanking. A student must spend the next two days studying for an examination or face the possibility of failure. A man must work at a job he intensely dislikes or take the chance of losing his income. Such conflicts are capsuled in the saying, "Caught between the devil and the deep blue sea." We all can think of things we do not want to do but must do or face even less desirable alternatives.

Two kinds of behavior are likely to be conspicuous in avoidance-avoidance conflicts. The first is *vacillation*. As we shall see, the strength of a goal increases the closer a person is to the goal. As he approaches a negative goal, he finds it increasingly repelling. Consequently he tends to retreat or withdraw. But when he does this, he comes closer to the other negative goal and finds it, in turn, increasing in negative valence. He is like a baseball player caught in a rundown between first and second base. He runs first one way, then the other. As he runs toward second base, he comes closer to being tagged out, but when he turns and runs back toward first base, he faces the same danger. Such vacillation is characteristic of avoidance-avoidance conflicts.

A second important feature of this kind of conflict is *an attempt to leave the conflict situation*. Theoretically, a person might escape avoidance-avoidance conflict by running away from it altogether. And people do indeed try this. In practice, however, there are additional negative goals in the periphery of the situation (the *field*, as it is called), and these ordinarily prevent us from leaving. A child who does not want either to do his arithmetic or to get a spanking may think of running away from home. This, however, has even more negative consequences, and so he does not do it. The person in avoidance-avoidance conflict may also try a quite different means of running away. He may rely on his imagination to free him from the anxiety aroused by the conflict. He may spend his time daydreaming instead of facing up to his problem. A student may daydream at times when he is supposed to be studying. A person may even conjure up an imaginary world, or re-create in his mind's eye the carefree world of childhood in which no unpleasant tasks have to be performed. In extreme cases, this way of leaving the conflict situation is called regression (see page 379).

APPROACH-AVOIDANCE CONFLICT The third type of conflict, approach-avoidance, is often the most difficult to resolve. In this kind of conflict a person is repelled and attracted by the same goal object (Figure 7.13).

A young bride, for example, may have been brought up in an atmosphere where sexual activities were treated as ugly and sinful things. As a consequence, sexual matters have a negative valence for her. At the same time, her normal sexual drive, as well as other social values involved in marriage, provides the marital situation with a positive valence. Now as she enters marriage, she experiences anxiety because she is caught between her sexual motives and the attitudes learned in her early environment.

This example gives us a hint about the way in which an approach-

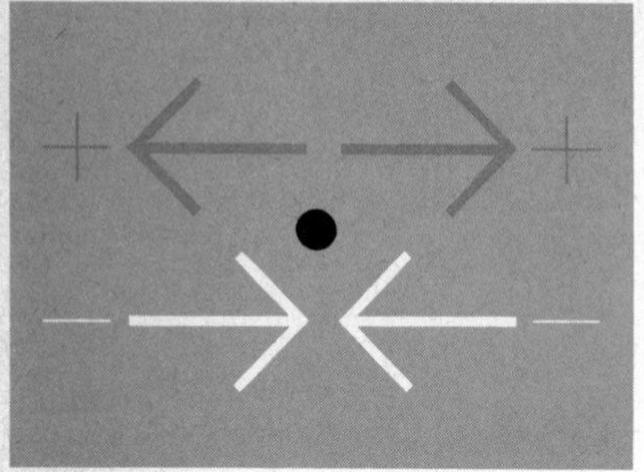

IN REAL LIFE, MANY FRUSTRATIONS ARE DUE TO SEVERAL SITUATIONS THAT ARE BOTH ATTRACTIVE AND REPULSIVE

Figure 7.14 *Double approach-avoidance conflict. Many conflicts that appear to be approach-approach or avoidance-avoidance conflicts are really double, or even multiple, approach-avoidance conflicts.*

avoidance conflict can develop. Note that it arose because of the social values acquired in early training. These values come to serve as obstacles to the satisfaction of motives. Since they are within the person, the process of acquiring them, which we considered in Chapter 6, is regarded as one of *internalizing obstacles.* Such obstacles frustrate a person in the same way that the environmental obstacles in early childhood do. But the fact that they are internal rather than external makes them much more difficult for the person to handle. He may find ways of circumventing environmental obstacles, but he can hardly circumvent or get away from something within himself. Coping with the anxiety caused by such inescapable conflict can create major problems of adjustment (see Chapter 12).

Such an analysis of frustration permits us to reduce frustrating situations to their simplest elements. In everyday life, however, things are seldom so simple. It is more typical to have conflicts in which there are many different goals, especially negative ones, that surround a person with pressures he wishes to avoid. In addition, there are some complex combinations of the kinds of conflicts we have described. One is the *double approach-avoidance conflict,* diagrammed in Figure 7.14. Here, two goals have both positive and negative signs. Consider, for example, the student who experiences a conflict between making good grades and making the college football team. Superficially this appears to be a simple case of approach-approach conflict—conflict between two positive goals. But the student may have considerable social pressure from his family and associates to achieve both goals. He may incur the disapproval of his parents if he fails to make good grades, and he may lose the esteem of his comrades if he does not make the football team. Thus failure at either one carries a threat. Each goal has a negative valence as well as a positive one, so that the student finds himself in a double approach-avoidance conflict.

APPROACH AND AVOIDANCE GRADIENTS As we have indicated, the strength of positive and negative goals varies with psychological distance. The strength of a goal—the amount that it attracts or repels—is stronger the nearer one is to it. This fact is represented by the gradients in Figure 7.15. However, as the figure also illustrates, a difference exists between the *approach gradient* and the *avoidance gradient:* The avoidance gradient is the steeper of the two (Brown, 1948). This means that, other things being equal, when a person is *some distance* from a goal having both positive and negative valences, the positive valence seems stronger. On the other hand, when he is *near* such a goal, the negative valence seems stronger. At the point where the two gradients cross, the valences are equal. In other words, the figure indicates that a person in an approach-avoidance conflict will tend to approach the goal; but then, as the tendency to avoid becomes stronger, he will come to a stop some distance from it. He is thus trapped and immobile at the point where the two goal strengths are equal. He gives up near the goal without resolving the conflict, leaving himself beset with anxiety.

Common conflicts When we consider the number of needs that people have and the many ways of satisfying them, we realize that all sorts of

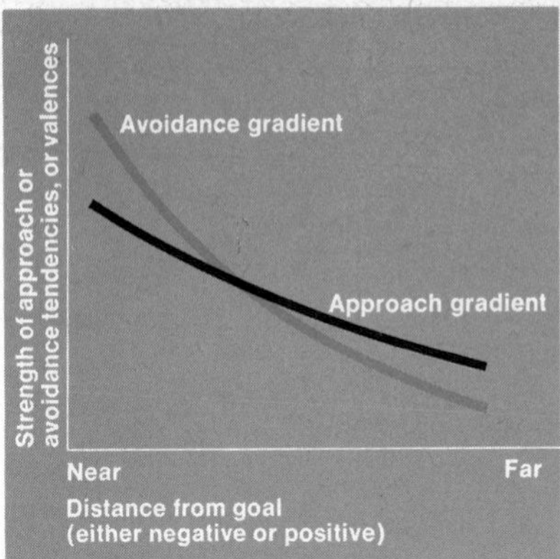

Figure 7.15 *Gradients of tendencies to avoid or approach positive and negative goals. Other things being equal, tendencies to avoid and approach are stronger the closer a person is to the goals. Negative tendencies, however, are somewhat stronger than positive ones when a person is near the goal. Positive tendencies are stronger than negative ones when he is far from the goal. This fact accounts for a person's being trapped in approach-avoidance conflict; he approaches the goal, then stops at the point where the gradients intersect, being afraid to go any closer. (After Brown, 1948.)*

frustrations and conflicts are possible. Moreover, we can expect conflict to occur whenever pleasure and pain, or reward and punishment, are associated with the same thing. That is what we mean when we refer to the conflict between positive and negative goals. Four such conflicts are common in American culture. (In foreign cultures, and even at other times in our own culture, other patterns of conflict may be more typical.)

ACHIEVEMENT NEED VERSUS FEAR OF FAILURE In Western countries, particularly the United States, achievement is highly valued. Children are expected to make good grades in school, to excel in sports, music, or the like, and generally to "succeed" in life. Individuals are praised, given medals and awards, and most of all, paid money for superior achievement. It is not surprising that the achievement motive is regarded as one of the individual's strongest motives in our society (see page 211).

The opposite of achievement is failure, which is punished in one way or another—by lack of approval, by failure to get promoted, sometimes by ridicule and ostracism. Hence the things one does to achieve his goals take on both positive and negative valences. People get caught between the desire to achieve and the fear of failure.

INDEPENDENCE VERSUS AFFILIATION NEEDS We saw in Chapter 6 that children learn to depend on others; they must in order to satisfy their needs. The people they depend on, however, have considerable authority over them, determining what they can and cannot do. When children reach adolescence, they typically develop a strong drive to be independent—to kick over the traces. This puts them in conflict, because it is difficult to be both independent and dependent. Indeed, independence means standing on one's own feet, and this the adolescent (and frequently the adult) may be afraid to do or may not know how to do. Parents themselves sometimes aggravate such a conflict because they themselves are in conflict about it—they criticize the adolescent one moment for being a "baby" and resent his show of independence a moment later.

Independence also conflicts with more general affiliative needs. A person may have a strong need to stand on his own feet, fend for himself, and go it alone. At the same time, he may feel an equally strong need to be approved by his parents, to be accepted by a group, and to have the moral support of others.

SEXUAL DESIRE VERSUS FEAR OF SEX Among many mid-Victorians, the conflict that arose between sexual drives on the one hand and social or religious scruples on the other was particularly strong. Today, this conflict is not so prevalent, but it is still common. It may be a conflict between religious precepts and sexual interests. It may be a milder conflict between sexual interests and early training. It may concern fears of pregnancy. Or it may involve the social approval of others. In any case, sex is frequently the center of an approach-avoidance conflict.

HOSTILITY VERSUS NEED FOR SOCIAL APPROVAL Another typical conflict arises between the need to express hostility and the fear of punishment for expressing it. Many situations occur from day to day which arouse an impulse to show anger or to fight back. Early in life, however, we have learned, usually by being punished or scolded, not to engage in physical combat or even to lose our temper. As adults, we find ourselves in almost the same situation, except that, generally, all we provoke by displays of anger is some mild social disapproval. Still, the constraints on showing anger and hostility are strong. Consequently, we are in conflict between expressing ourselves and fearing the consequences of doing so.

These are merely examples of typical approach-avoidance conflicts. There are, of course, almost as many sources of conflict as there are situations and people. The kind of conflict and its severity vary from one individual to another and from one culture to another, because conflicts are firmly rooted in the individual's training and acquired motives.

Synopsis and summary

We have not tried to give a psychological account of all the moods and shades of emotion to which man is subject; nobody could do this. Our aim instead has been to describe the major dimensions of emotion and to concentrate on some of the stronger emotions such as pleasure, fear and anxiety, and anger.

1. An emotion is many things: a state of arousal, a physiological change in the body, something physically expressed, a motivating force, and a feeling of pleasantness or unpleasantness.
2. A central dimension in emotion and other motivational states is the sleep-arousal (or sleep-tension) dimension.
3. Several stages in the depth of sleep can be distinguished by means of the electroencephalogram (EEG). These range from a regular rhythm (alpha) of 10 "brain waves" per second in relaxed waking to a slow rhythm (delta) of 1 to 3 waves per second in deep sleep. But in paradoxical sleep, which is marked by rapid eye movements (REMs), the EEG corresponds to that of a person who is awake or in a light sleep, while the subject is actually in deep sleep as judged by the difficulty of waking him. This is the stage in which most dreaming occurs.
4. Different states of arousal in waking can also be distinguished. In arousal as measured by the EEG, the alpha rhythm is blocked and gives way to a fast-wave activation pattern. The orienting reaction is another sign of arousal. Other common indications are widening of the pupils and an increase in skin conductance.
5. In general, the more intense an emotion or a motive, the higher the state of arousal. For simple tasks, the higher the arousal, the better the performance. But in complex tasks involving the discrimination of cues, there is an optimal level of emotional arousal. With emotional arousal above the optimum, the person is disorganized and his performance suffers.
6. When an individual experiences intense emotion, many changes occur within the body as a result of impulses from the autonomic nervous system, particularly from the sympathetic part of the system. One action of the sympathetic system is to cause secretion of the hormones epinephrine and norepinephrine, which in themselves cause a number of bodily changes.
7. Bodily changes in emotion can be measured with appropriate instruments. In general, these measured changes are similar for different emotions. One exception is directional fractionation, which occurs when a person is listening or "taking in" information rather than actively reacting. In this state his heart rate goes down while his skin conductance goes up.
8. Several theories attempt to relate bodily changes in emotion to emotional feelings. The James-Lange theory assumes that bodily changes give rise to feelings. The emergency theory states that both feelings and bodily changes are simultaneously triggered by the emotional situation. The cognitive theory assumes that bodily changes are about the same for different emotions, and that feelings are produced by the individual's interpretation of the situation which produced his bodily state.
9. Chronic emotional reactions caused by prolonged stress lead to psychosomatic illness when they result in a fast heart rate, high blood pressure, increased secretion of hormones, and other reactions that continue over an extended period. Disorders sometimes caused or aggravated in this way include peptic ulcers, high blood pressure, asthma, dermatitis, and obesity.
10. Three stages in the body's reaction to severe stress, which taken together constitute the general-adaptation syndrome, are (*a*) the alarm reaction, consisting of typical emotional reactions, (*b*) a stage of

increased resistance to stress, and finally, if the stress is great and prolonged, (*c*) a stage of exhaustion in which resources for dealing with the stress are depleted and which can end in death.

11. Tranquilizing drugs are sedatives of the emotions; they specifically calm anxieties and emotional reactions.

12. The kind of emotion expressed by a person's face, voice, and hands can be classified on a three-dimensional scale: sleep-tension, unpleasantness-pleasantness, and attention-rejection. Best results are obtained when the observer not only sees the person's entire behavioral pattern but also knows the situation giving rise to the emotion.

13. In general, the satisfaction of a drive or the achievement of a goal gives pleasure. Fear is aroused in the infant by any strange stimulus suddenly presented. Later in childhood, fear comes from threats of harm; and in adolescence, it is primarily connected with social situations. Anger is aroused by any frustration or interference with goal-directed activity.

14. Society attempts to suppress the expression of anger, but in doing so, it actually provokes anger and hostility. Both fear and anger are easily generalized.

15. In children, the frustration of motives is primarily caused by environmental obstacles. Later, frustration may be caused by goals that are so far above a person's level of performance that he cannot attain them. In adults, much frustration comes from a conflict between motives in which one motive cannot be satisfied without frustrating another. The frustration of motives causes anxiety.

16. Three basic types of conflict can be distinguished: approach-approach, avoidance-avoidance, and approach-avoidance. Actually, most conflicts are more complicated than these; they consist of multiple approach-avoidance combinations.

17. Some typical conflicts appearing in late adolescence and early adulthood are achievement need versus fear of failure, independence versus affiliation needs, sexual desire versus fear of sex, and hostility versus the need for social approval.

Related topics in the text

Chapter 3 Principles of Learning Classical conditioning, discussed in Chapter 3, is especially important in the association of emotional states with particular situations.

Chapter 6 Motivation Since emotions can function as motives, a review of the definition and principles of motivation may be helpful.

Chapter 11 Personality Defense mechanisms for coping with the anxiety produced by conflict are described in Chapter 11.

Chapter 12 Behavior Disorders The crippling effects of intense fear and anxiety, as well as other extreme emotional responses, are detailed in Chapter 12.

Chapter 13 Therapy for Behavior Disorders Various techniques are described for alleviating painful emotional states, such as anxiety.

Chapters 17 and 19 in Part Five, Biology of Behavior Some of the brain structures important in producing physiological states in emotion are discussed.

Suggestions for further reading

Arnold, M. *Emotion and personality.* New York: Columbia, 1960. 2 vols.
A comprehensive work reviewing much of the psychological (vol. 1) and physiological (vol. 2) research on emotion.

Candland, D. K. (Ed.) *Emotion: Bodily change.* New York: Van Nostrand Reinhold, 1962. (Paperback.)
A set of readings consisting of original papers on emotion, with special attention given to physiological changes.

Darwin, C. *The expression of the emotions in man and animals.* Chicago: University of Chicago Press, 1965.
A reprint of a classic and readable book, with an introduction by Konrad Lorenz.

Dunbar, F. *Mind and body: Psychosomatic medicine* (Rev. ed.) New York: Random House, 1955.
A popular account, written by a physician, of the role of emotions in health and disease.

Jacobsen, E. *Biology of emotions.* Springfield, Ill.: Charles C Thomas, 1967.
A review of emotions emphasizing biological changes.

King, R. A. (Ed.). *Readings for an introduction to psychology.* (3d ed.) New York: McGraw-Hill, 1971. (Paperback.)
A book of readings designed to accompany this text.

Lazarus, R. S. *Psychological stress and the coping process.* New York: McGraw-Hill, 1966.
A description and a theory of the effects of psychological stress.

Webb, W. B. *Sleep: An experimental approach.* New York: Macmillan, 1968.
A summary of experimental research on sleep by a psychological expert on the subject.

Why do things look as they do?
Kurt Koffka

Part of what we perceive comes through our senses from the object before us, another part . . . always comes . . . out of our own head.
William James

We live in a constantly changing world of experience; we see things, hear them, feel them, taste and smell them. Most of us take this amazing fact with nonchalance; we are so used to the world of experience that we do not regard it as the remarkable thing it is. Think about it sometime, and consider the wonder that is man.

Perception as Experience

Many definitions and points of view exist about perception. Let us say that perception refers to the way the world looks, sounds, feels, tastes, or smells. A person's perceived world is the world of his immediate experience.

Why should psychologists, especially those interested in psychology as a science of behavior, be concerned with the world of experience—how things "seem" to us? The answer is simply that perception—how things "seem"—is an important factor in the determination of behavior. Think about the following slice of life:

It's a Saturday afternoon and you have a blind date for the football game. (We shall look at this from the man's point of view—it's easier that way for the authors.) You meet your date and you look each other over, keeping within the rules of social propriety, of course. You notice her face, the way she is dressed, her figure, the way she talks, her style of behavior; and you probably make judgments about them. She looks a little scrawny and she seems nervous, but she has a nice face and talks well.

You are going to drive to the game. You get into the car and weave your way through the heavy traffic, keeping your body upright as you go around corners and compensating for the car's acceleration as you pick up speed. At one point, your knee happens to touch your date's knee; she does not pull away. You think about it; she doesn't think about it at all because she does not notice it. She is intent upon the conversation and creating a good impression.

It's a beautiful day: the sun is out, the grass is green, the band is playing. About the only thing that spoils the picture is a drunk behind you who blows cigar smoke in your face every so often. You think about telling him off, but he looks mean and tough—the scar across the cheek, the glass eye, and the curled-down lip don't make you very confident about the outcome of such a confrontation.

As you watch the game, it seems to you that the officials are blind. Can't they see what you can plainly see? The players on the other side are constantly interfering with the pass receivers; the rough play on the line is all started by the other side.

The game ends, off you go.

Some examples of perception at work in the guidance of behavior are obvious in this example. In sizing up your date, you were using visual and auditory sensory information coming through the sensory channels; you were adding other information, perhaps stored memory information, to make judgments about this new acquaintance. In driving to the game, perception of the environment was essential; you would not have made it without depth perception, form perception, movement perception, and so on. Automatic perceptual mechanisms kept the body upright in the face of forces put upon it. Another perceptual phenomenon, that of attention, is illustrated by the knee-touching episode. Not all sensory information enters into experience; we are conscious only of a small part of the sensory bombardment. For you, that touch of the knee was in the focus of attention; for her, something else was in the focus and the touch on the knee was far out in the margin of attention. At the game you saw the grass, heard the bands, and smelled the cigar smoke. You perceived the source of the annoying smoke, but you also perceived other things about the source of that smoke and moderated your behavior accordingly. You did not see things the way the referees saw them; you wanted your team to win, and motivation—or wishes—influenced what was perceived.

All this behavior was made possible by information in the sensory channels. Everything we know about the world around us comes through the sensory channels of vision, hearing, feeling, taste, smell, and so on. Of course, some of the sensory information is stored in memory to be used at a later time, but even this stored memory information originally came in through sensory channels. And some of our experience of the world is shaped by activity in the sensory channels themselves.

Perception and sensory channels The sensory channels consist of the receptor organs and the nerve fibers from the receptors to the brain. The physical energy in the world around us is coded by the receptors into a pattern of activity in the nerve fibers. Thus the characteristics of the physical energy are converted into a kind of input code in the nerve fibers. This input code is known as the *afferent,* or input, *code for experience.* In Chapter 18 we shall consider the detailed processes by which the physical energy is changed, or *transduced*, into the activity of the nerves that contains the information necessary for perception. For now, we need not be concerned with such mechanisms; it is enough to know they exist.

Some of our experience is very closely tied to the activity in the channel, or the afferent code, itself. In vision, for instance, our perceptions of brightness and color are largely determined by information coming directly from the receptor. And in hearing, perceptions of loudness and pitch are closely linked to the afferent code.

More complex aspects of experience are also a consequence of the code in the sensory channel. Our perception of visual depth, for instance, may be closely tied to the pattern of input from the eye (Gibson, 1966).

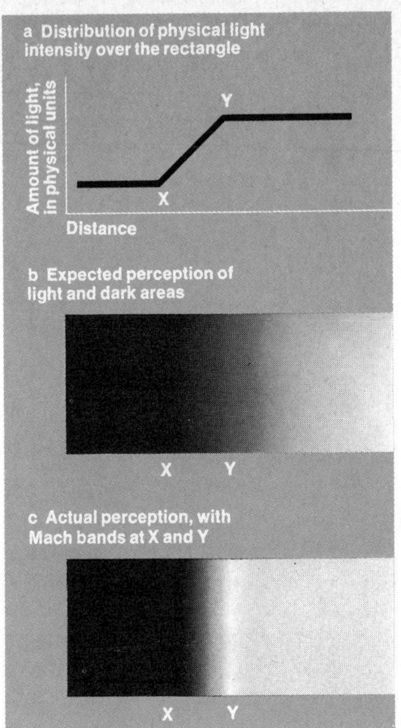

PERCEPTION IS SOMETIMES THE RESULT OF COMPLEX ACTIVITIES AT THE RECEPTOR

Figure 8.1 *Mach bands.*
(a) *Graph of the spatial distribution of light intensity.*
(b) *The expected perception based on physical light intensity.*
(c) *The actual perception. Note the dark and light bands, known as Mach bands. They are exaggerated in clarity here. Note that the Mach bands appear at the points of abrupt intensity change. Such bands are believed to represent complex interactions of inhibition and excitation at the receptor. They also illustrate the general principle that we cannot predict what we will experience from knowledge of the stimulus alone. (Based on Ratliff, 1965.)*

The receptors are not just passive receivers; they organize and elaborate the information going into the sensory channel, as the following example shows (Ratliff, 1965):

Suppose we do an experiment in which there is a fairly abrupt change in the physical intensity of light over an area that we are looking at. The physical situation is plotted in Figure 8.1*a*: the graph shows the amount of light as it might be measured by a light meter. Figure 8.1*c* depicts the pattern of light and dark that is actually perceived. Rather than an even change from dark to light, as would be predicted from the physical situation, we perceive a dark band and a light band at the points where the physical light intensities change abruptly. Such bands are called *Mach bands*, after the German physicist Ernst Mach (1838–1916) who investigated them.

It is believed that Mach bands are the result of complex events—interactions of activation and inhibition—at the receptor, which in this case is the retina. They demonstrate that what we experience is not a "copy" of the physical stimulus—it is not a picture in the head. Rather, our experience depends upon what comes up the sensory channel, and this is often the result of activities at the receptor.

To summarize: Some of our experience is closely tied to the afferent code in the sensory channel, and some of this experience may be quite complex. But in most cases, the information in the sensory channel merely provides the "raw data" that is reworked, transformed, or combined with stored information in the brain to create the world as the individual actually experiences it.

Perception and the brain As we know, and as as our introductory example illustrated, we do not live in a visual world of changing brightness and color or an auditory world of varying loudness and pitch. Instead, we live in a perceptual world of stable objects and of sounds that have meaning for us. In most cases, the psychological reality of experience is the result of drastic organization and transformation of the sensory input in the central receiving areas of the brain (see Chapters 17 and 18). The world of perceptual experience is characterized by (1) selectivity of input, (2) organization of input, (3) constancy of experience in the face of varying input, (4) a dimension of depth constructed out of cues from the input, (5) movement, (6) the simultaneous influence of other inputs, or the *context* of the situation, (7) the importance of relationships between inputs as opposed to absolute characteristics of inputs, and (8) effects produced by learning and motivation. We shall now discuss each of these major characteristics of our perceived world of experience. Since we know more about visual perception as a factor in behavior than about most other types of perception, the majority of examples will be visual ones.

Selectivity of Perception

One of the more obvious characteristics of perception is its selective nature. At any given moment our sense organs are bombarded by a multitude of stimuli. Yet we perceive only a few of these clearly at one time. There are other stimuli, or events, that we perceive less clearly, and the rest form a sort of hazy background of which we are only partially, if at all, aware. This is another way of saying that, of the various events around us, we attend to only a few. So *attention* is a basic factor in perception.

Focus and margin Attention divides our field of experience, so to speak, into a *focus* and a *margin.* The events that we perceive clearly are in the focus of experience. Because we attend to them, they stand out from the background. Other items in the margin are dimly perceived. We are aware of their presence, but only vaguely so. Imperceptibly shading off from the margin are still other items which are outside our field of attention and of which, for the moment, we are consciously unaware.

To illustrate the nature of attention, let us go back to the football game with which we began this chapter. While you are somewhat dimly aware of the tangle of players at the scrimmage line and of the activity of the blockers, it is the ball carrier and his movements that stand out most clearly. Your attention is focused on him. You are at the same time being bombarded by a number of other stimuli: Your feet may be aching with the cold; unpleasant sensations may be coming from your stomach as a result of the last hot dog you ate; and the fellow behind you is still smoking that cigar. While the play is going on, you are not aware of any of these things that are in the margin of your attention. Only when the play is finished or time out is called do you perceive how cold your feet are and smell the cigar smoke.

Shifting of attention The fact that you do at some times notice the cigar smoke and feel your cold feet illustrates another quality of our field of attention. Attention is constantly shifting. What is at the focus one minute is marginal the next, and still later may have passed completely from conscious awareness. Even when one activity dominates our attention, its dominance usually is not perfectly continuous. Other perceptions come fleetingly into the focus of our awareness and are replaced again by the dominant item.

What determines what things we attend to at a given time? Although attention shifts, it has a certain orderliness. If it were completely chaotic, we would be unable to carry out any extended activity. Actually, as a good advertising man could explain, certain principles determine the direction of our attention—the *principles of attention getting*. These govern what will be most clearly perceived and what may be only dimly perceived or not perceived at all. Two general classes of factors are concerned: external factors in the environment, and internal factors such as motives, set, and expectancy.

External factors in attention getting External factors governing attention may be considered under four headings: (1) intensity and size, (2) contrast, (3) repetition, and (4) movement. The factor of novelty might be added to the list, but this has been discussed earlier in connection with motivation (see chapter 6).

INTENSITY AND SIZE The louder a sound, the more likely a person is to attend to it. The brighter a light, the more it tends to capture his attention. By the same token, a full-page advertisement is more likely to be noticed than a half-column one. This factor of intensity or size is most pronounced when the person is experiencing something new or unfamiliar; the items in the environment that are biggest, loudest, or brightest will attract his attention first. In general, if two stimuli are competing for attention, the one that is more intense will be noticed before the other.

CONTRAST We tend to adapt or become used to the stimulation around us. The ticking of the clock may seem loud when we enter a room, but after a while it is not noticed at all. The room may feel hot or cold when we first come in, but after a few minutes we are hardly aware of the temperature. On the other hand, if the clock abruptly stops ticking, we notice the sudden silence. As we drive a car we are not aware of the hum of the engine, but if a cylinder misfires, the noise of the engine will occupy the center of our attention.

Contrast, or change in the stimulation to which we have become adapted, immediately captures our attention. If we are reading in our room and someone turns on the radio in the adjoining room, we are apt to be acutely aware of it. But after a short while it drops from our awareness as we again become absorbed in our reading. When the radio is turned off, its absence arouses our ATTENTION for a moment. Both the onset and the termination of a stimulus tend to promote attention, because both contrast with what has preceded them.

The word in capital letters in the paragraph above is another illustration of contrast. Most of you noticed the word as soon as you looked at this part of the page. However, if all the text were in capitals, the word would have gone unnoticed. It attracted attention because it contrasts with the words in lowercase letters.

REPETITION At times the repetition of a stimulus is attention-getting. A misspelled word is more likely to be noticed if it occurs twice in the same paragraph than if it occurs only once. We are more likely to hear a burst of gunfire than a single shot, or to hear our name if it is called twice. When his mother calls Junior in for dinner, she calls his name not once but several times.

The advantage of repetition is twofold: First, a stimulus that is repeated has a better chance of catching us during one of the periods when our attention to a task is waning. Second, repetition increases our sensitivity or alertness to the stimulus.

MOVEMENT Human beings, as well as most other animals, are quite sensitive to objects that move within their field of vision. Our eyes are involuntarily attracted to movement in much the same way that the moth is attracted to a flame. Soldiers on a night patrol soon learn this fact and freeze in their tracks when a flare bursts. To fall flat or duck behind shelter may make their detection more likely than if they remain motionless out in the open.

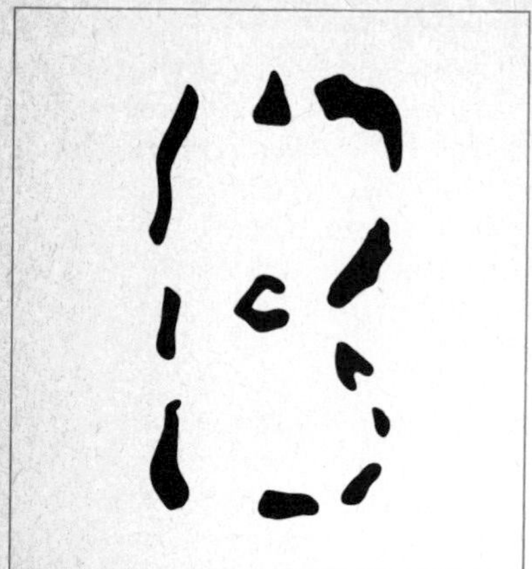

WHAT A PERSON SEES DEPENDS UPON WHAT HE IS SET TO SEE

Figure 8.2 *The effect of set on perception. The drawing can be perceived either as a B or a 13, depending on what a person expects.*

The field of advertising, of course, makes good use of movement as an attention getter. Some of the most effective advertising signs are those which involve movement—blinking lights or animated figures.

Internal factors in attention getting Intensity, contrast, repetition, and movement, all of which attract attention, are external stimulus factors. Of equal importance are internal factors, such as motives, interests, and other states within the person.

MOTIVES Our needs and interests govern not only what will attract our attention but also what will hold it. Even the sleepiest student in the class can be made to sit on the edge of his chair if the instructor announces that he is going to talk on the topic "Sex Practices of American Females." Appeal to the sex drive is particularly effective in our culture because the drive is traditionally suppressed. Thus advertisements use shapely girls in bathing suits very effectively to sell items as unrelated as spark plugs and cigars. In a society where food is scarcer than it is in ours, advertisements showing foods probably would outnumber those which play up to sex appeal.

Not only are basic motives such as sex and hunger important in directing attention; so too are any of the great variety of human motives and interests. If a geologist and a bird fancier take a walk through the same field, the geologist will notice the detailed features of the terrain and the different kinds of rocks, whereas the bird lover will notice the number and variety of birds. If you ask the geologist about the birds, he is apt to say that he did not notice any, much less how many or what kind. And of course the bird lover is not likely to have been aware of the geological features that characterize the terrain.

SET, OR EXPECTANCY Besides our interests and motives, set, or expectancy, plays a major role in selecting what we shall perceive. The geologist would have been able to report more about the bird life on his walk had he known beforehand that he would be asked about it. A doctor may hear the phone ring in the night, but not hear the baby crying. His wife, on the other hand, may sleep through the ringing but come wide awake at the slightest sound from the child.

When the drawing in Figure 8.2 is included in a series of two-digit numbers, subjects will report that they have seen the number 13. Another group of subjects who have been exposed to letters of the alphabet will report this drawing as the letter B. In the one case, the subjects have acquired a set, or expectancy, for numbers; in the other, for letters.

Of the various factors that determine attention, and thus perception, expectancy is probably the most important. It is mainly our sets and expectancies that direct and order the successions of our perceptual experiences. Without them, perceiving would be largely at the mercy of random fluctuations in the environmental stimuli.

The physiology of attention Some evidence indicates a possible physiological mechanism for the selectivity of perception (Hernández-Péon et al., 1956). When one sensory channel is engaged, others may be inhibited, or "gated out." The focus of attention is produced by sensory

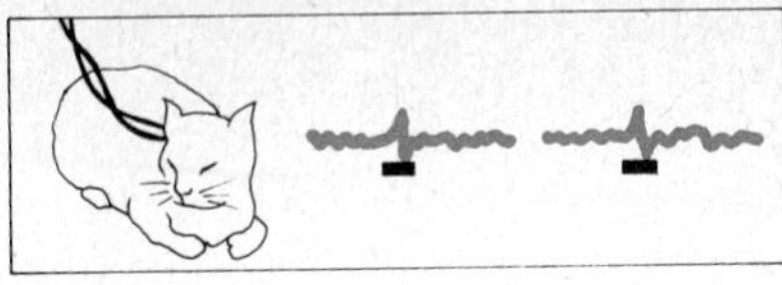

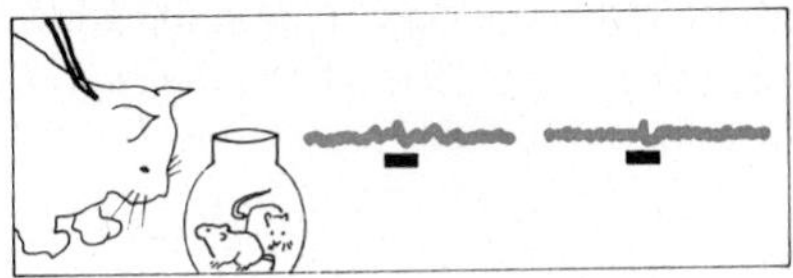

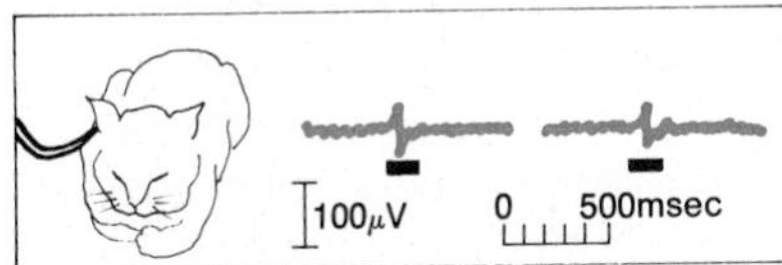

EXTRANEOUS SENSORY INPUT MAY BE "GATED OUT" IN ATTENTION

Figure 8.3 *Neural activity of the cochlear nucleus in attention. Top, two clicks are sounded, and the activity of the cochlear nucleus is recorded. The duration of the clicks is shown by the short black lines below the record of cochlear nucleus activity. This is a control record. Middle, the clicks are sounded while the cat is looking at mice in a bottle. Note the reduction of cochlear nucleus activity; the auditory input is being partially gated out. Bottom, another control record. Cochlear nucleus activity is the same as in the first record. (Based on Hernandez-Péon et al., 1956.)*

input which reaches the sensory parts of the central nervous system; the input in the margin of attention is gated out. For instance, when you are watching a ball carrier at a football game, the visual input from the image you see reaches the central nervous system—the visual channel is thus engaged. Other sensory channels are gated out—you do not feel your cold feet.

Evidence for this idea comes from experiments in which recordings are made from the sensory channels themselves (Hernández-Péon et al., 1956).

One experiment using cats recorded the electrical activity in the cochlear nucleus of the auditory system. The top row of Figure 8.3 shows the activity in the cochlear nucleus when a click stimulus was sounded and the cat was relaxed. In the middle row, the cat is looking at mice in a bottle—the visual channel is engaged. The activity in the cochlear nucleus is much diminished—the auditory input has been "gated out" to a large extent. The bottom row shows that after the mice have been removed and the cat is again in a relaxed state, the response to the clicks is about the same as it was initially.

However, more recent experiments have cast doubt on this interesting idea (Thompson, 1967). They found a lessening of responding in the nervous system for *all* stimuli, even those involved in the focus of attention.

Organization in Perception

Perceptual experience is filled with groups and patterns of stimuli which we call objects. The stimulation that people are constantly perceiving comes into their awareness as shapes and patterns. As we said earlier, people do not ordinarily perceive the world around them as patches of color, variations in brightness, and loud or high-pitched sounds. They see tables, floors, walls, and buildings, and hear automobile horns, footsteps, and words.

Some of this perception of objects is a matter of learning as we will discuss later in the chapter. But much of it is probably an unlearned property of our sense organs and nervous system. These structures tend to organize sensory inputs into perception of simple patterns or objects.

Organizing tendencies in perception have been much studied by the gestalt psychologists (see Chapter 1). Gestalt theorists have pointed to the existence of such tendencies to strengthen their argument that the perceived world is not simply the sum of "simple" sensory experiences (Koffka, 1935). Organizing tendencies take several different forms: (1) figure-ground perception, (2) grouping, (3) contour, and (4) closure.

Figure-ground perception Perhaps the most fundamental organizational tendency is the perception of figure and ground. We see the objects that fill our everyday perceptions as standing out from the general background of our experience. Pictures hang *on* a wall, words are *on* a page. In this case, the pictures and words are seen as *figure*, whereas the wall and the page are seen as *ground*. This primitive capacity to distinguish an object from its general sensory background is basic to all object perception.

AN OBJECT IS PERCEIVED AS A FIGURE ON A GROUND

Figure 8.4 *A figure-ground involves the simplest kind of perception.*

In glancing at Figure 8.4, you automatically see the dark area as an object. Despite the fact that it may look like no object you have ever seen, you still perceive it as a unitary whole or figure which is distinct from the page. If we examine carefully our general experience of figure-ground relations, we note certain characteristics that distinguish the figure from the ground in our perception. The figure seems to have some sort of shape or object quality, while the ground tends to be formless. The ground seems to extend continuously behind the figure, or in other words, the figure appears to be in front and the ground behind (Rubin, 1921).

Figure 8.5 shows a reversible figure-ground relation. The figure is perceptible either as a vase or as two profiles. To see the vase, the light area must be perceived as the figure against a dark ground. To see the profiles, the dark area must be perceived as a figure upon a light ground. It is seldom possible to see both vase and profiles simultaneously.

The figure-ground relation is also found in senses other than vision. When we listen to a symphony, the melody or theme is perceived as the figure while the chords are perceived as ground. In rock music, the guitarist uses repetitive chords as ground against which he sings a more or less varied song, or figure. In observing a person's movements, we might consider the overall posture as the ground for, say, the finer movements of the hands and arms.

SOMETIMES A FIGURE BECOMES A GROUND, AND VICE VERSA

Figure 8.5 *A reversible figure-ground, which may be perceived as either a vase or two profiles.*

Grouping Another kind of organizing tendency in perception is called *grouping*. Whenever several different stimuli are present, we tend to perceive them as grouped into some pattern. Figure 8.6 shows several different ways in which grouping takes place.

The role of *nearness*, or *proximity*, is illustrated by 8.6*a*. Instead of six vertical lines, we see three pairs of parallel ones. Items which are close together in space or time tend to be perceived as belonging together or constituting a group.

In 8.6*b* and *c* we can see the importance of *similarity* in grouping. In *b* most people see one triangle formed by the dots with its apex at the top and another triangle formed by the circles with its apex at the bottom. We perceive triangles because similar items—the dots and the circles—tend to group together. Otherwise we would see *b* as a hexagon or a six-pointed star, as is the case with *c*, where the stimuli are all the same. Another illustration of grouping according to similarity is *d*. If people are shown this figure and then asked to copy it, most of them will draw the two Xs close together and the two circles close together, with extra space separating the circles from the Xs.

Grouping according to similarity, however, does not always occur. The figure in 8.6*e* is more easily seen as a hexagon than as one figure composed of dots and another figure composed of circles. In this case, similarity is competing with the principle of *symmetry*, or *good figure*. Neither the circles nor the dots by themselves form a symmetrical pattern. In either case, certain members must be left out—a fact which most people find disturbing. In general, the tendency to group is a tendency to form a balanced or symmetrical figure that includes all the parts.

Our last principle of grouping is *continuation*, which is illustrated by

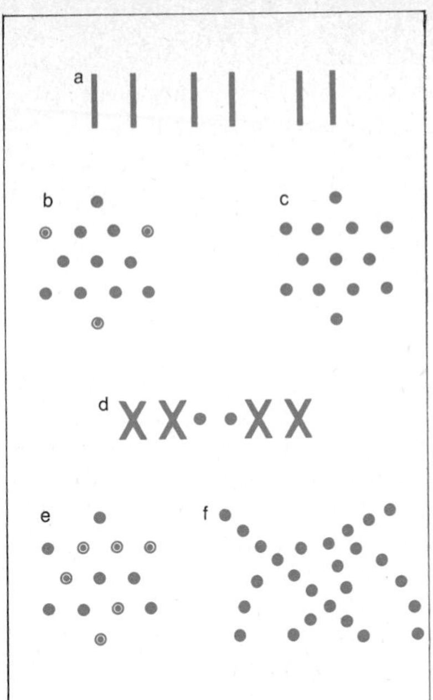

WE TEND TO PERCEIVE SEVERAL DIFFERENT STIMULI AS GROUPED INTO A PATTERN

Figure 8.6 *Examples of perceptual grouping in vision. Grouping processes operate for all the senses.*

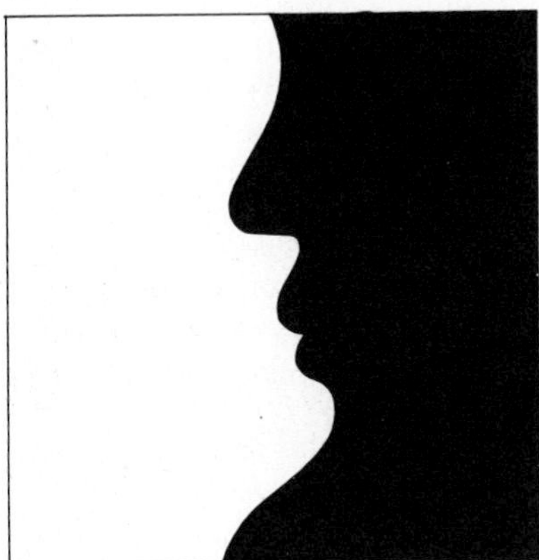

OBJECTS WITH DIFFERENT SHAPES MAY BE FORMED BY THE SAME CONTOUR

Figure 8.7 *Two different faces shaped by the same contour.*

the tendency to see a line that starts out to be a curve as continuing on a smooth course. Conversely, a straight line is seen as continuing straight, or if it does change direction, as forming an angle rather than a curve. The figure in 8.6*f* illustrates continuation; we see the dots as several curved and straight lines. Even though the curved and straight lines cross and have dots in common, it is only with effort that we can perceive a straight line suddenly becoming curved at one of these junctions.

Although the examples in Figure 8.6 are visual, the same principles of grouping can be observed in the other senses. The rhythm we hear in music also depends upon grouping according to proximity in time and similarity of accents. In the sense of touch, too, grouping occurs. For example, ask a friend to shut his eyes. Mark off three equally distant points on the back of his hand, touch a pencil to the first two points, and pause slightly before you touch the third. Your friend will report that the first two points were closer together than the second and third. This illusion illustrates the grouping of tactile stimuli according to nearness, or proximity, in time.

The principles of grouping, taken together, partially explain our perception of complex patterns as units or objects. Indeed, we see objects as objects, or units as units, only because grouping processes operate in perception. Were this not so, the various objects we perceive—a face on the TV screen, a car, a tree, a book, a house—would not "hang together" as objects. They would be merely so many dots, lines, or blotches.

Contour We are able to separate objects from the general ground in our visual perception only because we can perceive *contours*. Contours are formed whenever a marked difference occurs in the brightness or color of the background. If we look at a piece of paper which varies continuously in brightness from white at one border to black at the opposite border, we can perceive no contour. Such a paper appears uniform to us, and if asked to say where the sheet stops being light and starts to become dark, we can only guess or be arbitrary. On the other hand, if the change is marked rather than gradual—suppose several shades are skipped—we see the paper as divided into two parts, a light and a dark. In perceiving the division at the place where the brightness gradient abruptly changes, we have perceived a contour.

Contours give shape to the objects in our visual field because they mark off an object from other objects or from the general ground. We must be careful not to conclude, however that contours are shapes. The reversible faces in Figure 8.7 show clearly the differences between contour and shape. Although both faces are formed by the same contour, obviously they do not have the same shape. Contours *determine* shape, but by themselves they are shapeless.

Contour formation, although it might seem at first to be an immediate fact of perception, is rather complex. For one thing, it takes a surprising amount of time, as the following experiment demonstrates (Werner, 1935):

Subjects were shown the patterns of Figure 8.8 in a device called a *tachistoscope* —an apparatus for presenting perceptual materials for very brief intervals. It

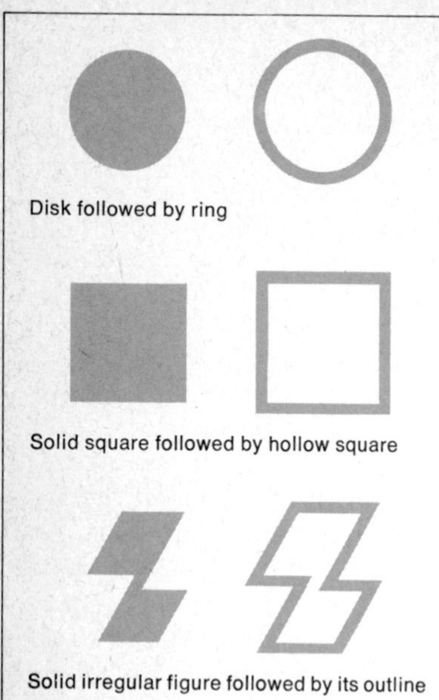

CONTOUR PERCEPTION IS NOT IMMEDIATE—IT TAKES TIME

Figure 8.8 *Representative figures used in one study of contour perception. In each case the figure on the left was flashed in a tachistoscope and then, after varying intervals, the figure on the right was flashed. If the time interval between the flash of each paired figure was less than 150 msec, the first figure was not seen—apparently because it takes longer than that for the central nervous system to elaborate the border, or contour, surrounding the first figure. Presentation of the second figure within 150 msec of the first seemingly interfered with the elaboration of the first. (Based on Werner, 1935.)*

was found that a fairly long time was necessary for the elaboration of a contour. For instance, if the filled circle is flashed on the tachistoscope screen for 12 to 20 msec (1 msec=1/1,000 second) and then is followed 150 msec later by the hollow ring, the filled circle will *not* be seen. The inner border of the hollow ring must fall at the place where the outer border of the filled circle had been flashed for this effect to appear. It is as if up to 150 msec are required for the elaboration of the border, or contour, surrounding the filled circle, and the presentation of the inner border of the hollow ring interferes. This is quite a long period on the time scale of the central nervous system.

Closure Our perception of objects is much more complete than the sensory stimulation we receive from them. Perceptual processes tend to organize the world by filling in gaps in stimulation so that we perceive a whole object, not disjointed parts. This filling in is termed *closure*, or the tendency to complete in perception what is physically an incomplete pattern or object. In Figure 8.9, for example, the two top drawings are seen as a "circle with gaps in it" and a "square with gaps in it," not as so many disconnected lines. If these incomplete figures were to be presented very rapidly, in a tachistoscope, they might even be perceived as complete figures without gaps—which would provide another instance of closure. The same principle applies to perception of the pattern in the lower part of Figure 8.9. There again, we fill in the gaps and perceive an object rather than disconnected lines. (Most people see a man on horseback.)

The closure process also fills gaps in the visual field which are due to certain characteristics of the receptor or other parts of the sensory channel. The retina, for instance, contains a blind spot where there are no sensitive cells (Chapter 18). Visual perception extends right across this blind spot, and we are not aware of its existence unless we take special pains to focus light on it alone. Indeed, images falling on either side of the blind spot are seen as continuous. Moreover, people with small blind spots, *scotomas*, due to brain lesions may close the visual field right through these spots (Teuber et al., 1960).

Perceptual Constancy

The world as we perceive it is a stable world. The size of a man does not appear to change much as he walks toward us. The dinner plate does not look like a circle when viewed from one angle and like an ellipse when viewed from another. The location of a sound does not appear to shift when we move our heads. To the layman nothing about this is very surprising. Why shouldn't the world of objects always look the same or remain constant?

Considered more carefully, however, this question raises some interesting problems, for often the physical stimuli from objects are not constant despite the fact that they appear to be. Indeed, as we move about in the world, the stimulation that we receive continually changes. Even the stimuli coming from the same object change markedly as we change our position with respect to it. When we stand directly in front of a window, its image on the retina is a rectangle. But when we move to one

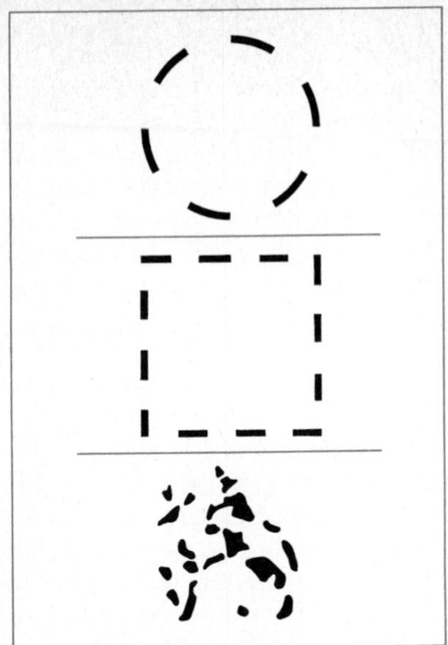

WE TEND TO PERCEIVE A COMPLETE OBJECT EVEN THOUGH IT MAY NOT BE ALL THERE

Figure 8.9 *(Above) Perceptual closure fills in the gaps.*

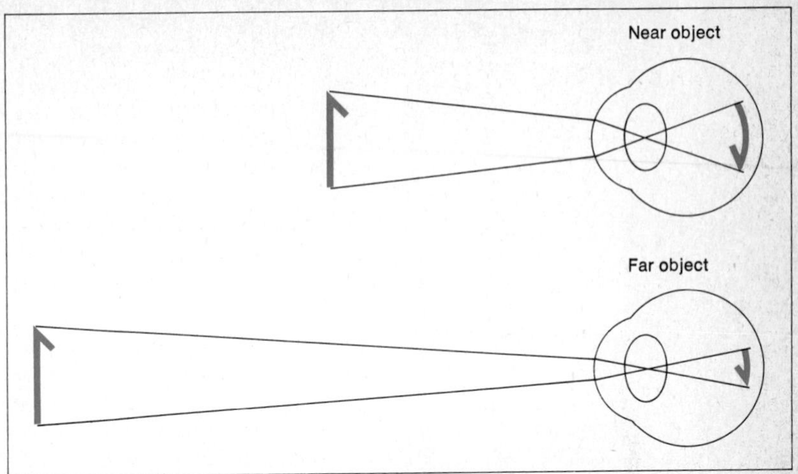

THE SIZE OF AN IMAGE ON THE RETINA VARIES WITH DISTANCE OF AN OBJECT FROM THE EYE

Figure 8.10 *(Right) The farther away the object, the smaller its image on the retina.*

side of the window, the image becomes a trapezoid. This is simple geometry. Despite the change in the shape of the retinal image, however, we continue to perceive the window as rectangular. *Perceptually*, therefore, its shape has not changed, even though its image on the retina has.

The general point is that the perceived shape of objects tends to remain the same irrespective of the positions or conditions under which we view them. This phenomenon is called *shape constancy*. And constancy in perception is not limited to shapes. The perceived *sizes* of objects, their *colors*, and their *brightness* also show perceptual constancy. We shall now consider these problems in a little more detail, for they illustrate not only the general problem of constancy, but also some of the means by which perceptual constancy is achieved.

Constancy of size We know that the eye works somewhat like a camera. Therefore the size of the image on the retina depends upon how far away the object is: the more distant the object, the smaller the image. The geometry of this fact is illustrated in Figure 8.10. The figure also implies that the same size image can be produced on the retina either by a nearby small object or by a larger object as some distance.

Knowing this much about the size of retinal images, we might expect the perceived size of an object to change as we approach it. At 50 feet, it should appear much larger than it did at 100 feet. But this does not happen. Within limits, the object appears to be about the same size irrespective of its distance. When it is perceptibly far away, we do not perceive it as smaller; we perceive it as being the same size—but farther away.

When depth cues are artificially reversed, however, familiar objects that ordinarily appear constant in size are perceived as vastly different (see Figure 8.11). Thus the constancy of object sizes in perception is closely related to our perception of distance. If the cues to depth or distance perception are gradually eliminated, our perception of the size of an unfamiliar object begins to correspond to the retinal image. And with all depth cues gone, constancy is completely eliminated, and our

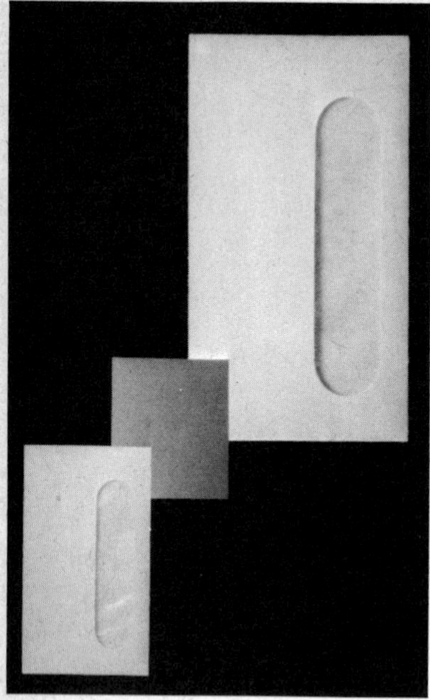

SIZE CONSTANCY DEPENDS UPON DEPTH CUES

Figure 8.11 *Size constancy destroyed by reversal of the depth cue called* interposition. *These envelopes are the same size, and they would be so perceived if the depth cues had not been reversed. The "large" envelope is actually much closer than the "small" one, but it is perceived as farther away because it seems to be behind the gray card which is, in turn, behind the "small" one. But in fact the gray card is not interposed between the two envelopes; it is behind both of them. It seems to be in front of the "large" envelope because the corner of this envelope has been cut out. (Fundamental Photographs.)*

perceptions and judgments of size are what one would expect them to be from the geometry of the retinal image.

For familiar objects, however, the elimination of depth cues does not completely destroy constancy, because we know approximately the objects' true sizes. Under certain conditions, this knowledge gives us some degree of size constancy even in the absence of depth cues. In fact, when comparisons between the relative retinal sizes of familiar objects are possible, the sizes of the retinal images may serve as a cue to distance for these objects. Such a cue is one of the monocular depth cues—linear perspective—which will come up later in the chapter.

Brightness constancy Visual objects also appear constant in their degree of whiteness, grayness, or blackness. Such brightness constancy, as we call it, tends to be independent of the illumination under which viewing occurs. Objects or surfaces which appear white in a bright light still are perceived as white in dim illumination. Similarly, what looks black in dim light still looks black in more intense light. Coal looks black even in very bright sunlight, while snow continues to look white even at night. Another example of brightness constancy is the appearance of a white paper that lies partly in a shadow. We perceive the paper as uniformly white; we do not perceive the shadowed portion as gray, but rather as white-in-the-shadow.

The following experiment, by showing that the perceived brightness of an object depends upon the *ratio* between the illumination of the object and its background, helps to explain brightness constancy (Wallach, 1963):

Light projectors were arranged in a dark room so as to project rings and disks superimposed, with the disk fitting exactly inside the ring (see Figure 8.12). The physical intensity of the light in the disks and rings could be varied independently. The absolute value of the disk's light intensity was kept constant, but the subjects' *perception* of its brightness depended upon the intensity of the light in the surrounding ring. As the physical intensity of light in the ring increased, *perception* of the constant physical intensity of the disk changed so that the disk looked darker.

Figure 8.12 represents the ring and disk as they might be *perceived*. The physical arrangement of intensities is indicated by the ratios: 1/3:1 means that the amount of physical light energy in the ring is one-third that of the disk; 2:1 means that the ring contains twice the light energy of the disk, and so on. Remember that the amount of physical light energy in the disk is constant in all four stimulus arrangements; it is the ring which varies physically. But note the change in *perception* of the brightness of the disk as represented in Figure 8.12. When the ratio of ring to disk is 1/3 to 1, the disk is perceived as rather bright; when the ratio is 8 to 1, the disk, with the same physical intensity of light on it as before, is perceived as rather dim.

This experiment shows that a change in the ratios of intensity between an *object* (the disk) and its *surround* (the ring) is necessary for a change in perception of object brightness. In most situations outside the laboratory, however, the ratio between an object and its surround stays constant because the illumination over the whole field changes; when the

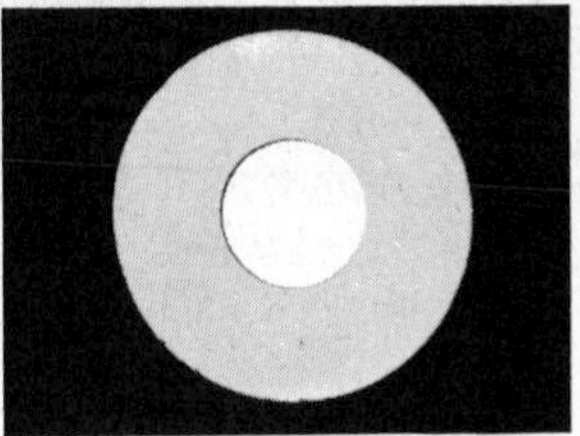
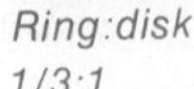
Ring:disk
1/3:1

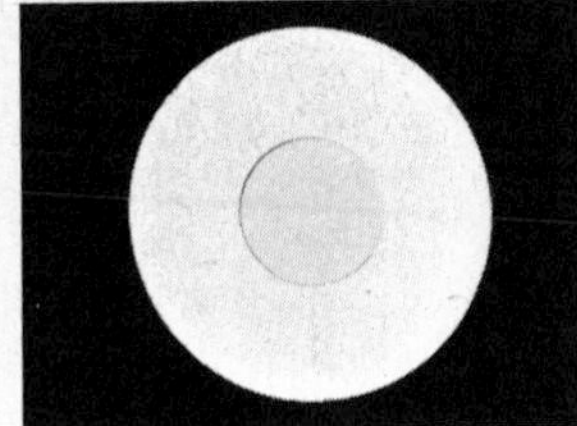
Ring:disk
2:1

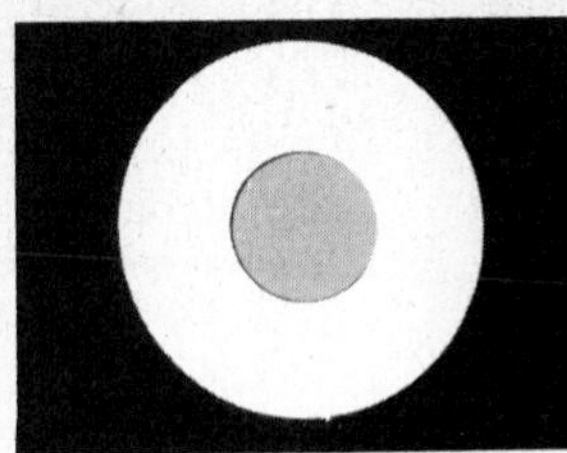
Ring:disk
4:1

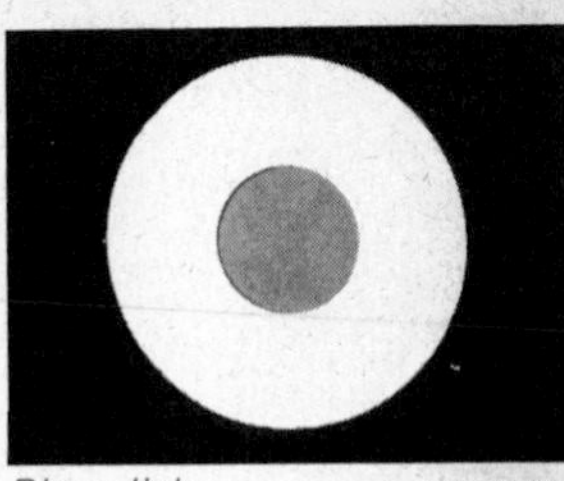
Ring:disk
8:1

RATIOS OF INTENSITY ARE RESPONSIBLE FOR PERCEIVED BRIGHTNESS

Figure 8.12 *Sample stimulus arrangements from an experiment on perceived brightness. Projectors were arranged so that a disk of light could be surrounded by a ring of light. Physical stimulus intensity was kept constant for the disk, but was varied for the ring. The ratios of ring to disk intensity are given above. The stimulus arrangements shown here represent the* perceived brightness*—what the stimulus looked like. They do not represent the physical brightness. With a ratio of ring intensity to disk intensity of 1/3 to 1, the disk was seen as light; with a ratio of 8 to 1, the disk was seen as dark. The point is that such a change in perception occurred even though the physical intensity of the disk remained the same. Perception of disk brightness depended on the* ratio *of physical energy between the ring and the disk. (From Wallach, 1963; Sol Mednick,* Scientific American.*)*

illumination on the object changes, the illumination of the surround changes too. If I turn up the lights in my room, the cover of the book on my desk looks just as bright as it did before, because the ratio of the illumination falling on the book cover and its surround has not changed. In other words, unchanged brightness ratios give constant brightness experiences, or brightness constancy. This rule must be accepted with some reservations, however, because it probably does not hold for the entire range of stimulus intensities (Jameson and Hurvich, 1964; Hochberg, 1964). But the constant ratio rule is still a useful first step toward an explanation of brightness constancy.

Perceptual stability Perceptual constancies are not perfect. Even in the most favorable circumstances, our visual perceptions are a compromise between what we know the object to be and the sensory image on the retina. Objects do appear to become slightly smaller as they move away from us, and white objects do not look quite as white when they are in shadow. In this sense, then, constancies are only relative. But our perceptions of objects correspond more closely to the true object than to the sizes of images on the retina or to the sensory stimulus in general.

We enjoy several advantages because of perceptual constancy. It would be exceedingly difficult to operate in a world where sounds changed their location when we moved our heads, and where objects changed their shapes and sizes when we saw them from different positions and distances. Imagine what it would be like if your friends and associates had a multitude of sizes and shapes that depended upon how far away they were and from what angle you viewed them. Imagine how difficult life would be if the colors of things varied markedly with changes in sunlight and weather. The relative constancy of our perceptions of shape, size, brightness, and color gives our world a perceptual stability it otherwise would not have.

Perception of Depth

Depth perception was a source of puzzlement to scientists and philosophers for hundreds of years. They could not understand how we can see a three-dimensional world with only a two-dimensional retina in each eye. Our retina is able to register images only in terms of right-left or up-down; yet we perceive the world as having the extra dimension of depth.

Figure 8.13 Three monocular factors in depth perception. The buildings and the street converge in the distance (linear perspective); more distant heights show less detail than the closer areas (clearness); and some parts of buildings are behind others (interposition). (Fundamental Photographs.)

Today we are a little more sophisticated about the problem. We realize that the ability to perceive depth is no more amazing than any other perceptual accomplishment. As we have seen, all awareness of ourselves and of the world depends upon physical energy in various forms striking special sense organs. Our brain receives various patterns of neural impulses, not tiny copies of various objects.

The problem of depth perception can be put this way: How do physical stimuli manage to stimulate our sense organs so that our brain is provided with proper cues for a perceptual experience of depth? Part of the answer is that differences in shadows, in clearness, and in the size of the image provide cues on the retina which are as informative as if the retina were able to register the third dimension directly.

Perhaps this idea can be made clearer by using an analogy. When a mathematician solves a problem involving speed and weight, he may let x stand for miles per hour and y for weight in pounds. Of course, neither x nor y has any physical resemblance to what it is representing. But as long as the manipulator of these symbols is consistent in his operations, his results will correspond with the physical world. His symbols will be adequate substitutes for the real objects.

In the case of depth perception, different cues, such as shadow and clearness, are the symbols that represent the physical world. Visual cues for depth perception are usually classified into monocular and binocular cues—that is, those which can be utilized by one eye alone and those which require two eyes.

Monocular cues Monocular cues, as the name suggests, are cues for depth that operate when only one eye is looking. These cues were first known to the ancient Greeks; they were exploited by the Renaissance painters who were concerned with techniques of giving depth to their paintings. The problem they had in presenting a three-dimensional world on a two-dimensional canvas is essentially the same problem which must be solved by our retinas. If the artist is able to paint the scene on his canvas so that it looks essentially the way it looks when its image is focused on the retina, he succeeds in achieving realistic depth in his pictures. Most of the following principles are used by the artist as well as by the eye to construct the third dimension.

LINEAR PERSPECTIVE Objects which are far away project a smaller image on the retina than near objects do. In addition, the distance separating the images of far objects appears to be smaller. Imagine that you are standing between railroad tracks and looking off into the distance. The ties seem gradually to become smaller, and the tracks to run closer together until they appear to meet at the horizon. Figure 8.13 owes part of its depth effect to such linear perspective.

CLEARNESS In general, the more clearly we can see an object, the nearer it seems. The distant mountain appears farther away on a hazy day than on a clear day because the haze in the atmosphere blurs the fine details so that we see only the larger features. Ordinarily, if we can see the details, we perceive an object as relatively close; if we can see only its outline, we perceive it as relatively far away (Figure 8.13).

Figure 8.14 Shadows and the perception of depth. If the picture is turned upside down, the buildings, especially the quonset huts, look like towers. (Wide World Photos.)

INTERPOSITION Still another monocular cue is interposition, which occurs when one thing obstructs our view of another thing. When one object is entirely in sight, but another is partly covered by it, the first object is perceived as being the nearer (Figure 8.13).

SHADOWS As Figure 8.14 shows, the pattern of shadows or of highlights in an object is very important in giving an impression of depth. When this aerial photograph of a group of quonset huts is turned upside down, the quonset huts look like towers. If you note carefully the differences between the quonset huts and the "towers," you will discover that the shadows are responsible for this effect. The reason is that we are accustomed to light coming from above. Thus when the picture is turned upside down, we do not perceive the quonset huts as illuminated from below. Instead we see towers with black-painted tops, because the dark areas are now of such a size and in such a position that they cannot possibly be shadows. We do not, of course, reason this out. The perception is immediate, based on whether or not the dark areas appear to be shadows.

GRADIENTS OF TEXTURE A *gradient* is a continuous change in something—a change without abrupt transitions. In some situations we can use the continuous gradation of texture of the visual field as a cue for depth (Gibson, 1950). The regions closest to the observer have a coarse texture and many details; as the distance increases, the texture becomes finer and finer (see Figure 8.15). This continuous transformation of texture provides the central nervous system with depth information.

MOVEMENT Whenever you move your head, you can observe that the objects in your visual field move relative to you and to one another. If you watch closely, you will find that the objects that are nearest to you

GRADIENTS OF TEXTURE ARE A FACTOR IN DEPTH PERCEPTION

Figure 8.15 *Left, an artificial texture gradient; right, a plowed field—a natural texture gradient. Note the impression of depth in both. (Gibson, 1950.)*

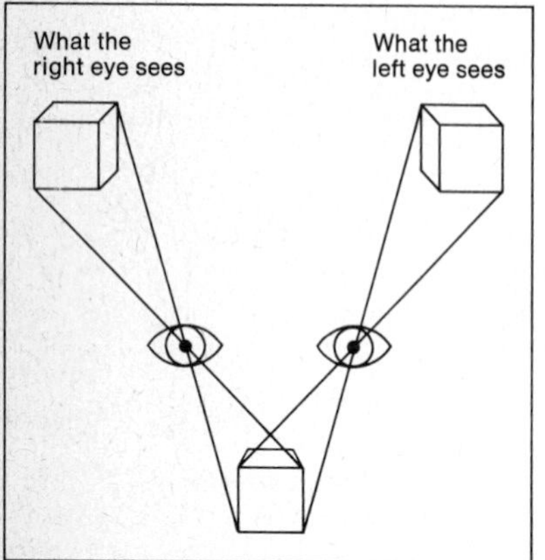

BECAUSE OUR EYES ARE SEPARATED BY SEVERAL INCHES, THE IMAGE OF AN OBJECT IS NOT EXACTLY THE SAME ON BOTH RETINAS

Figure 8.16 *The geometry of retinal disparity, an important cue to depth perception.*

appear to move in the opposite direction, whereas distant objects appear to move in the same direction as your head. This, of course, is an obvious cue to the relative distance of objects. Furthermore, whether we see real movement or move our heads, the relative amount of movement is less for far objects than for near ones.

ACCOMMODATION Accommodation is the adjustment of the shape of the lens of the eye in order to bring an image into focus on the retina. This adjustment is made by the ciliary muscles, which are attached to the lens and allow it to bulge when they contract, thus accommodating for near objects. Conversely, they let the lens become thinner when they relax, thus accommodating for far objects.

Many muscles of the body contain kinesthetic receptors which respond to the stretch and contraction of the muscles (see Chapter 18). It is possible that kinesthetic impulses from the ciliary muscles provide a cue to depth, although this has not been proved. Such a cue would be monocular, for it would operate in each eye and would not depend on seeing with two eyes at once. It would be important only for distances up to about 20 feet, since accommodation is negligible beyond that.

Binocular cues Some cues to depth perception depend on the fact that we have two eyes rather than one. These are called binocular cues.

RETINAL DISPARITY Retinal disparity is the difference in the images falling on the retinas of the two eyes. It can be explained by considering the geometry of the situations in which the two eyes view an object (see Figure 8.16). The fovea in the center of each retina is much more sensitive than the rest of the retina. When we look at an object we fixate our eyes—point them, in a manner of speaking—so that the image of the object falls mostly on each fovea. But since the two eyes are separated from each other by several inches, they get slightly different views of the object, and the two images are not exactly the same. (Compare the two

RETINAL DISPARITY HELPS US LOOK INTO THE THIRD DIMENSION

Figure 8.17 *Use a mirror whose shortest edge is at least as long as the height of the pictures. Put the mirror's edge in the space between the two pictures. Hold it at right angles to the page, with its reflecting side to the right. Close your left eye and, moving as close as is comfortable, look into the mirror with your right eye. Focus on the woman. Now open the left eye, and adjust the angle of the mirror until the two images of the woman converge. You will now see one three-dimensional picture. (Realist, Inc.)*

cubes in Figure 8.16.) Moreover, the images are more dissimilar when the object is very close, say a few inches away, than when it is far in the distance. In other words, a gradient of disparities is established as the point of fixation changes from the horizon to very near objects. From this gradient we get information about depth.

With the pictures in Figure 8.17 and a small mirror, you can demonstrate to yourself how retinal disparity contributes to the solid appearance of objects. The figure shows a scene photographed by a stereoscopic camera, a câmera that has two lenses about as far apart as the two eyes. The picture on the left was photographed by the left lens and the one on the right by the right lens. When you look at the mirror reflection of the right-hand scene according to the directions, the reflection appears to be physically located on top of the left-hand picture. When you open both eyes, one eye sees one picture and the other eye sees the other picture. Thus you achieve the illusion of depth. Although the right-left orientation of the objects in the right-hand scene has been reversed for the demonstration, close scrutiny of the pictures shows that they also differ in other details—those which result from retinal disparity.

CONVERGENCE We know that retinal disparity serves very effectively as a binocular cue to depth, but we are not so sure about another possible binocular cue. This is a kinesthetic cue from the muscles that turn and point the eyes. For objects farther away than 70 feet, the lines of sight of the eyes are essentially parallel. For nearer objects, however, the eyes turn more and more toward each other; that is they converge. If such convergence aids in depth perception, the cue is probably kinesthetic impulses from sense organs in the muscles which make the eyes converge.

Conflicting cues In general, the various cues to depth and distance perception work together and are mutually supporting. But there are cases where they conflict, and then we cannot see depth so clearly. When we look at a photograph, for example, most of the monocular depth cues are present; yet we do not perceive all the depth of the real scene because the binocular cues tell us that the photograph is flat. Thus our perception is a compromise.

It is possible, however, to eliminate the conflicting binocular cues and see more depth in a photograph. To do that, roll a piece of paper into a tube. Close one eye and look with the other eye through the tube at the photograph in Figure 8.13. You will find that the picture seems to have much more depth. By closing one eye, you eliminate the conflicting binocular cues, and by using the tube, you avoid seeing the edge or frame of the picture. The frame, of course, is a conflicting cue since real scenes do not have frames around them. You can further increase the apparent depth by having someone else hold the picture for you. In this case, you eliminate conflicting cues coming from your arms and body.

Perception of Motion

It may not seem that movement is a perceptual problem. After all, objects moving through the visual field, or along the skin, stimulate different parts of the receptor. Cannot motion perception be attributed to this changing stimulation? The answer is that, although such movement of energy across the receptor surface is important in the perception of some movements, it is neither necessary nor sufficient to explain the perceived phenomenon. It is not necessary because perceived motion often occurs without any energy flux across the receptor surface. This type of motion is called *apparent motion*. Further, it is not sufficient to explain our perception of motion because evidence shows that higher centers in the nervous system contribute to the reworking of the sensory input. Thus *real motion* is a perceived event involving perceptual organizing processes.

Apparent motion Many kinds of apparent motion, in which there is no actual movement of the stimulus pattern over the receptor, have been studied. These include stroboscopic movement, the autokinetic effect, induced movement, and movement in stationary patterns.

STROBOSCOPIC MOVEMENT This kind of apparent movement is what you see at the movies. A movie projector simply throws successive pictures of a moving scene onto the screen. If you take the film and examine the separate frames, you will see that each is slightly different from the preceding one. When the frames are presented at the right speed, continuous and smooth motion is perceived. Movies made with time-lapse photography illustrate this nicely: A slow event, such as the growth of a plant, can be made to seem like a continuous movement by taking separate pictures at different stages in the growth cycle. Then they are put together and shown in a movie projector. You have probably seen such movies, and the apparent motion is impressive—sometimes grotesque. This motion is perceived movement without any real movement of the energies over the receptor.

A variety of stroboscopic movement, sometimes called *optimal movement* or *beta movement*, is seen in experiments carried out in a more controlled and simplified situation (Wertheimer, 1912):

Two vertical bars of light are arranged a certain distance apart in a dark room and alternately turned on and off. The time interval between the flashes is the crucial thing. When it is too short (less than approximately 30 milliseconds), the lights are seen as simultaneous. When it is too long (more than approximately 200 milliseconds), they are seen as successive. But when the interval is right—60 milliseconds, for example—optimal movement is obtained, and a light is seen to move across the open space between the two stimulus lights. At slightly greater intervals, *pure movement*, or *phi movement*, is obtained. Phi movement is movement without an object, if it is possible to imagine such a thing. In other words, phi movement is an experience of movement without the experience that an object is moving.

In addition to the time interval, beta movement is strongly influenced by the intensity of the stimulating lights and the distance between them (Korte, 1915). It might be expected that such findings would lead to a physiological theory of stroboscopic motion, but in spite of efforts in that direction, no generally accepted theory of brain events in stroboscopic motion has been developed.

AUTOKINETIC EFFECT A small stationary spot of light in a completely dark room will appear to move if a person fixates on it. The movement can be large and dramatic, and it can be influenced by suggestion (Sherif, 1958). Movements of the eyes affect, but do not seem to account for, this phenomenon, which again demonstrates perception of movement, without real movement.

INDUCED MOVEMENT A stationary spot may be perceived as moving when its background or frame of reference moves. For example, the moon is often seen as racing through the sky when it is observed through a thin layer of moving clouds. The movement of the framework of clouds "induces" movement in the relatively stationary moon. Induced movement can be demonstrated in the laboratory: In a dark room, a fixed luminous spot in a luminous rectangle is seen to move if the rectangle is moved. When the framework is moved, the motion is induced in the stationary object (Duncker, 1929).

MOVEMENT IN STATIONARY PATTERNS Look at Figure 8.18 for a minute or so. The perceived undulation of the lines, although intriguing, is so strong as to be annoying for most people. Perhaps the mild conflict is part of the appeal of the picture. This painting provides another example of apparent motion without movement of an image over the retina. The movement seems to be the result of complex and shifting patterns of negative after images (see Chapter 18).

LIGHT OF DARKNESS

Figure 8.18 *Perceived motion in a stationary pattern. (Reproduction of the painting "Light of Darkness," by Julian Stanczak, 1960. Collection of Mr. and Mrs. Robert B. Mayer. Courtesy of the Martha Jackson Gallery.)*

Real movement We have said that movement of the stimulus pattern over the sensory surface does not account for all the phenomena of real motion. For instance, real motion is not simply there or not there—perceived real motion undergoes complex changes as the speed of the moving object varies. Furthermore, the perceived speed of an object depends upon the context in which it is seen. Finally, constancy of velocity must be considered.

In experimental studies of real motion, several kinds of movement are perceived when the velocity of the moving object (black squares on an endless belt, in this case) is increased (Brown, 1931; Teuber, 1960). As the threshold for perception of movement is passed, there is a stage in which the test objects appear to move backward. With further increases in speed, an apparent multiplication of the test objects takes place. Finally, at higher speeds, the objects fuse into a blur. Thus real movement is perceptually complex.

The background against which a test object moves (that is, the context) influences the perceived speed. Movement through a complex, structured field seems faster than that through a homogeneous field. And movement seems faster when the moving object is small: this is called the "scurrying mouse effect" (Teuber, 1960).

Finally, when two identical displays, with objects moving at the same velocity, are arranged so that one is some distance behind the other, the velocity of the two will seem to be about the same (Wallach, 1939; Teuber, 1960). This is true in spite of the fact that the velocity of movement over the retina from the near and far displays is quite different. Thus constancy, of the sort already described, must be at work here.

"Well, which is it? Was he very tall or very short?"

Figure 8.19 *Adaptation level in everyday life. (By special permission of the* Saturday Evening Post. *© 1964 by the Curtis Publishing Company. Also by permission of Charles Rodrigues.)*

Context and Relational Determinants

How we experience an object or event and then react to it depends upon the context in which it appears. An event is perceived against a background of other events. For instance, it has been reported that punishment used to suppress children's undesirable behavior is much more effective when it comes from loving parents (Sears et al., 1957). The punishment received from loving parents is perceived and reacted to differently from that given by callous, indifferent parents. This should give the general idea of the effect of context, but other experiments and concepts show it more explicitly.

Adaptation level The concept of *adaptation level* has been developed to quantify and provide a general theory concerning context effects (Helson, 1948, 1964). The central idea of the adaptation level theory is that the context or background acts to set a standard against which events or objects are perceived. For instance, although a mediocre student will look like a poor one in a class of good students, he may seem quite good in a class of dolts. The following experiment shows the way perception can be affected by the distribution of stimuli, or the context, to which a subject is exposed (Helson, 1964):

The perceived or judged size of squares was investigated under several different context conditions. The subjects judged squares on a scale extending from very, very small to very, very large. The context was manipulated by using *anchors*—extreme stimuli which bias a distribution of stimuli in one direction or another. The seven sizes of squares to be judged ranged from 1.0 to 3.82 inches on a side, and the two extreme anchors were squares of 0.30 and 9.00 inches on a side. These anchors were used to distort the distribution of square sizes and to provide a particular background or context against which the stimuli were perceived and judged. With the large 9.00-inch square, the other stimuli might be expected to look small by contrast; with the small anchor, we might expect the stimuli to look relatively large. This is what happened. The stimuli with the large anchor were judged to be smaller than those with the small anchor.

The concept of adaptation level is a general one which has been extended from its initial base in sensory perception to social stimuli (Helson, 1964). An example is shown in Figure 8.19. In analyzing adaptation level phenomena, there is a fine line between perception and judgment. Is it immediate experience—that is, perception—which is changed? Or is it merely the judgment of where stimuli should be placed in a series which is changed? When we attempt to extend the adaptation level theory to social situations, this type of question becomes more and more troublesome.

Figural aftereffects The idea of relational determinism has been put forward most strongly by gestalt psychologists, who use studies of the

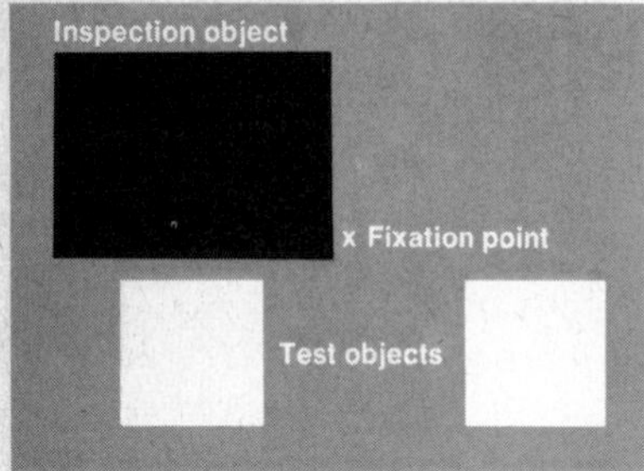

FIGURAL AFTEREFFECTS: THE INFLUENCE OF AN EARLIER PERCEPTION ON A LATER ONE

Figure 8.20 *Figures used for the production of visual figural aftereffects. The experiment is done in two parts. First, the subject fixates the X while the inspection object is present; next, the inspection object is removed and, with the same fixation point, the subject reports the appearance of the test objects. After inspection, the figural aftereffects are present and the test object on the left appears paler, farther back in space, and displaced downward when compared with the test object on the right. (Modified from Köhler and Wallach, 1944.)*

phenomena of *figural aftereffects* as demonstrations (Köhler and Wallach, 1944):

The subject first fixates a point (point X in Figure 8.20) close to an inspection object (the black box in the figure) for several minutes. After this, the inspection object is removed, the test objects (white boxes) are presented with the same fixation point X, and the subject reports how they look to him. The white box on the left of Figure 8.20 will be reported as displaced downward relative to the one on the right. The left box may also appear paler and farther back in space. The idea is that the previous fixation of the inspection object has altered the relations in the perceptual field so that the test object on the left appears different.

A theory of brain function has been proposed to account for, and make concrete, these relational effects. In brief, it states that there is a long-lasting "satiation" effect of a portion of the visual brain due to the inspection of the black box. When the left-hand white box is presented, activity from it is projected close to the visual region of the cerebral cortex which was already satiated by the inspection object. This is supposed to cause distortions in the brain processes corresponding to the white box and to perceived experience of the white box.

This brief account hardly does justice to the theory, but the important point for us is that events in one part of the perceptual field may affect perception in another part.

Transposition The importance of the perception of relations is shown in certain discrimination learning experiments (see Chapter 3). Suppose we teach a person a discrimination, using the stimuli in Figure 8.21. The learner's task is to find out which circle is correct. If we reinforce choices of the larger of the two circles, and never reinforce choices of the smaller, he will soon learn that the larger circle is the correct one. Now suppose we present him with two stimuli, one of which is the old positive stimulus while the other is a new larger one (see Figure 8.21). Now if we ask him which is correct, he will probably choose the new larger stimulus, despite the fact that the smaller stimulus in the new pair was the one which was reinforced in the first learning period. In other words, the person is responding in terms of a perceived relationship—"larger." Responding in terms of relationships is known as *transposition*.

The nature of transposition has been much argued. Some theorists have rejected the idea that it is caused by perceived relationships and have substituted explanations in terms of complex conditioning processes. However, in the light of certain animal experiments, the perceptual explanation seems to be the most plausible one (Lawrence and De Rivera, 1954).

Effects of Learning and Motivation on Perception

The degree to which perceptual experience can be modified by learning is an ancient problem. One group—the *empiricists*—have long argued that learning plays a very important role in perceptual organization; another group—the *nativists*—have argued that perceptual organization is largely inborn, or innate (see Chapter 2). This argument is still being

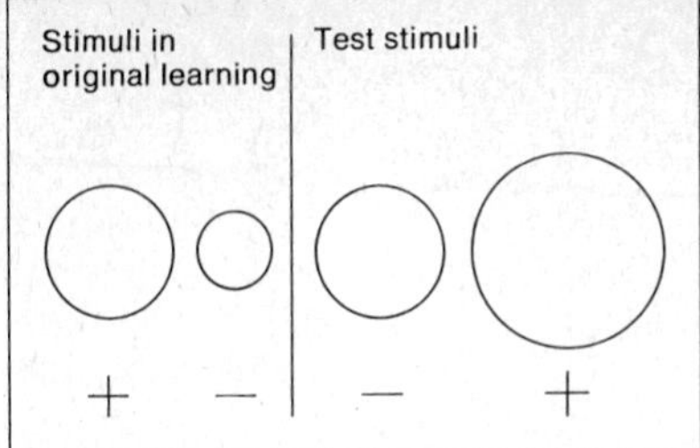

RELATIONS, NOT ABSOLUTE VALUES, ARE IMPORTANT IN TRANSPOSITION

Figure 8.21 *Sample stimuli which might be used in a transposition experiment. After learning that the larger of the first two circles is the correct response, the subject is presented with that circle and an even larger one. He then chooses the new larger circle—indicating that he was responding in terms of a perceived relationship: "larger."*

contested; good evidence exists for both points of view. The best we can do here is present some of the more interesting data on both sides.

Learning In discussing perceptual learning in Chapter 3, we were concerned with the learning of new associations between already established perceptions of objects and events. A gun may be perceived quite differently by a woman whose husband has been killed in a hunting accident and a child who is fascinated by cowboys. To the child, the perception of the gun is associated with pleasurable excitement, with fantasies of range wars and galloping horses. To the bereaved wife, the perception of the gun is associated with sadness and fear. We can think of many other examples. The sound I hear, for instance, is not just a sound; it is the creaking of the stairway which signals my wife's return from the store. The scent of freshly cut grass may recall memories of languid summer afternoons, childhood baseball games, golf, and other experiences.

While some might dispute that associations occur between already established perceptions, the crux of the empiricist-nativist argument about perception is not here. The argument turns on the issue of whether learning can affect the way the sensory input is organized into the perceived world of experience. Can learning affect this organization so that the world actually looks or sounds different? Consider the following observations from the empiricist tradition (Kohler, 1962):

The subject wore goggles with prisms in them which distorted the input in various ways. The question was whether people can learn to organize the world differently so that they see it as they usually do in spite of the distortions. One of the first things that happened when the prism goggles were put on was that the prisms broke up the light into its components, and colored fringes were seen in the visual field. These fringes went away within a few weeks. This should not surprise us too much, because the lens of the eye also tends to refract light in such a way as to produce colored fringes—*chromatic aberration.* We learn not to see the aberration colors produced by our own lens.

The prisms also bent light in such a way that straight lines were curved and right angles were obtuse or acute. When the subjects first wore the prism goggles, they perceived lines and angles in accordance with the geometry of the situation. But in time the distortions disappeared. And at first, eye and head movements produced curious effects when the prisms were on: The world expanded, contracted, and looked "rubbery" as the eyes swept over the visual field. These effects also disappeared in time.

If a person wore the goggles until the distortions disappeared in the perceived world and then removed them, colored fringes reappeared, lines and angles were again distorted, and the world once again looked "rubbery" as the eyes roved over it. The colored fringes, the distortions of lines and angles, and the expansion and contraction of the perceived world were now *opposite* in direction from the original distortions. It was as if the subject had canceled the original distortions with counterdistortions. Now he had to readapt and learn to reorganize without any counterdistortions.

Convincing counterarguments against these observations have not

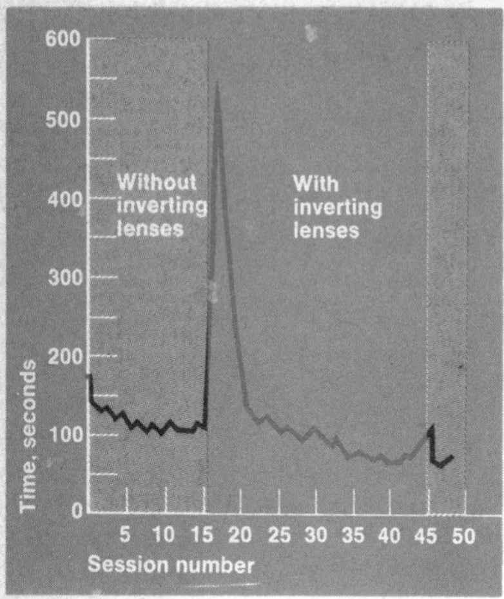

PEOPLE CAN ADAPT TO AN UPSIDE-DOWN WORLD

Figure 8.22 *Effect on a psychomotor task of wearing glasses that inverted the visual world. The graph shows the average time required for sorting packs of cards into boxes. (After Snyder and Pronko, 1952.)*

yet come from the nativists. Their arguments instead concern certain observations made in the "reversed world" and perceptual development experiments which we shall consider here and in the next section.

REVERSED WORLDS The reversed world experiments, in which goggles are worn with lenses that interchange up and down or right and left, are among the most famous experimental attempts to show the modifiability of perceptual input by experience (Stratton, 1897). Reports of what happens vary a little from one subject to another, but a general picture can be described.

When the lenses are first put on, the effect is bewildering. The individual is severely disoriented, and his eye-body coordination is badly disrupted. Every time he moves his head, the world appears to swim. Walking and moving around are difficult. When he tries to avoid walking into a chair that appears to be on the left, he steps to the right and bumps into it. To pick up an object that appears to be on his left, he must learn to reach to his right.

In most of these experiments the subjects report that, although they gradually get accustomed to the reversed world, it never looks entirely normal to them. They are able to adapt to it by making appropriate responses, and psychomotor performance may become almost as good as it was before the reversing glasses were put on (see Figure 8.22). Walking about and locating objects in the topsy-turvy world becomes easier and more automatic. The subject can turn his head without the world seeming to move. Sounds now seem to be coming from the place where the object actually is. One subject, an Austrian professor, rode his bicycle as usual to classes and carried on his ordinary routine (Kohler, 1964).

This *motor* adjustment to the reversed world may be complete. *Perceptual* adjustment, however, is not so simple. One of the subjects described it this way when he was asked whether a particular scene looked upside down to him:

> I wish you hadn't asked me. Things were all right until you popped the question at me. Now, when I recall how they *did* look *before* I put on these lenses, I must answer that they do look upside down *now*. But until the moment that you asked me, I was absolutely unaware of it and hadn't given a thought to the question of whether things were right side up or upside down (Snyder and Pronko, 1952, page 113.)

In other words, perceptual adjustment, in the sense of seeing the world as it was, is less complete and may be "unreasonable" in that only some parts of the perceived world are seen in their normal orientation; other parts are still seen as reversed (Kohler, 1951; Teuber, 1960). For instance, with spectacles which reverse the up and down dimension, subjects may report that snow is seen as falling past trees that are upside down.

Consequently some investigators believe that the perceptual world changes in these reversed world experiments, and to some degree this seems to happen (Kohler, 1964). To the extent that the world does come to look different, the empiricist point of view about the role of learning on a perception is supported. But other psychologists believe that most of the adaptation in such experiments is due to a change in the perception of the position, or proprioceptive, sense (see Chapter 18). According to this point of view, it is the proprioceptive sense which is plastic and moldable; it changes to match the distorted visual world so that the organism can adapt (Harris, 1965). A person with a changed position sense can now move accurately in the environment because the information received about body position matches the visual information. The world may still look distorted, but he can move accurately. Such an idea stresses the innate organization of visual perception and the plasticity of the position sense.

SENSORY DEPRIVATION The modification of perception by special experiences can also be shown by depriving people of sensory experience (Bexton et al., 1954; Heron et al., 1956). In these experiments, described in Chapter 6 (see page 200), subjects were isolated from as much sensory input as possible. Each lay in a partially soundproof cubicle and wore translucent goggles, gloves, and cardboard cuffs which covered the lower arm and hand. After several days of isolation, they reported some dramatic effects on perceptual organization. As illustrated in the following report, apparent movement was one.

> The whole room is undulating, swirling. . . . You were going all over the fool place at first. The floor is still doing it. The wall is waving all over the place—a horrifying sight, as a matter of fact. . . . The centre of the curtain over there—it just swirls downward, undulates and waves inside. . . . I find it difficult to keep my eyes open for any length of time, the visual field is in such a state of chaos. . . . Everything will settle down for a moment, then it will start to go all over the place. (Heron et al., 1956, page 15.)

In addition, there were distortions of shape and color: vertical and horizontal edges, when not directly fixated, were seen as curved. Colors appeared glowing and luminescent, and especially bright and saturated.

Besides these changes in perceptual organization, there were vivid reports of visual imagery in the absence of well-defined sensory input—in other words, the subjects had hallucinations. One subject, for instance, said that, with his eyes closed, he saw "a procession of squirrels with sacks over their shoulders marching 'purposely across a snow field and out of the field of 'vision' " (Bexton et al., 1954). Other experimenters have failed to find such extreme effects of sensory deprivation. But the experiments as a whole may show the plasticity of visual perception.

Perceptual development These examples showing possible effects of learning on visual perception are only samples from a voluminous literature. Can it be that all perceptual organization is the result of learning during development? The answer, which is far from complete, seems to be no; some, if not most, perceptual organization seems to be innate.

Psychologists have puzzled about, and at times argued about, the roles of heredity and environment in perception. "How much," they have asked, "is the way we perceive the world due to learning, and how much to the way our brain and nervous system are put together?" The general answer is the same as the general answer for other psychological

Figure 8.23 *The "visual cliff," a test of depth perception that can be used with almost any organism, human or animal, as soon as it can crawl or walk. At this stage, most organisms tested have good visual depth perception; they avoid the "deep side" even though they can tell by touch that the glass would support them. (From Gibson and Walk, 1960; William Vandivert,* Scientific American.*)*

abilities (see Chapter 2): Some aspects of perception arise mainly from the nervous system and the maturing of its structures; other aspects develop mainly through learning; in the middle ground is an interaction between learning processes and the perceptual abilities developed through maturation.

More specifically, however, the question is: Which perceptual abilities are to be accounted for in these various ways?

MATURATION Almost certainly the limits of sensory discrimination are established by neural and sensory structures. We cannot learn to see better in the dark or to improve our eyesight. All we can do is use our sensory capacities to the best advantage. The attention value of an intense stimulus, the figure-ground relation, the grouping of stimuli according to nearness and similarity, the perceiving of certain types of illusions—all these are phenomena that seem to depend upon the way our nervous system is structured. We say "seem" because we cannot prove conclusively that they do. We can only argue from the evidence that small children, primitive peoples, and even many of the lower animals show signs of having perceptions similar to ours in these respects.

Experiments on the maturation of depth perception have been done with an apparatus called a "visual cliff" (Walk and Gibson, 1961):

The visual cliff is a drop-off from a platform to the floor. In one version of the cliff (see Figure 8.23), the shelf of the platform and the floor are covered with a checkered pattern which enhances the perception of depth. A sheet of heavy glass, from which reflections have been reduced to a minimum, is placed over the shelf, and it extends out over the floor. Visually speaking, this creates a shallow side, the shelf, and a deep side. To a person with depth perception, there seems to be a sharp drop-off at the edge of the shelf. Between the shallow and deep sides is a starting strip on which the subject is placed. A test simply consists of seeing whether he moves to the shallow or deep side. If he perceives depth, he will avoid the drop-off on the deep side. The test can be given to any animal as soon as it is capable of crawling or walking. It has been used with human infants, kittens, monkeys, rats, lambs, kids (goats), and several other animals. The results are fairly consistent. Any animal mature enough to test is able to perceive depth, as indicated by its unwillingness to cross the glass when the well beneath it looks deep. It is interesting that babies and other organisms tested refuse to cross the "high cliff" even though they can touch the glass and tell that it can support them. Apparently they trust their eyes rather than their sense of touch.

From experiments such as these we conclude that depth perception matures in time to be useful to the organism when it can move about. For instance, in animals such as lambs that can walk on the day of birth, depth perception is present on the first day. It may be innate, or it may depend on experience acquired during the first few hours of life.

In species in which locomotion is delayed—humans, for instance—the situation is even more complicated, because there is more time for learning. The effects of maturation (or nature) and learning (or nurture) are more entangled. One way to separate the influence of nature and nurture in such situations is to try to hold nature, or environment, constant. For example, "isolation experiments" prevent animals from com-

THE DEVELOPMENT OF DEPTH PERCEPTION MAY DEPEND ON ACTIVE MOVEMENT BY THE PERCEIVER

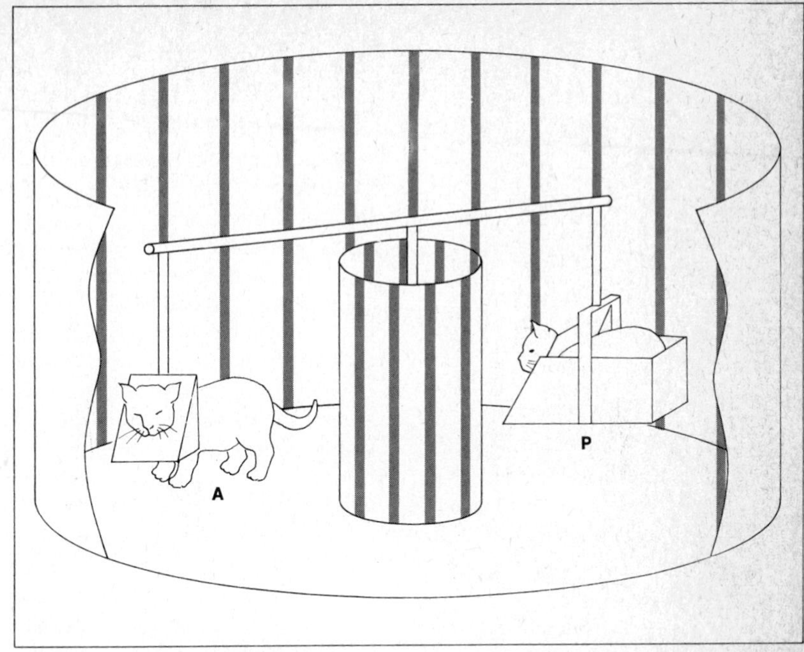

Figure 8.24 *An apparatus for studying the role of self-produced movement in the development of perception. Two groups of kittens, A (active) and P (passive), were raised in the dark except for short periods of exposure to visual stimulation in this apparatus. The* A *kittens could move rather freely around the box; the* P *kittens were closely confined by the suspended car and were passively moved through the apparatus by the* A *kittens. Thus both groups of kittens' visual experiences were about the same, but only the* A *kittens had the opportunity to develop visual-motor coordination. Subsequent tests on the visual cliff (Figure 8.23) showed that the* A *kittens developed normal depth perception but that the* P *kittens did not. (Modified from Held and Hein, 1963.)*

ing into contact with certain elements of the environment (see Chapter 2). Thus this approach involves the experimental manipulation of sensory experience.

SENSORY EXPERIENCE The role of learning in depth perception is sometimes studied by raising animals in the dark without visual experience until they are mature enough to be tested on the visual cliff. Rats raised in the dark show depth perception immediately after being brought into the light (Nealey and Edwards, 1960); no visual experience seems necessary for them to develop depth perception. With other animals—cats, for instance—the situation is different. Dark-reared cats require several days in the light with normal movement before they begin to avoid the deep side of the visual cliff apparatus. Some experiments seem to indicate that self-produced movement is necessary for the development of depth perception in cats (Held and Hein, 1963):

Two groups of kittens, one designated *P* for passive and the other *A* for active, were raised in the dark except for 3 hours a day of exposure to visual stimuli in the apparatus shown in Figure 8.24. A *P* kitten was placed in a little suspended car which moved when an *A* kitten, harnessed to the other side of the apparatus, moved. The *P* kitten's movement was much restricted by the car, but it had about the same amount of visual stimulation as the *A* kitten, because the *A* kitten's motion through the apparatus was transferred to the car in which the *P* kitten rode. Thus the visual experience of the *P* kittens was about the same as that of the *A* kittens. But unlike the *A* kittens, the *P* kittens had no opportunity to establish visual-motor coordination, because they were not free to run about in the apparatus. When tested later on the visual cliff (see Figure 8.23), the *P* kittens showed no evidence of depth perception, while the *A* kittens showed normal depth perception.

This and other experiments have been interpreted as demonstrating that self-produced movement is necessary for visual depth perception to develop. The experiment does not prove that depth perception is learned, but it does give support to the empiricists' viewpoint by suggesting that certain types of stimulation are necessary for the development of depth perception.

In other types of visual deprivation experiments, young animals are raised from birth in the dark or with occluding lenses over their eyes. One of the problems with these methods is that certain important cells of the retina degenerate if not exposed to light (Chow et al., 1957). This seems to be especially true of chimpanzees which have been used in visual-deprivation experiments, but to a lesser degree it is also true of the cat. The problem is overcome by using translucent occluders which allow diffuse light to enter the eye, but which prevent pattern vision. The results from animals raised with translucent diffusing lenses tend to show that experience with patterned light is necessary for the organization of sensory input which underlies form perception (Riesen, 1961).

Species differ in the necessity for having patterned light experience in order to develop form perception. Rats raised in the dark, for instance, even though they are possibly subject to a slight amount of retinal degeneration, show unimpaired form discrimination when they are tested (Hebb, 1937). Cats and chimpanzees, on the other hand, show impairment.

As might be expected, man also seems to require experience with patterned light stimulation to develop form perception (Senden, 1932; English edition, 1960). Observations which tend to confirm this were made on people who were seeing for the first time after operations had removed cataracts present from birth. The cataracts had sometimes allowed a little diffuse light to reach the retina, and this prevented retinal degeneration. In a sense, these patients had been wearing translucent occluding lenses from birth. Other patients, however, were probably completely blind from birth. Although some retinal degeneration occurred, it is generally believed that this was not nearly severe enough to account for the observed effects (Riesen, 1960).

For these people with newly acquired sight, what is the perceptual world like? One physician reported:

It would be an error to suppose that a patient whose sight has been restored to him by surgical intervention can thereafter see the external world. The eyes have certainly obtained the power to see, but the employment of this power, which as a whole constitutes the act of seeing, still has to be acquired from the very beginning. The operation itself has no more value than that of preparing the eyes to see; education is the most important factor. . . . (Moreau, 1910. Case cited in Senden, 1960, page 160.)

Accounts show that patients are overwhelmed by the flood of visual input. At first they are able to perceive vague figures against ground;

Figure 8.25 *The subject in one experiment on the effect of restriction of sensory input on perception. Note the cardboard tubes taped to the arms and legs. (After Nissen, Chow, and Semmes, 1951. Yerkes Regional Primate Research Center of Emory University.)*

they can see colors and follow moving figures with their eyes. Thus they perceive that something is there, and they can scan it with their eyes; but form perception is almost nonexistent. It is reported that they cannot distinguish shapes before they have had visual experience. They can learn to distinguish a triangle from a square, for example, by scanning the figures with their eyes and counting the corners, but it takes weeks or months of such scanning to develop the visual recognition of shape. Perceptual organization gradually improves, and vision becomes more nearly normal.

Vision is not the only sense in which the effects of deprivation on perceptual development can be demonstrated (Nissen et al., 1951):

A chimpanzee was restricted by having cardboard mailing tubes attached to its arms and legs at 15 weeks of age (see Figure 8.25). When it was 23 months old, training began on a tactual discrimination problem. The experimenters attempted to teach the chimpanzee to turn its head to the left or right depending on whether the left or right index finger had been squeezed lightly. For instance, if the left index finger was squeezed, the animal was rewarded for turning its head to the left and punished for turning it to the right. After more than 2,000 trials the chimpanzee had failed to learn this response. An unrestricted chimpanzee learned to do it reliably in slightly more than 200 trials. As a check to see whether the tactual restriction had impaired the subject's general ability to learn, its visual discrimination learning was studied and found to be normal.

Thus the development of perception is a function not only of maturation but also sensory experience. This should be no surprise, since we have seen that the nature-nurture question has no all-or-none answer.

CELL ASSEMBLIES AND PHASE SEQUENCES The physiological basis for the learning of perceptual organization is obscure. One theory, based in part upon data from cataract patients, proposes that the perceptual organization corresponds to acquired organization of cells in the brain (Hebb, 1949; Milner, 1957). For instance, as an infant, or a patient seeing for the first time after a cataract operation, scans a simple figure with his eyes, certain cells in the brain fire in sequence. The main idea of the theory is that such sequential firing may lead to establishment of a functional connection between the cells. Thus if cell A fires and this is followed by the firing of cell B as the person scans the figure, cells A and B will become linked together functionally, so that the firing of one will initiate the firing of the other.

Such a functional organization of cells has been called a *cell assembly*. Cell assemblies might be the neural representation of simple parts of figures, such as corners or angles. Cell assemblies themselves may be organized into larger units by the same process of sequential firing—first one cell assembly, then another, and so on. For instance, as a person scans a figure, the cell assemblies of the corners and lines may be sequentially activated and organized into a larger functional unit called a *phase sequence*. These may be the neural representation of whole figures—a triangle, for example. Note that according to this theory, the cell assemblies and phase sequences are developed through learning.

The theory involves more than our simple account would imply, but cell assemblies and phase sequences are two of the main ideas. When the theory was proposed, there was no direct evidence for it. Now, as more data about the functioning of the central nervous system are becoming available, we find evidence that some of the perceptual organization which was thought to be due to learned cell assemblies may actually be innate (Hubel and Wiesel, 1963). Whatever the outcome of future attempts to obtain direct evidence for learned cell assemblies and phase sequences, the theory has done its job. Many ideas for valuable experiments and for the organization of diverse data have come from it.

Motivation It seems reasonable to think that our needs and motives, both learned and unlearned, have an influence on perception. When people are motivated or emotionally involved, they tend to see what they want to see, hear what they want to hear, and believe what they want to believe. Many experiments have attempted to show that this commonsense notion is correct. Unfortunately, some of them have had serious inherent faults. One of the best demonstrations of the effects of motivation on perception involved estimates of size (Lambert et al., 1949):

Nursery school children, aged 3 to 5, were presented with a machine which had a crank on it. They received a poker chip for turning the crank 18 turns. By putting this poker chip into a slot, they could obtain candy. Before the experiment began, each child estimated the size of the poker chip by comparing it with a spot of light, the size of which could be varied by the experimenter until the child said the two objects matched. Again, after the children had been rewarded with candy for cranking out poker chips, estimates of size were made. The poker chips now seemed significantly larger to the children. The experimenters then instituted an extinction procedure during which the children got no candy for their efforts in cranking. Estimates of size were again made. The chips had shrunk back to their former apparent size. After that, the children were again rewarded with candy, and the chips again increased in apparent size.

This experiment, which is only one of several well-designed studies that might have been described, indicates that when the poker chip acquired value—that is, when it came to represent something the child wanted—it was perceived as larger than when it had no value. The experiment supports the general conclusion that a person's motivation affects his perception even of such physical characteristics as size.

Generally speaking, however, it is in the perceiving of such complex things as social and interpersonal relationships that our own internal needs and biases have their greatest effect. The concrete objects in our world do not allow us too much freedom in perception; everyone perceives them in much the same way. The occasional atypical individual who sees the table, the chair, or the bookcase differently winds up in a psychiatrist's office. On the other hand, such social situations as parties, conversations, and contacts with friends are often indefinite and ambiguous. Our perceptions of them are less definite and stable than our perceptions of physical objects. How many times have we pondered over what a friend "meant by that remark"? We all remember cases in which a remark was perceived as an insult or slight by one person but was regarded as a compliment by another. And most of us, at one time or another, have suffered because something we said or did was misperceived or misinterpreted by others.

Synopsis and summary

Because everyone behaves in accordance with the way he perceives the world, perception provides one key for unlocking the riddle of behavior. We have seen that the perceived world is a construction and an achievement. Information comes in through the sensory channels, and the perceptual processes act upon it to form it into the world of experience. Perceptual experience is characterized by the following general features: selectivity of input, organization of input, constancy of experience in spite of varying inputs, a dimension of depth, movement, the effect of context, the importance of relationships between inputs, and the influence of both learning and motivation.

1. Perception refers to the world of immediate experience—the world as seen, heard, felt, smelled, or tasted.

2. Our perceptual experience depends to a large extent upon organization by the brain of the input coming through the sensory channels—the receptors and nerve trunks from them. But some organization takes place in the channels themselves; Mach bands are an example of organization at the receptor level.

3. Attention, or selection of input, is an important determinant of what is perceived. It has a focus in which events are clearly perceived and a margin in which things are less clearly perceived, and it constantly shifts from one stimulus to another.

4. External factors controlling attention are (*a*) intensity and size of stimuli, (*b*) contrast between a stimulus and its background, (*c*) the repetition of stimuli, and (*d*) movement. Internal factors controlling attention are (*a*) motives, needs, or interests, and (*b*) a set, or expectancy, for a particular kind of stimulus.

5. Objects are usually seen as figures on a ground. It is, in fact, almost impossible to "see" them any other way. Such figure-ground perception depends, in turn, on the perception of contours marking off an object from its background.
6. A person's perceptual processes organize the world into objects and groups of objects. Thus he tends to perceive as a group (*a*) those objects that are close together, (*b*) those that are similar to each other, (*c*) those that are symmetrically arranged, and (*d*) those that form some continuous line or pattern.
7. Perception also tends to close gaps, so that a person perceives an object even when some of its parts are missing.
8. One of the most adaptive things about perception is that it tends to be relatively constant despite a considerable change in the stimulation of the sense organs. For example, shapes usually appear about the same, whether we view them from an angle or head-on; sizes tend to appear relatively constant, whether objects are near or far away; brightness remains comparatively constant even under different illuminations.
9. Even though the retina of the eye is flat and receives a two-dimensional picture, people perceive three-dimensional depth by using several depth cues. Most of these cues are monocular, but some are binocular.
10. The principal monocular cues are (*a*) linear perspective, (*b*) clearness, (*c*) interposition, (*d*) shadows, (*e*) gradients of texture, and (*f*) movement.
11. The chief binocular cue to depth is retinal disparity, that is, the slight difference in the images projected on the two eyes when they view the same situation.
12. Both apparent and real motion are matters of perception. The major types of apparent motion—motion without a moving flux of energy across a receptor—are (*a*) stroboscopic motion, (*b*) optimal, or beta movement, (*c*) pure, or phi, movement, (*d*) autokinetic movement, (*e*) induced movement, and (*f*) movement in stationary patterns. The perception of real movement cannot be attributed only to the movement of energy across a receptor.
13. Adaptation level, figural aftereffects, and transposition are examples which show that the context surrounding an object or event is important in determining perception.
14. Perception can be modified by experience. Learning influences the organization of the basic sensory data into the perceptual world of immediate experience.
15. Experiments with goggles, "reversed world" experiments, and experiments in sensory deprivation illustrate the importance of experience in the organization of sensory input.
16. Both innate and experiential factors contribute to the development of perception. The importance of sensory experience has been studied by raising animals under conditions of reduced sensory input and by studying cases of patients seeing for the first time after removal of cataracts.
17. Perception is influenced by motivation. To a considerable extent, we perceive what we want to perceive.

Related topics in the text

Chapter 3 Principles of Learning Perceptual learning—the learning of new ways of perceiving the world through the association of already existing perceptions—is considered at length.

Chapter 14 Social Influences on Behavior Our perceptions of social situations and people determine our responses to them. For example, our perception of the person and the situation he is in determine what motives we attribute to him.

Chapter 15 Attitudes and Beliefs The strength of an attitude is, in part, a matter of the context in which it is placed; to this degree, attitudes may have something in common with context effects in perception.

Chapter 18 Sensory Processes
This chapter discusses the mechanisms of operation of the sensory channels and some of the codes—the afferent codes—for perception which are closely tied to receptor action.

Suggestions for further reading

Bartley, S. H. *Principles of perception.* (2nd ed.) New York: Harper & Row, 1969.
A basic textbook on perception.

Beardslee, D. C., and Wertheimer, M. (Eds.) *Readings in perception.* New York: Van Nostrand Reinhold, 1958.
Selected classic articles from the literature on perception.

Dember, W. N. *The psychology of perception.* New York: Holt, 1960.
A description and review of many of the basic topics in perception, written with emphasis on a psychological, not a physiological, point of view.

Gregory, R. L. *Eye and brain.* New York: McGraw-Hill, 1966. (Paperback.)
A colorful and intriguing book written in a popular style. It provides good coverage of the field of perception and presents an interesting theory of the origin of certain illusions.

Haber, R. N. (Ed.) *Contemporary theory and research in visual perception.* New York: Holt, 1968.
A collection of important papers summarizing current work in visual perception. The papers are not easy, and the beginner may wish to start elsewhere and work up to this book.

Hochberg, J. E. *Perception.* Englewood Cliffs, N.J.: Prentice-Hall, 1964. (Paperback.)
An interesting and well-written introduction to the phenomena of perception.

King, R. A. (Ed.) *Readings for an introduction to psychology.* (3d ed.) New York: McGraw-Hill, 1971. (Paperback.)
A book of readings designed to accompany this text. Some articles on perception are included.

Solley, C. M., and Murphy, G. *Development of the perceptual world.* New York: Basic Books, 1960.
An interesting book that stresses perceptual learning as a process involving expectancy, attending, reception, trial-and-check, and final perceptual organization.

Vernon, M. D. (Ed.) *Experiments in visual perception: Selected readings.* New York: Penguin, 1966. (Paperback.)
Some interesting and important experiments in visual perception are included in this collection of readings.

Von Fieandt, Kai. *The world of perception.* Homewood, Ill.: Dorsey, 1966.
Includes some unusual examples concerning the perception of pictorial art and perception of the self.

Zubek, J. P. *Sensory deprivation: Fifteen years of research.* New York: Appleton Century Crofts, 1969.
An account of the major discoveries in experiments on sensory isolation and deprivation.

PART TWO INDIVIDUAL DIFFERENCES

I often say that when you can measure what you are speaking about, and express it in numbers, you know something about it; but when you cannot express it in numbers, your knowledge is of a meagre and unsatisfactory kind. . . .

Lord Kelvin

Progress in science often depends upon the development of quantitative methods. Without such methods, science is limited to crude observation and classification. With them, it can greatly extend and refine the conclusions it can draw from its data. To take a simple example, people have always known that stones fall when they are dropped, but physics made little progress as a science until early scientists began to measure how fast stones fall, how far they fall in a given period of time, and whether stones fall as fast as apples or feathers.

Similarly, even the ancients recognized that some people were slow-witted and others nimble-witted, some courageous and others timid. But psychology began to be a science only when it found ways of measuring such differences, attaching meaningful numbers to them, and then making useful predictions about them.

Although the problems of measurement are much the same in all sciences, psychologists and behavioral scientists are probably more concerned about the logic of measurement than most physical scientists. The reason is that many of the things they want to measure are complex and cannot be measured on physical scales. Courage, for example, is not the same sort of thing as the length of a table; there is no simple yardstick for measuring a man's courage. Not everything psychological is so difficult to measure as courage, but much of it is. Psychologists and behavioral scientists have therefore had to invent new methods of measurement and new ways of describing the results of measurement.

The specific techniques developed for measuring things such as personality, intelligence, and aptitudes are described in Chapter 10. This chapter covers two related areas: (1) the general rules of psychological measurement, and (2) the statistics used in analyzing such measurements. The term *statistics* can be used either to mean a collection of measurements, or to mean the methods used to analyze the measurements. The term is used mainly in the latter sense here.

Kinds of Measurement

Measurement, formally defined, is the assignment of numerals (numbers) to objects or events according to rules. The rules can be complex, as they often are in engineering and physics; but the first step in every case is the *classification* of objects into categories. Three kinds of categories can be employed: (1) qualitative differences, (2) ranking according to some attribute, and (3) position along a numerical scale denoting

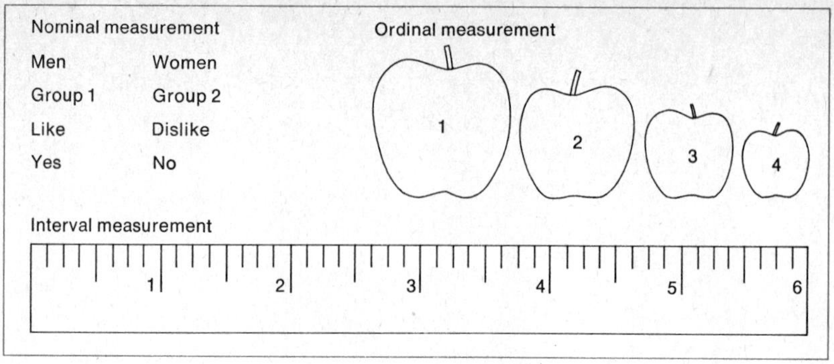

Figure 9.1 *Three kinds of measurement.* Nominal measurement *is classification according to qualitative differences, for example, men and women.* Ordinal measurement *is classification according to rank on some attribute, such as size or brightness.* Interval measurement *is classification according to position on a scale of magnitude along which equal differences in numbers are truly equal.*

Table 9.1 *Paired comparisons of preferences for vegetables: 100 individuals were asked to express their preference between pairs of vegetables. All possible combinations of pairs were presented. The number in each column is the proportion of the choices in which the vegetable named at the top was preferred over the one named at the side. In comparisons of carrots-carrots, spinach-spinach, etc. the preference value is obviously .50.*

Source: Based on Guilford, 1954.

	Carrots	Spinach	String beans	Peas	Corn
Carrots	.50	.49	.57	.71	.76
Spinach	.51	.50	.63	.68	.63
String beans	.43	.37	.50	.53	.64
Peas	.29	.32	.47	.50	.63
Corn	.24	.37	.36	.37	.50
Total preference	1.97	2.05	2.53	2.79	3.16

magnitude. Depending on the type of classification used, the measurement is known as (1) nominal, (2) ordinal, or (3) interval measurement, respectively (see Figure 9.1).

Nominal measurement A *nominal measurement* is nothing more than a classification of things into mutually exclusive categories so that all the things in one category are alike in some particular respect. If we took a basket of mixed fruit and sorted it into separate piles of bananas, oranges, or apples, we would be making the kind of classification involved in nominal measurement.

In scientific use, nominal measurements are often employed to designate groups, as indicated in Figure 9.1. Group 1 may be the experimental group that is given some particular treatment not given to group 2, a control group. In making comparisons of sex differences, men would constitute one category and women another. Or in comparing achievement of the graduates of different colleges, the categories might be college 1, college 2, college 3, and so on. Nominal measurements may be employed to designate dependent variables (see page 14). Simple categories such as "pass-fail," "for-against," or "like-dislike," which are often dependent variables in a study, are also essentially nominal measurements.

Probably the most important use of nominal measurements in psychology and the social sciences is in tests from which more sophisticated measurements are compounded. For example, the items on almost any objective examination, or on psychological tests of intelligence and personality, involve nominal measurements. Each item calls for the

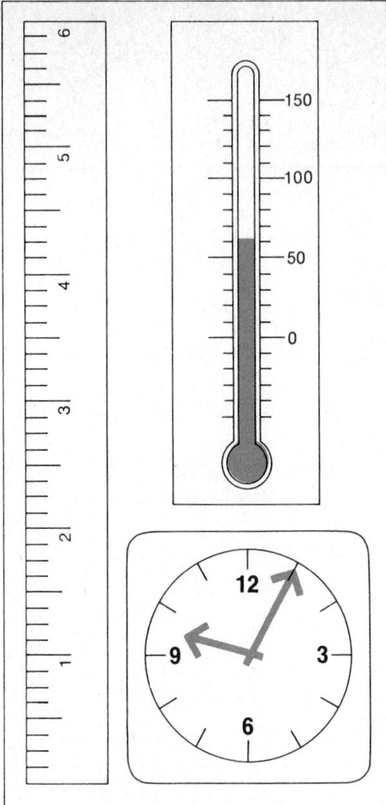

ON AN INTERVAL SCALE, EQUAL DIFFERENCES ARE EQUAL

Figure 9.2 *Three examples of interval scales: A ruler, a thermometer, and a clock. On each of these scales, equal differences between numbers represent equal differences in what is being measured—length, temperature, or time. The ruler is the only example here of an interval scale with a true-zero point. Neither a Fahrenheit nor a Celsius temperature scale has a true-zero point; 60° is not twice as hot as 30°. That is, an object at 60° does not contain twice as much heat as one at 30°, nor does it contain twice as much at 2° as at 1°. This should be clear when one considers that an object at some reading below 0°C or F also contains a certain amount of heat.*

choice of a simple category, such as *a, b, c,* or *d,* or "like" or "dislike," or "worry" or "don't worry." By making a choice, the individual places himself in one category or another on that particular item.

In the typical test, of course, a person makes a good many such choices. These can be counted according to some scoring system, and his score can be compared with another person's score. In this case, the outcome is no longer nominal measurement; it becomes either ordinal or interval measurement, as discussed below.

Ordinal measurement *Ordinal measurement* is the *ranking* of things according to some attribute they possess—size (for example, the four sizes of apple in Figure 9.1), brightness, attractiveness, or whatever. Suppose that I ask you to rank-order your preference for apples, oranges, bananas, pears, apricots, and prunes. You assign oranges your number 1 preference, bananas your number 2, pears your number 3, and so on. You have thus made an ordinal measurement of your preferences for this particular list of fruits. Because of its simplicity, this method of making ordinal measurements in commonly used in psychology and the social sciences.

In general, however, it is not so reliable as another method, the method of *paired comparisons.* This is primarily because a person in making each ranking cannot pay equal attention, and hence cannot do justice, to all other members of the list. The paired-comparisons method has the virtue of requiring that an objective judgment be made of only two things at a time. As will be demonstrated in Table 9.1, it also has the virtue of allowing the scientist to convert ordinal measurements into the more precise interval form of measurement.

In making paired comparisons, the first step is similar to the categorization described above. Things are compared two at a time, and some judgment is made of "greater" or "less," "like" or "dislike," "agree" or "disagree." Having done this for one pair, a person can make a similar comparison between one member of the pair and a third item. This process can be continued for all the items to be considered (see Table 9.1). When it has been completed, the number of times each item has been ranked above or below another item can be counted, and all the items can be ranked. This particular method has often been used by psychologists for the construction of attitude scales and other tests.

Interval measurement An *interval measurement* is a classification according to the magnitude of the difference between one thing and another. In other words, it is a classification according to position on a scale, as on the ruler, thermometer, and clock shown in Figure 9.2.

Take the thermometer as an example. Two scales are available for reading temperature: the Fahrenheit scale, used in households and commerce, and the Celsius (centigrade) scale, used in scientific measurements. The Fahrenheit thermometer is marked off so that 32°F represents the freezing point of water and 212°F the boiling point. The numbers between these points arbitrarily designate a given expansion or contraction of the indicator liquid. A change in the height of the liquid in the thermometer, say 1.2 millimeters, always means a change of 1° in temperature—no matter whether the difference is between 0 and 1°, between 53 and 54°, or between 154 and 155°. Equal differences along the scale represent equal differences in the behavior of the temperature-indicating liquid (see Figure 9.2). The same is true of the Celsius thermometer.

Uses of measurements These kinds of measurement clearly differ in the amount of information they convey. A nominal measurement merely tells us in what qualitative category a thing belongs. Ordinal measurements tell us more; they indicate that one thing possesses more or less of a characteristic than other things; but they do not reveal how much more or how much less. Interval measurement, on the other hand, does exactly that: It gives the magnitude of the difference between things.

At times we want as much information as we can get in order to describe a person or to make a prediction precisely. In those cases, we like to use interval scales. We automatically have interval measurements when we measure human behavior in physical units such as time. On the other hand, strictly *psychological* measurements made with such instruments as intelligence tests or attitude scales do not automatically give us interval measurements.

If we want interval measurements, we must start off with nominal measurements (which is what the individual items on most psychological tests provide), or with ordinal measurements (which are used in rating scales). Then through the compounding of such measurements, and sometimes through special statistical techniques, we convert nominal or ordinal measurements into interval scales. One way in which this can be done has already been indicated (see page 291).

Two other points should be made about the use of measurements. One is that nominal or ordinal measurements alone may be sufficient for some purposes. If we want to know, for example, whether individuals of high aptitude are more apt to succeed than those of low aptitude in a particular course of training, nominal or ordinal measurements may be as good as more precise interval measurements. In fact, in order to simplify computations, research workers sometimes reduce what was originally a set of interval measurements to ordinal ones, and get about the same result.

The other point is that the kinds of statistics we can use to summarize results, or to indicate a particular person's performance, depend on the kinds of measurements made. Some statistical measures, such as the arithmetic average, are simply not appropriate for ordinal measurements. This is brought out later when we describe ways of summarizing groups of measurements.

Distribution of Measurements

For most purposes, one lone measurement is of little value. It may do for reading a thermometer, but only because we have read thermometers many times and know how a particular reading compares with other possible readings. Thus we already have a frame of reference for interpreting a reading. In psychology, however, we usually need a fair number of measurements of some kind. For instance, if we are trying to describe personality characteristics of a person, we must first have enough measurements to provide a frame of reference for comparing any one measurement with a group of measurements. In doing research, we may need a relatively large number of measurements, if for no other reason than to avoid getting results that are a matter of chance or that are biased in one way or another. This is especially the case when the method of systematic observation is used (see page 18). When the experimental method is used and when the control is good—especially when a baseline has already been established (see page 16)—a few measurements may be enough, and elaborate statistical manipulation may not be required.

If we have obtained a large number of measurements of any given type, the problem of what to do with them arises. Indeed, it frequently happens that a person untrained in statistics collects a lot of measurements, and then comes to a psychologist or statistician and asks, "What do I do with them?" It is a little late to be asking the question at that point, because the kind of measurements one makes hinges on what he expects to do with them. They can be processed in several different ways, depending on the kind of measurements they are. The rest of this chapter is concerned with the processing, that is, the statistical treatment, of psychological measurements.

Counting frequencies The first step, usually, is to find some way of organizing measurements so that the researcher can see what they are like. To do this, he *counts frequencies*. This means that he determines how many measurements of a given kind he has. For nominal measurements, this step is easy. All he needs to do is count the cases falling into each of the categories used in making the measurements. Such counting is the common way of handling and presenting many measurements of popular interest: the number of automobiles purchased in March, the number of people who say they will vote Republican in the next election, the number of people who prefer Aroma soap, and so on. One can make counts of ordinal and interval measurements, but this involves another step that we come to in a moment.

After making a count of nominal measurements, the investigator usually finds it desirable to present his figures in some kind of chart so that others can immediately grasp the results. There are as many kinds of charts as there are artists to invent them, but two basic forms are commonly employed. First, the *pie chart* is suitable for depicting counts converted to percentages. One merely takes a circle, slices "pieces of pie" that correspond to the percentage of cases falling into a given category, and then labels the categories. From a pie chart, a reader can quickly see the relative proportions of cases, dollars, or whatever, in each category. Another common form is the bar graph, or more technically, the *histogram*. It can be used either for raw counts or for percentages. It simply represents the counts or percentages by relative heights of bars.

Frequency distributions The method of counting frequencies, and then of representing them with a histogram, is also the simplest way of handling interval measurements. This requires, as we indicated, an additional step: The scale on which the measurements were made must be

Figure 9.3 *An apparatus for measuring braking reaction time. (American Automobile Association.)*

Table 9.2 *Braking reaction time, in seconds, of 200 normal young men on a test of automobile driving. (The scores are arbitrarily presented in blocks of five for convenience.) The following measures of central tendency were computed from this set of scores: arithmetic mean, 0.60; median, 0.60; mode, 0.62 from this table, or 0.61 from the frequency distribution in Table 9.3. The standard deviation is 0.10.*

0.65	0.42	0.66	0.77	0.61	0.82	0.44	0.68	0.48	0.60
0.61	0.48	0.64	0.58	0.43	0.55	0.71	0.62	0.54	0.62
0.75	0.67	0.46	0.66	0.57	0.54	0.72	0.43	0.76	0.53
0.70	0.77	0.58	0.51	0.55	0.73	0.41	0.56	0.53	0.48
0.74	0.46	0.57	0.48	0.90	0.60	0.63	0.64	0.75	0.55
0.69	0.62	0.64	0.57	0.73	0.56	0.49	0.66	0.70	0.59
0.72	0.62	0.66	0.56	0.59	0.60	0.57	0.49	0.64	0.66
0.45	0.83	0.69	0.78	0.51	0.58	0.66	0.61	0.64	0.56
0.53	0.60	0.62	0.65	0.62	0.44	0.61	0.60	0.74	0.64
0.85	0.49	0.51	0.39	0.58	0.64	0.69	0.68	0.52	0.74
0.55	0.68	0.61	0.40	0.56	0.59	0.45	0.59	0.65	0.62
0.46	0.64	0.36	0.72	0.41	0.74	0.51	0.58	0.69	0.55
0.50	0.55	0.56	0.49	0.65	0.51	0.62	0.67	0.48	0.48
0.60	0.63	0.61	0.64	0.58	0.60	0.73	0.95	0.69	0.52
0.78	0.70	0.54	0.58	0.65	0.51	0.72	0.63	0.54	0.45
0.42	0.47	0.55	0.65	0.56	0.74	0.54	0.66	0.58	0.70
0.59	0.57	0.49	0.63	0.66	0.46	0.57	0.88	0.61	0.46
0.47	0.62	0.55	0.66	0.51	0.53	0.52	0.59	0.53	0.56
0.70	0.47	0.68	0.57	0.54	0.67	0.48	0.57	0.68	0.58
0.63	0.72	0.62	0.39	0.63	0.67	0.57	0.68	0.61	0.52

Table 9.3 *Frequency distribution of the data in Table 9.2. A large number of scores may be summarized by grouping them into classes, then counting the frequency (f) of scores—in this case, the number of men—falling in each class.*

Class intervals, seconds	Tallies	Frequency (*f*) [tallies totaled]
0.93–0.95	I	1
0.90–0.92	I	1
0.87–0.89	I	1
0.84–0.86	I	1
0.81–0.83	II	2
0.78–0.80	II	2
0.75–0.77	卌	5
0.72–0.74	卌 卌 III	13
0.69–0.71	卌 卌 I	11
0.66–0.68	卌 卌 卌 IIII	19
0.63–0.65	卌 卌 卌 卌 I	21
0.60–0.62	卌 卌 卌 卌 卌	25
0.57–0.59	卌 卌 卌 卌 IIII	24
0.54–0.56	卌 卌 卌 卌 II	22
0.51–0.53	卌 卌 卌 I	16
0.48–0.50	卌 卌 III	13
0.45–0.47	卌 卌 I	11
0.42–0.44	卌 I	6
0.39–0.41	卌	5
0.36–0.38	I	1

marked off into a reasonable number of equal *intervals*. In order to illustrate this step, let us take a study of the reaction time of automobile drivers. The measurements in this case were all made in terms of time, which for our purposes may be treated as an interval scale.

The study was conducted in a mock-up of an automobile, consisting of a seat, steering wheel, accelerator, and brake pedal (see Figure 9.3). In front of the driver was a panel on which a red light could be made to appear without warning. The subject was instructed to place his foot on the brake the moment the red light appeared. An electrical circuit connected the red light and the brake, and an electric clock recorded the exact time—the *reaction time*—between the moment the light turned red and the moment at which the brake pedal was depressed by 1 centimeter. One braking reaction-time measurement was made on each of 200 men. The measurements obtained are listed in Table 9.2.

We can look over the data in Table 9.2 and guess that the average reaction time was between 0.55 and 0.65. We can also estimate that the reaction times varied from about 0.45 to 0.75 second. Looking over the "raw figures," however, is not a very satisfactory way, and certainly not a precise way, of finding out what the data are like. A better method is to construct a *frequency distribution* of the measurements.

There are two steps in forming a frequency distribution from raw data such as those in Table 9.2. The first is to choose class intervals into which the scale of measurement can be divided (see the first column of Table 9.3). Such class intervals may be selected arbitrarily so long as

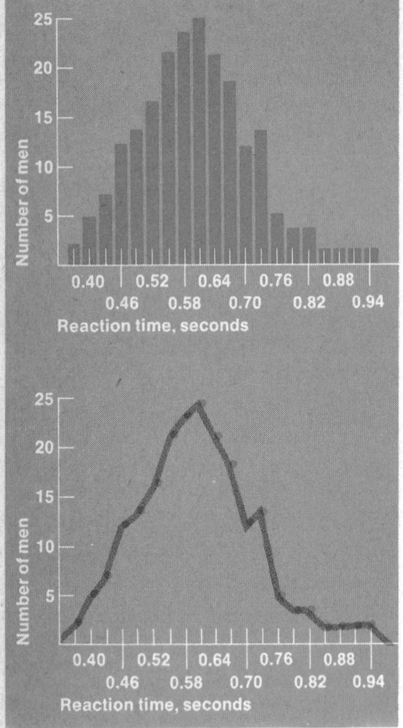

A GROUP OF MEASUREMENTS CAN BE PLOTTED AS A HISTOGRAM OR A FREQUENCY POLYGON

Figure 9.4 *A histogram (top) and a frequency polygon (bottom) presenting the data in Tables 9.2 and 9.3.*

(1) the number of intervals is sufficiently large to permit us to see the general distribution of the measurements, and (2) all the class intervals are equal in extent from the beginning of one interval to the beginning of the next; that is, as shown in Table 9.3, each interval spans 0.03 second. Usually 15 to 20 intervals is a good number to take, because this number yields just about the same results as a larger, more cumbersome number of class intervals. In the case given in Table 9.3, exactly 20 class intervals covered the distance from 0.36 to 0.95.

The second step in constructing a frequency distribution is to tabulate or count the number of cases falling into each of the class intervals. This can be done, as illustrated in Table 9.3, by making a tally alongside each interval for each score falling within that interval. The result is a frequency distribution. It is so called because it gives the frequency or count of measurements in each interval and shows how the frequencies are distributed along the scale of measurement, which in this case is a time scale. Once the counts have been made, they can be shown in either a *histogram* or a *frequency polygon* (see Figure 9.4). The difference between the two is simply that the histogram displays frequencies with bars and the polygon does it with points connected by lines. Otherwise, they represent the same information.

In most frequency distributions of scores on psychological traits, the great bulk of the scores falls in the middle of the distribution, and fewer and fewer scores are found toward the high and low extremes (see Figure 9.4). The distribution also tends to be symmetrical: about as many scores are found at the high end—called the "positive end"—as at the low—or "negative"—end. If for some reason scores tend to pile up at one end or the other of the distribution, it is called a *skewed distribution* (see Figure 9.5). Skews are termed *positive* or *negative* depending upon the direction of the longer "tail" of the distribution. Thus if scores pile up at the low end of a frequency polygon, the tail is toward the high, or positive, end, and the distribution is said to be positively skewed. If scores accumulate at the high end, the frequency polygon is negatively skewed. Distributions are often skewed when a particular subsample of a larger population is tested. For instance, the frequency polygon for intelligence test scores from college students is negatively skewed.

Normal curve All frequency polygons constructed from real measurements show some unevenness. In general, the more measurements we take, the smoother the graph becomes, because many of the irregularities are the result of chance variations in the population measured. It can be shown both mathematically and by experiments in probability that as the number of measurements increases and as other conditions of measurement are controlled, many frequency polygons eventually approach a shape known as the *normal curve*. The outline of this curve is shown in Figure 9.6. It is no longer a polygon, but rather a smooth and symmetrical bell-shaped affair.

The normal curve depicts exactly the same thing as the frequency polygon. Any point along the curve represents the relative frequency of measurements occurring within an interval along the scale. Scale intervals are not depicted, for they are arbitrary; the exact frequencies are not given, because they depend on the number of measurements taken.

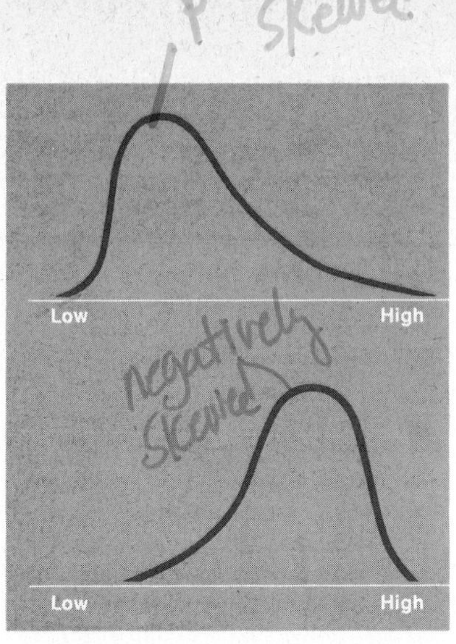

DISTRIBUTIONS OF MEASUREMENTS MAY BE POSITIVELY OR NEGATIVELY SKEWED

Figure 9.5 *A skewed curve has a longer "tail" on one side than on the other. The curve on the top is positively skewed—the "tail" is toward the high end of the distribution. The curve on the bottom is negatively skewed.*

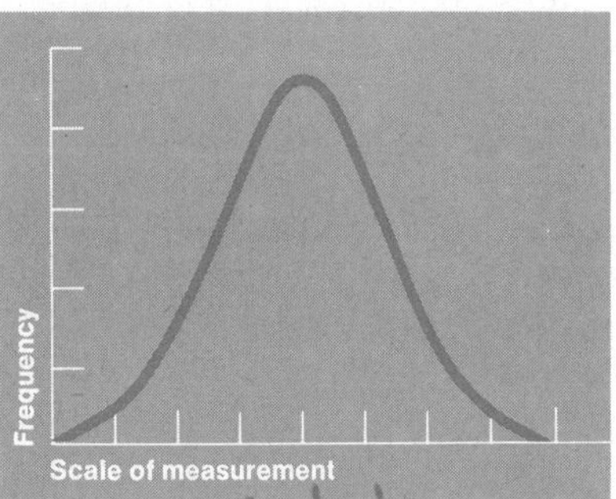

FREQUENCY DISTRIBUTIONS OF PSYCHOLOGICAL MEASUREMENTS OFTEN APPROXIMATE THE NORMAL, OR BELL-SHAPED, CURVE

Figure 9.6 *An idealized frequency distribution known as the normal probability curve. The height of the curve at any point represents the relative frequency of measurements having the particular value indicated on the abscissa.*

The *shape* of the curve—that is, the heights of the points along the curve *relative* to each other—is the important thing.

Many psychological traits are distributed so that they tend to form normal distributions when large groups of people are tested. Intelligence test scores, for instance, are normally distributed in the population. This simply means that few people make extremely high or low scores—most scores fall near the middle—and the shape of the distribution is describable by the mathematical formula for the normal curve.

Frequency polygons constructed from measures of psychological traits usually tend to become more and more like the normal curve as more and more measures are obtained. Since we thus know the shape that the distribution would have if all measurements could be made—for example, if all people could be tested—the normal curve provides a model distribution against which other distributions can be compared.

Measures of Frequency Distributions

In the preceding section, we described ways of organizing measurements into frequency distributions so that we can "get a good look at them." For some purposes, such as writing popular magazine articles or inspecting someone else's data, this may be enough. For other purposes, especially any sophisticated use of measurements, it is not. A more precise measure of the characteristics of the distribution is needed. Such a measure, sometimes called a *statistic,* can be derived mathematically from the distribution and can be used to characterize it in an exact way. There are two general kinds of measures of frequency distributions: (1) measures of central tendency and (2) measures of variability.

Measures of central tendency Measures of *central tendency,* sometimes called measures of central value, are numbers that fix the center of the distribution. The center, of course, must be a place on the scale. Hence it is a measurement, not necessarily of any one individual, but at least of a hypothetical individual. To measure the center of the distribution, we must know how to define the center, and this depends on the kind of measurements we have.

ARITHMETIC MEAN The measure of central tendency that can be used with interval measurements is the arithmetic mean. It is frequently called the *average,* but since "average" is often used loosely, the former term is more useful. To obtain the arithmetic mean, simply add all the measurements and divide by the total number. If, for example, you have a different income each month and you want to state your mean income over a 12-month period, you add the income received for each of the 12 months, divide by 12, and thus compute the arithmetic mean of your monthly income. You also can obtain the arithmetic mean of a group of interval measurements. For instance, the arithmetic mean of the reaction times in Table 9.2 is 0.60. Although this result can be obtained without making any use of the frequency distribution, special formulas do exist for computing the arithmetic mean from such a distribution.

Note: Some basic formulas for calculating the arithmetic mean, other measures of central tendency, and measures of correlation are given in Appendix 3, "Statistical Formulas and Calculations."

The arithmetic mean can be used only with interval measurements, because it gives equal weight to every measurement in the distribution. Hence it implies that all magnitudes of the difference between measurements are to be trusted. Since that is not the case with nominal or ordinal measurements, for these we must use one of the following measures of central tendency.

MEDIAN The median, very simply, is the *middle score in a group of measurements* when they have been rank-ordered from largest to smallest. If the number of measurements is even, there is no one real middle measurement. In this case, the median is the average of the two middle measurements. The median of the reaction times in Table 9.2 also happens to be 0.60.

The median is the proper and ideal measure of central tendency for ordinal measurements, because the middle score is the middle rank. The median may also be used, if one wishes, with interval measurements. In fact, with data that are normally distributed, it makes little difference whether one uses the median or the arithmetic mean. In the normal curve they are identical. For skewed distributions, on the other hand, the median is the preferred measure because it is not influenced so much by extreme measurements.

MODE The term mode means "most." As a measure of central tendency, it is the *most frequent score*. In a frequency distribution, it is the midpoint of the interval with the most cases in it. The mode is the only measure one can use with nominal measurements, for there is no proper way to calculate the arithmetic mean or the median.

The mode can also be used with other kinds of measurements, if there is any point to it—that is, if one really wants to know what the most frequent score is. But since the mode can shift around quite a bit with chance differences in scores, especially when cases are few, the median or mean, whichever is appropriate, is almost always a better measure of central tendency. The mode of the data in Table 9.2 is 0.62; that in Table 9.3 is 0.61. In the normal distribution, the mode will be exactly the same as the median or mean.

Measures of variability Measures of central tendency summarize only one feature of a distribution, namely, where its center is. Distributions also differ from one another in their variability—the spread of scores around the central point. In Figure 9.7 two hypothetical distributions are shown, one fat and the other slender. They both have the same means and medians; they are both based on the same number of measurements. To measure the difference between them, we need a measure of their relative "fatness" or "leanness." Though hypothetical, they depict situations often encountered. Waitresses, for example, have about the same mean intelligence as the general population; yet the general population includes greater proportions of highly intelligent persons and of mentally retarded persons than does a representative sampling of waitresses. Students in one school may, on the average, have the same aptitude as those in another, but in the second school there may be more students with both higher aptitude and lower aptitude. In each

THE SPREAD OF A DISTRIBUTION INDICATES ITS VARIABILITY

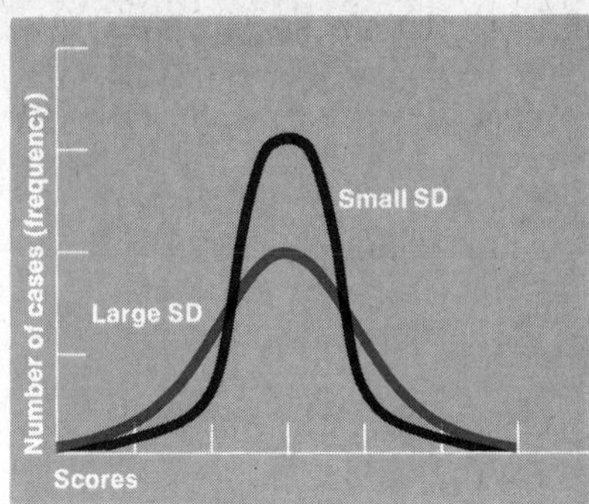

Figure 9.7 *(Left) Two distributions differing in variability. Both have the same central tendency, but one is narrow and the other is wide. Consequently they have different variability. Variability is measured by the standard deviation (SD).*

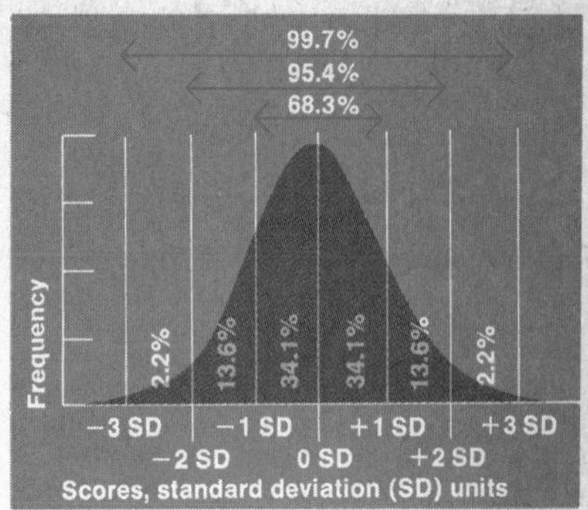

Figure 9.8 *(Right) The distribution of scores in a normal curve. Since the normal curve has a known shape, it is possible to state the percentage of scores that lie between +1 and −1 standard deviation, or between any other two points expressed in SD units. This normal curve might represent the distribution of IQ scores in the United States—in which case the mean would be 100 and the standard deviation would be approximately 15.*

GIVEN THE MEAN AND STANDARD DEVIATION, THE COMPLETE DISTRIBUTION OF SCORES IN A NORMAL DISTRIBUTION CAN BE KNOWN

case, the means are the same, but the *variability* of the measurements is different. Hence we need measures of variability.

RANGE Of the several possible measures we might use, the simplest, but not the best, is the range. This is the difference between the highest and lowest scores. For ordinal measurements, the range is of little value, since differences in scores do not mean anything; only ranks are important. For interval measurements, the range is a very crude and unstable measure, for it is based on only two measures: the very extreme ones. These, in most distributions, are erratic, and only a small change in them changes the size of the range. So statisticians do not use the range unless all they need is a quick and crude estimate of variability.

STANDARD DEVIATION The most useful measure of variability, the one generally preferred by behavioral scientists, is known as the standard deviation. We shall use the abbreviation SD to refer to the standard deviation as a statistic which describes a distribution of measurements made on an interval scale. The SD is a measure of the spread of the distribution. If scores are grouped closely around the mean, the SD is relatively small; if they are spread out in each direction, the SD is relatively large (see Figure 9.7). Put another way, the SD is a measure of how much the various scores deviate from their mean.

The first step in computing a standard deviation is, in effect, to convert the various scores in a distribution to *deviation scores.* To do this, simply subtract the mean from each score. Second, square each deviation score; third, average the squared deviation scores by summing and dividing by the number of scores. Fourth, as a compensation for having squared the individual deviation scores, take the square root of this average. In short, the SD is the root mean square of the deviations.

The reason for performing this set of operations, which may seem to be a roundabout process, is that the SD computed in this way has important mathematical properties in normal curves. The SD is such a good measure of variability that, if the frequency distribution is reasonably normal, we can reconstruct it if we know only two numbers: the mean and the SD. This is true because mathematicians have a precise formula for the normal curve, and the only two unknowns in it are the mean and the SD. Given these, one can draw the normal curve whose height and width best fit a particular frequency distribution. Thus, if a distribution is normal, the mean and the SD completely describe and specify it.

This mathematical nicety has important uses. In the normal probability curve, the SD can be used as a measuring rod to lay off distances along the scale of the distribution. The exact number of cases (the frequencies) that will be included in any given number of standard deviations is known from tables that have been constructed from the formula for the normal curve. The information supplied by the tables is summarized in Figure 9.8. It shows that 68.3 percent of the cases in a normal frequency distribution lie between 1 SD above and 1 SD below the mean. About 95 percent lie in the range between 2 SD above and 2 SD below the mean. And 99.7 percent fall between +3 SD and −3 SD. It is possible to determine from the tables the percentage of cases to be expected between any other two measurements given in terms of standard deviation units along the scale.

Standard scores The standard deviation can also be used to state individual measurements in a "universal language." All we have to do is to express a particular score in standard deviation units. Scores stated in terms of standard deviation units are called *standard scores;* the basic standard score is called the *z score.* In order to compute a *z* score, we take the difference between a particular score and the arithmetic mean of the distribution and then divide this difference by the standard deviation of the distribution:

$$z \text{ score} = \frac{\text{score} - \text{arithmetic mean}}{\text{standard deviation}}$$

The principle involved in this conversion of a score into standard deviation units is illustrated in Figure 9.13 (see page 314). There the distribution has an arithmetic mean of 45 and a standard deviation of 11. A score of 56, for instance, is 11 units above the mean and corresponds to a *z* score of +1; a score of 34 is 11 units below the mean and corresponds to a *z* score of −1. Similarly, any other score may be converted.

Other standard scores can be formed from the basic *z* score. Since in a normal distribution half the *z* scores will be negative, we can add a constant to the *z* scores to get rid of these minus signs. For convenience, we can also multiply the *z* score by a constant. The resulting score is called a *T score.* Frequently the constant we add is 500 and the constant we multiply the *z* score by is 100. (Another form of *T* score is shown in Figure 10.3. The CEEB [SAT] score of Figure 10.3 is the *T* score used here.) Here is the correspondence between *z* scores and *T* scores in a normal distribution:

z score	*T* score
−3	200
−2	300
−1	400
0	500
+1	600
+2	700
+3	800

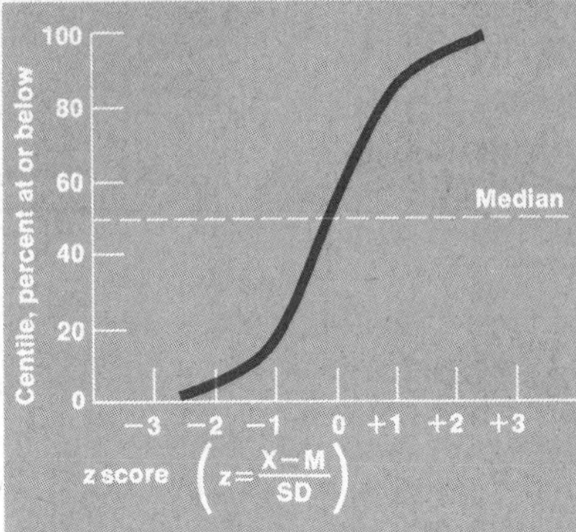

CENTILE SCORES CAN BE OBTAINED FROM Z SCORES IN A NORMAL DISTRIBUTION

Figure 9.9 *The relationship of z scores and centile scores in a normal distribution. From the curve, or from a table of the normal probability curve, one can determine the percentage of cases falling at or below any particular z score. This percentage is often called the centile score.*

For example, consider the Scholastic Aptitude Test (SAT), which students customarily take before entering college. The makers and administrators of this test go through exactly the steps we have described. They obtain raw scores that do not look at all like the scores given to students who have taken the test. They then convert these scores via the standard deviation into *z* scores, and next, after adding and multiplying by appropriate constants, they obtain *T* scores. This is why the mean on each part of the SAT tends to be approximately 500 and a combined score of 1000 for the verbal and quantitative parts is about average. It is also why the standard deviation approximates 100.

We had to say "approximately" and "about" in this example because the scoring system is developed on a sample population of testees, not on the entire group in the nation taking the SAT at any one time. Once developed, the same system is used to express the results for all persons taking the test. Naturally, however much the sample population differs from the total tested population (or from any other subpopulation), by that same degree the means and standard deviations will stray from 500 and 100 respectively. And of course, if we apply the system to quite different populations—such as to students who go on to college, or to those who succeed in college—the measures will depart even more from normal values calculated on the basis of the sample population.

Centile scores Comparisons among individuals and tests can also be made by means of centile scores. A *centile score* is the percentage of scores falling at or below a particular person's score in the distribution. Put another way, it is a person's rank in 100. It is obtained by dividing his rank by the total number of measurements in the distribution, and multiplying by 100.

A centile score (sometimes called the percentile score) has several uses. If distributions are badly skewed, or if there is no justification for assuming that they are distributions of interval measurements, then a centile score is a better way of indicating a person's standing in the distribution than a *z* score. At other times, we may have to present a score to people who do not understand the standard score or standard deviation and who do not have the time or willingness to learn. In such cases, it is better to use the centile score, since in a normal distribution one is easily converted into the other (see Figure 9.9). Notice, incidentally, that the median (*z* score = 0) is the 50th centile score; the −1 SD point is the 16th centile; the +1 SD point is the 84th centile; and so on.

We shall not describe in detail the measures of variability that are appropriate for ordinal measurements, because such measures are seldom used. The easiest way to indicate the variability of interval scores that are not symmetrical, is to state the 25th, 50th (median), and 75th percentile points. The greater the skewness of the distribution, the greater the difference between the 25th and 50th centiles and the 50th and 75th centiles. In a normal distribution, these differences are equal.

Correlation

So far we have been concerned with the statistical treatment of frequency distributions considered one at a time. Now we come to the topic of *correlation*. This is the relationship between two distributions of measurements. In one way or another, most of science is concerned with such co-relations. In physical science, however, they are usually called *functions;* the behavior of one variable (that is, one set of measurements) is related to the behavior of another variable (another set of measurements). Usually the relationship is precise enough so that a smooth curve can be drawn through nearly all the points joining the two variables and the relationship can even be neatly summarized in a mathematical formula.

Psychology sometimes has this precision too. Examples are to be found here and there throughout this book, particularly in the chapters on the senses. More often, however, psychologists are unable to define a function. Their job then becomes to determine whether or not there is a correlation between two variables, and if so, how much of a correlation there is.

To make clear what it is that psychologists are trying to do in the statistics of correlation, let us take a simple example of heights and weights. We know from casual observation that people differ a lot in both. If we wish, we can take any particular group of people and find their average heights and weights. We can also measure the variability of their heights and the variability of their weights. But beyond this, we know that there must be a relationship, or correlation, between height and weight. In general, people who are tall weigh more than those who are short. Yet obviously the correlation is not perfect, for some people only 5 feet tall weigh more than some who are 6 feet tall. So the correlation is one of degree—a statistical matter—and we therefore need a measure which expresses that degree.

For mathematical convenience, the degree of a correlation is expressed by a number between 0.00 and 1.00. Zero represents no correlation at all; 1.00 represents a perfect correlation—one comparable to the very precise functions often encountered in the physical sciences. In general in psychology, a correlation of .50 to .70 between two different variables (for example, aptitude and grade point average) is relatively high; one of .30 to .50 is medium; and correlations below .30 are low. With a battery of tests, however, correlations of less than .30 can be useful, because the individual correlations combine to give a fairly high correlation between the battery and another variable (such as grade point average).

It is possible to obtain a measure of correlation for any two sets of measurements of the same kind, whether they are two nominal, ordinal, or interval sets. It is also possible to obtain such a measure with any combination of sets, for instance, one nominal and the other interval, and so on. Each combination requires its own particular formula for calculating the answer. For simplicity, we shall discuss only the pure cases of nominal-nominal, ordinal-ordinal, and interval-interval.

Contingency When the measurements being correlated are all in the nominal class, one measure of correlation that may be used is the *coefficient of contingency*. To illustrate this, we shall take an example from a study of social classes (Siegel, 1956):

Table 9.4 *The curriculum taken by high school students of different social classes in one town. It is clear from this table that there is some correlation between social class and curriculum.*

Source: Siegel, 1956; after Hollingshead, 1949.

	Social class				
Curriculum	I–II	III	IV	V	Total
College preparatory	23	40	16	2	81
General	11	75	107	14	207
Commercial	1	31	60	10	102
Total	35	146	183	26	390

Of all the families in a community called Elmtown, 360 having children in high school were classified into one of five social classes. Various criteria were employed in the classification. There were too few families in each of the two upper classes (I and II) for statistical purposes; so these were lumped together, leaving only four categories of social class. Each child in high school was enrolled in one of three designated courses: college preparatory, general, or commercial. To obtain a correlation, counts were made of each child according to his social class and his high school course. Since there were four social classes and three high school curricula, 12 combinations were possible.

Table 9.4 shows the number (frequency) of individuals in each combination—statisticians call them "cells." It is clear from the table that there is some correlation between social class and type of high school course. The overwhelming proportion of those in the college preparatory curriculum came from classes I-II and III, and the great majority of those in classes III, IV, and V were not in college preparatory. The greatest proportion of those in the commercial curriculum were in classes III and IV. Computation of one particular index of correlation, the coefficient of contingency, gave a value of .39, a number which expresses the degree of correlation.

The contingency method of measuring correlation, then, makes use of data in nominal categories.

Rank-difference correlation Where ordinal measurements are the data for determining a correlation, the procedure is different. In this case, a formula has been devised that makes use of the differences in ranks on the two sets of measurements. One example comes from research in the field of humor (Guilford, 1956):

Fifteen individuals were shown at different times a series of 15 cartoons and a series of 15 limericks. When shown a cartoon, the subject was asked to rate its humor on a 5-point scale, giving 5 for "very humorous" and 1 for "not funny at all." He did the same thing for the limericks. When all the responses had been recorded, the points given by each individual on cartoons were added up to find a "cartoon score." Similarly, each individual received a "limerick score" (see the second and third columns in Table 9.5). The question was, How well did these scores correlate? Or what was the relationship between seeing humor in cartoons and seeing it in limericks? Since there was no reason to believe these scores met the criteria of interval measurements, the scores were transmuted to ranks. The

Table 9.5 *Humor scores on a cartoon test and a limerick test for 15 individuals. At the right are the rank orders of these two sets of scores and the differences in ranks (D).*

Source: After Guilford, 1956.

Individual	Cartoon score	Limerick score	Cartoon rank	Limerick rank	*D*
A	47	75	11	8	3
B	71	79	4	6	2
C	52	85	9	5	4
D	48	50	10	14	4
E	35	49	14.5	15	0.5
F	35	59	14.5	12	2.5
G	41	75	12.5	8	4.5
H	82	91	1	3	2
I	72	102	3	1	2
J	56	87	7	4	3
K	59	70	6	10	4
L	73	92	2	2	0
M	60	54	5	13	8
N	55	75	8	8	0
O	41	68	12.5	11	1.5

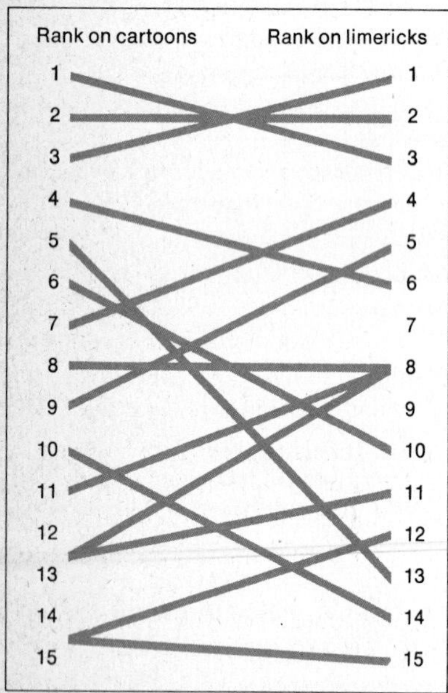

A RANK-DIFFERENCE CORRELATION CAN BE DEPICTED IN THIS WAY

Figure 9.10 *Each line connects the two ranks of one individual. The correlation coefficient, computed from the differences in ranks, was .70. (Data from Table 9.5.)*

subject scoring highest received a rank of 1, the one scoring next highest a rank of 2, and so on down through 15. Each individual's rank on the other set of scores was determined in the same way, as shown in Table 9.5. Then the correlation coefficient, known as *rho,* was computed from the differences in ranks (*D*). It was found to be .70, which is fairly high as correlations on psychological measurements go.

One can see in Figure 9.10 that the correlation is reasonably good. Although there are some inversions, those who ranked high on one index of humor tended to rank high on the other measurement. The conclusion is that people show some consistency in how funny they find things in two different situations, cartoons and limericks. This experiment was of some value in research leading to the development of tests of humor.

Thus the way to measure the correlation between two sets of ordinal measurements is to run a rank-difference correlation, a procedure that is devised to make use of the ranking afforded by ordinal measurements.

Product-moment correlation coefficient For measurements made on an interval scale, still another method of computation is used. In this case, the index of correlation is called the *product-moment correlation coefficient.* Its symbol is *r,* sometimes called *Pearson's r* after the English statistical psychologist who devised it.

An example of data yielding a high product-moment correlation can be drawn from the field of intelligence testing (Terman and Merrill, 1937). The 1937 Stanford-Binet test of intelligence has two forms: Form L and Form M. A group of children was given the two forms of this test on two different occasions. Hence two scores or measurements of intelligence were available for each child. These scores were plotted on the graph in Figure 9.11 by letting each point represent a pair of scores. They are all plotted in class intervals, just as were the data for reaction time in Figure 9.4. With the two scales, one for Form L and the other for Form M, at

THE SCATTERGRAM, IN WHICH EACH PERSON'S SCORE ON TWO TESTS IS PLOTTED AS A SINGLE POINT, IS ONE WAY OF PRESENTING A CORRELATION VISUALLY

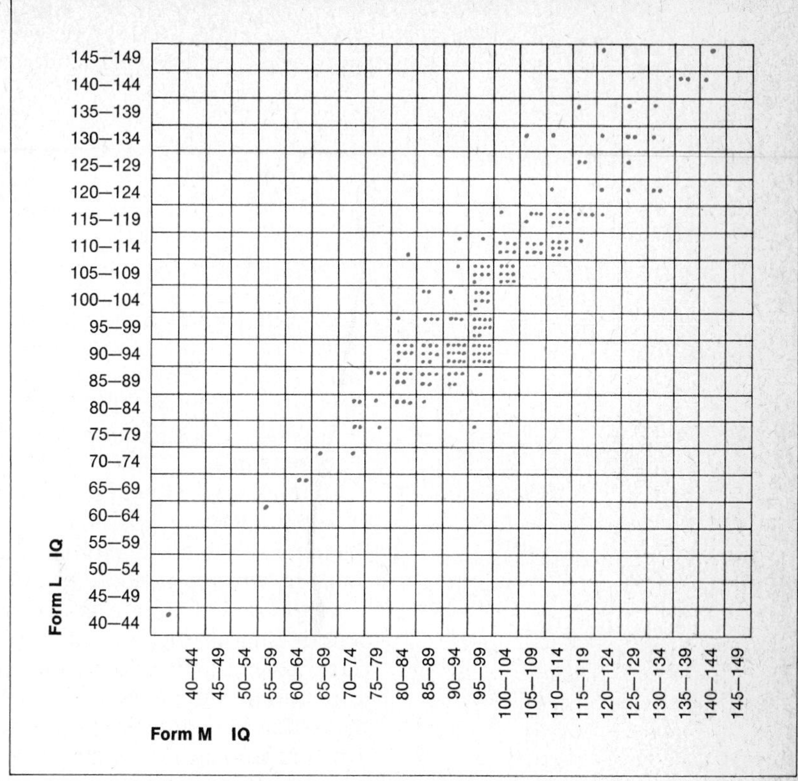

Figure 9.11 *A scattergram of IQs obtained on Forms L and M of the 1937 Stanford-Binet Intelligence Scale. A high degree of correlation exists between scores on the two tests—children scoring high on Form L also score high on Form M; those scoring low on Form L also score low on Form M. High correlations between equivalent forms of a test indicate that the reliability of the test is high; see page 311. (After Terman and Merrill, 1937.)*

right angles to each other, the two sets of class intervals form boxes or cells. A child scoring 87 on Form L and 90 on Form M has a single point entered in the cell made by the intersection of the class interval 85–89 on Form L and the class interval 90–94 on Form M. This procedure continues until all pairs of scores are plotted.

The Stanford-Binet test was so constructed that the same person would, ideally, make the same score on each form. If it turned out this way, the correlation between the two forms would be perfect and the correlation coefficient would be 1.00. This perfect correlation, represented graphically, would be a perfectly straight line of dots forming a diagonal from the graph's lower left corner to its upper right corner. In Figure 9.11, the scores fall around the hypothetical straight line but tend to stray in one direction or another a little off the diagonal. What this means is that a person tends to make slightly different scores on the two forms. Thus the correlation is not quite perfect, but is, in fact, very high—actually about .90.

Plots such as the one shown in Figure 9.11 are called *scatter diagrams* or *scattergrams.* They provide a visual picture of the degree of a correlation, because the amount of scatter, and its direction, varies with the correlation (see Figure 9.12). When a correlation is zero, the points on the scatter diagram are randomly distributed and do not line up in any particular direction. More points appear in the center of the scatter than

A GLANCE AT A SCATTERGRAM REVEALS THE DIRECTION AND APPROXIMATE DEGREE OF CORRELATION

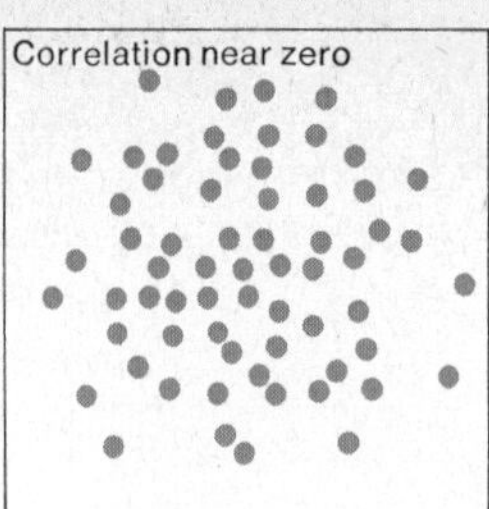

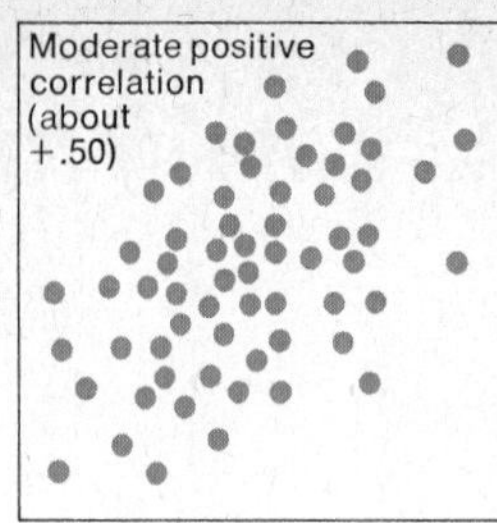

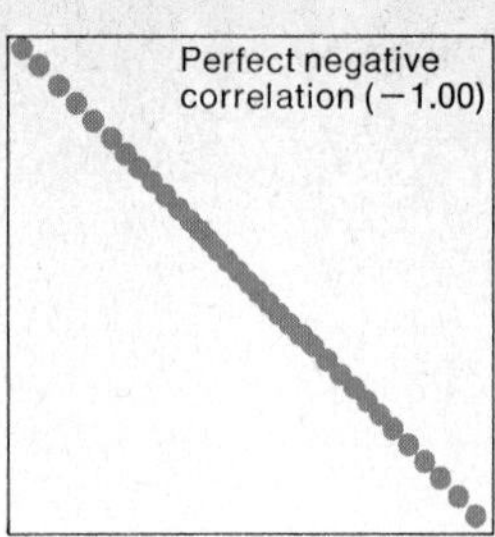

Figure 9.12 *Scattergrams depicting different amounts of positive and negative correlation.*

around its fringes simply because measurements of each of the contributing frequency distributions pile up more in the center than on the "tails." If the correlation is moderate, say .50, the scatter narrows in one direction or another. The scatter diagrams of a perfect positive correlation of 1.00 and a perfect negative correlation of −1.00 are both straight diagonal lines.

Another way to say this is to describe the shape of the scatter diagram. It is circular when the correlation is zero. It becomes more and more elliptical as the correlation increases, and it narrows down to a straight line when the correlation is perfect.

Note, too, in Figure 9.12 that the direction of the ellipse or line of the scatter diagram indicates the sign of the correlation, that is, whether it is positive or negative. Assuming that the scales of the diagram have been arranged in the conventional way, so that high scores are at the top of the ordinate and on the right of the abscissa, positive (+) correlations are indicated by a direction from the lower left-hand corner to the upper right-hand corner. Negative correlations (−) are indicated by ellipses or lines running from the upper left-hand corner to the lower right-hand corner.

All degrees of negative correlation from 0.00 to − 1.00 can occur, just as degrees of positive correlation can run from 0.00 to + 1.00. Minus signs and plus signs in front of a correlation coefficient of a particular size represent equally close relationships. It is the number, not the sign, which indicates the degree of correlation. The sign merely tells us the direction of the relationship. In negative correlations, high scores on one measure are associated with low scores on the other measure, and low scores with high scores. In positive correlations, high scores on one measure are associated with high scores on the other measure, and low scores with low scores.

Causation and correlation It is easy to think that a high correlation between two sets of measurements means that one of the factors measured causes the other. This, however, is usually not so. When there is a high correlation, both sets of individual differences are generally caused by some common factors. In the case of height and weight, for example, we cannot say that a person's height causes his weight, for both height and weight are caused by individual differences in genetic inheritance, nutrition, and disease. A correlation, in short, simply tells us that individual differences in two sets of measurements tend to vary together, not necessarily that one causes the other.

The need for care in the interpretation of correlation coefficients is amply shown by the following examples:

There is reported to be a positive correlation between the number of storks' nests and the number of births in northwestern Europe. Only the most romantic would contend that this indicates that the stork legend is true. A more prosaic interpretation is this: as population and hence the number of buildings increases, the number of places for storks to nest increases.

During the Italian campaign of World War II, it was found that there was a positive correlation between the number of propaganda leaflets dropped on the Germans and the amount of territory captured from them. While this is consistent with the hypothesis that the leaflets were effective, it is also consistent with other hypotheses, for example, that leaflets were dropped when major offensives were about to begin. (Wallis and Roberts, 1956, page 79.)

This is not to say that we never can tell anything about causation from correlation. We can. To decide what causes what, however, requires a great number of correlations and a careful logical analysis of which variables may be the basic ones.

Sampling

The measures we have described up to this point all fall under the general heading of *descriptive statistics*, because they describe accurately the characteristics of a set of measurements. Descriptive statistics, however, are of limited use by themselves. We want to know what they mean, that is, we need to interpret them. To do so we must employ another family of statistics known as *inferential statistics*. These are statistical measures which let us determine whether the differences or correlations found between two groups are significant (that is, are to be taken seriously), or whether they are due merely to chance fluctuations. This question takes us to the topic of *sampling*.

Representative sampling Sampling is the first concept that is essential to interpreting statistical descriptions. All measurement implies sampling. We usually cannot measure all cases of anything, whether it be animal learning, perception, intelligence, attitudes, public opinion, or anything else. There are always too many animals or people in the world and too many events to allow us to measure all cases in which we might be interested. So when we measure, whether we realize it or not, we are selecting a sample of the total possible measurements we might make.

All possible measurements, if made, would constitute a *population* of a particular kind. In political behavior, for example, it might be all individuals who vote in an election. A *sample* is a group selected to be representative of that population in characteristics such as age, socioeconomic class, geographical distribution, history of voting, etc.

Sometimes, when control is good, a very small sample may be used (see page 518). More often, control is less good and we try to select a sample that is large enough and representative enough to tell us about a much larger set of measurements we were unable to make. When, for example, psychologists try to measure public opinion regarding presidential candidates, they try to get a representative sample or cross section of the population and then try to take enough measurements to represent this population. From their measurements they predict, or infer, the opinions of the electorate at large. In our example of intelligence test scores, those who made the measurements were interested in getting a sample of schoolchildren representative enough to reflect the frequency distribution of intelligence among schoolchildren at large.

BIASES OF SAMPLES It is not always easy to get representative samples. In fact, the most frequent fault of a set of measurements is that it is not representative, so that we cannot properly make the inferences from it that we would like to. We run into this difficulty because many "biasing" factors are always at work. It may happen that, owing to factors we are not aware of, the schoolchildren in one geographical area are brighter or duller than schoolchildren in general. If we try to sample political opinion by calling people on the telephone, it may happen that people who own telephones are more often of one political opinion than another. If, as many psychologists are forced to do, we use college students for a set of measurements, it may be that they are not representative of the population in general. So various kinds of biases make it difficult to get a representative sample.

METHODS OF SAMPLING We have developed a number of different methods to try to ensure representative sampling. (Some of these are described in detail in Chapter 15.) In general, they take two different forms. One we term *random sampling,* even though selection is not completely by chance. We use this form when we know little or nothing about biasing factors in our measurement. To obtain a representative random sample, we try to see that only chance determines what is included in our sample. In making surveys of radio listening, for example, we may select every two-hundredth name in the telephone directory. Or to study learning in rats, we select 1 out of every 10 rats in the laboratory. This method may not yield a representative sample, however, if there is any bias (for example, the bias of socioeconomic level) in the construction of tests. Or to measure intelligence, we may draw at random 2 out of every 100 names of children in each of the schools of a state.

The other general method of obtaining a representative sample is to do *controlled sampling.* In this case we select certain factors, such as age, sex, economic status, educational level, or type of employment, and deliberately balance these factors in making up our sample. In sampling public opinion, for example, we may try to see that people are selected from small towns and large towns, from poor and rich classes, from the West and East, from labor and management—all in proportion to their numbers in the population at large. This kind of sampling, if it is done correctly, makes reasonably certain that biasing factors are controlled. Thus controlled sampling is the most economical sampling method, because it is usually possible to make correct inferences from a smaller number of cases selected by controlled sampling than by random sampling.

Sampling error Even when we have done our best to obtain a representative sample, we are still left with a *sampling error.* This, as its name implies, is an error due to the fact that we have measurements from only a sample of a population rather than from an entire population. The error arises from chance differences in the selection of individuals from the total population. When our sample is relatively small, the error tends to be relatively large. As the sample size increases in proportion to the population, the error decreases. As a rough general rule, the sampling error is inversely proportional to the square root of the number of measurements. In other words, the error of sampling 10 cases is about ten times as large as the error of sampling 1,000 cases.

The mean, median, standard deviation, indices of correlation, and other measures we have described always have some error, depending on the size of the sample used. By error, we mean that the measure differs somewhat from the value we would get if we had the "true" measure of the population sampled. This fact is easy to demonstrate in practice by taking more than one sample of measurements. If, in our example of measuring braking reaction time, we had taken a second set of 200 measurements on different people, the two frequency distributions would have been somewhat different. Hence their means and standard deviations would also have been different.

Mathematicians have worked out formulas for establishing sampling errors. By using these formulas, we obtain numbers indicating the amount by which different samples might be expected to differ simply by chance. Whether or not we know and use such formulas, however, we must always keep in mind that any measure we use has an error. This means that if we made the measurements over again on a new sample, each measure would have a slightly different value. That is why we should never put much stock in small differences in means, percentages, or other measures of a distribution.

Statistical decisions This brings us to statistical decisions and the concept of *significance.* If we are comparing two groups of measurements in an experiment, we will almost always obtain a difference between their means. Similarly, in correlating any two sets of measurements, we seldom get a correlation of zero. The question is, When is a difference or a correlation significant? By this we mean, When is the difference from zero greater than we would expect by chance?

This question must always be answered in terms of probabilities. There are no absolute certainties in statistics. If, for example, we flip 10 pennies and get 10 heads, we may ask whether this result can be expected by chance or whether it means that the coins are biased. From tables of probability, we know that 10 heads on 10 flips can be expected once in every 1,024 times, 20 heads in 20 flips once in about a million times. This may be very unlikely, but if we flip pennies several million times, we can expect this sequence to occur sometime by chance. So the question of whether something is significantly different from chance must be answered in terms of chance.

In practice, we arbitrarily select two different levels of significance. One is a loose criterion of $P = 0.05$; another is a stricter criterion of

$P = 0.01$. P is the probability, expressed as a number between 0.000 and 1.00, that a result occurs by chance. These probability values may help us to make decisions about the outcome of an experiment. Suppose we make observations and we find that there is a difference between the means of the control and experimental groups. How do we interpret this difference? For instance, in making observations of children from culturally impoverished homes, we might obtain a mean score of 150 (a score, not an IQ) on a test of general intelligence. A matched control group of children from homes which were not culturally impoverished might obtain a mean score of 200. Is this difference between means of 200 and 150 a real one? Or is it simply the result of chance variation in the samples of children we have chosen for our groups?

We can answer these questions by the use of techniques which help us to interpret the difference that was obtained. When the techniques are applied to this example we might, depending upon the size of the samples and the variability of scores within each sample, obtain a P value of 0.01. This would mean that there was 1 chance out of every 100 that the difference between the means of 200 and 150 was due to chance alone. Looked at from the other side, we can be rather certain that a real difference does exist between the intelligence test scores of children from the two types of homes.

What if the P value had been 0.05? Here there is 1 chance in 20 that the difference between means is due to chance, and we face a difficult decision. Our strategy will be dictated by the immediate importance of being right or wrong. If it is important that we know here and now whether or not there is a real difference between the two types of homes, we will probably repeat the observation with better control; we will hope to bring out the difference more clearly. If the cost of being wrong is not very great, we will probably accept the 1 out of 20 chance of being wrong. Then we will proceed to other experiments as if there were a real difference between the two groups. If the obtained difference is really due to chance, that is, if it really turns out to be the 1 wrong time out of 20, we will probably find it out in the course of future experiments. In the meantime, nothing much has been lost. Finally, if the probability of the difference being due to chance is greater than 1 out of 20, say 0.10 or 1 out of 10, we will probably decide that the finding cannot be trusted without replicating it in further work. Good experimenters will still worry about the differences, and they may try to refine their controls in further experiments so that any real differences will come out clearly. We can never be sure from probability figures that there is no difference; we can say only that we have not been able to demonstrate beyond a reasonable doubt that there is a difference.

Thus the purpose of these techniques is not to substitute for judgment, but to help the experimenter in planning his strategy for future research. They aid in the interpretation of results by allowing him to make inferences about the state of affairs in a large population on the basis of small samples from that population. For this reason, the methods are termed *inferential techniques*. The statistics, such as the standard error of the mean, that are used in the application of these techniques are termed *inferential statistics*.

Differences which might look large to the unsophisticated may not be statistically significant. A difference of 5 IQ points, or a difference of 20 percentage points, for instance, may fall far short of statistical significance. A correlation of .25, although it seems large, is unlikely to be significantly different from zero. Not much importance will be attached to these results by the statistically sophisticated person. Most of the results reported in this book, when evaluated statistically, were significant at the *P* level of 0.01 or better.

Characteristics of "Good" Psychological Tests

If we wish to measure the dimensions of a room or the amount of weight we have gained, we are accustomed to look for whatever ruler, scales, or appropriate measuring device is handy and to make our measurements without more ado. We do not ask any questions about the instrument; we assume that it is all right. Unfortunately, this attitude tends to carry over into things psychological. The public has heard a great deal about psychological tests and is inclined to "run to the nearest test" for the measurement of intelligence, personality, vocational aptitude, or whatnot. Such an attitude has been cultivated by the unwarranted use of tests of unknown value in popular periodicals.

Tests of any kind, psychological or physical, must be used intelligently. They are invented to do a particular job. Some succeed in doing it; some do not. Even tape measures and bathroom scales can prove unreliable. In more sophisticated measurement, many tests prove to be worthless. Others are exceedingly valuable, but only when they satisfy certain requirements and are used for the purposes for which they were intended. This is especially true of psychological tests. Therefore it is important to know just what the characteristics of a good test are.

Reliability A good test, first of all, must be *reliable.* In other words, it must be consistent in the answers it gives. If you cannot measure something twice with it and get about the same answer each time, its measurements are not worth very much. This is not the same as the problem of sampling error discussed above. In sampling, we measure two different things, or people, from the same population. The sampling error is due to chance differences in the things or people measured. Here we are talking about measuring the same thing, or person, twice and having the two measurements agree fairly well.

The concept of reliability can be illustrated by considering an example that, we hope, is unrealistic. A professor has given his class an examination, and now his somewhat odious task is to grade it. In this case he has no sampling problems, because he has obtained papers from all members of the class. All he has to do is choose a measuring stick—that is, a method of scoring them. One possible method is to throw them down the stairs and, assigning a number to each step, grade each paper according to the step on which it falls. If he does this, he will obtain a frequency distribution for which a mean and a standard deviation can be calculated.

Two obvious faults are inherent in this method of grading: it is invalid, and it is unreliable. The method would be unreliable simply because it would not give the same answer twice. If the professor gathered up the papers and threw them downstairs a second time, he would not get the same score for the same paper. Assuming that the papers landed randomly on the steps, the score a person got on the second grading would bear no relation to the score on the first grading.

The statistical method for inferring quite precisely the relative reliability or unreliability of a set of measurements is the correlational method which we have already described. By correlating one set of scores with another set obtained by the same method, we obtain a measure of the reliability of the measurements. Suppose we give the same psychological test to the same people at two different times which are far enough apart so that the people being tested do not remember specific questions from the test. If people get about the same score both times, the correlation will be high and positive, as it is in the case of intelligence tests. In such cases, we can assume that our measuring instrument is measuring something reliably. If results do not correlate well, our measurements are unreliable—we might as well be throwing papers down the stairs.

Reliability is a *sine qua non* of psychological measurement. If measurement is not reliable, it cannot be much of anything else. If, in other words, we cannot get the same set of scores, or almost the same set, for people on two successive independent measurements, we are not really measuring. Flipping pennies, rolling dice, or spinning roulette wheels would be just about as good. To put the matter another way, if a measuring instrument cannot be correlated rather well with itself, it is useless for making inferences about anything else.

Validity A good test or measurement must also be *valid.* It must correlate with something in addition to itself so that it is measuring something meaningful. In the simplest case, validity refers to how well a test measures what it is intended to measure. The professor who graded papers by throwing them downstairs was using an invalid method of scoring: it did not measure how well his students had mastered the course. If we are trying to measure anything—say, intelligence—our test should measure that thing, namely, intelligence, and not reaction time, cultural background, or something else. If it does not measure intelligence, we say that it is not a valid test of intelligence.

Speaking more generally, however, a test is valid to the extent that it correlates with something else we want to measure, and usually to predict. A test that correlates highly with reaction time would be a good test of reaction time, but if it does not correlate with intelligence, it is not a valid test of intelligence.

This problem of validity of measurement is a serious one for psychologists. It is relatively easy, although not so easy as one might suppose, to devise measuring instruments that are reliable. It is much harder to devise valid measures. To determine the validity of measurements, once their reliability has been established, we must use the correlational method. In this case, however, we must have some standard, or *criterion,* against which the test may be correlated.

One of the major criteria of intelligence, for example, is ability to learn and to solve problems, or to put it more generally, the ability to profit by education. Thus the criterion of an intelligence test *might* be success in school. To assess the validity of an intelligence test, we might therefore correlate a person's scores on intelligence tests with his educational progress—his grades, or how far he has progressed for his age. If the correlation is high, we can say that the intelligence test is valid; if it is low, the test is not so valid.

To take another example, if our purpose is to select pilots, our criterion would be whether they succeed or fail in their training for flying. When we have tests that correlate well with such success or failure, we say they are valid. If they do not correlate with the criterion, no matter how reliable they may be—that is, no matter how well they correlate with themselves—they are invalid.

Although other types of validity exist, validity typically is an index of the degree to which a test correlates with a criterion (Cronbach, 1960). Usually the criterion is what we say we want to measure. Sometimes it turns out that a test is not valid for the chosen criterion, but correlates well with some other criterion. To be valid, however, it must correlate with the criterion which it is used to measure. Hence it can be used properly to measure or predict only that criterion.

Sampling of tasks Good tests are samples of the many tasks that go to make up the criterion. A lot of things, for example, go into intelligence. Hence many different measurements correlate with intelligence: speed in problem solving, ability to memorize, size of vocabulary, and so on. A test of any one of these things has validity as a test of intelligence. To stick to one of them, however, is to limit the validity to a very low level. The highest validity is obtained by having in the test a fair sample of all the behaviors involved in the criterion.

Ideally, to develop the most valid test of intelligence, we should have to measure an almost infinite number of things. But this would be far too expensive and impractical, and after we had devised such a test, it would take so much time to give that we seldom would be able to administer it properly to those who should take it. In practice, we must construct tests with a reasonable number of items, sometimes compromising the highest validity we might ideally obtain in order to have a usable test. Nevertheless, the good test—the valid test—is one that includes as fair a sample as possible of the tasks which make up the criterion.

Standardization group Finally, a good test for general use as a measuring instrument should be based on a large and well-defined standardization group. The *standardization group* is a sizable representative sample of people to whom the test has been given. The various scores made by people in this group are called *test norms.* Such norms are essential for tests used in counseling, guidance, and making general predictions about people.

The reason for having a standardization group and test norms is that in psychological measurement we are primarily interested in *comparing* people. We are interested in the differences between them, or in their rank order (see the earlier sections on interval and ordinal measurements). A psychological trait is not like pounds and inches; it is a rela-

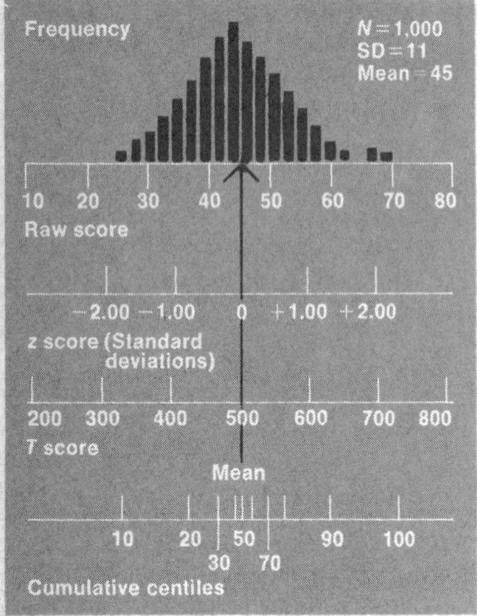

THE SCORES OF A STANDARDIZATION GROUP CAN BE EXPRESSED IN MANY WAYS

Figure 9.13 *Frequency distribution and scores of a hypothetical standardization group. The mean of this distribution is 45; the standard deviation is 11. In this example, raw scores are expressed in standard deviation units (z scores and T scores); they are also expressed as centiles.*

tive thing. It does us no good to know that John completed 83 questions on an intelligence test unless we are also told that the average number completed by other people was 60 and that fewer than 10 percent of them completed more than 83 questions. With this information, we have a rather good idea of how John rates in comparison with other people. Without it, we simply have a meaningless fact.

The test norms tell us what the average score is and also how much variability there is among scores. They allow us to compare a particular score with scores obtained by the standardization group. There are various ways of reporting such norms, and it is often possible to convert from one way of reporting to another. This can be seen in Figures 9.13 and 10.3 (see page 329), which show the relationships among several different ways of reporting norms. Figure 9.13 gives a distribution of scores made by a standardization group on a hypothetical test of ability. The scores range from 25 to 70. Below the scores are three scales. One shows the scores corresponding to different standard deviation units above and below the mean. The next scale shows *T* scores. The last scale shows the percentage of persons scoring at or below any particular score.

To illustrate these scales, let us suppose that a person made a score of 59 on our hypothetical test. By consulting the test norms, we discover that his score is about 1.3 SD above the mean, that it is a score as high as, or higher than, the score made by 90 percent of the standardization group, and that it represents a *T* score of 630. Test norms are expressed in any, and sometimes all, of these ways. Age norms are usually given when the test is to be used for people of heterogeneous ages. They are omitted if the test is to be used for a relatively homogeneous group, for instance, young adults. Norms may also be given for grades in school, occupational groups, or any other classification of individuals that may be relevant.

If our comparison of a person's score with test norms is to be fair, we must know the characteristics of the standardization group. Not any group will do. If John is 10 years old and we give him an intelligence test, it is not fair to use test norms from a standardization group of adults. The group should be children of John's own age. If we give an intelligence test to a person who grew up on a farm in the South, it is not proper to use norms obtained from people living in Northern cities. To interpret test results accurately, we must make sure that our test norms represent the kind of people with whom it is proper to compare a person's score.

Also, the standardization group should be reasonably large—at least several hundred and preferably a few thousand. If the group is too small, norms may be too high or too low just as a matter of chance in the selection of people for the group. Moreover, norms must be obtained, and the tests must be given, under standard conditions. For example, instructions and time limits may affect performance if they are allowed to vary. Therefore these and other aspects of test administration must be standardized.

Prediction from measurements It should be pointed out that the purpose of a good test is to make successful predictions. We would not go

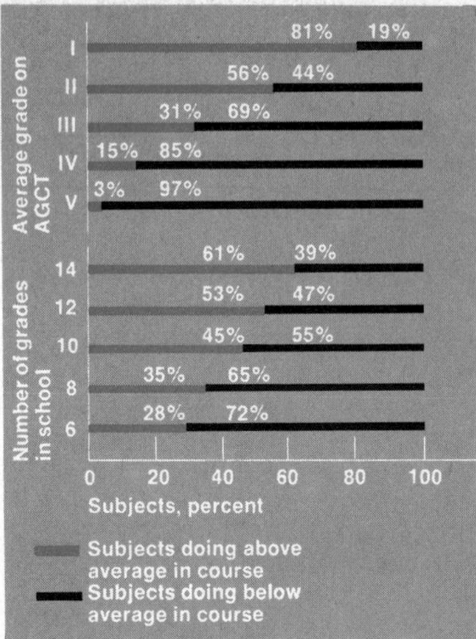

GOOD PREDICTIONS CAN BE MADE FROM VALID TESTS

Figure 9.14 *Predicting success in tank mechanics training from scores on the Army General Classification Test (AGCT) and from the number of grades completed in school. In this case, the AGCT predicts success in a tank mechanics course better than the number of grades in school. (After Boring, 1945.)*

to the trouble of constructing or administering tests just to predict something we already knew or could easily measure in the first place. Sometimes the prediction is for research or scientific purposes. Often it has important practical advantages. Several cases of such prediction are described in later chapters, but one example here illustrates the point:

During World War II, the Army was faced with the general problem of selecting men for specialized training—in this particular case, training in a tank mechanics course. Naturally it wanted to pick men who were most likely to succeed in such training. As can be seen from the lower chart in Figure 9.14, there was some correlation between the number of grades a man had completed in school and his success in the tank mechanics course. Those who had completed 14 grades of school had 6 chances in 10 of doing above-average work in the course. Those who had only 6 grades of school had less than 3 chances in 10 of doing so well. Consequently, the correlation between grades completed and success in the course provided some basis for prediction.

But a somewhat higher correlation existed between the Army General Classification Test and success in the tank mechanics course. This test is a test of intelligence especially designed for the Armed Forces. The upper part of Figure 9.14 shows that men in the highest-scoring group (I) on the test had 8 chances in 10 of doing above-average work in the course. Those in the lowest-scoring group (V) had hardly any chance of doing well. This prediction was considerably better than that afforded by number of grades completed.

Give a statistician a correlation coefficient between a test and a criterion, and he can make up a diagram like that in Figure 9.14 which predicts a person's chances of success from any particular score on the test. He can do this because he has the appropriate formulas that have been proved, both mathematically and in actual experience, to predict from one set of measurements to another. The use that can be made of such predictions depends upon many practical considerations, such as what it costs to train people with a low chance of success, or how much choice one has in selecting people. The important point is that valid measurements lead to useful predictions.

Synopsis and summary

Most of us are consumers of statistics and statistical arguments. For example, many, if not most, of the psychological facts and principles in this text are based upon statistical arguments. The major purpose of this chapter has been to help make you a more sophisticated consumer of statistics.

Carefully formulated statistical arguments allow us to draw sound conclusions. For instance, the conclusions of the Surgeon General's report on smoking were based on statistical data (Advisory Committee to the Surgeon General, 1964). It was found that the number of men in a given age range dying of lung cancer was far greater in the group of heavy cigarette smokers than in the group of light smokers or nonsmokers. Of course, the individual case is lost in the statistics, but the odds are that a heavy smoker is more likely to die of lung cancer than a light smoker. You will recognize that this is a correlational argument and that some other factor may be causative. As sophisticated statistics consumers, we conclude that a relationship does exist between cigarette smoking and lung cancer, but that further studies are necessary before it may be concluded with assurance that cigarette smoking actually causes lung cancer. However, the high relationship between cigarette smoking and lung cancer is enough for practical decisions.

Unfortunately, it is also possible to mislead with statistics (Huff, 1954).[1] A common trick is the presentation of graphs which magnify very small differences. Suppose your product is very slightly better than that of a competitor on a particular characteristic. You might tell a statistical fib by magnifying the top part of a bar diagram which shows only the difference. The use of arbitrary values on the ordinate often helps. Another trick is to make statistically meaningless statements such as "product X is 10 times more powerful."

Some of you may go on in psychology or other fields where you will become users of statistics. So another purpose of this chapter has been to present some of their uses. For instance, in describing groups, scores may be spread over a wide range. This is often the case in the biological and behavioral sciences, and descriptive statistics are needed to characterize the distribution of scores. Distributions of scores are also obtained in comparing control and experimental groups. Descriptive statistics can be computed and then inferential statistics used to find what the probability is that the difference between the control and experimental group means is due to chance. Inferential statistics allow us to feel more or less confident about the reality of an obtained difference between means. They also provide a basis for making decisions about which experiment should be done next.

The following specific points have been made in this chapter:

1. Three kinds of measurements are commonly used in psychology: (*a*) nominal measurements, in which numbers identify different categories; (*b*) ordinal measurements, in which numbers designate rank order among the things being measured; and (*c*) interval measurements, in which numbers represent differences in magnitude.
2. The first step in organizing a set of measurements is usually to count the frequencies of measurements in each category or interval. The resulting counts may be represented graphically in a bar diagram or histogram; they constitute a frequency distribution.
3. To make a frequency distribution of interval measurements, the scale is divided into 15 or 20 intervals of equal size, and the measurements falling in each interval are tallied.
4. Frequency distributions of many psychological and biological characteristics approximate an ideal distribution known as the normal probability curve. This is bell-shaped, being perfectly symmetrical and having more measurements near the center of the distribution than in the "tails."
5. Asymmetrical distributions are called skewed distributions. These have more of a tail on one side than on the other and are not perfectly centered.
6. A number or statistic derived mathematically from a frequency distribution and used to characterize it in an exact way is called a measure or descriptive statistic. Two general kinds of measures are commonly employed: measures of central tendency and measures of variability.
7. Three kinds of measures of central tendency are the arithmetic mean, the median, and the mode. The arithmetic mean is the sum total of the measurements divided by the number of cases. The median is the middle score when measurements have been ranked. And the mode is that score which occurs most frequently.
8. Two measures of variability of a distribution are the range and the standard deviation. The range is the difference between the highest and lowest scores; it is a very crude measure. The standard deviation is the root-mean-square deviation of measurements from the arithmetic mean; it is a more useful measure of variability.
9. A measurement may be converted into a z score by dividing its deviation from the mean by the standard deviation. This is one type of standard score and is a way of stating measurements in "universal" terms, independently of the particular scale of measurement or scoring used. Other standard scores may be derived from the z score.
10. A score may be expressed as a centile by dividing the rank of a score in a distribution by the total number of measurements and multiplying by 100, thus reducing all scores to a rank in 100. Since this is readily understood by nearly everyone, it is a popular way of expressing scores on psychological tests.
11. A correlation coefficient states quantitatively the degree to which pairs of scores in two distributions are related. If the correlation is perfect, which it almost never is, the coefficient is 1.00. If there is no relation between the scores in the two distributions, which there almost never is, the coefficient is 0.00. Between these values, any correlation coefficient is possible. For many practical purposes, a high correlation is one between .50 and .70; medium, between .30 and .50; and poor, below .30. The sign of the coefficient, which may be + or −, merely indicates whether the correlation is high-high and low-low, or high-low and low-high, respectively.
12. Different methods of computing correlations are appropriate for different kinds of measurement: a contingency coefficient for nominal measurements, a rank-difference correlation (*rho*) for ordinal measurements, and the product-moment correlation coefficient (r) for interval measurements.
13. In many cases of psychological

[1] "There are three kinds of lies: lies, damned lies, and statistics." Disraeli.

measurements, we need a measure that is representative of a much larger population. To achieve this, we must be careful either to take a completely random sample or to use one of several methods that have been devised for controlling possible biases in the sample.

14. Any set of measurements is subject, by the laws of chance, to a sampling error that makes the sample depart somewhat from the true population. For this reason, measures may differ from sample to sample. Inferential statistics allow us to state the probability (P) that a difference between measures is statistically significant.

15. In order to be a worthwhile measuring instrument, a psychological test should have certain characteristics. Foremost are reliability and validity. To be reliable, a test must be able to give essentially the same results on repeated measurements of the same person or thing. To be valid, it must measure what it is intended to measure, that is, correlate well with some criterion.

16. In addition, psychological tests should be administered under standardized conditions and should have norms based on a large, representative standardization group.

Related topics in the text

Appendix 3 Statistical Formulas and Calculations Provides formulas and instructions for calculating the measures of frequency distributions, correlations, and sampling error discussed in this chapter.

Chapter 1 The Science of Psychology Both the decision to use statistics and the type of statistics used in an experiment depend upon the experimental design. For instance, correlation is much more common in studies done by the method of systematic observation; inferential statistics are much more common in experimental studies.

Chapter 10 Psychological Testing An understanding of statistics is essential for further study of intelligence, aptitude, and personality testing.

Suggestions for further reading

Adkins, D. C. *Statistics.* Columbus, Ohio: Charles E. Merrill Books, Inc., 1964. (Paperback.)
An introductory textbook with emphasis on statistical techniques used in the behavioral sciences.

Guilford, J. P. *Fundamental statistics in psychology and education* (4th ed.). New York: McGraw-Hill, 1965.
A comprehensive textbook on psychological statistics.

Hammond, K. R., and Householder, J. E. *Introduction to statistical method.* New York: Knopf, 1962.
Standard statistical topics are soundly presented.

McCollough, C., and Van Atta, L. *Statistical concepts: A program for self-instruction.* New York: McGraw-Hill, 1963. (Paperback.)
A programmed textbook for learning elementary psychological statistics.

McNemar, Q. *Psychological statistics.* (4th ed.) New York: Wiley, 1969.
A thorough and authoritative treatment of psychological statistics.

Spence, J. T., Underwood, B. J., Duncan, C. P., and Cotton, J. W. *Elementary statistics.* (2d ed.) New York: Appleton Century Crofts, 1968.
A brief, readable textbook of fundamental statistics.

Wallis, W. A., and Roberts, H. V. *The nature of statistics.* New York: Macmillan-Free Press, 1965.
Examples are given from many fields, making this an interesting way to learn statistics.

Young, R. K., and Veldman, D. J. *Introductory statistics for the behavioral sciences.* New York: Holt, 1965.
An introductory textbook with a program for self-learning at the end of each chapter.

A psychological test is essentially an objective and standardized measure of a sample of behavior.
Anne Anastasi

Intelligence, operationally defined, is the aggregate or global capacity of the individual to act purposefully, to think rationally and to deal effectively with his environment.
David Wechsler

People obviously differ from one another in a great many ways—in aptitudes, attitudes, achievements, interests, motivations, personality traits, and skills. Some of these characteristics can be measured, and this is the aim of psychological testing. The measurement of human traits is not done out of idle curiosity—it is a highly practical business. In assigning people to training programs, in hiring people for specialized jobs, in measuring school achievement, in counseling, and in operating a psychological clinic, tests are being relied upon more and more.

Tests are primarily used in the study of a particular individual. This study of the characteristics of one person has been called the *idiographic* approach. But tests are also used in *nomothetic* psychology—the attempt to discover general laws of behavior. For instance, scores on psychological tests might be regarded as the dependent variable after control and experimental groups have been put through an experimental procedure. In the light of our increasing reliance upon them, psychological tests bear a thorough examination.

The Uses of Psychological Tests

Tests, while they provide scores, are only aids to decision making. Trained persons must interpret the scores and make recommendations on the basis of their interpretations. Although the general public can scarcely be expected to have studied the standards set up by the American Psychological Association (1966) for the proper use of psychological tests, people often show astonishing naïveté about tests. Remarks such as these are all too common:

"May I have a Stanford-Binet blank? I'd like to find my little sister's IQ. The family think she's precocious."

"Last night I answered the questions in an intelligence test published in our newspaper and I got an IQ of 80—I think psychological tests are silly."

"I'd like to borrow the Ishihara color-blindness test to show to my brother. He's applying for a Navy commission and would like some practice so he can pass that test."

"My roommate is studying psych. She gave me a personality test and I came out neurotic. I've been too upset to go to class ever since."

"I represent the school paper. We'd like a list of the IQ's of the entering freshmen to publish in our first Fall issue." (Anastasi, 1968, page 30.)

When interpreted by trained people, tests can be quite useful. Often several types of tests are given, and from these a counselor can obtain a picture of an individual's strengths and weaknesses. In the following example, the centile standings on the different types of tests show how this is done.

The case of Thomas Stiles[1]

When is an engineer an engineer? Tom was 17 years old, in good health, of average height and weight, a high school senior when he came to the counselor. He was enrolled in the academic course, in which he liked the work in mathematics and science better than anything else, and cared least for English and history. His leisure-time activities consisted largely of spectator sports; he liked also to read popular scientific and adventure story magazines. As a younger boy he had done odd jobs at home, and since then had had part-time and summer jobs working as a helper on a truck, operating machines in a shoe factory, helping in a garage, and working in a machine shop. Some of these jobs had been for no pay; others, the more recent, had been paid work.

The student's father was an operative in a shoe factory; the mother kept house, and several siblings, all younger than Tom, were still in school.

Tom stated that he was interested in machines, having lived among various types of machinery all his life; his junior high school ambition had been to be a diesel engineer or marine engineer, an ambition which had broadened to include work with almost any type of engine. He thought he would like engineering training, but was not certain of his choice. Asked what he would like to be ten years hence he replied: "Foreman or superintendent in an airplane factory."

The cumulative record in the school office showed that Tom's high school work was mediocre (see table of grades). As shown in the accompanying chart, he had failed junior English, did poorly in physics, had made only C's in mathematics after the tenth grade, and was doing no better in chemistry. His IQ on the Henmon-Nelson Test of Mental Ability, administered at the beginning of his junior year and recorded on the school record, was 106. The profile of test results obtained by the counselor during the first semester of Tom's senior year in high school is shown on the following page.

Tom's questions were: "Should I go into engineering? I am interested in engines. Should I continue my education in order to prepare for such work? What about engineering college?"

The Counselor's appraisal. Tom's intellectual level, as shown by his Otis IQ of 101 and confirmed by an A.C.E. score which put him at the 14th percentile point of a typical college freshmen class, was about average when compared with the general population. Occupational intelligence norms from both World Wars indicate that this is the ability level typical of skilled tradesmen and of the most routine clerical workers, [an] observation confirmed by various studies made with the Otis test in industry. His mastery of school skills and subjects as shown by his scores on the achievement tests was about that to be expected from one

[1]Adapted from pp. 643–645, including Figures 12 and 13 retitled "Grades" and "Test Profile," respectively (Figure 13 modified subject to authors' approval), and pp. 652–653 of *Appraising Vocational Fitness*, rev. ed., by Donald E. Super and John O. Crites. Copyright 1949 by Harper & Brothers. Copyright © 1962 by Donald Super and John O. Crites. By permission of Harper & Row.

Notes: The percentiles give the percentage of people in the normative group who score the same or lower than the person being tested. For instance, Thomas Stiles earned an A.C.E. score which was only as high as or higher than that earned by the lowest 14 percent of college freshmen. In the letter scores on the vocational-interest test, an A rating means that Tom's interests are essentially like those of people in a particular occupation; a C rating means that Tom's interest pattern does not correspond to that of people in an occupation.

Grades: *Thomas Stiles*

Subjects	9th grade	10th grade	11th grade	(1st sem.) 12th grade
English	C	D	E	C
Latin I		C		
Civics	B			
World history	B			
Prob. of democracy			C	
U. S. history				C
Algebra I		B		
Plane geometry		B		
Review math.			C	
Math. (gen.)	B			
Solid geometry				C
Physics			D	
General chem.				C
Phys. education		D		

Test profile: *Thomas Stiles*

	Test used	Norms	Percentile
Scholastic aptitude	A.C.E. Psych. Exam.	College freshmen	14
	Otis S.A. IQ 101	Students	19
Reading	Nelson Denny: Vocabulary	Freshmen	1
	Paragraph	Freshmen	30
Achievement	Coop. Social Studies	Freshmen	11
	Coop. Mathematics	Freshmen	74
	Coop. Natural Sciences	Freshmen	5
Clerical aptitude	Minn. Clerical: Numbers	General clerks	6
	Names	General clerks	6
Mechanical ability	O'Rourke Mechanical Aptitude	Men in general	67
Spatial relations	Minn. Paper Form Board, Rev.	College freshmen	65
Personality	Calif. Pers.:	Freshmen	35
	Social	Freshmen	40
	Total	Freshmen	40

Vocational interests	
1. Biological sciences	B+
2. Physical sciences	A
3. Technical:	
Carpenter	A
Policeman	A
Farmer	B+
4. Social sciences	C
5. Business detail	B−
6. Business contact	B
7. Literary	B

of his mental ability level, and decidedly below that of the college freshmen with whom he was compared, except for a superior score on the mathematics achievement test—his favorite subject. This suggested that he might have abilities useful in technical occupations at the skilled level which seemed appropriate to his mental ability. His school marks, however, were not so encouraging, being only B's in mathematics prior to his junior year, and C's since then. The explanation may have lain in his being in the more abstract college preparatory course.

On the special aptitude tests Tom appeared to lack speed in recognizing numerical and verbal symbols such as is required of even routine clerical workers.

Combined with his marginal intellectual ability for office work, this strengthened the basis for questioning the choice of a clerical occupation. On the other hand, Tom's scores on the tests of spatial visualization and mechanical aptitude seemed to confirm the implications of the mathematics achievement test. His inventoried interests, too, were in the physical science and subprofessional technical fields; the latter field seemed more in keeping with his intellectual level and with his poor achievement scores and fair grades in the natural sciences.

Tom's family background, leisure activities, and expressed vocational ambitions were all congruent with the implications of the test results. His father was a semiskilled worker, indicating that work at the skilled level might well be accepted by the family as a step upward. There were no older siblings who might have established a higher record for him to compete with. His leisure activities were nonintellectual, but they did show interest and achievement in mechanical and manual activities, as well as familiarity with work at those levels. He stated that he wanted to work with engines. It was true that, under the influence of a college preparatory course in the academic high school of a substantial middle-class community, he raised the question of going to college to study engineering, but in most contexts his discussions of work with engines were pitched at the skilled level.

The counselor who worked with Tom therefore felt that Tom would be wise to aim at a skilled trade, either by means of a technical school of less than college level, through apprenticeship, or through obtaining employment as a helper in an automotive maintenance shop and taking night school courses.

This example shows one of the most important uses of tests—as an aid in counseling and decision-making processes (Cronbach and Gleser, 1965). Note that the tests were not used alone: information about Tom's home life and his schoolwork was also important in the counselor's appraisal. Tests are often used to confirm impressions formed from interviews and other sources of information. Second, several tests were obtained on the same characteristic: the counselor's rough estimate of Tom's general intellectual ability was based on a previously given test and two tests given in conjunction with the present evaluation. Third, the counselor did not seize upon a single test result or set of results, but instead looked for consistencies within the total battery of tests. The idea is not so much to obtain a score as it is to make sense out of patterns of scores from tests of different abilities and tests of personality traits.

Measurement of Human Characteristics

Having considered one use of tests in some detail, let us now take a closer look at the general nature of tests. Many characteristics are appraised by particular psychological tests—intelligence, special aptitudes, interests, achievements, motivations, attitudes, personality characteristics—but certain general attributes of these tests can be described.

First of all, what is the definition of a test? Second, what are some of the characteristics of "good" psychological tests? Finally, what are some of the general ways in which psychological tests can be classified?

Definition of a test We all make informal subjective ratings of a person's characteristics from samples of his behavior. Often this sample is inadequate; for instance, first impressions can be quite inaccurate. The informal sample of behavior has another shortcoming: we are usually able to sample another person's behavior only in rather special situations, such as at work. Tests, in one way or another, attempt to provide more objective and more representative samples of behavior than we can obtain in most face-to-face relations and other unstandardized situations. One definition of a psychological test, then, is that it is "an objective and standardized measure of a sample of behavior" (Anastasi, 1968).

Characteristics of a good test In the last chapter we discussed the characteristics a test should have to be considered a "good" test—one that can be used with confidence to make decisions about particular individuals in a group, or about differences between groups. Let us review these characteristics briefly.

1. A test should be *reliable*. Different forms of the same test, or repeated measurements made with the test on the same individual, should give substantially the same results.
2. A test should be *valid*. It should correlate with the criterion which the test is used to measure. This means that it should measure what it is intended, or alleged, to measure. A test cannot be valid unless it is also reliable. Furthermore, a test that is highly valid and reliable with one group or in one situation may have low reliability with another group or in another situation.
3. A test should be administered according to *standardized procedure*. If it is not, both the reliability and the validity of the test may be in question.
4. A test should have norms based on a *standardization group*, which should be relatively large. This group should also be similar in character to the group of individuals with whom the test is subsequently used. The norms of the standardization group provide a frame of reference for interpreting the results obtained on any particular individual or group. Many tests should have more than one set of norms so that comparisons can be made with whatever group is appropriate.

Many of the tests described in this chapter possess these characteristics; some of the personality tests, however, are weak in one or more of them. The perceptive student will mark the flaws as well as the virtues of personality tests.

Kinds of tests Tests may differ in many general ways; following are a few of the more significant.

APTITUDE VERSUS ACHIEVEMENT *Aptitude* refers to the potentiality that a person has to profit from a certain type of training. It indicates how well he would be able to do something after training, not what he has done or will necessarily do. *Achievement*, on the other hand, refers to what a person has done. These terms are used to distinguish two different kinds of tests: *aptitude tests* and *achievement tests*.

Note, however, that any test, by definition, measures what a person

Figure 10.1 *The Stanford-Binet Intelligence Scale, Form L-M, year III. The child is asked to build a bridge of three blocks. (New York University Testing and Advisement Center.)*

actually does, for there is no other way of testing him. Put another way, we test a person only by asking him to do something, and what he does is an achievement. Hence aptitude tests and achievement tests are both, in a sense, tests of achievement. The difference between them depends on how we use the results.

An aptitude test is used to predict future achievement or achievement in another situation. Such a test given to a student before he goes to college, for example, is used to predict how well he will do there—his future college achievement. This aptitude test itself is a measure of achievement. It contains questions of knowledge or problems to solve, just as examinations in courses do. But a score on such a test has little merit by itself; the test is not used to assign a grade or to "pass" a person. Its value lies in its power to predict achievement in college or a similar situation—in other words, to measure aptitude. On the other hand, an examination given to a student in a course is designed to measure the knowledge he gained in the course. It is therefore an achievement test, even though we might be able to make reasonably good predictions about future achievement from it.

Sometimes we use the word *ability* as a general term referring either to a potential for the acquisition of a skill or to an already acquired skill (Super and Crites, 1962). Thus ability includes both aptitude—the potential—and achievement—the developed skill. For instance, if a general term is needed, intelligence tests might be called tests of *intellectual ability*. But if the emphasis is on intelligence as a characteristic enabling a person to benefit from training, intelligence tests might be called tests of *intellectual aptitude*.

In situations where they wish to *predict* achievement, test constructors often deliberately mix measures of aptitude and of achievement in one test. Such a mixed test usually predicts better than a test emphasizing either aptitude or achievement alone. Tests of this sort are regarded as tests of *educational development.* An example that will be familiar to many college students is the National Merit Scholarship Qualifying Test (NMSQT), now taken by about 750,000 high school students annually in the United States. Even though this test is given to students without regard to the particular subjects they have taken, it measures both general knowledge and aptitude. Its effectiveness in predicting success in college is quite high.

GROUP VERSUS INDIVIDUAL Some tests must be given by a trained tester to one person at a time; these are *individual tests.* Some may be given to groups of individuals by almost anyone who can follow directions and use a stopwatch; these are *group tests.* The interpretation of both kinds of tests, however, must be made by properly trained psychologists.

VERBAL VERSUS PERFORMANCE Most tests use written language in the instructions and in the questions to be answered by the examinees. These are called *verbal tests,* because they involve words. On the other hand, some tests have been devised for preschool children, illiterates, or foreign-born people who cannot read English. These are called *performance tests.* Instructions may be given verbally by the tester, but the test itself does not employ words or handicap a person who cannot read (see Figure 10.1).

SPEED VERSUS POWER *Speed tests* are limited in time, and the person who can do things quickly makes the best score. *Power tests* are designed to test the ability of a person to solve difficult problems irrespective of the time required. Sometimes power tests have time limits, but if so, they are only for administrative convenience and have been established so that the time limit makes no significant difference in a person's performance.

TESTS OF MAXIMUM PERFORMANCE VERSUS TESTS OF TYPICAL PERFORMANCE In many tests we are interested in the best a person can do. For instance: How fast can he solve simple problems in arithmetic? How many items can he get right on an achievement test? These are the aptitude, achievement, and ability tests. In personality tests, we are interested in what a person typically does (Cronbach, 1970). For instance, does he display hostility toward his supervisor? Does he usually make friends easily? Is he habitually anxious?

Tests may differ in other ways. For example, some tests give one overall score, whereas others provide separate scores for different abilities or traits. Some are designed only for a certain age group. Some are designed for the mentally retarded, others for the especially intelligent. Today there are literally hundreds of tests, and the testing business is a multimillion-dollar industry.

Intelligence Tests

Tests that measure general ability or aptitude for intellectual performance are called *intelligence tests.* Actually, intelligence tests measure not just one ability or aptitude but several—those that predict achieve-

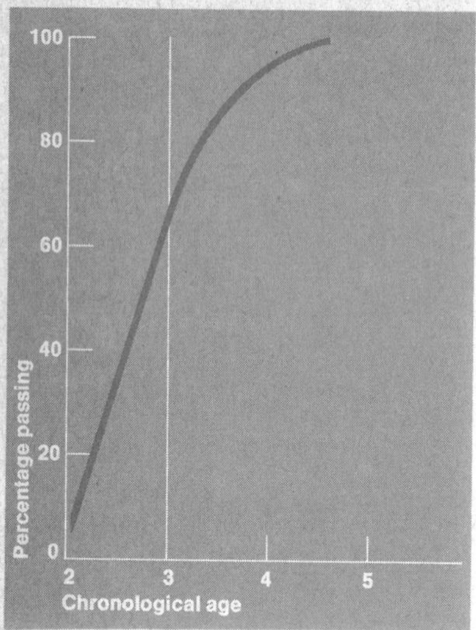

ITEMS FOR THE AGE LEVELS OF THE STANFORD-BINET SCALE ARE CHOSEN BY INSPECTION OF PERCENTAGE-PASSING CURVES

Figure 10.2 *The percentage of children passing the block bridge-building item of the Stanford-Binet Intelligence Scale at different ages. This item is at the 3-year-old level. Before 3, few children pass the item; at 3 and afterwards, most children pass it. (Modified from Terman and Merrill, 1960.)*

ment in a wide variety of real situations. For convenience we lump these aptitudes together as "intelligence." Such general aptitude tests may be contrasted with tests of the *special aptitudes* required in specific occupations or activities—mechanical, clerical, arithmetic, musical, and artistic aptitudes, to name just a few.

The wide variety of tests that exist for the measurement of intelligence may be confusing to a person who is accustomed to think of intelligence as a single "real" ability, as many people do. Why, he may ask, should we not have just one test of intelligence that "really" measures intelligence?

The reasons for having many tests of intelligence are threefold. One reason, as we shall see, is that intelligence is not a single ability; rather it is several abilities. Another reason is time: In an industrial setting, we may want a test that can be given quickly; in other situations, we may want tests that are detailed and analytical, no matter how much time they take. A third reason has to do with our purpose: For research purposes, one kind of test may be best; to evaluate possible brain damage in a patient, another kind may be best; and to carefully study a child who is doing poorly in school, still another may be best.

The Stanford-Binet Intelligence Scale The first test of intelligence to be devised was intended for schools and thus stressed the aptitudes involved in primary education. It was published in 1905 by Alfred Binet, a French psychologist, who designed the test at the request of the Paris school authorities to enable them to pick out children of low intelligence who could not profit from attending school. The test served its purpose and immediately caught the attention of American psychologists. In 1916, Terman (1877–1956) of Stanford University brought out a revision of Binet's test intended for schoolchildren in the United States. His revision came to be known as the Stanford-Binet test (Terman and Merrill, 1937) and became the model for many intelligence tests developed since then, including its own revision in 1960 (Terman and Merrill, 1960).

MENTAL AGE The 1960 Stanford-Binet Scale is an individual test which is used primarily with children. It consists of a series of subtests arranged according to age levels. There are separate age-level subtests for every half year from 2 through 5, for every year from 6 through 14, and for four adult levels. The items on the subtests at each age level are chosen so that the children that age or older can pass them, but younger children cannot. For instance, an ideal item for the 3-year-old subtest would be one which no child could pass until he was 3; after 3, all children should be able to pass the item. Of course, the items only approximate this ideal. Figure 10.2 shows the percentage of children passing the 3-year-old block bridge item (see Table 10.1) at different ages (Terman and Merrill, 1960).

When a child is being tested, the examiner first finds the highest level of subtest on which the child passes all the items. The age level specified by the scale for that subtest is called the child's *basal age*. The examiner then continues to give subtests appropriate to older and older ages until the child cannot pass any of the items on a particular subtest. This age level is called the child's *ceiling age*. When the results are

Age	Type of item	Description
2	Three-hole form board	Places forms (circle, triangle, square) in correct holes.
	Block building: tower	Builds a four-block tower from model after demonstration.
3	Block building: bridge	Builds a bridge consisting of the side blocks and one top block from model after demonstration.
4	Naming objects from memory	One of three objects (e.g., toys, dog, or shoe) is covered after child has seen them; child then names objects from memory.
	Picture identification	Points to correct pictures of objects on a card when asked, "Show me what we cook on," or "What do we carry when it is raining?"
7	Similarities	Answers such questions as, "In what way are coal and wood alike? Ship and automobile?"
	Copying a diamond	Draws three diamonds, following a printed sample.
8	Vocabulary	Defines eight words from a list.
	Memory for stories	Listens to a story, then answers questions about it.
9	Verbal absurdities	Must say what is foolish about stories similar to, "I saw a well-dressed young man who was walking down the street with his hands in his pockets and twirling a brand new cane."
	Digit reversal	Must repeat four digits backward.
Average adult	Vocabulary	Defines 20 words from a list (same list as at 8, above).
	Proverbs	Explains in own words the meaning of two or more common proverbs.
	Orientation	Must answer questions similar to, "Which direction would you have to face so your left hand would be toward the south?"

Table 10.1 *Some items from the Stanford-Binet Intelligence Scale. On the average, these items should be passed at the ages indicated.*

Source: Terman and Merrill, 1960.

tallied, the score the child obtains tells his *mental age* (MA). For example, if a child passed all tests for age 4, half those for age 5, and none of those for age 6, his mental age would be 4½ (54 months). In other words, even if his chronological age (CA) was only 4, he would have the intellectual ability of an average 4½-year-old. Thus mental ages are a type of norm. Usually the computation is not so simple as this example, but it illustrates the principle.

Table 10.1 presents some of the items from the Stanford-Binet Scale. Notice the kinds of abilities that are tested at various age levels. At lower levels, the tests stress information about objects and pictures, as well as perception of forms. In the higher age brackets, the tests emphasize the use of words, numbers, and relationships in reasoning problems.

A child's mental ability obviously increases as he grows older. When we test him at a certain age and obtain a mental-age score, we know merely the level of his ability at that age. On the average, we would expect a child's mental age to increase at the same rate as his chronological age. Indeed, the test norms were established so that it could hardly be otherwise. The bright child, on the other hand, should show a more rapid increase in mental ability, so that his mental age would be greater than his chronological age. The reverse would be true of the dull child.

INTELLIGENCE QUOTIENT This brings us to the idea that relative intelligence is a ratio between mental age and chronological age. If two children both score an MA of 5 years on the intelligence test, but one is only 4 years old and the other is 5, obviously the younger child is the brighter—in fact, much the brighter—of the two. To express this kind of difference precisely with numbers, we have the concept of the intelligence quotient (IQ). The IQ is a ratio of mental age (MA) to chronological age (CA) multiplied by 100 to avoid the inconvenience of decimals. The formula is

$$IQ = \frac{MA}{CA} \times 100$$

Looked at in this way, the IQ shows how fast a child's abilities are growing in relation to his chronological age. Applying the IQ formula to the two children mentioned above, we find that the brighter one has an IQ of 125 and the other an IQ of 100.

This definition of IQ was used in the interpretation of scores obtained on the 1937 Stanford-Binet Scale, and it gives the basic idea of all intelligence quotients. But other definitions of IQ are possible, and in the 1960 version of this scale, *standard-score*, or *deviation*, IQs are used. (For a discussion of deviation IQs, see the following section on the Wechsler Adult Intelligence Scale.) The IQ is a convenient yardstick of mental ability relative to age because it enables us to compare children of different chronological ages even though they have different mental ages and pass subtests that are quite different in difficulty. Great care had to be taken in selecting test items and in establishing age norms. In fact, the test was so constructed that the distribution of IQs is about the same for all age groups.

This *ratio* IQ, as it is called, conveys the idea that in children an IQ indicates the *rate* of intellectual growth. It tells us, for example, that a child of 13 with an IQ of 125 and a child of 5 with the same IQ are equally bright (quite bright, in fact, since only about 5 percent of children have IQs higher than that). There have, however, proved to be difficulties with the ratio IQ. One is that it breaks down in the middle teens when intellectual growth tapers off while the CA continues to advance. Another is that it is difficult to construct tests that evenly measure intellectual growth from year to year. For these reasons, the ratio IQ has given way in the most recent standardization of the Stanford-Binet (1960) and in the Wechsler test to another kind of IQ called the *deviation* IQ. This is basically a standard score (page 299) derived by determining where a person stands relative to his standardization group in standard deviations above or below the mean test score.

The Stanford-Binet has proved most useful with children, because the single IQ score that it furnishes is all that is needed to make predictions about ability to do schoolwork in the lower grades. With adults, however, we often want some breakdown of an IQ score. For this purpose, the Wechsler scale has proved more useful.

Wechsler Adult Intelligence Scale The most widely used test for adults is one developed by Dr. David Wechsler (1955) of the Bellevue Psychi-

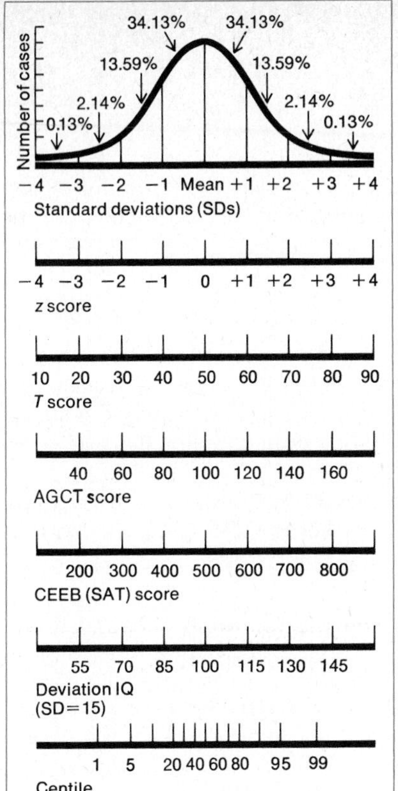

TEST SCORES CAN BE EXPRESSED IN MANY EQUIVALENT WAYS

Figure 10.3 *Equivalence between derived test scores and the percentage of cases falling at or above a particular score. From the normal curve at the top of the figure the percentage of cases falling at or above a particular derived score can be found. This can be done by reading up to the normal curve along a vertical line through the derived score. For instance, a WAIS deviation IQ of 115 is at or above 84.13 percent of cases. (Modified from Anastasi, 1968.)*

atric Hospital. It is called the Wechsler Adult Intelligence Scale (WAIS). The WAIS, like the Stanford-Binet, is an individual test requiring many props and expert testers. Also like the Stanford-Binet, it is made up of a wide variety of subtests. However, the WAIS is not scaled according to age. Instead, the subtests are grouped into two sets of categories: verbal and performance. There are six verbal subtests and five performance subtests.

Verbal subtests	Performance subtests
Information	Picture arrangement
General comprehension	Picture completion
Memory span	Block design
Arithmetic reasoning	Object assembly
Similarities	Digit symbol
Vocabulary	

The subtests can be separately scored so that a person's abilities in the various categories can be compared. Moreover, the verbal and performance sections of the test can be independently scored to give separate IQs on each. This feature is often helpful in testing people of foreign background or of poor education who have not had a fair opportunity to develop their verbal abilities. Such individuals frequently do better on performance tests than on verbal tests. It is also helpful in testing brain-injured persons or the mentally ill, because it sometimes makes clearer just where a person's trouble lies.

The method of computing IQs for the WAIS is different from the method we described for the 1937 Stanford-Binet. Instead of using MA and dividing that by CA (which at best is appropriate only for children), a WAIS IQ is obtained by a standard-score method (see page 300). This method, you will recall, requires that the mean and standard deviation of a distribution of scores be obtained and that standard-score equivalents be established. In this case, the standard scores are called IQs.

For standardization groups, Wechsler used a total sample of 1,700 people in seven age subgroups, ranging from 16 to 64, all selected from different geographical and racial groups according to the proportions found in census data. The distribution of scores for each age subgroup tested in this way served as the norms for assigning standard-score, or deviation, IQs.

Wechsler set the mean of the scores equal to an IQ of 100; he also set one standard deviation in score points equal to 15 IQ points. In other words, a simple transformation was made. The typical, or average, score—the mean—was given an IQ value corresponding to a typical, or average, IQ—100. One standard deviation in the scores was given an IQ value close to the value of the standard deviations which had been obtained from other earlier IQ tests—namely, 15. Thus a person having a score one standard deviation below the mean would obtain an equivalent IQ score of 85; an individual having a score one standard deviation above the mean would be assigned an IQ of 115 (see Figure 10.3).

All this is just another way of saying that each raw score has an equivalent IQ value. By defining IQs in this way, the distribution of IQs is tied

Table 10.2 *Distribution of intelligence quotients on the Wechsler Adult Intelligence Scale.*

Source: Modified from Wechsler, 1958.

IQ	Verbal description	% of adults
Above 130	Very superior	2.2
120–129	Superior	6.7
110–119	Bright normal	16.1
90–109	Average	50.0
80–89	Dull normal	16.1
70–79	Borderline	6.7
Below 70	Mentally retarded	2.2

directly to the normal curve. And the percentages of individuals having IQs above, below, or between any particular IQ values are readily predicted from the normal curve (see Figure 10.3). The resulting distribution of adult IQs and the descriptive terms applied to the IQs within different ranges are given in Table 10.2.

It may be of interest to the college student to have a more detailed breakdown of the distribution of above-average IQs. The percentage of the population with IQs of 110 and higher is as follows:

Wechsler IQ	110	113	119	125	128	135
Percent higher	25	20	10	5	3	1

These figures mean that about 1 percent of people have IQs above 135, 10 percent above 119, and so on.

In the revised Stanford-Binet Scale of 1960, data have been provided for making the same type of IQ computation as Wechsler used in the WAIS.

Group tests of intelligence In counseling situations in hospitals and schools, where intelligence testing is usually only part of the analysis of an individual's problem, it is convenient to use individual tests of intelligence. In these situations too, expert personnel trained in test administrations are frequently available to give the Stanford-Binet Scale, WAIS, or some other individual test. But in many other situations a group test is either desirable or absolutely essential. In the armed services, hundreds of thousands of people need to be tested each year. In many colleges and other schools of higher education, entering students must be tested in mass. Group tests have been devised to meet such needs.

World War I furnished the impetus for the first large-scale effort to develop group tests. Hundreds of thousands of young men were inducted into the service. We needed some quick method for weeding out the mentally unfit and for selecting the most able for officer training. And to utilize manpower effectively, we needed to assign people to different battalions and technical training schools according to their abilities.

Psychologists met these needs in World War I by devising the Army Alpha Test and the Army Beta Test. The Army Alpha, designed for the typical individual who can read and write, yielded scores for classifying men roughly according to intelligence. Table 10.4 shows some examples

Table 10.3 *Some items from the Army Alpha Test.*

A. If 5½ tons of bark cost $33, what will 3½ cost? (   )

B. A train is harder to stop than an automobile because
( ) it is longer, ( ) it is heavier ( ) the brakes are not so good

C. If the two words of a pair mean the same or nearly the same thing, draw a line under *same.* If they mean the opposite or nearly the opposite, draw a line under *opposite.*

comprehensive	restricted	same	opposite
allure	attract	same	opposite
latent	hidden	same	opposite
deride	ridicule	same	opposite

D. If, when you have arranged the following words to make a sentence, the sentence is true, underline *true;* if it is false, underline *false.*

people enemies arrogant many make	true	false
never who heedless those stumble are	true	false
never man the show the deeds	true	false

E. *Underline which*

The pitcher has an important place in
tennis   football   baseball   hand ball

F. *Underline which*

Dismal is to dark as cheerful is to
laugh   bright   house   gloomy

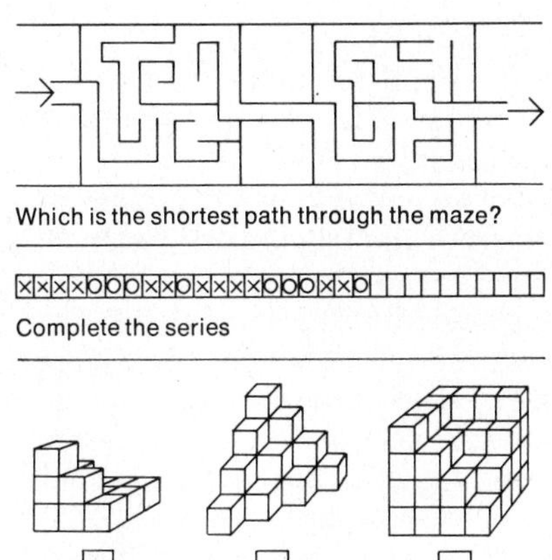

How many cubes in each pile?
Write number in appropriate square.

NONVERBAL PERFORMANCE TESTS ARE USED WITH ILLITERATES AND OTHERS HANDICAPPED IN THE USE OF ENGLISH

Figure 10.4 *Items from the Army Beta Test developed during World War I. The Beta test was used with illiterates and others for whom the verbal Alpha test was unfair. The instructions shown here were given orally by the examiner. (National Academy of Science.)*

of the problems on this test. Between the two wars, the Army Alpha was frequently revised for use with both servicemen and civilians. The Army Beta was designed as a test that could be given to illiterates and immigrants not proficient in English. It emphasized nonverbal problems for which simple instructions could be given orally. Examples of items from the Army Beta are shown in Figure 10.4.

When World War II came along, Army psychologists took advantage of extensive research in mental testing to make a drastic revision, which they named the Army General Classification Test (AGCT). This was given to several million servicemen upon induction into the Armed Forces. It was prepared in four different interchangeable forms, each requiring about an hour to give. In addition, longer forms of the test were devised to break down a person's performance into four different categories: (1) verbal ability, (2) spatial comprehension, (3) arithmetic computation, and (4) arithmetic reasoning.

The AGCT, like the Stanford-Binet, is scored so that the average person is assigned 100. The standard deviation, however, is 20 (see Figure 10.3). For purpose of rough classification, the Army divided people into five groups according to score. The spread or distribution is much like that on individual tests of intelligence, but the AGCT score and the IQ are not exactly comparable. The Navy developed and used a similar

NGCT, with this difference: Navy tests have an average score of 50. In recent years, one test, the Armed Forces Qualification Test (AFQT), has replaced the AGCT and the NGCT.

After World War I, several group tests were devised for use with civilians—primarily to help in selecting people for jobs in business and industry (see Chapter 16). One of the best known is the Otis Self-Administering Test of Mental Ability (Otis SA). This is a short four-page pencil-and-paper test that can be administered simply with a stopwatch and under testing conditions that are relatively easy to keep standard. It can be taken and scored with either a 20-minute or a 30-minute time limit. Scores on the test have been correlated with those on the Stanford-Binet so that it is possible, if one wishes, to convert them to equivalent IQs. The test is so constructed that it emphasizes verbal and reasoning factors but does not sample performance factors very well.

A number of other tests designed in connection with higher education follow the general pattern of the group tests of intelligence. For instance, the Scholastic Aptitude Test (SAT) of the College Entrance Examination Board is used in the selection of college students. The mean of this test is standardized at 500, and the standard deviation is 100 (see Figure 10.3). Still other tests are used at a more advanced level for students seeking entrance to medical and graduate schools. Since these are designed for the fairly specific purpose of predicting success in a particular kind of education, they have many of the earmarks of special aptitude tests, and are discussed later under the heading of special aptitudes.

The nature of intelligence It seems natural to think of intelligence as a single ability or attribute. When we call Mary "bright" and John "dumb," we are applying unitary labels to a person. Seldom do we think of Mary as being bright in school, but very dumb in other ways—that is we usually do not notice that there are different kinds of intelligence. The fact that most of our tests of intelligence produce one overall score, or IQ, further determines our thinking about intelligence as a unitary thing. Is there a general intelligence as distinguished from specific abilities, or is there just a collection of abilities? What actually is intelligence?

The method of factor analysis furnishes a way of answering this question. To perform a factor analysis, research workers give a good many different tests to the same people to see how well the tests correlate with each other. For this purpose they compute correlations between subtests, not just the overall scores, in order to isolate the elements of intelligence as best they can. Having a lot of correlations, they then proceed, by statistical analysis, to see which items form clusters and which ones are independent of each other. It may turn out, for example, that all sorts of subtests involving words may correlate with one another but not with other subtests involving numbers. In this way the researchers isolate *factors* in a number of tests. In the example just cited, they would conclude that a verbal factor is relatively separate from a numerical factor.

A great deal of such research has been done. Each investigator obtains somewhat different results, depending on the tests he uses and the sample of people he gives them to. Various studies agree, however, that there are a number of different factors in intelligence (see Guilford,

1967). Some of the most extensive investigations in the United States were carried out by Thurstone (Thurstone and Thurstone, 1941). After finishing an elaborate factor analysis of dozens of tests given to schoolchildren, he emerged with seven factors. Each factor represents a cluster of correlations between subtests and thus specifies what is common to them:

1. *Verbal comprehension (V)* Ability to define and understand words
2. *Word fluency (W)* Ability to think rapidly of words, as in extemporaneous speech or solving crossword puzzles
3. *Number (N)* Ability to do arithmetic problems
4. *Space (S)* Ability to draw a design from memory or to visualize relationships
5. *Memory (M)* Ability to memorize and recall
6. *Perceptual (P)* Ability to grasp visual details and to see differences and similarities among objects
7. *Reasoning (R)* Ability to find rules, principles, or concepts for understanding or solving problems

After discovering these factors, Thurstone rearranged his subtests, grouping together those which represented the same factor. Actually, in many instances he tried to improve on this technique by devising new subtests that seemed to be good measures of the factors he had discovered. Now, with a new set of tests of *primary mental abilities* (PMA), he could come to grips with the question of whether or not such a thing as general intelligence exists. Because he had obtained seven factors, he concluded that intelligence is partly made up of separate abilities. The question was, Is there a general factor, apart from the specific ones?

To settle this problem, he obtained scores on each of the tests of primary mental abilities from a large group of children and intercorrelated the scores with one another. If there were no such thing as general intelligence, each factor measured by a test should be independent of every other, and there should be no, or very low, correlations among them. Thurstone found, however, that the different tests *are correlated,* some relatively highly and some not so much. The correlations indicate that some general ability is common to all the tests of primary ability. He therefore came to the conclusion that "each of the primary factors can be regarded as a composite of an independent primary factor and a general factor which it shares with other primary factors." Since then, other investigators' findings have been in general agreement with Thurstone's. The answer to our original question—What is intelligence?—is that it is both some general ability and a number of specific abilities.

Interpretation of tests This conclusion is extremely important in the interpretation of intelligence tests. Though each test may measure "general intelligence" in some degree and thus in part measures what other intelligence tests are measuring, it also reflects its own particular sample of specific abilities. None of the individual or group tests of intelligence now in common use measures these specific abilities in equal degree. Some weight several abilities more heavily than others.

Actually, most intelligence tests, particularly the Stanford-Binet and the Otis, are heavily weighted with verbal content. In the case of the Stanford-Binet, this came about because achievement in school, which is mostly a verbal matter, was used as a criterion for selecting many of the items on the test. Group tests such as the Otis are weighted with verbal and numerical content partly because it is much easier to make up tests of these abilities than of others. In drawing conclusions about individuals' abilities from an intelligence test, the fact that such abilities are given greater weight must be kept in mind.

Another important thing to remember about intelligence tests is that they measure present ability, not native capacity. People have different opportunities to acquire abilities. Poor people do not have the same cultural and educational opportunities as those who are financially more fortunate. Moreover, many of the problems used in intelligence tests presuppose a common background. In the United States, the common background on which intelligence tests are based is that of the white middle and upper classes. The poor and disadvantaged, in which minority groups are heavily represented, lack familiarity with many of the words and objects employed in intelligence testing.

We shall later discuss hereditary and environmental influences on intelligence, but here let us note that in any test of ability three components are involved: innate ability, environmental influences, and motivation at the time of testing. Any change or difference due to any one of these will affect the test score. At the same time, the test score provides no way of disentangling these influences. All that it does is what it was intended to do, namely, give us some prediction of performance in situations to which the ability test is relevant.

Intelligence and creativity A question often asked about intelligence is whether or not it is the same thing as creativity. One would think that they would be related, and they are in principle, for we regard creativity as being an important component of intelligence. In practice, however, it turns out that our way of constructing intelligence tests causes us to discard items that measure creativity. Intelligence tests measure *convergent* thinking—thinking that is like other people's thinking—yet creativity is a matter of *divergent* thinking, which is unlike other people's (Guilford, 1965).

Considerable research has been done on creative thinking. Out of it have come several batteries of tests designed to measure creativity. Examples are association tests, in which a subject gives as many definitions as possible of fairly common words; tests of the "uses of things," in which the subject thinks of as many possible uses of a common object, such as a brick; a fables test, in which the last line of an incomplete fable is furnished by the subject. With tests such as these, investigators have set out to determine how closely creativity and intelligence are related. One such study is as follows (Getzels and Jackson, 1962):

Tests of intelligence and creativity were administered to 500 public school students in grades 6 through 12. A rather low correlation was obtained between the two types of tests. Then the experimenters selected a group of students who were in the upper 20 percent on creativity but *not* in the upper 20 percent on intelligence. These were compared with a group consisting of students in the top 20 percent on intelligence but *not* in the top 20 percent on creativity. The two groups, despite a difference of 23 points in mean IQ, performed about equally well in school. However, students in the high-intelligence group were more highly approved by their teachers and considered to be more "achievement oriented." Students in the high-creativity group, on the other hand, were rated by teachers as showing more originality, more humor, more playfulness (and more violence) than those in the high-intelligence group.

From studies like this we have learned that creativity and intelligence as measured by tests are not highly correlated, at least above an average level of intelligence. Creativity and intelligence, as we measure them, therefore are not the same thing. Individuals may be quite creative, performing well in school and contributing innovations to society, without being highly intelligent. This is something we should keep in mind in thinking about individual differences in intelligence (see below).

Individual Differences in Intelligence

Differences in intelligence make a difference in the occupational and educational achievements which can be expected from people. This is one aspect of the problem of individual differences in intelligence. Refer again to Table 10.2 presenting the distribution of WAIS IQs in the United States. The scores are arbitrarily grouped into seven categories: below 70, 70–79, 80–89, 90–109, 110–119, 120–129, and over 130. For convenience, each of these arbitrary categories has been given a characteristic name, such as average, superior, and so on. On the basis of intelligence test scores, what occupational and educational achievements can be expected from members of these different groups? The clearest predictions can be made for the two extreme groups of "exceptional" people—namely, those with IQs below 70 and above 130.

Mental subnormality People with IQs below 70 are regarded as mentally subnormal, or mentally retarded, and those between 70 and 80 as borderline (Robinson and Robinson, 1965). (The term "feebleminded," once much used, has now gone out of favor.) On the basis of intelligence tests, between 2 and 3 percent of the United States population is in the subnormal category (see Table 10.2). In the past, the subnormal were subdivided into three groups; morons, IQ 50–69; imbeciles, IQ 20–49; and idiots, IQ below 20. This classification is no longer used; more descriptive terms, such as mild, moderate, severe, and profound mental retardation, have been substituted (see Table 10.4).

Knowing the IQs for different degrees of retardation as shown in the table, we can forecast the ultimate mental age of the retarded adult. To do that, recall that the IQ is a ratio of mental age to chronological age and that mental growth, as measured by the Stanford-Binet Scale, comes to a maximum at about 16 years of age. From this knowledge, we can expect the mildly retarded person's ultimate mental age to be approxi-

Degrees of mental retardation	Preschool age (0–5) Maturation and development	School age (6–20) Training and education	Adult (21 and over) social and vocational capabilities
Profound (IQ below 20)	Gross retardation; minimal capacity for functioning in sensorimotor areas; needs nursing care.	Some motor development present; cannot profit from training in self-help; needs total care.	Some motor and speech development; totally incapable of self-maintenance, must have complete care and supervision.
Severe (IQ 20–35)	Poor motor development; speech is minimal; generally unable to profit from training in self-help; little or no communication skill.	Can talk or learn to communicate; can be trained in elemental health habits; cannot learn functional academic skills; profits from systematic habit training.	Can contribute partially to self-support under complete supervision; can develop self-protection skills to a minimal useful level in controlled environment.
Moderate (IQ 36–52)	Can talk or learn to communicate; poor social awareness; fair motor development; may profit from self-help; can be managed with moderate supervision.	Can learn functional academic skills to approximately 4th grade level by late teens if given special education.	Capable of maintaining himself in unskilled or semiskilled occupations; needs supervision or guidance when under mild social or economic stress.
Mild (IQ 53–69)	Can develop social and communication skills; minimal retardation in the sensorimotor areas; is rarely distinguished from normal until later age.	Can learn academic skills to approximately 6th grade level by late teens. Cannot learn general high school subjects; needs special education, particularly at secondary school age levels.	Capable of social and vocational adequacy with proper education and training; frequently needs supervision and guidance under serious social or economic stress.

Table 10.4 *Classification and developmental characteristics of the mentally retarded.*

Source: Modified from Kisker, 1964.

mately 8 to 12; that of the moderately retarded, 6 to 8 years; that of the severely retarded, 3 to 6 years; and that of the profoundly retarded, below 3 years. Knowing these limits, we can fill in the capacities of the retarded, as summarized in Table 10.4.

SOCIAL MATURITY Descriptions of the *intellectual* level of the retarded, however, do not give a fair account of their abilities. Because IQ tests tend to weight verbal factors, they are not such an effective measure of capabilities in more mundane daily affairs. An evaluation of social skills is of more use than an IQ. In such skills, the retarded generally rate better than one would expect from an IQ. Moreover, social development usually continues for a somewhat longer period into adulthood than does mental growth as tested by the Stanford-Binet. Hence we find many people of subnormal intelligence functioning quite adequately in day-to-day living situations.

CAUSES Mental retardation has two general causes: one is a matter of inheritance, the other injury or disease. In the first case the individual is sound physically; the only thing wrong with him is his intellectual deficit. In such a case other members of his family are also frequently subnormal, and therefore this kind of retardation is sometimes called *familial.*

Mental retardation may also be caused by several medical conditions: toxemia of the mother during pregnancy (proper treatment of this can prevent damage to the infant); inborn errors of metabolism or of glandular function; diseases such as syphilis or German measles contracted by the mother early in pregnancy; and injury to the brain at birth. Retardation caused by injury or disease is often termed *mental deficiency.*

TREATMENT OF MENTAL RETARDATION The treatment of mental retardation is a serious problem in our society—some five to six million are afflicted in the United States. All these people are handicapped in the kind of lives they can lead and in the kind of work they can do. What can be done about mental retardation?

Well-educated parents who are confronted with the fact that their child is mentally retarded are likely to think that something can be done to raise the child's IQ. Dramatic stories in the newspapers or magazines sometimes give this impression because they seem to show that it is possible to do much with a mentally retarded child. This possibility has been carefully investigated in several psychological studies, and the evidence unfortunately is against it (Kirk, 1958). Special training produces slight changes in IQ and in social intelligence, but seldom any dramatic transformation. Mental retardation in most cases is a matter of capacity; one can do little to alter the intelligence of the defective child. People usually deceive themselves if they think otherwise.

However, much can be done to make the most of the limited capacity of the mentally retarded. The majority of mentally deficient persons are only mildly or moderately retarded; a minority are severely or profoundly retarded. Whatever the degree of deficiency, the training may be long and tedious, but it is worth the effort. Gradually the individual can be taught some of the social skills, such as washing himself, helping with duties around the house, and doing many minor tasks that keep him from being such a burden to others. If his defect is not too severe, he can be taught some vocational skills, such as woodworking, printing, and weaving (see Table 10.4). The better institutions for the mentally deficient have facilities and teachers for training in these social and occupational skills, and each year they return to society many individuals who are capable of earning a living and looking after themselves reasonably well.

The mentally gifted At the top end of the distribution of IQs are the very superior (130–140) and the "near genius" (above 140). Psychologists have studied the very gifted in two ways: (1) by estimating the intelligence of gifted people who lived years ago, and (2) by following the accomplishments and problems of gifted children into adulthood.

GIFTED MEN OF HISTORY Enough is recorded about the lives of some of the people who have been prominent in history to make fairly reliable estimates of IQ scores if they had lived in a day when they could have taken the Stanford-Binet Scale. If we know at what age a child

Francis Galton	200
John Stuart Mill	190
Johann Wolfgang von Goethe	185
Gottfried Wilhelm von Leibniz	185
Samuel Taylor Coleridge	175
John Quincy Adams	165
David Hume	155
Alfred Tennyson	155
René Descartes	150
Wolfgang Amadeus Mozart	150
William Wordsworth	150
Francis Bacon	145
Charles Dickens	145
Benjamin Franklin	145
George Frederick Handel	145
Thomas Jefferson	145
John Milton	145
Daniel Webster	145

Table 10.5 *The IQs of some eminent men, estimated from biographical data.*

Source: Cox. 1926

began to read, at what age he made certain words a part of his vocabulary or mastered certain problems in arithmetic, and so on, we can match these accomplishments with the standards of the Stanford-Binet Scale.

This sort of thing has been done for a long list of people. Table 10.5 names some eminent men and gives their estimated IQs.

GIFTED CHILDREN Even more information was obtained in a monumental study conducted over a period of 35 years by Terman, the creator of the Stanford-Binet Scale (Terman and Oden, 1947, 1959). Terman and his associates, having tested many thousands of children, picked out for further study a group of more than 1,500 who had IQs of 140 or more: approximately the highest 1 percent of children.

Terman was able to follow most of these children into their adulthood. Periodically he sent them questionnaires or found out in other ways what they were doing, and built up a detailed picture of their achievements. Some of Terman's associates are continuing to follow up these gifted "children," many of whom are now middle-aged.

One interesting thing about them is the homes they came from. About a third were the children of professional people, about half came from homes of the higher business classes, and only a small proportion (7 percent) came from the working classes. This marked disproportion to the numbers of people in each class indicates that relatively more gifted children come from the higher socioeconomic classes. Such a fact is undoubtedly accounted for by both heredity and environment. These classes can provide a better environment for the development of intellectual abilities; and because the more successful people tend to be the more gifted, they also pass on such gifts to their children through heredity.

The later success of Terman's gifted children is a second striking discovery of his studies. About 700 people from the original study could be contacted 25 years later. Of these, about 150 were very successful judged by such criteria as (1) being listed in *Who's Who* or *American Men of Science,* (2) holding responsible managerial positions, or (3) receiving recognition for outstanding intellectual or professional achievement. Most of the others were less outstanding but still much more successful than people of average intelligence. On the other hand, some were conspicuously unsuccessful—some had committed crimes, some had dropped out of school early, and some became vocational misfits who had been unsuccessful at a number of jobs. Careful comparisons of those who were very successful with those who were least successful showed that factors in personality made the difference. The least successful were more poorly adjusted emotionally and more poorly motivated to succeed. Despite the exceptions, however, the fact was that children of superior ability generally made an outstanding record of social and intellectual achievement.

Contrary to some popular misconceptions about the very bright, Terman's gifted children were above average in height, weight, and physical appearance. But in other studies it has been shown that the intellectually normal brothers and sisters of gifted children are also physically above average (Laycock and Caylor, 1964). This suggests

OCCUPATIONAL GROUPS DIFFER IN INTELLIGENCE, BUT A GREAT DEAL OF OVERLAP OCCURS

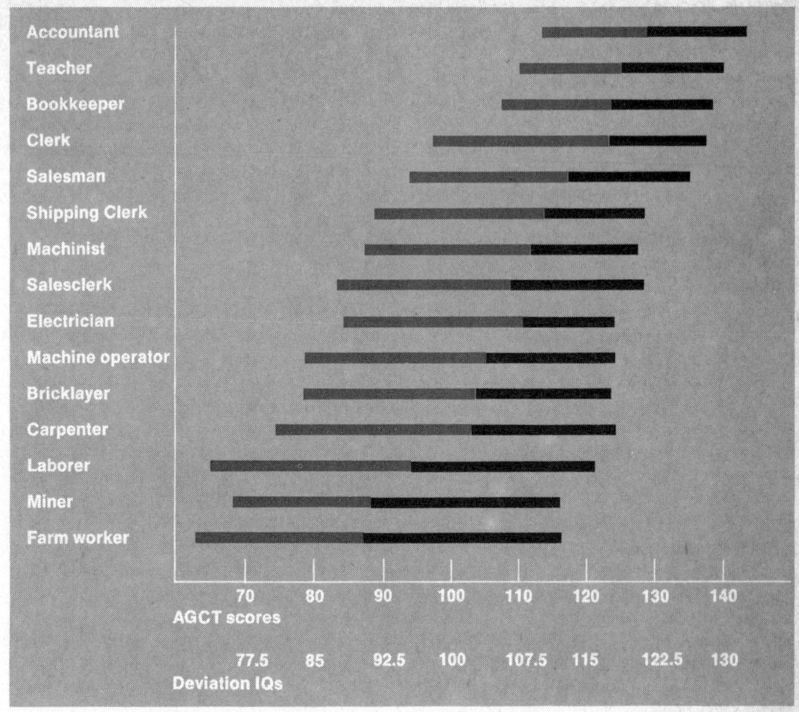

Figure 10.5 *The ranges of AGCT scores for selected occupations. Each bar shows the range between the 10th and 90th centiles for a sample of hundreds of men in each occupation. Scores below the median are shown in color; those above the median, in black. (Modified from Anastasi and Foley, 1958.)*

that above-average physical attributes of the superior children are not so much a concomitant of general superiority as a reflection of the good care they and their siblings receive at home. The very bright also are generally better adjusted and more socially adaptable, and they have more capacity for leadership than average children. Thus Terman disproved the notion that the "genius" is likely to be peculiar, maladjusted, and socially backward. Some very intelligent people, of course, are like that—and so are some average people—but in general the very bright are less so.

The middle groups The occupational achievements of people with IQs between 70 and 130 provide a good basis for predicting what can be expected from individuals at various levels in this middle group.

People in some occupations are, on the whole, more intelligent than those in others. Of the many studies that show this, the most extensive comes from data obtained during World War II (Stewart, 1947). As Figure 10.5 shows, accountants and teachers are quite high on the AGCT test. (The figure also gives a rough idea of the correspondence between AGCT scores and deviation IQs.) Lawyers and engineers, although their data are not shown in this chart, also had high AGCT scores. At the bottom of the list are farmhands, miners, and teamsters (not shown), with median scores of about 90. The variability, however, is large. Some people in every occupation scored over 130 and some scored 100

Table 10.6 *IQs of children averaged according to the occupational grouping of their fathers.*

Source: McNemar, 1942.

Father's occupation	Age of child 2–5½	6–9	10–14	15–18
Professional	115	115	118	116
Semiprofessional & managerial	112	107	112	117
Clerical, skilled, & business	108	105	107	110
Rural owners	98	95	92	94
Semiskilled	104	105	103	107
Slightly skilled	97	100	101	96
Day laborers	94	96	97	98

or below. Thus though there is an average difference in intelligence between occupational groups, there is a great deal of overlap.

It is not hard to understand how these occupational differences come about. In general, the higher-ranking occupations require considerably more schooling than the lower-ranking ones. The child with low intelligence tends not to stay in school as long, and when he does, he usually makes a poor grade record. Furthermore, colleges and professional schools tend to admit those with higher grades and to screen out those with low ones. Frequently these schools also use special tests of intelligence for deciding whom they will admit. This introduces a *spurious correlation:* if intelligence is the basis for admitting a person to certain occupations, persons in these occupations will average higher in intelligence, even if there is no necessary relation between that occupation and intelligence.

A more interesting and not so easily explained difference in intelligence is among the children of parents of different occupational groupings. The children of people in the higher occupational classes tend to have higher IQs than children of those at lower levels. The data in Table 10.6 taken from one study of this question show that the IQs of professional people's children average about 115, while children of day laborers average about 95. Perhaps part of the explanation for these differences lies in the relatively enriched home and cultural environments of the children of professional parents.

Group Differences in Intelligence

Everyday thinking is influenced by notions about the abilities of different *groups* of people. Many think that Negroes and foreigners are not so intelligent as white Americans. We regard older people as much wiser than, if not so quick as, younger people. Employers think women and young people more suitable for certain positions, men and older people for others.

Psychological research indicates that differences among various groups do exist. But often these differences are not the ones that the layman imagines, or not so great as he may think. Let us see what the facts are about differences in intellectual abilities.

Stability of IQ As background, we should first examine the question of stability of IQ. On the *average,* taking any representative group, IQs are constant throughout childhood and adolescence. This is true largely because the tests of IQ were designed to make it so. The constancy for groups, however, masks several kinds of changes that may take place in individuals.

For one thing, the IQ is not very stable in the preschool years (Sontag et al., 1958), largely because the tests are not so reliable for younger age groups. To the extent that IQs are stable from individual to individual, they may gradually shift in one direction or another as the child grows older. In about half the cases this difference is as much as 10 to 15 points. During the preschool period, IQs do not correlate with much of anything—with socioeconomic status, with biological parents, or in the case of adoptees, with foster parents. IQs finally stabilize fairly well around the second or third grade (at 7 to 8 years CA), when basic language skills have been acquired. Even from this point on, however, there can be sizable shifts upward or downward depending on the influence of factors we shall now discuss.

Sex differences If one compares the overall IQs of males and females at any age, one finds that they are virtually the same. In part, this is because intelligence tests were constructed to make them equal. In part, however, it is due to the averaging out of differences on subtests of the intelligence scale. On these subtests there are consistent differences in the average performance of males and females. Girls generally do better on verbal problems, on perceiving details quickly and accurately, and on making rapid, accurate manual movements. Boys surpass girls on items that involve spatial, numerical, and mechanical tasks. These differences come as no surprise, for they correspond to our common impressions of what the sexes do best. But whether the differences are due to inheritance or to the different roles the two sexes are taught from infancy is still largely unanswered at this point.

Studies of changes in IQ during childhood and adolescence reveal other interesting differences. On the average, the IQs of males tend to rise slightly starting at age 6, while those of females tend to decline somewhat (Sontag et al., 1958; Haan, 1963). If we pick out the cases that display these trends best and study them in detail, we find that trends correlate with changes in motivation and personality. In brief, the changes involve achievement motivation (see Chapter 6). Children with increasing IQs tend to show increasing achievement motivation, those with decreasing IQs an opposite trend. And because greater achievement is expected from boys, males tend to increase in this dimension while females decline. (This is just one example, as we shall see, of the influence of cultural and environmental factors on the IQ.) There is also a tendency for females to reach their maximum mental age and flatten out in intellectual growth earlier than boys. This correlates with the earlier physical maturation of girls and probably has a biological basis.

Age differences in ability Because people are living longer and longer, it is important that we have an accurate evaluation of the abilities of the

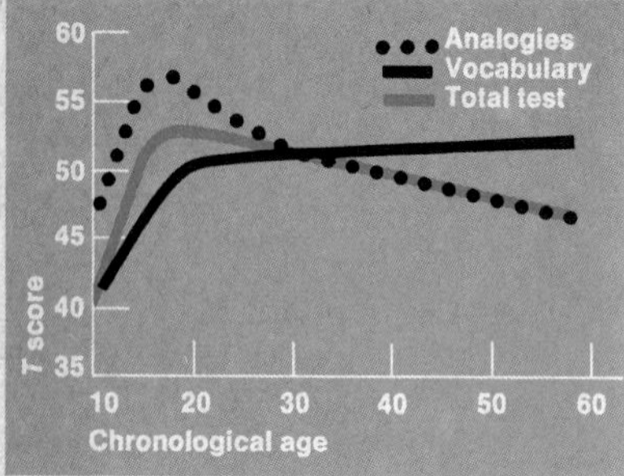

OLDER PEOPLE DO AS WELL AS YOUNG PEOPLE ON VOCABULARY TESTS, BUT LESS WELL ON TESTS INVOLVING NOVEL PROBLEMS SUCH AS ANALOGIES

Figure 10.6 *The relation of mental ability to age. (After Jones and Conrad, 1933.)*

elderly. The most general statement we can make about the change in abilities with age is this: As an individual approaches maturity, all his abilities increase to a peak level and then begin to decline. Just where the peak occurs, and how rapid the decline is, depend on what is being tested.

A famous study was performed by giving the Army Alpha test to virtually all the inhabitants aged 10 to 60 in a group of New England villages (Jones and Conrad, 1933). Results from the various subtests of the Army Alpha were then analyzed to sort out different abilities. The results on two subtests, as well as on the total test, are graphed in Figure 10.6. The solid colored line shows that general mental ability, as measured by the Army Alpha, rises to a peak somewhere between the ages of 16 and 20 and then declines steadily. Subtests, however, show that not all abilities behave in the same way. Tests of vocabulary, which weight previous verbal learning, show a slight rise if anything. The subtests on analogies, which weight reasoning, reach a fairly sharp peak followed first by a rapid decline, then by a slower one.

Roughly the same results were obtained in another more recent study designed to provide norms by age groups for the Wechsler Adult Intelligence Scale. However, this study indicates that the peak of intelligence is reached at a somewhat later age—usually in the late twenties. Due to the fact that the WAIS provides separate performance and verbal IQs, it is possible to analyze those two aspects of intelligence separately. It turns out that the peak of "performance intelligence" occurs earliest, in the mid-twenties, while the peak for "verbal intelligence" comes in the early thirties. And after these peaks, performance intelligence declines more rapidly than verbal intelligence, a finding which fits with the older study.

In all such studies we have difficulty being sure that the samples are comparable at different ages, because they can be biased, say, by a tendency of younger, brighter people to migrate from one particular area to another. Nevertheless, the main trends seem trustworthy. As a general conclusion, we can say that the peak of intelligence is reached between the teens and the early thirties, depending upon the type of intelligence being tested. Further, older people do as well as younger people in vocabulary and general information tests, but they do worse in tests which require them to work quickly or to adapt to situations which are different from those they are used to.

Note that the differences we have been discussing are *average* differences between the groups. A great deal of variability occurs within the younger and older groups, and in practically all the studies on aging many individuals in the older group do as well as, or better than, the average of the best younger group. In other words, the distributions of the two groups overlap to a considerable extent.

Overlap is statistically defined as the percentage of people in the lower group who achieve higher scores than the median of the higher group. For instance, a 40 percent overlap between an older and a younger group would mean that 40 percent of the individuals in the older group obtained scores higher than the median of the younger group. Note that a 40 percent overlap does *not* mean that only 40 percent of the lower group overlap any portion of the higher group. Sometimes results are reported, especially when controversial issues such as the difference between blacks and whites are involved, in such a way as to mislead the statistically unwary.

The great degree of overlap between the older and younger groups is important, because usually the practical problem is not to choose between groups but rather to select a small number of individuals for a particular job. Then the decision of who should be chosen is not determined by sex, race, nationality, age, or other "group" factors but by the *tested abilities of the individuals*.

Differences due to home environment Obviously the intellectual environment of children of professional parents is quite different from that of children of day laborers. When we find a difference in intelligence between two such groups of children, we are confronted by the age-old question of heredity versus environment. Are children of two groups of parents different in intelligence because they have different inheritances or because they have different intellectual environments? The question is as important as it is difficult, and psychologists have carried out extensive studies in an attempt to answer it. Even so, we do not have as conclusive an answer as we should like. Here are just a few of the most important facts.

Table 10.6 shows the IQs of children tested in different age groups from 2 to 18 and arranged according to seven major paternal occupational groups. The differences in the youngest group (2 to 5½ years) are just about the same as those in the oldest group (15 to 18). From these data, we must conclude either that the differences are hereditary or that they are established very early in life.

In Chapter 2, when we dealt with the general question of heredity and environment, we discussed two other kinds of studies bearing on the point (see page 50). One consisted of correlations of IQs between blood relatives with different degrees of similarity of heredity and environment. The other was a comparison of the IQs of identical twins, all reared apart and separated at different ages after birth. Both studies strongly supported heredity as a factor in intelligence.

It is also demonstrable that when children are taken from their true parents and placed in foster homes—as many thousands are every year—their intelligence seems more closely related to the intelligence and educational level of the true parents than to those of the foster parents. In one study, the correlation of children's IQs with the intelligence of their true parents was on the order of .30 to .40, while the correlations with the intelligence of their foster parents were in the neighborhood of zero (Skodak and Skeels, 1949). From this we can conclude that relative differences in intelligence are set principally, but not entirely, by inheritance rather than by the intellectual influences of the foster home.

We must say "but not entirely" because there is substantial evidence that the intelligence of children placed in superior foster homes is considerably higher than one would predict from the IQs of their true parents. In one of the more dramatic studies, children whose true mothers had an average IQ of 91 showed an average intelligence of more than 109 when measured at an average age of 13, usually 10 years or more after they had been placed in the superior foster homes (Skodak and Skeels,

1949). Since we are not certain how high their IQs would have been had they been reared by their true parents, we cannot be sure how much of a gain this is. It is probably fair to say that children may gain as much as 10 to 15 IQ points when reared in superior homes. This finding, unlike those we described in preceding paragraphs, points to the influence of the intellectual environment. Even so, it appears that the gain is not so much as it would be were it not limited by inheritance.

Facts and researches on the influence of the home environment could fill a book, but those we have cited are typical. What can we make of them? Clearly, both heredity and environment, interacting together determine measured intelligence. A good environment can improve intelligence; yet poor inheritance cannot be overcome by a good environment. So, even though no amount of favorable influence can fully overcome poor inheritance, a good environment can develop a person's latent intelligence to its fullest potentialities and can make a considerable difference in what he may be able to do.

Differences due to cultural environment If the home environment of a child contributes to his intelligence, we might wonder whether other features of his culture also contribute. After all, the child lives in other environments outside the home, especially as he grows from infancy into childhood. At 2 or 3 he starts to play with other children, and by the age of 7 he is spending a good part of his day in school. As he grows up, he is affected by intellectual influences from his playmates, his school, and even the community's library facilities. What effect do these influences have on intelligence?

One way of approaching the question is to compare *rural* and *urban* children, since the two kinds of environment differ considerably in richness of intellectual influences. And indeed we find that urban children, on the average, score higher on intelligence tests than rural children. Just how much higher depends upon which particular groups are compared, but it is frequently several IQ points. Such differences might be explained in part by the migration of the brighter families to the city, leaving the less intelligent behind. They might also be due in part to a cultural bias of the intelligence tests; it could be that the tests include items more familiar to city children than to farm children.

Undoubtedly there is something to be said for both these points, and our present data are somewhat inconclusive. However, it does seem fairly certain that the stimulating environment of the city, like that of a superior home, can raise substandard intelligence. We have some striking evidence for this view in a study conducted on Negro city boys 12 years old (Klineberg, 1935):

Over 400 boys who had moved to the city were given intelligence tests and compared with 300-odd boys who had been born and reared in the city. The longer the boys had lived in the city, the higher the intelligence scores. Those who had been in the city only 1 to 2 years averaged only 40 (test score, not IQ), whereas those born in the city averaged 75. This is a sizable difference, difficult to account for by the hypothesis of selective migration. (The general result has also been confirmed in other studies: see Lee, 1951.) Apparently, city influences affect measured intelligence.

The problem of cultural influences enters into all attempts to determine whether racial differences in intelligence do exist. As you probably realize, it has long been a question whether some "races" are inferior to others in intelligence. When psychologists attempt to settle the question through research—and they have made many studies—they immediately encounter the fact that races do not have the same cultural environments. There is also the fact that different groups migrating to this country come from varying socioeconomic and cultural groups in their country of birth. So most studies on this question are inconclusive.

DIFFERENCES BETWEEN BLACKS AND WHITES The racial group differences which have been most thoroughly studied are those between American Negroes and American whites. All have the same country of birth and all speak the same language—though the language habits of most whites differ considerably from those of many Negroes. Suppose we test a large group of blacks and compare their intelligence test scores with those of an equally large group of whites. In most comparisons between representative samples (see page 307) of Negroes and whites, the mean of the Negro group is lower—often by 10 or 15 IQ points—than that of the white group (Shuey, 1958). The question is not whether such a difference exists; it is how to interpret and evaluate the difference.

Some strong evidence for the influence of cultural factors in producing this difference comes from the intelligence tests given during World War I. In general black draftees did more poorly than whites. However, all Southern draftees were poorer on the average than all Northern draftees. And some blacks from some Northern states averaged better than whites from some Southern states. Moreover, as we saw above, city Negroes and city whites did better than rural Negroes and rural whites. It is therefore very difficult to separate the factors of race, geography, rural-urban origin, and educational advantages. The last three, however, may all be considered cultural influences, as distinguished from biological differences in the races. From these studies it can be concluded that the difference between Negro and white groups is partially due to the cultural disadvantages suffered by Negroes. Blacks on the average still have inferior educational advantages and usually, after centuries of systematic economic exploitation and demoralization, inferior intellectual environments.

However, when attempts are made to equate Negro and white groups with respect to socioeconomic class, the difference between the groups does not disappear (McGurk, 1951). Also—and this is contrary to what would be expected from a cultural explanation of Negro and white differences—the difference was greater on noncultural test questions than on cultural questions (McGurk, 1953). Is it likely that this difference represents a true innate difference between the two groups?

Even assuming that an adequate definition of race can be given, this is an unanswerable question at present. The main problem is that blacks and whites form distinct castes in the United States (Dollard, 1949; Dreger and Miller, 1960). Even when they are roughly equal in socioeconomic class, the cultures of Negroes and whites remain markedly different, and there is no way to remove these differences. They are intertwined with the variable, Negro or white, under study. For instance,

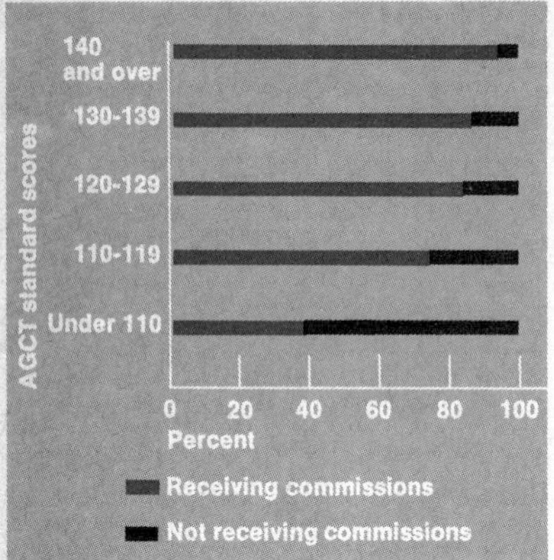

GENERAL INTELLIGENCE TESTS ARE OFTEN USEFUL IN PREDICTING SUCCESS IN SCHOOL

Figure 10.7 *The prediction of success in officer-candidate school from AGCT scores. The colored portion of the bars indicates the chances in 100 that an officer candidate making a certain score on the AGCT would receive a commission. Data are for 5,520 men in 14 schools. (After Boring, 1945.)*

lower-class Negroes and whites, although similar in some ways, differ in such things as the demands made upon children for achievement (Merbaum, 1961). It does not seem too farfetched to think that this, and other caste differences, will account for the small differences which exist after the groups have been equated on socioeconomic variables.

Fortunately, this unanswerable question on innate racial differences is academic. As already mentioned, we are not required to make decisions about groups; the problem is to make decisions about individuals. The question is simply whether an individual has the intellectual aptitude to benefit from a course of training, or whether he has the intellectual ability to do the job for which he is being considered. This is completely in accord with the philosophy of psychological testing. As we saw in the case of Thomas Stiles at the beginning of this chapter, tests are to be used to make decisions about *individuals*.

Special Aptitudes and Interests

No sharp line exists between intelligence tests and aptitude tests. We use intelligence tests to provide a general assessment of intellectual ability and aptitude tests to measure more specialized abilities required in specific occupations and activities.

Interests, although they definitely are not aptitudes, must also be taken into account in making predictions from aptitude tests. To succeed in a given activity, a person must have both an aptitude for the activity and an interest in it. Hence, for practical use and purposes, aptitude and interest tests go hand in hand.

Scholastic aptitudes It has become customary to speak of "aptitudes" and "aptitude testing" when we are trying to predict success or failure in specific training or in a line of work. If we are trying to predict success in academic training, we speak of *scholastic aptitude;* if in one of the vocations, we refer to *vocational aptitudes.*

Some aptitude tests serve two purposes—as a general intelligence test and as a scholastic aptitude test. The data in Figure 10.7, for example, are from the Army General Classification Test, which is designed as a test of general intelligence. It also predicts fairly well whether a person is likely to succeed in officer-candidate school. Hence it can be used as a scholastic aptitude test as well.

Figure 10.7 gives data from World War II. If a person scored 140 or over on the AGCT, his chances of succeeding in officer-candidate school were better than 9 in 10. If his score was less than 110, his chances of succeeding were less than 4 in 10. This illustrates the kind of prediction it is possible to make from a good scholastic aptitude test, though such predictions depend also on the cultural backgrounds of individuals with whom it is used and on the types of training involved.

A number of scholastic aptitude tests have been developed for various kinds of training. Probably one of the most widely used is the series known as the School and College Ability Tests (SCAT), which is administered to students entering the liberal arts colleges of the United States. Similar tests are available for schools of medicine, dentistry, nursing, and several other professions. More are being devised each year. Another called the Graduate Record Examination (GRE) has been designed for students who plan to do graduate work for the master's or doctor's degree in such specialties as psychology, economics, engineering, and physics, as well as a number of other fields in the arts and sciences. The Miller Analogies Test (MAT) is also used to predict success in graduate school. There is an increasing tendency for graduate and professional schools to require all students who apply to them to take the appropriate aptitude test.

Vocational aptitudes Scholastic aptitude tests measure a person's aptitude for success in relatively prolonged training. The great majority of jobs in business and industry, however, do not require such training. Success in these jobs or in the training for these jobs can be forecast from a knowledge of specific vocational aptitudes without too much regard for intelligence or scholastic aptitude.

Several hundred tests of vocational aptitude are available today. Not all of them are good tests in the sense that they have been proved to be good predictors of vocational success, but some are. Many are slight variations of another test which have been developed to serve some particular purpose. In fact, if time, money, and expert psychological talent are available, it usually is wise to modify existing tests to meet the needs of a particular business or industry.

VALIDATION OF TESTS To evaluate the ability of vocational aptitude tests to predict an applicant's success on the job, the following steps are necessary:

1. Give the test to *all* applicants for the kind of job in question until a large number of applicants, preferably several hundred, have been tested.
2. Select applicants for employment *without* considering the test results.
3. After those who are employed have been on the job long enough to be evaluated, divide them according to performance into two or more *criterion groups.* The division may be into satisfactory and unsatisfactory, or it may be into several groups, such as excellent, good, fair, and poor.
4. Compare the test results of the different groups.

This process is designed to determine the predictive validity of the test for the purposes intended. It is actually a way of obtaining a correlation between the test and the criterion, as described in Chapter 9. If there is such a correlation, the criterion groups will differ on their aptitude scores. And only when there is such a difference, and the difference is considerably more than one could expect by chance, is the test valid and worth using for selection purposes.

To construct a new test, the steps are essentially the same as for evaluating a test, except that the analysis must be made for each individual item rather than for the test as a whole. Such an analysis is called an *item analysis.* The items that discriminate between the criterion groups are selected for use in the final test; other items are discarded.

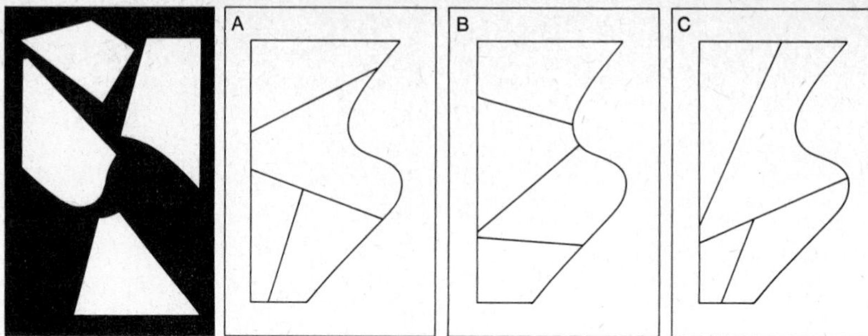

MECHANICAL APTITUDE CAN BE TESTED WITH A PAPER FORM BOARD

Figure 10.8 *A sample from the Minnesota Paper Form Board Test, a mechanical aptitude test. The examinee looks at the pieces on the left and indicates whether they fit together to make A, B, or C.*

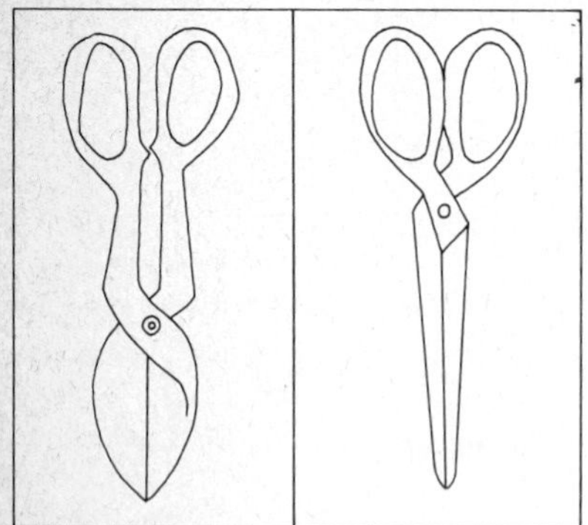

WHICH SHEARS WOULD BE BETTER FOR CUTTING METAL?

Figure 10.9 *An example of the type of item on the Bennett-Fry Test of Mechanical Comprehension. Items on the test, however, are generally more difficult. (The Psychological Corporation.)*

MECHANICAL ABILITY TESTS Many tests that are intended for mechanics, machine operators, assembly-line workers, repairmen, and similar workers involve mechanical knowledge or ability to manipulate objects. Our experience with such mechanical ability tests indicates that a relatively unique factor is common to the tests. People who score high on one mechanical ability test tend to do so on another. On the other hand, different jobs require different combinations of mechanical abilities; hence there are many different tests. Some examples are given in Figures 10.8 and 10.9.

PSYCHOMOTOR TESTS So far there is little evidence of a general motor ability comparable to perceptual or mechanical ability. A person who has good manual dexterity, for example, is not necessarily good at the kind of coordination involved in running a tractor or an airplane. So psychomotor tests must be conceived, developed, and proved for particular jobs and occupations. These tests involve such psychomotor tasks as manual dexterity, steadiness, muscular strength, speed of response to a signal, and the coordination of many movements into a unified whole.

APTITUDES FOR LOGICAL THINKING The usual aptitude tests are designed for the conventional occupations of the industrial world, particularly manufacturing and office occupations. Modern technology, however, is creating occupations that primarily require logical thinking and problem solving. Complex automatic systems develop malfunctions which must be diagnosed by technical troubleshooters. Computers must be programmed by people who can think through intricate sequences of steps. Development engineers must design machines for all sorts of purposes.

Until recently, we have not had satisfactory tests for measuring the aptitudes involved in such jobs. We still have a long way to go. But research is being pushed vigorously, with some promising results. One test, for example, is the LAD (Logical Analysis Device), shown in Figure 10.10. It consists of an operator's display unit plus a central logic unit, problem plugboards, and control and recording units. An examiner can set up various standardized problems of varying complexity for an operator to solve. The operator's problem is to discover the rules for responding logically in a correct sequence.

The LAD has fairly high validity in the selection of programmers for

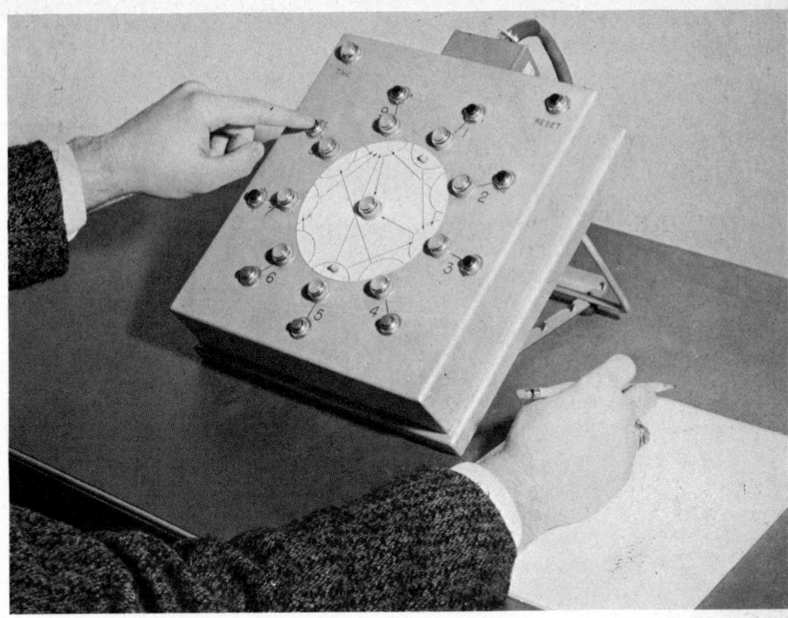

Figure 10.10 *Operator's display panel for LAD, or Logical Analysis Device, which is designed to measure aptitude for logical thinking and problem solving. This aptitude figures in such occupations as computer programming, engineering development, and trouble shooting. (The Psychological Corporation.)*

computers. Research on its validity, and on the validity of similar techniques for assessing problem-solving aptitudes in engineers, technicians, and maintenance men, should in time give us suitable aptitude measures for the newer occupations of our modern technology.

THE USE OF APTITUDE TESTS Aptitude tests are used both by the employer to select employees and by the vocational counselor to help a person assess his aptitudes for different types of work. The same tests are usually not suitable for both purposes. The employer, knowing exactly what jobs he has in mind, wants a test that will forecast success in them as accurately as possible. He therefore would like a test designed specifically for his purposes, for instance, to select electronics technicians, electrical welders, or lathe operators. The counselor, on the other hand, is trying to help a person make a choice—usually a fairly general choice—among different lines of work. For this purpose, the counselor wants more generalized tests that sample many different aspects of specific aptitudes. He has a large number to choose among.

Vocational aptitude tests, as well as the vocational interest tests described below, are frequently available in schools and communities. If a college has a psychological clinic or student counseling service, this office is usually prepared to administer such tests. The U.S. Employment Service and the Veterans Administration provide testing services for those who qualify for assistance. In the larger cities there are usually several independent agencies and individuals that offer competent testing facilities for a reasonable fee.

Test batteries For the purposes of counseling, it is often desirable to give several tests measuring different aptitudes. Some of these tests

Figure 10.11 *Sample items from the eight tests of the Differential Aptitude Tests (DAT) battery. These items are generally easier than those on the tests themselves. (The Psychological Corporation.)*

Verbal reasoning

Each of the fifty sentences in this test has the first word and the last word left out. You are to pick out words which will fill the blanks so that the sentence will be true and sensible.

Example X: ____ is to water as eat is to ____

A. continue . . . drive
B. foot . . . enemy
C. drink . . . food
D. girl . . . industry
E. drink . . . enemy

C is correct

Numerical ability

This test consists of forty numerical problems. Next to each problem there are five answers. You are to pick out the correct answer.

Examble X: Add 13 12

A 14
B 25
C 16
D 59
E none of these

B is correct

Abstract reasoning

Each row consists of four figures called problem figures and five called answer figures. The four problem figures make a series. You are to find out which one of the answer figures would be the next, or the fifth one in the series.

Example Y:

PROBLEM FIGURES ANSWER FIGURES

A B C D E

B is correct

Space relations

This test consists of 60 patterns which can be folded into figures. For each pattern, four figures are shown. You are to decide which *one* of these figures can be made from the pattern shown.

Example Y:

A B C D

D is correct

Mechanical reasoning

This test consists of a number of pictures and questions about those pictures.

Example X: Which man has the heavier load? (If equal, mark C.)

A B

B is correct

Clerical speed and accuracy

This is a test to see how quickly and accurately you can compare letter and number combinations. You will notice that in each Test Item one of the five is *underlined.* You are to look at the *one* combination which is underlined, find the *same* one after that item number on the separate answer sheet, and fill in the space under it.

TEST ITEMS

V. AB AC AD AE AF
W. aA aB BA Ba Bb
X. A7 7A B7 7B AB
Y. Aa Ba bA BA bB
Z. 3A 3B 33 B3 BB

SAMPLE OF ANSWER SHEET

V. AC AE AF AB AD
W. BA Ba Bb aA aB
X. 7B B7 AB 7A A7
Y. Aa bA bB Ba BA
Z. BB 3B B3 3A 33

Language usage: Spelling

This test is composed of a series of words. Some of them are correctly spelled; some are incorrectly spelled. You are to indicate whether each word is spelled right or wrong.

EXAMPLES

W. man Y. catt
X. gurl Z. dog

SAMPLE OF ANSWER SHEET

W. R W Y. R W
X. R W Z. R W

Language usage: Grammar

This test consists of a series of sentences, each divided into four parts lettered A, B, C, and D. You are to look at each sentence and decide which part has an error in grammar, punctuation, or spelling.

Some sentences have no error in any part. If there is no error in a sentence, fill in the space under the letter E.

Example X: Ain't we (A) / going to (B) / the office (C) / next week? (D)

SAMPLE OF ANSWER SHEET

X. A B C D E

have been combined into batteries which give information about *both* scholastic and vocational aptitudes.

One such battery, designed especially for counseling high school students and noncollege adults, is called the Differential Aptitude Tests (DAT). Tests of verbal reasoning, numerical ability, abstract reasoning, space relations, mechanical reasoning, clerical speed and accuracy, spelling, and the use of language in sentences are included in this battery. Sample items are shown in Figure 10.11. The scores on each of these tests are plotted as a *profile of scores* on a special chart (see Figure 10.12).

The sum of the scores on the verbal reasoning and numerical ability tests can be used by counselors as an index of scholastic aptitude. The predictive validity of this sum of scores is quite high; that is, high positive correlations with grades are usually obtained. The other scores, either singly or in various combinations, can be used to predict success in tasks requiring specific aptitudes. However, since even more specific aptitude tests are available, the aptitude tests of the DAT battery are not normally chosen to predict success on a particular job. Furthermore, these aptitude tests do not predict school success well (McNemar, 1964). Instead, the counselor typically determines an individual's strengths and weaknesses from the profile and uses this as a basis for discussion and recommendation (Bennett et al., 1951). In other words, he uses the DAT much as the counselor used the tests in the case of Thomas Stiles (see page 320).

THE RESULTS FROM THE DIFFERENTIAL APTITUDE TESTS ARE PLOTTED AS A PROFILE

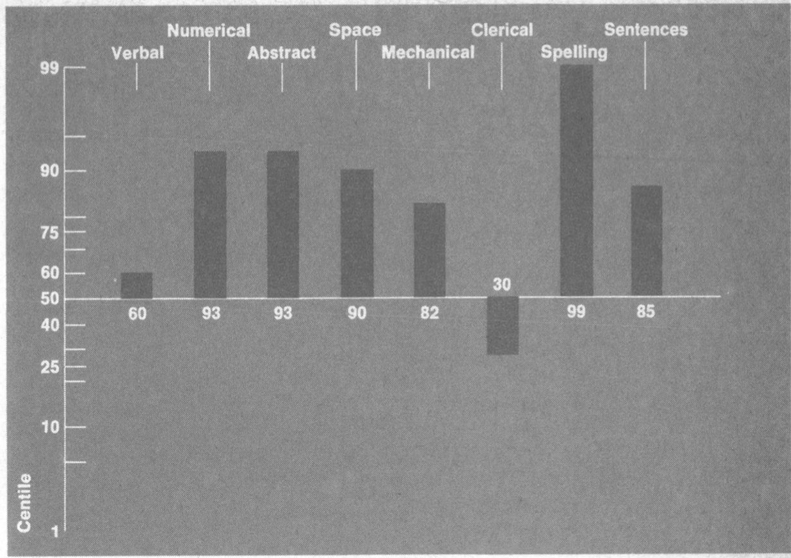

Figure 10.12 *A Differential Aptitude Tests (DAT) profile. The centile scale is bunched in the middle and stretched on the ends because many more cases fall in the middle of a normal distribution than at its ends. This profile was obtained from a girl interested in majoring in science in college. If you were a counselor, would you advise her to go ahead? (Modified from Bennett et al., 1951.)*

Vocational interests To succeed at a job or a course of training, a person must have not only the aptitudes required for it but also a set of interests that enable him to enjoy its various aspects. Psychologists have tried two general approaches in developing tests of interest that might serve in vocational guidance. One, devised by Strong, has been called the *empirical approach;* the other, developed by Kuder, has been called the *theoretical approach.* Each approach has its advantages and its limitations.

STRONG VOCATIONAL INTEREST BLANK The empirical approach to determining the interests required for a vocation involves measuring the interests of successful people already in the vocation. We find out what the interests of each vocational group are and then choose only those which *distinguish* successful people in this group from successful persons in other groups. We make the assumption that these distinctive interests are actually necessary for success in the vocation. On the basis of this reasoning, Strong constructed the Strong Vocational Interest Blank (Revised, 1966).

He began by selecting several hundred items that might conceivably distinguish interests in different occupations: items concerning preferences for amusements, school subjects, activities, kinds of people, and so forth. He organized most of his pencil-and-paper test so that a person can indicate whether he dislikes (D), likes (L), or is indifferent (I) to an item.

Strong developed his interest test by contrasting a representative sample of people in general with groups of successful people in many different occupations. He tried out a large number of items but retained for his test only those items that distinguished between people in general and one or more of the successful occupational groups. One item might

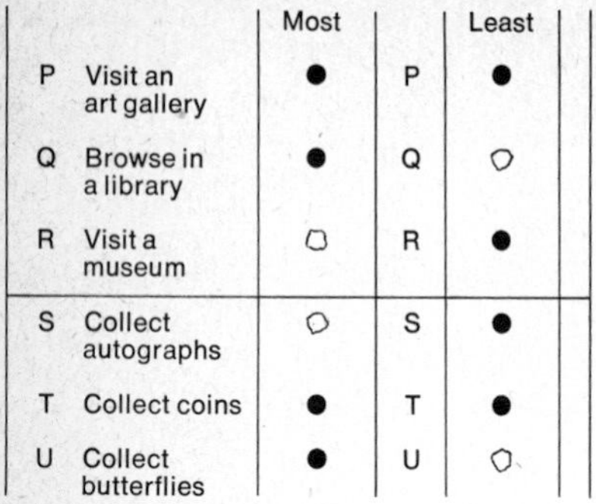

		Most		Least
P	Visit an art gallery	●	P	●
Q	Browse in a library	●	Q	○
R	Visit a museum	○	R	●
S	Collect autographs	○	S	●
T	Collect coins	●	T	●
U	Collect butterflies	●	U	○

THE KUDER PREFERENCE RECORD GIVES A GENERAL PICTURE OF A PERSON'S INTERESTS

Figure 10.13 *Two groups of items on the Kuder Preference Record. With a pinprick the subject indicates which of the three alternatives in each group he likes most and which he likes least. In group P, Q, and R, he likes Q least and R most, according to the pinpricks shown here. In group S, T, and U, he likes S most and U least. (G. F. Kuder and Science Research Associates.)*

discriminate well for certain occupations, moderately well for others, and not at all for still others. Another item might discriminate in different degrees between people in general and another set of occupations. To reflect the different contribution of each item to scores for different occupations, Strong constructed a different scoring key for each occupation. In this way, items are given different weights for the interests of the various occupations for which scales were constructed. Strong also provided different scoring keys for women and men in those occupations in which a sizable number of both work. Scores are given as grades—A, B+, B, B−, or C. If a person receives an A, his interests correspond quite well with those of successful people in the occupation, and the prognosis of success, so far as interests go, is excellent. On the other hand, a grade of C means that his interests do not correspond at all well with those of people in the occupation and that his chances of success, so far as interests go, are poor. Grades of B+, B, and B− are less certain and are interpreted as giving intermediate degrees of interest correspondence. Some of the occupations for which Strong scales are available are listed in Table 10.7.

KUDER PREFERENCE RECORD Nowadays many different interest tests are available for various purposes, but we will mention only one besides the one devised by Strong. This is the Kuder test. Actually, Kuder has developed a family of tests that include the Kuder Preference Record: Vocational; the Kuder Preference Record: Personal; and the Kuder Occupational Interest Survey. The first two can be scored by hand. The last is designed for scoring with a computer.

The general idea of the Kuder tests that distinguishes them from the Strong blank is that a limited number of general areas of interest are measured—mechanical interests, artistic interest, computational interests, and so on (see Figure 10.13). By obtaining a profile of such interests for the various areas, a counselor can guide a person in the direction of occupations for which his pattern of interests is most appropriate. For this reason, the Kuder tests, especially the Kuder Preference Record: Vocational, are most often used with high school students who usually need only general guidance. The Strong blank, on the other hand, is more often used when a person wishes to choose between specific occupations for which the Strong blank has scoring keys.

THE USE OF INTEREST TESTS Interest tests, like aptitude tests, are not infallible. People sometimes succeed in an occupation with few, if any, of the interests held by others in the field. All a counselor can conclude from interest tests is that the odds are strongly favorable, strongly unfavorable, or perhaps about even. Follow-up studies of people who have taken interest tests show that many more fail to succeed in a profession when their interest test indicates a poor prognosis than when the interest pattern appears highly favorable. Anyone who chooses an occupation after receiving strongly unfavorable advice based on interest tests is taking a considerable chance and may later regret his choice.

Personality Measurement

Aptitude and achievement tests are tests of maximum performance, since people try to do their best on them. Personality measures, on the other hand, are tests of typical performance (Cronbach, 1970). There are no right or wrong answers on personality tests; instead, people are asked about what they usually do or what is typical of them.

Personality testing is done for many reasons. Personnel psychologists may want to select people whose personality characteristics make them good salesmen. A military psychologist may want to measure neurotic tendencies that make people unfit for a sensitive assignment. Experimental psychologists may want to measure anxiety in order to control its influence in their experiments on perception or learning. A variety of methods suit these specific purposes (see Buros, 1970).

Pencil-and-paper tests The most convenient type of measure to use for almost any psychological purpose is a pencil-and-paper test which can be given cheaply and quickly to large groups of people. Hence pencil-and-paper tests are popular, and during the last 60 years psychologists have constructed a wide variety of them (James et al., 1969).

QUESTIONNAIRES Pencil-and-paper tests of personality characteristics are usually questionnaires in which the persons being tested must answer questions or say "yes" or "no" to simple statements, such as:

I generally prefer to attend movies alone.

I occasionally cross the street to avoid meeting someone I know.

I seldom or never go out on double dates.

In some questionnaires a person may also be allowed to answer "doubtful" or "uncertain."

This kind of personality test first gained widespread use during World War I, when it was used to weed out emotionally unstable draftees. The statements in the test were chosen to reflect psychiatric symptoms that might predict future emotional breakdown. They included such items as:

I consider myself a very nervous person.

I frequently feel moody and depressed.

Do items like these really test what the examiner thinks they test? The validity question is especially acute in personality testing.

THE PROBLEM OF VALIDITY In the case of personality tests, valid measurement means measurement that correlates with one or more personality characteristics. No test has perfect validity, but here the question is whether or not a test has sufficient validity to be useful in drawing any conclusions from its results. In other words, Can we make better decisions with the test than without it?

Since World War I, the use of personality questionnaires has greatly expanded. They are mostly designed to measure emotional maladjust-

Accountant
Advertising man
Architect
Artist†
Author†
Aviator
Banker
Buyer*
Carpenter
Chemist
City school superintendent
Coast guard
Dentist†
Dietitian*
Engineer
Farmer
Forest service
Housewife*
Laboratory technician
Lawyer†
Librarian*
Life insurance sales†
Mathematician
Minister
Musician
Nurse*
Occupational therapist*
Office worker†
Personnel manager
Pharmacist
Physician†
Policeman
Printer
Production manager
Psychologist†
Public administrator
Social science teacher
Social worker*
Stenographer-secretary*
Veterinarian
YMCA-YWCA secretary†

Table 10.7 *Some of the occupations for which the Strong Vocational Interest Blank can be scored. The test is scored separately for each occupation and for men and women. The occupations accompanied by an asterisk (*) are scored for women only, and those accompanied by a dagger (†) are scored for both men and women. The rest are scored for men only.*

Table 10.8 *Typical items from the MMPI. The response (true or false) which is scored positively is shown in parentheses. Such a response contributes to a high score on the scale with which the item is associated. Some of these items are scored on more than one scale.*

Hypochondriasis (Hs) scale
I am bothered by acid stomach several times a week. (True)

Depression (D) scale
I am easily awakened by noise. (True)

Hysteria (Hy) scale
I like to read newspaper articles on crime. (False)

Psychopathic deviate (Pd) scale
I am neither gaining nor losing weight. (False)

*Masculinity-femininity (Mf) scale**
When I take a new job, I like to be tipped off on who should be gotten next to. (False)

Paranoia (Pa) scale
I have never been in trouble with the law. (False)

Psychasthenia (Pt) scale
I am inclined to take things hard. (True)

Schizophrenia (Sc) scale
I get all the sympathy I should. (False)

Hypomania (Ma) scale
I never worry about my looks. (True)

Social introversion (Si) scale
People generally demand more respect for their own rights than they are willing to allow for others. (True)

Source: Items from Dahlstrom and Welsh, 1960.
*High score indicates feminine interests and values.

ment or such general traits as extroversion-introversion. When constructed by psychologists who are conscious of the validity problem, the tests have usually been validated in some way, so that the degree of validity is known.

But many of the questionnaires in popular magazines designed to tell you whether you are a good husband, a happy person, an introvert, and so forth, have not been validated. Neither is there any known validity in some of the tests made up by individuals or "testing agencies" for use in selecting executives or employees in industry. Even though the items on a test may look valid, this is no guarantee that they actually are. Indeed, since validity is so hard to come by, the best assumption is that a personality test is invalid until it is proved otherwise.

Another problem in developing valid personality tests is the possibility of an individual *faking* his answers on the test. For example, a person who knows that a high score on emotional maladjustment will keep him out of the Army can deliberately get a high score. A group of World War I draftees who made abnormal scores on a personality test at the time of induction were able to make normal scores on it after the war was over. Conversely, a person who may be quite maladjusted usually can make a normal score if that is necessary to get the job he desires.

MINNESOTA MULTIPHASIC PERSONALITY INVENTORY Despite instances of this sort, it is possible to construct personality tests with *empirical va-*

lidity. First, the test must be shown to correlate with a criterion when the people taking the test are being honest in their answers. Second, the test must be so constructed that answers are hard to fake or that faking, when it is done, can be detected. A few such tests are available; a good example is the Minnesota Multiphasic Personality Inventory, or MMPI (Hathaway and McKinley, 1951; Dahlstrom and Welsh, 1960).

The MMPI was constructed by comparing responses of normal subjects with those of abnormal individuals classified into several diagnostic categories. The items, which could be answered "true," "cannot say," or "false," were fairly typical of pencil-and-paper personality questionnaires (see Table 10.8). Items were given weights on different scales according to their ability to distinguish between people low and high in the trait measured by each scale. In addition, by determining the items which distinguished between men and women, it was possible to construct a scale to differentiate people with masculine and feminine interests, values, and ways of expressing emotion. Some men may have feminine patterns; some women may have masculine patterns. A scale of social introversion has also been constructed from items which differentiate the socially introverted from the socially nonintroverted. The 10 personality scales that are usually scored on the MMPI are as follows:

1. *Hypochondriasis (Hs)* Exaggerated anxiety about one's health, and pessimistic interpretations and exaggerations of minor symptoms
2. *Depression (D)* Feelings of pessimism, worthlessness, hopelessness
3. *Hysteria (Hy)* Various ailments such as headaches and paralyses which have no physical basis
4. *Psychopathic deviation (Pd)* Antisocial and amoral conduct
5. *Masculinity-femininity (Mf)* Measure of masculine and feminine interests; especially a measure of feminine values and emotional expression in men
6. *Paranoia (Pa)* Extreme suspiciousness of other people's motives, frequently resulting in elaborate beliefs that certain people are plotting against one
7. *Psychasthenia (Pt)* Irrational thoughts that recur and/or strong compulsions to repeat seemingly meaningless acts
8. *Schizophrenia (Sc)* Withdrawal into a private world of one's own, often accompanied by hallucinations and bizarre behavior
9. *Hypomania (Ma)* Mild elation and excitement without any clear reason
10. *Social introversion (Si)* Avoidance of other people and removal of oneself from social contacts

The process of empirical validation can be extended to many personality traits and other personal characteristics. In fact, 200 to 300 scales have been constructed from items of this test. These scales range all the way from a scale for measuring personality patterns similar to those of professional baseball players (LaPlace, 1954), to several for measuring anxiety (Taylor, 1953; Welsh, 1956) and one for measuring ego defensiveness (Byrne, 1964).

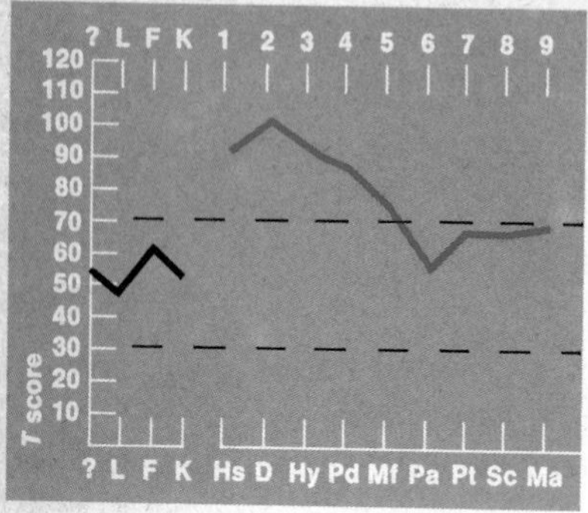

A GLANCE AT THE PROFILE SHEET OF THE MMPI REVEALS PATTERNS OF SCORES

Figure 10.14 *A profile of an individual's scores on the Minnesota Multiphasic Personality Inventory (MMPI). The four "validity" scales are plotted on the left; nine "clinical" scales are plotted on the right. Scores on the scales are T scores with a mean of 50 and a standard deviation of 10. Dashed lines are drawn on the chart at scores of 70 and 30, two standard deviations above and below the mean of the normative group. This profile was obtained from a person with a psychosomatic neurotic complaint. Note the marked elevation of the three scales which measure tendencies toward neurotic behavior—Hs, D, Hy. The pattern of scores within this "neurotic triad" is also important; in this case, the D score is higher than the Hs and Hy scores. The Pd score is also elevated. (Modified from Dahlstrom and Welsh, 1960.)*

In addition to the 10 personality scales which are usually scored, several "validity" scales are commonly employed. A ? scale is based on the frequency of "cannot say" responses; an L scale detects a tendency to give socially desirable responses; an F scale evaluates items not usually accepted by normal subjects; and a K scale distinguishes between normal subjects and abnormal subjects who otherwise yield normal profiles. These scales are designed to (1) provide a check on the individual's frankness in answering the items, (2) check on his thoroughness and conscientiousness in answering; and (3) assess defensiveness, or other sets or attitudes, with which he approaches the test. With these validity scales, malingering and attempts to create an unusually good or bad impression can be uncovered. The validity scales thus provide a check on faking. Another hindrance to the person who deliberately attempts to fake the test is due to the empirical validation of the test. What an item says does not necessarily mean that it will be on a particular scale; the test has empirical validity, not face validity. Trying to create a particular impression may backfire. As one writer has expressed it, "This is not a test for the amateur to trifle with" (Whyte, 1956).

The scores on the scales are plotted as *T* scores—mean of 50 and standard deviation of 10 (see pages 300 and 329)—on a profile sheet (see Figure 10.14). Scores above 70 and below 30, two standard deviations above and below the mean of the normal reference group, are of special interest. The pattern of peaks and the slopes of the profile are also of diagnostic importance. For example, the first three scales, Hs, D, and Hy, are sometimes called the "neurotic triad," and the pattern of scores on these is diagnostic of neurotic behavioral problems. The profile in Figure 10.14 has elevated scores on the neurotic triad and a pattern in which the Depression score is relatively higher than the Hypochondriasis and Hysteria scores. This profile was of a person with a neurotic psychosomatic illness.

ALLPORT-VERNON-LINDZEY SCALE The Allport-Vernon-Lindzey Study of Values (Allport et al., 1960) is another pencil-and-paper personality test. It measures a person's major values and interests: theoretical, economic, esthetic, social, political, and religious (see Figure 10.15).

In the first part of the test, the subject must give a "yes" or "no" answer to a series of statements, such as, "The main objects of scientific research should be the discovery of pure truth rather than its practical applications." If he agrees with this statement, his response helps make up a high score on theoretical interests. In the second part of the test, the subject must rank four alternatives in the order of his agreement with them. He would, for example, express his agreement with these statements by indicating a rank order for them:

Do you think that a good government should aim chiefly at

(a) More aid for the poor, sick, and old?
(b) The development of manufacturing and trade?
(c) Introducing more ethical principles into its policies and diplomacy?
(d) Establishing a position of prestige and respect among nations?

THE RELATIVE STRENGTH OF VALUES IS MEASURED BY THE ALLPORT-VERNON-LINDZEY STUDY OF VALUES TEST

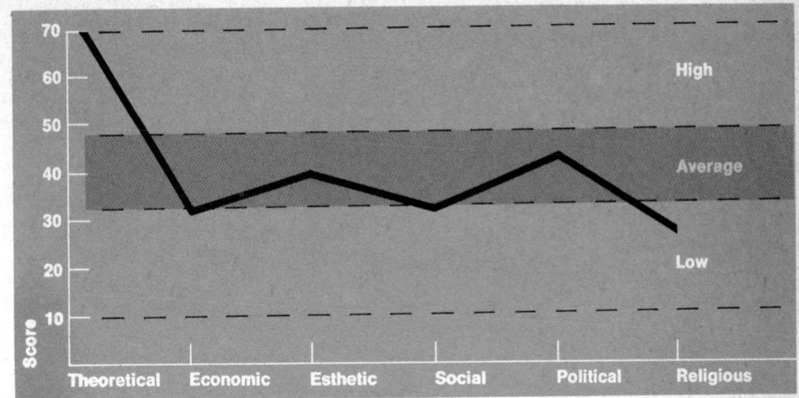

Figure 10.15 *A profile of scores from the Allport-Vernon-Lindzey test. Note the highest and lowest scores. What do you suppose some of the other characteristics of this person might be?*

As in the case of the MMPI, it is possible to construct a profile of the results. One person's profile for this scale's six major value areas is shown in Figure 10.15.

EDWARDS PERSONAL PREFERENCE SCHEDULE Another personality test widely used in recent years is the Edwards Personal Preference Schedule (Edwards, 1954). This inventory does not measure abnormal traits, as does the MMPI. Rather, it is designed to characterize the dominant motives or needs found in Murray's list of basic needs (see page 369): achievement, deference, order, exhibition, autonomy, affiliation, intraception, succorance, dominance, abasement, nurturance, change, endurance, heterosexuality, and aggression.

In constructing his test to measure these needs, Edwards wanted to avoid a bias found in many personality inventories: the tendency for a subject to make responses that show him in a socially desirable light. Consequently Edwards presents items in pairs that research has found to be, on the average, equally desirable. The subject is forced to choose one or the other of the two items in each pair. Altogether, 225 pairs of items make up the Edwards test. Although not validated so rigorously as we might like, it has proved quite useful in counseling situations. As one might expect, however, the MMPI is a better instrument in hospital work, because since it is constructed to measure abnormal tendencies, it helps considerably in the diagnosis of hospital patients.

Interviews and rating scales The tests described so far are *objective:* The subject must choose among a limited number of specifically worded alternative responses, and the tester must score these responses according to a key that dictates what the "right" answers are. Thus the subject's score is not affected by who does the scoring. Such tests are to be distinguished from subjective tests—a familiar example is the essay examination—which require the scorer to make judgments. Several types of subjective measures are used in personality evaluation. The data are usually obtained in an interview in which the subject answers questions or makes oral responses to standard stimuli. The latter situation is known as a *projective test* and will be discussed below.

RATING SCALES ARE EASILY USED AND CAN BE ADAPTED TO MANY SITUATIONS

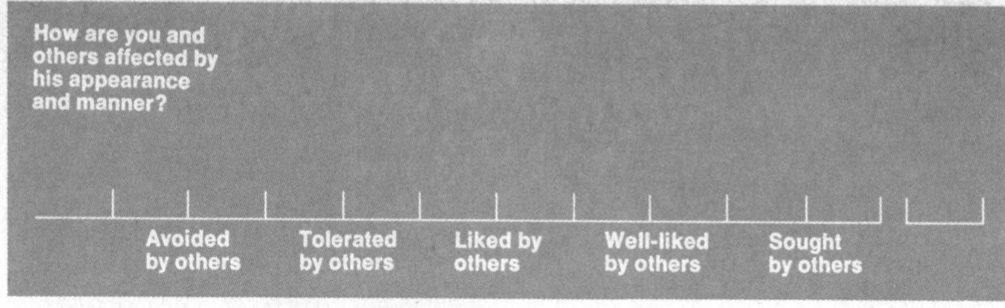

Figure 10.16 *An item on a rating scale. The rater checks a point on the scale to indicate his opinion of the subject. The open box at the end means "no opportunity to observe."*

Figure 10.17 *An item similar to those used on the Thematic Apperception Test (TAT). The subject is shown a card and instructed to tell a story about what it pictures. He is asked to explain the situation it represents, discuss events that led up to the situation, indicate the feelings and thoughts of the characters in the picture, and describe the outcome of the story. (After Murray, 1943.)*

The interview is one of the oldest methods for attempting to evaluate personality. The interviewer tries to sample as wide a range as possible of the person's feelings and attitudes by getting him to talk about his personal experiences. The interviewer not only notes what he hears but also observes more intangible behavior: the way a person talks about certain topics (the catch in the voice, for example, whenever mother is mentioned, or the tenseness that appears whenever certain topics are brought up) and in many cases, what the person is careful *not* to talk about. From these varied observations the clinician attempts to reconstruct a picture of a person's major motives, his sources of conflict, his modes of adjustment, and his overall adequacy of adjustment. Having done this, he tries to reduce his observations to some simple conclusions, often by writing a summary. He may go a step further and use a rating scale in order to put his conclusions into a more quantitative form that indicates how the patient is high or low on certain characteristics.

There are several forms of rating scales. One of the simpler types lists a number of personality characteristics, such as honesty, reliability, sociability, industriousness, and emotionality, and asks the rater who knows the person being evaluated to give a rating—say, between 1 and 7—on each characteristic (see Figure 10.16). Another method is to provide the rater with a number of alternative descriptions and ask him to check which alternative applies best to the person being rated. It is usually possible to convert the results into numerical scores on 5- or 7-point scales. An example of such a scale is one for aggression, which you see in Table 10.9.

Rating scales are so simple that we can use them to record our impressions of almost any aspect of a person's personality. Their simplicity, however, should not fool us. Like any form of personality measurement, they can be unreliable and invalid. In the hands of amateurs, they usually are. Rating-scale techniques must be subjected to the same rigorous analysis of validity as other more objective types of personality measurement.

Projective methods The last form of personality measurement to be discussed is the *projective method*. It is called projective because the subject is presented with an ambiguous situation, usually a visual object or picture, which induces him to reveal some of his personality characteristics by projecting them into the situation. He is presented with the object or picture and asked to say what he sees or to tell a story about it.

Table 10.9 *An example from a rating scale used to measure aggressive behavior toward other persons.*

Instructions: Place a check mark after the category that most closely describes the subject's behavior.

A. The degree to which the subject displays hostile or aggressive behavior in his relations with others:
   1. Avoids aggression even when it is called for. Never becomes angry or criticizes others.
   2. Seldom becomes angry or critical of others. Will do so, however, if strongly prodded or actually attacked.
   3. Shows normal amount of aggression when the circumstances seem to call for it. Is neither reluctant nor overready to show hostility.
   4. Frequently engages in quarrels or arguments. Is often sarcastic. Tends to be critical of many things.
   5. Almost always aggressive. Has trouble getting along with people because he is ready to argue or fight at the drop of a hat.

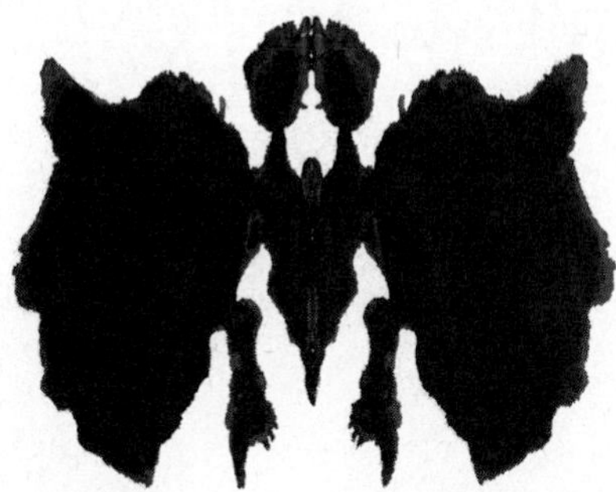

Figure 10.18 *An example of the type of inkblot figure used on the Rorschach Test. Blots similar to this one are shown to a subject with the instruction to describe what he sees in them. After all the subject's responses are recorded, the examiner inquires into them more deeply in an attempt to find out what it was about each card that determined the responses.*

In his narration, he ascribes certain characteristics to the things and people he talks about and thus reveals his own characteristics. At least that is the theory of the projective test, and that is why it is called projective. Of the several different projective tests, the Thematic Apperception Test (TAT) and the Rorschach Test are two that are widely known and frequently used by clinical psychologists.

The Thematic Apperception Test consists of a series of 20 pictures (Murray, 1943). Each picture is ambiguous enough to permit a variety of interpretations. Figure 10.17 shows an example of the kind of picture used, though it is not one of the test pictures. When presented with a picture, the examinee is asked to make up a story of what is happening. The story is supposed to begin with events leading up to the scene in the picture and end with an outcome. Most people, when they make up such stories, identify themselves with one of the characters in the picture, and their stories may be little more than thinly disguised autobiographies. In this way the examinee may reveal feelings and desires he would otherwise hesitate to discuss openly or, in some cases, would be unwilling to admit to himself.

As generally used, the TAT has no standardized scoring. The tester interprets it by noting recurring themes in the stories—the characteristic needs and frustrations of the hero, the relations of the hero with members of the opposite sex, with parents, or with persons in positions of authority—and the overall emotional tone of the stories, whether depressed or overly optimistic, and so on.

The Rorschach Test is relatively more objective and at the same time more ambiguous than the TAT. The Rorschach consists of 10 inkblots similar to the one in Figure 10.18, although some of the blots have colored parts (Rorschach, 1942). Each card is presented to the subject with the question, "What might this be?" or "What does this remind you of?" After responding for all 10 cards, the subject goes through them again, indicating what parts of the inkblot suggested his responses.

Some of the scoring is done objectively. For instance, the number of times the subject responds to *part* of the blot, compared with the number of times he responds to the blot as a *whole,* can be counted. Counts can also be made of other things, such as the number of responses to color and the number of responses suggesting movement. On the other hand, the clinician interprets not only the number of responses in different categories, but also the pattern of the responses, and this can become somewhat subjective. Even more subjective are interpretations based on other cues, such as spontaneous remarks made during the test, signs of emotional upset, and the symbolic meaning of the responses.

Clinicians regularly use projective tests such as the Rorschach and TAT because they believe that they learn about an individual's personality from them. Perhaps they do. After all, the projective test is a subtle kind of interview. The reliability of judgments made from projective tests, however, is not high compared with that of objective tests. In addition, convincing proof of the validity of the tests is lacking. We must therefore withhold judgment about their value as devices for personality measurement.

Synopsis and summary

A test is "an objective and standardized measure of a sample of behavior." In order for these measures to be useful in both practical and experimental situations, they should have the characteristics of reliability, validity, and standardization. Hundreds of more or less reliable, valid, and standardized tests are published (see Buros, 1970). Some of the most used tests of intelligence, special aptitudes, interests, and personality traits have been presented in this chapter.

Like many other useful devices, tests can be, and have been, abused. Criticism has come from within the psychometric subfield of psychology as well as from journalistic sources (Gross, 1962). The use of inadequately standardized tests, too much testing, and the inability of some test users to interpret the test results wisely and flexibly are all justified criticisms of psychological testing. Remember that tests are designed to help us make decisions about individuals, and even the objective tests merely give us a score or a set of scores. The use made of these scores is the crucial thing, and this requires a good deal of sophistication in statistics and counseling. As the standard of training and sophistication of test users improves, it is hoped that abuses of tests will become less frequent.

1. Psychological tests are quite useful in helping others, or the examinee himself, to arrive at decisions. They are intended to be administered and interpreted by trained people, and they are commonly used in conjunction with other information available about a person.
2. Ability is a general term which refers either to the potential for acquiring a skill or to an already acquired skill. Aptitude refers to the potentiality that a person has to profit from a certain type of training. Achievement refers to what a person has already learned. Tests can measure each of these aspects of performance. In aptitude tests, the emphasis is on predicting achievement in other situations.
3. Tests also differ in whether they (*a*) are individual or group tests, (*b*) emphasize verbal factors or nonverbal performance factors, or (*c*) measure the speed with which a person can solve problems or measure his ability to solve difficult problems irrespective of time.
4. Tests that measure general ability or aptitude for intellectual performance are called intelligence tests. Those that measure special aptitudes for a particular kind of training or for a vocation are called special aptitude tests.
5. The Stanford-Binet Scale is an individual intelligence test devised especially for children of school age. It yields a score called mental age (MA), and from this an IQ may be derived. The Wechsler Adult Intelligence Scale (WAIS) is an individual test for adults.
6. Group tests of intelligence may be used for testing large numbers of people at the same time. One well-known test of this type is the Army General Classification Test, or AGCT (it has been superseded by the Armed Forces Qualification Test).
7. Intelligence is not only a single general ability. By factor analysis, it has been demonstrated that several abilities are involved in conventional intelligence tests. Some tests weight certain of these abilities more than other tests do. Thus intelligence is some general ability and a number of specific abilities. It does not correlate well with separate tests of creativity.
8. People who have an IQ of less than 70 are called mentally retarded. They are classified into four retardation groups: mild, moderate, severe, and profound. Mental retardation

may have a genetic basis, in which case there may be no obvious organic defect; or it may be caused by some obvious organic disturbance.

9. At the high end of the distribution of IQs are the mentally gifted. Those with IQs between 130 and 140 are considered very superior; those above 140 are regarded as "near genius." Many of the outstanding leaders of history have been mentally gifted. In general, the gifted are far more successful, more physically fit, and better adjusted than those of average intelligence, though there are notable exceptions.

10. In the middle intelligence groups, a strong relationship exists between tested intelligence and job achievement.

11. Differences in intelligence among various groups in the population can be measured. Although men and women are equal in intelligence, the old do less well than the young on intelligence tests, and Negroes tend to score lower than whites (in part, certainly, for reasons having little to do with innate ability). Group differences in intelligence require careful interpretation and have little practical significance because of the large amount of overlap between groups and because decisions must be made about individuals, not groups.

12. Both a person's inheritance and his home and cultural environment play a role in determining the ability called intelligence.

13. Special aptitude tests have been developed to estimate ability to succeed in college or other advanced training. Other special aptitude tests assess the likelihood of success in some particular vocation. Those for training are called scholastic aptitude tests; those for vocations are called vocational aptitude tests.

14. Vocational interest tests serve as additional aids in vocational choice. They measure how close the subject's interests are to the interests found most frequently among persons already in a vocation.

15. Vocational aptitude tests and tests of general intellectual ability are often combined into test batteries.

16. Measurements of typical performance, or personality tests, have been devised both for research on personality and for use in practical situations. Serving both purposes are a great variety of pencil-and-paper tests. The Minnesota Multiphasic Personality Inventory (MMPI) is one which has been empirically validated.

17. Interviews are often used in an attempt to evaluate personality. Somewhat more objective and valid are rating scales which require the rating of the presence or degree of particular characteristics.

18. Projective tests such as the Rorschach Test and the Thematic Apperception Test (TAT) have come into widespread use, particularly in clinical work.

Related topics in the text

Chapter 9 Psychological Measurement and Statistics An understanding of the statistics discussed in Chapter 9 is essential. Means, standard deviations, standard scores, centiles, and correlation coefficients must be studied before one can make much sense of a chapter in psychological testing.

Chapter 11 Personality Personality tests are ways of measuring some of the traits which make people different. Even ability, aptitude, and interest tests may be thought of as measuring personality traits. In the chapter on personality, we take up the origin and patterning of traits.

Suggestions for further reading

Anastasi, A. *Psychological testing.* (3d ed.) New York: Macmillan, 1968.
A review of the principles and types of psychological tests.

Buros, O. K. (Ed.). *The sixth mental measurements yearbook.* Highland Park, N.J.: Gryphon Press, 1964.
The tester's "bible." It contains critical reviews of almost all published tests.

Cronbach, L. J. *Essentials of psychological testing.* (3d ed.) New York: Harper & Row, 1970. *A comprehensive introduction to the field of psychological testing.*

Guilford, J. P. *The nature of human intelligence.* New York: McGraw-Hill, 1967. *An excellent treatment of the theoretical foundations of intelligence testing.*

Lyman, H. B. *Test scores and what they mean.* Englewood Cliffs, N.J.: Prentice-Hall, 1963. (Paperback.)
A very readable presentation of some of the fundamentals involved in using and interpreting psychological tests.

Mischel, W. *Personality and assessment.* New York: Wiley, 1968.
A textbook on personality and its measurement.

Robinson, H. B., and Robinson, N. M. *The mentally retarded child: A psychological approach.* New York: McGraw-Hill, 1965.
A description of the measurement, treatment, and causes of mental retardation.

Super, D. E., and Crites, J. O. *Appraising vocational fitness by means of psychological tests.* (Rev. ed.) New York: Harper & Row, 1962.
The use of tests in vocational counseling and selection.

Telford, C. W., and Sawrey, J. M. *The exceptional individual: Psychological and educational aspects.* Englewood Cliffs, N.J.: Prentice-Hall, 1967.
An analysis of the social, psychological, and educational problems of both very superior and retarded children, intended for the nonspecialist.

Tyler, L. E. *Tests and measurements.* Englewood Cliffs, N.J.: Prentice-Hall, 1963. (Paperback.)
A lucid primer on tests and the statistics used with them.

People is mostly alike,
but what difference they is
can be powerful important.
Vermont farmer,
quoted by Henry Murray

To understand other people and ourselves better is one of the main reasons why we study psychology. Many areas within psychology, including learning, behavioral inheritance, motivation, perception, and measurement, help us to improve this understanding. So does the study of personality—the branch of psychology directly concerned with differences in behavior between individuals, and with the consistencies of behavior within an individual. In this chapter we shift from the disembodied examination of general psychological principles—the "laws of learning," for example—to apply some of these principles to the individual person: you, me, and Charlie Brown.

The Nature of Personality

The personality psychologist has a difficult task. Individual behavior does not fit into easily classified molds; its variation is almost infinite, and the psychologist must attempt to find a way to describe the great multiformity of personality characteristics and patterns. In other words, he must attempt to deal with what is called the *structure* of personality. He can measure characteristics of people and can find differences between people, but if that is all he accomplishes, he is likely to end up with nothing but a huge catalog of characteristics. To bring some order and meaning into these various measurements, personality psychologists have made inferences about the ways in which the characteristics cluster together and about which ones are the most important. Some investigators, for instance, emphasize a person's feelings about himself, or his self-concept; others emphasize sexual motivation; others stress the measurement of characteristics by personality tests; and so on. Because it has been difficult to reach agreement about these inferences, there are many theories and ideas about what is important in personality structure.

A second problem for the personality theorist arises from the fact that personality is more than just a collection of static characteristics. Personality is *dynamic*—it leads to behavior, especially to consistencies of behavior. A theme runs through an individual's behavior; day after day he acts in consistent ways that can best be understood by inferring an organization of characteristics—namely, personality—that guides his behavior. The raw data is there; one person typically acts aggressively in many situations, another seeks power over others, still another withdraws from contacts with others. As with the structure of personality, the inferences made about the personality characteristics behind these themes vary widely, and little consensus has been reached. This is another reason for the diversity of personality theories.

Yet in order to describe the behavior of an individual adequately and to account for his consistencies of behavior, it has been found valuable to construct the idea of personality. In the words of a leading personality theorist, "Personality *is* something and *does* something" (Allport, 1961). Thus the problem of the personality psychologist is to discover useful ways of describing the *structure* and *dynamics* of personality.

A definition of personality Perhaps we can give a better idea of what is meant by the construct, or idea, of personality by presenting a more specific definition. Here again personality psychologists differ, but most definitions of personality have certain general aspects that can be pointed out. The term *personality,* as used by the psychologist, commonly refers to the distinctive characteristics of individuals, the stable and changing relationships between these characteristics, the origins of the characteristics, the ways in which they help or hinder the interaction of a person with other people, and the characteristic ways in which a person thinks about himself.

While no definition of personality is completely satisfying, the following one is widely accepted: *Personality is the dynamic organization within the individual of those psychophysical systems that determine his characteristic behavior and thought* (Allport, 1961). In this definition, the words *dynamic organization* refer to the idea that the characteristics of personality interact with and modify each other. The word *psychophysical* means that personality contains both mental and physical elements. And the word *determine* refers to the idea that personality is considered to be a cause of behavior.

Character and temperament In ordinary speech it is customary to use the term *character* as a synonym for personality, and sometimes European psychologists adopt this usage. To American psychologists, however, character and personality are not synonomous; when they speak of character they generally are referring to the ethical or moral characteristics of an individual. Quoting again from Allport: "We prefer to define *character* as *personality evaluated;* and personality, if you will, as *character devaluated*" (1961).

In everyday speech, the word *temperament* is also sometimes a synonym for personality. But the psychologist uses temperament to refer to a subset of personality characteristics—namely, the emotional aspects of personality: a person's ease of emotional arousal, his characteristic forms of emotional expression, and his typical emotional mood state, for example. In this sense temperament is supposed to be determined largely by genetic, or constitutional, factors (see Chapter 2).

Structure of Personality

When we attempt to study an individual in a real-life setting, we are immediately struck by the tremendous number of things we might observe. Every moment in the day he is doing something—sleeping, eating, writing, working, playing, talking, walking. Any attempt to describe and understand everything he does involves us in a tremendously complicated, and in the end impossible, task. Once, for example, a group of psychologists attempted to record in detail the activities of a 7-year-old boy for just one day (Barker and Wright, 1951). The result was a book of 435 pages! Think how voluminous the report would be if we attempted such a record for many individuals over a longer period.

In attempting to understand personalities, we obviously must make some choices of what to study. To a certain extent, these choices are arbitrary, and they are made according to what we are most interested in knowing about a person. In some circumstances, we may be satisfied with only general traits of behavior. In others, we may want most to characterize a person's attitudes, or his motives, or his way of dealing with personal problems.

No matter what personality characteristics are chosen for study, two requirements must always be met if the selection is to be meaningful and useful. First, a personality characteristic must be *characteristic* and relatively *consistent over time*. It does us little good, for example, to know that Mr. A was angry on a certain Tuesday morning. He may have been facing a situation that would have made anyone angry, and he may not have been angry at any other time for a month. What we would rather know about Mr. A is whether he is characteristically an angry or hostile person, or whether he usually has a serene, sunny disposition and is provoked to anger only in the most exasperating circumstances. If he is usually serene, and only occasionally angry, we characterize him as a serene person.

Second, the aspects of personality that we choose for study should be *distinctive*. Almost all men in the United States work for a living. Therefore it does us little good to note that a man works for a living, for this is not a characteristic that distinguishes him from most other men. On the other hand, some people work harder than others; this difference does distinguish people from one another, so that we might regard "industriousness" as a distinguishing personality characteristic. The measurement of some characteristic and distinctive personality traits was described in Chapter 10.

Confining ourselves to those aspects of personality which are characteristic, consistent, and distinctive simplifies the problem of studying personality considerably. Even so, the possible number of distinctive characteristics is enormous. Moreover, they are not always easily separated from each other. Is there a clear-cut distinction, for example, between honesty, on the one hand, and conscientiousness, integrity, or dependability, on the other hand? What is the difference between a person's need to depend on others and his need for affection? In these and many other instances, we find that personality characteristics often overlap and are highly correlated with each other. Hence several possible sets of characteristics may not be clearly different from one another. Each set, however, may serve some particular purpose in describing personality.

Traits and types When we talk about aspects of personality that are reasonably characteristic, consistent, and distinctive, we are talking

Table 11.1 *One set of primary traits of personality obtained by the method of factor analysis. A group of experienced judges rated adult men on 35 broad traits. Factor analysis was used on the results to identify the traits that for all practical purposes were duplicates, and the list of 35 was consolidated into these 12 primary traits.*

Source: Modified from Cattell, 1946.

1.	*Cyclothymia* Emotionally expressive, frank, placid	*vs.*	*Schizothymia* Reserved, closemouthed, anxious
2.	*General mental capacity* Intelligent, smart, assertive	*vs.*	*Mental defect* Unintelligent, dull, submissive
3.	*Emotionally stable* Free of neurotic symptoms, realistic about life	*vs.*	*Neurotic emotionality* Variety of neurotic symptoms, evasive, immature
4.	*Dominance* Self-assertive, confident, aggressive	*vs.*	*Submissiveness* Submissive, unsure, complaisant
5.	*Surgency* Cheerful, joyous, humorous, witty	*vs.*	*Desurgency* Depressed, pessimistic, dull, phlegmatic
6.	*Positive character* Persevering, attentive to people	*vs.*	*Dependent character* Fickle, neglectful of social chores
7.	*Adventurous cyclothymia* Likes meeting people, strong interest in opposite sex	*vs.*	*Withdrawn schizothymia* Shy, little interest in opposite sex
8.	*Sensitive, infantile emotionality* Dependent, immature, gregarious, attention-seeking	*vs.*	*Mature, tough poise* Independent-minded, self-sufficient
9.	*Socialized, cultured mind* Polished, poised, composed, introspective, sensitive	*vs.*	*Boorishness* Awkward, socially clumsy, crude
10.	*Trustful cyclothymia* Trustful, understanding	*vs.*	*Paranoia* Suspicious, jealous
11.	*Bohemian unconcernedness* Unconventional, eccentric, fitful hysterical upsets	*vs.*	*Conventional practicality* Conventional, unemotional
12.	*Sophistication* Logical mind, cool, aloof	*vs.*	*Simplicity* Sentimental mind, attentive to people

about *traits.* As constructs, or ideas, that bring order to the many facets of human personality, traits provide what is probably our most useful means of characterizing a person. The problem, as we have said, is to decide which traits we should select to rank people on. Webster's unabridged dictionary contains approximately 18,000 adjectives that describe how people act, think, perceive, feel, and behave (Allport and Odbert, 1936). It also contains about 4,000 words that might be accepted as trait names—such words as humility, sociability, honesty, and forthrightness. Of course, many of these are synonyms or near synonyms, and others are so rare and unusual that they are of little value. When the synonyms and rare words are weeded out, we are left with about 170 words—still an unwieldy number for scientific purposes. It must be further reduced and refined.

But the process of reduction should not be carried to the point of setting up personality types based on a single trait, or on only a few traits. We often hear someone say, for instance, "John is the submissive type," "Harry is the extroverted type," or "Dick is the Don Juan type." Such statements may convey *one* of a person's distinctive traits, but they

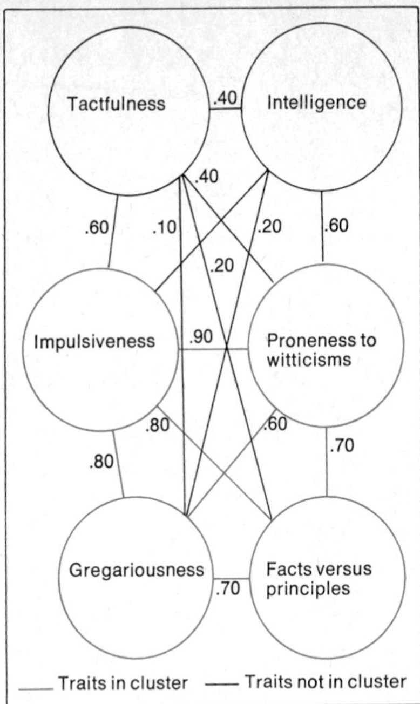

FACTOR ANALYSIS CAN BE USED TO FIND CLUSTERS OF RELATED TRAITS

Figure 11.1 *The clustering of traits. Each circle represents a possible trait on which individuals were rated. After the ratings were completed, they were correlated with each other. The number along the line joining two circles is the correlation obtained. In this case, impulsiveness, gregariousness, proneness to witticisms, and facts versus principles are highly correlated and can be considered essentially one trait. (After Cattell, 1950.)*

vastly oversimplify the structure of personality. It is true that types based on patterns of interrelated traits that are known as *syndromes* are sometimes useful in characterizing people (see page 371); it is the types based on extremes of one or a few traits that are misleading.

Notions of personality types based on these extremes arise in several ways. They can stem from observations of a few dramatic instances of somebody's behavior, from contact with relatively rare personalities, or from exposure to fictional characters who have purposely been overdrawn to make them interesting. We then unthinkingly use these rare instances as models for people in everyday life. The big bully who beats up all the kids in the neighborhood becomes a model for an "aggressive type." The relatively rare person who is the life of the party may be the model for the "extroverted type." And distinctive fictional characters like Hamlet, Pollyanna, and Scrooge serve as models for their types. Actually, such models are so rare that they are hardly valid in describing real people.

Another objection to typing people is that it lumps together a number of different personality traits. The "introverted type" is supposed to be withdrawn, sensitive to criticism, and inhibited in emotional expression; the "extroverted type" is supposed to be outgoing, thick-skinned about personal failures, and spontaneous in emotional expression. It happens more often, though, that one person is as sensitive as the introvert, yet as sociable as the extrovert. Another person may be as thick-skinned as the extrovert, but as ill-humored and unfriendly as the introvert. A personality is not simple enough to be put into a single basket; people are characterized by a number of traits. Some of these may be introvertive and some extrovertive; seldom do they all fit the pattern of any one type. Even in the rare case where they appear to fit one pattern, it is very unlikely that all of them will be so extreme. Most people are not extreme types, nor do they exhibit extreme traits; they fall somewhere between.

Examples of traits Although it is usually incorrect to reduce a complex personality to a simple type, for purposes of study we must distinguish certain general, unifying traits from the welter of human differences.

FACTOR-ANALYTIC STUDIES Factor analysis is one of the tools used to reduce the large number of personality traits by identifying clusters of related traits. For instance, in one study it was found that 171 trait names gathered from a dictionary could be reduced to 12 clusters or factors (Cattell, 1946). As a first step, all the traits that correlated highly with another set of traits were combined under one trait name. This produced 35 broad traits or trait clusters. Then a small group of experienced judges rated a large group of adult men whom they knew reasonably well on each of the 35 traits. All the ratings were put through a factor analysis that reduced the 35 traits to a basic 12 (see Table 11.1). In other words, 12 basic or primary traits proved to be almost as good as 35 in describing personality, because a person's rating on each of the 35 traits could be predicted from his ratings on the 12. (See Figure 11.1 for an example of the way a cluster is derived from factor analysis.)

But one should not jump to the conclusion that there are just 12 basic personality traits; the study cited is only an example among many. The final number of traits obtained from a factor-analytic study depends on several conditions, including the kinds of people observed, the settings or walks of life in which they are studied, the judges doing the rating, and the number of possible traits the judges use in making their ratings.

Psychologists have not settled on any one set of traits, nor are they likely to. Just as there is no one "correct" picture to take of a person or a scene, so no one set of traits should be considered final. The important thing is to have a set that is significant for a particular purpose and that can be used for making comparisons among individuals.

ABILITIES, ATTITUDES, AND INTERESTS Any description of personality characteristics is incomplete if it does not include such things as abilities, attitudes, and interests. It may, for example, be characteristic of a person that he is intelligent, conservative, and sports-loving. Such characteristics are commonly included in the list of traits used for rating personality, as can be seen from Table 11.1.

Abilities, attitudes, and interests, however, are different from other personality traits in two important respects. First, they are more often measured by objective tests, that is, by tests that can be mechanically scored and that make no use of the interpretations or ratings of a judge (see Chapter 10). Second, they are often measured for special purposes, such as for selecting students or employees, for vocational counseling, or for surveying public opinion (see Chapters 15 and 16).

MOTIVES We can also describe a person in terms of his motives and goals—why he does what he does. Motives (see Chapter 6) are one example of general traits: "general" means that the motive is assumed to lead to many different types of specific behaviors. In the following examples, the specific behaviors can vary considerably, but they are all expressions of a more general trait—a motive.

George is friendly and attentive, thereby exhibiting desirable traits, but his reason is that he wants to sell me an insurance policy. Dave, on the other hand, shows the same traits simply because he likes my company. Ferdinand wants very much to be my friend, but he seems reserved and aloof because he does not have the social skills needed to show his friendship. I may mistake his motive entirely if I judge him by his superficial traits alone.

We therefore need to have concepts of personality that are cast in terms of general traits, of which motives are an example, as well as in terms of specific traits and behaviors. As in the case of specific traits, psychologists have not yet agreed on any particular set of motives as the standard for comparing different individuals. The set they use depends on their theoretical orientation and what they are attempting to find out about a particular individual or group. One set that has been widely accepted, particularly in interpreting the Thematic Apperception Test (see Chapter 10), is given in Table 11.2.

This set of motives was not chosen by factor analysis or any statistical method (Murray, 1938). It was arrived at in an extensive investigation of personality conducted at the Harvard Psychological Clinic. A number of young men were thoroughly tested, interviewed, and studied by a group of clinical psychologists. The investigators found that the set shown in

Table 11.2 *A classification of major personal motives, based on extensive tests and interviews of a large number of young men.*

Source: After Murray, 1938.

Motive	Goal and effects
Abasement	To submit passively to others. To seek and accept injury, blame, and criticism.
Achievement	To accomplish difficult tasks. To rival and surpass others.
Affiliation	To seek and enjoy cooperation with others. To make friends.
Aggression	To overcome opposition forcefully. To fight and revenge injury. To belittle, curse, or ridicule others.
Autonomy	To be free of restraints and obligations. To be independent and free to act according to impulse.
Counteraction	To master or make up for failure by renewed efforts. To overcome weakness and maintain pride and self-respect on a high level.
Deference	To admire and support a superior person. To yield eagerly to other people.
Defendence	To defend oneself against attack, criticism, or blame. To justify and vindicate oneself.
Dominance	To control and influence the behavior of others. To be a leader.
Exhibition	To make an impression. To be seen and heard by others. To show off.
Harmavoidance	To avoid pain, physical injury, illness, and death.
Infavoidance	To avoid humiliation. To refrain from action because of fear of failure.
Nurturance	To help and take care of sick or defenseless people. To assist others who are in trouble.
Order	To put things in order. To achieve cleanliness, arrangement, and organization.
Play	To devote one's free time to sports, games, and parties. To laugh and make a joke of everything. To be lighthearted and gay.
Rejection	To remain aloof and indifferent to an inferior person. To jilt or snub others.
Sentience	To seek and enjoy sensuous impressions and sensations. To enjoy the arts genuinely.

the table provided a satisfactory way of classifying and rating the subjects' motives.

Motives such as those in Table 11.2 exist in each of us in varying degrees. Since the original study was conducted, psychologists skilled in the study of personality have devised techniques for rating the strength of each of the motives, or needs, of a person fairly reliably. For instance, an objective test, the Edwards Personal Preference Schedule (EPPS), has been developed for the assessment of many motives (Edwards, 1954).

MODES OF ADJUSTMENT AND DEFENSE MECHANISMS Another way of characterizing people is by their typical modes of adjustment. *Adjustment* refers to the process of accommodating oneself to circumstances, and more particularly, to the process of satisfying needs, or motives, under various circumstances. There are a number of characteristic modes or ways of adjusting. Most individuals at one time or another use all of them. Yet each person relies more on some than on others.

Defense mechanisms are important adjustment techniques. The concept of defense mechanisms comes to us from Sigmund Freud, though others have modified it in various ways (Dollard and Miller, 1950). We shall consider specific defense mechanisms in detail later. Here we note only that a defense mechanism is a device—a way of behaving—which a person uses unconsciously and automatically to protect himself against the fear, anxiety, or feelings of worthlessness that are the emotional consequences of motive frustration (see Chapter 7). Each of us has his own characteristic and distinctive pattern of defense mechanisms; as such, these mechanisms are important traits of personality. In addition, as we shall see later, they are important in personality dynamics.

Personality Organization: The Individual and the Self

The measurements we can make of a person's traits are merely windows through which we catch brief glimpses of the underlying personality. How can we synthesize these glimpses into a coherent picture of his individual organization? Although there is no set of rules for understanding a personality as a whole, each of us struggles to do this day by day as we deal with the people we know intimately.

Individuality A person is not simply a profile of disembodied traits measured by tests or ratings, nor is he a piece of putty molded by environmental circumstances. Personality tests provide only samples of behavior (see page 313), and environmental influences combined in different ways to affect personalities quite differently.

UNIQUENESS OF PERSONALITY One thing to realize is that each person is unique; no two people—not even identical twins reared together—can be exactly alike. Every individual has his unique set of abilities and habits and, except for identical twins, his unique hereditary endowment. Two people with similar rearing are different because their endowments cause them to react differently to environmental influences. People with similar endowments are different because they have at least slightly different environmental influences. In dealing with individuals it is unwise to generalize glibly from one to another. Because Cheryl and Sally have similar backgrounds and even superficially similar personalities, it does not follow that the two girls are to be understood in the same way. An intimate knowledge of their individual motives, traits, and modes of adjustment almost always reveals significant differences that make each a unique personality.

CONTINUITY OF PERSONALITY Besides uniqueness, personality has a basic continuity. Habits and motives that are learned over a number of years are not easily forgotten or supplanted by new ones. Thousands and thousands of learning trials make up the history of any particular individual. Continuity is also provided by biological factors, of which the individual is partly a product; these do not change greatly, at least in the adult.

In addition to learning and biological endowment, the roles a person is called upon to play give continuity to his personality. His family, friends, social class, and economic circumstances all are relatively constant. They continue to make demands on him for certain ways of behaving, called roles (see Chapter 14). These roles do not change very rapidly as a person goes through life.

Thus three factors—learning, biological endowment, and social roles—lead us to expect a certain continuity, consistency, and permanency in a personality. What a person will be tomorrow is an extension of what he is today. If he seems to be a Dr. Jekyll and Mr. Hyde, his appearance is probably deceptive. Beneath the exterior, his motives and habits make sense in terms of his past history.

PERSONALITY CHANGES Over a period of time, however, personality usually does change. Some people change more than others, but nearly everyone gradually acquires some new habits to supplant old ones. Often people discover ways of satisfying motives that were previously frustrated. Sometimes they change their way of life, and this leads to satisfactions they did not know before or to new roles they can play. For example, marriage (although it is usually no cure for a personality problem) occasionally produces marked personality changes, because it involves a new way of life and exposes a person to a different set of influences. Sometimes, too, relatively sudden personality changes take place as a result of intense religious experience, changing jobs, moving to a new community, achieving success in a line of work, and so on. In these dramatic, but comparatively rare, instances, the change takes place because something fundamental has happened to change motives, satisfy motives, teach new habits—in short, to alter a person's fundamental modes of adjustment.

Most personality changes occur gradually and with no conscious intent. Sometimes, however, a deliberate attempt is made to bring about change. A person may change himself, or someone close to him may effect a change. Psychotherapy and counseling are organized methods for bringing about such changes when a person faces a problem he feels unable to solve, or when he becomes so incapable of making social adjustments that an important personality change is urgently needed (see Chapter 13). When successful, psychotherapy and counseling enable the individual to discard old habits and learn new ones that reduce his motivational conflicts and provide satisfactions for his needs. Such personality changes may therefore be regarded as cases of relatively rapid learning.

Personality syndromes Although each individual's personality is unique, a person may display a *syndrome* which is similar in many respects to the syndrome found in other individuals. In medical terminology, this word refers to a pattern of causes and symptoms of disease. In the field of personality, a syndrome means a pattern of origins and characteristics of the personality. Syndromes can be patterns of desirable or undesirable traits, although the undesirable patterns have traditionally been given the most attention.

Several personality syndromes have been described and measured. One purpose of some personality tests, such as the Minnesota Multiphasic Personality Inventory (MMPI), is to detect such syndromes (see page 354). For example, a *hypochondriacal syndrome,* which may consist of many specific characteristics, is one of abnormal concern over bodily health. A *psychasthenic syndrome* is characterized by excessive doubt, compulsions, obsessions, and unreasonable fears. Both these syndromes are measured on the MMPI. Another syndrome, called the *authoritarian personality,* is marked by highly conventional behavior, desire for power, hostility, prejudice, and intolerance. This kind of personality pattern appears to have its origins in rejection or excessive domination of a child by his parents.

Thus in a syndrome, some personality characteristics tend to be highly correlated and to form patterns, and people who display similar syndromes can be compared. But our use of the concept of syndrome does not imply the classification of all people into a few types. First of all, many syndromes exist; secondly, not everyone has a particular personality syndrome. Hence syndromes cannot be used to classify all people. But if we are aware of a syndrome when it exists in a person, we have a better overall understanding of him.

The self Each of us has a concept of his *self,* and for most of us, this is the real essence of the personality. Unfortunately, the self is elusive from the point of view of the scientist; many problems stand in the way of an objective study. Nevertheless, some conclusions can be drawn about the self which are helpful in understanding personality.

ORIGIN OF THE SELF In psychological terminology, *the self represents the individual's awareness or perception of his own personality.* We learn to perceive our own body and behavior in much the same way that we learn to perceive other objects and events in the world about us (see Chapter 8). The beginnings of the perceived self can be traced to early infancy, when the baby first starts to learn distinctions between his own body and other objects in his environment. At birth, he is probably aware only of vague feelings of comfort or discomfort. As his capacity for learning and memory develops and as his experience widens, the child sees that parts of his body are common to all his experiences. Muscular and organic sensations accompany all his activities, and he discovers that pinching objects, such as his doll, does not cause pain, whereas pinching any part of his own body does. By the time the child is 2 years old, his distinction between his own body and other objects is generally well established.

SELF-PERCEPTION The perception of the body as a unit distinct from the changing background is probably the core around which all later self-perception takes place. Given this core, a number of other influences contribute to the development of self-awareness. The child is given a name, he is held responsible for his behavior, and a distinction is made between possessions that are his and possessions that belong to his parents, brothers, and sisters. Since the family and society treat the child as a unit, he comes to perceive himself in this way.

The kinds of experiences that the child has are very important in determining what his self-perception will be like. He finds that his behavior and appearance elicit kindness or hostility, respect or rebuke, attention or indifference from parents and playmates. He hears himself described by other people in terms of various personality traits, and when these traits are consistently applied, he often accepts them as descriptions of himself. Praise and love from his parents and respect and attention from his playmates help him to form a picture of himself as a desirable person. Rejection and excessive criticism at home and indifference from others can lead to a derogatory self-picture, with resulting inferiority feelings.

Of course, the treatment a child receives has some relation to his traits and abilities. The physically strong child is more apt to win the admiration of his playmates than the weak one. The intelligent child has a greater opportunity for gaining success and praise in school. Hence we would expect that the individual's perception of his own personality would tend to coincide with the way others perceive him. But this is not always true; in fact, we probably never see ourselves exactly as others see us.

In some cases the differences between the perceived self and the personality as perceived by others are very sharp. Suppose that a strong, healthy, intelligent child is reared by parents who feel indifferent to him and who constantly criticize and belittle him. He may learn to perceive himself as an inadequate, undesirable person. Most of us have known people who constantly underrate their own performance. We have also known people with a grossly exaggerated view of their accomplishments and capabilities. Children surrounded by an admiring and doting family who excessively praise even poor performance are often found to have inflated self-evaluations (see page 402).

THE SELF AND EMOTIONAL ADJUSTMENT In many instances, knowing a person's self-picture helps us to understand his behavior. This is particularly true where a marked discrepancy exists between the way he sees himself and the way others see him. Behavior is largely determined by how the person perceives a situation with reference to himself. We may think that John should be popular with the girls—after all, he is handsome and witty—but if John does not see himself as having these attributes, he may be just another wallflower.

If the person's self-picture is too different from the true or objective personality, serious adjustment problems can arise. He is constantly called upon to explain or ignore evidence which is incompatible with his view of himself. The mediocre student who pictures himself as an intellectual giant is faced with the objective evidence of his poor grades and failures. Often, instead of changing his self-evaluation, he will use rationalizations to explain the evidence away. For example, he may tell himself that bright people like him are not interested in getting grades because they have broader interests. Or he may completely ignore the evidence by repressing his perception of the discrepancy. Thus defense mechanisms are often used to maintain distorted self-perceptions.

Personality Dynamics and Defense Mechanisms

The term *personality dynamics* has two aspects, the first of which refers to the *interactions* among personality characteristics. In this area, conflicts among motives are especially important (see Chapter 7); people develop characteristic, consistent, and distinctive ways of adjusting to these conflicts. The second aspect refers to the *behavioral expression* of such personality characteristics as the traits, aptitudes, and motives in the process of *adjustment* to stresses from the environment.

Adjustment is thus the key idea in both aspects of personality dynamics. Faced with external and internal stresses, a person may gradually learn to cope with them. He may learn new ways of avoiding situations that arouse anxiety, and he may learn more satisfactory ways of achieving goals and of getting along with people (see the case of Joseph Kidd, page 402).

In addition to such gradual learning, adjustment to internal and external forces is accomplished by the more or less automatic *defense mechanisms.* In general, we can say that these mechanisms are used to reduce the anxiety and unpleasant emotions arising from motive frustration, to defend against the feeling of worthlessness that arises when motives are blocked, or to obtain a combination of anxiety reduction and self esteem. Let us consider some of the defense mechanisms in greater detail.

Repression Repression is one of the most common and powerful defense mechanisms. It is both a way of reducing the emotional consequences of motive frustration and a kind of "forgetting." Through repression a person conveniently forgets the things that might make him uncomfortable. I can easily forget to pay a bill because paying it might bring me uncomfortably close to insolvency. I can forget my appointment with the dentist because I am afraid of his drill. This kind of forgetting, however, is a matter of motivation more than a true memory loss, for the memories can be recovered when the fear or anxiety connected with them is reduced or eliminated. I remember the bill when I get my next pay check; I remember the dentist's appointment after the date is past. So, although repression often takes the form of forgetting, it goes deeper than that. It is a process of "pushing down" memories or thoughts that might be expressed openly, or acted upon, if they did not arouse fear or anxiety. Sometimes the repressed memories or thoughts are expressed in disguised fashion in dreams. This idea provides one scheme for the interpretation of dreams. Within such a framework, dreams may give significant clues to the personality psychologist and psychotherapist (see Chapter 13).

The thing repressed may be a memory, a motive, a goal, a barrier, a conflict—almost anything connected with a frustration-producing situation. Repression of strong, persistent, deep-seated, and insoluble conflicts is the most significant kind of repression. Through repression, a person fools himself into believing that a conflict, and everything connected with it, does not exist. This, of course, does not really resolve the conflict, but it does partially relieve him of anxiety. The following incident illustrates repression as it may take place in most of us:

A young man who had recently become engaged was walking along the street with his fiancée. Another man greeted him and began to chat in a friendly fashion. The young man realized that he must know this apparent stranger, and that both courtesy and pride required that he introduce the visitor to his fiancée. The name of the other man, however, eluded him completely; indeed, he had not even a fleeting recognition of his identity. When in his confusion he attempted at least to present his fiancée, he found that he had also forgotten her name.

Only a brief behavior analysis was necessary to make this incident comprehensible as an example of normal . . . repression. The apparent stranger was in fact a former friend of the young man; but the friendship had eventually brought frustration and disappointment in a situation identical with the one described. Some years before, our subject had become engaged to another woman, and in his pride and happiness he had at once sought out this friend and introduced the two. Unfortunately the girl had become strongly attached to the friend and he to her; at length she broke her engagement and married the friend. The two men had not seen each other until this meeting, which repeated exactly the earlier frustrating situation. It is hardly surprising that the newly engaged man repressed all recognition of his former friend, all hints as to his identity, and even the name of the fiancée. (Cameron and Margaret, 1951, pages 367–368.)

Such complete repression serves effectively as a defense mechanism against anxiety. However, repression may be less complete; it may disguise only some aspect of one of the conflicting motives. For example, it may disguise only the nature of the motive, who has the motive, what the goal of the motive is, or which motive is behind a particular form of behavior. Each one of these ways of dealing with conflict is regarded as a different defense mechanism and has its own name.

Reaction formation A person may disguise his motivation and conflict by believing that his motive is exactly the opposite of his real motive. This defense mechanism is called *reaction formation*. We see it in the case of the daughter who unconsciously hates her mother but appears to be oversolicitous of her mother's health and comfort. To admit to herself that she hates her mother may be so abhorrent and may create so many anxieties that she tries to overcome the anxiety by showing excessive affection. The well-known quotation from Shakespeare, "The lady doth protest too much, methinks," refers to this disguise. When a person is *too* solicitous or *too* modest or *too* affectionate, it is very likely that he harbors aggression or other hostile impulses that are being repressed and disguised by the opposite kind of behavior.

The following example of reaction formation is taken from a letter received from a "kindly, warm-hearted" antivivisectionist by Jules Masserman after his work on alcohol addiction in cats had been publicized:

I read . . . your work on alcoholism. . . . I am surprised that anyone who is as well educated as you must be to hold the position that you do would stoop to such a depth as to torture helpless little cats in the pursuit of a cure for alcoholics. . . . A drunkard is just a weak-minded idiot who belongs in the gutter and should be left there. Instead of torturing helpless little cats why not torture the drunks or better still exert your would-be noble effort toward getting a bill passed to exterminate drunks. . . . If people are such weaklings, the world is better off without them. . . . If you are an example of what a noted psychiatrist should be I'm glad I am just an ordinary human being without a letter after my name. I'd rather be just myself with a clear conscience, knowing I have not hurt any living creature, and can sleep without seeing frightened, terrified dying cats—because I know they must die after you have finished with them. No punishment is too great for you, and I hope I live to read about your mangled body and long suffering before you finally die—and I'll laugh long and loud. (Masserman, 1946, page 35.)

The person who wrote this letter professed to be interested in the welfare of cats. The love of cats, however, appears to be a reaction formation serving as a disguise for bitter hostility toward people.

Projection Another common disguise that protects a person against anxiety-producing impulses is *projection,* in which the individual disguises the source of conflict by ascribing his own motives to someone else. If a student has a strong desire to cheat on an examination but is unwilling to admit it to himself because of his moral code, he may become unduly suspicious of others and accuse them of cheating when they are innocent. Or if he feels like being nasty to other people and yet knows that this tendency is "wrong," he may accuse other people of being nasty to him when in fact they have not been.

Projection is well illustrated in a study of the attitudes of 97 fraternity members (Sears, 1936):

The students were asked to rate certain of their fraternity brothers on four undesirable traits: stinginess, obstinacy, disorderliness, and bashfulness. After rating others, each student rated himself. Thus it was possible for the investigator to compare a student's rating of himself with other members' ratings of him. Some subjects seemed to have an accurate idea of their own traits, for their self-ratings agreed well with the ratings made by other members. From the ratings of the group, however, it appeared that certain students had one or more traits in an undesirable degree. These students rated other students higher on their own undesirable traits than they did themselves. Thus they failed to acknowledge undesirable traits in themselves and assigned them—that is, projected them—to their fraternity brothers.

Examples of projection abound in human behavior. When a person believes incorrectly that other people are out to do him wrong, one can suspect that he is harboring strong aggressive impulses and is projecting them to other people. The unattractive spinster who will not leave her house because she is sure that men are waiting to attack her must be suspected of projecting to others her own thwarted sex desires. Similarly, the white supremacist who eventually reduces all arguments about civil rights to a sexual level must be suspected of projecting his own unacceptable sexual impulses to Negroes. To recognize such desires in himself would make him anxious, and so he defends himself by projecting them to someone else. In the extreme form, this projection is the mark of the behavior disorder called paranoia.

Displacement In *displacement,* the object or goal of an anxiety- producing motive is disguised by substituting another object in place of it. For example, the man who gets angry at his boss but is afraid to tell him off comes home and bawls out his wife. Or consider the little girl who finds her baby brother the new center of attention. Her jealousy makes her want to harm the baby. The family, however, forbids it and teaches

Figure 11.2 *The displacement of aggression. A rat that had learned to strike an "innocent bystander" rat turned to another "innocent bystander," the rubber doll, and struck it when the second rat was no longer present. (Miller, 1948b.)*

her that hurting the baby is naughty. Unable to express her aggression against the baby, she substitutes a safer object, a doll, and may succeed in totally destroying it. Thus by displacing her aggression, she finds an acceptable outlet for it. The displacement of aggression has been demonstrated in experiments carried out with rats (Miller, 1948b):

Two rats were placed in a box having a grill for the floor (see Figure 11.2). One rat was the "subject" in the experiment; the other rat was put there merely as an "object of aggression." Periodically the grill floor was electrified. The shock applied in this way made the subject both fearful and angry. As it thrashed around, it struck the other rat, whereupon the shock was turned off. This procedure was repeated until the subject had learned to strike the second rat as a means of terminating the shock. Then the second rat was removed and replaced by a rubber doll. In this situation, the subject turned to the new "innocent bystander," the doll, and struck it. Thus aggression was displaced from the unavailable object to an available object. A learned aggressive response—striking a rat to turn off the shock—was displaced to a neutral object, the doll.

Displacement is related to the concept of generalization (see page 00). When a motive cannot be satisfied directly, its expression will be directed toward situations which are similar in some way to the original situation. In other words, the expression generalizes from the original situation. Many factors influence the degree of generalization. For instance, if the drive toward a situation, or goal, is strong, and the negative aspects of the goal are weak, the new goal will be rather similar to the original one; if the reverse is true, of course, the new goal will be quite different from the original one.

Rationalization In *rationalization* an individual explains his behavior in such a way as to assign a socially approved motive to it and conceal the unacceptable motive it actually expresses. This mechanism is among the most common socially accepted ways of reducing anxiety. A student who is motivated to have a good time may rationalize his school failures by attributing them to inadequate teaching, an instructor's unfairness, or too little time to study. A mother whose real motive is to hold onto her son as long as possible may not permit him to go out on dates, rationalizing that his schoolwork will be hampered or that he will fall into unwholesome company. A father may beat his child because—he rationalizes—the child deserves or needs it, but his real motive may be aggression. By rationalizing his behavior, he can gratify his needs without taking the blame.

Sublimation and compensation Two similar forms of defense have been given special names by Freud and others. One is *sublimation,* or the use of a substitute activity to gratify a motive. For example, when a sexual motive cannot be directly satisfied because of external obstacles or internal conflict, Freud claimed that the individual satisfies the motive by finding some other outlet which seems to reduce tension. Freud believed that the frustrated urge can be partially gratified by channeling it into art, religion, music, or some aesthetic activity that is socially acceptable. Because of the passionate way in which some people embrace their aesthetic activities, Freud argued that the substitute activity is a means of satisfying sexual drives. This interpretation of sublimation is open to question, for it is doubtful whether physiological motives can be relieved by substitute activities. It is more likely that the motives involved in aesthetic activities are not sexual. On the other hand, the general idea that motives can be gratified by substituting one set of activities for another seems to be sound.

In *compensation* also, a frustrated motive is satisfied by means of a substitute activity. But compensation usually involves failure or loss of self-esteem in one activity, which is then compensated for by efforts in some other area. The concept of compensation does not carry with it the implication of an outlet for sexual frustration. The unattractive girl may become a bookworm and eventually a distinguished scholar, thereby commanding the respect and prestige that she is unable to win with good looks. The short man may develop his skill in boxing in order to secure the respect for his masculinity that his small stature had denied him. Life is full of compensations through which a person achieves satisfaction that he otherwise cannot obtain. When a person's frustration stems from a feeling of social inferiority, compensation is very likely to be expressed in attempts to gain attention, as in the following example:

One high school girl, Alva B., was notably unattractive because she was overweight and had large, coarse features. Her father was a bartender, an occupation not esteemed in a conservative small town's social scheme. All these circumstances barred her from desired social relationships. In response, Alva took to an excessive use of make-up. She appeared in school well coated with cosmetics, her eyebrows plucked and penciled, and her lips drawn in a most exaggerated manner. The painting did not render her beautiful, but it made her noticed, and this was an effective substitute for social recognition. Later Alva became a cheer leader and was an excellent one, the position being perfectly suited to her need for attention. (Shaffer and Shoben, 1956, pages 171–172.)

Fantasy Sometimes a frustrated motive can be partially gratified by *fantasy* or daydreaming. Fantasy is common among most people, and is particularly prominent during adolescence. As a form of adjustment, it rarely leads to constructive action, and thus may leave a person's basic conflicts unsolved. On the other hand, if it is not overdone, daydreaming about success, sexual conquests, and the like can produce a certain amount of satisfaction. A person who has been embarrassed in a social situation feels somewhat better if he indulges in a little fantasy about all the things he could have said. If a girl does not get an invitation to the junior prom, she can at least have some fun dreaming about what it would be like. It has been estimated that more than 95 percent of college students spend some time daydreaming. Their most frequent subjects for daydreaming are academic honors, success with the opposite sex, and a future of fame and fortune.

Regression Closely related to fantasy is a reaction called *regression*. This is a retreat to early or primitive forms of behavior. We say "early or primitive" because there is some question as to whether regression is one or both of these. On the one hand, regression seems to be a relapse to habits and ways of behaving that the person learned in childhood; on the other, it seems merely to represent a simpler, more primitive, and less intellectual approach to solving a problem. Whatever its interpretation, regression takes the form of a childish, rather than an adult, adjustment to frustration. It is a defense mechanism because the person retreats in imagination and behavior to a time before the anxiety-producing conflict was present. It may also help to restore self-esteem and confidence in the face of frustration.

Regression is frequently encountered in children 4 or 5 years old, for at this age they are beginning to face an increasing variety of complex frustrations (Barker et al., 1941). The particular occasion that evokes regressive behavior may be the birth of another child, or it may be the beginning of school adjustments. In any event, the child at this stage frequently reverts to baby talk and acts like a 2-year-old.

Regression is not limited to children—adults often regress too. Childish fits of anger, or pouting when one fails to get his way, may be regressions to reactions acquired in childhood. A person who goes to bed with the slightest cold or who seems to enjoy being sick may be regressing to behavior which, in childhood, brought him affection and attention.

Extreme frustration of the sort encountered in Nazi concentration camps during World War II can produce regression in otherwise normal people. A more or less general regression to infantile behavior was reported as characteristic of the inmates of the Dachau and Buchenwald camps:

> The prisoners lived, like children, only in the immediate present . . . they became unable to plan for the future or to give up immediate pleasure satisfactions to gain greater ones in the near future. . . . They were boastful, telling tales about what they had accomplished in their former lives, or how they succeeded in cheating foremen or guards, and how they sabotaged the work. Like children, they felt not at all set back or ashamed when it became known that they had lied about their prowess. (Bettelheim, 1943, page 443.)

Identification In addition to the reduction of anxiety, some defense mechanisms are also used to enhance self-esteem. *Identification,* in which we imagine that we are like another person, is a method of doing both. When we identify with a successful individual or a victorious football team, we feel more worthwhile. Conversely, it is difficult to enhance self-esteem by identifying with a losing team. Perhaps this is one of the reasons for the great stress on winning in school and professional athletics. By identification we may also satisfy, in fantasy, some of our longings and motives. The unattractive girl who identifies with a glamorous movie star is the classic example.

Identification is a defense because, in some situations, we may reduce anxiety by taking on the characteristics of another person. One example is identification with the aggressor. Bettelheim notes in his study of prisoners in concentration camps that they not only regressed, but sometimes took on the brutal characteristics of their guards. According to Freudian psychoanalysis, a similar type of identification occurs in the resolution of the so-called Oedipal conflict (see page 389). In the Oedipal conflict, the son is supposed to be threatened by his father with severe punishment for his attentions to his mother. The boy removes the threat of punishment by identifying with the father, thus taking on many of his characteristics. The logic of identification with the aggressor is something like this: "If I am the aggressor, I cannot be aggressed against."

Use of defense mechanisms The student has probably recognized a number of these defense mechanisms in himself. Almost everybody uses them some of the time. Indeed, in moderation they can be a harmless and convenient way of disposing of minor conflicts. If defense mechanisms make us feel better and make others more comfortable, as they often do, their value in reducing tension and letting us get on with important problems more than offsets the trivial self-deceptions they entail.

Defense mechanisms are not always so harmless, however. If they are used excessively to sidestep persistent and severe sources of conflict, they can get us into a great deal of trouble. Defense mechanisms, when used to excess, have at least two major weaknesses.

First, they fail to solve the underlying conflict of motives. Defense mechanisms are directed mainly at the symptom—anxiety—rather than at the motivational conflicts that give rise to anxiety. Thus they merely conceal or disguise the real problem which is still there, ready to produce anxiety again and again. A man harboring homosexual tendencies, for example, may avoid anxiety by repressing them; yet they may be reawakened by a wide variety of stimuli. Whenever he is confronted with a situation which excites the tendencies, the latent conflict is reinstated. For that reason, during World War II many men with latent homosexual impulses who in civilian life had simply avoided the intimate company of other men developed severe anxieties when thrust into the close group living of the armed services. If a conflict is serious and persistent, defense mechanisms merely postpone its solution; the conflict is still intact and will probably rise again to plague the person.

Second, defense mechanisms may not function to protect the individual when the conflict is prolonged, or when its severity or salience is increased by a new situation. Under these conditions, the defense mechanisms may not be adequate protection against anxiety. They may break down, causing the person to experience a "flood" of anxiety. These breakdowns of defense mechanisms are called *anxiety attacks* (see page 406), and they can be extremely uncomfortable.

Everyone has conflicts and frustrations; there is nothing abnormal about them. Nor, as we have said, is there anything abnormal about using defense mechanisms. On the other hand, if the mechanisms are not effective—if the person continues to suffer from a great deal of anxiety—that *is* abnormal. Actually, no sharp line can be drawn between normal and abnormal behavior. Only when a person suffers from anxiety to an unusual extent or when he becomes a nuisance or a danger to other people can he be considered abnormal. Abnormal behavior is considered in detail in the next chapter. The point here is that people adjust by using different defense mechanisms, and the ones they characteristically use constitute important personality traits.

Development and Shaping of Personality

Personality traits and the self-concept do not emerge all at once; they have a developmental history. Starting from the genetic endowment bequeathed at birth, and continuing to death, personality is a developing system. Personality change and development tend to be most rapid early in life but personality growth never ceases. To a great degree, personality development is cumulative and interactive; what happens at an earlier stage of development influences what happens later (see page 56). When we study an individual's personality *longitudinally*—that is, when we look at it from time to time in his life—we can trace the continuity from earlier forms of personality organization to later ones. But if we do not have a complete record, we may also find apparent discontinuities as different personality characteristics emerge relatively rapidly (see page 371). Such jumps, breaks, or discontinuities in the record of development are most likely to be seen if we look at a *cross-section* of personality development at a particular age. The cross-sectional method has its uses; for instance, we might study the personality characteristics of a sample of 9-year-olds and ask the question: What are the common personality characteristics at this age in our culture?

In the course of development, we can distinguish a number of forces at work molding personality. Some of these are more important at earlier stages, some at later. For instance, the defense mechanisms tend to develop most rapidly during the childhood years of 6 to 12. On the other hand, the development of the self-concept tends to be a continuing lifelong process. Defense mechanisms originate in the dynamic interplay and conflict of motives; the self-concept emerges from our perception of how other people respond to us.

But what can be said in general about forces that operate to shape personality through the course of development? We have covered some of these influences in other parts of the book. Chapters 2, 3, 5, 6, 7, and

8 deal with fundamental processes in behavior, many of which are at work in the shaping of personality. Chapters 14 and 15 on the influence of social groups on behavior and attitudes also relate to the development of personality. Our aim in this section is to focus on a few specific factors that are among the major determinants of personality structure and organization: biological inheritance, cultural forces, and experiences within the family circle.

Inherited predispositions As is the case with most things psychological, personality is not directly inherited. What is inherited is a *predisposition* to develop in certain ways (see Chapter 2). Whether the individual actually develops the kind of personality to which he is predisposed —and if he does, to what degree he develops it—depend on environmental factors.

You can see some of these predispositions at an early age in infants before much chance for learning has taken place. Indeed, striking differences can often be observed among infants. One baby is extremely active, another sluggish. One cries and fusses most of the time, whereas another is so placid that its mother calls the pediatrician to see if anything is wrong. It seems obvious that such differences are to some extent innate. These innate personality characteristics are sometimes called *temperamental traits,* and they might have been included in our discussion of personality structure. In addition to activity, or the tempo of actions, characteristic moods and mood changes are often considered temperamental traits (Allport, 1961).

Some of the best scientific evidence that inherited predispositions develop into certain kinds of personalities comes from studies of certain behavior disorders, particularly schizophrenia (see page 54). The abilities are another example of inherited predispositions; each person is endowed with certain abilities that gradually develop. There can be little doubt that inheritance partly determines these (see Chapter 2).

Psychologists refer to the more general abilities to learn, abstract, and solve problems as *intelligence;* they call special abilities, such as a talent for music or mechanical things, *aptitudes* (see Chapter 10). As we have pointed out, abilities are to a certain extent a part of personality. They are also important influences on personality development. For instance, superior intelligence helps a person make better social adjustments. Since personality can be regarded, in part, as the composite of such adjustments, superior intelligence should be a factor in the development of a "better" personality. The brighter a child is, the sooner he can learn to understand that his mother may be cross and grouchy because she has a headache rather than because he is a naughty, unlovable child. And the more intelligent child can learn sooner to see into the future—to forgo a satisfaction now for a greater one tomorrow.

Intelligence and aptitudes also influence personality by providing a person with a means of gaining recognition. The bright child is rewarded by parents and teachers for his accomplishments. The child with mechanical ability receives recognition for building a ham radio set. Thus intelligence and special abilities permit a child or an adult to develop areas of competence from which he acquires confidence and feelings of self-worth and self-esteem.

Abilities also seem to provide their own motivation. A person with a special talent usually has a strong motive to exercise it. The great musician Handel, for example, had a father who strongly opposed his son's interest in music. Nevertheless, even when faced with severe punishment, Handel as a child would sneak to the garret at night to practice the harpsichord. As a consequence of such strong drives to exercise their talents, children with outstanding abilities usually show them at an early age.

Culture To shift from the influence of nature to the influence of nurture, an individual's personality also depends upon his circumstances in life. Whether he is reared in the United States or in the jungles of New Guinea, whether he lives in the city or on the farm, whether he is reared in an upper or lower socioeconomic class—these and many other conditions constitute the culture or subculture in which he lives (see Chapter 14). Culture largely determines the experiences a person has, the frustrations and adjustments he must deal with, and the standards of conduct required of him. Each culture has its distinctive values, morals, and ways of behaving. It lays down the rules for child training and the relationships within a family. Thus culture influences personality because it dictates many of the characteristics a person will acquire. The process of acquiring the personality traits typical of members of a particular culture is called *socialization*.

Personality differences caused by differences in socialization are most convincingly demonstrated in cultures of primitive societies. The Balinese, for example, have been described as an introverted people who seem emotionally blunted. They do not form warm personal attachments; each member seems to live within himself. The Navaho Indians are passive and forbearing in the face of physical discomfort. The Eskimos are rugged individualists. The Arapesh of New Guinea seem to lack egotism and competitiveness.

In the Balinese people, the lack of emotional response has been attributed to child-rearing practices. Most of the baby tending is done by little girls, and each child may be cared for by a number of little "mothers." Such practices prevent intense family relationships from building up. In addition, the Balinese mother may deliberately tease her child: she will play with him up to the point of evoking love or anger, then lose interest in him or become indifferent. In these circumstances the Balinese child soon learns to inhibit emotional responses to other people.

Family As the dominant factor in the environment during the individual's early years when his personality is being molded most rapidly, the family is the major agent of the socialization process. The family socializes the child both through specific training procedures and through the atmosphere it creates. Some of the most important characteristics of personality that are socialized by family influences include the learning of socially valued skills, such as manners and social poise; the learning of socially condoned values about right and wrong, good and bad; and the inhibition of socially unwanted behaviors and values, such as aggressive behavior, tantrums, and hatred of others (Janis et al., 1969). Families in different cultures, of course, differ on the specifics, but the power of family influences in the shaping of personality is strong in most cultures.

FAMILY WARMTH One significant way in which the family influences personality is by giving or withholding affection. This is especially important, the evidence indicates, during babyhood. If a child receives fondling and affection during this period, he is more likely to be emotionally responsive later in life. Conversely, if he lacks fondling then, his emotional responsiveness may be blunted. Studies show that children who are reared from birth in orphanages, where they receive every physical care but little personal handling and attention, are less responsive than children who are placed in an orphanage after they are 2 years old (Goldfarb, 1947).

LEARNING IN THE FAMILY Parents are teachers. By reinforcing some kinds of behavior and discouraging others, they help determine the personality traits, goals, and values of the child. One child may discover that his mother will let him have his own way if he throws a temper tantrum. Another child in another family may find that temper tantrums do not work, but that feigning illness does. The techniques a child develops in dealing with his parents naturally carry over into his contacts with others. The grown man who sulks because he is angry with his wife probably learned this response in dealing with his mother.

The training given by parents can be seen clearly in the process of *sex-typing*—the development of responses and interests appropriate to one's sex (Janis et al., 1969). In most families, continuous pressure is directed toward sex-typing the child. Boys are reinforced for rather rough and aggressive play, for inhibiting emotional displays, and for showing an interest in the workings of mechanical things. Girls are usually reinforced for being more submissive, "sweet," and emotionally expressive, and they are discouraged from developing interests in mechanical devices. This pressure is not, of course, often applied consciously by the parents, but it is nevertheless actively and powerfully present. Later, as the child grows older, much of the socialization process, including sex-typing, becomes the province of the peer group. Conformity to its standards carries forward the process of learning the roles and traits characteristic of one's sex.

PARENTAL ATTITUDES Probably parents' attitudes toward their children are as important as anything else in the way personality develops in children. Parents who are well adjusted and who love and respect their child as a person do much to give him a feeling of self-worth and self-confidence. This in turn is a great advantage to the child in facing his problems. Unfortunately, many parents reject their children, enmesh them in the cross-fire of their own emotional problems, or take out on the children the ill-treatment that they experienced in their own childhood. In fact, studies have shown that many mothers and fathers unconsciously relive their own childhood problems through their children (Hilgard, 1953). A mother may unconsciously react to her son with the same emotions and feelings that she herself felt as a child toward her older brother. If she resented and disliked her brother, some of

LIKE FATHER, LIKE SON

Figure 11.3 *Imitation in the family. The boy here is learning to act like his father, who was a college and professional football player. Perhaps more important, he is learning to value many of the same things. (Courtesy of Henry Ford.)*

her feelings toward her son may be similar. She may find herself competing with him and thus unable to give him encouragement, love, and praise. It is easy for children in such a situation to feel unwanted and unloved and to develop a lack of confidence and emotional security that carries over into adulthood.

Parental attitudes also express themselves in the so-called "home atmosphere" (Baldwin, 1948):

Homes were rated on whether the dominant atmosphere was one of democracy or control. In the families classified as democratic, the children were given explanations of decisions, and they were allowed to participate to some extent in forming decisions about policies which would affect them. In general these families were characterized by a high degree of permissiveness. The controlled atmosphere was one in which permissiveness was low and clear-cut sets of dos and don'ts were established.

Definite differences were observed in the superficial personality traits of the children from the different atmospheres. The democratic families tended to produce children who were rated as outgoing—aggressive, fearless, full of plans, and high in leadership, curiosity, and nonconformity. Children from the controlled atmospheres tended to be much less outgoing—socially unaggressive, more fearful, and rather low in planning ability and tenacity. In short, they tended to be conforming, well-behaved children.

These results would be predicted from what we know about learning (see Chapter 3). In the democratic atmosphere, outgoing responses are being reinforced. In the controlled atmosphere, other responses are being reinforced. Although it is difficult to avoid making value judgments about these findings, it should be pointed out that one pattern is not intrinsically better than the other. The outgoing children from the democratic homes were no doubt obnoxious and cruel at times, but they were more socially successful and curious and thus would seem to be more likely to get things done and to be creative. The less outgoing children from the controlled homes were easier to be with and would seem to have developed control over impulsiveness.

IMITATION Parents influence personality development by being *models*. A child learns much, both in the way of general attitudes and specific responses, by imitation (Bandura and Walters, 1963). By watching his father, a son learns how to act like a man (see Figure 11.3), and by watching her mother, daughter learns how to act like a woman. An example of the learning of specific aggressive responses through imitation comes from an experiment illustrated on the next page, in Figure 11.4 (Bandura et al., 1963).

The photographs in the top row show specific aggressive responses made by an adult model. Children watched the behavior of the model and then were tested. The middle row of pictures show the imitative aggressive behavior of a little boy after he had seen the model. Note that he displays aggressive responses very much like those of the model. The same is true for the little girl in the bottom row of pictures.

Figure 11.4 Imitation of aggressive behavior. Top row: An adult model acts aggressively toward a large plastic doll. Middle row: A boy, who has watched the aggressive behavior of the adult model, shows similar aggressive behavior. Bottom row: A girl, having seen the aggressive behavior of the model, also imitates the model's behavior. (After Bandura et al., 1963.)

Thus children find models, good ones or poor ones, with whom to identify. In so doing, they may copy many of the personality traits of their parents, taking over their moral and cultural standards as well as their mannerisms and typical ways of adjusting to problems. The principles of learning provide explanations of the way in which imitation may come about. For instance, it may be that children are reinforced for making responses similar to those of the family member who serves as the model (see page 76). Or imitation learning may be an example of perceptual learning, in which reinforcement plays little or no role (see page 96). It seems likely that both reinforced learning, or operant conditioning, and perceptual learning occur in imitation and in the consequent shaping of personality. In addition to learning explanations of this sort, the psychoanalytic theory of personality provides another explanation of the mechanisms behind some identification—as we shall see in the next section.

Theories of Personality

So far, we have described various facets of personality and some influences bearing on the development of personality. But how do the pieces fit together? What causes what? What is our general theory of personality?

The truth is that psychologists do not agree on any general theory. Personality has proved too complex, its manifestation too varied, and its determinants too numerous for us to put the pieces together into one clear picture; instead, we have a great many theories (see Hall and Lindzey, 1970). None, however, manages to explain the subject to everyone's satisfaction, for none is complete enough to encompass all that we know about personality. Each stresses certain factors and ignores others.

One day the problem will no doubt be solved through research and new attempts to formulate a general theory. In the meantime, the best we can do is to present several different theories that have had an important influence on our present conceptions of personality.

Psychoanalytic theory When we mentioned psychoanalysis in Chapter 1, we said that it involves both a method of psychotherapy and a theory of personality. As a method, it is covered in Chapter 13. As a theory, it has been the most influential of all theories of personality. Psychoanalytic theory has three main themes: a theory of personality structure, a theory of personality development, and a system of personality dynamics (Freud, 1933).

PERSONALITY STRUCTURE Freud, the founder of psychoanalysis, believed that personality has a three-part structure: the *id, the ego,* and the *superego.* The id can be thought of as a sort of storehouse of biologically based motives and "instinctual" reactions for satisfying motives. The major motives, or "instinctive drives," in psychoanalytic theory are the sexual and destructive urges. The energy of these motives is termed *libido.* Left to itself, the id energy, or libido, would satisfy fundamental motives as they arose, without regard to the realities of life or to morals of any kind.

The id, however, is usually bridled by the ego. This consists of elaborate ways of behaving and thinking that are learned for dealing effectively with the world. It delays the satisfaction of motives, and it channels motives into socially acceptable outlets. It keeps a person working for a living, getting along with people, and generally adjusting to the realities of life. Indeed, Freud characterized the ego as working "in the service of the reality principle."

The superego corresponds closely with what we commonly call conscience. It consists of restraints, acquired in the course of personality development, on the activity of the ego and the id. The superego may condemn as wrong certain things which the ego would do in order to satisfy the id's motives. In addition, the superego keeps a person working toward the ideals—the ego ideals—he acquired in childhood.

Freud's conception of personality structure sums up three major aspects of personality. In early chapters, particularly Chapter 6, we described these aspects in different terms. The first aspect, equivalent in some ways to the id, consists of unlearned biologically based motives and unlearned reactions for satisfying them. The second, corresponding to the ego, is made up of learned instrumental acts for satisfying motives and also of the perceived self discussed earlier in this chapter. The third, represented by the superego, is the set of socially derived motives that affect, and sometimes conflict with, the first two factors. Thus Freud's

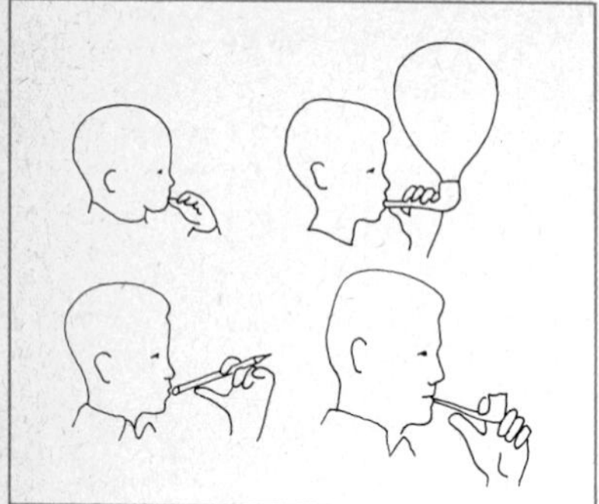

THE ORAL STAGES OF MAN

Figure 11.5 *The expression of orality. Changes occur in the normal expression of oral behavior as a person grows older. Fixation at the oral stage may produce an oral syndrome characterized by excessive oral behavior and such traits as greediness, dependence, and passivity. (After Wattenberg, 1955.)*

basic ideas of personality structure, although clothed in different terminology, are in general accord with the conclusions of experimental psychology.

The objection has been made that the Freudian view of personality structure divides personality into three compartments, each of which seems to be a separate personality. It is indeed easy to slip into this way of viewing the id, ego, and superego, but this was not what Freud intended. The three terms represent convenient concepts for summarizing major aspects of personality that have no clear lines separating them. They provide a general picture which, when considered in detail, becomes very complicated.

Two of Freud's additional points about personality structure should be kept in mind here. First, the libido—that is, the energy of the motives or instincts of the id—is frequently blocked by the ego and superego. When it is, this energy may be *displaced* in other directions to seek outlets that are acceptable to the ego and superego. Second, because the id is frequently in *conflict* with the ego and superego, *anxiety* is aroused. The person then seeks ways to reduce his anxiety. The methods of reducing anxiety that he learns are the defense mechanisms we discussed earlier.

PERSONALITY DEVELOPMENT Freud conceived of personality as developing from infancy to adulthood through several overlapping stages. The first are the *pregenital stages:* the oral stage, the anal stage, and the phallic stage. Then comes a *latency stage,* and finally the *genital stage* is entered at puberty. It is possible, according to Freud, for the person to become fixated in any one of the pregenital stages if he experiences unusual frustration, insecurity, or anxiety at that point in his development. Fixation in a pregenital stage is characterized by certain personality syndromes, or patterns, in the adult.

The *oral stage* occupies much of the first year of life. The infant receives pleasure from sucking and other activities involving his mouth. If he is prevented from sucking, or is made anxious about it, he may acquire an *oral fixation.* Later in life the *oral syndrome* is considered to include excessive oral behavior (see Figure 11.5) and such adult personality traits (or *character traits,* as the Freudians call them) as greediness, dependence, and passivity.

The *anal stage* is most prominent during the second and third years of life. According to Freud, the child focuses his interest on anal activities largely owing to parental attempts to toilet-train him and to suppress "naughty" behavior connected with excretion. If training is too strict and arouses anxieties about these activities, it may be that the adult *anal syndrome* is one of compulsiveness and excessive conformity or self-control.

After toilet training is mastered, the child focuses his interest on his sexual organs. In the pregenital *phallic stage,* the child typically develops "romantic" feelings toward the parent of the opposite sex: the girl toward her father, the boy toward his mother. For boys, Freud called this the *Oedipus complex*, after the mythical story of Oedipus, who unwittingly killed his father and, upon becoming King of Thebes, just as unwittingly married his mother.

The phallic stage with its accompanying Oedipal complex is perhaps the most crucial one in development, according to Freudian theory. In this stage, the child is supposed to feel that he is threatened with dire punishment for the romantic attachment to the parent of the opposite sex. For boys, this punishment is supposed to be a direct or symbolic threat of castration by the jealous father. The threat produces anxiety and defenses against this anxiety. In the normal case, the defense which eventually emerges is an *identification* with the threatening parent. It is as if the little boy said to himself; "If I become like daddy, I can express my affection toward mother as he does." So the boy begins to become like the father, and in the process of doing so, takes on the behavioral patterns and ideas, especially ideas about right and wrong, which are characteristic of his culture. For girls, the situation is a little different and more complicated, but the principles are similar. In other words, identification and, through it, indoctrination into the culture are supposed to be the outcomes of resolution of the Oedipal conflict. In terms of psychoanalytic theory, the superego, or conscience and ego ideal, develops from resolution of the Oedipal situation. On the other hand, if the Oedipal situation is not resolved by the child, the adult may end up with a weak conscience and distorted relations with his friends and with members of the opposite sex.

Following the pregenital stages, and beginning at about age 6, the *latency period* is said to begin. In this period, running from 6 to about the onset of puberty, no important new psychological mechanisms are said to emerge. It is a period of elaboration and strengthening of the defense mechanisms which arose in the pregenital stages to protect the individual against anxiety-producing conflicts. It is also a period in which the ego expands as the child learns about the world around him during the school years.

The latency period is followed by the *genital stage* at puberty. When a person enters the genital stage, instead of centering interest upon himself as he did in the earlier stages, normal heterosexual interests emerge, and interests begin to focus more and more on others and on playing the normal roles of an adult in society.

PERSONALITY DYNAMICS The psychoanalytic theory of personality is both a deterministic and a dynamic theory. The theory states that thoughts and behavior are caused by motives. The motives are the id instincts and urges which seek expression. However, many of these impulses would arouse a great deal of anxiety if they were expressed directly, because they are in conflict with ego and superego forces. Therefore the id urges are repressed and are expressed only in disguised form, if at all. When disguised, the id instincts may gain expression without causing so much anxiety. Thus because of repression, we are not usually aware of the id motives, and for this reason they are called *unconscious motives.* Unconscious motivation is, perhaps, the underlying dynamic force in Freudian psychoanalytic theory.

For example, the Freudian interpretation of dreams is based on the idea of unconscious id urges. Dreams are supposed to be the disguised manifestations, sometimes called "wish fulfillments," of id motives (see page 387). In everyday life, the existence of id urges may be revealed by slips of the tongue and selective forgetting. In a book called *The Psychopathology of Everyday Life,* Freud analyzed the disguised manifestation of id motives. (Freud, 1914). The following examples are from the edition of this book translated by A. A. Brill:[1]

A woman wrote to her sister, felicitating her on the occasion of taking possession of a new and spacious residence. A friend who was present noticed that the writer put the wrong address on the letter, and what was still more remarkable was the fact that she did not address it to the previous residence, but to one long ago given up, but which her sister had occupied when she first married. When the friend called her attention to it, the writer remarked, "You are right; but what in the world made me do this?" to which her friend replied: "Perhaps you begrudge her the nice big apartment into which she has just moved because you yourself are cramped for space, and for that reason you put her back into her first residence, where she was no better off than yourself." "Of course I begrudge her the new apartment," she honestly admitted. As an afterthought she added, "It is a pity that one is so mean in such matters."

Ernest Jones reports the following example given to him by Dr. A. A. Brill. In a letter to Dr. Brill, a patient tried to attribute his nervousness to business worries and excitement during the cotton crisis. He went on to say: "My trouble is all due to that d— frigid wave; there isn't even any seed to be obtained for new crops." He referred to a cold wave which had destroyed the cotton crops, but instead of writing "wave" he wrote "wife." In the bottom of his heart, he entertained reproaches against his wife on account of her marital frigidity and childlessness, and he was not far from the cognition that the enforced abstinence played no little part in the causation of his malady.

The psychoanalyst is adept at interpreting many behaviors and trains of thought in terms of unconscious id motives. In so doing, he assumes that behavior is determined by unconscious motives and that the particular behavior or thought which is expressed is a disguised expression of an id urge.

PSYCHOANALYSIS AND SCIENCE Although some psychoanalysts would disagree, psychoanalytic theory, and for that matter many of the other theories of personality mentioned here, are not scientific theories in the usual sense of the term. Psychoanalytic theory is based on clinical impressions and not on careful measurement under controlled conditions. The theory is intuitive—literary and verbal—a set of seemingly plausible guesses about the structure, origins, and dynamics of personality. The intuitive and literary nature of psychoanalysis is both its strength and its weakness. The guesses of Freud and others about unconscious motives, the development of such motives, their frustrations, and the defense mechanisms which result can all be made to fit almost everyone by appropriate manipulation of the symbols and terms of the theory. But do the terms of the theory describe facts—situations or entities which can be measured and demonstrated under controlled conditions without elaborate interpretation? For instance, is there really a phallic stage in development which has the properties attributed to it by psychoanalytic

[1] From *The Basic Writings of Sigmund Freud,* trans. and ed. by A. A. Brill. Copyright 1938 by Random House, Inc. Copyright renewed 1965 by Gioia B. Bernheim and Edmund Brill. Reprinted by permission.

theory? Evidence on this and similar points is at best moderately convincing.

Thus most psychologists find themselves in an ambivalent position with regard to psychoanalysis—it cannot be tested the way they would like to see it tested, but at the same time, some aspects of it seem like valid hunches. The ideas of unconscious motivation, repression, and defense mechanisms have found their way into many branches of academic psychology and, for that matter, into much of Western thought. Perhaps the best advice which can be given about psychoanalysis and related theories is that one should approach them with caution.

Superiority and compensation Freud's theory emphasizes the biological drives—sex, in particular. Most other theories place somewhat greater emphasis on social factors. One of these, proposed by Alfred Adler, an early disciple of Freud who later rejected Freudian theory, emphasizes a drive or striving for *superiority,* or power. (A discussion of the theory as it relates to therapy is given in Chapter 13.)

It is to Adler that we owe the concept of the *inferiority complex,* a phrase now part of everyday speech. Because we strive for power, argued Adler, we are always seeing ways in which we fall short of our aspirations, and hence ways in which we are inferior. This itself is healthy, for feeling our weakness in first one respect and then another provides things for us "to work on." We are forever striving to overcome our inferiorities. But an inferiority complex develops when a person regularly fails to overcome his weaknesses, or when for any reason he comes to put too much emphasis on any particular inferiority.

From Adler, too, we have the concept of *compensation* (see page 378). Being aware of a weakness, we may strive especially hard to overcome it. The person who, like Theodore Roosevelt, is fragile and sickly as a child may throw himself into physical activities and *overcompensate* for handicaps or inferiorities. In many instances, because of overcompensation, people ultimately become superior in areas where they were originally inferior. In addition, people may compensate for inferiority by achieving distinction in some other area. For example, a frail boy may become superior in academic things when he fails in athletics. This kind of compensation resembles Freud's idea of displacement; the difference lies in the motivation. Freud's displacement is an outlet for libidinal motives; Adler's compensation is a means of satisfying the striving for superiority.

Anxiety theory Most theories give anxiety an important place in their scheme of things. Freud considered anxiety the outcome of conflicts between the id, ego, and superego. Another theorist, Karen Horney, made the concept of *basic anxiety* central to her theory (Horney, 1937). Moreover, she believed that this anxiety arises from social influences in the development of the child, rather than from the conflict between biological motives and the ego or superego.

According to Horney, basic anxiety is first aroused in the child by any social situation which tends to make him fearful. It can be instigated by threats or domination by the parent, by tension and conflict between the parents, by being required to do too much, by being mistrusted, by criticism, coldness, or indifference, and so on. Once anxiety is aroused, the child attempts to alleviate it by trial-and-error behavior, as any organism might try to solve a problem. In this way he learns certain methods of dealing with anxiety; these in turn form a pattern of "neurotic needs."

A neurotic need is thus a learned need. If the child learns to cope with anxiety by running to his mother for affection and approval, he may develop a neurotic need for affection and approval. If he managed to cope with some anxiety-producing situations by obtaining prestige or personal admiration, he may have a neurotic need for these things. According to this theory, there can be any number of neurotic needs, depending on the things the child learned to need to reduce anxiety. In any given culture, however, certain patterns of needs can be expected to arise. This is because the sources of anxiety tend to form a repetitive pattern from one family to another and from one child to another. Hence Horney has formulated a list of 10 needs, which include needs for such things as affection, dependency, power, prestige, achievement, and self-sufficiency.

Horney's theory, like Freud's and most others, has a place in it for *conflict.* To Horney, however, the major conflict is between needs, simply because some needs are incompatible. If a person develops both a need to have someone to depend on and a need to be self-sufficient and independent, these needs will often conflict. Almost everyone possesses neurotic needs in some degree, but when a person is unable to resolve conflicts between them, some needs tend to dominate his life. He then becomes a "neurotic."

Psychological needs Another theorist, Henry Murray, has an even longer list of needs than Horney, but he arrived at them in a different way (Murray, 1938). Although influenced considerably by Freud, he came to feel that any approach to personality which emphasizes one source of motivation (such as Freud's id, Adler's striving for superiority, or Horney's basic anxiety) oversimplifies matters. He preferred to determine, as empirically as possible, the needs that could be distinguished in a representative sample of people. From extensive material—life histories, projective test data, and interviews—gathered on 51 young men, he formulated a list of 28 needs. (Some of these have already been presented in Table 11.2.) He felt that a large number of needs is required to account for the strivings observed in people.

According to Murray's theory, the psychological needs he has distinguished can be found in almost everyone, but they vary in strength. In one individual, one pattern of needs may be strong; in another individual, another pattern may predominate. It is the strength of the needs and the pattern they form that characterize any particular individual's personality. The Thematic Apperception Test (TAT) was devised to measure these needs (see page 359).

Self-actualization Another theorist, Abraham Maslow, has outlined a theory that for brevity is called the *self-actualization* theory (Maslow, 1954). At first glance, it might seem to be a single-factor theory like Adler's striving for superiority, but it is not. It is a multiple-factor theory which posits five levels of needs arranged in a hierarchy. From lower to higher levels, they are:

Physiological needs, such as hunger, thirst and sex
Safety needs, such as security, stability, and order
Belongingness and love needs, such as needs for affection, affiliation, and identification
Esteem needs, such as needs for prestige, success, and self-respect
Need for self-actualization, or self-fulfillment (see page 546)

The order in which these needs are listed is significant in two ways. This is the order in which they are said to appear in the normal development of the person. It is also the order in which they need to be satisfied. And if earlier needs are not satisfied, the person never gets around to doing much about the later needs. It might be expected from this theory that people in a poor society will be mostly concerned with physiological and safety needs. Those in an "affluent" society, on the other hand, will manage to satisfy the needs lower in the hierarchy and in many cases will be preoccupied with the need for self-actualization.

The need for self-actualization refers to the person's need to develop his full potentialities. Naturally, the meaning of this need varies from person to person, for each has different potentialities. For some, it means achievement in literary or scientific fields; for others, leadership in politics or the community; for still others, merely living their own lives fully without being unduly restrained by social conventions. "Self-actualizers" are found among professors, businessmen, political leaders, missionaries, artists, and housewives. But not all individuals in any of these categories are able to achieve self-actualization; many have numerous unsatisfied needs, and because their achievements are merely compensations, they are left frustrated and unhappy in other respects.

Trait theory Trait theory, which has been developed by Gordon Allport, gives us no finite list of needs or traits (Allport, 1937, 1961). It assumes a multiplicity of needs that are never quite the same from one individual to the next. (This chapter's earlier discussion of the definition of personality and of personality traits was guided by Allport's theory.) It can be distinguished from other theories in two important respects.

One is the concept of the *uniqueness of personality.* Each person, with his unique background of childhood experiences, develops a set of traits that are unique to him.

A second, related feature of the theory is the concept of *functional autonomy of motives.* In the course of development, each person acquires, or learns, motives as part of satisfying other motives (see Chapter 6). These motives, according to Allport, continue to function autonomously without further reinforcement of the physiological conditions originally concerned in their acquisition.

Examples of what seems to be the functional autonomy of motives abound in everyday life. The poor boy who earned his first pennies to ward off hunger and discomfort continues to work day and night at amassing a large fortune long after he has acquired enough money to meet his physical needs. A businessman who approaches retirement age with ample reserves insists on staying at his job, probably because he finds that the job now satisfies his needs for companionship and activities, even though his original motivation for working was to earn a living. Even the persistence of sexual interests in middle age, after hormones are no longer of much importance, has been cited as an example of functional autonomy.

Learning theory of personality Certainly learning plays a major role in the development of the characteristics which differentiate personalities. We have seen that social motives, which are important aspects of personality, are learned. In addition, abilities, attitudes, and interests are shaped by reinforcement (see Chapter 3). Our discussion of the role of the family in the determination of personality traits also stressed the role of learning.

Not only are many of the characteristics of personality learned, but according to learning theory, many modes of adjustment—the defense mechanisms, for example—are learned habits. After all, the defense mechanisms are techniques for reducing anxiety, and the reduction of anxiety is reinforcing (Dollard and Miller, 1950). Thus some of the terms and dynamics of Freudian psychoanalysis can be translated into the terms of experimental psychology. The advantage of this is that some experimental rigor can be applied to the intuitions of psychoanalysis. (A discussion of learning in psychotherapy is given in Chapter 13.)

Other personality theories Several "neoanalytic" theories of personality give far more importance to social factors in development than Freud did (see Monroe, 1955). Erich Fromm, for instance, has stressed the fact that the infant as he grows up eventually becomes free from his parents. However, this new freedom produces a sense of isolation and separateness, and the individual attempts to "escape from freedom" (Fromm, 1941). Fromm lists several basic mechanisms of escape by which the person attempts to relate himself to primary groups in order to lose his feeling of separateness. These escape mechanisms are important aspects and themes of personality as it is seen by Fromm.

According to Harry Stack Sullivan, the learning that takes place in interpersonal situations is basic in the development of personality (Sullivan, 1953). Personality arises in stages as the individual interacts with other people who are significant in his life. For instance, an infant may develop anxiety if the "mothering one" expresses anxiety when caring for him; there seems to be a kind of empathic communication of anxiety from mother to infant. Such early social learning may form the nucleus for later evaluations of, and reactions in, symbolically similar interpersonal situations. (A more detailed discussion of this theory as it relates to psychotherapy is given in Chapter 13, page 450).

Erik Erikson has stressed the search for *ego integrity* as a basic human motive (Erikson, 1963). The search for integrity involves identification with figures in the culture, and this is supposed to be difficult in modern Western society where models for identification are weak and goals of the society are vague. The development of ego identity procedes through eight stages. At each of the first seven stages, a particular problem must be solved before ego integrity is reached in the eighth stage. Even in this eighth stage, however, ego identity is still threatened. The eight problems and stages are (1) trust versus basic mistrust, (2) autonomy versus shame and doubt, (3) initiative versus guilt, (4) industry versus inferiority, (5) identity versus role diffusion, (6) intimacy versus isolation, (7) generativity "doing things" versus stagnation, (8) ego integrity versus despair.

In recent years, psychoanalytic theory has been concerned more with rational aspects of personality—the ego, in other words—than with the expression of id instincts and motives (Hartmann, 1964; Kris, 1950). Many other variants of psychoanalytic theory exist, and the interested student will find it rewarding to consult other references.

Scientific validity of personality theories What can we make of all these theories that attempt to explain our distinctive and consistent characteristics—our personalities? One of the first things to say is that they differ in their purpose and in their comprehensiveness. Trait theory, for example, tries to provide a way of ordering much of the complex data about human personality; but this is a limited goal. Psychoanalytic personality theory, on the other hand, attempts to present a comprehensive theory of personality development. But none of the theories is really comprehensive. All are based on a very limited set of observations, and they ascribe a great deal to a limited set of motive forces.

A second, and perhaps more important point is that most of the theories are not based upon controlled observations; instead they represent the intuitive best guesses of a number of brilliant and sensitive people. In that respect, personality theories are a bit like some aspects of literary criticism. But maybe this is as it must be. The complexities of human personality have not been easy to study by controlled experimentation and observation, and we should probably be grateful to the theorists who are willing to take a chance in speculating about this important aspect of human existence. Certainly some of their speculations have been useful. In the last few decades, however, there have been an increasing number of controlled studies in the areas of learning, child development, motivation, socialization, and behavior disorders. It seems likely that in the next 50 years of psychology there will be less theorizing that is general and intuitive and more that is factually based.

Synopsis and summary

The unique organization of characteristics which comprises the human personality is not easy to study, but some progress has been made. Experimental psychology has contributed knowledge about motivation, learning, and frustration and conflict. Child psychology has contributed experimental and observational studies on the development of personality characteristics. Psychological testing, or psychometrics, has contributed techniques for the measurement of personality characteristics. Psychiatry has contributed the insights of psychoanalytic and other theories of personality. In time, we hope, these areas of inquiry will bring us to a more complete understanding of the structure and dynamics of personality.

1. In psychology the study of personality is concerned with the behavioral differences between people and the consistency of individual behavior. Personality study focuses on the behavior of particular individuals rather than on general laws of behavior.

2. One often quoted definition of personality is that it is "the dynamic organization within the individual of those psychophysical systems that determine his characteristic behavior and thought" (Allport, 1961).
3. Psychologists frequently distinguish personality from character and temperament. In American usage, character refers to the ethical or moral qualities of an individual. Temperament refers to a person's ease of emotional arousal, his characteristic form of emotional expression, and his typical mood state.
4. Characteristics which distinguish individuals from one another are important in the study of personality. One set of characteristics may serve one purpose in describing personality, another set another purpose.
5. We can characterize personalities by studying people's traits, their abilities, attitudes, and interests, their typical motives, and their typical modes of adjustment and defense mechanisms.
6. Personality is not just a collection of specific traits; the traits are organized in distinctive ways so that they uniquely characterize a person. The organization of personality traits is consistent and persistent and changes only slowly. Although each personality is unique, there are certain organizations of personality traits, called personality syndromes, that are common to many people.
7. The self—the individual's self-awareness or perception of his own personality—develops through his being treated as a single entity during childhood. The self is what we subjectively experience as our personality. A person's perception of the self has an important bearing on his relations with others and on his emotional development.
8. Personality has a dynamic aspect as well as a static nature, or structure. Adjustment to motivational, situational, and personal conflicts is a key concept of personality dynamics. Such adjustment may be accomplished by gradual learning or by the more or less automatic defense mechanisms. These mechanisms are important modes of adjustment serving to reduce anxiety arising from motive frustration and to enhance the evaluation of the self.
9. Some major defense mechanisms are (*a*) repression—which is a kind of protective and automatic "forgetting," (*b*) reaction formation—in which the person disguises anxiety-producing motives by fooling himself into thinking that the motive driving his behavior is the opposite of the true motive, (*c*) projection—in which the person disguises an unacceptable motive by ascribing his own motives to other people, (*d*) displacement—which involves disguising the object or goal of the motive by shifting it to a substitute goal, (*e*) rationalization—in which unacceptable motives are disguised by explaining them away in socially approved ways, (*f*) sublimation and compensation—which use substitute, less anxiety-arousing, activities to satisfy motives, (*g*) fantasy—in which frustrated motives are gratified in imagination, (*h*) regression—which is a retreat to more primitive behaviors that may restore self-confidence in the face of a threat to self-esteem, (*i*) identification—in which the individual enhances self-esteem by imagining that he is like some more powerful person or group.
10. If not used to an exaggerated degree, defense mechanisms are normal and useful ways of reducing conflict. But they do not solve problems; they only disguise the real problem. And they may not work in new situations or in situations in which anxiety is severe. For these reasons defense mechanisms should not be used to excess.
11. Personality traits and the self-concept have a developmental history. The major determiners of personality characteristics in development are biological inheritance, culture, and the individual's experiences within the family circle.
12. As the agent of socialization, the family exerts its influence on its developing members through the type of emotional climate it creates, through the learning situations it presents, through the attitudes of the parents, and through the models of behavior it provides.
13. Theories of personality are attempts to integrate the diversity of data about human personality by providing sets of basic principles from which particular facts can be derived. The major theories described in this chapter include psychoanalytic theory (Freud), superiority and compensation theory (Adler), anxiety theory (Horney), psychological need theory (Murray), self-actualization theory (Maslow), trait theory (Allport), the learning theories, and other "neoanalytic" theories of personality.
14. Freud conceived of three major aspects of personality structure: (*a*) the id as a storehouse of motives and instincts, (*b*) the ego as the part of personality that attempts to cope realistically with the world, and (*c*) the superego as a conscience that restrains the ego and the id and keeps a person working toward ideals acquired in childhood.
15. Freud also conceived of personality development as proceeding through the following stages: (*a*) oral, (*b*) anal, (*c*) phallic, (*d*) latency, and (*e*) genital.
16. The dynamic aspects of Freudian psychoanalytic theory are perhaps its most important feature. Many behaviors and thoughts are interpreted as disguised expressions of unconscious motives. It is this aspect of psychoanalytic theory that has made it an appealing explanation of much human behavior.

Related topics in the text

Chapter 2 Behavioral Inheritance
Many personality characteristics that differentiate people are due to differences in their inherited potentialities for behavior.

Chapter 3 Principles of Learning
Many personality traits, some aspects of adjustment, are learned.

Chapter 6 Motivation Motives are important aspects of the structure and dynamics of personality.

Chapter 7 Arousal, Emotion, and Conflict The sources of motive frustration, especially conflicts between motives, and the emotional reactions to frustration, are discussed in Chapter 7. The defense mechanisms serve in part to protect the individual against these emotional consequences of frustration.

Chapter 10 Psychological Testing The measurement of personality traits is an important aspect of scientific work on personality.

Chapter 12 Behavior Disorders Deviant or abnormal personalities are the result of many causes, biological and environmental.

Chapter 13 Therapy for Behavior Disorders Some of the personality theories are discussed more fully as they relate to psychotherapy.

Chapter 14 Social Influences on Behavior The influence of culture and social class on personality is elaborated.

Suggestions for further reading

Allport, G. W. *Pattern and growth in personality.* New York: Holt, 1961.
A revision of one of the classic texts on personality, first published in 1937. It is nontechnical and easily read.

Baughman, E. E. *Personality: The psychological study of the individual.* Englewood Cliffs, N.J.: Prentice-Hall, 1972.
An important and interesting text stressing the uniqueness and the consistency of personality.

Brenner, C. *An elementary textbook of psychoanalysis.* Garden City, N.Y.: Doubleday, 1957. (Paperback.)
A book which is intended, in the words of the author, "to provide a clear and comprehensive exposition of the fundamentals of psychoanalytic theory."

Byrne, D. *An introduction to personality: A research approach.* Englewood Cliffs, N.J.: Prentice-Hall, 1966.
Stresses experimental studies of personality structure, dynamics, and change.

Dollard, J., and Miller, N.E. *Personality and psychotherapy: An analysis in terms of learning, thinking and culture.* New York: McGraw-Hill, 1950. (Paperback available.)
Learning theory as applied to the dynamics of personality.

Freud, S. *New introductory lectures on psychoanalysis.* New York: Norton, 1933. (Paperback available.)
Lectures to a lay audience which illustrate Freud's style of reasoning and some of the most important points of his theory.

Freud, S. *The basic writings of Sigmund Freud.* (Trans. A. A. Brill.) New York: Random House, 1938.
Selections from some of the most important works of the founder of psychoanalysis.

Hall, C. S. *A primer of Freudian psychology.* Cleveland: World, 1954. (Paperback.)
A clearly written, systematic description of Freudian theory which tries to emphasize his contributions to the psychology of normal people.

Hall, C. S., and Lindzey, G. *Theories of personality* (2d ed). New York: Wiley, 1970. *A comprehensive treatment of the major personality theories.*

Janis, I. L., Mahl, G. F., Kagan, J., and Holt, R. R. *Personality: Dynamics, development, and assessment.* New York: Harcourt, Brace & World, 1969.
A factual approach to personality. The authors summarize much of the current knowledge about stress and frustration, conflict and defense, personality development, and the assessment of personality. The book does not emphasize personality theories.

Lindzey, G., and Hall, C. S., (Eds.). *Theories of personality: Primary sources and research.* New York: Wiley, 1965.
A book of readings on personality theories.

Lundin, R. W. *Personality: A behavioral analysis.* New York: Macmillan, 1969.
The study of personality from the point of view of modern behaviorism, or behavior theory.

McCurdy, H. G. *The personal world.* New York: Harcourt, Brace & World, 1961.
A text that departs from the usual mold of personality books. It covers many interesting topics and brings new insights and ideas to bear on the study of personality.

Mussen, P. H., Conger, J. J., and Kagan, J. *Child development and personality.* (3d ed.) New York: Harper & Row, 1969.
A textbook on child psychology. Some of the chapters deal with socialization and the learning of personality characteristics in infancy and childhood.

Sarason, I. G. *Personality: An objective approach.* New York: Wiley, 1966.
A general book on personality from an empirical point of view. Contains sections on personality theories, personality assessment, the experimental study of personality, personality development, and deviant behavior.

White, R. W. *Lives in progress: A study of the natural growth of personality.* (2d ed.) New York: Holt, 1966. (Paperback available.)
Intensive case study analysis of personality development in a few individuals. In the case histories, many important factors that shape personality can be seen at work.

PART THREE
DISTURBED BEHAVIOR

Everyone is queer save thee and me, and sometimes I think thee a bit queer too.
Quaker proverb

In the last chapter we considered normal personality development and structure. As people go through life, their natures, or constitutions, interact with their environment. Certain traits emerge, certain motives are learned, and normal methods are developed for adjusting to the inevitable conflicts and problems of life. But in some people, nature and nurture interact in ways that produce behaviors labeled "abnormal."

What is abnormal behavior? In most cases, no sharp line divides normal from abnormal behavior; the distinction is just a matter of degree. Only when a person is markedly unhappy, or when he fails to use his talents, or when he suffers from anxiety to an unusual extent, or when his behavior becomes a nuisance or a danger to other people is he considered abnormal.

Abnormal behavior is difficult to classify, probably because it grades into normal behavior and because each individual has his unique history and has developed his particular pattern of reacting to the environment. Another problem in classifying abnormal behavior is that what is considered abnormal differs from cultural group to cultural group. The patterns of behavior called "normal" are those which are culturally approved; those called "abnormal" are those which are not culturally approved. Hence abnormal behavior cannot be neatly pigeonholed the way infectious diseases can be identified by the organism causing the disease. On the other hand, certain general patterns of disordered, or abnormal, behavior that are characteristic of our culture can be named and described in some detail. This chapter employs terms from the 1952 and 1968 editions of the *Diagnostic and Statistical Manual of Mental Disorders* of the American Psychiatric Association and from other sources. It does not catalog all behavior disorders or follow a rigorous diagnostic system; its more modest aim is to acquaint the student with some of the major types of behavior disorders, of which certain very general types can be distinguished.

This chapter discusses several of these general kinds of behavior disorders. For instance, many people have relatively mild life adjustment problems. Other people, whose problems are labeled *neuroses*, are usually anxiety-ridden and may develop exaggerated defense mechanisms to reduce their anxieties. People with *personality disorders* may express aggression by pronounced stubbornness, they may be generally withdrawn, they may behave sexually in ways which are considered deviant, they may be addicted to alcohol or drugs, or they may lack conscience and feeling for the rights of others. People who have another

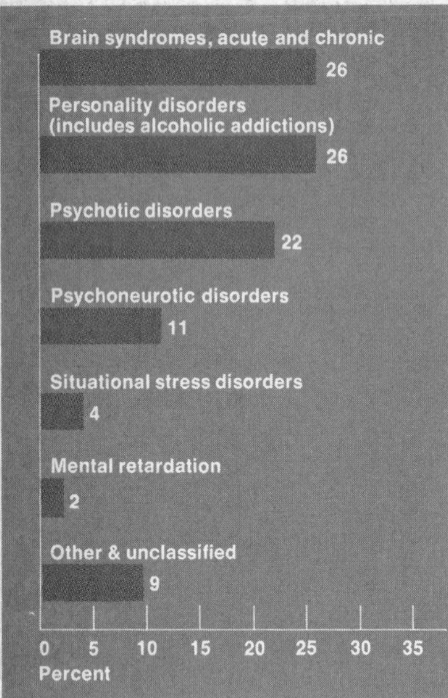

MOST PATIENTS ADMITTED FOR THE FIRST TIME TO MENTAL HOSPITALS HAVE BRAIN SYNDROMES, PERSONALITY DISORDERS, OR PSYCHOTIC DISORDERS

Figure 12.1 *Percentages of patients in particular diagnostic categories upon first admission to state and county mental hospitals, 1968. First admissions for all categories that year totaled 175,637. The order of the three largest categories changes occasionally, but they consistently remain at the top. (Biometry Branch, National Institute of Mental Health.)*

general type of behavior disorder—a *psychosis*—may experience hallucinations and delusions and act in bizarre ways. Still other people, who are said to be suffering from *chronic brain syndromes,* may have brains so severely damaged that they do not function adequately. Chronic brain syndrome patients, psychotic patients, and those with personality disorders compose the majority of first admissions to mental hospitals, as can be seen from Figure 12.1. These are some of the major types of behavior disorders, but psychologists and psychiatrists today are not content with mere categorization. Rather, they are trying to find causes and ways of preventing and alleviating these behavior disorders.

The extent and distribution of the more severe behavior problems are discussed in greater detail at the beginning of Chapter 13. The general picture is that about one person in ten will, at some time in his life, be treated in a mental hospital. This statistic, of course, does not cover people with mild problems of adjustment—problems characterized by symptoms of unhappiness, aimlessness, and unproductiveness. Most of us experience these symptoms during certain periods in our lives, and fortunately, for most of us they are transitory. We know that problems of adjustment, such as the case described in the following section, are very common, but we cannot even guess at their exact frequency.

Mild Adjustment Problems

The course of life is never smooth. Motives must be satisfied, but frustrating situations and competing motives inevitably arise. Unhappiness, feelings of worthlessness, anxiety, behavior which is unproductive, self-defeating, and contradictory—all are symptoms of the sorts of mild adjustment problems which may develop when learned and social motives (see Chapters 6 and 7) are frustrated. The case of Joseph Kidd illustrates the symptoms in a typical mild, transient adjustment problem. It also shows how the causes of a disturbance can be analyzed.

Joseph Kidd's case Although the roots of Joseph Kidd's problem lay in the frustration of a learned motive, notice as you read his case that the pattern of frustration involved many particular maladaptive behaviors. Also note that in order to analyze his problem, he must be seen as a complex individual with certain abilities, habits, personality traits, and attitudes, as well as a particular family background. All these factors interacted with the frustration to produce his behavior, so that the clinician attempting to understand his symptoms had to bring information to bear from many sources.

Present difficulties At his lowest point, during his junior year at college, Joseph Kidd suffered from acute distress in all relations with people. He was bothered by severe self-consciousness, feeling always a painful uncertainty as to his standing in the opinion of others, and with this went an irresistible submissiveness designed to avoid conflict with people and win their favor. He could neither control this submissiveness nor accept it. If anyone showed him friendliness he immediately, as he put it, "began acting like his son or kid brother," but he was ashamed of this afterwards and wished that he could behave like a man. "I can't make a decision on my own and back it up," he wrote at one point; "it's always guided by some factor outside my own intellect." With his girl he was equally troubled. He was completely dependent on her affection and very jealous if she so much as danced with somebody else. Realizing that he acted toward her "too much like a spoiled child, crying for my own way," he yet could not bring himself to take a more manly and independent attitude. In consequence it became increasingly clear that the girl was bored with him and did not really respect him.

Why did he not take a different attitude? He wanted to, and there was every inducement to do so, but in this respect he was not free. The pattern of his personality was such as to resist this particular change. He expected people to give him a great deal of easy appreciation; when they did not do so, he was worried and hungrily asked for it. Kidd felt that he had no personality of his own, and he tried the following rather desperate expedient:

"I began trying to fit a personality to my make-up. I began acting out personalities, and tried observing people and copying them. But these personalities were all short-lived because they pleased some and not others and because they didn't produce that underlying purpose of making people like me; and every time, unconsciously, I would resort to my childish attitude to make myself noticeable. Examples of these personalities are independence (but I couldn't keep it up); arrogance (but people were arrogant back at me); hatefulness (people paid no attention to me); extreme niceness (people took advantage of it, kidded me about it); humorous nature (but I was only being childish, silly); quiet and studious (but people were only passing me by and I kept feeling I was missing something). I became a daydreamer so intensively that now I find I'm daydreaming almost all the time. I became conscious of a person's approach and would become flustered, would try to make a friend of him no matter who he was, but I overdid it."

Clearly Kidd's problem was not an unusual one. It is a universal problem to develop adult independent attitudes. Everyone learns from experience how to adapt successfully to the people around him; everyone finds out gradually what roles are congenial to himself and others. It is also a universal problem to develop a stable conception of oneself, an enduring sense of personal identity. Kidd's case is peculiar not in kind but in degree. It will be noticed that he was satisfied with a "personality" only if it pleased everybody; he was unwilling that anyone should fail to notice and like him. From his own description we can see that he was making a frantic search for affectionate esteem. His overwhelming motive was to make people like him, and his well-practiced method, when all else failed, was to make himself noticeable. Failure cast him into despondency and alarm. At times he lapsed into passive daydreaming, but at other times he struggled to learn new and more appropriate attitudes. Eventually, as we shall see, his struggle met with success.

Personal history Whenever it appears that a disorder lies in the sphere of motives and the acquired methods for satisfying them, we must look for enlightenment in the past history. Joseph Kidd was the second son of hard-working, socially ambitious parents. He was a very pretty child with blue eyes and long golden curls, far more attractive than his older and younger brothers. His delighted parents showered him with notice and praise. His early memories were crowded with scenes in which he was patted on the head, dressed up, shown off, placed in the center of attention; once the teacher stood him on her desk so that all the pupils might see his new velvet suit with lace collar. He basked happily in this warm light of admiration. The effect on his subsequent development was not so happy. For one thing, his constant exposure to the eyes and praises of other people laid the foundation for that intense self-consciousness which later harassed him. For another thing, he was receiving praise for gratuitous qualities—for good looks and fine clothes, or at best for slight accomplishments—so that he felt little incentive to work for what he got. He formed a habitual expectation of high esteem income received at no greater cost than making himself noticeable.

In school Kidd progressed well, and through the machinations of his ambitious mother he was given a double promotion from the fourth to the sixth grade. This put him in the same class as his older brother and automatically made him the youngest and smallest of his immediate group. To keep up his popularity he fell into the role of what he called "a clown and a stooge"; he made the other boys laugh and did errands for them. Entering high school in a distant neighborhood, he found these roles no longer productive of esteem. His income in this respect was sharply lowered when he realized that his new companions were contemptuous of his childish ways. Filled with resentment at this turn of events, he began to feel that everyone was against him; so he withdrew from sports and social activities and spent his time at home listening to the radio. He experienced great shame over masturbation, which further increased his feeling of inferiority and unwillingness to mingle with others. Even his interest in studies dwindled, so that he barely passed his examinations for college.

At college he found nothing in the curriculum that awakened enduring interest. His failure to make friends soon cost him the esteem of his parents, who looked upon college as a means of social advancement and compared him unfavorably with his sociable brothers; in addition, he seriously offended his parents by espousing the theory of evolution which they considered at variance with their religious faith. As we have seen, his girl began to withhold her esteem. He sought consolation in promiscuous sexual episodes, which gave him at least a momentary feeling that he was acceptable as a man and could get what he wanted. But when he regaled his fellow students with these proofs of his enterprise and manhood, he got much less admiration than he expected. He who had been rich was now indeed destitute of esteem.

Spontaneous recovery Under these circumstances it is not surprising that his mediocre academic record went completely to pieces and that he was presently looking for a job. It was at this point that his suffering was most acute and that he fully realized the failure of the various "personalities" he had been trying to assume. After a while, however, things began to go more favorably. He took the step of leaving home to escape the now irksome parental supervision, and he parted with his girl. He found a small business position, acquitted himself well, and enjoyed the company of other young people in the office, most of whom were college graduates. It was a white-collar job which met his parents' social expectations, so that he was somewhat restored in their favor. He resumed his interest in sports and began to read instead of daydreaming. Another girl came upon the scene. Starting the relation on a better footing, he was soon the happy recipient of a fair esteem income from her. His life was again moving forward, and he began to be mildly satisfied with himself.

Having made a good work record for a year, he was permitted to return to college. Ultimately he graduated, but at the cost of a setback in his personal development. Many of the old problems reappeared, particularly his distaste for study and his hunger for the good opinion of his fellow students. When he entered military service it was with a decided sense of relief: at last he could put school behind him and silence his parents' clamor for further professional training. As a private in a health survey unit he was not exposed to the dangers of combat, and he found great satisfaction in the comradeship of the other men in the unit. He resumed the social growth that had been brought to a standstill by his double promotion at school and subsequent estrangement from other boys. He became more assertive, but not to the point of welcoming the role of officer, in which he did so badly that he was at one point demoted. "I like to be *with* fellows," he said, "not *over* them." Some years later he looked back to his period in the Army as the happiest time in his life.

Returning to the family home, he was at first immersed in some of the old conflicts, but the changes in his personality proved to be enduring. He was no longer at the mercy of parental desires, nor was he enslaved by his hunger for esteem. When an opportunity arose to reorganize his father's dwindling business he took charge of the project and carried it to a successful conclusion. This accomplishment substantially increased his self-respect as well as his income of esteem from others; it also permitted him to feel that he had repaid his parents for their earlier sacrifices on his behalf. Throughout these developments his environment was fairly kind to him, but he displayed initiative and took an active part in overcoming his difficulties. Under moderately favorable circumstances he proved capable of developing new channels for satisfying his needs and promoting his growth. It is this that distinguishes Kidd's maladjustment from the more severe psychological disorders. (Robert W. White, *The Abnormal Personality,* 3d ed. Copyright © 1964 The Ronald Press Company. Pages 55–58.)

Analysis of the case Joseph Kidd was lucky because his problems, although a bother to himself and his family, lasted for a relatively brief time and he did eventually make a good adjustment. But why, after so promising a beginning, did he have difficulties?

This case has been analyzed in terms of the interaction between Kidd's learned motives and his abilities (White, 1964). Need for esteem was especially great because of the learning experiences of childhood. Kidd had come to expect to be appreciated for just being around—not for any particular talent or skill. In high school and college, things changed. No longer was esteem given for being a "cute" little fellow, and Kidd, in whom this motive was strong, had no other skills for obtaining esteem. He was not particularly clever, strong, or given to active participation in sports—all talents esteemed in high school and college. He tried various artificial ways of meeting his esteem needs, but through lack of ability, he did not succeed. Kidd also began to develop some hostility toward those who were frustrating his needs for esteem—those whom he wanted to have as his friends. This, of course, made it less likely than ever that his esteem motive would be satisfied. In trying to find himself, he was preoccupied with his own problems, and his college work suffered.

Kidd began to lead a happier and more productive life after he had experiences which made him feel valued. His army experience, his better relationship with a new girl friend, and his success with his father's business all satisfied his esteem needs, gave him a feeling of success, and enabled him to find a pattern of life that made esteem possible. By the time Kidd had reached his forties, he had become a successful and very stable person. He had managed to use his considerable talents in a constructive way to satisfy his esteem needs by success in business and politics; his feelings of inferiority were gone (White, 1966). However, some of his early problems can still be seen in his relationship with his family. With his own boys, Kidd does not want to repeat the mistakes that were made with him; he has some difficulty deciding on the type of role model he should be. On the one hand he does not want the boys to be too dependent on him; on the other he does not want to reject them. But life is never free of conflicts, and Kidd has shown considerable ability to cope with problems before.

This case is an example of the sort of mild adjustment problems which are due to motivational conflicts and frustration. It also illustrates the kind of spontaneous recovery that often occurs in such situations, and finally, it shows the way a case can be analyzed in terms of basic psychological processes and ideas which we have already discussed—motivation, learning, and abilities.

Psychoneurotic Reactions

People suffering from *psychoneuroses*—or *neuroses,* as they are more commonly called—are anxious people. Often the anxiety is obvious. The person may be constantly apprehensive, worried, or full of complaints; he may have spells when he is overcome by anxiety. Sometimes the anxiety is not so obvious; the person may appear to be relatively free of it, but his reactions can nevertheless be traced to anxiety and his mechanisms for avoiding it (Fenichel, 1945). In these cases, his unusual symptoms and defense mechanisms furnish the clues to his constant battle with anxiety. We shall make no attempt to classify or describe all the variants of neurotic behavior, for they would fill a book. The following descriptions provide a general idea of some typical neurotic reactions.

Anxiety reactions Although anxiety, or the attempt to deal with it, is the mark of neurosis, in many of the neuroses it is concealed by other symptoms. Not so in *anxiety reactions.* In these neuroses, intense and observable anxiety is the principal symptom (see Figure 12.2). The anxiety may be persistent and uncomfortably high most of the time. Or it may come as a sudden attack that lasts from a few hours to several days. An abnormal state of anxiety can make a person thoroughly miserable, force him to the border of panic, and upset his health.

Usually neither the person himself nor those around him can assign a cause to the anxiety. The anxiety may become more intense in, or be precipitated by, a stressful situation or a difficult problem. Yet the precise reason for the intense anxiety is not clear—at least not until the patient's history and the situations that make him anxious have been analyzed. The following case illustrates an anxiety attack as well as the analysis of its causes:

A successful business executive developed acute anxiety attacks which occurred about once every two or three months. The patient's wife was eight years older than he, and he was no longer physically attracted to her. He had found himself increasingly interested in younger women and had begun to think how much more enjoyable it would be to have a younger, more companionable wife. During

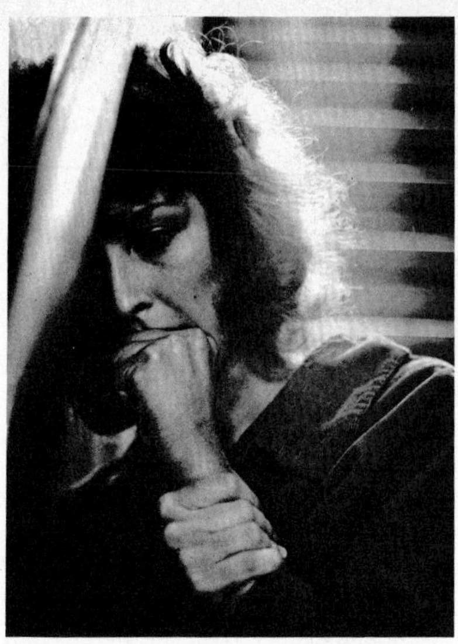

Figure 12.2 The anguish of the anxiety neurotic. (Meade Johnson Laboratories.)

this period, he met a girl with whom he was sure he had fallen in love. It was shortly thereafter that the anxiety attacks began to occur. They were preceded by a period of several days of increased tenseness and anxiety, but the attacks came on suddenly and were very intense.

This man was . . . at a complete loss to explain his attacks. But the explanation was not difficult to find. The patient had had a poverty-stricken and insecure childhood and felt basically inferior, insecure, and threatened by a hard world. These feelings had been intensified when he had failed college courses in his second year, even though the failure had resulted primarily from excessive outside work. He had been able to achieve some security, however, by marrying an older and very strong woman who had instilled considerable self-confidence and initiative in him. The relationship had proved very fruitful financially and the patient was living in a style which as a youth, "I hadn't dared to imagine in my wildest dreams!" His persistent thoughts about divorcing his wife, on whom he felt dependent for his security and style of life, thus represented a severe threat to the moderate adjustment he had achieved. The anxiety attacks followed. (From *Abnormal Psychology and Modern Life,* 3d ed., by James C. Coleman. Copyright © 1964 by Scott, Foresman and Company. Page 199.)

An anxiety neurotic may sometimes find a little relief from his anxiety by adopting certain physical symptoms. If he becomes excessively concerned with his physical welfare or constantly complains of minor ailments, he is called a *hypochondriac.* His complaints are either groundless or grossly exaggerated, but by worrying about his health, he manages to take his mind off the feelings of guilt or inadequacy that otherwise cause him to be unbearably anxious. If the person complains of general nervousness, fatigue, and insomnia, he is called a *neurasthenic.* The word literally means "nervous weakness," and it refers to the person's chronic inability to do anything. The neurasthenic, indeed, frequently claims that he is unable to work because he feels fatigued and worn out all the time. But, of course, the nervous weakness is not due to physical deterioration or disease of the nervous system; the symptoms are psychogenic—they are caused by anxiety. These symptoms, although they incapacitate him, do accomplish something, for they provide him with an excuse and a disguise for some underlying source of anxiety. The following case illustrates a persistent anxiety neurosis with physical symptoms:

Thomas R., an eighteen-year-old high school senior . . . was referred to a counselor because he was failing in his studies and had an attitude of apprehension and despair which was readily noticed by his teachers. Interviews showed that the boy's anxieties were not limited to any definite situation, but widely generalized. He was concerned about his academic standing, and especially about his father's reaction to it. Referring to his possible school failure, he said, "It will be the end for me." He felt an acute social incompetence, and said in a vague manner that he did not know much about the world, and that he had many things to learn. Thomas had little association with girls and appeared to be afraid of them, or rather of his inability to impress them as favorably as the other boys. During the preceding year he had had a few dates with a girl a little older than himself, on which he placed a high value, considering himself in love. The girl went away to

college, and Thomas felt afraid of "losing" her. He was utterly unable to make decisions. The simplest problem caused him to seek advice or to feel incompetent to face the difficulty.

In addition to his anxiety, Thomas had visceral symptoms, centering around his heart. At times his heart beat very rapidly and his pulse pounded in his ears. Although several physicians examined him carefully and reported that he had no organic disorder, Thomas often rested in bed from early Saturday evening until Sunday noon because of his supposed heart disease. The intensity of Thomas's anxiety was best revealed by notes he scribbled from time to time and gave to the counselor. He wrote, "I can never be at rest and am never satisfied. I fear of not being able to control my mental and physical actions. Something is always elusive. I am more afraid of life than the basest coward. Why can't I understand people? Why can I remember only my fears, the vacant mental situations and the lonely places in my life? I seem to exist isolated. All the clean wholesome desires which make a man want to live seem to be crushed. Will I snap out of this, or will I never be a man?"

Thomas's anxiety reaction may be interpreted as a nonadjustive response to all the principal problems of late adolescence. He faces the issues of establishing his independence as a sufficient person, of financial self-support, of the choice of a vocation, and of social and sexual adjustment, quite unable to achieve a satisfactory course of action in any of them. Such an inability to adjust must have its roots in his past learning experiences. In Thomas's case, as in most, the basis was found in the attitudes and personalities of his parents. (Shaffer and Shoben, 1956, pages 277–278.)

Phobic reactions An intense and irrational fear of something is a *phobia.* There are many kinds of phobias, depending upon the object of the fear. *Claustrophobia,* for example, is an intense, unreasonable fear of small, enclosed places; *acrophobia,* an intense, unreasonable fear of high places; *nyctophobia,* fear of the dark; *zoophobia,* fear of animals (see Figure 12.3).

Some people who are otherwise normal and healthy have phobias. The phobias may be mild and rarely evoked; if so, they cause little difficulty. On the other hand, a phobia may be so powerful and irrational that it alters the whole course of a person's life.

One often-quoted example of an intense phobia is the case of the poet and professor at the University of Wisconsin, William Ellery Leonard (1927):

Leonard had a phobia of going more than a few blocks away from his home and the university. For years his phobia kept him a virtual prisoner in this small geographical area. Although he knew of his fear, he did not know its underlying cause. During the course of psychoanalysis, he was able to remember a frightening incident in his childhood. He had wandered away from his home and gone over to the railroad tracks, where a passing train had scalded him with steam. His fear, it developed, originated in this incident, and it proved to be the real motive for his staying near home. The phobia was so powerful that it dominated his whole life. It was never completely eradicated even though he recognized its source and could be objective enough to write a book about it—*The Locomotive God.*

A PHOBIA IS AN INTENSE IRRATIONAL FEAR OF SOMETHING

Figure 12.3 *Four relatively common phobias are represented here. From top to bottom, the photographs at left dramatize fear of high places and fear of small places; those above illustrate fear of darkness and fear of snakes. (Photographs, Alfred Gescheidt; oil painting done during analysis, collection of Dr. Jolande Jacobi, with permission of the painter; drawing, Kubin-Archiv.)*

Such intense fears can best be understood through the concept of classical conditioning. Phobias may have their origin in fears learned by the association of painful or unpleasant events with particular situations. In Chapter 3 we saw how such fears develop through classical conditioning and how this kind of learning may provide the model for the initial development of the fear. The life histories of people with phobias almost always provide examples of especially frightening events, or "traumatic" events, as they are sometimes called. These may, as in Leonard's case, be isolated episodes, but more often they are frightening situations which are repeated many times throughout the person's early life.

Although the fear may be rational when it is initially learned, it subsequently diffuses. The actual source of the fear may come to be repressed (see page 374), so that the fear seems to be an irrational one. From the point of view of the learning theorist, the spread of the fear to other situations can be considered an example of stimulus generalization (see Chapter 3). Thus phobias may get their start in a learning experience (that is, classical conditioning), but the fear may be displaced to objects which symbolize the originally feared object or situation.

No matter what their origin, phobias serve a purpose—like most other psychoneurotic symptoms. Although it may seem paradoxical at first, such intense, irrational fears may actually reduce anxiety. They do this by keeping the person away from situations in which he would be overwhelmed by much more intense fear (Dollard and Miller, 1950). A person with a phobia makes a bargain—he accepts one fear because it keeps him away from situations in which his fear of something else would be much more intense. Leonard, in the case cited earlier, accepted his fear of going away from home because it kept him away from railroads, the real source of his fear.

Obsessive-compulsive reactions Another neurotic set of symptoms, or syndrome, includes obsessions and compulsions. An *obsession* is an idea that constantly intrudes into a person's thoughts. It is usually foolish and groundless, at least at the time it is felt. The person may be obsessed with the notion that he has cancer or syphilis, or with the fear that he will kill himself or someone else. In less extreme cases, senseless phrases or ideas may run through his mind over and over again. Current opinion holds that obsessions represent a defense against anxiety, but it is not always easy to tell exactly what the anxiety is. Many obsessions defend against anxiety-provoking sexual urges, others against aggressive tendencies, but they may appear in any situation or experience that makes a person very anxious.

Compulsions are similar to obsessions, except that they are *acts*, rather than ideas, that repeatedly intrude into a person's behavior. One compulsive person may wash his hands every few minutes; another must count all the steps he climbs; another assiduously avoids stepping on cracks in the sidewalk. Some people do not have conspicuous, particular compulsions, but are compulsive in a more general way. They find ambiguity and uncertainty extremely uncomfortable, and they strive for orderliness of thought, of dress, or of work. Indeed, any unusual emphasis on "doing things the right way" may be regarded as compulsive. However, these people might better be considered to have *compulsive personality disorders* (see the next section, page 416).

The following case illustrates a typical compulsion:

A successful executive who, for various reasons, unconsciously hated the responsibilities of marriage and fatherhood was troubled many times a day with the idea that his two children by his divorced wife were somehow ill or in danger, although he knew them to be safe in a well-run private school to which he himself took them every morning. As a result, he felt impelled to interrupt his office routine thrice daily to make personal calls to the school authorities. After several months the principal began to question the sincerity of the patient's fatherly solicitude and thus intensified his obsessive-compulsive rituals by bringing the issue more nearly into the open. The same patient could not return home at night unless he brought a small present to his second wife and each of his children, although, significantly, it was almost always something they did not want. (Masserman, 1961, page 45).

Obsessions and compulsions are means of reducing anxieties while they repress the motives that arouse them. In the case just cited, the symptoms acted in much the same way as a reaction formation to help the patient deny his real motives (see page 375). His overt solicitousness—his compulsions, in other words—served to disguise the basic hostility. In other cases, obsessions and compulsions may be ways of attempting to reduce anxiety and expiate guilt over past acts. If someone is obsessive about developing cancer, for example, it may be because he has anxieties over some past act or misconduct for which he may fear punishment. Similarly, the compulsive person who washes his hands every few minutes may have anxieties over sexual transgressions, and the hand washing may be an unconscious attempt to cleanse himself of guilt. In this way, obsessive and compulsive individuals find some measure of relief from anxiety. But it is not complete. In fact, a cycle is set up in which mounting anxiety evokes the obsession or compulsion, and this in turn temporarily relieves the anxiety until, in the course of time or circumstances, it returns again. The mechanism, however, is a defense that keeps anxiety from reaching unbearable proportions.

The connection between the obsession or compulsion and the original experience from which the reaction stems is often rather difficult to discover. Occasionally the person has some insight into the connection. More often, he rationalizes his obsessions and compulsions to make them appear reasonable and appropriate, and thus he disguises to himself their real basis. In such circumstances, it probably will require extensive probing by an experienced clinician to find the source of the anxiety.

Conversion reactions Occasionally, when a conflict is unusually severe and repression is relatively complete, the conflict may be converted into a physical symptom. Hence this reaction to conflict is called a *conversion reaction*. The particular symptom that appears varies with the individual, his conflict, and his habits. It may be a paralysis of almost any part of the body, a localized loss of feeling, blindness or deafness, or almost any other sort of incapacity. The symptom is convenient in that it removes the individual from an intolerable and insoluble anxiety-producing situation. The soldier with "combat fatigue" is an example. Some soldiers in the avoidance-avoidance conflict situation where they risk death if they obey commands, and incur disgrace or imprisonment if they do not, develop symptoms that resolve the conflict by removing them from the whole situation. For instance, a soldier might become paralyzed so that he is no longer fit for combat. But understand that his is not conscious malingering—he really cannot move, although nothing is wrong with the nerves and muscles. Of course, he does not realize the conflict-based cause of the paralysis. If he were aware of the real cause, he would feel guilty, and the paralysis would not serve its purpose as a successful defense—guilt would replace anxiety.

It should be emphasized that the symptoms of conversion reactions do not have a biological cause: they are not caused by a lesion, germ, or other detectable physical agency. A physician cannot find the cause of this kind of disorder in a physical examination, no matter how thorough. The symptom—which is real enough, however—is a device for coping with conflict and anxiety. Another name for a conversion reaction is *hysteria*. But note that this meaning of hysteria (namely, the conversion of a motivational conflict into a physical symptom) is not the same as the common meaning of hysteria (an outbreak of uncontrolled emotional behavior). The following illustrates a case of hysteria or conversion reaction:

A woman was admitted to a hospital with a paralysis of the legs. Her legs were extended rigidly and close together, like two stiff pillars. Neurological examination indicated no physical disorder, so physicians looked into other aspects of her problem. They discovered that she was the mother of several children, that she had reason to fear having any more, that her husband desired frequent intercourse, and that she had strong prohibitions against both practicing birth control and denying her husband's sexual demands. Here were all the elements of a complex conflict situation. After interviewing the woman at length and investigating the case thoroughly, physicians concluded that her paralysis was an unconscious device for eliminating conflict.

Hysterical reactions are good illustrations of the process of *repression*, for in them repression is complete. In other reactions some, but not all, aspects of a conflict are repressed; but in hysteria the entire conflict is put out of consciousness. The individual completely rejects any thoughts and motives that may be involved, and he does this effectively by resorting to physical symptoms that dispose of them all. The woman with the paralyzed legs no longer had to worry about birth control, resisting her husband's sexual demands, or having more children. With her hysterical symptom, she had completely eliminated any occasion for the conflict.

The particular symptom that the hysteric employs may first occur by accident or as the result of a real physical illness. For example, a person may suffer a temporary paralysis as a result of an automobile accident. Although the injury is a handicap, it may also prove advantageous in satisfying other wants. It may make the patient's wife, husband, or parent become very attentive, thus giving him the love and care he has lacked. Or it may punish those who have the work and expense of taking care of him, so that it indirectly expresses aggression. Or it may protect the individual from anxiety-producing situations, such as a job, school, or social relations. The point is that the patient may experience a "secondary gain" from the ailment. Thus what begins as a physical ailment may be prolonged because it reduces both the conflict and the attendant anxiety. The patient does not consciously realize that he is doing this; he has repressed the conflict and his need to defend himself from anxiety.

An experienced doctor usually can recognize the hysterical personality, even if no full-blown physical symptoms have appeared in his patient. One of the signs is unusual naïvete. The individual is naïve because the anxiety he feels in many situations makes him avoid them, and thus he either misses or represses experiences that are normal for other people. Another sign is that he is easily disturbed emotionally. When confronted with an unpleasant situation, his thoughts become blocked and confused, and he may grow so disturbed that he becomes dizzy or ill, or actually faints. On a small scale, this is the kind of symptom that protects the hysteric against anxiety. In addition, the person who is using a conversion reaction as a defense against anxiety may be indifferent to his very real physical symptoms. In marked contrast to the patient with a biologically caused illness, the hysteric does not seem really concerned about his illness. He displays what has come to be called *la belle indifférence.*

Dissociative reactions Other reactions which, like conversion reaction, represent a great deal of repression are known as the *dissociative reactions.* They are so called because some personality traits and memories appear to be dissociated, or separated, from each other. In a mild, relatively harmless form, dissociative reactions may involve no more than a compartmentalization of a person's thinking and way of living. The businessman who is a vigorous competitor and not too scrupulous in his business affairs may be kind to his family, a fervent churchgoer, and active in the philanthropic affairs of his community. He may see no conflict whatever between these two modes of living. He compartmentalizes his thinking and his activities so that his two personalities do not consciously get in each other's way. In more extreme forms, however, dissociative reactions are bizarre and incapacitating. They furnish the most dramatic instances of neurotic behavior.

AMNESIA One well-publicized type of extreme dissociative reaction is amnesia. The amnesiac is the subject of numerous plays, "psychological" stories, and news items. A person suffering from amnesia usually forgets his own name, where he has come from, who his relatives are, and what he has been doing for some weeks, months, or years. Amnesia can be caused by a blow to the head or an injury to the brain. As a neurotic disorder, however, amnesia represents repression in the extreme. To cope with a painful conflict, the person unconsciously represses the memory of his own identity and things closely connected with it.

Donald G., twenty-two, attended college at night while working to support his forty-five-year-old mother. He was in love with a girl whom he hoped to marry. Donald's mother did not like the girl and tried to break them up.

The girl could see that Donald would never be able to support both her and his mother. She also knew that the three of them could never get along together under the same roof. She gave Donald a month to decide what to do about it. A week before the deadline, he suddenly disappeared. He was found two weeks later in another state, completely unable to say who he was, where he was, or what he was planning to do. He could not recall, or even recognize, the name of either his mother or his girl friend. Obviously, he had developed a case of amnesia as a solution to his conflict.

This behavior was not inconsistent with his previous history. In his earlier school days, he had frequently forgotten his homework and been absent-minded. Forgetting things was already a convenient habit for him. When a major conflict developed, this mode of adjustment became a full-blown amnesia. (Adapted from Ernest W. Tiegs and Barney Katz—*Mental Hygiene* in *Education,* page 53. Copyright © 1941 renewed © 1969, The Ronald Press Company, New York.)

As in other instances of repression, the memories are not forgotten; they are merely made unavailable to consciousness. Hence, if the source of the conflict can be discovered and if something is done to make the conflict less painful for the person, he frequently can be helped to recover his memory.

Some amnesias are temporary lapses accompanied by flight. The person suddenly disappears, wanders around aimlessly, or takes a long journey. During the period of flight or wandering, he suffers from amnesia. Days or perhaps weeks later, he recovers his memory partially or fully. At this point, he may go to the police or someone else for help; or, if he is fully recovered, he may contact his friends or relatives. Temporary amnesia, accompanied by flight, is called a *fugue,* from the Latin word meaning "to flee."

MULTIPLE PERSONALITY Occasionally, repression works in such a way as to dissociate two or more relatively complete personalities, as in the fictional case of Dr. Jekyll and Mr. Hyde. In this story, one personality is evil, the other good. The transformation is accomplished by drinking a potion. In real cases of multiple personality, however, the transformation is tripped off by stress or emotional trauma, and it stems from a deep-seated conflict of motives. Though often dramatized and talked about, split or multiple personality is relatively rare. Only a few cases have been studied in detail by competent clinical authorities. One famous case is reported in the book *The Three Faces of Eve* (Thigpen and Cleckley, 1957), later made into a movie.

Depressive reactions Neurotic depression is often a reaction to some severe loss that the patient has sustained. Neurotic depression is differentiated from psychotic depression, which we discuss later, by the absence of such symptoms as hallucinations, delusions, and severe thought disturbances.

> The neurotically depressed individual gives the outward general appearance of being dejected, discouraged, and sad. He may have an extremely sorrowful expression on his face or a dull, masklike one. He seems to see only the dark side of everything, seems uninterested in any pleasurable activities, may stay by himself, may just sit and stare. Although his thinking is not slowed up, he may complain of difficulties in concentrating. He may have trouble sleeping, feelings of restlessness, irritability, and inward tension. Vague hostile feelings may be detected. (Kutash, 1965, page 967.)

The neurotic depressive reaction tends to be short in duration. Suicide is a danger while the patient is in the depths of the depression, but spontaneous recovery is the rule rather than the exception in this type of neurotic disorder.

Persons who suffer from neurotic depression are often found to have feelings of guilt connected with some aspects of the loss which brought on the depression. For instance, the depressed person might have had strong ambivalent feelings toward a deceased parent or spouse; he sometimes hated them and sometimes loved them. The depression—occasioned, for example, by the death of the person toward whom the ambivalent feelings were directed—may sometimes be diagnosed as a way in which the depressed person punishes himself for the hostile feelings he had.

Personality Disorders

A large number of people admitted to public mental hospitals in the United States for the first time are diagnosed as suffering from personality disorders (see Figure 12.1). The deviant behaviors which fall in this class are a little hard to describe, because many different kinds of symptoms and symptom syndromes (collections of symptoms) are shown. But some general characteristics are typical of this group. In contrast to psychotics (who are discussed in the next section), these patients show little of the thought disturbance and bizarre behavior typical of many psychotic disorders. The basic problem seems to be the development of deviant lifelong personality trait patterns:

> These disorders are characterized by developmental defects or pathological trends in the personality structure, with minimal subjective anxiety, and little or no sense of distress. In most instances, the disorder is manifested by a lifelong pattern of action and behavior, rather than by mental or emotional symptoms. (American Psychiatric Association, 1952, page 34.)

The general category of personality disorders may be further divided into the following groups: *personality pattern and trait disturbances* and *sociopathic personality disturbances* (American Psychiatric Association, 1952; and Kisker, 1964).

Personality pattern and trait disturbances Individuals who can be placed in this group manage a marginal adjustment, and most of them stay out of mental hospitals. They seem to most of us to lead rather unrewarding lives, but they themselves generally do not feel that way.

We shall define this class of personality and trait disturbances by discussing some of the most common symptom syndromes.

SCHIZOID PERSONALITY The schizoid personality is characterized by withdrawal from other people, eccentric thinking, and a lack of normal aggressiveness in relations with others. As *The Diagnostic and Statistical Manual* of the American Psychiatric Association phrases it, people with schizoid personalities are recognized by:

> . . . coldness, aloofness, emotional detachment, fearfulness, avoidance of competition, and day dreams revolving around the need for omnipotence. As children, they were usually quiet, shy, obedient, sensitive, and retiring. At puberty, they frequently become more withdrawn, then manifesting the aggregate of personality traits known as introversion, namely, quietness, seclusiveness, "shut-inness," and unsociability, often with eccentricity. (American Psychiatric Association, 1952, page 35.)

The general picture is that of the eccentric fellow who lives down the block in the back room of the big house on the corner. He is rarely seen in the neighborhood, preferring to come and go when other people are not about. If approached, he shies away and flees back to his room.

Another personality pattern is termed the *paranoid* personality. Those in whom it appears have many of the traits of the schizoid personality, but in addition they show a marked suspiciousness of other people and their motives. Note that people who display the schizoid and paranoid patterns are *not psychotic*—they are not suffering from the psychosis *schizophrenia;* nor are they suffering from a psychotic *paranoid reaction.* Some of the symptoms of these personality pattern disturbances resemble those of psychosis, but contact with reality is maintained far more adequately than in the psychotic behavior disorders.

PASSIVE AND AGGRESSIVE PERSONALITIES Three varieties of passive and aggressive personalities are commonly described: the *passive-dependent* variety, the *passive-aggressive* variety, and the *aggressive* type. The passive-dependent person clings to others in the same way that a dependent child clings to adults. Such people are helpless, and they expect, and want, other people to dominate them. The helpless little wisp of a girl who must rely on her big strong boyfriend to do almost everything comes to mind as the exemplification of this disorder. However, passive-dependent personalities are by no means exclusive to women.

The passive-aggressive person expresses his feelings of rebellion and resentment by passive means such as "pouting, stubbornness, procrastination, inefficiency, and passive obstruction" (American Psychiatric Association, 1952, page 37).

The aggressive person burns with resentment and irritability and is prone to temper tantrums and violent aggressive attacks. These people act out their hostility by striking out at the world, and they can be dangerously aggressive at times. They are especially dangerous because the aggressive attack is often apparently unprovoked.

OBSESSIVE-COMPULSIVE PERSONALITY It has been jokingly, if incorrectly, said that this personality pattern characterizes the successful graduate student or scientist. Here is what the *Diagnostic and Statistical Manual* of the American Psychiatric Association has to say about the disorder:

This behavior pattern is characterized by excessive concern with conformity and adherence to standards of conscience. Consequently, individuals in this group may be rigid, over-inhibited, over-conscientious, over-dutiful, and unable to relax easily. This disorder may lead to an *obsessive compulsive* neuroris from which it must be distinguished. (American Psychiatric Association, 1968, page 43.)

Many other types of personality pattern and trait disturbances might be mentioned, but these are some of the major ones. They give an idea of the kinds of behavior included in this category.

Sociopathic personality disturbances People with sociopathic personality disturbances are not mentally ill in the sense that they experience anxiety or have bizarre thoughts. Rather, they are people who feel little guilt over their violations of the rules, regulations, laws, or mores of their culture. Several classes of sociopathic personality disturbance are distinguishable—the *antisocial reaction, sexual deviations,* and *drug addictions.*

ANTISOCIAL REACTION Persons in this category have little feeling for others or for the rights of others. They display no sense of responsibility and are incapable of loyalty. They are, generally speaking, without conscience, and to use one of the older terms, they might be called "morally insane." Another older term is "psychopathic deviate." They tend to be selfish and adept at rationalizing their immoral behavior. Within this framework, there are several patterns of antisocial behavior which can be discerned.

One common pattern is that of the suave "con man." Superficially, these people are convincing, their behavior is bland, they are glib talkers, and they are even quite charming. But they do not feel constrained by conscience.

Impulsive behavior is typical of another antisocial pattern; the person acts impulsively without regard to his responsibilities or his obligations to others. The New York bus driver who became bored with his route one day and drove across the George Washington Bridge and down the East Coast to Florida was manifesting such behavior. When apprehended by the police, the driver explained his 1,500-mile trip by saying, "I just wanted to get away from New York." (Kisker, 1964, page 231).

Perhaps more typical of this behavior disorder is a pattern of irresponsible, impulsive episodes which culminate in arrest after arrest.

Calvin F. was admitted to the psychiatric hospital at the age of eighteen with the diagnosis of antisocial personality. Two months after admission he escaped from an attendant, but was returned by the police. The following month he escaped again by breaking a screen on a porch, and the next day he was arrested while driving a stolen car. He was transferred to a maximum security hospital where he remained for three years. At the end of this time he was returned as "improved." A month later, he escaped by sawing the iron bars on a window. Four months later he was arrested in Montana for wearing the uniform of an Army officer, and was placed on Federal probation for five years. Six months later he was arrested in Spokane, Washington for stealing automobiles. He was hospitalized in Spokane for a short time, and was then returned to the psychiatric hospital. Two months after his return he attacked an attendant with a soft drink bottle, taped his mouth, stole his money, and escaped. (Kisker, 1964, page 232.)

What can be said about the psychological causes, or *psychogenics*, of the antisocial disorder? Perhaps the antisocial syndrome is related to psychological rejection within the family: perhaps the child who has not been given affection does not learn how to express affection. This may simply mean that the child does not have an opportunity to learn that affectionate relationships and concern for others are accepted and important aspects of interpersonal behavior. Because he is treated as an object to be manipulated, he may learn to deal with other people in this way.

SEXUAL DEVIATIONS Various types of sexual deviations are considered sociopathic behaviors. Without going into great detail, here are a few of these.

Exhibitionism involves exposing one's sexual organs to the view of others. *Voyeurism* is the compulsion to look at scantily clothed or naked bodies, usually of the opposite sex. *Fetishism* occurs when sexual excitement is produced by the sight, touch, or smell of an article of clothing or some part of the body not usually associated with sexual activity. *Sadism* and *masochism* are the terms used for sexual pleasure derived from giving pain to another (sadism) or receiving pain from another (masochism). *Homosexuality* is the sexual desire for members of the same sex. *Pedophilia* involves sexual interest in heterosexual or homosexual activity with a child. *Zoophilia* involves a desire for sexual relations with animals.

The psychodynamics of these sexual deviations are quite complicated. It might be mentioned that there is disagreement as to whether or not some of them are really deviations. For instance, some forms of voyeurism are socially approved and even encouraged, as any glance around the beach in summer will show. Voyeurism is widespread, and most members of the male population have such tendencies. Homosexuality is another example of sexual behavior which is fairly widespread in our culture and which may not be a deviation in the statistical sense. For instance, 37 percent of all men interviewed in the Kinsey report stated that they had had definite homosexual relations (Kinsey et al., 1948). This survey is reasonably accurate, and its findings indicate that homosexuality is not rare. Although we might still wish to pass moral judgment on such behavior, it is difficult to apply the term "deviation" to it. Perhaps we might say that voyeurism and homosexuality are deviations only when they are symptomatic of fundamental problems or when they cause the individual to make a nuisance of himself.

Table 12.1 *Drug addiction versus drug habituation.*

Source: After Jones Shainberg, and Byer, *Drugs and Alcohol* (Harper & Row, 1969. Modified from Seevers, 1962.)

Drug addiction	Drug habituation
Drug addiction is a state of periodic or chronic intoxication produced by the repeated consumption of a drug (natural or synthetic). Its characteristics are:	Drug habituation is a condition resulting from the repeated consumption of a drug. Its characteristics are:
1. An overpowering desire or need (compulsion) to continue taking the drug and to obtain it by any means	1. A desire (but not a compulsion) to continue taking the drug for the sense of improved well-being or effect it produces
2. A tendency to increase the dose	2. Little or no tendency to increase the dose
3. A psychic (psychological) and generally a physical dependence on the effects of the drug	3. Some psychic dependence on the effect of the drug, but no physical dependence and hence no abstinence syndrome.
4. A detrimental effect on the individual and on society	4. Detrimental effects, if any, primarily on the individual

DRUG DEPENDENCY Excessive dependency on drugs is an important category of behavior disorders. It may take the form of *habituation* or *addiction*, the major differences between which are shown in Table 12.1. In both cases the person has a need for the drug, or a psychological dependence. But in the case of addiction, a physical need for the drug develops; the physiology of the body is altered so that there are *withdrawal symptoms* when drug use is discontinued. A person who is physically addicted may become so agitated, depressed, or otherwise miserable that he can think of nothing but getting another dose of the drug. The need for it has become a powerful physiological drive. Some drugs, such as heroin, are strongly addictive; after a few doses, or a period of days on the drug, the person is "hooked." Other drugs, such as marijuana, do not seem to be addicting; their intermittent use engenders habituation but not addiction. Almost any drug taken in quantity over a long period, however, profoundly affects the nervous system, so that, eventually, the need for it can be considered an addiction.

The major drugs used by people in Western societies are treated in some detail in Chapter 19. Here we shall briefly note the behavior associated with alcoholism and drug addiction in general.

The term *alcoholic,* or *alcoholism,* refers to habituation or addiction to alcohol; depending on the degree of usage, alcohol can be considered either an addicting or a habituating drug. The line between the heavy social drinker and alcoholism is not easy to draw, but the crucial factors seem to be dependence on alcohol to "solve" basic problems of adjustment, and loss of control over drinking (Jellinek, 1952). Getting drunk occasionally does not make a person an alcoholic; it is only when he is constantly or regularly drunk and craves alcohol that he can be called an alcoholic—that is, alcohol-dependent.

The behavior of the alcoholic is variable, just as the behavior of nonalcoholics who have had too much to drink varies considerably. Depending upon situational factors and his personality structure, the alcoholic may be depressed, hostile, or euphoric; he may act out his aggressive or sexual motives—alcohol is a notorious "solvent of the superego." As this sort of behavior persists, trouble accumulates. He probably loses his job, his marriage suffers, and his relationships with people in general are deranged. He begins to function at lower levels of psychological adjustment; he tends to lack foresight; he may become slovenly in appearance. As one tie after another with the past is severed, he may end up on "skid row."

The causes of alcoholism are a question of considerable debate, and in recent times, of large-scale research. One important factor appears to be the reduction of anxiety; alcohol seems to calm anxiety and thus certain social inhibitions connected with anxiety. Another factor is that alcohol often permits a person to act out his hostilities and sexual wishes, so that it provides a means through which strong aggressive and sexual motives can be gratified (Kisker, 1964). Many other explanations have been offered. Hence there is little agreement on the cause of alcoholic dependency.

About the same comments apply to other kinds of drug dependency which are becoming more widespread. The first use of LSD or marijuana, like the first use of alcohol, is partly a matter of curiosity—to see "what it is like"—and partly a social matter in which drugs are used to "release inhibitions." Of course, since alcohol is legal in most places and other drugs are not, there is in drug taking an element of rebellion against the prohibitions laid down by the law and authority figures.

For most people, the occasional use of nonaddictive drugs does not establish dependency. For others, drugs like alcohol, become crutches for calming anxieties and releasing strong needs. We do not yet have enough data concerning dependency on nonlegal drugs such as LSD and marijuana to know how many people are becoming dependent on them or how the dependency arises. The best guess is that the development of dependency resembles that for alcohol. (For descriptions of the effects that various specific drugs have on behavior, see Chapter 19.)

Psychotic Reactions

For a long time it was thought that neurosis and psychosis were two completely different kinds of disorder. "Once a neurotic, never a psychotic" was almost an axiom. This meant that neurosis and psychosis were such different reactions that they could not develop in the same person. Today we are not so sure about this. Certainly many patients encountered in clinical practice are difficult to classify—they appear to be somewhere in between. For the present we must consider this question unresolved.

Figure 12.4 *An example of the autistic thought of the psychotic. What seems to make little sense probably has deep private and personal significance for the psychotic patient who made this drawing. (Courtesy of CIBA,* State of Mind.*)*

In practice, however, we can make a distinction. Whereas the neurotic individual is characterized by anxiety or strenuous defenses against anxiety, the psychotic individual typically has lost considerable contact with reality. He may simply withdraw and fail to respond to things going on around him. Or he may be so excited or depressed that his reactions are inappropriate to circumstances. In many instances, his thought processes, and hence his communication with others, are seriously disturbed (see Figure 12.4). A psychotic person may also have *hallucinations*—experiences for which no sensory input exists—or *delusions*—ideas, sometimes used to explain the presence of hallucinatory experience, which have no foundation in actual happenings. In any case, the psychotic tends to live in a world of his own—that is, he is said to be *autistic*—rather than in the real world around him. For this reason, psychosis is more severe than neurosis, and the psychotic person is more likely to require hospitalization and protective care. Most of the inmates of our mental hospitals, particularly those who stay a long time, are psychotic, not neurotic.

The psychotic reactions can be described under five main headings: affective reactions, paranoid reactions, schizophrenic reactions, involutional reactions, and chronic brain syndromes.

Affective reactions The major characteristic of one variety of psychosis is *extremes of mood.* Hence it is called *affective psychosis*—one in which marked disturbances of mood or emotion take place—or sometimes *manic-depressive psychosis.* Affective reactions often appear as relatively short psychotic episodes in the otherwise normal behavior of a person. These episodes, which may be either manic or depressed, tend to last about 6 months. On the average, the depressed episodes are more prolonged than the manic ones. Most sufferers from this disorder experience several such psychotic episodes in their lives.

SYMPTOMS As the term manic-depressive implies, sometimes the psychosis is cyclical. The patient is manic for a period and then swings into a depression. The cycle may be repeated rapidly, or a period of months may intervene. It may be repeated more than once. On the other hand, manic states may never swing over into depressive ones, and vice versa. Almost any pattern of affective disturbance may be encountered; cycles of mania followed by depression, mania with no depression, or depression alone. All are possible symptom sequences.

The manic individual is unduly elated and active. He may sing, dance, run, talk a lot, and generally expend more energy than one would think humanly possible. He may also exhibit obsessions and delusions. Frequently he is aggressive and obstreperous. He may break chairs, attack people, use vile language, and generally put life and property in jeopardy. Or he may try so hard to be helpful that he becomes extremely troublesome. The following case illustrates some of the typical characteristics of manic excitement.

A thirty-five-year-old biochemist was brought to the clinic by his frightened wife. To his psychiatrist the patient explained: "I discovered that I had been drifting; broke the bonds and suddenly found myself doing things and doing them by telegraph. I was dead tired, and decided to go on a vacation; but even there it wasn't long before I was sending more telegrams. I got into high gear and started to buzz. Then a gentle hint from a friend took effect and I decided to come here and see if the changes in my personality were real. . . ."

When his wife had left, the patient soon demonstrated what he meant by "high gear." He bounded down the hall, threw his medication on the floor, leaped up on a window ledge and dared anyone to get him down. When he was put in a room alone where he could be free, he promptly dismantled the bed, pounded on the walls, yelled and sang. He made a sudden sally into the hall and did a kind of hula-hula dance before he could be returned to his room. His shouting continued throughout the night. . . .

The following morning, after almost no sleep, the patient was more noisy and energetic than ever. He smashed the overhead light with his shoes and ripped off the window guard. He tore up several hospital gowns, draped himself in a loin cloth made of their fragments, said he was Tarzan, and gave wild jungle cries to prove it. "I've tasted tiger's blood!" he roared. "I'm a success and I'm the man for my boss's job. I've made a killing and this time I will keep going." He made amorous remarks to the nurses, accused them of flirting with him, and announced loudly, "At the present time I am not married; but my body is not for sale, regardless of price." From his talk it could be inferred that, far from being happily relaxed and irresponsible, the patient was in reality deeply disturbed over job competition, sexual conflicts, and his own hospitalization. A study of his personal background confirmed this inference and indicated that, as might be expected, affectional relationships and personal status had presented recurring problems throughout his life. (Cameron and Margaret, 1951, page 332.)

In contrast to the individual who develops the manic variety of affective reaction, the depressed person feels melancholy, worthless, guilty, and hopeless. Some depressed patients cry a good deal of the time, some keep talking about terrible sins they imagine that they have committed, and some are so depressed that they will take no food or water, have to be forcibly fed through a tube, and refuse to dress or take care of their toilet needs. The extremely depressed patient is often on the verge of suicide and must be watched closely to see that he does not harm himself. The following case is typical:

Pauline B. is a fifty-seven-year-old widow who graduated from high school, attended business school, and had training as a nurse. She has had three commitments to mental hospitals for her depressions. When seen at the hospital on her most recent admission, the patient presented the typical picture of depression. She appeared sad, talked in a somewhat whining voice, and showed psychomotor retardation. She had numerous self-condemnatory ideas, and was preoccupied with thoughts of suicide. Her general attitude was one of hopelessness. She said that life is not worth living, and that she would be better off dead. She had no interest in anything, and there was nothing left to live for. Between her depressive episodes, the patient is regarded as a happy outgoing person, although subject to rather wide swings of mood. (Kisker, 1964, page 374.)

CAUSES AND TREATMENT The dramatic behavior seen in manic-depressive psychoses immediately arouses our curiosity about the *etiol-*

ogy of the disorder, that is, its causes. Unfortunately, the causes of manic-depressive reactions are not really known; we have only some shrewd guesses about their origins. On the one hand, it seems clear that a strong genetic basis, and therefore probably a biochemical basis, exists for the disorder. On the other hand, there are several psychogenic theories. Perhaps the most common psychological explanation holds that the basic disorder is depression and that mania is a flight into activity to ward off depression. The problem then becomes one of explaining depression. Depression can be caused or aggravated by any number of factors—lack of love, feelings of guilt, thwarted ambitions, shame, or feelings of frustration and futility. But whatever the psychogenic basis of manic-depressive psychosis, the biochemical and genetic basis must still be considered, and the relationship between the psychological and the physical factors is unclear.

Without any special treatment, about 70 percent of manic-depressive patients recover sufficiently within one year to be released from the hospital (Coleman, 1956). With treatment, nearly 100 percent of manic-depressive patients can be released within the first year of hospitalization (Coleman, 1964).

Physical treatment is employed more often than psychotherapy for this type of disorder. Electroconvulsive shock therapy (ECT) is frequently used with some success. Its major effect seems to be that the length of time of the psychotic reaction is shortened (Bond, 1954; White, 1964). Drugs are also used to manage depression (see Chapter 19).

Paranoid reactions Paranoid psychosis is relatively rare. It takes several forms, which are considered collectively in the following discussion.

SYMPTOMS Paranoid reactions, one of the main varieties of which is called *paranoia,* are marked by *delusions.* The delusions may be imaginings of grandeur or persecution. A paranoid patient may tell you that he is Napoleon or George Washington and spin quite a tale to prove it. He also may have the delusion that someone is persecuting him, that someone has invented a machine which is slowly destroying him by a kind of wave, or that someone is hatching a nefarious plot to deprive him of his rights as the President of the United States.

Except for his delusional system, the paranoid psychotic usually shows almost no disorder in thinking; he appears normal until something happens to precipitate the delusional thinking. In general the delusional system is well worked out, and it often seems plausible. The intact thinking and the more or less logical delusions are in marked contrast to the disordered thinking encountered in the variety of schizophrenia which is labeled paranoid.

The following letter from a person with a paranoid reaction illustrates the "logical" delusion typical of paranoia:

Washington, D.C.

Dear Dr. ———:

I have a neighbor who owns and operates an ultrasonic machine. The transducer is projected toward us, i.e., we are in the direct beam of its energy! This neighbor has tried at various times to kill us but we have always managed to run from the apartment, thereby getting out of its beam before it affects us too much! Most of the time, he has just turned it on us to give us various feelings (not all of them at once, of course) headaches, fever, extreme fatigue or nervousness, tiredness, irritability, dizziness, nausea, sometimes fainting and a feeling of "impending doom."

There is absolutely nothing in the world we can do about it, or at least there hasn't been so far. That is what makes our case so unique! They could murder us, as they did a neighbor of ours, and even a post mortem would only show an ordinary heart attack. No one can even prove it on our neighbor, because it would only show what an ordinary heart attack would show. His widow knows this fact and so do we. She couldn't even tell the authorities because they would think she was crazy or too unbalanced by her grief.

Really, there is no telling how many more of these machines our neighbor owns throughout the country. He certainly wouldn't stop with one since he has long since recognized his strength and secret treachery. No one has caught him yet and no one is able to except for one thing that I shall write later.

Why is this man doing this? He used to be our neighbor and he hated us for what we are and what we have—those are the only things that we have been able to figure out other than he has a complex he can't outgrow. He just *happened* onto this machine and he has followed us around the country with it, moving in just next door with it wherever we have moved to get away from him.

Since there is no obvious law governing machines of this sort, there is nothing we can do to stop him. Can you imagine a flat-foot cop having the knowledge of an ultrasonic machine? There aren't any! It doesn't come under the jurisdiction of the F.B.I. since there is no federal offense committed, nor the F.C.C. because they are only interested in radio waves.

To prove all this in a mechanical way, that this neighbor actually has an ultrasonic machine, and that he projects it on our apartment, we would have to order CUSTOM-BUILT (from a reputable electronics firm) a model GA 1007 sound pressure equipment with built-in calibrator, and with a M-123 microphone, cost around $1350. Who has money like that nowadays to spend on such a thing? WHAT WOULD YOU DO?

Sincerely,

P.S. Call me long distance, reverse the charges. I'll be glad to give you any more information, after 5 P.M. (Kisker, 1964, page 368.)

CAUSES AND TREATMENT Physiological and genetic causes do not appear to be important in this disorder; it seems entirely psychogenic. Two factors are prominent in the paranoid's peculiar mode of adjustment. One is *aggression.* In general, his attitudes, acts and thoughts are full of aggression, and we may surmise that he has failed to adjust normally because he has been unable to give vent in normal ways to strong aggressive impulses. The other factor is *projection.* His hallucinations and delusions usually represent a projection to others of his own aggressive or sexual impulses, and that is why he believes someone is plotting against him or persecuting him. The paranoid's aggression is so strong and he believes his projection of it so firmly that he is often dangerous. If not kept in custody, he may do someone harm. The treatment of the paranoid reactions is very difficult, and the *prognosis,* or the expected course of the disorder, is not very good.

Schizophrenic reactions The word "schizophrenia" is constantly misused. It is often applied to people who behave in inconsistent, but by no means psychotic, ways. Newspapers will label the inconsistent behavior of politicians, for example, as schizophrenic. The term is also incorrect when it is used to mean "split," or multiple, personality. We have seen that multiple personality is a relatively rare neurotic disorder characterized by repression and dissociation.

Since schizophrenia does not mean these things, what does it mean? Perhaps the formal medical language of the description by the American Psychiatric Association will give a more precise idea of the symptomatology of the various syndromes which are lumped together under the term schizophrenia.

This large category includes a group of disorders manifested by characteristic disturbances of thinking, mood, and behavior. Disturbances in thinking are marked by alterations of concept formation which may lead to misinterpretation of reality and sometimes to delusions and hallucinations, which frequently appear psychologically self-protective. Corollary mood changes include ambivalent, constricted and inappropriate emotional responsiveness and loss of empathy with others. Behavior may be withdrawn, regressive and bizarre. The schizophrenias, in which the mental status is attributable primarily to a *thought* disorder, are to be distinguished from the *major affective illnesses* which are dominated by a *mood* disorder. The *paranoid states* are distinguished from schizophrenia by the narrowness of their distortions of reality and by the absence of other psychotic symptoms. (American Psychiatric Association, 1968, page 33.)

Schizophrenia used to be called *dementia praecox,* which means "youthful insanity," because it tends to develop early in life. Although it may occur at any age, the highest rate of admission to mental hospitals for this disease is among people in their late teens and early twenties. Schizophrenia is no rarity. It is the most common of all the psychotic disorders, affecting about 1 percent of the population; it tends also to be one of the most crippling.

Although the situation has improved with the introduction of intensive modern therapeutic techniques, a substantial number of schizophrenic patients steadily "deteriorate" so that they must be taken care of for many years. About 15 to 20 percent of people admitted to mental hospitals in the United States for the first time are diagnosed as schizophrenic, and the average length of stay in the hospital is approximately 13 years (Wolman, 1965; Lemkau and Crocetti, 1958).

A still clearer picture of this disorder may be gained by considering some of the types which have been distinguished. The American Psychiatric Association lists ten major forms of schizophrenic reaction, but we shall take up only four: the *simple* type, the *hebephrenic* type, the *catatonic* type, and the *paranoid* type. The distinction between these is not always clear. In fact, the diagnosis of schizophrenia is not highly reliable; its classification into types is less so. We shall examine the simple type in more detail in order to give a picture of schizophrenic thinking, while we describe the other three types only briefly.

SIMPLE TYPE Simple schizophrenia has been defined by the American Psychiatric Association as follows:

This psychosis is characterized chiefly by a slow and insidious reduction of external attachments and interests and by apathy and indifference leading to impoverishment of interpersonal relations, mental deterioration, and adjustment on a lower level of functioning. In general, the condition is less dramatically psychotic than are the hebephrenic, catatonic, and paranoid types of schizophrenia. Also, it contrasts with schizoid personality, in which there is little or no progression of the disorder. (American Psychiatric Association, 1968, page 33.)

These characteristics are easily seen in the following case.

Dr.: Do you know who I am?
Pt.: A doctor, I suppose.
Dr.: How do you feel?
Pt.: Oh—OK, I guess.
Dr.: Do you know where you are?
Pt.: It's a hospital.
Dr.: Why are you here?
Pt.: I don't know. . . . I don't think I should be here. I'm all right.
Dr.: Where would you rather be?
Pt.: I don't care, just out . . . I don't know. Maybe with some fellows or something. I don't care. There were some guys I used to know.
Dr.: What did you do with those fellows?
Pt.: I don't know—just go around.
Dr.: How do you like it here?
Pt.: I don't know. I don't care. It's all right, I guess. I liked the boys though. I used to know them.
Dr.: And you used to like them?
Pt.: Yes—they were all right, I guess.
Dr.: Who is "they?"
Pt.: Some men. I don't know them by name.
Dr.: Can you think of any reason why you should be here?
Pt.: No, I'm all right. I feel all right. I'd like to be with the fellows I used to know.
Dr.: Are there any fellows here you like?
Pt.: I don't know. They're all right, I guess.
Dr.: Do you think the men who brought you here had it in for you?
Pt.: No. They were nice to me. They were all right. They didn't have it in for me or hate me or anything.
Dr.: Do you ever hear strange noises?
Pt.: No, I never do that. I'm not crazy.

This patient was hospitalized on the complaint of his sister-in-law, who stated that he had tried to force her at the point of a gun to have sexual relations with him. On admission to the hospital the patient appeared rather indifferent about the whole matter and explained that it must have been some "temporary impulse" which overcame him.

Although 30 years of age, the patient had been living with his parents and was completely dependent upon them. His educational background was good. He made an A average in high school, but during his first year of college he lost interest in his studies and refused to attend classes despite his parents' pleadings. His parents then did their best to help him achieve some vocational adjustment, but the patient seemed indifferent to their efforts and hopes for him. After leaving college he did take several part-time jobs, including one in a grocery store, which he lost soon after because of his listless attitude and indifference to his duties. Thereafter he would not either look for nor accept work and was quite content to remain dependent upon his parents. Although rather handsome, he had never gone out with girls. When questioned on this subject he stated that "I'm not interested in girls. All they ever do is get you in trouble." (From *Abnormal Psychology and Modern Life,* 3d ed., by James C. Coleman. Copyright © 1964 by Scott, Foresman and Company. Page 277.)

The withdrawal from the world and lack of appropriate emotional responsivity that is characteristic of simple schizophrenics are easily observed in this patient. It has been noted that "no type of patient is more colorless and more unlike the popular idea of a lunatic" (White, 1964). Occasionally, however, violent aggressive behavior or episodes of sexual misbehavior occur, and it is usually these that get the patient in sufficient trouble for him to be hospitalized.

HEBEPHRENIC TYPE In this type of schizophrenic disorder, the individual seems to regress to childish levels of behavior. He may giggle incessantly; in fact, everything may seem funny or foolish to him. It is typical that his mood seems to bear no relation to the situation. He may talk about the death of his mother and laugh in a silly way. Or he may, for no apparent reason, begin to cry. Sometimes, while he is crying, he may report that he has no real feeling of sadness. He may revert to a child's vocabulary and accents. His habits of eating and his toilet habits may be childishly sloppy.

CATATONIC TYPE Although catatonic schizophrenia is not so common as the other forms, it is perhaps the most dramatic. The catatonic is extremely negativistic, often doing exactly the opposite of what he is asked to do. He may completely ignore people around him and refuse to say anything under any circumstances. Perhaps the most striking thing about him, though, is his *catatonia,* which is a state of muscular rigidity. For many minutes, or even hours, he may stay fixed in some strange position, for example, in a crouch or with arms outstretched. In fact, it is hard to see how catatonic postures can be maintained for so long; no normal person could hold them for even a short while.

PARANOID TYPE Like the victim of a paranoid reaction, the paranoid schizophrenic has delusions of grandeur or persecution. But unlike the person with a paranoid state, the paranoid schizophrenic often has hallucinations and *unsystematized* delusions—delusions that are not very coherent and that he does not defend with such elaborate rationalizations. He may shift with little apparent reason from one delusion to another, showing bizarre attitudes and behavior.

CAUSES OF SCHIZOPHRENIA Since schizophrenia in all its forms is such an important mental health problem, much research effort is being expended to find its causes. They are sought in genetics, biochemistry, and psychological stresses (Jackson, 1960). As yet, none of the answers is really convincing, and the best that can be done is to cite a few of the promising research leads.

Genetics almost certainly plays some role. The *concordance ratio*—the percentage of relatives of a schizophrenic person who also have schizophrenia—is approximately 46 percent in the case of identical twins (see Table 2.5). Although not absolutely convincing in itself, this and other similar findings point strongly toward a genetic and biochemical basis for schizophrenia.

Psychological stress also seems to play a role in the genesis of schizophrenia. Attention has been focused on the *pattern of interaction* within the family between the parents and the preschizophrenic child. This interaction pattern seems to be marked by schism and inconsistency (Lidz and Fleck, 1960; Bateson et al., 1956). In a study of 16 families of schizophrenics, the relationship between the mother and father was characterized as follows:

> Most of the marriages upon which the families were based were gravely disturbed. The majority were torn by schismatic conflict between the parents that divided the family into two hostile factions, with each spouse seeking to gain the upper hand, defying the wishes of the other, undercutting the worth of the spouse to the children, seeking to win the children to his side and to use them as emotional replacements for the spouse. The remaining families developed a skewed pattern because serious psychopathology of the dominant parent was passively accepted by the other, leading to aberrant ways of living and of child rearing. Their acceptance and masking of the serious problems that existed created a strange emotional environment that was perplexing to the child. (Lidz and Fleck, 1960, page 332.)

In addition to such disordered family interaction patterns, other theorists claim that inconsistent demands are made on preschizophrenic children by their parents. One theory which discusses these inconsistencies is known as the *double-bind* theory (Bateson et al., 1956). The psychological stress involved in schizophrenia is, according to this school of thought, due to the inconsistencies in the communications which the child receives from his parents. The theory maintains that the communication process goes on at two levels—the ordinary verbal one and the level of action. The inconsistency between the two levels creates the stress and the confusing situation that leads to schizophrenia. For instance, a parent may tell a child that he is loved and then, by his actions, communicate to the child that just the opposite is true. The family interactions of preschizophrenics and their parents are, according to this

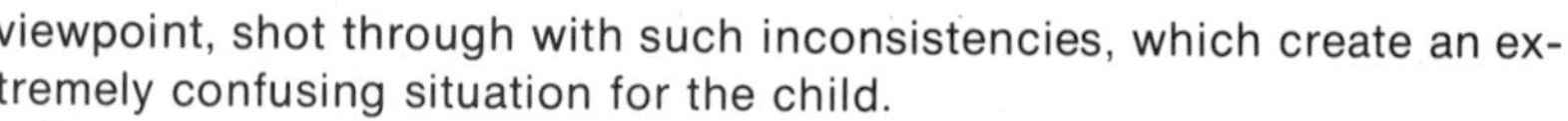

viewpoint, shot through with such inconsistencies, which create an extremely confusing situation for the child.

Perhaps it is possible to tie together the studies that show parental discord with the theory that emphasizes the inconsistencies in the double bind. First, it may simply be that family derangement facilitates inconsistent communication. Second, the fact that the families are so disharmonious, but are still living together, is itself a confusing inconsistency—perhaps a basic one (Weakland, 1960).

Still other authorities attempt to find relationships between the genetic evidence and the psychological evidence. One theory states that an inherited biochemical brain defect must exist as a necessary condition for schizophrenia; without it, schizophrenia is not possible (Meehl, 1962). In the usual life situation, the biochemical defect manifests itself in a syndrome of personality traits known as the *schizotypic* syndrome. Schizotypic people have many of the traits of schizophrenics, but in a much milder form which is not severely incapacitating. They show mild confusion of thought and a tendency toward withdrawal from other people, inappropriate emotional expression, and ambivalence—liking and disliking the same thing to an exaggerated degree. According to this theory, the brain defect alone is not sufficient to produce full schizophrenia; it results only in schizotypic behavior, unless the type of family stress discussed above is also present. The brain-chemistry disorder and the family stress act together to produce full schizophrenia. Either by itself will not; the biochemical brain defect will cause schizotypic behavior, while stress from a disordered family or the double-bind situation might induce neurotic behavior, but not schizophrenia.

TREATMENT AND PROGNOSIS In the absence of firm knowledge as to the causes of schizophrenia, a wide variety of treatments has been proposed. These range all the way from physical therapies, such as prefrontal lobotomy and insulin shock, to various forms of psychotherapy (see Chapter 13).

Figure 12.5 *Mental hospitals are no longer "bedlams." Instead, especially since the introduction of tranquilizing drugs, most are quiet, orderly places. In many institutions today, patients engage in activities much like those outside, and by so doing they learn new ways of adjusting to situations and other people. Therapy that strives to make the environment a stimulating and interesting place in which learning can occur is sometimes called* milieu, *or environmental, therapy. (State of New York Department of Mental Hygiene.)*

In the bad old days, not so many years ago, little was done for the schizophrenic patient in the mental hospital. Perhaps he was given insulin shock treatment or electroconvulsive shock therapy, but he received very little understanding care—to say nothing of psychotherapy. Sometimes these physical treatments help, but they are most effective when used as adjuncts to some type of psychotherapy.

The current tendency is to make the mental hospital a more meaningful therapeutic environment. Tranquilizing drugs are used to produce partial remission of symptoms, reduction of anxiety, and some clearing of thought (see Chapter 19). Perhaps the most important thing about these drugs is that they help the patient reestablish some contact with the external world; thus they also enable him to pay attention to, and perhaps to benefit from, psychotherapy.

In addition to drug therapy, a concerted effort has been made in recent years to change the underlying philosophies of the mental hospital and its staff and to create new routines in the care of schizophrenics and other patients (see Figure 12.5). It is felt that the hospital should be a milieu, or environment, in which the patient can establish contact with the world as we know it. Generally, this has been done by shifting from a custodial pattern of care to a pattern which provides for more activities and allows more free choice among them. Thus the formation of friendship groups among the patients becomes possible. Opportunities for structured social interactions are also provided in sports programs and dances. Sometimes, depending upon the home situation, visits home are arranged. All this is sometimes called *milieu,* or environmental, therapy. Of course, much of this has been made possible by massive use of the tranquilizing drugs. Here again, we see how these drugs, although they may not be curative agents in themselves, prepare the way for successful therapy.

The prognosis for schizophrenic disorders depends upon a number of factors. One of the most important is the adjustment the person had made before he became sick enough to be hospitalized. If the onset of the schizophrenic symptoms was rapid, if the patient suffered some pronounced shock, or trauma, just before the schizophrenic break, and if he was moderately well adjusted before the break, the prognosis is rather good. In other words, the chances of recovery are fairly high for what has been called *reactive schizophrenia.* On the other hand, if the onset of the disorder was slow and the symptoms gradually increased in severity, if there was no precipitating trauma, and if the patient's adjustment before being diagnosed as schizophrenic was marginal, the prognosis is poor. In other words, the chances of recovery are not good for what has been called *process schizophrenia.* Early treatment is another extremely important factor in the prognosis for schizophrenia. Rather than being hidden and protected by their families—perhaps because of some ill-formed fears on the family's part, or perhaps because of the general disorganization of the families of schizophrenics—people with schizoid symptoms should receive early treatment.

The treatment of schizophrenia is at best a chancy business—there is no assurance of a cure. As with all health problems, it is advisable to stay well in the first place. How much better it would be if we could prevent schizophrenia and other behavior disorders! As we learn more about the family conditions which seem to be at the roots of schizophrenia, and as community mental health clinics become more and more accessible, we shall be on the way toward partial eradication of this most crippling of the psychotic disorders.

Involutional reactions Whereas schizophrenia is a psychosis which develops in young people, involutional psychoses begin later in life. They may occur in women during the involutional period of menopause at 45 to 55 years of age. In men the onset is at 55 to 65.

The syndromes of the psychotic episodes which occur during the involutional periods are of two main types—agitated depression or paranoia. For the paranoid type of involutional disorder, the symptoms are similar to the paranoid reactions described in an earlier section. Agitated depression is characterized by crying, moaning, lamentations, wailing, restless pacing, wringing the hands, and attacks on one's own body—hair pulling, for example. The following case illustrates agitated depression:

Laura A. is a 50-year-old woman who was admitted to the psychiatric hospital after complaining at home that she was "losing her mind." For days she made this complaint, spoke of a "visual fog," and said her mind was a "blank." She had involuntary episodes of crying over a period of several months, and was sent to a private hospital where she received treatment which did not alleviate her symptoms.

When seen at the psychiatric hospital, Laura was a short woman who looked many years older than her age. Her eyes were sunken and her long straight hair was disheveled. She had the appearance of a sad and somewhat ghostly person who constantly repeated her symptoms in a flat sing-song voice. She complained that she "had no head," that her mind was gone, and that a nerve in her forehead was making her "holler." She cried out repeatedly, "Help me! Keep me from hollering!" Her moaning and occasional screaming could be stopped temporarily by distracting her, and it was possible with some effort to get her to talk about herself. She was well oriented in all areas, although her thinking was somewhat rambling and egocentric. While her mood was one of dejection, she was restless and disturbed.

The patient was seen on a number of subsequent occasions, and there appeared to be some degree of deterioration. She did not remember the examiner, and she became increasingly hostile and vicious. At the time of her admission to the hospital she had been a rather gentle person in spite of her agitation. The patient was placed on medication, and two weeks later was sitting quietly on the ward in a rather relaxed state. She did not remember talking previously to the examiner, but she repeated the ideas that her mind was gone, her head was no good, and that she was "crazy." She said that she talks too much, walks up and down too much, and "acts like an animal." She concluded by saying there was no hope for her. While these ideas were similar to those expressed when she was admitted to the hospital, they were now expressed in a relatively calm and unemotional way. Several months later the patient was able to leave the hospital and make a satisfactory adjustment. She returned to work as a secretary, and managed her home efficiently and with growing interest in her activities. (Kisker, 1964, pages 377–378.)

In spite of the fact that these psychoses occur at the time of the involutional period, their causes seem to be mainly psychological. This is a time of crisis for both men and women. For some women, menopause is a sign that life is coming to an end and that their sexual attractiveness is fading. By the time of menopause, many of the previous life adjustments are no longer appropriate. For instance, after years of having children in the house, suddenly, it seems, they are grown, and the mother may feel lonely and left out. For both men and women, worries about such things as financial security in old age, regrets over opportunities lost, and so on, may also be pressing. The depressed patient tends to blame himself for the predicament in which he finds himself, whereas the paranoid patient blames others.

The prognosis is moderately good for the depressed involutional psychosis, but the depression typically lasts for several years. Various tranquilizing drugs and electroconvulsive shock therapy often help. The prognosis is less good for the paranoid type of involutional psychosis, and these patients often show increasing deterioration as they grow older.

Chronic brain syndromes Our concern here is with the agents and conditions which produce long-lasting, or chronic, brain damage rather than those which precipitate acute, or short-lasting, alterations in brain function and behavior. Among the causes of brain damage which can result in behavior disorders are syphilis of the brain, physical blows to the head, disturbances of the blood supply in the brain, brain tumors, disorders of metabolism, physical changes in the brain with old age, and chemical agents, drugs, or alcohol. Behavior disorders due to brain changes with old age, or *senile psychosis,* and those due to the overuse of alcohol are by far the most common types of chronic brain syndromes.

SENILE PSYCHOSIS Old people may develop psychotic behavior that is characterized by delusions, defects of memory, and general disorientation. For example, the person may imagine that he has been talking to someone who really was not there, or he may imagine that people are boring holes in his head. As his memory grows worse, he may forget what he has just said, at the same time insisting that he remembers things which never happened. Very frequently in senile psychosis the person hardly knows where he is, where he has been, or what is going on—in other words, he is generally disoriented.

Senile psychosis is due to brain damage. Some of this damage is caused by deficiencies of the blood circulation in the brain. Accumulating fatty deposits make some of the small arterioles supplying the brain cells become smaller in diameter. When the blood flow to a portion of the brain ceases, or is markedly diminished, the cells die and that part of the brain is said to be atrophied. Other brain damage in senile psychosis has less specific causes; for instance, it seems that as we grow older we are constantly losing nerve cells which are not replaced. This cell loss seems to be simply a consequence of age.

INTOXICATION PSYCHOSIS (ALCOHOL) The long-term effects of prolonged heavy drinking—for example, a pint to a fifth of whiskey a day for 10 to 30 years—can bring on this psychosis. It is quite distinct from the marked

changes in behavior that take place in acute cases of alcoholic intoxication—*delerium tremens,* for instance.

Chronic alcoholism produces irreversible damage to brain cells, and this in turn causes a typical pattern of symptoms called *Korsakoff's syndrome.* It includes disorientation, confusion, memory disorders, impulsiveness, and some physical symptoms such as inflammation of the peripheral nerves. *Confabulation*—the filling in of gaps in memory with plausible guesses—is characteristic of the memory disorder which forms part of Korsakoff's syndrome. A similar syndrome, but without the nerve inflammation and other specific physical symptoms, tends to occur whenever there is any generalized and widespread damage to the cerebral cortex. A severe blow to the head, for example, can cause such a syndrome.

Synopsis and summary

Here ends our tale of anguish and misery. Sometimes students and authors tend to depersonalize the people who are described in discussions of behavior disorders. But these are real people who, in most cases, are suffering a great deal of misery and anguish. Perhaps the student will object that this accusation of depersonalization does not apply to him. Quite the contrary, he may say. He has found some mild forms of these symptoms in himself; he may, then, have a little insight into some of the feelings of those with behavior disorders. This discovery of mild forms of symptoms, where no problem really exists, is sometimes called the "medical student's disease." It is only natural, and perhaps it helps to establish empathy with the sufferers we have been describing.

One of the prerequisites in any discussion of behavior disorders is objectivity. We need not lose appreciation for people and their problems, but we should regard behavior disorders as natural phenomena with causes which are no less real than those of other diseases. Three large problems seem to impede progress in finding causes. In the first place, the causes are complex, and interactions of nature and nurture, although important in all diseases, are perhaps even more intricate and confusing in the behavior disorders. In the second place, a large portion of the causation must be sought in psychological mechanisms—disordered opportunities for learning, disorganized family situations, and so on—and objective investigation of these situations is difficult. In the third place, all the ignorance, fear, and superstition about behavior disorders must be overcome.

One of the purposes of this chapter has been to emphasize that behavior disorders have natural and understandable origins. To put it another way, given a certain nature, or constitution, and given particular forces interacting with this nature, a behavioral disorder will be the expected and natural outcome. When we understand the origins, or etiology, of the behavior disorders, and even before we understand them completely, great strides can be made toward preventing them and the anguish that attends them.

1. Mild adjustment problems, which often involve frustration of motives, can produce unhappiness and can interfere with a person's efficiency and strivings toward self-actualization. Such adjustment problems are common, but they tend to be short-lived, and recovery in the course of ordinary living is the rule.
2. The psychoneurotic reactions, or neuroses, are characterized by anxiety and attempts to reduce anxiety. The psychoneurotic symptoms may be considered, in some cases, special varieties of defense mechanisms.
3. Some of the major types of psychoneurotic reactions are (*a*) anxiety-reactions, in which anxiety, chronic or acute, is the prominent symptom, (*b*) phobic reactions, involving intense irrational fears, (*c*) obsessive-compulsive reactions, in which ideas or acts involuntarily intrude into the ongoing stream of behavior, (*d*) conversion reactions, involving the conversion of a motivational conflict into symbolically meaningful physical symptoms, (*e*) dissociative reactions, in which a person represses many ideas, and which may result in such disorders as amnesia or multiple personality, (*f*) depressive reactions, in which the major symptom is profound depression, usually after a person has experienced a severe loss.
4. People with personality disorders are characterized by "developmental defects or pathological trends in personality structure." In contrast to the psychoneurotic reactions, anxiety is at a minimum. And in contrast to the psychotic reactions, little thought disturbance is present. Two varieties of personality disorder are the personality pattern and trait disturbances and the sociopathic personality disturbances.

5. Among the personality pattern and trait disturbances are (*a*) the schizoid personality, in which the major symptoms are withdrawal and autistic thinking, (*b*) passive and aggressive personalities, in which dependency motives and aggressive tendencies are expressed in various ways, and (*c*) the compulsive personality, in which the major symptoms are excessive concern with standards of conduct and conscience.
6. People with sociopathic personality disturbances show many symptom patterns. Among these are (*a*) the antisocial reaction, in which the major symptoms are little concern over right and wrong, inability to be loyal or responsible, and impulsive criminal acts, (*b*) sexual deviations, and (*c*) drug dependency, of which alcoholic addiction is the most common.
7. Psychotic reactions are those in which the individual has, for a time, lost contact with reality. He often has hallucinations (reported experiences for which no sensory input exists) and delusions (ideas which have no foundation in actual happenings). The thinking of many psychotics tends to be private, or autistic, and bizarre associations are characteristic.
8. Among the major types of psychotic reaction are (*a*) affective reactions, involving extreme moods of excitement or depression, (*b*) paranoid reactions, characterized by systematized delusions of persecution or of grandeur, (*c*) schizophrenic reactions, marked by disorientation, confused thinking, withdrawal, and delusions, (*d*) involutional reactions, in which depression or paranoid-like delusions originate in late middle age, and (*e*) chronic brain syndromes.
9. Of the ten major types of schizophrenia, four of the most dramatic and common ones are (*a*) the simple type, involving withdrawal from other people and deterioration of behavior with time, (*b*) the hebephrenic type, in which behavior regresses to a childish level, (*c*) the catatonic type, involving negativism and the prolonged assumption of postures and unresponsiveness to surroundings, and (*d*) the paranoid type, characterized by unsystematic delusions of persecution.
10. Because schizophrenia is such a common, tragic, long-lasting, and crippling disorder, research into its causes has been pursued vigorously. Among the ideas advanced concerning the causes of schizophrenia are genetic hypotheses and psychogenic interpretations. The psychogenic interpretations stress faulty social learning in disordered family situations and contradictory patterns of communication within the family. The trend in theorizing about the origins of schizophrenia is toward a recognition of some pattern of interaction between genetic and psychological causes.
11. The behaviors included under chronic brain syndromes are caused by damage to the brain. The most common syndromes result from brain changes as a result of old age and as a result of chronic alcoholism—the senile and alcoholic psychoses.

Related topics in the text

Chapter 2 Behavioral Inheritance The genetic nature of schizophrenia is discussed here.

Chapter 11 Personality Some of the defense mechanisms are described. Since one idea of the neuroses is that they are special defense mechanisms, you should review the origins and functions served by normal defense mechanisms.

Chapter 13 Therapy for Behavior Disorders Some methods of treatment for the neurotic and psychotic disorders are discussed.

Chapter 19 Brain and Behavior Some of the addictions are examined in the section on drugs.

Suggestions for further reading

Buss, A. H. *Psychopathology.* New York: Wiley, 1966.
A text emphasizing theories of behavior disorder.

Coleman, J. C. *Abnormal psychology and modern life.* (3d ed.) Chicago: Scott, Foresman, 1964.
A popular textbook on abnormal psychology.

Kaplan, B. (Ed.) *The inner world of mental illness: A series of first-person accounts of what it was like.* New York: Harper & Row, 1964.
Persons who have suffered from behavior disorders report on their experiences.

Kisker, G. W. *The disorganized personality.* New York: McGraw-Hill, 1964.
A textbook on abnormal psychology stressing description of the syndromes of behavior disorders.

Rabkin, L. Y., and Carr, J. E. (Eds.) *Sourcebook in abnormal psychology.* Boston: Houghton Mifflin, 1967.
A selection of stimulating articles on the behavior disorders and psychotherapy.

Stone, A. A., and Stone, S. S. (Eds.) *The abnormal personality through literature.* Englewood Cliffs, N.J.: Prentice-Hall, 1966.
An interesting introduction to the behavior disorders; composed of excerpts from the writings of famous authors.

White, R. W. *Lives in progress.* (2d ed.) New York: Holt, 1966.
An analysis of the personality growth of three normal people. Mild adjustment problems are well illustrated by some of these growth patterns.

Sometimes I feel like
I has no friend
Sometimes I feel like
I has no friend
Sometimes I feel like
I has no friend
And a long ways from home,
A long ways from home.
Spiritual

The last chapter dealt mainly with the causes and nature of maladjustments in behavior. This chapter deals with remedies, or at least with ways and means of treating these maladjustments when they occur, and with action that may prevent them. Unfortunately, neither the prevention nor the cure of disturbed behavior is easy, quick, or sure. The problems in both areas are still largely unsolved, and we are not at all certain of the effectiveness of the methods which are now being used to attack them. Nevertheless, the treatment of behavior disorders is of such importance that every intelligent person should know as much about it as he can.

The Problem of Mental Health

The term *behavior disorder*, as used in the previous chapter, is in some ways preferable to *mental illness* for describing maladjustments. However, mental illness is a common expression, and so are *mental disease* and *mental disorder.* In a way, all these terms are unfortunate, but they are entrenched in the psychological literature.

Behavior disorders in the United States Mental health is a problem that concerns everyone. So many people suffer from behavior disorders that none of us can escape some personal contact with them.

Except for the number of people in hospitals, figures for the incidence of various behavior disorders are at best only estimates which are based on studies of certain communities. These estimates vary with the particular criterion used for deciding whether a person is maladjusted enough to be judged as suffering from a behavior disorder.

Neurotics undoubtedly make up the largest single group. Those people who are neurotic enough to be severely handicapped in social adjustment probably constitute about 5 percent of the adult population. (Extremely conservative figures give something less than 1 percent, whereas more liberal estimates run as high as 37 percent.) Another 2 or 3 percent are addicted to alcohol or are problem drinkers. Roughly a million individuals, or about 0.5 percent of adults, can at any one time be classified as psychotic. If we add another 3 million or so who have personality trait disorders or display antisocial reactions, the number of people with behavior disorders approximates 10 percent of the population.

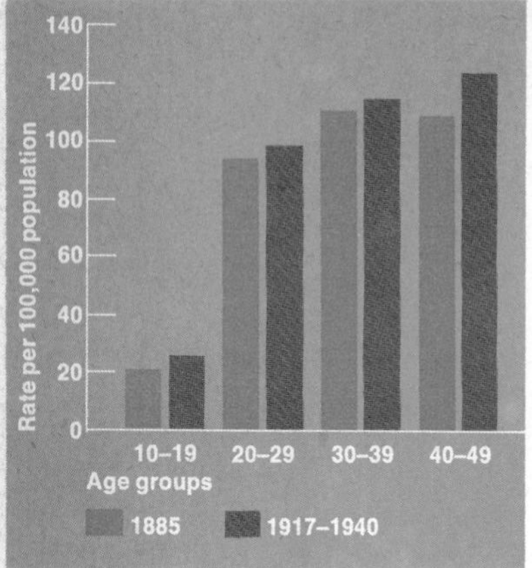

DO STRESSES OF MODERN LIFE CONTRIBUTE TO BEHAVIOR DISORDERS? FOR PERSONS UNDER 50, STATISTICS HAVE CHANGED LITTLE OVER THE YEARS

Figure 13.1 *Admission rates to mental hospitals in Massachusetts for the year 1885 and the period 1917–1940. (After Goldhammer and Marshall, 1953.)*

These figures represent only one given point in time. Over a period of years, the incidence of maladjustment is even higher. In the past the chances of a person spending some part of his life in a mental hospital have been about 1 in 17, or 6 percent. And it is primarily psychotics, rather than neurotics, who are admitted to mental hospitals. Now that modern medicine has dramatically extended the life span, many more people will live long enough to become victims of the senile psychoses. In view of this fact, we now estimate that about 1 individual in 10 will at some time be admitted to a mental hospital.

The number of patients in mental hospitals gives us another idea, and a shocking one, of the prevalence of behavior disorders. *Almost half* the hospital beds in the United States are occupied by mental patients; thus the number of people hospitalized for behavior disorders, or mental diseases, is equal to the number hospitalized for all other diseases combined. There are roughly 1 million beds in mental hospitals. Since most mental hospital facilities are provided by state and local governments, a sizable share of our local taxes is used to care for those with behavior disturbances.

Of all patients admitted to public mental hospitals for the first time, about 75 percent are diagnosed in three major categories—brain syndromes, personality disorders, and psychotic disorders. The rank of these three categories, whether first, second, or third, changes occasionally, but they consistently remain at the top (see Figure 12.1).

Most of the patients diagnosed as suffering from brain syndromes are older people in whom brain damage has been caused by the diseases of old age. Patients diagnosed as having a personality disorder are people who display antisocial reactions, sexual deviations, or alcoholic and drug addictions. Of these, the alcoholic addiction group is by far the largest. In the psychotic category are persons with the bizarre behavior described in Chapter 12. Much the largest psychotic group consists of people displaying schizophrenic behavior. Hospitalization is usually a long-term affair for patients with chronic brain syndromes and for certain types of schizophrenia. This fact, together with high initial admission rates for these disorders, accounts for the very large proportion of mental hospital patients who are suffering from either brain syndromes or schizophrenia.

Neurotics constitute the fourth-largest group of first admissions to public mental hospitals. The reason why their group ranks below the top three is that most neurotics are treated as outpatients or as private patients by psychiatrists. (Refer back to Figure 12.1 for a summary of the first-admission data on the major categories of behavior disorders.)

It is frequently assumed that the stress of modern life is an important factor in behavior disorders. Some observers feel that because life has become more complex, a greater number of individuals are unable to solve conflicts, thus becoming maladjusted and seriously disturbed. Whether or not this is true for all types of behavior disorders we cannot say. It may be so for neurotics. On the other hand, it does not seem to explain the number of admissions to mental hospitals. For people under 50 years old, the statistics on admissions have remained surprisingly constant for nearly a century (Goldhammer and Marshall, 1953). Consider the figures compiled from Massachusetts' records which are given in

TOTAL ADMISSIONS TO MENTAL HOSPITALS ARE UP, BUT PATIENTS ARE BEING RELEASED FASTER

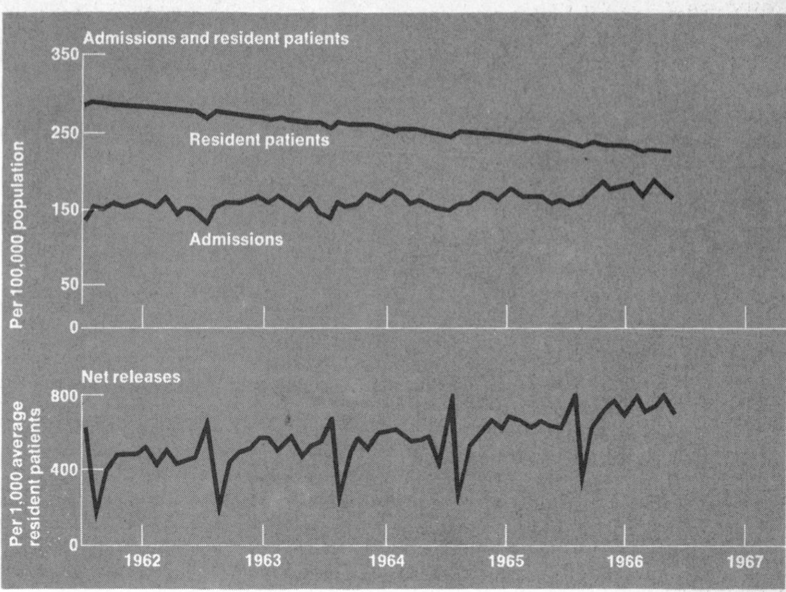

Figure 13.2 *The admission rate for all ages has increased, mainly because the life span is longer and more people develop the senile psychoses. But new forms of therapy for behavior disorders have also increased the discharge rate. Above, rate of admissions and number of resident patients per 100,000 people in state and local mental hospitals; below, rate of release from state and local mental hospitals. The sharp fluctuations in the rate of release between the beginning and end of each year reflect administrative practices. What is important is the trend over the whole period. (Based on Health, Education, and Welfare Indicators, 1967.)*

Figure 13.1. There the rate of admission at various ages below 50 was about the same in the period 1917–1940 as it was in 1885. Data from other sources show almost the same thing. Perhaps this is not surprising in view of the genetic factor in some of the psychoses (see Chapter 12). In any case, the precipitating factors in psychoses apparently have not been altered appreciably by changes in our culture over the years.

Although the admission rate for patients under 50 does not seem to have increased markedly since 1885, the admission rate for all ages has risen mainly because of the higher incidence of senile psychoses as more people live to be older (see Figure 13.2, top). However, another look at the upper part of Figure 13.2 shows that the number of patients per 100,000 population has dropped steadily. The lower part of Figure 13.2 indicates that this drop is due to the discharge rate, which on the average has gradually increased. New techniques of therapy, new drugs, and greater use of out-patient treatment have speeded the discharge of patients from mental hospitals. The long-range trend shows a dramatic drop in number of resident patients per 100,000 since 1954 (see Figure 13.3). But note that, although the *rate* is decreasing, the country's total population is increasing; thus the pressure on mental health facilities is still great.

Trends in therapy Over the years we have moved away from the primitive idea that persons with behavior disorders are witches or have been possessed by demons; behavior disorders are natural, not supernatural, events. And we no longer regard the sufferers as subhuman beings to be "put away" and left in an asylum. Now we think of a behavior disorder as a natural, but tragic, outcome of the play of natural forces on an individual, and we attempt to correct, or treat, his condition.

THE RATE OF HOSPITALIZATION FOR BEHAVIOR DISORDERS IS DROPPING RAPIDLY

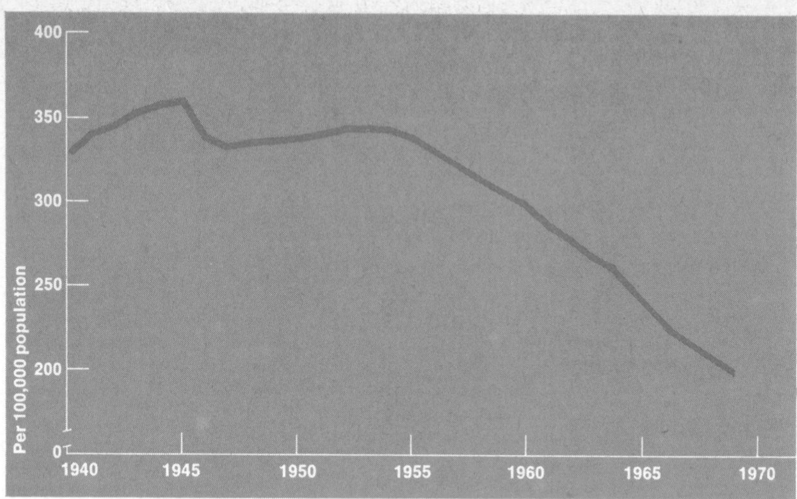

Figure 13.3 *Figures from state and local hospitals show the long-range trend in the rate of hospitalization for behavioral disorders. But while the rate is decreasing, total population is increasing, and hospital facilities are in short supply. (Based on data from the Department of Health, Education, and Welfare.)*

Therapy is the general name for any method used in treating an illness. As we have seen, behavior disturbance, or mental illness, may be a neurosis, a personality disorder, a psychosis, or a chronic brain syndrome due to brain damage. Different forms of therapy are employed to treat these different disorders.

Some therapies aim at eradicating the underlying physical disease. Others involve brain surgery, shock induced by electrical means or drugs, or the use of drugs that restore the patient to a more normal state. Such therapies, naturally, are administered by medical specialists and are therefore classified as *medical therapy.*

Other therapeutic methods are aimed at the emotional and psychological aspects of the patient's problem. They employ interviews, discussions, play acting, and changes in the patient's environment. Since these methods of treatment involve psychological, rather than medical, techniques, and are often in the hands of psychologists, they are called *psychotherapy.*

Medical therapy is much more drastic than psychotherapy and is ordinarily restricted to severe cases of disturbed behavior, or mental illness, particularly to the psychoses. Psychotherapy, on the other hand, is used not only for psychotics and neurotics, but also for persons with a wide range of adjustment problems—delinquents and maladjusted children, and people with marital, scholastic, or occupational difficulties.

At the start of this century, attempts to treat behavior disorders were confined mainly to severe psychotic disorders requiring hospitalization. Therapeutic methods were largely medical. As the understanding of behavior disorders grew, more reliance came to be put on psychotherapeutic procedures. Psychotherapy was extended first to severe neuroses, then to milder neurotic reactions encountered in people outside hospitals. The psychoanalytic movement, launched by Freud, had a great deal to do with this trend, for psychoanalysis, as one particular kind of therapy, is aimed largely at milder neurotic disorders.

The trend toward the use of psychotherapy in treating the milder behavior disorders has occurred for several reasons: (1) The severely and chronically ill cost more to treat, and are less likely to benefit from treatment, than less maladjusted individuals. (2) Psychotherapists have been in short supply, and they therefore have put their efforts where they might do the most good. (3) The treatment of less neurotic individuals offers the greatest benefit to society, for they are still active in social, economic, and political affairs. Any improvement in their adjustment is quickly reflected in their influence on associates and everyday affairs. (4) The successful treatment of mild disorders *prevents* the development of more serious ones.

Of course, if we eventually achieve some dramatic breakthrough in treating more severe cases of neurosis or psychosis, this trend may be reversed. If we do not, the trend is likely to continue and to expand into widespread counseling, individual psychotherapy, and group psychotherapy, with the aims of holding down the incidence of more severe disorders and of making life happier for many people.

Kinds of Therapy

A physician treats many different things when he treats physical diseases. If he can diagnose the underlying cause and has the means of combating it, he will treat that. If he knows, for example, that the patient has scarlet fever, which is caused by a particular microorganism, he fights it with the drug most likely to kill the organism.

We run into problems when we approach the behavior disorders with this medical model of diagnosis followed by treatment. For we are not even sure that classifications such as those given in the previous chapter are accurate designations of different basic processes. While we categorize and label people by the symptoms they display, we do not really know whether the symptom categories represent the same underlying causes. We may be grouping symptoms together simply on the basis of superficial resemblances—something like grouping birds and bees together because they both fly. So we are not sure that categorization, or diagnosis, really helps much with therapy. This problem of categories merely reflects the fact that the causes of behavior disturbances are poorly understood. Consequently many of the therapies for behavior disorders are aimed at relieving symptoms; often the therapist does what "works" without knowing why it works.

Medical therapy Medical therapies for treating behavior disorders can be grouped into four main classes: psychosurgery, shock therapy, narcosis, and drug therapy.

PSYCHOSURGERY Ancient man sometimes drilled holes in skulls to let out the "evil spirits" in behaviorally disturbed people. Although the technique was crude, the reasoning incorrect, and the results of questionable value, the general idea that behavior can be altered by brain operations would seem to have merit. In the 1930s, an operative method was adopted for treating a wide variety of behavior disorders. The method was called *psychosurgery* because it consisted of surgery of the brain for the purpose of relieving mental and behavioral symptoms (Freeman and Watts, 1950).

The most common form of psychosurgery involved the *prefrontal lobes* (see Chapter 19). The neurologists who developed the psychosurgical operation on the prefrontal lobes believed that these lobes were somehow more involved in foresight, planning, and anticipation of the future than were other parts of the brain. The prefrontal lobes were also supposed to have something to do with emotional expression because they are anatomically connected with some of the areas of the lower brain which are important in emotion. Thus it was thought that removal of tissue from the frontal lobes (lobectomy) or the severing of the connections between the frontal lobes and the lower areas of the brain (lobotomy) would make the individual less worried about future events.

It should be noted that the evidence for these supposed functions of the frontal lobes in man is very flimsy. Opponents of the operation have claimed that psychosurgery of the prefrontal lobes produces a rate of remission of symptoms which is no higher than the cures which occur spontaneously (Mettler, 1949). In addition to its questionable efficacy and flimsy rationale, the operation is dangerous. These reasons, together with the development of more effective methods of treatment (the use of tranquilizers, for instance), account for the nearly total disuse into which prefrontal lobe psychosurgery has fallen.

SHOCK THERAPY Shock therapy includes several different kinds of treatment which put the patient into an unconscious state for a time (Jessner and Ryan, 1941). In most cases, this state is preceded by convulsions similar to epileptic convulsions. The usefulness of the method was discovered by accident when a mental patient who was also a diabetic received an overdose of the antidiabetic substance *insulin*. Subsequently he showed remarkable improvement in mental symptoms. Today no one is quite sure why or how shock treatment works. All we know is that some patients improve after a series of shock treatments.

The first form of shock treatment, used in the 1930s, involved relatively large doses of insulin. Although insulin treatment often had beneficial results, it was dangerous; at the very least, it was hard on the patient. After that, the convulsive drug *Metrazol* was employed in place of insulin. But Metrazol is also dangerous, sometimes producing convulsions so violent that bones are broken. In addition, patients characteristically experience a terrifying emotional upset just before the convulsion. A third form of shock therapy is *electroshock*. A brief, carefully regulated jolt of electrical current is passed through the patient's brain. This, like other shock methods, causes a convulsion followed by a period of unconsciousness. Except for feelings of apprehension before the shock, a patient has little unpleasant experience connected with it, and indeed has little memory of the events immediately preceding the shock session. Because of its safety, its simplicity, and its acceptability to patients, electric shock therapy is now the most widely used shock method.

Shock therapy, and particularly electroshock treatment, is most effective with individuals suffering from depression. It seems to alleviate their guilt feelings, suicidal tendencies, and self-deprecation. Sometimes the patient seems entirely normal after a series of electroshock treatments and can be discharged without further therapy. Often, however, shock treatment is combined with psychotherapy. The effects of the shock may be only temporary, but they sometimes leave the patient lucid and approachable enough for a therapist to make progress with psychotherapeutic techniques.

NARCOSIS Narcotic drugs in sufficient dosage put a person to sleep. They differ from one another in several ways: speed of action, length of effect, and degree of effect. Many years ago, before the days of shock therapy, narcosis was administered extensively to keep agitated patients under control. It served this purpose, but it was not safe to use repeatedly and over long periods. By itself, moreover, it had little or no therapeutic value. Now that tranquilizers are available, narcosis is almost never prescribed merely to calm or control patients.

Narcosis is currently used, however, for *narcoanalysis*—that is, analysis of the patient's problems while he is under the effects of certain narcotics such as *Sodium Amytal.* Injected in small doses, this drug makes the patient groggy for several minutes before he falls into a deep sleep. During the groggy or twilight state, he can reenact traumatic experiences and discuss unpleasant subjects (Orr, 1949). Thus the medical therapist can uncover deep-seated problems which have been repressed, and the patient can sometimes relieve his tensions. Narcoanalysis has proved particularly valuable in analyzing disorders caused by a traumatic experience, such as a pilot's terrifying experience in combat. It is also a substitute for hypnosis, because it is quicker and more dependable. Sodium Amytal has sometimes been called a "truth serum," for it enables a patient to remember things otherwise deeply buried by repression. It has little or no value, however, in eliciting confessions in criminal cases.

CHEMOTHERAPY Chemotherapy has been so effective in the alleviation of symptoms in severe behavior disorders that it might be called a biochemical revolution in their management. The main types of chemotherapeutic drugs are the tranquilizers and the psychological activators. We discuss the details of these and other drugs in Chapter 19.

The tranquilizers seem to quiet an anxious person and keep him from feeling so tense and miserable. By themselves, however, they do not reduce worry or deal with the sources of anxiety. They treat the symptom, not the cause.

Nevertheless, the quieting effect of tranquilizers is invaluable in certain forms of behavior disturbance. It enables some patients to be released from the hospital, for it was their agitated behavior that brought them there in the first place. In other cases the quieting effect enables people to deal with the patient, and hence makes it possible for the therapist to establish a relationship within which psychotherapy can be carried on. As a matter of fact, tranquilizers are probably largely responsible for the increased discharge rate from mental hospitals already noted (see Figures 13.2 and 13.3).

The activators are the opposite of the tranquilizers in a behavioral sense; they can activate patients who are severely depressed. These drugs certainly treat the symptoms—and some authorities think that they go farther and actually correct biochemical abnormalities in the brain which are responsible for the disturbed behavior. If so, then the medical model of diagnosis and treatment of cause that we mentioned earlier can be applied to the use of activators in depressive disorders.

Psychotherapy Psychotherapy can be a simple or a very complex process, depending upon the nature of the individual's problem, how severe it is, the type of therapy, and the goals of the treatment.

The aims and overall strategy of psychotherapy should be decided on jointly by the patient and therapist early in the treatment. They may, however, change during the course of therapy. The therapist usually draws upon several sources of information to form his opinion of what can be accomplished in therapy. One source is the *life history* of the person as it is given by the patient himself and by his friends and relatives. Another is a *physical* examination. A third consists of *psychological* examinations of the person, including tests of intelligence, personality, and vocational abilities. Finally, the therapist draws upon the picture he forms of the person's problems in the course of the first few interviews.

The psychotherapist may conclude that the patient's problem stems from (1) environmental frustrations, (2) personal frustrations, (3) motivational conflicts, or (4) faulty learning. Usually all four elements are present, but the therapist must decide on the particular aims of treatment. If environmental frustrations are to be the focus, then changing the situation of the patient will be a psychotherapeutic aim. If the emphasis is on personal frustrations, then temporarily providing support and reassurance will be the primary aim. If motivational conflict is at the heart of the problem, as it very often is, then the principal aim will be to help the patient achieve insight and self-understanding. If faulty learning is the critical factor, extinction and relearning techniques may be tried. Let us consider briefly each of these kinds of therapy.

CHANGING THE SITUATION This is the simplest goal of treatment. It does not involve an attempt to bring about any major change in the patient; rather, an effort is made to manipulate his situation in such a way as to relieve the stress on him. He may be advised to take a vacation, change his occupation, change his educational goals, and so on. Although this may be the only treatment possible in some instances, it is not likely to be satisfactory for most persons. Major changes in the environment are frequently difficult or impossible, and they sometimes make matters even worse for the patient. When the major difficulty is motivational conflict within the person, manipulating the environment is apt to bring only minor relief—he carries the problem with him.

Situational changes, of course, can be important, but they are usually secondary to the treatment of the individual. For children, situational changes are frequently necessary. In simple adjustment problems of adults, too, such changes may provide security for the patient. However, for the great majority of persons who come for treatment, a good deal

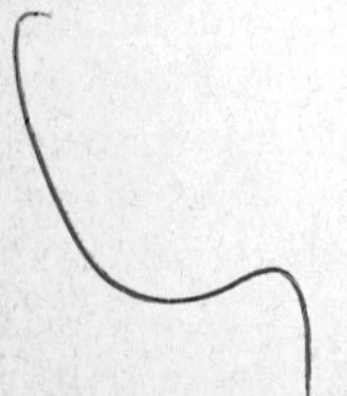

Figure 13.4 *The psychotherapeutic situation. The patient talks with the psychotherapist, and together they work to understand certain facts preceding the illness and to develop ways of working out the underlying problems. (Lee Lockwood, from Black Starr.)*

more is necessary. To begin by changing the situation may completely block progress toward other goals of therapy.

PROVIDING SUPPORT When treatment is arranged to give support to the patient but not to bring about permanent personality changes, it is called *supportive therapy.* The aim here is to help the individual through a crisis. Much of what is called *counseling* is supportive psychotherapy (Bordin, 1955). It helps relatively normal people face specific problems of adjustment. The counselor gives information, listens to the person's problems, suggests courses of action, and reassures him about what he has done or proposes to do. In this way, the counselor may support the person sufficiently to enable him to make a satisfactory adjustment.

Giving support and reassurance, however, requires an expertness that is not easily acquired. The counselor must do it subtly or he will increase rather than decrease the person's anxiety. It is usually wise to use supportive therapy only in certain special cases. One type is the chronic case in which illness is of such long standing, the resources for health are so poor, and the environmental blocks are so great that the chances of effecting a permanent change in the person are small. In such cases, supportive therapy may strengthen his ability to deal with some of his problems. Another type of case is that in which the person has been well adjusted most of his life but temporarily develops a neurotic disturbance in a crisis. Here, supportive therapy may help reestablish healthy modes of adjustment.

ACHIEVING INSIGHT For deeply seated motivational conflicts, insight or uncovering therapy may be appropriate. Its aim is to uncover the causes of a person's difficulty, to rid him of his neurotic defenses, and thereby to free him for flexible adaptive behavior. Insight is not obtained through simple intellectual discovery. Rather, it is a long and painstaking procedure in which the patient exposes himself to various emotional attitudes and situations. He must focus on the emotional situations he has been unable to face—those which he has repressed and around which he has developed his neurotic defenses (see Figure 13.4).

LEARNING AND EXTINCTION One way of looking at some deviant behaviors is to consider them as bad habits which are the result of unfortunate learning experiences. The therapist with this point of view will use special techniques to promote unlearning, or extinction, of the bad habits. Or the techniques may aim at replacing deviant habits by learning new adjustments. Most psychotherapy is not directly learning-oriented in this way, but learning is an implicit feature of almost all psychotherapeutic techniques.

In actual practice, almost all psychotherapy includes some support, some insight, some unlearning and relearning, and eventually even some situational change. However, when the primary effort is to develop insight and to gain continuous emotional growth, the therapy is called *insight therapy.* When the effort to support the self system is greater than the effort to obtain insight, the treatment is called *supportive,* and when the therapy centers on learning and extinction, it is called *behavior modification* or *behavior therapy.*

Psychotherapy with Individuals

Over the years many psychotherapeutic techniques have been developed for use with individuals. Early psychotherapists mainly gave advice and experimented with such directive techniques as hypnosis. Then came psychoanalysis, with its emphasis on motivation and the unconscious. During the last decades of the nineteenth century and the early twentieth century, Freud and his followers developed psychoanalytic techniques of therapy that are still in use. There have been many modifications of their basic psychoanalytic techniques, and new systems of psychotherapy based on different premises have come into prominence in recent years. We shall sample some of the major types which represent important trends.

Psychoanalysis The main objective of psychoanalysis is to help the patient achieve a deep understanding of his own mechanisms of adjustment and thereby to help him solve his own basic problems. It is designed primarily for the treatment of neuroses, but has been used with a great variety of disorders. Although there are shorter versions of psychoanalysis, it is generally a time-consuming therapy that requires at least an hour per week for many months or years. Therefore it is usually worthwhile only for patients with extreme, deep-seated problems who can afford the time and expense of long treatment.

The term *psychoanalyst* refers to, and should be reserved for, a psychotherapist who follows certain teachings of Sigmund Freud. The theory properly called *psychoanalysis* includes some fairly specific ideas about personality and related techniques of therapy. In Chapter 11 we discussed psychoanalysis as a theory of personality which emphasizes structure, development, and dynamics. In the therapeutic setting, psychoanalysis emphasizes free associations, resistances, dreams, and the transference situation as it develops.

The basic aim of psychoanalytic therapy is to make the patient aware of the sources of his anxiety. According to psychoanalytic theory, anxiety is basically due to the presence in us all of certain threatening sexual or aggressive id urges, wishes, or motives—call them what you will. These taboo sexual and destructive urges are, according to the theory, in conflict with the ego and superego systems of personality. Therefore they cannot be expressed directly; the fear of expected punishment is too great, and the urges and the conflicts are repressed. After repression, the id urges are unconscious—we cannot think about them or verbalize them—but they are still there in conflict with the ego and superego and dynamically driving for expression. The individual still fears to express them; but after repression he no longer knows why he feels the fear, because the motive and the conflict are unconscious. This fear of "I know not what" is called anxiety, and various normal defense mechanisms and abnormal defense mechanisms (that is, some neurotic symptoms) develop to reduce it (see Chapters 11 and 12).

The aim of psychoanalytic therapy is to lessen anxiety and the need for exaggerated defense mechanisms through self-understanding and knowledge of the sources of anxiety. By making it possible for a neurotic to gain *insight* into the repressed urges responsible for his anxiety, the psychoanalyst hopes to help him face his conflicts and solve them more rationally. In other words, the attempt is to take someone who is "stupid," because of repression, about the origins of his anxiety and defensive symptoms, and "wise him up" (Dollard and Miller, 1950). This takes time. The analysis of the motives themselves is time-consuming, and the patient usually resists any direct interpretation of his symptoms —that would be too threatening. He must be led gradually to believe in the explanations of his anxiety, symptoms, and behavior as they unfold through his own insights in the course of therapy. This goal is accomplished through the psychoanalytic techniques of therapy.

FREE ASSOCIATION Psychoanalysis begins with the therapist's explanation of the general procedure, aims, and purposes of the therapy. The patient is told that he should not expect recovery in a specific period of time, that his behavior and attitudes may depend upon emotional factors of which he is unaware, and that these must be traced back to their unconscious motivations, chiefly through *free-association.* He is required to say whatever he thinks of, regardless of how irrelevant or objectionable it may be. Since letting thought be free is quite different from ordinary thinking, patients frequently take some time to learn how to free-associate. To facilitate free association, patients lie relaxed on a couch during many psychoanalytic sessions. The following is an example of free association taken verbatim from an interview:

The same thing applies to the fact that they told me some time ago about loss of sleep in the beginning of the night or the last part of the night and I insisted the first was . . . I noticed for two or three nights I began waking up at 2:30 and laying awake most of the night . . . of semi-conscious . . . two—three nights . . . is that done because I'm a creature of habit on account of the suggestion of my mind . . . or am I with a nervous disease. (Pause) Thought about nearly everything . . . in general—can't recall it—nothing relating to sex . . . tried to put it out of my mind and I fight to keep it out. Got the habit of thinking about things and would dream about them . . . tried to keep things out of my mind . . . like fighting on account of the past. My mind traced right on through these lights to the fifth floor and a blond woman . . . shows my mind runs on to sex and injury . . . things like how to avoid going up in high buildings . . . afraid of how high I'd go. Didn't want to tell anybody what my trouble was. Saw it was only a four- or five-story building so I consented. It didn't bother me . . . didn't seem a real test because it wasn't high. Still no confidence in myself . . . still in the dark as to my conflicts . . . two things, one "yes" and one "no." Decided I'd adopt the good because the bad was lashing me. (Cameron and Margaret, 1951, page 511.)

RESISTANCE During free association the patient often shows *resistance,* that is, the inability to remember important events in his past or to talk about certain anxiety-charged subjects. A great part of the analyst's task is to deal with these resistances. By continuous free association, the patient goes beyond his unknown resistances and overcomes them. The situation cannot be forced, but the analyst may suggest some interpretations, which are considered tentative and are revised as the free associations continue. The interpretations are not offered to provide solutions but rather to clear the path of the associations and to provide for the possibility of free flow for further understanding.

DREAMS At any time during psychoanalysis, the patient may report dreams for analysis and interpretation. *Dream analysis* is considered important because dreams are believed to provide a shortcut to the unconscious. The theory holds that the unconscious id motives and conflicts are expressed in disguised and symbolic form in the *manifest content* of the dream—that is, the material of the dream itself. In other words, the manifest content is supposed to be symbolic of unconscious motives and conflicts, which are known as the *latent content*. Such motives and conflicts are too threatening to be expressed directly in the dream. Thus dreams are to be interpreted, according to psychoanalytic theory, as *disguised urge or wish fulfillments*. In certain dreams, extreme anxiety may be generated because the disguise has worn a little thin. From the analysis of dreams the psychoanalyst can sometimes come to understand the particular urges which have been repressed in his patient.

Of course, the interpretation of dreams as disguised fulfillments of sexual and aggressive urges is not the only way of analyzing them. For example, another somewhat different rationale is known as the *cognitive theory* of dream interpretation (Hall, 1953). This method of dream interpretation emphasizes the discovery of themes which run through sequences of dreams. These themes usually concern problems which are significant for the individual, and they are not necessarily conflicts over sexual or aggressive urges. The symbols in dreams, according to this theory, are to be understood as attempts at clear and economical representation of what the referent *means* to a person. For instance, someone who views motherhood as a life-giving and nurturant process may dream about a cow to symbolize this idea of motherhood. It is often only after many dreams have been analyzed that the person's ideas about a referent, and his symbols for it, can be understood.

The interpretation of dreams in terms of wish fulfillments or important problems is a difficult art at best, and it is complicated by several factors. One problem is secondary elaboration of the dream. For instance, parts of the dream may not have been clear, and other parts may have been forgotten—repression may be active enough to wipe out even disguised urge expressions. The reported dream, then, is not the dream which was actually experienced by the person—it is a construction.

TRANSFERENCE Another important phenomenon in psychoanalytic therapy is the transference that gradually develops as the analysis proceeds. *Transference* involves the transfer of attitudes from one person to another; more specifically, it is a reenactment of previous relationships with people, principally of the parent-child relationship. It really amounts to a generalization to the therapist of attitudes acquired toward other people. It appears when the patient and therapist have established good rapport. The therapist may, for example, become a *father figure* and be regarded emotionally by the patient much as he regarded his father. When the emotions directed toward the therapist are those of affection and dependence, the transference is called *positive*. A hostile attitude may be dominant, however, and this is referred to as *negative* transference.

Transference is significant in two ways. First, if it is positive, it can help the patient overcome his resistances. It gives him a feeling of protection so that he has the courage to uncover repressed thoughts. Second, it helps the analyst understand the patient's problem. The transference substitutes a conflict between the patient and the analyst for the conflict that has gone on within the patient. Thus the therapist gets a better look at the problem. He can then analyze the transference and explain its nature to the patient. The following case illustrates some aspects of the transference relationship:

At one stage in therapy, the patient in this case began to make excessive demands of the therapist, requesting special examinations, medications, extra appointments, and similar types of preferment. When attempts were made to discuss this pattern of behavior, the patient immediately accused the therapist of having no interest in him, of being rejecting, and of not really trying to understand him. In this instance the patient was exhibiting patterns of behavior which he had manifested previously in other life situations. He was relating to the therapist as he had related previously to significant persons in his past life, and was perceiving the therapist as he had perceived other figures in the past who could not comply with his insatiable demands. Part of the therapeutic task was to help the patient understand this behavior and the motivations back of it. (Garfield, 1957, page 258.)

The last stages of analysis are reached when the patient gives evidence of insight into the sources of his anxieties. But the analysis cannot be terminated until the transference situation has been broken and a normal doctor-patient relationship reestablished. This is sometimes a very difficult thing to do.

Client-centered therapy In contrast to psychoanalysis, in which the role of the therapist as a "healer" is central, a number of other therapies place more emphasis on the potentialities of the patient, or client, for mental health. Such therapies tend to be *nondirective*—the therapist does not take active charge of the therapy. The client is put into a permissive situation where he has freedom to explore and express his attitudes, hopes, and fears, and the therapist keeps interpretation of these expressions to a minimum. One of the best-known nondirective techniques is called *client-centered therapy*. Rather than attempting to solve any particular problem of the patient, it is designed to provide an opportunity for him to develop his own improved methods of adjustment. The following statement expresses this attitude:

When the counselor perceives and accepts the client as he is, when he lays aside all evaluation and enters into the perceptual frame of reference of the client, he frees the client to explore his life and experience anew, frees him to perceive in that experience new meanings and new goals. But is the therapist willing to give the client full freedom as to outcomes? Is he genuinely willing for the client to organize and direct his life? Is he willing for him to choose goals that are social or antisocial, moral or immoral? If not, it seems doubtful that therapy will be a profound experience for the client. . . . To me it appears that only as the therapist is completely willing that *any* outcome, *any* direction, may be chosen—only then does he realize the vital strength of the capacity and potentiality of the individual for constructive action. (Rogers, 1951, pages 48–49.)

In general, client-centered therapy can be described as a therapy in which (1) the individual, not the problem, is the focus, (2) feelings rather than intellect are attended to, (3) the present receives greater attention than the past, and (4) emotional growth takes place in the therapeutic relationship.

The therapy begins with some explanation of the roles of the counselor and the client and the indication that they will work out difficulties together. The therapist takes pains to establish a relationship that is warm and permissive, without pressure to follow any prescribed course and without criticism or judgment of what the patient says. The counselor's main aim is to help the person express his feelings freely. In this process, the client gains the ability to accept his feelings without fear and gradually finds it possible to express feelings that were formerly repressed. He then begins to see new relationships among his emotional attitudes and to react positively to situations in which he formerly responded negatively.

The following interchange between patient and therapist illustrates the emphasis upon emotional attitudes which distinguishes nondirective therapy. The patient is a young man who complained of recurring periods of tension and depression at a time when his imminent induction into the Army threatened his close relationship with his mother.

P. I went home, you know. I think I have, well, a better way of getting along with Mom. I mean, take the V-12 tests, for example. She seems to understand better or something. I mean, she said I could even enlist in the Air Corps if I wanted to, and she used to just cringe when I mentioned it.

T. So it seems as if you have a new understanding with her.

P. Well, I think we've reached a pretty good understanding now. It was funny . . . once around her, I got the same old feeling back I used to have when I was younger. For the past year or so, I just haven't been feeling anything, and now I got the same old feeling of love. I didn't think I could. I thought I was just cynical and hardened or something. With a different attitude you find things easier to take. (Pause) I don't know. (Long pause)

T. Feeling pretty tense about it, aren't you?

P. Yes. Is it that obvious?

T. I am aware of it, though I guess you'd rather I weren't.

P. Well . . . of course, maybe it was just because I spent such a short time at home, and Mom thought, well, I was going away pretty soon, so she was more willing to hear my side. I don't know, really. I feel I am getting back to the understanding I had as a very small person.

T. Things feel more like they used to.

P. It's just a more pleasant relationship, that's all. Take an example like this.

Mom used to scream if she saw me with a cigarette—tell me I couldn't smoke, and give me all sorts of reasons and everything. And this time when I was home she offered me one! I was simply bowled over. I just couldn't understand why. (Pause) I decided maybe she just realized I was growing up or something. Oh, she let me do little things. When I was fifteen, I worked one summer at a stock exchange. She let me do that all right, she let me go, but she didn't direct me to do it. There's never been any encouragement or guidance in getting out on my own—I just went. She let me go with a tear in her eye, you know.

T. When you wanted to do things yourself, get out on your own, there was always a tear. . . .

P. Boy, that's sure the truth! I never thought about that before, but it's sure the truth. You know, a kid doesn't realize how much effect his childhood has on him, does he? You think, well, I don't have those conflicts, I didn't have a tough adolescence, you think you're apart from all that, above it, somehow. . . . (Pause) So many of the other fellows act more, well, more cold toward their folks, I think I'll always need some sort of ties, somebody to come home to that I love. (Cameron and Margaret, 1951, pages 564–565.)

Client-centered therapy has been effective in counseling college students, in helping normal people with problems of adjustment, such as marital and vocational problems, and in treating mild neuroses. It has not been so successful with dependent people or with people suffering from extreme behavior problems.

Other individual therapies Besides the psychoanalytic and client-centered approaches, there are many other forms of therapy for the individual. Psychoanalysis itself has given rise to new schools, while existential therapies and directive therapies are based on altogether different premises about treatment of behavior disorders. In addition, special play and release therapies have been developed for use with children.

VARIETIES OF PSYCHOANALYTIC THERAPY Many therapists have been impatient with the theoretical bases and the slowness of orthodox psychoanalysis, and new schools of psychoanalytic thought have been established over the years (see Chapter 11). Starting with different theories of behavior and personality, these newer psychoanalytic schools have developed various approaches to therapy. The first new schools were formed by some of the students of Freud: Alfred Adler, Carl Jung, and Otto Rank, for instance. Adler split from the main body of orthodox psychoanalytic thought about 1911, Jung about 1912, and Rank about 1920. As founders of new theoretical systems, these men tended to put less emphasis on the sexual basis of behavior and more emphasis on other basic motives, or strivings. Adler stressed the importance of striving for power, Jung propounded a relatively nonsexual form of libido, or "life energy," and Rank emphasized the importance of the shock of being born, the "birth trauma." As therapists, they tended to be more concerned than the orthodox psychoanalysts with the immediate, present-day situation and problems of the client. We shall take Adlerian therapy as our example of these early offshoots of Freudian analysis.

The approach to therapy developed by Alfred Adler and his school is much more directive than that of orthodox psychoanalysis. The therapist takes a considerably more active role in conversing with the client; he does not make much use of free association; he tries to reeducate the client and teach him the meaning of his present behavior. The therapy session is conducted face-to-face, and the therapist interrupts the client from time to time. We have said that Adlerian theory stresses *power motivation*, not sexual motivation, as the dominant human striving. Adlerian therapy concerns itself with analysis of the ways in which a person handles this basic motive and expresses it in his *life style.* An individual's particular life style stems from his attempts to overcome, or *compensate* for, feelings of *inferiority.*

According to Adler, we are driven to gain power and mastery, but since we start off as weak, helpless infants who do not have the ability to satisfy this motive, we develop feelings of inferiority. Some of us compensate for these inferiority feelings and gain success and some measure of control over other people. Others—the neurotics—are not successful in compensation and retreat into fantasy, overdependency, and other forms of neurotic behavior. These neurotic life styles are the concern of the Adlerian therapist, whose job is to help the client understand his neurotic life style in terms of power motivation and to teach him other ways of expressing this striving constructively. Since so much emphasis is put on the life style of a particular person, Adlerian therapy is sometimes called *individual therapy.*

In more recent times, approximately the period from 1920 to 1950, therapists developed other varieties of psychoanalytic thought which are called the *neoanalytic schools.* In general, these schools have continued the deemphasis of sexual motivation and have stressed the importance of social forces as the dominant influences shaping behavior and personality. The schools of Karen Horney, Erich Fromm, and Harry Stack Sullivan illustrate this trend. We shall consider Sullivanian therapy as an example.

Sullivan regards relationships with other people as crucial in personality development in general and in the development of anxiety and behavior disturbances in particular. As we grow up, he says, we pass through certain stages—the infancy stage, the childhood stage, the juvenile era, the preadolescent stage, the early adolescent stage, and the late adolescent stage. In each of these periods we form fantasy pictures, or distorted ideas, of important people in our lives—mother, father, other family members, friends, and so on. It is to the fantasies or distortions, called *parataxic distortions* by Sullivan, that we respond; we do not respond to the persons as they actually are. Parataxic distortions, then, occur when we conceive of others and respond to them in nonrealistic ways. They limit our effectiveness in relationships with others and, although they may have reduced anxiety when they were originally developed, they serve to perpetuate anxiety in later life.

The client is usually not aware that he holds distorted conceptions of others. In other words, he has distorted views of interpersonal relationships, but he is not aware that these ideas are inaccurate. The Sullivanian therapist attempts to reveal the distortions to him and to change them with his help. The client and the therapist engage in much mutual communication as they attempt to replace the distortions with more realistic conceptions of people. Finally the therapy is terminated with a summary of discoveries and predictions about the client's future behavior in terms of the new interpersonal perceptions which have emerged.

EXISTENTIAL THERAPY This therapy, which has its roots in the existential philosophical viewpoint developed by Heidegger, Sartre, and Buber, is more a group of ideas than a set of specific therapeutic techniques. As applied to psychotherapy, the main existential idea is that life is arbitrary: We are born and die; nothing we can do will alter this; and between birth and death we search for meaning and values in what is basically a meaningless existence. While seeking meaning in a meaningless life, we are constantly threatened with death, or "nonbeing." The existentialists consider both lack of meaning and the threat of nonbeing as the major sources of human anxiety and unhappiness. They believe that we are driven to relieve our anxiety by engaging in various neurotic, or "unauthentic," behaviors which help us escape these bitter truths. We turn to frenzied activity and exploit our fellow man in order to escape; we try to fool ourselves. But the result of this restless, or cover-up, activity is that we fail to become the "real," "authentic," people we really might be. We fail to reach our human potential, and we are not able to establish deep, meaningful, loving relationships with other people.

These existential ideas may be incorporated into many types of psychotherapy. Regardless of the specific technique used, the mark of the existential therapist is that he accepts the patient as he is and tries to understand the ways he seeks for meaningfulness and values in life. The existential therapist tries to serve as a model to help the patient overcome his fear of "nonbeing" and to realize his full human potentiality. The model presented by the therapist is that of an "authentic" person who has found some meaning in life, or at least who knows and accepts the basic meaninglessness of existence, and who is not afraid of death. He tries to communicate to the patient, in both a direct and an empathic manner, his "way of being in the world."

DIRECTIVE THERAPIES In marked contrast to therapies that stress the potentials of the clients are the directive therapies, in which the therapist is an authoritative prescriber. In this type of treatment the therapist is dominant; he gives the client instructions which may help if they are followed. With the advent of psychoanalysis and the realization of the importance of unconscious mechanisms and resistance, directive therapies have declined in importance. But one extreme form, *hypnotherapy*, persists because it can be useful in the alleviation of symptoms and the uncovering of repressed memories. Although considerable debate swirls around the exact nature of hypnosis (see Barber, 1970), in this state resistance to direction and suggestion seem to be low. Through *posthypnotic suggestions*—suggestions which are effective after the hypnotic session has been terminated—the therapist can sometimes direct the patient in ways that lead to better adjustment. A person suffering from hysterical paralysis of the right arm, for example, might be told under hypnosis, "When you wake up, you will be able to use your right arm. It will be completely normal again." Such suggestions often are efficacious; the patient finds that he is not paralyzed when he "awakes."

One drawback of hypnosis as an aid in therapy is that many people are difficult to hypnotize. A more important shortcoming of both suggestion and hypnosis is that the symptom relief tends to be short-lived. This may be either because the suggestions are not very effective or because hypnosis does not treat the underlying causes of the symptom. Consequently, suggestion techniques are useful only in certain situations where it is important to give the patient temporary relief. If a pregnant woman has an intense fear of childbirth, for example, it may be possible by suggestion to get her through the experience without any serious disturbance.

Hypnosis has some diagnostic value in psychotherapy apart from the use of suggestion (Dorcus, 1956). A person in a hypnotic state can often remember events that he has repressed and cannot recall in the normal state. Indeed, the therapist may be able to get the patient, under hypnosis, to relive terrifying experiences of the past that are now causing him trouble. In this way the therapist obtains necessary information to use in other phases of the treatment. Through posthypnotic suggestion he may also be able to induce the patient to carry over the terrifying memories into the normal state. Thus hypnosis is a valuable technique in therapy, even though it generally does not itself effect any basic cure. The following case in which repressed memories were recovered under hypnosis is somewhat unusual because of the insight that developed after recall. Note that further therapy was able to build on the insight.

A neurotic patient, Betty R., age forty-two, visited a psychiatrist with the complaint that she had to clear her throat every few minutes. She had had this compulsive symptom for many years. Besides being an annoyance and an embarrassment, it had kept her, she said, from becoming a successful singer. As a consequence, she was forced into employment in office work, which she hated.

Under hypnosis, she was able to trace the symptom back about twenty years. She was regressed to a time at about twenty-two years of age when she had had no throat trouble, then instructed to recount any emotional experiences she could recall. She remembered attending a picnic with her fiancé, whom she was soon to marry. The two had gone canoeing on a lake, the canoe had tipped over, and she, being unable to swim, had almost drowned. She was saved when her fiancé pulled her to the canoe, which she held onto until other help arrived. He, however, was a poor swimmer and, exhausted by his efforts, himself drowned.

Reliving this experience under hypnosis, the patient began choking as though she were swallowing water. After that, she started crying and said, "I love him so, I can't stand losing him, I just can't swallow it; it sticks in my throat." Then it dawned on her, "Why, that's the reason I clear my throat!" Whereupon the therapist ended the trance.

The insight achieved through hypnosis in this case greatly aided subsequent therapy. In time the symptom disappeared, and the patient's adjustment greatly improved. (Based on Lecron and Bordeaux, 1947, pages 211–212.)

Figure 13.5 *Release therapy. Emotionally disturbed adolescents release some of their feeling in finger painting. (Life Magazine, Time, Inc.)*

PLAY OR RELEASE THERAPY Most of the therapies considered so far were designed for adults; but children have behavior problems too. They cannot be expected to participate in the abstract verbal exchanges necessary in psychoanalysis or even client-centered therapy. Recognizing that play provides unusual opportunities for relieving tension and achieving insight, therapists have devised techniques known as *play* or *release therapy* (Axline, 1947). These techniques utilize play with toys, puppet shows, drawing, modeling, and many other activities (see Figure 13.5).

The greatest value of play technique is in the study of personality. The child often cannot or will not explain himself in the first person; yet he may reveal much of his inner life if allowed to play freely with toys. The child who will not tell about his own fears and conflicts may readily project these feelings into dolls. Feelings of rejection, insecurity, ambivalent attitudes toward parents, repressed hatreds, fears, and aggressions may all be freely revealed in play. Consequently the play technique, when properly handled, offers opportunities for understanding the child that are otherwise difficult to create.

The play situation can also be therapeutic. In the security and permissiveness of play, the child may relieve tension by releasing feelings without fear of reprisal. A carefully conducted play situation allows the child's feelings to come to the surface and thus helps him learn to face them, control them, or abandon them. To the extent that the play situation is a miniature of the child's life, emotional conflicts can be worked out and new learning can take place.

Effectiveness of traditional psychotherapies How successful are the psychotherapeutic techniques we have described in this section? It might seem at first that this would be an easy question to answer. Using the records of psychotherapists, can't we find the number of patients treated and compare this with the number of cures? Unfortunately, a multitude of problems complicate this simple-sounding program. First is the problem of records; many, if not most, psychotherapists do not keep the kinds of records which lend themselves to scientific evaluation. Second and far more troublesome is the criterion problem and its related difficulties. For instance, can we decide what constitutes a "cure"? By what standards are patients to be evaluated? Third is the so-called base-rate problem. What is the number of patients who get better spontaneously? In other words, we need to be able to estimate the rate of spontaneous recovery in order to have a basis for comparison of the effects of psychotherapy. A fourth problem is that of selection, for psychotherapists, especially those in private practice, select the patients with whom they expect to be most successful. Are the figures which we obtain on the rates of "recovery" inflated because of this selection of the most favorable cases? What can be said about all cases if we are looking only at the results of the most favorable?

For all these reasons the question of the effectiveness of psychotherapeutic techniques is likely to remain just that—a question. Even so, some brave investigators have attempted to study the issue. In one evaluation of many of these studies, the effectiveness of psychotherapy was found to be low (Eysenck, 1952):

A careful attempt was made to establish an adequate base rate for spontaneous recovery. One way in which this was done was to find the percentage of neurotics who had been discharged from mental hospitals within a year of admission. These patients received custodial care in the hospital, but very little psychotherapy. Therefore their recovery may be considered "spontaneous." Several difficulties with using this as a base rate arise because, for one thing, only the most severe neurotics are admitted to institutions. Consequently the figure may be biased so that the base rate of recovery is too low—perhaps less disturbed neurotics would show a higher spontaneous recovery rate. There are many other difficulties with this estimate of the spontaneous recovery rate. Recognizing them, and attempting to allow for them, the investigator arrived at an estimate that about 67 percent of neurotics improved markedly, and spontaneously, in a year.

What about improvement in psychotherapy? A study was made of two types of psychotherapy: (1) the psychoanalytic and (2) the eclectic, in which different traditional approaches are used. The results were not encouraging for psychotherapy—44 percent of patients treated by psychoanalytic therapy were "cured," "much improved," or "improved"; 64 percent of those treated by eclectic methods were "cured," "much improved," or "improved." Since many of the patients in psychoanalytic therapy broke off treatment, the figures may be corrected to exclude them. When this is done, approximately 66 percent of the patients treated by psychoanalysis were "cured," "much improved," or "improved." Summing all this up, we can say that it looks as if no difference exists between the recovery rates of untreated neurotics and those treated by the traditional methods of psychotherapy.

Many authorities would not agree that this study is completely accurate, but it does make clear that the usual kinds of psychotherapy are not panaceas. Prevention would seem to be the most rational course of action.

Perhaps the fact that the overall figures are not encouraging is due less to the therapeutic technique than to the therapists. Some people seem to make better therapists than others. When we look at average figures, we are lumping the "good" therapists together with the "not-so-good" therapists. It has been pointed out that "the therapist's contribution to the treatment process is a dual one: it is personal *and* technical" (Strupp, 1958, page 66). It is the personal aspects of the therapist's contribution which we are stressing here. In one study, for instance, the following characteristics were found to be typical of competent, or "good," psychotherapists:

The competent therapists were (1) self-confident, outgoing, aggressive persons; (2) individualistic, nonconforming, and spontaneous, although they remain within the limits of acceptable social behavior; (3) introspective and empathic persons who can admit to personal deficiencies without loss in self-esteem; (4) more open and consistent in their relationship to authority figures and tend toward inner control rather than external conformity. (Modified from Fox, 1962, page 58.)

Perhaps this set of characteristics would not be the best for every type of psychotherapeutic situation. The main point, however, is that some therapists are more effective than others. Thus in addition to the many problems inherent in studies of psychotherapeutic effectiveness, the lumping together of good and not-so-good therapists may make the figures seem less encouraging than they should be. No final conclusion can be reached about the effectiveness of traditional methods of psychotherapy—success or failure would seem to depend on the patient, the therapist, and their interaction.

Group Therapy

In contrast to the somewhat artificial setting of individual therapy, in which the patient expresses himself to one other person, the circumstances of group therapy more closely resemble the real social environment. In a group therapy session the patient can behave more as he does in everyday relationships, with the therapist and the other members of the group representing people who have special meanings for him.

It has also been found that sessions providing certain kinds of group experience can benefit mentally healthy people, giving them greater sensitivity and depth of feeling for others. These groups conducted for the mentally healthy are one of the newer developments in psychology. So too is family therapy, in which the behavior problems of an individual are approached through the entire pattern of relationships within his family. Another form of group therapy is psychodrama, in which the patient acts out his problems rather than merely talking about them.

Group experience as therapy As a therapy, group experience is sometimes a supplement to individual therapy, sometimes a substitute for it, and sometimes a sequel to it. A patient who has been in individual therapy may begin or continue group therapy when it seems to be doing him more good than individual treatment.

There are many variations of group therapy. The usual type consists of the group's assembling under the guidance of a therapist for meetings of about an hour. The therapist attempts to remain in the background, permitting individuals in the group to talk freely. While he does not dominate the session, the traditional group therapist tries to keep the discussion focused and may throw out some interpretations of behavior for discussion by the group. As the group conversation progresses, certain members may discuss their own problems and symptoms. The other members give their points of view, and gradually each one interposes some of his own experiences, attitudes, and feelings. Some members inevitably profit more than others, but most receive some benefit. Merely learning that their problems are not unique is helpful. The opportunity to view situations and attitudes from a variety of perspectives is also valuable. It may assist the individual to relieve his feelings of isolation and rejection, overcome his self-consciousness, modify a too strict conscience, give vent to aggressions, and obtain substitute gratifications.

Another value of the group method is the support it can provide. In individual therapy, some patients find it intolerable to be dependent on the therapist and are unable to accept his support. Others accept support too readily and react unfavorably when it is withdrawn. In group therapy, the members of the group support and depend upon one another, without having an obligation to any single person.

Group experience for learning and emotional growth Group experience for mentally healthy people has recently become an exciting and rapidly developing area of psychology. Of the many varieties, the best known are probably the *laboratory method,* or the *T (training)-group method, sensitivity,* and *encounter groups* (Bradford et al., 1964; Rogers, 1967; Burton, 1969). The emphases of these methods differ; for example, the laboratory method is somewhat more structured than the various types of encounter groups. Generally speaking, however, all have the following aims:

1. To bring people closer together in order to ease the lost and lonely feeling that many of us are said to experience in the depersonalized modern world. In other words, to provide some help for modern man's "existential neurosis" of alienation, meaninglessness, and loneliness—to bring some joy into life.
2. To open up areas of thought and feeling previously sealed off in order to foster greater personal freedom and deeper relationships with others. To overcome "hang-ups"; this may mean giving greater attention to bodily feelings.
3. To improve mutual communication by making people more sensitive to the emotional reactions and feelings of others.
4. To provide an experience of trust and openness in relating to other people; to create a situation in which one learns that others are not really frightening.
5. To produce conditions in which the new learnings about openness and the importance of emotions will carry over to relationships with people outside the group—in marriage, at work, and so on.

Can we analyze the processes by which these goals are approached? So many variations of group techniques exist, and so much is new and unformulated, that we can only give a general description. The groups, usually of about 5 to 20 people, have a minimum of structure. The leader, facilitator, or trainer, as he is variously called, does not follow an agenda and does not usually work within the framework of ideas provided by traditional psychotherapy; that is, he does not try to use his knowledge to bring about a "cure," or a change in behavior. Instead, he attempts to create an atmosphere in which emotions and feelings are stressed. It is an atmosphere in which people can break through the front, or facade, that they usually put up before others.

When facades are dropped and emotions are stressed, many things can happen. Early in the history of such groups negative attitudes, aggressive behavior, and confrontations between people are common. Part of the process of growth in encounter groups is supposed to consist of working through these negative feelings about others. There is constant feedback from the group, so that the individual has many opportunities to see how he appears to other people and what kinds of emotional responses he arouses. As the group interactions proceed—usually a matter of some weeks or months—the members work through their negative feelings. As they come to know each other better emotionally, positive feelings emerge; previously unloved, lonely people may begin to experience positive regard from others in the group. Such is the joyous, positive part of the group encounter—one of its major goals.

The path to this goal is difficult, however. The expression of negative feelings and aggression may be upsetting; the breaking down of facades is likely to result in a weakening of defenses against anxiety. Another difficulty is that the increased freedom of expression developed within the group may not work with people outside the group; for example, a person's husband or wife who is not in the group may not share this new emotional freedom.

Being a leader of such a group may look easy, but it is not; he must be highly skilled in meeting the difficult interpersonal problems that may arise. He must also be adroit in handling the anxiety that may develop in some members of the group. Anyone thinking about joining such a group should investigate to make sure it is being conducted by competent people.

Family therapy This form of therapy is another reflection of the trend toward greater emphasis on the relationships between people and away from exclusive concern with the individual (Haley, 1963). In family therapy a person's behavior problems are seen in terms of relationships and conflicts among family members rather than in terms of conflicts within the person himself. The disturbed behavior of a child, for example, is one of the most common problems brought to the family therapist. The therapist will try to change the child's behavior by altering the patterns of interaction within the family—the ways the child is controlled by others and the ways he uses his disturbed behavior to gain power over other family members. By changing the family pattern of relationships, the therapist seeks to remove some of the root causes of disturbed behavior, or at least to make the family members aware of the actual patterns—the power plays and techniques of control.

Family therapists use many settings and tactics. The family may be brought together as a unit, or the therapist may start by talking to the parents or children and then only gradually introduce other members of the family into the conversations. The therapist may visit the home or hold all sessions in his office. He may be present while the family talks together, or he may observe their interactions through a one-way window and offer only occasional comments. Television tapes of family interactions may be made and played back for analysis and comment with the family present.

During the therapy session the family therapist may work individually with a single family member while other members look on. Or he may serve as a "funnel" through which all communications from one family member to another must pass. Or, most often, he may encourage intense communication between members of the family. Such communication and discussion of feelings frequently has therapeutic value,

Figure 13.6 *Psychodrama, a special technique in psychotherapy. Under the guidance of members of the professional staff, patients use psychodrama to work out various problems in human relationships, often in front of a small audience of other patients. (Moreno Institute, Inc.)*

because some families do very little of it naturally. In this way the therapy session provides an opportunity to work out differences that were not apparent before.

Whatever the particular tactics used, the family therapist avoids taking sides and becoming involved in the power struggles and coalitions among family members. He tries to be perceived as a person interested in helping the whole family solve its problems. Because he does not allow himself to be manipulated by the usual family control tactics, he presents a model for different ways of handling the family's problems.

Family therapists often try to keep their directions to the family vague and to blunt direct comments by putting them into "feeling" language. For instance, if one family member is critical of another, the therapist may raise the question of how the family members "feel" about that. Family therapists also attempt to overcome resistance by emphasizing the positive aspects of the family's behavior.

Thus instead of attempting to bring about change in a family by direct instructions, the family therapist tries to provide a model for new ways of handling interpersonal problems. The setting he creates is designed to minimize resistance and encourage the family to explore these new ways of getting along with each other.

Psychodrama The drama in some form has been used in mental healing since ancient times. Its therapeutic values were mentioned by many philosophers, and there is evidence that, in the ancient theater, plays were sometimes presented for their therapeutic effects. *Psychodrama,* however, is a specialized technique designed to permit patients to act out roles, situations, and fantasies related to their problems (Moreno, 1946). It thus affords something not normally provided by therapies in which the patient is treated alone and is able to express his feelings only in words. Psychodrama enables him to express himself in realistic situations by acts rather than words. It also treats the individual in social situations resembling those which have been a source of his difficulties.

In psychodrama the patient usually is encouraged to act out real situations or fantasies freely, spontaneously, and without limitation (see Figure 13.6). Trained therapeutic actors help him get started and play the roles of people significant in his problems. The patient may act out not only situations he has experienced, but those he has feared and evaded. At times he may portray himself; at other times he may take the part of someone who is influential in his life. As the therapy proceeds, it may become evident that he avoids certain roles and situations, and it may be necessary to direct him to live through scenes that are painful or undesirable. Psychodrama thus provides some of the same opportunities for free association and reliving of experiences as does psychoanalysis, but psychodrama uses the vehicle of the play to do it. From time to time, the therapist may analyze and interpret the situations that have been acted out.

The therapy may be carried on with or without an audience. In some situations the audience, often composed of people with problems similar to those of the actors, participates in the performance and consequently serves as an aid to the therapy. In other instances the audience may be made up of patients who themselves are the object of the therapy, since many of their own problems are being dramatized. Much of the success of this therapy depends upon an astute chief therapist and a carefully trained staff of assistants. Even under these circumstances, however, many patients find it impossible to participate in such a dramatic procedure.

Community mental health While it is not group therapy in the sense of giving therapy to small groups, the community mental health movement is concerned with issues affecting the mental health of very large groups of people. This movement brings public health to the field of mental health. Just as public health physicians work to eradicate epidemics, community mental health authorities hope someday to develop techniques that will help communities reduce the incidence and virulence of maladaptive behavior.

Individual and small-group therapies, by themselves, are not appropriate for this task. First, the number of people who can be reached by them is quite limited. In the second place, these therapies are usually restricted to people who can afford them (as a rule individual psychotherapy is expensive) and to people who are skilled in talking about their intimate feelings and experiences. Most people have neither the money nor the verbal skills and attitudes necessary for individual or small-group psychotherapy; these therapies are essentially middle-class ones. Therefore individual and small-group psychotherapies do not reach many people; in particular, they are not geared to help those who are overwhelmed and defeated by the burdens and crises of poverty. Finally, individual and small-group psychotherapies are aimed at individuals with specific problems. They are not concerned with the factors within communities that contribute to motive frustrations, broken families, or psychological tensions that are at the root of many, if not most, psychological problems.

One aim of community mental health is to make inexpensive long-term individual or group psychotherapy more readily available. Another aspect of community mental health is that it attempts to provide emergency psychological aid for people during crises. But this movement is also concerned with the prevention of behavior disorders and with such social questions as these: How can the unfavorable attitudes that groups of people have about other groups be changed? If the blacks of a community hate the whites and the whites hate the blacks, what can be done about it? What will help a community in such crisis situations as school integration? How can public officials—the police, for instance—be made more sensitive to the feelings and motives of those with whom they deal?

Thus the community mental health movement is concerned not only with providing psychological services for the poor, who might not otherwise have them, but also with alleviating tensions in the community that may lead to maladaptive behavior. In doing this, the movement encroaches on some sensitive areas of life. Mental health workers who try to change attitudes within a community, for instance, may be dealing with strongly held emotional beliefs and may encounter a great deal of hostility. Progress is often slow, and tension reduction is often accomplished only after the members of the community come to trust the mental health workers. In spite of the problems, the need is so great that community mental health will probably be a rapidly growing area of psychology in the future.

Behavior Modification

Dissatisfaction with traditional forms of psychotherapy has been growing for some years now. First, as our earlier discussion indicated, they are not effective enough. Second, the theoretical basis of many therapeutic systems is questionable and often bears little resemblance to the therapy as actually practiced. Third and perhaps most important, methods have recently been developed for the direct modification of specific behaviors.

These newer therapeutic procedures utilize techniques and principles from classical conditioning, operant conditioning, and perceptual learning (see Chapter 3). Their rationale is that the symptoms of the behavior disorders were learned in the first place and, with proper training techniques, can be unlearned—that is, extinguished. Extinction may involve either weakening the responses or learning new responses that are incompatible with the ones being extinguished.

Therapists who use learning techniques do not believe that theories about underlying dynamic mechanisms (for instance, the various psychoanalytic mechanisms) are useful in treatment of behavior disorders. These therapists are content to concentrate on the disordered behavior itself in the attempt to alter it (Bandura, 1965). After all, their argument runs, it is the behavior, not some unconscious mechanism, that has gotten the person into the difficulty from which he now seeks relief. They usually deny the traditional explanations given for the underlying causes of disorders—the theories about anxiety, and so on. And they point out that changing the patient's behavior results in improved adjustment; he is better able to derive satisfaction from his environment. For instance, a phobic person is uncomfortable in many situations, and his life tends to be dominated by the active avoidance of the situations which provoke the phobia. Remove the phobic responses, and he will lead a more satisfying life. Or consider a person whose sexual behavior is deviant—a fetishist, for instance (see page 417). The behavior which centers on the fetish object will get him into trouble with his friends and, perhaps, the police; but remove the behavior and he has fewer difficulties.

Thus behavior therapy is a direct attack on deviant behavior, with the aim of eliminating or altering it. The behavioral changes that result tend to be relatively long-lasting, in contrast to the more temporary symptom relief produced by hypnosis. This difference is probably due to the greater power of learning techniques, for as we saw in Chapter 3, they create relatively permanent changes in behavior. Changes based on suggestion, as in hypnosis, seem to be much less permanent.

Classical conditioning techniques One of the major classical conditioning techniques in behavior therapy is *counterconditioning.* The idea here is that disordered behavior is conditioned to a particular set of stimuli or a stimulus situation. Therapy consists of conditioning responses to the same stimuli which are incompatible with the undesirable responses, as in the following case (Raymond, 1956):

The patient had a strong fetish—he was sexually excited by the sight of baby carriages and women's handbags. He could have satisfactory sexual intercourse with his wife only when imagining handbags. His fetish was a problem because he often attacked baby carriages. Since, in general, other methods of therapy are not successful with this type of disorder, counterconditioning behavior therapy was tried. Handbags, baby carriages, and a movie of baby carriages being pushed were used as the conditioned stimuli. At the same time that the patient was shown these stimuli, he was made nauseous by the injection of a drug; the aim was to condition sight of the sexually exciting objects to nausea. The treatment was successful in removing the fetish: After some days the patient, referring to the handbags and baby carriages, said over and over, "Take them away." A follow-up 19 months later showed that he had continued to be free of his fetish.

Thus when nausea was conditioned to the stimuli which triggered the sexually deviant responses, the sexual response became aversive. Generally, this type of counterconditioning therapy is called *aversion therapy.* It is sometimes used as a first step in treatment of alcohol addiction.

Other counterconditioning techniques aim at *desensitization,* that is, making the person feel comfortable in situations where he has previously been anxious or fearful. For many patients certain circumstances have been associated with pain, shame, or insecurity. The counterconditioning therapy in these instances is to have the patient, under special "safe" conditions, face the anxiety- or fear-arousing situations so that other responses can be conditioned to them.

A special variety of counterconditioning to desensitize fears and anxieties is known as therapy by *reciprocal inhibition* (Wolpe, 1958). The main idea is to present the conditioned stimuli for the fear or anxiety responses when the patient is making responses which are incompatible with fear or anxiety responses. For instance, thorough relaxation is typically used as an incompatible response. When the patient is relaxed, stimuli which might be expected to produce fear or anxiety are presented in a graded series: those which will arouse only a little fear or anxiety are presented first, and more powerful stimuli are presented after the patient is desensitized to the weaker ones. In other words, the therapist works along the generalization gradient from stimuli which produce weak conditioned responses to stimuli which are close to the conditioned stimulus and therefore produce strong responses (see page 73). Eventually, even the strongest responses are desensitized through inhibition by incompatible responses, as in this example (Clark, 1963):

A 31-year-old woman suffered from a phobia of birds and feathers. She could not go for walks, take her child to the park or the zoo, or go to the beach because of her fear that birds would come near her, or even worse, swoop over her. The reciprocal inhibition therapy consisted of inducing her to relax through suggestion and mild hypnosis. Records of her galvanic skin response (GSR) were taken as an index of emotional reactivity (see page 231). With the patient relaxed, and her GSR showing responses indicative of this relaxation, she was presented with a stimulus far out on the generalization gradient for her fear—a single feather, shown 12 feet away. The therapist had a good idea of the relative potencies of stimuli in eliciting the fear because the patient had ranked them before the therapy began. Next the feather was moved closer and closer and the GSR reaction watched for signs of emotional upset. If any occurred, the feather was immediately moved back. After the patient showed no emotional reaction to the single feather when it was only a foot away, the next item in the stimulus hierarchy was presented. Going from weak to strong, these consisted of assorted feathers, bags of feathers, a bundle of feathers, stuffed birds, and finally, live birds. In addition to this therapy at the hospital, the patient, after some desensitization had already taken place, was instructed to visit places where birds or feathers were likely to be found. While there she was instructed to try to remain calm, but to retreat immediately if she felt any fear. By the time the therapy was completed, she "could have handfuls of feathers flung at her, could plunge her hands into a bag of down and no longer feared going out of doors or birds in the garden and hedgerows."

Here, then, is a case in which a specific piece of behavior was altered. This type of therapy seems to be most successful when the deviant behavior is fear or anxiety which is limited to rather specific situations.

Operant conditioning techniques Another type of learning that has been applied in behavior modification is operant conditioning. It has been found that disordered behavior can be modified by the appropriate use of positive and negative reinforcers.

REINFORCEMENT We know from Chapter 3 that behavior is modified, or shaped, in operant conditioning when a reinforcer follows as a consequence of behavior. One rough definition of a *reinforcer* is that it is a stimulus or event which changes the rate of behavior when it follows that behavior. Another way of describing operant conditioning is to say that in it behavior is modified when reinforcement is *contingent* upon, or depends upon, the behavior.

Many things can reinforce behavior. A rough distinction can be made between positive and negative, or aversive, reinforcers. Positive reinforcers are those that the subject ordinarily approaches or prefers. Examples are praise, food when one is hungry, and tokens that serve as symbols for desired objects. Negative, or aversive, reinforcers are events or objects which the subject will work to avoid. Examples are painful shocks and the removal of positive reinforcers. The crucial factor in operant conditioning is that reinforcement is arranged so that it is contingent upon certain behaviors. In behavior modification, the trick is to arrange such reinforcement in real-life, or natural, settings.

In addition to the ordinary types of positive and negative reinforcers, one behavior is able to reinforce another. Thus a high-rate behavior, or a preferred behavior, can be employed to reinforce a low-rate, or nonpreferred, behavior (Premack, 1965). Consider a 9-year-old piano-baseball player: His parents usually say, "Play the piano and then you can play ball," and they often justify this command with some vague ethical principle, such as "Business before pleasure." But they may actually be reinforcing the piano playing by making a preferred, or high-rate, behavior—baseball playing—contingent upon piano practice. Maybe there is some folk wisdom in "Business before pleasure." Situations of this type are often complicated by many other reinforcers and by the

WITHDRAWAL OF POSITIVE REINFORCEMENT IS AVERSIVE AND WILL SHAPE BEHAVIOR

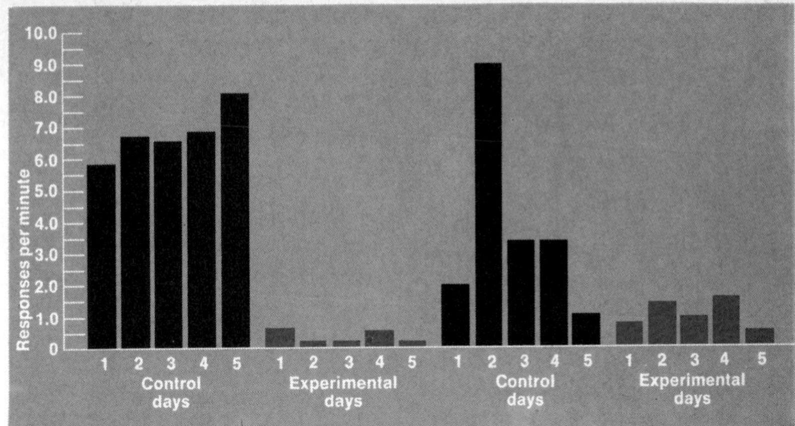

Figure 13.7 *In this experiment a psychotic boy went on walks hand in hand with the therapist. On the experimental days, whenever the boy began his usual behavior of banging his head and slapping himself, the therapist removed his hand from the boy's. Hand holding was a positive reinforcement, and its withdrawal was aversive. In the experimental conditions, withdrawal of positive reinforcement was extremely effective in reducing the boy's self-destructive behavior. On control days there was no withdrawal of positive reinforcement, and behavior occurred at a high rate*

Note that there was a tendency for the undesirable behavior to decrease in the second group of control days; perhaps this indicates a spread of effect from the experimental days. Some loss of behavioral control occurred in the second experimental conditions. (Modified from Tate and Baroff, 1966.)

unwise use of punishment to control behavior. But if handled correctly, such reinforcers are powerful because they make use of strong behavior tendencies and motivations that are already present.

REINFORCEMENT IN THE ELIMINATION OF SYMPTOMS By combining positive and negative reinforcement, a behavior therapist can do much to eliminate annoying and disruptive responses that are symptomatic of behavior disorders. This treatment has been found effective in many cases of psychosis (Ayllon, 1963):

One woman, diagnosed as a schizophrenic, had been in the hospital for 9 years. Several of her deviant behaviors were selected for treatment by operant techniques: overeating and stealing food, hoarding towels, and wearing up to 25 pounds of clothing in the form of extra layers of garments and a peculiar headdress. All these behaviors were gradually removed by use of principles of operant conditioning.

For example, here is how the patient was conditioned to discard her extra layers of clothing. The crucial factor is that the therapist had complete control over her environment; he could regulate when and whether she was reinforced. In this case, he made eating contingent upon the amount of clothing she wore. She was weighed before each meal with all her clothes on, and her actual body weight was subtracted from her clothed weight. Whether or not she was allowed to eat depended upon the weight of extra clothing she wore. At first, the level was set at 23 pounds or less of clothing—a reduction of 2 pounds over her usual clothing weight. If she had more than this on, she did not eat. Of course, she went hungry for a few meals, but she eventually met this standard. Then the limit was set lower and lower, until after several weeks the clothing weight stabilized at 3 pounds. In addition to taking off her excess clothing, the patient now removed her headdress and began to arrange her clothes more normally.

One of the outcomes of the removal of these deviant behaviors was that the patient's family, for the first time in 9 years, asked to have her come home for a visit.

Negative and positive reinforcers have also been used to control self-injurious behavior (Tate and Baroff, 1966):

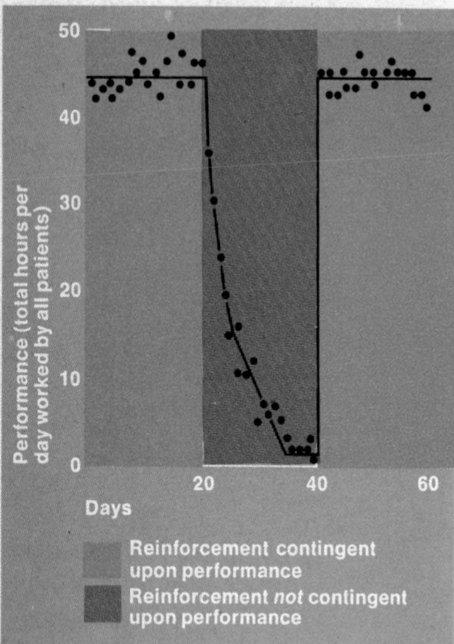

CONTINGENT REINFORCEMENT CAN BE A POWERFUL SHAPER OF BEHAVIOR

Figure 13.8 *Job performance as a function of contingent and noncontingent reinforcement in a group of 44 schizophrenic patients. Each dot represents the total hours worked each day by all patients. Note how reinforcement controlled their behavior. When reinforcements (tokens) were awarded for the work they did, output was high; when reinforcements were given whether or not the patients worked, output fell drastically. (Modified from Ayllon, T., and Azrin, N. H. The measurement and reinforcement of behavior of psychotics.* Journal of the Experimental Analysis of Behavior, *1965, 8, 357–383. Copyright © 1965 by the Society for the Experimental Analysis of Behavior, Inc. Additional information and related experiments can be found in* The Token Economy: A Motivational System for Therapy and Rehabilitation, *by T. Ayllon and N. H. Azrin, published by Appleton-Century-Crofts, 1968.)*

The patient, a psychotic boy, was accustomed to bang his head and slap his face so vigorously that he had to be kept in bed under restraint. In the experiment, the therapist and the boy took walks hand in hand. When the boy began his usual self-destructive behavior during a walk, the therapist removed his hand from the boy's. Since hand holding was a positive reinforcer, its removal was aversive for the patient. The results of the therapy, depicted in Figure 13.7 on the previous page, indicate that this aversive consequence markedly reduced the boy's self-injurious behavior on the experimental days.

Other negative reinforcers that have been used to shape the behavior of autistic and self-destructive children include verbal reprimands and electric shock (Lovaas, 1968). Negative reinforcers must be handled with care, however; their unwise use may result in fear conditioning and increased emotionality.

THE TOKEN ECONOMY Behavior modification techniques that stress contingent positive reinforcement can be effective with relatively large groups of people in social situations. In the *token economy,* for example, whole mental hospital wards can be managed through moneylike tokens that are used to reinforce certain performances. The hospital thereby becomes more like the world outside, and patients are led to interact with other people in socially useful ways. This aspect of the token economy can be a large part of the milieu therapy discussed in Chapter 12 (see page 429). Patients earn tokens contingent upon particular behaviors and can spend them for such important things as privacy, leave from the hospital, or little luxuries.

Figure 13.8 depicts the results of a set of observations on 44 schizophrenic patients who were reinforced by tokens for serving in such jobs as waitress, janitor, recreational assistant, secretarial assistant, and so on. When reinforcement by tokens was contingent upon the performance of their work, their output was high. But when tokens were given noncontingently—that is, when the patients were simply issued tokens whether or not they completed their work—output dropped drastically. When the contingency condition was reimposed, the amount of work the patients did returned to the previous level. This may not seem a surprising result in itself, but it is important in demonstrating the degree of control exerted over human behavior by contingent positive reinforcement.

Thus by using positive reinforcers in a token economy, mental hospital personnel are able to channel behavior into patterns conducive to rehabilitation. Patients relearn behaviors that will fit them for social life outside the hospital; they do not sit and deteriorate. With such techniques we can probably expect a continued drop in the rate of hospitalization for behavior disorders (see Figure 13.3).

Modeling The imitation, or *modeling,* of behavior is a behavior modification technique that is related to perceptual learning (see Chapter 3). In the following experiment, snake phobias were treated by modeling (Bandura, et al., 1969):

Figure 13.9 *Frames from a movie shown to subjects with snake phobia. Viewing the movie gave them some relief from the phobic condition. (Modified from Bandura et al., 1969.)*

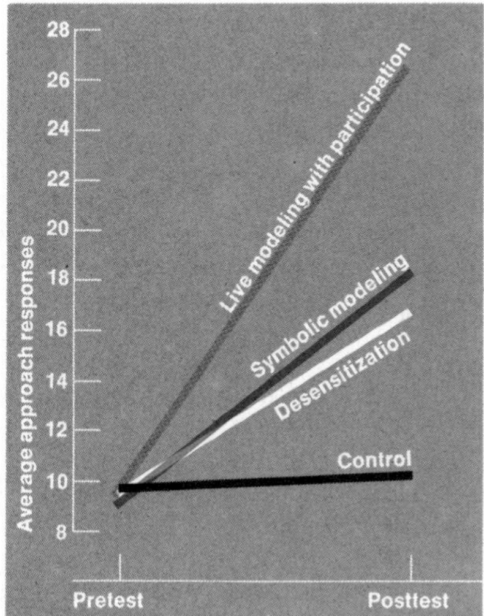

MODELING CAN BE USED THERAPEUTICALLY TO REDUCE FEAR

Figure 13.10 *Results of three treatments for snake phobia. In live modeling, the experimenter handled a real snake and gradually induced the subjects to handle it. In symbolic modeling, subjects watched a movie of people handling snakes (see Figure 13.9). In desensitization, the subjects relaxed while being presented with gradually stronger snake stimuli. The graph shows that all three treatments were helpful, but live modeling was the most effective. (Modified from Bandura et al., 1969.)*

The subjects suffered from such severe snake phobias that they restricted their daily routines to situations in which there was virtually no chance that they would see a snake. They were given a pretest to measure their degree of fear and were assigned to four groups so that fear of snakes was about equal in all four.

Subjects in one group, called the *live-modeling* group, watched the experimenter, or model, handle a king snake. The experimenter next guided the subjects in touching the snake with gloves on, then with bare hands, then near the head. Finally the experimenter let the snake crawl over him, and the subjects were persuaded to do likewise. Each step of this procedure was carefully graded from conditions producing the least fear to those producing the most fear. At all times the model acted fearlessly.

The second experimental group was presented with *symbolic modeling*—in this case, movies of models handling snakes (see Figure 13.9). The subjects could control the movie projector, and whenever too much fear was aroused, they stopped it and reversed it to the beginning of a sequence.

The third group was a *desensitization* group (see page 461). These subjects relaxed while being presented with fear-inducing snake stimuli that were graded from weak to strong. The fourth group was a control group that received no treatment for snake phobia.

After the three experimental groups had been given their treatments, the approach responses of all subjects to snakes were counted. As Figure 13.10 shows, approach responses increased markedly with all three treatment techniques, but the live-modeling procedure was the most effective. In addition to the subjects' actual approach behavior toward snakes, their attitudes about snakes were evaluated by means of the semantic differential technique (see page 161). It was found that attitudes also became more favorable in the three experimental conditions.

In addition to its use in the direct treatment of symptoms, modeling often serves as a technique to *prompt* behavior. A subject may be induced to make a desired response by having him imitate a model. The response thus evoked can then be reinforced and strengthened by operant conditioning principles. In this way modeling and operant conditioning can be combined.

As the cases described have indicated, behavior modification, whether by classical conditioning, operant conditioning, or modeling, shows great promise in the treatment of behavior disorders. Its application of principles from the psychological laboratory to human behavior has been effective with many types of disorder; its limits have yet to be explored.

Prevention of Behavior Disorders

A few of the major techniques of psychotherapy have been covered in this chapter, and many more might have been added. Some of them apparently have some effectiveness, but none of them can relieve the misery of mental illness without laborious effort. It is obvious that the best public and private course of action is to prevent behavior disorders. In public terms, prevention rather than treatment and custodial care would result in considerable savings of tax money; in private terms, prevention would save intense and unnecessary suffering.

How does one prevent mental illness? The answer is easier stated than applied, since the roots of many behavior disorders are to be found in certain maladjustments in the intimacy of the family circle. Many parents, perhaps because it is the accepted cultural pattern in their subgroup, literally abandon their children to the streets; others functionally abandon them by being too busy to spend time with them. Somehow, as a start, parents must be made to believe that it is important to take an interest in their children. After this minimum requirement has been met, parents must not be too inconsistent, too harsh, or too demanding; nor should they give a child absolute freedom—they should set realistic limits for his behavior. It is really not too difficult to rear children who are free from neuroses or personality disorders. Even in the psychotic disorders, the virulence of the symptoms can probably be lessened by reasonable, understanding, consistent, and loving techniques of child rearing.

Of course, we are caught in a vicious circle when we try to prevent mental illness. Neurotic parents or those with personality disorders are not likely to set reasonable limits or to provide the kind of love children need to grow into healthy adults. Perhaps some outside assistance in the form of community mental health clinics can be of help. They can attempt to educate people toward the goal of prevention. A sound understanding of the material presented in textbooks like this one may also give people an understanding of the basic elements in mental health.

Synopsis and summary

The prevalence of behavior disorders makes psychotherapy a vital human concern. This chapter has described a few of the major psychotherapeutic techniques.

1. Behavior disorders are perhaps the largest and most burdensome of all the health problems in the United States; persons suffering from mental illness occupy about one-half of all hospital beds.
2. The relative proportion of the population under 50 years old which is admitted to mental hospitals appears to have remained relatively constant over the years. This seems to indicate that the genetic and environmental causes of behavior disorders are fairly constant.
3. The admission rate to mental hospitals for all ages has risen, but the discharge rate has increased enough so that the proportion of the population in mental hospitals has declined. However, since the population is growing, the pressure on mental hospital space is still great.
4. Except for the increasing use of tranquilizers, the trend in therapy is toward psychological methods of treatment. The trend is also toward the prevention of severe disorders by concentrating therapeutic effort on patients who are mildly ill and patients who have disorders that are more readily treated.
5. The two kinds of therapy for behavior disorders are medical therapy and psychotherapy. Medical therapies consist of psychosurgery, shock therapy, narcosis, and chemotherapy. Of these, the most widely used are electric shock therapy for depressed patients and chemotherapy for patients with many kinds of disorders. Chemotherapy has transformed mental hospitals from "bedlams" to quiet places where therapeutic work can be done.
6. The main aim of psychotherapy is to change disordered behavior. The techniques used to do this may involve some combination of (*a*) changing the situation, (*b*) providing emotional support, (*c*) achieving insight, and (*d*) learning and extinction.
7. Many kinds of psychotherapeutic techniques have been devised for use with individual patients. One of the major types is psychoanalysis, developed by Freud. Free association, resistance, the analysis of dreams, and transference are important aspects of psychoanalytic therapy.
8. Client-centered therapy, one of the nondirective therapies, provides a permissive situation in which the patient is encouraged to talk out his feelings about matters of crucial importance to him. The therapist tries to clarify these feelings. The hope is that the patient has sufficient strength to work out his problems with the help provided by the therapist.
9. A number of therapies have arisen from Freud's basic psychoanalytic idea. Adler, Jung, and Rank set up their own systems of therapy relatively early in this century. Adlerian therapy, for example, stresses power motivation and attempts to overcome inferiority feelings.
10. The more recent varieties of psychoanalytic therapy have emphasized the importance of interpersonal relationships. For instance, Harry Stack Sullivan's approach to the genesis and treatment of behavior disorders stresses the individual's distorted perceptions of other people.
11. Existential therapy tries to apply some of the ideas developed by the existentialist philosophers to the treatment of behavior disorders. These therapists believe that human anxiety comes from the meaninglessness of life and the threat of death. Therapy consists of teaching the patient not to be afraid of death and to strive to reach his full human potential.
12. Directive therapies give patients specific directions about how to solve their personal problems.

One form of directive therapy is hypnotherapy, which is sometimes helpful in relieving symptoms and uncovering repressions.

13. Play or release therapy is a special technique developed for children, who cannot benefit from the highly verbal therapies which are useful for adults.

14. Studies of the effectiveness of psychotherapy are very difficult to carry out. The few that have been done may be interpreted as indicating that psychotherapy is far less effective than we would like it to be. One implication is that the prevention of behavior disorders must assume greater importance.

15. Therapy can be conducted with groups of people as well as with individuals. In addition, group experience can be valuable for mentally healthy people. Training groups, sensitivity groups, and encounter groups are examples of group experiences for mentally healthy people which are designed to lead to greater personal freedom and greater depth of feeling for others.

16. Family therapy is a type of therapy in which individual problems are treated as part of the set of relationships within a family. The family therapist attempts to bring about changes in the family's patterns of interaction which will benefit both the patient and the rest of the family.

17. Psychodrama is a special variety of group therapy that permits a patient to act out roles, situations, and fantasies in his life.

18. The community mental health movement attempts (*a*) to make psychological services more readily available, and (*b*) to reduce tensions within communities that may lead to maladaptive behavior.

19. Behavior modification therapy concentrates on the disordered behavior itself, not on theories about the underlying causes. Techniques from classical conditioning, operant conditioning, and perceptual learning are used to change disturbed behavior.

20. The classical conditioning techniques used in behavior modification are basically forms of counterconditioning. Specific varieties of counterconditioning are aversion therapy, desensitization, and reciprocal inhibition therapy.

21. Behavior modification by operant conditioning, like all operant conditioning, relies upon reinforcement. Both positive and negative, or aversive, reinforcement may be helpful in eliminating the symptoms of behavior disorders. The "token economy" is one application of reinforcement principles to the control of large groups of people in mental hospitals.

22. Modeling, or imitative behavior, is a variety of perceptual learning which can be used to eliminate some behavior disorders, such as phobias.

Related topics in the text

Chapter 3 Principles of Learning Since behavior modification depends heavily on learning principles, a review of Chapter 3 would be helpful.

Chapter 7 Arousal, Emotion, and Conflict Motivational conflicts and their alleviation are involved in the treatment of behavior disorders; some important types of conflict are discussed in this chapter.

Chapter 11 Personality Some of the therapies used for behavior disorders are based on theories of personality discussed in Chapter 11.

Chapter 12 Behavior Disorders Mild adjustment problems, neuroses, personality disorders, and psychoses are described.

Chapter 19 Brain and Behavior The drugs used in chemotherapy for the behavior disturbances are discussed in some detail.

Suggestions for further reading

Bandura, A. *Principles of behavior modification.* New York: Holt, 1969. *A complete textbook with many interesting examples that should be intelligible to the beginner who has read something about various kinds of conditioning.*

Bromber, W. *The mind of man: A history of psychotherapy and psychoanalysis.* New York: Harper & Row, 1959. (Paperback available.)
A survey of man's attempts to deal with the perplexing problems posed by the behavior disorders.

Burton, A. (Ed.) *Encounter.* San Francisco: Jossey-Bass, 1969.
A number of people prominent in the encounter group movement discuss their experiences.

Dorcus, R. M. (Ed.) *Hypnosis and its therapeutic applications.* New York: McGraw-Hill, 1956.
A modern, authoritative treatment, written by experts, of the nature and uses of hypnosis.

Egan, G. *Encounter: Group processes for interpersonal growth.* Belmont, Calif.: Brooks/Cole, 1970. (Paperback.)
Informative coverage of the recent trend toward the use of group experience for interpersonal growth and learning.

Freud, S. *An outline of psychoanalysis.* New York: Norton, 1949.
A short description of some of the basic ideas of psychoanalysis as a theory and as a therapy. A good book for the beginner because it gives the fundamentals.

Garfield, S. L. *Introductory clinical psychology.* New York: Macmillan, 1957.
An elementary textbook describing methods of appraising personality and behavior disorders, as well as psychotherapeutic methods.

Harper, R. A. *Psychoanalysis and psychotherapy.* Englewood Cliffs, N.J.: Prentice-Hall, 1959. (Paperback.)
This book succinctly summarizes many of the systems of psychotherapy.

Hilgard, E. R. *The experience of hypnosis.* New York: Harcourt, Brace & Jovanovich, 1968. (Paperback.)
An informative summary of many important facts about the hypnotic state.

Rogers, C. R. *On becoming a person: A therapist's view of psychotherapy.* Boston: Houghton Mifflin, 1961.
A personal account, by the founder of the system, of the processes involved in client-centered therapy.

Rotter, J. B. *Clinical psychology.* Englewood Cliffs, N.J.: Prentice-Hall, 1964. (Paperback.)

A description of some of the methods of clinical psychology and psychotherapy.

Tussing, L. *Psychology for better living.* New York: Wiley, 1959.
An easily read text in which an attempt is made to apply psychological facts to the problems of life and adjustment.

Wiener, D. N. *A practical guide to psychotherapy.* New York: Harper & Row, 1968.
A helpful book describing systems of psychotherapy, suggesting ways to find the kind of therapist who will be best for you, and discussing what you can expect in therapy.

PART FOUR GROUP PROCESSES

Custom and convention govern
human action.
Pyrrho

Although you know that other people influence your behavior, have you ever stopped to think how powerful their influence really is? Even if you are twenty-one and relatively independent of parental control, you cannot free yourself from the control of society. Its pressure is brought to bear on all your behavior, prescribing everything from what you should wear to how you should live. Parents and elders exhort you to moral behavior, policemen enforce traffic regulations, employers determine how you spend most of your waking hours—in many subtle and not-so-subtle ways, other people dictate what you do, where you go, and how you enjoy yourself.

Many of society's subgroups also have a compelling influence on your behavior. In your family you first learned about interpersonal relations and the behaviors which are appropriate and acceptable to society. And your friends and associates have taught you how to respond to many situations, for peers are often more important than parents in determining behavior. Even when—or perhaps especially when—a person attempts to escape from the social pressures of one group, a new set of group pressures is developed. "Hippies," whose conformity to their own group in type of dress, hair styling, and drug usage is well known, are a good example.

The person who joins a new group may help to determine the behavior of the group; but often instead, to be accepted as a group member he must go along with the plans of the group even if he is not convinced that the group is right. Mob behavior can be an important determiner of individual behavior. The juvenile delinquent conforms to the standards of his gang and grows up with vastly different social forces shaping his life than the child outside the gang.

So steady, so insistent, and so pervasive are cultural influences on our behavior that we rarely stop to perceive or analyze their nature. *Social psychology* studies the behavior of the individual in his society, "as it is influenced by the presence, beliefs, actions, and symbols of other men" (McGrath, 1964). *Sociology* concentrates on the study of the behavior of groups of people taken as a whole. These fields overlap, but the focus in social psychology is on the social forces which shape and determine individual, rather than group, behavior.

Socialization and Culture

Socialization is the name given to the social learning process through which the infant is trained in the attitudes, beliefs (see Chapter 15), and behaviors appropriate to his culture. As Ruth Benedict, the social anthropologist, has put it:

> The life-history of the individual is first and foremost an accommodation to the patterns and standards traditionally handed down in his community. From the moment of his birth the customs into which he is born shape his life experience and behaviour. By the time he can talk, he is a little creature of his culture, and by the time he is grown and able to take part in its activities, its habits are his habits, its beliefs are his beliefs, its impossibilities are his impossibilities. Every child that is born into his group will share them with him, and no child born into one on the opposite side of the globe can ever achieve the thousandth part. (Benedict, 1959, page 2.)

The socialization process ensures that new members of a society—the young and developing children—learn what that society has to say about how to get along in the world and with other people. In a word, they learn the culture of the society into which they are born. The term *culture,* used in its scientific sense, refers to the customs and traditions of a people and to the attitudes and beliefs they have about important aspects of their life. Occasionally culture has been called "social heritage," but this gives the somewhat false impression that culture is inherited unchanged from generation to generation. More accurate, though more imposing, definitions of culture have been provided by anthropologists. One such definition is "Culture is the configuration of learned behaviors and results of behavior whose component elements are shared and transmitted by members of a particular society" (Linton, 1945, page 32). As psychologists, our interest focuses on the behaviors, attitudes, and values which are transmitted and shared.

Culture influences behavior through the socialization process. The following passage describes how the culture of a society affects socialization.

> The cultural environment (or, more exactly, the members of the community) starts out with a human infant formed and endowed along species lines, but capable of behavioral training in many directions. From this raw material, the culture proceeds to make, in so far as it can, a product acceptable to itself. It does this by training: by reinforcing the behaviors it desires and extinguishing others; by making some natural and social stimuli into [discriminative stimuli], and ignoring others; by differentiating out this or that specific response or chain of responses, such as manners and attitudes; by conditioning emotional and anxiety reactions to some stimuli and not others. It teaches the individual what he may and may not do, giving him norms and ranges of social behavior that are permissive or prescriptive or prohibitive. It teaches him the language he is to speak; it gives him his standards of beauty and art, of good and bad conduct; it sets before him a picture of the ideal personality that he is to imitate and strive to be. In all this, the fundamental laws of behavior are to be found. (Keller and Schoenfeld, 1950, page 365.)

Each cultural group has worked out certain ways of handling various universal problems, such as caring for and training children, feeding

Figure 14.1 *Cultural patterns differ. Both of these boys are being formally initiated into full-fledged membership in their groups. Left, a caste ceremony in India. Right, a Bar Mitzvah ceremony. (Left, Margaret Bourke-White,* Life Magazine, *© Time Inc. Right, Maxwell Coplan, Design Photographers International, Inc.)*

and sheltering the group members, and so on, and the successful practices are adopted and passed on to successive generations as the culture of that society. Language, traditions, norms, values, and the expectations and sanctions associated with them are taught by the culture through the social learning process (see Figure 14.1). It has been stated that "Culture influences the person in a massive and pervasive way and thus makes for the stability of a society and the continuity of its culture; the person also influences his culture and thus makes for social change" (Krech et al., 1962, page 341).

Social Structure

Not only is each culture characterized by a distinctive pattern; each also has its own *social structure* that is involved in the socialization of individuals. Each of the components of the social structure contributes something to the socialization of the person. When we refer to social structure, we mean that the culture assigns ranks to people; it expects certain people to do one kind of work and others to do other kinds; it expects its families to be constituted in a certain way; and it expects its members to have certain attitudes and beliefs. In some societies, this social structure is rigid; in others, it is more flexible. But there is no society without some degree of structuring.

Much of the structuring arises from differences among people in the goods and services they produce. One person makes trinkets, an-

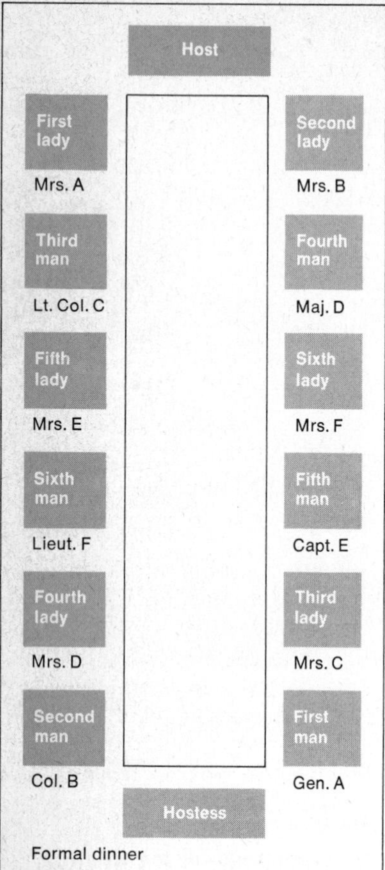

A MILITARY ORGANIZATION IS AN EXTREME EXAMPLE OF A STATUS SYSTEM

Figure 14.2 *Status as it is represented in a formal seating arrangement. The diagram, adapted from one published in a manual for Army officers, gives the proper seating arrangements for formal dinners. (Fort Benning, Ga., Infantry School.)*

other makes shoes, another controls the production of a whole factory. The dependence of people upon one another is not equally distributed; some people are much more important to the society than are others.

Of all the distinctions which can be made in the value of services to a society, those based upon sex and age are most common. These differences, therefore, provide some kind of structure in all societies. Infants obviously contribute little and demand much, and in most societies mothers are assigned to take care of them. Children may contribute something, but not very much, and they are expected to treat adults with the respect appropriate to their more crucial roles. In nearly all societies, young men are expected to be warriors in time of danger. Old men are often regarded as the sources of wisdom and leadership. Thus people's differences in their ability to meet society's needs have much to do with the social structure. Technological differences in societies also affect the social structure. Societies which are more highly industrialized and have more work specialties also contain more elaborate social structures.

Status and role Division of labor is only one factor shaping social structure; many others, such as positions in the family unit and memberships in social groups also contribute. A social structure is established when members of a society categorize people according to differences that are important to their society's needs. Thus they assign to each person in the society what social scientists call a *status*—or rather, several statuses—age status, sex status, occupational status, social status, and so on. Each status is a position representing differences that are important in the exchange of goods and services and in the satisfaction of needs in the society. Status may depend on an individual's occupation, his power to affect others in his everyday relationships with them, his economic resources, or his ascribed rank in the social-class system of the community (see Figure 14.2).

Different people may occupy a particular status at different times, and their statuses may change from time to time. Along with each status goes a *role*. This is a pattern of behavior that a person is expected to exhibit in a particular status. At a very early age, boys and girls in our society learn that different behaviors are expected of them. A father as "head of a household" has a role, or mode of behavior, which he must act out in that status. So does a person in the status of employer, or mother, or teacher. Status and role are key concepts in understanding social structure, and they must be clearly distinguished. Status applies to position in the social structure; role applies to the behavior which goes along with that position.

Multiple status The system by which statuses are arranged in a social structure usually permits any particular person to be categorized in many ways: for instance, as head of a household, teacher, employee, church member. A person therefore comes to have several statuses in a social structure. For some part of his life, he occupies one status; for another part, another status. In each of these statuses, he has a role to play which goes along with the particular status, so that he finds himself in multiple roles.

Role conflict Serious trouble can arise when a person is caught in a conflict of roles; it is a common occurrence in a society as complex and as mobile as ours. The foreman who drives his men with an iron hand may find his methods unsuccessful when he is promoted to executive status. The student leader accustomed to the role of class president in a small-town high school may be unhappy when he becomes just another freshman in a large university. The middle-class professor used to the manners and repartee of cocktail parties may find himself uncomfortable in a gathering of the poor.

Such changes in status put a person in a conflict of roles. He finds that the role he learned in one status is no longer appropriate in a new status. He becomes uncertain what role he should play, and when he is forced to decide on one, he may have little confidence in his choice. Thus he may be thrust into motivational conflict of the sort we described in Chapter 7. The consequences may be frustration, anxiety, hostility, and failure to adjust. Many of the problems of an adolescent in our society are related to difficulties in adjusting to the changing behaviors, or roles, expected of him as he progresses from child to adult (McGrath, 1964).

For many people, conflicts in role are infrequent. This may be because people usually perceive only the particular status that is most appropriate to their immediate situation. An unscrupulous businessman who is also a regular churchgoer probably sees no incompatibility between his business behavior and the beliefs he professes on Sundays in church. During the week, functioning in the status of a businessman, he does not think in terms of his status as a churchgoer. In a sense, he usually does not become aware of other statuses he holds until he is reminded of them by situational demands or other cues (Charters and Newcomb, 1958).

Conflicts of roles may be important problems in the lives of some individuals, however. For some time now there has been much discussion of the role conflict of a well-educated woman who assumes the duties of housewife and mother. Unless she is able to inject intellectual stimulation into her life, she may become bogged down in her multiple roles of maid, babysitter, chauffeur, cook, handyman, and companion. She may experience role conflict as she adjusts to the changing behaviors expected of her as a consequence of marriage and raising a family.

Social classes We have described social structure in terms of statuses and roles, but there is more to social structure than a mere assortment of statuses. In every society, these statuses are arranged on *a scale of prestige.* That is to say, the people in the society regard some statuses more favorably than others, or they rank statuses according to their desirability. Then the awards that the community has to distribute, such as wealth, power, respect, and honors, are parceled out according to this prestige scale. Naturally, there is no one-to-one correlation, say, between wealth and prestige, for people with equal prestige may receive somewhat different shares of the wealth. But taken together, the awards of the community correspond fairly well to status on a prestige scale. Studies have shown that when asked to rank different occupations according to social status, most groups give about the same rankings. For example, occupations such as physician, banker, and manager of a business are highly rated; clerks and salespersons have an intermediate rank, and unskilled factory workers are ranked low (Cattell, 1942).

Thus the prestige scale becomes the basis for forming social classes or strata. Those high on it are largely in one class; those low on it are mainly in another class. In a number of societies, the class system has become so formalized that it permeates all social organization and behavior. In many ancient kingdoms the classification of all members into one of three strata—nobility, freemen, and slaves—was unequivocal. Each person belonged to one of the three. Frequently his class membership was indicated by his speech, dress, or some other symbol clear to any observer. Each class was restricted to certain occupations and indeed to certain kinds of social behavior; freemen, for example, behaved in one way toward nobility, in another toward freemen, and in another toward slaves.

Our own society does not formalize classes so rigidly. It is not always easy to pick out a person's social class, and members of a class are certainly not confined so strictly to that class and its particular occupations as are, say, members of a caste in India. In other words, we have more class mobility. There is nevertheless a definite class structure in American society.

To a large extent, social class determines the social environment of the individual:

The social-class system maintains cultural, economic, and social barriers which prevent intimate social intermixture between the slums, the Gold Coast, and the middle class. We know that human beings can learn their culture only *from other human beings,* who already know and exhibit that culture. Therefore, by setting up barriers to social participation, the American social-class system actually prevents the vast majority of the children of the working classes, or the slums, from learning any culture but that of their own group. *Thus the pivotal meaning of social class* to students of human development is that it defines and systematizes different learning environments for children of different classes. (Davis and Havighurst, 1946, page 699.)

The socioeconomic level of the neighborhood, whether crowded tenement or spacious subdivision, will certainly affect the probability that a young person will ever complete high school or get to college. Social class affects vast aspects of an individual's experiences—for example, how he spends his leisure time, what sorts of things he considers important, what kind of job he will try to get, and even how he perceives others and is perceived by them.

The division of society into classes has been scientifically investigated. One study, made in a town pseudonymously called Yankee City, revealed the class structure depicted in Figure 14.3 (Warner and Lunt, 1941). The chart is based partly on a large number of interviews in which citizens were asked to rate their fellow townsmen on social status. For the most part, they did not think of social classes by the names used in

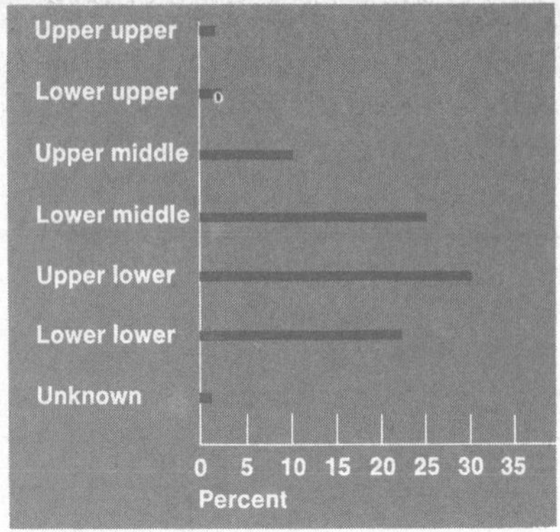

EACH SOCIETY AND COMMUNITY HAS A SOCIAL CLASS STRUCTURE

Figure 14.3 *The class structure of "Yankee City," which is the pseudonym for a New England community of about 15,000 people. They were stratified in three major classes, each with a lower and an upper part, on the basis of interviews and other information concerning their socioeconomic status and social activities. (Data from Warner and Lunt, 1941.)*

the illustration. These were furnished by the research workers afterward. Yet it was clear that people distinguished three major classes, each with a lower and an upper part. Using these categories they were able to classify almost everyone in town. The percentages shown in Figure 14.3, however, would vary from one city, state, or section of the country to another.

What criteria do the members of a community use when they rate social class? The answer is never simple. The type of occupation and economic criteria are perhaps the most important, but many other factors enter into the evaluation. In Yankee City, for example, people used the following yardsticks: kind of income (whether salary, commissions, dividends, or the like), moral standing, family geneology, social relationships and organization affiliations, and type of residential area.

Social classes and behavior The social classes differ not only in status and the things that go along with status; they also differ in the attitudes and personalities of their members. In regard to attitudes, political scientists, sociologists, and public opinion pollsters have long known that the social classes differ in their political beliefs and social philosophies. One of the simplest and clearest correlations is that the higher a person is, either on the occupational scale or in the social class he thinks he belongs to, the more likely he is to hold conservative political opinions. This is by no means universally true, however.

One of the "Kinsey reports," an investigation of sexual behavior in the American male, revealed a significant relationship between sexual conduct and social class as measured by occupation (Kinsey et al., 1948). The semiskilled-labor group showed a relatively frequent incidence of premarital intercourse and relatively infrequent masturbation. This pattern was reversed among professional persons, and the lower-white-collar group showed an intermediate or transitional pattern of sexual behavior. It is interesting to note what happens when an individual moves from one class to another. One of the unexpected findings of the Kinsey study was that "a person born into the skilled-labor class who *ultimately* moves into the professional class shows a youthful sexual pattern congruent with the *class into which he will eventually move!* Similarly, if a person born into the skilled-labor class ultimately locates in the unskilled-labor class, his pattern of sexual conduct closely resembles the pattern of persons born into that class" (Krech et al., 1962, page 334). Thus knowledge of the social environment of the individual facilitates understanding of his sexual attitudes and behavior.

It is not widely recognized that members of the various social classes tend to have somewhat different personalities. Indeed, the kind of home or neighborhood in which one lives, the kind of work, the kind of play, the facilities that are available, and even the minimum necessities for satisfying basic needs all go along with social class and help to determine personality patterns. Even more important, however, the training and education of a child differ according to social class.

Several studies of social class differences in child-rearing practices provide information on this point (Bronfenbrenner, 1958). In the 1930s and 1940s, research generally showed that middle-class parents were stricter and more frustrating in their child-rearing practices than working-class parents. Studies conducted during the 1950s, however, reached the opposite conclusion. By then, middle-class parents had become more permissive in training their young. The reason for the change, it seems, is that the middle-class parent more often follows the advice of the "experts" in child behavior. When, in the 1930s, these experts prescribed rigid schedules for children, the mother of higher status was more likely to follow suit. Similarly, when the experts later advised that children be permitted greater freedom, she followed that advice too. Since most child specialists now tend to be somewhat more conservative, advising permissiveness but within definite limits, we can expect middle-class parents to follow this pattern before their counterparts among the working class do so.

There is another important difference between working-class and middle-class parents: The working-class parent is more likely to use physical punishment in disciplining his child, whereas the middle-class parent more frequently employs "psychological discipline" in which he tries to reason with the youngster and make him feel guilty for doing disapproved things. Psychological discipline, the evidence indicates, is more effective in training and controlling the child (see Chapter 3). As one psychologist puts it, "These findings mean that middle-class parents, though in one sense more lenient in their discipline techniques, are using methods that are actually more compelling . . . which are likely to be effective in evoking the behavior desired in the child" (Bronfenbrenner, 1958, page 419).

The social classes also differ, of course, in their occupational goals for their children; the higher-class parent more often wants his children to train for business and professional occupational status. The cause of this difference is partly economic. If a working-class parent cannot afford to send his son to college and then to medical school, and in addition must have his boy's income as soon as possible to help support the family, there is little sense in the child thinking about becoming a doctor. But in addition, more profound differences in motivation exist among the social classes.

Research with high school students has indicated, for example, that boys from the upper and middle social strata tend to have a higher level of achievement motivation (see page 211) than those from the lower classes (Rosen, 1956). Teen-agers from the higher classes more often want to do well relative to standards of excellence. The upper- and middle-class teenagers, moreover, are more likely to have some of the personal values and attributes conducive to occupational success. More of them believe that it is possible for an individual to improve his status in life; more of them also think it worthwhile to postpone present pleasures for future goals.

We see, then, that a number of important differences occur among individuals from the different social classes: They differ in attitudes and beliefs, in child-rearing practices, in educational goals, and even in certain motivations.

Structure of Social Groups

We have now seen that every society has a culture and a social structure. Each is also characterized by *social groups.* Not only does every member of a society have his statuses, roles, and social class, but he also belongs to a large number of groups. For at least part of his life he is a member of a family group. A person's peer group changes through the years, but peer groups are important, and the pressures these groups exert are determiners of behavior. A college student may belong to a dormitory or other living group, a fraternity, a debating club, the basketball team, a political group, and a bowling league, as well as classroom groups. His behavior affects these groups in small or large ways, and the groups affect and sometimes control his behavior.

Characteristics of groups Social groups may differ in a number of dimensions:

1. Size, or the number of members.
2. The degree to which they are organized and operate in a formal manner.
3. The degree to which they are stratified, that is, the extent to which group members are related to one another in a hierarchy.
4. The degree to which they exercise or attempt to exercise control over the behavior of their members.
5. The degree of participation which is permitted, expected, or demanded of members.
6. The ease of access to membership in the group and the ease with which a member can leave or be expelled from the group.
7. The degree of stability of the group over time and the continuity of its membership over time.
8. The degree to which group members relate to one another intimately, on a personal basis and with respect to a wide range of activities and interests, rather than in a formal manner and only with respect to a narrowly defined set of activities.
9. The degree to which the group is subdivided into smaller groups or cliques, and the extent to which such cliques are in conflict with one another. (McGrath, 1964, page 65.)

The study of the nature of groups has been given the name *group dynamics* (Lewin, 1951). This field of investigation seeks to learn more about how groups develop and function and what factors affect the relationships between groups and individuals and between groups and other groups. The rest of this chapter and much of the following chapter on attitudes could be considered to deal with the field of group dynamics.

Interaction patterns Particular attention has been paid by researchers to the patterns of communication and social interaction in small groups. Several systems have been devised to help in the description and analysis of behavior in these groups (Bales, 1950, 1970). Figure 14.4, on the next page, shows one such method. Using this scheme, an observer behind a one-way window classifies each statement made by a member of the group into one of 12 categories, recording also who spoke to whom. The categories are (1) shows solidarity, (2) shows tension release, (3) shows agreement, (4) gives suggestion, (5) gives opinion, (6) gives information, (7) asks for information, (8) asks for opinion,

A SYSTEM FOR STUDYING GROUP BEHAVIOR

Figure 14.4 *The Bales interaction scheme. An observer records responses of people in a problem-solving group and classifies them into 12 categories. These are grouped into social-emotional and task area classes. Various problem areas, a through f, can also be studied. (Adapted from Bales, 1950.)*

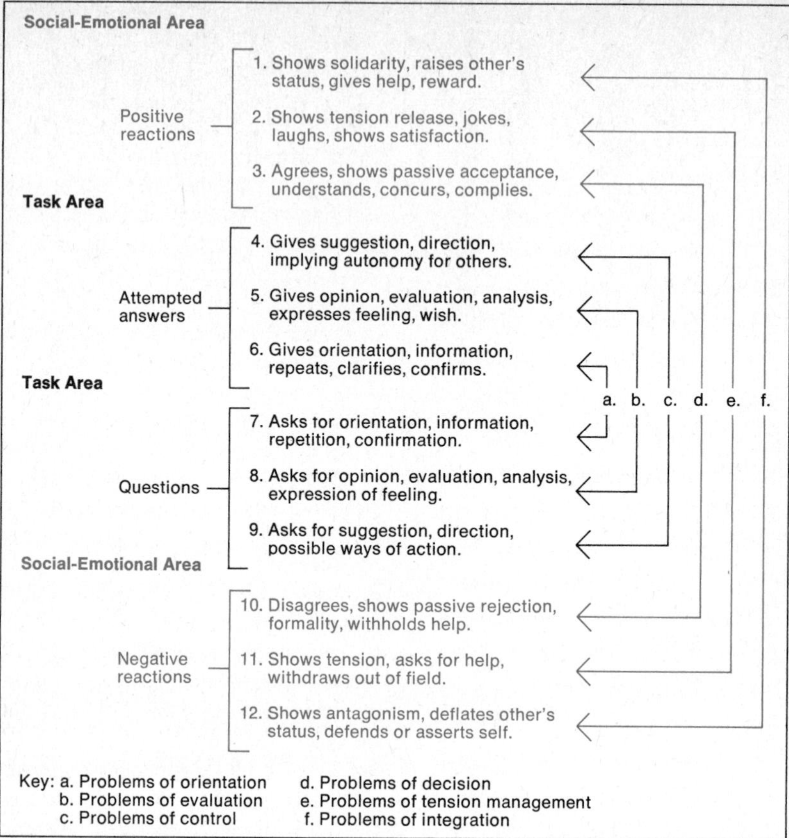

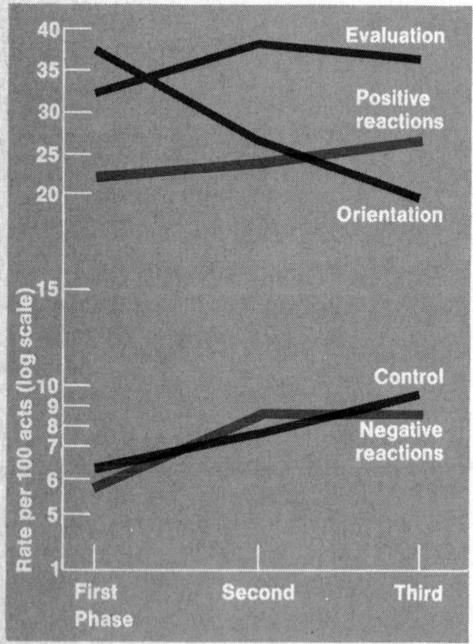

CHARTING THE COURSE OF GROUP INTERACTION

Figure 14.5 *Changes in the frequency of types of communication in a problem-solving group. The changes were studied with the Bales method. From the first to the third phase of the meeting, control, positive reactions, and negative reactions rise, evaluation rises and falls, and orientation drops sharply. (Adapted from Bales, 1952.)*

(9) asks for suggestion, (10) shows disagreement, (11) shows tension, (12) shows antagonism. These categories are divided into active task contributions (attempted answers) and passive task contributions (questions), and into positive and negative reactions not specifically related to the point under consideration.

The study of changes in communications during a problem-solving session clarifies the nature of the problem-solving process and facilitates comparison of groups. Combining observations from 22 different groups which had met to deal with various problems yielded the data shown in Figure 14.5. Reactions pertaining to the task—orientation, evaluation, and control—are graphed in black; positive and negative socioemotional reactions are shown in color. In the first phase of the problem-solving process, discussion tends to emphasize orientation and clarification of information pertaining to the problem. The middle of the group session emphasizes analysis and evaluation of the task. The final portion of the meeting is focused on seeking resolution of the problem. The relative frequency of positive and negative reactions tends to increase from beginning to end of most group sessions, with laughing and joking highest at the end.

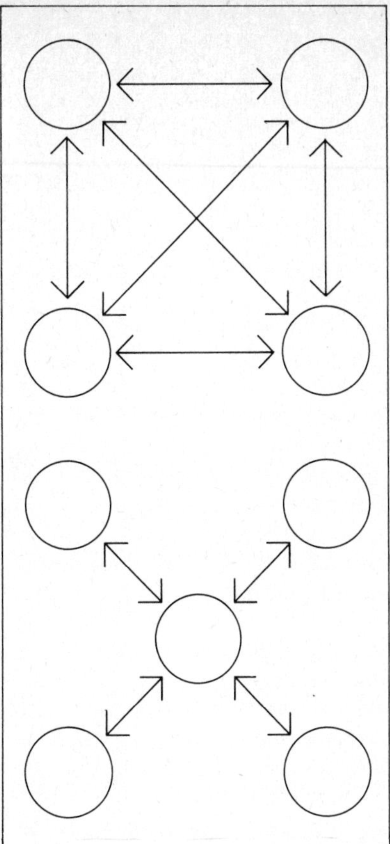

THE COMMUNICATION STRUCTURE OF A GROUP IS ITS PATTERN OF COMMUNICATION CHANNELS

Figure 14.6 *Two types of communication structure. Top, a completely connected free-communication pattern in which each person may communicate with everyone else. Bottom, the "star" pattern in which group members may communicate only with a central person.*

The Bales analysis shows that two types of leaders usually emerge in group problem-solving situations (see page 484). The conventional leader is the one with the best ideas: the one who usually makes the most contributions toward getting the group to work on the task at hand. The best-liked person keeps the group in good spirits by providing the "light-touch" of humor or encouragement when needed. These two roles are seldom held by the same person, as they are somewhat incompatible.

Communication patterns Communications within a group are affected not only by whom the individuals in the group *wish* to talk to, but also by whom they are *permitted* to talk to. Most groups do not allow free-for-all discussions. They have chairmen to govern who may talk and when. They may also have rules about who may talk to whom. The workingman seldom gets a chance to talk to the company president. A junior executive may talk to his boss, but ordinarily cannot go over his boss's head to the boss's boss. Thus the channels of communication are usually limited in certain ways. The pattern of closed- and open-communication channels in a group is known as the *communication structure*.

Let us take as an example two different groups of men, each organized to solve a particular business problem. In one group, each member is free to talk to anyone else. In the other, each member can communicate only with a central person. If members want to send messages to each other, they must do it through the central person, who can relay it on or not as he sees fit. This pattern is usually known as a "star" communication structure. Obviously there can be many other kinds of structures, but for simplicity we shall discuss only these two (see Figure 14.6).

Is one structure better than another for getting a job done? Unfortunately, there is no simple answer. Many experiments have been done comparing the two structures, and the results seem to depend upon a number of factors. Two of the most significant are the difficulty or complexity of the job to be done and the work load given to each group member. We can say with assurance, however, that people feel better in the free-communication structure than in the star pattern. People in the free-communication structure generally find their jobs more satisfying and have higher morale than the noncentral members of the star pattern (Shaw, 1955).

The reason usually given for this difference is that the free-communication pattern allows the group members more *independence* (Shaw, 1955). A person can talk to whomever he wishes; he can get the information or opinion he wants from any member at any time. This is not the case in the star structure; members must depend upon the central person for the information needed to get their work done. Most people in our society, however, desire some degree of independence in their jobs. Communication structures that frustrate this desire tend to make them dissatisfied. (Trow, 1957).

Leadership Groups, as we have seen, have patterns of interaction and patterns of communication, both of which can be charted. They also have leaders to delegate and take authority and responsibility. The social psychology of leadership is still relatively undeveloped. Different types of leaders have been distinguished, and some information exists about the personality patterns of leaders; but we still cannot predict who will emerge as a leader in a particular group.

PERSONALITIES OF LEADERS It is difficult to make definitive statements about the personality traits (see page 365) of leaders. Libraries are filled with well-meaning books containing highly opinionated advice on the subject, usually intended for the young males of our society who are about to be initiated into the glories of adulthood. Opinions unrelated to facts are next to worthless for a science, and that is what most popular writing on leadership is.

Of the scientific studies that have been conducted on leadership, many have tried to isolate personality characteristics which are possessed by leaders but not by nonleaders. By and large, the results of the research have been inconsistent (Jenkins, 1947), partly because too many different kinds of "leaders" have been grouped together, as if there were only one kind of leadership. Clearly, the person who is the leader of an intellectual group concerned with abstract ideas must be different from the person who leads, say, an athletic club. To get a picture of leaders and leadership, we must consider the group situation in which the leader operates.

This is not to say that leaders of different groups will have no traits in common, or that the person who emerges as the leader of one group is unlikely to become the leader of any other group. Indeed, it is possible to list some general qualities that often distinguish people who emerge as leaders: by and large, they are more likely to be active participators in their groups, and they tend to be dependable, persistent, verbally facile, self-confident, and socially popular (Stogdill, 1948). Having these qualities does not ensure leadership in every group; but in many situations the person who possesses such a combination of traits will probably be a prominent contender for the leader's position.

FORMAL AND INFORMAL LEADERS Before we can understand why these traits may be important and in what situations they are most effective, we must understand more clearly who a leader is. Basically, of course, a *leader* is a person who influences a group to follow the course of action he advocates. We generally restrict the term to people who do this not once, but often; the leader is the group's major influencer. Even when another person comes up with an idea that influences the group throughout one of its meetings, the leader's approval is necessary to sanction the idea.

A *formal leader* influences his group primarily because he occupies a formally recognized status. He is the president, chairman, or king. It is his usual role to attempt to influence, and it is the followers' role to follow. Frequently, of course, the followers accept the formal leader's ideas because the leader has authority over them; he dispenses rewards and punishments.

As we have seen, influence based upon the threat of punishment is not likely to be lasting. The followers will obey orders only so long as they fear getting caught. Thus such leadership is not the most effective kind, though in some situations (in battle, for instance) it may be necessary. Generally, a leader is most effective when his followers accept his ideas because they truly believe in them. In any case, the formal leader ultimately derives his authority and influence from the position he occupies.

The following experiment demonstrates how an individual's formal status can affect other group members' acceptance of his proposals (Raven and French, 1958):

One person, the investigator's confederate, attempted to influence the real subjects under two different conditions. In one condition, the confederate apparently usurped the leadership role when it was not "legally" granted him by the group. In the other condition in a different group, he supposedly was elected to this role. His attempts to influence the group were much more successful when he was elected and thereby given formal status as the leader.

An *informal leader's* influence on the group is not derived from an explicit position of authority. More than anything else, the group follows his lead because his personal qualities convince them that they can satisfy their own needs by accepting his ideas. For this to happen, the group members must be unsure of how to attain their goals on their own. Since they cannot cope with the problems facing the group, they turn to the informal leader for ways of achieving the group goals.

Why does a group in this situation turn to one particular person? What are the important qualities he must possess? One certainly is proficiency, as the group perceives it, in handling the tasks confronting the group. Of course, it often happens that a group has no sure way of knowing this. In the absence of any objective means for evaluating an individual's task competence, the group frequently relies on his past performance. This is probably one reason why a person who has done well in the past is more likely to be a successful influencer than a person who has not (Mausner, 1954).

Past performance, however, is not the only basis for accepting an informal leader's ideas. In addition, a person who is well liked has a much better chance of having his ideas accepted, and thus of influencing people, than one who is less popular. Partly for this reason, social skills and personal popularity often characterize the person chosen for a position of leadership. Moreover, the leader's job frequently involves promoting and maintaining harmonious relations among the members of his group, and a socially skillful, popular person is well qualified to do this.

The person who is highly popular with the members of one group is also more likely to be popular with other groups. Of course, he may not appeal to everybody, but a person who has social skills and is likable can recruit friends from a wide range of people. This means that the individual who emerges as leader in one group may well become a leader in other groups, assuming that the tasks and the people involved are relatively similar (Bell and French, 1950).

Finally, evidence shows that an assertive person is more likely to be chosen leader than an unassertive one, at least in the first stages of the group's existence. The assertive person talks a great deal and advances a relatively large number of ideas. If he is not arrogant and aggressive in asserting himself, his active participation makes him stand out in the group. This, of course, increases his chances of being chosen as the leader. Talking and participating in the group give the group members ideas for coping with its problems. Further, since the assertive person usually presents his ideas with a great deal of confidence in them, the members of the group come to feel that his ideas are indeed correct.

There are dangers, of course, in being too assertive. The individual who continues to dominate a group's activities over a number of sessions may well begin to frustrate some of its members' needs for independence. As a group proceeds with its work, many of its original problems are solved and the situation becomes less ambiguous. When this happens, other members want to have more control over their own activities. They no longer need as many ideas as they did at first. At this point, the very assertive person may lose his popularity if he continues to assert himself. The adroit leader will realize that it is time to let the other members of the group have more say in what they do.

EFFECTIVENESS OF LEADERS Leadership effectiveness has been studied by investigating relationships between leaders and their coworkers in such diverse groups as basketball teams, steel mill work crews, student surveying crews, and Air Force bomber crews, as well as in experimentally created groups (Fiedler, 1954). These experiments suggest that, in relatively relaxed situations, a leader who is attuned to the personal feelings of the group members will have a more productive and successful group than a leader who is very much concerned with getting the job done. However, in difficult situations, a group led by a more objective and task-oriented leader performs better than a leader who is overly concerned about maintaining good interpersonal relationships.

Groups and Behavior

Belonging to a group affects behavior profoundly. Groups have a major role in determining our attitudes, beliefs, actions, decisions, and behavior toward other people. To examine this pervasive influence, we shall consider the general question of conformity to group norms and how it affects what we do; then the development of agreements and norms within groups; and finally the influence of larger groups—crowds and cities—on individual behavior.

Conformity Conformity is a general term that simply means "going along with" the behaviors, attitudes, and beliefs of a group (see Chapter 15 for more information about attitudes and beliefs). We may go along either because we believe in what the group does and stands for, or because we are bowing to group pressures without feeling convinced of the group's "rightness." The term *private acceptance* is sometimes used when we make the group's values and behaviors our own. The word *compliance* is sometimes used when we go along with the group because of group pressures without changing our private attitudes and beliefs.

These aspects of conformity, private acceptance and compliance, are very difficult to disentangle; there is probably an element of both in most conformity behavior. Thus when we speak of conformity, we are only describing a tendency of people to go along; usually we cannot say why they do. But in the real-life and experimental situations discussed below, we shall see the strength of this tendency.

CONFORMITY IN REAL LIFE We are all members of social groups that influence our behavior and attitudes. Groups exert this influence powerfully and pervasively through *group norms.* A norm, as the term implies, is a standard of behavior, but it is more than that. To understand its precise nature, we must refer again to the concepts of role and status.

A role, we have seen, is the behavior expected of us in a particular status. The accent should now be placed on the word "expected." A group can *expect* certain behavior from us because it can turn its disapproval on us if we do not do what is expected. Since most of us acquire the need for social approval, and hence do not wish to incur disapproval, we conform to our group's expectations. For example, as members of many groups—family, university, community, church, commune, and so on—we have many expected roles we must play. We must somehow *conform* to the expectations of the group or suffer the disapproval of the group members. These expectations constitute group norms, which may be defined more formally as widely shared expectations among most members of a group, class, or culture.

Group norms seem to emerge, like statuses and social structure, whenever a group is formed. A group exists when interaction occurs among individuals. By interaction we mean any conversation, exchange of goods and services, or joint efforts which cast group members into any kind of status. The longer people interact, and the more they interact, the more they tend to adopt common ways of perceiving the world. From shared perceptions, it is only a short step to shared rules or norms governing the behavior of group members in each status position. The difference is that norms have a *demand* quality. Not only does an individual tend to see the world and act the way other group members do, but he *must* do so or suffer the social consequences. To enforce this demand, the group devises different degrees of punishment ranging all the way from capital punishment for major crimes to something as innocuous as a social snub. In between are many tangible and effective methods of demanding conformity to group norms. Adolescents and young adults, for instance, may be forced to leave home if they do not conform to the major behaviors, attitudes, and beliefs of their families. The person who marries someone of another religion or race may suffer ostracism and other social punishment from the groups whose norms he violated. Even hair styles and dress styles, if they deviate from the group norm, can be the occasion for social demands and pressures. It is strange but true: most groups do not tolerate much deviation from their norms before social sanctions are brought to bear.

CONFORMITY IN EXPERIMENTAL SITUATIONS Some of these generalizations about conformity and the influence of group norms in real-life situations have come from experiments in which group norms were artificially manipulated. For instance, the development of group norms and their influence upon conformity behavior were studied in an early, now classic, experiment in social psychology (Sherif, 1935):

The subjects were placed in a pitch-dark room and were asked to judge how far a stationary point of light seemed to move. (Perceived motion of a stationary light in a totally dark room is known as the *autokinetic effect.* It is one example of perceived motion—see Chapter 8.) Since the walls of the room were not visible, no physical frame of reference was available to aid in making these judgments. In part of the experiment, individuals were shown the light for the first time in a group situation, and each person expressed his opinion aloud for the others to hear. The group members soon came to influence one another. Their estimates at first did not agree very well, but as they listened to one another's opinions, they began to agree that the light moved within a certain range. Each group developed its own range of judgments, that is, its own way of perceiving this situation. Later, when each of the group members was asked to make his estimates alone, he still judged the movement to be within the range that had been agreed upon in the group. Thus in the group, the subjects learned to interpret the ambiguous situation in a given way, and the learning carried over into their judgments when they were alone.

A slightly different, and perhaps more Machiavellian, type of experiment studies conformity in a situation where group norms clash with the individual's judgment. Will a person conform to group norms that clearly differ from his own? This question has been asked in many experiments that were done in many different ways, and the answer seems to be yes, to some extent, if the conditions are right. One famous series of experiments was conducted by Asch (1956):

Subjects were asked to estimate the lengths of lines. To do this they were given one standard and three comparison lines: For instance, in some cases the standard line was 5 inches and the comparisons were 5, 4, and 6 inches. Control subjects who made their judgments by themselves without group pressure were accurate 99 percent of the time; therefore it was a simple task.

In the experimental sessions, judgments were made by subjects in groups. Each session typically employed only one actual subject in a group of seven to nine other people who had been coached to make their judgments differ from the standard. The subject heard the judgments of all but one of these confederates, or "stooges," before making his own decision. Thus with nine stooges, the subject would hear eight of them say that a standard line of 5 inches looked like 4 inches to them.

What did the subjects do when the majority judgment differed from their own? In general, they showed some tendency to conform to the group: about 33 percent of their judgments were wrong because they were influenced by the majority opinion (see Figure 14.7). But there were wide differences between subjects in yielding; some conformed on almost every trial, while others almost never yielded. And subjects were notably consistent in their responses. If they conformed to the majority early, they continued to do so; if not, they tended to disagree with the group repeatedly. Subjects conformed most often when their judgments were "public"—that is, when the majority could hear their answers.

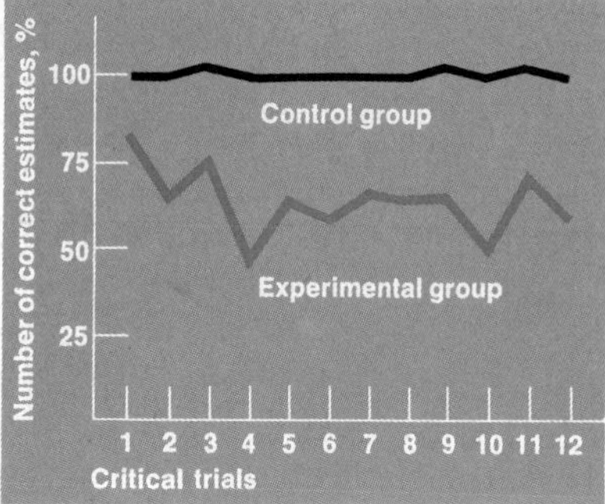

GROUP PRESSURES MAY MAKE US CONFORM

Figure 14.7 *Results of a series of conformity experiments in which the task was to estimate the length of various lines. Each control group subject was alone when he judged the lengths of the lines; each experimental subject judged the length of the lines when he was with a group of people who were in league with the experimenter and chose the incorrect line. (After Asch, 1956.)*

Since the subjects conformed more under public conditions than under private, theirs seems to be a case of compliance rather than private acceptance. This general conclusion can be reached about many similar experiments (Deutsch and Gerard, 1955). But why did the subjects comply at all? We shall discuss several reasons shortly when we take up the factors leading to conformity.

Some interesting experiments have been done on another aspect of conformity—obedience to authority. In them the authority figure can be regarded as a representative of a group who is indirectly applying group pressures toward conformity. Some of the obedience experiments have been widely quoted because of their resemblance to certain real-life situations. But the experimenters are careful to point out the limitations of such generalizations. Here is one of the best-known obedience experiments (Milgram, 1963):

The subjects were skilled and unskilled workers, sales, business, white-collar, and professional men in their twenties, thirties, and forties. They were recruited by newspaper ads in the New Haven, Connecticut, area and were paid $4.50 for coming to the laboratory. It was made clear to them, however, that the payment did not depend upon their going on with the experiment—they could quit any time they liked and still be paid.

Each subject met the director of the experiment and another person who was introduced as a subject, though he was actually an accomplice. The subject was told that the experiment was an important one on the effects of electric shock, or punishment, on learning. The director gave an elaborate rationale as to why that was a vital subject to study. The basic idea of the experiment was that one person—called the teacher—would shock the other person—called the learner—when the learner made mistakes in learning a list of paired-associate words (see page 116).

The subject and the accomplice subject drew lots to see who would be the learner and who the teacher. (It was a rigged drawing; both slips of paper had "teacher" on them, but the accomplice reported that his said "learner.") The teacher and learner then examined the electric chair. The learner—accomplice subject—was strapped into the chair while the teacher—the real subject—was assured that the shocks to be given, while painful, would cause no permanent tissue damage. The accomplice subject was left strapped in the chair while the real subject was shown the electric shock apparatus that was located in another room. (This too was bogus; no shocks were given.)

The shock apparatus was an impressive-looking device, with a panel on which 30 lever switches and various lights and warning labels were mounted. Supposedly the first switch gave a 15-volt shock, the second a 30-volt shock, and so on to the last switch that gave a 450-volt shock. Labels such as *Slight shock, Moderate shock, Danger: Severe shock,* and so on, indicated the general level of the shocks. The last two shock switches were labeled XXX. To make the situation even more real for the subject, he was given a 45-volt sample shock before he started the "learning" part of the experiment.

The teacher—the real subject—was told to shock the learner—the accomplice—whenever he made a mistake in learning. After some practice trials, the experiment began. The learner responded appropriately, making a mistake from time to time and receiving shock, until the shock level reached 300 volts. At this point, the learner pounded on the wall; then he stopped giving answers—so that all responses from the learner's room ceased. The teacher was instructed to treat no answer as a wrong answer and to continue with the shock. If the subject (that is, the teacher) said he wanted to quit the experiment, the experimental director applied social pressure in the form of a standard and graded series of "prods." The measure of obedience was the number of switches depressed—that is, the amount of shock the subject thought he was giving to another person.

The results run counter to what most of us might expect. At least, they contradict the judgment of a group of Yale seniors who were asked to predict the results. The students estimated that, on the average, only 1 percent of people would continue to give shocks until the 450-volt level was reached. But in fact, 26 out of the 40 subjects, or 65 percent, went to the maximum. None of the subjects quit shocking the learner until 300 volts had been reached. At 300 volts, 5 out of 40 quit; between 300 and the limit, 9 more did. The teacher subjects showed a great deal of tension—trembling, stuttering, groaning, nervous laughter, and so on—as they increased the shock. These were men caught in a conflict between the demands of the experiment and their consciences. The demands of the situation for obedience and conformity won out, but the conflict was intense.

As we pointed out, caution is necessary in generalizing the results of such an experiment. But it does have certain important features that resemble real-life situations. For instance, it was because this experiment was carried out by presumably competent authority figures that obedience was obtained. The subjects thought that the experiment was being conducted for a worthy cause by people who knew what they were doing.

REASONS FOR CONFORMITY Researchers have proposed a number of hypotheses to account for conformity behavior and have investigated many specific factors involved in conformity. One suggested hypothesis is that an individual simply "goes along" with the opinions of his group because they seem to be correct. If the situation is ambiguous and he does not know exactly what is expected of him, he seeks to compare his behavior with that of others who are in the same situation. This sort of *social comparison* does not always lead to conformity, but where objective evaluation of environmental situational cues is difficult, going along with someone else is often chosen as the appropriate behavior (Festinger, 1954; Schachter and Singer, 1962).

Another hypothesis stresses the individual's tendency to avoid the social disapproval and social censure that can come from violating group norms. Pressure to conform, however, is not exerted only by people who clearly have the power to enforce the norms. The desire for social approval is so ingrained and so generalized to members of the group or community that we may even desire approval from complete strangers. This fact was demonstrated in one of the earliest experiments in social psychology (Allport, 1924). Subjects in the experiment tended to give less extreme judgments when they were with other people, even when they did not know them, than when they were alone. Presumably they feared that extreme judgments would bring disapproval from the others.

A third hypothesis emphasizes the unpleasant conflict the person experiences between what he perceives and what others tell him. This conflict is an example of cognitive dissonance (see page 219), which exists when two ideas, or cognitions, are in disagreement. It motivates us to try to reduce the dissonance between ideas—which we can do by changing one of the ideas. In conformity situations such as Asch's experiment with people who estimated the length of lines, the subjects had to agree or disagree with the majority. On the early trials of experiments like this, agreement or disagreement sets up certain consequences that tend to bring about consistent yielding or nonyielding on later trials (Gerard, 1965). In other words, the pattern of conformity behavior in Asch-type situations is apt to be bimodal—either the subject yields on almost every trial, or he almost never yields. The dissonance idea is said to work something like this to produce consistent patterns of yielding or nonyielding: It predicts that conformers will like their groups because they believe that their conformity makes them liked by members of the group. We tend to think well of those whom we believe think well of us. On the other hand, the people who deviate will believe they are being judged negatively and will not like the other group members. The person who yields and evaluates the group positively now has a reason for going along with the group: they are "good guys," and their judgments can't be far wrong. Thus the positive evaluation of the group that stems from his conformity tends to smooth out his dissonant ideas. The nonconformer, on the other hand, smoothes out the conflict by devaluing the group; he sees them as "bad guys" whose judgment is not to be trusted. In so doing, he reduces the dissonance between what he sees and what the group says. If he has devalued the group and decided that their opinions can be disregarded, the conflict is over, and he can "call them as he sees them."

These three hypotheses—social comparison, avoidance of social disapproval, and dissonance reduction—are only a sample of the general concepts that have been proposed to explain conformity behavior. Although it is difficult to separate the general from the specific in this field, a number of specific factors in conformity have been studied, of which we shall discuss four.

1. *Orientation to the group.* Orientation can vary in a number of ways. One is in the individual's strength of attraction to the group. In examining the hypothesis of dissonance reduction, we saw that a person who feels drawn to the group, either because he likes it or because he somehow sees it as meeting his needs, is more inclined to conform to it than a person who is not attracted. And the greater the attraction, that is, the more a person wants to belong to the group, the more likely he is to agree with the opinions of the other members. Fear of disapproval is certainly one of the reasons for this behavior; the punishment we may suffer by being rejected or disapproved of is more serious if it is meted out by a group to which we would really like to belong.

People's tendency toward conformity in groups which are attractive to them can be observed both in daily experience and in the laboratory. In general, we all have a higher regard for the opinions of people we like than for those of people we do not like. This is particularly the case if we have no objective way of determining whether the opinions are correct, as we often do not.

A second way in which orientation can vary is in group orientation versus task orientation. Some people are much more concerned with the task the group has to accomplish—with getting things done—than with their personal relations in the group. This may be because the individual is typically task-oriented rather than group-oriented, because he is seriously interested in the purposes of the group, or because people in the group somehow make him feel this way. In any case, research shows that the task-oriented person is much less affected by group pressures for conformity than the group-oriented person who is concerned about his personal relations with the group (Thibaut and Strickland, 1956).

2. *Need to be liked and accepted.* Another factor, which is closely related to group attractiveness, is the need of a person to be liked and accepted by the group he values. A teen-ager, for instance, wants to be accepted by his peers and may find it difficult to resist group pressures to conform. The group may require him to wear certain clothes, adopt certain hair styles, know the latest dances, and own a car; or the conformity behavior may involve drinking, shoplifting, sex exploration, and experimentation with drugs. Fear of social disapproval by one's peers can provide strong motivation to conform—at least, to comply if not to privately accept.

A certain sameness is sometimes noted among members of a fraternity chapter; conformity produces some of these standard behaviors. Even the extreme "nonconformists" who exist on the fringes of many university communities have easily identifiable habits and modes of dress which are norms in their own groups. Though they wish to be considered nonconformists, they often slavishly conform to the behaviors expected of them by their friends.

Thus we may conform because we need to be accepted. Similarly, we may use conformity as a technique to make other people like us. Experiments have shown that conformity is a common "tactic of ingratiation . . . a means of currying favor with a more powerful individual" (Jones, 1965). By subtly agreeing with the opinions of the more powerful person, we may make him like us more. Commonly the ingratiator steers a course between being an obvious "yes man" and outright disagreement. He achieves this compromise in several ways: (1) by agreeing with the more powerful person, but expressing low confidence in his own opinion, (2) by agreeing with the substance but disagreeing with specific details of the more powerful person's arguments, and (3) by agreeing only on those occasions when the other person seems open to argument.

3. *Perceived consensus within the group.* If an individual sees that all the other group members are agreed on a certain opinion or course of behavior, he is more likely to conform to their views than if he believes they are not unanimous. In experiments similar to the Asch experiment described earlier, in which a subject seated with a group of confederates

of the experimenter is asked to express his estimate of the length of certain lines, conformity was high when the other people in his group had been coached to give a unanimous opinion (Asch, 1958). However, the subject was much less likely to conform to the group judgments when at least one other person also differed from the group. One reason for this result, it seems, is that deviation from a unanimously agreed-upon point of view may bring greater disapproval than nonconformity to a less agreed-upon opinion.

4. *Gradual conformity induction.* This is the foot-in-the-door technique: a person who is first induced to comply with a small request will often comply later with a much larger request. It seems to be a common technique in marketing. It was also a prominent part of the Korean War brainwashing—an attempt to produce private acceptance of certain ideas, or attitude change. Prisoners who signed mild confessions could be induced later to sign more incriminating documents. Experiments have shown that gradual induction is an important variable in compliance (Freedman and Fraser, 1966):

The experimenters, posing as researchers for *Guide,* a bogus consumer magazine, telephoned housewives, talked to them about *Guide,* and, depending on which of four experimental groups they were in, made a small request—they asked the women to answer some questions about the kind of household soap they were using. Women in the first group, called the performance condition, answered questions about the soaps on the first call. Those in the second group, called the agree-only condition, did not actually answer any questions, but they agreed to answer questions at a later time. In the third group, called the familiarization condition, the experimenter gave a description of *Guide,* but said nothing about questions. Women in a control group, called the one-contact condition, were contacted only once, at the time of the second (the large-request) contact in the other conditions.

This contact was made several days later, when the experimenters telephoned the women again and asked them to allow several men from *Guide* to come into their homes for several hours to inventory all the household products. The men were to have freedom to rummage through the cupboards and cabinets for these products—a really outrageous request! What happened? Of the housewives in the performance group, 53 percent complied with the large request, while only 22 percent of the control (one-contact) subjects agreed. The other conditions produced intermediate degrees of compliance, with the familiarization condition producing only a little more than the one-contact condition.

One reason for the effectiveness of gradual induction may be found in the dissonance theory of conformity described earlier. This theory predicts that conformity behavior will persist after it first occurs. The small request in gradual induction may just be a way of securing the first compliance, thus setting the stage for further compliance because of the dissonance mechanisms.

Bargaining and norm formation People must reach agreement with each other if they are to live together in social groups. They must establish rules about who is to do what, how it is to be done, how the results are to be shared, and so on. These rules are really norms—agreements and expectations by the group members about how one should behave. We have already seen that norms arise in the process of socialization; but they also arise as people bargain and interact with each other. This section will trace the relationship between small-group bargaining and the development of norms.

REWARDS AND COSTS One influential analysis of this relationship is in terms of rewards and costs (Thibaut and Kelley, 1959). It has been proposed that, in general, people attempt to maximize rewards and reduce costs in social situations. *Rewards* are events that produce gratification—events that result in material gain, enhance self-esteem, bring social approval, and so on. *Costs* are events that result in loss of material things or that lower self-esteem, increase tension and anxiety, and so on. An individual consciously or unconsciously weighs the various alternatives in a situation and decides what he will do. He tries to anticipate which course of action will be most rewarding to him, with the least cost. He may compare the attractiveness of the situation or relationship with other possible opportunities. For instance, a college freshman may decide to choose no one "best" friend until he has had an opportunity to get to know many of the others in his dormitory.

Once a relationship between two or more persons is begun, each is somewhat interdependent upon the other to receive satisfactory *outcomes.* Generally, each person expects the rewarding outcomes to be proportional to costs in an exchange relationship. A person may be angry if he does not get what he feels is due him; he may feel guilty if he is overrewarded (Homans, 1950).

The theory says that people seek to maximize rewards and minimize costs (seek pleasure and avoid pain) in the present, and that they plan actions to bring rewards and minimize costs in the future. The definition of rewards and costs in the theory depends upon what is called the *comparison level,* which is a kind of subjective standard. Positive outcomes exceeding this standard, which provides a sort of neutral point, are satisfactory; outcomes falling below it are unsatisfactory. The setting of the comparison level depends upon many things—among them, what the person's past experience has been, and what he has heard about others in similar situations. If the interactions a person has with the members of a group generally exceed the comparison level, he will tend to maintain contact with that group. And if most of the group members derive rewards from group interaction, the group will tend to be a stable one. The theory that people seek rewards which exceed their comparison levels has interesting consequences for the formation of norms in small groups.

REWARDS, COSTS, POWER, AND NORMS A two-person group, or *dyad,* is perhaps the simplest situation that can be studied. The analysis of interaction in dyads in terms of rewards, costs, and power has led to certain predictions about the conditions under which norms will be established. Suppose two people are mutually interdependent so that both must work together to produce favorable outcomes—outcomes ex-

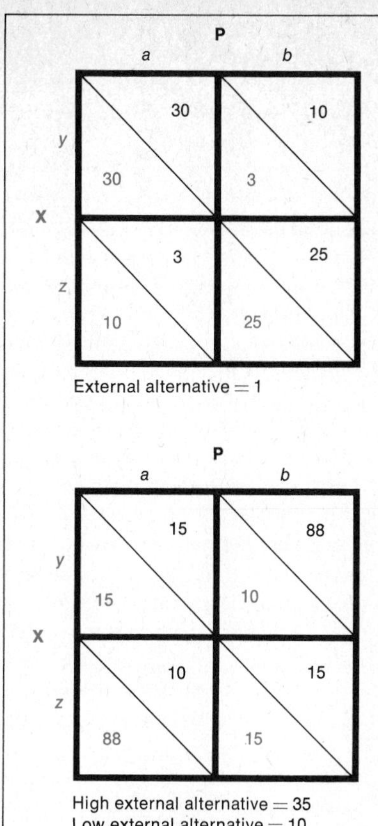

BARGAINING AND NORM FORMATION CAN BE STUDIED WITH GAMES

Figure 14.8 *Two of the matrices used in a bargaining experiment. Top, a sample matrix designed to acquaint the subjects of the experiment with the task. Bottom, an actual game matrix used in the set of experimental conditions described in the text. (From Thibaut and Faucheux, 1965.)*

ceeding the comparison levels of each. Even when one member of the dyad has more power than the other and can exert a disproportionate influence on the outcomes, the dyad will stay together because of its strong interdependence—no one will get anything if the two members do not cooperate.

But it is instructive to see what happens when stress is introduced into this kind of stable social situation. In the experiment discussed next, stress was created by increasing the power of one of the members, by reducing the amount of interdependence, and by making attractive alternatives available outside the dyad. Under these conditions bargaining occurs, and norms are developed governing the possible range of permissible behaviors. In other words, in harmonious situations of high interdependence, no norms are necessary to limit action in order to keep the dyad together. But when stress is introduced—when interdependence is weakened, when the power of one of the members is increased, and when attractive alternatives outside the dyad are made available—then the group will break up unless the partners develop agreements, or norms, specifying and limiting possibilities of action (Thibaut and Faucheux, 1965):

The basic situation was one in which bargaining games were played between groups of students. The nature of the games can be specified by various matrices. The subjects bargained openly about what to do with each matrix, or game. In the matrix shown in Figure 14.8 (top) the two players are designated P and X. P played the columns, *a* or *b;* X played the rows, *y* or *z;* their two choices then intersected in one of the four boxes. The outcomes from playing the various options are shown in each box. The number in black gives the outcomes for P, the number in color the outcomes for X. For example, if P played *a* and X played *y,* P would get 30 points and so would X. For the members of each pair in these games did not compete with each other; they tried to help each other make more points than other P and X players who were playing at the same time. The P players were instructed to get as many points as they could relative to P players in other dyads, and so were the X players relative to other X players.

P was the "high-power" player. Power was defined as follows: In the boxes (called cells) where there was a discrepancy between the two players' outcomes (as in the *by* and *az* cells of Figure 14.8, top), P was allowed to take any number of points up to the largest number, leaving the remaining points to X. For instance, in boxes *by* and *az* of Figure 14.8 (top), P could take 10 points, leaving X 3; or P could take 8 points, leaving X 5, and so on. This condition was introduced so that bargaining could occur.

Also shown in the top of Figure 14.8 is another feature of the experiment—the external alternative. In this matrix, the alternative was worth 1 point. Either player could elect to take it rather than taking his points in the matrix, and then the other player would get nothing. But while the external alternative was a "sure thing," it was of very low value in this particular matrix; not many points would be gained in comparison with other P or X players by taking it.

The rational choice for both players in the matrix at the top of Figure 14.8 is easy to see—P should take *a* and X should take *y*; that way they both can get 30 points. P is powerless in this type of situation; he can only use his power at the cost of gaining fewer points. If he chooses a discrepant cell—*by,* for instance—

P will get a maximum of 10 points; but he could have had 30 points by agreeing with X on *ay*.

But now consider what happened when stress was added to this harmonious situation. In the matrix shown in Figure 14.8 (bottom), a large conflict between the outcomes in the discrepant cells was introduced so that P could use his power. External alternatives of both high and low attractiveness were also made available. Thus high conflict within the matrix was paired with external alternatives of both high and low attractiveness, creating pairs which we shall call HH and HL groups. In other words, the dyadic relationships were stressed by increasing the power differential and the attractiveness of the outside alternatives. (Other groups were provided with low conflict and high or low attractiveness of alternatives, but for simplicity we shall restrict ourselves to the HH and HL groups.)

Suppose you were going to play the bottom matrix in Figure 14.8 using the high external alternative of 35 points—that is, under the HH condition. If you were P, you would probably use your power and play column *b*, but unless you modified your power in some way, X would go outside the dyad to maximize his gains by taking 35 points, leaving you with zero. You, as P, will have to compensate X by not taking all the points you can, and a bargain, or norm, will be established. Now consider the HL condition, where the external alternative is only 10 points. If you were P, you could exercise your power (play column *b*) and get away with it; there is less stress on the dyad. X could not go outside the dyad to maximize his gains because he would only get 10 points; by staying in the dyad he can play row *z* and get 15 points. So you, as P, can suit yourself. Not much bargaining will be necessary to hold the dyad together; X will stay in without any bargaining, because he can get the most that way. But if something better should become available to X—watch out!

The results indicated that 100 percent of the HH dyads engaged in vigorous bargaining and established norms. Only 50 percent of the HL dyads bargained, and the bargaining was less intense.

This experiment is an artificial case, of course. In real life things are not static; new alternatives are always becoming available, and people in a dyad do not usually strike bargains over one thing at a time. Rather, many factors are brought to bear in a bargaining situation. But the results of such an analysis are instructive because they indicate some of the conditions under which norms will develop.

Speaking loosely now, the HH condition is somewhat like a modern marriage in the United States, in which the husband may be the boss but the wife has many external alternatives open to her: she can get a divorce, she can go to work, and so on. Bargaining and the formation of norms will be intense. The HL condition is, perhaps, somewhat like a Victorian marriage in that the husband was the absolute boss, and the wife had few attractive alternatives open. Under these circumstances norm formation would be inhibited. Or to extend the idea to groups in conflict, not dyads, consider black power. In social psychological terms, black power might be regarded as an attempt to establish an attractive alternative to the powerful "establishment." When people have alternatives, normative agreements will ensue. This speculation probably extends things too far beyond the simple dyadic groups on which the ideas were founded, but the reward-cost-power analysis of norm formation does seem to be a fruitful approach.

Crowds and cities We have all heard much lately about riots, panics, vandalism, social callousness, and other mass social phenomena. Social psychologists have attempted to analyze some of the social forces underlying these behaviors.

CROWDS In crowds people tend to do things they would not do alone. Of course, being in a crowd provides a setting, or stimulus situation, in which certain behaviors are appropriate that are not appropriate when we are alone or in a small group. If I jump up at my desk and cheer loudly when I am alone, I am acting inappropriately in the light of agreed-upon social norms. (See the discussion of the social definition of behavior disorders in Chapter 12.) But if I jump up and cheer when I am in a crowd of people at a basketball game, I am acting appropriately. The crowd has provided a setting in which I behave differently from the way I behave when alone.

But people do things in crowds that they would not do alone for many other reasons. One factor in much violent crowd behavior is that a strong motive, or drive, is being expressed; the drive is strong enough to override the usual social controls. Fear drive in panics and aggressive drives in certain riots are examples. Another factor in violent social crowd behavior is often an ambiguous situation in which rumors can be believed. If there is no way to check the accuracy of a rumor, we may believe it if it sounds plausible and if strong motives have been aroused. The rumor may serve as a trigger to initiate crowd behavior. For instance, against a background of hostility and frustration, the rumor that the police have shot an innocent person may trigger a riot.

Thus strong drives and an ambiguous situation contribute to violent crowd behavior—riots, lynchings, panics, and the like. In addition, it is satisfying to express impulses that are usually not expressed: violent crowd behavior can be fun for the participants. To some extent emotional contagion is also a factor in riots: people behave violently and emotionally because they see others behaving this way. Another very important factor in crowd behavior is anonymity: acting as a faceless and nameless part of a larger unit allows a person to escape guilt feelings because responsibility is diffused to the crowd.

SOCIAL PSYCHOLOGY OF CITY LIVING In recent years, much attention has been given to cities and to certain social-psychological factors—*anonymity,* or deindividuation, *social inhibition,* and *cognitive overload*—that seem to be strongest in cities.

1. *Anonymity, or deindividuation.* These are terms referring to the namelessness and facelessness often found in large groups. Their opposite is *individuation,* in which people are known as individuals by name and characteristics (Zimbardo, 1970). We have seen that anonymity is a factor in crowd behavior, but in urban communities it goes beyond crowd behavior to become a pervasive part of life. Anonymity tends to free people from the usual social constraints of feeling responsible for, and being held responsible for, their actions. Here is a sobering account of an experiment in which two cars—one in New York

City, the other in Palo Alto, California—were left parked on the street with their hoods open and license plates off:[1]

What happened in New York was unbelievable! Within ten minutes the 1959 Oldsmobile received its first auto strippers—a father, mother, and eight-year-old son. The mother appeared to be a lookout, while the son aided the father's search of the trunk, glove compartment, and motor. He handed his father the tools necessary to remove the battery and radiator. Total time of destructive contact: seven minutes.

In less than three days what remained was a battered, useless hulk of metal, the result of 23 incidents of destructive contact. The vandalism was almost always observed by one or more other passersby, who occasionally stopped to chat with the looters. Most of the destruction was done in the daylight hours and not at night (as we had anticipated), and the adults' stealing clearly preceded the window-breaking, tire-slashing fun of the youngsters. The adults were all well-dressed, clean-cut whites who would under other circumstances be mistaken for mature, responsible citizens demanding more law and order. The one optimistic note to emerge from this study is that the number of people who came into contact with the car but did not steal or damage it was twice as large as the number of actual vandals.

In startling contrast, the Palo Alto car not only emerged untouched, but when it began to rain, a passerby lowered the hood so that the motor would not get wet!

---

2. *Social inhibition.* It has been claimed that city dwellers are callous because they are deindividuized. This is probably part of the story; but in addition, city people may act as they do in crowds because they are socially "confused" and socially inhibited. By social confusion we mean that the situation is sometimes so complex that the decisions about what to do are difficult and unclear. By social inhibition we mean that people have a tendency to refrain from acting in certain situations when they are members of groups.

The famous case of Kitty Genovese is often cited as an example of the callousness of city people. Miss Genovese was murdered on a residential street in New York City while people living in the buildings on all sides heard her screams and did nothing to help. Yet this may not have been callousness at all; it may have been a matter of confusion about what to do. We take cues from others in social situations, and if the others do not react, then the situation may seem ambiguous so that we do not know quite what to do. In the case of Miss Genovese people may also have thought that someone else had reported the incident. Moreover, it seems that simply being in a group tends to inhibit individual action. Social confusion and social inhibition are demonstrated in the following experiment (Latané and Darley, 1969):

The subjects, male undergraduates at Columbia University, thought they were participating in a market research survey. When they came to the laboratory to

[1]Zimbardo, P. G. The human choice: Individuation, reason, and order versus deindividuation, impulse, and chaos. In *The Nebraska Symposium on Motivation, 1969,* W. J. Arnold and D. Levine (Eds.). Reprinted by permission of The University of Nebraska Press. Copyright © 1970 by The University of Nebraska Press.

take the survey, they waited in a room under one of the following conditions: (1) alone, (2) with a passive confederate (stooge) of the experimenter, (3) with a stranger, or (4) with a friend.

A simulated emergency was created as follows: The subjects, while waiting in the room under one of the four conditions, were given questionnaires to fill out by an attractive young woman—the supposed representative of the market research firm. The students could see that her office was piled high with papers and precariously balanced filing cabinets. Their room was divided from hers by a collapsible curtain. She gave them the questionnaire and then returned to her room, saying that she would be back in 10 minutes. She made sure the subjects could see that the curtain between the two rooms was not locked and could be opened easily.

After a few minutes, the simulated emergency began. The young woman turned on a tape of an accident in which she was supposedly involved: There was a loud crash, followed by agonized comments such as "Oh, my foot!" "I can't move, get this thing off of me!" In condition 2, the passive stooge simply shrugged his shoulders and went on with the questionnaire.

What action did the subjects take? Of those who waited alone, 70 percent offered to help her. By contrast, only 7 percent of the subjects with the passive stooge intervened. When two strangers were together, only 40 percent offered to help. When friends were together, social inhibition, while still present, was less than in the "stranger" or "stooge" conditions.

Other experiments have also found social inhibition in group behavior: people respond to emergency situations less when they are together than when they are alone. Why? One explanation is that people take cues from other people in an emergency situation. Our perception of what others do defines what we should do. If no one does anything, we may interpret the situation as not too much of an emergency and so may not act. If we do not act, others, perceiving our inaction, will not act. Thus a state of "pluralistic ignorance" builds up, and nothing happens. It seems likely that friends are less susceptible to pluralistic ignorance because they can more easily talk the situation over. But as the experiment above discovered, social inhibition still exists for groups of friends. Another explanation of social inhibition concerns the diffusion, or spreading, of responsibility. We expect someone else to take responsibility when we are in a group—"Someone else will do something; I don't need to," we say.

Groups of people are more likely to be present at emergency situations in cities than in rural areas. So according to this analysis, the behavior of city people is not intentionally callous; it is just that the presence of other people may be socially inhibiting.

3. *Cognitive overload.* People in cities may act abruptly and irritably because of what has been called cognitive overload (Milgram, 1970). *Overload* is a term used in communication engineering; if a communication channel has more information than it can carry at a given time, priority must be given to certain messages, while others are rerouted or not sent at all. By analogy, people who are exposed to more information than they can assimilate and process must give priority to certain per-

ceptions and thoughts (cognitions). Other perceptions and thoughts that have a low priority may be blocked.

In large urban centers, the amount of stimulation is staggering. In riding to work on the subway, for example, a person's senses are bombarded with information. He can respond only to a limited amount of the sensory input—only that part which is immediately concerned with getting to work. He must disregard the other people on the subway as much as possible. This is adaptive; we must ignore low-priority messages in order to cut down the overload. Otherwise we would be swamped and could not do what we need to do. What looks like callousness, indifference, irritability, and so on may just be manifestations of the adaptive overload reduction that enables people to function in crowded city life.

Interpersonal Attraction

Why do people like or dislike each other? Part of the answer will be found in the next section on attribution. Here we shall present other answers that have been given to this complex question. Folklore is full of sayings about it. "Birds of a feather flock together," and "A person is known by the company he keeps," express the idea that people who are similar in certain ways like each other. But what about the saying, "Opposites attract"? With certain exceptions, as we shall see, people are not like electrical charges, and opposites do not attract. Similarity of attitudes and beliefs (see Chapter 15) seems to be the factor that accounts for much of our liking of others. But other factors also play a role, and many theories about interpersonal attractiveness have been proposed.

Satisfaction of needs One idea is that we like those who satisfy our needs. Such people, in terms that might be used by a psychologist interested in learning, are secondary reinforcers (see Chapter 3). People who comfort us, people who enhance our self esteem, or people who reduce our anxieties are people we are probably going to like.

Another idea about needs and attractiveness is that of *need complementarity.* It has been proposed that people with needs which complement each other will be attracted. For instance, a nonassertive person might be attracted to an assertive one; or a person with a need to dominate might be attracted to people with needs to be dominated. The idea of complementarity comes close to the notion that "opposites attract." In general, the evidence for need complementarity is not very convincing (Tharp, 1963). But one interesting study indicates that complementarity may play some role in liking (Kerckhoff and Davis, 1962):

In a study of some of the factors involved in the selection of a steady girl friend, it was found that complementarity played a role for those who had been "pinned" for a relatively long period—18 months or more. For couples who had been "pinned" for less than 18 months, factors such as need satisfaction, similarity of attitudes, and similarity of religion and social class were more important than

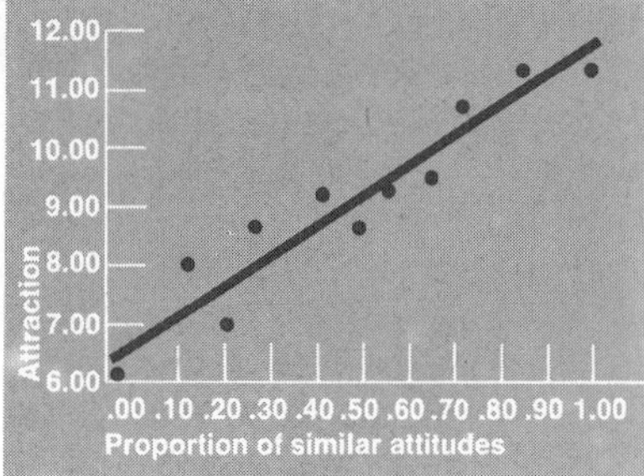

LIKE LIKES LIKE

Figure 14.9 *The relationship between the proportion of similar attitudes perceived to be held by another person and the degree of attraction felt. (After Byrne, 1969.)*

complementarity. Complementarity thus seemed more important in the formation of lasting relationships.

Similarity of attitudes and beliefs Although need complementarity may play some role in liking, strong evidence exists that we like people who think as we do. A number of field studies have indicated that husbands and wives, who presumably like each other at least a little, have similar attitudes. The degree of correlation tends to follow the rated happiness of the marriage: couples who are happily married show greater agreement than those who are unhappily married or divorced. But perhaps the best evidence for attitude and belief similarity as a factor in interpersonal attraction comes from experimental studies. Here is a composite of several such studies (Byrne, 1969):

College students filled out six-choice attitude scales of the following type:

Political Parties (Check one)

_____ I am a strong supporter of the Democratic party.
_____ I prefer the Democratic party.
_____ I have a slight preference for the Democratic party.
_____ I have a slight preference for the Republican party.
_____ I prefer the Republican party.
_____ I am a strong supporter of the Republican party.

Then the subjects were given false scales that had been prepared by the experimenter so that they agreed or disagreed with the subject's own attitude ratings. For instance, all the answers on the false scale might be as dissimilar as possible to those of the subject. If, in the political party example above, a subject had checked "I am a strong supporter of the Republican party," the false questionnaire would have a check for "I am a strong supporter of the Democratic party." Other subjects were given questionnaires that agreed completely with their own answers. Subjects were told that the questionnaires prepared by the experimenter came from strangers and were then asked to rate the strangers on a scale of attraction that gave scores ranging from 2 (not attractive) to 14 (very attractive).

The results indicated that subjects who received attitude scales that agreed with their own gave the "strangers" a high rating (an average of 13) on attractiveness; subjects who received the dissimilar scales gave the "strangers" a low attractiveness rating (averaging 4.41).

Moreover, the attractiveness of the hypothetical "stranger" was found to depend upon the *proportion* of the attitudes which the subject shared with the "stranger." This was discovered by giving the subjects "stranger" scales in which the proportion of similar attitudes varied from 1.00—complete agreement, or similarity—to 0.00—complete dissimilarity. The results, as shown in Figure 14.9, are striking. There is a linear (straight-line) relationship between the proportion of perceived agreement and ratings of attractiveness: As perceived agreement goes up, so does attractiveness. It is not so much a matter of the absolute number of items agreed upon as it is of the *proportion of the total* agreed upon. This finding seems to be true for many groups—not just college students.

So it seems clear that people like people who hold similar attitudes and beliefs. Why should this be so? One idea, in terms of what we have already discussed, is that social interaction with those who have attitudes similar to ours is rewarding. Another idea involves the *social comparison process*—that is, we seek confirmation of our ideas, especially when we are uncertain, by comparing them with the ideas of others (Festinger, 1954). We may tend to like people who confirm our beliefs and attitudes and therefore reduce our uncertainty. A third explanation involves what might be called *reciprocity.* The subject believes that the "stranger" with the similar attitudes would probably like him. Other experiments indicate that if a person knows someone likes him, he will reciprocate with liking. Since reciprocity and social comparison are important factors in their own right in interpersonal attraction, we shall discuss them next.

Reciprocity The advice is often given: "Be a friend to someone and he will be a friend to you." This idea is at the core of many books on how to be popular, and it has some truth. As we noted above, people tend to reciprocate perceived liking. Some experimental evidence verifies the general idea of reciprocity, but this same evidence goes on to indicate that it needs many qualifications (Backman and Secord, 1959):

Ten college students took a personality test and then met each other for the first time. Each subject had been privately told that the personality tests predicted he would be liked by three particular members of the group. After the group had met, records of liking were made, and it did turn out that people liked the group members who supposedly liked them. But in subsequent meetings, the reciprocity effect did not last. The persons whom the subjects liked initially were no longer especially liked after several group meetings. It seems probable that the subjects discovered that the three members of the group who were supposed to like them did not really like them. Then, too, the subjects had a chance to find out about attitude and belief similarity, and this important factor in liking may have canceled the reciprocity effect.

Social comparison Most of the things we need to know about the world, especially the world of social relationships, cannot be verified by direct observation. The social world we live in is ambiguous; we seek support for our attitudes and beliefs by comparing them with other people's, and we tend to like the people who support our attitudes and beliefs in the face of uncertainty. Such support may, of course, be one of the reasons for the relationship between attitude and belief similarity and attractiveness.

Social contact Another variable in attraction is simply the *amount* of social interaction that people have with each other (see page 537). A number of studies have shown that we tend to have stronger feelings of liking (and to some extent, of dislike too) for people who live near us. For instance, people tend to marry people who live near them. (Marriages are made on the block and not in heaven.) Thus liking, and dislike too, are to some extent matters of geographical accident. The following study illustrates this for liking (Festinger et al., 1950):

The friendship patterns of people in married student housing projects were investigated. In one project the apartments were arranged on two floors of a long building. The chart of friendship patterns showed that the strongest relationships were established between people living close to each other. In other words, there was an inverse relationship between the distance—as measured by the number of footsteps between apartments—and liking. In addition, people living at the end of the building where the stairways were located tended to have more friends upstairs than people who did not live near the steps.

Another housing development was arranged so that all except two of the individual units faced a central courtyard. Friendship was again found to be related to geographical distance. Moreover, the people in the two outward-facing units had fewer friends in the project than those facing the courtyard.

Geographical closeness, or propinquity, to other people sets the occasion for interaction and the sharing of common concerns. Propinquity may simply provide an opportunity for the attitude and belief similarity factor, the social comparison factor, and the reciprocity factors to operate. But liking and friendships are not the only consequences of geographical closeness; propinquity may also lead to the creation of enemies. Assaults and murders are most frequently committed by acquaintances, not by strangers. If you are going to get knifed, bashed, shot at, or raped, it will most likely be by someone you know well. The police are aware of this, and the first suspects in assault cases are often family members or close acquaintances.

Physical attractiveness We tend to like people we judge as physically attractive. Most of the factors thus far discussed that make for interpersonal attraction might be subsumed under the heading of "information exchange"; people come to like those with whom they exchange information. Physical attractiveness is a variable relatively unrelated to the exchange of information. Why it is important is something of a mystery, but important it is, especially in dating behavior (Walster et al., 1966):

More than 700 freshmen were signed up to attend a "mixer" dance where their partners would be selected by computer—or so they were told. Each freshman was secretly rated on a scale of physical attractiveness by a group of sophomores when he came to buy his ticket for the dance. Partners were then assigned at random. During an intermission at the dance, the freshmen filled out a questionnaire, supposedly concerning the computer matching, which included a scale on which they rated their liking for their date. Relatively high correlations were found between liking for the date and the ratings of physical attractiveness that had been made earlier by the sophomores: the higher the physical attractiveness rating, the greater the liking. This was true for both men and women.

Incidentally, in this experiment the reciprocity relationship did not hold. The correlation between liking the date and the date's returning the sentiment was essentially zero. Perhaps, as the authors point out, the artificiality of the situation had much to do with this.

Physical attractiveness is thus a factor in liking. But the generality of this finding to other groups is in some dispute. Age may be a factor, and older groups may not show such a strong reaction to physical attractiveness. The effects of this variable may also be less when the contacts between people are more prolonged than they were in this experiment.

Disliking people So far our discussion has mainly concerned liking for others; but enmity is also a common human phenomenon. An important cause of dislike, although not the only one (Berkowitz, 1969), is frustration—people's blocking of our motives (see Chapter 7). We are quick to anger when we are frustrated, and we often become angry with, and dislike, the people who do the frustrating. As with most human affairs, the frustration may be perceived rather than actual; but with people, perceiving makes it so.

Frustration is most effective in producing anger when it is perceived as a deliberate act by the frustrator; it is not so effective when it is perceived as due to chance or accident. Frustration does not necessarily cause aggression and dislike of others; instead, it leads to the emotional states of anger and fear. Whether the anger will result in overt aggression and dislike depends upon many factors, one ot which is the social cost of overt aggression. For instance, on the job, in school, or in the army, the cost of bawling out a subordinate might be negligible, but the social consequences of such aggressive behavior directed toward the boss, teacher, or sergeant might be very great. Another important factor in turning anger into aggression is the presence of cues in the situation that prompt one to channel behavior in the aggressive direction (Berkowitz and Lepage, 1967).

So we tend to be angry with, and dislike, those who are perceived as frustrating us. Whether we will be overtly hostile and aggressive depends on the social cost and on the cues that are present to channel behavior.

The Attribution Process

Our perception of other people, while not a new field of social psychology, has recently received increased emphasis. People are the most important stimuli in our world, and to have stability in our psychological world we must be able to make accurate perceptions about the causes of behavior (Heider, 1958). *Attribution* is the name given to this aspect of the perception of people; it is the process of attempting to find satisfactory causes for the behavior of others. We assign attributes to other people that are inferences from their behavior. Such attributes—or *dispositions,* as they are sometimes called—enable us to make predictions about people's behavior. If from his behavior I attribute to a person the tendency, or disposition, toward dominance, I have an explanation that satisfies me when he tries to direct, say, my choice of political candidates. Thus the process of attributing dispositions to people is an attempt to make their behavior more predictable.

One theory of attribution is that it consists of moving from "acts to dispositions" (Jones and Davis, 1965). This is simply another way of saying that we make inferences about the behavioral tendencies, or dispositions, of people from instances of their behavior. But not every instance of behavior conveys information about the underlying dispositions. For attribution to occur, the observed behavioral act must be perceived as intended by the actor; we do not use accidental actions as the basis for inference about dispositions. In order to decide whether the act was intentional, the perceiver must judge (1) whether the actor had the *ability* to perform the action or whether it was simply the result of chance or luck, and (2) whether the actor had *knowledge* of the probable effects of the action.

Besides the conditions outlined above, the evidence indicates that we take a person's role into account when we draw conclusions from his actions. We do not derive much information from things he does that are part of his role; it is only when his behavior does not conform to the expected role behavior that we have an act from which dispositions will be inferred. We would not think much about a person with alcohol on his breath at a party, but alcohol on the breath at 8 A.M. is another matter. Early-morning drinking deviates from the expected norm of behavior, and we would use it to attribute behavior dispositions if the other necessary condition of intentionality had been met.

In summary, we attempt to find stable dispositions, or tendencies to behave, in people in order to make the social world predictable. We infer stable behavioral tendencies from a person's intended actions that differ from his average, or expected, role behaviors.

We need a great deal more information about the important social process of attribution. For instance, how permanent are attributions, and under what conditions will they change after they are formed? But for now, the important thing to realize is that we do constantly make attributions about the most important stimuli in our lives—other people. It might be instructive to consider the deep human feelings of love and hate in terms of attribution. In any case, attributions have many similarities with attitudes, the topic of the next chapter.

Synopsis and summary

At the beginning of this chapter, we suggested that behavior is molded to a very large degree by social forces. Think back over all the things you did yesterday and see if anything happened that was not influenced by the social sea in which we all swim—poor fish that we are. Suppose you decided to cut chemistry lab yesterday afternoon to go for a walk with friends. Leaving aside the cultural determinism which lies behind the fact that you are in school at all, a number of social problems arise. What would the instructor say? Are there rules about this? If so, are you violating one? If you are, what form of social disapproval will be meted out if you are caught? What are the costs and rewards in this situation? How will this act be perceived? And we have only begun to touch on the social aspects of a fairly simple situation. Even the logical structure of thought about such a problem is culturally determined. If we add the values, beliefs, and attitudes, all social in origin, which are mobilized when you consider this or any course of action, you will probably agree that virtually all our behavior is social.

1. Socialization is the process of learning the attitudes, beliefs, and behaviors appropriate to one's culture.

2. Cultures of different societies tend to have characteristic patterns. These are widely shared ways of behaving, together with the beliefs that accompany them.
3. Social structures are made up of different statuses. Individuals occupying a particular status are expected to play an appropriate role. Since a person may have several statuses and roles, conflicts occasionally develop, but often statuses and roles supplement each other or are compartmentalized.
4. Characteristic statuses tend to be arranged on a prestige scale, which becomes the basis for a division into social classes. Members of social classes differ in their sexual behavior, in their child-rearing practices, in occupational goals, in their dominant motivations, and in many other ways.
5. Groups vary in many dimensions and have many characteristics. The important social fact about groups is that they help to determine the behaviors of their members.
6. A great deal of work has been done on the description of interaction patterns within groups. Category systems have been established in the attempt to describe the various behaviors engaged in during group meetings.
7. Communication patterns within groups are important, largely because they determine the satisfaction felt by the members of the group with their group membership.
8. Many groups have leaders, but it is difficult to specify the personality characteristics that make for a good leader. These depend upon the type of group and what it is organized to do. Groups can have formal or informal leaders. The formal leader is the one designated to be the leader by the rules of the group; the informal leader is the one the members of the group perceive as central to the functioning of the group. Different types of leaders are effective in relaxed and tense situations.
9. Conformity to the group is an important aspect of the influence of the group upon behavior. Conformity is the general term that subsumes compliance and private acceptance. Private acceptance is a change in personal attitude in the direction advocated by the group; compliance is a change in behavior without a corresponding change in attitude.
10. Group norms are expected ways of behaving that are widely shared by most members of a group. They have a demand quality; hence most people conform to them.
11. Conformity to group norms has been demonstrated in many experimental situations. Such experiments have involved the perception of ambiguous situations and obedience to authority figures.
12. A number of general factors affect conformity to group norms, including social comparison, avoidance of social disapproval, and dissonance reduction. Specific factors influencing conformity include orientation to the group, the need to be liked and accepted, the perceived consensus within the group, and the relative speed of conformity induction.
13. One important way in which norms are formed in groups is through bargaining. Behavior in groups has rewards and costs associated with it; we try to maximize rewards and minimize costs. In the process of maximizing rewards and minimizing costs, bargaining occurs and norms develop. This process was illustrated by a bargaining experiment, and some generalizations were made about real-life situations.
14. The effects of crowds and cities on behavior is a recent focus in social psychology. Crowd behaviors are due to a combination of factors, including presence of strong drives, ambiguity of the situation, emotional contagion, and anonymity. In cities, anonymity, or deindividuation, social inhibition, and cognitive overload are concepts invoked to explain vandalism, callousness, and the apparent lack of concern of city dwellers with other people.

15. Interpersonal attraction—the liking or dislike one person feels for another—is a focus in social psychology. Among the factors that make for liking are (*a*) the satisfaction of needs by other people, (*b*) similarity of attitudes and beliefs, (*c*) reciprocity, (*d*) social comparison, (*e*) social contact, and (*f*) physical attractiveness. A major reason for dislike is the frustration of motives and the channeling of the anger produced by frustration toward the frustrator.
16. As we perceive people's behavior, we try to find satisfactory explanations of it. Starting with particular actions of a person, we infer his attributes, or behavioral dispositions.
17. For an attribution to be made from an action, the action must have certain characteristics. First, it must be perceived as an intentional act, not one that is due to chance, and not one in which the actor does not know the consequences of his action. Second, the action must be nonconforming; it is only through actions which differ from expected role behavior that we learn much about an individual. These nonconforming, intentional actions are the ones that provide the basis for attributing dispositions to people.

Related topics in the text

Chapter 3 Principles of Learning
The principles of classical conditioning as well as the principles concerning punishment, apply to socialization because it is a learning process.

Chapter 15 Attitudes and Beliefs
The social determiners of behavior covered here in Chapter 14 make up one of the two large concerns of social psychology. The other is the study of attitudes and beliefs.

Suggestions for further reading

Backman, C. W., and Secord, P. F. (Eds.) *Problems in social psychology: Selected readings.* New York: McGraw-Hill, 1966. (Paperback.)
Important articles covering a wide range of topics in social psychology are reprinted here.

Benedict, R. *Patterns of Culture.* (2d ed.) Boston: Houghton Mifflin, 1959. (Paperback available.)
A classical description and analysis, written by a social anthropologist, of patterns of culture in primitive societies.

Berkowitz, L. *Roots of aggression: A re-examination of the frustration-aggression hypothesis.* New York: Atherton, 1969. (Paperback.)
A modification and elaboration of the frustration-aggression hypothesis to explain human aggressiveness.

Berscheid, E., and Walster, E. H. *Interpersonal attraction.* Reading, Mass.: Addison-Wesley, 1969. (Paperback.)
A summary of the social psychology of why people like and dislike each other.

Brown, R. *Social psychology.* New York: Free Press, 1965.
A text which presents basic concepts through discussions of current problem areas.

Jones, E. E., and Gerard, H. B. *Foundations of social psychology.* New York: Wiley, 1967.
An authoritative textbook on social psychology.

Kiesler, C. A., and Kiesler, S. B. *Conformity.* Reading, Mass.: Addison-Wesley, 1969. (Paperback.)
Major studies and theories of social conformity are discussed.

Schopler, J. and Insko, C. A. *Experimental social psychology: Readings and commentary.* New York: Academic Press, 1971.
Each chapter consists of a few readings and an extensive commentary that puts the readings in context.

Attitudes are important keys in understanding the long-range organization of behavior. . . .
Newcomb, Turner, and Converse

A man with a conviction is a hard man to change.
Festinger, Riecken, and Schachter

The attitudes of other people are never seen or felt—they are only inferred. Yet they make a great difference in almost everyone's life. A person may hold specific attitudes toward various groups, such as student activists, blacks, whites, or the mentally ill; or he may hold attitudes toward some event, such as marriage, moon shots, or rock festivals. To the person in business or politics, attitudes may mean the difference between success or failure. The businessman depends upon the favorable attitudes of his customers toward his products and services to keep his business going. The politician needs favorable attitudes from the electorate toward his personality, abilities, and political behavior in order to be reelected. For similar reasons we all try to create favorable, and eliminate unfavorable, attitudes toward ourselves among our friends and associates. Indeed, few actions are taken or decisions made in everyday life without considering the way they might affect the attitudes of others.

Nature and Theory of Attitudes

Definitions In order to understand clearly what an attitude is and how it operates, we need a definition not only of attitudes but also of several kinds of behavior that interact with attitudes—namely, beliefs, opinions, prejudices, and stereotypes.

ATTITUDE An attitude, like an emotion (page 223), is not easy to pinpoint, and psychologists do not wholly agree on a definition. The one we shall use combines the important aspects of several approaches: *An attitude is a learned orientation, or disposition, toward an object or situation which provides a tendency to respond favorably or unfavorably to the object or situation.* (Rokeach, 1968).

Considering this definition in parts, let us first emphasize that attitudes are learned. They are learned in the same way that other responses are learned—through classical and operant conditioning. Secondly, an attitude is an orientation, or disposition, we carry around with us, just as we carry around all our habits. At any given moment, the attitude may be latent, or inactive, but it is there ready to be tripped off by appropriate circumstances. Thirdly, if the relevant circumstances do arise, the orientation of the person provides a tendency to respond in some way. How likely he is to respond depends on the strength of the attitude and the circumstances; how he responds, and whether he does so openly or privately, will hinge on the situation. Finally, an attitude has an object. The object may be thought of as a goal of learned behavior.

This definition of an attitude makes it simply a form of learned behavior. In Chapter 3, we regarded the learning process as an increase in the tendency to respond in a certain way to achieve positive goals or to avoid negative goals. Thus attitudes and learned tendencies to respond are basically the same thing. In fact, all operant learning is essentially the learning of attitudes that are favorable or unfavorable toward certain goals.

If we consider the object of an attitude as a learned goal, we can see that we must be literally loaded with attitudes. Every bit of motivated learning we have experienced has endowed us with another attitude. Thus we end up with attitudes toward mothers, teachers, automobiles, toys, animals, water, and so on, endlessly. Any of these attitudes could be important in an individual's life. Attitudes that cause a person trouble can be the occasion for psychotherapy—the purpose of which is to change attitudes. In social psychology, however, we are not interested in all possible objects of an attitude. Rather, we are concerned with *social objects* of attitudes. These are either people or things that people are involved in. Examples are parents, racial and ethnic groups, schools, wars, and religions.

BELIEF Closely related to an attitude is a belief. In fact, attitudes influence beliefs and beliefs attitudes. A belief is the *acceptance of some proposition.* It does not, by itself, necessarily imply an attitude of being for or against something. Believing that the world is round does not necessarily engender an attitude one way or another (although we are likely to have an unfavorable attitude toward someone who does not share this belief). On the other hand, many beliefs do imply an attitude and, moreover, can alter our attitude. If we accept the proposition that Communists are conspiring to destroy our freedom, we then have an unfavorable attitude toward Communists.

Attitudes can also determine beliefs. We are much more likely to accept a proposition that agrees with our attitudes than one that does not. If we have a negative attitude toward the "Establishment," we are likely to believe all sorts of unfavorable statements made about it. Thus attitudes and beliefs, though distinguishable, go hand in hand: Beliefs shape attitudes, which determine what we will and will not believe.

OPINIONS An opinion lies between an attitude and a belief and has properties of both. If, for example, a person expresses the opinion, "We should pull out of the Vietnam War," he is reflecting an unfavorable attitude toward that war and also expressing a belief about it. An opinion, however, can be distinguished from an attitude in two ways: First, an opinion, like a belief, is verbalized, while an attitude may not be. We may harbor attitudes acquired in the distant past that we are unaware of until we confront some issue which brings them out. Even then we may have a difficult time expressing them. Opinions and beliefs, on the other hand, are statements that are expressed verbally. Second, attitudes are private affairs, while opinions are public. We speak, for example, of public opinion polls, in which the opinions of many individuals are counted. On the other hand, from these polls we infer something about the attitudes of people toward such issues as, say, the Vietnam War. So the distinction between the terms is not always rigidly maintained.

PREJUDICE The word prejudice is used by many people to mean a negative attitude toward some minority group such as Jews or Negroes. But this is a layman's definition, not a psychological one. From the psychologist's standpoint a prejudice is the same in its operation as any attitude, and it can be either positive or negative.

However, a prejudice can be distinguished from an attitude in that it is an *unjustified* attitude. Etymologically, the word prejudice means *prejudgment.* In this sense, a prejudice is the application of a previously formed judgment to some person, object, or situation. The preformed judgment may be inappropriate, and hence unfair, to its object.

On the other hand, very few attitudes are formed or held with full knowledge of all the facts analyzed in a dispassionate way. Hence most attitudes are forms of prejudice. This point will become clearer later, when we consider how attitudes are formed or changed.

STEREOTYPES Prejudiced attitudes lead to what has been called a stereotype. This is any widespread, oversimplified, and hence erroneous belief (Krech et al., 1962). Generally, too, a stereotype concerns a category of people. For example, the notion that redheads have fiery tempers is a stereotype because it is widespread, at least in some cultural groups, and oversimplified. Actually, some redheads are quick-tempered and some are not. Other stereotypes are prevalent about blonds, scientists, Italians, Negroes, and many other groups. One way of studying widespread prejudice, and one that we shall give examples of later, is to determine the stereotypes held by one group, say, whites, about another group, such as blacks.

Consistency theory With these definitions in mind, let us form a general picture of how attitudes operate. Most social psychologists now accept one overall theory of attitudes; they differ mainly on details that will not concern us here (McGuire, 1968). What they agree on is that an attitude provides some consistency for cognitions and tendencies to respond that otherwise would be discrepant, incongruous, or dissonant—all three terms are used in different theories (page 219). It follows that attitude change is a process of resolving discrepancies between previous attitudes and new information. Let us trace the theory step by step.

LEARNING, CATEGORIZING, AND THINKING Learning an attitude, as we have already pointed out, is like learning anything else: the person learns to approach (react favorably to) positive goals, and to avoid (react unfavorably to) negative ones. Later when he encounters one of these goals, his attitude toward it is whatever he has learned about it in the past.

A child, for example, learns a respectful attitude toward his father. When he encounters other men, stimulus generalization (page 73) takes place: he transfers his attitude of respect to them because they resemble his father in being male adults. Until or unless he has reason to discriminate between his father and other men, he will have a respectful attitude toward all of them.

This kind of stimulus generalization is customary in attitude formation. Because we encounter many kinds of people and situations for which we have no previously learned attitudes, we transfer our existing attitudes to them whenever these new stimuli resemble something for which we have attitudes. In other words, we place people in categories on the basis of similarities to goals we previously learned to approach or avoid.

Suppose that Mr. Smith has a new neighbor, Mr. Jones. Soon after their meeting, Smith hears Jones say some kind words about ex-President Lyndon B. Johnson. Chances are that one of Smith's first responses will be to classify his neighbor as a Democrat—that is, to put him in the category *Democrat*. Unless (or until) he gets to know his neighbor better, he will regard Jones as being fairly similar to other people in the same category.

Smith has previously formed some belief about Democrats: He thinks that they favor high taxes and socialism, goals toward which he has unfavorable attitudes. Out of this "generalization," Smith develops a mild dislike of Jones. Of course, Smith is not responding to Jones as a person in his own right; he doesn't know Jones well enough to know what his unique characteristics are. He is reacting to him as a Democrat for whom he already has unfavorable attitudes. Later, as he learns more about Jones and can categorize him in other ways, his attitude may change in one direction or another.

An important consequence of classifying people into categories is that it produces erroneous thinking and beliefs, for in everyday life no two persons or situations are quite the same. Since Smith does not regard Jones as a unique person but classifies him as a Democrat, and since Smith's notion of the category *Democrat* includes only people who favor high taxes and socialism, he is probably attributing characteristics to Jones that he does not have.

ATTITUDE AVERAGING We know so little about some people and some groups that our attitudes toward them, like Smith's attitude toward Jones, are formed from single impressions or bits of information. In other cases, fortunately, we know more—we have several kinds of information on which to base an attitude. As Smith gets to know Jones better, suppose he learns that Jones is a good father, a helpful neighbor, and a regular churchgoer—all of which Smith regards favorably. What will be Smith's attitude toward Jones then?

Psychologists have various models of what goes on in this case; we can say that, in general, an averaging model fits the circumstances (Anderson, 1968). The unfavorable attitude toward Jones as a Democrat is averaged out with the favorable attitude toward him as a father, neighbor, and churchgoer. Some people who are discriminating may be able to verbalize two attitudes simultaneously toward the same object—to regard a man favorably in one regard and unfavorably in another—but most of us do not do this consistently. Instead, our attitude toward a person or group has one dimension running from favorable to unfavorable, and the different components of the attitude add and subtract from each to form a given degree of attitude. In the end Smith, for example, feels mildly favorable toward Jones for his "good traits," but not quite so favorable as he would if he did not regard Jones as a Democrat. The averaging of attitudes is further illustrated by the following study (Anderson, 1965):

Before the experiment, several hundred adjectives had been rated by 100 raters on a scale of 0 to 6, with 0 representing extreme dislike and 6 extreme liking. In this way, adjectives with known scale values could be selected and used in the description of a hypothetical person. Four groups of adjectives were used: H (high) adjectives ranging from *truthful*, 5.45, to *reasonable*, 5.00; M+ (high medium) ranging from *persuasive*, 3.74, to *painstaking*, 3.45; M− (low medium) from *dependent*, 2.54, to *unpopular*, 2.22; L (low) from *abusive*, 1.00, to *spiteful*, .72.

Four adjectives from these groups were then selected to describe a hypothetical person, and subjects were asked to indicate how much they would like or dislike him. They were instructed to take 50 as a neutral point and use higher numbers for liking, lower ones for disliking. When all four adjectives were H, the subjects gave an average rating of 79; when all four were L, the rating was about 18. Hypothetical persons with adjective descriptions of M+ and M− fell in between. The rating for four adjectives in the combination HHM+M+ was 71, a value falling between 79 for HHHH and 63 for M+M+M+M+. This can be accounted for by the averaging of attitudes. A similar averaging took place with LLM−M− adjectives.

This study employed traits that were all in the same step or only one step apart on a four-step scale. (That is, L and H adjectives were never combined for the same hypothetical person.) If a similar experiment is done with traits that are two or more steps apart, the situation becomes more complicated. Suppose, for example, the adjectives rated LHHH are used as descriptive traits. (This is like Mr. Smith's impressions of Mr. Jones, in which one "bad" trait was mixed with three "good" ones.) In such a case, the order in which the adjectives are presented will make a difference, and so will the instructions given to subjects. But if order of presentation is randomized, and if the subject is instructed to give all traits equal weight, the ratings produced fit the averaging model very well. Such experiments have been done with three traits in the form of HHH, LHH, HLL, and LLL, in different orders (Anderson and Jacobsen, 1965). They have also been done with categories of economic status—income, education, and occupation (Himmelfarb and Senn, 1969). In each case the results fitted the averaging model.

COGNITIVE DISSONANCE The simple averaging model described above is useful in explaining the degree of favorableness or unfavorableness people have in many of their attitudes. There are two kinds of situations, however, in which something more is involved. In one, a large discrepancy exists between the favorable and unfavorable components of the attitude. In the other, a person is forced to make a decision between two objects about which he has mixed feelings. In both, cognitive dissonance is aroused—that is, the person recognizes a definite discrepancy between two things that he knows (Festinger, 1957). As we saw in Chapter 6 on motivation (page 219), such dissonance is not easily tolerated; we are motivated to somehow reduce the dissonance and "make things fit."

As an example of the first case, suppose that there is a very large discrepancy between two things we know, or think we know, about a person. Perhaps Smith learns that Jones is a crooked businessman—a category about which Smith has a strongly unfavorable attitude. How can this be made to fit with the favorable categories of good neighbor and churchgoer? It is hard to let this go with an attitude of, "He's crooked, but otherwise a fine guy." Smith is far more likely to think, "Jones goes to church to make people think he isn't crooked," and "He's nice to me as a neighbor in order to get my business." In this way, Smith revises his interpretation of the favorable facts so that they fit with his unfavorable attitude toward Jones as a crooked businessman.

In the second situation where cognitive dissonance requires more than a mere averaging of attitudes, a person is forced to decide between two objects about which he has mixed feelings. He thereby becomes committed to a course of action. For example, medical evidence in recent years has made a convincing case against cigarette smoking, yet many people are still "hooked." Surveys of attitudes toward the medical evidence show that smokers place less faith in it than nonsmokers. For the smoker, smoking enjoyment and the belief that smoking is harmful are dissonant perceptions. Accordingly, people who smoke heavily may reject the information that smoking is injurious to health and may try to avoid additional information that increases dissonance. In addition, smokers may reassure themselves that smoking is relaxing and therefore not harmful.

Thus the smoker is committed because he is addicted to cigarettes. Dissonance theory also applies, however, in cases where people make a "free" choice (Brehm and Cohen, 1962). Suppose a man is thinking of buying either a sedan or a station wagon and carefully considers the relative advantages of each. He finds certain features of each very attractive, but he settles on a station wagon. Having made a choice, he is bothered by perceptions of dissonance between the good features of the rejected sedan and those of the wagon. To reduce the dissonance, he will alter his attitudes so that he emphasizes the undesirable features of the sedan and the desirable features of the wagon. He may also begin to pay closer attention to advertisements of station wagons, especially his own brand, to convince himself that he made the correct choice. And he may seek the approval of other people to confirm his decision. Thus in various ways he modifies his attitudes and beliefs to reduce dissonance.

Attitude Measurement

An attitude, we have seen, is a *tendency to respond* favorably or unfavorably to an object or situation. This tendency to respond, if measurable, may be taken as a *prediction* of how a person will respond when

Table 15.1 *Statements from a Thurstone-type scale for measuring attitudes toward war. Low scale values represent prowar statements; high scale values antiwar statements.*

Source: Droba, 1930.

Scale value	Statement
1.3	1. A country cannot amount to much without a national honor, and war is the only means of preserving it.
2.5	2. When war is declared, we must enlist.
5.2	3. Wars are justifiable only when waged in defense of weaker nations.
5.6	4. The most that we can hope to accomplish is the partial elimination of war.
8.4	5. The disrespect for human life and rights involved in a war is a cause of crime waves.
10.6	6. All nations should disarm immediately.

he is required to. For that reason, leaders in government and public life want to measure attitudes in order to predict elections and responses to legislation. Businessmen want attitude measurements to predict responses to products and advertising. And both practical men and research workers want to measure the *changes* in attitudes produced by messages such as advertisements, speeches, and political actions. Thus the measurement of attitudes has long been a lively field of study.

In general, attitudes are measured in one of two ways: (1) by presenting a person with a statement and finding out whether or not, or to what degree, he accepts or agrees with it; (2) by presenting two or more alternatives and asking a person to choose between them. Either method can be crude or accurate, depending on how many questions there are and how much research goes into developing them. Both methods are used in attitude scaling and public opinion polling.

Attitude scales An attitude scale attempts to obtain a precise index of the degree of favorableness-unfavorableness a person feels about an issue. For maximum accuracy, a relatively large number of items is used. All the items, however, are related to one issue so that the final score is a measure of a single attitude. Of the literally hundreds of attitude scales that have been developed, we shall illustrate the general procedures by describing a Thurstone scale and a Likert scale.

THURSTONE SCALE In the Thurstone method, statements on some issue, such as war, are collected and given to judges to rate. The judges assign each statement a value of, say, 1 to 11, indicating the degree to which they think the statement reflects a certain attitude. Statements on which their ratings markedly disagree are discarded; those on which they agree are retained and given scale values obtained by averaging the ratings. In Table 15.1, for example, are some statements taken from a scale designed to measure attitude toward war.

Once constructed, this sort of attitude scale can be administered to anyone. The person taking it is instructed to check the statements with which he agrees. One way of scoring the results is to average the scale values of the items he checks. In this way, we get a numerical measure of the person's attitude on the issue in question.

LIKERT SCALE Like the Thurstone, the Likert method employs a number of items concerning a given issue; but it asks the individual to express his *degree* of approval of each statement. Usually it provides a five-point scale running from "strongly disapprove" to "strongly approve," with "disapprove," "undecided," and "approve" in between. The particular items selected for a scale are those to which people respond in the same way. For example, if people who strongly approve of one statement also strongly approve of another one on the same general issue, the two statements are considered to be relevant to the same attitude. In this way clusters of items are selected for a given scale. One scale may measure, say, attitude toward imperialism in foreign affairs, while another measures attitude toward internationalism.

Attitude scales constructed in these or similar ways are used mostly in research. They require too much time to develop and administer to be practical for public opinion polling. But in research they are valuable for studying various sorts of correlations—for example, between educational or religious background and attitudes toward war. Many of the statements concerning such correlations that are made in the following sections are based on research with attitude scales. These scales are also helpful in studying factors that bring about attitude change, as we shall see.

Public opinion polling Public opinion polling must usually be done face-to-face rather than by having subjects read and rate statements. And because people generally do not have time to give long interviews, questions in opinion polling tend to be brief. Typically, only two or three related questions are asked, and each one gives the individual a choice of two or three alternatives. In polls for the purpose of predicting elections, of course, the interviewee is simply asked to say which of the candidates he favors. On other issues—for instance, the President's popularity, which is regularly measured by pollsters in the United States—the person is asked a question like "Do you generally approve of the way the President is doing his job?" The respondent then answers "Yes," "No," or "Don't know."

WORDING OF QUESTIONS When questions concern issues rather than candidates in an election, the type of question used and the manner of phrasing it are extremely important. For example, take the following questions on the Vietnam War (Converse and Schuman, 1970):

In October 1968 two polling agencies, the Survey Research Center of the University of Michigan and the Gallup Poll, asked *parallel* questions: (1) "Do you think we did right in getting into the fighting in Vietnam, or should we have stayed out?" (2) "In view of the developments since we entered the fighting, do you think the U.S. made a mistake in sending troops to fight in Vietnam?" These questions are essentially the same and should produce comparable responses, but because of the slight differences in wording they led to somewhat different results. With the "mistake" versus "no mistake" phrasing, twice as many respondents were certain of their attitude as with the phrasing of "did right" versus "should have stayed out" (see Figure 15.1, top).

THE WORDING OF QUESTIONS AFFECTS AN OPINION POLL'S RESULTS

Survey Research Center (September-October 1968): "Do you think we did the right thing in getting into the fighting in Vietnam, or should we have stayed out?"

Gallup Poll (October 1968): "In view of the developments since we entered the fighting do you think the U.S. made a mistake in sending troops to fight in Vietnam?"

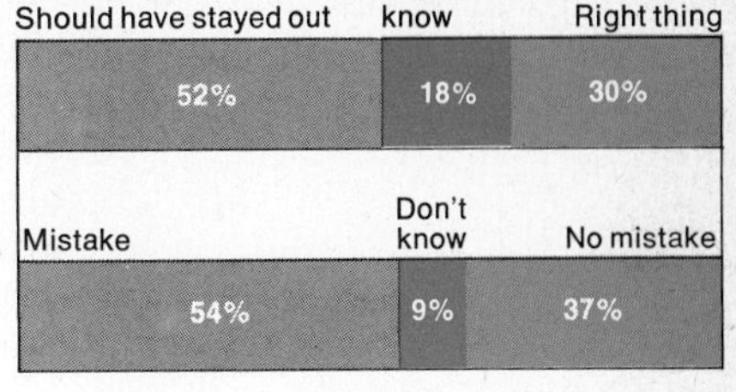

Gallup Poll (July 1966) asked if respondents approved of the bombing of oil storage dumps in Haiphong and Hanoi.
Gallup Poll (September 1966) noted a proposal that the United States submit the Vietnam problem to the United Nations and abide by whatever decision was reached there, and asked: "Do you think this is a good idea or not?"

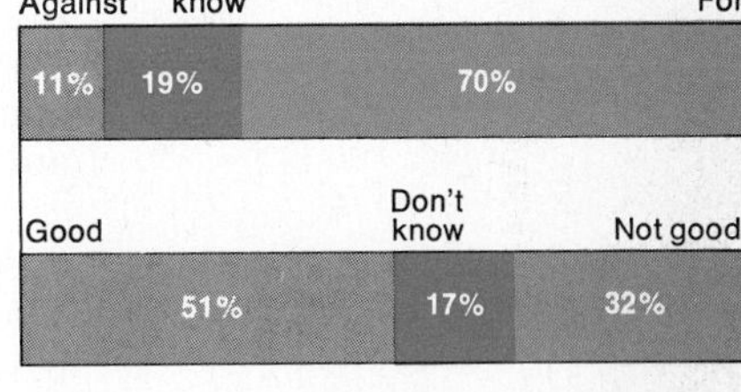

Gallup Poll (June 1969):["The President has] ordered the withdrawal of 25,000 troops from Vietnam in the next 3 months. [Do you think] troops should be withdrawn at a faster or slower rate?"
Harris Poll (September-October 1969): "In general, do you feel the pace at which the President is withdrawing troops is too fast, too slow, or about right?"

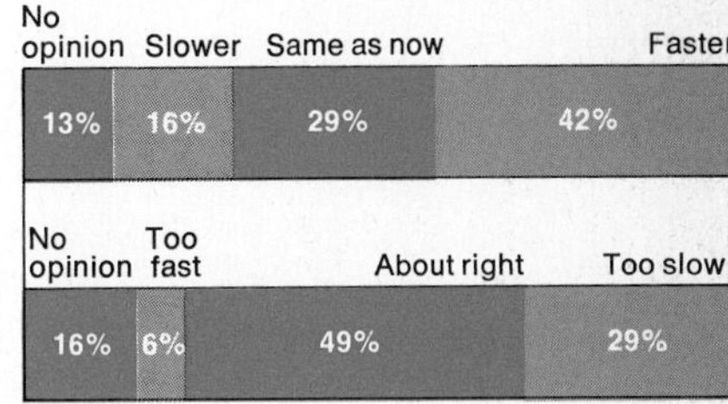

Figure 15.1 *Results obtained in opinion polls using various questions. Top, parallel questions by different polling agencies, when asked at about the same time, should produce about the same results (as these two do). Middle, different questions on the same broad issue must be interpreted cautiously: Here it might seem that many hawks have turned into doves within a short time, but such an interpretation would be faulty because the questions are quite different and cannot be presumed to measure the same thing. Bottom, the same question presented in slightly different ways. The Gallup version provided only the alternatives "faster" and "slower"; the Harris version also offered the alternative "about right." This seemingly slight difference made a great difference in the polls' findings on the "same" question. (After Converse and Schuman, 1970,* Scientific American.*)*

Presenting *different* questions on the same issue can give even more diverse results. The Gallup Poll in 1966 asked people their opinion on the United States bombing of oil storage dumps in Haiphong and Hanoi. Another Gallup question 2 months later asked whether we should submit the Vietnam problem to the United Nations. While there was no reason to believe that the two samples of people interviewed held different views or that opinion had changed in 2 months, the answers to the first question (70 percent in favor of the bombing) made the respondents look like "hawks," while the answers to the second (51 percent for submitting the issue to the United Nations) made them look like "doves" (Figure 15.1, middle).

In June 1969 the Gallup Poll asked a question that the Harris Poll repeated 4 months later, but the means of *presentation* was slightly different. In seeking opinions about the speed of troop withdrawals from Vietnam, the Gallup poll presented two alternatives (faster-slower), and accepted the answer "about the same" only if it was offered. The Harris Poll, on the other hand, presented all three alternatives. Making it easier for respondents to say that the current withdrawals were about right nearly doubled the number who chose that response (Figure 15.1, bottom).

Pollsters use various approaches to minimize the problems involved in interpreting answers to questions. One is to deliberately ask several kinds of questions on the same issue at about the same time in order to assess the effects of wording on responses. Figure 15.1 has just given examples of this approach. Another is to use the same question over a period of time, so that the pollster can trace changes in opinions even when he is not quite sure of the absolute percentages. The perennial opinion poll question on the President's popularity is an example of this second approach.

SAMPLING AND OPINION CHANGE We have already mentioned that when public opinion polling is used to forecast elections, the phrasing of the question is not crucial: people are merely asked which candidate they plan to vote for. But other problems do become important, two of which are the necessity for taking a representative sample and the difficulty of keeping track of opinion change right up to the time of the election.

All public opinion polling involves sampling, simply because the population being studied is so large that interviewing everyone would be prohibitively expensive. The polling agency wishes to draw conclusions about the whole population from the relatively small sample it selects. Fortunately, statisticians have worked out some dependable rules for making inferences about a population from a sample. Just how accurate the inferences are depends upon a number of factors. In general, it is possible to use a sample of several hundred cases and predict the response of the whole population with relative accuracy. To do this the sample must be chosen so that it is truly representative of the population. Practical people ignorant of statistical methods often wonder how conclusions can be drawn about a whole population from a small sample. Actually, there is no difficulty at all so long as the sample is representative. It is the matter of representativeness that is the major problem of the pollsters.

Representative samples can be constructed in a number of ways. The most efficient one, and the one most often used in forecasting elections, is *quota sampling*. This is based on the assumption that a sample will be an accurate miniature of a larger population if important sociological groups are represented in the sample in the same proportion that they occur in the population. The polling agency sets quotas for certain categories such as age, sex, socioeconomic status, and geographical region. Interviewers are then told how many interviews they must conduct with respondents in each category. The interviewers are left some discretion as to how they manage to fill their quota.

By establishing quotas in this way, the agency hopes to obtain a fair cross section of the population. When given a choice, however, interviewers usually select the person who seems somewhat more cooperative or the house that seems somewhat better kept. Thus biases can creep into the sample. Whenever such biases have anything to do with attitudes, the quota sampling method gives inaccurate results. This is one reason why attempts to predict national elections entail a certain amount of unknown error.

Because of biasing errors (page 308) and known errors in using a sample of a given size, pollsters ask for a leeway of about 6 percent in their forecasts. When elections are closer than that, as they frequently are, polls will be right more often than they are wrong; but this is not very satisfactory when accurate prediction is what is wanted. Even so, the prediction of votes has been quite good in most United States elections since modern polling methods were introduced. In the very close 1960 race of Kennedy against Nixon, the polls were within 2 percent of actual percentages. In the 1964 landslide of Johnson over Goldwater, the polls' predictions were only 3 percent off, and in the 1968 election, a three-way race between Nixon, Humphrey, and Wallace, the polls were just as close.

Occasionally polls seem to fall very wide of the mark in predicting an election. They were far wrong in the Dewey-Truman presidential race in the United States in 1948, and in the Conservative-Labor contest in Great Britain in 1970. In these cases the trouble came primarily from inaccurate prediction of the undecided vote (Campbell et al., 1960). In every election, the majority of voters make up their minds early—on the basis of party affiliation, socioeconomic interests, or liking for particular candidates. But in fairly close races, this majority does not decide the outcome; instead, the voters whom the polls show as undecided are the ones who swing the election. The polls usually assign the undecided vote in proportion to the decided vote, making certain adjustments based on past experience. When this method fails, the prediction fails.

The undecided voter, studies show, is a voter in conflict (Campbell et al., 1960). For instance, he may belong to one party but like the other party's candidate better. Or he may be strongly concerned with certain issues and feel uncertain how the respective parties will handle them. He experiences some incongruity in his attitudes and perhaps suffers severe cognitive dissonance. Such voters tend to decide at the last minute, so that their decisions are often missed by even the latest pre-election polls. More important, they are swayed by last-minute influences in the campaign, such as the impressions made by the candidates in the closing days, or by late news events. When these influences swing a larger than usual number of voters to one side or the other, and sometimes cause a few mildly committed voters to switch as well, the polls fail. They just can't win 'em all.

Development of Attitude

Attitude Formation The number of attitudes that a person may form as he grows to adulthood is virtually limitless, like the number of habits he can develop. To measure them, psychologists have constructed many different attitude scales; one book which lists only those that were considered sufficiently reliable and valid for use in research includes over 100 (Shaw and Wright, 1967). To come to any conclusions from the measurement of attitudes, however, we must reduce their number to a reasonably few clusters. For our purposes in examining how attitudes normally develop, we shall use a single continuum of *conservatism versus liberalism.*

In this continuum, conservatism is defined as follows: The conservative tends to emphasize strong family ties, with dominant parents and obedient children. In education he is for the three R's and for training in practical skills. He tends to be religious along fundamentalist lines; he opposes birth control and sexual relations outside of marriage; he is against smoking and the use of alcohol and is generally careful about his health. In economic matters he is for making each person "earn his own way," and he opposes big spending by government and programs for public welfare. In politics he favors as little intervention by the government as possible; he tends to be nationalistic and objects to international involvement (except possibly to fight Communism). He is for strict law enforcement and severe punishment of criminals. Finally, he tends to be racially prejudiced and status-conscious, feeling that his own kind of people are "better" than others. To define liberalism, we need merely say that it is the opposite of conservative.

Though people are seldom all liberal or all conservative, a few such individuals are found in any broad sample of attitudes. In between are people with various mixtures of views. The components of conservatism and liberalism tend to average, both in the sense of attitude averaging that we have already described, and in a statistical sense when a large group of people is measured. For these reasons, the conservative-liberal dimension is very valuable in attitude studies.

Parental influences To see the extent of parental influence on children's attitudes, we need do little more than ask children about their attitudes. For example, here are some responses of grammar school children in interviews aimed at eliciting their attitudes toward Negroes:

First-grade girl: Mamma tells me not to play with black children, keep away from them. Mamma tells me, she told me not to play with them.

Second-grade girl: Mother doesn't want me to play with colored children. . . . I play with colored children sometimes but Mamma whips me.

Second-grade boy: . . . mother and daddy tell me. They tell me not to play with colored people or colored persons' things.

Third-grade girl: Mother told me not to play with them because sometimes they have diseases and germs and you get it from them.

(Adapted from Horowitz and Horowitz, 1938, pages 333 and 335.)

Parental influence wanes as children grow older, and adolescents and adults seldom quote their parents in responding to attitude surveys. To determine the lasting effects of parental teaching on adult attitudes, we assess the amount of agreement between people's views and those of their parents. Investigations of this sort that have been conducted over the last 40 years all show considerable similarity between certain attitudes of parents and children (Hyman, 1959). One recent study, for example, found significant correlations between the religious and political party affiliations of high school seniors and those of their parents (Jennings and Niemi, 1968):

A national cross section of 1,669 high school seniors was interviewed. Separately 1,992 of their parents were surveyed as a check on what the seniors reported. Some of the questions concerned the religious and political party affiliations of children and parents. As in previous studies, the greatest agreement was on religious affiliation: 74 percent of the seniors had the same affiliation (Protestant, Catholic, or Jewish) as their parents. A negligible percentage had changed to another religion. A similar, but not so strong, agreement was found in political party affiliation: 60 percent of those naming a party chose the same one as their parents. Some had shifted to independent status, but less than 10 percent had defected to the other party. Moving back a whole generation, very similar results were obtained for the parents' agreement with their own parents.

Although the agreement in these studies is high on religion and political party, it is not so close on questions about specific issues. A child of a Protestant may remain a Protestant, but he is likely not to be as fervent or as conservative as his parent. The son of a Republican may become a Republican, but his attitudes on particular political issues are likely to diverge from those of his parent, usually in the direction of liberalism. Even so, there is more overall similarity than dissimilarity between children's attitudes and those of the parents. Hence children's attitudes do show long-lasting effects of parental influences.

Critical period From birth to puberty, the child's attitudes, what there are of them, are shaped predominantly by his parents. Beginning with adolescence and continuing through early adulthood to about 30, other social influences become increasingly important. During the period from 12 to 30 most of a person's attitudes take final form and thereafter change rather little. This has been called the "critical period" (Sears, 1969). During the critical period three main factors are at work: peer influences, information from news media and other sources, and education.

PEER INFLUENCE Peer influences begin to have an effect on attitudes during adolescence. The adolescent spends less time at home, less time communicating with his parents, and increasingly more time with friends and acquaintances. His peers become powerful influences because people most readily accept as "authorities" those they like and find it easy to talk to. This point is supported by a great deal of research, such as the following famous study of peer influence (Newcomb, 1943):

At Bennington, the women's college in Vermont, most of the students entering as freshmen in the mid-1930s came from the upper and middle socioeconomic class and held the conservative political and economic views of their families. The highly self-contained college community, however, was at that time strongly "New Dealish" and liberal in its political sentiments.

What happened to the freshman "conservatives" in this environment? Attitude surveys revealed that the longer the girls remained in college, the more liberal they generally became. Thus as juniors and seniors they were more liberal than they had been as freshmen and sophomores.

Of course, there were individual differences in the degree to which the girls adopted the attitudes of their peers. The girls who were regarded by their peers as most closely identified with the community were the ones who developed the most pro–New Deal beliefs. The girls who remained conservative despite the widespread liberalism among their fellow students generally were unable or unwilling to participate fully in college life. Often they were socially withdrawn, either because they were insecure and lacked social skills or because they had met frustrations at Bennington. Some girls did not enter into college life fully because they had strong attachments to other groups, such as their families. Whatever the reason, the girls who did not adopt the prevalent beliefs at Bennington usually participated least in the activities of their peers.

As the Bennington study shows, peer influences in American life 30 years ago were overshadowed by parental influence until late adolescence, when a child went to college or left home. Since then, changing social conditions, such as a decreasing emphasis on parental dominance and the increasing affluence and mobility of adolescents, have caused the period of peer influence to begin earlier and to assume a larger role in the individual's development.

INFORMATION News and entertainment have also become more important in recent years because of television which, since it is more vivid and immediate than radio or the newspapers, has made young people aware at a much earlier age of events going on in their world. Thus both peer groups and television are now influential sources of so-called information for the adolescent. Today's young people express attitudes earlier and more strongly than they used to. Unfortunately, these attitudes emerge in the absence of other information to which they used to be tied, such as the material learned in college courses or in the process of earning a living and supporting a family.

EDUCATION Education is the third major variable during the critical period of forming permanent attitudes. How important it is depends upon how far the individual goes in school, but he goes increasingly farther than his parents did. Of all the factors studied in connection with attitudes, educational level consistently stands out as a significant variable. It is almost as conspicuous as party and religious affiliations, and these are relatively superficial.

In study after study, education correlates most highly with the conservative-liberal dimension: the more education people have, the more liberal they tend to be. One such study is summarized in Table 15.2. In a more recent survey, a liberal attitude toward civil liberties was held by 66 percent of college graduates but by only 16 percent of grade school graduates (Sears, 1969).

Table 15.2 also shows that liberalism correlates with income level. In fact, many studies over the years indicate that socioeconomic status correlates with most, but not all, aspects of liberalism (Harding et al., 1969; Sears, 1969). Socioeconomic status, however, is a mixture of three variables: income, education, and occupation. It is the result of an attitude which is an average of impressions made by these variables (Himmelfarb and Senn, 1969). But the important variable of the three

Table 15.2 *A study of attitudes toward armed imperialism. The question was "Some people say we should use our Army and Navy to make other countries do what we think they should. How do you feel about that?" Disapproval increased with education and income level.*

Source: Social Science Research Council, 1947.

Respondents	General approval, %	General disapproval, %	No response, %	Number of respondents
Education:				
Grade school	19	57	24	500
High school	13	77	10	455
College	8	83	9	213
Income:				
Under $2,000	19	58	23	440
$2,000 to $3,999	16	73	11	478
$4,000 and more	8	86	6	216

is surely education, for people high in economic status but low in education tend to be conservative, especially in economic matters, while those with high status and high education tend to be liberal.

Later adulthood The period between 12 and 30, the critical time during which attitudes are being formed, might be subdivided into adolescence, when attitudes are taking shape, and young adulthood, when they are becoming crystallized (some say "freezing") to a point where they will change little in subsequent years.

COMMITMENT The period of young adulthood appears to be a time of commitments. An adolescent's attitudes may vary quite a bit and often seem like "so much talk." In his twenties, though, a person usually commits himself in many ways: He votes in elections, he marries, he finishes his education. These all imply decisions in which he acts on the basis of his attitudes. Young adulthood can be a period of some instability (though not so much as adolescence), for the person may be switching all sorts of plans, including his votes in a political election (Sears, 1969). Gradually, however, attitudes average out to some position which most people hold thereafter without many changes.

CONSERVATIVE DRIFT The relative permanence of attitudes from the early twenties on is one of the striking discoveries that have come out of attitude research. In a 1960 follow-up to the Bennington College research described above, the investigator located most of the girls he had studied in the late thirties and reassessed their attitudes (Newcomb, 1963). On most matters of liberal-versus-conservative significance, he found that they held virtually the same views as they had expressed 20 years before. One general change was that they were slightly more conservative than they had been upon graduating from college. This small shift toward conservatism, starting at around age 30, turns up repeatedly in such studies.

Generation changes In view of the talk in recent years about the "generation gap," let us examine the evidence on how attitudes change from one generation to the next. Several sources indicate that changes have indeed been taking place, but not for the reasons that many people think.

Table 15.3 *The fading of stereotypes in Princeton students.*

Source: Karlins et al., 1969.

Group trait		Students attributing trait to group, %		
		1932	1950	1967
Americans:	Industrious	48	30	23
	Intelligent	47	32	20
	Materialistic	33	37	67
	Ambitious	33	21	42
	Pleasure loving	26	27	28
Germans:	Scientifically minded	78	62	47
	Industrious	65	50	59
	Stolid	44	10	9
	Intelligent	32	32	19
	Extremely nationalistic	24	50	43
Japanese:	Intelligent	45	11	20
	Industrious	43	12	57
	Progressive	24	2	17
	Sly	20	21	3
	Imitative	17	24	22
Jews:	Shrewd	79	47	30
	Mercenary	49	28	15
	Industrious	48	29	33
	Grasping	34	17	17
	Ambitious	21	28	48
Negroes:	Superstitious	84	41	13
	Lazy	75	31	26
	Happy-go-lucky	38	17	27
	Ignorant	38	24	11
	Musical	26	33	47

FADING STEREOTYPES Earlier in the chapter a stereotype was defined as a widespread, oversimplified, and hence erroneous belief. It is a good example of prejudice. One 30-year study of Princeton University students shows us how stereotypes have been changing (Karlins et al., 1969). Although these stereotypes might be different in a different population, the trend is the significant thing.

Three different studies of Princeton students were made: one in 1932 (Katz and Braly, 1933), another in 1950 (Gilbert, 1951), and a third in 1967 (Karlins et al., 1969). In each case, approximately 200 students were used as subjects. They were carefully selected as a representative sample, although all were white Gentiles because the study concerned attitudes toward other ethnic groups. Approximately 80 adjectives (or phrases) were presented to them, and they were asked to select the 5 that they thought best described ten different ethnic groups.

Table 15.3, which gives the results for five of the ethnic groups, shows that the stereotypes held in 1932 have largely faded out. No longer are two or three adjectives, for the most part derogatory, often used to describe a group. Thus on the whole, the students have come to regard these groups as made up of people possessing many different traits. As for the attitudes toward separate groups, Americans fared the worst over the years, jumping from 33 to 67 percent on *materialistic* and sliding from 47 to 20 percent on *intelligent*. Jews and Negroes, on the other hand, made out well. Jews went down on *shrewd* and *mercenary* and up on *ambitious,* while Negroes fell on *superstitious* and *lazy* and rose on *musical.*

All the evidence we have confirms the conclusion of this study that prejudice is on its way down in the United States, especially among the more educated (Harding et al., 1969).

LIBERAL DRIFT Along with a change toward less prejudice in younger people goes a shift toward greater liberalism in other respects (Middleton and Putney, 1964):

A total of 1,440 college and university students was selected to represent a cross section of college students. Among other questions, they were asked how their political attitudes compared with those of their parents. Their answers showed that 33 percent saw themselves as being to the left of their parents, while only 8 percent regarded themselves as to the right. Approximately 60 percent called themselves socialists or liberals compared with 30 percent of their parents. On the other hand, 32 percent considered themselves mildly or strongly conservative, in contrast to 49 percent of their parents.

Although this study shows only the way the students saw themselves in comparison with their parents, the results are confirmed by direct observation of today's students and their parents' reactions to them.

STUDENT ACTIVISM Of several studies that have examined student activism, one surveyed delegates attending national conventions of right and left-wing student organizations (Braungart, 1966):

The subjects were a sample of 180 students attending the convention of Students for a Democratic Society (left wing) and a sample of 155 attending a convention of the Young Americans for Freedom (right wing). As Table 15.4 shows, the right-wing students were predominantly Protestant, churchgoers, and middle-class. Their parents most often worked in administrative or clerical jobs and were Republicans or some form of political conservatives, and most had not graduated from college. In contrast, the left-wing student activists were predominantly Jewish or nonreligious, usually were not churchgoers, and came mostly from the upper class. Their parents were college graduates more often than not, were concentrated in the executive and professional occupations, and usually belonged to Democratic or liberal parties.

This study presents in one profile the various factors correlated with conservative versus liberal attitudes. Upper-class status, a college education, a weak religious affiliation, and liberal parents are the prominent features of left-wing (liberal) activists; the opposite characteristics are features of right-wing (conservative) activists. These results support the other facts about changes between the generations that were brought out earlier. In addition, other studies show that student activists on the left have parents who are considerably more liberal than the usual liberalism characteristic of educated upper-class parents (see Flacks, 1967).

These data put to rest the notion that activism is typically a rebellion against parental attitudes and restraints. Although cases of rebellion

		Young Americans for Freedom (right wing), %	Students for a Democratic Society (left wing), %
Own religion:	Protestant	61	32
	Jewish or "none"	8	52
	Currently attend church or synagogue	82	26
Social class:	High	31	62
	Middle	38	23
	Low	31	15
Father's education:	College graduate	33	52
	Some college	22	21
	No college	45	27
Father's occupation:	Executive, proprietor, professional	29	58
	Administrative, clerical	49	28
	Skilled, unskilled labor	19	7
Parents' political affiliation:	Democrat, socialist, Communist	12	53
	Independent	25	31
	Republican, conservative	61	13
Student's political affiliation:	Democrat, socialist, Communist	—	55
	Independent	12	37
	Republican, conservative	88	—

Table 15.4 *Social and political backgrounds of right and left-wing student activists.*

Source: Braungart, 1966. (This table based on data in Sears, D. O. Political behavior. In Lindzey and Aronson, eds., *The Handbook of Social Psychology,* 2d ed., Vol. V, 1969. Addison-Wesley, Reading, Mass.)

undoubtedly occur, liberals generally come from liberal families; they are simply a little more liberal than their parents.

Attitude Change

Many of the influences that mold our attitudes are inadvertent; they occur without anyone deliberately attempting to bring about an attitude change. On the other hand, many individuals and organizations in modern society are busy deliberately attempting to change attitudes. Their attempts can be informal, as when people in a group discussion try to convince each other of their beliefs. Or they can be formal, as in the cases we shall examine in this section.

First, some definitions. *Propaganda* is a deliberate attempt to influence attitudes and beliefs. Since propaganda is so often used by dictators and others who have ulterior motives and socially questionable purposes, the term has come to have an odious connotation. In principle, however, propaganda is neither good nor bad. It can be used to bring attitudes and beliefs closer to the facts just as well as it can be used to tell lies.

Education is commonly distinguished from propaganda by saying that its purpose is to inculcate knowledge of facts and principles rather than to change attitudes and beliefs. In actuality, however, there is no clear line between them (see Figure 15.2). Education does change attitudes and beliefs, and the educator in interpreting the knowledge he teaches is frequently biased toward a point of view he wishes his students to adopt.

Figure 15.2 *Education or propaganda? A newspaper cartoon designed to build a favorable attitude toward increasing teachers' salaries. (Walt Partymiller;* Gazette and Daily, *York, Pa.)*

Advertising, of course, is clearly an attempt to change attitudes. Its ultimate purpose is to get people to buy the advertiser's product, but in doing this, it attempts to create favorable attitudes toward the manufacturer and his wares. Thus advertising is really no different from propaganda; one is concerned with attitudes toward commercial products, the other with attitudes toward social issues.

The process of changing attitudes, whether by education, advertising, or propaganda, has three main components: (1) the source of the message, that is, the person or group attempting the change, (2) the message or appeal used to effect the change, and (3) characteristics of the person who receives the message. Other components have been distinguished (McGuire, 1968), but these will serve as the framework for our analysis.

Source characteristics How likely we are to change our attitude when bombarded by messages depends in part on our attitude toward the source of the messages.

CREDIBILITY If we have good reason to believe the sender of a message, he is more likely to persuade us than if we think he is not telling the truth or does not know what he is talking about. One important factor in his credibility is his prestige. If he is a well-known authority on something, we are more apt to believe him than if he has no special credentials. A second factor in his credibility is whether we have found him to be credible before. In the 1960s the Johnson administration in the United States was said to have a "credibility gap," largely because various statements made by administration spokesmen, especially about the Vietnam War, turned out to be incorrect. It mattered little whether the errors were due to deliberate deceit or to mistakes in judgment on the part of military commanders. To some of the public, the fact that the administration had been wrong before made it less believable when it issued further statements.

ATTRACTIVENESS The person receiving a message is also likely to be influenced by the source's attractiveness, which can be broken down into three components: (1) similarity, (2) friendship, and (3) liking.

The more similar two people perceive themselves to be, the more inclined one is to believe the other. Women can persuade other women more easily than they can men. A student is more likely to be swayed by another student than by anyone else, including a professor. A workingman is more apt to be persuaded by fellow workingmen than by college professors. Other factors being equal, we tend to be influenced most by people we feel are just like us.

Friendship is also a potent factor in bringing about attitude change. Patterns of friendship were easily traced in a study of the voting process conducted in Elmira, New York, during the 1948 national election (Kitt and Gleicher, 1950):

In August before the election, citizens of Elmira were asked, among other things, how their three closest friends would vote. Most of the people who could answer this question reported that their friends were in agreement on one or the other of the candidates. When asked their own opinion, they tended to support the candidate their friends preferred. The investigators reported that "More than 90 percent of the respondents with three Republican friends show some degree of Republican vote inclination themselves." This figure declined to only 68 percent Republican for people who said that one of their three closest friends was a Democrat. Similar tendencies in favor of the Democrats were obtained among people whose friends preferred the Democratic candidate.

Later in the campaign, some of the people were interviewed to see whether their opinions had changed. In the majority of cases where they had, the shifts were in the direction that increased agreement among members of the friendship group. These findings are summarized in Table 15.5.

Thus we tend to form attitudes which agree with those of people we like—our friends. The process also works the other way: "We like those with whom we agree" (McGrath, 1964). This has been shown in a comprehensive study of the *acquaintance process* (Newcomb, 1961):

Seventeen new men students who did not know one another were invited to live, without charge, in a house at the University of Michigan. The men had to make their own living and study arrangements. In exchange for the free accommodations, the men were required to participate for an hour or so a week in research which was designed to investigate the nature of the acquaintance process. The most lasting friendships which developed were based on similarities of attitudes; early friendships usually did not last if the individuals discovered that they were not actually as similar or compatible as they had thought.

As part of this study of friendships, attitudes, and interpersonal perception, the students estimated how their preferred associates would respond to various attitude questionnaires. The experimenters compared these estimates of attitudes with the responses made by each person himself and found that all estimates tended to increase in accuracy with increased acquaintance, but that there was a tendency to overestimate agreement with best friends.

Friendships are formed, of course, on the basis of mutual liking, but liking can be an important factor outside of friendship. Dwight Eisenhower was a war hero, but more than that, he was a very likable man. He swept to victory as President on a slogan of "I like Ike" even though he was a member of a minority party, for his likableness persuaded many people to vote for him who usually voted Democratic. Experimental studies in which the likableness of the persuader is deliberately varied also indicate that attitude change depends in part on how much we like the person who is trying to change us.

POWER Other things being equal, we are more easily persuaded by people who have power over us than by those who do not. The power to coerce a given behavior is itself a persuader. In this case, however, it is necessary to distinguish between a real and a superficial change in attitude. If a person has power over us, we may do as he says even though we do not believe him. This was illustrated during the Korean War in the "brainwashing" of American prisoners by the Chinese. Brainwashing was an elaborate plan to make the prisoners favorable to Communism. Although many prisoners professed to be convinced, most showed no permanent attitude change when they were released. On the other hand,

Table 15.5 *August to October shifters in Elmira, New York, during the 1948 election.*

Source: Kitt and Gleicher, 1950.

Political inclination of 3 closest friends in August	Shifted toward Republicans by October, %	Shifted toward Democrats by October, %
R R R	56	44
R R D / D D R	49	51
D D D	39	61

a few soldiers did refuse repatriation, and there were signs of some attitude change in some of the prisoners (Schein et al., 1961).

CONFLICT OF CHARACTERISTICS A persuader may, of course, have some characteristics that are favorable to attitude change and some that are not. An older person may have credibility because of his age and education, but he may not be as attractive to young people as other young people. What happens when there is a conflict of characteristics in the source?

The answer depends upon whether we study this question in the laboratory or in the field (McGuire, 1968). In a conflict in the laboratory—say, between the credibility of superiors (professors, graduate students) and the attractiveness of peers—the superiors generally win out. Probably the fact that laboratory situations are contrived by superiors and use students as subjects creates a willingness to believe the superiors. Field studies, on the other hand, generally show peer influences to be most important. This is apparently because in everyday affairs people spend far more time talking with and listening to their peers than to authorities or persons with prestige.

Characteristics of the message Persuaders of all varieties work tirelessly on their messages to make them more effective in changing attitudes. What are the methods that can be used to create influential messages?

SUGGESTION One technique of the advertiser or propagandist is *suggestion.* To the psychologist, suggestion is the uncritical acceptance of a statement; that is, a person may accept a belief, form an attitude, or be incited to action on someone else's say-so, without requiring facts.

A common form of suggestion is *prestige* suggestion. Advertisers often exploit the fact that some famous person uses a product (indeed, they frequently pay him to use it). Politicians refer to Abraham Lincoln, John F. Kennedy, and other respected leaders in order to peddle their own ideas. Anyone who watches television for an hour or looks at billboards along a few miles of highway can see that prestige is used to influence people to buy products, vote for political tickets, and alter their attitudes and behavior in many ways.

Prestige suggestion can play on already existing negative attitudes and use them to form new negative attitudes. If people have a generally unfavorable attitude toward Communists, the suggestion may be made that such and such a political belief is "Communistic" or endorsed by the Communist press. This is a way of taking an existing attitude and turning it toward another—often innocent—victim. Much of the name-calling or "smearing" that occurs in politics consciously or unconsciously makes use of such suggestion.

Another important aspect of prestige suggestion is that it alters a person's perception of an object or situation. When a prestige suggestion is attached to a thing, he views it in a new light, as the following study illustrates (Asch et al., 1940):

Students were asked to rank such professions as business, dentistry, journalism, medicine, and politics according to (1) the amount of intelligence they thought the profession required and (2) its social usefulness. Before they began, various groups were given different suggestions; for example, one was told that another group had ranked politics highest, while a second group was told that another group had ranked politics lowest. A control group was given no suggestions.

The suggestions turned out to be effective in influencing the rankings. Students who were told that politics had been ranked low by others ranked it low, whereas those who were told that others had ranked politics high also ranked it high. When these groups were later asked what politicians they had in mind when making their rankings, the group ranking politics low said they had thought of politicians such as "Tammany Hall politicians" and the "usual neighborhood politicians." Those ranking politics high had concentrated on national politics and statesmanlike politicians. Thus the effect of the suggestions was to get the students to think of the better or poorer examples of politicians and to express their attitudes accordingly.

APPEALS TO FEAR A common technique in persuasive messages is to make the listener fear that something undesirable will happen to him if he disregards the message. Political candidates warn us that if the other side wins, we will have higher taxes, poorer services, inflation, or war. Most appeals to drive safely attempt to frighten people about the danger of not doing so, as in the slogan "Speed kills," and the statistics we hear daily about the number of traffic fatalities.

Are frightened people more likely to obey a message? The evidence is mixed. In some cases the appeal to fear may actually block, rather than aid, acceptance, as the following study demonstrates (Janis and Feshbach, 1953):

High school students listened to lectures on dental hygiene under one of three conditions: strong fear arousal, moderate fear arousal, or minimal fear arousal. Under the strong-fear condition, subjects were made very anxious about the state of their mouths, whereas under the minimal-fear conditions no attempt was made to create anxiety. In all conditions, the students were urged to adopt certain dental practices. The results demonstrated that the higher the level of fear arousal, the *less* likely the students were to accept the communicator's point of view.

The explanation for the results in such cases seems to be that fear arousal produces a *defensive avoidance* reaction. To defend themselves against the threat created by the message, the audience avoids accepting the communicator's conclusions. It is as if they believed that his dire predictions would affect other people but not themselves. Examples of defensive avoidance can be found in everyday life. For instance, there is the story of the cigarette smoker who was so disturbed by newspaper articles on how smoking produces lung cancer that he stopped reading the papers.

Appeals to fear do not always produce defensive avoidance, however. In one study, a more favorable attitude toward seat belts was created by arousing people's fear of injury or death in an automobile accident (Berkowitz and Cottingham, 1960). In another study, fear of death from tetanus infection caused people to regard tetanus inoculations more favorably (Leventhal et al., 1965). The best explanation of these differences in effects of fear appeals is that attitude change is an inverted U-shaped function of fear arousal (McGuire, 1968). This means that up to a point, fear produces the desired attitude change, but very high fear arousal triggers defensive avoidance that protects the attitude against change (see page 535).

LOADED WORDS The style of messages can be varied in many ways. The element of style that has received the most attention in attitude research is the question of explicit versus implicit argument. In explicit argument, the persuader states what side he is on, gives his reasons in favor of it, and perhaps answers objections to his point of view. Implicit messages attempt to persuade by appearing to take a neutral point of view, while they actually slant the argument by their terminology. In this case we speak of *loaded words.*

Loaded words are the stock-in-trade of the propagandist. If he wishes to evoke an unfavorable attitude, he may speak of "Communists," "dictatorship," "regimentation," "agitators," and "revolutionaries"—to which the overwhelming majority of Americans react with strongly negative attitudes. If he wishes to create a favorable attitude, he can describe the same set of events in terms of "democracy," "freedom," "regulation," "taxpayer," and "advisers."

If we happen to agree with the point of view being expressed, we may not even notice the loaded words. If we disagree with the point of view, we are more likely to spot them as propaganda or distortions. But the person who has no strong attitudes or beliefs on the subject can be influenced very easily by loaded words. One rather old but carefully done study examined loaded words used in newspapers (Sargent, 1939):

From the news columns of the *Chicago Tribune* the investigator selected 20 terms that the paper used in reporting policies it did not support and 20 it used for policies it did support. He added 10 neutral terms to these 40, mixed them up, and presented the list to several groups of people, including parents and teachers, college students, high school alumni, laborers, and white-collar workers. He asked the subjects to indicate whether they liked, disliked, or had no feeling about each word. From the results he could assign the word a score representing its "feeling tone": −100 was extremely unfavorable, +100 extremely favorable. Here

***Table 15.6** Two newspapers describe the same events in different, but equally loaded, words. Feeling-tone values for terms used by the* Chicago Tribune *and the* New York Times.

Source: Sargent, 1939.

Chicago Tribune		New York Times	
Term	Value	Term	Value
Radical	−53	Progressive	+92
Regimentation	−53	Regulation	+32
Government witch-hunting	−38	Senate investigation	+57
The Dole	−35	Home Relief	+27
Alien	−35	Foreign	0

are some of the feeling-tone values he obtained for words used by the newspaper:

For policies it did not support		For policies it did support	
Czarism	−84	Cooperation	+95
Dictatorship	−84	Freedom	+92
Domination	−79	Reemployment	+88

Unquestionably the *Chicago Tribune* successfully chose words that evoked the strongly unfavorable or favorable attitudes it wished to arouse in support of its own views.

In a follow-up study, the investigator chose 12 loaded terms from the *Chicago Tribune* and 12 that the *New York Times* used in reporting the same events. As before, he determined feeling-tone values for these words, some of which are given in Table 15.6. Again it was clear that the same news was being slanted one way by one newspaper and another way by the other. Loaded words were being used in the news columns to create the attitudes the paper desired.

ONE-SIDED VERSUS TWO-SIDED MESSAGES If we want to convince people of our point of view, is it better to present only one side of the issue, or both sides? Considerable research has been done on this question (McGuire, 1968). A classic study of propaganda in wartime illustrates the kind of results frequently obtained (Hovland et al., 1949):

When the German surrender in the spring of 1945 ended the war in Europe, American authorities believed that the war with Japan would go on for a long time (and undoubtedly it might have if the atomic bomb had not been used). Yet they knew that many United States soldiers, anxious to get home, would think that the war with Japan could be quickly won. To correct this attitude, two radio programs were prepared for American troops. The first, the one-sided approach, simply gave the reasons why the war would be long; the second program presented both sides. Some troops heard the first, some the second; a control group heard neither. Before and after the programs were put on the air, a large sample of men from the troops was asked to estimate how long the war would last.

When the results were analyzed, it appeared that the two programs were equally effective. On closer analysis, however, it turned out that the two-sided approach had been more successful with the men who had originally thought the war would be short. Said another way, the two-sided approach was most effective in changing the attitudes of those opposed to the message. The investigators interpreted this to mean that the men who were opposed gained confidence in the message when they heard arguments on their own side. Their confidence made them more willing to listen to, and thus be persuaded by, the other side.

If any rule can be formulated from research on this question, it is that a one-sided approach is most successful in strengthening neutral or already favorable attitudes, but a two-sided approach is more likely to win converts from an opposing point of view.

ATTITUDE DISCREPANCY A message can take an extreme stand on an issue or a moderate one. An extreme message presents an attitude that is highly discrepant with the attitudes of those strongly opposed to it. Which is more effective, the extreme message or the moderate one?

Here we encounter again the inverted U-shaped function (McGuire, 1968) which, in this case, means that there is more chance of an attitude change if the discrepancy between the message and the listener's attitude is moderate. With an extreme discrepancy, something like defensive avoidance is produced. The person who strongly disagrees with the message simply "tunes out" and refuses to believe it, as in the following study (Insko et al., 1966):

Subjects in groups of 3 to 6 were quickly shown a series of 16 posters containing a variety of objects of different sizes, shapes, and colors. The presentation time was too brief to allow the subjects to count the objects, but after each poster was shown, they were asked to write down their estimate of the number of objects it pictured. (One set of posters contained 30 objects; another set, 50 objects.) Just before making their judgments, however, the experimental subjects were shown a "sample" series of posters for which a "volunteer" called out his estimates. The volunteer deliberately gave estimates differing in varying degrees from the correct answer. Control subjects were not exposed to the volunteer's estimates or to the sample series.

When the estimates of experimental and control subjects were compared, it was found that the experimental subjects had clearly been influenced by the incorrect "volunteer" estimates, but only up to a point. When the volunteer estimate was so far off as to be clearly wrong, the experimental subjects gave estimates agreeing closely with the controls. Thus an inverted U-shaped curve describes the function relating the discrepancy between the volunteer estimate and the subject's perception of the "truth."

Characteristics of the recipient Besides the nature of the source and the form of the message, certain characteristics of the person who receives the message determine whether or not it will cause him to change his attitude.

INFLUENCEABILITY In general, personality traits do not correlate highly with the attitudes a person holds or with his resistance to change. There is, however, a trait that can be called influenceability; some people are more easily influenced than others. In fact, some people are downright gullible—bombarded with conflicting viewpoints, they believe for the moment almost anything they are told. As might be expected, there are group differences in this trait. Women are more influenceable, on the whole, than men. Children are more influenceable than adults. And poorly educated people are more influenceable than well-educated ones.

NEEDS AND GOALS As we said in discussing consistency theory early in this chapter, attitudes involve relationships between the category into which the object of an attitude is placed and the individual's goals or values. Things we regard favorably are related to pleasant events or to attaining some positive goal; things we regard unfavorably are associated with threats and unpleasant events. It follows that a persuader can develop or change an attitude by associating a category of objects or issues with an individual's goals or values. If necessary, he may even create such goals and values within the individual so that they can be related to the attitude category.

Several investigations have demonstrated that it is possible to alter people's attitudes toward an issue by changing their perceived relationships between the issue and their own goals and values. In one study the experimenter changed college students' attitudes toward racially desegregated housing (Carlson, 1956). He did it by convincing them that such housing would contribute to certain goals (such as improving American prestige abroad), and would not interfere with other goals (for example, it would not necessarily lower property values).

In another study, students who were high in achievement motivation were given talks on "teaching as a career" (Di Vesta and Merwin, 1960). A speech that highlighted the connection between teaching and the satisfaction of achievement needs influenced their attitudes more than speeches that gave other arguments in favor of teaching. Thus the speech that changed attitudes toward teaching most was one that made the audience aware of the relationship between this category and their own needs.

A third experiment shows that a similar principle can be applied to negative as well as to positive goals (Weiss and Fine, 1958):

One group of subjects was exposed to a humiliating and insulting experience designed to arouse their hostility, whereas another group was given a nonfrustrating and satisfying experience. In both groups, half the subjects then read a message urging harshly punitive treatment of juvenile delinquents. The other halves read a message arguing that America should be very lenient in dealing with her allies. The study showed that the angered people were more likely than the nonangered ones to accept the idea of treating delinquents harshly. They were also somewhat less likely to be convinced that the United States should be lenient toward her allies. People in the angered group apparently most readily adopted the opinions congenial to their emotional state.

SELECTIVE INTERPRETATION Whether or not a message gets through to alter an attitude in the desired direction depends in large measure upon how the listener interprets the message. He is very likely to interpret the facts presented by selecting those that fit in with his existing attitudes. This is especially true where there is a large discrepancy between his attitude and the message.

Selective interpretation of facts is one of the potent factors in freezing attitudes so that they resist change. If the bigot who thinks that Negroes are dirty sees a Negro coming home in dirty work clothes, this is likely to confirm his prejudice. He may not notice a white man who is in the

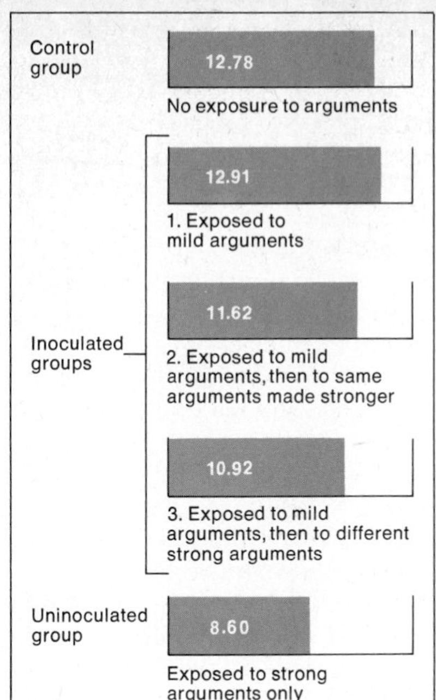

PEOPLE CAN BE "IMMUNIZED" AGAINST STRONG ATTACKS ON THEIR ATTITUDES

Figure 15.3 *Building defenses by refuting mild arguments against their position helps people resist strong attacks later. Each bar represents the average attitude (on a 15-point scale) of a group toward four commonsense health propositions. The difference between the control group and the uninoculated group indicates the change in attitude brought about by a strong attack on "uninoculated" people who had no experience in defending their position. The three inoculated groups, who were given practice in refuting mild attacks on their position, showed considerable resistance to strong attacks. (Adapted from McGuire, 1961.)*

same state, or if he does, he may see the man as a person coming home from a hard day's work. If someone who is strongly opposed to government spending sees the newspaper headline "Congress appropriates $50 billion for Armed Forces," he may view the 50 billion dollars as an instance of big government spending. Someone else who is strongly concerned about national defense may see in this headline an instance of Congress providing for our safety; he may not especially notice the amount of money involved. Of the facts presented in a message, a person tends to perceive those which fit in with, or are relevant to, his attitudes and beliefs and to pay little attention to other facts. In this way his attitudes and beliefs are reinforced and strengthened, rather than changed, by his perceptions.

AVOIDANCE OF INFORMATION Another difficulty in trying to change attitudes is that some people will not listen to the message. They are so reluctant to alter their attitudes and beliefs that they attempt to avoid information which is inconsistent with these attitudes and beliefs. Plenty of situations in everyday life illustrate the tendency to withdraw from everything that conflicts with what one already believes. A confirmed liberal may refuse to read conservative magazines or newspapers. The person who is prejudiced against Jews may have nothing to do with them, thus never giving himself a chance to acquire facts that might change his mind. People in general tend to expose themselves only to viewpoints that agree with their own, thereby strengthening the attitudes and beliefs that they already hold.

IMMUNIZATION The final individual factor to consider in attitude change has been called immunization, by analogy to the medical practice of immunizing a person against a disease by inoculating him with a small dose of it. Applied to attitudes, this analogy is that a mild exposure to an opposing attitude can immunize a person against it so that he will never accept further facts or arguments for it, no matter how strong they are. There is some evidence that such a process takes place (McGuire, 1961):

In this study, changes in attitudes toward four commonsense health propositions were measured. (They were propositions that most people would tend to regard favorably, such as "Everyone should see his doctor at least once a year for a routine medical checkup.") Of the five groups of subjects in the experiment, one was a control group whose members rated the propositions without persuasion of any kind (their average rating, shown in Figure 15.3, was 12.78 out of a possible 15).

For subjects of three other groups, the "inoculated" groups, the experiment was carried out in two stages. In the first stage, all three groups were presented with mild arguments against the propositions, and then were permitted to try and refute the arguments. In the second stage, one of the three groups (group 1 in Figure 15.3) made ratings of the original propositions without hearing further arguments against the propositions. This group maintained about the same degree of approval (12.91) as the control group, showing that they had refuted the arguments to their satisfaction. Group 2 in Figure 15.3 was again presented with the same arguments, but in much stronger terms. This group's average rating of the original propositions was 11.62—slightly below the control group's 12.78.

Figure 15.4 Interaction among members of various ethnic groups, especially groups of children working together, usually tends to reduce prejudice. (Susan Johns.)

Group 3 was also presented with strong arguments, but the arguments were new ones. This produced a slightly lower approval rating of 10.92. However, in contrast to the "inoculated" group, the last group, an "uninoculated" group which had not been exposed to the mild arguments and so had no chance to build up a defense, was the most susceptible when presented with the strong arguments: its ratings of the original propositions fell to 8.60.

Obviously the effectiveness of inoculation will depend on many factors, including the attitudes involved, the counterarguments made, and the source of attacks. Experiments such as this one, however, indicate that subjects can be immunized against strong attacks by building their defenses against mild ones. Such immunization accounts for some of the resistance to attitude change frequently found in people.

Racial Attitudes and Conflicts

The word *race*, in ordinary usage, means a group of human beings having common and distinctive innate physical characteristics. However, when we talk of "racial conflict," we refer to social conflict resulting from prejudice against any social group that has some distinctive common characteristic, whether the characteristic is race, religion, or national origin. Most of the examples discussed here will draw upon anti-Negro prejudice in the United States, both because this kind of prejudice is most intense in our country and because it has been intensively studied. But the same principles which apply to conflict between blacks and whites also apply to other "racial" conflicts.

Acquiring prejudices What is a prejudice? At the beginning of the chapter we defined it as a previously formed judgment applied to some person, object, or situation. As we use it in this section, however, prejudice refers to a hostile attitude toward some social group. Thus any attitude of hostility toward whites, blacks, Germans, politicians, Communists, or any other group is a prejudice. It does not matter whether the prejudice has some objective basis or not; if it is hostility toward a group, it is a prejudice.

Just like any other attitudes, prejudices obey the principles of attitude formation and maintenance which were discussed earlier. In particular, prejudices are *learned.* It is very important to ask how they are learned, since one of the best ways of eradicating them is to prevent their being learned in the first place.

Logically, a prejudice can be learned in two possible ways: (1) from contact with the object of the prejudice or (2) from contact with others who have the prejudice. Prejudices are, in fact, learned in both ways, but various studies indicate that they are more commonly acquired by contact with people who have them.

CONTACT WITH PREJUDICED PEOPLE Many studies have shown that there is a high correlation between the prejudices of parents and those of their children. The correlation exists because parents often train their children to be prejudiced. For example, a study of rural Tennessee children showed that their parents warned them to avoid Negro children and

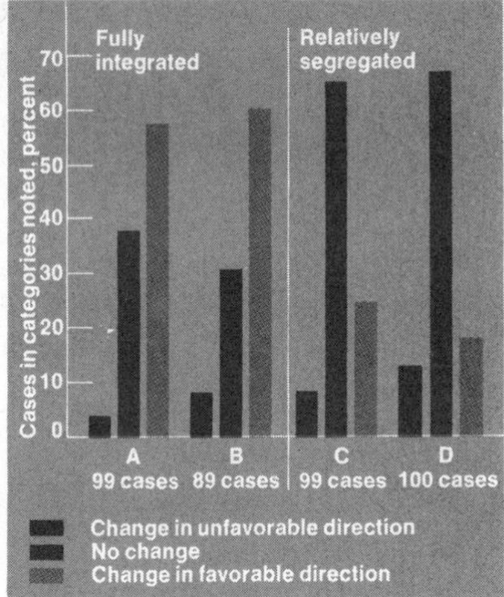

PREJUDICE TENDS TO DIMINISH WITH DIRECT CONTACT AND SHARED EXPERIENCE

Figure 15.5 *Changes in attitudes toward Negroes held by white housewives in integrated and relatively segregated housing projects. (From Newcomb et al., 1965; adapted from Deutsch and Collins, 1951.)*

even objects which had been handled by Negro children, and that the parents sometimes punished their children severely for violating these warnings.

Parents are not the only teachers of prejudice. Schoolmates, teachers, and general communication media such as newspapers and television are also responsible. In addition, most of the people we meet try to influence our attitudes. Hence we are continuously exposed to carriers of prejudice.

A dramatic demonstration of the fact that prejudice is usually learned from contact with the prejudiced rather than from contact with people against whom it is directed is the very strong anti-Communist prejudice held by so many Americans. Very few Americans have ever met a Communist; what they know about Communists they have learned from newspapers, television, and other public information media. If it became desirable—as it was during World War II, when the Russians were our allies—to create a more favorable attitude toward Communists, the mass media would probably be mobilized to do this.

CONTACT WITH OBJECTS OF PREJUDICE Prejudice may grow out of personal experience with the group against which it is directed, but this source of prejudice is probably rare. In fact, direct contact and shared group experience are sometimes a cure for prejudice (see Figure 15.4).

During World War II, the Army experimented with the creation of mixed Negro and white units. Both before and after the whites saw service in these units, their attitudes toward Negroes were measured. In almost all cases, the whites were less prejudiced after their experience in mixed units than they had been before. Moreover, the blacks in mixed units proved to be effective combat troops, unlike many blacks in segregated units (Rose, 1946).

White housewives' attitudes toward Negroes became much more favorable after the women had lived in biracial housing projects (Deutsch and Collins, 1951). Two of the housing areas in this study were fully integrated, while two were relatively segregated, with black and white families in the same project but in different buildings or separate parts of the project. Figure 15.5 shows that there was little attitude change toward blacks in an unfavorable direction. Furthermore, in the fully integrated projects where the families had the greatest opportunity for contact and friendship, there was substantial change in a favorable direction. Interviews with some of the housewives provided additional information about the processes of attitude change.

"I started to cry when my husband told me we were coming to live here. I cried for three weeks . . . I didn't want to come and live here where there were so many colored people. I didn't want to bring my children up with colored children, but we had to come. . . . Well, all that's changed. I've really come to like it. I see they're just as human as we are. They have nice apartments, they keep their children clean, and they're very friendly. I've come to like them a great deal. . . . I'd just as soon live near a colored person as a white, it makes no difference to me."

"I thought I was moving into the heart of Africa. . . . I had always heard about how they were . . . they were dirty, drink a lot . . . were like savages. Living with them, my ideas have changed altogether. They're just people . . . they're not any different."

(Deutsch and Collins, 1951, pages 98–99.)

Thus for the people who lived near Negroes, new information that did not fit their prejudiced stereotype led to a generally favorable attitude change. The results might also be explained by dissonance theory (see page 219) in this way: Prejudiced people in the integrated housing developments had to cooperate with Negroes and could not indulge their prejudices publicly; thus behavior and attitude were dissonant, and attitudes were changed to restore internal harmony.

Supports for prejudice Once learned, prejudices are not allowed to die out through forgetting or disuse. Rather they continue to serve the purpose of *gratifying an individual's needs.* In addition, they so alter his perception and memory, as we have already indicated, that his everyday experiences tend to support his prejudices. Consequently, between his needs and his perceptions, an individual usually maintains his prejudices at full strength.

NEEDS Probably the need best served by prejudice is the need for a feeling of superiority. A prejudice creates a social hierarchy in which the prejudiced person has a superior status. If he is prejudiced against Negroes, for example, he believes that they are inferior to him. Some people need to think well of themselves—to think that they are better than others (see Chapter 6). The poorest, least-educated, most unimportant white in a backwoods Southern town has the consolation of "knowing" that he is mentally, morally, and socially superior to most of the blacks of his area.

Prejudice also serves the need to express *aggression.* Psychologists have good reason to believe that hostility and aggression usually originate in the frustration of needs (see Chapter 7). This notion is certainly consistent with ordinary experience, for we frequently see people become irritated or angry when they have failed to get what they want or when something or somebody has obstructed their efforts.

Aggression resulting from frustration can often be vented directly at whatever is doing the frustrating. When a person of superior status or a situation beyond one's control is the frustrator, however, the aggression must be expressed in some other way. The consequence is *displaced aggression.*

In an experiment in which psychologists deprived students for a prolonged period of sleep, food, cigarettes, and even permission to talk, one subject vented his aggression in hostile drawings (Sears et al., 1940). In other instances, aggression may be expressed in prejudice against some "inferior" group that cannot retaliate. Displaced aggression is displayed when the lieutenant bawls out the sergeant, the sergeant works it out on the private, and the private kicks the dog. It was illustrated scientifically in an experiment with boys at a summer camp who were frustrated by not being allowed to go to the movies. Before and after the frustration, their attitudes toward Mexicans and Japanese were measured. These measurements showed that the boys were considerably more prejudiced after they had experienced frustration than before (Miller and Bugelski, 1948).

SCAPEGOATING Displaced aggression is particularly significant in racial conflict, where it is called *scapegoating.* The prejudiced person who suffers economic, social, or political frustrations may displace his aggression to some convenient object, and the most convenient object is often a group against whom he is already prejudiced. This is particularly likely if he can so distort the facts that the group seems to be responsible for his frustrations. An infamous example is the German persecution of the Jews in the 1930s. Hitler was able to convince his followers—who were presumably anti-Semitic to begin with—that the Jews were responsible for most of Germany's economic and social problems. Thus he made Jews the scapegoats of displaced aggression.

Scapegoating, however, is not the inevitable result of frustration; aggression that cannot be directed against the frustrator is not necessarily displaced onto a minority group. For example, many people would not exhibit the displaced aggression and prejudice displayed by the boys in the summer camp. When that experiment was repeated in other populations, prejudice against minority groups did not always increase.

One way of understanding scapegoating better is through the concept of *stimulus generalization* (see Chapter 3). A frustrator who arouses hostility in a person can be regarded as an original stimulus giving rise to the response of aggression. As we have seen in our discussion of stimulus generalization in conditioning experiments, once the organism has learned to make this response, then other stimuli can elicit it. The greater the similarity between the other stimuli and the original stimulus, the greater the likelihood that they will produce the response. Thus people similar to the original frustrator may arouse hostility within the frustrated person.

The similarity need not be a physical one. Hostility may be generalized when little or no physical resemblance exists between the original frustrator and the people it is turned toward. To the angered person, the similarity may be qualitative; for example, the only thing the frustrator and another group of people may have in common is that he dislikes them both (Berkowitz and Holmes, 1959). This analysis suggests that the boys at camp may have had some previous dislike for Mexicans and Japanese, and that the same result would not be obtained from subjects who had no such dislike.

The main point is that hostility will be displaced from the frustrator to the person most similar to him when the frustrator is not available for direct attack. A somewhat different prediction must be made when the angered person is *afraid* to strike at the frustrator because the frustrator might retaliate. In this case, the person may inhibit his aggression both toward the frustrator and toward other people very similar to him. Instead, he will be most likely to attack others who appear to possess some intermediate degree of similarity to the frustrator.

PERCEPTION AND JUDGMENT Our earlier discussion of selective interpretation gave some examples of how prejudice alters perception so that the prejudiced person sees what he wants to see or what he believes

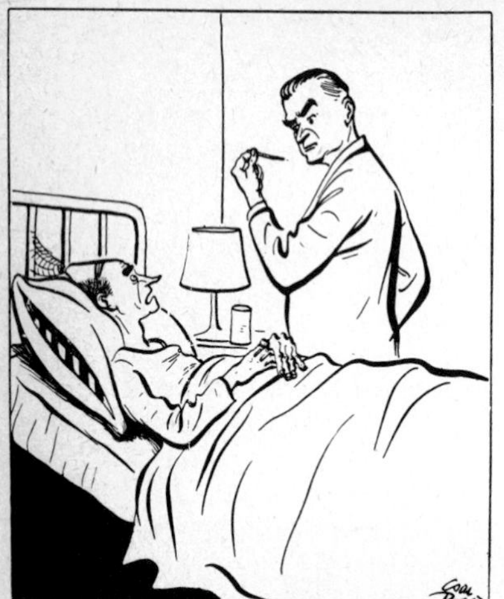

"In case I should need a transfusion, doctor, I want to make certain I don't get anything but blue, sixth-generation American blood!"

Figure 15.6 *One of several Mr. Biggott cartoons used in a study of prejudice. (American Jewish Committee and Carl Rose.)*

he is going to see. If a man feels that Jews are "pushy," he takes special note of instances he considers "pushy" which involve Jews, while in cases involving Gentiles, he pays little attention or else characterizes them differently. With practice, we all become skilled at perceiving only things that are consistent with our prejudices.

One experiment illustrates the way in which prejudice can distort judgment and the interpretation of situations (Cooper and Jahoda, 1947). Subjects were shown a series of cartoons involving a character named Mr. Biggott and were asked to give their reactions. One subject who was intensely prejudiced in favor of "blue-blooded Americans" looked at the cartoon shown in Figure 15.6 and remarked that if Mr. Biggott is only a sixth-generation American, he is a newcomer and is not entitled to put on airs.

SOCIAL HANDICAPS To the extent that prejudice is permitted to operate in social affairs, it produces a world that is exactly what the prejudiced person expects it to be. People with racist attitudes believe that blacks are inferior to whites; and believing this, they prevent blacks from getting adequate schooling, library facilities, housing, and other social advantages. The result is a social handicap for blacks that prevents them from being as well educated as whites. Thus the prejudice becomes "true." This is obviously a vicious circle in which the effects of prejudice help to maintain the prejudice by providing an observable basis for it.

Social effects of prejudice Another effect of prejudice—in fact, the means through which social handicaps are created—is segregation. Wherever prejudice has been strong and widespread—against Jews in the Middle Ages, against blacks in South Africa, or against groups in the United States—the oppressed group has been segregated in schools, in housing, and in jobs. Segregation is a means of depriving them of the facilities and opportunities enjoyed by the oppressor. Any attempt to combat prejudice must begin with efforts to abolish segregation. Civil rights legislation of the 1960s has attempted to do this and has had some beneficial results, but removing all forced segregation in education, housing, and employment will be a long, uphill battle.

Still another social effect of prejudice is that the oppressed may *hate* their oppressors. So long as the oppressed are thoroughly cowed, the hate may not be observable. In the days of complete segregation in the South, for example, there were relatively few civil disturbances. But when some of the restraints are removed, and when the oppressed begin to have some hope of attaining equality, the hate becomes visible and often erupts into violence, as we have seen in the race riots in the United States.

This chapter has shown you that psychological forces for maintaining prejudice are powerful, and that its social effects on the targets of prejudice are oppressive. As a consequence, prejudice produces the most disruptive tensions to be dealt with in our society. White Americans are becoming less prejudiced, a trend that is most pronounced among the young and the better educated. They are leading the movement to eradicate prejudice and its oppressive social effects. How well it will succeed, and with what cost in racial conflict, remains to be seen.

Synopsis and summary

Attitudes tinge practically everything we do. We are continually making evaluations of people and events as good, bad, or in between. In fact, much of our daily round of activities consists of trying to create in other people favorable attitudes toward ourselves, of trying to convince other people to change their attitudes, and of justifying our own attitudes. Most differences of opinion can be traced back to differences in attitudes.

We learn many of our attitudes from our family and our peers. Once learned, attitudes are quite resistant to change, yet we are bombarded with communications which attempt to change them. The attitude-change business is enormous, encompassing many facets of human communication. Newspapers, radio and television news broadcasts, advertising, and education are all fields in which attempts, some more benign than others, are made to induce attitude change. Some attempts at attitude change are extremely subtle. For example, the popular entertainment business, including the creation of "glamorous" personalities, is mainly an exercise in attitude manipulation. Some of it is fun, but we should keep our eyes open and try to realize when we are being manipulated. It is often to our advantage; usually someone else gains from our acceptance of propaganda.

Attitudes have a motivational function—they lead us to and away from certain goals. We like many things, and we approach these; but we also "can't stand" many other things, and these we avoid. Usually the motivational function of attitudes is harmless enough, but when prejudices are involved, it can lead us to do things which can be classed only as wrong.

1. An attitude is a tendency to respond positively or negatively to certain objects, persons, or situations. A belief is an acceptance of a proposition. Beliefs shape attitudes, and attitudes determine what one is willing to believe. Prejudice is a case of a negative attitude, the object of which is usually a minority group.
2. An opinion has characteristics of both an attitude and a belief. It is verbalizable and public, whereas an attitude may not be easily verbalized and is a private affair.
3. Attitudes are learned tendencies to approach positive goals or to avoid negative goals. Thus attitudes place their objects into categories, usually oversimplified, related to these goals. As a result, attitudes may produce erroneous thinking.
4. When a number of things differing in favorableness or unfavorableness are known about a person or object, the resulting attitude tends to be an average of the components. In this way, otherwise discrepant attitudes are made consistent.
5. When there is a large discrepancy between the favorable and unfavorable components of an attitude, or when a person is forced to commit himself to something about which he has mixed feelings, cognitive dissonance is aroused. This motivates the person to alter his beliefs and hence his attitudes in order to achieve consistency.
6. Several methods of measuring attitudes have been developed. An attitude scale provides a precise measure of the degree of an attitude toware an issue, but it can be used only with people who have the time and interest to take it. For many practical purposes, we are limited to the public opinion poll, which consists of a series of questions answered in a brief personal interview. The phrasing of questions and representative sampling are extremely important to the results obtained.
7. A very large number of attitudes can be distinguished and measured. They form various clusters that can be used for various purposes, but most social attitudes can be lumped into one continuum of conservatism versus liberalism.
8. Parental attitudes help shape

children's attitudes so that the attitudes of parents and children are similar, especially in religious and party affiliation.

9. The critical period in the formation of attitudes is between the ages of 12 and 30. During this period, the important influences are (*a*) peers, (*b*) information, and (*c*) education. By the end of this period, attitudes become quite stable and persist with little change for the rest of life. In later adulthood, however, there is small drift toward conservatism.

10. Among educated people, stereotyped prejudices have been fading in successive generations. Each generation has moved to the liberal side of its parents. The attitudes of student activists, on the whole, resemble their parents, but are more extreme on the liberal side.

11. Propaganda and advertising are deliberate attempts to change attitudes and beliefs in a direction favorable to the source. Education is an attempt to inculcate knowledge, but in the process attitudes and beliefs are changed.

12. The degree to which attitudes are affected by messages depends upon a number of factors. These may be classified into (*a*) characteristics of the source, (*b*) the nature of the message, and (*c*) factors within the individual.

13. Important characteristics of the source are credibility, attractiveness, and power. The higher the source stands in any of these characteristics, the more likely it is to bring about an attitude change.

14. Several characteristics of messages are effective in changing attitudes: prestige suggestion, appeals to fear, loaded words, and two-sided arguments. However, if the appeal to fear is too strong or if the message is too inconsistent with the listener's existing attitude, little change may occur.

15. Factors within the listener that are important to whether or not his attitude is changed by a message include: his influenceability, the relation of the message to his needs and goals, his selective interpretation, his tendency to avoid information, and his immunization, if any. If he has been previously inoculated with mild counterarguments to his attitude, the attitude may withstand strong attacks without changing.

16. Prejudices may be learned either from the object of the prejudice or, more commonly, from contact with others who have the prejudice.

17. Once learned, prejudices are preserved and supported by (*a*) the needs they help satisfy, (*b*) the fact that they provide a means of scapegoating, that is, of displacing aggression for which there might otherwise be no outlet, (*c*) distortion in perception and judgment that makes the prejudice seem "true," and (*d*) creating social handicaps for minority groups which appear to justify the prejudice.

18. The principal social consequences of prejudice are segregation, inferior facilities for minority groups, and possible hatred of the oppressor.

Related topics in the text

Chapter 3 Principles of Learning Since attitudes are learned, and since stimulus generalization is an important concept in explaining prejudice, a review of these topics in Chapter 3 would be helpful.

Chapter 8 Perception Attitudes seem to result in selective perception —we perceive and interpret those things toward which we have favorable attitudes in a different way from those things toward which we have unfavorable attitudes. Some of the basic facts of perception—especially the influence of learning on perception—should be reviewed.

Chapter 7 Arousal, Emotion, and Conflict Information about motivational conflicts and aggression are presented. These phenomena are related to prejudice and scapegoating.

Chapter 14 Social Influences on Behavior The general role of culture and social groups in influencing behavior is discussed. Conformity to group norms is an important determiner of attitudes, and the section in Chapter 14 on conformity is especially pertinent.

Suggestions for further reading

Allport, G. W. *The nature of prejudice.* Reading, Mass.: Addison-Wesley, 1954.
A readable summary and analysis of the literature on group prejudice.

Brown, J. A. C. *Techniques of persuasion: From propaganda to brainwashing.* Baltimore, Md.: Penguin, 1963. (Paperback.)
Attitude formation and change are the focus of this survey of various kinds of persuasion, including advertising, political propaganda, and psychological warfare.

Campbell, A., Converse, P. E., Miller, W. E., and Stokes, D. E. *The American voter.* New York: Wiley, 1960.
A discussion of factors affecting voting behavior as discovered by attitude survey techniques.

Greenwald, A. G., Brock, T. C., and Ostrom, T. M. (Eds.) *Psychological foundations of attitudes.* New York: Academic Press, 1968.
A collection of articles emphasizing the role of learning in attitude formation and describing theories other than the consistency theory discussed in this chapter.

Hollander, E. P., and Hunt, R. G. (Eds.) *Current perspectives in social psychology: Readings with commentary.* Fair Lawn, N.J.: Oxford, 1963 (Paperback.)
A carefully selected book of readings presenting an overview of empirical problems, research findings, and current theoretical viewpoints.

Insko, C. A. *Theories of attitude change.* New York: Appleton-Century-Crofts, 1967.
Major viewpoints on the theoretical reasons for attitude change are discussed.

Kiesler, C. A., Collins, B. E., and Miller, N. *Attitude change.* New York: Wiley, 1969.
A compact, balanced text covering theory and facts of attitude change.

Krech, D., Crutchfield, R. S., and Ballachey, E. L. *Individual in society: A textbook of social psychology.* New York: McGraw-Hill, 1962. Chaps. 5–7.
A text with a comprehensive section on the nature and measurement of attitudes, the formation of attitudes, and attitude change.

McGrath, J. E. *Social psychology: A brief introduction.* New York: Holt, 1964. (Paperback.)
An overview of the major concepts of social psychology.

McGuire, W. J. *Attitudes and attitude change.* In G. Lindzey and E. Aronson (Eds.), *Handbook of social psychology.* (2d ed.) Reading, Mass.: Addison-Wesley, 1968.
A comprehensive summary of research on the factors influencing attitude change.

Newcomb, T. M., Turner, R. H., and Converse, P. E. *Social psychology: The study of human interaction.* New York: Holt, 1965. Chaps. 2–5.
A general introduction which attempts to integrate different psychological approaches. Contains a comprehensive section on attitudes.

Secord, P. F., and Backman, C. W. *Social psychology.* New York: McGraw-Hill, 1964, Chaps. 3–6.
A text that presents an inclusive section discussing social influence processes, with emphasis on attitudes and communication.

Shaw, M. E., and Wright, J. M. *Scales for the measurement of attitudes.* New York: McGraw-Hill, 1967.
A reference work covering methods of constructing attitude scales that are useful in research.

We are today in a period when the development of theory within the social sciences will permit innovations which are at present inconceivable. Among these will be dramatic changes in the organization and management of economic enterprise.
Douglas McGregor

An adult in Western society is a member of many different groups, and is influenced by many more. His interaction with these groups was the subject of the two preceding chapters. One prominent group they did not cover, however, is the work group. Of people between 20 and 65, the vast majority of men, as well as millions of women, spend 40 hours or so a week in such a group. Because it takes up so much of their time and because they must almost always be a member of a work group to make a living, this kind of social group is one of the most important of all.

The psychological study of people at work has long been known as *industrial psychology.* Psychologists moved into industry as early as World War I, and since then have made it a major area of research. Today much of their work is done from the "outside," that is, by separate firms of psychologists who contract with organizations to study and advise on certain problems. But whether done from the "inside" or the "outside," this work has produced a considerable body of knowledge.

Industrial psychology has many subdivisions, as well as areas in which it overlaps other fields. Personnel psychology, dealing with the selection, placement, and training of personnel, was one of the first to emerge. It was closely followed by consumer psychology, studying the needs, attitudes, and reactions of consumers to products and to advertising. Later, after World War II, came engineering psychology, which deals with man's relation to machines—in particular, complicated machines with many dials and controls. The latest to emerge (Leavitt, 1962) is organizational psychology, which studies the relationships between people in organizations, primarily industrial groups (Bass, 1965; Schein, 1964). Organizational psychology covers much of the same territory as industrial psychology, but its emphasis is on the social and motivational aspects of organizations rather than on more mechanical matters. Because our focus here is social, we have chosen this term as a chapter title. We shall, however, briefly cover such topics as personnel selection, work and fatigue, and man-machine relations not normally included in organization psychology. The chapter will start with the worker and what he wants in a job, then consider industrial organization and the management of workers, and end with a summary of the psychological factors involved in productive work.

Job Satisfaction

If we ask people holding jobs why they work, they almost always say, "To make a living." That is the pat answer, but it is far from the whole truth. Even if it were true, most people have considerable latitude in the kind of work they do and where they do it. They exercise this choice through the kind of education they elect for preparation, where they look for jobs, which jobs they stick to, and what jobs they aspire to in any particular kind of employment. Apparently, for each person, some jobs are more desirable and more satisfying than others. Let us see why.

Hierarchy of needs In Chapter 6 we described man's various needs, from those rooted in his physiological makeup to those that are personal and social. Arranging these needs in a hierarchy is a useful way of looking at the satisfaction people can or do achieve in their work (Maslow, 1968). In outline, the hierarchy is:

1. Physiological needs
2. Safety needs
3. Social needs
4. Egoistic needs
5. Self-fulfillment needs

Some of these terms are different from terminology we have used before. Physiological needs for food, water, comfort, etc., are the same. Safety needs refer to the motivation to be protected from danger, threat, and deprivation; they represent the desire to be assured that other needs, particularly of the physiological variety, will in the future be met. The social needs are those for affiliation, for social approval, and for giving and receiving friendship—needs for interacting with other people. The egoistic needs are of two general types: self-esteem, that is, needs for self-respect, self-confidence, and competence; and status, that is, needs for recognition, appreciation, and respect from other people. Finally, the need for self-fulfillment is the need to realize our potentialities, to do what we are good at and find interesting.

This hierarchy represents an order of dominance of the needs when they go unsatisfied. Physiological needs come first because they must be satisfied before other needs appear. A starving man is not concerned with social approval or status; he is preoccupied with obtaining food. If he is really hungry, he doesn't even wonder where tomorrow's meal is coming from (safety need); only today's meal counts. But once he is assured of eating today—that is, of having his physiological needs satisfied over the short run—he can begin to worry about the future and ask whether his physiological needs will always be met. Thus he moves on to safety needs.

The same system of priorities operates at each step up the ladder. Once a man has a steady job, or knows he can get another if he loses the one he has, his other needs come to the fore. In general, the sequence is social needs, egoistic needs, and self-fulfillment needs, as listed above in the hierarchy. This sequence, however, is not rigid. People vary considerably in the strength of these complex motives; some individuals are high in egoistic needs and low in social needs, and vice versa. Although the scale does not apply strictly to each person, it does represent the spectrum of needs to be considered in job satisfaction.

	Women factory workers	Union workers	Nonunion workers	Men	Women	Employees of five factories
Steady work	1	1	1	1	3	1
Type of work				3	1	3
Opportunity for advancement	5	4	4	2	2	4
Good working companions	4			4	5	
High pay	6	2½	2	5½	8	2
Good boss	3	5½	5	5½	4	6
Comfortable working conditions	2	2½	3	8½	6	7
Benefits		5½	6	8½	9	5
Opportunity to learn a job	8					
Good hours	9	7½	7	7	7	
Opportunity to use one's ideas	7	7½	8			
Easy work	10					

Table 16.1 *What industrial workers say they want in a job. The numbers are the ranks they gave to the various factors. (A summary of several different surveys. Different language and varying numbers of alternatives were used in the surveys, and the factors named at the left have been paraphrased.)*

The authenticity of this hierarchy of needs is generally confirmed in many psychological studies of the satisfactions people derive, or fail to derive, from their work. (There are several methods of asking employees what they consider most important: questionnaires, rating scales, interviews, "My Job" contests, etc.) Although the results naturally vary from one locality to another and from one occupation to another, we are justified in drawing the following conclusions that apply to most people at work.

Pay For those of us who work for a living, pay or income is what enables us to buy the material things we want. Without it we could not live; yet pay does not usually head the list of things people consider important in their jobs (Smith, 1964). When asked to rank pay along with several other features of their jobs, most people place it relatively low, and very few rank it first (see Table 16.1).

Even when they rank pay high, they usually indicate that it is not just high pay that they want. Rather, they want to be paid as well as other people doing the same work, or as well as other people in the same industry. Thus most people are more concerned about fair treatment than about the amount of money received.

The fact that pay is seldom listed as the most important factor in working should not lead us to think that it is unimportant. Probably most people assume that they will be paid enough to take care of their basic necessities. Above that point, then, pay becomes relatively unimportant. If the pay scale were dropped far below its present level for a particular person, pay would become important again. It is interesting to see, though, how often people decide which job to take or which to keep on grounds other than the pay they receive.

Security Probably the factor most often ranked first in importance is job security. People want to know that they will have steady work and that the work will continue for many years. They also want security in the sense that they want to work on safe jobs. They do not want to run the risk of disability because of accidents.

The importance of security in job satisfaction partly explains why pay is not ranked higher than it is. Most people prefer a low salary which is guaranteed over a long period to a high salary which may not last long. Such concerns are typical of the human species. People are able to look well beyond immediate satisfactions and to anticipate satisfying their needs at some time in the future.

Good working conditions Good working conditions are frequently listed as important considerations. People like to work in clean and neat surroundings. If it is an industrial plant, they want to feel that it provides a pleasant environment they can be proud of. Other working conditions that are frequently preferred over higher pay are short hours and jobs which are not too taxing.

The large class of white-collar workers provides the best example of people to whom working conditions are more important than high pay. Office workers, clerks, and stenographers often earn much less money than they could if they were doing skilled manual labor, and yet they do not often change their job category. In addition, of course, white-collar workers usually have steady work and can look forward to a future of continued employment.

Opportunity for advancement Another proof that people are frequently more concerned about the future than the present is that they usually give a high rating to opportunity for advancement in status. A man often turns down a higher-paying job to take one which starts at a lower salary but ensures early advancement. Sometimes people's concern about advancement takes the form of wanting a guaranteed rate of promotion after a fixed period of time. In other instances, they simply want to be assured that they will be told about the opportunities for advancement and can compete for them. Or a job applicant may be most interested in the company's training opportunities for employees, because he wants to learn the skills necessary for advancement.

Regardless of the particular form the concern about advancement takes, it is clear that concepts of fair play are important when people ask for equal opportunity for advancement or opportunity to learn. In such instances, they are not asking for a guarantee of advancement, but only for a fair chance. A "fair chance" for many workers, especially in blue-collar jobs for which many could qualify, means advancement or job security based on seniority. In any case, nobody wants to work where the boss's son-in-law gets promoted regardless of his qualifications.

Group relations Also important to most people are the social relations they have in their jobs (McGregor, 1960). People want companions and co-workers whom they like. They will work for a good boss, and quit when they don't like him. They want help from management in their work, and they want to know how their work is progressing. They want to be sure that they have somebody to whom they can take their grievances, and that they will get a fair deal. For that reason, the organization which provides special means of handling grievances will always have an advantage in attracting workers. Finally, people want recognition of the importance of their work, and of their efforts to do better work.

This desire for appreciation of work has raised a good many problems for psychologists who have tried to do experiments in industry. In the famous experiments in the Hawthorne plant of the Western Electric Company, several girls were studied over the course of 2 years (Roethlisberger and Dickson, 1939):

The girls were put in a separate room where many different working conditions could be controlled. First, the illumination was changed, and production immediately went up. Then other factors were changed: The girls were given rest periods, sometimes for 5 minutes and sometimes for 10. They were given free lunches, and at one time were allowed to go home early. Every time a change was made, production improved. Then all the rest periods, free lunches, and so forth, were taken away, *and production went up still higher.*

What had happened here? The answer, it was learned later, was in the *attention* the girls were getting. Every time a change was made, the girls saw that other people were concerned with what they were doing, and this appreciation was what really made production go up.

In summary, people work for many things besides money. They want security, future opportunity, pleasant working conditions, and good relations with their co-workers and their bosses. We should never forget that people have complex motives which require satisfaction.

Industrial Organization

Having examined industry from the point of view of the worker, let us now look at it as the owners and managers do. What are their needs, or goals, and how do they go about satisfying them? How can the needs of both groups be met in the working situation?

Organizational goals Just as it is commonplace for a worker to say he works for a living, so businessmen regularly point out that they run a business for profit. That statement, like the first, is only partly true. Both groups have more than one need or objective in mind when they perform their respective functions in industry. This fact has been established by many studies—for example, by a large survey of 145 businesses selected as a cross section, representing firms of all sizes, engaged in different kinds of production, and located in various parts of the United States (Dent, 1959).

In confidential interviews, the chief executives or principal deputies of the 145 businesses were asked: "What are the aims of top management in your company?" It was found that the answers given could be condensed into one or more of five categories: profit, growth, public service, employee welfare, and good products. Three-quarters of the executives listed more than one of these goals. A sizable number, about one-sixth, mentioned four or more. Only about one-third

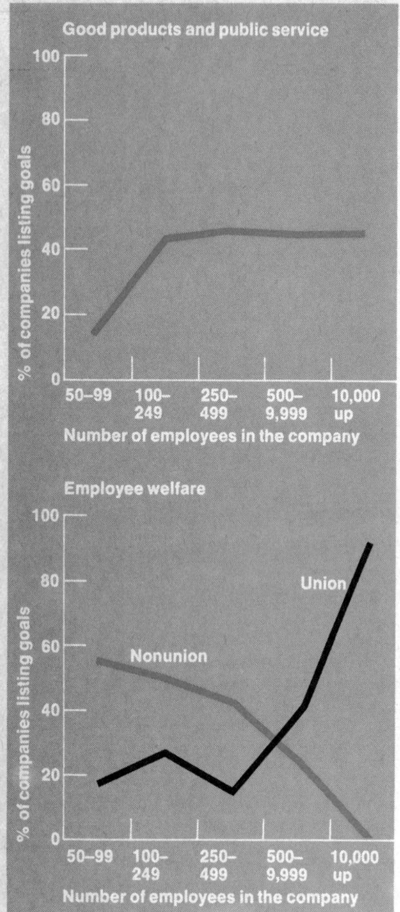

STATED COMPANY GOALS VARY WITH SIZE AND UNIONIZATION

Figure 16.1 *Percentage of managers in a survey of 145 industries listing good products and public service and employee welfare as major company goals. (Dent, 1959.)*

gave profit as their chief goal, and only about one-half named it as a goal at all. (Perhaps this result is an understatement; some executives may have been embarrassed to say that profit was their primary motive.)

The goals listed by the executives correlated with certain characteristics of the companies involved (Figure 16.1). Large companies named good products and public service as goals more often than small companies. Large companies that were unionized gave employee welfare more emphasis than large companies that were not unionized. On the other hand, small companies without unions considered employee welfare more important than companies of the same size with unions. Another finding, not shown in Figure 16.1, was that growing companies more often listed good products and public service than static firms.

The general point is that industrial organizations, like employees, have a number of goals they attempt to achieve in their operations. Moreover, there is a rough parallel between their goals and the hierarchy of human needs. The businesses most concerned with profits are small companies that are still trying to meet "physiological needs." Larger firms give more weight to social needs (public service, employee welfare) and to self-esteem and achievement (good products). Even with smaller employers, the desire for profits is generally limited to a "fair" or "reasonable" profit rather than extending to the maximum possible.

A stockholder, who expects a return on investment, may wonder how managers "get away with" having social goals as distinguished from profit goals. To find the answer, we must ask who really sets the goals. Although in the American corporate structure these are formally established by the board of directors, the board itself tends to be dominated by managers. As early as 1935, about half of America's largest corporations had a majority of salaried executives among their directors (Gordon, 1945). Hence the goals of an organization, once some acceptable profit is produced, are set by the managers more than by the stockholders or by the stockholders' representatives on the board.

Management and human motivation Not only are managers influential in setting the goals of their organizations, but they are the people charged with achieving the goals. They design their organizations in ways that they think will best do the job, and these designs reflect their theory of human motivation as well as their responses to engineering and economic problems (Schein, 1964). Does a manager feel convinced that employees need to be controlled and driven, as managers used to believe in the days when almost the only needs satisfied by work were those for food and shelter? Or does he think that work should be arranged to meet some of his employees' social and "higher" needs? These are contrasting philosophies that have been formulated as follows:

Theory X

The average human being has an inherent dislike of work and will avoid it if he can.

Because of this human characteristic of dislike of work, most people must be coerced, controlled, directed, threatened with punishment to get them to put forth adequate effort toward the achievement of organization objectives.

The average human being prefers to be directed, wishes to avoid responsibility, has little ambition, wants security above all.

Theory Y

The expenditure of physical and mental effort in work is as natural as play or rest.

External control and the threat of punishment are not the only means for bringing about effort toward organizational objectives. Man will exercise self-direction and self-control in the service of objectives to which he is committed.

Commitment to objectives is a function of the rewards associated with their achievement.

The average human being learns, under proper conditions, not only to accept but to seek responsibility.

The capacity to exercise a relatively high degree of imagination, ingenuity, and creativity in the solution of organizational problems is widely, not narrowly, distributed in the population.

Under the conditions of modern industrial life, the intellectual potentialities of the average human being are only partially utilized. (McGregor, 1960, pages 33 and 47.)

A manager who believes theory X will emphasize wages and security. He will not understand that most of his employees are really trying to satisfy other motives, such as those relating to self-esteem and the realization of potential, or self-fulfillment (see page 393). His policy will be directed toward manipulating subordinates through the use of incentives—money, for instance—which are largely ineffective in improving production. After all, most of these incentives can only be used *off the job,* and the job often seems to be a barrier preventing the enjoyment of its own rewards (McGregor, 1960).

The theory Y manager, on the other hand, attempts to unite the goals of the individual and the organization, so that the employee does not need to be coerced into work. This does not imply that the theory Y manager is a "softy" or a "backslapper"; he has a view of human motivation which is potentially a very powerful one.

Classical organization theory Classical organizational design is based on theory X. It can be summarized in eight precepts (Bass, 1965):

1. Some one person should be responsible for each essential activity.
2. Responsibility for each activity should not be duplicated and should not overlap.
3. Each position should have a limited number of clearly stated duties.
4. Every person should know exactly what his duties are.
5. Authority for making decisions should be commensurate with responsibility for them.
6. Authority should be delegated to persons close to the point of action.
7. Managers should have a limited number of subordinates—say, four to seven.

8. Every manager should know whom he reports to and who reports to him: the chain of command should be clearly defined.

If some combination of these principles were not followed to some degree, no organization would exist, and little would be accomplished. Followed rigidly, however, they produce an organization with serious deficiencies.

The basic drawback of a classically organized company is that it fails to develop each individual's potential. A chain of command encourages dependency and stifles initiative. People come to regard it as their job to get work out of others rather than out of themselves. Yet few superiors can wrest the amount and quality of work out of people under them that the people can produce for themselves when properly motivated.

Another fault of such a system is that essential activities are neglected at times, leading to major "boo-boos" or even to organizational disasters. No one component in a piece of equipment is perfectly reliable, and neither is any one person. There are times when a manager is preoccupied with one set of activities and neglects others, particularly if they are supposed to be done by a subordinate. As space engineers have found, to be highly reliable any system must have built-in redundancy, that is, it must have overlapping and backup components. If one fails, another comes into play to make certain a function is executed. In human systems, this means there must be overlapping of functions and responsibilities so that if one person forgets, another remembers. In addition, the old adage that "two heads are better than one" applies; if two or more people share responsibility for something, they may cross-train each other or develop ideas between them that neither one could have created alone.

A third disadvantage of classical organization theory is that it creates an extremely vertical structure. To maintain a strict chain of command, layer upon layer of management must be built. In consequence the time involved in making decisions can become too long. More important, communication suffers so that perceptions are distorted up and down the line. Like the game of Gossip and the qualitative changes that take place in memory when something is passed through several minds (page 141), messages become scrambled as they are relayed through a chain. It is not uncommon in a long chain for people at different ends to have exactly opposite views of the same problem.

The fourth deficiency of classical organization theory is that it simply does not work according to the charts it creates. Anyone who has been associated with a large organization for some time knows that people follow the chain of command only in the most official matters. Otherwise they find out who "gets things done" and deal with him. This can be demonstrated by formal sociometric studies in which each person in an organization is asked to indicate which other people he most frequently contacts. One such study of a small naval unit is illustrated in Figure 16.2. The colored lines show the formal organization, the black lines the actual working relationships. The two are quite different.

Integrative organization theory A different theory of organization, developed in the 1950s through the efforts of many psychologists work-

CLASSICAL ORGANIZATION CHARTS DO NOT SHOW ACTUAL WORKING RELATIONSHIPS

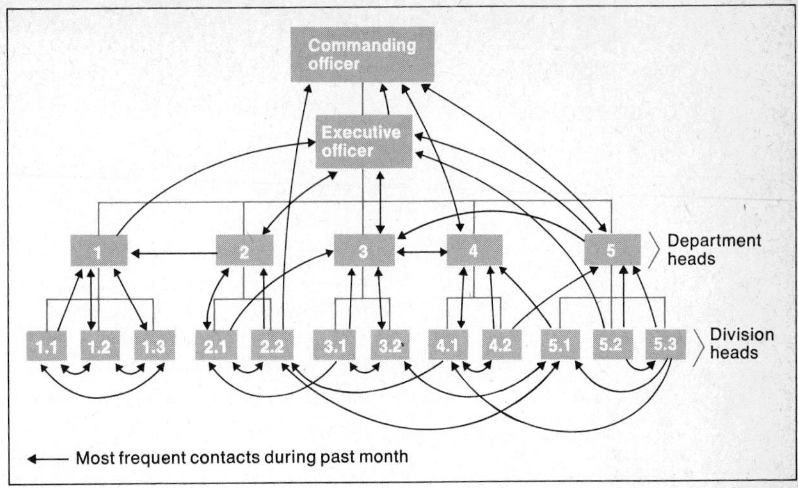

Figure 16.2 *Colored lines show formal relationships within a small naval unit as outlined in the table of organization. The black lines, however, indicate the most frequent working contacts during one month of study. (Stogdill, 1949.)*

ing in industry, is best expressed in a book by Douglas McGregor entitled the *Human Side of Enterprise* (1960). McGregor gave the name *integrative management* to the new theory. By "integrative" he meant a management that attempts to integrate the needs and goals of the company with those of the employees (including the managers).

The basic aim of integrative management is to develop self-control—that is, control from inside the person—rather than control from outside, as classical organization theory would have it. There is no firm set of rules for doing this; each manager must deal in a different way with different people, depending on their strengths and weaknesses. Integrative management, however, does stress certain departures from classical theory.

One is "shared leadership," both across and down the organization chart. Each manager helps others with whom he works to develop their own goals in their areas of responsibility rather than simply carrying out objectives handed down from above.

Second, emphasis is placed on "open communication" throughout the system. This means more informal communication among those working closely together. It also means that as much information as people are interested in is spread throughout the system.

A third aim is to build confidence. By sharing leadership and information, managers instill confidence in each other and their employees. Confidence increases self-esteem and motivates the person to function on his own without depending on orders.

Management development What is a manager, exactly? According to classical organization theory, managers are different from supervisors. A supervisor, often called a foreman, is the person directly over employees doing the work, while the term manager is reserved for persons with a larger sphere of influence in the organization. This distinction fades somewhat in integrative theory, because management attempts to get everyone, from top to bottom, to undertake as much "self-management'' as possible. Nevertheless, the distinction has some merit, for the people who must develop successful integrative approaches are the managers at the highest level of the organization. The following passage describes what such a manager does:

We can partially differentiate managerial from other jobs by emphasizing the *change* quality of managerial problems as against the relatively static quality of tasks at lower levels. The manager deals largely with unknowns instead of knowns. He is a solver of *unprogrammed* problems.

We can also differentiate the manager's job from the executive's job. For the word ''executive'' implies that the executing function is primary. The managerial job should be *more than an executive one.* It should also include information-gathering and problem-defining functions. Once programs have been worked out, the manager is likely either to ''execute'' them himself or pass them on to other ''executives.''

The manager ought to do more than search for problems and alternative solutions to them. He must translate his understanding into *decisions for action* and thence into *action* itself. (Leavitt, 1964. pages 297–298.)

How does a company develop managers who can carry out these functions in an integrative way? The training techniques are somewhat different for beginning managers and for senior managers.

TRAINING BEGINNING MANAGERS Perhaps the most common method in most companies is *job rotation*—the trainee works for a few months in several key departments before being assigned to his permanent job. This technique is designed to acquaint the young manager with various aspects of the company's operation, and it probably does. Its big drawback is that the manager-to-be does not get practice in solving the sorts of problems which will be coming his way later (Leavitt, 1964). He is, in many training programs, a passive onlooker, without responsibility, in the department to which he is temporarily assigned.

Another training method, which may give the responsibility necessary for development of managerial skills, is *problem-centered group training* (Leavitt, 1964). The idea is to set a realistic problem for a group of trainees —perhaps a problem with which the senior managers have been grappling. In working on it, the trainees should be allowed to draw on the experiences of, and information available to, the senior managers. Young managers can learn a great many things about the company in this way, because motivation to learn is high. In addition, the problem-centered approach provides the trainee with invaluable experience in working with people in groups. Perhaps a good training program should include some aspects of both job rotation and the problem-solving approach.

TRAINING SENIOR MANAGERS Organizations employ a variety of training programs for the development of their middle- and upper-level managers (Flippo, 1966; Fleishman, 1967). Among them are courses established by the firm and taught by members of it (such as the General Motors Institute of Technology) and university courses to which executives are sent for varying periods of time (for example, the Sloan Fellowship Program, Massachusetts Institute of Technology). Although the contents and purposes of such programs are diverse, in recent years most of them have placed increasing emphasis on training in decision making and training in human relations.

A popular form of training in decision making utilizes a simulation technique in which information is provided about a simulated organization—production, costs, research, inventories, sales, etc. Trainees are then asked to make decisions based on this information. Often they are divided into competing teams in order to provide experience both with teamwork and with the success or failure of alternative decisions. This kind of training is frequently set up as a game, with a computer supplying information and processing the results of various decisions. Or it may simulate real life by giving trainees various papers to be processed through "in" and "out" baskets. Whatever the particular method, the purpose is to broaden the manager's grasp of the complex interactions of business decisions and teach him the value of long-term planning.

Training in human relations takes several forms. One is *role playing,* which is an offshoot of the sociodrama or psychodrama techniques pioneered by Moreno (1953). In this kind of training a problem is presented to a group, and then the members of the group act out the roles of the characters in the problem-solving situation. For instance, a manager might act the role of a union leader. The hope is that the manager will gain some insight into the way the situation is perceived from the union's viewpoint.

A second, increasingly popular training method in the area of human relations is *sensitivity training.* It is carried out in small, unstructured groups in which the leader's job is not to teach, but to help the members gain a greater awareness of how human beings relate to each other. Extreme frankness is encouraged, so that each person can become conscious of how he is affecting others. For example, one person may learn that what he thinks is a "dignified manner" is regarded by another trainee as "pompousness." Or a forceful leader may find that his "leadership" is considered to be "railroading" by other members of the group (Flippo, 1966, page 226). In this way members of the group develop sensitivity to others and learn to discard styles of behavior that impede effective work in groups.

Communication As we have seen, communication is the crucial link in successful integrative management. An essential requirement is that the channels of communication remain open and be used. Beyond that, however, communications should be effective; they should really communicate. Unfortunately, managers may be skillful in many ways without being good at communication. Today a number of firms have set up special training programs for improving the skills of their managers in sending and receiving information. Here are some principles that are useful for everyone to know.

1. The manager should make sure to tell his employees what they need to know. He does not leave it to them to "read his mind" or to "pick up" the necessary facts. He sees to it that they are promptly and accurately informed of anything relevant to their work.

2. The manager should dispense his communications in small doses, for most people can absorb only a limited amount of information at one time. Long, involved communications are seldom read or listened to, and if they are, they are rarely digested. Only a few important points should be communicated at a time.

3. The manager should learn to phrase his communications in simple, direct style. His employees are usually not so well educated or experienced as he. Even if they are, they are more likely to perceive the intended message correctly if it is phrased in the most straightforward manner.

USING SIMPLE LANGUAGE On this last point, individuals differ widely in ability. Some succeed in making themselves relatively easy to understand; others make the task unbearably difficult. Research workers in language and psychology have studied this problem in some detail. The results of one study are described in *The Art of Plain Talk* by Rudolf Flesch (1946). Flesch has analyzed those elements of language expression which, in general, make for ease of reading and comprehension:

Number of words in a sentence. The shorter the sentence, the more easily it is comprehended.

Number of syllables in a word. The shorter the words—as measured by syllables but not necessarily letters—the easier they are to understand.

Number of personal words and sentences. The greater the percentage of personal words and/or personal sentences, as distinguished from impersonal or abstract constructions, the more comprehensible the language.

Flesch has combined these elements into an index which anyone can compute by following his rules (Flesch, 1946, 1954). The index is a fairly good measure, although not a perfect one, of the relative difficulty of written or spoken language. Flesch gives many examples of good versus poor communication as judged by his index. Here is one almost unintelligible piece of legal prose:

Ultimate consumer means a person or group of persons, generally constituting a domestic household, who purchase eggs generally at the individual stores of retailers or purchase and receive deliveries of eggs at a place of abode of the individual or domestic household from producers or retail route sellers and who use such eggs for their consumption as food.

Flesch comments:

That's a lot of words; let's try to cut down on them. Let's say just "people" instead of "a person or group of persons." Then let's leave out all those clauses with the word "generally" in them (they don't belong in a definition anyway); then let's say "eat" instead of "use for consumption as food." Now let's see what we have:

Ultimate consumers are people who buy eggs to eat them. (Flesch, 1946, page 170.)

Note how well Flesch followed his own precepts in explaining how the communication could be made more comprehensible.

Work Performance

Everything we have said up to this point has a bearing on the willingness of people to work and the likelihood that they will work effectively. In this section, we shall focus on the specific question of efficiency in work as it has been studied by psychologists over the years. We shall discuss the principal factors that affect the amount and quality of the work an employee does.

Personnel selection To get a job done well, choose the right person to do it. This is the area in which psychologists first contributed to industrial problems. Their work began, as is often the case, with problems posed by war. They were given the task in World War I of selecting suitable personnel for the Army from those made available by the draft. The tests they developed for this purpose proved useful in industry after the war was over (see Chapter 10). Once psychologists were involved in personnel selection, their research on methods of doing it got well under way in the 1920s. Since then, an elaborate science of personnel selection has been developed.

Since employers have been selecting employees for centuries and scientific methods have been available for only a few decades, it is natural that present-day methods of selection are a mixture of opinions and facts. Some of the facts are based on long employment experience and some on modern scientific research.

APPLICATION BLANKS The most generally used source of information about the characteristics of a job applicant is the application blank. This may be made out by the applicant or by someone in an employment office who asks the applicant questions and records the answers on the blank. When used wisely, it is by far the simplest method of obtaining *some* of the desired information about the worker, such as age, sex, education, and most recent employment. Application blanks, however, are frequently loaded with items that have no relevancy to the job concerned, such as birthplace, height, weight, and number of brothers and sisters. Application blanks, moreover, do not enable the employer to appraise the *quality* of such things as education and previous employment. Some applicants may have had considerable education and work experience, but may not have profited from them as much as they should have. So the application blank has its limitations.

Because the application blank is used so widely in selecting employees, a job applicant should always be prepared to supply certain standard information that it may require. Even the best of memories may not be able to cope with all the questions on the blank. So it is an excellent idea to list in advance the items that it may include, such as the beginning and ending dates of employment, name of supervisor, name of position held, and salaries received. Table 16.2, on the next page, is a composite of many typical application blanks.

Name	Dates of employment	Business and evening schools:
Address	Salary	Major course
Birthplace	Title of your job	College:
Age	Brief description of work	Major course
Height	Supervisor	Degree received
Weight	Personal references:	Special abilities
Sex	Name	Honors received or offices held
Health	Address	Membership in organizations, societies, etc.
Physical defects	How long known and in what capacity	Hobbies
Father's occupation	Occupation	Places traveled
Number of brothers and sisters	Education:	Reason for wanting a job with company
Most recent employment:	Grade school:	Date available for work
Employer	Name	
Address	Years	
	High school:	
	Major course	

Table 16.2 *Some information often requested on the application blank.*

INTERVIEWS A second timeworn device is the employment interview. A survey of personnel selection practices in 325 prominent industrial concerns showed that 96 percent of them included an interview (Spriegel and Wallace, 1948).

Despite its widespread use, the interview is often not so good a selection device as employers may think (see the related discussion in Chapter 10). One classic psychological study illustrates what can happen under some circumstances (Hollingworth, 1929).

Twelve sales managers interviewed 57 applicants for an actual job under realistic yet controlled conditions. The sales managers were experienced interviewers because their regular positions required frequent interviewing, but they were not *trained.* They were allowed to conduct the interviews as they saw fit. They were required to rank the applicants in order of desirability for the job, and when the interviewing was completed, their rankings were collected and compared. The results, some of which are given in Table 16.3, show very little agreement. Applicant A was ranked sixth by one interviewer and fifty-sixth by another. Applicant B was ranked as the best man by one interviewer and the worst by another.

These results are fairly typical of many studies; there is often little agreement among interviewers (Uhrbrock, 1948; Yonge, 1956). If the interview is to serve effectively as a selection method, certain precautions must be taken. Three factors can make the difference between good interviewing and practically worthless interviewing:

1. The interviewer should have a thorough knowledge of the job to be filled.
2. He should acquire good technique. This is usually somewhat nondirective (see Chapter 15); he must draw out the applicant rather than ask direct questions. On the other hand, he must be able to keep the

Table 16.3 *Interviewers often disagree. Twelve sales managers interviewed 57 applicants, then ranked them for suitability for the job. These are the ranks assigned to three applicants.*

Source: Hollingworth, 1929.

	Interviewer											
Applicant	1	2	3	4	5	6	7	8	9	10	11	12
A	33	46	6	56	26	32	12	38	23	22	22	9
B	53	10	6	21	16	9	20	2	57	28	1	26
C	43	11	13	11	37	40	36	46	25	15	29	1

interview on the track, and by the time he completes it he must know the answers to a predetermined list of questions.

3. He should be carefully selected for the task. Some people cannot put applicants at ease or establish rapport with them; others are simply poor judges of people under any circumstances.

If these important conditions are met, the interview can be a valuable aid in selection (Ghiselli and Brown, 1955).

LETTERS OF RECOMMENDATION The letter of recommendation, like the application blank and interview, is a traditional technique, particularly in selecting students for colleges and professional schools and in selecting clerical, white-collar, and professional personnel.

Though widely used, the letter of recommendation has the same limitations as the application and interview, and a few others as well. The writer of the letter is usually a busy person who tosses them off as one of many chores in a day's work. He may not know very much about the job the applicant wants or about the standards of performance required. He is inclined to be lenient in his evaluation, because the applicant will be working for *someone else.* Since he is often asked to write the letter because he is a high-ranking figure, he may not know very much about the applicant. Finally, the words that are used to describe such traits as honesty, reliability, and initiative are vague and mean different things to different people. It is difficult to use them in a way that discriminates between well-qualified and unqualified applicants.

Users of recommendations have taken steps to remedy some of their shortcomings. The "letter" now often includes a checklist of traits on which the recommender is asked to rate the applicant. This has the advantages of brevity and of obtaining ratings that can be compared for different applicants. It has the disadvantages, however, of being stereotyped, of permitting the recommender to omit important information, and of encouraging leniency in rating. To offset these limitations, recommendation blanks that call for ratings on traits also often ask the recommender to make comments freely, as he would in a letter. Even so, the recommendation is seldom a highly reliable source of information for selecting employees.

TRADE TESTS Applications, interviews, and recommendations are the three most common sources of information used in selecting employees, especially for the better-paying occupations. The benefits of scientific tests are not so widely exploited as they might be, but they are being used more and more each year for all sorts of occupations from the

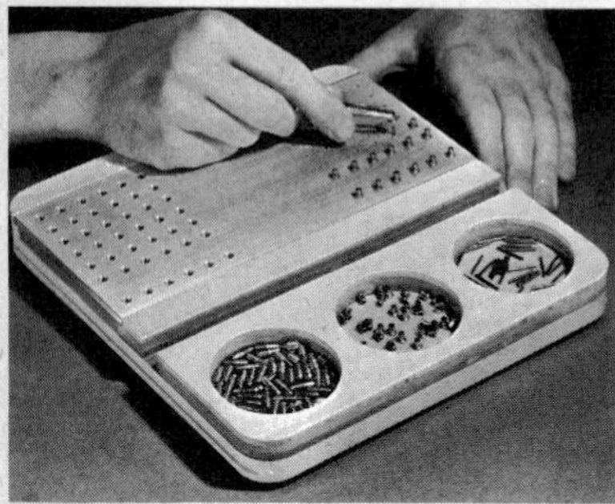

Figure 16.3 *Examples of vocational-aptitude tests. Left, the Crawford Small Parts Dexterity Test. In Part I (top) the subject, working as rapidly as possible, inserts small pins in close-fitting holes and places small collars over the pins. In Part II (bottom) he puts small screws in threaded holes and screws them down until they drop through. Right, The Minnesota Spatial Relations Test. Here the task is to place the forms correctly in the various spaces, again as rapidly as possible. (Left, The Psychological Corporation. Right, American Guidance Service, Inc.; YMCA Counseling and Testing Service, New York; Susan Johns.)*

semiskilled to the executive classes. Of the many tests which are available, the two kinds that have proved most valid are the trade tests and the aptitude tests.

A trade test is an achievement test; it measures, or attempts to measure, just how good a person is at his trade. It is usually given orally by an employment interviewer, but it may be administered as a pencil-and-paper test. Commonly it consists of a few items that correlate well with degree of knowledge and experience in a particular job. Of the large number of trade tests available today, many were constructed by expert job analysts in the U.S. Employment Service as part of a program to provide a relatively complete array of tests.

Some of the questions on a trade test require definitions. A carpenter, for example, may be asked, "What do you mean by a shore?" (Answer: An upright brace.) Some deal with methods used in the trade. A plumber may be asked, "What are the most commonly used methods of testing plumbing systems?" (Answer: Air, water, smoke, peppermint.) Other questions deal with use, procedures, location, names, purpose, and number. An example of a number question is, "How many jaws has a universal chuck?" (Answer: Three.)

Questions and tests of this type have been prepared, standardized, and validated for most of the common trades. They usually have a high validity in that they distinguish well between the different levels of accomplishment within the trade: the expert, who has had long experience;

DIFFERENT OCCUPATIONAL GROUPS SHOW DIFFERENT PATTERNS OF ABILITY

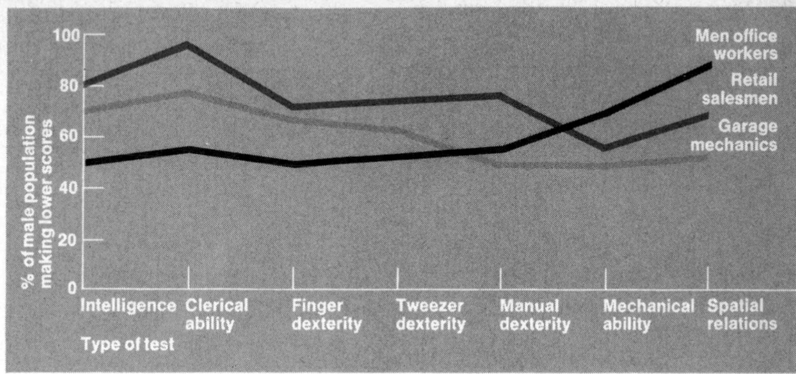

Figure 16.4 *Profiles of abilities (job psychographs) for three occupations. The scale is a centile scale based upon a standard sample of men drawn from all occupational levels. The scores for each occupational group are average scores translated into the general centile scale. Thus the average male office worker is at the 80th centile of the general population in intelligence, and the average garage mechanic stands at about the 80th centile of the general population in spatial-relations ability. (After Ghiselli and Brown, 1955.)*

the apprentice, who is in the process of learning the trade; and the related worker, who by working with or around experts and apprentices has picked up a limited knowledge of it.

APTITUDE TESTS We have already described aptitude tests in Chapter 10. They can be used both to advise a person about his vocational abilities and to help the employer determine who is best suited for his jobs (see Figure 16.3).

The employer is faced with the problem of deciding which of hundreds of possible aptitude tests is most valid for a particular job. To do that he must consider the characteristics essential for persons doing the work. This problem has been met by the construction of *psychographs.*

Two kinds of psychographs are job psychographs and individual psychographs. *Job psychographs,* illustrated in Figure 16.4, show the traits and abilities required on a job or a family of jobs. They are drawn up in terms of percentages of the population. The amount of a trait or ability required in a job is defined by the percentile ranks of workers in that job. To make this kind of representation as simple as possible, the U.S. Employment Service has distinguished three grades of abilities. The A grade is the amount possessed by only the upper 2 percent of the population; the B grade, the amount possessed by the next 28 percent; and the C grade, the amount possessed by the remaining 70 percent.

Quite a few occupations have been investigated to determine whether or not a particular pattern of abilities can be distinguished for each one. In Figure 16.4 we see the profiles of three occupations: office clerk, garage mechanic, and retail salesman. The centiles on the psychograph are based upon a standard sample of men drawn from all occupational levels. Clerks seem to score higher than the average person on tests of intelligence, clerical ability, and manual dexterity, but they are about average in mechanical ability. Contrast this score with that of the garage mechanic.

To select an employee, one must know whether an applicant's abilities correspond with those on the profile, or job psychograph, of required abilities. This means that some way must be found to construct

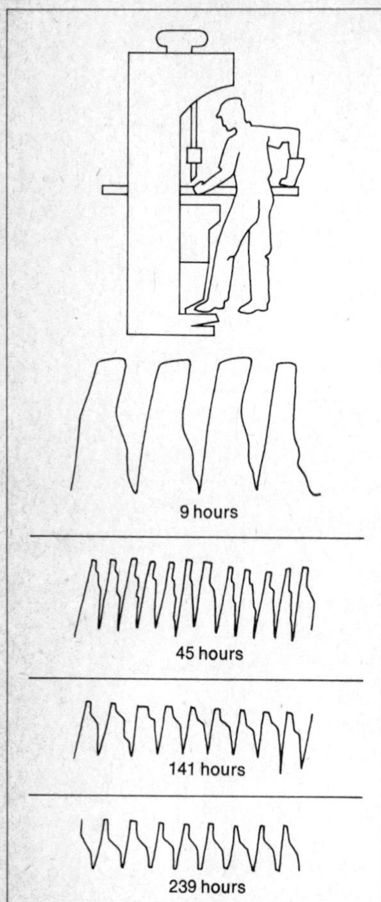

KNOWLEDGE OF RESULTS AIDS TRAINING

Figure 16.5 *The records are of foot-action patterns in the operation of a disk-cutting machine. The person being trained has the record of an experienced operator as a guide and attempts to duplicate the record. Notice the great improvement in the course of 239 hours of supervised training. (After Lindahl, 1945.)*

an *individual psychograph* for the applicant and match it with the job psychograph. In some circumstances, this can be done by rating him on the basis of information obtained from the application blank, interview, and recommendation. But it is better done with tests selected to measure the required abilities. This can be done by picking those tests, from the hundreds available, that have proved through past research to measure the particular aptitudes indicated by the job psychograph to be most important for success in the job.

VALIDITY IN SELECTION Whatever method or combination of methods is used to select employees, the validity of the selection procedure is always a problem (see Chapter 9). In the practical world, it may often prove too expensive or may require too much research to determine whether one's selection procedures are valid. Nevertheless, it must be recognized that one can be sure of validity only when he has properly followed the necessary procedures for predicting a criterion with a particular population (see page 312). Anything less is risky. Sometimes one can make a good guess from knowing that the procedures have proved valid in a seemingly similar set of circumstances. Research experience, however, indicates that procedures are not necessarily valid simply because they look valid to the employer or to a psychologist. It is best, therefore, to be cautious and to make strenuous efforts to measure the actual validity of the procedures used in selecting employees.

Training Once an employee has been selected for a job, no matter what his qualifications, he always needs some training before he becomes proficient. This training is ordinarily given by his immediate supervisor. The most important part of the training, of course, occurs during the first few weeks that an employee is on the job, but it goes on after that, month in and month out. Whether he learns his job slowly or rapidly, correctly or incorrectly, and whether he keeps up as the technology of the work changes, depend very much on the skill of the supervisor as a teacher.

Perhaps the main principle a supervisor should keep in mind—and often does not—is that learning proceeds best when a person has knowledge of results (Figure 16.5). To know what he should be doing and to correct his mistakes, the trainee should know what he has just done and whether it is right or wrong. This point has been stressed in Chapter 4 on human learning.

In his role as trainer the supervisor should remember several other principles drawn from the psychology of learning:

1. In general, guidance is much more effective early in learning than later; it is better to show somebody how to do things right in the first place than it is to wait until after he has learned bad habits.
2. People usually master one thing at a time better than they master many things at a time. Training should be limited to a reasonable number of tasks and to a reasonable degree of complexity in any one period.
3. Transfer of training is a powerful ally. When a person has learned one task, that is the time to show him other similar tasks, or other tasks

that involve the same principle. In this way the teacher can capitalize on positive transfer and avoid negative transfer (see Chapter 4).

Work motivation Assuming that a person has been carefully selected and trained for a job, how well he performs will hinge largely on his motivation. We might suppose that if he likes his job—has high job satisfaction—he will be motivated to perform. But this is not necessarily true; in fact, correlations between job satisfaction and performance are often low (Bass, 1965). In other words, people who don't like to work are frequently satisfied with jobs in which high performance is not required. Besides satisfaction, there must be motivation to work in the particular job.

One factor in motivation is whether or not the employee is task-oriented. Some people, more than others, like to "get things done." This desire, a variety of the achievement need, develops through learning: at home and at school the person has been rewarded for jobs well done. On the other hand, one of the reasons why the "disadvantaged" are often labeled unemployable is that they have not acquired this kind of work motivation.

Aside from intrinsic work motivation, several external factors influence work performance. One, as we have seen, is the attitude of the employee toward his employer. If he feels that the employer is concerned with his welfare, and if he feels that he is an active participant in achieving the company's goals, he is more highly motivated to work.

Another factor is the establishment of performance goals. When imposed by management, these may take the form of intensely unpopular quotas; but if the company goals become the employee's goals so that he wants a lot of work done, he is more likely to do it and like it, too. One procedure conducive to this motivation is to break the work load into small lots—to batch it. Most people work harder when they are close to a goal than when it is far off. (This principle, which also applies to animals in mazes, is known as the *goal gradient*.)

The inherent interest of the work is also a powerful motivator. This depends not only on the job but on the worker; what is boring and repetitive to one person may seem interesting to another. To improve efficiency, however, there has been a tendency to narrow jobs so much that they become dull for the people who do them. Bored workers do not perform well and thus defeat the goal of increased efficiency through specialization. Enlightened management is moving toward *job enlargement*. This is deliberate variation or rotation of a job in order to make it more interesting, as in the following example (Davis, 1957):

For years a hospital appliance had been assembled by nine workers, each doing a specific task, spaced along a conveyorized assembly line. The first step in the study was to remove the conveyor belt. Production dropped precipitously, but then recovered so that the overall loss for a period of two weeks was only 10 percent. In the next stage of the study the entire job was redesigned: each worker performed all nine tasks and so made the whole product himself. With this change, production did not fall; instead it gradually returned toward the quantity previously produced on the assembly line. More important, the quality of the work

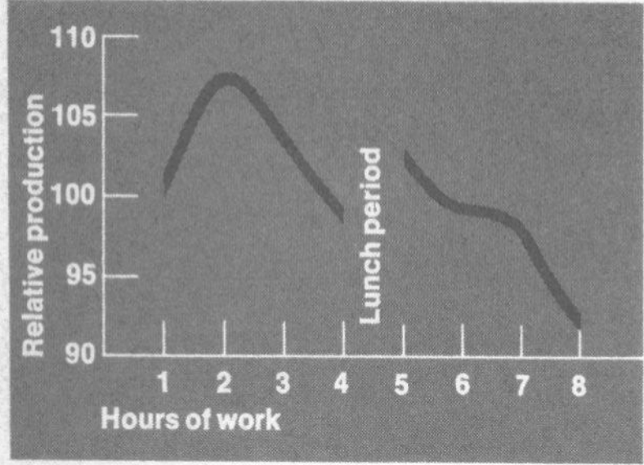

THE TYPICAL WORK CURVE PEAKS AROUND MIDMORNING

Figure 16.6 *A typical work curve for heavy handwork. It begins at the end of the first hour and continues to the end of the eighth hour, with an hour off for lunch. The figures have been adjusted so that 100 stands for the average rate of production for the 8-hour day.*

improved enormously, with rejects decreasing to one-fourth their original total.

Other studies of job enlargement show widely varying results, both in production and in job satisfaction (Hinrichs, 1970). Production and satisfaction may go up; both may go down; or one may go up and another down. Some workers, especially in the blue-collar ranks, prefer job specialization to job enlargement. Hence job enlargement is not a cure-all for boredom in repetitive jobs, but it is sometimes quite effective.

The work curve People seldom work at the same pace over a long period of time; work has its ups and downs. For example, you probably do not study so well at the end of a long session as you do at the beginning. And you may not study so well at the beginning as you do after you have been at it for a little while.

When we have some measure of the efficiency of work and plot our measurements against the minutes or hours of the work period, the graph that results is called a *work curve.* Work curves are somewhat different for different types of work, but ones similar to that in Figure 16.6 have been found in many industries and for many tasks.

The work curve in this figure was obtained for a job involving heavy handwork. Notice that production was slightly better than the daily average for the first hour of the day, and it improved during the second hour. During the third hour it dropped considerably, but it was still better than average. It dropped even more during the fourth hour. After the lunch period, production increased again, but then it dropped steadily for the rest of the afternoon.

The precise shape of a work curve depends on a number of factors. By studying the effect of these factors on the work curve, research workers have been able to analyze the curve into four components. They are waıming up, beginning spurt, end spurt, and fatigue.

WARMING UP A warm-up effect may be one of the features that appears in a work curve. It is illustrated in Figure 16.7. Most of us are familiar with the idea of warming up and deliberately make use of it. A boxer warms up before a fight by dancing around and shadow-boxing. A runner runs back and forth lightly. Football players run a ball before going into a game. In these cases, the athlete warms up before he enters the game because he knows that he will not be at his top performance if he does not.

Warming up takes place in other types of activity, even in intellectual occupations such as studying for an examination or writing a term paper. When you first start to work, you are poorly organized; you are not really set for the job, and perhaps you fidget or even get up and walk around. The warming-up period may take longer for some people than for others, and it may take longer for some activities than for others. But warming up is of value in almost every type of activity.

Referring back to Figure 16.6, we can see that warming up accounts for the fact that production is greater during the second hour than the first. If the warming up is very slow, the work curve may rise throughout the whole morning period. If it is very fast, it may be over in the first few

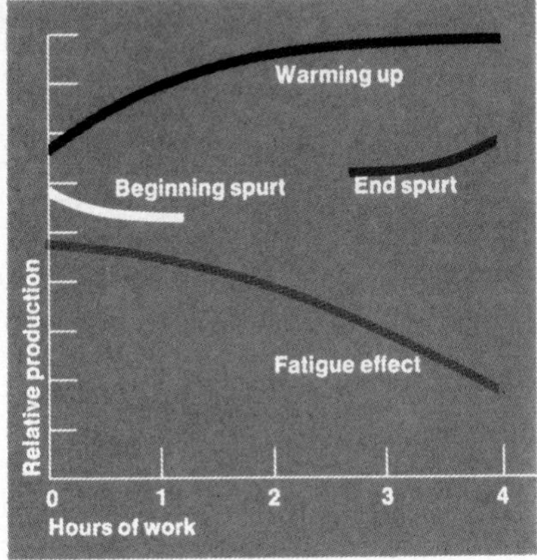

A WORK CURVE CAN BE ANALYZED INTO FOUR COMPONENTS

Figure 16.7 *The shape of any particular work curve will depend on the relative importance of the various components.*

minutes and so will not have any appreciable effect on the total productivity for the first hour.

BEGINNING SPURT Another curve in Figure 16.7 illustrates the beginning spurt. This is exactly the opposite of the warming-up effect and can completely cancel it. We may start a particular job with a great deal of enthusiasm and put our full effort into it. Then we realize that the job is going on for a long time, and we slow down to a steadier pace more suitable for the long haul. After people have worked on the same job a good many times, they are less likely to show a beginning spurt. It is characteristic of a new job or activity and does not occur at all in some jobs.

END SPURT When activity is increased at the end of a job, we call it an end spurt. The end of the day brings with it an increased enthusiasm, and a final burst of energy sends production up. The end spurt is also common in athletic events. There, it probably represents the athlete's willingness to use up all the energy he has left, because he knows he need not save it anymore. A long-distance runner usually manages an extra burst of speed at the end of a run, and a boxer frequently fights most vigorously in the last round.

Occasionally the end spurt in a job is so large that it results in a peak of production for the day. When this happens, it is clear that the worker has not really been working at top effort all along. As we shall see in the discussion on fatigue, it is important to recognize the difference between what a man can do and what he is willing to do.

Effects of fatigue The most important component of a work curve is usually fatigue. This is the general downward trend throughout the whole period of work. It is on this trend that the effects of other factors such as warming up, beginning spurt, and end spurt are superimposed. Fatigue makes the efficiency of work fall far short of what one might expect by looking at the peaks of the work curve.

Because fatigue is a common word, we are inclined to think that we know what it means. Certainly we feel fatigue, and we have many words to describe this feeling—tired, weary, exhausted, spent, worn out, beat, dead. Such subjective reports of fatigue probably are the best definition that can be offered at the present time. *Fatigue* is usually (but not always) a feeling of being tired. As we shall see, there is no completely consistent way of measuring fatigue.

OUTPUT Sometimes fatigue is reflected in a decrement in performance. The decrement may be measured either by a decreased *output* of work, when the work is primarily physical, or by increased *errors.* Decreased output is the usual decrement. If a person is shoveling coal, he shovels less coal when he is fatigued than when he is not. If he is typing, he usually types fewer words per minute when he is tired than when he is rested. Here we are talking about the amount of work accomplished, and it is easy to measure. We can weigh the coal shoveled or count the number of words typed. When output can be measured, our first attempt to measure fatigue is always in terms of the amount of work done.

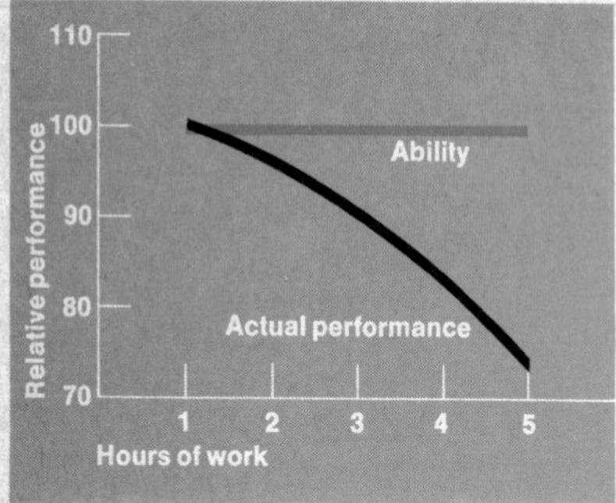

FATIGUE MAY REDUCE MOTIVATION RATHER THAN ABILITY

Figure 16.8 *Tests may tell us that a worker's ability has not changed during the course of the working period; the fact that his actual performance has declined indicates a change in his motivation.*

Typically, the amount at first drops slowly, if at all. Then it drops faster and faster, as shown in Figure 16.7. If the work is kept up long enough, fatigue eventually becomes so great that no work can be done, and we say the person is completely exhausted.

ERRORS In psychomotor work such as typewriting or assembling—work which involves skill, speed, or accuracy, as distinguished from physical work such as shoveling snow—there frequently is no decrement in amount of work done as fatigue increases. Sometimes this is because the output cannot be measured. Studying for an examination is an activity that can hardly be measured in terms of amount. At other times, the physical effort involved in the work is so slight that no change in amount occurs. In such cases, however, a measurement of errors frequently reveals fatigue when a measurement of amount does not. For example, when a person is receiving telegraphic code, his fatigue is reflected in an increase in the number of errors.

In one study, telegraphers made three to four times as many errors in the third hour of receiving code as they did in the first (Mackworth, 1950). In a study of typing errors, the time required to type successive lines was measured, and although the time required per line (a measure of amount of work) went up at first, it later went back down (Robinson and Bills, 1926). An analysis of the errors made, however, showed that the number of errors per line continued to increase long after the time per line leveled off.

Whether fatigue shows up as increased *time* taken to do a certain amount of work or as increased *errors* depends in part on the attitude or set of the worker. If he has been instructed to work for accuracy, he can do so over a long period of time. Then as he becomes more and more fatigued, he must slow down in order to keep from making errors. If he has been instructed to work primarily for speed, he may continue to work at the same rate for long periods but will make more and more errors.

Thus we must be careful, in looking for the effects of fatigue, to examine all possible changes in performance. If we measure one thing and neglect another, we may find that there is no change in what we are measuring. The change may take place instead in some aspect of performance that we fail to measure. This is especially true when the worker knows what is going to be measured, for then he strives to keep his performance up in that respect. But if he is really fatigued, his work will deteriorate in some other way.

PHYSIOLOGICAL EFFECTS Fatigue may be reflected in physiological performance. Muscle tension may increase; so may heart rate, blood pressure, and other measures of exertion. The amount of oxygen required to do a given amount of work may also increase. Hence physiological measures of these changes may indicate fatigue when there is little or no evidence in the person's behavior.

FATIGUE AS A CHANGE IN MOTIVATION Suppose that you observe men at work over a long period until their production steadily declines. You then have clear evidence of fatigue. Suppose that you now stop the men

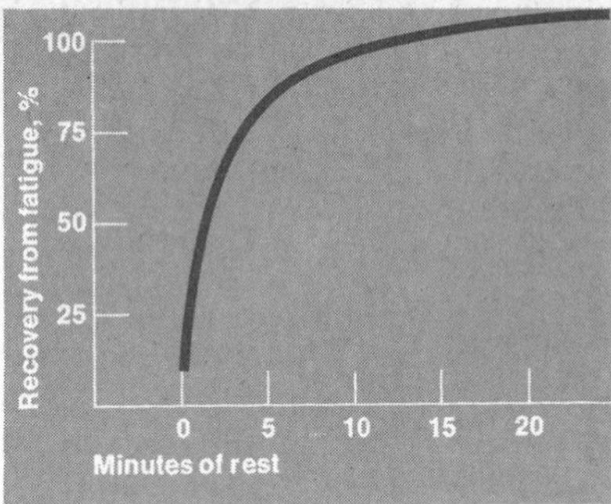

RECOVERY FROM FATIGUE IS MOST RAPID DURING THE FIRST FEW MINUTES OF REST

Figure 16.9 *These are the results of a test for recovery from fatigue. Subjects lifted a weight with their fingers until they were so tired they could no longer lift it. Then, after various periods of rest, they were required to lift the weight again. The curve shows how high, relative to first lifting, they could lift the weight after rest. (After Manzer, 1927.)*

and give them some tests of ability. You may find that their ability to perform on these tests is as good after many hours of work as it was when they were fresh. You may also find that their work is being done with no loss in physiological efficiency. So the men are still able to work as well after many hours as when they first began, but they are actually not working so well.

What accounts for the decline in their production? You might be justified in supposing that it is due to a change in *motivation* rather than fatigue—that the men simply are not trying so hard as they might. Alternatively, you might say that to compensate for fatigue, more motivation is required. Both statements are correct. The situation is shown schematically in Figure 16.8. The curve of work output continues to drop, but the curve of ability as measured by laboratory tests does not go down. What has changed is the person's feeling of what is necessary—his willingness to work.

This effect of fatigue is common in everyday life. If you have been driving an automobile for several hours and are stopped and given a driving test, you will probably do as well as if you had not been driving for a long time. However, while you are driving, you probably change your idea of what is necessary. You are less alert, you do not slow down quite so soon when you approach an intersection, and you take more chances when you pass another car—not because you are unable to do the correct thing, but because it no longer seems quite so necessary. The term *vigilance* has been used to describe what diminishes, and it is very apt. You can do as well, but you are less vigilant.

The very nature of this effect of fatigue makes it important. If you have been digging a ditch for several hours, you are fatigued, and you know it. If you are driving a car, however, you may be more fatigued than you think, because the only effect of the fatigue, especially at first, has been to make you relax your standards of what you consider good performance. You do not drive so well because you think you do not have to; and if you have an accident because of carelessness, you are sure that you have done everything just as you should. But when you are tired, what you *think* you should do and what you *really* should do are often two different things.

Work and rest We have seen that many factors affect how we work. Fatigue, the most important, shows itself in many different ways, and we are greatly concerned with methods of preventing it and of overcoming it.

RECOVERY FROM FATIGUE Perhaps the best way of learning how to prevent or overcome fatigue is to find out just how fast we recover from it. Figure 16.9 shows the results of a classic experiment performed with university students (Manzer, 1927).

The students were required to lift a weight with their fingers, and the height to which they lifted it was measured on each trial. They continued lifting the weight until they could no longer lift it at all. Then they were given rest periods for various lengths of time, after which they lifted the weight again. The height to which they could lift it on the first trial after rest was a measure of the relative recovery from fatigue. If they still could not lift it at all, they had not recovered at all. If they could lift it as high as they had on the first trial, then the recovery from fatigue was 100 percent.

Figure 16.9 shows that recovery from fatigue is fairly rapid at first but then slows down considerably. Even after 20 minutes of rest, the students had not completely recovered from the fatigue. In fact, at the rate they were recovering, a total of 40 minutes would be required for them to get back to normal.

If the students were stopped and given rest periods before they had reached complete fatigue, recovery was much faster. For example, they might have been stopped when they were lifting the weight only 50 percent as high as they had on the first trial. In this case, recovery would be complete in a much shorter period of time. In fact, recovery from fatigue is so much faster after short periods of work than after long periods that much greater overall efficiency can be obtained with short work periods.

Suppose you have a certain amount of snow that has to be shoveled. If you start right in and keep going until you can barely lift the shovel, you will have to stop and take a rest. It will require a long rest, however, for you to recover from your fatigue and get back to work. On the other hand, if you shovel for a little while, then rest for a little while, then shovel, and so on, you never need very long rest periods, because recovery from fatigue is rapid when only a little work has been done. In this way, you can shovel steadily for a much longer period of time, and you actually can get the whole job done much sooner than if you keep shoveling until you are completely fatigued.

REST PERIODS There is a definite moral to this story: To stave off fatigue and still get work done, schedule rest periods often enough to keep from getting very tired. How often they should be and how long they should be depend on the kind of work. Heavy manual labor requires frequent and reasonably long rest periods. For sedentary work, they can be shorter and less frequent. (See the related discussion in Chapter 4 on periods of practice in learning.)

Increasing numbers of industrial firms have applied these principles by providing for regular rest periods throughout the workday. They have learned by experience as well as experiment that rest periods allay fatigue and increase productivity. In other words, necessary rest is not time lost but work gained. As a practical matter, however, an employer may not know how long to make the periods and when to schedule them. Usually, periods of 10 to 15 minutes prove beneficial. By studying production records carefully, it is possible to schedule the periods just before production tends to fall off. In the case of clerical and sedentary workers, one break about midmorning and another about midafternoon are usually effective.

LENGTH OF THE WORKDAY AND WORKWEEK Another factor in work efficiency is the length of the working day. The facts of this matter are very interesting. Many people assume that if we want to get more from a worker, the thing to do is to increase the number of hours per day or per week that he works. It has become increasingly clear, however, that there is a real limit to the number of hours most people can work in a day or week and still work with reasonable efficiency. Perhaps it is obvious that a man becomes less efficient *per hour* if he works 10 hours a day than if he works 8 hours. What was not realized for a long time, however, is that he can become so much less efficient that the total work done in a 10-hour day is less than the total done in an 8-hour day.

A number of studies demonstrate both points (Ghiselli and Brown, 1955). If maximum production per hour is what we want, then a workweek between 36 and 44 hours is best. But if we want the maximum production per workweek, a workweek between 48 and 54 hours is best. (This fact was discovered during World War II, when workers were in short supply and maximum production was urgently needed.) The reason for this difference is that the hourly efficiency drops when the workweek is increased from 40 to 50 hours, but the drop in efficiency is not large enough to offset the greater number of hours. If, however, the workweek is increased beyond this point, then the drop in hourly efficiency is so large that it completely offsets the increased number of hours.

Engineering for Human Use

In this technological age, another aspect of the adjustment of people to their work must be considered—their relationship to machines. Machines are taking over countless tasks formerly done by people, as well as doing things that were never before possible. It takes people, however, to run these machines, and the machines in turn control people's behavior. The net result is that people are doing more and more of their work with or through machines. They must somehow "get along" with machines, and do it well, in order to work safely and efficiently and to make machines do what they are intended for.

Man-machine problems This relationship of man to machines is generating new problems—problems of matching men and machines. One set of problems, which we have already mentioned, concerns selecting and training people for operating machines. Another set of problems concerns the design of machines for human use—designing them so that the man together with the machine gets the job done (see Figure 16.10). The field of knowledge concerned with the solution of these problems has various names. One is *human engineering*, but this is often expanded to *human-factors engineering* in order to make clearer what is meant. Such engineering involves a number of disciplines; the one of interest here is *engineering psychology*. This is a rapidly growing field of psychology, mostly experimental psychology, applied to problems of engineering design.

During World War II, wartime demands brought psychologists into contact with engineering problems (Chapanis et al., 1949). Today most of the larger industries concerned with designing complex systems, such as airplanes, rockets, communication systems, computers, and the like, employ engineering psychologists as members of their teams of engineers charged with designing such systems.

The operation of machines may involve various kinds of work—physical, psychomotor, or mental. Typically, it falls into the psychomotor class. There are two general ways to measure performance in such tasks: errors and amount of work. When a man-machine combination fails to perform effectively, the failure may be due to errors made by the operator or to his being overloaded with more work than he can do. These two factors interact, of course. By slowing down, a man usually can be more accurate; by speeding up, he usually can handle a larger load of work but at the sacrifice of accuracy. Hence the two factors and their interaction are the problems that concern the engineering psychologist. He attempts to design, or redesign, machines in such a way as to minimize errors and maximize output. The relative importance of each depends on the machine and its purpose.

The work of engineering psychology can also be divided in another way, into displays and controls. Man may be regarded as a component in a man-machine system. As such, he receives "inputs" from the machine component as well as from his physical environment. In other words, he receives information through his senses. Such information is presented to him through some kind of *display*. On the other hand, his "output" consists of things he does to and with the machine to control its behavior. The "things" he uses for this purpose are *controls*. Thus most of the problems the engineering psychologist works with involve either displays or controls or both.

Man compared with machines How does man compare with machines in ability to perform different tasks?

SENSING Man as a sensor is restricted in the range of the spectrum of light or sound to which he responds, whereas machines can be built to sense signals—infrared energy, for example—of which man is completely unaware. On the other hand, human sensitivity to many forms of physical energy is exceedingly acute, often better than that of sensing devices. Moreover, man's senses operate through a much wider range of intensities, giving good performance for very weak as well as very strong stimuli, as compared with sensing devices. It is important, however, to realize that one sense may be much better for assimilating a particular kind of information—for example, the eye is far superior to the ear in handling spatial information—and this fact may determine whether one should use a visual or an auditory display.

DATA PROCESSING In processing data (remembering and interpreting information), man is superior to machines in that he does not need extensive programming, as a computer does, for example. He is more flexible and can deal with unforeseen situations. He can exercise judgment and quickly recall facts and methods of solving problems. However, machines are superior to men in the amount of detailed information they can store or remember, in the speed and accuracy with which they can arrive at answers, in sorting and classifying data, in giving reliable results in routine operations, and in working longer at high speed without being subject to fatigue, prejudice, or other factors that distort judgment and decision.

Figure 16.10 *A problem in human engineering: this instrument panel has been designed so as not to overload the flight crew. Psychologists specializing in the field of human engineering rearrange and simplify levers, knobs, and dials so that the man who uses them can do his job more easily, more efficiently, and more safely. (Pan American World Airlines, Inc.)*

CONTROLLING When it comes to controlling things, man is generally inferior to machines, and the controls he uses must be designed to take his limitations into account. He is relatively weak and slow. He is limited in the kind of movements he can make and in the number of controls he can operate simultaneously or in quick succession. The amount of time he can work without fatigue or wavering of attention is relatively short. For these reasons, the tasks assigned to human control must be carefully chosen and designed.

Handbooks are available that give specific data for determining how well human beings can perform on various sensing, judging, and control tasks (Morgan et al., 1963). When the data at his command do not answer specific questions, the engineering psychologist runs tests and experiments to obtain the answers. Then, together with other members of the design team, he draws up an overall design of the man-machine system that roughly prescribes what is expected of the man and of the machine. It serves as a guide to the development of specific components of the system.

After he knows at least approximately what the man will be expected to do in a man-machine system, the engineering psychologist can concentrate on the design of the displays and controls involved in the man's tasks. He must obtain a complete job description of the man's duties, specified in terms of the information needed (for display) and the actions that must be taken (for control). Having accomplished that, the engineering psychologist moves on to the design of the displays and controls of the system. We shall consider only displays here.

Design of displays To design the displays that a man must use in any complicated system, the engineer must consider the chance of overloading one or more of the senses. The sense that is most often overloaded is vision; after that, hearing. In the airplane cockpit shown in Figure 16.10, the visual sense obviously has plenty to do. However, this

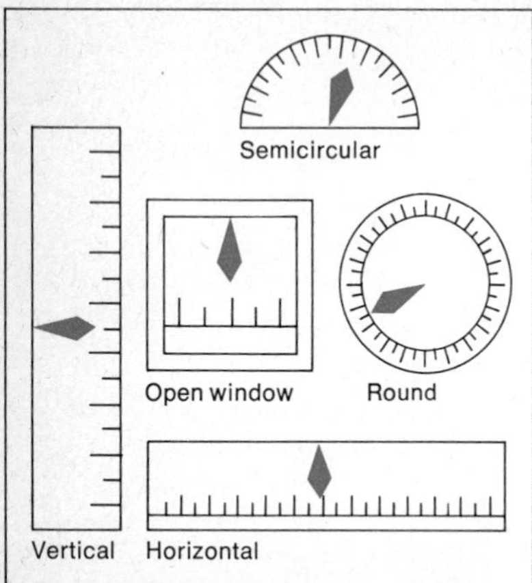

SOME DIALS ARE BETTER THAN OTHERS FOR A PARTICULAR PURPOSE

Figure 16.11 *Five different shapes used in an experiment to compare dial types. It was found that the open-window, fixed-pointer dial was read with the greatest accuracy and the vertical, moving-pointer dial with the greatest number of errors. This result was obtained under a particular set of experimental conditions and it cannot be generalized to every situation. But it shows how a designer may go about selecting the proper type of dial for a particular task. (Sleight, 1948.)*

is a scientifically designed flight deck, incorporating many principles of human engineering, including the patterning of dials (see below). Years ago, before such principles were developed and applied, many accidents or near-accidents occurred because too many dials, improperly arranged, overloaded the capacity of cockpit personnel to attend to them.

Where one sense is overloaded, the engineering psychologist can devise ways of delivering some of the information through another sense. Simple warning signals, for example, are often better conveyed as auditory signals, perhaps as buzzers.

When a decision has been made about the mode of presenting information, the next step is to work out the type of display to be used. Since most displays are visual, let us restrict ourselves to them. Any complicated man-machine situation, such as a flight deck, may contain dozens of visual displays, and in designing them the engineering psychologist must make several decisions.

PICTORIAL VERSUS SYMBOLIC DISPLAYS A *pictorial display* is one that reproduces with some realism the situation it represents. Maps, for example, are pictorial displays. In an aircraft, an artificial horizon indicator may be a pictorial display, for it pictures the position of a plane and its orientation with respect to a horizon. *Symbolic displays* are instruments that present information indirectly, usually by dials, pointers, or lights. The speedometer on a car is a symbolic display.

Symbolic displays have the advantages of being simple, versatile, compact, and above all, accurate. Pictorial displays, on the other hand, can usually be interpreted more quickly than symbolic displays, and with little or no training. To decide which type of display to use, the engineering psychologist must know what kind of people will be using it and what will be required of them.

KINDS OF INDICATORS Many interesting problems are involved in the design of pictorial displays, but symbolic displays are most frequently used, primarily because they are compact. Most practical problems, therefore, arise in connection with symbolic displays, particularly dials. In designing a symbolic display, the designer must first ask what its purpose is. In general, each display serves one of three purposes:

1. *Check-reading indicators.* A check-reading indicator tells the operator whether something is on or off, working or not working. For example, some automobiles use a red light to indicate whether oil pressure or battery charging is adequate.

2. *Qualitative indicators.* Some indicators serve the purpose of telling the operator whether things are all right, and if not, in which direction they are wrong. The temperature gauge on most automobiles is such an indicator. It does not say exactly what the temperature is, for that does not matter; but it does tell whether the car is cold, is warmed up and in the normal range, or is getting too hot.

3. *Quantitative indicators.* Some information must be relatively precise. If, for example, we are to obey posted speed limits when driving, we need to know how fast we are going. The customary speedometer gives this information quantitatively.

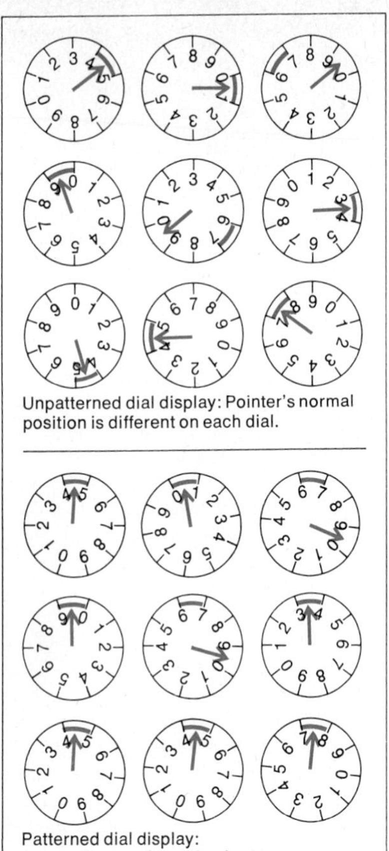

PATTERNING MAKES DIAL CHECKING MUCH EASIER

Figure 16.12 *The patterning of dials. Patterning helps the operator to see at a glance which dials are not indicating their normal readings.*

In order to avoid overloading an operator, it is important to know just what kind of indicator is necessary. If all that is required is check reading, an indicator showing more information than that should not be used. Similarly, a quantitative indicator should not be used when a qualitative one will do.

DIAL DESIGN Once the type of indicator has been chosen, the problem narrows down to the details of designing each dial for its intended purpose. This is not too difficult for check-reading or qualitative indicators, but it may be a problem for quantitative indicators. For one thing, a choice must be made between a *counter* and a *dial.* (The odometer showing accumulated mileage is a counter; the speedometer is usually a dial.) Experiments indicate that counters can generally be read more quickly and accurately than dials. On the other hand, they may be impossible to use if the operator must set them to a prescribed number or read them while their readings are changing. Hence the choice again depends on the nature of the operator's task. If the designer decides on a dial, there are many types of dials from which he can select (see Figure 16.11).

Many other problems occur in the design of dial displays, especially when the information to be delivered is complex and involves a large range of numbers. Let us consider a common problem presented by a large number of dials. In the upper part of Figure 16.12 is a display of dials as they might appear when arranged on a flight deck panel without regard to their use by people. Indeed, such displays can be found in many situations. Since each dial contains a different sort of information, the normal place of the pointer differs from dial to dial. One can see that it would be difficult and time-consuming for an operator to read each of these dials and determine whether things were all right or, if not, how wrong they were.

The task can be greatly simplified by *patterning the dial display:* orienting each dial so that the normal or usual position of a pointer is the same on every dial (Morgan et al., 1963). Only when the dial indicates something different or unusual does the pointer move away from the usual position. At a glance, the operator can see which dials are "out of line" and then read them to find out what the discrepancy means. This principle is being incorporated in airplanes and other systems that involve displays of many dials.

These are just a few of many ways in which psychology is being applied in the design of machines for human use. Sometimes the engineering psychologist does little more than employ common sense. He is then a watchdog to see that human factors are not overlooked in meeting engineering objectives. More important, he also draws on a stockpile of knowledge about human capacities and limitations and goes ahead to obtain more information through further experiments.

Comparatively, the number of engineering psychologists is not large. On a liberal count, there are only a few hundred. Several years ago, however, there were only a handful; so growth has been very rapid. Engineering psychology is encountered and utilized in many phases of modern technology.

Synopsis and summary

Many of the topics studied in earlier chapters are applicable to the problems of industrial organization. Aspects of learning, thinking, motivation, sensory perception, psychological testing, psychotherapy, and social psychology all can be useful to industry. Large companies of consulting psychologists apply basic discoveries in these branches of psychology in giving advice and assistance to business firms.

1. Man's needs can be arranged in a hierarchy from low to high: physiological needs, safety needs, social needs, egoistic needs, and self-fulfillment needs. In general, the lowest unsatisfied needs dominate behavior.
2. In Western society, physiological and safety needs are usually adequately supplied. Hence social, egoistic, and self-fulfillment needs become important motivations in work.
3. Surveys of factors in job satisfaction show that this is true. Pay is usually not the principal satisfaction; people are also concerned with security, working conditions, advancement, and group relations.
4. The goals of management include not only adequate profits, but also growth, public service, employee welfare, and good products.
5. Classical organization theory stresses the chain of command. This makes people dependent, stifles initiative, and in fact is not actually followed by employees as they do their work.
6. Gradually replacing the classical theory is a new one of integrative management. This attempts to integrate the goals of the company and those of the employee by developing self-control at all levels of organization.
7. The most common technique for training new managers is job rotation, although problem-centered group training is being increasingly used. Training programs to develop senior managers with an integrative philosophy focus on decision making and human relations. Techniques include simulation, role playing, and sensitivity training.
8. Good communication is crucial to integrative management. Managers need to communicate their instructions promptly and intelligibly and keep employees informed on matters that concern their work.
9. Traditional methods of selecting employees through application blanks, interviews, and letters of recommendation are relatively unreliable, unless precautions are taken to obtain the best results.
10. Trade tests, if properly designed and interpreted, are helpful in selecting skilled workers. Aptitude tests also can be valid in choosing many types of employees.
11. The principal factors involved in work motivation are task orientation, attitudes toward the employer, establishing realistic performance goals, and the intrinsic interest of the work.
12. Work curves that are typical of the amount of work done during the course of a day have their ups and downs. They can be analyzed into four principal components: (*a*) a warm-up effect, (*b*) a beginning spurt, (*c*) an end spurt, and (*d*) a fatigue effect.
13. Fatigue can be measured in a number of ways: (*a*) by the amount of work produced, (*b*) by errors or quality of work, (*c*) by physiological effects, and (*d*) by changes in motivation.
14. Often, when there is not a measurable effect of fatigue on volume of production, fatigue shows up as a lowered motivation for work or as a lowered standard of performance.
15. Recovery from fatigue is generally faster when the fatigue is mild than when it has become severe. Thus it is better to take short rests frequently than to take long rests infrequently.
16. If we attempt to lengthen the workday or the workweek, we find that beyond a certain point total

production declines. Consequently there is an optimum workday and workweek.

17. Engineering psychology is the field in which psychological methods and research are used to improve the design of machines so that they are better suited to the capabilities of the human operator.

Related topics in the text

Chapter 6 Motivation Since learned human motives influence both managers and workers, Chapter 6 provides an important background for the points made here.

Chapter 10 Psychological Testing Tests are widely used in the selection and evaluation of employees.

Chapter 14 Social Influences on Behavior A discussion of the influence of groups on individual behavior, a topic that is particularly relevant to organizational psychology because managers and workers spend much of their time directing and participating in groups.

Suggestions for further reading

Anastasi, A. *Fields of applied psychology.* New York: McGraw-Hill, 1964.
A text giving a fuller account of all the topics in this chapter, as well as some other aspects of applied psychology.

Bass, B. M. *Organizational psychology.* Boston: Allyn and Bacon, 1965.
A textbook that covers many of the topics in this chapter in more detail.

Chapanis, A. *The design and conduct of human engineering studies.* Baltimore: Johns Hopkins, 1959.
A readable account of the methods used in human engineering.

Flippo, E. B. *Principles of personnel management.* New York: McGraw-Hill, 1966.
A textbook covering various aspects of personnel management.

Guion, R. M. *Personnel testing.* New York: McGraw-Hill, 1965.
A basic text presenting principles of mental measurements, instruments of prediction, and applications of testing to selection and placement.

Haire, M. *Psychology in management.* (2d ed.) New York: McGraw-Hill, 1964.
A brief and interesting psychological analysis of the role of the manager and supervisor.

Leavitt, H. J. *Managerial psychology.* (2d ed.) Chicago: University of Chicago Press, 1964.
A very readable book on the principles of psychology in the management of large and small groups.

McCormick, E. J. *Human factors in engineering.* (2d ed.) New York: McGraw-Hill, 1964.
An introductory textbook in human engineering.

McGregor, D. *The professional manager.* New York: McGraw-Hill, 1967.
A brief, lively presentation of McGregor's philosophy of integrative management and some applications of it.

Schein, E. H. *Organizational psychology.* Englewood Cliffs, N.J.: Prentice-Hall, 1964. (Paperback.)
A readable textbook which treats many of the most important developments in the psychology of industry.

Smith, H. C. *Psychology of industrial behavior.* (2d ed.) New York: McGraw-Hill, 1964.
A textbook emphasizing the role of motivational and social factors in industry.

PART FIVE BIOLOGY OF BEHAVIOR

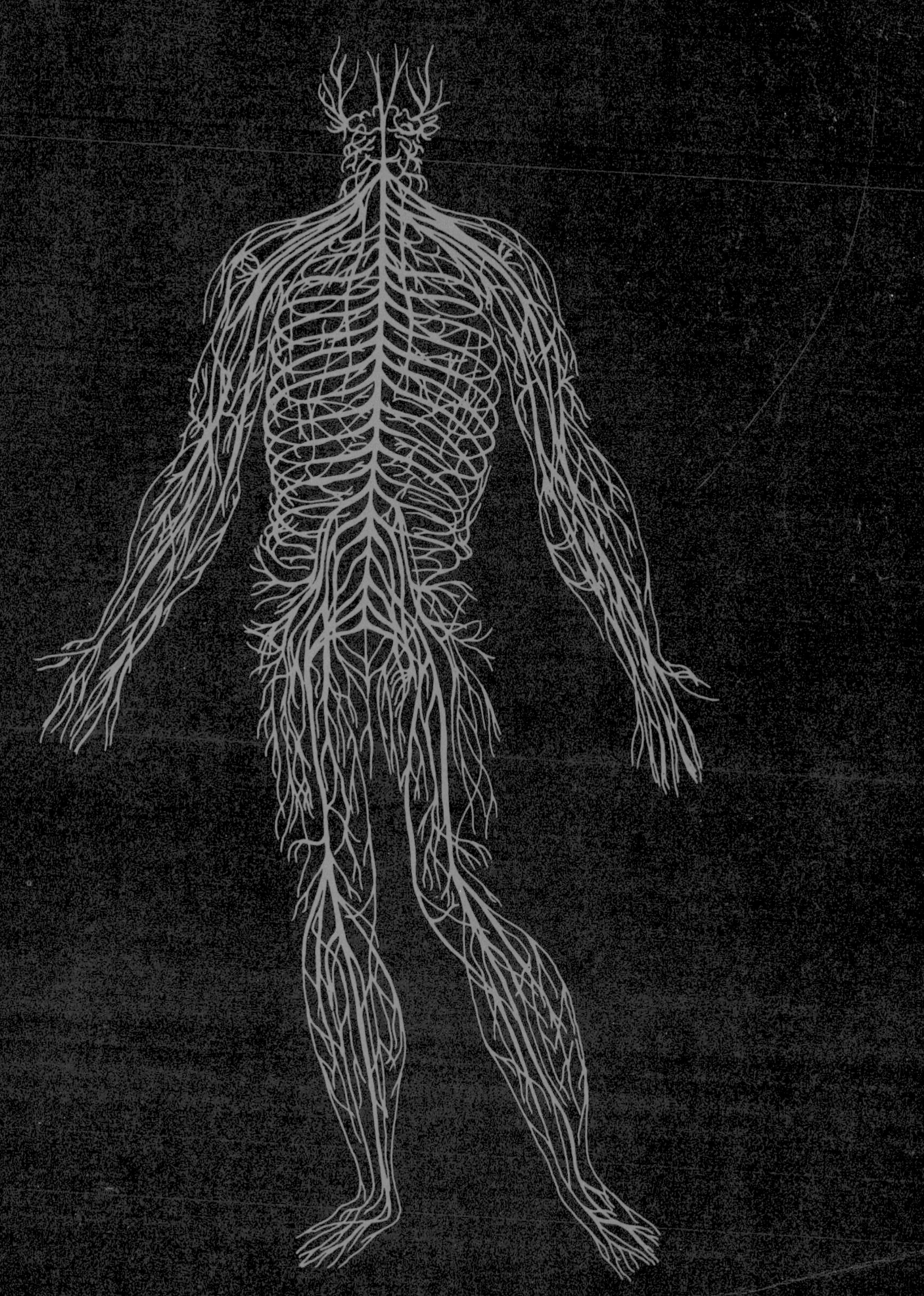

A scheme of lines and nodal points, gathered together at one end into a great ravelled knot, the brain, and at the other trailing off to a sort of stalk, the spinal cord.

C. S. Sherrington

We come now to an area that many students will be surprised to find included in psychology. It is a branch of experimental psychology that studies the relationship between physical structure, function, and biochemistry on the one hand, and behavior and experience on the other. This field and its subareas have various names. The one most commonly used is *physiological psychology.* The broader term *biological psychology,* or more simply *biopsychology,* is more accurate because it includes structures as well as functions which relate to behavior. For that reason, and because of its relative simplicity, we shall use the term *biopsychology* throughout this chapter.

Biopsychology is not the exclusive province of psychologists. Other scientists such as neurologists, psychiatrists, physiologists, anatomists, pharmacologists, and biochemists have occasion to study correlations between events in the nervous system and behavior. But biopsychology is the brain science, or neuroscience, that makes the role of the nervous system in behavior its main study.

We shall take three chapters to cover the field of biopsychology. Here in Chapter 17 we shall describe the nervous system and events that take place in it. The next two chapters consider the correlations between nervous function and the psychological events this book has already discussed. Chapter 18 covers sensory processes, and Chapter 19 deals with more complex processes such as motivation, emotion, learning, and speech.

Methods of Biopsychology

In his attempt to establish correlations between neural events and behavior, the biopsychologist must know and use the methods both of psychology and of other neurosciences. This chapter begins with a survey of the methods of the neurosciences as they are used in biopsychology. First we provide a general picture of the nervous system and how it is constructed; later we shall fill in some details.

Overview of the nervous system The basic unit of the nervous system is a cell called a *neuron.* All neurons have two parts, a *cell body* and some *fibers* leading to and going away from the cell body. Cell bodies are gathered together in clumps that have various names; for the present we shall call them *centers.* The fibers similarly are found in groups that make *pathways* through the nervous system from the sense organs on the one end to the muscles and other organs of response on the other end. Fibers leaving one set of cell bodies connect up with fibers leading into another set of cell bodies in junctions known as *synapses*. Thus, basically the nervous system consists of many centers and pathways connected at various points in synapses.

The greater part of the nervous system is enclosed in the bony case provided by the skull and backbone; this is called the *central nervous system* (CNS). It is subdivided into *brain* (in the skull) and *spinal cord* (in the backbone). Naturally the biopsychologist is most interested in the brain, because that is where the important psychological processes take place. The brain of man and higher animals is further subdivided into *cerebral cortex* and *subcortical structures*.

The part of the nervous system lying outside the skull and backbone is called the *peripheral nervous system* (PNS). It consists mostly of *sensory nerves* leading to the central nervous system and *motor nerves* emerging from it.

The nervous system functions through two basic processes: electrical and chemical. The principal electrical process is a *nerve impulse* that travels from one end of a neuron to the other. This is the means by which messages are sent through the pathways of the nervous system. Transmission of messages across synapses, however, is chemical: a substance emitted by the end of one fiber when the nerve impulse reaches it excites another nerve impulse in the fiber on the other side of the synapse. In much of the nervous system, this chemical transmission is carried out by a substance known as acetylcholine (ACh) which, after it has done its work, is quickly destroyed by enzymes known as acetylcholinesterase (AChE) and cholinesterase (ChE).

The terms we have just introduced are those you will need in what follows. Now we are ready to take a look at the way a biopsychologist studies the correlations between brain function and behavior. The methods he uses fall into four main groups: brain changes, brain damage, electrical recording, and stimulation.

Brain changes One general method is to see whether some psychological manipulation is followed by detectable changes in the brain. The manipulation may be sensory deprivation, sensory enrichment, handling and gentling, stress, or learning a habit. The changes in the brain that might conceivably occur through such experiences can be either structural or chemical. To detect structural alterations, we can measure any changes in the size or weight of the brain as a whole or in part. For example, we can measure changes in the cerebral cortex, or even in some relevant part of the cortex—say, its visual area in the case of a visual experience. To detect modifications in brain chemistry, we can look for changes in the concentrations of substances such as acetylcholine or cholinesterase known to function in synaptic transmission.

Put another way, the biopsychologist asks questions such as, "Can experience with the environment actually cause growth and chemical changes in the brain?" "If experience actually changes the brain, can we then relate the brain changes to behavior?" Such questions have been posed for hundreds of years, and we still do not have answers that apply to human beings. We do, however, have the beginnings of answers for such lower animals as the rat (Rosenzweig, 1966; Krech, et al., 1962):

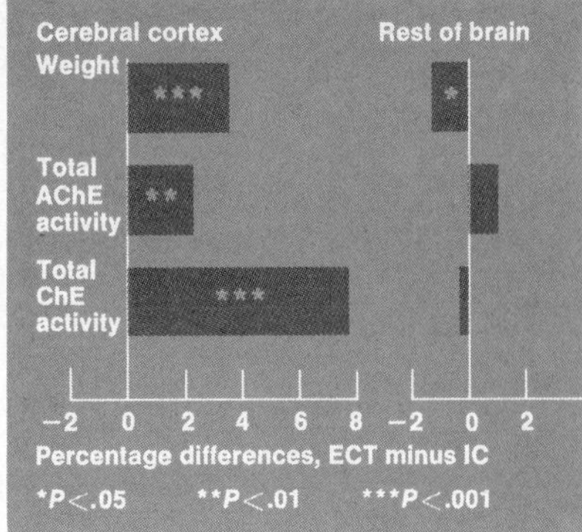

AN ENRICHED ENVIRONMENT CAN ALTER A RAT'S BRAIN STRUCTURE AND MAKE IT "SMARTER"

Figure 17.1 *Percentage differences in brain weight and brain chemical activity of rats raised in an enriched environment (ECT) and rats raised in impoverished conditions (IC). The percentage differences were calculated from pairs of littermates raised under the different conditions. ECT rats have also proved to be better than IC rats at learning complex visual-discrimination problems. The P values refer to the level of statistical significance; see Chapter 9. (Modified slightly from Rosenzweig, 1966.)*

For several years a group of biopsychologists at the University of California in Berkeley has been doing experiments in which rats raised in enriched environments (environmental complexity and training, or ECT, group) are compared with those raised in impoverished conditions (IC group). The ECT group is housed, several rats to a cage, in large cages which are full of rat "playthings"—ladders, running wheels, platforms, and boxes. These enriched-environment animals are also given training in mazes. The impoverished-environment animals, littermates of the enriched-environment animals, live alone in cages in a quiet, uniformly lit room. The animals cannot see or touch other animals.

The rats grow up in these different environments from weaning at about 25 days old to 105 days of age. Then their brains are examined for chemical activity and weighed. The chemical analysis has focused on the study of enzymes important in the process of nervous conduction: acetylcholinesterase (AChE) and cholinesterase (ChE).

Percentage differences between the enriched-environment (ECT) and impoverished-conditions (IC) littermates are shown in Figure 17.1. Weight of the cerebral cortex was relatively greater in the ECT animals, while weight of the rest of the brain was relatively less. Both AChE and ChE chemical activity increased in the cerebral cortex of the ECT animals relative to the IC littermates; no significant changes were found in chemical activity in the rest of the brain.

The results of the experiment, and many others, show that the environment can have an influence on the weight and chemical activity of the brain in developing rats. The next question is whether these brain changes are related to changes in behavior. Some data indicate that rats from the enriched environments do not differ from impoverished-environment rats in learning a simple light-dark discrimination problem (see Chapter 3). But the rats from the enriched environment with their heavier cerebral cortices are markedly better than rats from the impoverished environment in learning more complex visual-discrimination problems. Since other work has shown that the cerebral cortex is involved in an important way in the learning of the complex discriminations, this finding seems to relate the increased weight of the cerebral cortex to greater learning ability by the rats from the enriched environment. Experience with the environment, then, does cause growth and chemical changes in the brain, and these changes are related to behavior.

Destruction One of the oldest methods of studying both the structure of the nervous system and the function of its parts in behavior is to destroy some portion of it. In using this method to study the *structure* of the brain, the neuroanatomist takes advantage of the *degeneration* that occurs when only a part of a neuron is destroyed. Under appropriate conditions, it is necessary to sever only the end of a neuron's fiber to cause the whole neuron to die slowly and later to disappear. In the course of dying, distinctive changes take place in the cell body that can be seen under the microscope when an appropriate stain is used.

This fact permits neuroanatomists to trace many of the pathways in the brain. For example, when the visual area of the cerebral cortex, lying in the back of the head, is destroyed, the ends of fibers coming to it in the visual system are also destroyed. This causes the cells of which these fibers are a part to degenerate and die. By studying sections of

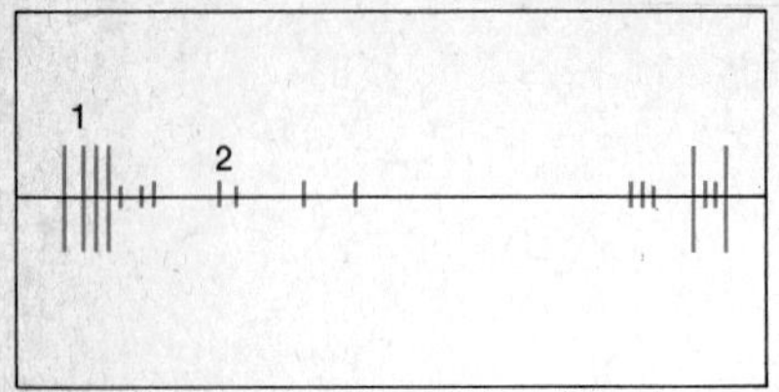

THE ACTIVITY OF SINGLE CELLS AND FIBERS CAN BE RECORDED BY MICROELECTRODES

Figure 17.2 *Record of the firing of single cells. Note that two cells seem to be contributing to the record. Large spikes apparently come from one cell, small spikes from another. (Modified from Hubel and Wiesel, 1962.)*

the brain under a microscope, the neuroanatomist can discover the arrangements of brain pathways. In this case, it turns out that the cells lie in a structure known as the *thalamus,* and they are arranged in a *topographical way,* that is, much like a map of the visual field.

With knowledge such as this provided by neuroanatomists, the biopsychologist can use the method of destruction to study, say, visual functions. He can destroy known centers of the visual system and test the subjects both before and after on a visual discrimination taught to the animal in one of the ways described in Chapter 3. Or after destroying an area, he can determine whether the animal has more than the normal difficulty in learning a particular task; or he can find out whether a task taught before the destruction is remembered. In this way he can study the role of various parts of the brain in vision, learning, memory, and other functions. Chapters 18 and 19 give examples of such experiments.

Destruction is accomplished in a number of ways. It should be noted in general that operations performed to destroy portions of an animal's brain or other organs are carried out under anesthesia, with precautions comparable to those employed in human surgery. One of the simplest and oldest methods of destruction is to cut out the tissue being studied. This method, however, has its limitations: It can cause profound bleeding that may damage neighboring areas, and it cannot be used for structures lying deep within the brain, because other tissues must be damaged to get at them. Nowadays, other techniques of destruction are often preferred. One is *thermocoagulation:* destruction of tissue by heat, which also clots blood and prevents undesirable bleeding. Another is the *electrolytic* method: destruction by passing electric current through a tissue. This method is particularly useful in pinpointing structures deep in the brain by lowering an electrode that conducts only at its tip, so that damage to other structures is negligible. Another method that is finding increasing favor is one in which certain chemicals—potassium chloride, for instance—are used to render an area temporarily nonfunctional. If done properly, this procedure has the advantage of destroying function but not structure; normal functioning later returns. So far, however, the chemical method can only be used with certain areas of the brain. Each of these techniques of tissue destruction has its place in the study of brain functions and behavior.

As we have learned more and more about the brain, particularly about its deeper and more minute structures, we have found that small areas or centers have considerable importance in certain kinds of behavior. To get at these areas, we employ the electrolytic method mentioned above along with a *stereotaxic instrument* to position the electrode. This instrument, coupled with an *atlas* of the brain, which gives the coordinates of all brain structures, permits exact destruction of areas as small in diameter as a millimeter or less.

Electrical recording Another method used by the biopsychologist to study the brain and behavior is to record electrical changes in the brain. As mentioned earlier, one of the main processes by which the neurons, or nerve cells, of the nervous system communicate with each other is through electrical impulses. Using various techniques, we can record

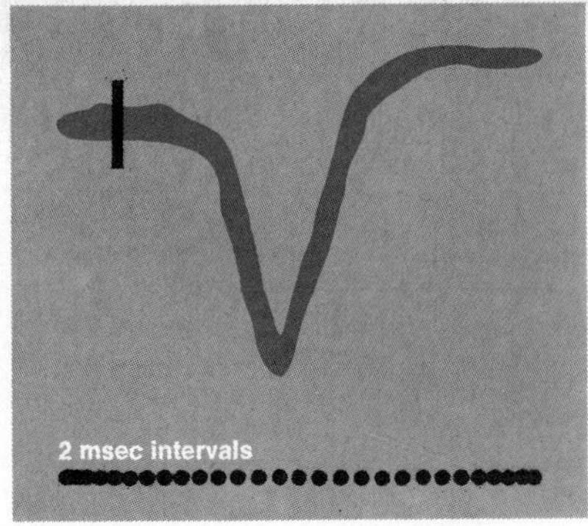

EVOKED POTENTIALS FROM THE CENTRAL NERVOUS SYSTEM CAN BE RECORDED BY LARGE ELECTRODES

Figure 17.3 *An evoked potential from the sensory cortex of a cat. The interval between each dot represents 2 milliseconds (msec); the vertical black line at the beginning of the record indicates the point at which the evoking stimulus was presented. By stimulating the sensory pathway and recording the electrical activity evoked by this at distant points in the nervous system, detailed pathways can be traced. (From Towe, 1965.)*

these impulses as they occur in single cells, or in large groups of cells that are simultaneously active. The measured electrical changes are basically voltage differences, or differences of electrical potential, and are sometimes called *potentials*.

For recording the electrical activity (often called *firing*) of single cells or fibers, very fine electrodes known as microelectrodes have been developed. Larger electrodes are required for groups of cells. In recording from groups, electrical changes can be evoked by a stimulus, in which case they are called evoked potentials. Or they can reflect the spontaneous activity of the cells, as recorded in an electroencephalogram (EEG).

MICROELECTRODE RECORDING The most refined of all electrical recording methods is the *microelectrode technique,* in which the electrode has been drawn out so finely that its tip is smaller than the diameter of a single cell body. Hence when the electrode is inserted into the nervous system, the experimenter can record electrical potentials from individual neurons. Sometimes the tip of the electrode is close to a small cluster of neurons, and their activity is recorded together on a single record. In such a case the experimenter can usually distinguish between the individual neurons because the voltages recorded from each are typical of that neuron (see Figure 17.2). By recording impulses in this way, while presenting specific stimuli either to the animal's sense organs or to other regions of its nervous system, we can study the "fine grain" of the nervous system and the responses of particular neurons to particular types of stimulation. The method has been most useful in research on sensory and perceptual mechanisms, as Chapter 18 will demonstrate. Recently, experimenters have begun to use microelectrode techniques to investigate changes in the nervous system when new responses are learned (Olds, 1969). Such studies may bring us closer to an understanding of learning and memory at the cellular level.

EVOKED POTENTIALS In the cruder method of recording *evoked potentials,* larger electrodes are used than in microelectrode recording. We place one, the active electrode, directly on or in the part of the nervous system being studied and a second electrode at some more distant, neutral point. Then we "evoke" potentials by stimulating a sense organ or sometimes by electrically stimulating a nerve or some other point in the pathway. The passage of impulses in the region near the active electrode is signaled by a change in electrical potential shown by the recording instrument (see Figure 17.3).

Electrical recording of this sort is valuable in "mapping" the nervous system. We can, for example, place an electrode on the cerebral cortex and then touch the skin at different spots. By determining which electrode placements show the greatest electrical activity when a particular skin spot is stimulated, we can roughly establish the limits of the skin sensory area of the cortex. Incidentally, there are several such skin "maps" on the cortices of most animals. Such maps have also been made for several of the other senses, and multiple maps or representations seem to be the rule rather than the exception.

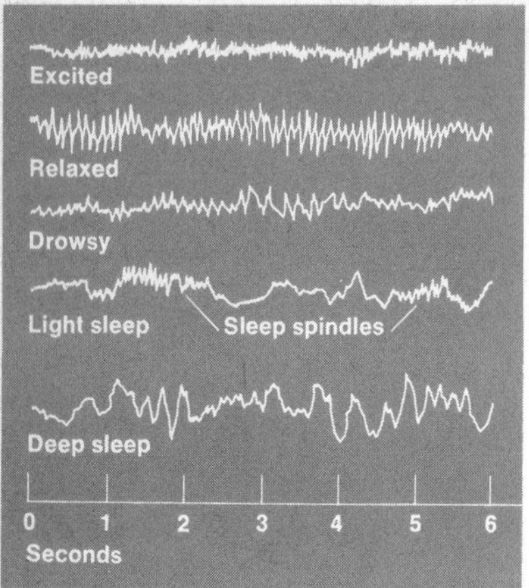

THE ELECTRICAL ACTIVITY OF THE BRAIN IS DIFFERENT IN WAKING, DROWSINESS, AND SLEEP

Figure 17.4 *Electrical activity of the human brain ("brain waves") typical of various states of alertness. (After Jasper, 1941.)*

ELECTROENCEPHALOGRAPHY Swinging from the most refined to the crudest of recording methods, we come to the technique called *electroencephalography*. In this, electrodes are attached to the skull, leaving the brain intact and untouched. We are not quite sure what is being recorded in an EEG, or electroencephalogram—whether it is the summation of millions of impulses or whether it reflects some other slowly changing electrical activity of the cells. In any event, the electroencephalograph records wavelike changes in voltage, known informally as "brain waves," varying from 1 or 2 per second to as many as 50 per second and averaging around 10 per second. (By recent international convention, cycles per second are known as hertz, or Hz, and technically these waves vary from 1 to 50 hertz.) A number of correlations have been obtained between changes in brain waves and behavior. For example, it has recently been found that the overall electrical activity of the brain is remarkable during dreaming. (Dement, 1965).

For many years it has been known that types of EEG activity are correlated with various degrees of alertness, or arousal (see Chapter 7). A few of these correlations are shown in Figure 17.4. In general, low-amplitude (voltage), high-frequency waves are associated with arousal and alertness; high-amplitude, low-frequency waves are correlated with sleep. The relaxed wakeful state is characterized by activity in which waves of moderate amplitude come at 8 to 12 cycles per second (hertz).

As a person or animal falls asleep, characteristic changes take place in the EEG; four stages of EEG activity are recorded. Stage 1 consists of a preponderance of low-amplitude, high-frequency activity mixed with some slower activity (less than 8 hertz)—see Figure 17.4. Stage 2 is characterized by bursts of high-amplitude 12 to 14 hertz waves; these bursts, called *sleep spindles,* appear against a relatively low-amplitude EEG background. Stage 3 is characterized by slow activity in the 4 to 7 and 1 to 3 hertz ranges; the 4 to 7 hertz waves predominate, but sleep spindles are also present; the amplitude of the slow activity is relatively great. Stage 4 is characterized by very slow (1 to 3 hertz) activity of high amplitude which is present more that 50 percent of the time (not shown in Figure 17.4).

Figure 17.5 diagrams the progression through these stages during a night's sleep. One of the striking things it shows about EEG stages of sleep through the night is their cyclical nature; EEG changes go from stages 1 to 4 and back again several times. Note that stage 4, the deep-sleep stage, may not be reached during the later sleep cycles: sleep later in the night tends to be lighter.

Dreaming occurs when the EEG activity has returned from stage 4 to low-amplitude, high-frequency activity. But this activity is *not* the same as that of stage 1, even though it looks somewhat like it in the EEG record. It is a new stage called the *paradoxical stage,* because the EEG activity looks very much like that of waking (low amplitude, high frequency), but the person is very deeply asleep, judging by the intensity of stimulation needed to awaken him. Periods of paradoxical sleep are shown by the shaded areas of Figure 17.5. Here is an apparent exception to the regularity of the correlation between EEG activity and the state of arousal. The paradox is between the EEG record and behavior—the depth of sleep. But we know that the EEG activity is probably being controlled by different regulating systems of the brain in paradoxical and regular sleep.

During paradoxical sleep, something else happens: the eyes begin to move rapidly from side to side. For this reason the paradoxical-sleep stage is sometimes

DREAMS OCCUR IN CYCLES

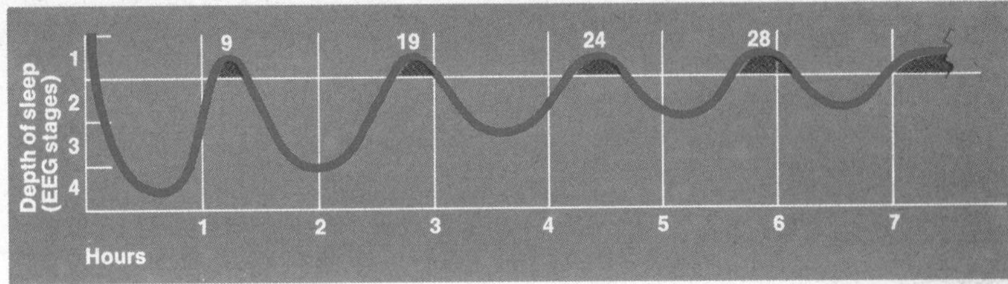

Figure 17.5 *EEG stages of sleep during a typical night. Note that this graph does not represent actual EEG recordings; it is a diagram to show the EEG stages at various times during a night's sleep. Periods of paradoxical, or REM, sleep are indicated by the shaded areas. It is in these periods that most dreaming occurs. The numbers over the paradoxical periods indicate the length of the period in minutes. (Modified slightly from Dement and Wolpert, 1958.)*

called the *rapid-eye-movement (REM) stage.* But perhaps of greatest interest is the fact that the paradoxical, or REM, stage is the period of dreaming. Although figures differ somewhat, about 80 to 90 percent of the times when subjects are awakened during or immediately after paradoxical sleep, they report that they had been dreaming. At other portions of the sleep cycle, dreams are reported in less than 15 percent of the awakenings. Note that several dreams occur each night—four complete dream periods are shown in Figure 17.5—and the dreams later in the night are longer. Dreams occur in "real" time—they are not over in a "flash." As the diagram shows, some last about 30 minutes.

Here is a set of close correlations between brain activity and behavior; but every advance in knowledge brings further questions and opportunities for analysis. For instance, we would like to know more about the systems of the brain which control the EEG activity that is recorded. We would also like to know more about the conditions which cause the switch from one controlling system to another as we go into paradoxical sleep.

Stimulation The fourth method of exploring the correlations between brain function and behavior is to stimulate the brain, commonly by electrical means, and observe any changes in behavior. Electrodes can be used to stimulate, as well as to record from, neural tissue. In fact, the same electrodes may sometimes serve at different times both for stimulation and for recording. More often, one pair is inserted in one place for stimulation, and another pair at a different site is used for recording. In this way, activity in the nervous system can be traced from one point to another. The stimulus is usually an electrical pulse or series of pulses generated by a specially designed stimulator.

One of the first uses of the method of electrical stimulation was in the excitation of the so-called "motor areas" of the cortex. In fact, these areas were first mapped by means of electrical stimulation. A neutral, or inactive, electrode is attached to the skull or body, and the active electrode is touched to a point on the surface of the cerebral cortex, which has been exposed by surgery. Because there is a pathway leading from the motor cortex downward to the muscles of the body, stimulation of the motor area of the cortex causes the subject to make various kinds of movements. Stimulation at one point in the cortex causes a movement in a particular part of the body; stimulation at another point causes another movement somewhere else. By keeping track of the movements evoked by stimulation at various points, one can construct a map of the parts of the body controlled by different parts of the motor cortex.

This method has also been used in conscious human subjects to ex-

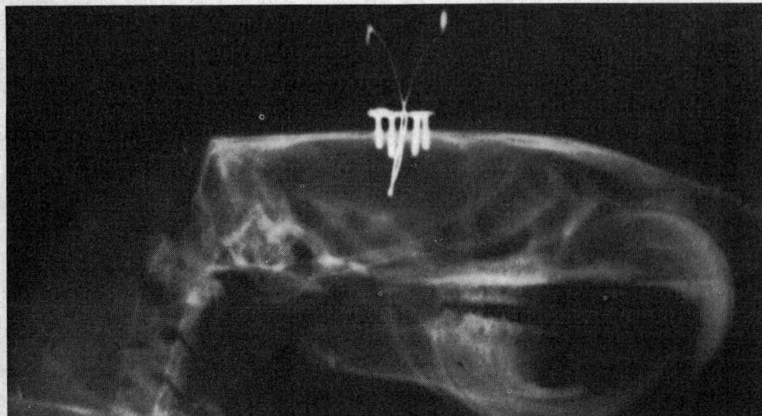

WITH PERMANENTLY IMPLANTED ELECTRODES, THE BRAIN CAN BE STIMULATED WHILE THE ANIMAL IS BEHAVING

Figure 17.6 *Left, an x-ray photograph of an electrode permanently implanted in the brain of a rat. Right, the electrode is in a self-stimulating circuit, and the rat is pushing a bar to stimulate his brain. (Olds, 1956; University of Michigan.)*

plore areas of the cortex concerned in sensation and memory (Penfield and Rasmussen, 1950). This is done, of course, only when a patient is being operated on for some other reason, usually for removal of a brain tumor. The stimulation is carried out under local anesthesia so that the patient feels no pain but is fully conscious. Electrodes are then used to stimulate various points on the cortex while the patient reports what he experiences. The method has yielded much information about the functions of the cerebral cortex. It also enables a surgeon to perform the operation with a minimum of damage to the areas most concerned in sensory experience, speech, and memory.

A method of permanently implanting electrodes in experimental animals for purposes of stimulation has been developed. A fine wire or needle, similar to the ones used for recording, is inserted into the brain while the animal is anesthetized. The electrode is anchored to the skull and equipped with a socket or connection which protrudes through the skin (see the x-ray photograph in Figure 17.6). After the operation, the animal is able to live a normal life. If the experimenter wishes to stimulate the spot at the tip of the electrode, he merely hooks up the connector to a stimulator. This method is now commonly used to study the behavioral functions of some of the deeper parts of the brain. The stimulus applied through the electrode may be controlled either by the experimenter or by the animal itself. In certain sites, electrical stimulation of the brain is "pleasant"—as the drawing in Figure 17.6 shows, an animal will close a switch to deliver stimulation to itself (Olds and Milner, 1954). Stimulation through electrodes placed in other regions of the brain results in "unpleasant" sensations; at least, animals will respond in order to stop stimulation in these areas (Olds and Olds, 1963).

Although the method of local stimulation in the intact animal usually involves an electrical stimulus, chemical stimuli can also be used. A small pipette is inserted instead of an electrode, and the experimenter delivers small amounts of chemicals through the pipette in order to study the response of the particular area to different substances. This method has been valuable in experiments on the mechanism of thirst and hunger motivation (Grossman, 1960).

THE NEURON IS THE UNIT OF THE NERVOUS SYSTEM

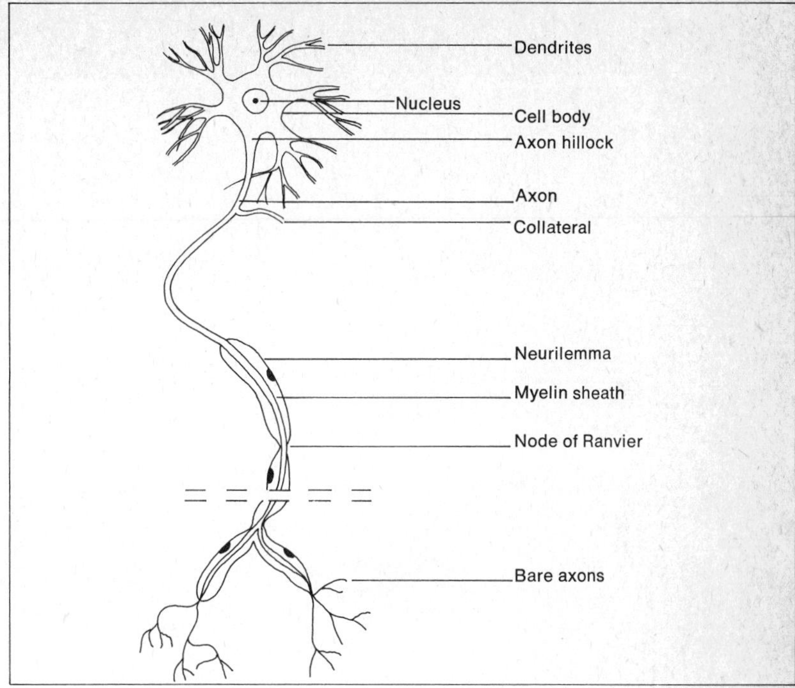

Figure 17.7 *An idealized diagram of a neuron. In this motor neuron from the spinal cord, the cell body lies in the ventral horn of the spinal cord, and the axon extends to muscles in the periphery of the body. The* collateral *is a branching fiber; the* myelin sheath *is the fatty white covering of the axons of some neurons; the* neurilemma *is an outer covering of the fiber in the peripheral nervous system over the myelin sheath of a myelinated fiber, or the axis cylinder of an unmyelinated fiber. (Modified from Brazier, 1968.)*

Neurons and Synapses

As we have already pointed out, the function of the individual nerve cells, or neurons, is to conduct information from one part of the body to another. This they do by means of electrical impulses, or nerve impulses, that travel along the nerve fibers. The connection between individual nerve cells is functional rather than physical: a small gap, called the synapse, separates individual nerve fibers at the region of functional contact. When the nerve impulse of one fiber reaches the end of that fiber, it triggers the release of a chemical, or *transmitter substance,* that spreads across the synaptic gap to influence the next cell. Thus, to repeat a point made earlier, information transmission along a nerve fiber is electrical; communication from cell to cell in the mammalian nervous system is chemical.

The chemical process at the synapse can either excite or inhibit activity in the cell being influenced. As we shall see, the synaptic processes of excitation and inhibition add a great deal of flexibility to the functioning of the nervous system.

Neurons A schematic drawing of a neuron appears in Figure 17.7. Neurons actually vary a great deal in size and shape; the one shown is typical of a motor neuron that extends out from the spinal cord to a muscle. The diagram, however, brings out the essential features of neurons. They all have two general parts: a cell body and fibers. The cell body contains structures that keep the neuron alive and functioning normally. Neuron fibers are of two types: *dendrites,* which are stimulated

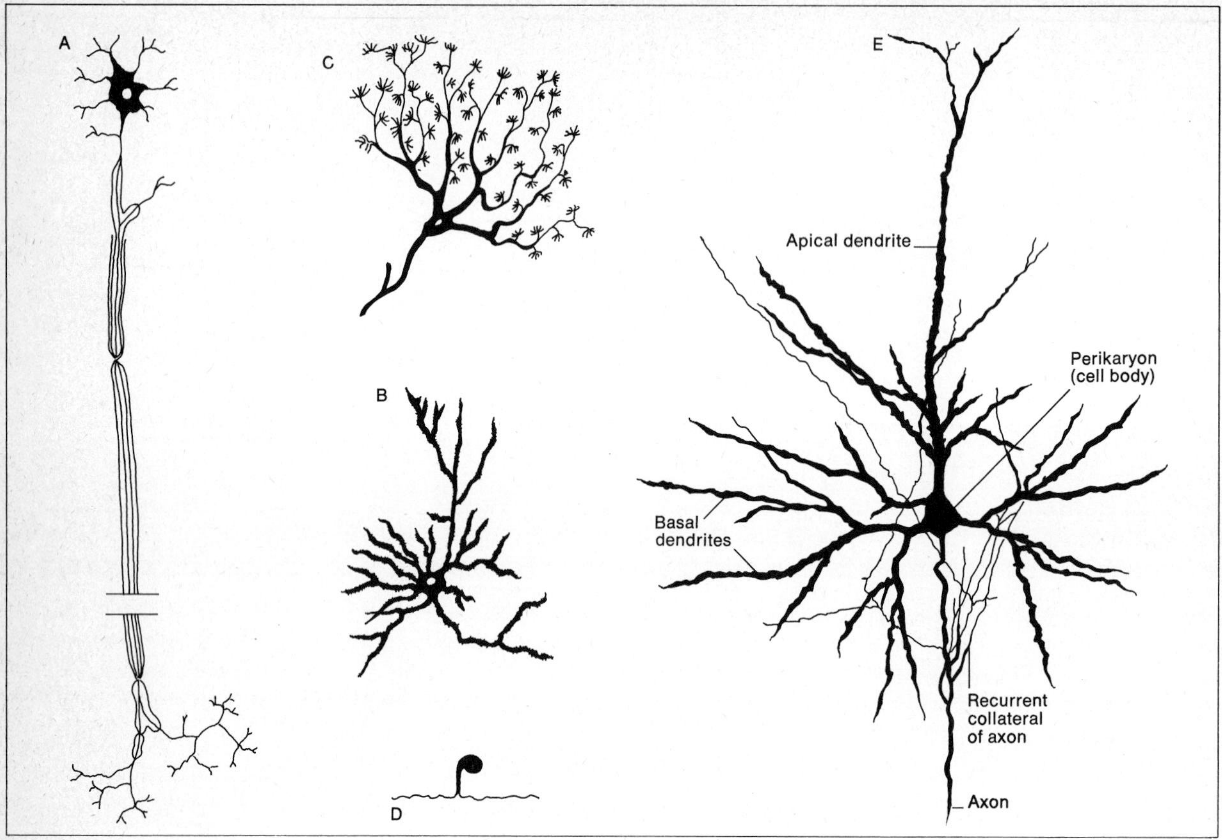

NEURONS COME IN MANY VARIETIES

Figure 17.8 *Representative types of neurons.*
(a) *Motor neuron of spinal cord.*
(b) *Golgi II neuron—a short connecting neuron.*
(c) *A bushy cell.*
(d) *Bipolar cell such as is found in some sensory pathways.*
(e) *Pyramidal cell of the cerebral cortex. Note that some branches of the axon, the* recurrent collaterals, *return to the region of the cell body and are often inhibitory: activity in this cell might be followed by its inhibition for a period of time.*
[*(a) to (d) adapted from C. L. Evans,* Principles of Human Physiology *(12th ed.). London: Churchill, 1956, by permission; (e) from E. A. Sholl,* The Organization of the Cerebral Cortex. *London: Methuen, 1956. By permission.*]

by neighboring neurons or by physical stimuli; and *axons,* which deliver nerve impulses to adjacent neurons or to an effector, such as a muscle. Dendrites and axons may be relatively long or very short, depending on the cells with which they connect (see the various neurons illustrated in Figure 17.8). Many of the neurons within the brain that serve as connectors between closely packed neurons have very short fibers. Other neurons within the brain have relatively long dendrites and axons. Still others, such as motor neurons connected with the muscle fibers of the limbs, toes, or fingers, have very long axons and short dendrites.

In its function as a conductor of electrical nerve impulses from one part of the body to another, perhaps the most important part of the neuron is the cell *membrane* which surrounds the cell body, dendrites, and axon core. The membrane is a very thin structure—approximately 75 to 100 angstrom units, or 75 to 100 ten-millionths of a millimeter, thick. The membrane may be thought of as containing very small pores which enable certain *ions*, or charged particles, to move through it.

Nerve impulses The nerve impulses conducted by the neuron are very brief electrical pulses traveling along the membrane of the cell body and

THE INSIDE STORY OF THE ACTION POTENTIAL

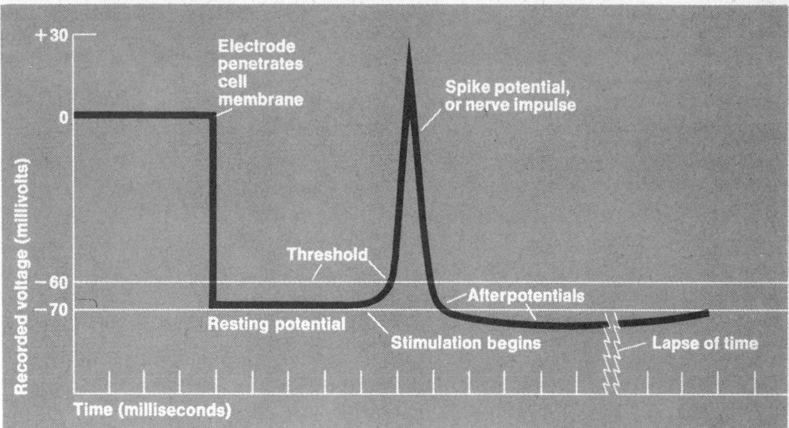

Figure 17.9 *A schematic record of the voltage changes* inside a nerve *cell during an experiment in which the cell is stimulated.*
At first, the electrode is outside the cell and the recorded voltage is zero. When the electrode penetrates the cell membrane, the voltage drops suddenly to the resting potential, *which is −70 millivolts in this experiment.*
Next, stimulation begins, and at first the change of voltage is slow. When the threshold *is reached, sodium ions rush into the cell and the change of voltage is very rapid. The inside of the cell becomes positive, about +30 millivolts, for a brief period. Then the voltage declines and, after going through a period when* afterpotentials *appear, finally comes to the resting potential again.*
The whole sequence of voltage changes, from the beginning of stimulation, that includes the spike potential and the afterpotentials is called the action potential. *(Modified from Ruch and Patton, 1965.)*

fibers. The rate of travel depends upon the type of fiber and its diameter. For small fibers the rate is comparatively slow—approximately 0.6 to 2.0 meters per second; for fibers of large diameter, it may be as much as 120 meters per second. The pulses themselves are due to rapid and reversible changes in the permeability of the membrane to certain ions, especially sodium (Na^+) and potassium (K^+) ions. The resulting flows of ions through the membrane give rise to the electrical nerve impulse which can be recorded by the various methods described earlier.

RECORD OF A NERVE IMPULSE The following example, which is a composite of many neurophysiological recordings, illustrates the microelectrode technique for recording nerve impulses (Ruch and Patton, 1965; Eccles, 1957):

The first step is to take a microelectrode—one with a tip approximately 1 micron, or 1 millionth of a meter, in diameter—and gradually lower it with a device called a micromanipulator toward the neuron from which we wish to record. At first, when the tip of the microelectrode is in the solution surrounding the cell, the recorded voltage is zero. But when the microelectrode penetrates the cell membrane, the voltage changes abruptly and now reads about −70 millivolts, or thousandths of a volt (see Figure 17.9). In other words, the inside of the cell is charged negatively, when compared with the outside of the cell membrane, by 70 millivolts. In fact, the nerve cell is like a tiny battery in that it is *polarized,* with the inside of the cell being the negative pole of the battery and the outside of the membrane being the positive pole. This voltage, or potential, of the neuron in the inactive state is called the *resting potential.* Now, suppose we stimulate the cell so that the inside of the cell is made a little less negative, or, from the other point of view, a little more positive. The rate of change of voltage is at first rather slow and depends upon the strength of the stimulus. But then a voltage is reached at which there is suddenly a very rapid voltage change in the positive direction. The voltage level at which this rapid change begins is about 10 millivolts more positive than the resting potential, making it about −60 millivolts in this case, and is called the *threshold.* After threshold has been reached, the voltage rapidly shoots toward zero and then overshoots zero to become positive by about 30 millivolts. There-

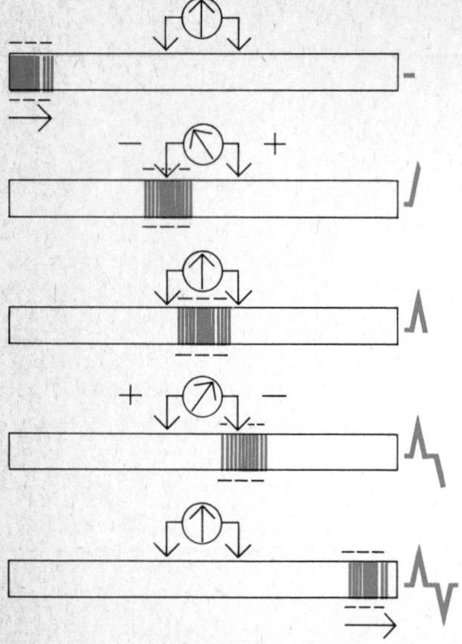

THE NERVE IMPULSE TRAVELS DOWN THE FIBER

Figure 17.10 *The arrow in the circle represents the needle of a voltmeter making a circuit with the nerve fiber through two electrodes (arrows in contact with membrane). The colored graph lines at the far right are the records of the swing of the needle as the impulse passes first one electrode, then the other. The active electrode is the one to the left; when it is negative relative to the other electrode, the graphed record swings upward; when it is positive with respect to the other, the record swings downward. In records such as this one, where the recording is made from outside the cell, it is traditional to record negative voltages in the upward direction. However, records made from inside cells, such as that in Figure 17.9, show positivity with upward swings. (After Gardner, 1968.)*

after the voltage declines back to the resting potential, or even a little beyond it for a period. The whole sequence of voltage changes is called the *action potential.* The particular part in which the internally recorded voltage rapidly changes toward positivity and then declines is the *spike potential,* or nerve impulse, which only lasts for approximately 0.5 to 1.0 milliseconds—thousandths of a second. The later parts of the action potential are known as the *afterpotentials.*

If we had recorded from the outside surface of the fiber instead of from the inside, the voltage changes of the action potential would have been opposite in sign. For example, the spike potential would have been recorded as a rapid negative shift of voltage. The spike potential, or nerve impulse, is then seen to travel down the nerve fiber (Figure 17.10). Thus the spike potential appears from the outside as a wave of negativity moving along a fiber.

THE ALL-OR-NONE LAW This law states that the size of the nerve impulse does *not* depend on the strength of the stimulus which initiates it; instead, the size of the impulse and the speed with which it travels down a fiber depend upon characteristics of the fiber itself. It is easy to see that all-or-none behavior of a neuron is related to the idea of the threshold which was just illustrated in Figure 17.9. The stimulus either causes threshold to be reached, or it does not; if reached, the voltage changes go to completion. All that is necessary is that threshold be reached; after this, a self-propagating series of events, which cannot be stopped, takes place in the membrane of the fiber. Consider the mousetrap as an analogy. It makes no difference to the trap whether a big mouse or a little mouse steps on the trigger. It is only essential that the weight of the mouse—the stimulus—be sufficient to exceed the threshold of the trigger.

One implication of the all-or-none law is that information in the nervous system is not carried by graded sizes of the voltages of spike potentials. If a particular neuron is stimulated, and if it is in a relatively normal state, its spike potential will always be about the same. Different neurons have different-sized spikes—for instance, the spike potential is greater in the fibers with larger diameters—but the size of the spike depends upon the neuron and not on the strength of the stimulus. Thus, information about stimulus strength must be carried by the frequency of firing, and the pattern of fibers which fire; it is not carried by the sizes of spikes.

EXCITABILITY OF NERVE FIBERS While a region of a fiber is actively conducting a spike, it cannot be stimulated to fire another impulse—the fiber is said to be in the *absolute refractory period.* Since the nerve impulse lasts for approximately 1 millisecond, the fiber is absolutely refractory for that long. This puts a limit of about 1,000 impulses per second on the rate at which a single nerve fiber can respond. The limit on the frequency of firing in turn limits the amount of information which can be carried. As we shall see in the next chapter, frequency by itself is far less important as an information carrier in the nervous system than the patterns of firing in different nerve fibers.

Immediately after the absolute refractory period, the fiber is in a state

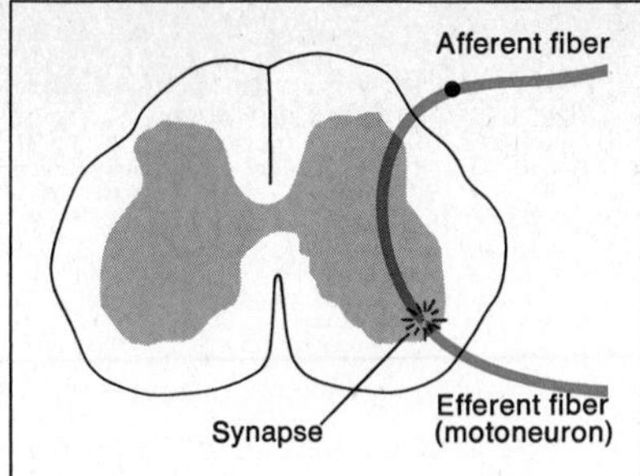

THE SIMPLEST REFLEX ARC

Figure 17.11 *Afferent fibers, efferent fibers, and the synapse between them constitute the simplest arrangement for a behavioral response to a stimulus. This is a cross section of the spinal cord; compare with Figure 17.17.*

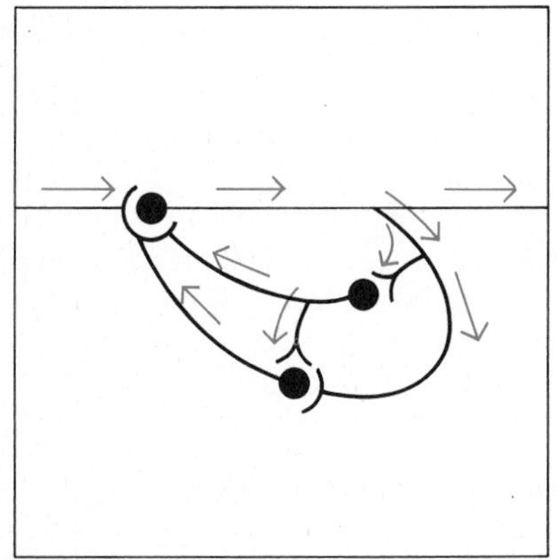

NEURONS MAY FORM SELF-EXCITING CIRCUITS

Figure 17.12 *A reverberating circuit. Such reverberating, or recurrent, circuits can maintain activity for quite some time and may, according to some sources, form a basis for short-term memory. (After Lorente de Nó, 1938.)*

where it can be stimulated, but only by a very strong stimulus. This stage is called the *relative refractory period.*

Synaptic connections We have seen that nerve impulses travel along fibers. Where do they come from, and where do they go? This question has several answers. One is that impulses originate in the receptors of the various senses. Some receptors, such as the free nerve endings in the skin, are themselves fibers of neurons. In such fibers, an external stimulus evokes a response directly. In the receptors for many other senses, neurons are stimulated by a complex process that changes physical energies into nerve impulses. (This transduction process, as it is called, will be described in more detail in Chapter 18.) In any case, no matter how a neuron from a sensory organ is stimulated, it will carry nerve impulses into the central nervous system (CNS), that is, the spinal cord and brain.

Fibers carrying information into the central nervous system are called *afferent* fibers. The fibers of some afferent neurons extend all the way from the sense organs—no matter how far away these may be—to the central nervous system. When impulses in the afferent fibers reach the CNS, they excite other neurons, and information is carried further through the nervous system.

Many routes through the central nervous system are possible. For instance, the afferent neuron may pass information directly, or through intervening neurons called *association neurons,* to a motor, or *efferent neuron*—one leading out of the central nervous system to muscle fibers—and movement may occur. Such a simple connection from afferent to efferent, whether through an association neuron or not, is called a *reflex arc* (see Figure 17.11). This is the simplest complete arrangement for a behavioral response to a stimulus. Of course, the input into the CNS through the afferent fiber may not result in muscle movement. It may, for example, be relayed to excite those cells which give rise to our experience of the world (see Chapter 8). Or the input may excite neurons which loop to form *recurrent nerve circuits,* or *reverberating circuits* (see Figure 17.12). Such circuits may be the neural basis for short-term memory storage, as will be discussed in Chapter 19.

Whatever its eventual fate, the information as it speeds through the CNS is passed from neuron to neuron—typically from the axon of one neuron to the dendrites or cell bodies of the next one. It is transmitted across the gap, or synapse, between the ends of the axon of one neuron and the dendrites of the next neuron by intricate processes that involve both excitation and inhibition of firing. This excitatory and inhibitory activity at the synapse is important because it subjects a cell to fine control by preceding cells. Actually, events in the synaptic region may be the basis for the plasticity of the nervous system, which we previously considered in discussing learning (Chapter 3) and perception (Chapter 8).

SYNAPTIC ANATOMY The region that includes the end of the axon of one neuron, the small gap, and the membrane of the next cell is called the *synaptic region.* The neuron along which a nerve impulse comes to the synapse is called the *presynaptic neuron;* its membrane in the synaptic

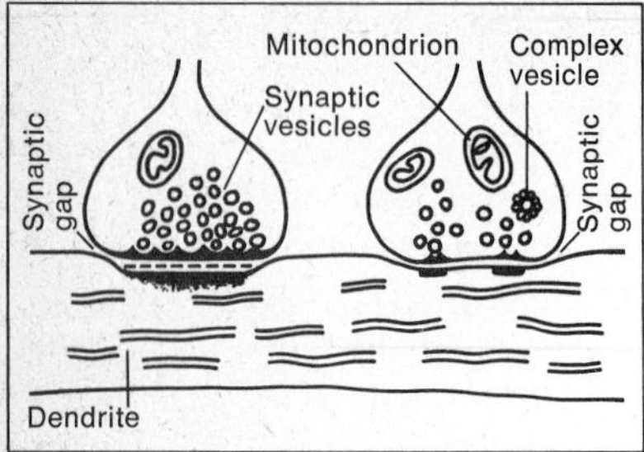

SYNAPTIC REGIONS ARE AREAS OF FUNCTIONAL CONNECTION BETWEEN NEURONS

Figure 17.13 *Two types of synapses. The synaptic knobs of the presynaptic fibers are shown above; the postsynaptic fiber—a dendrite—is below. A type 1 synapse—possibly excitatory—is shown on the left; a type 2 synapse —possibly inhibitory—is shown on the right. (Modified slightly from Eccles, 1964.)*

region is called the *presynaptic membrane.* The neuron to which the information is being transmitted is called the *postsynaptic neuron;* its membrane in the synaptic region is the *postsynaptic element.*

A schematic diagram of two types of synaptic regions is shown in Figure 17.13. Note the swellings of the presynaptic fibers—the ends of axons—in the synaptic region. These swellings are often called *synaptic knobs,* or *boutons*—"buttons." The two structurally different synaptic regions in the figure are called *type 1* and *type 2* synapses (Eccles, 1964). In type 1 synapses, the postsynaptic membrane is thickened and the gap appears to be a little wider than in type 2 synapses. In both types, little hollow spheres may be seen clustering around the presynaptic membrane; no such spheres are seen at the postsynaptic membrane. These little spheres—called *synaptic vesicles*—are thought to contain transmitter substances—the chemicals responsible for carrying the information across the synaptic gap.

SYNAPTIC PROCESSES As we have seen, the synpatic region is not a place of physical but of *functional* contact between the membranes of the presynaptic and postsynaptic neurons. Let us examine some processes in this region as they can be studied through the microelectrode technique (Eccles, 1957, 1964).

Suppose we combine a number of experiments into one description. First we impale a postsynaptic cell with a microelectrode. Then we stimulate a presynaptic fiber (A_1), which has synaptic knobs on the cell from which we are recording. If we stimulate the presynaptic fiber rather gently, we may see (in step 1, Figure 17.14) that the inside of the postsynaptic cell becomes slightly less negative—it begins to be depolarized—but threshold is not reached. If the stimulation of the presynaptic fiber is now turned off, the potential of the postsynaptic cell drops back to the resting potential (step 1). However, if we stimulate the presynaptic fiber vigorously—and additionally stimulate another fiber (A_2) which synapses on the same cell—we obtain a greater amount of depolarization. This time the depolarization reaches threshold, and a nerve impulse is initiated in the postsynaptic cell (step 2).

The relatively slow depolarization which results from stimulation of the presynaptic fiber is called the *excitatory postsynaptic potential* (EPSP). The EPSP, in contrast to the spike potential, is graded—it can be large or small, and can have a fast or slow rate of rise, depending on the strength of stimulation of the presynaptic fiber. EPSPs caused by impulses arriving over several different fibers (A_1 and A_2) which synapse on a single postsynaptic cell can sum up to cause threshold to be reached.

If, on the other hand, we stimulate certain presynaptic fibers (see *B*, left panel, Figure 17.14), we find that the postsynaptic cell becomes *hyperpolarized*—the inside becomes more negative (step 3). The result of hyperpolarization is to drive the potential of the postsynaptic cell farther from threshold, and this makes it harder to excite. In other words, the cell is *inhibited.* In this case, the potential is called the *inhibitory postsynaptic potential* (IPSP). IPSPs can combine with EPSPs to control the excitability of the postsynaptic cell.

When we look at the types of synapses which depolarize a given postsynaptic cell, we see that they are type 1 synapses. Activity at type 2 synapses seems to hyperpolarize—that is, it is inhibitory.

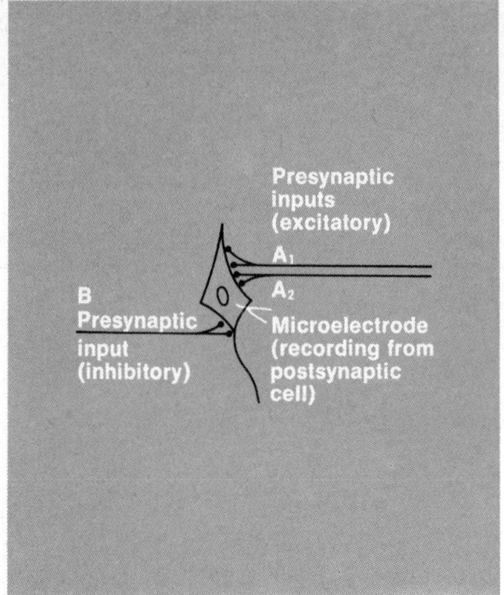

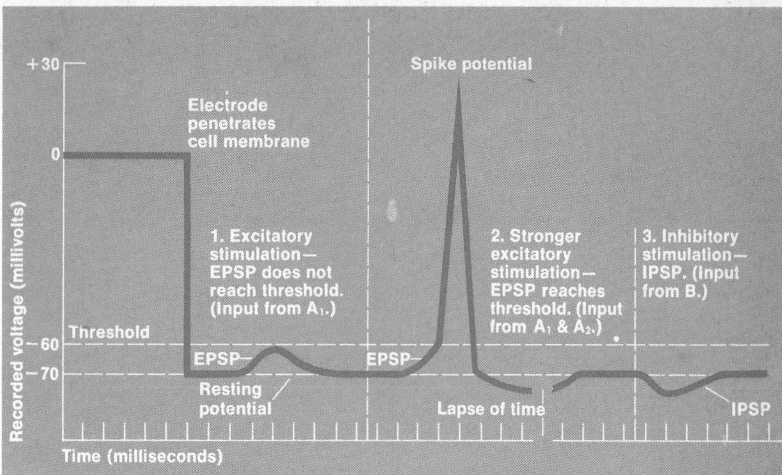

EXCITATORY AND INHIBITORY INPUTS CONTROL CELLS

Figure 17.14 *A schematic record of the voltage changes* inside a *post-synaptic neuron when the neuron is experimentally stimulated—first through excitatory presynaptic fibers and then through inhibitory presynaptic fibers (see left panel).*
(1) The excitatory input, *which makes the inside of the fiber less negative, produces a graded change—not an all-or-none change—in voltage and drives the cell toward threshold. If the excitatory input is too weak, the threshold is not reached, and the excitatory postsynaptic potential (EPSP) falls back to the resting potential when the stimulation is turned off.*
(2) If the EPSP is strong enough, the threshold is reached and the cell fires an all-or-none spike potential (nerve impulse).
(3) The inhibitory input *makes the inside of the cell more negative, thus driving the inside voltage farther from the threshold voltage and making cell firing more difficult. When the inhibitory input is removed, the inhibitory postsynaptic potential (IPSP) returns to the resting potential. (Modified from Ruch and Patton, 1965.)*

Any particular neuron is covered by both inhibitory and excitatory synapses. The inhibitory synapses are at the ends of one set of presynaptic fibers, the excitatory synapses at the ends of other presynaptic fibers. Thus inhibitory and excitatory influences from many sources can play upon any given cell. This means that impulses arriving from many parts of the nervous system can impinge upon a postsynaptic cell and, if the timing is right, delicately control its excitability. Another way of expressing this is to say that the excitatory inputs add to the total inputs driving the cell toward threshold and firing, while the inhibitory inputs add to the total inputs driving the cell away from the firing level. Thus a single cell can integrate excitatory and inhibitory inputs; if the excitatory input is great enough, threshold will be reached and the cell will fire.

Consider, for instance, a *motoneuron* of the spinal cord. Firing of this cell will cause a group of muscle fibers to twitch. But the firing of the cell is controlled by the excitatory and inhibitory inputs on it. Many excitatory and inhibitory inputs converge on the cell from other parts of the nervous system; all these inputs have the cell in common, and it is the last cell in the chain before the muscle fibers are excited. Such a cell is sometimes called the *final common pathway.* The principle behind the control of activity in a motoneuron holds throughout the nervous system. It is perhaps not too much of an oversimplification to say that action, and even feelings and thought, are the result of the interplay of the two antagonistic processes of excitation and inhibition upon various groups of neurons.

CHEMICAL EVENTS AT THE SYNAPSE Knowing about excitatory and inhibitory electrical events in the postsynaptic element (the EPSPs and IPSPs), can we begin to understand them at a more fundamental level? In part we can. The sequence of events seems to be something like this: In some way, the electrical impulses arriving in the presynaptic knobs cause transmitter substances to be released from the vesicles into the synaptic gap. These substances are thought to combine with the post-

THE SOMATIC AND AUTONOMIC GANGLIA OF THE PERIPHERAL NERVOUS SYSTEM

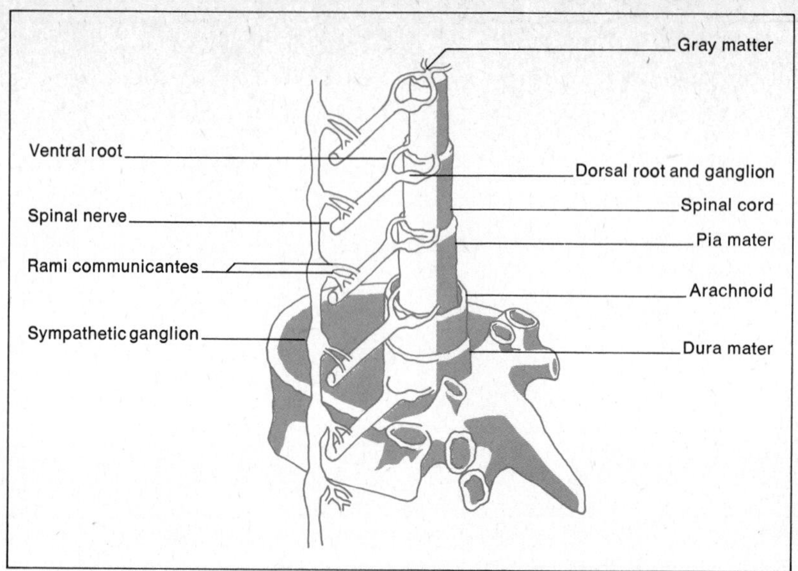

Figure 17.15 *The relationships between the spinal cord and the somatic and autonomic ganglia. The spinal nerve divides into two roots just before the fibers enter the spinal cord. One of these roots, the dorsal root, is sensory; the other, the ventral root, is motor. The cell bodies of the sensory dorsal root are clustered in a ganglion on the dorsal root: the dorsal root ganglion.*
In addition, certain fibers from the spinal nerve feed into the sympathetic ganglia where synapses are made (see Chapter 7). From the sympathetic ganglia, after a synapse, fibers rejoin the spinal nerve to run to certain smooth muscles, blood vessels, and glands.
The branches connecting the spinal nerve with the autonomic ganglia are called the rami communicantes. *The coverings of the spinal cord—the* pia mater, *the* arachnoid, *and* dura mater*—are also shown. (From Gardner, 1968; and Morgan, 1965.)*

synaptic membrane so that the permeability of a patch of membrane on the postsynaptic cell is changed.

In excitatory, or type 1, synapses there are probably several different transmitter substances; one in particular is acetylcholine, which was mentioned earlier in the chapter. There is also an enzyme, acetylcholinesterase, which destroys acetylcholine. One may think of acetylcholine as being released by presynaptic nerve impulses, having its action on the postsynaptic patch of membrane, and then being destroyed by acetylcholinesterase, so that the cycle can be repeated again. Many inhibitory substances are probably released from the vesicles in the synaptic knobs of inhibitory neurons. It has been suggested that *gamma-aminobutyric acid* (GABA) acts as such a substance in the mammalian nervous system, but the evidence is inconclusive. The coalition of two lines of research—electrical studies of synapses and chemical studies of transmitters—will in the future give us much more information about the bases for learning, memory, motivation, emotion, and the effects of drugs on the nervous system.

Structures of the Nervous System

The anatomy of the nervous system is wonderfully complex, and some knowledge of its "geography" is indispensable to an understanding of its role in behavior. Here we shall present a broad outline of some of the major structures of the nervous system, while Chapters 18 and 19 will give more detailed accounts of structure where they are needed.

The nervous system can be divided for analysis in several ways. One way is to describe portions of it in terms of function; another way is to describe portions of it in terms of the place in the body where a particular division is located.

Two major functional divisions of the nervous system are the *somatic* and the *autonomic nervous systems.* The somatic nervous system serves the sense organs and is responsible for movement of the skeletal, or striped, muscles, which are involved in posture, limb and jaw movement, and instrumental behavior in general. The autonomic nervous system controls the smooth muscles of the internal organs of the body, the blood vessels, heart, and certain glands. The autonomic nervous system itself has two main functional divisions: the *sympathetic division* and the *parasympathetic division* (see Chapter 7, Figure 7.4).

In classifying the nervous system by place in the body, a distinction is made between the central nervous system (CNS) and the peripheral nervous system (PNS). The CNS is the part of the nervous system which lies within the bony case formed by the skull and spine. The parts lying outside this case make up the PNS.

These two methods of classifying the nervous system overlap, of course. For instance, a portion of the nervous system can be described as belonging to the somatic nervous system—classification by function—and the peripheral nervous system—classification by place. We shall use the distinction between the peripheral and central nervous systems to organize the discussion which follows.

Peripheral nervous system The peripheral nervous system may be thought of as a channel that carries information to and from the central nervous system. In part, the PNS consists of fibers of sensory and motor neurons. The sensory, or *afferent,* fibers run from sense organs into the central nervous system; the motor, or *efferent,* fibers run out from the central nervous system to excite muscles or glands. Collections of fibers are gathered together to form *nerves.* Most of these collections are mixed in function; in other words, they contain both sensory and motor fibers. However, some of the nerves entering or leaving the head region, the *cranial nerves,* are only sensory or only motor in function. Except for the head region, the mixed nerves are divided just outside the central nervous system into two roots: a sensory and a motor root. The efferent fibers leave the CNS through the *ventral,* or motor, *root;* the afferent fibers enter the CNS through the *dorsal,* or sensory, *root* (see Figure 17.15). But in the portion of the peripheral nerve extending toward the muscles, glands, and receptors, the sensory and motor fibers are mixed together.

So far, this discussion has been concerned with the *fibers* of the peripheral nervous system, which includes fibers of both the somatic and the autonomic divisions. Although the PNS is primarily a channel, some integrative activity does take place in it, and both the autonomic and somatic systems contain cell bodies as well as fibers. The cell bodies are collected together in groups called *ganglia.* Arranged along the spinal column are two series of ganglia. One consists of some of the ganglia of the autonomic nervous system—the sympathetic ganglia—containing cell bodies of some of the autonomic sympathetic motor fibers; the other consists of the *sensory ganglia,* or *dorsal root ganglia,* of the somatic system (see Figure 17.15). Cell bodies of certain sensory neurons in the somatic system (the cell bodies of the retina of the eye, for instance) are also located outside the central nervous system. Except

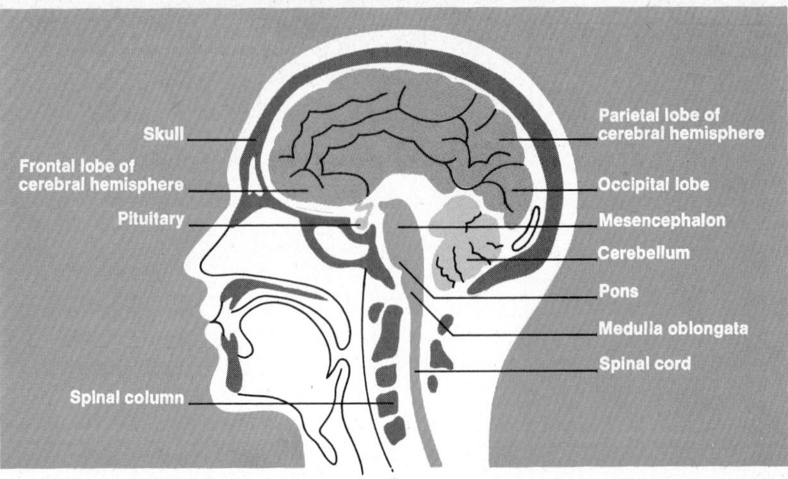

Figure 17.16 The relationship of the brain and spinal cord to the bony skull and spinal column. (Modified from Ranson and Clark, 1959.)

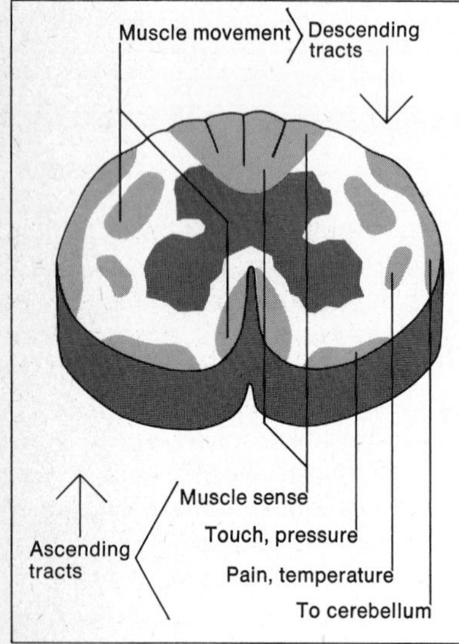

THE SPINAL CORD EFFECTS REFLEX ACTION AND CONDUCTS IMPULSES TO AND FROM THE BRAIN

Figure 17.17 A cross section of the spinal cord.

for these and a few other ganglia, the cell bodies of the PNS neurons are located inside the CNS and send only their fibers out into the PNS. For instance, the cell bodies of the somatic motor fibers, or motoneurons, which innervate the striped muscles of the body, are located in the central nervous system.

Central nervous system As we have just seen, the peripheral nervous system brings information into and carries information away from the CNS. On receiving information from the peripheral nervous system, the central nervous system reorganizes and transforms some of it, collates it with other information, stores some of it, and sends out signals through the motor part of the peripheral nervous system. The reorganizing, transforming, collative, and storage functions of the central nervous system are parts of its integrative activity; thus, in contrast to the PNS, the CNS is especially organized as an integrator of information.

To accomplish such integration, the neurons within the central nervous system are more or less segregated into centers and pathways. The pathways consist of bundles of fibers, and the centers are made up of cell bodies. Frequently, however, the cell bodies in the centers have very short fibers that connect with neighboring neurons within the center. Fibers in the pathways also usually connect with other neurons in these centers. A center, therefore, is something of a mixture of cell bodies and fibers. Centers have specific names depending on where they are and how they are arranged. Sometimes they are called *nuclei,* in other cases *ganglia,* and in still others simply *areas.* We shall have occasion to use all three terms, but it should be remembered that they refer to centers, or collections of cell bodies, where connections are usually made.

A coincidence of nature makes it relatively easy to distinguish centers and pathways of the CNS as one looks at it either with the naked eye or under a microscope. The normal color of a neuron is gray. Many of the fibers in the nervous system have a fatty, white sheath—the myelin sheath—around them. But the cell bodies do not have this sheath. Consequently, to the observer, pathways appear white and collections of

THE FOREBRAIN IS HIGHLY DEVELOPED IN MAN AND THE HIGHER ANIMALS

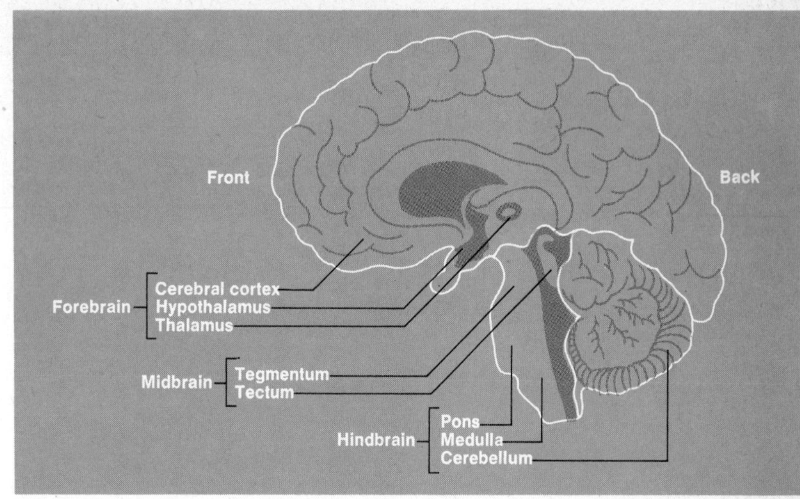

Figure 17.18 *Some of the principal parts of the human brain—highly schematic. This is a medial view. In other words, the brain has been cut in half along the longitudinal fissure and we are looking at the medial surface of the right brain. The hindbrain, midbrain, and forebrain, up through the thalamus, form a kind of stalk or stem and are sometimes collectively referred to as the* brainstem.

cell bodies appear gray. Thus we often refer to pathways as *white matter* and to centers as *gray matter.*

The spinal cord The central nervous system is organized regionally into two principal parts: the *spinal cord* within the spinal column and the *brain* within the skull (see Figure 17.16). A cross section of a spinal cord is shown in Figure 17.17. Notice that its center is gray and its outside is white. The central gray thus consists of cell bodies of neurons, and the white conducting pathways are outside. Notice also that motor pathways bringing impulses down from the brain are toward the front and sides of the cord. The sensory, or ascending, pathways are in several bundles in the white matter. Pathways for muscle, or *kinesthetic,* sensibility and some aspects of touch sensibility are toward the back of the cord; those for temperature, pain, and other aspects of touch sensibility are in two bundles at the side and front.

The spinal cord, generally speaking, has two functions: as a conduction path to and from the brain, and as an organ for effecting reflex action. Most spinal reflexes are affected by impulses descending from the brain, yet some can be seen as purely spinal affairs when the brain is disconnected from the cord in experimental animals.

The brain Of the two principal parts of the nervous system, the brain is more interesting than the spinal cord to psychologists because it plays the central role in all complex activities: learning, thinking, perception, and so on. Its part in these processes is the subject of study in Chapters 18 and 19. In order to understand it, we must get to know the general structure of the brain. Its principal divisions, which are diagrammed in Figure 17.18, may be considered in three main groups: the hindbrain, midbrain, and forebrain.

1. Within the *hindbrain* are the *cerebellum,* the *pons,* and the *medulla.* The medulla contains vital centers for breathing and heart rate, but it

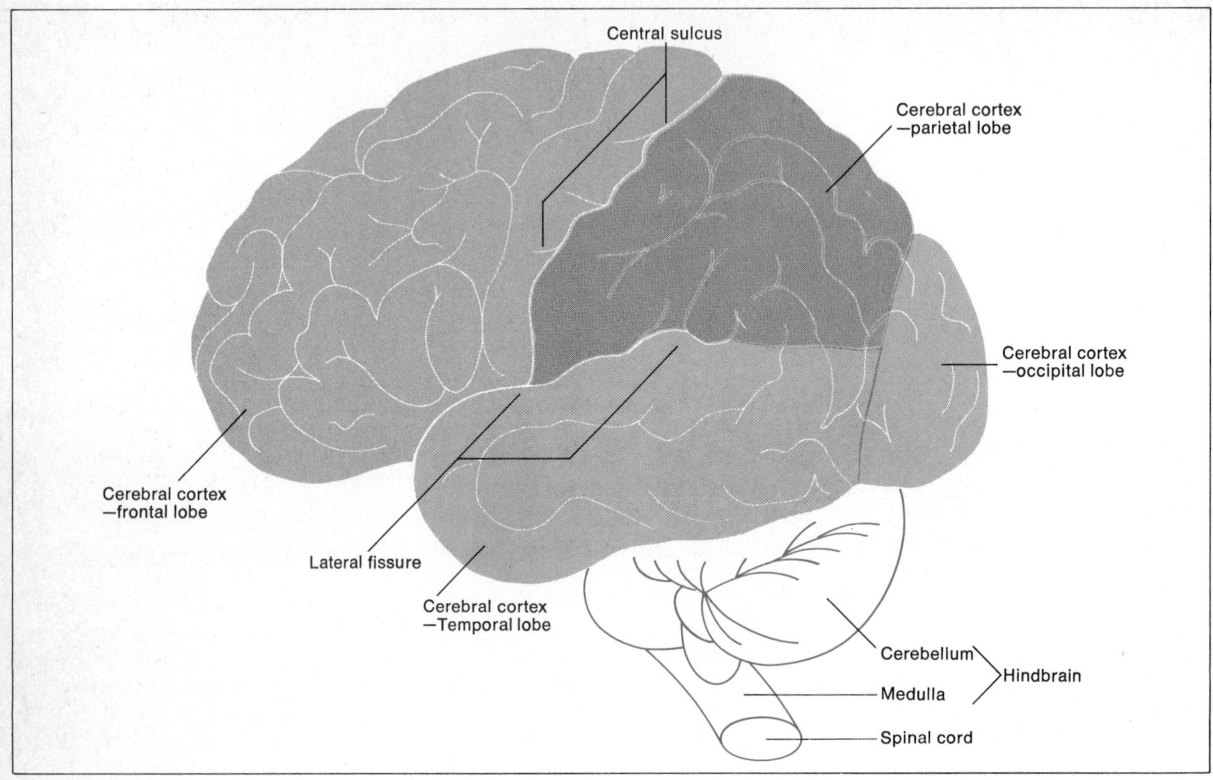

THE LARGE EXTENT OF THE CEREBRAL CORTEX OF THE HUMAN BRAIN

Figure 17.19 *A lateral, or side, view of the brain—highly schematic. The cerebral cortex dominates this view. The lobes of the cerebral cortex—temporal, frontal, parietal, and occipital—are shown; the central sulcus and the lateral fissure are prominent landmarks of the lateral cerebral cortex. Note the many sulci, or grooves, and gyri, or ridges, of the cerebral cortex.*

also includes centers that relay sensory impulses upward to the midbrain and forebrain. The cerebellum is one center, but not the only center, for motor coordination; it helps make our movements smooth and accurate. By utilizing vestibular and kinesthetic impulses, it also is an organ essential for maintaining posture and balance. The pons consists of fibers connecting the portions, or hemispheres, of the cerebellum on one side with those on the other side. It also contains upward- and downward-coursing tracts and various nuclei of the central nervous system.

2. The *midbrain* contains a number of tracts which convey impulses upward and downward; it also has important centers controlling reflex postural changes of the body in response to visual and auditory stimulation. In addition, the midbrain contains a number of motor nuclei—some of those responsible for eye movement, for example. The two main portions of the midbrain are the upper "roof," or *tectum,* and the lower portion, or *tegmentum* (see Figure 17.18).

3. The *forebrain* is the "highest" part of the brain. Although it was slow to develop in the course of evolution, it has become a prominent part of the brain in the higher animals and man. Thought, perception, speech, and several types of learning are functions of the forebrain. Its mass is considerably greater than that of the midbrain or the hindbrain (see Figures 17.18 and 17.19). Many areas of the forebrain are

ANOTHER VIEW OF THE BRAIN

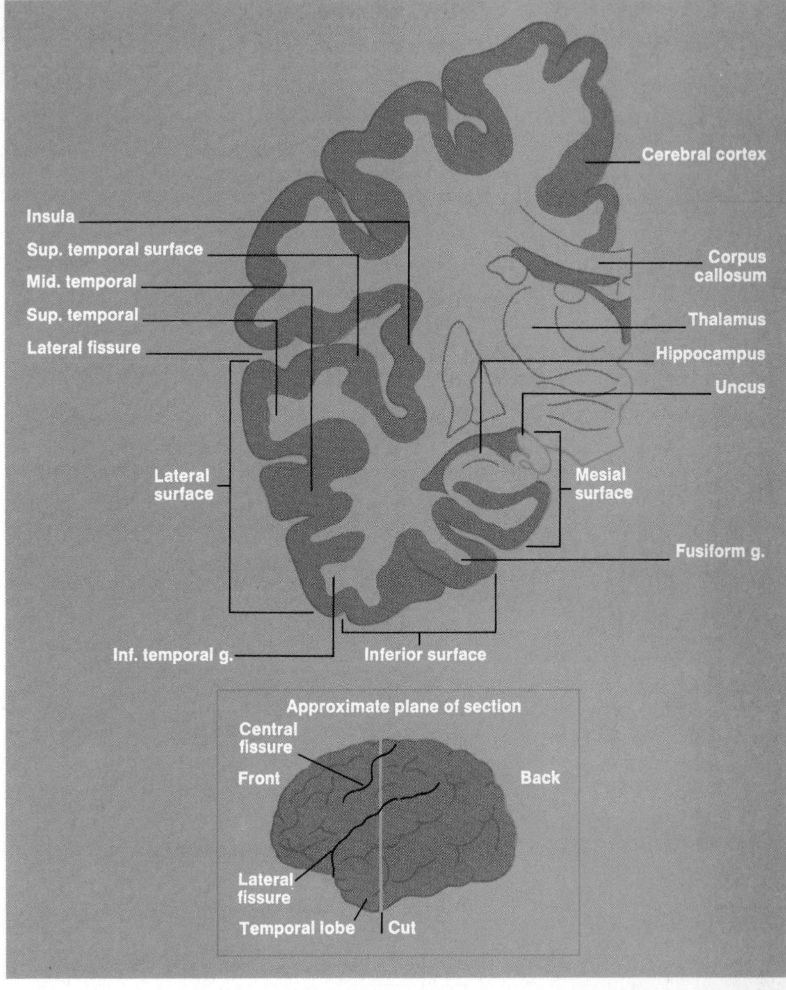

Figure 17.20 *A cross section of the brain through one cerebral hemisphere. The plane of the section is approximately as shown in the inset. Note the temporal lobe under the lateral fissure. Some of the gyri (g) of this lobe are labeled. The shaded area shows depth of the cortex. Other structures—the insula, thalamus, corpus callosum, and hippocampus—appear. (Modified from Penfield and Roberts, 1959.)*

known to take part in complex behavior, but those of greatest interest to us fall into three main groups: the *cerebrum,* which is covered by the "bark of the cerebrum," or the *cerebral cortex;* the *thalamus;* and a group of closely related structures forming the *limbic system.* The cerebral cortex and thalamus are shown in a frontal section of the brain in Figure 17.20. Frontal, or coronal, sections are cut at right angles to the medial sagittal, or front-to-back, section shown in Figure 17.18. Outside the forebrain, running through the hindbrain and midbrain, is another set of structures, the *reticular activating system,* which has an important influence on forebrain activity.

CEREBRUM AND CEREBRAL CORTEX The cerebrum consists of an inner core of white matter and an outer layer of gray. The inner white is composed of fibers running to and from the cells in the outer layer, or the cerebral cortex. A drawing of the human brain, such as the one in Figure 17.19, is more a picture of the cerebral cortex than of anything else, because the cerebrum, which encloses almost all the forebrain and midbrain, is covered by the cortex. The cortex looks like a rumpled piece of cloth that has many ridges and valleys. Anatomists call a ridge a *gyrus* (plural, gyri); a valley, or crevice, is sometimes called a *sulcus* (plural, sulci) and sometimes a *fissure*.

The large sulci, or fissures, can be used to mark off the cerebral cortex. Along the midline dividing the forebrain into symmetrical halves, called *cerebral hemispheres*, is the *longitudinal fissure*. Running from this fissure across the top and down the sides of the two hemispheres is the *central sulcus*. All the cortex in front of this sulcus is known as the *frontal lobe*, which can be called an *expressive* part of the brain because it contains motor centers for controlling movements and actions. The cortex behind the central sulcus has been termed the *receptive* part of the cortex because it contains the centers at which incoming sensory impulses arrive (see Chapter 18). (Although there are many exceptions to these statements, they serve as a reasonably good way of dividing the functions of the cerebral cortex.)

Finally, along the side of each hemisphere is a crevice known as the *lateral fissure*. The cortex below it and to the side of it makes up the *temporal lobe*. Two other lobes of the cerebral cortex are not set off by any major fissures on the outside cortical surface; these are the *parietal lobe* and *occipital lobe*. The parietal lobe lies immediately behind the central fissure, and the occipital lobe is the part of the cortex lying under the back of the skull.

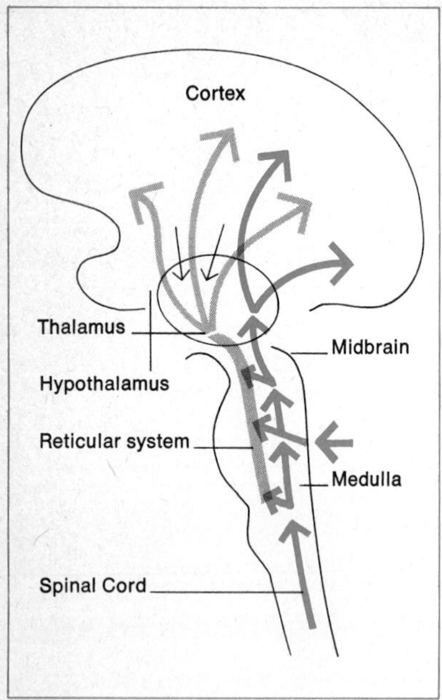

THE RETICULAR ACTIVATING SYSTEM SEEMS TO BE A GENERAL ACTIVATING SYSTEM FOR THE CEREBRAL CORTEX

Figure 17.21 *A schematic diagram of the reticular activating system. The system (gray region) comprises an indirect sensory pathway (gray arrows) to several areas of the cortex; it receives branches from the direct sensory pathway (colored arrows). Pathways also lead back (black arrows) from the cortex to the reticular system, thus forming a loop.*

THALAMUS The thalamus lies just above the midbrain, enveloped by the cortex and other structures of the forebrain (see Figures 17.18 and 17.20). It is best thought of as a relay station, although some of its parts have other functions. Impulses from receptors, coming into the spinal cord, hindbrain, and midbrain, make their way, after intervening connections, to centers in the thalamus. Thalamic centers relay impulses from below to various parts of the receptive cortex. These thalamic nuclei are sometimes called the *extrinsic thalamic nuclei*. Other thalamic nuclei do not receive input from the receptors; instead, these centers, known as *intrinsic thalamic nuclei*, receive input from other thalamic nuclei and send impulses on to the cortex. (Rose and Woolsey, 1949; Pribram, 1958).

The function of another relay, or projection, system, the *reticular activating system* (RAS), is mentioned here because its function parallels that of the thalamus. It is not properly a part of the forebrain; but like the thalamus, it is a relay station on the way to the cerebral cortex (Lindsley, 1958; Zanchetti, 1967). The thalamus relays impulses directly to the cerebral cortex, and its projection is relatively specific. Visual impulses, for example, arrive at a visual center in the thalamus, the lateral geniculate body, and are relayed to a visual area of the cortex. Hearing and many of the other senses similarly have their own thalamic nuclei and their respective areas of projection on the cerebral cortex. This is not the case, however, with the RAS, which is a relatively diffuse system. It receives impulses from sensory systems "on the side" as sensory fibers ascend to the thalamus (see Figure 17.21). It relays impulses to the cerebral cortex, but to a relatively large part of it. The RAS does not keep different sensory systems entirely separate from each

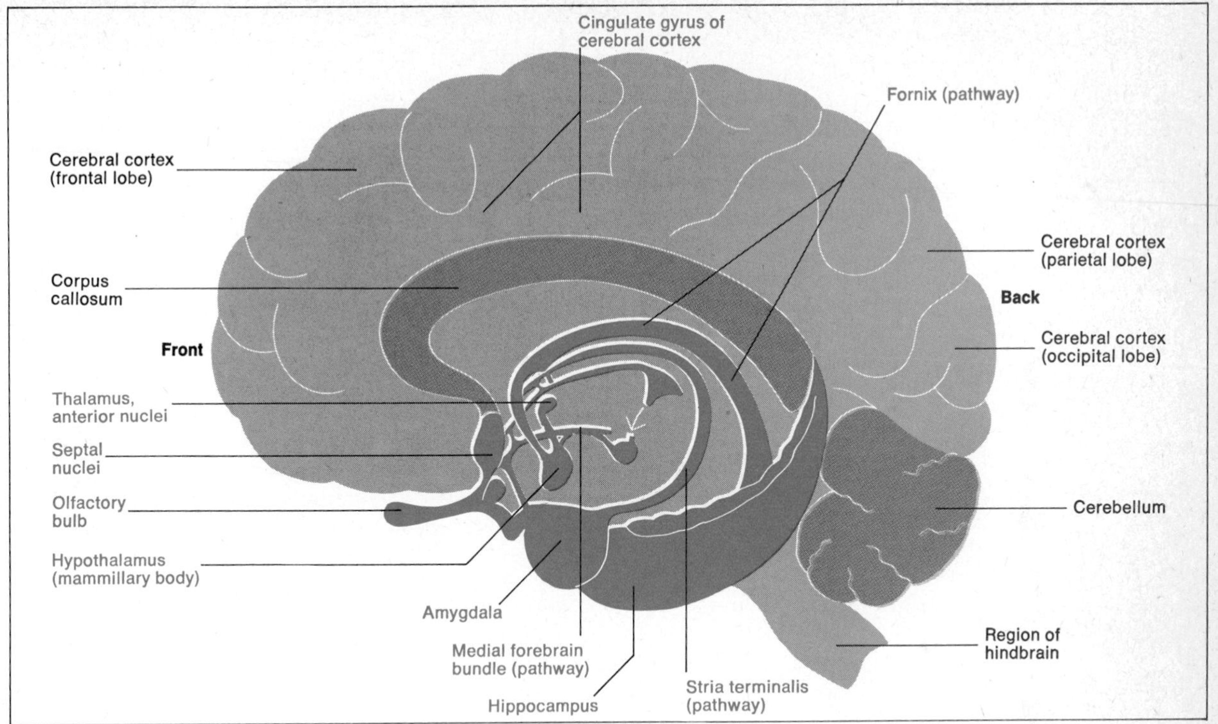

THE LIMBIC SYSTEM IS IMPORTANT IN EMOTION

Figure 17.22 *A schematic drawing of the limbic system. Limbic system structures are labeled in color. Note particularly the cingulate gyrus, the septal nuclei, the amygdala, the hippocampus, and the fornix pathway. A few other limbic and nonlimbic structures are shown so that the location of the limbic system can be better visualized. (Modified from MacLean, 1949.)*

other; rather, it seems to activate wide regions of the cerebral cortex—hence its name.

The part of the RAS that relays sensory impulses to the cerebral cortex is called the ascending reticular activating system. Another part, a descending system, sends impulses downward to the spinal cord. In addition, the cerebral cortex also sends back impulses to the RAS. Thus the RAS and the cerebral cortex form a closed loop in which impulses in the RAS arouse the cerebral cortex, but those in the cortex in turn arouse the RAS. We shall examine later the part that may be played by the RAS in sleep and alertness.

LIMBIC SYSTEM Another region of the forebrain—the limbic system—contains a complex arrangement of pathways and centers (see Figure 17.22). We need note only the structures in this system which are most important in behavior, particularly in emotion and motivated behavior. These include portions of the *hypothalamus,* the *septal area,* the *amygdala,* the *hippocampus,* and the *cingulate gyrus.* The cingulate gyrus is a cortical part of the limbic system. The general size and position of the hypothalamus can be seen in Figure 17.22. As "hypo" (under, below) implies, it lies underneath the thalamus, in a nook in the floor of the skull. Its comparatively small size—it is hardly larger than a peanut—stands in marked contrast to the large number of its very important functions.

The relation of the hypothalamus to the septal area, the amygdala, and the hippocampus is diagrammed in Figure 17.22. The septal area, which is a relatively small structure in man, lies in front of and above the hypothalamus in the median plane. The amygdala, or amygdaloid complex, lies somewhat to the side of the hypothalamus and at the front end of the hippocampus. As the figure indicates, these noncortical parts of the limbic system are complexly interconnected with each other and with the cingulate gyrus of the cortex. Figure 17.22 shows the limbic system structures in only one-half of the brain. Actually, all the limbic structures, like most others in the brain, are symmetrically paired. The septal area and the hypothalamus, although paired, lie along the midline so that their two sides are adjacent.

Some of the major pathways connecting the structures of the limbic system are shown in Figure 17.22. Many recent experiments have begun to unravel the behavioral functions of this system. It is generally considered to control emotional expression, and there is some evidence that it is involved in subjective feelings of emotion (MacLean, 1949).

Synopsis and summary

The task of biopsychology is to find correlations between behavior and experience on the one hand and events in the body—especially in the nervous system—on the other. People persist in this very difficult task because, for some, understanding behavior and experience in physical terms is intellectually exciting. In addition to this intellectual satisfaction, the reduction of behavior to its underlying molecular events would put the explanation of behavior and experience into the domains of other sciences—physiology, anatomy, chemistry, and physics, for example. Many of the established laws and principles of these sciences would then have a bearing on behavior. Unfortunately, we are still a long way from understanding even the relatively simple behaviors—classical conditioning, for example—in physiological, anatomical, or chemical terms.

In this introduction to biopsychology, we have considered some methods for the study of correlations between the nervous system and behavior, we have studied the mechanisms of communication within the nervous system; and we have given a general picture of the anatomy of the nervous system. Our purpose has been to provide a basis for the next chapters. In Chapter 18 we consider the biology of sensory processes, and it helps to know about nerve impulses and synaptic mechanisms. In Chapter 19 we deal with the correlations between nervous system activity and such psychological processes as emotion and memory, and it helps to have a general picture of the anatomy and communication processes in the nervous system.

1. The task of physiological psychology, or biopsychology, is to find correlations between bodily—especially nervous system—events and behavior and experience.
2. The methods of studying neural function most often used to establish correlations with behavior and experience are (*a*) study of chemical or structural brain changes after psychological manipulations, (*b*) study of behavior after destruction of a portion of the nervous system, (*c*) recording of the electrical activities of the nervous system while a particular kind of behavior is taking place, (*d*) electrical, and sometimes chemical, stimulation of selected regions of the nervous system to discover behavioral functions of the regions stimulated.
3. The basic unit of the nervous system is the neuron. It consists of a cell body, an axon, and one or more dendrites; axon and dendrites together are known as nerve fibers.
4. Stimulation of a nerve fiber to threshold generates a nerve impulse which obeys an all-or-none law; the nerve impulse either occurs at full size or does not occur at all.
5. The nerve impulse, or spike potential, is due to a flow of sodium ions into the fiber.
6. Between the end of one nerve fiber and the fibers or cell body of another neuron is a gap called a synapse. The synaptic region contains a number of complex structures.
7. Transmission across synapses in the nervous system of mammals is chemically mediated. When the nerve impulse reaches the end of the presynaptic fiber, a chemical transmitter substance is released into the synaptic gap. This transmitter substance crosses the gap and stimulates or inhibits the fiber on the far side of the gap, the postsynaptic fiber.
8. The excitatory and inhibitory synapses have distinct electrical potentials associated with them. The transmitter substance of the excitatory synapses stimulates by partially depolarizing the postsynaptic fiber and produces an excitatory postsynaptic potential (EPSP) in this fiber. The transmitter substance of inhibitory synapses inhibits by hyperpolarizing the postsynaptic fiber. This hyperpolarization is recorded as an inhibitory postsynaptic potential (IPSP).
9. If the synaptic activity depolarizes the cell to threshold, it will fire and an all-or-none spike potential

will then be propagated down its fibers.

10. The discussion of the anatomy of the nervous system was organized around two of its major divisions: (*a*) the peripheral division, consisting of all the nervous system other than the central nervous system, and (*b*) the central division in the bony cavities of the skull and spine. The nervous system may also be divided into somatic and autonomic divisions; the autonomic system, in turn, consists of sympathetic and parasympathetic portions.

11. The peripheral nervous system is, for the most part, a channel conveying impulses to and from the central nervous system. The CNS consists of nuclei and pathways in the brain and spinal cord. The spinal cord conveys impulses to and from the brain, but it is also responsible for spinal reflexes.

12. The brain has three principal divisions: hindbrain, midbrain, and forebrain. The hindbrain is necessary for the reflex movements in breathing, and it plays a role in the regulation of heart rate and blood pressure. The hindbrain is also important in the coordination of bodily movements. The midbrain contains areas involved in bodily movement and reflex responses to light and sound. Within the forebrain, the areas of greatest interest to psychologists are the cerebral cortex, the thalamus, hypothalamus, and the limbic system. Cortical and thalamic functions include perception, thinking, and many types of learning. Hypothalamic and limbic functions include the control of motivation and emotion.

Related topics in the text

Chapter 2 Behavioral Inheritance
Many of the instinctive behaviors of lower animals are due to the inherent organization of activity in the nervous system. It also seems likely that the limitations and potentialities of human behavior are set by fundamental properties of the human nervous system.

Chapter 18 Sensory Processes
The receptor organs studied in this chapter are capable of changing various forms of energy into nerve impulses that form the basis of our knowledge about the worlds around and within us. Understanding something about the nature of nerve impulses may help us appreciate the sensory processes in general and the sensory, or afferent, codes for experience in particular.

Chapter 19 Brain and Behavior
Important aspects of the biological correlates of such psychological processes as perception, speech, motivation, emotion, learning, and memory are discussed in this chapter. It draws upon basic information about nervous system structure, neuron activity, and methods of investigation that were developed in this Chapter (17).

Suggestions for further reading

Brazier, M. A. B. *The electrical activity of the nervous system: A textbook for students.* (3d ed.) Baltimore: Williams and Wilkins, 1968.
An elementary but authoritative treatment of the electrical phenomena of the nervous system.

Brazier, M. A. B. The historical development of neurophysiology. In J. Field (Ed.), *Neurophysiology.* Vol. 1. Washington, D.C.: American Physiological Society, 1959.
An interesting history of some of the highlights of the study of nervous function. It describes the gradual development of ideas, puts these in the context of human history, and shows how recent is our understanding of some basic phenomena of the nervous function—especially as nervous function relates to behavior.

Butter, C. M. *Neuropsychology: The study of brain and behavior.* Belmont, Calif.: Brooks/Cole, 1968.
A brief, understandable treatment of the relationship between brain and behavior. Its Chapters 1 to 3 parallel the topics of this chapter.

Gardner, E. *Fundamentals of neurology.* (5th ed.) Philadelphia: Saunders, 1968.
An introductory text on the structure and function of the nervous system.

Katz, B. *Nerve, muscle, and synapse.* New York: McGraw-Hill, 1966.
Presents the fundamentals of information transmission in the nervous system in a comprehensive and understandable fashion.

McGaugh, J. L., et al. (Eds.) *Psychobiology: Readings from the Scientific American.* San Francisco: Freeman, 1966.
A collection of some significant articles from the Scientific American on the relationship between brain and behavior.

Morgan, C. T. *Physiological psychology.* (3d ed.) New York: McGraw-Hill, 1965.
A text stressing the physiological mechanisms of behavior; contains readable accounts of the basic anatomy and processes described in this chapter.

Netter, F. H. *The CIBA collection of medical illustrations.* Vol. 1. *The nervous system.* CIBA Pharmaceutical Company, 1962.
A collection of anatomical drawings of the nervous system. Very helpful as a general introduction.

Thompson, R. F. *Foundations of physiological psychology.* New York: Harper & Row, 1967.
A biological psychology text with good chapters on the basics of nervous system structure and function.

Stevens, C. F. *Neurophysiology: A primer.* New York: Wiley, 1966.
A readable and authoritative introduction to neuronal and synaptic physiology.

For there is no conception in a man's mind, which hath not at first, totally, or by parts, been begotten upon the organs of sense.
Thomas Hobbes

Behavior as we know it, our own private experience, and the reported experience of others would be impossible without information about the world around us. The senses are the channels through which we receive this information. Vision enables us to find our way through crowded streets, to appreciate the riches of an art museum or the delicate new foliage of spring. Hearing makes possible the use of speech for communication between people—the lover's tender words, the bigot's venom, the professor's wry humor. Through the skin senses we feel the pain of a bruise, or appreciate the tingle of a cold day and the warmth of a fire. Through taste and smell we avoid spoiled foods, and savor the delights of French cooking. These are the so-called "five senses" of man: vision, hearing, skin sense, taste, and smell. But this does not exhaust the list.

In the last few decades, biological investigation has made great strides in solving the riddles of the senses. As we shall see in this chapter, man is beginning to understand the ingenious processes by which he is able to perceive the world around him.

The Senses of Man

The number of senses man possesses is closer to ten than to five. The skin sense is not a single sense; there are at least four skin senses: *cold*, *warmth*, *pain*, and *touch.* Sense organs in the muscles, tendons, and joints give us information, most of it utilized without our awareness, about the position of our limbs in space and the state of tension in our muscles. These are the kinesthetic sense organs—they serve the sense called *kinesthesis.* The *vestibular sense* gives information about the movement and stationary position of the head; it is the key sense in maintaining balance.

In summary, a minimal list of man's senses includes *vision*, *hearing*, *cold*, *warmth*, *pain*, *touch*, *smell*, *taste*, *kinesthesis*, and the *vestibular sense*. These sensory systems may be classified in various ways, other terms may be substituted, and other senses may be added by subdivision of the basic ones; but we shall use the list given here.

Each sensory system is a kind of channel which, if stimulated, will result in a particular type of experience. The visual channel, for instance, is usually stimulated by light, but it may also be stimulated by such things as pressure applied to the eyeball. Regardless of the source of stimulation, activity produced in a sensory channel will re-

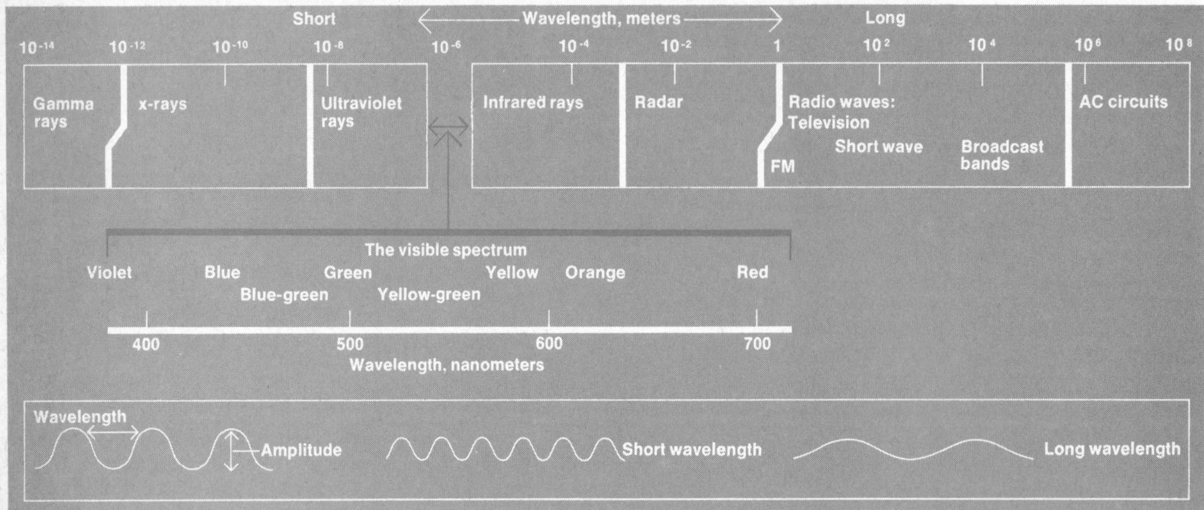

THE HUMAN EYE CAN SEE ONLY A SMALL PART OF THE ELECTROMAGNETIC SPECTRUM

Figure 18.1 *The electromagnetic and visible spectra. Electromagnetic waves have a spectrum from as short as 10^{-14} meters to as long as 10^{8} meters. The part of the spectrum that is visible and is called light is only a tiny fraction in the neighborhood of 10^{-6} meters.*

sult in a certain type of experience. In other words, what we experience is the activity in the nervous system (Müller, 1838); we do not experience the stimulating world directly. Thus it is not quite accurate to say, as we often do, that we sense objects. Instead, we experience the pattern of activity in the nervous system corresponding to the objects.

Activity in a sensory channel usually results from a particular kind of stimulation—light in vision, for instance—because the channel is more sensitive to this type of stimulation than any other. The kind of stimulation which commonly excites a sensory channel is called the *adequate stimulus* (Sherrington, 1906).

Each sensory channel consists of a sensitive element, called the *receptor,* nerve fibers leading from this receptor to the central nervous system, and the various relay stations and places of termination within the central nervous system. A receptor is a cell, or group of cells, specialized to respond to relatively small changes in a particular kind of energy. Some receptors, such as those for sight and smell, are really nerve cells that migrated out from the brain in the course of evolution and have become specialized for their particular function. Other receptors, such as those for pain, are merely the relatively unspecialized ends of nerve fibers. In other cases, such as taste, hearing, kinesthesis, and the vestibular sense, the receptor has developed from the same sort of cells that produce skin.

Each of these receptors responds primarily to a certain kind of physical energy. Chemical receptors for smell and taste respond to chemical substances. Warmth and cold are thermal senses—they respond to thermal energy. Four senses—touch, kinesthesis, the vestibular sense, and hearing—are mechanical senses: some kind of mechanical movement is required to activate them. The pain sense is stimulated by tissue destruction and by extremes of chemical and thermal energy. The remaining sense, sight, responds to a certain range of electromagnetic energy.

The range of stimuli to which each kind of receptor responds is relatively restricted. Electromagnetic energy, for example, covers a tremendous spectrum from gamma rays through x-rays, ultraviolet rays, infrared rays, radar, and radio waves to the alternating current in house wiring (see Figure 18.I). Yet our visual receptors respond only to energy lying in the spectrum between the ultraviolet and infrared waves. Our hearing receptors, similarly, respond to vibrations of matter between about 20 and 20,000 cycles per second, even though ultrasonic energies go up into the millions of cycles per second. Our chemical senses also respond only to certain chemical molecules; we cannot smell or taste others. Later, we shall specify more exactly the energies to which different receptors respond. The point here is that they respond to only a very small portion of the energy changes taking place in the world around us. Most of the energy changes in the external world are never perceived by human beings without the aid of special instruments, which are basically extensions of the senses.

Sensory Mechanisms

The study of the senses is a natural meeting ground for many sciences, especially psychology, neurophysiology, and physics. As such, it has had a long history. For instance, both Kepler (1571-1630) and Descartes (1596-1650) attempted to answer some of the questions concerning the working of vision. These men were completely mechanistic. Kepler tried to answer the question of how images are formed in the eye; Descartes tried to show the relationship between sensory input and response. Descartes "allowed only one kind of question: What physical motions follow each preceding physical motion?" (Crombie, 1964). In later centuries this mechanistic conception of the senses, in the hands of men such as Helmholtz (182I-1894), has been fruitful. We can do no better than to be mechanistic also. Our basic question will always be: What are the mechanics of sensory experience? The answer is, of course, very complex, and many of its aspects are imperfectly understood. We shall begin by considering three preliminary questions. Then we shall analyze the mechanisms of sensory experience for the specific senses, with special emphasis on vision and hearing.

Transduction Our first question is *What is the process by which physical energy is converted into information that can be used by the nervous system?* As already mentioned, we do not experience physical energy itself; we sense activity in the nervous system. This process of converting physical energy into activity in the nervous system is known in sensory psychology as *transduction*. Transduction takes place at the receptors—structures which, we have already seen, are specialized for best conversion of one particular type of energy: the adequate stimulus. The transduction process itself seems to involve several steps. In general, the specialized cells of the receptor act to convert physical energy into a rather slowly changing electrical potential, the *generator potential*. The generator potential, in turn, acts upon nerve cells and fibers to produce the nerve impulses which travel through the central portions of the channel and eventually result in an experience.

To explain this in terms familiar from Chapter 17, the generator poten-

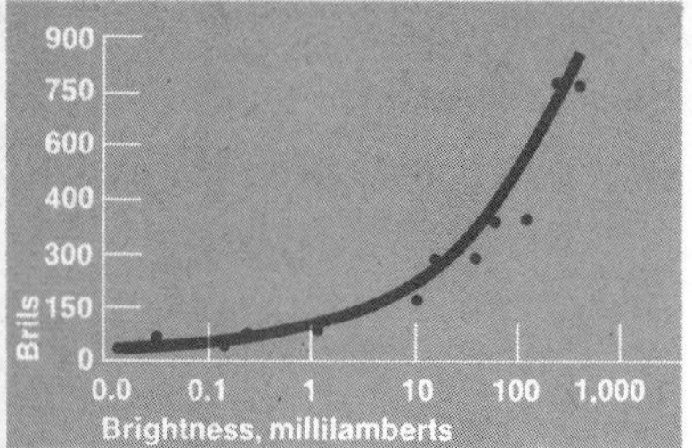

SUBJECTIVE BRIGHTNESS IS NOT DIRECTLY PROPORTIONAL TO PHYSICAL INTENSITY

Figure 18.2 *A subjective scale of brightness. Brils are the subjective (psychological) units, and millilamberts the physical units. In the middle of the curve, a stimulus that is ten times as intense as another is perceived as being about twice as intense. (After Hanes, 1949.)*

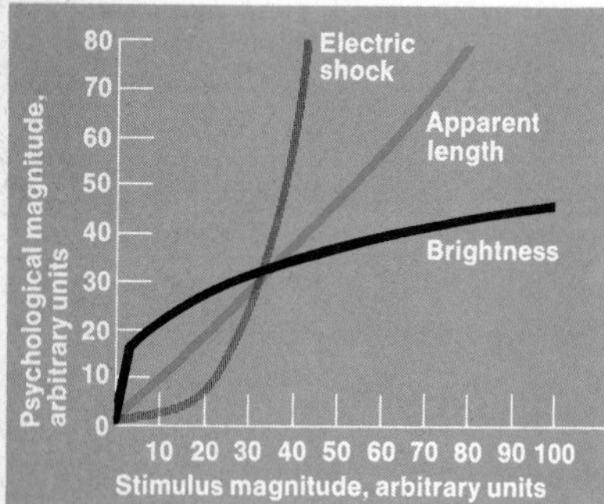

SUBJECTIVE EXPERIENCE IS EQUAL TO $k\Phi^n$

Figure 18.3 *The relationship between physical stimulus intensity and subjective experience according to one investigator. The size of the exponent n determines the shape of the curve. The exponent for the brightness curve is less than 1; that for the apparent length curve is 1; that for the electric shock intensity curve is greater than 1. (From Stevens, 1961.)*

tial acts like an excitatory postsynaptic potential, or an EPSP, to depolarize the endings of the nerve fibers which lead into the central nervous system. Depolarization to threshold levels causes nerve impulses to be triggered in the sensory channel. In some sensory systems—kinesthesis, for instance—the idea of such a general process is supported by a mass of evidence. In other systems—such as hearing—the idea is attractive but less definitely supported by evidence.

Nervous system and experience Let us suppose that nerve impulses have been generated in a sensory channel by the transduction process. The second question is this: *What is the relationship between activity in the sensory channel and experience?* We are asking about the *afferent code,* or pattern of activity in the sensory nervous system, which is the basis of the experience reported by a person (Pfaffmann,1959). Much of sensory psychology has been directed toward breaking this code to find the correlates between neuron activity and experience.

In order to discover the pattern or code, we need techniques for the investigation of single cells or fibers ("units") in the sensory channels. And in order to correlate pattern with reported experience, we need accurate reports of experience. On the one hand, such reports are best obtained from human beings; on the other hand, the recordings from single cells or fibers are obtained with physiological techniques which cannot be used on human beings. By giving animals a special experimental language, it is possible to get accurate "reports" from them (Blough, 1958). In the future we may be able to combine methods of unit recording from alert animals with methods of obtaining accurate reports from animal subjects. The technical problems are, however, enormous, and as yet largely unresolved. The current expedient is to study the relationship between characteristics of the physical energy and the patterns of nerve firings in the nervous system.

Physical energy and experience: Psychophysics Suppose we pass over the relationship between neural activity and experience for a while and go on to a third question: *What is the relationship between the characteristics of physical energy and reported experience?*

Psychophysics studies this relationship between physical energy and experience by means of *psychophysical methods.* Our emphasis here is not on the detailed methods of psychophysics. (For a description of these methods, see Guilford, 1954; Green and Swets, 1966.) Rather, we are interested in some of the general concepts.

PSYCHOPHYSICAL RELATIONSHIPS Sensory experience and physical energy are related, and the characteristics of the relationship must be discovered by experiments using psychophysical methods. As we shall see, the relationship is regular, or lawful—so much of a change in experience for so much of a change in physical energy. On the one hand is the physical energy, which is measured and referred to in physical terms; on the other hand is the experience, which is referred to in psychological terms.

For instance, the relationship between perceived brightness and the amount of energy in the physical stimulus appears in Figure I8.2. Here

Table 18.1 *Some approximate detection threshold values.*

Source: Modified from Galanter, 1962.

Sense modality	Detection threshold
Vision	Candle flame seen at 30 miles on a dark clear night (about 10 quanta)
Hearing	Tick of a watch under quiet conditions at 20 feet (about 0.0002 dyne/cm^2)
Taste	Teaspoon of sugar in 2 gallons of water
Smell	Drop of perfume diffused into the entire volume of a three-room apartment
Touch	Wing of a bee falling on your cheek from a distance of 1 centimeter

the scale of perceived brightness is labeled "brils," and the amount of physical energy is measured in millilamberts. In the middle of the curve, a stimulus that is ten times as intense as another is not perceived as ten times greater, but more like two times greater. Furthermore, the exact relationship between perceived brightness and physical energy varies with the intensity of the physical stimulus. In any case, perception of a change in intensity does not correspond in a one-to-one fashion with the physical change in intensity. Similar types of relationships between perception and physical energy exist in other sensory channels.

Several attempts have been made to formulate a general relationship between physical energy and perceptual experience which holds for most, if not all, sensory channels. To some extent, such general laws depend upon certain assumptions and upon the method used to measure intensity of experience. The most direct methods of measurement seem to give a power function as the general law. The *power function law* relating intensity of experience to intensity of stimulation states that the strength of experience is equal to some constant times the magnitude of the physical stimulation raised to some power (Stevens, 1961). The constant and the power must be discovered for each sensory channel by experiment. In mathematical terms, the power law states that $\Psi = k\Phi^n$, where Ψ is intensity of *experience,* k is a constant, Φ is the intensity of the *physical energy,* and n is a power to which Φ is raised. Figure 18.3 shows this general relationship for several sensory modalities with differing exponents and constants. The important point is that the shape of the functional relationship can be fitted best to the general power equation.

ABSOLUTE AND DIFFERENTIAL THRESHOLDS Even though receptors are extremely effective transducers, each seems to require some minimum level of activating physical energy before sensory experience is possible (see Table 18.1). In our attempt to relate physical energy and experience, we want to know the answer to the question: What is the least amount of physical energy which can be experienced? This basic question in psychophysics has turned out to be much more complicated than it might seem at first glance. The classic answer is that there is an *absolute threshold* for each sense. When physical energy levels are below certain values—that is, when they are below the threshold—the stimuli are not detected; when they are above this value, detection and differential response are possible. There are difficulties with this view, however, and doubts have been raised about the possibility of measuring absolute threshold points (Swets, 1961).

So far we have been considering the absolute threshold and the least amount of energy required for detection. Another important question in psychophysics is: What is the smallest difference between two stimuli—two light intensities, for instance—necessary before we can discriminate a difference between them? The smallest difference which can be discriminated is known as the *differential threshold,* or the *just noticeable difference* (JND). One of the most important things about the differential threshold is that it is not constant. Suppose you are in a room which is illuminated by one 25-watt bulb, and another 25-watt bulb is turned on. The addition of this amount of extra light will be immediately detectable—it is well above the differential threshold. If, however, you are in a room which is illuminated by a thousand 25-watt bulbs, the addition of the light from one more bulb will not be noticed. The amount of energy added in the brighter room is the same, but that amount is below the differential threshold. Thus the value of the differential threshold depends upon the intensity of the stimulus to which more energy is added. It has been found, however, that, for relatively moderate intensities, a constant *ratio* exists between the amount of energy which must be added, called ΔI, to reach the differential threshold, and the intensity, called I, of the stimulation. In other words, $\Delta I/I$ is a constant for the middle range of intensities. This has been called *Weber's law,* and it holds fairly well for all but the extreme intensities of stimulation.

In this chapter on the nervous system and behavior, our interest centers on questions about the nervous system and experience. Thus we come back to the first two questions we raised at the beginning: What do we know about the way physical energy is converted into nerve impulses, the common coin of experience? And what is the relationship between activity in the nervous system and experience, or put another way, what is the afferent code for various experiences in the various sensory channels? A great deal of progress has been made toward answering these questions, in the course of which several Nobel prizes have been awarded to biologists.

Vision

The fact that we experience the world visually is wonderful and amazing, but how can it happen? Neurophysiologists and psychologists do not know all, or even very many, of the details of the process. But a coherent explanation of vision, and of some other senses as well, is beginning to emerge.

The outline of the story for vision is really fairly simple. The *electromagnetic energy* which we call visible light strikes specialized *receptor cells* in the eye—namely, the *rods* and *cones* of the *retina*—and initiates a series of chemical changes in the light-sensitive substances of these

THE VISIBLE SPECTRUM

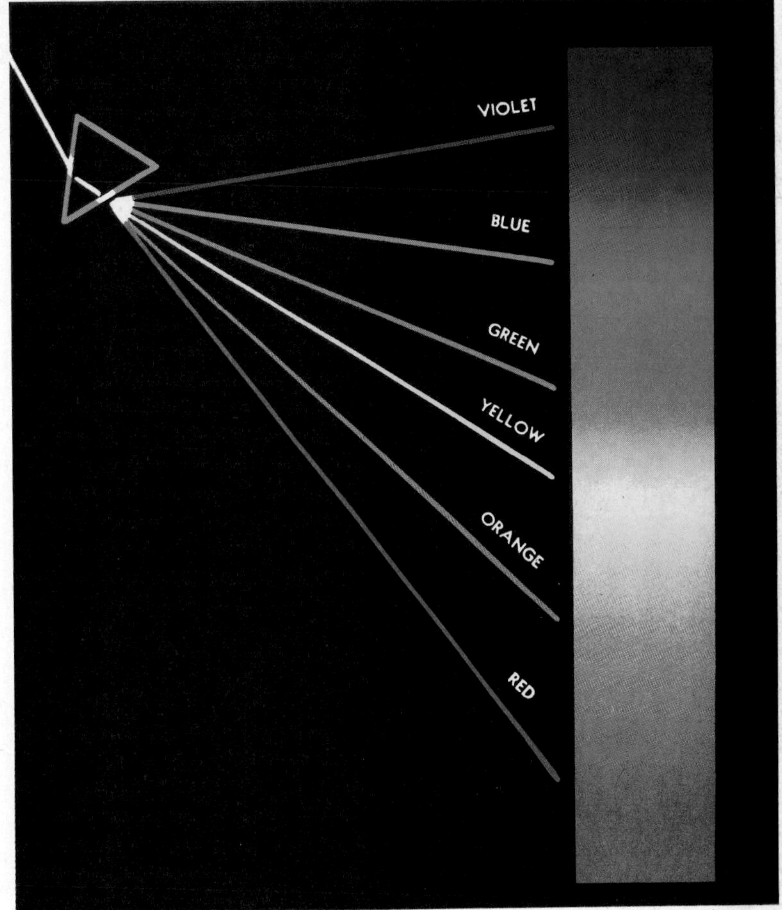

Figure 18.4 *All the colors of the visible spectrum are produced when a prism is used to break up white light into its components. (From Bustanoby, 1947.)*

cells. The outcome of the series of reactions is an electrical event, a voltage change, called the *generator potential.* The generator potential is the event which causes barrages of nerve impulses to be triggered, and it is this barrage which constitutes the input into the central nervous system responsible for seeing. What we see depends, of course, on the objects transmitting light to the retina. But from the point of view of our analysis, what we see depends upon the characteristics of the barrage of nerve impulses which reach the central nervous system.

The physical stimulus for vision We see objects because they emit radiant energy or because radiant energy is reflected from them. This energy, which physicists call electromagnetic radiation, may be thought of as electric charges moving through space at approximately 186,000 miles per second. It is difficult to explain just what these charges or electromagnetic radiations are like. But they exhibit wavelike characteristics, and it is conventional to speak of these radiations as *electro-*

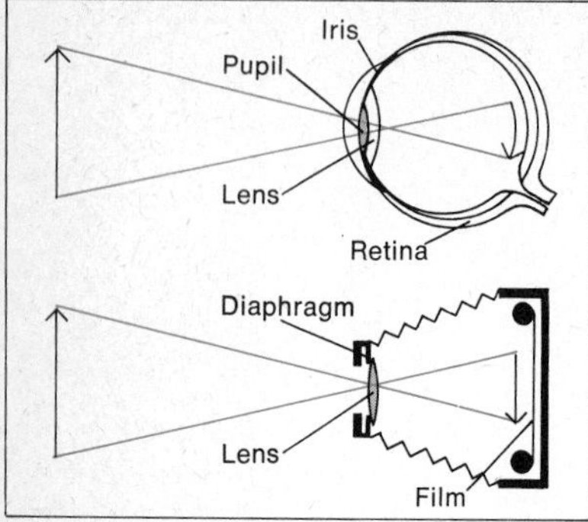

THE EYE IS LIKE A CAMERA

Figure 18.5 *Both the eye and the camera are dark chambers that admit light through an opening. In both, the image is focused by a lens and is projected upside down and reversed on the photosensitive surface. The amount of light entering each is adjustable. The eye, however, has many features which make it a different and far more complex instrument than a camera.*

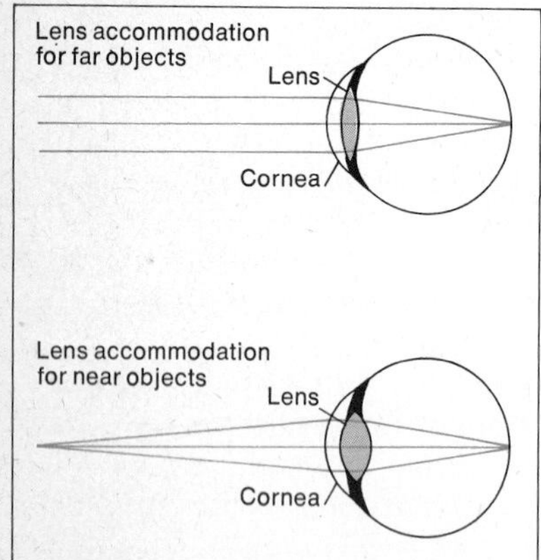

THE LENS CHANGES SHAPE TO FOCUS OBJECTS ON THE RETINA

Figure 18.6 *The accommodation of the lens. The lens flattens to focus images of objects far away, and it thickens to focus images of nearby objects. Note that much of the refraction, or bending, of the light is done by the cornea, which does not change shape.*

magnetic waves. Radiant energy can be measured and classified in terms of the distance from the peak of one wave to the peak of the next—that is, in terms of *wavelength.* Some electromagnetic radiations have wavelengths as short as 10 trillionths of a meter (the gamma rays), some have wavelengths of thousands of meters (radio waves), and all sorts of wavelengths occur in between (see Figure 18.1). The entire range of wavelengths is called the *electromagnetic spectrum.*

Although it is true that all radiant energy—all wavelengths of the electromagnetic spectrum—is very much the same physically, only a small portion of it is visible. Somewhere in the middle of the range of radiant energies are the wavelengths that we can see (Figure 18.1). These wavelengths are known as the *visible spectrum.* Because the word *light* implies seeing, it is only these visible wavelengths that are called light waves. To express wavelength, we use the metric scale; in the visible spectrum, the wavelengths are expressed in billionths of a meter, or *nanometers* (nm). The visible spectrum extends from about 380 to 780 nanometers.

As Isaac Newton discovered in 1666, it is possible to break up the visible spectrum into its component wavelengths.[1] The trick is to pass a beam of white, or mixed, light through a glass prism (see Figure 18.4). Such a prism bends short wavelengths (which appear violet) more than long wavelengths (which appear red). A prism, in fact, spreads all the wavelengths out in a broad band so that we can see and measure each wavelength in a mixed beam of light. Wavelengths in the visible spectrum are related to color experience.

Structure of the eye and visual system Now let us turn to the anatomy of the eye and visual portions of the central nervous system, so that we can have it in mind when we consider the transduction process and afferent coding. In certain respects, the eye looks and behaves like a camera (see Figure 18.5). Both are essentially dark chambers which admit light through an opening in front. Immediately behind the opening is a lens which focuses images of outside objects onto the rear surface. In the eye, the surface on which the image is projected is called the retina; in the camera, it is the photographic film. Just as in a camera, the images falling on the retina are inverted and reversed from right to left.

Both the camera and the eye can be adjusted to control the amount of light falling on this surface. To control light entering a camera, the photographer adjusts the diaphragm in front of the lens. When he wants less light he decreases the size of the opening in the diaphragm; when he wants more light to enter the camera, he increases the size of the opening. The eye, however, has its own automatic, or reflex, mechanism for making this adjustment. Its diaphragm is the *iris,* which is the colored part of the eye. The iris controls the size of the opening, known as the *pupil,* which admits light to the eye. In dim light, the iris expands the pupil, thus increasing the amount of light admitted; in bright light, it contracts the pupil. This adjustment permits a person to see in dimmer and in brighter illuminations than would otherwise be possible. You can

[1] This work was not published in full until Newton presented his *Opticks* in 1704.

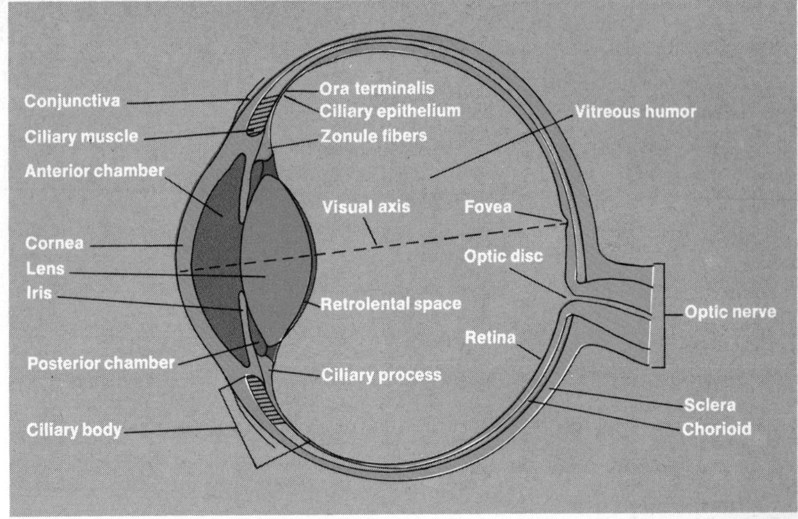

Figure 18.7 *The anatomy of the eye, showing some of the principal parts. (Based on Walls, 1942.)*

easily observe the contraction of the pupil by having a person close his eyes for a while and then open them. The normal pupil has a maximum range of adjustment of 2 to 8 millimeters in diameter—corresponding to a sixteenfold change in area.

Although it is instructive to compare the eye to the camera, this comparison must not be pushed too far. The details of the processes are different, and there are other fundamental differences. First, it is misleading to think that we see directly the small images which form on the retina—what we see is the result of a long series of events (see Chapter 8). It is true that the light falling on the retina is patterned, but we do not see this. As mentioned earlier, the activity of the nervous system is what we "see." The neural input is subject to much reorganization on its way through the retina and from the retina to the brain, and the eventual spatial and temporal pattern of nervous activity which underlies visual experience is quite different from the light patterns on the retina.

Second, the eye has a double lens system: the *cornea* and the lens itself (see Figures 18.6 and 18.7). As a matter of fact, most light bending, or *refraction*, in the eye is done by the cornea; the lens simply adds enough bending to the basic corneal refraction to bring near objects into sharp focus on the retina.

Furthermore, the eye focuses light on the retina differently from most cameras. The typical camera method of adjusting focus for objects at different distances is by moving the lens back and forth. In the human eye, focus is achieved by changing the shape of the lens—a process made possible by an arrangement of muscles and ligaments. The lens becomes thicker in order to focus objects which are close; it becomes thinner for distant objects (see Figure 18.6). These lens changes are termed *accommodation*. Correction of accommodation defects is the major reason for wearing glasses.

Finally, the eye is not a passive receiver—it is never at rest. Extremely small tremors of the eye muscles produce small and continual move-

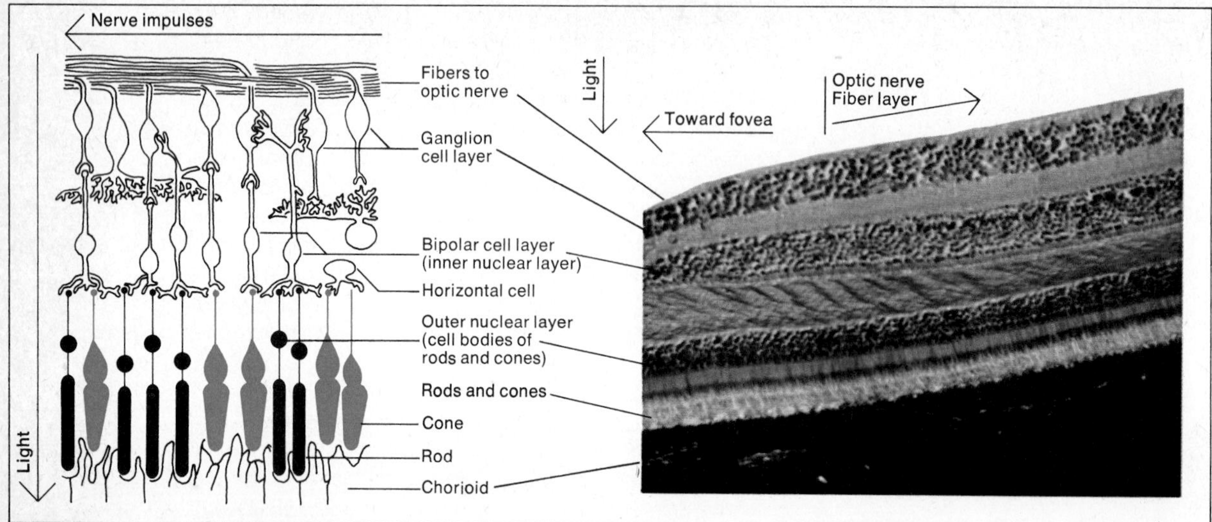

LIGHT EXCITES THE RODS AND CONES, WHICH SEND NERVE IMPULSES VIA THE BIPOLAR AND GANGLION CELLS TO THE BRAIN

Figure 18.8 *A schematic diagram and a photomicrograph of a cross section of the retina. Three cell layers are clearly shown in the photograph; the cell bodies appear as dark dots. These three sets of cells are on the "direct line" to the brain for transmitting information about light.*
From the top in both the photograph and the drawing, the first layer of cell bodies is the ganglion cell layer; the next is the bipolar cell layer (inner nuclear layer); the third cell layer (outer nuclear layer) consists of the cell bodies of the light-sensitive elements themselves—the rods and cones. Between the cell layers are the fiber connections.
In the photograph, the ganglion cell layer becomes thinner toward the left. This is because the fovea—the area for sharpest vision—is to the left, and there are no ganglion cells at the fovea. (The cell bodies of the ganglion cells serving the fovea lie around the fovea.)
(Photograph from Mitchell Glickstein, Brown University.)

ments of the eyeball. These small movements, called *physiological nystagmus,* are essential to vision. In experiments where special lens systems are used to prevent the play of excitation over the retina, objects disappear from vision (Riggs et al., 1953). By spreading excitation over a fairly wide area, physiological nystagmus probably prevents fatigue of the receptor elements.

SCLERA, CHORIOID, AND RETINA A closer look at the eye reveals an organ of enormous complexity—so complex that the drawing in Figure 18.7, which is complicated enough, shows only its essential features. The eye is roughly a sphere, and its walls consist of three separate layers: the sclera, the chorioid, and the retina.

1. The outer layer, the *sclera layer,* is a tough fibrous material that protects the eyeball and maintains its shape. In the front of the eye, this sclera layer becomes transparent and bulges out to form the *cornea.* The *extraocular muscles* which turn the eyeball are attached to the sclera layer.
2. Underneath the sclera layer is the *chorioid layer,* which corresponds roughly to the opaque backing on a photographic film or to the blackening on the inside of a camera. This dark layer absorbs stray light in the eyeball and prevents light from entering the eye except through the cornea and lens.
3. The *retina layer,* the innermost layer of the eyeball, is like a photographic film, as we have said; it is the sensitive tissue that enables us to see.

RODS, CONES, AND THE FOVEA Since the retina is the sensitive element for seeing, we shall give it closer attention than the other structures of the eye. Examining it with a microscope, we can see that it is made up of many layers of cells and fibers (see the photograph in Figure 18.8). Two

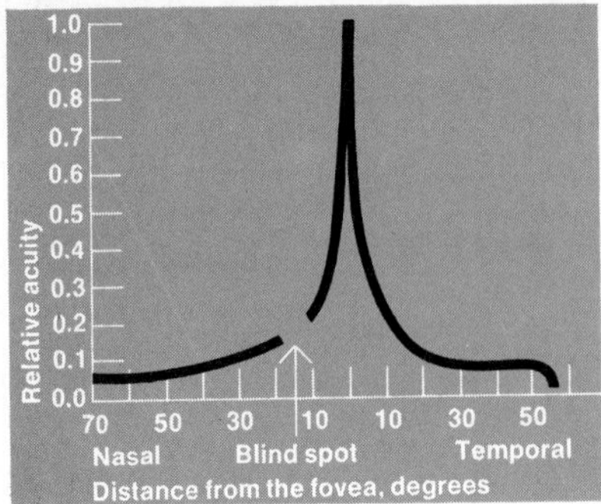

VISUAL ACUITY IS MORE ACUTE AT THE FOVEA

Figure 18.9 *Visual acuity varies with the part of the retina used in viewing. It is greatest at the fovea and drops off rapidly toward the periphery of the retina. Note the position of the blind spot on the side of the retina toward the nose.*

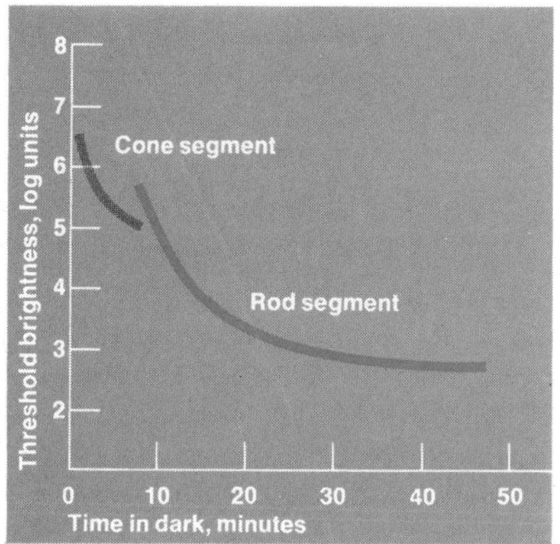

GIVEN ENOUGH TIME, THE EYE BECOMES THOUSANDS OF TIMES MORE SENSITIVE IN THE DARK

Figure 18.10 *A typical curve of dark adaptation. After a subject has been in normal or bright illumination for some time, he is placed in the dark and asked to indicate the weakest light (threshold intensity) that he can see. Thresholds are taken repeatedly, minute after minute, and the results are plotted in a curve of dark adaptation. Notice the two segments of the curve; after 7 or 8 minutes the rods, which are responsible for our dim-light vision, take over from the cones, which function in bright light.*

types of cells—rods and cones—are the light-sensitive elements (see the drawing in Figure 18.8). Note that the rods and cones are placed on the side of the retina away from the light; light must go through the nearly transparent layers of the retina before reaching the rods and cones. For this reason, the human retina is known as an *inverted* retina. The rods are cylindrical in shape, and the cones are rather tapered. Our best estimate is that the eye contains between 110,000,000 and 125,000,000 rods and between 6,300,000 and 6,800,000 cones (Østerberg, 1935). This tremendous number of rods and cones, however, is not spread uniformly over the entire retina. In the *blind spot,* for instance there are no rods or cones, and no vision is possible. The blind spot is the region of the retina where the optic nerve fibers leave the retina and where the blood vessels enter and leave (see Figure 18.7).

Cones are most numerous in a highly specialized region of the retina known as the *fovea.* The rods occur most frequently about 20 degrees away from the fovea. As Figure 18.7 shows, the fovea, or *fovea centralis,* is a slightly depressed area of the retina. It is the region of the retina responsible for the most acute, or distinct, vision and is the part that we use most in looking at objects which we wish to see clearly. Figure 18.9 shows that visual acuity, or sharpness, is greatest at the fovea, nonexistent at the blind spot, and graded from the fovea out toward the periphery of the retina.

In addition to their role in visual acuity, cones have other characteristics which distinguish their function in vision from that of rods. In fact, it has sometimes been said that we really have two visual systems, a cone system and a rod system; this idea is known as the *duplicity theory* of vision. Cones, for instance, are the retinal elements active in bright light, or daylight vision; rods are the retinal elements active in dim light conditions. In careful studies of visual function, it is often possible to find evidence for the activity of both cone and rod systems, as the following example shows.

We all know that the eye becomes more sensitive in the dark. But the curve of increasing sensitivity is not a smooth one; it contains a break as function shifts from cone elements to rod elements. We measure the course of dark adaptation by first having a person fully adapt his eyes to bright light. Then he is put in the dark, and his absolute threshold—the least amount of light he can reliably detect—is measured several times over a period of minutes in the dark. Typical results from such an experiment are shown in Figure 18.10. As might be expected, the absolute threshold decreases over time in the dark. But notice that a break occurs in the function after about 7 or 8 minutes in the dark. Around this time, the rod elements of the retina, which had been rendered nonfunctional by the previous light adaptation, begin to operate. The detection of very dim lights after longer periods in the dark is a rod function.

Not only are cones the elements responsible for the greatest acuity and for daylight vision; they are also the retinal elements necessary for color vision. Stimulation of the peripheral portions of the retina that are many degrees from the fovea does not produce an experience of color, but only black and white vision. Color-blind persons have deficiencies in the cone mechanisms.

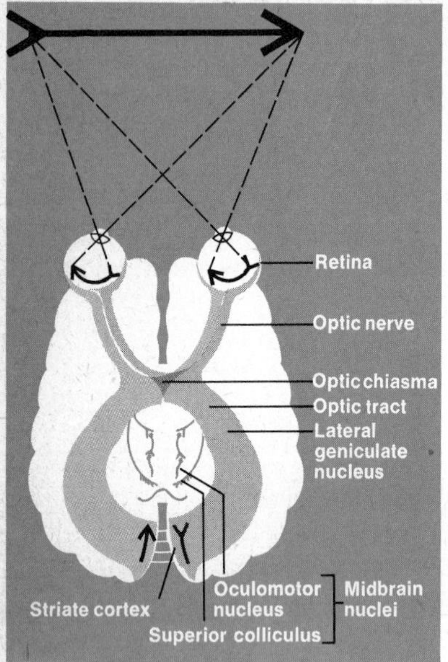

HERE'S LOOKING AT YOU

Figure 18.11 *A diagram of the visual system. The view is, generally, of the base of the cerebrum. The projections through the system are shown. Note that the right half of the visual field—the point of the arrow—projects to the left half of the brain; this projection is shown by the blue pathway. The left half of the visual field—the back of the arrow—projects to the right half of the brain; this projection is shown by the gray pathway. At the optic chiasma, the two projections from the nasal sides of the retinas cross. Certain areas of the midbrain which receive an input from the optic nerve are also shown: The oculomotor nucleus controls some movements of the eyes and the pupillary reflex; the superior colliculus is a midbrain area for reflexes in which the body is oriented toward visual stimuli. (From Polyak, 1957, as modified by Butter, 1968. By permission of The University of Chicago Press and Brooks/Cole Publishing Company.)*

CONNECTIONS OF THE CONES AND RODS From the rods and cones, tiny nerve fibers make connections with still other types of cells, as seen in Figure 18.8. Two kinds, the *bipolar* cells and the *ganglion* cells, shown in both the photograph and the drawing of this figure, are in a direct line with the central nervous system. Indeed, the fibers of the ganglion cells make up the optic nerve which conveys impulses from the retina to the brain. Hence the three sets of cells in the retina which are on the "direct line" for transmitting information about light are (1) rods and cones, (2) bipolar cells, and (3) ganglion cells.

Note from the drawing in Figure 18.8 that other cells make interconnections at the retinal level: not all the cells are on the direct line to the brain. Such interconnectedness at the retinal level means that before the information leaves the retina, it has already been partially processed at the receptor itself. Some fairly complex phenomena of vision can be explained by this processing. And as we know, the information is further transformed at higher levels of the nervous system (see Chapter 8).

CENTRAL NERVOUS SYSTEM CONNECTIONS OF THE VISUAL SYSTEM Suppose we follow the course of axons of the retinal ganglion cells into the brain. Figure 18.11 shows the visual pathway from the retina to the brain. Fibers from the ganglion cells make up the *optic nerves.* Those fibers coming from the sides of the retinas nearest the nose, the nasal half-retinas, cross to the other side of the brain at the *optic chiasma,* or crossover of the optic nerves. Fibers from the outside, or temporal half-retinas, do not cross at the optic chiasma but project back to the same side of the brain as the retina from which they started. The collection of crossed and uncrossed fibers after the chiasma is known as the *optic tract.* After running through the optic tract, the fibers reach the relay center for vision in the thalamus, the *lateral geniculate body.* Here the ganglion cell axons terminate in synapses, and new fibers project upward in the *optic radiation*—the tract from the lateral geniculate body to the visual sensory area of the cerebral cortex located along the midline in the back of the brain (see Figure 18.11). On their way to the brain, some fibers go to visual centers in the midbrain that are involved in reflex actions.

One of the interesting things about the projection of some of the sensory systems to the brain is the *topographical arrangement* which exists. The projection regions—that is, the regions of the brain on which the sensory information is projected—are arranged like maps of the sensory surface. In the case of vision, for instance, the lateral geniculate body in the thalamus and the cortical area are arranged so that points on them represent particular points on the retina. By recording with electrodes and by using degeneration methods and staining techniques, it can be shown that for every point on the retina there is a corresponding region in the thalamus and a cortical area. This arrangement is sometimes called a *point-to-point projection.*

Some of the details of this projection pathway are shown in Figure 18.11. First of all, the arrow in the visual field is reversed in the right-left dimension by the lens system of the eye. It is also reversed in the up-down dimension, but in order to simplify the diagram, this reversal of the visual field on the retina is not shown. Next, the information from

DAMAGE TO THE VISUAL SYSTEM PRODUCES SPECIFIC BLINDNESSES

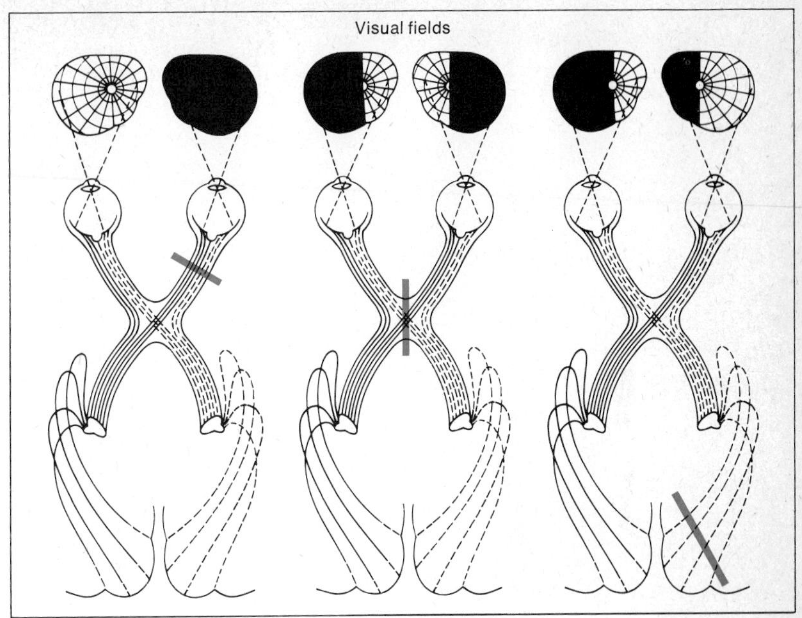

***Figure 18.12** The effects of cuts in various parts of the human visual projection pathway. In each diagram, the visual fields are shown at the top, the retinas and pathways in the middle, and the visual regions of the cerebral cortex at the bottom. (After Teuber et al., 1960.)*

the surface of the retina is projected, through the tracts already detailed, back to the brain in the following manner: The fibers from the halves of the retina toward the temples (the temporal half-retinas) do not cross; they project back to the side of the brain on which they originated. The fibers from the halves of the retina nearest the nose (the nasal half-retinas) cross at the optic chiasma to the opposite side of the brain. Point-to-point projection is maintained between the retinas and the lateral geniculate bodies; this is not shown in the diagram. Point-to-point projection is also maintained between the retinas and the primary visual areas of the cortex; the projection of the arrow along the *calcarine fissure* is shown in the figure. Owing to the partial crossing of the visual projection system in man and the higher primates, the right visual field projects to the left visual cortical area, and the left visual field projects to the right visual cortical area. Another point of interest is that half of the arrow is represented on each side of the brain, and a gap in the cortex exists between projections of the two halves of the arrow. Yet we do not see this gap in our experience of the visual world; the world looks continuous. This is a bit of evidence for the conclusion that visual, or any, sensory experience depends upon reorganization of the information arising in the receptors (see Chapter 8).

To understand the visual pathway a little better, we might consider what would happen if a person had *lesions,* or damage, in various parts of the visual system. First of all, if the optic nerve has been destroyed on the right side (see Figure 18.12, left) the patient will, of course, be completely blind in his right eye. Second, if a cut has been made through the optic chiasma (Figure 18.12, middle), the crossed fibers from the nasal halves of the two retinas are cut. Since the temporal parts of the

LIGHT BREAKS DOWN VISUAL PURPLE, BUT IN THE DARK, VISUAL PURPLE RE-FORMS FROM THE BREAKDOWN PRODUCTS

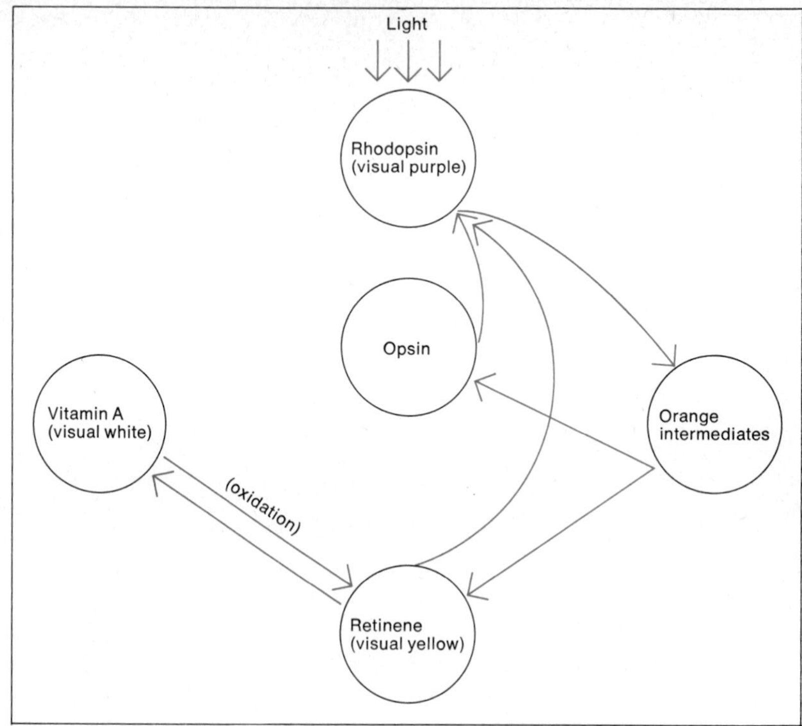

Figure 18.13 *The visual cycle. (Morgan, 1965.)*

visual field project onto the nasal retinas, the person will be blind in the two temporal, or outside, parts of the visual fields. Finally, if the right optic radiation is completely cut, or the right visual cortex destroyed, the patient will be blind on one side of his visual field—the left side, in this case (Figure 18.12, right). Blindness of this sort in the right or left half of the visual field is called *homonymous hemianopia.*

Transduction in vision Now that we know something about the structures involved in vision, we can turn to the functioning of the system. How do the light-sensitive rods and cones change electromagnetic energies of certain wavelengths into the nerve impulses flowing through the visual system that are necessary for our visual perception? The entire process of transduction is extremely complex when all the details are considered, but its outline is simple. It takes place in three main stages: The first consists of chemical events in the light-sensitive pigments found within the rod and cone cells. The second is the creation of a generator potential as a result of the photochemical activity. The third is the generation and propagation of nerve impulses along the fibers of the visual pathway to the brain.

PHOTOSENSITIVE PIGMENTS When electromagnetic energy in the visible spectrum strikes photosensitive pigments in the rods and cones, chemical changes occur that initiate the chain of processes in seeing. The

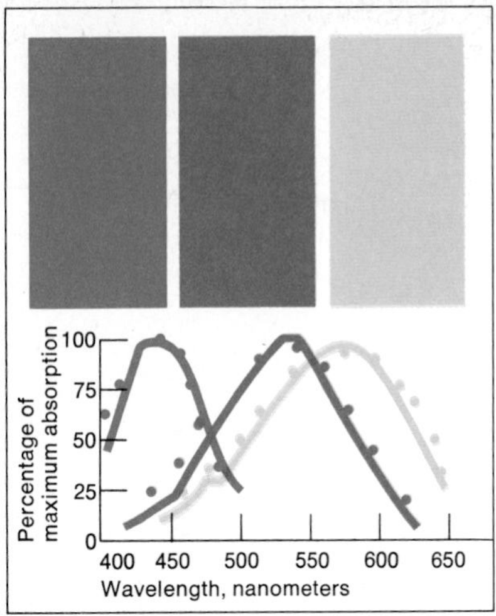

CONES OF THE HUMAN RETINA SEEM TO BE MOST SENSITIVE TO THREE WAVELENGTHS

Figure 18.14 *The human retina seems to contain "blue" cones, "green" cones, and "yellow" cones. The lower curves show the absorption of light by the three types of human cones. For instance, the "blue" cones absorb the short wavelengths most effectively; the "green" cones absorb the middle wavelengths; and the "yellow" cones absorb the long wavelengths most effectively. The peak absorptions are at 447 nanometers, 540 nanometers, and 577 nanometers for the three types of cones. The colors corresponding to the wavelengths of these peak absorptions are shown above. (MacNichol, 1964;* Scientific American.*)*

fact that photosensitive pigment is involved in vision was first discovered by Franz Boll in 1876. He noticed that the retina of a frog which had been in the dark for some time had a reddish-purple color, but that when the eye was exposed to light, the pigment bleached to a yellowish color. Thus the photosensitive substance was first called "visual purple," and after exposure to light, it was called "visual yellow." Subsequent research has shown that the rods and cones have different photosensitive pigments with different properties. *Rhodopsin* is the major pigment in the rods; *iodopsin* is the general term which has been applied to the cone pigments of certain animals (Wald, 1959). It has been shown that three types of cone pigments probably occur in the human retina. This fits well with the three-color theory of color vision which we discuss later.

Originally called visual purple, the *rod pigment,* or rhodopsin, is found in the rods of most vertebrate animals. When struck by electromagnetic energy in the visible range, rhodopsin is broken into orange intermediates and then into two substances, *retinene* and *opsin* (see Figure 18.13). Retinene is yellowish and was originally called visual yellow. Retinene and opsin spontaneously change back into rhodopsin. The whole sequence of chemical changes is called the *visual cycle.* In this cycle, an equilibrium is established between the breakdown of rhodopsin and its synthesis from retinene and opsin. The rates of the reactions depend upon the intensity of the illumination. Under dim illumination, the rhodopsin-retinene-rhodopsin reaction is the prominent one, but under intense illumination, some of the retinene is converted to vitamin A. This reaction is also reversible; after the intense illumination is over, the vitamin A will be converted back into retinene, which will then change back into rhodopsin (Figure 18.13).

Cone pigments have been identified by the study of spectral-absorption curves. Spectral-absorption curves are obtained because the electromagnetic energy which is active in decomposing the visual pigments is absorbed in the process. Some substances absorb some wavelengths best, other substances absorb other wavelengths. For example, in the chicken retina, the general cone substance, iodopsin, has a peak of absorption at wavelengths near 555 nanometers; rhodopsin, the major rod substance, has an absorption peak near 505 nanometers.

That three different types of cone substances seem to exist in human and monkey retinas has been discovered by using a device called a microspectrophotometer, in which the absorption of light in single cones can be studied (MacNichol, 1964). The substance in one type of cone seems to have an absorption peak at approximately 447 nanometers; that in another type, a peak at approximately 540 nanometers; and that in the third type, a peak at about 577 nanometers (see Figure 18.14). The cones of the primate retina thus seem to fall into three clusters or populations. Since we see blue when stimulated by wavelengths at 477 nanometers, green when stimulated at 540 nanometers, and yellow at 577 nanometers, the different types of cones might be called "blue," "green," and "yellow" cones. Although the peak sensitivity of the yellow cones is in the part of the spectrum perceived as yellow, they are also sensitive to longer, or "red," wavelengths.

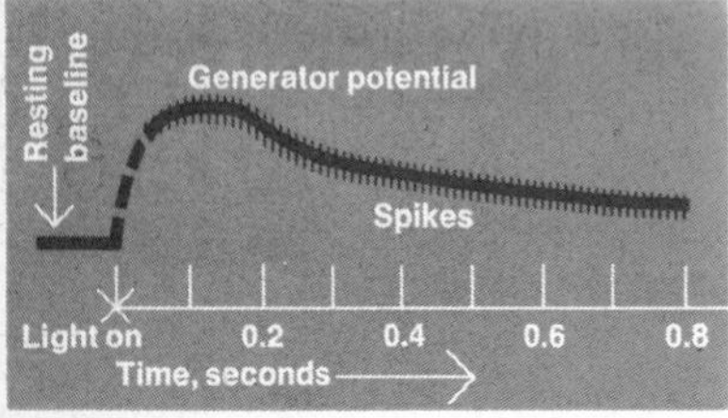

SLOW VOLTAGE CHANGES (GENERATOR POTENTIALS) AND FAST VOLTAGE CHANGES (SPIKES) ARE RECORDED FROM THE EYES OF MANY ANIMALS

Figure 18.15 *Generator potential and nerve impulses recorded from the eye of the horseshoe crab,* Limulus. *The light is turned on at the X on the lower line and remains on for the duration of the recording. Shortly after it goes on, a slow and prolonged change of voltage occurs—the generator potential. It seems to be responsible for the fast voltage changes, that is, nerve impulses, which appear as spikes superimposed on it. The details of this sort of process are discussed in Chapter 17. (Based on Hartline et al. Reproduced from Volume XVII:* Cold Spring Harbor Symposia, 1952.*)*

GENERATOR POTENTIALS The next event after light strikes the eye is the production of slow, graded, generator electrical potentials in the retina. They are probably related to the chemical changes in the pigments, but the exact relationship is not clear.

In the eyes of some animals—*Limulus,* the horseshoe crab, for example—the generator electrical potential following light stimulation is relatively easy to measure (Hartline et al., 1952; Benolken, 196l). The prolonged deflection of voltage above the baseline shown in Figure 18.15 is the generator potential. The generator potential makes the neural elements more electrically negative—it depolarizes these elements and triggers nerve impulses, or *spikes* (see Chapter 17). Generator potentials are characteristic of other sensory systems also (Granit, 1955).

Electrical activity similar to generator potentials has been discovered in the eyes of other creatures. These have been called the S, or slow, potentials (Tomita, 1963). The slow potentials are like generator potentials in that they are graded—their size depends upon the intensity of the stimulus. The stronger the stimulus, the greater the size of the electrical S potentials. The nerve impulses, or spikes, which arise on top of the slow potentials are not graded—their size does not depend upon the strength of the stimulus (see Chapter 17). The exact site of the generation of these slow potentials is not certain. Experiments have shown that they do not originate in rods or cones or at the ganglion cells—they arise between these elements. The current opinion is that they do not originate in the bipolar cells, as one might expect, but in large glial (supporting or nourishing) cells within the retina.

NERVE IMPULSES We have already seen nerve impulses, or spikes, arising from the generator potential. These impulses are recorded from the ganglion cells (shown in Figure 18.8) with microelectrodes. A strong relationship exists between the size of the generator potential and the rate at which nerve impulses are produced: the greater the size of the generator potential, the greater the frequency of nerve impulses. This seems to be true in general, but it has been shown most clearly in the eye of *Limulus.*

It seems clear that nerve impulses arise in ganglion cells when light strikes the retina. But the picture is more complicated than this. The activity of an individual ganglion cell can be increased or decreased by stimulating various points over a wide region of the retina. This brings us to the idea of a receptive field. The *receptive field* of any sensory cell (a ganglion cell, in this case) is the area of the receptor surface (the rod and cone layer of the retina, in this case) from which its firing can be influenced—either increased or decreased. The receptive fields of many ganglion cells are organized as shown in Figure 18.16. Stimulation of the center part of the field results in an "on" response—the ganglion cell gives nerve impulses, it "fires." Stimulation of the peripheral part of the field results in an "off" response—the same ganglion cell fires when the stimulus goes off. The reverse of this situation is also quite common. An intermediate zone between the inner and outer "on" and "off" zones gives "on-off" responses.

These receptive fields of the ganglion cells indicate that the output of the retina is organized and patterned at the first stage of projection to the

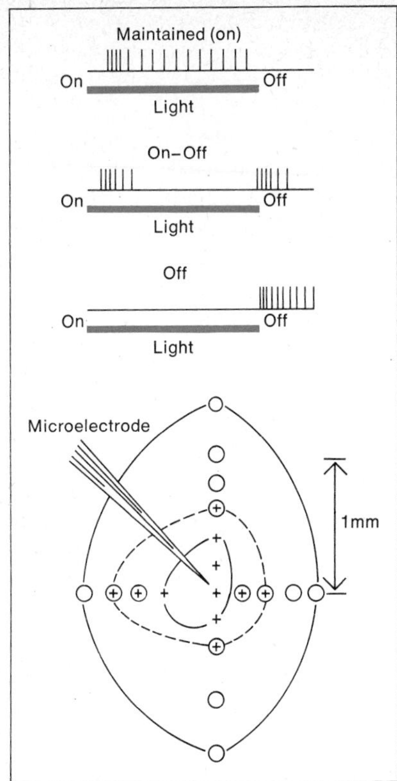

GANGLION CELLS OF THE RETINA MAY RESPOND TO LIGHT IN SEVERAL WAYS

Figure 18.16 *Top, "on," "on-off," and "off" responses from ganglion cells of the retina, as measured by microelectrodes. Bottom, types of ganglion cell response from different parts of the receptive field. Stimulation restricted to the center of this receptive field produces "on" responses, indicated by +; stimulation of an intermediate zone produces "on-off" responses, indicated by ⊕; stimulation at the periphery of the field produces "off" responses, indicated by ○. (Top, modified from Hartline, 1938; bottom, after Kuffler, 1953.)*

cortex. The firing rates of the ganglion cells are complexly determined by influences from other parts of the retina. Some of the code for visual sensory experience, the *afferent code*, is in these ganglion cell firing patterns. The point here is that the ganglion cells in the retina fire in response to light and that the nerve impulses from these cells influence the next cells in the visual system, the lateral geniculate cells (located in the lateral geniculate body, shown in Figure 18.11). The lateral geniculate cells can be excited or inhibited, as we shall see, by the output of the retinal ganglion cells. In other words, a barrage of nerve impulses from ganglion cells can increase or decrease the firing of lateral geniculate cells. The activity of these lateral geniculate cells is more closely related to visual experience and more directly involved in the afferent code for visual experience than the ganglion cell activity. Therefore we shall consider activity in the lateral geniculate cells, and the cortex too, shortly when we discuss the afferent code for visual experience.

Psychophysical relationships Before studying the nervous system code, or afferent code, underlying visual experience, we must examine the relationships between the physical stimulus and various aspects of experience. A visual experience may have *form, brightness,* and *hue;* and the hue may be more or less mixed with white, or more or less *saturated.* The psychophysics of form perception depend upon differences in the amounts of energy focused on the retina. Thus some parts of the perceived scene are lighter than others and have an outline separating the darker from the lighter. Basically, leaving aside complications (see Chapter 8), it is the pattern of energies projected on the retina which determines form in vision. Hue, saturation, and brightness are determined by other aspects of the stimulating light energy.

HUE Hue is the perceived dimension of color we refer to when we use common color names such as red, green, yellow, blue, or combinations of them. Thus when we say that something is red, we mean that it has a red hue; greenish-blue, a greenish-blue hue; and so on.

Hue depends primarily on the wavelength of light. If several wavelengths are mixed together, as is usually the case with all colors except those made by a prism (see Figure 18.4), hue depends on the wavelength that is dominant in the mixture. Although wavelength primarily determines the experience of hue, the intensity of the stimulation also contributes something to it. In addition, hue depends upon *contrast* effects. For instance, two adjacent colored areas may induce what appear as mutual changes in hue in each other near the border between the two areas—this is called *simultaneous contrast.* Hue can also be induced in colorless areas from a colored surround (see Figure 18.17). But under arbitrarily standardized viewing conditions, the hue perceived can be precisely related to wavelength.

The relationship of hue to wavelength is depicted in Figure 18.18, in which hues and their corresponding wavelengths are arranged in a circle called the *color circle.* This circle shows the wavelengths of the "pure" or *unique* colors—the hues that observers consider untinged by any other hue. Thus a unique yellow is one judged not to be tinged with green on the one side or red on the other, and it appears on the spectrum

Figure 18.17 *Simultaneous contrast. The gray squares are all exactly the same gray, but they do not look the same. The perceived differences are caused by* induction *from the backgrounds of the colored squares. The lavender background induces a greenish-yellow in its gray square; the green background induces a lavender in its gray square. The induced colors are the complements of the inducing color. This demonstration works with various colors, but these give a particularly striking effect.*

to the right of center, at 582 nanometers. Unique blue is located at 477 nanometers—near the short end—and unique green to the left of center at 515 nanometers. Unique red is interesting because it has no corresponding simple wavelength. The reddest red in the physical visible spectrum at 700 to 780 nanometers—the hue hardly changes at all between these two points—is still not red enough to be perceived as "pure," or unique. It requires a little blue from the other end of the physical spectrum to get rid of a slightly yellowish tinge and to be judged as a pure red. For that reason, unique red is said to be "extraspectral," which means that it does not occur in the physical spectrum obtained by bending light waves (Dimmick and Hubbard, 1939). The color circle was devised by psychologists as a model to represent perceived color experience, or hue; it stands for the *perceived* world of color experience, not the physical spectrum. The extraspectral location of unique red on the color circle provides a clue to one of the basic laws of color vision: the *law of complementary colors*. Complementary colors are hues which are perceived as gray or white when mixed together. Gray or white refers to the dimension of brightness—another dimension of color perception, extending from black at one extreme to white at the other. The law of complementary colors states that for every hue there is a complementary hue, and that complementary hues, when mixed in the appropriate proportions, produce gray or white. As can be seen in Figure 18.18, the yellows and the blues have single complementaries in the visible spectrum, represented by unshaded sectors. Those in the green region have no spectral complementary hues. Their complementaries are extraspectral, which is to say, they are formed out of mixtures of the red and the blue ends of the spectrum. This point is represented in Figure 18.18 by the shaded sectors, of which the darker one represents the extraspectral hues. It should now be apparent why the hues are arranged in the form of a circle. This way of showing them reflects the law of complementary colors, which operates in all our everyday perceptions in color.

What happens if, in mixing wavelengths, we do not use wavelengths that are complementaries of each other? This is a common occurrence: we do not ordinarily have lights that are pure enough in wavelength to make complementary matches. The resulting hue lies in an intermediate position on the color circle.

For hues that are not too far apart, we can find approximately the resulting hue on the color circle by first drawing a line connecting the two hues that are mixed and then making a point on the line that represents the proportions in which they are mixed. Thus if we mix a yellow and a green, in equal parts, we can draw a line between their respective positions on the circle and mark the point halfway between. If we have mixed one part of green with two parts of yellow, we mark off one-third of the distance on that line from yellow to green, obtaining a yellowish-green. A line from this point through the center of the circle intersects the circle at the resulting hue. If we want to know what will happen when we mix any two wavelengths, we can use this procedure to figure it out. The same procedures can be used, though they become more complicated, for predicting the dominant hue when three, four, or even more different hues are mixed.

THE HUES OPPOSITE EACH OTHER ON THE COLOR CIRCLE ARE COMPLEMENTARY

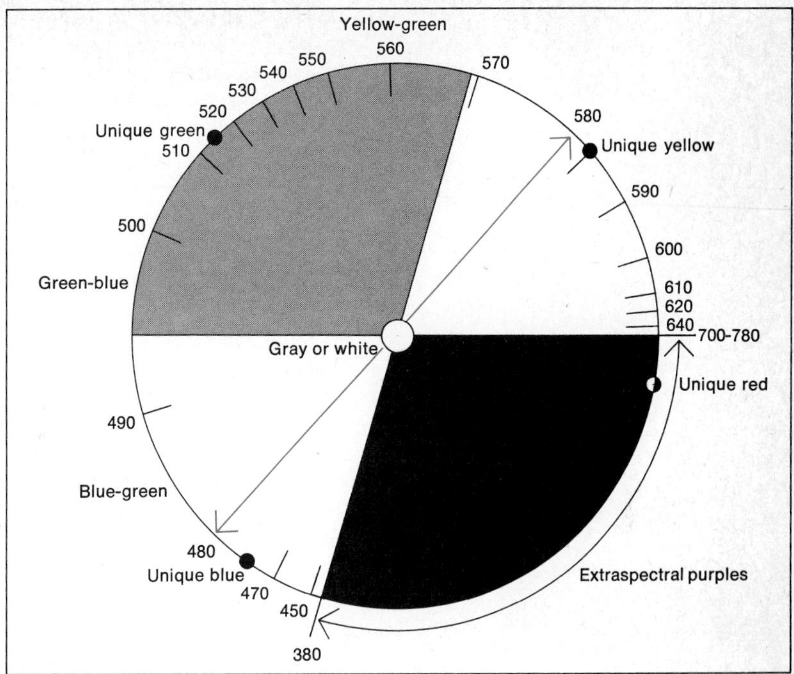

Figure 18.18 *The color circle. This diagram shows the arrangement of various hues and their corresponding wavelengths on a circle. Points opposite each other on the unshaded sectors represent complementary hues in the visible spectrum. Those on the lightly shaded sector have no complementary wavelengths in the visible spectrum.*

It will occur to some of you that the rules for mixing wavelengths do not seem to be the same as those for mixing paints. This is true. The perception of a mixture of yellow and blue wavelengths, for example, is gray or white; but the perception of a mixture of blue and yellow paints is green. Why?

Paints do not emit light; they reflect or absorb it. But they never reflect all the light that strikes them. If a paint or any other substance contains a pigment, it absorbs some wavelengths; the remaining reflected wavelengths give it its perceived color. For example, yellow paint generally absorbs violet and blue wavelengths; it reflects some green and red, somewhat more yellow-green and orange, and a lot of the yellow wavelengths. Blue paint, on the other hand, absorbs red, orange, and yellow wavelengths, and reflects the yellow-green, green, blue, and violet ones. When these two paints are mixed, the result is one of subtraction as well as addition. Each of the paints absorbs its part of the spectrum, and what is left to be reflected depends upon both the absorption and the reflectance of the two paints. In the case of a mixture of yellow and blue paints, most of the reflected wavelengths are green. Consequently, the rules for the color mixing of paints do not violate the rules of color mixture. When one mixes paints, the important thing is to figure out what wavelengths finally reach the eye.

SATURATION So far we have explained the hue dimension of color and have mentioned in passing another dimension, brightness, which is treated more fully in the next section. The other dimension of perceived color is *saturation*.

When hues are mixed, the resulting color is different not only in hue, but also in saturation. Saturation refers to the *purity of color,* and in fact is sometimes called purity. By purity, we do not mean uniqueness of hue or hues. We can have a very pure purple or pure yellow-green, even though these are not unique hues. By purity, or saturation, we refer to the degree to which a hue is diluted or not diluted by grayness or whiteness.

The following example should make this clear. A yellow of 580 nanometers is the complementary hue of a blue of 480 nanometers. Each one alone, when produced by a prism, is as pure or highly saturated as it can be. When these two hues are mixed, however, the resulting color lies somewhere along the line joining the two wavelengths in Figure 18.18. If the proportions are right, this color will lie in the center designated as gray or white. At that point it has no saturation or purity at all, simply because it has no detectable hue. At a point, say, one-third of the way from the center out to the 580 point on the circle, it has some hue—indeed, exactly the same hue as the component 580 wavelength. The saturation of the color, however, is low because the color contains a lot of white. The blue has counterbalanced some, but not all of the yellow, thus mixing white and yellow.

Saturation, then, may be regarded on the color circle as the position of a color on the spokes of the circle. The farther out it is on a spoke, the higher its saturation, or purity. The closer it is to the gray or white neutral point in the center, the lower its saturation, or purity. Translating this into more familiar terms, the pastel, or weak, colors are colors that are relatively unsaturated. To make them, the mixer of paints puts a relatively small amount of dye into a base of white paint. The deep, or strong, colors, on the other hand, are the ones that are highly saturated. To make them, the paint mixer uses a large amount of dye in proportion to the white base paint. In fact, the most highly saturated colors are made by using only color pigments and avoiding any white at all.

BRIGHTNESS The third dimension of perceived color is brightness: The intensity of the physical stimulus is one of the major determiners of perceived brightness. As we shall see, another major determiner is the state of adaptation of the rods and cones of the retina.

The dimension of brightness extends from black to white through various shades of gray. To represent it along with the dimensions of hue and saturation requires that the two-dimensional color circle be extended into a three-dimensional color solid (see Figure 18.19). To make a color solid, color circle is piled on color circle like so many layers of cake. In this solid, the up-and-down dimension represents brightness. The colors at the top are bright, those at the bottom dark. The center line of the solid runs through the centers of the various color circles and represents the points at which there is neither hue nor saturation, only varying brightnesses.

The relation of brightness to hue and saturation can be illustrated again by the example of paint mixing. We can vary the grayness of paint by mixing black pigment with white pigment. By using all white pigment and no black, we obtain the brightest paint possible. Conversely, by using all black and no white, we obtain a paint of low brightness. In between, varying mixtures produce different shades of gray. This gives the up-and-down dimension to the solid. Gray can in turn be mixed in varying proportions with pigments of different hues. When the proportion of colored pigment to gray pigment is low, the resulting colors are near the center of the solid and are of low saturation. When the proportion is high, the resulting color is out closer to the periphery of the circle, and its saturation is high. The remaining dimension, hue, of course, determines the position of the color around the circle.

Afferent codes in vision Although scientists are a long way from understanding the afferent code for all aspects of vision, a good start has been made on some of the basic qualities of visual experience that we have just described. Enough is known now, for instance, to construct plausible hypotheses about the nervous system code for hue, saturation, and brightness. The beginnings of an analysis of the code for form have also been made.

AFFERENT CODE FOR HUE Before the necessary techniques of direct neurophysiological observation were perfected, two major rival theories of color vision had been proposed. As we shall see, some aspects of both have been supported by modern observations.

The *Young-Helmholtz theory,* named after Thomas Young (1773-1824) and Hermann Helmholtz (1821-1894), proposed the existence of three kinds of cones in the retina: "red," "green," and "blue" cones (Helmholtz, 1924). As already described, we now have good evidence for three types of cones in the primate retina. According to the Young-Helmholtz theory, the code for hue is such that the effects generated in these cones add and combine to produce the perceived hues. For instance, an equal amount of activity in all three cones is supposed to produce the experience of white.

The strongest support for a theory based on a minimum of three cones comes from the data on hue mixture. We can mix hues by taking three primary wavelengths: one in the blue region of the spectrum, one in the red region, and another in the middle, the green or yellow region. It is possible to mix three wavelengths chosen from these regions in various proportions and to reproduce any hue or saturation that human observers see. In the right mixture, they add together to produce white.

The *Hering theory,* named for its chief advocate, Ewald Hering (1834-1918), is another attempt to explain color vision. It is often now called the *opponent-process theory* (Hurvich and Jameson, 1957). As originally stated, the Hering theory assumed three sets of cones—white-black, red-green, and yellow-blue—all able to function in opposing ways. Thus the theory stated that the cones for hue are separate from those for brightness. It further stated that the processes for red oppose, or cancel, those for green, and that the processes for yellow oppose those for blue. Hue experience was supposed to be due to the total amount of excitatory activity in the color cones at a given time. The original version of the theory held that a separate cone was responsible for each pair of processes. It now seems more likely that three color cones exist which

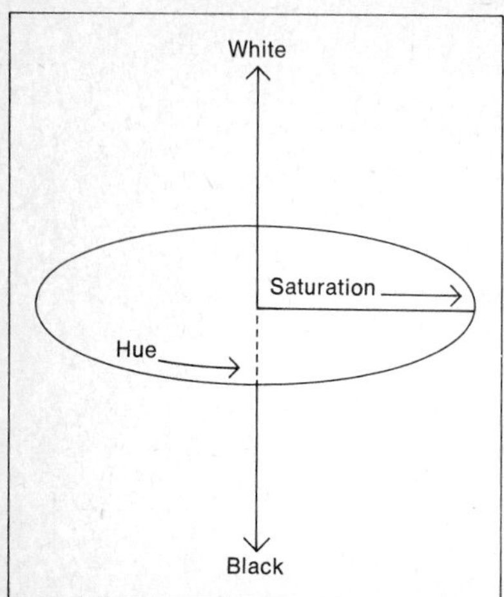

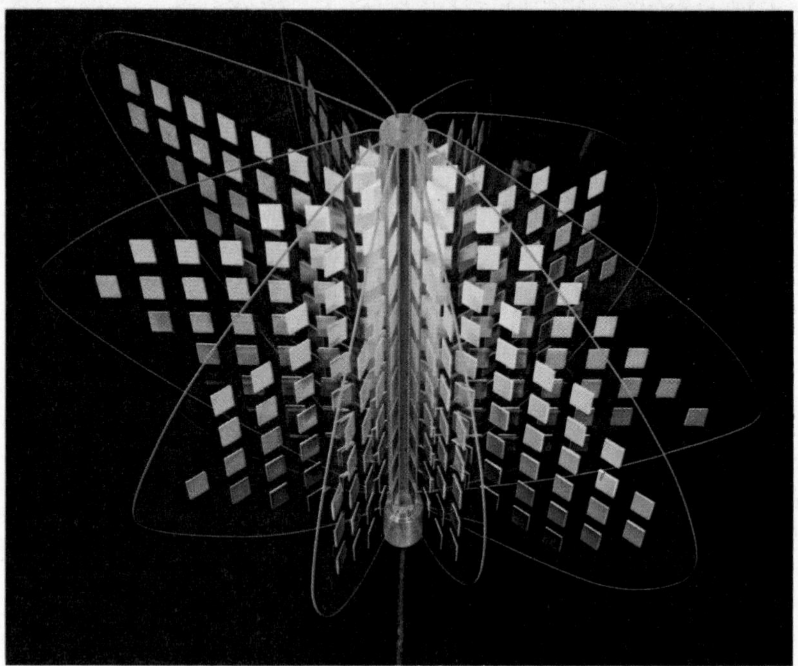

Figure 18.19 Both the drawing and the photograph illustrate the principle of the color solid. When all the colors are arranged in three dimensions, they form a color solid. The photograph shows ten segments from the complete solid. At the top are the highest brightnesses; at the bottom, the lowest brightnesses. Around the circle are the different hues. The distance out from the center axis of the solid represents saturation. (Photograph courtesy The National Bureau of Standards, 1965.)

are linked to cells further on in the visual system in such a way that they function, by exciting or inhibiting these cells, in opponent pairs. Furthermore, the pairs seem to be a little different from those originally postulated by Hering, as we shall see.

In summary, direct neurophysiological observations indicate that three color cones exist, as postulated in the Young-Helmholtz theory. These, however, are linked to the nervous system in such a way as to produce the opponent processes postulated by the Hering theory. Hence both early theories of color vision anticipated some of the results of direct observations on the hue-producing parts of the visual system, and both are substantially correct.

Support for an opponent-process mechanism at work comes from direct observations of the responses of cells in the lateral geniculate body (Figure 18.11). According to one series of studies, activities in these cells provide the afferent code for hue. Here are some sample results from one set of experiments in which single-cell recordings were made (DeValois et al., 1966):

Microelectrodes were placed in the lateral geniculate body of monkeys. When a single cell was encountered, its responses were recorded for a large number of wavelengths encompassing most of the visual spectrum. Energies striking the retina were kept as constant as possible; thus wavelength was the independent variable.

Since nerve cells are spontaneously active, firing when they are not stimulated, it is possible to measure *inhibition* of activity caused by stimulation; a

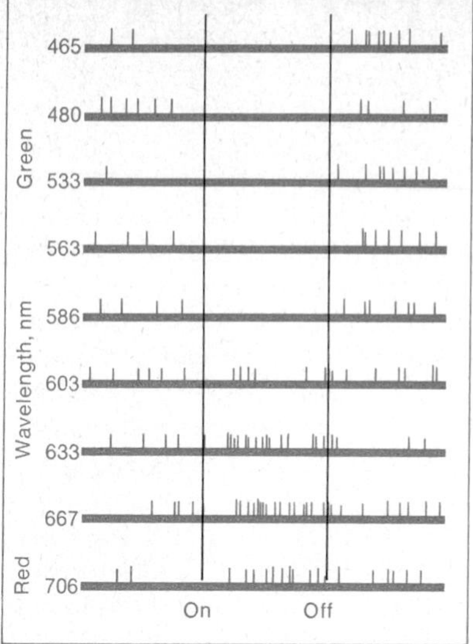

THE KEY TO THE AFFERENT CODE FOR HUE MAY LIE IN THE OPPONENT CELLS OF THE LATERAL GENICULATE BODY

Figure 18.20 *The responsiveness to light of an opponent cell in the lateral geniculate body of a monkey. Each short spikelike line represents a single firing of the cell. Stimulation by lights of different wavelengths affects the firing rate differentially. The vertical black lines frame the duration of the stimulus.*
The bottom line, for instance, shows the firing rate before, during, and after stimulation by red light of 706 nanometers wavelength. The firing before stimulation is the spontaneous, or unstimulated, firing of the cell.
Note that wavelengths of 586 nanometers or less inhibit the spontaneous firing rate—no responses occur during the period of stimulation at those wavelengths. Stimulation by a wavelength of 603 nanometers produces very little, if any, effect. Stimulation by longer wavelengths, however, causes a marked increase in the firing rate.
The opponent cell which produced this record is classified as a red-excitatory, green-inhibitory, or +R −G, cell. (Based on DeValois et al., 1966.)

decrease in the rate of firing when the stimulation started was the measure of inhibition used in these observations. An increased rate of firing to the stimulation was the measure of *excitation* used.

In general, two types of cells were discovered: *nonopponent* and *opponent* cells. Nonopponent cells showed excitation for all the wavelengths tested. Opponent cells were excited by light from one portion of the spectrum and were inhibited by light from another portion. For instance, Figure 18.20 shows one common type of opponent cell, a red-excitatory, green-inhibitory (+R −G) cell; this cell was excited by the longer, or red, wavelengths and inhibited by the shorter, or green, wavelengths.

The nonopponent cells of the lateral geniculate body are probably connected to the three cone types of the retina in such a way that all three types can produce excitatory effects. Thus the nonopponent cells are excited over the whole range of the spectrum covered by the retinal cones. The opponent cells of the lateral geniculate body probably receive inputs from the retinal cones in such a way that some cone types excite and other cone types inhibit. For the cell shown in Figure 18.20, the "red" cones send excitatory inputs to the lateral geniculate cell being recorded, while the "green" cones send inhibitory inputs to this same cell.

Comparisons with certain human psychophysical data seem to indicate a strong correlation between the activity of the opponent cells of the lateral geniculate body and color experience. The tentative conclusion is that the afferent code for color is to be found in the activity patterns of these opponent cells.

AFFERENT CODES FOR BRIGHTNESS AND SATURATION A good match exists between the amounts of activity in the nonopponent cells of the lateral geniculate body and the sensitivity of daylight vision. Perceived brightness can be coded by the amount of activity in the nonopponent cells.

Tentative conclusions can also be drawn about the afferent code for saturation. If activity of nonopponent cells represents brightness, or whiteness, and activity in opponent cells supplies codes for hue, we might expect that mixing a great deal of nonopponent cell activity with opponent cell activity would reduce saturation. On the other hand, reducing the relative amount of nonopponent cell activity might be expected to increase saturation. Thus the afferent code for saturation may be the relative amounts of nonopponent and opponent activity. Such a conclusion seems supported by comparisons between relative nonopponent and opponent firing rates and certain human psychophysical data. For instance, other things being equal, judged saturation is least at about 570 nanometers—yellow is the least saturated hue—and greatest at the lower and upper ends of the spectrum. The relative amount of nonopponent firing is greatest at 570 nanometers and decreases progressively toward the high and low ends of the spectrum, matching the curve of judged saturation quite closely.

The cerebral cortex and form vision Studies of brain lesions in the higher primates and rats have shown that the visual cerebral cortex is necessary for form vision (Klüver, 1942; Lashley, 1939). Remove this area and a rhesus monkey, for instance, cannot distinguish a triangle from a circle, or horizontal stripes from vertical ones (see Figure 18.21). But the animal can still react to a light going on or off and can distinguish which of two areas is lighted. The ability to distinguish brightness (or more properly, in the case of the brain-lesioned animal, the total amount of light energy—*luminous flux*) is thus not entirely a cortical function in the monkey. This is in keeping with the idea that an important part of the afferent coding for amount of energy in the visual stimulus occurs in noncortical components of the visual system. In human beings, on the other hand, total blindness is said to ensue from complete visual cortex lesions, but the data are not completely clear on this point.

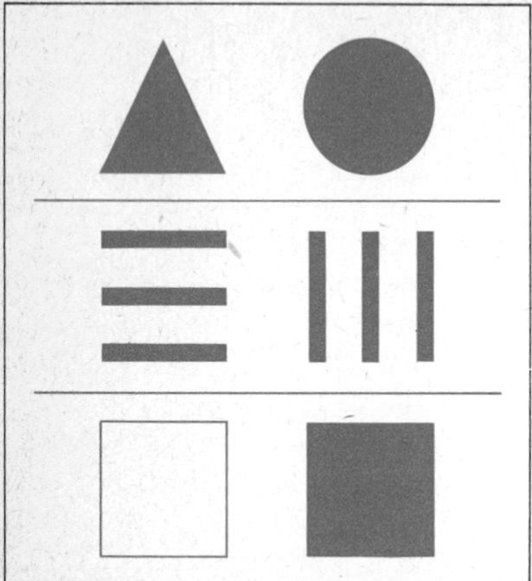

MONKEYS LACKING THE VISUAL CORTEX CAN DISCRIMINATE LUMINOUS FLUX BUT NOT PATTERNS

Figure 18.21 *In the absence of the visual cortex, monkeys cannot distinguish between the patterns in the top and middle rows. They can, however, distinguish between the elements in the bottom row, for they are able to perceive the differences in brightness—or more correctly, in luminous flux.*

With the evidence from lesion studies in mind, it seems reasonable to look in the cerebral cortex for cells which respond differentially to different forms. For such a complex attribute of vision as form, it is difficult to specify the coding process from evidence now at hand. Yet it seems clear that cells of the visual cerebral cortex are differentially sensitive to orientations of stimuli in space. Perhaps this fact may provide the beginning of an understanding of how the central nervous system codes visual form. Perhaps too, such observations may give a clue to the neural basis for certain of the perceptual phenomena mentioned in Chapter 8. The following is a condensation of some recent experiments showing the spatial responsiveness of cells of the visual cortex (Hubel and Wiesel, 1962, 1968):

In this series of experiments on the visual cortex of cats and monkeys, records of single cell responses, or *unit* responses, were obtained from microelectrodes pushed into the cortex (see Figure 18.22). When the retina was stimulated by patterns of light and dark, such as bars of light or dark bars, some cells in the cortex responded.

The responses depended upon the orientation of the stimulus, or its shape. Only certain orientations, or shapes, of stimuli would cause certain cells to fire. Figure 18.23 shows a unit from a cat that responds to a slit of light with vertical, or nearly vertical, orientation on the retina. Units which are fired by such highly specific types of stimulation are called *"simple" units.* A simple unit fires to a particular type of stimulus projected onto a particular part of the retina.

Other units, called *"complex" units,* also fire only to specific shapes or orientations, but they are influenced by stimuli of this shape or orientation over a relatively large area of the retina. A record of the activity of a complex unit from a monkey's visual cortex is given in Figure 18.24. On the left, a black bar is shown projecting on a rectangular patch. The patch represents the area of the retina that forms the receptive field of the complex unit. The bar is oriented in successively different positions over the patch; in each position it is moved back and forth without changing its orientation. On the right, the response of the complex unit is shown for each orientation and direction of movement. Notice that the unit fires most rapidly when the bar is presented at a particular orientation and is moved through the receptive field from lower left to upper right; other orientations and directions of movement are far less effective in firing this particular complex unit.

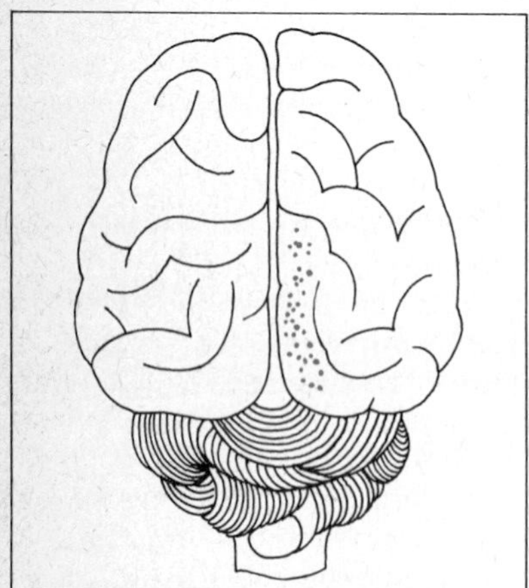

Figure 18.22 *Dorsal, or top, view of the cat brain. The dots show the sites in the visual cortex from which single cell recordings were made. (Modified from Hubel and Wiesel, 1962.)*

The visual cortex is supposed to be organized so that simple cells fire the complex cells. Several simple cells which fire to stimuli with a particular orientation

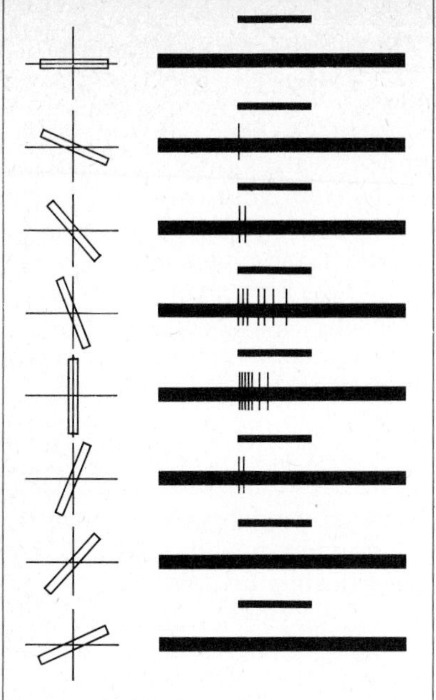

ORIENTATION IN A PARTICULAR PART OF THE VISUAL FIELD IS CRUCIAL FOR THE FIRING OF "SIMPLE" CORTICAL UNITS

Figure 18.23 *Left, the orientation of a bar of light in the visual field of a cat; right, responses from a single cortical unit, or cell. The period during which the stimulus is present is shown by the black line above the records. The spikelike records, made with a microelectrode, show the electrical activity or firing of a single cortical cell. (After Hubel and Wiesel, 1959.)*

may, for instance, feed into a complex cell. This means that the firing of the complex cell will be influenced by stimulation over a wide region of the retina. *"Hypercomplex" units* have also been found; these are supposed to be fired by complex cells. Corners of figures and other discontinuous stimuli are effective in firing hypercomplex units.

In summary, the firing of cortical cells in response to particular orientations of stimuli on the retina may provide some of the information needed to code visual form. The rapid rate of firing of complex cells when stimuli move through their receptive fields in the proper orientation may provide some of the afferent code for movement.

Besides the simple, complex, and hypercomplex units, there are other types of receptive fields (Spinelli, 1969). Analysis of these types may give valuable information concerning the coding of visual form and other aspects of perception. For instance, the firing pattern of one class of units may provide the basis for perceptual size constancy (see Chapter 8). Some units have been found which maintain a constant rate of firing even though the stimulus pattern on the retina increases or decreases markedly in size. These units may be part of the basis for the relatively constant perception of the size of an object even though the size of its projection on the retina changes manyfold. Perhaps other types of cortical cells will be found which provide the basis for other perceptual phenomena.

Hearing

We have seen that we are visually sensitive to only a small portion of the electromagnetic spectrum (Figure 18.1). Actually, this is the most important fraction for us to perceive, since it is the portion that reaches the surface of the earth most readily. For all creatures the ability to detect changes in the surrounding flux of energy is necessary for survival. In the billion or so years of their evolution, living organisms have developed receptor structures to deal with the major kinds of energy which they encounter on the earth, in the air, or in the sea. Whenever we use our eyes, we draw on a billion-year heritage from our slimy, scaly, and furry ancestors.

Of course, electromagnetic energy is not the only type of energy which is abundantly present on earth. For instance, pressure changes occur in the gaseous atmosphere and the liquid sea. Devices to detect the pressure changes were soon developed by primitive creatures, and we owe our ability to hear, and therefore to behave adaptively to certain transient changes of pressure in the air, to these prehistoric pioneers.

Hearing is probably second only to vision in providing a channel through which we can know, learn about, and appreciate our world. Through hearing, we can understand speech—our chief medium for imparting and acquiring knowledge. Through hearing, too, we receive a great many signals and cues—the warning automobile horn, the chime of the clock, the fire engine's siren, the footsteps of a person approaching from behind. Through hearing, we also derive one of our great aesthetic pleasures from listening to music.

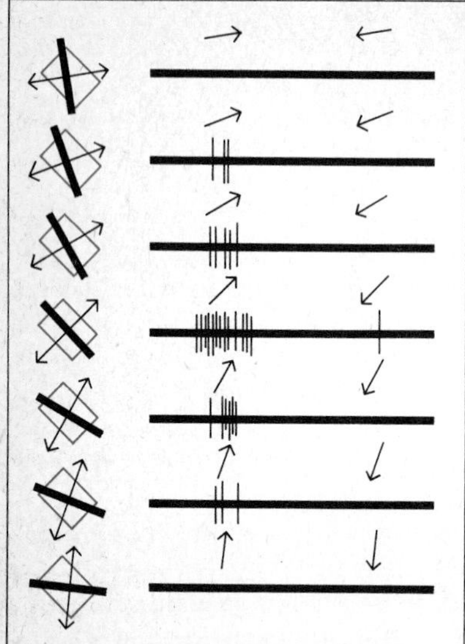

"COMPLEX" CORTICAL UNITS RESPOND TO STIMULI WITH A PARTICULAR ORIENTATION OVER WIDE REGIONS OF THE RETINA

Figure 18.24 *Left, orientation of a black bar within the receptive field of a complex cortical unit. The rectangles represent the area of the retina that forms the receptive field of the unit. Arrows indicate the direction of movement of the bar across the receptive field.*
Right, response of the complex cortical unit at each of the bar positions. The arrows above the response record show the time during which the stimulus is presented and the direction of movement of the stimulus. The unit fires most rapidly when the bar is tilted at a particular angle in the receptive field and when it moves across the field from lower left to upper right. (Based on Hubel and Wiesel, 1968.)

The physical stimulus for hearing Before we can understand the sense of hearing we must study its physical stimulus, which in many ways determines what we hear.

SOUND WAVES The air is not a vacuum but a collection of molecules that are always moving about at random, colliding with one another and exerting pressure on one another. The more closely packed together they are, the greater the air pressure; the fewer they are, the less the pressure. When there is no sound or wind, the molecules are evenly distributed in the air around us, and thus they have a uniform pressure. When there is a sound, however, changes in pressure occur which move through the air as waves do along the surface of water. It is, in fact, such changes in pressure that constitute the physical basis of sound perception.

Sound waves are ordinarily generated by the vibration of a physical object in the air. When such an object vibrates, the molecules close to the object are pushed together, and thus are put under *positive pressure.* The molecules that are under positive pressure push against the molecules close to them, and these in turn transmit the pressure to neighboring molecules. A wave of positive pressure moves through the air in much the same way that ripples move on the water (see Figure 18.25, left.) But sound-pressure waves travel much faster than waves of water; at sea level and at a temperature of 20°C, they travel about 760 miles per hour, or approximately 1,130 feet per second.

However, most objects do not move in just one direction when they are struck. A plucked violin string, for example, vibrates back and forth. As the string moves in one direction, a positive-pressure wave begins to propagate through the air; but when the string swings back to its original position and beyond, a little vacuum, or *negative pressure,* is created just behind the wave of positive pressure. The vacuum moves with the speed of sound, just as the positive-pressure wave does. The alternations in air pressure moving in all directions from the source are called a *sound wave,* and this sound wave is the physical stimulus for everything we hear. Different vibrations produce different sound waves. To understand the physical stimulus for hearing, then, we must understand the characteristics of sound waves.

SINE WAVES Common observation tells us that there is an infinite variety of possible sound waves. One kind of wave, called a *sine wave,* is regarded as the simplest, because it can be used in different ways to duplicate or analyze any other kind of wave. Figure 18.25 shows diagrams of the sine wave, which is so called because it can be mathematically expressed by the sine function of trigonometry. It is produced when a single vibrating object moves back and forth freely and changes the pressure of the air. The sound that we hear when we listen to a sine wave is called a *pure tone.* Since sine waves can be produced only with special equipment, a pure tone is usually heard only in the laboratory. However, some musical instruments, such as the flute, can sound notes that are almost pure tones.

The height or amplitude of the sine wave is a measure of the intensity of the pressure wave. As the peaks of positive pressure pass, the sine

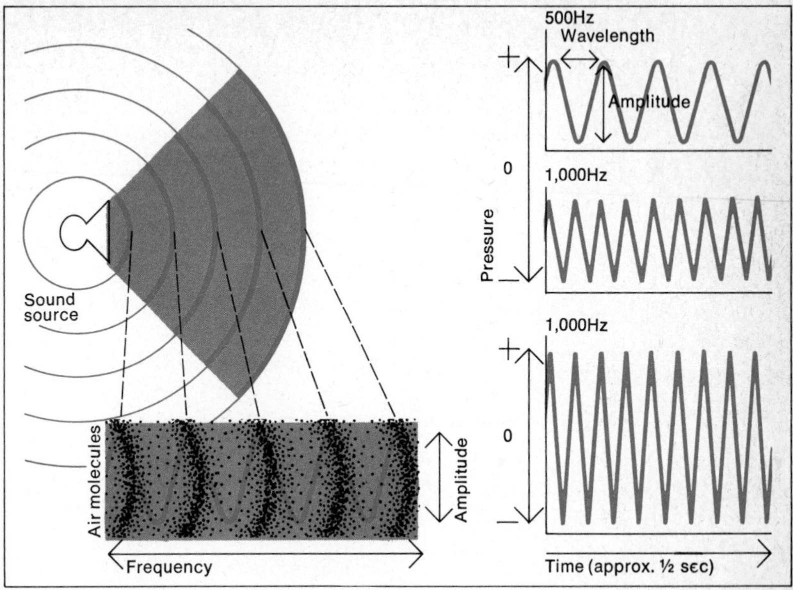

SOUND WAVES ARE GENERATED BY PRESSURE WAVES AND CAN BE REPRESENTED GRAPHICALLY

Figure 18.25 *Top left, a pressure wave generated by a sound source. As the sound source vibrates, it alternately compresses and rarifies the air around it, generating a pressure wave which is transmitted outward in all directions by the air molecules impinging on one another. Such a pressure wave is perceived as a sound wave.*
Bottom left, a sound wave corresponding to a given pressure wave can be represented graphically. The sound wave's amplitude *is the strength of the pressure wave—the difference in pressure between its densest and most rarified points. The sound wave's* frequency *is the number of pressure waves generated per second.*
Right, three sine waves, or simple sound waves, with different amplitudes and frequencies. The upper and middle sine waves have the same amplitude, or pressure, but the middle one has a frequency twice that of the upper one. The middle and lower sine waves have the same frequency, but the lower one has an amplitude twice that of the middle one.

waves reach their high points; as the troughs of negative pressure pass, the sine waves reach their low points (see Figure 18.25). The rate of change from peak to trough is defined by the ascending and descending limbs of the sine curves. The distance between the successive peaks of positive pressure, or the distance between the peaks of the sine waves, is the wavelength. In hearing, however, frequency, and not wavelength as such, is used as the measure of this particular dimension. The frequency of a sine wave is simply the number of cycles—alternations between positive and negative pressure—in a given period of time. We ordinarily use 1 second as the time unit and express frequency as cycles per second. One cycle per second is called a Hertz, a unit named after Heinrich Rudolph Hertz, a German physicist of the late nineteenth century. The abbreviation is Hz, and we shall use this abbreviation to stand for cycles per second. At the right of Figure 18.25, the sound wave at the top alternates fewer times per second than the middle and lower two sine waves—it has a lower frequency. To be more specific, if a sine wave goes to positive pressure, then to negative pressure, and back again 500 times in a second, its frequency is 500 Hz, for the sine wave has completed that many cycles in 1 second.

There are several ways of *seeing,* as well as of hearing, sound waves. The one used most often in the laboratory is a cathode-ray oscilloscope, which has a screen very much like a television screen. If we have a microphone, that is, a transducer, with which to convert sound waves into electrical signals, we can lead its wires into the oscilloscope and see the waves on the screen, which portrays them graphically like the waves in Figure 18.25.

MEASUREMENT OF PHYSICAL SOUND INTENSITY In Figure 18.25 intensity is shown as the height of the wave, and this height represents the wave's

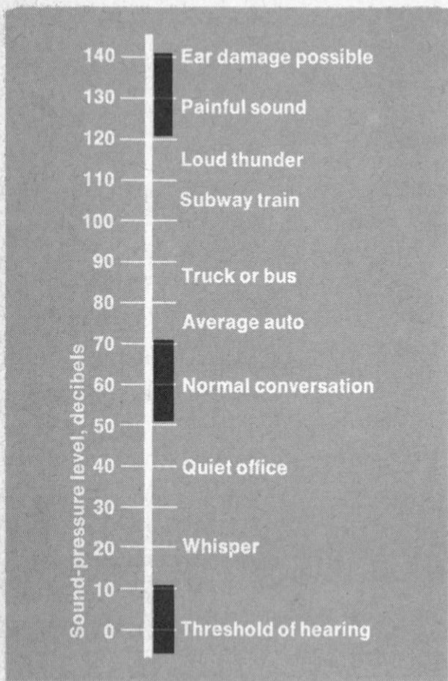

NORMAL CONVERSATION IS ABOUT 60 DECIBELS ABOVE THE THRESHOLD OF HEARING; LOUD THUNDER IS ABOUT 120 DECIBELS ABOVE

Figure 18.26 *The sound-pressure level (SPL) of familiar sounds. Each of the sounds indicated on the right has a SPL, or intensity, of approximately the number of decibels shown at the left.*

pressure. At the right of the figure the middle and lower sine waves have the same frequency but different amplitudes or intensities. Thus while frequency gives us a measure of how often the sound wave changes from positive to negative pressure, intensity gives us a measure of how great the pressure changes are.

Scientists have developed a special scale for measuring the intensities of sound energies. The range of intensities that people can hear is very large. The loudest sound that people can listen to without experiencing discomfort has a pressure about one million times as great as the weakest sound that is just audible. So if we were to measure intensities in actual sound pressures, we should have to deal with a very large scale of numbers. Consequently, we use the *decibel* (db) as our unit of measurement.

The decibel as a unit for expressing sound, or any other intensity, has two main features. First, it represents a *ratio* of two intensities, or pressures. When these are expressed in decibels, the numbers tell us that one intensity, or pressure, is so many times the other, but they do not say what either one is. Second, a decibel is so defined that 20 decibels represents a ratio of 10 times; 40 decibels, 100 times; 60 decibels, 1,000 times; and so on up to 120 decibels, which represents a ratio of 1,000,000 times. A person familiar with logarithms can figure out for himself what any number of decibels means if he keeps in mind that the number is equal to 20 times the logarithm of the ratio of two sound pressures:

$$\text{db} = 20 \log \frac{P1}{P2}$$

For such a scale to be meaningful, it must have a starting point. Scientists have arbitrarily agreed to use a pressure of 0.0002 dyne per square centimeter—a dyne is a unit of pressure—as a starting point because this is close to the absolute threshold. In other words, *P*2 in the previous equation is equal to 0.0002 dyne per square centimeter. When this point is used as reference, we talk about the decibel scale as the scale of *sound-pressure level* (SPL).

For most practical purposes we can simply regard a decibel scale as a set of numbers, like a scale of temperature, and then learn that certain numbers correspond to certain loudnesses. To give you an idea what the numbers mean, Figure 18.26 shows the scale of sound-pressure levels for some sounds with which you are familiar. If you are not sure what different sound-pressure levels mean, reference to this chart will at least provide a rough idea of the correspondence of SPL and loudness. Remember that loudness is *not* a measure of the physical intensity of a sound; loudness is psychological and is perceived, while pressures and the SPL are measured in terms of the physical energy itself. Figure 18.26 is designed to give an idea of some of the psychophysical relationships between SPL and perception.

COMPLEX WAVE FORMS Sine waves are extensively used in the laboratory for the study of hearing, but they are seldom encountered outside it. The sounds produced by objects in our normal environment are made

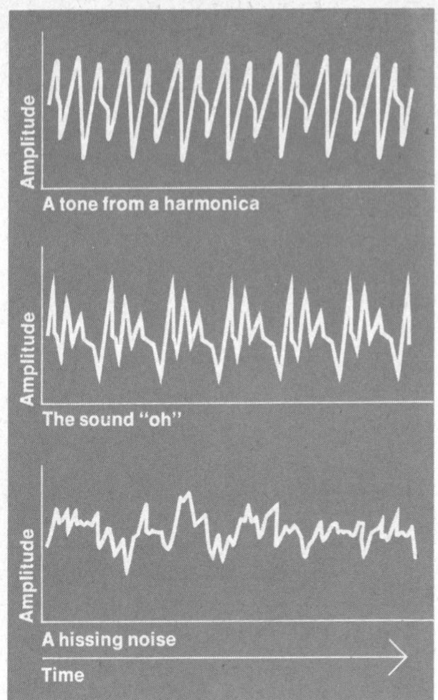

A MUSICAL TONE OR A SUSTAINED "OH" IS PERIODIC; A HISSING NOISE IS APERIODIC

Figure 18.27 *Oscillographic pictures of three complex sound waves. The wave at the top is a musical note played on a harmonica. The middle wave is the sustained vowel "oh." These two sound patterns are periodic; the same pattern repeats itself. The sound wave at the bottom is aperiodic; the record of a hissing noise, it is completely irregular.*

up of *complex waves.* Three examples of such waves, as seen on an oscilloscope, are shown in Figure 18.27. They may be almost any conceivable shape, but in general they are either *periodic* or *aperiodic.* This means that either they have a repetitive pattern occurring over and over again, or they consist of waves of various heights and widths in more or less random order. In Figure 18.27, the top and middle tracings are periodic waves; the lower tracing is an aperiodic wave.

In 1822, a French mathematician named Fourier showed that any periodic function can be expressed as the sum of a number of different sine waves. This fact provides a very simple technique for describing a complex periodic wave. To describe a sine wave, all we need to know is its frequency and intensity. For a complex wave, we simply need to know the frequency and intensity of each of the sine-wave components of the complex wave. Thus we might describe the tone of a musical instrument by saying that it has a sound-pressure level of 70 decibels at 400 Hz, 62 decibels at 800 Hz, 43 decibels at 1,200 Hz, 29 decibels at 1,600 Hz, and so on. Such a description of a complex tone is known as a *Fourier analysis.*

Notice that in this example each of the frequencies involved is some multiple of the lowest frequency. All musical instruments produce complex tones of this type. The lowest frequency is called the *fundamental,* and all other frequencies are called *harmonics.* The frequency which is twice as great as the fundamental is called the second harmonic; that which is three times as great, the third harmonic; and so forth. The complexity of a periodic tone, then, is a matter of the number and the intensities of the different sine waves that make up the complete tone.

The auditory receptor and transduction So far we have been discussing the physical energy which impinges upon the ears. Later we shall take up the psychological attributes of pitch, loudness, and timbre to which this energy gives rise. Before doing that, however, let us bridge the psychophysical gap between the physical stimulus and reported experience by discussing the structures of the auditory system, the transduction process taking place in the structures of the system, and the auditory pathway.

STRUCTURE OF THE AUDITORY RECEPTOR Figure 18.28 shows the major features of the ear. The ear consists of three principal parts: the external ear, which collects the energy; the middle ear, which transmits the energy; and the inner ear, which transforms the energy into nerve impulses.

The *pinna* of the outer ear collects energy which travels through a small air-filled duct, called the *auditory canal*, or *meatus*, to the eardrum. The *eardrum* is a thin membrane stretched tightly across the inner end of the canal. Alternations in the pressure of the sound wave move this small membrane back and forth. The oscillation of the eardrum in turn moves three small bones, the *ossicles,* so that vibration is conducted through the middle ear to the entrance of the *cochlea* in the inner ear. The bones of the middle ear are connected like a series of levers. Hence energy is mechanically transmitted, and amplification takes place through the middle ear.

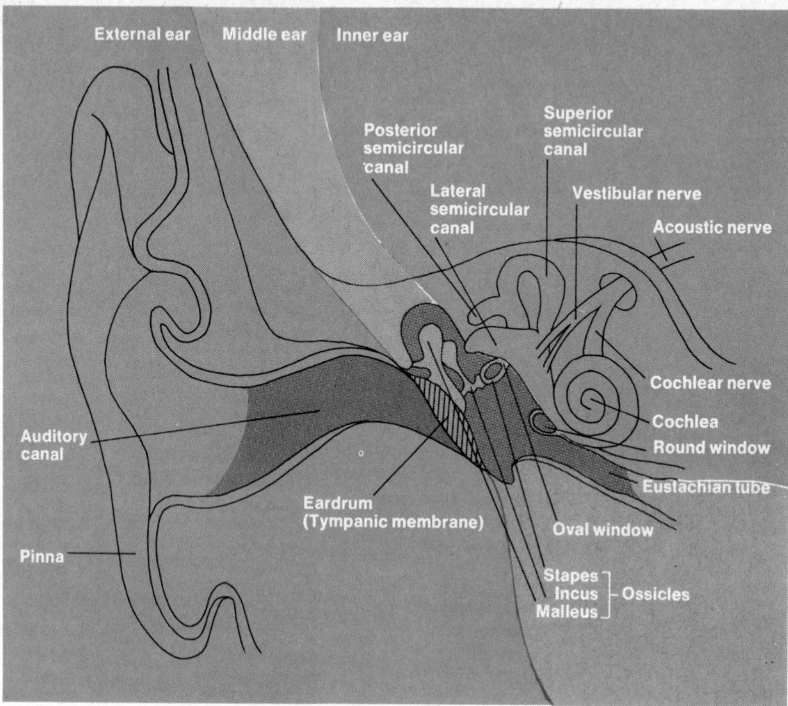

Figure 18.28 *The human ear. The ear has three major parts: the external ear, the middle ear, and the inner ear. The external ear consists of the pinna and a canal that conducts pressure changes to the eardrum. The eardrum, marking the division between the external and middle ears, is set into vibration by the pressure changes. This vibration is transmitted and amplified by the bones, or ossicles, of the middle ear—the malleus, the incus, and the stapes. The amplified vibrations push on the oval window and thus are transformed into waves of pressure in the fluid-filled cochlea (see Figure 18.30). By distorting the organ of Corti on the basilar membrane (see Figure 18.29, two drawings at lower right), the fluid waves in the cochlea stimulate the hair cells located on this membrane. After the fluid wave has traveled through the cochlea, the pressure is relieved by bulging of the round window. (After a modification from M. Brödel in E. Gardner,* Fundamentals of Neurology, *5th ed., Saunders, 1968. Labels are somewhat different.)*

The inner ear is by far the most complicated of the three major parts of the ear. It consists of two kinds of sense organs, one concerned in the sense of balance and the other in hearing. The organs for balance are called the vestibular sense organs. (Of these, only the semicircular canals are labeled in Figure 18.28. They are discussed later in the chapter.) The sense organs for hearing are contained in a bony structure which is spiraled like a snail and thus called the cochlea, which means snail shell. The cochlea has three different fluid-filled ducts or canals spiraling around together and separated from each other by membranes. Figure 18.28 shows a side view of the cochlea. Figure 18.29 (lower right, second from bottom) gives a cross section of the cochlea showing the ducts: the *scala vestibuli* (vestibular canal), *cochlear duct,* and *scala tympani* (tympanic canal).

THE AUDITORY ROUTE TO THE CEREBRAL CORTEX

Figure 18.29 *(opposite page) Input originating in the cochlea eventually reaches the superior surface of the temporal lobe—the lower bank of the lateral fissure. The sections on the left are cross sections of the medulla, midbrain, and cerebrum (frontal section). The drawing of the brain at the top right shows the temporal lobe pulled down and out to expose the superior surface; the supposed tonotopic organization of the human cortex is also shown. The drawings at the lower right show (1) a cross section through the cochlea, (2) below, a magnification of the organ of Corti. (Modified from Netter, 1962; Copyright* The CIBA Collection of Medical Illustrations by Frank H. Netter, M.D.*)*

As the ossicles of the middle ear move back and forth, the foot of one of them, the *stapes,* presses on a membrane, the *oval window,* which is located at the end of the vestibular canal. Thus when pressure waves move the ossicles back and forth, this movement is transferred to the fluid of the cochlea. Figure 18.30 shows the direction taken by the wave in the cochlear fluid as it moves from the oval window through the vestibular canal and is transmitted across the cochlear duct, *organ of Corti,* and *basilar membrane* to the tympanic canal and the round window.

The important event that takes place in the cochlea is the stimulation of sensitive cells—called *hair cells* because they have hairs on their ends—located in the organ of Corti on the basilar membrane (see Figure 18.29, bottom right). This is the membrane separating the tympanic canal

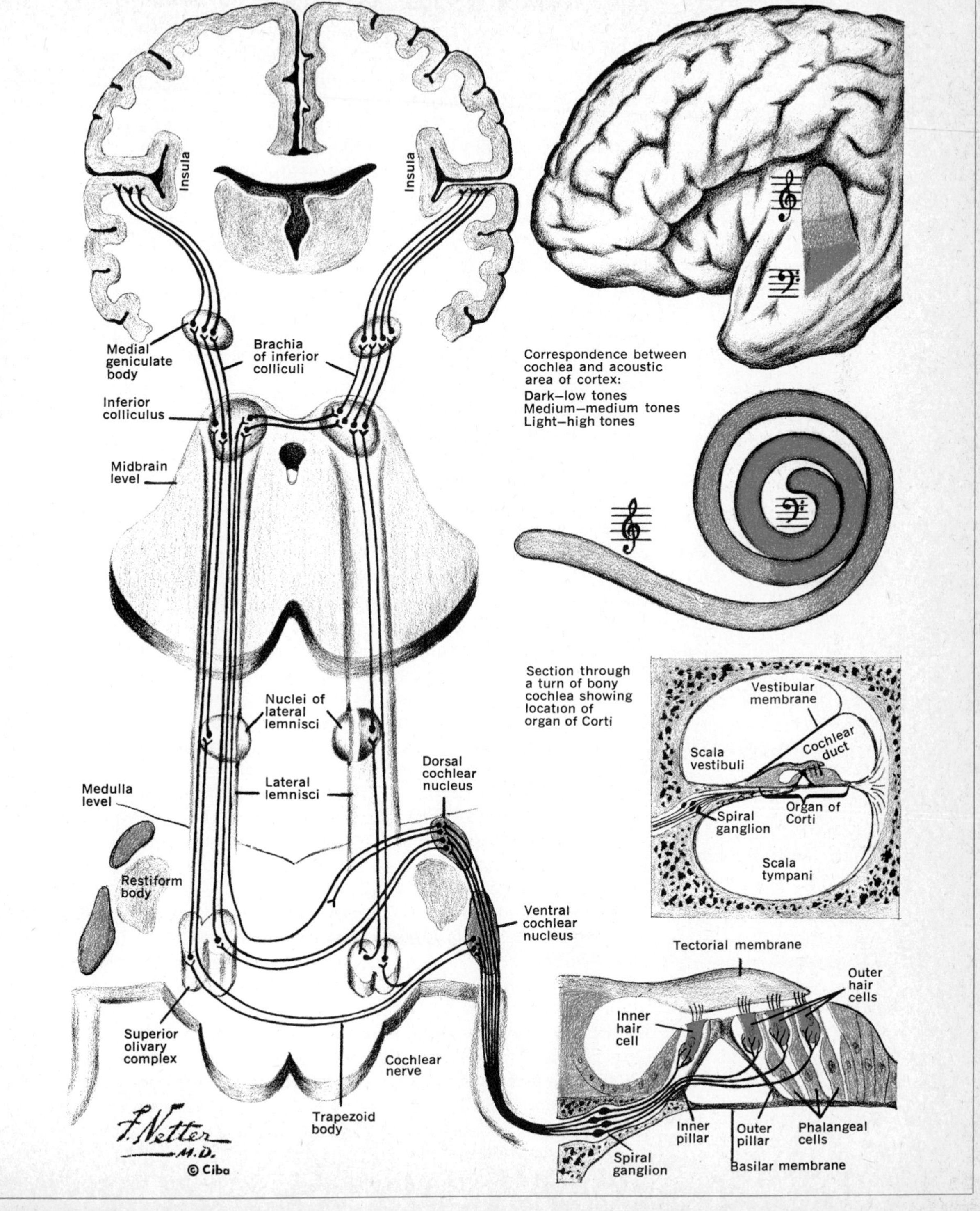
Insula
Insula
Medial geniculate body
Brachia of inferior colliculi
Inferior colliculus
Midbrain level
Nuclei of lateral lemnisci
Lateral lemnisci
Medulla level
Dorsal cochlear nucleus
Restiform body
Ventral cochlear nucleus
Superior olivary complex
Cochlear nerve
Trapezoid body
F. Netter M.D.
© Ciba
Correspondence between cochlea and acoustic area of cortex:
Dark—low tones
Medium—medium tones
Light—high tones
Section through a turn of bony cochlea showing location of organ of Corti
Vestibular membrane
Cochlear duct
Scala vestibuli
Spiral ganglion
Organ of Corti
Scala tympani
Tectorial membrane
Outer hair cells
Inner hair cell
Inner pillar
Outer pillar
Phalangeal cells
Spiral ganglion
Basilar membrane

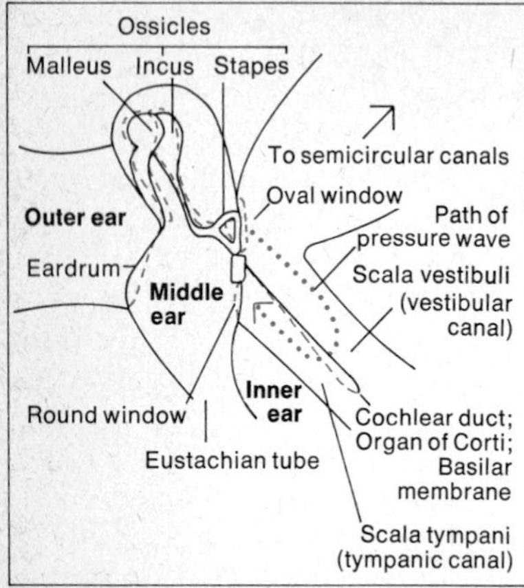

THE VIBRATING MEMBRANES AND BONES OF HEARING

Figure 18.30 *Diagram of the middle and inner ears to show some of the movements taking place when we hear something, or more accurately, when pressure waves strike the eardrum and are transduced into nerve impulses. (For greater clarity in illustrating these movements, the cochlea of the inner ear is drawn straight, not coiled.) The dashed lines show how the eardrum, the middle-ear bones, and the oval window move when pressure strikes the eardrum. The arrow shows the pressure waves in the fluid of the inner ear that are set up by movement of the oval window. These waves travel first in the scala vestibuli (vestibular canal). Their energy is then transmitted across the cochlear duct, the organ of Corti, and the basilar membrane to the scala tympani (tympanic canal) and round window. The greatest movements, or displacements, of the organ of Corti and basilar membrane take place at various points along their length, depending on the frequency of the pressure wave striking the eardrum. Figure 18.31 shows how this point of maximum displacement, measured from the foot of the stapes, varies with the frequency of the pressure wave. (Based on Davis and Silverman, 1970, as modified from Stevens and Davis, 1938.)*

and cochlear duct. Pressure changes in the fluid of the canals cause a bending movement of the hairlike processes at the ends of the hair cells. These hairlike processes protrude into the *tectorial membrane* above them, and the structure of the basilar membrane is such that waves in the fluid bend these hair cells with respect to the overlying tectorial membrane. This movement stimulates the hair cells to produce generator potentials, which in turn stimulate the nerve fibers that carry information to the auditory areas of the brain.

Movements of the basilar membrane during artificial stimulation have actually been observed (Békésy and Rosenblith, 1951). Measurements show that the maximum amplitude of displacement of the basilar membrane varies with the frequency of stimulation: the end away from the stapes and oval window is stimulated most by low-frequency stimulation; as the frequency increases, the point of maximum stimulation becomes more restricted and moves toward the stapes (see Figure 18.31). This is one of the major bits of evidence for the *place theory* of pitch perception discussed later.

TRANSDUCTION IN HEARING To summarize, when pressure changes in the fluid of the cochlea are finally translated into bending movements of the hair cells on the basilar membrane, the transduction process of converting mechanical energy into nerve impulses begins with a generator potential. Several different potentials can be recorded from the ear, but the one that many biologists believe is probably the generator potential is the *cochlear microphonic potential.* This potential is recorded as a fluctuating voltage which, as shown in Figure 18.32, follows the wave form of the physical stimulus quite closely (Wever and Bray, 1930). Figure 18.32 also demonstrates that the microphonic tends to occur at the places of maximum displacement of the basilar membrane. The cochlear microphonic is unlike nerve impulses in that it has almost no threshold, occurs almost immediately after stimulation, and follows the frequency of the stimulus at a much higher rate than would be possible for a nerve fiber. The supposition is that the stimulation of the hair cells changes them in such a way that an electric current can flow through them. This current is driven by a steady voltage, the *endocochlear potential,* which exists between the cochlear duct and the other inner ear canals (see Figure 18.33). By Ohm's law, a flow of current through a resistance will be recorded as a voltage, and this voltage, according to the theory, is the cochlear microphonic. The flow of current across the basilar membrane may excite the ends of nerve fibers that are in very close contact with the hair cells. This theory is still controversial, but at least it does one of the important things expected of a theory—it helps to organize many diverse facts.

Auditory pathways Input from the auditory receptors of the organ of Corti in the inner ear is projected to the cerebral cortex (see Figure 18.29, left). The major region of projection in humans is to the top of the temporal lobe—the lower bank of the lateral fissure.

The auditory pathway is complex, and we need not be concerned with all its details. One notable point, however, is that the fibers from each

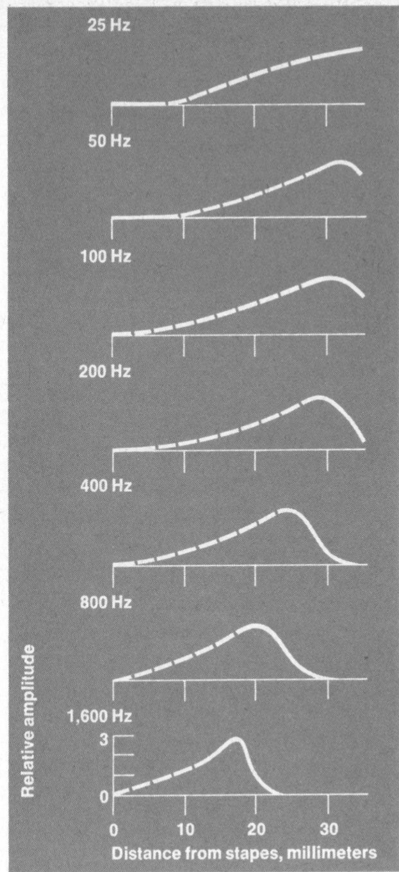

FREQUENCY OF THE PRESSURE WAVE DETERMINES THE PLACE OF MAXIMUM DISPLACEMENT OF THE ORGAN OF CORTI AND THE BASILAR MEMBRANE

Figure 18.31 *Measurements of displacement of the basilar membrane with different stimulation frequencies. Note that the point of maximum displacement shifts toward the stapes and the oval window as the frequency increases. The solid lines represent actual measurements; and the dotted lines represent extrapolations. (Modified from Békésy and Rosenblith, 1951.)*

ear project to the same, or ipsilateral, and the opposite, or contralateral, sides of the cerebral cortex. The functional significance of this crossing is that a lesion in the auditory area of one cerebral hemisphere does not produce deafness in either ear.

Topographic organization may exist in hearing, but the arrangement is not nearly so precise and clear-cut as that for vision. We have already seen that different frequencies of sound waves stimulate different portions of the organ of Corti in the cochlea (Figure 18.31). This so-called *tonotopic* organization may be preserved, in a rough way, in the cortex. For instance, Figure 18.29 (two drawings at top right) shows that the base of the cochlea, which is stimulated by high frequencies, is projected toward the back of the cortex on the floor of the lateral fissure; the apex of the cochlea, which is stimulated most by the lower frequencies, is projected to the front portion of the primary auditory cortex. The middle range of frequencies is projected to the middle region of the auditory projection area.

There is little doubt that the tonotopic organization on the cortex of the human, if it exists at all, is more complex than this, but our knowledge is based on clinical cases and accumulates slowly. Experimental analyses of lower animals, the cat and monkey especially, have shown that several primary sensory areas seem to exist for audition and that each has its own rough tonotopic organization.

The role of various portions of the auditory pathway in hearing has been extensively investigated. The detection of differences in intensity seems to be primarily a subcortical auditory function; at least, such detection is possible when the cortical auditory areas have been removed. In the animal most studied, the cat, frequency differences, or pitch differences, can be perceived without the auditory cortex (Butler, Diamond, and Neff, 1957). Another important aspect of hearing experience, the ability to tell where a sound is coming from, seems to involve structures at several levels of the auditory pathway. The two major aspects of stimulation which enable us to localize sounds in space are (1) differences in time of arrival of stimulating pressures at the two ears—one ear is likely to be farther from the source of the sound; (2) differences in intensity at the two ears—the head creates a "sound shadow" for the ear farthest from the source of stimulation. In any case, either because of the time difference or because of the decreased intensity of stimulation, the ear farthest from the source of stimulation sends out nerve impulses slightly later than the ear nearer the sound source. Such time differences can be detected low in the auditory pathway just after it enters the brain, and a nucleus at this level is important in the localization of sound in space (Masterton, Jane, and Diamond, 1967). But there is also evidence that the cerebral cortex plays a role in sound localization (Masterton and Diamond, 1964).

Some psychophysical relationships in hearing Let us consider a few of the correlations between stimulating energies and auditory experience before coming to the question of afferent codes. In hearing, we are especially concerned with the physical correlates of pitch, loudness, and timbre.

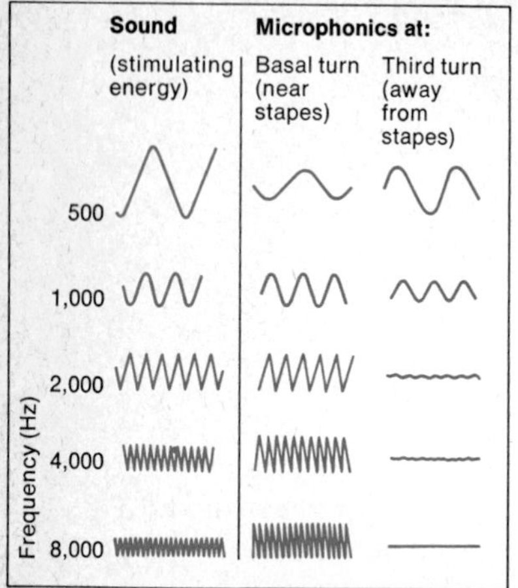

THE WAVE FORMS OF THE STIMULATING ENERGY AND OF THE COCHLEAR MICROPHONIC ARE QUITE SIMILAR

Figure 18.32 *The cochlear microphonic for different frequencies and places on the basilar membrane. Note the similarity between the wave forms of the stimulating energy and of the microphonic. The higher frequencies do not produce microphonics in the part of the basilar membrane at the third turn. This is at some distance from the stapes and fits with the data which show that the basilar membrane is not distorted here when high-frequency stimulation is used (see Figure 18.31). Such data give strong support for the place theory of hearing. (After Tasaki, 1954.)*

FREQUENCY AND PITCH The frequency of stimulation is the major, but not the only, determiner of the experience of pitch. In the earlier sections on psychophysical relationships, we saw that physical energy and reported experience can be measured separately. Sensory experience is *not* a kind of carbon copy of the physical stimulus; a lawful relationship exists between them, but this relationship must be discovered. The measurement of the relationship between frequency and pitch is illustrated in the following experiment (Stevens and Volkmann, 1940):

An observer is provided with a set of earphones through which tones of different frequency can be presented to him. He is given two switches which he may depress. Pressing one turns on a standard tone of a frequency set by the experimenter. Pressing the other turns on a comparison tone whose frequency can be set by the observer merely by twisting a knob. He is instructed to set the frequency of the comparison tone so that it is perceived by him to be twice the *pitch* of the standard tone. He does this by listening first to the standard tone, then to the comparison tone, in alternation. He then adjusts the comparison tone until he is satisfied that he has set it at twice the pitch of the standard tone. The experimenter notes the frequency chosen.

The procedure is repeated with different standard tones. For example, the first standard tone might be 400 Hz, and the observer's choice of a tone that is twice its pitch might be roughly 1,000 Hz. This might serve as a standard in the next observation, when the observer might choose 3,500 as being twice the pitch of 1,000 Hz, and so on. The numbers are only approximate, but they illustrate the point. Observations are repeated until there are many measures of "twice the pitch" throughout the audible range.

From measurements of this kind, a scale can be constructed showing quantitatively the relation between frequency and pitch (see Figure 18.34). Such a scale, called a *pitch scale,* is not a straight line but a curved one. Pitch rises slowly below 1,000 Hz and above 4,000 Hz. Between 1,000 and 4,000 Hz, it is more nearly proportional to frequency. Even so, a tone of 4,000 Hz has little more than twice the pitch of a 1,000 Hz tone. From 4,000 to 20,000 Hz—a fivefold change in frequency—pitch increases by only 50 percent. This fact demonstrates conclusively that pitch and frequency are not the same, because pitch does not increase or decrease in exact proportion to frequency.

This conclusion is strengthened by another fact: The pitch of a tone depends not only on its frequency, but also on its intensity (Morgan et al., 1951). The relationship between the two is complicated, but in general the pitch of a low frequency falls as it is made more intense, and that of a high frequency rises as its intensity increases. Thus the experience of pitch can be made to vary without changing frequency.

LIMITS OF HEARING There is a limit to the range of frequencies which can be detected by human beings. Generally speaking, we can say that the audible range is between 20 and 20,000 Hz in man. Other animals have different ranges. The bat, for instance, has an upper limit which extends into the neighborhood of 150,000 Hz (Griffin, 1959). As can be seen from Figure 18.35, the range depends upon the intensity of stimulation. Tones at the extremes of the range of frequencies can be heard

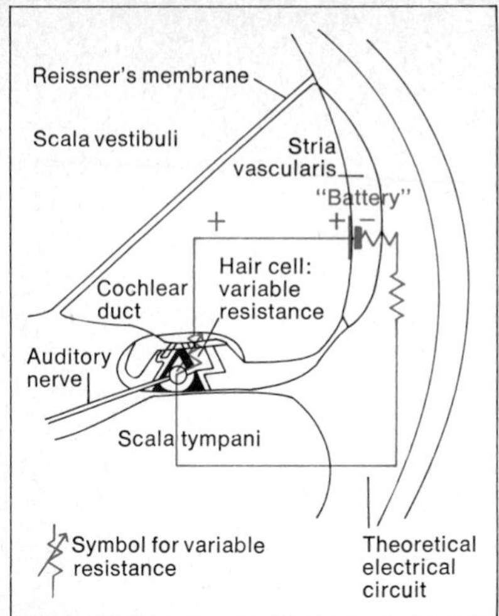

THE "BATTERY" IN THE COCHLEAR DUCT MAY BE A CRUCIAL PART OF THE TRANSDUCTION PROCESS IN HEARING

Figure 18.33 *Cross section of the cochlea (see Figure 18.29, lower right) and a theoretical scheme to explain the excitation of the auditory nerve fibers. The theory starts with the fact that the fluid of the cochlear duct is positively charged with respect to the other ducts of the inner ear. Positive and negative charges are separated as they are in a battery. The theory goes on to suppose that the pressure wave and bending movements of the hair cells cause them to lower their electrical resistance. If the resistance of the hair cells decreases, a current will flow between the poles of the cochlear battery. This flow of current through a resistor, the hair cells of the organ of Corti in this case, can be recorded as a voltage, and it may be this voltage that is the cochlear microphonic. (The electric current flowing across the hair cells is also believed to liberate a chemical mediator, or neurohumor, from the bases of the hair cells. This neurohumor then stimulates the nerve endings.) (Modified from Davis, 1959.)*

only at very high intensities, and at lower intensities the range is considerably smaller.

In order to give a more realistic idea of the frequency limits of hearing, the tones of a piano are also indicated in Figure 18.35. From this we can see that the range of notes is considerably narrower than the range of frequencies we can actually hear, particularly at the higher frequencies. It is, in fact, generally true that we seldom hear frequencies near the higher limits. Tones at these very high frequencies hardly sound like tones at all; rather they sound weak, very thin, and almost without a real pitch. You may have noticed that even the highest notes on a piano have very little tonal character compared with notes in the middle range of frequencies.

At very low frequencies, we can still hear sounds, but they are not tonal. Instead, we actually hear the individual pressure changes rather than a tone corresponding to the frequency of the sound. A tone of 8 or 10 Hz, for example, is a throbbing sound. In practice, it is very difficult to measure the frequency at which we no longer hear a tone. A related difficulty is that these very low-frequency tones have harmonics, which may sound tonal even though the fundamental frequency does not.

INTENSITY AND LOUDNESS Like frequency, intensity is a physical characteristic; it is not the same as the psychological characteristic of loudness. Loudness, like pitch, is an attribute of auditory experience. Although closely correlated with the intensity, or amplitude, of the physical stimulus, loudness does not increase or decrease in exact proportion to changes in amplitude. We know this because we have been able to construct loudness scales that are comparable to the pitch scale illustrated in Figure 18.34. The shape of the relationship is different, but the general point is the same: in each case, the attribute can be measured on a psychological scale that is different from the related physical scale.

Just as frequency corresponds most closely to the pitch of tones, intensity corresponds most closely to the loudness of tones. Once again, the two do not correspond perfectly—the relationship is not a linear one. Also, as we shall see, frequency, in addition to intensity, is quite important in determining perceived loudness.

It is probably obvious that intensity limits a person's hearing. If a tone is too weak, we cannot hear it at all, and even though physical measurement might show that a sound wave exists, a wave that is too weak cannot be an adequate stimulus. A sound pressure level of zero decibels (0.0002 dyne per square centimeter) is approximately the lowest intensity of sound, at an optimum frequency, that normal human beings ever hear. However, as Figure 18.35 shows, the intensity of many frequencies must be even greater than that to reach the absolute threshold, that is, the just-audible intensity.

The curve of Figure 18.35 depicts absolute thresholds for tones of different frequencies. From it we can see that hearing is best for frequencies between 1,000 and 4,000 Hz. At a frequency of 50 Hz, for example, a sound pressure about 1,000 times as great is required for a tone to be heard as for a frequency of 2,000 Hz. Similarly, at higher frequencies, greater intensities are required for hearing.

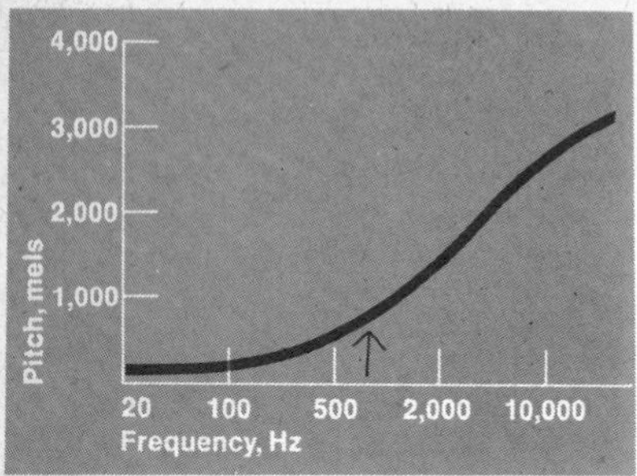

PITCH IS A PSYCHOLOGICAL EXPERIENCE; FREQUENCY IS A PHYSICAL DIMENSION

Figure 18.34 *The pitch scale. Units of pitch are called mels. The pitch of a 1,000-cycle stimulus is arbitrarily assigned a value of 1,000 mels (the arrow indicates the 1,000-mel point on this graph.) Tones that sound twice as high in pitch are assigned 2,000 mels; those that sound half as high, 500 mels. In this way a pitch scale, relating pitch to frequency, has been constructed.*
Note, for example, that an experience of "twice as loud," or 2,000 mels, is produced by physical energy of more than twice *the starting frequency, 1,000 cycles per second. As frequencies are increased and decreased from the starting frequency, experience does not follow in a one-to-one fashion. (After Stevens and Volkmann, 1940.)*

COMPLEXITY OF WAVE FORM AND TIMBRE The psychological counterpart of wave complexity is *timbre,* or *tonal quality,* which enables us to distinguish different musical instruments and different voices. A pure tone, for example, sounds very thin and lacking in tonal quality compared with the complex tone produced by an instrument such as the violin. In contrast, we would describe the violin tone as rich. The difference is that the violin tone has many strong harmonics. It is not just more timbre or less timbre, however, that distinguishes different instruments. Rather, the combinations of harmonics produced by a violin are different from the combinations produced by any other instrument.

There are, of course, other sounds that have little or no tonal quality. These are called *noises.* The hissing noise pictured at the bottom of Figure 18.27 was made by blowing air across a microphone. Notice that the trace of the noise is not periodic; it does not repeat itself in any regular pattern as do the sounds of musical instruments. Such a noise is made up of many different frequencies which are not multiples or harmonics of one another. Rather, the frequencies are mixed more or less randomly. When the mixture is really random, we speak of *random noise.* In other instances, such as clicks or tapping sounds, the noises are not completely random—they have certain dominant frequencies. They are nevertheless noises because they contain many frequencies that are not multiples of one another.

Afferent codes in hearing Just as in vision, when nerve impulses are finally produced in the transduction process, we would like to know which properties of the afferent, or neural, barrage are correlated with reported auditory experience. In other words, what are the afferent codes for the perceived characteristics of loudness, pitch, and timbre?

The afferent code for *loudness* is based on the fact that sense organs usually generate more and more nerve impulses as the intensity of a stimulus increases. The number of impulses generated is not usually directly proportional to the intensity of a stimulus, but a relationship does exist between the two. Hence it is reasonable to assume that the loudness of a tone is determined by the number of impulses generated and propagated down the auditory nerve to the brain. The evidence we have for hearing supports this conclusion.

According to the preponderance of data, perceived *pitch* depends upon the fact that a part of the basilar membrane of the cochlea is stimulated maximally by a given frequency (Békésy, 1960). Somehow the central nervous system uses a place code—that is, nerve impulses arising from a given region of the basilar membrane are perceived as a particular pitch. Since place is so important, this type of afferent coding in hearing is sometimes called the *place theory.* Some of the best evidence for the place theory is given in Figures 18.31 and 18.32. The emphasis on place is carried into the auditory cortex, where a rough spatial arrangement exists with respect to parts of the auditory cortex most sensitive to the various frequencies (Ades, 1959). Thus the afferent code for pitch really seems to be a spatial one.

The afferent code for *timbre* is quite complex, and so far little evidence is available on it. You can imagine how complex the neural activity would be as it coded all the harmonics of a guitar note.

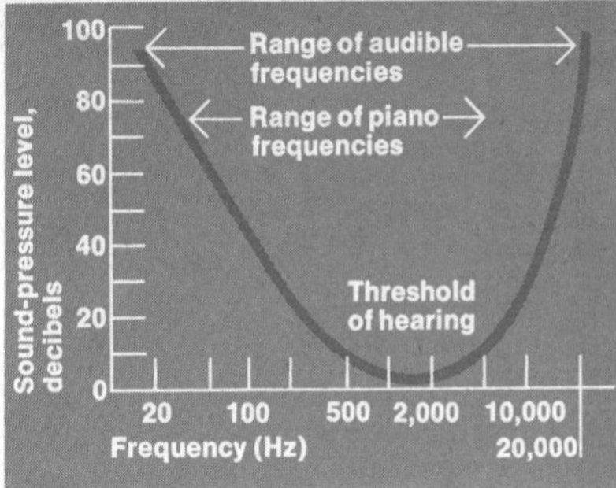

THE TONE A NORMAL PERSON HEARS BEST IS A FREQUENCY BETWEEN 1,000 AND 4,000 Hz

Figure 18.35 *The absolute threshold of hearing for sine waves, or pure tones, of different frequencies.*

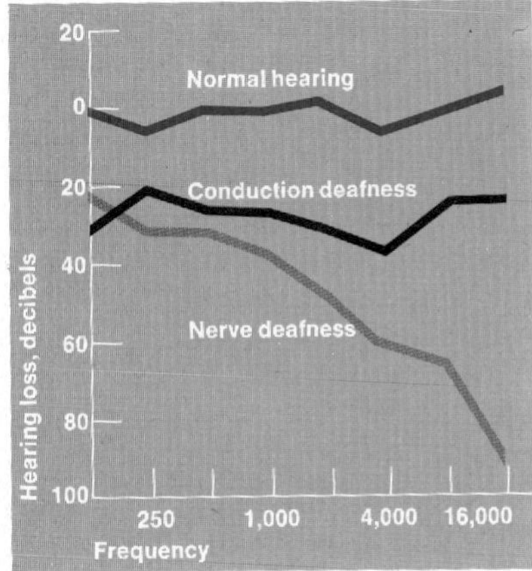

IN CONDUCTION DEAFNESS, ALL FREQUENCIES ARE AFFECTED; IN NERVE DEAFNESS, THE HIGH FREQUENCIES ARE MOST AFFECTED

Figure 18.36 *Audiograms for normal hearing and two major kinds of deafness. The average threshold for normal people at different frequencies is taken as zero. Any particular individual does not have exactly this threshold, but he does not depart from it by more than a few decibels. The person with conduction deafness has a fairly uniform hearing loss at all frequencies. The person with nerve deafness has a greater hearing loss at high frequencies than at low ones.*

Deafness Deafness is a serious problem in a civilization that depends so much on spoken communication. Everything must be written out for the deaf person, or he must "hear" by sign language. Some hard-of-hearing people become proficient at reading lips, but this is at best a poor substitute for actually hearing speech.

Deafness is fairly common in our society, and until very recent years any kind of deafness was a severe handicap. It was not until the advent of the modern electronic hearing aid that partially deaf people had a sensory aid almost as good as eyeglasses for people with vision defects. A totally deaf person cannot hear with a hearing aid, however, any more than a totally blind person can see with glasses.

Deafness is a two-way problem; it handicaps a person as a speaker and as a listener. Because he can never hear his own voice, he eventually loses his ability to speak well. That is why many deaf people speak in a peculiar tone—they have no way of knowing whether or not their voices sound like the voices of other people. In addition, deafness can create serious emotional problems. The deaf person tends to withdraw from people because of the difficulty he has in communicating with them and because of the irritation they show when he cannot understand them.

MEASURING DEAFNESS Deafness is measured clinically by an instrument known as the *audiometer,* which is simply a device for testing the intensity and frequency limits of hearing that were described earlier in this chapter. The audiometer produces pure tones at several different frequencies and provides accurate control of the sound pressure at each frequency. The examiner uses it to find the minimum intensity of sound, in decibels, that a person can hear at each frequency. From this data a special graph, called an *audiogram,* is constructed. It shows the *hearing loss in decibels relative to average normal hearing.* On the average, the curve for a normal person will be close to zero hearing loss for all frequencies; the curve for a person with deafness will be below the zero line—he will show hearing loss.

The top curve in Figure 18.36 is a typical audiogram for a person with normal hearing. (Notice that a particular normal person does not hear all tones at exactly the same sound-pressure level as the *average* normal person, for there are always individual variations from the average.) The other two curves in Figure 18.36 are for two individuals who are partially deaf—that is, who have sizable hearing losses. The two curves show two kinds of deafness which result from different causes and are characterized by different patterns of hearing loss in their respective audiograms.

KINDS OF DEAFNESS Conduction deafness, as Figure 18.36 shows, involves roughly the same hearing loss at all frequencies—the person suffering from it is no more deaf at one frequency than he is at another. The term conduction deafness is used because the deafness originates in deficiencies of mechanical conduction in the ear. The ear may be stopped up, the eardrum may be broken, or the ossicles of the middle ear may be damaged. The effect of conduction deafness is much the same as that of stuffing cotton in one's ears.

The lowest curve in Figure 18.36 represents a second kind of hearing loss, *nerve deafness*. As its name suggests, in this type of deafness something is wrong with the auditory nervous system. Either the nerves themselves have been damaged, or damage has been done in the cochlea, particularly to the basilar membrane. (For example, very intense sounds can cause cochlear damage.) It is characteristic of nerve deafness that hearing loss is much greater at higher frequencies. This means that the nerve-deaf person can hear low-pitched sounds reasonably well but hears high-pitched sounds very poorly or not at all. Such a person has a great deal of trouble understanding speech because the relatively high frequencies are very important in speech comprehension. He can hear the low tones, but he is not able to distinguish easily between the word sounds. For this reason, nerve deafness has sometimes also been called *perception deafness*.

Nerve deafness is very common in older people. In fact, nearly all of us can expect to have at least mild nerve deafness by the time we are 60, just as most of us can expect to be a bit farsighted by that age. But for most people, the deafness is not serious enough to require a hearing aid.

Other Senses

So far, we have covered the two senses that many people consider to be the most important: vision and hearing. We shall deal more briefly with the others: the chemical senses (smell and taste), the skin senses, and the proprioceptive senses.

Smell The receptors for smell respond to chemical substances, but only if those substances are volatile. Liquids, for example, do not stimulate the sense of smell. Smell receptors are located high up in the nasal passages leading from the nostrils to the throat. They lie in two small patches, one on the left and one on the right, in the roofs of these passages. They are a little off the main route of air as it moves through the nose in normal breathing, and consequently our sense of smell is relatively dulled when we are breathing quietly. A sudden sniff or vigorous intake of air, however, stirs up the air in the nasal passages and brings it more directly to the receptors, which is why animals and people sniff when they are trying to identify an odor.

BASIC ODORS Recalling the odors that you encounter in one day, you will realize that they have many shades and qualities. This is also true, of course, for color. In both cases, scientists have raised the question of whether such a multitude of experiences might not result from mixtures of a relatively few primary qualities. Color vision has indeed worked out that way: three hues mixed in various proportions can account for all perceived differences in color. Perhaps in smell there are also a few unique odors which, mixed in different proportions, account for the various discriminable odors.

Attempts have been made to discover or devise such a scheme, but they have not been very successful. Although research workers have devoted considerable effort to the problem, we are not yet certain what the primary odors are, or even whether their number is limited. One scheme that does reasonably well is known as the Henning smell prism.

Devised by the German research worker Henning, it is called a prism because Henning chose six basic odors and represented them in prismatic shape—that is, he assigned one basic odor to each of the six corners of the prism. He assumed that the six basic odors could be mixed in various proportions to account for the different odors we meet in daily experience. As with the color circle, all mixtures of basic elements—odors, in this case—can be regarded as falling somewhere on the prism's surfaces between the points representing the basic odors.

Industrial chemists, who are faced with the problem of making artificial perfumes and scents, prefer a simpler fourfold classification of odors (Crocker, 1945). According to this classification, the four basic smells are fragrant (musk), acid (vinegar), burnt (roast coffee), and caprylic (goaty or sweaty). Still other systems of primary odors have been proposed. Each may serve some particular purpose well, but there is little assurance that in any of them we have found the "real" primaries, in the sense that psychological primaries for color have been clearly established. Probably the biggest stumbling block to our accepting any scheme of primary odors as final is the difficulty of getting individuals to agree consistently, either with themselves or with each other, in classifying different odors.

SMELL SENSITIVITY In hearing and vision, we are able to state precisely how much energy is required for a person to detect, or discriminate, a stimulus. In the case of smell, our measures of sensitivity are not so precise. There are several reasons for this; the chief one is that the smell receptors are recessed away from the main path of air through the nasal passages. The best way to get odors to the smell receptors is by sniffing; yet sniffs vary from one person to another and from one sniff to another.

Despite such limitations in measuring smell sensitivity with precision, many measurements have been made of the amounts of odorous material needed for a person to detect its presence. Thresholds of detection vary considerably for the different odors, but the impressive thing about them is that they are often incredibly low. Anesthetic ether, which is one of the less odorous materials, requires only 6 milligrams per liter of air—approximately 40 millionths of an ounce to a quart of air—to be detected. Artificial musk, one of the most odorous of substances, can be sensed in extraordinarily small dilutions. Only 0.00004 milligram of it in a liter of air can be smelled. This dilution is so enormous that no physical or chemical means can be used to measure it; the nose must be responding to no more than a few chemical molecules per sniff. However, impressive as this may be, the sense of smell in many animals surpasses that in man.

THEORIES OF SMELL Disagreement concerning the basic types of odors has not prevented scientists from theorizing about transduction and the psychophysical characteristics of smell. Of the many theories proposed, none has yet been widely accepted.

A current hypothesis is the stereochemical theory (Amoore et al., 1964). The basic idea is that certain odors are produced by molecules with particular shapes. It is called a "lock-and-key" theory because these

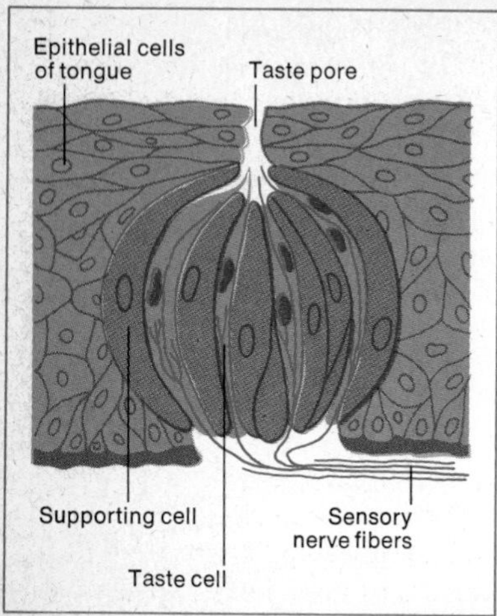

TASTE CELLS ARE LOCATED IN THE TASTE BUDS

Figure 18.37 *Portrait of a taste bud. These buds are located on the top and sides of the tongue, at the back of the mouth, and in the throat. They are especially dense on the bumps, or papillae, of the tongue.*

molecules are supposed to fit into "sockets" in the olfactory receptors. For example, the molecules of camphor, and substances which have a camphorlike odor, are assumed to have a spherical shape and fit into a bowl-shaped depression in the olfactory receptor. Five of the odors considered basic in this theory—camphoraceous, musky, floral, pepperminty, and ethereal—are supposed to have distinctive shapes. Two other so-called basic odors, pungent and putrid, are assumed to arise from molecules having distinctive patterns of electrical charge allowing them to fit into sockets in the olfactory receptor.

The evidence for this theory is suggestive. For instance, it is possible to synthesize substances with particular molecular shapes and to see whether they would have the odor predicted by the theory. In some tests they do. Thus transduction in smell may depend upon the shape of, and the charges on, the molecule; but the evidence is not yet conclusive.

Taste The receptors for taste are specialized cells which are grouped together in little clusters known as *taste buds* (see Figure 18.37). These buds are located mostly on the top and sides of the tongue, but a few of them are at the back of the mouth and in the throat. If you examine your tongue closely in a mirror, you will notice a number of bumps on it, some large and some small. These bumps, called *papillae*, are richly populated with taste buds. To stimulate the taste receptors, substances must be in solutions which wash around the papillae and penetrate to the taste cells within them.

PRIMARY TASTE QUALITIES We have said that we are not yet certain of the primary odors. Fortunately we are clearer about the primary taste qualities. Several lines of evidence point to four qualities: *salty, sour, sweet,* and *bitter*. Part of the evidence for these qualities is the fact that the tongue is not uniformly sensitive to all stimuli. If, for example, we apply minute drops of a bitter solution, such as quinine, to different parts of the tongue, we find the bitter taste most pronounced when the drops are put at the back of the tongue. The taste of sweetness, on the other hand, is most noticeable when sugar solutions are placed on the tip of the tongue. The sides of the tongue respond mainly to sour stimuli, and the tip and part of the sides respond to salty solutions. This, together with other data, supports the idea that there are four primary taste qualities.

If we now try to state what kinds of solutions give rise to the different qualities, we run into trouble. Sugars, such as common table sugar, taste sweet. But so do many other chemical compounds, such as saccharine, which chemically have little in common with sugar. The taste of bitter presents a similar problem. A class of compounds that the organic chemist calls *alkaloids,* which includes quinine and nicotine, tastes bitter. But so do substances such as some of the mineral salts which have little in common with the alkaloids. However, all this may prove only that we have not yet discovered which aspects of a chemical substance are the keys to determining taste quality. We cannot at present give definite rules for the kinds of chemical substances that produce sweet and bitter qualities of taste.

In the cases of sour and salty tastes, a somewhat better correlation

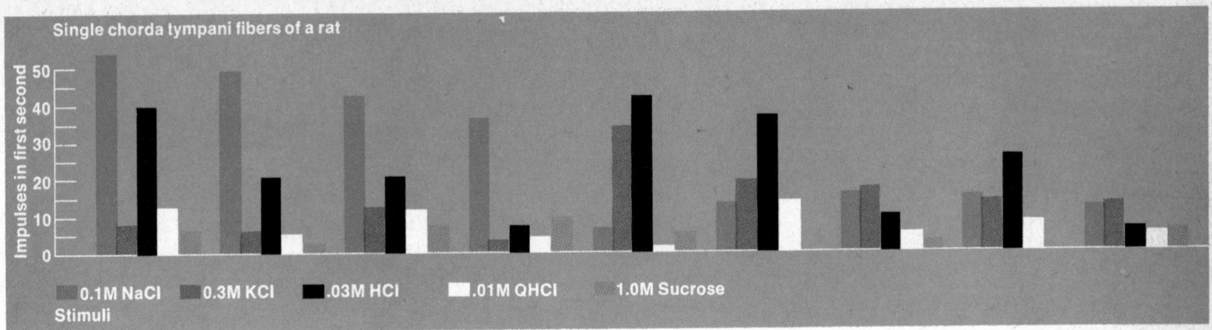

SINGLE TASTE FIBERS RESPOND TO MANY STIMULI

Figure 18.38 *Recordings from nine single fibers of a taste nerve, the chorda tympani, of the rat. Various stimuli were applied to a spot on the tongue, and nerve impulses were recorded from single nerve fibers. The stimuli were 0.1 molar sodium chloride, 0.3 molar potassium chloride, 0.03 molar hydrochloric acid, 0.01 molar quinine hydrochloride, and 1.0 molar sucrose (common table sugar). Note that the nine fibers fired, in varying amounts, to many of the stimuli. (Modified from Erickson, 1963.)*

exists between chemical composition and taste. All the stimuli that taste sour are acids. Moreover, the degree of sourness that we taste is fairly proportional to the total number of acid (H+) ions present. Salty taste, similarly, is usually aroused by what the chemist calls salts—that is, the chemical product of acids and alkalies. Common table salt, however, is about the only salt that has a uniquely salty taste; most other salts produce experiences of bitter or sweet in addition to that of salt.

AFFERENT CODE FOR TASTE What is the input, or afferent, code in the taste nerves for taste? It can be seen clearly from studies of electrical responses of single taste nerve fibers that almost all of them respond to several taste stimuli (Pfaffmann, 1964). For instance, a single taste fiber may respond to any of the five stimuli shown in Figure 18.38 (Erickson, 1963). Thus the firing of a single fiber is not unique—it may be fired by many stimuli—and therefore a single fiber does not carry reliable information regarding the stimulating agents to the central nervous system. As far as the brain "knows," the fiber could be firing because any of a number of stimuli have come in contact with the tongue. However, several elements together may make a unique combination. It seems that the "neural message for gustatory quality is a *pattern* made up of the amount of neural activity across many neural elements" (Erickson, 1963).

TASTE SENSITIVITY Just as it is difficult to measure a person's threshold for odors, so it is difficult to measure thresholds for taste. All stimuli for taste must be in solution and must reach the taste cells lying beneath the surface of the papillae. For an experimenter to control taste stimuli precisely, he must make sure that all saliva is removed from the surface to be stimulated and that the surface is washed free of any solutions which have been used in preceding tests. The temperature of the tongue and the size of the area stimulated must also be carefully controlled.

When an investigator takes all these precautions, he can measure taste sensitivity. From measurements that have been made, it is clear that taste sensitivity is not nearly so good, relatively, as smell sensitivity. It takes from 4 parts of a taste stimulus in 100 to 1 part in 1,000 to be easily detected. In general, our sensitivity is greater for acids and bitter substances than it is for sweet and salty substances.

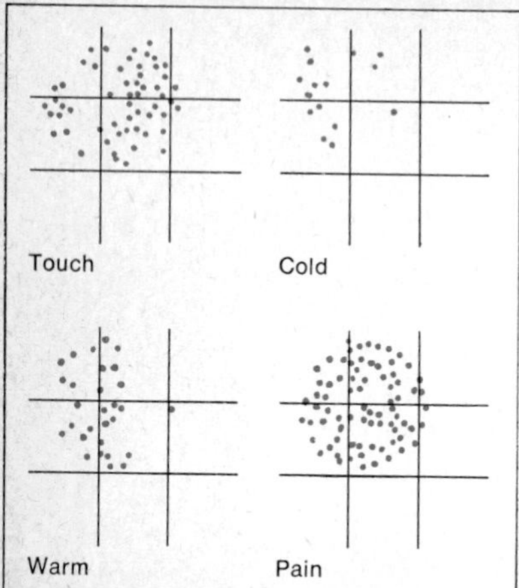

DIFFERENT POINTS ON THE SKIN ARE MOST SENSITIVE TO TOUCH, COLD, WARMTH, AND PAIN

Figure 18.39 *Mapping the sensitivity of the skin. By marking a grid on an area of the skin and then systematically stimulating different spots, we can construct a map of the sensitive spots. Maps for touch, cold, warmth, and pain, stimuli are usually different, indicating that there are four distinct skin senses. (Diagram from Gerard, 1941.)*

TASTE OR SMELL? Although we all believe that we taste with our tongues and smell with our noses, most of us do not realize that we commonly confuse taste and smell. Indeed, we often think that we are identifying a flavor by taste when smell is the more important.

You can prove this by asking a friend to hold his nose while you place drops of familiar beverages on his tongue. If you place a drop of lemon juice on it, the chances are that he will say merely that it is something sour. If you drop a little Coca-Cola on it, he may know only that it is something bittersweet. If you give him a piece of potato, he may be unable to distinguish its taste from that of an apple. If you repeat the experiment without your friend holding his nose, he will immediately identify the substances correctly.

Some smells, like tobacco smoke, so mask a flavor that gourmets have been known to refuse to eat in smoke-filled restaurants. The part played by smell explains why food is "tasteless" when a person has a stuffy head cold that greatly reduces his sensitivity to odors.

The four skin senses Vision, hearing, and the chemical senses are the sensory channels used most in conscious perception of the world. If these channels are functioning properly, we hardly need any other senses to appreciate what is going on around us. For this reason we tend to ignore what we could do, if we had to, with our skin senses. In general, we rely on our skin senses only for such simple experiences as itches and tinglings, feelings of hot and cold, and painful sensations of injury. Actually, the skin senses are capable of telling us much more than that. We could, for example, identify many objects by their touch or even read braille, as the blind must do.

Let us begin our account of these senses with an experiment that has now become common in the psychological laboratory (Woodworth and Schlosberg, 1954).

A subject is seated and asked to roll up the sleeve of his shirt, baring his forearm. On the undersurface of the arm, a grid is stamped. The experimenter then takes a hair that can be applied with known pressure and touches the end of it first to one spot on the grid and then to another. Each time the hair is applied, the blindfolded subject reports whether or not he feels pressure. The experimenter keeps a chart corresponding to the grid stamped on the subject's arm and marks on the chart each position at which the subject reports having felt pressure (see Figure 18.39).

Having plotted all the points on the grid where pressure, or touch, is reported, the experimenter now takes a rod that has been cooled to a temperature, say, of 28°C, and kept at that temperature throughout the experiment. With this rod, he goes again from square to square and charts the points at which the subject reports "cold." He then does the same thing with a rod that has been maintained at a temperature above normal, say 35°C, and he maps all the spots for which "warm" is reported. Finally, with a fine sharp needle applied with a constant light pressure, he goes over the entire grid again and plots the "pain spots."

Now let us look at Figure 18.39, where all these points are plotted. First, you can see that not all areas are equally sensitive. In some places the subject reports "touch"; in others he does not. Thus you see that the

THE SKIN IS A COMPLEX ORGAN

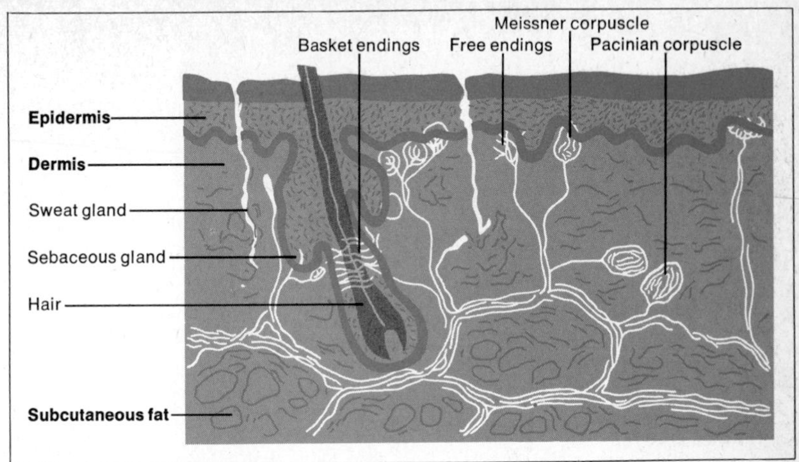

Figure 18.40 *Cross-sectional diagram of the skin. Note the most important sensory elements: the Meissner corpuscles, the Pacinian corpuscles, free nerve endings, and the basket nerve endings—the nerve fibers around the bases of the hairs.*

skin has a *punctate sensitivity*—it is sensitive at some points and not others. (Actually, detailed analysis shows that the skin is simply *more* sensitive or *less* sensitive from one point to another.) Second, you will notice different maps for the different stimulators. The spots of greatest sensitivity to touch, cold, warmth, and pain are, on the whole, different. From data such as these it should be apparent that there is not one skin sense, but four.

PRESSURE OR TOUCH The experience a subject reports when he is touched lightly with a hair is called either pressure or touch. The amount of pressure required to elicit this experience varies greatly for different parts of the body. The tip of the tongue, the lips, the fingers, and the hands are the most sensitive areas. The arms and legs are less sensitive, whereas the trunk and calloused areas are the least sensitive of all. We experience pressure, it should also be noted, not only when some object touches the skin but also when hairs on the body are slightly moved.

Psychologists have studied carefully what it is about a stimulus that elicits the experience of pressure. They wanted to know in particular whether it was the weight of an object on the skin, or simply a bending of the skin, that aroused sensation. They have concluded that it is the latter—the deforming or bending of the skin. A *gradient of pressure,* not uniformly distributed pressure, is the adequate stimulus for touch experience.

For more than fifty years many attempts have been made to determine the receptors for pressure. Seldom have scientists worked so assiduously at a problem with so little success. We think that a fairly complex structure called the *Meissner corpuscle* (see Figure 18.40) serves the pressure sense in the hairless regions of the body—the palms of the hands, for example. We think that another structure, the *basket nerve ending,* does the same for the roots of hairs. We also have good reason to believe that simple *free nerve endings*—endings not associated with any special structure—convey touch impulses, because people can feel pressure in some areas of the skin where no receptors other than free nerve endings are to be found. A final answer to this problem awaits further research. In addition to the sense of touch or pressure on the surface of the body, we are sensitive to deep pressure. The receptors for this sense seem to be small capsules called *Pacinian corpuscles*.

TEMPERATURE SENSATION: COLD AND WARMTH Experiences of warmth and cold are elicited by any change in the normal gradient of skin temperature—that is, by any change in the difference between the temperature of the skin surface and the temperature of the blood circulating beneath it. This gradient in the case of the forearm, for example, is about 5°C. The surface of the skin is usually about 32 or 33°C and that of the blood beneath it 37.5°C. A stimulus of 28 to 30°C, which is definitely felt as cold, increases this gradient a little, whereas a stimulus of 34°C, which can be felt as warm, decreases it a little. Thus it takes a change in skin temperature of only 1 or 2°C to be experienced as warmth or cold.

In the experiment charted in Figure 18.39, the maps of "cold" spots and "warm" spots were different. This fact has been taken to mean that there are two different senses for experiencing warmth and cold. It might be expected that different receptors underlie the warm and cold spots. However, there do not seem to be any obvious receptors for thermal sensitivity which can be demonstrated anatomically. Instead, free nerve fibers, some of them physiologically specialized, appear to be responsible for signaling perceptions of temperature. Increasing the temperature gradient by cooling the skin 5 to 10°C causes certain fibers to increase their rate of firing. These fibers might be called "cold" fibers. Similarly, decreasing the temperature gradient by warming the skin causes an increase in the firing of certain fibers, up to a point (Zotterman, 1959). These might be called "warm" fibers. Thus the input, or afferent, code for experiences of cold and warmth appears to be the rate of firing in "cold" and "warm" fibers.

It is interesting that some "cold" fibers show an increase in firing rate when very warm stimuli, say, 45 to 50°C (113 to 122°F), are applied to the skin. This may be the physiological basis for the psychological phenomenon of *paradoxical cold*—reports by a subject that a small, hot stimulus spot feels cold.

PAIN Many diverse stimuli produce pain—a needle prick, scalding steam, a hard blow to the skin, or strong acid. One laboratory method of producing pain is to use a device that radiates heat to a given area of the skin (Wolff and Wolf, 1948). As the radiant heat is increased in intensity, the person first reports warmth, and then at a particular intensity reports pain. Other methods which are not quite so precise make use of pinpricks and chemical solutions.

The biological utility of pain is most clearly illustrated in cases of the rare individuals who have no pain sensitivity. Sometimes these people unknowingly incur grave injuries. One 7-year-old girl accumulated multiple scars, bruises, fractures, self-mutilations, dislocations, and other local deformities (Boyd and Nie, 1949). On several occasions her parents smelled burning flesh and found her leaning casually on a hot stove.

Because of the close relationship between pain and bodily injury, scientists have been inclined to believe for a long time that injury to tissues is the common immediate stimulus for the sensation of pain. Some experiments with heat radiation make this view plausible (Hardy et al., 1951). When an observer is asked to report pain while heat is radiated to a patch of skin on his forehead, he will usually report a sensation of pain when the temperature of his skin reaches the point at which tissues begin to break down. The amount of pain felt is not directly related to the *amount* of tissue damage, however. Rather, it is related to the *rate* of destruction. A painful sensation results when stimulation produces a critical state in which destructive forces just begin to exceed the rate of repair.

Other experiments have shown that the receptors for pain are almost certainly unspecialized free nerve endings. These are abundant in most parts of the skin, particularly where sensitivity to pain is greatest.

Proprioceptive senses Hidden away in our muscles, and in our joints and tendons, are a large variety of sense organs. In addition, there are sensory cells in the semicircular canals and otolith organs of the inner ear. All these sense organs give us information about the position of the body in space. The general term for the body-position sense is *proprioception.*

KINESTHETIC SENSE A bodily sense that physiologists now know a good deal about is one that many people have never heard of: *kinesthesis.* In some ways it is the most important sense we have, because it provides an automatic system for coordinating our muscles in walking and in all our skilled movements. One can see how important it is only by observing a person who has been deprived of it. This sometimes happens in a form of syphilis, known as tabes dorsalis, which attacks the sensory pathways from the kinesthetic sense organs. The patient gets no information from his muscles about their movement. He is able to walk, balance a ball, or carry out other skills only by carefully watching what his arms and legs are doing. If syphilis invades the brainstem and interrupts kinesthetic impulses from the face and mouth, uncoordinated movements of the face may also occur, together with a slurring of speech which may be severe enough to make the patient unintelligible.

The kinesthetic receptors are found in three distinct places. One is in the muscles, where free nerve endings surround small, specialized muscle fibers called *muscle spindles* (see Figure 18.41). These kinesthetic receptors signal the *stretch* of a muscle. A second location of kinesthetic receptors is in the tendons that connect muscles to bones. The receptors here are nerve endings that serve a specialized organ known as the *Golgi tendon organ* (see Figure 18.41). They are stimulated when a muscle contracts and puts tension on the tendon. Finally, some receptors are to be found in the linings of the joints. These are stimulated whenever a limb moves, changing the relative positions of two bones in the joint. We are still not certain about the receptors in the joints, but it is possible that they are *Pacinian corpuscles*—the same receptors that yield perception of deep pressure when regions below the skin are stimulated.

KINESTHETIC RECEPTORS ARE FOUND IN THE MUSCLES, TENDONS, AND JOINTS

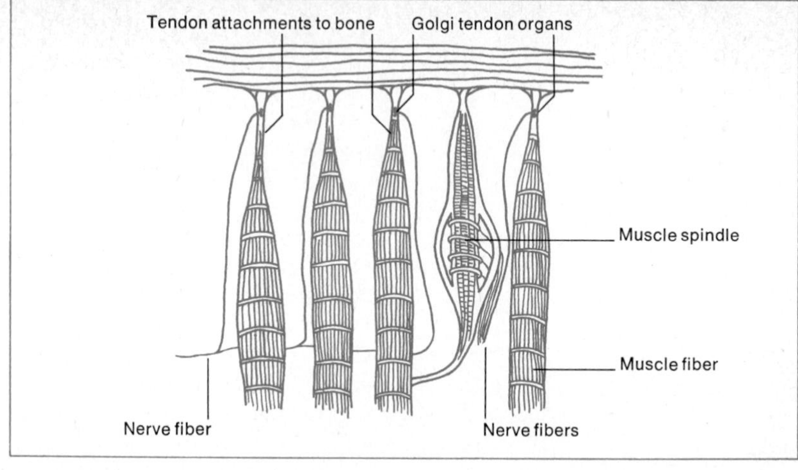

Figure 18.41 *Kinesthetic receptors in muscle and tendon. The two kinesthetic receptors shown are the muscle spindle and the Golgi tendon organ. The sensory muscle spindles signal the stretch of a muscle. They are on special types of muscle fibers which lie parallel with the muscle fibers whose main function is movement of a part of the body. The Golgi tendon organs also signal the muscle stretch. They lie in the attachments of muscle fibers to bone—that is, in the tendons. (After Richard F. Thompson,* Foundations of Physiological Psychology, *Harper & Row, 1967.)*

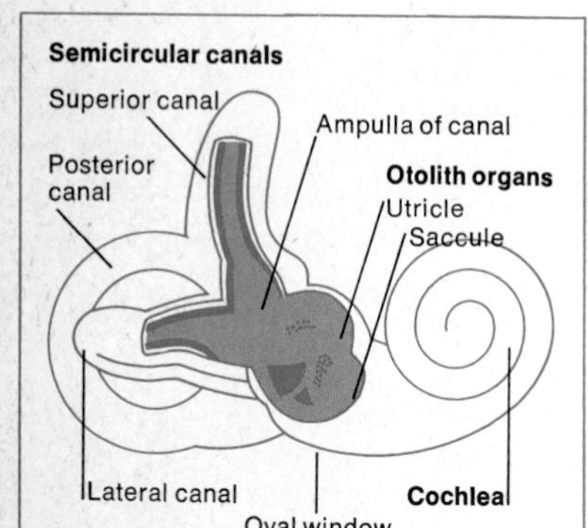

SENSE OF BALANCE IS PROVIDED BY THE SEMICIRCULAR CANALS AND THE OTOLITH ORGANS

Figure 18.42 *Diagram of the vestibular sense organs. The three semicircular canals are so arranged that one is in each plane (see also Figure 18.28). Organs in the ampullae of these canals respond to rotation of the head. On the other hand, the otolith organs, located in the saccule and utricle, are stimulated by the position of the head; they respond to tilt of the head and do not require rotation for stimulation.*

VESTIBULAR SENSE Like kinesthesis, the vestibular sense is important in balance and movement, but it does not provide direct experiences of which we are ordinarily aware. The organs of the vestibular sense are well known because they are highly specialized, are reasonably large, and can be studied in detail under the microscope. They are, in fact, part of the inner ear. The inner ear is a series of cavities, only one of which, the cochlea, is concerned with hearing. The rest of the cavities constitute the vestibular organs. They divide into two main groups: the *semicircular canals* and the *otolith organs.* The semicircular canals can be seen in the drawing of the ear in Figure 18.28; Figure 18.42 provides a detailed drawing of the canals and the otolith organs.

The three semicircular canals, each roughly perpendicular to both the others, are so oriented as to represent three different planes of movement. In an enlarged part of each canal, the *ampulla,* is a set of hair cells similar in general structure to those in the cochlea. These cells are encompassed by the fluid that fills the canal and are stimulated when pressure is exerted on this fluid. Such pressure occurs mainly when the head is rotated, and thus the canals are sense organs for rotation. It appears, however, that the receptors do not respond to continuous rotation—continuous pressure—but to changes in rate of rotation, that is, to acceleration or deceleration. So when a person is rotated, or rotates himself as a dancer does, for example, it is only while he is increasing speed or slowing down that the semicircular organs are stimulated.

Dancers and acrobats who do a lot of spinning have learned tricks which help them overcome the dizziness that comes from prolonged stimulation of the vestibular organs. Watch a ballet dancer spinning, and you will see that he keeps his head as motionless as possible by temporarily fixing his eyes on some object in the environment. The head whips around to pick a new fixation point while the body is still turning.

Two other cavities make up the organs of the vestibular sense. On the walls of these cavities are thickenings which contain receptor cells.

They protrude into a gelatinous mass that contains small crystals, the *otoliths* (*oto* means "ear"; *lith* means "stone"). These receptors appear to be positional, or static, receptors, for they respond merely to the tilt or position of the head and do not require rotation to be stimulated.

The canals and the otolith organs together provide a sense of balance. Impulses from these organs help a person right himself when he has been thrown off balance. More specifically, they control a number of reflexes that automatically compensate for loss of balance. One such reflex is a movement of the head back to a normal position whenever it has been turned away from it. Another is a reflex twisting of the trunk and body to return the whole body to normal position.

Motion sickness, which causes some people so much misery, is an effect of vestibular stimulation. We know that the vestibular organs are responsible for motion sickness for two reasons: first, the occasional individual whose vestibular system is not functioning properly does not suffer motion sickness; second, we can induce motion sickness experimentally by producing the vestibular neural impulses that evoke reflex reactions in the alimentary tract (Wendt, 1951). Other factors such as anxiety can augment such reactions, and they therefore contribute to the direct effects of vestibular stimulation. There are now well-publicized drugs, Dramamine, for instance, which reduce or prevent motion sickness, but it is not known yet whether they work on the vestibular sense, alimentary tract, or some other part of the nervous system involved in the reaction.

Synopsis and summary

All behavior and experience depend heavily upon sensory processes. For this reason the study of the senses has had a long history in psychology and biology. In psychology, the structuralist school studied the senses in order to find the elements, or indivisible units, of experience. Although many valuable observations were made, this endeavor did not prove very fruitful, and interest in the senses waned in psychology. In biology, the study of the senses forms a continuing tradition, and great strides have been made in unraveling the mystery of the correlations between physical energy, the afferent code in the nervous system, and experience. It is for this reason that we treat the senses as a part of the biology of behavior.

This chapter stresses vision and hearing, perhaps the two most important senses for man. The discussion of each of these senses follows similar lines: First the physical stimulus, then the structure of the receptor and pathway, next the transduction process in which physical energy is converted into nerve impulses, then some of the major psychophysical relationships, and finally some of the important features of the afferent code as it is known today.

1. Man has ten or more sensory channels, the most important of which are vision, hearing, cold, warmth, pain, touch, smell, taste, kinesthesis, and the vestibular sense. Each of the sensory systems can be thought of as a channel with the sensitive receptor at the receiving end, conducting nerve fibers in the middle, and the central nervous system at the other end.
2. Three preliminary questions set the stage for an analysis of particular sensory mechanisms. The first is the question of transduction: What is the process by which physical energy is converted into nerve impulses? The second is the question: What is the relationship between activity in the nervous system and experience? The third is the psychophysical question: What is the relationship between the physical energy and reported experience?
3. Transduction involves the action of physical energy on the specialized receptor cells to produce a slowly changing electrical potential: the generator potential. The generator potential, in turn, depolarizes the sensory neurons of the receptor so that nerve impulses are produced.
4. The relationship between the nervous system and experience involves the afferent code for experience. As a result of the transduction process, various patterns of activity are set up in the nervous system; the patterns form the afferent, or input, code necessary for experience.
5. Psychophysics is the study of the relationships between characteristics of the physical energy and experience. Much of psychophysics is

concerned with techniques for studying two kinds of threshold: the absolute threshold (the least amount of stimulus energy necessary for the stimulus to be detected), and the differential threshold (the least amount of change of energy necessary for an experience of stimulus change).

6. The physical stimulus for vision is electromagnetic energy in the wavelength band between approximately 380 and 780 nanometers (nm). Portions of the electromagnetic spectrum above and below this band are not visible; hence the band between 380 and 780 nm is termed the visible spectrum.

7. The visual receptor, the eye, is in many ways like a camera. It has a lens system for focusing light on a photosensitive surface, the retina at the back of the eye; it has a mechanism for controlling the amount of light allowed to fall on the retina. But the eye is not like a camera in some important respects: We do not see the image on the retina; the patterns of light and shadow on the retina only initiate the processes leading to nerve impulses. Second, the eye has a double lens system, the cornea and the lens itself; the eye focuses light by changing the shape of the lens. Finally, the eye is not a passive receiver but is constantly in motion.

8. The sensitive elements of the retina are the rods and cones, which contain photosensitive pigments. Rods and cones are connected to the brain through a relatively intricate pathway. The cones are more concentrated in the center of the retina, in the fovea. They are important in visual acuity and in daylight and color vision. The rods are concentrated more toward the periphery of the retina and are important for vision in dim light.

9. The transduction process in vision, as in most other sensory channels, consists of several steps. In vision, the first step is a photochemical change that generates a second process, the generator potential. Third, the generator potential produces nerve impulses in the fibers from the ganglion cell layer of the retina. These nerve impulses travel to the lateral geniculate body. From the lateral geniculate body, fibers of the visual system then travel to the visual cortex which, in man, is in the posterior portion of the cerebral cortex. A point-to-point, or topographical, projection is maintained in the visual projection system.

10. Psychophysical relationships in vision include relationships between characteristics of the physical energy and the experiences of brightness, hue, or color, and saturation. Hue is what is commonly meant by color: blue, green, yellow, red, or shades in between. Saturation is the relative amount of color, as distinguished from gray, in a stimulus. Brightness refers to the relative lightness or darkness of a stimulus.

11. The wavelength of the stimulating energy is the primary physical determiner of hue. Hues can be arranged in a circle, the color circle, with saturations as distances along the radii of the circle. The color circle helps summarize the results of mixing colors.

12. The amount of energy in the physical stimulus is the primary determiner of brightness experience.

13. Long before it was possible to make direct electrophysiological recordings, two theories of the afferent code for hue in vision were proposed. The Young-Helmholtz theory postulated three different types of cones that were most sensitive in the blue, green, and red regions of the spectrum. The Hering theory postulated three pairs of receptor elements: white-black, yellow-blue, and red-green. Direct study of cone pigments indicates that three distinct types exist as postulated by the Young-Helmholtz theory; furthermore, recordings from the nerve fibers from the retina indicate that these cones function in an opponent-process manner as postulated in the Hering theory.

14. In many animals, the visual cerebral cortex seems necessary for form vision. Single cells, or units, in the visual cortex are hooked to the receptor cells so as to be differentially sensitive to the orientations of stimuli in space. Such physiological connections may furnish part of the afferent code for form.

15. The stimulus for hearing is provided by alternations of air pressure, called sound waves. The experience of a pure tone is caused by sine waves. Complex waves consisting of many frequencies provide the experience of noise if they are aperiodic; if the complex waves are periodic, they provide a complex tonal experience.

16. The pressure waves enter the canal of the outer ear and cause the eardrum to vibrate. This vibration is transmitted via the bones of the middle ear to the inner ear, which contains the cochlea and the organ of Corti.

17. The crucial event in auditory transduction takes place in the organ of Corti on the basilar membrane of the cochlea. Here the pressure wave in the fluid of the cochlea causes a bending motion of the hair cells. One theory states that this motion changes the electrical resistance of the hair cells and allows current to flow across the basilar membrane. The current is recorded as the cochlear microphonic, and it is considered by some authorities to be the generator potential in hearing. In any case, nerve impulses are generated by the transduction process, and they ascend through the auditory pathway to the cerebral cortex.

18. Pitch, loudness, and timbre are the psychological attributes of sound energy. Pitch is correlated with the frequency of the physical energy. Loudness is correlated with the intensity of the physical stimulation. Timbre is correlated with the complexity of the wave form. However, intensity also affects pitch, and frequency also affects loudness.

19. The place theory states that the afferent code for perceived pitch is

a spatial one; much evidence indicates that nerve impulses from the place of maximal stimulation of the basilar membrane code the experience of pitch. Loudness is coded by the number of impulses in the system.

20. Deafness is fairly common. Two types can be distinguished: conduction deafness involves some loss in the conduction of sounds to the inner ear; nerve deafness involves some defect in the organ of Corti or the auditory nerve. Nerve deafness tends to be greater for high tones than for low tones, and it is common in old age.

21. The number of qualities in the sense of smell is uncertain, although combinations of as few as four or six will account for most odors. Taste seems to have four basic qualities: sweet, salty, sour, and bitter.

22. Smell is much more acute than taste, sometimes requiring only a few molecules per liter of air for detection.

23. Four basic senses are associated with the skin: warmth, cold, pressure or touch, and pain. Although there seem to be specialized receptors for touch, free nerve endings in the skin can probably serve as the receptors for each of these sensory modalities. It is well established that such free nerve endings are the receptors for warmth, cold, and pain.

24. Proprioception consists of the kinesthetic and vestibular senses. The kinesthetic receptors are found in muscles, tendons, and joints. Impulses from these receptors make posture and coordination automatic. The vestibular sense organs are located in the inner ear. They respond to the rotation of the head or to changes in its position, thus providing a sense of balance.

Related topics in the text

Chapter 8 Perception The discussion in this chapter of the physiological basis of sensory experience contributes to an understanding of how we come to know the world. But many other factors are involved in experience of the world as it actually looks, sounds, smells, tastes, and so on. These other factors, and some theories about the complex organization of inputs from the world which make experience possible, are discussed in Chapter 8.

Chapter 17 The Nervous System
The basic anatomy of the nervous system, the nature of nerve impulses, and the mechanisms of conduction at synapses are detailed. These topics are basic to an understanding of sensory projection systems and afferent coding in the sensory systems.

Chapter 19 Brain and Behavior
The neural bases of emotion, motivation, learning, memory, psychopathology, and so on, are discussed to round out Part Five's treatment of the biology of behavior.

Suggestions for further reading

Alpern, M., Lawrence, M., and Wolsk, D. *Sensory processes.* Belmont, Calif.: Brooks/Cole, 1967. (Paperback.)
A short textbook on sensory mechanisms, with emphasis on peripheral receptor processes.

Bergeijk, W. A. van, Pierce, J. R., and David, E. E., Jr. *Waves and the ear.* Garden City, N. Y.: Doubleday, 1960. (Paperback.)
A popular and interesting account of many aspects of hearing and speech sounds.

Boring, E. G. *Sensation and perception in the history of experimental psychology.* New York: Appleton Century Crofts, 1942.
An authoritative history of experimental work on sensory perception.

Buddenbrock, W. von. *The senses.* Ann Arbor, Mich.: University of Michigan Press, 1958. (Paperback.)
An interesting discussion of the sense organs of many animals, including man.

Gregory, R. L. *Eye and brain: The psychology of seeing.* New York: McGraw-Hill, 1966.
An interesting and colorful account of visual sensation and perception.

King, R. A. (Ed.) *Readings for an introduction to psychology.* (3d ed.) New York: McGraw-Hill, 1971. (Paperback.)
Several papers on sensory processes are included in this book of readings designed to accompany your text.

Lowenstein, O. *The senses.* Baltimore: Penguin, 1966. (Paperback.)
A survey of sensory mechanisms with special attention to the sensory capacities of lower animals.

Mueller, C. G. *Sensory psychology.* Englewood Cliffs, N.J.: Prentice-Hall, 1965. (Paperback.)
A short but authoritative survey of basic sensory processes.

Mueller, C. G., and Rudolph, M. (Eds.). *Light and vision.* New York: Time-Life, 1966.
An elementary treatment of many of the main topics in vision; the illustrations are dramatic, interesting, and worth the bleaching of some visual pigment.

Wright, R. H. *The science of smell.* New York: Basic Books, 1964.
A readable summary of modern knowledge about the sense of smell.

Wyburn, G. M., Pickford, R. W., and Hirst, R. J. *Human senses and perception.* Edinburgh: Oliver & Boyd, 1964.
An interesting book because it discusses perception from the physiological, psychological, and philosophical points of view.

The thoughts of which I am now giving utterance and your thoughts regarding them are the expression of molecular changes in that matter of life which is the source of our other vital phenomena.

T. H. Huxley

We have discussed the tasks and techniques of biological psychology, some basic ideas about the functioning and anatomy of the nervous system, and some ways in which people come into contact with the world through their sensory channels. Now we are ready to give examples of the biological basis of more complex behaviors—the biology of learning and memory, of motivation, and of activation and emotion, for instance. In addition, we shall discuss the biological activity of certain drugs which affect behavior.

The Biology of Learning and Memory

We said earlier that an important characteristic of the nervous system is its plasticity in forming new associations. How is the nervous system changed so that new responses can be made to stimuli, so that stimuli can be associated with each other, and so that perceptual organization can be changed? What is the physical basis for the retention of the changes? That the changes take place in the nervous system is agreed, but their nature is still in dispute.

Two general approaches to these significant problems can be distinguished. One traditional procedure—the *structural* approach—is to study the location of the changes in the nervous system and the pathways involved. The second approach is more molecular; it takes up the problem in finer detail. This *molecular* approach stresses the changes which may take place within cells, and between cells, in learning and memory. Both approaches have been fruitful in research into nervous system activity, and we shall consider both.

Learning systems of the brain Where does learning occur in the nervous system? The learning capacity, or plasticity, of lower areas of the nervous system—the spinal cord, the medulla, the pons, and the midbrain—is very limited. Plasticity and learning are important properties of the nervous system only at the higher levels. The lower areas function in the transmission of sensory information and the reflex action necessary for life. Higher areas also do this, but they are involved as well in the processes necessary for adjustment to a rapidly changing environment. Learning is one of these processes.

Within the higher levels of the brain there is some localization of function, but the brain area involved in the learning and memory of any association is relatively large. It is not restricted to one cell or to a

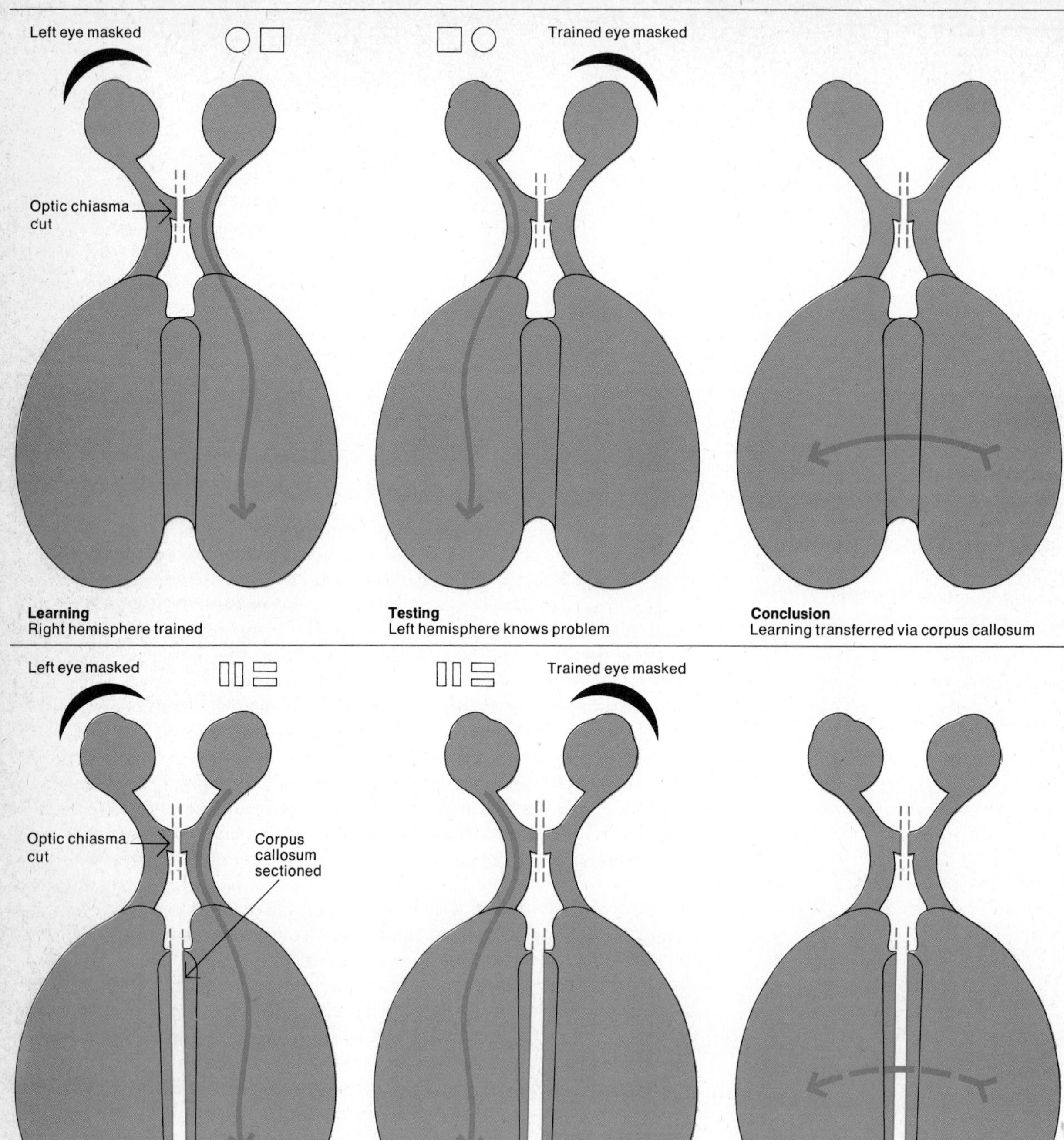
Left eye masked
Trained eye masked
Optic chiasma cut
Learning
Right hemisphere trained
Testing
Left hemisphere knows problem
Conclusion
Learning transferred via corpus callosum
Left eye masked
Trained eye masked
Optic chiasma cut
Corpus callosum sectioned
Learning
Right hemisphere trained
Testing
Left hemisphere does *not* know problem
Conclusion
Transfer pathway was blocked

ONE HEMISPHERE OF THE CEREBRUM MAY KNOW WHAT THE OTHER HEMISPHERE HAS LEARNED

Figure 19.1 *Diagrams of "split brain" experiments.*
Above: Visual input was restricted to one hemisphere by cutting the optic chiasma, but the other hemisphere had also learned the problem of discriminating between a circle and a square.
Below: Another experiment in which both the optic chiasma and the corpus callosum were cut. In this case the other hemisphere did not learn the visual discrimination problem, leading to the conclusion that the corpus callosum is the pathway for transfer of learning in the two hemispheres. (From Glickstein, 1965; in Ruch and Patton, 1965.)

small network of cells. In such a region of the brain a memory is duplicated over and over again; one part of the region stores the information as well as another part. In other words, the region is *equipotential* for the learning and memory of the particular response.

One of the first scientists to reach this conclusion was Karl Lashley (1890–1958), who was among the founders of biological psychology. From his studies of maze learning in rats, he concluded that the animal's whole cerebral cortex was involved in the learning of the correct path through the maze—that the rat's cerebral cortex was *equipotential* for maze learning (1929). Such a conclusion has since been slightly qualified, for the whole cerebral cortex is not truly equipotential. But the principle still holds within more narrowly confined regions of the brain.

Perhaps the clearest demonstration that wide regions of the brain participate in the learning and memory of a particular association comes from studies of *interocular,* or between-eye, *transfer*. These studies show that both hemispheres of the brain participate in the learning of the association of a stimulus to a response, even when the information necessary for learning is confined to one hemisphere by surgical operations (Myers, 1955, 1956):

The visual input to the cerebral cortex was restricted to one hemisphere by cutting the *optic chiasma* to eliminate crossed fibers in the visual pathways, then covering one eye during learning. Thus the information necessary for learning a visual discrimination—circle versus square, in this case—was restricted to one hemisphere of the cerebral cortex (see Figure 19.1, top). After the animals had learned the discrimination, the eye which had been uncovered during training, the "trained" eye, was covered; the eye which had been covered during training, the "untrained" eye, was uncovered. Testing on the discrimination problem showed that with the input now coming in from the "untrained eye" to the "untrained hemisphere," the animal was still able to choose the correct stimulus. The conclusion was that learning had taken place in both cerebral hemispheres even though the stimulus input necessary for learning had been restricted to only one of them.

This is an example of interocular transfer, or, with reference to the hemispheres, interhemispheric transfer. It demonstrates the equipotentiality of large regions of the brain in the learning of visual discriminations. What is learned is duplicated throughout both hemispheres. These studies also concluded that the *corpus callosum,* the band of fibers connecting the two hemispheres, was responsible for the transfer of the learned changes from one hemisphere to the other. When both the optic chiasma and the corpus callosum were cut, no interhemispheric transfer occurred (see Figure 19.1, bottom). The conclusion was that the corpus callosum is the fiber pathway necessary for the reduplication of learning in the two hemispheres. In the intact brain, of course, both hemispheres receive inputs, and interhemispheric transfer occurs, so that learning and memory of particular associations are functions of wide regions of both hemispheres.

With the understanding that learning is widespread within regions of the brain, let us look at some of the evidence that particular regions

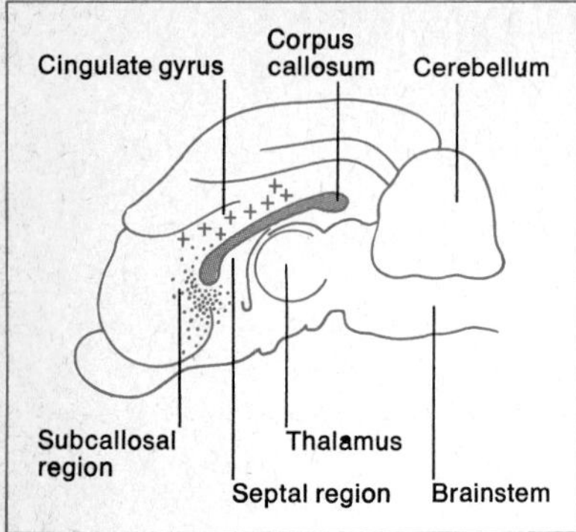

LESIONS OF THE LIMBIC SYSTEM MAY AFFECT AVOIDANCE BEHAVIOR

Figure 19.2 *A medial view of the cat brain. Lesions of the subcallosal and septal regions, shown by dots, interfered with the learning of passive avoidance tasks; lesions of the cingulate gyrus, shown by plus marks, interfered with active avoidance learning. (Modified from McCleary, 1961.)*

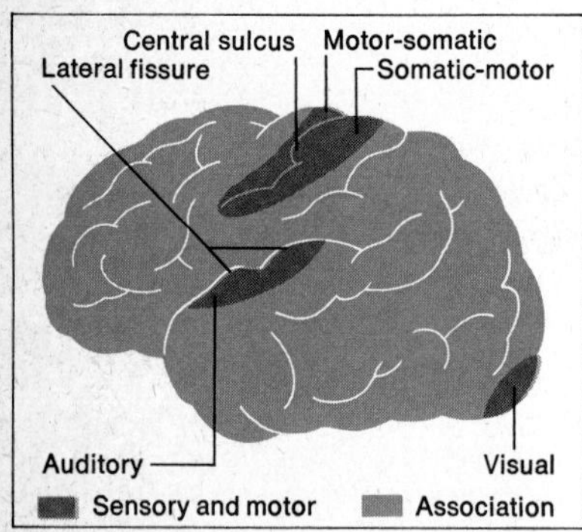

THE CEREBRAL CORTEX MAY BE DIVIDED INTO SENSORY, MOTOR, AND ASSOCIATION AREAS

Figure 19.3 *A lateral view of the human cerebral cortex. Note the relatively large area of the association cortex. The lateral fissure and central sulcus are also shown. (From Morgan, 1965; as modified from Cobb, S.* Foundations of Psychiatry. *Baltimore: Williams & Wilkins, 1941. Copyright © 1941, The Williams & Wilkins Co., Baltimore, Md. 21202, U.S.A.)*

of the brain are most involved in certain types of learning. We shall consider the roles taken in learning by the limbic system and the association cortex.

Limbic system and learning The structure of the limbic system has already been discussed in Chapter 17 (see Figure 17.22). Within this system the cingulate gyrus, subcallosal cortex, and septal nuclei are important structures which seem to be necessary for different types of avoidance learning (see Chapter 3). Passive avoidance is the avoidance of a place where a noxious, or unpleasant, event has occurred; such learning seems to involve inhibition of response. Active avoidance learning involves learning to make a response in order to get away from stimuli which signal a noxious event. Different parts of the limbic system seem to be involved in these two types of avoidance learning (McCleary, 1961):

The effects of lesions in different parts of the limbic system of the cat were studied using both active and passive avoidance learning tasks. In active avoidance learning, cats had to learn to shuttle from one box to another at the presentation of a signal indicating that shock would be coming. In passive avoidance learning, other cats had to learn to avoid going into a compartment of the box where they had been shocked. Thus the learning task for the active avoidance cats was to run away from a signal to a safe place; that for the passive avoidance cats was to refrain from moving to another place where they had been shocked.

The control animals—those without lesions—did learn the appropriate response in each case. The experimental animals had lesions in regions of the limbic system shown in Figure 19.2. It was found that the cats with lesions of the cingulate gyrus were greatly impaired in learning the active avoidance response. On the other hand, cats with lesions of the subcallosal region were greatly impaired in learning the passive avoidance response.

This experiment illustrates the concept of *double dissociation.* A lesion in place A (for instance, in the cingulate gyrus) interfered with response X (active avoidance, for instance); but this lesion did not interfere with response Y (passive avoidance, for instance). Conversely, a lesion in place B (in the subcallosal cortex) interfered with response Y (passive avoidance learning), but not with response X (active avoidance). This is a general principle; double dissociation is a strong test for localization of particular types of learning in certain regions of the brain.

Association cortex and learning Although it is somewhat artificial, a distinction is often made between the primary sensory and motor cortex on the one hand, and the association cortex on the other (see Figure 19.3). We have discussed the sensory and motor cortex in previous chapters. By exclusion, that cortex which is not primarily motor or primarily sensory is called the *association cortex.* The learning and memory functions of the association cortex have long been a puzzle—one that is beginning to be solved (Pribram, 1969).

Most studies which attempt to decipher the functions of the association cortex in learning and memory are lesion studies. After surgically

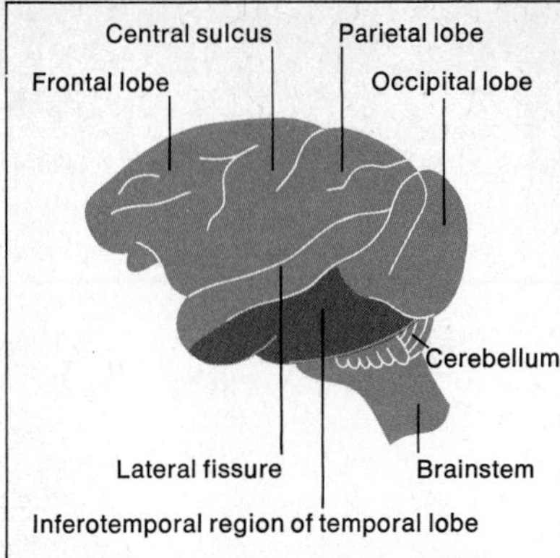

COMPLEX VISUAL LEARNING IS IMPAIRED BY INFEROTEMPORAL LESIONS

Figure 19.4 *Lateral view of monkey brain showing the approximate position of the inferotemporal region. Lesions here produce deficits in complex visual learning.*

removing a portion of an animal's association cortex, the experimenter measures any deficit in behavior which results. In general, investigators agree on the behavioral changes caused by such lesions, or ablations, but disagree somewhat in interpreting the changes.

TEMPORAL LOBE ASSOCIATION CORTEX The association areas of the temporal lobe are sometimes called the *inferotemporal* region because they are low, or ventral, in the temporal lobe. In the last 30 years many studies have focused on this portion of the association cortex. One of the first was done by Klüver and Bucy (1937), who removed the ventral portion of both temporal lobes, and associated structures, of several rhesus monkeys (see Figure 19.4). They found two major changes in behavior: one in the emotional behavior of the animals which we shall discuss later, the other a visual deficit. The visual deficit has since been analyzed in some detail. It is an impairment of visual form-discrimination learning (Chow, 1951), but it is not due to blindness or loss of visual acuity (Wilson and Mishkin, 1959). Monkeys with the discrimination deficit can learn to pull in food attached to fine strings, which indicates that their visual acuity is normal. However, they do poorly on visual discrimination problems, especially on visual discrimination learning sets (see Chapter 3).

Analysis of these and many other experiments has led to the conclusion that the difficulty stems not from failure to store information, but from a deficiency in the animal's sampling of all the stimulus possibilities (Pribram, 1969). It is as if the inferotemporal monkey is "paying attention" to only a limited range of the stimuli available to it. Thus the learning deficit is really a result of a deficiency in the processing of information. The information-processing interpretation of the functions of the inferotemporal lobe has been generalized by some investigators to the entire association cortex (Pribram, 1969).

In man, the inferior temporal lobes and associated structures such as the hippocampus (see Figure 17.20) have sometimes been removed as a therapeutic measure in stubborn cases of epilepsy. These patients suffer certain visual deficits and an impairment in immediate memory. The immediate-memory deficit, which occurs when the person is distracted immediately after some sensory input, is probably due to damage to the hippocampus (Milner, 1959). The visual deficit is not one of visual acuity; it may be similar to that of the monkey in the experiments discussed above (Milner, 1954).

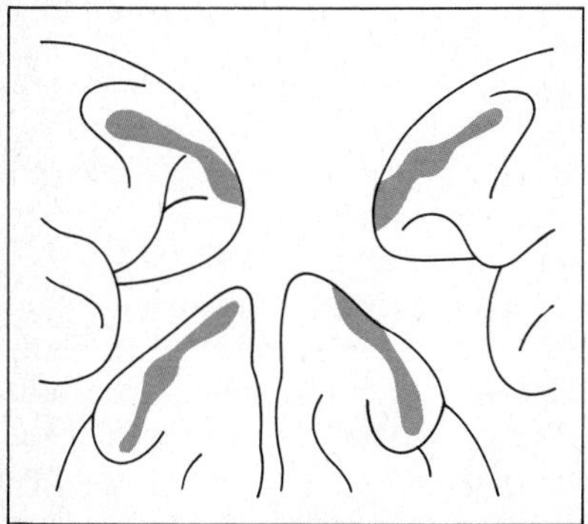

REMOVAL OF A SMALL AREA OF THE FRONTAL LOBES DESTROYS ABILITY TO DO CERTAIN TYPES OF DELAYED-RESPONSE PROBLEMS

Figure 19.5 *The cortical areas necessary for performing a delayed response correctly. Right, left, and top views of the frontal lobes of the cerebrum of a monkey; the colored areas show the extent of the lesion. (Modified from Mishkin, 1957.)*

FRONTAL ASSOCIATION CORTEX In monkeys, the ability to solve certain types of discrimination problems which involve a delay of response is destroyed by lesions of the frontal lobes (see Figure 19.5). Many types of *delayed-response* problems are possible. A typical task is illustrated in the following experiment, which was one of the earliest investigations of frontal function in monkeys (Jacobsen, 1935):

A monkey is shown that food is placed in a small well under one of two identical wooden blocks. Then a screen is lowered in front of him so that he cannot solve the problem by keeping his eyes fixed on the block with the food under it. (An apparatus similar to the one used in this experiment is shown in Figure 3.25.

There, however, the monkey is being taught a discrimination problem, not a delayed-response problem, and the blocks are not identical.) After an interval—perhaps between 5 and 50 seconds—the screen is raised, and the monkey's task is to select the correct block after the delay. Normal monkeys can do this after delays up to several minutes. Monkeys with operations in the crucial part of the prefrontal association cortex shown in Figure 19.5 cannot solve this problem even if the delay is no more than a few seconds.

Again there is agreement on the fact of a deficit; the problem is the interpretation. Earlier investigators concluded that the loss was due to a deficit of "immediate memory." But this cannot be the case, because frontally operated monkeys can solve certain other types of delayed-response problems (Mishkin and Pribram, 1956).

One current interpretation is given in terms of information processing. The idea is that a function of the frontal cortex is to break experience into discrete periods—a process called the *parsing of experience.* Monkeys with lesions in the frontal cortex may not be able to differentiate when an experience occurs in time: if they cannot do this, previous experiences run together. In terms of the delayed-response problem it is as if all the previous trials had been run together: the monkey cannot pull out and use the crucial information which was given to him a few seconds before. As Pribram says, the frontally lesioned monkey's experience may resemble a page of print in which all the words are run together (1969).

Another interpretation is in terms of the tendency of frontally lesioned monkeys to *perseverate*—to repeat the same response over and over regardless of the consequence. A third interpretation is based on another effect produced by frontal lesions in monkeys: an increase in activity, or motor movement. In delayed-response tasks such as the one described above, this hyperactivity may reduce the monkey's ability to bridge the time gap by orienting his body toward the block with the food under it during the delay interval.

In man, the prefrontal area is one about which much has been claimed but little has been proved. For instance, it has been claimed that lesions of the prefrontal lobes result in a decrease in drive, a decline in ability to direct behavior toward goals, and inability to synthesize, or put together, elements of experience. Other investigators have reported personality changes characterized by loss of social inhibition. But the results are variable, and many of them may arise from damage to subcortical structures underlying the frontal lobes. It has sometimes been claimed that the prefrontal areas play a special role in general intelligence; but marked intellectual deficits on intelligence tests do not usually show up after damage to the prefrontal lobes (Teuber, 1964). It has been found, however, that certain intellectual abilities are affected after prefrontal lesions.

One apparently reliable discovery is that patients with prefrontal lesions perseverate—they cannot shift easily from one mode of attack on a problem to another (Milner, 1964). Other studies have found that abstract thinking ability of such patients seems to be impaired (Goldstein, 1950).

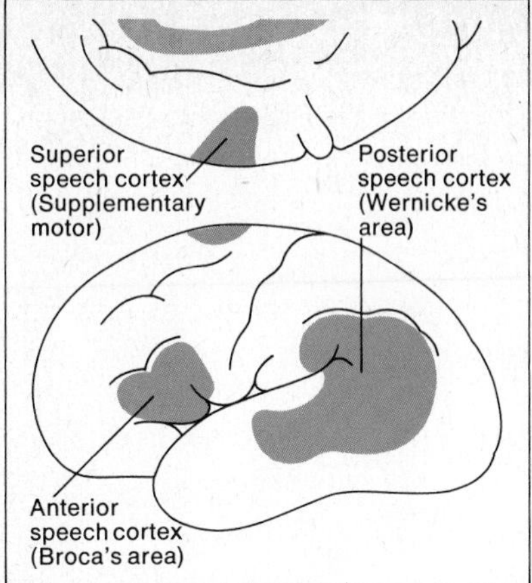

MUCH OF THE HUMAN BRAIN IS INVOLVED IN SPEECH

Figure 19.6 *The speech areas of the human cortex. Stimulation of these regions in conscious patients produces aphasic disturbances in speech. Lesions in some of these areas also produce aphasic disturbances. The upper part of the drawing shows the medial portion of the cortex in an upside-down position; the lower part is a lateral view of the cortex. (Modified from Penfield and Roberts, 1959.)*

PARIETAL ASSOCIATION CORTEX The parietal association cortex seems to make it possible to recognize objects by touch. Although there may be some sensory loss from lesions of the parietal association cortex, the loss of ability for touch recognition cannot be completely explained on the basis of a loss of touch sensitivity. The following experiment shows a loss of touch recognition ability (Ruch et al., 1938):

A chimpanzee was taught to discriminate a cone from a pyramid by touch alone. The animal could not see the objects and had to discriminate them by handling them. It also learned a more difficult discrimination between a wedge and a pyramid. Then its posterior parietal association area was removed. After the operation, the animal lost both habits, but upon retraining, it was again able to discriminate the pyramid from the cone. No amount of retraining, however, enabled the animal to make the more subtle and complex discrimination between the wedge and the pyramid. Thus it appears that the touch recognition of subtle distinctions requires the intact parietal association cortex.

In man, a portion of the parietal cortex, largely confined to the left hemisphere, is devoted to symbolic speech. In the right hemisphere, the corresponding portions seem to be involved in the perception of the body. Patients with lesions here often fail to take account of their bodily parts; for instance, in dressing they may neglect to dress half of their body (Hécaen et al., 1956).

SPEECH AREAS Although they cannot talk as we do, animals such as chimpanzees can learn to use a type of symbolic communication. In an experiment which was described in Chapter 2, for example, a chimpanzee is being taught to use sign language (Gardner and Gardner, 1969). However, this learning has taken place under special conditions. The use of symbolic speech for communication can be considered a species-specific human characteristic (Beach, 1960); it constitutes a large part of that which makes us distinctively human. In addition to our use of speech to communicate with each other, the symbols we manipulate in the process of thinking are mainly speech symbols (see Chapter 5). Thus man has been intensely interested in locating the areas of the association cortex which are crucial to the use of symbolic speech.

Areas of the association cortex in the frontal, parietal, and temporal lobes seem to be involved in the symbolic use of speech (see Figure 19.6). Regardless of whether the person is right- or left-handed, the speech areas are usually in the left hemisphere of the cerebral cortex (Penfield and Roberts, 1959). These discoveries are the result of careful sifting of clinical cases by many neurologists. In addition, some information comes from the stimulation of the human cortex (Penfield and Roberts, 1959). The stimulation studies were done on epileptic patients as part of operations to remove foci, or areas, of the brain from which epileptic seizures seemed to originate. The symptoms of epilepsy are caused by abnormal, massive discharges of millions of cortical neurons. Sometimes this discharge seems to begin in a particular region—the focus—and then spreads over the cortex. In patients whose abnormal

STIMULATION OF THE BRAIN TELLS US ABOUT ITS FUNCTION

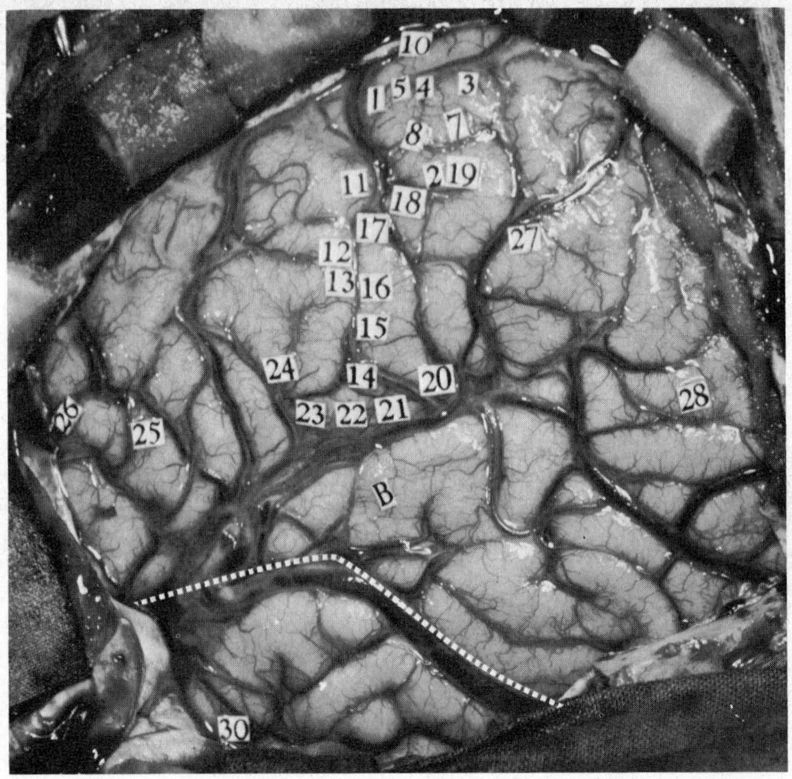

Figure 19.7 *Lateral view of human cerebral cortex exposed during an operation. The numbered tickets show points of stimulation; most of them are scattered along the central sulcus. The temporal lobe is at the bottom of the picture, around and below B. (From Penfield and Roberts, 1959.)*

discharge of the focus cannot be held in check by drugs, surgical removal of the focus helps. But the surgeons do not wish to remove the focal zone if it is involved in significant behavioral functions. Hence careful mapping is first done, with the patient under local anesthesia, to discover the functions of the focal and the adjacent regions.

Stimulation applied to the anterior speech region of the frontal lobe, sometimes called Broca's area, or the posterior speech region which roughly corresponds to what has been called Wernicke's area, produces *aphasic* speech—deficits in symbolic speech. Mild aphasic symptoms are also obtained from a region called the supplementary motor area (see Figure 19.6). Aphasic symptoms are hard to classify; they involve speech problems such as the use of inappropriate words, inability to recall words and the names of things, inability to understand speech, circumlocutions, and perseveration, or saying the same thing over and over. Some aphasic defects are illustrated in the following account of a patient who was shown pictures to identify while various parts of his brain were being stimulated (numbers refer to those in Figure 19.7):

25 The patient hesitated and then named "butterfly" correctly. Stimulation was carried out then below this point and at a number of points on the two narrow gyri that separate 24 and 25, but the result was negative—no interference with the naming process.

26 The patient said, "Oh, I know what it is. That is what you put in your shoes." After withdrawal of the electrode he said, "foot."
27 Unable to name tree which was being shown to him. Instead he said, "I know what it is." The electrode was withdrawn then and he said, "tree."
28 The patient became unable to name as soon as the electrode was placed here. When asked why he did not name the picture shown, he said, "No." He continued to be silent after withdrawal of the stimulating electrode.
(Modified slightly from Penfield and Roberts, 1959, P. 117.)

The production of speech sounds, but not necessarily the symbolic use of speech, is largely a function of the lower part of the primary motor area on the precentral gyrus, the adjacent cortex in the frontal lobes, and the cortex of Broca's area. Stimulation of the lower part of the motor area and the anterior adjacent cortex produces a prolonged vowel sound. In addition, the supplementary motor area on the medial surface of the cerebral hemisphere is involved in production of speech sounds (see Figure 19.6).

Molecular approaches to learning and memory We have just considered some of the regions of the brain where learning, memory, and information processing seem to occur. As we noted at the beginning of the chapter, this is the so-called structural approach to the biology of learning and memory. But the next questions are: What is happening in these brain structures, or regions, when learning takes place? What changes do the cells and the connections between the cells undergo? Such are the main questions of the molecular approaches to learning and memory. We are a long way from answering these questions, but they provide an exciting and active field of research.

MEMORY CONSOLIDATION A theory that guides some current research in this field is called *consolidation* theory. It says that memories are stored permanently only after a period of consolidation, or fixation, of the memory trace has occurred. In its simplest form, the sequence of events is as follows: The input to be remembered sets up a series of changes in the appropriate regions of the nervous system. The changes are labile, that is, easily disrupted, and are subject to interference. This is the stage of short-term memory (see page 145), and the labile events are the "carriers" of short-term memory. If these first changes are allowed to go on undisturbed for some time, the memory trace, or *engram,* as it is sometimes called, becomes fixed and relatively permanent. The permanent memory trace is sometimes called long-term memory. Thus according to consolidation theory, it takes time, perhaps some minutes, for the initial activity to become consolidated, or fixed, into a permanent memory. The following experiment makes clear what is meant by consolidation (King, 1965):

Rats were taught to avoid a box where their feet received electric shock; only one avoidance trial was necessary for learning. Unless something was done to interfere with this learning, the animals would not enter the box where the single shock had been delivered.

Animals of the various experimental groups were given a single electrocon-

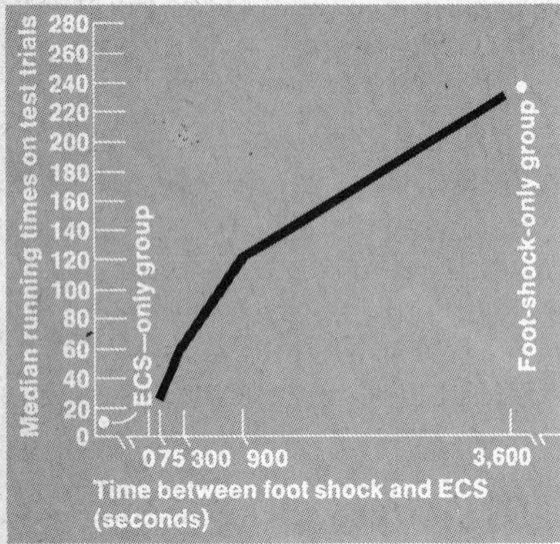

EVIDENCE FOR A CONSOLIDATION PROCESS IN MEMORY

Figure 19.8 *In this experiment, rats received foot shock followed by a single electroconvulsive shock (ECS) to the brain at the time indicated on the abscissa. The results indicate that ECS given shortly after the foot shock prevented consolidation of the foot shock memory; there was not enough time for the short-term memory trace to become fixed in the brain. "Forgetting" of foot shock is indicated by failure of avoidance and short running times; "memory" of the foot shock is indicated by avoidance and long running times. A gradient of effect is shown: If the time between foot shock and ECS is short, "memory" is impaired—running times are short. With increasing times between foot shock and ECS, "memory" of foot shock is better—running times are longer. Note that ECS by itself has no effect on running times. Memory is complete when 1 hour (3,600 seconds) elapses between foot shock and ECS: there is no difference between the group receiving ECS at 3,600 seconds and the foot-shock-only group. (Based on King, 1965.)*

vulsive shock (ECS) to the brain at 75, 300, 900, and 3,600 seconds *after* the learning trial. The ECS was given to disrupt the consolidation process needed for permanent memory. Animals of one control group were given no ECS. In another control group, animals received ECS but no foot shock in order to discover whether ECS might possibly affect avoidance behavior when given alone. The next day the rats were tested for memory of the learning experience.

Results are shown in Figure 19.8. Control animals that had received only foot shock had long running times—they remembered the avoidance response. Other control animals had been given only ECS and ran quickly into the foot-shock box; hence ECS by itself did not have much effect on running time. The experimental animals that had received ECS within 75 seconds of the foot shock also had short running times—they had forgotten the avoidance response. As the period between foot shock and ECS increased—as more time was given for consolidation to occur—greater evidence of memory of the avoidance response was seen: Running times increased. In cases where 1 hour had elapsed between foot shock and ECS, memory was complete: The animals stayed out of the shock box. According to consolidation theory, fixation of memory had already occurred by this time, and ECS was unable to disrupt the fixed, or permanent, memory trace.

This is only one example of hundreds of experiments which indicate that a memory consolidation period exists (McGaugh and Herz, 1970). But the question remains: What is happening to the cells and their connections during the consolidation period? We do not know the answer, but several interesting leads have developed.

BIOCHEMICAL CHANGES IN MEMORY One suggestion made is that changes in ribonucleic acid (RNA) molecules in the cells may be the physical basis of memory. RNA controls formation of proteins and enzymes, especially those involved in the growth of cells and the production of transmitter substances (see Chapter 17). Some evidence has been found that RNA may be involved in learning and memory, for RNA in the brain appears to increase after learning experiences (Zemp et al., 1966); but it is still scanty and needs further investigation.

Another group of experiments supports the general idea that proteins are important in the permanent nervous system changes which take place in memory. In these experiments, memory disruption is produced by substances that interfere with the biochemical synthesis of proteins. Such substances impair memory when they are injected *after* the learning experience, but the results so far are too confusing to draw any general conclusions (Deutsch, 1969). A great deal more research must be done before we know whether RNA or protein synthesis plays the major role in the consolidation of memory traces.

The Physiological Drives

The term *drive* has a rather complex definition (see Chapter 6). Speaking generally, it can be considered an impetus to, or an instigator of, behavior. People become hungry, thirsty, or sexually aroused, and these drive states result in behaviors aimed at satisfying them. For any drive state rooted in the physiology of the body, we can ask several questions:

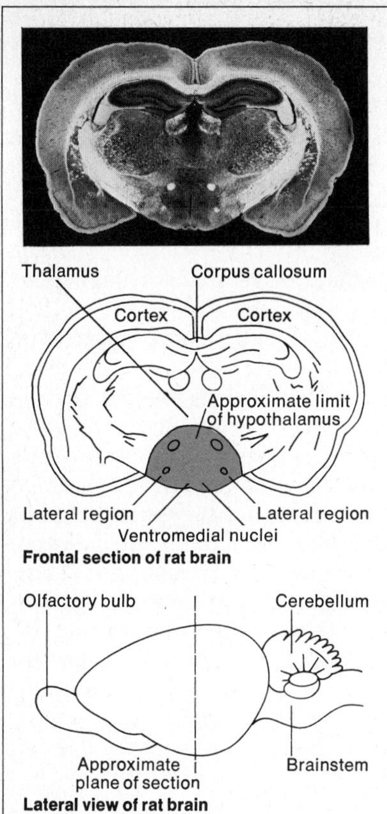

THE HYPOTHALAMUS IS A SMALL REGION WITH MANY IMPORTANT FUNCTIONS

Figure 19.9 *A cross section of a rat brain showing the hypothalamus. The approximate plane of the section is indicated in the lateral view drawing. (J. F. R. König and R. A. Klippel,* The Rat Brain: A Stereotaxic Atlas of the Forebrain and Lower Parts of the Brain Stem. *Baltimore: The William & Wilkins Company, 1963. Copyright © 1963, The Williams & Wilkins Co., Baltimore, Md. 21202, U.S.A.)*

What are some of the necessary conditions which initiate the drive state? What centers in the nervous system are necessary for the drive? What guides the behavioral expression of the drive state? What causes the drive state to cease? Some of the general answers were given in Chapter 6; now we shall be more specific.

The internal environment The internal environment consists of all the chemical, temperature, and stimulus conditions within the body that form the environment for its organs and systems, just as the outside world constitutes the body's external environment. The internal environment tends to remain relatively constant—a tendency known as *homeostasis* (see page 190). If, for instance, the amount of water in the body falls, the body automatically reacts by decreasing water excretion; if the body temperature rises too high, perspiration and other automatic mechanisms begin to lower it.

This tendency toward maintaining the homeostatic balance is a prime instigator of drive states. Low body water, for instance, leads to a drive state and the behavior of drinking. In this case the *behavior* stemming from the drive state, not an automatic physiological mechanism, restores the homeostatic balance. If the body temperature rises, physiological mechanisms go into action to reduce temperature; but a drive state also results and may lead to the appropriate behaviors—opening the window, taking off a coat, and so on—which help to restore homeostatic balance.

To generalize: Drive states result when homeostatic balance is disturbed. The driven behavior aims at restoring the homeostatic balance.

Sensory stimuli and motivation Sensory stimuli, both learned and unlearned, can directly arouse drive states. Perhaps the clearest case of this is the sexual drive; other examples were given in Chapter 6. Sensory stimuli also guide behavior in certain patterns, and it is these patterns of motivated behavior that lead to the restoration of homeostatic balance. In other words, sensory stimuli can be thought of as cues which guide behavior in ways appropriate to the particular drive aroused. Food is sought when hunger stimuli are present; water is sought when the mouth is dry.

The hypothalamus and physiological motivation We have learned that conditions in the internal environment and the various sensory stimuli converge in the part of the brain known as the hypothalamus to produce drive states. The hypothalamus is a small area at the base of the brain (see Figure 19.9). It has a rich blood supply and is in close contact with the pituitary gland, the so-called "master gland," which secretes hormones controlling the activities of other glands.

The picture we have formed of hypothalamic events in physiological motivation is this: Drive states occur when the outgoing nerve impulses from the excitatory regions of the hypothalamus exceed some critical amount. The level of this outgoing neural traffic is in turn controlled by (1) conditions in the internal environment, (2) sensory stimuli, and (3) inhibitory nuclei within the hypothalamus, when these nuclei are present (see Figure 19.10). Activity from the inhibitory nuclei depresses the outflow of activity from the excitatory nuclei. When they are present, the

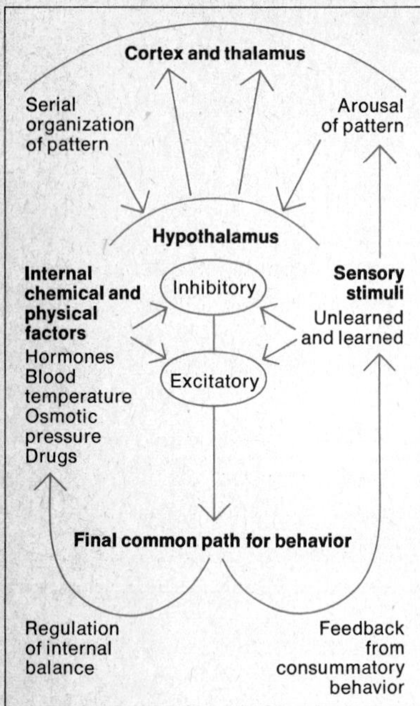

A THEORY OF HYPOTHALAMIC FUNCTION

Figure 19.10 *Activity in the excitatory nuclei of the hypothalamus may determine motivated behavior. The activity of the excitatory areas is controlled by the internal environment, sensory stimuli, and inhibitory nuclei. In addition, cortical influences affect activity of the excitatory hypothalamic nuclei. (From Stellar, 1954.)*

inhibitory nuclei are also under the control of the internal environment and sensory stimuli.

To summarize: Drive is controlled by activity coming out of the excitatory nuclei; such excitatory nuclei might be called the final common pathways for drive states. But the excitatory activity itself is controlled by the inhibitory nuclei, the internal environment, and sensory stimuli.

Thirst drive We constantly need water because we are losing it in evaporation from the skin, in breathing, and in the formation of urine. But what is it about the need for water that makes us thirsty and therefore motivated to drink? In Chapter 6 we discussed this problem and concluded by saying that thirst is caused by the effect lack of water has on certain cells in the hypothalamus.

To be more specific, lack of water makes all the cells in the body give up water; this is *absolute dehydration.* Some cells within the region of the hypothalamus seem especially sensitive to loss of water; these cells are the *osmoreceptors.* The osmoreceptors are concentrated in certain regions of the hypothalamus, and these regions are the excitatory centers for thirst. Through connections with other parts of the brain, the osmoreceptors regulate thirst according to the amount of water in the body.

The existence of the osmoreceptor regions has been shown by experiments in which salt solutions have been injected directly into the hypothalamus (Andersson, 1953). If the injected salt solution is more concentrated than the bodily fluids—that is, if it is a *hypertonic solution*—the osmoreceptors lose fluid, and thirst drive and drinking ensue. A recent demonstration of the role of the internal environment in thirst comes from the work of Corbit (1969):

The amount of fluid in the body of rats was kept about the same, but the extracellular fluid (blood and plasma) was made more concentrated by the injection of various concentrations of salt solution. Such an increase in external cellular concentration pulls water away from the insides of cells, the osmoreceptors included. As we have seen, if the osmoreceptors are dehydrated, thirst drive will ensue.

The amount of salt solution injected in the rats indicates the increase in concentration of the extracellular fluid. From this figure calculations can be made of the amount of water the rat needs to drink in order to dilute the extracellular fluid enough to cancel the difference in concentrations between the external fluid and the intracellular fluid. In Figure 19.11 the amount the injected rats actually drank is plotted on the ordinate, and the amount they needed to establish equilibrium is plotted on the abscissa. As the amount needed to establish equilibrium increased, the amount drunk increased. (Note, however, that the animals do not drink quite as much as would be needed to establish equilibrium. A perfect relationship of 1.00 is indicated by the gray line; the actual relationship is about .77. This departure from absolute agreement between the amount drunk and the amount needed to restore equilibrium is probably due to the excretion of some of the salt by the kidneys.)

To summarize: Dehydration produces changes in the tension of the walls of the osmoreceptors in the hypothalamus. This initiates excitatory neural activity which results in the thirst drive. The drive persists

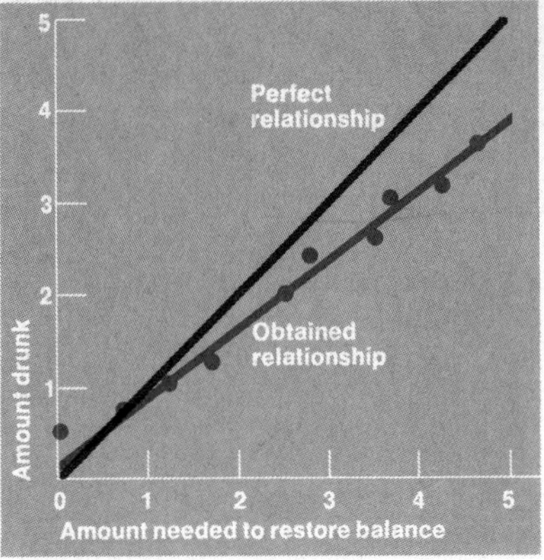

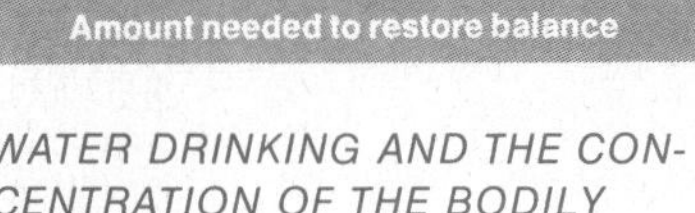

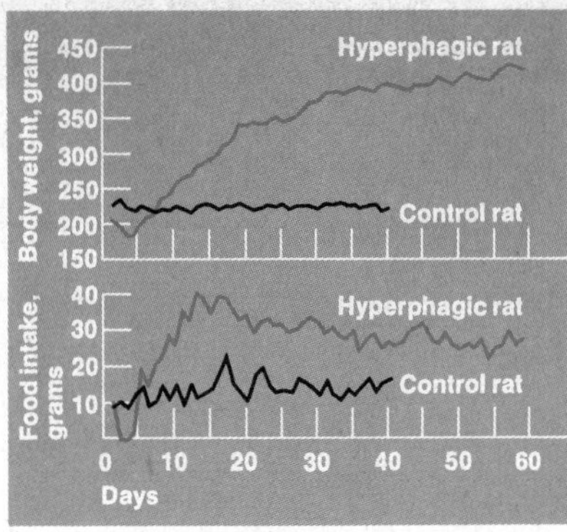

WATER DRINKING AND THE CONCENTRATION OF THE BODILY FLUIDS ARE RELATED

Figure 19.11 (Left, above) *The relationship between the amount of water consumed by rats and the amount of water needed to dilute the bodily fluids to normal after an injection of salt solution. The colored line is the relationship actually obtained; the gray line represents what would be perfect correspondence. Evidence such as this strengthens the osmoreceptor theory of thirst. (Modified from Corbit, 1969.)*

EATING INCREASES DRASTICALLY IF A SMALL LESION IS MADE IN A PORTION OF THE HYPOTHALAMUS

Figure 19.12 (Middle and right, above) *The graphs show changes in a rat's body weight and food intake after it had received ventromedial hypothalamic lesions. The hyperphagic animal overate and gained weight rapidly at first, reaching a weight plateau 30 to 40 days after the operation. The photograph, from a similar experiment, was taken some weeks after lesions had been made in the ventromedial nuclei; the hyperphagic rat had about doubled its normal weight. (Graphs modified from Teitelbaum, 1961.)*

until the water balance is restored and the osmoreceptors are no longer shrunken. Thus there is no inhibitory center for thirst in the hypothalamus; there is only an excitatory center, which is turned on or off by the state of the osmoreceptors within it.

Hunger motivation In Chapter 6 we concluded that the source of the hunger drive is probably some product of metabolism circulating in the blood, but that we have not yet found out what it is. We do know, however, that the hunger drive and eating are controlled by two centers in the hypothalamus, and we have considerable information about them.

One is an excitatory center located in the lateral region of the hypothalamus (see Figure 19.9). When a lesion is made in this area, animals never touch food again unless they are given special care. Left alone they suffer from *aphagia*—failure to eat—and eventually die of starvation (Teitelbaum and Stellar, 1954). By maintaining the animals through artificial means, such as stomach tubes, and by offering them water and especially desirable food, such as chocolate bars, experimenters have found that some of the animals become able to eat again.

The other hunger-controlling center, located a millimeter or so toward the midline of the hypothalamus, is called the *ventromedial nucleus* (see Figure 19.9). It seems to be the inhibitory center in the hypothalamus for the hunger drive. [At least this is the widely accepted view at present, but as with many generalizations in science, the situation is somewhat more complicated (Reynolds, 1965).] When the ventromedial hypothalamus is lesioned, animals develop voracious appetites, or *hyperphagia* (Brobeck, 1946; Hoebel, 1965). Even before they have completely recovered from the operation giving them the lesions, they attack food ravenously and eat large quantities. Their hunger drive is somewhat different from that of normal animals; they are more finicky in their choice of food. But given food they find palatable, they overeat until they weigh two to three times as much as comparable unlesioned animals (see Figure 19.12). After a time, a new baselevel of weight is reached, food intake slacks off, and the animals maintain themselves at a new heavy weight.

Experimenters have studied animals with lesions of the ventromedial hypothalamus to see what has gone wrong with them. Their metabolism is normal, and so is just about everything else in the machinery of the body. Apparently the main disturbance is that their appetites have gotten out of hand. It may be that the ventromedial hypothalamic center is deficient in some obese human beings, but this is probably rare. It seems more likely that obesity in humans is a matter of bad eating habits, lack of activity, and personality difficulties.

Sexual motivation In Chapter 6 we said that hormones are crucial in sexual motivation for lower animals; the existence of sex behavior depends on them. On the other hand, in man and the higher primates, learned stimuli, habit, and experience are important determiners of sexual behavior. Now let us look at the neural mechanisms of the sex drive.

In sexual behavior, as in the other drives we have discussed, the hypothalamus seems to play a central integrating role. Factors in the internal environment (hormones) and in the external environment (sensory stimuli) combine to produce activity in excitatory centers of the hypothalamus (see Figure 19.10). In sexual behavior, the hypothalamus can exert its activity in two ways: It controls the secretion of hormones from the pituitary gland, and it regulates the outflow of nerve impulses from excitatory sexual centers. Our concern here is primarily with the excitatory sexual centers, not with the hypothalamic, hormonal control of sexual behavior.

Early experiments in which the brainstem of lower animals was cut through, or transected, at various levels taught us that the hypothalamus is an important area for the control of sexual behavior. If the hypothalamus was cut off from the rest of the brainstem, mating behavior was abolished. Following this kind of experiment, the next logical step was to make restricted lesions in the hypothalamus in order to localize the area of the hypothalamus necessary for integrated sexual behavior. This was done in both males and females of several species. The general conclusion was that the area for integration, though not sharply defined, lies in the more anterior portion of the hypothalamus (Larsson and Heimer, 1964). Giving hormones to animals with lesions in the anterior hypothalamus does not usually restore their mating behavior. This test shows that a crucial nervous system area necessary for sexual behavior has been eliminated, so that alteration of the internal environment by hormones cannot restore the integrated behavior. If the conclusion from lesion studies is correct, it might be expected that stimulation of the anterior hypothalamus would induce sexual behavior; and this does seem to be true (Vaughan and Fisher, 1962). But stimulation of the posterior hypothalamus has also been found to produce integrated sexual behavior (Caggiula and Hoebel, 1966). Much remains to be discovered about the hypothalamic control of integrated sexual behavior.

Activation and Emotion

Activation and emotion are related: the brain structures are similar and some psychologists consider activation to be the basic phenomenon in emotionality (see Chapter 7). A great deal of work in physiology and biopsychology has disclosed some of the brain mechanisms apparently responsible for activation, emotion, and perhaps what we commonly call consciousness.

Activation An organism's level of activation varies continuously from extreme alertness and arousal at one end of the scale to deep sleep at the other. Cycles of activation occur even during sleep itself (see Chapter 17). Some of the electroencephalographic (EEG) changes associated with levels of activation and sleep are shown in Figure 17.4. So far, this book has only described the EEG characteristics and their relationships to behavior. In addition, it is known that certain areas of the brain control the state of arousal of the cerebral cortex which is measured by the EEG. Such controlling areas might be called activating and sleep areas.

ACTIVATING AND SLEEP AREAS It was first suggested many years ago about patients who were somnolent—that is, who had abnormal tendencies to sleep—that there may be centers for sleep in the brain. Some of these patients had tumors or diseases in the posterior hypothalamus. Following this lead, experimental scientists focused on the posterior hypothalamus and made controlled lesions in animals to duplicate the effects seen in patients. This work was rewarding, for they found a relatively small region in the posterior hypothalamus whose destruction causes pronounced somnolence. Monkeys, for example, sleep almost continuously for 4 to 8 days after destruction of this region and are extremely drowsy for months afterward (Ranson, 1939). They can be aroused briefly by noises or other strong stimulation, but when left alone they quickly fall asleep again. Since similar results have been obtained with other animals, there is little doubt that such an area exists in the brains of other species (Nauta, 1946). Because the destruction of this center causes somnolence, we assume that it keeps the animal awake when it is functioning normally; therefore it has been called a waking, or activating, region. It seems likely that this region is not a special set of hypothalamic nuclei; rather, the lesions in the posterior hypothalamus seem to disrupt fibers of the reticular activating system (see Chapter 17).

Although it is not so conclusive as the data on the activating region, there is evidence that a sleep center also exists (Nauta, 1946). Lesions have been made in the anterior hypothalamus of rats that kept them from sleeping. The animals seemed relatively normal, but they never slept. They stayed awake for several days, gradually became more exhausted, fell into a coma, and died. Stimulation of this region seems to have an opposite effect: cats stimulated electrically through electrodes implanted in the anterior hypothalamus go to sleep when the current is turned on (Clemente and Sterman, 1963).

Thus in the case of sleep, although we do not have conclusive evidence that the sleep center inhibits the waking center, we do have some evidence that there are two centers with opposed action.

RETICULAR ACTIVATING SYSTEM The two sleep centers, however, are not the whole story about the neural control of sleep and waking. Another part of the story concerns the reticular activating system

(RAS), which is shown in Figure 17.21. Experiments have discovered that the reticular activating system exerts a great deal of control over the activation of the cortex through its projections to wide regions of the cortex (see Chapter 17). Thus the RAS seems to be the system of the brain largely responsible for controlling the EEG patterns of the cerebral cortex which are associated with different degrees of arousal (see Figure 17.4). The following experiment demonstrates the role of the RAS in cerebral cortical activation (Moruzzi and Magoun, 1949):

The investigators explored the effects of direct electrical stimulation of the brain by placing electrodes in various positions and noting the effects of stimulation. They were surprised to find that stimulation of the RAS did two things: First, it woke up a cat that was sleeping or drowsy, and alerted one that was already awake. Second, it altered the EEG, producing the same changes in the EEG that accompany waking or arousal. It appeared that the RAS was directly involved in the mechanism of waking and sleeping.

Further research has shown that the activation of the RAS itself comes from sensory input. Thus two channels to the cortex exist for sensory input: One, the direct, or *specific sensory system,* carries the information about the environment responsible for perception. The other, the indirect, or *nonspecific system,* is the projection from the RAS, which has been activated by branches from the specific sensory system. The specific sensory system projects to the relatively restricted sensory projection areas of the cerebral cortex; the nonspecific projection from the RAS is widespread over much of the cerebral cortex. The roles of the specific and nonspecific projection systems in activation have been studied in experiments like the following, in which one or the other of the systems is cut (Lindsley et al., 1950):

The investigators cut the sensory pathways to the cortex, leaving those from the RAS to the cortex intact, and found that this operation had no effect on the sleep and waking pattern of a cat. The EEG pattern, as well as observation of the cat, indicated the typical waking state. On the other hand, when the RAS was severed, the cat went to sleep and tended to stay asleep for long periods of time. How deep and prolonged the somnolence became depended on the level at which the RAS was cut. If the cut was made relatively high, near the junction of the midbrain and hypothalamus, blocking off practically all impulses from the RAS to the cerebral cortex, the somnolence was severe. If the cut was made lower down, leaving some of the RAS linked with the cortex, the somnolence was relatively slight.

From studies of this sort, it seems clear that the RAS is a basic arousal mechanism for the brain. Without activation of the cortex by the RAS, an organism remains somnolent, and even though impulses in the sensory systems reach the cortex by the direct route, they are not decoded by the cortex. According to this view, then, the RAS determines the organism's general state of arousal. This conclusion is generally accepted, but other studies have shown that the situation may be more complicated. When the RAS is cut in stages, with time elapsing between each cut, marked somnolence does not occur. In addition, if the animals are carefully nursed after the RAS has been cut all at once, they may recover from coma in the second month after the operation (Adametz, 1959).

Emotion A number of structures in the brain core are involved in the expression of the stronger emotions—especially the emotions of rage and fear (Papez, 1937; MacLean, 1949). These structures are interrelated and are collectively known as the *limbic system* (see Figure 17.22). We shall summarize the action of several of the limbic system regions that are important in emotion: the *septal nuclei,* the *amygdaloid nuclei,* and the *cingulate gyrus* of the cerebral cortex. Although some ambiguities of classification exist, we shall also treat the *hypothalamus* as part of the limbic system.

HYPOTHALAMUS The role of the hypothalamus in emotion was first proved by the now classic experiments of Cannon (1927) and Bard (1928):

Using cats as their experimental animals, they made a series of sections through the forebrain, each time slicing off a little more until they had severed the entire forebrain from its connections with the midbrain and hindbrain. Before and after an operation, the experimenters attempted to provoke each animal to angry behavior by pinching its tail, showing it a dog, blowing a bugle, and so on. The characteristic behavior of angry cats includes growling, hissing, spitting, fur ruffing, biting, lashing the tail, thrashing the forelegs, protruding the claws, urinating, and breathing rapidly. The investigators found that the essential pattern of angry behavior was always present as long as the hypothalamus was intact. When the hypothalamus was eliminated by the operation, leaving only the midbrain and hindbrain, the pattern of rage response was broken up. The subjects sometimes displayed fragments of emotion, such as growling, hissing, or fur ruffing, but without the hypothalamus the characteristic pattern of angry behavior appeared to be lost.

The investigators concluded that the hypothalamus is the area in which the various elements of hostile behavior are organized into a pattern. This idea has been strengthened by stimulation studies: Electrical stimulation of the hypothalamus produces irritation, rage, and sometimes attack behavior (Hess, 1954).

SEPTAL AREA AND AMYGDALA The roles in emotion of the septal area and the amygdala have been studied by making lesions in them and observing the effects upon behavior. Such experiments performed on rats, cats, and monkeys give results like the following (King, 1958):

A scale for rating the emotionality of a rat was developed that translated into a point system the judgment of skilled raters of an animal's emotionality when subjected to several standard situations, such as having a pencil thrust at it. Ratings of emotionality were made of rats before and after they were operated on, and a control group not subjected to any operation was also rated. One operated group was given lesions in the septal region; another, lesions in the amygdaloid nuclei. All lesions had to be made bilaterally because of the symmetrical pairing of the structures.

Rats with lesions in the septal region showed a great increase in ferocity. Formerly tame animals had to be handled with heavy gloves; they quickly attacked and bit a pencil thrust into their cage, and they were generally jumpy and ferocious. The effects of such lesions have been found to be relatively temporary, however. Lesions made in the amygdaloid area had just the opposite effect. Animals who were not very wild to begin with nevertheless became unusually placid; they would accept all kinds of provocation and rough handling without showing any rage.

In another experiment, some animals were subjected first to a septal operation, which made them ferocious, and then to an amygdaloid operation, which made them calm and placid. Thus the two regions oppose each other, but lack of both has about the same effect as lack of the amygdaloid area only.

Since the destruction of an area should produce opposite results from those of its normal functioning, we can tentatively conclude that the septal area normally inhibits ferocious behavior, while the amygdala normally excites it. But the situation is more complicated than this. If lesions of the amygdala are combined with lesions of other structures, an increase in enraged behavior occurs. For instance, lesions of the amygdala and the ventromedial nucleus of the hypothalamus produce an increase in ferociousness. Similarly, lesions of the amygdala and the cingulate gyrus increase rage behavior and in some experiments, even removal of the amygdala alone has intensified, not reduced, the animal's ferocity.

CINGULATE CORTEX One of the areas of the cerebral cortex that are included in the limbic system is the cortex of the cingulate gyrus (see Figure 17.22). By itself, this cortical area seems to have little effect upon emotional behavior. But when it is removed together with all of the neocortex, ferocious behavior markedly increases. These conclusions have been drawn from experiments in which the cerebral cortex was eliminated in stages (Bard and Mountcastle, 1947). In the first stage, the cortex of the cingulate gyrus was spared, but the rest of the cerebral cortex was cut away—the animals were partially *decorticated.* The animals became more placid after this stage—they were harder to enrage. In the second operation the cingulate gyrus was removed, so that the animals were almost completely decorticated. They then exhibited the ferocious behavior known as "decorticate rage," which had been seen in earlier experiments where nearly complete decortication had been carried out in one step (Bard, 1934).

Despite such experimental evidence, the ways in which these structures function together are not known. For instance, removal of the cingulate gyrus alone, leaving the rest of the cerebral cortex intact, has no marked effect on emotional responsiveness. Apparently the inhibitory functions of the cingulate gyrus are not present when the rest of the cortex is intact. This points to the general principle that the control of emotional expression cannot be understood by studying the action of isolated regions. Rather, the interactions of many areas of the brain

Table 19.1 *Limbic system lesions and rage behavior.*

Structure	Effects of removal on integrated rage behavior*
Neocortex	↓
Cingulate cortex	none
Neocortex + limbic cortex (cingulate cortex)	↑
Amygdala	↑ or ↓
Septal area	↑
Amygdala + limbic cortex (cingulate cortex)	↑
Amygdala + ventromedial nucleus (hypothalamus)	↑
Hypothalamus	↓
All tissue above hypothalamus	↑

*↑ means increase in rage; ↓ means decrease in rage.

Source: After Richard F. Thompson, *Foundations of Physiological Psychology* (Harper & Row, 1967).

must be studied together—a very difficult task. A summary of some effects of limbic system lesions on integrated rage behavior is given in Table 19.1.

Drugs and Behavior

Drugs which affect behavior have been with us throughout recorded history. For example, the effects of opium in relieving pain and altering mood have been known since 5000 B.C. But recently, spurred by many influences, interest in the effects of drugs on behavior has risen sharply. One such influence was the discovery in the 1950s that certain drugs could be used to calm, or tranquilize, emotionally disturbed people. A second influence was the increase during the 1960s in the use of various hallucinogenic drugs. A third influence, from the academic sector, was the development of operant methodology—the "Skinner box"—for controlled investigations of drug effects on behavior (see Chapter 3). For these and other reasons, the field which explores the effects of drugs on behavior—*psychopharmacology,* as it is sometimes called—has grown at a rapid rate. Because the action of drugs on behavior is complex, its study has many biological, psychological, and social ramifications.

A *drug* may be defined as any substance which, by its chemical nature, alters the structure or function of a living organism. A drug that has important effects on behavior is called a *psychoactive drug.* The target cells for psychoactive drugs are the neurons of the central nervous system. But psychoactive drug effects are due to much more than their chemical action on certain parts of the central nervous system. What a drug does also depends upon the individual's previous experience with it, the situation in which it is taken, and the characteristics of the response being investigated. In addition, the amount taken, the user's expectations about what the drug will do to him, and many other factors, such as the route of administration, the user's age, and the presence or absence of disease, are important. Such effects represent *drug-environment interactions.* In summary, the effects of psychoactive drugs are relatively complex and depend upon the characteristics of the person taking the drug as much as, or more than, upon the drug itself.

Hundreds, perhaps thousands, of such drug compounds exist. We shall discuss some of the most common psychoactive drugs with an emphasis on those which have social significance.

Stimulants *Caffeine* is among the most widely used stimulants in Western civilization. In the United States, coffee, tea, and cola-flavored drinks are the most common sources of caffeine. Neurons at all levels of the central nervous system are made more excitable by this drug. The "psychological lift" that we feel after a cup of coffee is probably due to stimulation of cells of the cerebral cortex, but the exact mechanism by which caffeine acts on the neurons is not known. In healthy persons, and with moderate doses, caffeine is not known to be harmful, but it is *habituating.* We discussed the meaning of habituation and addiction in the section on drug dependency in Chapter 12. Table 12.1 shows the differences between a habituating drug such as caffeine and addicting drugs such as heroin.

The *amphetamines* are chemically related to certain naturally occurring chemical transmitters (see Chapter 17). Chemical transmitters are the substances released from the endings of nerve fibers which stimulate the next cells in the chain of neurons. One action of amphetamines is to stimulate cells in the sympathetic portion of the autonomic nervous system (see Chapter 7). The drugs are not, however, abused—that is, used to excess—because of this action, but rather because they produce a feeling of euphoria and elation, increase a person's ability to concentrate, and reduce feelings of fatigue. Such effects come from their action on the central nervous system. The amphetamines probably work either by mimicking natural transmitters, or by causing stored transmitters to be released for action.

Many amphetamines exist. Among these are amphetamine sulfate, *d*-amphetamine sulfate, and methamphetamine hydrochloride. Common trade names for these are, respectively, Benzedrine ("bennies"), Dexedrine ("dexies"), and Methedrine ("meth" or "speed"). These drugs are often abused (taken to excess), and dependency results. Excessive use of amphetamines results in periods of extreme activity followed by great fatigue and long periods of sleep. Normal social behavior and life styles are, of course, impossible with such a pattern of behavior. Amphetamines are dangerous to society as well as to the individual. The manic and antisocial behavior of some people when high on amphetamines can be dangerous for other people.

Narcotics and analgesics *Narcotics* are drugs which can produce sleep as well as lessen pain. Those used primarily as pain-killers are called *analgesics.* Note that the term narcotic is *not* synonymous with "illegal drug," although it is often used in this way. As examples of narcotics, we shall consider opium and its derivatives, morphine and heroin. Among the analgesics we shall restrict ourselves to cocaine, which is useful as a local anesthetic but is often abused because of its effects on the central nervous system.

Table 19.2 *Some common drug terms.*

Source: Based on several authorities, chiefly Goodman and Gilman, 1965; Jones et al., 1969; Lindesmith, 1968; Lingeman, 1969.

Acid LSD; Lysergic acid diethylamide.

Bag A small quantity of drugs, often in a folded paper. May then be called a *paper* or a *deck*. The unit in which drugs are sometimes sold: so many bags, papers, or decks.

Cap Heroin in a capsule.

Cold turkey To stop taking drugs suddenly. Refers especially to withdrawal, usually enforced, from narcotics such as heroin.

Crash Withdrawal symptoms from the amphetamines. The crash is from the high produced by the drug.

DMT A hallucinogenic drug that is easily manufactured. Tends to produce a quick, relatively short high.

Dropped To take a pill orally. Usually refers to barbiturate pills.

Goofballs Pills containing barbiturates.

Hash Hashish. One of the many varieties of drug derived from the hemp plant. Contains a high concentration of the active ingredient, tetrahydrocannabinol (THC).

High The feeling of euphoria and well-being sometimes produced by certain drugs.

Horse, H Heroin.

Joint A marijuana cigarette, also a *reefer*.

Junk Heroin.

Mainline To inject a drug, usually heroin, directly into a vein.

Mary Jane Marijuana. Also grass, pot, tea, weed.

Outfit The necessary equipment for a vein shot, or mainlining. Usually consists of a spoon for dissolving and heating the heroin, cotton for straining it, and a hypodermic needle. Also called *works*.

Pusher A seller of illicit drugs. Often sells drugs to support his own drug dependency, or *habit*. He may induce others to try drugs to increase sales.

Red devils Barbiturate pills which are relatively short-acting; also *yellow jackets*.

Roach The butt of a marijuana cigarette. The device for holding the butt is a *roach holder*.

Skin pop An injection into the muscle.

Speed Any amphetamine, but most often Methedrine.

Speedball A mixture of heroin and cocaine injected by an addict.

STP A very potent, artificially synthesized, hallucinogen; psychotic reactions common. Seems to give users feeling of great power and strength.

Trip A high on drugs, usually on LSD.

Cocaine ("snow") has a stimulating effect on the brain, especially on the higher centers—the cerebral cortex, for instance. Excitement, restlessness, euphoria, talkativeness, and suspiciousness (paranoid ideas) are examples of central nervous system effects of cocaine. A depression of activity follows the cocaine "high" fairly quickly.

Opium comes from the sap of the seed capsules of a species of poppy native to the Near and Far East; *morphine* is the active ingredient of the sap. *Heroin*, derived from morphine, is more potent and is extremely addicting. It produces euphoria, a dreamy state, drowsiness, and slowing of thought processes.

Heroin addicts show great *tolerance* for the drug: that is, in order to obtain these psychological effects, they require large doses. The drug is expensive because it is illegal, and many addicts resort to criminal activities, including drug "pushing," to get the money. But the heroin addict, although he does not perform as efficiently as he might, is not often the "hophead" of popular imagination. Except for the need for money and his own personal problems, the heroin addict may lead a somewhat miserable but more or less normal existence. The drug, however, is extremely dangerous because it is so addictive and deaths from overdoses are not uncommon. At the very least, some personal misery is bound to accompany its use.

The withdrawal symptoms of heroin addiction are acute: irritability, sleeplessness, vomiting, chills, sweating, muscle spasms, yawning, sneezing, and a craving for the drug are common for about a week. Abrupt withdrawal is the "cold turkey" treatment. In other forms of treatment, less addicting substitute drugs are gradually introduced, and withdrawal is not so painful. But whatever the treatment, the outlook for permanent abstention from heroin is not good; the habit is reinforced by many social factors, and most addicts eventually go back to the drug. In this way personal maladjustment accumulates, and the addict continues to pour money into the criminal organizations that support traffic in the drug. Heroin addiction is an unmitigated social evil. On the other hand, morphine and its derivatives are beneficial drugs when used medically to alleviate pain.

Hypnotics and sedatives These drugs, which include the *barbiturates,* depress the activity of the central nervous system and produce drowsiness and sleep. Although it is not exactly a sedative or hypnotic, we shall discuss *alcohol* here also, because its basic action is to depress CNS activity.

BARBITURATES In this large class of drugs are such compounds as phenobarbital (trade names include Luminal), pentobarbital (trade names include Nembutal), secobarbital (trade names include Seconal), and thiopental (trade names include Pentothal). In general, barbiturates depress the central nervous system. The reticular activating system, already discussed as the system which controls the level of activation of the cerebral cortex, seems especially sensitive to the barbiturates. These drugs are contained in "sleeping pills." When they are taken in doses not large enough to produce sleep, their effects resemble those of alcoholic intoxication: drowsiness, relaxation, and thick speech.

Tolerance for a barbiturate develops over time: more and more of the drug is needed for an effect. Barbiturates are also addicting if abused, and severe withdrawal symptoms with convulsions may follow rapid cessation of usage. Barbiturates are dangerous drugs because they are so widespread and because they are sometimes taken with alcohol—a dangerous practice, since it combines the effects of two depressant drugs.

ALCOHOL Sometimes it seems that alcohol stimulates the nervous system, for people under its influence may become talkative, show upswings of mood, lose their self-restraint, and have difficulty with such mental functions as concentration and memory. Yet alcohol is basically a depressant of the central nervous system (although it might also be classed as an hallucinogenic drug). The reason it may seem to stimulate is simply that it first depresses the inhibitory mechanisms, thus giving the appearance of activation. With increasing concentrations of alcohol in the blood, however, excitatory mechanisms are also depressed, so that drowsiness and general depression result. Such depression of function, which can be seen in impairment of motor coordination, begins to be pronounced when the alcohol concentration in the blood reaches .10 percent—the percentage set in most states to define the legal beginning of drunkenness. In a person weighing 180 pounds, such a concentration is produced if he quickly drinks five to six 1¼-ounce shots of 80-proof whisky, or five to six bottles of beer. A 120-pound person needs less: four to five shots of whisky, or four to five bottles of beer.

Alcohol can be addicting, and people who consume a great deal develop tolerance for it. Withdrawal symptoms after chronic, or prolonged, intoxication can be severe. Dependence upon alcohol, called *alcoholism,* was discussed in Chapter 12.

Tranquilizers and antidepression drugs Perhaps the greatest breakthrough in the treatment of the psychoses—severe behavior disorders—has been a chemical one. Drugs such as *chlorpromazine* (trade names include Thorazine) calm agitated psychiatric patients and make psychotherapy and home treatment possible for those who would otherwise be unmanageable. The drop in the resident population rate in mental hospitals (see Chapter 13) is partly due to the widespread use of these drugs. They do not by themselves cure psychosis, but they make it much easier to deal with the problems created by psychotic patients.

Other milder tranquilizers have been developed for the relief of anxiety and tension. Chief among these is meprobamate (trade names include Miltown and Equanil). Depressed patients are sometimes treated with drugs called monoamine oxidase (MAO) inhibitors. Apparently these drugs act by raising the level of certain naturally occurring brain transmitter chemicals such as serotonin and norepinephrine. Recently it was shown that *lithium* may be an effective drug in the treatment of manic behavior, and a great deal of research is now being done to investigate the mechanism by which this element works.

Hallucinogenic, or perception-distorting, drugs Even though drugs such as lysergic acid diethylamide (LSD), mescaline, and marijuana are sometimes called hallucinogens, it might be more accurate to say that they produce distortions of perception, for they rarely cause true hallucinations—perceptual experiences with no sensory input. The sensory distortions seem to be one of the major reasons for the relatively widespread use of these drugs.

LSD Lysergic acid is an artificially synthesized product. It is a tasteless and odorless compound; it is effective in very small amounts; and it produces many sensory and behavioral changes.

LSD is a powerful stimulant of the autonomic nervous system and often produces nausea, chilling, and muscle aches. But these "side effects" are overlooked by the people who take it for its sensory and psychological effects. Colors are especially enhanced—they seem to glow from within—and textures become fascinating and beautiful.

Beauty is seen in the most commonplace objects. Distortions of sensory perception, such as the loss of certain constancies of perception (see Chapter 8), occur, and visual hallucinations have been reported.

LSD, which has become a part of various religious cults, produces great disturbances in thought and mood. Thought is typically fragmented and confused. Moods may range from euphoria to extreme depression (suicides have occurred under LSD) and catatonia, or almost complete immobility (see Chapter 12). Paranoid ideas are common. The mood changes depend on the situation in which the drug is taken and on the user's general personality pattern.

LSD is a dangerous drug because of the biochemical changes it may produce in the brain. Although its mechanism of action is not known, it is thought to affect various biochemical systems within the brain which are involved in synaptic transmission. Prolonged usage of the drug, especially in the increasingly heavy doses necessitated by the tolerance the user develops, can result in extended periods of delirium and confusion. In addition, so-called flashbacks may occur in which druglike symptoms appear when the drug has not been taken. Heavy usage markedly interferes with the ability of a person to function in the world. Rather than promoting increased creativity which, after all, depends upon work, LSD seems to lead its heavy users into a state in which very little creative work can be done. Fortunately, LSD is not addicting, and there are no withdrawal symptoms (except for possible flashbacks) when its use is discontinued.

MARIJUANA Marijuana is the name given in the United States to the drug produced from the hemp plant, *Cannabis sativa.* The use of cannabis derivatives is widespread throughout the world, where they go by such names as hashish, charas, bhang, and ganja. The most active ingredient of the crude plant derivative seems to be tetrahydrocannabinol (THC). The flowering parts of the plant contain the greatest amounts of THC. These are usually dried and smoked, although they may be made into a drink somewhat like tea.

Many behavioral and sensory effects follow marijuana smoking. Sensory experience may become more intense: smells are richer, textures feel more sensuous, objects are seen as more beautiful, sounds are more brilliant and stirring. Ideas flow freely, but they may be disjointed. The person may experience an emotional high in which he feels great joyousness, tranquility, and a sense of well-being.

In contrast to most other drugs which have psychoactive effects, some evidence indicates that tolerance does not develop for marijuana. In fact, experienced users may need less to get high than nonexperienced users (see page 16). Marijuana is apparently not addicting and only mildly, if at all, habituating (see Table 12.1). It has been claimed that the use of marijuana is the first step on the road to "hard" drugs such as heroin. But the evidence for this assertion is ambiguous. On the one hand, not many users of marijuana become heroin addicts; on the other hand, almost all heroin addicts started with marijuana.

The effects of marijuana, like those of other drugs, are very much influenced by the setting. Taken in a pleasant, relaxed social situation, marijuana can lead to euphoria; but taken under conditions of stress,

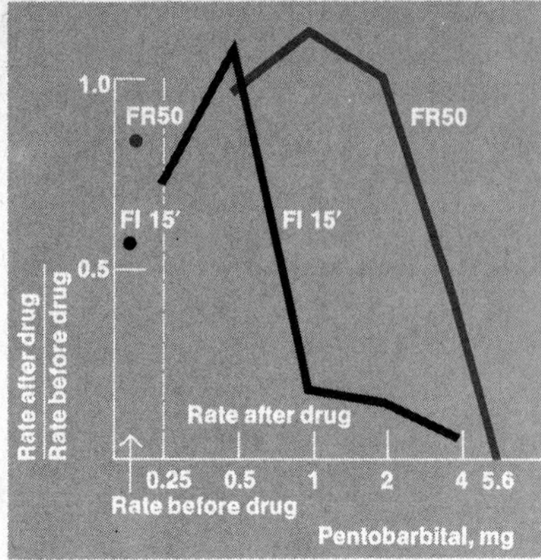

BEHAVIORAL RESPONSE TO A DRUG IS ONLY PARTIALLY DEPENDENT ON THE DRUG'S PHYSIOLOGICAL EFFECTS

Figure 19.13 *An example of drug-schedule interaction: the rate of a key-pecking response in pigeons after various doses of pentobarbital. The measure used is the* ratio of the *response rate after injection of the drug to the response rate before injection. Two schedules of reinforcement, a 15-minute fixed-interval schedule, or FI 15', and a fixed-ratio 50 schedule, or FR 50, were used. The rates before drug injection are given at the left. At the right, the graph shows what happened to response rates after pentobarbital injections. For instance, at 1 mg of pentobarbital, the FI rate dropped markedly and the FR rate increased. Thus the effect of a drug on behavior depends upon the on-going behavioral background into which it is introduced. In this case, the drug increased high-rate (FR) behavior and decreased relatively low-rate (FI) behavior. (Modified from Dews, P. B. Studies on behavior. I. Differential sensitivity to pentobarbital of pecking performance in pigeons depending on the schedule of reward.* Journal of Pharmacology and Experimental Therapeutics, *1955, 113, 393–401. Copyright © 1955, The Williams & Wilkins Co., Baltimore, Md. 21202, U.S.A.)*

the effects may be quite unpleasant. Personality patterns also affect the drug experience. Paranoid, suspicious, or aggressive users may find these patterns enhanced; calm better-adjusted users are more apt to experience a good, or euphoric, high.

Drug-environment interactions The fact that the behavioral effect of a drug depends upon the situation in which it is taken and the personality of the user is a specific example of an important general principle of psychopharmacology. The principle is simply that the physiological effect of the drug on the body is only one of the factors which determine the behavioral response to it. This basic principle is shown clearly in certain animal experiments with drugs. The same dosage can result in entirely different behavioral effects, depending upon the type and strength of behavior going on when the drug is administered (Dews, 1955):

Pigeons were trained to peck a key in a Skinner box (see Figure 3.14) in order to receive small amounts of food which were delivered on different schedules of reinforcement. One schedule was a fixed-interval, 15-minute (FI 15') schedule: Food was delivered for the first response after each 15-minute interval, producing a cumulative response record in which there is little responding during the first portion of the fixed interval and a great deal during the last (see Figure 3.13b). The other schedule was a fixed-ratio 50 (FR50) schedule: Food was delivered after every 50 responses. With this type of schedule the rate of responding tends to be high and, except for some pauses after each reinforcement, rather steady (see Figure 3.13a).

After stable baseline rates had been established, various amounts of pentobarbital were given (see Figure 19.13). Although large doses of this drug caused a drop in response rate under both schedules, consider what happened at a dose of 1 milligram (mg): Responses went sharply down on the FI schedule but increased on the FR schedule. Thus the same response—keypecking, in this case—was increased under one set of schedule conditions and decreased under another set.

From many experiments of this general sort, the conclusion has emerged that "the effects of drugs on behavior depend upon the pattern of behavior maintained" (Kelleher and Morse, 1968). With certain exceptions, behaviors of humans or animals which occur at a high rate or have great strength will be affected one way by a drug; behaviors which occur at a low rate will be affected in another way by the same dosage. Such a principle is very useful in predicting the effects of a drug on behavior.

We considered another example of drug-environment interaction in the chapter on emotion (see page 232). The cognitive theory of emotions states that a person's experience of emotion depends upon his interpretation of a stirred-up bodily state. Drugs may produce this stirred-up state, and the person may then interpret it in various ways. His interpretation will, in turn, be strongly influenced by the situation in which he takes the drug and by his personality pattern.

To summarize: The prediction of drug effects upon behavior is a fascinating and complex problem. Not only must the physiological effects of the drug be considered, but situational and personality patterns must be taken into account. Drug influences on behavior, however, are only part of the interesting field of the physiology of behavior, in which knowledge is rapidly accumulating.

Synopsis and summary

This chapter completes the survey of the biology of behavior that we began in Chapter 17. As discussed there, the task of biopsychology is to find correlations between events in the nervous system and behavior. We explored these correlations in our discussion of the biology of sensory processes in Chapter 18. Here in Chapter 19 we have considered the biological basis of learning, memory, motivation, activation, and emotion. We also discussed some of the drugs which affect the nervous system and behavior.

1. Brain changes in learning take place in relatively large regions of the higher portions of the central nervous system.
2. The limbic system seems especially involved in both active and passive avoidance learning.
3. The association cortex includes all the cortical areas which are not primary sensory or motor areas; this is most of the cerebral cortex of the human.
4. Inferotemporal regions of the temporal lobe association cortex are necessary for visual form-discrimination learning in monkeys. Related visual effects have been seen in man.
5. Delayed-response problem solving is impaired after lesions of the frontal association cortex in monkeys. In man, various consequences follow damage to the frontal association cortex, including perseveration of behavior, decrease in the goal-directedness of behavior, and impairment of abstract thinking ability.
6. Loss of the ability to learn discriminations based on the sense of touch results from lesions of the parietal association cortex. In man, the body image may be distorted following damage to this area.
7. The speech areas of the human brain are located around the lateral fissure in the frontal, parietal, and temporal association cortex. Damage or stimulation in these areas causes impairment of speech, or aphasia.
8. Molecular and biochemical approaches to learning and memory have attempted to discover the cellular changes taking place during learning.
9. A period of memory fixation, or consolidation, seems necessary after a learning experience if long-term memories are to be formed. But the cellular changes occurring in this period are not yet known. Various hypotheses about changes in brain proteins have been put forward as the molecular basis of memory.
10. The physiological drives are part of the mechanism by which the balance of systems within the internal environment of the body is maintained. This balance of systems is termed homeostasis. Drive states result when homeostatic balance is disturbed.
11. Sensory stimuli, both learned and unlearned, can trigger drive states.
12. The hypothalamus is a major integrating center in physiological drive states. Cells in the hypothalamus are sensitive to changes in the internal environment and are influenced by sensory stimuli. The hypothalamus is "the final common pathway" for physiological motivation.
13. When the amount of water in the blood drops, the osmoreceptors of the hypothalamus initiate the neural activity which results in the thirst drive.
14. Hunger drive is probably aroused by unknown substances in the blood circulating through the hypothalamus. Both excitatory and inhibitory hypothalamic centers are active in the control of the hunger drive.
15. The anterior regions of the hypothalamus seem to be the integrating regions for sexual motivation.
16. The organism's level of activation, or arousal, varies continuously from alert wakefulness to deep sleep. Such degrees of activation are reflected in EEG patterns and are controlled by the reticular activating system.
17. Limbic system structures play an important though complex role in emotional behavior. Many structures of the limbic system, and some nonlimbic structures as well, act together to control emotional expression. As a general rule, the role of the brain in emotional expression cannot be understood by studying particular areas in isolation.
18. Many drugs affect the nervous system and behavior. The study of the effects of drugs upon behavior is termed psychopharmacology; the drugs which affect behavior are called psychoactive drugs.
19. Some drugs—caffeine and the amphetamines, for instance—are stimulants that increase arousal and the tempo of behavior.
20. Analgesics and narcotics are drugs that relieve pain. Besides this, the narcotics are usually extremely addicting and have many effects upon behavior: some produce a relaxed, dreamy feeling; others a euphoric high.
21. Hypnotics and sedatives depress the activity of the central nervous system. The barbiturates, often found in sleeping pills,

are common examples.
22. Tranquilizers and antidepression drugs have been very useful in the therapy of behavior disorders. Common examples of tranquilizers are chlorpromazine and meprobamate.
23. Hallucinogenic drugs such as lysergic acid (LSD) and marijuana cause changes in sensory experience, mood, and thought.
24. The behavioral effects of drugs are dependent upon the environmental situation and the state of the user at the time the drug is taken.

Related topics in the text

Chapter 2 Behavioral Inheritance Many of the behaviors controlled by the central nervous system do not occur at birth; they await maturation, or growth, of the central nervous system.

Chapter 3 Principles of Learning Operant conditioning is a valuable topic to review when studying animal experiments in the area of psychopharmacology.

Chapter 6 Motivation Stresses stimulus factors in the control of physiological motives; discusses the general nature and role of motivation in behavior.

Chapter 7 Arousal, Emotion, and Conflict Psychological and physiological aspects of motivation are treated. The physiological discussion centers on the peripheral autonomic nervous system.

Chapters 12 and 13 in Part Three, Disturbed Behavior Describes some of the neurotic and psychotic behaviors on which drug therapy is effective.

Chapter 17 The Nervous System Aspects of the basic anatomy and physiology of the nervous system are discussed. In a way, Chapters 17 and 19 form a unit.

Suggestions for further reading

Butter, C. M. *Neuropsychology: The study of brain and behavior.* Belmont, Calif.: Brooks/Cole, 1968. (Paperback.)
An introductory treatment of biological psychology.

Isaacson, R. L. (Ed.) *Basic readings in neuropsychology.* New York: Harper & Row, 1964. (Paperback.)
A collection of some of the most important original papers in the field of biological psychology.

Jones, K. L., Shainberg, L. W., and Byer, C. O. *Drugs and alcohol.* New York: Harper & Row, 1969. (Paperback.)
A lucid account of the effects of behaviorally active drugs, together with a discussion of some of the social problems connected with their use.

King, R. A. (Ed.) *Readings for an introduction to psychology.* (3d ed.) New York: McGraw-Hill, 1971. (Paperback.)
A book of readings to accompany this text containing some articles on biological psychology.

Lingeman, R. R. *Drugs from A to Z: A dictionary.* New York: McGraw-Hill, 1969. (Paperback.)
An annotated dictionary of drug terms. Contains many interesting notes on the derivation of certain terms.

McGaugh, J. L., et al. (Eds.) *Psychobiology: The biological bases of behavior.* San Francisco: Freeman, 1966. (Paperback.)
A collection of reprints from The Scientific American. *Interesting summary papers by major investigators in the field of neurobiology.*

Morgan, C. T. *Physiological psychology.* (3d ed.) New York: McGraw-Hill, 1965.
One of the standard texts on the physiological mechanisms of behavior.

Teitelbaum, P. *Physiological psychology.* Englewood Cliffs, N. J.: Prentice-Hall, 1966. (Paperback.)
A short, readable introduction to the biological basis of behavior.

Thompson, R. F. *Foundations of physiological psychology.* New York: Harper & Row, 1967.
A standard text in biological psychology that emphasizes physiological mechanisms and behavior. Intended for somewhat more advanced students—juniors and seniors.

Thompson, T., and Schuster, C. R. *Behavioral pharmacology.* Englewood Cliffs, N. J.: Prentice-Hall, 1968.
Describes the techniques and some of the major findings of experimental psychopharmacology.

Wooldridge, D. E. *The machinery of the brain.* New York: McGraw-Hill, 1963. (Paperback.)
A popularly written book explaining some of the physiological mechanisms of behavior in nontechnical language.

As a student you may be taking psychology for many reasons: to satisfy a college requirement, because of an interest developed through high school courses or general reading, or as part of training in a related field—education, social work, nursing, business, and so forth. After this beginning course, you may find your interest satisfied—or perhaps, dissipated; but, more likely, your interest in some aspects of psychology has been whetted. If so, after taking a few more psychology courses to be sure, you may decide to major in psychology.

What can a psychology major do? Two routes are open: He can go to graduate school and become a professional psychologist, or he may go off into the business world after finishing college. Suppose we examine the latter path first.

Psychology offers little or no opportunity for professional employment if one has only a bachelor's degree. There are some positions here and there as assistants, which may be attractive to a girl who plans later to make a career of marriage or to a man who needs temporary employment before going on to other things. But such jobs usually offer little future. Some industrial positions also exist, chiefly in personnel work, which are open to those holding undergraduate degrees in psychology. In general, if one plans to make a career of psychology, he must go to graduate school.

If an undergraduate psychology major does *not* prepare a student for professional work in psychology, what can he do? Actually, he is in practically the same position as any student who has majored in any one of the arts or sciences. A major in English, history, political science, and, for that matter, even chemistry or mathematics does not by itself lead to a professional career—further training is necessary. But industry and government are interested in people who have taken a general education course with a major in any of the arts or sciences. This interest is summed up in the following quotations from employers in government and business: "We look for bright people even though they are not fully trained," or more succinctly, "If you educate them, we will train them."

What of the student whose interests and talents lead him to a career in professional psychology? He has a long but rewarding preparation before him. While still an undergraduate, he should take a broad program in the natural and social sciences. Psychology bridges these groups of sciences and requires some knowledge of each. Hence it is advisable to take some training in mathematics, physics, chemistry, biology, sociology, and anthropology. Students who are most interested in psychology as an experimental science should, of course, emphasize the natural sciences—especially physiology, zoology, chemistry, and mathematics. Those most interested in the clinical, social, educational, and industrial subfields should take further work in the social sciences. In any case, one should not concentrate too much in psychology; specialization can be left to graduate training.

In addition to the training we have been talking about, the psychology major, or anyone for that matter, is probably well advised to develop a skill or interest unrelated to his field. It is fun for most people to be able to do something well, or to know a great deal about some subject. The undergraduate psychology major might develop his skill in music, his interest in some aspect of history, his skill in art, or languages, and so on. This, of course, applies to the psychology majors who are going into the profession as well as those who are not. For the professionally oriented major, skill in languages will be a useful asset in later training because most graduate schools require a reading knowledge of one or two languages for the Ph.D. degree.

Graduate training, we have said, is a necessary part of the preparation for a professional career in psychology. Standards for admission to graduate school in psychology are quite high. To be admitted, the candidate usually must have aptitudes considerably above those of the average college student—most graduate schools require that the applicant take special tests of aptitude—and his grade record must be good. The majority of those admitted have B to A averages, especially in the junior and senior years of college, and most graduate schools do not admit C or low B students unless something in their records indicates that they can do the quality of work required in graduate school. Such indications might be a marked improvement to the A or B level in the junior and senior years of college and marks of brilliance in the record—for example, excellent grades in the more demanding science courses.

One does not have to be rich, or even able to afford the usual cost of higher education, to go to graduate school in psychology. Numerous assistantships and fellowships are available; most graduate students in psychology receive some financial support during their course of study. Many opportunities for employment as research assistants and technicians are also available to graduate students in psychology. These jobs are often very valuable because they give the student training in skills that he will later put to use in his professional career.

Several degrees are available to graduate psychology students. These degrees are at two levels—the master's level and the doctoral level. The master's degree—Master of Arts (M.A.) or Master of Science (M.S.)—is the only degree offered by some of the smaller graduate schools. It requires one to two years of full-time work or its equivalent. The program for this degree usually includes a core curriculum taken by all graduate students in the department; it also provides an opportunity to specialize somewhat in the field in which the person expects to be employed. Sometimes the master's degree is part of the training for the doctor's degree—that is, the student on the way to this higher degree more or less automatically meets the requirements for the master's degree. Usually, however, students work directly for the doctorate which is required for the highest level of professional work in psychology. The doctorate is usually the Doctor of Philosophy (Ph.D.), but it may, at a small number of universities, be the Doctor of Psychology (Psy.D). The Ph.D. program usually provides a course of study stressing research and professional skills; the training programs leading to the Psy.D. degree stress the applied practice of psychology. Whatever the degree, the doctorate usually requires 3 to 5 years of full-time work or its equivalent. It involves considerably more advanced and specialized work than the master's degree, and often requires that the candidate complete a significant piece of research. In most graduate schools, the advanced psychology graduate student is treated as an apprentice and works in the laboratory or clinic under the close supervision of a staff member, or a committee of staff members. For those specializing in clinical psychology, one of the years of graduate training, typically the third, is an internship year in which the student works in a clinical setting—for example, a counseling center or hospital—in a professional capacity.

Many employment opportunities exist in public and private schools, in clinical settings, in industry, and in government for the holder of the master's degree. He must expect, however, to receive a substantially lower salary than he could earn if he held a doctor's degree, and his opportunities for promotion are often limited. In some areas, however, particularly in government and industry, he has about the same opportunity to succeed as the person with a doctorate. On the other hand, for most regular teaching positions in colleges and universities and for a position of responsibility in a research organization or clinical setting, the doctorate is now almost mandatory. In general, a person who expects to make a life-long career of teaching and/or research in psychology is well advised to earn the doctor's degree.

The pay for positions in psychology varies considerably from one situation to another. In general, it is lowest in teaching positions, somewhat higher in government, and highest in industry. On the whole, the financial rewards in psychology compare reasonably well with those of other professional pursuits, and the positions that are not so lucrative often have the compensation of allowing more freedom for research, writing, and independent work.

For additional information on careers in psychology, the student should consult his professor or one of the helpful pamphlets published by the American Psychological Association, the professional organization of the psychologist. These pamphlets are available at a nominal cost from the American Psychological Association, 1200 Seventeenth St., N.W., Washington, D.C. 20036. Here are two especially useful ones: *A Career in Psychology.* Washington, D.C., 1970. *Graduate Study in Psychology* (revised every year). Washington, D.C.

APPENDIX 2 HOW TO LOOK IT UP

Some of the topics mentioned in this text may have aroused interest; we hope so. Many other interesting subjects on the fringes of psychology have been deliberately omitted. But if you want to know more, here are a few general guides.

Perhaps the first place to look is in the *Psychological Abstracts.* Here you will find a list of subjects and authors, together with references to the journals and books in which they appear. The *Psychological Abstracts* are arranged by year, so you may have to look through several volumes before you have a fairly complete set of references. Similar index sources are available in other fields related to psychology: *Sociological Abstracts, Education Index,* and the *Public Affairs Information Service* provide a listing in several related fields. The *Index Medicus* and *Biological Abstracts* list articles in the biologically related fields. And references to related articles of general scientific interest may be found in such sources as the *Science Citation Index.* The chances are, however, that if the article has any psychological relevance at all, it will be listed in *Psychological Abstracts.* Incidentally, *Psychological Abstracts* was not started until 1927; a list of references before that date can be found in the *Psychological Index,* a supplement of the *Psychological Review.* In addition, the *Readers' Guide to Periodical Literature* may help the student find popular articles on many psychological subjects. These are often useful in the first stages of becoming acquainted with a topic, but serious interest should not stop here. Most of these reference sources will be available in any reasonably complete college library. If they are not available, you should complain to the librarian and to your professor.

The general card catalog of the library may be of some help if books have been written about the topic in which you are interested. It often happens, however, that a shorter article is more valuable than a whole book, at least in the initial stages of study. You may also use the Suggestions for Further Reading, which are given at the end of each text chapter, for locating books on a subject.

Finally, when you locate a book or article, look at the list of references at the end of it. These references often prove to be invaluable in calling attention to significant work in an area, for the author has done much of the winnowing for you. For this purpose it is, of course, usually useful to have a recent book or article.

With these hints, and the other resources and techniques you will develop for yourself, you should have no trouble finding information about almost any psychological subject. From here on, it is up to you to select and evaluate the relevance of the articles and books you find. We hope this text and your beginning psychology course have enabled you to begin to do a reasonably good job of this. Always be a little skeptical—there is still a tinge of charlatanism in psychology.

For a list of the symbols used in this section and their respective definitions see below.

Measures of frequency distributions The formula for the *arithmetic mean* is

$$M = \frac{\Sigma X}{N} \tag{1}$$

The formula for the *standard deviation* may be written in several ways. Among them are

$$SD = \sqrt{\frac{\Sigma x^2}{N}} \tag{2}$$

and

$$SD = \sqrt{\frac{\Sigma X^2}{N} - M^2} \tag{3}$$

Computation of the mean by formula (1) and the standard deviation by formula (2) is illustrated in Table 1. The work proceeds by first obtaining the sum of the measurements (ΣX) and then calculating the mean (M). Next the column of xs can be filled in by subtracting the mean from each measurement ($X - M$), and from that the column of x^2 values can be obtained. From the sum of the deviations squared (x^2), one can then obtain the standard deviation by dividing by the number of cases (N) and taking the square root.

If a desk calculator is available, the computation of the mean is the same as just described in formula (1), but that of the standard deviation is faster by formula (3), which eliminates the step of converting each measurement into a deviation.

The formula for a *z score* is

$$z = \frac{x}{SD} \tag{4}$$

Definition of symbols

X or Y	The numerical value of a measurement
M	Arithmetic mean
Σ	Greek capital sigma used to mean "sum of"
N	Number of cases in a distribution or set of measurements
SD	Standard deviation of a distribution—a descriptive statistic
x or y	The deviation score, that is, a measurement expressed as a deviation from the arithmetic mean, ($X - M$) or ($Y - M$).
z	The result of the deviation score divided by the standard deviation, x/SD or y/SD
O	Obtained frequency, or the number of cases counted, in the cell of a contingency table
E	Expected frequency, or the number most likely to fall in the cell if the frequencies in all cells were determined by chance and hence if there were no correlation

Table 1 *Computation of the arithmetic mean and standard deviation. The computation proceeds by getting first the sum of X; next the mean is obtained from the sum of X. Then the column of xs can be filled in and the x^2 values computed. From the sum of x^2, one can then obtain the standard deviation (SD). For large samples, desk calculators are usually used and convenient formulas are available.*

X	$X - M = x$	$(X - M)^2 = x^2$
40	22.5	506.25
35	17.5	306.25
33	15.5	240.25
20	2.5	6.25
19	1.5	2.25
19	1.5	2.25
19	1.5	2.25
16	−1.5	2.25
14	−3.5	12.25
11	−6.5	42.25
10	−7.5	56.25
9	−8.5	72.25
7	−10.5	110.25
7	−10.5	110.25
4	−13.5	182.25
$\Sigma X = 263$		$\Sigma x^2 = 1{,}653.75$

$N = 15$

$$M = \frac{263}{15} = 17.5$$

$$\text{SD} = \sqrt{\frac{1653.75}{15}} = \sqrt{110.25} = 10.5$$

ρ — Rho, the rank-difference coefficient of correlation, a measure of correlation when measurements have been made on an ordinal scale or are expressed as ranks

r — Pearson product-moment coefficient of correlation, a measure of correlation when measurements have been made on an interval scale

SE_M — Standard error of a mean, a measure of the variability that may be expected among the means of different samples of the same size drawn from the same population

Measures of correlation To calculate the *coefficient of contingency,* it is first necessary to obtain the quantity known as chi-square (χ^2). This calculation can be illustrated by Table 1, which is based on the data in Table 9.4. The first step is to determine the number that would be expected in each cell if there were no correlation between (in this instance) class and high school curriculum. This is done by multiplying the totals of the row and column intersecting on the cell and dividing by the grand total. Thus, the expected number, by chance, in the cell formed by "college preparatory" versus "class I–II" is $\frac{35 \times 81}{390} = 7.3$. For the next cell to the right, $\frac{81 \times 146}{390} = 30.3$, and so on. When all the expected values—expected by chance if there were really no correlation—have been computed in this way,

Table 2 *The computation of chi-square (χ^2) and the contingency coefficient. (Note: Numbers in boldface are those expected by chance; other numbers are those obtained. See text for explanation.)*

Source: From Siegel, 1956, p. 177.

Curriculum	Social Class I–II		III		IV		V		Total
College preparatory	**7.3**		**30.3**		**38.0**		**5.4**		
		23		40		16		2	81
General	**18.6**		**77.5**		**97.1**		**13.8**		
		11		75		107		14	207
Commercial	**9.1**		**38.2**		**47.9**		**6.8**		
		1		31		60		10	102
Total		35		146		183		26	390

the following formula is used to complete the computation of chi-square:

$$\chi^2 = \Sigma \frac{(O - E)^2}{E} \tag{5}$$

where O is the observed value—the one actually obtained in the study—and E is the expected value just computed. Chi-square turns out to be 69.2. To find the contingency coefficient, one then uses the formula:

$$C = \sqrt{\frac{\chi^2}{N + \chi^2}} \tag{6}$$

The formula for the *rank-difference coefficient* (*rho*) is

$$\rho = 1 - \frac{6\Sigma D^2}{N(N^2 - 1)} \tag{7}$$

The D in the formula refers to a difference in ranks (see Table 9.5). Hence to compute ρ, one squares each rank difference, sums the squares, multiplies by 6, and divides by $N(N^2 - 1)$, subtracting the result from 1.

The coefficient of correlation r, called the *product-moment correlation coefficient* because of the way it is obtained, has a formula that may be written in any one of several ways, depending on what other measures are also being calculated and whether a calculator is available. The general formulas are

$$r_{xy} = \frac{\Sigma xy}{NSD_xSD_y} \quad \text{or} \quad \frac{\Sigma z_x z_y}{N} \quad \text{or} \quad \frac{\Sigma xy}{\sqrt{\Sigma x^2 \Sigma y^2}} \tag{8}$$

Written this way it makes clear that the coefficient is essentially the average of the products of z scores. If a person's z score on one measurement is randomly related to his z score on another, that is, is uncorrelated, the average product moment will be zero because negative z scores will tend to cancel out positive ones. On the other hand, if the correlation is positive, the products of negative z scores being positive, they tend to add to the products of positive scores and hence give a positive correlation.

When a good calculating machine is available, the best formula to use is one that looks forbidding, but is nevertheless easy to solve:

$$r_{xy} = \frac{N\Sigma XY - (\Sigma X)(\Sigma Y)}{\sqrt{[N\Sigma X^2 - (\Sigma X)^2][N\Sigma Y^2 - (\Sigma Y)^2]}} \tag{9}$$

If one has previously computed the standard deviations of the two distributions by formula (3), the only additional quantity to be obtained from the measurements themselves is the sum of the products of X and Y. The rest is simple arithmetic.

It should be noted that the different coefficients C, ρ, and r are not exactly equivalent. In other words, a C of .50 does not have exactly the same meaning, for mathematical reasons, as an r of .50. The differences, however, are usually not very large, and methods of correction are available for determining the r that is equivalent to, say, a particular C or ρ.

Sampling *Sampling error of a mean* may be estimated by the formula

$$\mathrm{SE}_M = \frac{\mathrm{SD}}{\sqrt{N - 1}} \tag{10}$$

where the result is the standard deviation of a distribution of means that one could expect to obtain by chance if successive samples of measurements of the same number of cases were drawn from the same population. This is the basic measure involved in methods for determining whether an obtained difference in the means of two groups of measurements is significant in the sense of being greater than one would expect to obtain by chance.

The numbers in parentheses at the end of each reference indicate the pages of this text where the works are cited. The names of journals most frequently cited are spelled out in the list at right.

Amer. J. Orthopsychiat.	The American Journal of Orthopsychiatry
Amer. J. Psychiatr.	American Journal of Psychiatry
Amer. J. Psychol.	American Journal of Psychology
Amer. Psychol.	American Psychologist
Annu. Rev.	Annual Review of Psychology
Behav. Res. Ther.	Behaviour Research and Therapy
Brit. J. Psychol.	British Journal of Psychology
Cand. J. Psychol.	Canadian Journal of Psychology
Child Developm.	Child Development
Child Develop. Monogr.	Child Development Monographs
EEG clin. Neurophysiol.	Electroencephalography and Clinical Neurophysiology
Genet. Psychol. Monogr.	Genetic Psychology Monographs
J. abnor. soc. Psychol.	Journal of Abnormal and Social Psychology
J. appl. Psychol.	Journal of Applied Psychology
J. comp. physiol. Psychol.	Journal of Comparative and Physiological Psychology
J. consult. Psychol.	Journal of Consulting Psychology
J exp. anal. Behav.	Journal of the Experimental Analysis of Behavior
J. exp. Psychol.	Journal of Experimental Psychology
J. exp. soc. Psychol.	Journal of Experimental Social Psychology
J. genet. Psychol.	The Journal of Genetic Psychology
J. gen. Psychol.	The Journal of General Psychology
J. Neurophysiol.	Journal of Neurophysiology
J. Neurosurg.	Journal of Neurosurgery
J. Pers.	Journal of Personality
J. Pers. soc. Psychol.	Journal of Personality and Social Psychology
J. Physiol.	Journal of Physiology
J. Psychol.	Journal of Psychology
J. soc. Psychol.	Journal of Social Psychology
J. verb. Learn. verb. Behav.	Journal of Verbal Learning and Verbal Behavior
Monogr. soc. res. Child Develm.	Society for Research in Child Development Monographs
Psychol. Bull.	Psychological Bulletin
Psychol. Monogr.	Psychological Monographs
Psychol. Reps.	Psychological Reports
Psychol. Rev.	Psychological Review
Psychon. Sci.	Psychonomic Science
Sci. Amer.	Scientific American

Adametz, J. H. (1959). Rate of recovery of functioning in cats with rostral reticular lesions. *J. Neurosurg.,* 16, 85–98 *(671)*

Adams, J. A. (1967). *Human Memory.* New York: McGraw-Hill. *(147)*

Adamson, R. E. (1952). Functional fixedness as related to problem solving: A repetition of three experiments. *J. exp. Psychol.,* 44, 288–291. *(166)*

Ades, H. W. (1959). Central auditory mechanisms. In J. Field, H. W. Magoun, and V. E. Hall (Eds.), *Handbook of physiology.* Vol. 1. Washington, D.C.: American Physiological Society. Pp. 585–613. *(640)*

Adkins, D. C. (1964). *Statistics.* Columbus, Ohio: Charles Merrill. *(317)*

Adolph, E. F. (1941). The internal environment and behavior. III. Water content. *Amer. J. Psychiatr.,* 97, 1365–1373. *(191, 192)*

Advisory Committee to the Surgeon General (1964). *Smoking and health.* Washington, D.C.: U.S. Department of Health, Education, and Welfare. *(315)*

Allport, F. H. (1924). *Social psychology.* Boston: Houghton Mifflin. *(76, 180, 490)*

Allport, G. W. (1937). *Personality.* New York: Holt, Rinehart and Winston. *(393)*

Allport, G. W. (1954). *The nature of prejudice.* Cambridge, Mass.: Addison-Wesley. *(543)*

Allport, G. W. (1961). *Pattern and growth in personality.* New York:

Holt, Rinehart and Winston. (*364, 382, 393, 396, 397*)

Allport, G. W., Vernon, P. E., and Lindzey, G. (1960). *A study of values: A scale for measuring the dominant interests in personality* (3d ed.). Boston: Houghton Mifflin. (*356*)

Allport, G. W., and Odbert, H. S. (1936). Trait names, a psycho-lexical study. *Psychol. Monogr.,* 47 (Whole No. 211). (*366*)

Alpern, M., Lawrence, M., and Wolsk, D. (1967). *Sensory processes.* Belmont, Calif.: Brooks/Cole. (*653*)

American Psychiatric Association (1952). *Diagnostic and statistical manual: Mental disorders.* Washington, D.C.: Amer. Psychiat. Assoc. (*414, 415*)

American Psychiatric Association (1968). *Diagnostic and statistical manual of mental disorders* (2d ed.). Washington, D.C.: Amer. Psychiat. Assoc. (*416, 424, 425*)

American Psychological Association (1967). *Standards for educational and psychological tests and manuals.* Washington, D.C.: American Psychological Association. (*319*)

American Psychological Association (1970). *A career in psychology.* Washington, D.C.: American Psychological Association. (*29*)

Amoore, J. E., Johnston, J. W., Jr., and Rubin, M. (1964). The stereochemical theory of odor. *Sci. Amer.,* 210 (2), 42–49. (*643*)

Anastasi, A. (1964). *Fields of applied psychology.* New York: McGraw-Hill. (*575*)

Anastasi, A. (1968). *Psychological testing* (3d ed.). New York: Macmillan. (*319, 323, 329, 361*)

Anastasi, A., and Foley, J. P., Jr. (1958). *Differential psychology* (3d ed.). New York: Macmillan. (*339*)

Anderson, N. H. (1965). Averaging versus adding as a stimulus-combination rule in impression formation. *J. exp. Psychol.,* 70, 394–400. (*513*)

Anderson, N. H. (1968). A simple model for information integration. In R. P. Abelson, E. Aronson, W. J. McGuire, T. M. Newcomb, M. J. Rosenberg, and P. H. Tannenbaum (Eds.), *Theories of cognitive consistency.* Chicago: Rand McNally. (*512*)

Anderson, N. H., and Jacobsen, A. (1965). Effect of stimulus inconsistency and discounting of instructions in personality impression formation. *J. Pers. soc. Psychol.,* 2, 531–549. (*513*)

Andersson, B. (1953). The effect of injections of hypertonic NaCl solutions into different parts of the hypothalamus of goats. *Acta Physiol., Scand.,* 28, 188–201. (*666*)

Appley, M. H. (1962). Motivation, threat perception, and the induction of psychological stress. *Proc. Sixteenth Internat. Congr. Psychol., Bonn, 1960.* Amsterdam: North Holland Publ. Co. (Abstract). (*218*)

Appley, M. H. (1970). Derived motives. *Ann. Review of Psychology,* 21. Pp. 485–518. (*187*)

Applezweig, M. H., Moeller, G., and Burdick, H. (1956). Multimotive prediction of academic success. *Psychol. Reps.,* 2, 489–496. (*212*)

Arnold, M. (1960). *Emotion and personality.* Vol. I. *Psychological aspects.* New York: Columbia Univer. Press. (*251*)

Arnold, M. (1960). *Emotion and personality.* Vol. II. *Neurological and physiological aspects.* New York: Columbia Univer. Press. (*251*)

Asch, S. E. (1956). Studies of independence and conformity: A minority of one against a unanimous majority. *Psychol. Monogr.,* 70, Whole No. 416. (*488, 489*)

Asch, S. E. (1958). Effects of group pressure upon the modification and distortion of judgments. In E. E. Maccoby, T. M. Newcomb, and E. L. Hartley (Eds.), *Readings in social psychology* (3d ed.). New York: Holt, Rinehart and Winston. Pp. 174–183. (*493*)

Asch, S. E., Block, H., and Hertzman, M. (1940). Studies in the principles of judgments and attitudes. II. Determination of judgments by group and by ego standards. *J. soc. Psychol.,* 12, 433–465. (*530*)

Atkinson, J. W. and Litwin, G. H. (1960). Achievement motive and test anxiety conceived as motive to approach and motive to avoid failure. *J. abnor. soc. Psychol.,* 60, 52–63. (*212, 213*)

Atkinson, J. W. (1964). *An introduction to motivation.* New York: Van Nostrand Reinhold, 1964. (*221*)

Atkinson, J. W., and Feather, N. T. (Eds.) (1966). *A theory of achievement motivation.* New York: Wiley. (*211, 213, 214, 221*)

Atkinson, R. C. (Ed.) (1964). *Studies in mathematical psychology.* Stanford, Cal.: Stanford University Press. (*221*)

Atkinson, R. C., Bower, G. H., and Crothers, E. J. (1965). *An introduction to mathematical learning theory.* New York: Wiley. (*103*)

Atkinson, R. C., and Shiffrin, R. M. (1968). Human memory: A proposed system and its control processes. In K. W. Spence and J. T. Spence (Eds.), *The psychology of learning and motivation,* Vol. 2. New York: Academic Press. Pp. 89–195. (*145*)

Axline, V. M. (1947). *Play therapy.* Boston: Houghton Mifflin. (*453*)

Ayllon, T. (1963). Intensive treatment of psychotic behaviour by stimulus satiation and food reinforcement. *Behav. Res. Ther.,* 1, 53–61. (*463*)

Ayllon, T. and Azrin, N. H. (1965). The measurement and reinforcement of behavior of psychotics. *J. exp. Anal. Behav.,* 8, 357–383. (*464*)

Bachrach, A. J. (1965). *Psychological research: An introduction* (2d ed.). New York: Random House. (*29*)

Backman, C. W., and Secord, P. F. (1959). The effect of perceived liking on interpersonal attraction. *Human Relations,* 12, 379–384. (*502*)

Backman, C. W., and Secord, P. F. (Eds.) (1966). *Problems in social psychology: Selected readings.* New York: McGraw-Hill. (*507*)

Bahrick, H. P. (1954). Incidental learning under two incentive conditions. *J. exp. Psychol.*, 47, 170–172. *(114)*

Baker, C. H., and Young, P. (1960). Feedback during training and retention of motor skills. *Canad. J. Psychol.*, 14, 257–264. *(122)*

Baker, R. A. (Ed.) (1963). *Psychology in the wry.* Princeton, N. J.: Van Nostrand. *(29)*

Baldwin, A. L. (1948). Socialization and the parent-child relationship. *Child Developm.*, 19, 127–136. *(385)*

Bales, R. F. (1950). A set of categories for the analysis of small-group interaction. *Amer. sociol. Rev.*, 15, 257–263. *(481, 482)*

Bales, R. F. (1952). Some uniformities of behavior in small social systems. In G. E. Swanson, T. M. Newcomb, and E. L. Hartley (Eds.), *Readings in social psychology* (Rev. ed.). New York: Holt, Rinehart and Winston. Pp. 146–159. *(482)*

Bales, R. F. (1970). *Personality and Interpersonal Behavior.* New York: Holt, Rinehart and Winston. *(481)*

Bandura, A. (1965). Personal Communication. *(460)*

Bandara, A. (1969). *Principles of behavior modification.* New York: Holt, Rinehart and Winston. *(468)*

Bandura, A., Ross, D., and Ross, S. A. (1963). Imitation of film-mediated aggressive models. *J. abnorm. soc. Psychol.*, 66, 3–11. *(385, 386)*

Bandura, A., and Walters, R. H. (1963). *Social learning and personality development.* New York: Holt, Rinehart and Winston. *(385)*

Bandura, A., Blanchard, E. B., and Ritter, B. (1969). Relative efficacy of desensitization and modeling approaches for inducing behavioral, affective, and attitudinal changes. *J. Pers. soc. Psychol.*, 13, 173–199. *(464, 465)*

Barber, T. X. (1970). Who believes in hypnosis? *Psychology Today,* 4, No. 2. *(451)*

Bard, P. (1928). A diencephalic mechanism for the expression of rage with special reference to the sympathetic nervous system. *Amer. J. Physiol.*, 84, 490–515. *(671)*

Bard, P. (1934). On emotional expression after decortication with some remarks on certain theoretical views. *Psychol. Rev.*, 41, 309–329. *(672)*

Bard, P., and Mountcastle, V. B. (1947). Some forebrain mechanisms involved in the expression of rage with special reference to suppression of angry behavior. *Res. Publ. Ass. nerv. ment. Dis.*, 27, 362–404. *(672)*

Bare, J. K. (1949). The specific hunger for sodium chloride in normal and adrenalectomized white rats. *J. comp. physiol. Psychol.*, 42, 242–253. *(191)*

Barker, R., Dembo, T., and Lewin, K. (1941). Frustration and regression, an experiment with young children. *Univer. Iowa Stud. Child Welf.*, 18, No. 386. *(379)*

Barker, R. G., and Wright, H. F. (1951). *One boy's day.* New York: Harper & Row. *(365)*

Barron, F. (1963). *Creativity and psychological health.* Princeton, N.J.: Van Nostrand. *(171)*

Bartlett, F. C. (1932). *Remembering: An experimental and social study.* London: Cambridge Univer. Press. *(141)*

Bartley, S. H. (1969). *Principles of perception* (2nd ed.). New York: Harper & Row. *(285)*

Bass, B. M. (1965). *Organizational psychology.* Boston: Allyn and Bacon. *(545, 551, 563, 575)*

Bateson, G., Jackson, D. D., Haley, J., and Weakland, J. H. (1956). Toward a theory of schizophrenia. *J. Behav. Sci.*, 1, 251–256. *(427)*

Baughman, E. E. (to be published, 1972). *Personality: The psychological study of the individual.* Englewood Cliffs, N.J.: Prentice-Hall. *(397)*

Beach, F. A. (1947). A review of physiological and psychological studies of sexual behavior in mammals. *Physiol. Rev.*, 27, 240–307. *(193)*

Beach, F. A. (1960). Experimental investigations of species-specific behavior. *Amer. Psychologist,* 15, 1–18. *(661)*

Beach, F. A. and Jaynes, J. (1954). Effects of early experience upon the behavior of animals. *Psychol. Bull.*, 51, 239–263. *(34)*

Beard, R. M. (1969). *An outline of Piaget's developmental psychology for students and teachers.* New York: Basic Books. *(185)*

Beardslee, D. C., and Wertheimer, M. (Eds.) (1958). *Readings in perception.* New York: Van Nostrand Reinhold. *(285)*

Békésy, G. von (1960). *Experiments in hearing.* New York: McGraw-Hill. *(640)*

Békésy, G. von, and Rosenblith, W. A. (1951). The mechanical properties of the ear. In S. S. Stevens (Ed.), *Handbook of experimental psychology.* New York: Wiley. Pp. 1075–1115. *(636, 637)*

Bekhterev, V. M. (1932). *General Principles of Human Reflexology.* New York: International. *(71)*

Bell, G., and French, R. (1950). Consistency of individual leadership position in small groups of varying membership. *J. abnorm. soc. Psychol.*, 45, 764–767. *(485)*

Benedict, R. (1959). *Patterns of culture* (2d ed.). Boston: Houghton Mifflin. *(474, 507)*

Bennett, E. M. and Cohen, L. R. (1959). Men and women: Personality patterns and contrasts. *Genet. Psychol. Monogr. 59,* 101–155. *(18)*

Bennett, G. K., Seashore, H. G., and Wesman, A. G. (1951). *Counseling from profiles: A casebook for the Differential Aptitude Tests.* New York; Psychol. Corp. *(350, 351)*

Benolken, R. M. (1961). Reversal of photoreceptor polarity recorded during the graded receptor potential response to light in the eye of *Limulus. Biophys. J.*, 1, 551–564. *(620)*

Bereiter, C., and Englemann, S. (1968). An academically oriented preschool for disadvantaged children: Results from the initial experimental group. In D. W. Brison & J. Hill (Eds.) *Psychology and early childhood education.* Ontario Institute for Studies in Education, No. 4. Pp. 17–36. (*60*)

Bergeijk van, W. A., Pierce, J. R., and David, E. E., Jr. (1960). *Waves and the ear.* Garden City, N.Y.: Doubleday. (*653*)

Berko, J. (1958). The child's learning of English morphology. *Word,* 14, 150–177. (*177, 178*)

Berkowitz, L. (1969). *Roots of aggression: A re-examination of the frustration-aggression hypothesis.* New York: Atheron. (*218, 221, 507*)

Berkowitz, L. (Ed.) (1969). *Advances in Experimental Social Psychology.* Vol. 4. New York: Academic Press. (*504*)

Berkowitz, L., and Holmes, D. S. (1959). The generalization of hostility to disliked objects. *J. Pers.,* 27, 565–577. (*539*)

Berkowitz, L., and Cottingham, D. R. (1960). The interest value and relevance of fear arousing communications. *J. abnorm. soc. Psychol.,* 60, 37–43. (*531*)

Berkowitz, L., and LePage, A. (1967). Weapons and aggression-eliciting stimuli. *J. Pers. soc. Psychol.,* 7, 202–207. (*504*)

Berlyne, D. E. (1960). *Conflict, arousal, and curiosity.* New York: McGraw-Hill. (*221*)

Berscheid, E., and Walster, E. H. (1969). *Interpersonal attraction.* Reading, Mass.: Addison-Wesley. (*507*)

Bettelheim, B. (1943). Individual and mass behavior in extreme situations. *J. abnorm. soc. Psychol.,* 38, 417–452. (*379*)

Bexton, W. H., Heron, W., and Scott, T. H. (1954). Effects of decreased variation in the sensory environment. *Canad. J. Psychol.,* 8, 70–76. (*200, 277*)

Bills, A. G. (1927). The influence of muscular tension on the efficiency of mental work. *Amer. J. Psychol.,* 38, 227–251. (*227*)

Bilodeau, E. A. (Ed.) (1966). *Acquisition of skill.* New York: Academic. (*147*)

Bilodeau, I. McD. (1966). Information feedback. In E. A. Bilodeau (Ed.). *Acquisition of skill.* New York: Academic Press. (*122*)

Bindra, D. (1959). *Motivation: A systematic reinterpretation.* New York: Ronald. (*221*)

Birney, R. G., and Teevan, R. C. (Eds.) (1961). *Instinct.* Princeton, N.J.: Van Nostrand. (*61*)

Birney, R. G., and Teevan, R. C. (Eds.) (1961). *Reinforcement.* New York: Van Nostrand Reinhold. (*107*)

Blough, D. S. (1958). A method for obtaining psychophysical thresholds from the pigeon. *J. exp. anal. Behav.,* 1, 31–43. (*608*)

Bond, E. D. (1954). Results of treatment in psychoses—with a control series. *Amer. J. Psychiat.,* 110, 881–887. (*422*)

Bonner, D. M. (1961). *Heredity.* Englewood Cliffs, N.J.: Prentice-Hall. (*45, 61*)

Bordin, E. S. (1955). *Psychological counseling.* New York: Appleton-Century-Crofts. (*443*)

Boring, E. G. (1942). *Sensation and perception in the history of experimental psychology.* New York: Appleton-Century-Crofts. (*653*)

Boring, E. G. (Ed.) (1945). *Psychology for the armed services.* Washington, D.C.: Combat Forces Press. (315, 346)

Boring, E. G. (1950). *A history of experimental psychology* (2d ed.). New York: Appleton-Century-Crofts. (*29*)

Boring, E. G. (1953). A history of introspectionism. *Psychol. Bull.,* 50, 169–189. (*24*)

Bousfield, W. A. (1961). The problem of meaning in verbal learning. In C. N. Cofer (Ed.), *Verbal learning and verbal behavior.* New York: McGraw-Hill. (*127*)

Bower, G., Clark, M. C., Lesgold, A. M., and Winzenz, D. (1969). Hierarchical retrieval schemes in recall of categorized word lists. *J. verb. Learn. verb. Behav.,* 8, 323–343. (*128, 129*)

Boyd, D. A., Jr., and Nie, L. W. (1949). Congenital universal indifference to pain. *Arch. Neurol. Psychiat., Chicago.* 61, 402–412. (*648*)

Bradford, L. P., Gibb, J. R., and Benne, K. D. (Eds.) (1964). *T-group theory and laboratory method.* New York: Wiley. (*456*)

Brady, J. V. (1958). Ulcers in "executive" monkeys. *Sci. Amer.,* 199, (4), 95–100. (*235*)

Braine, M. D. S. (1963). The ontogeny of English phrase structure: The first phase. *Language,* 39, 1–13. (*154*)

Braungart, R. G. (1966). SDS and YAF: Backgrounds of student political activists. Paper presented at meeting of the American Sociological Association, Miami. (*525, 526*)

Brazier, M. A. B. (1959). The historical development of neurophysiology. in J. Field (Ed.), *Neurophysiology.* Vol. 1. Washington, D.C.: American Physiological Society. (*603*)

Brazier, M. A. B. (1968). *The electrical activity of the nervous system. A textbook for students.* (3d ed.). Baltimore: Williams & Wilkins. (*587, 603*)

Brehm, J. W., and Cohen, A. R. (1962). *Explorations in cognitive dissonance.* New York: Wiley. (*219, 514*)

Brenner, C. (1957). *An elementary textbook of psychoanalysis.* Garden City, N.Y.: Doubleday. (*397*)

Bridgman, P. W. (1927). *The logic of modern physics.* New York: Macmillan. (*12*)

Broadbent, D. E. (1958). *Perception and communication.* New York: Pergamon Press. (*134*)

Broadbent, D., and Heron, A. (1962). Effects of a subsidiary task on performance involving immediate memory by younger and older men. *Brit. J. Psychol.,* 53, 189–198. (*134*)

Brobeck, J. R. (1946). Mechanism of the development of obesity in animals with hypothalamic lesions. *Physiol. Rev.*, 26, 541–559. (*667*)

Bromber, W. (1959). *The mind of man: A history of psychotherapy and psychoanalysis.* New York: Harper & Row. (*469*)

Bronfenbrenner, W. (1958). Socialization and social class through time and space. In E. E. Maccoby, T. M. Newcomb, and E. L. Hartley (Eds.), *Readings in social psychology* (3d ed.). New York: Holt, Rinehart and Winston. (*479, 480*)

Brown, J. (1958). Some tests of the decay theory of immediate memory. *Quart. J. exp. Psychol.*, 10, 12-21. (*134, 184*)

Brown, J. A. C. (1963). *Techniques of persuasion: From propaganda to brain-washing.* Baltimore, Md.: Penguin. (*543*)

Brown, J. F. (1931). The visual perception of velocity. *Psychol. Forsch.*, 14, 199–232. (*272*)

Brown, J. S. (1948). Gradients of approach and avoidance responses and their relation to motivation. *J. comp. physiol. Psychol.*, 41, 450–565. (*248, 249*)

Brown, R. (1958). *Words and things.* New York: Free Press. (*185*)

Brown, R. (1965). *Social Psychology.* New York: Free Press. (*507*)

Brown, R., Cazden, C., and Bellugi, U. (1970). The child's grammar from I to III. In Bar-Adon and Leopold (Eds.), *Readings in child language.* Englewood Cliffs, N. J.: Prentice-Hall. (*176*)

Bruce, R. W. (1933). Conditions of transfer of training. *J. exp. Psychol., 16,* 343–361. (*130, 131*)

Bruner, J. S., Goodnow, J. J., and Austin, G. A. (1956). *A study of thinking.* New York: Wiley. (*155, 156*)

Brunswick, E. (1956). *Perception and the representative design of psychological experiments.* Berkeley, Calif.: Univ. Calif. Press. (*112*)

Buddenbrock, W. von (1958). *The senses.* Ann Arbor, Mich.: Univ. Michigan Press. (*653*)

Bugelski, B. R. (1938). Extinction with and without subgoal reinforcement. *J. comp. Psychol.*, 26, 121–133. (*81*)

Buros, O. K. (Ed.) (1964). *The sixth mental measurements yearbook.* Highland Park, N. J.: Gryphon Press. (*361*)

Buros, O. K. (Ed.) (1970). *Personality tests and reviews: Including an index to the Mental Measurements Yearbooks.* Highland Park, N. J.: Gryphon Press. (*353*)

Burt, C., and Howard, M. (1956). The multiple factorial theory of inheritance and its application to intelligence. *Brit. J. statist. Psychol.*, 9, 95–131. (*51*)

Burton, A. (Ed.) (1969). *Encounter.* San Francisco: Jossey-Bass. (*456, 469*)

Burtt, H. E. (1941). An experimental study of early childhood memory. *J. genet. Psychol., 58,* 435–439. (*135*)

Buss, A. H. (1961). *The psychology of aggression.* New York: Wiley. (*217, 218*)

Buss, A. H. (1966). *Psychopathology.* New York: Wiley. (433)

Bustanoby, J. H. *Principles of color and color mixing.* New York: McGraw-Hill, 1947. (*611*).

Butler, R. A. (1953). Discrimination learning by rhesus monkeys to visual-exploration motivation. *J. comp. physiol. Psychol., 46,* 95–98. (*198*)

Butler, R. A. (1954). Incentive conditions which influence visual exploration. *J. exp. Psychol.*, 48, 19–23. (*105, 198*)

Butler, R. A., Diamond, I. T., and Neff, W. D. (1957). Role of auditory cortex in discrimination of changes in frequency. *J. Neurophysiol.*, 20, 108–120. (*637*)

Butter, C. M. (1968). *Neuropsychology: The study of brain and behavior.* Belmont, Calif.: Brooks/Cole. (*603, 616, 681*)

Byrne, D. (1964). Repression-sensitization as a dimension of personality. In B. A. Maher (Ed.), *Progress in experimental personality research,* vol. 1. New York: Academic Press. Pp. 169–220. (*355*)

Byrne, D. (1966). *An introduction to personality: A research approach.* Englewood Cliffs, N. J.: Prentice-Hall. (*397*)

Byrne, D. (1969). Attitudes and attraction. In L. Berkowitz (Ed.), *Advances in experimental social psychology.* Vol. 4. New York: Academic Press. (*501*)

Caggiula, A. R., and Hoebel, B. G. (1966). "Copulation-reward site" in the posterior hypothalamus. *Science, 153,* 1284–1285. (*668*)

Cameron, N., and Magaret, A. (1951). *Behavior pathology.* Boston: Houghton Mifflin. (*375, 421, 445, 449*)

Campbell, A., Converse, P. E., Miller, W. E. and Stokes, O. E. (1960). *The American voter.* New York: Wiley. (*519, 543*)

Campbell, B. S., and Misanin, J. R. (1969). Basic drives. *Annu. Rev.*, 20, 57–84. (*194*)

Campbell, D. T. (1960). Blind variation and selective retention in creative thought as in other knowledge processes. *Psychol. Rev.*, 67, 380–400. (*169*)

Candland, D. K. (Ed.) (1962). *Emotion: Bodily change.* Princeton, N.J.: Van Nostrand. (*251*)

Cannon, W. B. (1927). The James-Lange theory of emotions: A critical examination and an alternative theory. *Amer. J. Psychol.*, 39, 106–124. (*232, 671*)

Cannon, W. B. (1929). *Bodily changes in pain, hunger, fear and rage* (2d ed.), New York: Appleton-Century-Crofts. (*232, 235*)

Cannon, W. B. (1932). *The wisdom of the body.* New York: Norton. (*190*)

Cannon, W. B. (1934). Hunger and thirst. In C. Murchison (Ed.), *A handbook of general experimental psychology.* Worcester, Mass.: Clark Univer. Press. Pp. 247–263. (*190, 191*)

Carlson, E. R. (1956). Attitude change and attitude structure. *J. abnorm. soc. Psychol.*, 52, 256–261. (*534*)

Carmichael, L., Hogan, H. P., and Walter, A. A. (1932). An experimental study of the effect of language on the reproduction of visually perceived form. *J. exp. Psychol.*, 15, 73–86. (*141, 142*)

Caron, R. F., and Caron, A. J. (1968). The effects of repeated exposure and stimulus complexity on visual fixation in infants. *Psychon. Sci.*, 10, 207–208. (*199*)

Carroll, J. B. (1964). *Language and thought.* Englewood Cliffs, N.J.: Prentice-Hall. (*163, 164, 185*)

Cason, H. (1930). Common annoyances: A psychological study of every-day aversions and irritations. *Psychol. Monogr.*, 40 (Whole No. 182). (*243*)

Cates, J. (1970). Psychology's manpower: Report on the 1968 national register of scientific and technical personnel. *Amer. Psychologist*, 25, 254–263. (5)

Cattell, R. B. (1942). The concept of social status. *J. soc. Psychol.*, 15, 293–308. (*478*)

Cattell, R. B. (1946). *Description and measurement of personality.* Yonkers, N.Y.: World. (*366, 367*)

Cattell, R. B. (1950). *Personality.* New York: McGraw-Hill. (*367*)

Chapanis, A., Garner, W. R. and Morgan, C. T. (1949). *Applied experimental psychology.* New York: Wiley. (*132, 569*)

Chapanis, A. (1959). *The design and conduct of human engineering studies.* Baltimore: Johns Hopkins Press. (*575*)

Charters, W. W., Jr., and Newcomb, T. M. (1958). Some attitudinal effects of experimentally increased salience of a membership group. In E. E. Maccoby, T. M. Newcomb, and E. L. Hartley (Eds.), *Readings in social psychology* (3d ed.). New York: Holt, Rinehart and Winston. Pp. 276–281. (*477*)

Chomsky, N. (1965). *Aspects of the theory of syntax.* Cambridge, Mass.: M.I.T. Press. (*176*)

Chow, K. L. (1951). Effects of partial extirpations of the posterior association cortex on visually mediated behavior in monkeys. *Comp. Psychol. Monogr.*, 20, 187–217. (*659*)

Chow, K. L., Riesen, A. H., and Newell, F. W. (1957). Degeneration of retinal ganglion cells in infant chimpanzees reared in darkness. *J. comp. Neurol.*, 107, 27–42. (*280*)

Church, R. M. (1963). The varied effects of punishment on behavior. *Psychol. Rev.*, 70, 369–402. (*94*)

Clark, D. F. (1963). The treatment of monosymptomatic phobia by systematic desensitization. *Behav. Res. Ther.*, 1, 63–68. (*461*)

Clemente, C. D., and Sterman, M. B. (1963). Cortical synchronization and sleep patterns in acute restrained and chronic behaving cats induced by basal forebrain stimulation. *EEG clin. Neurophysiol.*, Supplement 24, 172–187. (*461, 669*)

Cobb, S. (1941). *Foundations of psychiatry.* Baltimore: Williams & Wilkins. (*658*)

Cofer, C. N., and Appley, M. H. (1964). *Motivation: Theory and research.* New York: Wiley. (*196, 210, 212, 218, 221, 227*)

Coleman, J. C. (1956). *Abnormal psychology and modern life* (2d ed.). Chicago: Scott, Foresman. (*422*)

Coleman, J. C. (1964). *Abnormal psychology and modern life* (3d ed.). Chicago: Scott, Foresman. (*406, 422, 426, 433*)

Converse, P. E., and Schuman, H. (1970). "Silent majorities" and the Vietnam War. *Sci. Amer.*, 222, 17–25. (*516, 517*)

Cooper, E., and Jahoda, M. (1947). The evasion of propaganda: How prejudiced people respond to anti-prejudice propaganda. *J. Psychol.*, 23, 15–25. (*540*)

Corbit, J. D. (1969). Osmotic thirst: Theoretical and experimental analysis. *J. comp. physiol. Psychol.*, 67, 3–14, (*666, 667*)

Cox, C. M. (1926). *Genetic studies of genius.* Vol. II. Stanford, Calif.: Stanford Univer. Press. (*338*)

Crocker, E. C. (1945). *Flavor.* New York: McGraw-Hill. (*643*)

Crombie, A. C. (1964). Early concepts of the senses and the mind. *Sci. Amer., 210* (5), 108–116. (*607*)

Cronbach, L. J. (1960). *Essentials of psychological testing* (2d ed.). New York: Harper & Row. (*313*)

Cronbach, L. J., and Gleser, G. C. (1965). *Psychological tests and personnel decisions* (2d ed.). Urbana, Ill.: Univer. Illinois Press. (*322*)

Cronbach, L. J. (1970). *Essentials of psychological testing* (3d ed.). New York: Harper & Row. (*325, 353, 361*)

Crowne, D. P., and Marlowe, D. (1964). *The approval motive: Studies in evaluative dependence.* New York: Wiley. (*216, 221*)

Dahlstrom, W. G. and Welsh, G. S. (1960). *An MMPI Handbook: A guide to use in clinical practice and research.* Minneapolis, Minn.: Univer. Minnesota Press. (*354, 355, 356*)

Darwin, C. (1965). *The expression of the emotions in man and animals.* Chicago: University of Chicago Press. (Reprint) (*251*)

Dashiell, J. F. (1949). *Fundamentals of General Psychology* (3d ed.). Boston: Houghton Mifflin. (*76*)

Davis, A., and Havighurst, R. J. (1946). Social class and color differences in child-rearing. *Amer. social. Rev.*, 11, 698–710. (*478*)

Davis, F. C. (1932). The functional significance of imagery differences. *J. exp. Psychol.*, 15, 630–661. (*151*)

Davis, F. C. (1933). Effect of maze rotation upon subjects reporting different methods of learning and retention. *Univer. Calif. Los Angeles Publ. Educ., Phil., Psychol.*, 1, 47–63. (*151*)

Davis, H. (1959). Excitation of auditory receptors. In J. Field et al. (Eds.). *Handbook of physiology,* Vol. 1. Washington, D.C.: American Physiological Association. (*639*)

Davis, H., and Silverman, S. R. (Eds.) (1970). *Hearing and deafness* (3d ed.). New York: Holt, Rinehart and Winston. (*636*)

Davis, K. (1947). Final note on a case of extreme isolation. *Amer. J. Sociol.*, 52, 432–437. (42)

Davis, L. E. (1957). Job design and productivity: A new approach. *Personnel,* 33, 418–430. (*563*)

Davis, R. C. Garafolo, L., and Kveim, K. (1959). Conditions associated with gastro-intestinal activity. *J. comp. physiol. Psychol.,* 52, 466–475. (*190*)

Deese, J. (1970). *Psycholinguistics.* Boston: Allyn and Bacon. (*185*)

Deese, J., and Hulse, S. H. (1967). *The psychology of learning.* (3d ed.) New York: McGraw-Hill. (*102, 107, 113, 123, 147*)

Dember, W. N. (1960). *The psychology of perception.* New York: Holt, Rinehart and Winston. (*285*)

Dember, W. N., and Jenkins, J. J. (1970). *General psychology.* Englewood Cliffs, N.J.: Prentice-Hall. (*204*)

Dement, W. (1965). An essay on dreams: The role of physiology in understanding their nature. In *New directions in psychology II.* New York: Holt, Rinehart and Winston. 137–257. (*584*)

Dement, W., and Wolpert, E. (1958). The relation of eye movements, body motility, and external stimuli to dream content. *J. exp. Psychol.,* 55, 543–553. (*585*)

Dennis, W. (1940). The effect of cradling practices upon the onset of walking in Hopi children. *J. genet. Psychol.,* 56, 77–86. (*40*)

Dent, J. K. (1959). Organizational correlates of goals of business managements. *Personnel Psychol.,* 12, 365–393. (*549, 550*)

Dethier, V. G., and Stellar, E. (1970). *Animal behavior: Its evolutionary and neurological basis* (3d ed.). Englewood Cliffs, N.J.: Prentice-Hall. (Paperback.) (*35, 61*)

Deutsch, J. A. (1969). The physiological basis of memory. *Annu. Rev. Psychol.,* 20, 85–104. (*664*)

Deutsch, M., and Collins, M. E. (1951). *Interracial housing: A psychological evaluation of a social experiment.* Minneapolis, Minn.: Univer. Minnesota Press. (*537, 538*)

Deutsch, M., and Gerard, H. (1955). A study of normative and informational social influences upon individual judgment. *J. abnorm. soc. Psychol.,* 51, 629–636. (*489*)

DeValois, R. L., Abramov, I., and Jacobs, G. H. (1966). Analysis of response patterns of LGN cells. *Journal of the Optical Society of America*, 1966, 7, 966–977. (*626, 627*)

Dews, P. B. (1955). Studies on behavior. I. Differential sensitivity to pentobarbital of pecking performance in pigeons depending on the schedule of reward. *J. Pharmocol. exp. Therapeutics,* 113, 393–401. (*679*)

DiCara, L. V., and Miller, N. E. (1968). Instrumental learning of vasomotor responses by rats: Learning to respond differentially in the two ears. *Science,* 159, 1485–1486. (*86*)

Dimmick, F. L., and Hubbard, M. R. (1939). The spectral components of psychologically unique red. *Amer. J. Psychol.,* 52, 348–353. (*622*)

DiVesta, F. J., and Merwin, J. C. (1960). The effects of need-oriented communications on attitude change. *J. abnorm. soc. Psychol.,* 60, 80–85. (*534*).

Dollard, J. (1949). *Caste and class in a southern town* (2d ed.). New York: Harper & Row. (*345*)

Dollard, J., Doob, L. Miller, N., Mowrer, O., and Sears, R. (1939). *Frustration and aggression.* New Haven, Conn.: Yale Univer. Press. (*218*)

Dollard, J., and Miller, N.E. (1950). *Personality and psychotherapy.* New York: McGraw-Hill. (*27, 75, 370, 394, 397, 409, 445*)

Dorcus, R. M. (Ed.). (1956) *Hypnosis and its therapeutic applications.* New York: McGraw-Hill. (*452, 469*)

Dreger, R. M., and Miller, K. S. (1960). Comparative psychological studies of Negroes and whites in the United States. *Psychol. Bull.,* 57, 361–402. (*345*)

Droba, D. D. (1930). *A scale for measuring attitude toward war.* Chicago: Univer. Chicago Press. (*515*)

Dunbar, Flanders. (1955). *Mind and body: Psychosomatic medicine* (enlarged ed.). New York: Random House. (*251*)

Duncan, C. P. (Ed.) (1967). *Thinking: Current experimental studies.* Philadelphia: Lippincott. (*185*)

Duncker, K. (1929). Über induzierte Bewegung. *Psychol. Forsch.,* 12. 180–259. (*271*)

Duncker, K. (1945). On problem-solving. *Psychol. Monogr.,* 58 (Whole No. 270). (*166, 167*)

Ebbinghaus, H. (1885). *Memory: A contribution to experimental psychology* (trans. H. A. Ruger and Clara E. Bussenius). New York: Teachers College, Columbia Univ., 1913. (*116, 136*)

Eccles, J. C. (1957). *The physiology of nerve cells.* Baltimore, Md.: Johns Hopkins Univer. Press. (*589, 592*)

Eccles, J. C., (1964). *The physiology of synapses.* Berlin: Springer-Verlag. (*592*)

Edwards, A. L. (1954). *The Edwards personal preference schedule manual.* New York: Psychol. Corp. (*357, 369*)

Egan, G. (1970). *Encounter: Group processes for interpersonal growth.* Belmont, Calif.: Brooks/Cole. (*469*)

Engen, T., Levy, N., and Schlosberg, H. (1957). A new series of facial expressions. *Amer. Psychol.,* 12, 264–266. (*239*)

Engen, T., Levy, N., and Schlosberg, H. (1958). The dimensional analysis of a new series of facial expressions. *J. exp. Psychol.,* 55, 455–458. (*239*)

Erickson, R. P. (1963). Sensory neural patterns and gustation. In Y. Zotterman (Ed.), *Olfaction and Taste.* Oxford: Pergamon. Pp. 205–213. (*394, 645*)

Erikson, E. H. (1963). *Childhood and society* (2d ed.). New York: Norton. (*394*)

Erlenmeyer-Kimling, L., and Jarvik, L. F. (1963). Genetics and intelligence: A review. *Science,* 142, 1477–1479. (*51*)

Estes, W. K. (1964). Probability Learning. In A. W. Melton (Ed.) *Categories of human learning.* New York: Academic Press. Pp. 90–128. *(113)*

Evans, C. L. (1956). *Principles of human physiology.* (12th ed.) London: Churchill. *(588)*

Eysenck, H. J. (1952). The effects of psychotherapy: An evaluation. *J. consult. Psychol.,* 16, 319–324. *(453)*

Falk, J. L. (1967). Control of schedule-induced polydipsia: Type, size, and spacing of meals. *J. exp. Analysis Behav.,* 10, 199–206. *(192)*

Fechner, G. T. (1860). *Elemente der Psychophysik. Leipzig:* Breitkopf und Härtel. *(23)*

Fenichel, O. (1945). *The psychoanalytic theory of neurosis.* New York: Norton. *(406)*

Ferster, C. B. and Skinner, B. F. (1957). *Schedules of reinforcement.* New York: Appleton-Century-Crofts. *(82, 83, 84)*

Festinger, L. (1954). A theory of social comparison process. *Hum. Rel.,* 7, 117–140. *(490, 502)*

Festinger, L. (1957). *A theory of cognitive dissonance.* New York: Harper & Row. *(514)*

Festinger, L., Schachter, S., and Back, K. (1950). *Social pressures in informal groups: A study of human factors in housing.* New York: Harper & Row. *(503)*

Festinger, L., Riecken, H. W., and Schachter, S. (1956). *When prophecy fails.* Minneapolis: University of Minnesota Press. *(2, 9)*

Fiedler, F. E. (1954). Assumed similarity measures as predictors of team effectivenes. *J. abnorm. soc. Psychol.,* 49, 381–388. *(486)*

Fields, P. E. (1932). Studies in concept formation. I. The development of the concept of triangularity by the white rat. *Comp. Psychol. Monogr.,* 9, No. 2. *(118, 156)*

Flacks, R. (1967). The liberated generation: An explanation of the roots of student protest. *J. soc. Issues,* 23, 52–75. *(525)*

Fleishman, E. A. (1967). *Studies in personnel and industrial psychology* (rev. ed.). Homewood, Ill.: Dorsey Press. *(554)*

Flesch, R. (1946). *The art of plain talk.* New York: Harper & Row. *(556)*

Flesch, R. (1954). *How to make sense.* New York: Harper & Row. *(556)*

Flippo, E. B. (1966). *Principles of personnel management.* New York: McGraw-Hill. *(554, 555, 575)*

Ford, C. S., and Beach, F. A. (1951). *Patterns of sexual behavior.* New York: Hoeber-Harper. *(221)*

Fox, R. E. (1962). Personality patterns of resident psychotherapists. Unpublished doctoral dissertation. Univer. North Carolina, Chapel Hill, N.C. *(454)*

Fox, R. E. and King, R. A. (1961). The effects of reinforcement scheduling on the strength of a secondary reinforcer. *J. comp. physiol. Psychol.,* 54, 266–269. *(80)*

Freedman J. L., and Fraser, S. C. (1966). Compliance without pressure: the foot-in-the-door technique. *J. Pers. soc. Psychol.,* 4, 195–202. *(493)*

Freeman, W., and Watts, J. W. (1950), *Psychosurgery* (2d ed.). Springfield, Ill.: Charles C Thomas. *(440)*

Freud, S. (1914). *Psychopathology of everyday life.* New York: Macmillan. *(390)*

Freud, S. (1933). *New introductory lectures on psychoanalysis.* New York: Norton. *(387, 397)*

Freud, S. (1938). *The basic writings of Sigmund Freud* (trans. A. A. Brill). New York: Random House, 1938. *(390, 397)*

Freud, S. (1949). *An outline of psychoanalysis. New York:* Norton. *(469)*

Fromm, E. (1941). *Escape from freedom.* New York: Holt, Rinehart and Winston. *(394)*

Fuller, J. L. (1962). *Motivation: A biological perspective.* New York: Random House. *(221)*

Fuller, J. L. (1967). Experiential deprivation and later behavior. *Science,* 158, 1645–1652. *(59)*

Fuller, J. L., and Thompson, W. R. (1960). *Behavior genetics.* New York: Wiley. *(61)*

Galanter, E. (1962). Contemporary psychophysics. In *New directions in psychology.* Vol. 1. New York: Holt, Rinehart and Winston. *(609)*

Gardner, E. (1968). *Fundamentals of neurology.* (5th ed.). Philadelphia: Saunders. *(590, 594, 603, 634)*

Gardner, R. A., and Gardner, B. T. (1969). Teaching sign language to a chimpanzee. *Science,* 165, 664–672. *(38, 661)*

Garfield, S. L. (1957). *Introductory clinical psychology.* New York: Macmillan. *(447, 469)*

Gates, A. I. (1917). Recitation as a factor in memorizing. *Arch. Psychol.,* 6 (Whole No. 40). *(123)*

Gerard, H. B. (1965). Deviation, conformity and commitment. In I. D. Steiner and M. Fishbein (Eds.), *Current studies in social psychology.* New York: Holt, Rinehart and Winston. Pp. 263–277. *(491)*

Gerard, R. W. (1941). *The body functions.* New York: Wiley. *(646)*

Gesell, A., and Thompson, H. (1929). Learning and growth in identical infant twins: An experimental study by the method of co-twin control. *Genet. Psychol. Monogr.,* 6, 1–124. *(40)*

Getzels, J. W., and Jackson, P. W. (1962). *Creativity and intelligence.* New York: Wiley. *(170, 334)*

Ghiselin, B. (Ed.) (1955). *The creative process: A symposium.* New York: Mentor. *(185)*

Ghiselli, E. E., and Brown, C. W. (1955). *Personnel and industrial psychology* (2d ed.). New York: McGraw-Hill. *(559, 561, 569)*

Gibson, E. J., and Walk, R. D. (1960). The "visual cliff." *Sci. Amer.,* 202 (4), 64–71. *(278)*

Gibson, J. J. (1929). The reproduction of visually perceived forms. *J. exp. Psychol.* 12, 1–39. *(141)*

Gibson, J. J. *The perception of the visual world.* Boston: Houghton Mifflin, 1950. (*267, 268*)

Gibson, J. J. (1966). *The senses considered as perceptual systems.* Boston: Houghton Mifflin, 1966. (*254*)

Gilbert, G. M. (1951). Stereotype persistence and change among college students. *J. abnorm. soc. Psychol.,* 46, 245–254. (*524*)

Glaze, J. A. (1928). The association value of nonsense syllables. *J. genet. Psychol.,* 35, 255–269. (*116*)

Gleitman, H. (1955). Place learning without prior reinforcement. *J. comp. physiol. Psychol.,* 48, 77–79. (*96, 97*)

Glickstein, M. Neurophysiology of learning and memory. In T. C. Ruch and H. D. Patton (Eds.), *Physiology and biophysics* (19th ed.). Philadelphia: Saunders, 1965. (*657*)

Goldfarb, W. (1947). Variations in adolescent adjustment of institutionally reared children. *Amer. J. Orthopsychiat.,* 17, 449–457. (*384*)

Goldhammer, H. and Marshall, A. W. (1953). *Psychosis and civilization.* New York: Free Press. (*436*)

Goldstein, K. (1950). Prefrontal lobotomy: Analysis and warning, *Sci. Amer.,* 182 (2), 44–47. (*660*)

Goodman, L. S. and Gilman, A. (Eds.) (1970). *The pharmacological basis of therapeutics* (4th ed.). N.Y.: Macmillan, 1965. (*675*)

Gordon, R. A. (1945). Business leadership in the large corporation. Washington, D.C.: Brookings Institution. (*550*)

Granit, R. (1955). *Receptors and sensory perception.* New Haven: Yale Univer. Press. (*620*)

Grant, D. A., Hake, H. W., and Hornseth, J. P. (1951). Acquisition and extinction of a conditioned verbal response with differing percentages of reinforcement. *J. exp. Psychol.,* 42, 1–5. (*113*)

Green, D. M., and Swets, J. A. (1966). *Signal detection theory and psychophysics.* New York: Wiley. (*608*)

Greenspoon, J. (1955). The reinforcing effect of two spoken sounds on the frequency of two responses. *Amer. J. Psychol.,* 68, 409–416. (*79*)

Greenwald, A. G., Brock, T. C., and Ostrom, T. M. (Eds.) (1968). *Psychological foundations of attitudes.* New York: Academic Press. (*543*)

Gregory, R. L. (1966). *Eye and brain: The psychology of seeing.* New York: McGraw-Hill. (*653*)

Griffin, D. R. (1959). *Echoes of bats and men.* Garden City, N.Y.: Anchor. (*638*)

Grossman, S. P. (1960). Eating or drinking elicited by direct adrenergic or cholinergic stimulation of the hypothalamus. *Science,* 132, 331–332. (*586*)

Guilford, J. P. (1954). *Psychometric methods* (rev. ed.). New York: McGraw-Hill. (*290, 608*)

Guilford, J. P. (1956). *Fundamental statistics in psychology and education* (3d ed.). New York: McGraw-Hill. (*303, 304*)

Guilford, J. P. (1965). *Fundamental statistics in psychology and education* (4th ed.). New York: McGraw-Hill. (*317, 334*)

Guilford, J. P. (Ed.). (1966). *Fields of psychology* (3d ed.). Princeton, N.J.: Van Nostrand. (*29*)

Guilford, J. P. (1967). *The nature of human intelligence.* New York: McGraw-Hill. (*332, 361*)

Guion, R. M. (1965). *Personnel testing.* New York: McGraw-Hill. (*575*)

Guthrie, E. R. (1952). *The psychology of learning* (rev. ed.). New York: Harper & Row. (*25, 105*)

Guttman, N. (1953). Operant conditioning, extinction, and periodic reinforcement in relation to concentration of sucrose used as reinforcing agent. *J. exp. Psychol.,* 46, 213–224. (*105*)

Haan, N. (1963). Proposed model of ego functioning: Coping and defense mechanisms in relationship to IQ change. *Psychol. Mongr.,* 77, (Whole No. 8). (*341*)

Haber, R. N. (Ed.). (1968). *Contemporary theory and research in visual perception.* New York: Holt, Rinehart and Winston. (285)

Haber, R. N. (1969). Eidetic images. *Sci. Amer.,* 220, No. 4, 36–44. (*151*)

Hailman, J. P. (1969). How an instinct is learned. *Sci. Amer.,* 221, No. 6, 98–106. (*57*)

Haire, M. (1964). *Psychology in management* (2d ed.). New York: McGraw-Hill. (*575*)

Haley, J. (1963). *Strategies of psychotherapy.* New York: Grune & Stratton. (*457*)

Hall, C. S. (1938). The inheritance of emotionality. *Sigma Xi Quart.,* 26, 17–27. (*53*)

Hall, C. S. (1953). A cognitive theory of dream symbols. *J. gen. Psychol.,* 48, 186–199. (*446*)

Hall, C. S. (1954). *A primer of Freudian psychology.* Cleveland: World. (*397*)

Hall, C. S., and Lindzey G. (1970). *Theories of personality* (2d ed.). New York: Wiley. (*387, 397*)

Hall, J. F. (1956). The relationship between external stimulation, food deprivation, and activity. *J. comp. physiol. Psychol.,* 49, 339–341. (*196, 197*)

Hall, J. F. (1966). *The psychology of learning.* Philadelphia: Lippincott. (*68, 102, 107, 120, 147*)

Hammond, K. R., and Householder, J. E. (1962). *Introduction to statistical method.* New York: Knopf. (*317*)

Hanes, R. M. (1949). The construction of subjective brightness scales from fractionation data: A validation. *J. exp. Psychol.,* 39, 719–728. (*608*)

Hanson, H. M. (1959). Effects of discrimination training on stimulus generalization. *J. exp. Psychol.,* 58, 321–334. (*85*)

Harding, J., Proshansky, H., Kutner, B., and Chein, I. (1969). Prejudice and ethnic relations. In G. Lindzey and E. Aronson (Eds.), *Handbook of social psychology* (2d ed.), Vol. VII. Reading, Mass.: Addison-Wesley. (*522, 525*)

Hardy, J. D., Goodell, H., and Wolff, H. G. (1951). The influence of skin temperature upon the pain threshold as evoked by thermal radiation. *Science,* 114, 149–150. *(649)*

Harlow, H. F. (1949). The formation of learning sets. *Psychol. Rev.,* 56, 61–65. *(101, 102)*

Harlow, H. F. (1958). The nature of love. *Amer. Psychologist,* 13, 673–685. *(201, 202)*

Harlow, H. F. (1962). The heterosexual affectional system in monkeys. *Amer. Psychologist,* 17, 1–9. *(57, 193)*

Harlow, H. F., and McClearn, G. E. (1954). Object discrimination learned by monkeys on the basis of manipulation motives. *J. comp. physiol. Psychol.,* 47, 73–76. *(199)*

Harlow, H. F., and Griffin, G. (1965). Induced mental and social deficits in rhesus monkeys. In S. F. Osler and R. E. Cooke (Eds.), *The biosocial basis of mental retardation.* Baltimore: The Johns Hopkins University Press. Pp. 87–106. *(58)*

Harper, R. A. (1959). *Psychoanalysis and psychotherapy.* Englewood Cliffs, N.J.: Prentice-Hall. *(469)*

Harris, C. S. (1965). Perceptual adaptation to inverted, reversed, and displaced vision. *Psychol. Rev.,* 72, 419–444. *(277)*

Hartline, H. K. (1938). The response of single optic nerve fibers of the vertebrate eye to illumination of the retina. *Amer. J. Physiol.,* 121, 400–415. *(621)*

Hartline, H. K., Wagner, H. G., and MacNichol, E. F., Jr. (1952). The peripheral origin of nervous activity in the visual system. *Cold Spring Harbor Symp. Quant. Biol.,* 17, 125–141. *(620)*

Hartmann, H. (1964). *Essays on ego psychology: Selected problems in psychoanalytic theory.* New York: International Univer. Press. *(395)*

Hartman, T. F., Grant, D. A., and Ross, L. E. (1960). An investigation of the latency of "instructed voluntary" eyelid responses. *Psychol. Rep.,* 7, 305–311. *(109)*

Hathaway, S. R., and McKinley, J. C. (1951). *The Minnesota Multiphasic Personality Inventory manual* (rev. ed.). New York: Psychological Corp. *(355)*

Hayes, K.J., and Hayes, C. (1951). The intellectual development of a home-raised chimpanzee. *Proc. Amer. phil. Soc.,* 95, 105–109. *(38)*

Health, Education, and Welfare Indicators (1967). Washington, D.C.: U.S. Dept. Health, Education, and Welfare. *(438)*

Hebb, D. O. (1937). The innate organization of visual activity. I. Perception of figure by rats reared in total darkness. *J. genet. Psychol.,* 51, 101–126. *(280)*

Hebb, D. O. (1949). *The Organization of behavior.* New York: Wiley. *(242)*

Hebb, D. O. (1955). Drives and C. N. S. (Conceptual Nervous System). *Psychol. Rev.,* 62, 243–254. *(228)*

Hebb, D. O. (1966). *A textbook of psychology* (2d ed.). Philadelphia: Saunders. *(228, 282)*

Hécaen, H., Penfield, W., Bertrand, C., and Malmo, R. (1956). The syndrome of apractognosia due to lesions of the minor cerebral hemisphere. *Arch. Neurol. Psychiat., Chicago,* 75, 400–434. *(661)*

Heider, F. (1958). *The psychology of interpersonal relations.* New York: Wiley. *(504)*

Held, R., and Hein, A. (1963). Movement-produced stimulation in the development of visually guided behavior. *J. comp. physiol. Psychol.,* 56, 872–876. *(279)*

Helmholtz, H. L. F. von. (1924). *Physiological optics.* (Trans. J. P. C. Southall). Vol. II. Rochester, N.Y.: Optical Soc. Amer. *(625)*

Helson, H. (1948). Adaptation-level as a basis for a quantitative theory of frames of reference. *Psychol. Rev.,* 55, 297–313. *(273)*

Helson, H. (1964). Current trends and issues in adaptation-level theory. *Amer. Psychologist.* 19, 26–38. *(273)*

Hernández-Péon, R., Scherrer, H., and Jouvet, M. Modification of electric activity in cochlear nucleus during "attention" in unanesthetized cats. *Science,* 123, 331–332. *(258, 259)*

Heron, W., Doane, B. K., and Scott, T. H. (1956). Visual disturbance after prolonged perceptual isolation. *Canad. J. Psychol.,* 10, 13–16. *(277)*

Hess, E. H. (1965). Attitude and pupil size. *Sci. Amer.,* 212, 4, 46–54. *(224, 226)*

Hess, E. H. (1968). Pupillometric assessment. In J. M. Shlien (Ed.), *Research in psychotherapy,* Vol. III. Washington, D.C.: American Psychological Association. *(225)*

Hess, E. H., and Polt, J. M. (1960). Pupil size as related to interest value of visual stimuli. *Science,* 132, 349–350. *(225)*

Hess, W. R. (1954). *Diencephalon: Autonomic and extrapyramidal functions.* New York: Grune. *(671)*

Heston, L. L. (1970). The genetics of schizophrenic and schizoid disease. *Science,* 167, 249–256. *(55)*

Hildum, D. C., and Brown, R. W. (1956). Verbal reinforcement and interviewer bias. *J. abnorm. soc. Psychol.,* 53, 108–111. *(79)*

Hilgard, E. R. (1931). Conditioned eyelid reactions to a light stimulus based on the reflex wink to sound. *Psychol. Monogr.,* 41, (Whole no. 184). *(110)*

Hilgard, E. R. (1968). *The Experience of hypnosis.* New York: Harcourt, Brace, & Jovanovich. *(469)*

Hilgard, E. R., and Bower, G. H. (1966). *Theories of learning* (3d ed.). New York: Appleton-Century-Crofts. *(107, 147)*

Hilgard, J. R. (1953). Anniversary reactions in parents precipitated by children. *Psychiatry,* 16, 73–80. *(384)*

Hill, W. F. (1956). Activity as an autonomous drive. *J. comp. physiol. Psychol.,* 49, 15–19. *(197)*

Hill, W. F. (1963). *Learning: A survey of psychological interpretations.* San Francisco: Chandler. *(107)*

Himmelfarb, S., and Senn, D. J. (1969). Forming impressions of social class: Two tests of an averaging model. *J. Pers. soc. Psychol.,* 12, 38–51. *(513, 522)*

Hinrichs, J. R. (1970). Psychology of men at work. *Annu. Rev.,* 21, 519–554. *(564)*

Hirsch, J. (1959). Studies in experimental behavior genetics: II. Individual differences in geotaxis as a function of chromosome variations in synthesized *Drosophila* populations. *J. comp. physiol. Psychol.,* 52, 304–308. *(50)*

Hirsch, J. (Ed.). (1967). *Behavior-genetic analysis.* N.Y.: McGraw-Hill. *(61)*

Hirsch, J., and Erlenmeyer-Kimling, L. (1962). Studies in experimental behavior genetics: IV. Chromosome analysis for geotaxis. *J. comp. physiol. Psychol.,* 55, 732–739. *(50)*

Hochberg, J. E. (1964). *Perception.* Englewood Cliffs, N.J.: Prentice-Hall. *(285)*

Hoebel, B. G. (1965). Hypothalamic lesions by electrocauterization: Disinhibition of feeding and self-stimulation. *Science,* 149, 452–453. *(667)*

Holland, J. G., and Skinner, B. F. (1961). *The analysis of behavior: A program for self-instruction.* New York: McGraw-Hill. *(107)*

Hollander, E. P., and Hunt, R. G. (Eds.) (1963). *Current perspectives in social psychology: Readings with commentary.* New York: Oxford Univer. Press. *(543)*

Hollingshead, A. B. (1949). *Elmtown's youth: The impact of social classes on adolescents.* New York: Wiley. *(303)*

Hollingworth, H. L. (1929). *Vocational psychology and character analysis.* New York: Appleton-Century-Crofts. *(558, 559)*

Homans, G. C. (1950). *The human group.* New York: Harcourt, Brace & World. *(494)*

Honig, W. K. (1966). *Operant behavior.* New York: Appleton-Century-Crofts. *(107)*

Horney, K. (1937). *The neurotic personality of our time.* New York: Norton. *(391)*

Horowitz, E. L., and Horowitz, R. E. (1938). Development of social attitudes in children. *Sociometry,* 1, 301–338. *(520)*

Housman, A. E. (1933). *The name and nature of poetry.* New York: Macmillan. *(169)*

Hovland, C. I. (1937). The generalization of conditioned responses. I. The sensory generalization of conditioned responses with varying frequencies of tone. *J. gen. Psychol.,* 17, 125–248. *(73)*

Hovland, C. I. (1938). Experimental studies in rote-learning theory. III. Distribution of practice with varying speeds of syllable presentation. *J. exp. Psychol.,* 23, 172–190. *(121)*

Hovland, C. I. (1951). Human learning and retention. In S. S. Stevens (Ed.), *Handbook of experimental psychology.* New York: Wiley. Pp. 613–689. *(137)*

Hovland, C. I., Lumsdaine, A. A., and Sheffield, F. C. (1949). *Experiments on mass communication.* Princeton, N.J.: Princeton Univ. Press. *(532)*

Hubel, D. H., and Wiesel, T. N. (1959). Receptive fields of single neurones in the cat's striate cortex. *J. Physiol.,* 148, 574–591. *(629)*

Hubel, D. H., and Wiesel, T. N. (1962). Receptive fields, binocular interaction and functional architecture in the cat's visual cortex. *J. Physiol.,* 160, 106–154. *(582, 628, 634)*

Hubel, D. H., and Wiesel, T. N. (1963). Receptive fields of cells in striate cortex of very young, visually inexperienced kittens. *J. Neurophysiol.,* 26, 994–1002. *(282)*

Hubel, D. H., and Wiesel, T. N. (1968). Receptive fields and functional architecture of monkey striate cortex. *J. Physiol.,* 195, 215–243. *(628)*

Huff, Darrell. (1954). *How to lie with statistics.* New York: Norton. *(316)*

Hull, C. L. (1920). Quantitative aspects of the evolution of concepts. *Psychol. Monogr.,* 28 (Whole No. 123). *(158)*

Hull, C. L. (1943). *The principles of behavior.* New York: Appleton-Century-Crofts. *(25, 104, 105, 144)*

Hull, C. L. (1951). *Essentials of behavior.* New Haven: Yale Univ. Press. *(104, 144)*

Hull, C. L. (1952). *A behavior system.* New Haven: Yale Univer. Press. *(144)*

Hull, C. L., Hovland, C. I., Ross, R. T., Hall, J., Perkins, D. T., and Fitch, R. B. (1940). *Mathematico-deductive theory of rote learning.* New Haven: Yale Univer. Press. *(109)*

Humphrey, G. (1948). *Directed thinking.* New York: Dodd, Mead. *(169)*

Hunt, H. F., and Brady, J. V. (1951). Some effects of electro-convulsive shock on conditioned emotional responses ("anxiety"). *J. comp. physiol. Psychol.,* 44, 88–98. *(88)*

Hurvich, L. M., and Jameson, D. (1957). An opponent-process theory of color vision. *Psychol. Rev.,* 64, 384–404. *(625)*

Hyman, H. (1959). *Political socialization: A study in the psychology of political behavior.* New York: Free Press. *(520)*

Insko, C. A. (1967). *Theories of attitude change.* New York: Appleton-Century-Crofts. *(543)*

Insko, C. A., Mirashima, F., and Saiyadain, M. (1966). Communicator discrepancy, stimulus ambiguity, and influence. *J. Pers.,* 34, 262–274. *(533)*

Isaacson, R. L. (Ed.) (1964). *Basic readings in neuropsychology.* New York: Harper & Row. *(681)*

Jackson, D. D. (Ed.) (1960). *The etiology of schizophrenia.* New York: Basic Books. *(427)*

Jacobsen, C. F. (1935). Functions of the frontal association areas in primates. *Arch. Neurol. Psychiat.,* Chicago, 33, 558–569. *(659)*

Jacobsen, E. (1967). *Biology of emotions.* Springfield, Ill.: Charles C Thomas. (*251*)

Jacobson, L. E. (1932). The electrophysiology of mental activities. *Amer. J. Psychol.,* 44, 677–694. (*153*)

James, W. (1890). *Principles of psychology.* New York: Holt, Rinehart and Winston. 2 vols. (*24, 232*)

Jameson, D., and Hurvich, L. M. (1964). Theory of brightness and color contrast in human vision. *Vision Res.,* 4, 135–154. (*265*)

Janis, I., and Feshbach, S. (1953). Effects of fear-arousing communications. *J. abnorm. soc. Psychol.,* 48, 78–92. (*530*)

Janis, I. L., Mahl, G. F., Kagan, J., and Holt, R. R. (1969). *Personality: Dynamics, development, and assessment.* New York: Harcourt, Brace, and World. (*383, 384, 397*)

Jasper, H. H. (1941). Electroencephalography. In W. Penfield and T. Erickson (Eds.), *Epilepsy and cerebral localization.* Springfield, Ill.: Charles C Thomas. (*584*)

Jellinek, E. M. (1952). Phases of alcohol addiction. *Quart. J. Stud. Alcohol.,* 13, 673–684. (*418*)

Jenkins, J. G., and Dallenbach, K. M. (1924). Oblivescence during sleep and waking. *Amer. J. Psychol.,* 35, 605–612. (*138*)

Jenkins, J. J., Russell, W. A., and Suci, G. J. (1958). An atlas of semantic profiles for 360 words. *Amer. J. Psychol., 71,* 688–699. (*163*)

Jenkins, W. D., McFann, H., and Clayton, F. L. (1950). A methodological study of extinction following a periodic and continuous reinforcement. *J. comp. physiol. Psychol.,* 43, 155–167. (*82*)

Jenkins, W. O. (1947). A review of leadership studies with particular reference to military problems. *Psychol. Bull.,* 44, 54–79. (*484*)

Jennings, M. K., and Niemi, R. G. (1968). The transmission of political values from parent to child. *Amer. polit. Sci. Rev.,* 62, 169–184. (*521*)

Jensen, A. R. (1969). How much can we boost IQ and scholastic achievement? *Harvard educ. Rev.,* 39, 1–123. (*60*)

Jersild, A. T., Markey, F. V., and Jersild, C. L. (1933). Children's fears, dreams, wishes, daydreams, likes, dislikes, pleasant and unpleasant memories. *Child Developm. Monogr.,* No. 12. (*242*)

Jessner, L., and Ryan, V. (1941). *Shock treatment in psychiatry.* New York: Grune & Stratton. (*440*)

Johnson, D. M. (1948). *Essentials of psychology.* New York: McGraw-Hill. (*157*)

Johnson, D. M. (1955). *The psychology of thought and judgment.* New York: Harper & Row. (*160*)

Jones, E. E. (1965). Conformity as a tactic of ingratiation. *Science.,* 149, 144–150. (*492*)

Jones, E. E. and Davis, K. E. (1965). From acts to dispositions: The attribution process in person perception. In L. Berkowitz (Ed.). *Advances in experimental social psychology.* Vol. 2. New York: Academic Press. (*504*)

Jones, E. E. and Gerard, H. B. (1967). *Foundations of social psychology.* New York: Wiley, 1967. (*507*)

Jones, H. E., and Conrad, H. S. (1933). The growth and decline of intelligence: A study of a homogeneous group between the ages ten and sixty. *Genet. Psychol. Monogr.,* 13, 223–298. (*342*)

Jones, K. L., Shainberg, L. W., and Byer, C. O. (1969). *Drugs and alcohol.* New York: Harper & Row. (*418, 675, 681*)

Jost, H., and Sontag, L. W. (1944). The genetic factor in autonomic nervous system function. *Psychosom. Med.,* 6, 308–310. (*54*)

Kagan, J. (1969). Inadequate evidence and illogical conclusions. *Harvard Educ. Rev.,* 39, 274–277. (*60*)

Kagan, J., and Berkun, M. (1954). The reward value of running activity. *J. comp. physiol. Psychol.,* 47, 108. (*197*)

Kallmann, F. J. (1951). Twin studies in relation to adjustive problems of man. *Trans. N. Y. Acad. Sci.,* 13, 270–275. (*54*)

Kallmann, F. J., and Jarvik, L. F. (1959). Individual differences in constitution and genetic background. In J. E. Birren (Ed.), *Handbook of aging and the* individual. Chicago: Univer. Chicago Press. Pp. 216–263. (*48*)

Kaplan, B. (Ed.) (1964). *The inner world of mental illness: A series of first-person accounts of what it was like.* New York: Harper & Row. (*433*)

Karlins, M., Coffman, T. L., and Walters, G. (1969). On the fading of social stereotypes: Studies in three generations of college students. *J. Pers. soc. Psychol.,* 13, 1–16. (*524*)

Katz, B. (1967). *Nerve, muscle and synapse.* New York: McGraw-Hill. (*603*)

Katz, D., and Braly, K. (1933). Racial stereotypes of one hundred college students. *J. abnorm. soc. Psychol.,* 28, 280–290. (*524*)

Katz, D., Maccoby, N., and Morse, N. C. (1950). *Productivity, supervision, and morale in an office situation.* Ann Arbor, Mich.: Survey Research Center. Part I. (*19*)

Katz, M. S., and Deterline, W. A. (1958). Apparent learning in the paramecium. *J. comp. physiol. Psychol.,* 51, 243–247. (*63*)

Kelleher, R. T., and Morse, W. H. (1968). Determinants of the specificity of behavioral effects of drugs. In R. Jung et al. (Eds.), *Reviews of physiology: Biochemistry and experimental pharmacology.* Berlin: Springer-Verlag, Pp. 1–56. (*679*)

Keller, F. S., and Schoenfeld, W. N. (1950). *Principles of psychology.* New York: Appleton-Century-Crofts. (*474*)

Kendler, H. H., and Kendler, T. S. (1962). Vertical and horizontal processes in problem solving. *Psychol. Rev.,* 69, 1–16. (*115*)

Kerckhoff, A. C., and Davis, K. E. (1962). Value consensus and need complementarity in mate selection. *Amer. sociol. Rev.*, 27, 295–303. (*500*)

Kiesler, C. A., Collins, B. E., and Miller, N. (1969). *Attitude change.* New York: Wiley. (*543*)

Kiesler, C. A., and Kiesler, S. B. (1969). *Conformity.* Reading, Mass.: Addison-Wesley. (*507*)

Kimble, G. A. (1961). *Hilgard and Marquis' conditioning and learning.* New York: Appleton-Century-Crofts. (*68, 107*)

Kimble, G. A. (1964). Categories of learning and the problem of definition. In A. W. Melton (Ed.), *Categories of human learning.* New York: Academic Press. (*110*)

Kimble, G. A. (1967). *Foundations of conditioning and learning.* New York: Appleton-Century-Crofts. (*72*)

Kimble, G. A., and Bilodeau, E. A. (1949). Work and rest as variables in cyclical motor learning. *J. exp. Psychol.*, 39, 150–157. (*120*)

Kimble, G. A., and Garmezy, N. (1968). *Principles of general psychology* (3d ed.). New York: Ronald. (*29, 70*)

King, F. A. (1958). Effects of septal and amygdaloid lesions on emotional behavior and conditioned emotional responses in the rat. *J. nerv. ment. Dis.*, 126, 57–63. (*671*)

King, J. A. (1958). Parameters relevant to determining the effects of early experience upon the adult behavior of animals. *Psychol. Bull.*, 55, 46–58. (*59*)

King, R. A. (1965). Consolidation of the neural trace in memory: Investigation with one-trial avoidance conditioning and ECS. *J. comp. physiol. Psychol.*, 59, 283–284. (*663, 664*)

King, R. A. (Ed.). (1971). *Readings for an introduction to psychology* (3d ed.). New York: McGraw-Hill. (*29, 107, 147, 251, 285, 653, 681*)

Kingsley, H. R., and Garry, R. (1957). *The nature and conditions of learning* (2d ed.). Englewood Cliffs, N.J.: Prentice-Hall. (*137*)

Kinsey, A. C., Pomeroy, W. B., and Martin, C. E. (1948). *Sexual behavior in the human male.* Philadelphia: Saunders. (*417, 479*)

Kirk, S. A. (1958). *Early education of the mentally retarded.* Urbana, Ill.: Univ. of Illinois Press. (*337*)

Kish, G. B. (1955). Learning when the onset of illumination is used as a reinforcing stimulus. *J. comp. physiol. Psychol.*, 48, 261–264. (*197*)

Kisker, G. W. (1964). *The disorganized personality.* New York: McGraw-Hill. (*336, 414, 416, 417, 419, 421, 423, 430, 433*)

Kitt, A., and Gleicher, D. B. (1950). Determinants of voting behavior: A progress report on the Elmira election study. *Publ. Opin. Quart.*, 14, 393–412. (*527, 529*)

Kline, L. W., and Johannsen, D. E. (1935). Comparative role of the face and of the face-body-hands as aids in identifying emotions. *J. abnorm. soc. Psychol.*, 29, 415–426. (*239*)

Klineberg, O. (1935). *Negro intelligence and selective migration.* New York: Columbia Univer. Press. (*344*)

Klineberg, O. (1954). *Social psychology* (rev. ed.). New York: Holt, Rinehart and Winston. (*240*)

Klopfer, P. A., and Hailman, J. P. (1967). *An introduction to animal behavior: Ethology's first century.* Englewood-Cliffs, N.J.: Prentice-Hall. (*61*)

Klüver, H. (1942). Visual mechanisms. In *Biological symposia.* Vol. VII. New York: Ronald. (*628*)

Klüver, H., and Bucy, P. C. (1937). "Psychic blindness" and other symptoms following bilateral temporal lobectomy in rhesus monkeys. *Amer. J. Physiol.*, 119, 352–353. (*659*)

Koch, S. (1951). The current status of motivational psychology. *Psychol. Rev.*, 58, 147–154. (*26*)

Koch, S. (1969). Psychology cannot be a coherent science. *Psychology Today,* 3. (*2*)

Koffka, K. (1935). *Principles of Gestalt psychology.* New York: Harcourt, Brace & World. (*26, 259*)

Kohler, I. (1951). Über Aufbau und Wandlungen der Wahrnehmungswelt: Insbesondere über "bedingte Empfindungen." *Osterreichische Akademie der Wissenschaften, Sitzungberichte,* 227, No. 1. (*276*)

Kohler, I. (1962). Experiments with goggles. *Sci Amer.*, 206 (5), 63–72. (*275*)

Kohler, I. (1964). The formation and transformation of the perceptual world (trans. H. Fiss). *Psychological Issues,* 3, Monograph 12. (*276*)

Köhler, W. (1925). *The mentality of apes* (trans. E. Winter). New York: Harcourt, Brace & World. (*101*)

Köhler, W. (1947). *Gestalt psychology* (rev. ed.). New York: Liveright. (*26*)

Köhler, W., and Wallach, H. (1944). Figural aftereffects: An investigation of visual processes. *Proc. Amer. philos. Soc.*, 88, 269–357. (*274*)

König, J. F. R., and Klippel, R. A. (1963). *The rat brain: A stereotaxic atlas of the forebrain and lower parts of the brain stem.* Baltimore: Williams and Wilkins. (*665*)

Korte, A. (1915). Kinematoskopische Untersuchungen. *Z. Psychol.*, 72, 193–206; 271–296. (*271*)

Krech, D., Crutchfield, R. S., and Ballachey, E. L. (1962). *Individual in society: A textbook of social psychology.* New York: McGraw-Hill. (*475, 479, 511, 543*)

Krech, D., Crutchfield, R. S., and Livson, N. (1969). *Elements of psychology* (2d ed.). New York: Knopf. (*47*)

Krech, D., Rosenzweig, M. R., and Bennett, E. L. (1962). Relations between brain chemistry and problem-solving among rats raised in enriched and impoverished environments. *J. comp. physiol. Psychol.*, 55, 801–807. (*580*)

Kris, E. (1950). On preconscious mental processes. *Psychoanal. Quart.*, 19, 540–560. (*395*)

Krueger, W. C. F. (1929). The effect of overlearning on retention. *J. exp. Psychol.*, 12, 71–78. (*137*)

Kuffler, S. W. (1953). Discharge patterns and functional organization of mammalian retina. *J. Neurophysiol.*, 16, 37–68. (*621*)

Kuo, Z. (1967). *The dynamics of behavior development: An epigenetic view.* New York: Random House. (*56*)

Kutash, S. B. (1965). Psychoneuroses. In B. B. Wolman (Ed.), *Handbook of Clinical Psychology.* New York: McGraw-Hill. Pp. 948–975. (*414*)

Lacey, J. I. (1967). Somatic response patterning and stress: Some revisions of activation theory. In M. H. Appley, and R. Trumbull (Eds.), *Psychological stress.* New York: Appleton-Century-Crofts. (*231, 232*)

Lambert, W. W., Solomon, R. L., and Watson, P. D. (1949). Reinforcement and extinction as factors in size estimation. *J. exp. Psychol.*, 39, 637–641. (*282*)

Landis, C., and Hunt, W. A. (1939). *The startle pattern.* New York: Holt, Rinehart and Winston. (*238*)

LaPlace, J. P. (1954). Personality and its relationship to success in professional baseball. *Res. Quart.*, 25, 313—319. (*355*)

Larsson, K. and Heimer, L. (1964). Mating behavior of male rats after lesions in the preoptic area. *Nature*, 202, 413–414. (*668*)

Lashley, K. S. (1924). Studies of cerebral function in learning. V. The retention of motor habits after destruction of the so-called motor area in primates. *Arch. Neurol. Psychiat.*, Chicago, 12, 249–276. (*98*)

Lashley, K. S. (1929). *Brain mechanisms and intelligence.* Chicago: Univer. Chicago Press. (*99, 657*)

Lashley, K. S. (1950). In search of the engram. *Symp. soc. exp. Biol.* Vol. IV. London: Cambridge Univer. Press. Pp. 454–482. (*66*)

Lashley, K. S. (1951). The problem of serial order in behavior. In L. A. Jeffress (Ed.), *Cerebral mechanisms in behavior.* New York: Wiley. (*67*)

Latané, B., and Darley, J. M. (1969). Bystander "Apathy." *Amer. Scientist*, 57, 244–268. (*498*)

Lawrence, D. H., De Rivera, J. (1954). Evidence for relational transposition. *J. comp. physiol. Psychol.*, 47, 475–481. (*274*)

Laycock, F., and Caylor, J. S. (1964). Physiques of gifted children and their less gifted siblings. *Child Developm.*, 35, 63–74. (*338*)

Lazarus, R. S. (1966). *Psychological stress and the coping process.* New York: McGraw-Hill. (*251*)

Leavitt, H. J. (1962). Unhuman organizations. *Harvard Bus. Rev.*, 40, 90–98. (*545*)

Leavitt, H. J. (1964). *Managerial psychology.* (2d ed.). Chicago: Univer. Chicago Press. (*554, 575*)

LeCron, L. M., and Bordeaux, J. (1947). *Hypnotism today.* New York: Grune & Stratton. (*452*)

Lee, E. S. (1951). Negro intelligence and selective migration: A Philadelphia test of the Klineberg hypothesis. *Amer. sociol. Rev.*, 16, 227–233. (*344*)

Lehrman, D. S. (1953). A critique of Konrad Lorenz's theory of instinctive behaviour. *Quart. Rev. Biol.*, 28, 337–363. (*34*)

Lehrman, D. S. (1961). Hormonal regulation of parental behavior in birds and infrahuman mammals. In W. C. Young (Ed.), *Sex and internal secretion* (3d ed.). Baltimore: William and Wilkins. (*194*)

Lemkau, P. V., and Crocetti, G. M. (1958). Vital statistics of schizophrenia. In L. Bellak (Ed.), *Schizophrenia: A review of the syndrome.* New York: Logos. (*424*)

Lenneberg, E. H. (1967). *Biological foundations of language.* New York: Wiley. (*179*)

Lenneberg, E. H. (1969). On explaining language. *Science*, 164, 635–643. (*42*)

Leonard, W. E. (1927). *The locomotive god.* New York: Appleton-Century-Crofts. (*408*)

Leventhal, H., Singer, R., and Jones, S. (1965). Effects of fear and specificity of recommendation upon attitudes and behavior. *J. Pers. soc. Psychol.*, 2, 20–29. (*531*)

Lewin, K. (1935). *A dynamic theory of personality* (trans. D. K. Adams and K. Zener). New York: McGraw-Hill. (*246*)

Lewin, K. (1951). *Field theory in social science: Selected theoretical papers.* (D. Cartwright, ed.). New York: Harper & Row, 1951. (*481*)

Liddell, H. S., James, W. T., and Anderson, O. D. (1934). The comparative physiology of the conditioned motor reflex. *Comp. Psychol. Monogr.*, 11 (Whole No. 51). (*71*)

Lidz, T., and Fleck, S. (1960). Schizophrenia, human integration, and the role of the family. In D. Jackson (Ed.), *The etiology of schizophrenia.* New York: Basic Books. (*427*)

Lindahl, L. G. (1945). Movement analysis as an industrial training method. *J. appl. Psychol.*, 29, 420–436. (*562*)

Lindesmith, A. R. (1968). *Addiction and opiates.* Chicago: Aldine. (*675*)

Lindsley, D. B. (1958). The reticular system and perceptual discrimination. In H. Jasper et al. (Eds.), *Reticular formation of the brain.* Boston: Little, Brown. (*600*)

Lindsley, D. B., Bowden, J. W., and Magoun, H. W. (1950). Behaviorial and EEG changes following chronic brain lesions in the cat. *EEG clin. Neurophysiol.*, 2, 483–498. (*670*)

Lindzey, G., and Kalnins, D. (1958). Thematic Apperception Test: Some evidence bearing on the "hero assumption." *J. abnorm. soc. Psychol.*, 57, 76–83. (*217*)

Lindzey, G., and Hall, C. S. (1965). *Theories of personality: Primary sources and research.* New York: Wiley. (*397*)

Lingeman, R. R. (1969). *Drugs from A to Z: A dictionary.* New York: McGraw-Hill. (*675, 681*)

Linton, R. (1945). *The cultural background of personality.* New York: Appleton-Century-Crofts. (*474*)

Lockman, R. F. (1964). An empirical description of the subfields of psychology. *Amer. Psychol.,* 19, 645–653. *(4, 5)*

Logan, F. A. (1959). The Hull-Spence approach. In S. Koch (Ed.), *Psychology: A study of a science,* Vol. II. New York: McGraw-Hill. *(104)*

Lorente de Nó, R. (1938). Analysis of the activity of the chains of internuncial neurons. *J. Neurophysiol.,* 1, 207–244. *(591)*

Lorenz, K. (1965). *Evolution and Modification of Behavior.* Chicago: The University of Chicago Press. *(34)*

Lorge, I. (1930). Influence of regularly interpolated time intervals upon subsequent learning. *Teach. Coll., Columbia Univer. Contr. Educ.* (Whole No. 438). *(120)*

Lovaas, O. I. (1968). Some studies on the treatment of childhood schizophrenia. In J. M. Shlien (Ed.), *Research in psychotherapy.* Washington, D.C.: American Psychological Association. Pp. 103–129. *(464)*

Lowell, E. L. (1952). The effect of need for achievement on learning and speed of performance. *J. Psychol.,* 33, 31–40. *(211)*

Lowenstein, O. (1966). *The senses.* Baltimore: Penguin. *(653)*

Luchins, A. (1954). Mechanization in problem solving: The effect of Einstellung. *Psychol. Monogr.,* 54 (Whole No. 6). *(165)*

Lundin, R. W. (1969). *Personality: A behavioral analysis.* New York: Macmillan. *(397)*

Lyman, H. B. (1963). *Test scores and what they mean.* Englewood Cliffs, N.J.: Prentice-Hall. *(361)*

McCarthy, D. A. (1946). Language development in children. In L. Carmichael (Ed.), *Manual of child psychology.* New York: Wiley. Pp. 476–581. *(175)*

McCleary, R. A. (1961). Response specificity in the behavioral effects of limbic system lesions in the cat. *J. comp. physiol. Psychol.,* 54, 605–613. *(658)*

McClelland, D. C., Rindlisbacher, A., and DeCharms, R. (1955). Religious and other sources of parental attitudes toward independence training. In D. C. McClelland (Ed.), *Studies in motivation.* New York: Appleton-Century-Crofts. *(214)*

McClelland, D. C., Atkinson, J. W., Clark, R. A., and Lowell, E. L. (1953). *The achievement motive.* New York: Appleton-Century-Crofts. *(210, 211, 215, 227)*

McCollough, C., and Van Atta, L. (1963). *Statistical concepts: A program for self instruction.* New York: McGraw-Hill. *(317)*

McCormick, E. J. (1964). *Human engineering* (2d ed.). New York: McGraw-Hill. *(575)*

McCurdy, H. G. (1961). *The personal world.* New York: Harcourt, Brace & World. *(397)*

McGaugh, J. L., Weinberger, N. M., and Whalen, R. E. (Eds.). (1966). *Psychobiology: The biological bases of behavior.* San Francisco: Freeman. *(603, 681)*

McGaugh, J. L., and Herz, M. J. (1970). Controversial issues in consolidation of the memory trace. Unpublished manuscript. *(664)*

McGeoch, J. A. and Irion, A. L. (1952). *The psychology of human learning.* (2d ed.). New York: Longmans, Green. *(70, 123, 130, 138, 139)*

McGrath, J. E. (1964). *Social psychology: A brief introduction.* New York: Holt, Rinehart and Winston. *(473, 477, 481, 528, 543)*

McGregor, D. (1960). *The human side of enterprise.* New York: McGraw-Hill. *(548, 551, 552)*

McGregor, D. (1967). *The professional manager.* New York: McGraw-Hill. *(575)*

McGuire, W. J. (1961). Resistance to persuasion conferred by active and passive prior refutation of the same and alternative counterarguments. *J. abnorm. soc. Psychol.,* 63, 325–332. *(535)*

McGuire, W. J. (1968). The nature of attitudes and attitude change. In G. Lindzey and E. Aronson (Eds.), *The handbook of social psychology* (2d ed.), Vol. III. Reading, Mass.: Addison-Wesley. *(511, 527, 529, 531, 533, 543)*

McGurk, F. C. J. (1951). Comparison of the performance of Negro and white high school seniors on cultural and non-cultural test questions. Washington, D.C.: Catholic Univer. Amer. Press. (Microcard). *(345)*

McGurk, F. C. J. (1953). On white and Negro test performance and socioeconomic factors. *J. abnorm. soc. Psychol.,* 48, 448–450. *(345)*

McNemar, Q. (1942). *The revision of the Stanford-Binet scale.* Boston: Houghton Mifflin. *(51, 340)*

McNemar, Q. (1964). Lost: Our Intelligence? Why? *Amer. Psychologist,* 19, 871–882. *(350)*

McNemar, Q. (1969). *Psychological statistics* (4th ed.). New York: Wiley. *(317)*

Macfarlane, D. A. (1930). The role of kinesthesis in maze learning. *Calif. Univer. Publ. Psychol.,* 4, 277–305. *(98)*

Mackworth, N. H. (1950). *Researches on the measurement of human performance.* London: Medical Research Council Report. No. 268. *(566)*

MacLean, P. D. (1949). Psychosomatic disease and the "visceral brain." Recent developments bearing on the Papez theory of emotion. *Psychosom. Med.,* 11, 338–353. *(601, 602, 671)*

MacNichol, E. F., Jr. (1964). Three-pigment color vision. *Sci. Amer.,* 211 (6), 48–56. *(619)*

Mandler, G. (1967). Organization and memory. In K. W. Spence and J. T. Spence (Eds.), *The psychology of learning and motivation.* New York: Academic Press. Pp. 327–372. *(127, 144)*

Manzer, C. W. (1927). An experimental investigation of rest pauses. *Arch. Psychol.,* 14 (Whole No. 90). *(567)*

Martin, E. (1965). Transfer of verbal paired associates. *Psych. Rev.,* 72, 327–343. *(130)*

Maslow, A. H. (1954). *Motivation and personality.* New York: Harper & Row. *(392)*

Maslow, A. H. (1968). *Toward a psychology of being.* (2d ed.). Princeton, N.J.: Van Nostrand. (*546*)

Masserman, J. H. (1946). *Principles of dynamic psychiatry.* Philadelphia: Saunders. (*376*)

Masserman, J. H. (1961). *Principles of dynamic psychiatry.* (2d ed.). Philadelphia: Saunders. (*410*)

Masterton, B., and Diamond, I. T. (1964). Effects of auditory cortex ablation on discrimination of small binaural time differences. *J. Neurophysiol.,* 27, 15–36. (*637*)

Masterton, B., Jane, J. A., and Diamond, I. T. (1967). Role of brainstem auditory structures in sound localization. I. Trapezoid body, superior olive, and lateral leminscus. *J. Neurophysiol.,* 30, 341–359. (*637*)

Mausner, B. (1954). The effect of one partner's success in a relevant task on the interaction of observer pairs. *J. abnorm. soc. Psychol.,* 49, 557–560. (*485*)

Max, L. W. (1937). Experimental study of the motor theory of consciousness. IV. Action-current responses in the deaf during awakening, kinesthetic imagery and abstract thinking. *J. comp. Psychol.,* 24, 301–344. (*153*)

Mechanic, A. (1962). The distribution of recalled items in simultaneous intentional and incidental learning. *J. exp. Psychol.,* 63, 593–600. (*114*)

Meehl, P. E. (1962). Schizotaxia, schizotypy, schizophrenia. *Amer. Psychologist,* 17, 827–838. (*428*)

Melton, A. W. (Ed.). (1964). *Categories of human learning.* New York: Academic Press. (*109, 147*)

Merbaum, A. D. (1961). Need for achievement in Negro and white children. Unpublished doctoral dissertation, Univer. North Carolina, Chapel Hill, N.C. (*346*)

Mettler, F. A. (Ed.) (1949). *Selective partial ablation of the frontal cortex.* New York: Hoeber-Harper. (*440*)

Middleton, R., and Putney, S. (1964). Influences on the political beliefs of American college students: A study of self-appraisals. *Il Politico,* 29, 484–492. (*525*)

Milgram, S. (1963). Behavioral study of obedience. *J. of Abnorm. soc. Psychol., 67,* 371–378. (*489*)

Milgram, S. (1970). The experience of living in cities. *Science,* 167, 1461–1468. (*499*)

Miller, G. A. (1956). Human memory and the storage of information. *IRE Trans. Inform. Theory,* IT–2, 129–137(a). (*146*)

Miller, G. A. (1956). The magical number seven, plus or minus two: Some limits on our capacity for processing information. *Psychol. Rev.,* 63, 81–97(b). (*134*)

Miller, G. A. (1965). Some preliminaries to psycholinguistics. *Amer. Psychologist,* 20, 15–20. (*153*)

Miller, N. E. (1948). Studies of fear as an acquirable drive. I. Fear as motivation and fear-reduction as reinforcement in the learning of new responses. *J. exp. Psychol.,* 38, 89–101(a). (*205*)

Miller, N. E. (1948). Theory and experiment relating psychoanalytic displacement to stimulus-response generalization. *J. abnorm. soc. Psychol.,* 43, 155–178(b). (*377*)

Miller, N. E. (1961). Analytic studies of drive and reward. *Amer. Psychologist,* 16, 739–754. (*105*)

Miller, N. E. (1969). Learning of visceral and glandular responses. *Science,* 163, 434–445. (*85*)

Miller, N. E., and Bugelski, R. (1948). Minor studies of aggression: II. The influence of frustration imposed by the in-group on attitudes expressed toward out-groups. *J. Psychol.,* 25, 437–442. (*539*)

Miller, N. E., and Banuazizi, A. (1968). Instrumental learning by curarized rats of a specific visceral response, intestinal or cardiac. *J. comp. physiol. Psychol.,* 65, 1–7. (*87*)

Millikan, G. A. (1948). Anoxia and oxygen equipment. In E. C. Andrus (Ed.), *Advances in military medicine,* Vol. 1, Chap. 24. Boston: Little, Brown. (*14*)

Milner, B. (1954). Intellectual function of the temporal lobes. *Psychol. Bull.,* 51, 42–62. (*659*)

Milner, B. (1959). The memory deficit in bilateral hippocampal lesions. *Psychiat. Res. Reps.,* 11, 43–52. (*659*)

Milner, B. (1964). Some effects of frontal lobectomy in man. In J. M. Warren and K. Akert (Eds.), *The frontal granular cortex and behavior.* New York: McGraw-Hill. Pp. 313–334. (*660*)

Milner, P. M. (1957). The cell assembly: Mark II. *Psychol. Rev.,* 64, 242–252. (*282*)

Minami, H., and Dallenbach, K. M. (1946). The effect of activity upon learning and retention in the cockroach. *Amer. J. Psychol.,* 59, 1–58. (*139*)

Mischel, W. (1968). *Personality and assessment.* New York: Wiley. (*361*)

Mishkin, M. (1957). Effects of small frontal lesions on delayed alternation in monkeys. *J. Neurophysiol.,* 20, 615–622. (*659*)

Mishkin, M., and Pribram, K. H. (1956). Analysis of the effects of frontal lesions in monkey: II. Variations of delayed response. *J. comp. physiol. Psychol.,* 49, 36–40. (*660*)

Monroe, R. L. (1955). *Schools of psychoanalytic thought.* New York: Holt, Rinehart and Winston. (*394*)

Moreno, J. L. (1946). *Psychodrama.* New York: Beacon House. (*458*)

Moreno, J. L. (1953). *Who shall survive? Foundations of sociometry, group psychotherapy, and sociodrama.* (2d ed.) Beacon, N.Y.: Beacon House. (*555*)

Morgan, C. T. (1965). *Physiological psychology* (3d ed.). New York: McGraw-Hill. (*221, 594, 603, 618, 658, 681*)

Morgan, C. T., Garner, W. R., and Galambos, R. (1951). Pitch and intensity. *Acoust. Soc. Amer.,* 23, 658–663. (*638*)

Morgan, C. T., Cook, J. S., III, Chapanis, A., and Lund, M. W. (Eds.). (1963). *Human engineering guide to equipment design.* New York: McGraw-Hill. (*571, 573*)

Morgan, C. T., and Deese, J. (1969). *How to study* (rev. ed.). New York: McGraw-Hill. (*123, 147*)

Morphett, M. V., and Washburn, C. (1931). When should children begin to read? *Elem. Sch. J.*, 31, 496–503. (*43*)

Moruzzi, G., and Magoun, H. W. (1949). Brain stem reticular formation and activation of the EEG. *EEG clin. Neurophysiol.*, 1, 455–473. (*670*)

Moulton, R. W. (1958). Notes for a projective measure of fear of failure. In J. W. Atkinson (Ed.), *Motives in fantasy, action and society*. New York: Van Nostrand. (*212*)

Mowrer, O. H. (1960). *Learning theory and the symbolic process.* New York: Wiley. (*179*)

Mueller, C. G. (1965). *Sensory psychology.* Englewood Cliffs, N.J.: Prentice-Hall. (*653*)

Mueller, C. G., and Rudolph, M. (Eds.) (1966). *Light and vision.* New York: Time Incorporated. (*653*)

Müller, J. (1838). *Handbuch der Physiologie des Menschen.* Coblentz: Hölscher. (*606*)

Munn, N. L. (1955). *The evolution and growth of human behavior.* Boston: Houghton Mifflin. (*61*)

Murray, E. J. (1964). *Motivation and emotion.* Englewood Cliffs, N.J.: Prentice-Hall. (*221*)

Murray, H. A. (1938). *Explorations in personality.* New York: Oxford Univer. Press. (*368, 369, 392*)

Murray, H. A. (1943). *Thematic apperception test.* Cambridge, Mass.: Harvard Univer. Press. (*358, 359*)

Mussen, P. H. (1963). *The psychological development of the child.* Englewood Cliffs, N.J.: Prentice-Hall. (*181*)

Mussen, P. H., Conger, J. J., and Kagan, J. (1968). *Child development and personality* (3d ed.). New York: Harper & Row. (*61, 397*)

Myers, R. E. (1955). Interocular transfer of pattern discrimination in cats following section of crossed optic fibers. *J. comp. physiol. Psychol.*, 48, 470–473. (*657*)

Myers, R. E. (1956). Function of the corpus callosum in interocular transfer. *Brain.*, 79, 358–363. (*657*)

Nauta, W. J. H. (1946). Hypothalamic regulation of sleep in rats: An experimental study. *J. Neurophysiol.*, 9, 285–316. (*669*)

Nealey, S. M., and Edwards, B. J. (1960). "Depth perception" in rats without pattern-vision experience. *J. comp. physiol. Psychol.*, 53, 468–469. (*279*)

Neisser, U. (1967). *Cognitive psychology.* New York: Appleton-Century-Crofts. (*150*)

Netter, F. H. *Ciba collection of medical illustrations.* Vol. I. New York: Ciba, 1962. (*603, 634*)

Newcomb, T. M. (1943). *Personality and social change.* New York: Dryden. (*521*)

Newcomb, T. M. (1961). *The acquaintance process.* New York: Holt, Rinehart and Winston. (*528*)

Newcomb, T. M. (1963). Persistence and regression of changed attitudes: long range studies. *J. soc. Issues,* 19, 3–14. (*523*)

Newcomb, T. M., Turner, R. H., and Converse, P. E. (1965). *Social psychology.* New York: Holt, Rinehart and Winston. (*537, 543*)

Newman, H. H., Freeman, F. N., and Holzinger, K. J. (1937). *Twins: A study of heredity and environment.* Chicago: Univer. Chicago Press. (*51, 52*)

Nissen, H. W., Chow, K. L., and Semmes, J. (1951). Effects of a restricted opportunity for tactual, kinesthetic, and manipulative experience on the behavior of a chimpanzee. *Amer. J. Psychol.*, 64, 485–507. (*281*)

Noble, C. E. (1952). An analysis of meaning. *Psychol. Rev.*, 59, 421–430(a). (*126*)

Noble, C. E. (1952). The role of stimulus meaning (*m*) in serial verbal learning. *J. exp. Psychol.*, 43, 437–466(b). (*126*)

Olds, J. (1969). The central nervous system and the reinforcement of behavior. *Amer. Psychologist*, 24, 114–132 (*583*)

Olds, J., and Milner, P. (1954). Positive reinforcement produced by electrical stimulation of septal area and other regions of rat brain. *J. comp. physiol. Psychol.*, 47, 419–427. (*586*)

Olds, M. E., and Olds, J. (1963). Approach-avoidance analysis of rat diencephalon. *J. Comp. Neurol.*, 120, 259–295. (*586*)

Olson, G., and King, R. A. (1962). Supplementary report: Stimulus generalization gradients along a luminosity continuum. *J. exp. Psychol.*, 63, 414–415. (*84, 85*)

Orr, D. W. (1949). Psychiatric uses of sodium pentothal. *U.S. Nav. med. Bull.*, 49, 508–516. (*441*)

Osgood, C E., Suci, G. J., and Tannenbaum, P. H. (1957). *The measurement of meaning.* Urbana, Ill.: Univer. Illinois Press. (*156, 159, 163*)

Østerberg, G. (1935). Topography of the layer of rods and cones in the human retina. *Acta ophthal., Suppl.* (Whole No. 6). (*615*)

Papez, J. W. (1937). A proposed mechanism of emotion. *Arch. Neurol Psychiat.*, Chicago, 38, 725–743. (*671*)

Pavlov, I. P. (1927). *Conditioned reflexes* (trans. G. V. Anrep). London: Oxford Univer. Press. (*69*)

Pavlov, I. P. (1928). *Lectures on conditioned reflexes* (trans. W. H. Gantt). New York: International. (*69*)

Pavlov, I. P. (1960). *Conditioned reflexes.* New York: Dover. A reprint of: Pavlov, I. P. *Conditioned Reflexes* (trans. G. V. Anrep). London: Oxford Univer. Press, 1927. (*69, 107*)

Penfield, W., and Rasmussen, T. (1950). *The cerebral cortex of man.* New York: Macmillan. (586)

Penfield, W., and Roberts, L. (1959). *Speech and brain-mechanisms.* Princeton, N.J.: Princeton Univer. Press. (*599, 661, 662, 663*)

Perin, C. T. (1942). Behavior potentiality as a joint function of the amount of training and the degree of hunger at the time of extinction. *J. exp. Psychol.*, 30, 93–113. (*104, 105*)

Peterson, L. R., and Peterson, M. J. (1959). Short-term retention of individual verbal items. *J. exp. Psychol.*, 58, 193–198. (*133*)

Pfaffmann, C. (1959). The afferent code for sensory quality. *Amer. Psychologist*, 14, 226–232. (*608*)

Pfaffmann, C. (1964). Taste, its sensory and motivating properties. *Amer. Sci.*, 52, 187–206. (*68, 105, 645*)

Piaget, Jean (1952). *The child's conception of number.* New York: Humanities Press. (*181*)

Poincaré, H. (1913). Mathematical creation. In *The foundations of science* (trans. G. H. Halsted). New York: Science Press. Pp. 383–394. (*169*)

Polyak, S. (1957). *The vertebrate visual system.* Chicago: University of Chicago Press. (*616*)

Postman, Leo. (1964). Short-term memory and incidental learning. In A. W. Melton (Ed.), *Categories of human learning.* New York: Academic Press. Pp. 146–201. (*114, 119*)

Postman, L., and Phillips, L. W. (1954). Studies in incidental learning. I. The effects of crowding and isolation. *J. exp. Psychol.*, 48–56. (*126*)

Premack, D. (1965). Reinforcement theory. In D. Levine (Ed.), *Nebraska symposium on motivation: 1965.* Lincoln, Nebr.: University of Nebraska Press. Pp. 123–180. (*105, 462*)

Pribram, K. H. (1958). Neocortical function in behavior. In H. F. Harlow and C. N. Woolsey (Eds.), *Biological and biochemical bases of behavior.* Madison Wis.: Univer. Wisconsin Press. Pp. 151–172. (*600*)

Pribram, K. H. (1969). The amnestic syndromes: Disturbances in coding? In G. A. Talland and N. C. Waugh (Eds.), *The pathology of memory.* New York: Academic. Pp. 127–157. (*658, 659, 660*)

Psychology Today. Del Mar, Calif.: Communications/Research/Machines, Inc. (*29*)

Rabinovitch, M. S., and Rosvold, H. E. (1951). A closed-field intelligence test for rats. *Canad. J. Psychol.*, 5, 122–128. (*49*)

Rabkin, L. Y., and Carr, J. (Eds.) (1967). *Sourcebook in abnormal psychology.* Boston: Houghton Mifflin. (*433*)

Ranson, S. W. (1939). Somnolence caused by hypothalamic lesions in the monkey, *Arch. Neurol. Psychiat.*, Chicago, 41, 1–23. (*669*)

Ranson, S. W., and Clark, S. L. (1959). *The anatomy of the nervous system: Its development and function* (10th ed.). Philadelphia, Pa.: Saunders. (*596*)

Raven, B., and French, J. R. P. (1958). Group support, legitimate power, and social influence. *J. Pers.*, 26, 400–409. (*485*)

Ratliff, F. (1965). *Mach bands: Quantitative studies on neural networks in the retina.* San Francisco: Holden-Day. (*255*)

Ray, W. S. (1967). *The experimental psychology of original thinking.* New York: Macmillan. (*185*)

Raymond, M. J. (1956). Case of fetishism treated by aversion therapy. *Brit. med. J.*, 2, 854–857. (*460*)

Reeves, J. W. (1965). *Thinking about thinking.* New York: Braziller. (*185*)

Rethlingshafer, D. (1963). *Motivation as related to personality.* New York: McGraw-Hill. (*221*)

Reynolds, R. W. (1965). An irritative hypothesis concerning the hypothalamic regulation of food intake. *Psychol. Rev.*, 72, 105–116. (*667*)

Reynolds, W. F. (1958). Acquisition and extinction of the conditioned eyelid response following partial and continuous reinforcement. *J. exp. Psychol.*, 55, 335–341. (*82*)

Rheingold, H. L., Gewirtz, J. J., and Ross, H. W. (1959). Social conditioning of vocalizations in the infant. *Journal of Comparative and Physiological Psychology*, 52, 68–73. (*180*)

Richter, C. P. (1927). Animal behavior and internal drives. *Quart. Rev. Biol.*, 2, 307–343. (*196*)

Richter, C. P. (1942–1943). Total self-regulatory functions in animals and human beings. *Harvey Lect.*, 38, 63–103. (*196*)

Richter, C. P. (1943). Total self-regulatory functions in animals and human beings. *Harvey Lect.*, 38, 63–103. (*190*)

Riesen, A. H. (1960). Statement in Appendix. In M. Von Senden, *Space and sight* (trans. P. Heath). New York: Free Press. Pp. 313–316. (*280*)

Riesen, A. H. (1961). Stimulation as a requirement for growth and function in behavioral development. In D. W. Fiske and S. R. Maddi (Eds.), *Functions of varied experience.* Homewood, Ill.: Dorsey. Pp. 57–80. (*280*)

Riggs, L. A., Ratliff, F., Cornsweet, J. C., and Cornsweet, T. (1953). The disappearance of steadily fixated visual test objects. *J. opt. soc. Amer.*, 43, 495–501. (*614*)

Robinson, E. S. (1927). The "similarity" factor in retroaction. *Amer. J. Psychol.*, 39, 297–312. (139)

Robinson, E. S., and Bills, A. G. (1926). Two factors in work decrement. *J. exp. Psychol.*, 9, 415–443. (*566*)

Robinson, H. B., and Robinson, N. M. (1965). *The mentally retarded child: A psychological approach.* New York: McGraw-Hill. (*335, 361*)

Roethlisberger, F. J., and Dickson, W. J. (1939). *Management and the worker.* Cambridge, Mass.: Harvard Univer. Press. (*549*)

Rogers, C. R. (1951). *Client-centered therapy: Its current practice, implications, and theory.* Boston: Houghton Mifflin. (*448*)

Rogers, C. R. (1961). *On becoming a person: A therapist's view of psychotherapy.* Boston: Houghton Mifflin. (*469*)

Rogers, C. R. (1967). The process of the basic encounter group. In J. F. T. Bugental (Ed.). *Challenges in humanistic psychology.* New York: McGraw-Hill. (*456*)

Rokeach, M. (1968). *Beliefs, attitudes, and values.* San Francisco: Jossey-Bass. (*509*)

Rorschach, H. (1942). *Psychodiagnostics.* Berne: Huber. (Reprint). (*359*)

Rose, A. M. (1946). Army policies toward Negro soldiers. *Ann. Amer. Acad. pol. soc. Sci.,* 244, 90–94. (*537*)

Rose, J. E., and Woolsey, C. N. (1949). Organization of the mammalian thalamus and its relationships to the cerebral cortex. *EEG clin. Neurophysiol.,* 1, 391–404. (*600*)

Rosen, B. (1956). The achievement syndrome: A psychocultural dimension of social stratification. *Amer. soc. Rev.,* 21, 203–211. (*480*)

Rosenthal, D. and Kety, S. S. (Eds.) (1968). *The transmission of schizophrenia.* Long Island City, N.Y.: Pergamon. (*54*)

Rosenthal, R. (1964). Experimenter outcome-orientation and the results of the psychological experiment. *Psych. Bull.,* 61, 405–412. (*15*)

Rosenzweig, M. R. (1966). Environmental complexity, cerebral change, and behavior. *Amer. Psychologist,* 21, 321–332 (*580, 581*)

Rotter, J. B. (1964). *Clinical psychology.* Englewood Cliffs, N.J.: Prentice-Hall. (*469*)

Rozin, P. (1967). Specific aversions as a component of specific hungers. *J. comp. physiol. Psychol.,* 64, 237–242. (*191*)

Rubin, E. (1921). *Visuell wahrgenommene Figuren.* Copenhagen: Gyldendalske. (*260*)

Ruch, T. C., Fulton, J. F., and German, W. J. (1938). Sensory discrimination in the monkey, chimpanzee, and man after lesions of the parietal lobe. *Arch. Neurol. Psychiat.,* Chicago, 39, 919–937. (*661*)

Ruch, T. C. and Patton, H. D. (Eds.) (1965). *Physiology and biophysics* (19th ed.). Philadelphia: Saunders. (*589, 593, 657*)

Sarason, I. G. *Personality: An objective approach.* New York: Wiley, 1966. (*397*)

Sargent, S. S. (1939). Emotional stereotypes in the *Chicago Tribune. Sociometry,* 2, 69–75. (*531, 532*)

Schachter, S. (1959). *The psychology of affiliation: Experimental studies of the sources of gregariousness.* Stanford, Calif.: Stanford Univer. Press. (*215*)

Schachter, S., and Singer, J. (1962). Cognitive, social and physiological determinants of emotional state. *Psych. Rev.,* 69, 379–399. (*232, 233, 490*)

Schein, E. H. (1964). *Organizational psychology.* Englewood Cliffs, N.J.: Prentice-Hall. (*545, 550, 575*)

Schein, E. H., with Schneier, I., and Barker, G. H. (1961). *Coercive persuasion: A socio-psychological analysis of the "brainwashing" of American prisoners by the Chinese communists.* New York: Norton. (*529*)

Schenkel, R. (1948). Ausdrucks-Studien an Wölfen: Gefangenschafts Beobachtungen. *Behaviour,* 1, 81–129. (*37*)

Schjelderup-Ebbe, T. (1935). Social behavior of birds. In C. Murchison (Ed.), *Handbook of social psychology.* Worcester, Mass.: Clark Univer. Press. Pp. 947–972. (*217*)

Schlosberg, H. (1954). Three dimensions of emotion. *Psychol. Rev.,* 61, 81–88. (*227, 239*)

Schopler, J., and Insko, C. A. (1971). *Experimental social psychology: Readings and commentary.* New York: Academic Press. (*507*)

Scott, J. P. (1958). *Animal behavior.* Chicago: Univer. Chicago Press. (*53*)

Sears, D. O. (1969). Political behavior. In G. Lindzey and E. Aronson (Eds.), *Handbook of social psychology* (2d ed.), Vol. VII. Reading, Mass.: Addison-Wesley. (*521, 522, 523, 526*)

Sears, R. R. (1936). Experimental studies of projection. I. Attribution of traits. *J. soc. Psychol.,* 7, 151–163. (*376*)

Sears, R. R., Hovland, C. I., and Miller, N. E. (1940). Minor studies in aggression. I. Measurement of aggressive behavior. *J. Psychol.,* 9, 277–281. (*538*)

Sears, R. R., Maccoby, E. E., and Levin, H. (1957). *Patterns of child rearing.* New York: Harper & Row. (*273*)

Secord, P. F., and Backman, C. W. (1964). *Social psychology.* New York: McGraw-Hill. (*543*)

Seevers, M. H. (1962). Medical perspectives on habituation and addiction. *J. Amer. med. Assoc.,* 181, No. 2, 92–98. (*418*)

Sells, S. B. (1936). The atmosphere effect: An experimental study of reasoning. *Arch. Psychol.,* 29 (Whole No. 200). (*173*)

Selye, H. (1950). *The physiology and pathology of exposure to stress.* Montreal: ACTA. (*235*)

Senden, M. von. (1932). *Raum- und Gestaltauffassung bei operierten Blindgeborenen vor und nach Operation.* Leipzig: Barth. (*280*)

Senden, M. von. (1960). *Space and sight: The perception of space and shape in the congenitally blind before and after operation* (Trans. P. Heath). New York: Free Press. (*280*)

Seward, J. P. (1949). An experimental analysis of latent learning. *J. exp. Psychol.,* 39, 177–186. (*99*)

Shaffer, L. F. (1947). Fear and courage in aerial combat. *J. consult. Psychol.,* 11, 137–143. (*228, 229*)

Shaffer, L. F., and Shoben, E. J., Jr. (1956). *The psychology of adjustment* (rev. ed.). Boston: Houghton Mifflin. (*378, 408*)

Shaw, M. E. (1955). A comparison of two types of leadership in various communication nets. *J. abnorm. soc. Psychol.,* 50, 127–134. (*483*)

Shaw, M. E., and Wright, J. M. (1967). *Scales for the measurement of attitudes.* New York: McGraw-Hill. (*519, 543*)

Sherif, M. (1935). A study of some social factors in perception. *Arch. Psychol.,* 27 (Whole No. 187). (*488*)

Sherif, M. (1958). Group influences upon the formation of norms and attitudes. In E. E. Maccoby, T. M. Newcomb, and E. L. Hartley (Eds.). *Readings in social psychology* (3d ed.). New York: Holt, Rinehart and Winston. Pp. 219–232. (*271*)

Sherrington, C. S. (1906). *The integrative action of the nervous system.* London: Constable. (*606*)

Shirley, M. M. (1931). *The first two years: A study of twenty-five babies.* Vol. I. *Postural and locomotor development.* Minneapolis: Univer. Minnesota Press. (*41*)

Sholl, D. A. (1956). *The organization of the cerebral cortex.* London: Methuen. (*588*)

Shuey, A. M. (1958). *The testing of Negro intelligence.* Lynchburg, Va.: J. P. Bell. (*345*)

Sidman, M. (1960). *The tactics of scientific research.* New York: Basic Books. (*16, 29*)

Siegel, S. (1956). *Nonparametric statistics for the behavioral sciences.* New York: McGraw-Hill. (*302, 303*)

Skaggs, E. B. (1925). Further studies in retroactive inhibition. *Psychol. Monogr.,* 24 (Whole No. 161). (*139*)

Skeels, H. M., and Dye, H. B. (1939). A study of the effect of differential stimulation on mentally retarded children. *Proc. Amer. Assoc. Mental Deficiency,* 44, 114–136. (*59*)

Skinner, B. F. (1938). *The behavior of organisms.* New York: Appleton-Century-Crofts. (*81, 92*)

Skinner, B. F. (1961). *Cumulative record* (enlarged ed.). New York: Appleton-Century-Crofts. (*26*)

Skodak, M., and Skeels, H. M. (1949). A final follow-up of one hundred adopted children. *J. genet. Psychol.,* 75, 3–19. (*343*)

Slater, E. (1968). A review of earlier evidence on genetic factors in schizophrenia. In D. Rosenthal and S. S. Kety (Eds.), *The transmission of schizophrenia.* New York: Pergamon. (*55*)

Sleight, R. B. (1948). The effect of instrument dial shape on legibility. *J. appl. Psychol.,* 32, 170–188. (*572*)

Smith, C. P., and Feld, S. (1958). How to learn the method of content analysis for *n* Achievement, *n* Affiliation, and *n* Power. In J. W. Atkinson (Ed.), *Motives in fantasy, action, and society.* Princeton, N.J.: Van Nostrand. Pp. 685–818. (*210*)

Smith, H. C. (1964). *Psychology of industrial behavior* (2d ed.). New York: McGraw-Hill. (*547, 575*)

Smith, S. M., Brown, H. O., Toman, J. E. P., and Goodman, L. S. (1947). The lack of cerebral effects of d-tubocurarine. *Anesthesiology,* 8, 1–14. (*153*)

Snyder, I. W., and Pronko, N. H. (1952). *Vision with spatial inversion.* Wichita, Kans.: Univer. Wichita Press. (*276*)

Social Science Research Council (1947). *Public reaction to the atomic bomb and world affairs.* Ithaca, N.Y.: Cornell Univer. Press. (*523*)

Solley, C. M., and Murphy, G. (1960). *Development of the Perceptual World.* New York: Basic Books. (*285*)

Solomon, R. L. (1964). Punishment. *Amer. Psychologist,* 19, 239–253. (*90, 95*)

Solomon, R. L., and Wynne, L. C. (1953). Traumatic avoidance learning: Acquisition in normal dogs. *Psychol. Monogr.,* 67 (Whole No. 354). (*89, 90*)

Solomon, R. L. and Turner, L. H. (1962). Discriminative classical conditioning in dogs paralyzed by curare can later control discriminative avoidance responses in the normal state. *Psych. Rev.,* 69, 202–219. (*153*)

Sontag, L. W., Baker, C. T., and Nelson, V. L. (1958). Mental growth and personality development: A longitudinal study. *Monogr. Soc. Res. Child Developm.,* 23, No. 2. (*341*)

Spence, J. T., Underwood, B. J., Duncan, C. P., and Cotton, J. W. (1968). *Elementary statistics* (2d ed.). New York: Appleton-Century-Crofts. (*317*)

Spence, K. W. (1951). Theoretical interpretations of learning. In C. P. Stone (Ed.). *Comparative Psychology* (3d ed.). Englewood Cliffs, N.J.: Prentice-Hall. Pp. 239–291. (*66*)

Spence, K. W. (1964). Anxiety (drive) level and performance in eyelid conditioning. *Psychol. Bull.,* 61, 129–139. (*119*)

Sperling, G. (1960). The information available in brief visual presentations. *Psychol. Monogr.,* 74, (Whole No. 498). (*150*)

Spielberger, C. D. (1962). The effects of manifest anxiety on the academic achievement of college students. *Ment. Hyg.,* 46, 420–426. (*119*)

Spinelli, D. N. (1969). Personal communication. (*629*)

Spriegel, W. R., and Wallace, R. F. (1948). Recent trends in personnel selection and induction. *Personnel.* 77–88. (*558*)

Staats, C. K., and Staats, A. W., (1957). Meaning established by classical conditioning. *J. exp. Psychol.,* 54, 74–80. (*164*)

Stellar, E. (1954). The physiology of motivation. *Psychol. Rev.,* 61, 5–22. (*666*)

Stephens, J. M. (1965). *The psychology of classroom learning.* New York: Holt. (*147*)

Stern, C. (1960). *Principles of human genetics* (2d ed.). San Francisco: Freeman. (*61*)

Stevens, C. F. (1966). *Neurophysiology: A primer.* New York: Wiley. (*603*)

Stevens, S. S. (1961). The psychophysics of sensory function. In W. A. Rosenblith (Ed.), *Sensory communication.* Cambridge, Mass.: The M.I.T. Press. (*608, 609*)

Stevens, S. S., and Davis, H. (1938). *Hearing: Its psychology and physiology.* New York: Wiley. (*636*)

Stevens, S. S., and Volkmann, J. (1940). The relation of pitch to frequency: A revised scale. *Amer. J. Psychol.,* 53, 329–353. (*638, 640*)

Stewart, N. (1947). AGCT scores of Army personnel grouped by occupations. *Occupations,* 26, 5–13. (*339*)

Stogdill, R. M. (1948). Personal factors associated with leadership: A survey of the literature. *J. Psychol.,* 25, 37–71. (*484*)

Stogdill, R. M. (1949). The sociometry of working relationships in formal organizations. *Sociometry,* 12, 276–286. (*553*)

Stone, A. A., and Stone, S. S. (Eds.) (1966). *The abnormal personality through literature.* Englewood Cliffs, N.J.: Prentice-Hall. (*433*)

Stone, C. P. (1932). Wildness and savageness in rats of different strains. In K. S. Lashley (Ed.), *Studies in the dynamics of behavior.* Chicago: Univer. Chicago Press. Pp. 3–55. (*53*)

Stratton, G. M. (1897). Vision without inversion of the retinal image. *Psychol. Rev.,* 4, 341–360; 463–481. (*276*)

Stroud, J. B. (1940). Experiments on learning in school situations. *Psychol. Bull.,* 37, 777–807. (*133*)

Strupp, H. H. (1958). The psychotherapist's contribution to the treatment process. *Behav. Sci.,* 3, 34–67. (*454*)

Sullivan, H. S. (1953). *The interpersonal theory of psychiatry.* New York: Norton. (*394*)

Super, D. E., and Crites, J. O. (1962). *Appraising vocational fitness by means of psychological tests* (rev. ed.). New York: Harper & Row. (*320, 324, 361*)

Swets, J. A. (1961). Is there a sensory threshold? *Science,* 134, 168–177. (*610*)

Taber, J., Glaser, R., and Schaefer, H. (1965). *Learning and programmed instruction.* Reading, Mass.: Addison-Wesley. (*124*)

Tasaki, I. (1954). Nerve impulses in individual auditory nerve fibers of guinea pig. *J. Neurophysiol.,* 17, 97–122. (*638*)

Tate, B. G., and Baroff, G. S. (1966). Aversive control of self-injurious behavior in a psychotic boy. *Behav. res. ther.,* 4, 281–287. (*463*)

Taylor, J. A. (1953). A personality scale of manifest anxiety. *J. abnorm. soc. Psychol.,* 48, 285–290. (*355*)

Teitelbaum, P., and Stellar, E. (1954). Recovery from the failure to eat produced by hypothalamic lesions. *Science,* 120, 894–895. (*667*)

Teitelbaum, P. (1966). *Physiological psychology.* Englewood Cliffs, N.J.: Prentice-Hall. (*681*)

Teitelbaum, P. (1961). Disturbances in feeding and drinking behavior after hypothalamic lesions. In M. R. Jones (Ed.), *Nebraska symposium on motivation.* Lincoln, Nebr.: University of Nebraska Press. (*667*)

Telford, C. W., and Sawrey, J. M. (1967). *The exceptional individual: Psychological and educational aspects.* Englewood Cliffs, N.J.: Prentice-Hall. (*361*)

Terman, L. M., and Merrill, M. A. (1937). *Measuring intelligence.* Boston: Houghton Mifflin. (*304, 305, 326*)

Terman, L. M., and Oden, M. H. (1947). *Genetic studies of genius.* Vol. IV. The *gifted child grows up.* Stanford: Stanford Univer. Press. (*338*)

Terman, L. M., and Oden, M. H. (1959). *Genetic studies of genius.* Vol. V. *The gifted group at midlife.* Stanford: Stanford Univer. Press. (*338*)

Terman, L. M., and Merrill, M. A. (1960). *Stanford-Binet Intelligence Scale: Manual for the third revision form L-M.* Boston: Houghton Mifflin. (*326, 327*)

Teuber, H.-L. (1960). Perception. In J. Field, et al. (Eds.), *Handbook of physiology,* Vol. 3. Washington, D.C.: American Physiological Society. Pp. 1595–1668. (*272, 276*)

Teuber, H.-L. (1964). The riddle of frontal lobe function in man. In J. M. Warren and K. Akert (Eds.), *The frontal granular cortex and behavior.* New York: McGraw-Hill. Pp. 410–444. (*660*)

Teuber, H.-L., Battersby, W. S., and Bender, M. D. (1960). *Visual field defects after penetrating missile wounds of the brain.* Cambridge, Mass.: Harvard University Press, 1960. (*262, 617*)

Tharp, R. G. (1963). Psychological patterning in marriage. *Psychol. Bull.,* 60, 97–117. (*500*)

Thibaut, J. W., and Strickland, L. (1956). Psychological set and social conformity. *J. Pers.,* 25, 115–129. (*492*)

Thibaut, J. W., and Kelley, H. H. (1959). *The social psychology of groups.* New York: Wiley. (*494*)

Thibaut, J. W. and Faucheux, C. (1965). The development of contractual norms in a bargaining situation under two types of stress *J. exp. soc. Psychol.,* 1, 89–102. (*495*)

Thigpen, C. H., and Cleckley, H. M. (1957). *The three faces of Eve.* New York: McGraw-Hill. (*413*)

Thomas, R. (1959). *The psychology of thinking.* Baltimore: Penguin. (*185*)

Thompson, W. R. (1954). The inheritance and development of intelligence. *Proc. Assoc. Res. nerv. ment. Dis.,* 33, 209–231. (*49*)

Thompson, R. F. (1967). *Foundations of physiological psychology.* New York: Harper & Row. (*603, 650, 673, 681*)

Thompson, T., and Schuster, C. R. (1968) *Behavioral pharmacology.* Englewood Cliffs, N.J.: Prentice-Hall. (*681*)

Thompson, W. R., and Melzack, R. (1956). Early environment. *Sci. Amer.,* 194 (1), 38–42. (*58*)

Thompson, W. R., and Solomon, L. M. (1954). Spontaneous pattern discrimination in the rat. *J. comp.*

physiol. Psychol., 47, 104–107. (*99, 100*)

Thorndike, E. L. (1911). *Animal intelligence.* New York: Macmillan. (*68*)

Thorndike, E. L. (1932). *The fundamentals of learning.* New York: Teachers Coll., Columbia Univer. (*122*)

Thorndike, E. L., Bregman, E. O., Tilton, J. W., and Woodyard, E. (1928). *Adult learning.* New York: Macmillan. (*118*)

Thorpe, W. H. (1963). *Learning and instinct in animals.* (2d ed.). London: Methuen. (*61*)

Thorpe, W. H. (1963). *Learning and instinct in animals* (2d ed.). London: Methuen. (*37*)

Thurstone, L. L., and Thurstone, T. G. (1941). Factorial studies of intelligence. *Psychometr. Monogr.* (Whole No. 2). (*333*)

Tiegs, E. W., and Katz, B. (1941). *Mental hygiene in education.* New York: Ronald. (*413*)

Tinbergen, N. (1951). *The study of instinct.* Oxford: The Clarendon Press. (*36, 61*)

Tolman, E. C. (1932). *Purposive behavior in animals and men.* New York: Appleton-Century-Crofts. (*25*)

Tomita, T. (1963). Electrical activity in the vertebrate retina. *J. opt. Soc. Amer.,* 53, 49–57. (*620*)

Torrance, E. P. (1962). *Guiding creative talent.* Englewood Cliffs, N.J.: Prentice-Hall. (*169*)

Towe, A. L. (1965). Electrophysiology of the cerebral cortex: Consciousness. In T. C. Ruch and H. D. Patton (Eds.), *Physiology and biophysics* (19th ed.). Philadelphia, Pa.: Saunders. Pp. 455–464. (*583*)

Trow, D. (1957) Autonomy and job-satisfaction in task-oriented groups. *J. abnorm. soc. Psychol.,* 54, 204–209. (*483*)

Tryon, R. C. (1940). Genetic differences in maze-learning ability in rats. *39th Yearbook Nat. Soc. Stud. Educ.* (Part 1). Bloomington, Ind.: 111–119. (*49*)

Tussing, L. (1959). *Psychology for better living.* New York: Wiley. (*469*)

Tyler, L. E. (1963). *Tests and measurements.* Englewood Cliffs, N.J.: Prentice-Hall. (*361*)

Uhrbrock, R. S. (1948). The personnel interview. *Personnel Psychol.,* 1. (*558*)

Underwood, B. J. (1957). Interference and forgetting. *Psychol. Rev.,* 64, 49–60. (*139, 140, 146*)

Underwood, B. J. (1961). Ten years of massed practice on distributed practice. *Psychol. Rev.,* 68, 229–247. (*121*)

Underwood, B. J. (1964). The representativeness of rote verbal learning. In A. W. Melton (Ed.) *Categories of human learning.* New York: Academic Press. Pp. 48–78. (a). (*117, 127, 143*)

Underwood, B. J. (1964). Forgetting. *Sci. Amer.,* 210 (3), 91–99. (b) (*137*)

Underwood, B. J., and Schulz, R. W. (1960). *Meaningfulness and verbal learning.* Philadelphia: Lippincott. (*116, 143*)

Underwood, B. J., and Keppel, G. (1962). One trial learning? *J. verb. Learn. verb. Behav.,* 1, 1–13. (144)

Vaughan, E., and Fisher, A. E. (1962). Male sexual behavior induced by intracranial electrical stimulation. *Science,* 137, 758–760. (*668*)

Vernon, M. D. (Ed.). (1966). *Experiments in visual perception: Selected readings.* New York: Penguin. (*285*)

Von Fieandt, Kai (1966). *The world of perception.* Homewood, Ill.: Dorsey. (*285*)

Wake, F. R. (1950). Changes of fear with age. Unpublished doctoral dissertation, McGill Univer. Cited in J. P. Zubek and P. A. Solberg (1954), *Human development.* New York: McGraw-Hill. (*241*)

Wald, G. (1959). The photoreceptor process in vision. In J. Field, H. W. Magoun, and V. E. Hall (Eds.), *Handbook of Physiology.* Vol. 1. Washington, D.C.: American Physiological Society. Pp. 671-692. (*619*)

Walk, R. D., and Gibson, E. J. (1961). A comparative and analytical study of visual depth perception. *Psychol. Monogr.,* 75 (Whole No. 519). (*278*)

Wallach, H. (1963). The perception of neutral colors. *Sci. Amer.,* 208 (1), 107–118. (*264, 265*)

Wallach, H. (1939). On constancy of visual speed. *Psychol. Rev.,* 46, 541–552. (*272*)

Wallas, G. (1926). *The art of thought.* New York: Harcourt, Brace & World. (*170*)

Walis, W. A., and Roberts, H. V. (1956). *Statistics: A new approach.* New York: Free Press. (*307, 317*)

Walls, G. L. (1942). *The Vertebrate Eye.* Bloomfield Hills, Mich.: Cranbrook Institute of Science. (*613*)

Walster, E. (1966). Assignment of responsibility for an accident. *J. of Pers. soc. Psychol.,* 3, 73–79. (503)

Wangensteen, O. H., and Carlson, A. J. (1931). Hunger sensations in a patient after total gastrectomy. *Proc. Soc. exp. Biol., N.Y.,* 28, 545–547. (*190*)

Ward, L. B. (1937). Reminiscence and rote learning. *Psychol. Monogr.,* 49 (Whole No. 20). (*137*)

Warner, W. L., and Lunt, P. S. (1941). *The social life of a modern community.* New Haven, Conn.: Yale Univer. Press. (*478, 479*)

Warren, J. M. (1965). Learning in paramecia and planaria. *Annu. Rev.,* 17, 95–118. (*63*)

Washburn, R. W. (1929). A study of smiling and laughing of infants in the first year of life. *Genet. Psychol. Monogr.,* 6, 397–539. (*240*)

Watson, J. B. (1925). *Behaviorism.* New York: Norton. (*25*)

Watson, J. B., and Rayner, R. (1920). Conditioned emotional reactions. *J. exp. Psychol.,* 3, 1–14. (*88, 89*)

Wattenberg, W. W. (1955). *The adolescent years.* New York: Harcourt, Brace & World. (*388*)

Weakland, J. H. (1960). The "double-bind" hypothesis of schizophrenia and three-party interaction. In D. Jackson (Ed.), *The etiology of schizophrenia.* New York: Basic Books. Pp. 373–388 (*428*)

Webb, W. B. (Ed.) (1962). *The profession of psychology.* New York: Holt, Rinehart and Winston. (*29*)

Webb, W. B. (1968). *Sleep: An experimental approach.* New York: Macmillan. (*251*)

Wechsler, D. (1955). *Wechsler adult intelligence scale, manual.* New York: Psychological Corporation. (*328*)

Wechsler, D. (1958). *Measurement and appraisal of adult intelligence* (4th ed.). Baltimore: Williams & Wilkins. (*330*)

Weil, A. T., Zinberg, N. E., and Nelsen, J. M. (1968). Clinical and psychological effects of marihuana in man. *Science,* 162, 1234–1242. (*15, 16, 17*)

Weiss, W., and Fine, B. J. (1958). The effect of induced aggressiveness on opinion change. In E. E. Maccoby, T. M. Newcomb, and E. L. Hartley (Eds.), *Readings in social psychology* (3d ed.). New York: Holt, Rinehart and Winston. Pp. 149–156. (*534*)

Welker, W. I. (1956). Some determinants of play and exploration in chimpanzees. *J. comp. Physiol. Psychol.,* 49, 84–89. (*198, 199*)

Welsh, G. S. (1956). Factor dimensions A and R. In G. S. Welsh and W. G. Dahlstrom (Eds.), *Basic readings on the MMPI in psychology and medicine.* Minneapolis: Univer. Minn. Press. (*355*)

Wendt, G. R. (1951). Vestibular function. In S. S. Stevens (Ed.), *Handbook of experimental psychology.* New York: Wiley. Chap. 31. (*651*)

Werner, H. (1935). Studies on contour. I. Qualitative analyses. *Amer. J. Psychol.,* 47, 40–64. (*261, 262*)

Werner, H., and Kaplan, E. (1950). Development of word meaning through verbal context: An experimental study. *J. Psychol.,* 29, 251–257. (*159*)

Wertheimer, M. (1912). Experimentelle Studien über das Sehen von Bewegungen. *Z. Psychol.,* 61, 161–265. (*26, 271*)

Wertheimer, M. (1923). Untersuchungen zur Lehre von der Gestalt. II. *Psychol. Forsch.,* 4, 301–351. (*24*)

Wertheimer, M. (1959). *Productive thinking* (rev. ed.). New York: Harper & Row. (*164, 167, 185*)

Wever, E. G., and Bray, C. W. (1930). The nature of acoustic response: The relation between sound frequency and frequency of impulses in the auditory nerve. *J. exp. Psychol.,* 13, 373–387. (*636*)

White, R. W. (1959). Motivation reconsidered: The concept of competence. *Psychol. Rev.,* 66, 297–333. (*204*)

White, Robert W. (1964). *The abnormal personality* (3d ed.). New York: Ronald. (*405, 422, 426*)

White, R. W. (1966). *Lives in progress: A study of the natural growth of personality* (2d ed.). New York: Holt, Rinehart and Winston. (*397, 406, 433*)

Whyte, W. H., Jr. (1956). *The organization man.* Garden City, N.Y.: Doubleday. (*356*)

Wiener, D. N. (1968). *A practical guide to psychotherapy.* New York: Harper & Row. (*469*)

Wilkins, L., and Richter, C. P. (1940). A great craving for salt by a child with cortico-adrenal insufficiency. *J. Amer. med. Assoc.,* 114, 866–868. (*188*)

Wilson, W. A., and Mishkin, M. (1959). Comparison of the effects of inferotemporal and lateral occipital lesions on visually guided behavior in monkeys. *J. comp. physiol. Psychol.,* 52, 10–17. (*659*)

Winterbottom, M. R. (1958). The relation of need for achievement to learning experience in independence and mastery. In J. W. Atkinson (Ed.), *Motives in fantasy, action and society.* Princeton, N.J.: Van Nostrand. Pp. 453–478. (*215*)

Wolf, M., Mees, H., and Risley, T. (1964). Application of operant conditioning procedures to the behavior problems of an autistic child. *Behav. Res. Ther.,* 1, 305–312. (*79, 80*)

Wolfe, J. B. (1936). Effectiveness of token rewards for chimpanzees. *Comp. Psychol. Monogr.,* 12 (Whole No. 60). (*206*)

Wolff, H. G., and Wolf, S. (1948). *Pain.* Springfield, Ill.: Charles C Thomas. (*648*)

Wolman, B. B. (Ed.). (1965). *Handbook of clinical psychology.* New York: McGraw-Hill. (*424*)

Wolpe, J. (1958). *Psychotherapy by reciprocal inhibition.* Stanford, Calif.: Stanford Univer. Press. (*461*)

Woodrow, G. (1946). The ability to learn. *Psychol. Rev.,* 53, 147–158. (*118*)

Woodworth, R. S., and Schlosberg, H. (1954). *Experimental psychology* (rev. ed). New York: Holt, Rinehart and Winston. (*646*)

Woodworth, R. S., and Sheehan, M. R. (1964). *Contemporary schools of psychology* (3d ed.). New York: Ronald. (*29*)

Wooldridge, D. E. 1963. *The machinery of the brain.* New York: McGraw-Hill. (*681*)

Wright, R. H. (1964). *The science of smell.* New York: Basic Books. (*653*)

Wyburn, G. M., Pickford, R. W., and Hirst, R. J. (1964). *Human senses and perception.* Edinburgh: Oliver & Boyd. (*653*)

Yerkes, R. M. (1943). *Chimpanzees.* New Haven: Yale Univer. Press. (*193*)

Yonge, K. A. (1956). The value of the interview: An orientation and a pilot study. *J. appl. Psychol.,* 40, 25–31. (*558*)

Young, P. T. (1961). *Motivation and emotion: A survey of the determinants of human and animal activity.* New York: Wiley. (*221*)

Young, P. T. (1944). Studies of food preference, appetite, and dietary habit. I. Running activity and dietary habit of the rat in relation to food preference. *J. comp. Psychol.,* 37, 327–370. (*191*)

Young, R. K., and Veldman, D. J. (1965). *Introductory statistics for the behavioral sciences.* New York: Holt, Rinehart and Winston. (*317*)

Zanchetti, A. (1967) Subcortical and cortical mechanisms in arousal and emotional behavior. In G. C. Quarton, T. Melnechuk, and F. O. Schmitt (Eds.), *The neurosciences: A study program.* New York: Rockefeller University Press. (*600*).

Zemp, J. W., Wilson, J. E., Schlesinger, K., Boggan, W. O., and Glassman, E. (1966). Brain function and macromolecules, I. Incorporation of uridine into RNA of mouse brain during short-term training experience. *Proc. National Acad. Sci.* 55, 1423–1431. (*664*)

Zimbardo, P. G. (1970). The human choice: Individuation, reason, and order versus deindividuation, impulse, and chaos. In W. J. Arnold and D. Levine (Eds.), *Nebraska symposium on motivation.* Lincoln, Nebr.: University of Nebraska Press. (*497, 498*)

Zotterman, Y. (1959). Thermal sensations. In J. Field, H. W. Magoun, and V. E. Hall (Eds.), *Handbook of physiology: Neurophysiology.* Vol. 1. Washington: American Physiological Society. Pp. 431–458. (*648*)

Zubek, J. P. (1969). *Sensory deprivation: Fifteen years of research.* New York: Appleton-Century-Crofts. (*200, 285*)

In addition to the acknowledgments given in the text and in the references section, we wish to give special credits to the following:

Table 1.1 Data from: Cates, J. Psychology's manpower: Report on the 1968 National Register of Scientific and Technical Personnel. *American Psychologist,* 1970, *25,* 254–263. Copyright 1970 by the American Psychological Association, and reproduced by permission.

Table 1.2 Data from: Weil, A. T., Zinberg, N. E., and Nelsen, J. M. Clinical and psychological effects of marihuana in man. *Science,* 1968, *162,* 1234–1242, 13 December 1968. Copyright 1968 by the American Association for the Advancement of Science.

Table 1.3 Data from: Bennett, E. M. and Cohen, L. R. Men and women: personality patterns and contrasts. *Genetic Psychology Monographs,* 1959, *59,* 101–155. Copyright 1959 by the Journal Press.

Figure 1.2 Adapted from: Lockman, R. F. An empirical description of the subfields of psychology. *American Psychologist, 19,* 1964, 645–653. Copyright 1964 by the American Psychological Association, and reproduced by pemission.

Figure 1.7 From: Weil, A. T., Zinberg, N. E., and Nelsen, J. M. Clinical and psychological effects of marihuana in man. *Science,* 1968, *162,* 1234–1242, 13 December 1968. Copyright 1968 by the American Association for the Advancement of Science. This figure originally appeared in: Mirsky, A. F. and Kornetsky, C. On the dissimilar effects of drugs on the digit symbol substitution and continuous performance tests. *Psychopharmacologia,* 1964, *5,* 161–177. Copyright 1964 by Springer-Verlag.

Table 2.1 Modified slightly from: Lenneberg, E. H. Explaining language. *Science,* 1969, *164,* 635–643, 9 May 1969. Copyright 1969 by the American Association for the Advancement of Science.

Table 2.2 Data from: Krech, D., Crutchfield, R. S., and Livson, N. *Elements of Psychology* (2d ed.). New York: Knopf, 1969. Copyright 1969 by Alfred A. Knopf, Inc.

Table 2.5 Based on: Heston, L. L. The genetics of schizophrenic and schizoid disease. *Science,* 1970, *167,* 249–255, 16 January 1970. Copyright 1970 by the American Association for the Advancement of Science.

Figure 2.1 Modified slightly from: Dethier, V. G., and Stellar, E. *Animal Behavior* (3d ed.). Englewood Cliffs, N.J.: Prentice-Hall, 1970.

Figure 2.2 Modified slightly from: Tinbergen, N. *The study of instinct.* Oxford: The Clarendon Press, 1951.

Figure 2.3 Based on: Schenkel, R. Ausdrucks-Studien an Wolfen. *Behaviour,* 1948, *1,* 81–129.

Figure 2.4 Courtesy of R. A. Gardner and B. T. Gardner, Department of Psychology, University of Nevada, Reno.

Figure 2.7 Based on: Morphett, M. V., and Washburne, C. When should children begin to read? *Elementary School Journal,* 1931, *31,* 496–503. Courtesy of the University of Chicago Press, the University of Chicago, Chicago, Illinois.

Figure 2.10 From: *Handbook of Aging and the Individual,* James E. Birren (Ed.). © 1959 by the University of Chicago. Published 1959. Composed and printed by the University of Chicago Press, Chicago, Ill., U.S.A. Used by permission of L. F. Jarvik, James E. Birren, and the publisher.

Figure 2.11 (Upper) Modified slightly from: Thompson, W. R. The inheritance and development of Intelligence. *Proceedings of the Association for Research in Nervous and Mental Diseases,* 1954, *33,* 209–231.

Figure 2.12 Modified slightly from: Hirsch, J. Studies in experimental behavior genetics: II. Individual differences in geotaxis as a function of chromosome variation in synthesized Drosophila populations. *Journal of Comparative and Physiological Psychology, 52,* 1959, 304–308. Copyright 1959 by the American Psychological Association, and reproduced by permission.

Figure 2.13 Based on data from: Erlenmeyer-Kimling, L., and Jarvik, L. F. Genetics and intelligence: A review. *Science,* 1963, *142,* 1477–1479, 13 December 1963. Copyright 1963 by the American Association for the Advancement of Science.

Figure 3.5 Modified from: Liddell, H. S., James, W. T., and Anderson, D. D. The comparative physiology of the conditioned reflex. *Comparative Psychology Monographs,* 1935, *11* (Whole No. 51). Reproduced by permission from The Johns Hopkins Press.

Figure 3.10 Modified from: Wolf, M., Mees, M., and Risley, T. Application of operant conditioning procedures to the behavior problems of an autistic child. *Behaviour Research and Therapy,* 1964, *1,* 305–312. Copyright 1964 by Pergamon Press.

Figure 3.12 Modied from: Jenkins, W. D., McFann, H., and Clayton, F. L. A methodological study of extinction following aperiodic and continuous reinforcement. *Journal of Comparative and Physiological Psychology, 43,* 1950, 155–167. Copyright 1950 by the American Psychological Association, and reproduced by permission.

Figure 3.13 Adapted from: Ferster, C. B., and Skinner, B. F. *Schedules of Reinforcement.* New York: Appleton-Century-Crofts, 1957. Copyright © 1957 by Appleton-Century-Crofts, Inc. Reprinted by permission of Appleton-Century-Crofts, a division of Meredith Publishing Company.

Figure 3.14 Adapted from: Ferster, C. B., and Skinner, B. F. *Schedules of Reinforcement.* New York: Appleton-Century-Crofts, 1957. Copyright © 1957 by Appleton-Century-Crofts, Inc. Reprinted by permission of Appleton-Century-Crofts, a division of Meredith Publishing Company.

Figure 3.15 Modified from: Olson, G. M., and King, R. A. Supplementary report: Stimulus generalization gradients along a luminosity continuum. *Journal of Experimental Psychology, 63,* 1962, 414–415. Copyright 1962 by the American Psychological Association, and reproduced by permission.

Figure 3.16 From: Miller, N. E., and Banuazizi, A. Instrumental learning by curarized rats of a specific visceral response, intestinal or cardiac. *Journal of Comparative and Physiological Psychology, 65,* 1968, 1–7. Copyright 1968 by the American Psychological Association, and reproduced by permission.

Figure 3.17 Slightly modified from: Hunt, H. F., and Brady, J. V. Some effects of electro-convulsive shock on a conditioned emotional response ("anxiety"). *Journal of Comparative and Physiological Psychology, 44,* 1951, 88–98. Copyright 1951 by the American Psychological Association, and reproduced by permission.

Figure 3.19 Modified from: Solomon, R. L., and Wynne, L. C. Traumatic avoidance learning: Acquisition in normal dogs. *Psychological Monographs, 67,* 1953 (Whole No. 354). Copyright 1953 by the American Psychological Association, and reproduced by permission.

Figure 3.21 Modified from: Gleitman, H. Place learning without prior performance. *Journal of Comparative and Physiological Psychology, 48,* 1955, 77–79. Copyright 1955 by the American Psychological Association, and reproduced by permission.

Figure 3.24 Based on: Thompson, W. R., and Solomon, L. M. Spontaneous pattern discrimination in the rat. *Journal of Comparative and Physiological Psychology, 47,* 1954, 104–107. Copyright 1954 by the American Psychological Association, and reproduced by permission.

Figure 3.25 Redrawn from: Harlow, H. F. The formation of learning sets. *Psychological Review, 56,* 1949, 51–65. Copyright 1949 by the American Psychological Association, and reproduced by permission.

Figure 3.26 Modified from: Harlow, H. F. The formation of learning sets. *Psychological Review, 56,* 1949, 51–65. Copyright 1949 by the American Psychological Association, and reproduced by permission.

Figure 3.27 Modified from: Perin, C. T. Behavior potentiality as a joint function of the amount of training and the degree of hunger at the time of extinction. *Journal of Experimental Psychology, 30,* 1942, 93–113. Copyright 1942 by the American Psychological Association, and reproduced by permission.

Page 75: Quotation from: Dashiell, J. F. *Fundamentals of General Psychology* (3d ed.). Boston: Houghton Mifflin, 1949. Copyright © 1949 by John Frederick Dashiell. Reprinted by permission of Houghton Mifflin Company.

Page 100: Quotation from: Köhler, W. *The Mentality of Apes* (2d ed.). New York: Harcourt, Brace, and Jovanovich, 1925. Reproduced by permission of: Springer-Verlag, Humanities Press, and Routledge and Kegan Paul Ltd., the original English-language publishers.

Page 98: Quotation from: Lashley, K. S. *Brain Mechanisms and Intelligence.* Chicago: University of Chicago Press, 1929. Copyright © 1929 by The University of Chicago.

Chapter 4 epigraph: Quotation from: James, W. *The Principles of Psychology.* Volume I. New York: Holt, Rinehart and Winston, 1890. Reprinted by permission.

Table 4.2 Modified from: Underwood, B. J. The representativeness of rote verbal learning. In A. W. Melton (Ed.), *Categories of Human Learning.* New York: Academic Press, 1964. Pp. 48–78. By permission of Academic Press.

Figure 4.1 (Left). Slightly modified from: Hilgard, E. R. Conditioned eyelid reactions to a light stimulus based on the reflex wink to sound. *Psychological Monographs, 41,* 1931 (Whole No. 184).

Figure 4.1 (Middle and right). Redrawn from: Kimble, G. A. The problem of definition. In A. W. Melton (Ed.), *Categories of Human Learning.* New York: Academic Press, 1964. By permission of Academic Press.

Figure 4.4 Modified from: Grant, D. A., Hake, H. W., and Hornseth, J. P. Acquisition and extinction of a conditioned verbal response with differing percentages of reinforcement. *Journal of Experimental Psychology, 42,* 1951, 1–5. Copyright 1951 by the American Psychological Association, and reproduced by permission.

Figure 4.5 Modified from: Kendler, H. S., and Kendler, T. S. Vertical and horizontal processes in problem solving. *Psychological Review, 69,* 1962, 1–16. Copyright 1962 by the American Psychological Association, and reproduced by permission.

Figure 4.7 Selection from: Glaze, J. A. The association value of nonsense syllables. *Journal of Genetic Psychology,* 1928, *35,* 255–269. Reprinted by permission from the Journal Press.

Figure 4.9 Redrawn from: Spielberger, C. D. The effects of manifest anxiety on the academic achievement of college students. *Mental Hygiene,* 1962, *46,* 420–426. Reprinted by permission from the National Association for Mental Health.

Figure 4.13 Redrawn from: Bower, G. H., Clark, M. C., Lesgold, A. M., and Winzenz, D. Hierarchical retrieval schemes in recall of categorized word lists. *Journal of Verbal Learning and Verbal Behavior,* 1969, *8,* 323–343. Reprinted by permission from Academic Press.

Figure 4.14 Modified from: Peterson, L. R., and Peterson, M. J. Short-term retention of individual verbal items. *Journal of Experimental Psychology, 58,* 1959, 193–198. Copyright 1959 by The American Psychological Association, and reproduced here by permission.

Figure 4.16 Modified from: Hovland, C. I. Human learning and retention. In S. S. Stevens (Ed.), *Handbook of Experimental Psychology.* New York: Wiley, 1951. Pp. 613–689. Reprinted with permission from Wiley.

Figure 4.18 Modified from: Robinson, E. S. The "similarity" factor in retroaction. *American Journal of Psychology,* 1927, *39,* 297–312. Copyright © 1927 by The American Journal of Psychology.

Figure 4.19 Modified from: Underwood, B. J. Interference and forgetting. *Psychological Review, 64,* 1957, 49–60. Copyright 1957 by The American Psychological Association, and reproduced by permission.

Figure 4.23 Modified from: Underwood, B. J., and Keppel, G. One-trial learning? *Journal of Verbal Learning and Verbal Behavior,* 1962, *1,* 1–13. Reprinted by permission from Academic Press

Page 113: Quotation from: Deese, J., and Hulse, S. H. *The Psychology of Learning.* New York: McGraw-Hill, 1967. Reprinted by permission.

Pages 130, 138, 139: Transfer diagram, retroactive interference diagram, and proactive interference diagram slightly modified from: McGeoch, J. A., and Irion, A. L. *The Psychology of Human Learning* (2d ed.). New York: Longmans, 1952. Used by permission of David McKay Company, Inc.

Page 134: Quotation from: Broadbent, D., and Heron, A. Effects of a subsidiary task on performance involving immediate memory by younger and older men. *British Journal of Psychology,* 1962, *53,* 139–198. By permission from the British Psychological Society.

Table 5.1 Based on: Luchins, A. Mechanization in problem solving: The effect of Einstellung. *Psychological Monographs, 54,* 1954 (Whole No. 6). Copyright 1954 by the American Psychological Association, and reproduced by permission.

Figure 5.1 Modified from: Sperling, G. The information available in brief visual presentations. *Psychological Monographs, 74,* 1960 (Whole No. 498). Copyright 1960 by the American Psychological Association, and reproduced by permission.

Figure 5.7 From: Carroll, J. B. *Language and Thought.* Englewood Cliffs, N.J.: Prentice-Hall, 1964. Reprinted by permission from Prentice-Hall.

Figures 5.8 and 5.9 From: Duncker, K. On problem-solving. *Psychological Monographs, 58,* 1945 (Whole No. 270). Copyright 1945 by the American Psychological Association, and reproduced by permission.

Figure 5.11 From: Berko, J. The child's learning of English morphology. *Word,* 1958, *14,* 150–177. Reprinted by permission.

Page 171: Quotation from: *Creativity and Psychological Health* by Frank Barron. Copyright © 1963, by Litton Educational Publishing, Inc., by permission of Van Nostrand Reinhold Company.

Page 169: Quotation from: Carroll, J. B. *Language and Thought.* Englewood Cliffs, N.J.: Prentice-Hall, 1964. Reprinted by permission from Prentice-Hall.

Page 169: Quotation from: Housman, A. E. *The Name and Nature of Poetry.* New York: Macmillan, 1933. Reprinted here by permission of the Cambridge University Press.

Page 169: Quotation from: Humphrey, G. *Directed Thinking.* New York: Dodd, Mead, 1948. Reprinted by permission of Dodd, Mead and Company. Copyright © 1948 by George Humphrey.

Chapter 6 epigraph: From: Young, P. T. *Motivation and Emotion.* New York: Wiley, 1961. Reprinted with permission.

Figure 6.2 Based on: Bare, J. K. The specific hunger for sodium chloride in normal and adrenalectomized white rats. *Journal of Comparative and Physiological Psychology, 42,* 1949, 242–253. Copyright 1949 by the American Psychological Association, and reproduced by permission.

Figure 6.7 Based on: Welker, W. I. Some determinants of play and exploration in chimpanzees. *Journal of Comparative and Physiological Psychology, 49,* 1956, 84–89. Copyright 1956 by the American Psychological Association, and reproduced by permission.

Figure 6.9 Based on Harlow, H. F. The nature of love. *American Psychologist, 13,* 1958, 673–683. Copyright 1958 by the American Psychological Association, and reproduced by permission.

Figure 6.11 Modified from: Miller, N. E. Studies of fear as an acquirable drive. I. Fear as motivation and fear-reduction as reinforcement in the learning of new responses. *Journal of Experimental Psychology, 38,* 1948, 89–101. Copyright 1948 by the American Psychological Association, and reproduced here by permission.

Figure 6.13 Modified from: Atkinson, J. W. and Litwin, G. H. Achievement motive and test anxiety conceived as motive to approach success and motive to avoid failure. *Journal of Abnormal and Social Psychology, 60,* 1960, 52–63. Copyright 1960 by the American Psychological Association, and reproduced by permission.

Figure 6.14 Modified from: Atkinson, J. W., and Feather, N. T. (Eds.) *A Theory of Achievement Motivation.* New York: Wiley, 1966. Copyright 1966 by John Wiley and Sons, and reprinted with permission.

Page 209: Quotation from Smith and Feld. From: Smith, C. P., and Feld, S. How to learn the method of content analysis for *n* achievement, *n* affiliation, and *n* power. In *Motives in Fantasy, Action, and Society* by J. W. Atkinson. Copyright © 1958, by Litton Educational Publishing, Inc., by permission of Van Nostrand Reinhold Company.

Chapter 7 epigraph: From: Hebb, D. O. *A Textbook of Psychology* (2d ed.). Philadelphia: Saunders, 1966. Reprinted by permission.

Table 7.1 Based on: Shaffer, L. F. Fear and courage in aerial combat. *Journal of Consulting Psychology, 11,* 1947, 137–143. Copyright 1947 by the American Psychological Association, and reproduced by permission.

Figure 7.1 From: Hess, E. H. Attitude and pupil size. *Scientific American,* 1965, *212,* 46–54. Copyright © 1965 by Scientific American, Inc. All rights reserved.

Figure 7.3 Modified from: Hebb, D. O. Drives and the CNS (Conceptual nervous system). *Psychological Review, 62,* 1955, 243–254. Copyright 1955 by the American Psychological Association, and reproduced by permission.

Figure 7.7 Based on: Schlosberg, H. Three dimensions of emotion. *Psychological Review, 61,* 1954, 81–88. Copyright 1954 by the American Psychological Association, and reproduced by permission.

Figure 7.15 Based on: Brown, J. S. Gradients of approach and avoidance responses and their relation to motivation. *Journal of Comparative and Physiological Psychology, 41,* 1948, 450–465. Copyright 1948 by the American Psychological Association, and reproduced by permission.

Figure 8.1 Modified from: Ratliff, F. *Mach bands: Quantitative studies on neural networks in the retina.* San Francisco: Holden-Day, 1965. Reproduced by permission.

Figure 8.3 Modified from: Hernández-Péon, R., Scherrer, H., and Jouvet, M. Modification of electrical activity in cochlear nucleus during "attention" in unanesthetized cats. *Science,* 1965, *123,* 331–332, 24 January 1956. Copyright 1956 by the American Association for the Advancement of Science.

Figure 8.12 From: Wallach, H. The perception of neutral colors. *Scientific American,* 1963, *208,* 1, 107–118. Copyright © 1963 by Scientific American, Inc. All rights reserved.

Figure 8.23 From: Gibson, E. J., and Walk, R. D. The "visual cliff." *Scientific American,* 1960, *202,* 4, 64–71. Copyright © 1960 by Scientific American, Inc. All rights reserved.

Figure 8.24 Based on: Held, R., and Hein, A. Movement-produced stimulation in the development of visually guided behavior. *Journal of Comparative and Physiological Psychology, 56,* 1963, 872–876. Copyright 1963 by the American Psychological Association, and reproduced by permission.

Page 277: Quotation from: Heron, W., Doane, B. K., and Scott, T. H. Visual disturbance after prolonged perceptual isolation. *Canadian Journal of Psychology,* 1956, *10,* 13–16. Quoted by permission.

Page 307: Quotation from: Wallis, W. A., and Roberts, H. V. *Statistics: A new approach.* New York: The Free Press, 1956. Reprinted by permission of The Free Press, a division of The Macmillan Company.

Chapter 10 epigraph: From: Anastasi, A. *Psychological Testing* (3d ed.). New York: Macmillan, 1968. Copyright © 1968 by The Macmillan Company, and reproduced by permission.

Chapter 10 epigraph: From: Wechsler, D. *The Measurement and Appraisal of Adult Intelligence* (4th ed.). Baltimore: Williams & Wilkins, 1958. Copyright © 1958 by David Wechsler, and reproduced by permission.

Table 10.1 Modified from: Terman, L. M., and Merrill, M. A. *Stanford-Binet Intelligence Scale: Manual for the Third Revision, Form L-M.* Boston: Houghton Mifflin, 1960. Copyright © 1960 by Houghton Mifflin Company, and reproduced by permission.

Table 10.2 Modified from: Wechsler, D. *The Measurement and Appraisal of Adult Intelligence* (4th ed.). Baltimore: Williams & Wilkins, 1958. Copyright © 1958 by David Wechsler, and reproduced by permission.

Figure 10.2 Modified from: Terman, L. M., and Merrill, M. A. *Stanford-Binet Intelligence Scale: Manual for the Third Revision, Form L-M.* Boston: Houghton Mifflin, 1960. Copyright © 1960 by Houghton Mifflin Company, and reproduced by permission.

Figure 10.3 Modified from: Anastasi, A. *Psychological Testing* (3d ed.). New York: Macmillan, 1968. Copyright © 1968 by The Macmillan Company, and reproduced by permission.

Table 10.8 Sample items from: Dahlstrom, W. G., and Welsh, G. S. *An MMPI Handbook: A Guide to Use in Clinical Practice and Research.* Minneapolis, Minn.: University of Minnesota Press, 1960. Reproduced by permission.

Figure 10.11 From: Bennett, G. K., Seashore, H. G., and Wesman, A. G. *Differential Aptitude Tests.* New York: The Psychological

Corporation. Copyright © 1947, 1961, 1962 by The Psychological Corporation, New York, New York. All rights reserved. Reproduced by permission.

Figure 10.12 Modified from: Bennett, G. K., Seashore, H. G., and Wesman, A. G. *Counseling from Profiles: A Casebook for the Differential Aptitude Tests.* New York: The Psychological Corporation. Copyright © 1951 by The Psychological Corporation. All rights reserved. Reproduced by permission.

Figure 10.14 Modified from: Dahlstrom, W. G., and Welsh, G. S. *An MMPI Handbook: A Guide to Use in Clinical Practice and Research.* Minneapolis, Minn.: University of Minnesota Press, 1960. Reproduced by permission.

Page 323: Quotation from: Anastasi, A. *Psychological Testing* (3d ed.). New York: Macmillan, 1968. Copyright © 1968 by The Macmillan Company, and reproduced by permission.

Figure 11.2 From: Miller, N. E. Theory and experiment relating psychoanalytic displacement to stimulus-response generalization. *Journal of Abnormal and Social Psychology, 43,* 1948, 155–178. Copyright 1948 by the American Psychological Association, and reproduced by permission.

Figure 11.4 From: Bandura, A., Ross, D., and Ross, S. A. Imitation of film-mediated aggressive models. *Journal of Abnormal and Social Psychology, 66,* 1963, 3–11. Copyright 1963 by the American Psychological Association, and reproduced by permission.

Figure 11.5 Adapted from drawings by Don Sibley. From *The Adolescent Years* by William W. Wattenberg, Copyright 1955 by Harcourt, Brace Jovanovich, Inc., and reproduced with their permission.

Page 390: Quotation from: *The Basic Writings of Sigmund Freud* (translated by A. A. Brill). Copyright © 1938 by Random House, Inc. Copyright renewed 1965 by Gioia B. Bernheim and Edmund Brill. Reprinted by permission.

Page 364: Quotations from: Allport, G. *Pattern and Growth in Personality.* New York: Holt, Rinehart and Winston, 1961. Copyright, 1937, copyright © 1961 by Holt, Rinehart and Winston, Inc. Copyright © 1965 by Gordon W. Allport. Reprinted by permission of Holt, Rinehart and Winston, Inc.

Page 407: Quotation from Shaffer and Shoben: From: Shaffer, L. F., and Shoben, E. J., Jr. *The Psychology of Adjustment* (2d ed.). Boston: Houghton Mifflin, 1956. Reprinted by permission.

Page 410: Quotation from Masserman: From: Masserman, J. H. *Principles of Dynamic Psychiatry* (2d ed.). Philadelphia: Saunders, 1961. Copyright © 1961 by W. B. Saunders Co., and reproduced by permission.

Page 414: Quotation from Kutash: From: Kutash, S. B. Psychoneuroses. In B. B. Wolman (Ed.), *Handbook of Clinical Psychology.* New York: McGraw-Hill, 1965. Reprinted by permission.

Pages 416, 424, 425: Descriptions of behavior disorders quoted from: American Psychiatric Association. *Diagnostic and Statistical Manual of Mental Disorders* (2d ed.). Washington, D.C.: American Psychiatric Association, 1968. Reprinted by permission.

Pages 416, 421, 422: Case descriptions from: Kisker, G. W. *The Disorganized Personality.* New York: McGraw-Hill, 1964. Reproduced by permission.

Page 420: Quotation from Cameron and Magaret: From: Cameron, N., and Magaret, A. *Behavior Pathology.* Boston: Houghton Mifflin, 1951. Reprinted by permission.

Page 427: Quotation from Lidz and Fleck: From: Lidz, T., and Fleck, S. Schizophrenia, human integration, and the role of the family. From *The Etiology of Schizophrenia,* edited by Don D. Jackson, Basic Books, Inc., Publishers, New York, 1960.

Chapter 13 epigraph: From: Lomax, J. A., and Lomax, A. *111 Best American Ballads. Folk song U. S. A.* New York: Duell, Sloan and Pearce. Copyright © 1947 by John A. and Alan Lomax under the title: *Folk song U. S. A.* Now property of Hawthorn Books, Inc. Reprinted by permission.

Figure 13.7 Modified from: Tate, B. G., and Baroff, G. S. Aversive control of self-injurious behavior in a psychotic boy. *Behaviour Research and Therapy,* 1966, *4,* 281–287. Copyright © 1966 by Pergamon Press.

Figures 13.9 and 13.10 Modified from: Bandura, A., Blanchard, E. B., and Ritter, B. Relative efficacy of desensitization and modeling approaches for inducing behavioral, affective, and attitudinal changes. *Journal of Personality and Social Psychology, 13,* 1969, 173–199. Copyright 1969 by the American Psychological Association, and reproduced by permission.

Page 461: Quotation from: Clark, D. F. The treatment of monosymptomatic desensitization. *Behaviour Research and Therapy,* 1963, *1,* 63–68. Copyright © 1963 by Pergamon Press. Wording slightly changed.

Figure 14.4 Adapted from: Bales, R. F. A set of categories for the analysis of small group interaction. *American Sociological Review,* 1950, *15,* 257–263. Reprinted with permission from the American Sociological Association and the author. The particular adaptation used is from: Secord, P. F., and Backman, C. W. *Social Psychology.* New York: McGraw-Hill, 1964. Used by permission.

Figure 14.5 From "Some Uniformities in Small Social Systems" by

Robert F. Bales, from *Readings in Social Psychology,* Revised Edition, edited by G. E. Swanson, T. M. Newcomb, and E. L. Hartley. Copyright 1947, 1952 by Holt, Rinehart and Winston, Inc. Reprinted by permission of Holt, Rinehart and Winston, Inc.

Figure 14.7 After: Asch, S. E. Studies of independence and conformity: I. A minority of one against a unanimous majority. *Psychological Monographs,* 1956 (Whole No. 416). Copyright 1956 by the American Psychological Association, and reprinted by permission.

Figure 14.8 From: Thibaut, J. W., and Faucheux, C. The development of contractual norms in a bargaining situation under two types of stress. *Journal of Experimental Social Psychology,* 1965, *1,* 89–102. Reprinted by permission of the senior author and the Academic Press.

Figure 14.9 After: Byrne, D., and Nelson, D. Attraction as a linear function of proportion of positive reinforcements. *Journal of Personality and Social Psychology, 1,* 1965, 659–663. Copyright 1965 by the American Psychological Association, and reprinted by permission.

Page 474: Quotation from Benedict: Benedict, R. *Patterns of Culture* (2d ed.). Boston: Houghton Mifflin, 1959. Copyright © 1959 by Houghton Mifflin Company. British Commonwealth rights in the English language held by Routledge and Kegan Paul, Ltd. Reprinted by permission.

Page 474: Quotation from Keller and Schoenfeld: Keller, F. S., and Schoenfeld, W. N. *Principles of Psychology.* New York: Appleton-Century-Crofts, 1950. Copyright © 1950 by Appleton-Century-Crofts, Inc. Reprinted by permission of Appleton-Century-Crofts, a division of Meredith Publishing Co.

Page 478: Quotation from Davis and Havighurst: Davis, A., and Havighurst R. J. Social class and color differences in child rearing. *American Sociological Review,* 1946, *II,* 698–710. Reprinted with permission from the American Sociological Association and the authors.

Page 481: Quotation from McGrath: McGrath, J. E. *Social Psychology: A Brief Introduction.* New York: Holt, Rinehart and Winston, 1964. Reprinted with permission from the author and Holt, Rinehart and Winston.

Table 15.3 Based on data reported in: Karlins, M., Coffman, T. L., and Walters, G. On the fading of social stereotypes: Studies in three generations of college students. *Journal of Personality and Social Psychology,* 1969, *13,* 1–16. Copyright 1969 by the American Psychological Association, and reproduced by permission.

Table 15.4 Based on data from: Braungart, R. G. SDS and YAF: Backgrounds of student political activists. Paper presented at meeting of the American Sociological Association, Miami, 1966. These data also appear in the following source, and Table 15.4 was based on it also: Sears, D. O. Political behavior. In G. Lindzey and E. Aronson (Eds.), *The Handbook of Social Psychology* (2d ed.), Volume 5. Reading, Mass.: Addison-Wesley, 1969. Pp. 315–458.

Figure 15.1 Data from: Converse, P. E., and Schuman, H. "Silent majorities" and the Vietnam war. *Scientific American,* 1970, *222,* 6, 17–25. Copyright © 1970 by Scientific American, Inc. All rights reserved.

Figure 15.3 Data from: McGuire, W. J. Resistance to persuasion conferred by active and passive prior refutation of the same and alternative counterarguments. *Journal of Abnormal and Social Psychology, 63,* 1961, 326–332. Copyright 1961 by the American Psychological Association, and reproduced by permission.

Figure 15.5 From: *Social Psychology: The Study of Human Interaction* by T. M. Newcomb, R. H. Turner, and P. E. Converse. Copyright © 1965 by Holt, Rinehart and Winston. Based on data from: Deutsch, M., and Collins, M. E. *Interracial Housing: A Psychological Evaluation of a Social Experiment.* Minneapolis, Minn.: University of Minnesota Press, 1951. Reprinted by permission.

Page 537: Quotation from Deutsch and Collins: Deutsch, M., and Collins, M. E. *Interracial Housing: A Psychological Evaluation of a Social Experiment.* Minneapolis, Minn.: University of Minnesota Press, 1951. Reprinted by permission.

Chapter 16 epigraph: From: McGregor, D. *The Human Side of Enterprise.* New York: McGraw-Hill, 1960. Reprinted by permission.

Figure 16.2 Stogdill, R. M. The sociometry of working relationships in formal organizations. *Sociometry,* 1949, *12,* 276–286. Reprinted by permission.

Page 554: Quotation from: Leavitt, H. J. *Managerial Psychology* (2d ed.). Chicago: University of Chicago Press, 1964. Copyright © 1964 by the University of Chicago Press. Reprinted by permission.

Page 551: Paraphrased from: Bass, B. M. *Organizational Psychology.* Boston: Allyn and Bacon, 1965. Used by permission.

Chapter 17 epigraph: Quotation from: Sherrington, C. S. *Man on his Nature* (2d ed.). Cambridge: Cambridge University Press, 1963. Copyright © 1963 by the Cambridge University Press.

Figure 17.1 Modified from: Rosenzweig, M. R. Environmental complexity, cerebral change, and behavior. *American Psychologist, 21,* 1966, 321–332. Copyright 1966 by The American Psychological

Association, and reproduced by permission.

Figure 17.3 From: Towe, A. L. Electrophysiology of the cerebral cortex: Consciousness. In T. C. Ruch and H. D. Patton (Eds.), *Physiology and Biophysics* (19th ed.). Copyright © 1965 by W. B. Saunders Company.

Figure 17.5 Modified from: Dement, W., and Wolpert, E. A. The relation of eye movements, body motility, and external stimuli to dream content. *Journal of Experimental Psychology, 55,* 1958, 543–553. Copyright 1958 by The American Psychological Association, and reproduced by permission.

Figure 17.7 Modified from: Brazier, M. A. B. *The Electrical Activity of the Nervous System* (3d ed.). London: Pitman Publishing Co., 1968. Reproduced with permission of the author and the Pitman Medical and Scientific Publishing Co., Ltd.

Figure 17.9 Modified from: Patton, H. D. Spinal reflexes and synaptic transmission. In T. C. Ruch and H. D. Patton (Eds.), *Physiology and Biophysics* (19th ed.). Philadelphia: Saunders, 1965. Reproduced by permission.

Figure 17.10 From: Gardner, E. *Fundamentals of Neurology* (5th ed.). Philadelphia: Saunders, 1968. Reproduced by permission.

Figure 17.13 Modified from: Eccles, J. C. *The Physiology of Synapses.* Berlin-Göttingen-Heidelberg: Springer, 1964. Reproduced by permission.

Figure 17.14 Modified from: Patton, H. D. Spinal reflexes and synaptic transmission. In T. C. Ruch and H. D. Patton (Eds.), *Physiology and Biophysics* (19th ed.). Philadelphia: Saunders, 1965. Reproduced by permission.

Figure 17.15 From: Gardner, E. *Fundamentals of Neurology* (5th ed.). Philadelphia: Saunders, 1968. Reproduced by permission.

Figure 17.16 Modified from: Ranson, S. W., and Clark, S. L. *The Anatomy of the Nervous System* (10th ed.). Philadelphia: Saunders, 1959. Reproduced by permission.

Figure 17.20 Modified from: Penfield, W., and Roberts, L. *Speech and Brain-mechanisms.* Princeton, N.J.: Princeton University Press, 1959. Copyright © 1959 by The Princeton University Press. Reprinted by permission of Princeton University Press.

Figure 17.22 Modified from: MacLean, P. D. Psychosomatic disease and the "visceral brain." Recent developments bearing on the Papez theory of emotion. *Psychosomatic Medicine,* 1941, *11,* 338–353. (The original figure was based on work of W. Krieg.) Reproduced by permission of the author and Harper & Row, Hoeber Medical Division.

Table 18.1 Modified from: "Contemporary Psychophysics" by Eugene Galanter, from *New Directions in Psychology,* Volume One, by Roger Brown, E. Galanter, E. H. Hess, and G. Mandler. Copyright © by Holt, Rinehart and Winston, Inc. Reprinted by permission of Holt, Rinehart and Winston, Inc.

Figure 18.3 Reprinted from *Sensory Communication,* W. A. Rosenblith (Ed.), by permission of The M.I.T. Press, Cambridge, Massachusetts. Copyright © 1961 by The Massachusetts Institute of Technology. The figure is from the article by S. S. Stevens, "The psychophysics of sensory function," which appeared in *Sensory Communication.*

Figure 18.7 Based on Walls, G. L. *The Vertebrate Eye.* Bloomfield Hills, Mich.: Cranbrook Institute of Science, 1942. Reprinted with permission.

Figure 18.11 Modified from: Polyak, S. *The Vertebrate Visual System.* Chicago: University of Chicago Press, 1957. Copyright © 1957 by The University of Chicago Press. Reprinted by permission of The University of Chicago Press. The version of the figure used here is modified from: Butter, C. M., *Neuropsychology: The Study of the Brain and Behavior.* Belmont, Calif.: Brooks/Cole, 1968. Copyright © by Wadsworth Publishing Company, Inc. Reprinted by permission of the publisher, Brooks/Cole Publishing Company.

Figure 18.12 Reprinted by permission of the publishers from: Hans-Lukas Teuber, William S. Battersby, and Morris B. Bender, *Visual Field Defects after Penetrating Missile Wounds of the Brain.* Cambridge, Mass.: Harvard University Press. Copyright 1960, by The Commonwealth Fund. By permission of Harvard University Press.

Figure 18.14 From: MacNichol, Edward F., Jr., Three-pigment color vision. *Scientific American,* 1964, *211,* 6, 48–56. Copyright © 1964 by Scientific American, Inc. All rights reserved.

Figure 18.20 Based on: DeValois, R. L., Abramov, I., and Jacobs, G. H. Analysis of response patterns of LGN cells. *Journal of the Optical Society of America,* 1966, *7,* 966–977. Reproduced by permission.

Figure 18.30 Based on: Davis, H. and Silverman, S. R. (Eds.) *Hearing and Deafness* (3d ed.). New York: Holt, Rinehart and Winston, 1970. The original version of this figure appeared in: Stevens, S. S., and Davis, H. *Hearing: Its Psychology and Physiology.* New York: Wiley, 1938. Reproduced by permission.

Figure 18.38 Modified from: Erickson, R. P. Sensory neural patterns and gustation. In Y. Zotterman (Ed.), *Olfaction and Taste.* Copyright © 1963 by Pergamon Press, Ltd.

Figure 19.1 From: Glickstein, M. Neurophysiology of learning and memory. In T. C. Ruch and H. D. Patton (Eds.), *Physiology and Biophysics* (19th ed.). Philadelphia: Saunders, 1965. Reproduced by permission.

Figure 19.2 Modified from: McCleary, R. A. Response specificity in the behavioral effects of limbic system lesions in the cat. *Journal of Comparative and Physiological Psychology, 54,* 1961, 605–613. Copyright 1961 by The American Psychological Association, and reproduced by permission.

Figures 19.6 and 19.7 Modified from: Penfield, W. and Roberts, L. *Speech and Brain-mechanisms.* Princeton, N.J.: Princeton University Press, 1959. Copyright © 1959 by The Princeton University Press. Reprinted by permission of Princeton University Press.

Figure 19.10 Modified from: Stellar, E. The physiology of motivation. *Psychological Review, 61,* 1954, 5–22. Copyright 1954 by The American Psychological Association, and reproduced by permission.

Figure 19.11 Modified from: Corbit, J. D. Osmotic thirst: Theoretical and experimental analysis. *Journal of Comparative and Physiological Psychology, 67,* 1969, 3–14. Copyright 1969 by The American Psychological Association, and reproduced by permission.

Figure 19.12 (Graphs) Modified from: Teitelbaum, P. Disturbances in feeding and drinking behavior after hypothalamic lesions. In M. R. Jones (Ed.). *Nebraska Symposium on Motivation.* Lincoln, Nebr.: University of Nebraska Press, 1961. Reproduced by permission.

Page 662: Quotation slightly modified from Penfield and Roberts: Penfield, W., and Roberts, L. *Speech and Brain-mechanisms.* Princeton, N.J.: Princeton University Press. Copyright © 1959 by The Princeton University Press. Reprinted by permission of Princeton University Press.

ability A general term referring to the potential for the acquisition of a skill or to an already acquired skill. Cf. *aptitude and achievement.*
abscissa The horizontal axis of a graph; measures of the independent variable (*q.v.*) are usually plotted on this axis.
absolute refractory period A brief period during the discharge of a nerve impulse when the neuron cannot be fired again. *Cf. relative refractory period.*
absolute threshold The smallest amount of a stimulus that can be perceived. *Cf. differential threshold.*
abstraction A learning process in which an individual learns to disregard some properties of objects and to respond only to certain properties that the objects have in common. It is the process through which concepts (*q.v.*) are formed.
accommodation (1) A change in the shape of the lens of the eye that focuses the image of an object on the retina. It compensates for the distance of the object from the observer. (2) According to Piaget, the use of schemas (*q.v.*) to adapt to the world.
acetylcholine (ACh) A transmitter (*q.v.*) chemical in the nervous system. *See Acetylcholinesterase.*
acetylcholinesterase (AChE) An enzyme that destroys the transmitter substance acetylcholine (*q.v.*).
ACh *See acetylcholine.*
AChE *See acetylcholinesterase.*
achievement Accomplishment on a test of knowledge or skill; also a personal motive.
achievement motive *See achievement need.*
achievement need A need to succeed and to strive against standards of excellence; it serves to motivate an individual to do well.
achievement test Any test used to measure present knowledge or skills—especially knowledge or skills developed through specific training.
achromatism Total color blindness (*q.v.*); extremely rare.
acquired fear A learned fear.
acquired need A learned motive.
acquisition The gradual strengthening of a learned response.
acquisition curve The graphic representation of the acquisition process in which the strength of the response is measured on the vertical axis and the number of learning trials on the horizontal.
action potential Alterations in electrical potential along a nerve fiber which accompany the conduction of an impulse.
activation pattern An EEG pattern accompanying arousal in which fast, irregular waves appear.
activator A drug used to increase the activity level of a person otherwise depressed or withdrawn.
active avoidance conditioning Learning to make a particular response to a warning signal, such as shuttling from one side of a compartment to the other, to avoid a noxious stimulus. *Cf. passive avoidance conditioning.*
activity A general term covering restlessness, exploration, and miscellaneous responses to environmental stimuli; considered to be a general unlearned drive (*q.v.*).
acute experiment In biological psychology, an experiment usually done on anesthetized, nonbehaving animals, often done over a relatively short time. *Cf. chronic experiment.*
adaptation A change in the sensitivity of a sense organ due to stimulation or lack of stimulation. In general, all senses become less sensitive as they are stimulated and more sensitive in the absence of stimulation. *See also dark adaptation.*
adaptation level A theory of context effects (*q.v.*) which holds that background acts to set a standard against which events or objects are perceived.
addictions States of periodic or chronic intoxication produced by a drug (*q.v.*), with an overpowering desire for the drug, a tendency to increase the dose, and a physical and a psychological dependence on the drug. *Cf. Habituation.*

adequate stimulus Stimulation of the type that typically excites a sensory channel. E.g., light is the adequate stimulus for vision. *See receptor.*
adjustment The relationship that exists between an individual and his environment, especially his social environment, in the satisfaction of his motives. *See also method of adjustment.*
adrenal glands A pair of endocrine glands located on the top of the kidneys. They secrete the hormones epinephrine (*q.v.*), nonepinephrine (*q.v.*), and cortin (*q.v.*).
adrenaline *See epinephrine.*
affectional drive A general unlearned drive (*q.v.*) to have contact with and be close to another organism.
affectional motive *See affectional drive.*
affective reactions Psychotic reactions marked by extremes of mood, e.g., depression or manic elation.
afferent code The pattern of neural input to the central nervous system (*q.v.*) that corresponds to various aspects of the external stimulating environment.
afferent fibers Nerve fibers which receive and carry impulses produced by internal and external stimuli to the central nervous system. *Cf. efferent fibers.*
affiliation (affiliative) need The need to associate with or belong with other people.
aggression A general term applying to feelings of anger or hostility. Aggression functions as a motive, often in response to threats, insults, or frustrations.
alarm reaction The first stage of the general-adaptation syndrome (*q.v.*), in which a person reacts vigorously to a stressful situation.
all-or-none law The principle that a nerve impulse (*q.v.*) is either evoked at full strength or not evoked at all. *See threshold.*
alpha rhythm One of the named rhythms of the EEG (*q.v.*); has a frequency of 8–12 Hz and a voltage of about 50 μV as measured at the surface of the skull.
alternation An experimental method in which the subject is required to alternate responses in a pattern such as left-right-left-right or left-left-right-right. The method has been used in the study of thinking in animals and children. *See also delayed alternation, delayed reaction.*
ambivalence Having both positive and negative feelings toward some object or individual at the same time.
amnesia Generally any loss of memory; specifically, a neurotic reaction in which a person forgets his own identity and is unable to recognize familiar people and situations. *See also dissociative reaction.*
amplitude The intensity at any given instant of energy, e.g., acoustic or electric energy.
amygdala A structure of the forebrain connected with the hypothalamus and concerned in emotion.
anal stage The stage, according to psychoanalytic theory, during which the child's interest centers on anal activities. *See pregenital stages.*
analgesics Drugs (*q.v.*) that lessen pain ("pain-killers").
animistic reasoning Reasoning based on coincidences in nature. For example, if there is a thunderstorm on the day a boy plays hooky from school, then according to animistic reasoning, the boy's truancy caused the thunderstorm.
anomalous color defect Color weakness in which a person is able to discriminate colors when they are vivid but is colorblind when they are poorly saturated.
antisocial reaction Little or no concern for other people and little feeling of right and wrong. *See sociopathic personality.*
anxiety A vague, or objectless, fear.
anxiety attack *See anxiety reaction.*
anxiety reaction One of the major classes of psychoneurosis, characterized by anxiety.
aperiodic sound A complex sound consisting of waves of various heights and widths appearing in random order. *See also random noise; cf. periodic sound.*

aphasia A language defect ordinarily due to damage or disease of the brain. It may be a sensory disorder consisting of some impairment in reading or understanding of speech, or it may be a motor disorder consisting of an impairment in the writing or speaking of language. *See also agnosia, apraxia.*

apparent motion Perceived motion in which no actual movement of the stimulus pattern over the receptor occurs.

approach-approach conflict Conflict in which a person is motivated to approach two different goals that are incompatible.

approach-avoidance conflict Conflict in which a person is both attracted and repelled by the same goal.

apraxia A disorder due to brain injury, characterized by inability to remember how to perform skilled movements such as driving a car, dressing oneself, or playing baseball. *See also agnosia, aphasia.*

aptitude Ability to profit by training. *See also scholastic aptitude, vocational aptitude.*

arithmetic mean One measure of central tendency (*q.v.*), commonly called the average, computed by summing all the scores in a frequency distribution, then dividing by the number of scores. *Cf. median, mode.*

arousal An increase in alertness and muscular tension.

art A skill or knack for doing something that is acquired by study, practice, and special experience. *Cf. science.*

assimilation A term used in Piaget's theory of thought, or cognitive development; refers to the ways schemas (*q.v.*) are modified through the incorporation of new information.

association A general term referring to any connection formed through learning.

"association" cortex A general term for areas of the cortex outside the primary sensory and motor areas.

association neuron A neuron, usually within the central nervous system, which occupies a position between sensory and motor neurons.

association theory A theory of learning in which the fundamental process in learning is assumed to be the gradual formation of an associative bond between stimuli or between a stimulus and a response.

associative process A process within the organism that is some part or fraction of an original, either unlearned or previously learned, process.

astigmatism Irregularities in the shape of the cornea or other structures of the eye transmitting light to the retina; these cause parts of an image projected on the retina to be out of focus.

atmosphere effect Distortion of reasoning due to the way in which the premises of a syllogism (*q.v.*) are worded. *Cf. Opinion effect.*

attention Focusing on certain aspects of current experience and neglecting others. Attention has a focus in which events are clearly perceived and a margin in which they are less clearly perceived.

attitude A tendency to respond either positively or negatively to certain persons, objects, or situations. *See also set.*

attitude scale A method of measuring attitudes which typically consists of a set of items, each having a preestablished scale value, to be checked with favor or disfavor by the examinee. *See also Thurstone scale and Likert scale.*

attribute The perceived quality or aspect of a stimulus or person; a psychological dimension of sensory experience

attribution An aspect of the perception of people in which we infer attributes, or characteristics, of people from certain types of nonrole behavior.

audiogram A graph representing the absolute threshold of hearing at different frequencies.

audiometer A device for obtaining an audiogram, used to detect deafness.

auditory canal The canal leading from the outside of the head to the eardrum; also called the external auditory meatus.

auditory nerve The nerve leading from the cochlea and conducting impulses to the brain.

authoritarian personality The traits that characterize an individual who seeks security in authority and wants a social hierarchy in which everybody has and knows his place. *See also ethnocentric personality.*

autistic Thoughts which do not correspond to perceptual reality and are strongly determined by a person's needs.

autokinetic effect Apparent movement (*q.v.*) of a small spot of light against a completely dark background in a completely dark room.

autonomic changes Changes in heart rate, blood pressure, and so forth, controlled by impulses in the autonomic system.

autonomic conditioning The conditioning of responses controlled by the autonomic nervous system, e.g. salivation, heart rate, dilation or constriction of blood vessels, intestinal contraction or relaxation.

autonomic system A division of the nervous system serving certain endocrine glands and the smooth muscles. It controls internal changes in the body during emotion as well as other functions that are essential to homeostasis. *See also parasympathetic and sympathetic systems.*

aversion therapy A form of behavior modification (*q.v.*) in which the stimuli eliciting the behavior to be eliminated are paired with unpleasant states of affairs; in time, these stimuli tend to be avoided.

aversive conditioning Any conditioning of a response to a noxious stimulus such as shock.

avoidance-avoidance conflict Conflict in which a person is caught between two negative goals. As he tries to avoid one goal, he is brought closer to the other, and vice versa.

avoidance learning Learning to avoid a noxious stimulus, e.g., shock, by responding appropriately to a warning signal.

axon A nerve fiber transmitting impulses from the cell body to an adjacent neuron or to an effector.

backward conditioning Presenting the CS after the US in classical conditioning; little or no conditioning results from such pairing of stimuli.

barbiturates A class of drugs (*q.v.*) that depress the central nervous system and produce sleep.

baseline A stable and reliable level of performance that can be used as a basis for assessing changes in behavior caused by the introduction of independent variables (*q.v.*).

basic anxiety A concept in Karen Horney's theory of personality; anxiety learned as a reaction to a variety of tension-laden situations giving rise to neurotic needs (*q.v.*).

basilar membrane The membrane in the cochlea on which the organ of Corti is located. Its motion is important in hearing.

basket nerve ending A specialized structure at the root of hairs on the body. It is regarded as a sense organ for pressure or touch.

beginning spurt The tendency for the work curve to be elevated briefly at the beginning of a period of work. *Cf. warming up.*

behavior Any observable action of a person or animal.

behavior disorder A general term referring to psychoneurotic reactions (*q.v.*), psychotic reactions (*q.v.*), personality disorders (*q.v.*), and chronic brain syndromes (*q.v.*). Means about the same thing as "mental disorder" or "mental illness."

behavior modification A form of psychotherapy which focuses on changing the behavioral problem by using techniques of classical conditioning (*q.v.*), operant conditioning (*q.v.*), and perceptual learning (*q.v.*). *See desensitization, counterconditioning, reciprocal inhibition, aversion therapy.*

behavior therapy *See behavior modification.*

behavioral sciences The sciences most concerned with human and animal behavior. The principal behavioral sciences are psychology, sociology, and social anthropology, but they also include certain aspects of history, economics, political science, and zoology.
behaviorism A viewpoint held early in the twentieth century by some experimental psychologists who were opposed to the method of introspection (*q.v.*) and proposed that psychology be limited to the study of observable behavior (*q.v.*).
belief The acceptance of a statement or proposition. It does not necessarily involve an attitude (*q.v.*), although it may.
belongingness and love needs Motives in the hierarchy of human motivation proposed by Maslow; needs for affection, affiliation, and identification. *See physiological needs for a list of other needs in the hierarchy.*
beta rhythm One of the named rhythms of the EEG (*q.v.*); has a frequency of about 13–25 Hz and relatively low voltage. Sometimes called low-voltage, fast (or high-frequency) activity.
binaural Pertaining to the simultaneous use of the two ears.
binocular Pertaining to the simultaneous use of the two eyes.
biopsychology A general term referring to the study of the relationships between bodily events on the one hand and behavior (*q.v.*) and experience (*q.v.*) on the other.
bipolar cell A neuron (*q.v.*) with a single axon and a single dendrite; in the eye, a cell connecting the rods and cones (*q.v.*), with ganglion cells (*q.v.*).
blind spot The region of the retina where fibers leave the eyeball to form the optic nerve. There are no photosensitive receptors at this point.
bouton "Buttons" or swellings of axon (*q.v.*) endings at synapses; they contain the transmitter (*q.v.*) chemicals.
brain The part of the nervous system cased in the skull. It is the site of centers for sensory experience, motivation, learning, and thinking.
brainwashing Systematic attempts to change attitudes, especially political attitudes (*q.v.*).
brain waves Electrical fluctuations in brain activity recorded from the skull. *See also electroencephalogram.*
brightness A dimension of color that refers to the relative degree of whiteness, grayness, or blackness of the color, as distinguished from hue and saturation (*q.v.*). The term is also used to refer to the perceived intensity of a light.
brightness constancy A phenomenon of perception in which a person perceives an object as having the same brightness despite marked differences in the physical energy stimulating the eye.

CA *See chronological age.*
castration Operative removal of the male gonads, used experimentally to study the effects of reducing sex hormones. *Cf. ovariectomy.*
catatonic type A kind of schizophrenia (*q.v.*) characterized by negativism and a state of muscular rigidity.
cell assembly A functionally organized group of neurons; thought, in one theory, to be the neural basis for simple perceptual experiences. *See phase sequence.*
centile score The percentage of the scores in a distribution that are equal to or less than the obtained score; sometimes called percentile score.
central nervous system The part of the nervous system enclosed in the bony case of the skull and backbone. *Cf. peripheral nervous system.*
central stimulation Electrical or chemical stimulation of some region of the brain, usually in the waking animal, by means of a permanently implanted electrode or pipette.
central sulcus A groove in the cerebral cortex dividing the frontal lobe from the parietal lobe.
central tendency A statistic (*q.v.*) used to represent the center, or

midpoint, of a frequency distribution (*q.v.*). *See arithmetic mean, median, and mode.*

CER *See conditioned emotional response.*

cerebellum A structure in the hindbrain concerned with the coordination of movements and balance.

cerebral cortex The gray matter covering the cerebrum.

cerebrum The largest structure of the forebrain consisting of white matter (fiber tracts), deeper structures, and covered by the cerebral cortex (*q.v.*).

chaining Learning of a series of responses in which the stimulus arising from one response is associated with the next response in the series.

character The ethical or moral traits of personality. *See personality.*

ChE *See cholinesterase.*

chemical senses The senses of taste and smell.

chemotherapy The treatment of a psychoneurotic or a psychotic reaction with a drug or chemical substance, e.g., with a tranquilizer (*q.v.*).

cholinesterase (ChE) An enzyme (*q.v.*) that destroys the transmitter (*q.v.*) acetylcholine (*q.v.*); its action is less rapid than that of acetylcholinesterase (*q.v.*).

choroid layer The middle layer of the wall of the eyeball, dark in color and opaque. *See retina and sclera.*

chromosome A long chain-like structure in the nuclei of body and germ cells containing genes.

chronic brain syndrome Behavior disorders produced by long-lasting disturbances in brain function.

chronic experiment In biological psychology, experiments usually done on awake, behaving animals, and often carried out over a long period of time. *Cf. acute experiment.*

chronological age (CA) Age in years. *Cf. mental age.*

ciliary muscle A muscle attached to the lens of the eye which thickens the lens when it contracts, and flattens the lens when it relaxes. It controls accommodation.

cingulate gyrus A cortical portion of the limbic system (*q.v.*) which lies in the longitudinal fissure (*q.v.*) above the corpus callosum (*q.v.*).

class *See social class.*

classical conditioning Learning that takes place when a conditioned stimulus is paired with an unconditioned stimulus.

classical organization theory A theory, sometimes called Theory X, that people need a "chain of command." *Cf. integrative organization theory.*

client-centered therapy A nondirective therapy (*q.v.*) developed by Carl Rogers which typically is not so intensive or prolonged as psychoanalysis.

clinical methods Methods of collecting data in which information is obtained about people who come to physicians and psychologists for assistance.

clinical psychology A branch of psychology concerned with psychological methods of recognizing and treating behavior disorders, and research into their causes.

closure The tendency for gaps to be perceived as filled in.

clustering The tendency in free recall (*q.v.*) for items to be recalled in groups that are similar in meaningfulness, hierarchy, or conceptual category.

cochlea A bony cavity, coiled like a snail shell, containing receptor organs for hearing. It contains three canals: vestibular, tympanic, and cochlear.

cochlear duct One of the canals in the cochlea.

cochlear microphonic potential A fluctuating voltage, or potential (*q.v.*), recorded from the inner ear that follows the stimulating energy very closely.

coefficient of contingency A measure of correlation that may be computed from nominal measurements, i.e., when individuals have been classified in categories. Symbol: *C*. *See also coefficient of correlation, rank-difference correlation, and product-moment correlation.*

coefficient of correlation A number between +1.00 and —1.00 expressing the degree of relationship between two sets of measurements arranged in pairs. A coefficient of +1.00 (or —1.00) represents perfect correlation, and a coefficient of .00 represents no correlation at all. *See also rank-difference correlations, product-moment correlation.*
cognition A thought or idea.
cognitive *See cognition.*
cognitive dissonance A motivational state produced by inconsistencies between simultaneously held cognitions (*q.v.*), or between a cognition and behavior.
cognitive map Tolman's term for the learned representation of a subject's environment.
cognitive overload A state in which there is more information directed at a person than he can process in thought at a particular time. *See cognition.*
cognitive theory of dreams A method of dream interpretation which views the actual dream, or the manifest content (*q.v.*), as an attempt by the dreamer to think about, and solve, important personal problems. *Cf. wish fulfillment.*
color blindness A defect that makes a person unable to tell the difference between two or more colors that most other people can easily distinguish.
color circle An arrangement of colors in which hues are spokes of a wheel and saturation is represented by radial distance on the spokes.
color constancy The tendency to perceive colors as unvarying despite changes in the sensory input.
color solid A three-dimensional diagram representing the relationships of hue, saturation, and brightness in the perception of color.
communication structure The pattern of closed and open channels of communication within a group of individuals.
community mental health The attempt to bring public health principles to the area of mental health. Community mental health stresses crisis intervention in psychiatric emergencies; it attempts to make inexpensive specialized psychotherapy available to poor people; and it attempts to resolve community problems that lead to behavior disorders.
comparative psychology The branch of psychology that compares the behaviors of one species with those of others.
comparison level A subjective standard for judging the outcomes of social interactions. Unsatisfactory outcomes fall below the comparison level, satisfactory outcomes are above it. *See adaptation level.*
compensation A defense mechanism in which an individual substitutes one activity for another in an attempt to satisfy frustrated motives. It usually implies failure or loss of self-esteem in one activity and the compensation of this loss by efforts in some other realm of endeavor.
competence motivation The motive to develop skills which make possible effective interaction with the environment; also, to exercise one's potentialities. *See general unlearned motive.*
complementary colors Pairs of hues that, when mixed in proper proportions, are seen as gray.
complex unit A type of neuron in the visual cortex which fires only when a particular shape, or kind, of stimulus is projected onto the retina. In contrast with the simple unit (*q.v.*), these units do not require that the stimulus be at a particular place on the retina; it is only necessary that they be of a particular shape. The unit will fire to stimulation produced by that particular shape over a fairly wide expanse of the retina.
compliance Behavior in accordance with group pressures without accepting the values and norms (*q.v.*) of the group as our own. *Cf. private acceptance.*
compulsion An irrational act that constantly intrudes into a person's

behavior. *See obsessive-compulsive reaction.*

compulsive personality Personality pattern disurbance characterized by rigidity of habits and excessive conscientiousness.

compulsive reaction Behavior disorder in which a person finds ambiguity and uncertainty extremely uncomfortable. Extreme emphasis is put on "doing things the right way."

computer-assisted instruction Programmed learning (*q.v.*) in which the program is stored in a computer which can respond to correct and incorrect answers by the learner.

concept An internal process representing a common property of objects or events, usually represented by a word or name.

concordance ratio The percentage of relatives of a person who show the same trait as the person in question. Concordance ratios are often computed for identical twins (*q.v.*) and fraternal twins (*q.v.*).

concrete operations The fourth stage in Piaget's characterization of mental development in which the child became able to use rules based on concrete instances, but is still unable to deal with abstract qualities.

conjunctive concept A concept defined by the joint presence of several characteristics. *See concept; cf. disjunctive concept, relational concept.*

conditioned emotional response (CER) Fear conditioned to stimuli associated with noxious events; often investigated by using a baseline technique in a Skinner box (*q.v.*)

conditioned reinforcement *See secondary reinforcement.*

conditioned response A response produced by a conditioned stimulus after learning.

conditioned stimulus The stimulus that is originally ineffective but that, after pairing with an unconditioned stimulus, evokes the conditioned response. *See also classical conditioning.*

conditioning A general term referring to the learning of some particular response. *See also classical conditioning.*

conduction deafness Deafness due to an impairment of the conduction of energy to the cochlea. *Cf. nerve deafness.*

cone A photosensitive receptor in the retina and most sensitive under daytime conditions of seeing. Cones are closely packed in the fovea and are the receptors in color vision. *cf. rod.*

confabulation The filling in of gaps in memory with plausible guesses; characteristic of chronic brain syndromes (*q.v.*), and a part of Korsakoff's syndrome (*q.v.*).

conflict *See approach-avoidance, approach-approach, avoidance-avoidance, motivational conflict.*

conflict of motives *See motivational conflict.*

conformity The tendency to be influenced by group pressure and to acquiesce to group norms (*q.v.*) *See private acceptance, compliance.*

connotative meaning The emotional and evaluative meaning of a concept. *Cf. denotative meaning.*

conscience *See superego.*

conservation Piaget's term for the ability of the child to ignore irrelevant transformations. For instance, the child judges things in terms of their immediate perceptual appearance.

consistency theory A theory of attitudes (*q.v.*) which states that attitudes provide consistency for cognitions (*q.v.*) and tendencies to respond that otherwise would be discrepant, incongruous, or dissonant.

consolidation The theory that memory traces, or engrams (*q.v.*), must go through a strengthening process before they can become a fixed part of long-term memory.

constancy *See perceptual constancy.*

constitution The genetic (*q.v.*) makeup of an individual.

consummatory response A response that tends to satisfy a primary drive, e.g. eating, drinking, copulation.

context Surroundings, background, or environment.
contiguity, law of The principle that two events must occur close together in time and space to be associated in learning.
contingency Generally, the state of affairs that exists when one thing depends upon another. More specifically, reinforcement is said to be contingent upon certain responses in operant conditioning (*q.v.*). *See also coefficient of contingency.*
continuation The tendency to perceive objects as forming a line, curve, or other continuous pattern. *See also grouping.*
continuity theory A theory which holds that learning occurs by a gradual strengthening of S-R bonds. *Cf. noncontinuity theory.*
continuous reinforcement Reinforcement of all correct responses.
contour The line of demarcation perceived by an observer whenever there is a marked difference between the brightness of color in one place and that in an adjoining region.
contrast A marked difference in stimulation, as between light and dark, silence and noise, and hot and cold; also, more specifically, the difference in brightness between an object and its immediate surround.
contrast threshold *See differential threshold.*
control Used in two senses: (1) The group or condition in an experiment that is similar in all respects to the experimental group or condition except that it does not include the independent variable. (2) Any stick, switch, wheel, or other device used by an individual to operate a device or machine.
controlled sampling Sampling (*q.v.*) according to some plan that provides for certain numbers of people in each category according to their incidence in the population sampled.
convergence Turning the eyes inward toward the nose as objects are brought closer to the eyes.
conversion reaction A psychoneurotic reaction (*q.v.*) in which motivational conflict has been converted into physical symptoms, so that the person appears to have various ailments that have no physical basis.
cornea The outermost, transparent layer of the front of the eye.
corpus callosum A band of fibers connecting the two cerebral hemispheres (*q.v.*).
correlation Generally, the relationship between any two events. *See coefficient of correlation.*
correlation coefficient *See coefficient of correlation; correlation.*
cortex A rind or covering. *See also cerebral cortex.*
cortical Pertaining to a cortex; usually refers to the cerebral cortex, but can also refer to the cortex of other structures, e.g., the adrenal gland.
cortin A general term for the hormones secreted by the cortical part of the adrenal glands (*q.v.*). It governs, among other things, levels of sodium and water in the internal environment.
costs In social psychology (*q.v.*) anything that would deter or inhibit behavior.
counseling *See counseling psychology.*
counseling psychology The branch of psychology stressing the giving of advice and assistance to individuals with vocational or personal problems. *See clinical psychology.*
counterconditioning The weakening of a conditioned response (*q.v.*) by conditioning the stimuli that elicit the response to other responses which are incompatible with the response to be eliminated. *See behavior modification.*
CR *See conditioned response.*
cranial nerves The nerves serving the brain. There are 12 cranial nerves, some sensory, some motor, and some of mixed function.
cretinism A physical disorder caused by insufficient thyroxin in infancy and childhood. It results in dwarfism and mental retardation, but it can be alleviated or cured by administration of thyroxin.

criterion In the evaluation of tests, the job or performance that a test is supposed to predict; in learning, the level of performance considered to represent relatively complete learning.
critical incidents A technique of making a job analysis by compiling instances that are critical for doing the job satisfactorily, as distinguished from those representing work that can be done by almost anybody and are not important in determining whether a job is done satisfactorily.
critical period A period of time in which an organism is most ready for the acquisition of certain responses.
cross-cultural method The approach which studies cultural patterns in a wide sample of societies.
cross-sectional method The study of groups of persons or a process at a particular stage of development; different groups are contrasted at each stage of development. *Cf. longitudinal method.*
CS *See conditioned stimulus.*
cue-producing response A response which serves as a kinesthetic stimulus for another response. It may be either an observable response or an implicit response.
culture The customs, habits, traditions, and artifacts that characterize a people or a social group. It includes the attitudes (*q.v.*) and beliefs (*q.v.*) that the group has about important aspects of its life.
culture pattern Widely shared ways of behaving in a society together with the beliefs that accompany them.
curiosity A tendency to prefer or to respond to novel stimulation; considered to be a general unlearned drive (*q.v.*) *See also exploratory drive, manipulative drive.*

Daltonism Color blindness (*q.v.*).
dark adaptation The increase in sensitivity of the eye that takes place when the eye is allowed to remain in the dark.
deaf-mute A person who is completely deaf and consequently unable to talk. Such a person, however, ordinarily can be taught how to talk.
decibel The unit of measurement used to express the intensity of a sound. It is essentially the logarithm of a ratio of pressures or energies; usually expressed by the formula

$$db = 20 \log \frac{P_1}{P_2}$$

A reference must be given. In hearing, the reference level is a pressure of 0.0002 dyne per square centimeter.
decorticate Lacking the cerebral cortex.
deduction A logical process for deriving conclusions from *a priori* assumptions.
defense mechanism A reaction to frustration that defends the person against anxiety and serves to disguise his motives, so that he deceives himself about his real motives and goals. Defense mechanisms also enhance self-esteem. For examples, *see displacement, reaction formation, repression.*
degeneration A neuroanatomical means for studying the course of fiber pathways.
deindividuation Anonymity; not knowing the names and personal characteristics of other people in a social situation. *Cf. individuation.*
delay conditioning A classical-conditioning situation in which the CS persists at least until the beginning of the US.
delayed alternation A variation on the alternation method in which a subject is required to wait for an interval between each response in a series of alternations. *See also alternation, delayed reaction.*
delayed reaction A type of experiment in which a subject is shown the correct stimulus, usually along with incorrect stimuli, but must wait for an interval before having an opportunity to make the correct choice.
delayed-response test One of several behavioral situations in which there is a delay between the presentation of a stimulus and the opportunity

to respond. *See delayed reaction.*
delta rhythm One of the named rhythms of the EEG (*q.v.*); has a frequency of about 1–3 Hz and its voltage is relatively great, about 150 μV as measured at the surface of the skull. Characteristic of deep sleep and sometimes called high-voltage, slow (low-frequency) activity.
delusion A groundless, irrational belief or thought, usually of grandeur or of persecution. It is characteristic of paranoid reactions (*q.v.*)
dendrite A nerve fiber that normally is stimulated by an external physical stimulus or by the impulse brought to it by an axon (*q.v.*).
denotative meaning The socially accepted definition of a concept. *Cf. connotative meaning.*
deoxyribonucleic acid (DNA) Large molecules found in the nuclei of cells, thought to be the chemical basis of reproduction. Genes (*q.v.*) are portions of the DNA molecule.
dependency need The need to depend on other people for advice, counsel, and moral support.
dependent variable The variable that changes as a result of changes in the independent variable (*q.v.*).
depolarization A decrease in the internal negativity of a nerve cell, especially when stimulated. If depolarization goes to threshold (*q.v.*), the cell will fire.
depressive disorder A mental disorder, characterized by anxiety, guilt feelings, self-depreciation, or suicidal tendencies.
depressive reaction Psychoneurotic reaction characterized by severe depression; often a reaction to a severe loss.
depth perception Perception of the relative distance of objects from the observer.
descriptive statistics Statistical measures that summarize the characteristics of a frequency distribution (*q.v.*), or the relationship between two or more distributions. *Cf. inferential statistics.*
desensitization Generally, a weakening of a response, usually an emotional response, with repeated exposure to a situation; more specifically, a method used in psychotherapy to enable a person to be comfortable in situations in which he was previously highly anxious. *See behavior modification.*
developmental psychology The branch of psychology studying changes in behavior (*q.v.*) that occur with changes in age.
deviation IQ An intelligence quotient (*q.v.*) based on standard scores (*q.v.*), so that IQs more nearly compare in meaning from one age to another.
deviation score The difference between the score obtained and the mean of the distribution that includes the obtained score. Symbol: ***x.***
dichromatism Partial color blindness (*q.v.*) consisting of two-color vision. All colors are seen as shades of two hues.
differential psychology The study and comparison of the differences between groups of people, e.g. men and women.
differential reinforcement Reinforcement of the response to one stimulus but not to another. Such reinforcement is used experimentally to establish a discrimination. *Cf. discrimination.*
differential threshold The smallest difference in a stimulus that can be perceived. *See also absolute threshold.*
directional fractionation An autonomic reaction in which heart rate goes down, as in a parasympathetic reaction, while other changes such as skin conductance change, as in a sympathetic response.
directive therapy Therapy in which the therapist prescribes remedies and courses of action much as a physician prescribes medicine. It was used extensively in the early history of psychotherapy. *Cf. nondirective therapy.*
discrimination learning Learning in which the subject learns to choose one stimulus and not another. Usually responses to one stimulus, the positive one, are reinforced

(*q.v.*), while responses to the other stimulus are extinguished (*q.v.*). *See simultaneous discrimination, successive discrimination.*

disjunctive concept A concept that contains at least one element from a larger class of elements. Something is a member of the concept class if it contains at least one of a particular pool of elements, e.g. a strike in baseball is defined in different ways. *See concept; cf. conjunctive concept, relational concept.*

displacement The disguising of the goal of a motive by substituting another in place of it.

display Any means of presenting information to a person.

dissociative reaction A neurotic reaction involving repression (*q.v.*) in which certain aspects of personality and memory are compartmentalized and function more or less independently, e.g., amnesia and multiple personality (*q.v.*).

distributed practice Periods of practice interspersed with periods of rest, often permitting more efficient learning than continuous practice.

distribution *See frequency distribution.*

dizygotic (DZ) twins *See fraternal twins.*

DNA *See deoxyribonucleic acid.*

dominant gene A gene whose hereditary characteristics are always expressed. *Cf. recessive gene.*

double-bind theory States that the psychological stress involved in schizophrenia (*q.v.*) is due to the inconsistencies in verbal and behavioral communication between parent and child.

double-blind technique A method used in the study of drug effects in which neither subject nor observer knows what drug is being administered.

double dissociation A logical requirement for showing that a function is localized in the brain. A lesion in one place should affect performance A but not performance B; a lesion in another place should affect performance B but not performance A.

dream analysis The analysis of the dream content to obtain information about the source of a person's emotional problems; sometimes used in psychoanalysis.

drive A term implying an impetus to behavior or active striving; often used synonomously with motive or need (*q.v.*). *See also general unlearned drive.*

drive-reduction theory The theory that the satisfaction or alleviation of a drive is necessary for a response to be learned.

drive-stimulus reduction theory A theory of reinforcement which says that reinforcement is due to the reduction of the intensity of unpleasant or uncomfortable stimuli. *Cf. drive-reduction theory.*

drug A chemical substance which alters the structure or function of a living organism.

drug dependence See *addictions, habituation.*

dyad A two-person group.

dynamics *See personality dynamics.*

ear drum A thin membrane which separates the outer ear from the middle ear and which vibrates when sound waves reach it.

educational psychology A field of specialization concerned with psychological aspects of teaching and the formal learning processes in school.

Edwards Personal Preference Schedule (EPPS) A test which purports to measure the major personal, or social, motives of individuals.

EEG *See electroencephalogram.*

effectors Organs of response (*q.v.*), muscles and glands.

efferent fibers Nerve fibers which carry impulses from the central nervous system to the organs of response. *Cf. afferent fibers.*

ego In psychoanalysis (*q.v.*), a term referring to the self and to ways of behaving and thinking realistically. The ego delays the satisfaction of motives when necessary; it directs

motives into socially acceptable channels. *See also id, superego.*
egocentrism In Piaget's theory, the inability of a child to take the perceptual frame of reference of another person.
eidetic imagery Extremely detailed imagery; a sort of projection of an image on a mental screen. *See image.*
electroconvulsive shock therapy (EST) A form of therapy used primarily with depressed patients; consists of administering electrical shocks to the brain sufficient to produce convulsions and to render the patient unconscious.
electroencephalogram (EEG) A record of electrical fluctuations in the brain (brain waves), usually obtained by placing electrodes on the skull. *See alpha rhythm, beta rhythm, delta rhythm, and theta rhythm.*
electroencephalography *See electroencephalogram.*
electrolytic lesion A lesion, usually in the nervous system, made by passing an electrical current through an area.
electromagnetic radiation A general term referring to a variety of physical changes in the environment, including light, radio waves, X rays, and cosmic rays. It travels at approximately 186,000 miles per second and can be specified in terms of either wavelength or frequency of vibrations.
electromagnetic spectrum *See electromagnetic radiation.*
electroretinogram (ERG) A record of electrical activity obtained from the eye when it is exposed to light.
embryo A young organism in the early stages of development in man, it refers to the period from shortly after conception until 2 months later. *Cf. fetus.*
emotion Affective states, often accompanied by facial and bodily expression, and have arousing and motivating properties.
empirical Founded on experiments, surveys, and proven facts, as distinguished from that which is asserted by argument, reasoning, or opinion.
empirical law of effect A statement of the fact that responses that produce certain changes in the environment increase in their probability of occurrence.
empirical validity Validity based on observations. *Cf. face validity.*
empiricist One who argues that behavior tendencies, especially perceptual organizing tendencies, depend upon learning and past experience (*q.v.*). *Cf. nativist.*
encounter groups One name for groups which bring mentally healthy people together to enrich life. In general, these groups try to: bring people together to ease the lost and lonely feeling of modern life; open up areas of thought and feeling previously blocked off; improve mutual communication with other people; provide an experience of trust and openness with others; and produce conditions to make the personality changes arising from these experiences long-lasting. Similar types of groups are the laboratory-method groups, or T (training) groups, and sensitivity groups.
end spurt A tendency to give a final spurt of effort at the end of a period of work. It is a factor in the shape of the work curve.
endocrine glands Glands that secrete substances called hormones directly into the blood. The thyroid gland is an example. *Cf. exocrine glands.*
engineering psychology An applied field of psychology concerned with psychological factors in the design and use of equipment. *See human engineering.*
engram The hypothetical memory trace.
enzyme An organic catalyst regulating particular chemical steps in metabolism.
epigenetics The intertwining of nature (*q.v.*) and nurture (*q.v.*) in such a way that there is a constant interplay between these factors in development. For instance, as

applied to behavior, genetically controlled behavior may be modified and shaped by the environment; this newly emergent behavior then interacts with other genetically controlled behaviors to modify them and to be modified by them, and so on.

epinephrine A chemical substance produced by the adrenal medulla that stimulates the sympathetic nervous system. Probably a transmitter (*q.v.*) at certain synapses of the sympathetic nervous system. (Preferred over adrenaline.) *See norepinephrine.*

EPSP *See excitatory postsynaptic potential.*

equipotentiality The idea that capacity for learning is not narrowly localized in the brain.

ERG *See electroretinogram.*

escape learning Learning to escape from a noxious or unpleasant situation by making an appropriate response.

esteem needs Motives in the hierarchy of human motivation proposed by Maslow: needs for prestige, success, and self-respect. *See physiological needs for a listing of the other needs in the hierarchy.*

ethnocentric personality The traits that characterize an individual who is generally hostile or prejudiced toward most groups to which he does not belong. *See also authoritarian personality.*

ethology The study of behavior, especially the instinctive behavior, of animals.

evoked potential The electrical activity recorded from the nervous system that is produced by a stimulus.

excitation (1) Arousal (*q.v.*); (2) increased tendency to respond; (3) depolarization (*q.v.*) or firing of nerve cells. *Cf. inhibition.*

excitatory postsynaptic potential (EPSP) An electric potential of nerve cells due to depolarization (*q.v.*); a decrease in the internal negativity of a nerve cell due to impulses arriving over excitatory fibers. If depolarization goes far enough, the cell fires.

exhaustion The third stage of the general-adaptation syndrome (*q.v.*), in which a person is no longer able to endure stress.

existential therapy A type of psychotherapy in which the therapist accepts the person as he is and tries to help him understand the ways he seeks for meaningfulness and values in life.

exocrine glands Glands that secrete through ducts into cavities of the body, e.g., salivary glands. *Cf. endocrine glands.*

exorcism The attempt to cast out demons or evil spirits by such acts as prayer, religious rites, medicines, or whipping.

experience (1) Refers to the past history of the organism; (2) the immediate perception (*q.v.*) of the present situation or the present content of consciousness.

experimental method A scientific method in which conditions that are likely to affect a result are controlled by the experimenter. It involves dependent and independent variables. *Cf. method of systematic observation.*

experimental psychology A subfield of psychology which seeks to learn more about the fundamental causes of behavior by investigating problems in the areas of sensation and perception, learning and memory, motivation, and the physiological basis of behavior. *Cf. clinical psychology.*

exploratory drive A tendency to explore a novel environment; is considered a general unlearned drive (*q.v.*) not clearly distinguishable from curiosity or manipulative drive (*q.v.*).

external auditory meatus *See auditory canal.*

extinction The procedure of presenting the conditioned stimulus without reinforcement to an organism previously conditioned; also the diminution of a conditioned response resulting from this procedure.

extinction curve A graph of the diminution of previously learned responses during the course of extinction (*q.v*).
extirpation The removal of a part, usually of the nervous system.
extraocular muscles Muscles attached to the sclera layer that turn the eyeball.

face validity The appearance of validity (*q.v.*) in a test because of the similarity of the test to the job to be performed. Face validity is not, however, necessarily true validity. Tests should always be examined with validating procedures to determine whether they are, in fact, valid.
factor analysis A general statistical method, involving coefficients of correlation, that isolates a few common factors in a large number of tests, ratings, or other measurements.
family therapy Therapeutic techniques which try to alter the disturbed behavior of a person in a family by changing the family's patterns of relationships and ways of interacting.
fantasy Daydreaming and imagining a world of one's own, often used as a defense mechanism (*q.v.*).
FAP *See fixed action pattern.*
father figure An instance of transference (*q.v.*) in which a person is regarded as though he were a father.
fatigue A general term referring to the effects of prolonged work or lack of sleep, probably best defined as a feeling of being tired.
feedback The situation in which some aspect of the output regulates the state of the system.
fetus A young organism in the later stages of prenatal development. In man, it refers to the period from 2 months after conception until birth. *Cf. embryo.*
fiber *See nerve fiber.*
field theory A type of psychological theory that stresses the importance of interactions between events in the person's environment.
figural aftereffect A perceptual phenomenon used by gestalt (*q.v.*) psychologists to demonstrate that events in one part of the perceptual field may affect perception in another part.
figure-ground perception Perception of objects or events as standing out clearly from a background.
final common pathway The last neuron before a response is made; usually considered to integrate excitatory and inhibitory influences (*q.v.*).
firing Electrical activity of single nerve cells. *See nerve impulse.*
fissure A relatively deep crevice in the cerebral cortex. *Cf. sulcus. See also central fissure, lateral fissure, longitudinal fissure.*
fixation A rigid habit developed by repeated reinforcement or as a consequence of frustration.
fixed action pattern (FAP) A complex organization of innate responses. *See instinctive behavior.*
fixed-interval schedule A schedule of partial reinforcement (*q.v.)* in which a response made after a certain interval of time is reinforced.
fixed-ratio schedule A schedule of partial reinforcement (*q.v.*) in which every *n*th response is reinforced.
flexion reflex A reflex in which a limb is bent. *Cf. extension reflex.*
forebrain The most forward of three divisions of the brain. It includes the **cerebrum, thalamus, and hypothalamus.** *See also hindbrain, midbrain.*
forgetting A partial or total loss of retention of material previously learned.
formal-discipline theory *See mental-faculty theory.*
formal group A social group that has a relatively permanent structure of positions, jobs, and roles.
formal operations The fifth stage in Piaget's characterization of mental development which is marked by the ability to use abstract rules. The stage of adult thought.
Fourier analysis The analysis of a complex tone into sine-wave components, each specified in terms of frequency and intensity.

fovea A central region of the retina where cones are closely packed together and visual acuity is at its best.

fraternal twins Twins who develop from two different fertilized eggs (ova), and who consequently may be as different in hereditary characteristics as ordinary brothers and sisters. Also called dizygotic (DZ) twins. *Cf. identical twins.*

free association The technique of requiring a patient in psychotherapy to say whatever comes to his mind, regardless of how irrelevant or objectionable it may seem.

free learning Learning a series of words, syllables, or other material without regard to order. Subjects may recall the material in any order it occurs to them. *Cf. serial learning.*

free nerve endings Nerve endings that are not associated with any special receptive structures. They are found in the skin, blood vessels, and many parts of the body. They are regarded as sense organs for pain and probably also for touch and temperature.

free-response method A method of measuring the meaning of concepts in which a person is asked to describe or define a concept.

frequency One of the dimensions of vibrational stimuli, such as light or sound. It is most often used with sound and is stated in number of cycles per second, or hertz (*q.v.*), which is the number of alternations in air pressure per second.

frequency composition The composition of complex tones as specified by Fourier analysis (*q.v.*).

frequency distribution A set of measurements arranged from lowest to highest (or highest to lowest) and accompanied by a count (frequency) of the number of times each measurement or class of measurements occurs.

frequency polygon A frequency distribution (*q.v.*) represented by plotting a point on a graph for each frequency of each score, or class of scores, and connecting the points with straight lines.

frontal association area The nonmotor areas of the frontal lobes said to be involved in certain complex behavioral functions. *See prefrontal lobotomy.*

frontal lobe The lobe of the cerebrum (*q.v.*) which lies in front of the central sulcus (*q.v.*). *See frontal association areas.*

frustration The thwarting of motivated behavior directed at a goal.

frustration tolerance Ability to tolerate frustration and its accompanying anxiety. It is characteristic of well-adjusted people and is something to be learned in achieving mental health.

fugue Temporary amnesia (*q.v.*) in a dissociative reaction (*q.v.*) accompanied by flight.

functional autonomy The ability of certain motives to continue functioning without further reinforcement of the conditions under which they were learned. *See also learned goal.*

functional fixedness A special type of set (*q.v.*) in which individuals cannot use objects in novel ways. It may hinder problem solving.

functionalism A viewpoint taking the middle course among structuralism (*q.v.*), behaviorism (*q.v.*), and gestalt psychology (*q.v.*). Functionalists proposed that all activities serving some adaptive function, including both behavior and experience, be studied by psychologists.

fundamental In hearing, the lowest frequency in a complex tone.

galvanic skin response (GSR) A change in the electrical resistance of the skin, occurring in emotion and in certain other conditions.

ganglion A collection of the cell bodies of neurons.

ganglion cell In the eye, the cells of the third cell layer of the retina. Fibers of the retinal ganglion cells make up the optic nerve.

gene The essential element in the transmission of hereditary characteristics, carried in chromosomes. *See also dominant gene, recessive gene.*

general adaptation syndrome (GAS) A sequence of physiological reactions to prolonged physical or emotional stress; consists of three stages: the alarm reaction, resistance to stress, and exhaustion (*q.v.*).

general motive *See general unlearned drive.*

general unlearned drive A drive that is unlearned but is not aroused by a specific physiological need.

generalization The phenomenon of an organism's responding to situations similar to the one to which it has been conditioned. *See also stimulus generalization.*

generator potential The voltage change that occurs in receptor cells when acted upon by physical energy. Generator potentials trigger nerve impulses from the receptor organ.

genetic *See genes.*

genetic constitution *See constitution.*

genital stage in psychoanalytic theory, the adult stage of personality. It begins around 12 years of age and is characterized by the expression of heterosexual interests. *Cf. pregenital stages, latency period.*

genotype The genetic constitution of an organism made up of dominant and recessive genes. *Cf. phenotype.*

germ cell An egg or sperm cell.

gestalt psychology A viewpoint, developed by German psychologists, that considered introspection (*q.v.*) and behaviorism (*q.v.*) too atomistic and emphasized the importance of configuration in perception (*q.v.*) and insight (*q.v.*) in learning.

gland An organ that secretes. There are two general types, endocrine glands and exocrine glands (*q.v.*).

goal The place, condition, or object that satisfies a motive.

goal gradient In the study of motivational conflict, the increasing strength of a goal, the nearer one is to the goal. Other things being equal, the avoidance gradient for negative goals is steeper than the approach gradient for positive goals.

Golgi tendon organs Receptors located in tendons that are activated when the muscle to which the tendon is attached contracts putting tension on the tendon. *See kinesthetic receptor.*

gonads The sex glands, which are the testicles in the male and the ovaries in the female. They determine secondary sex characteristics such as growth of the breasts, beginning of menstruation, growth of the beard, and change of the voice and also influence sexual motivation.

gradient A state of affairs in which a condition varies continuously and evenly in amount.

gradient of reinforcement The concept that the closer a response is in time and space to a reinforcement, the more the response is strengthened.

gradient of texture One of the principal monocular cues for depth perception. Consists of a gradation in the fineness of detail which can be seen at increasing distances from a person.

grammar The study of the rules for combining words into meaningful sentences.

gray matter Collections of cell bodies in the nervous system. *Cf. white matter.*

group *See social group.*

group dynamics The study of the development and functioning of groups, with special reference to the interactions between groups and the patterns of relationships between individuals within groups.

group norm A widely shared expectation or standard of behavior among most members of a group, class, or culture (*q.v.*).

group test A test that may be administered to a group of people at one time.

group therapy A specialized technique of psychotherapy, consisting of a group of patients discussing their personal problems under the guidance of a therapist.

grouping The tendency to perceive objects in groups rather than as

isolated elements. Grouping is determined by such factors as nearness, similarity, symmetry, and continuation of objects.
growth hormone A hormone secreted by the pituitary gland and controlling the general rate of growth of the body.
GSR *See galvanic skin response.*
gyrus A ridge in the cerebral cortex of the brain. *Cf. sulcus.*

habit A learned response.
habit formation, law of An equation in Hull's mathematic learning theory that expresses the relation between habit strength and number of reinforcements.
habituation (1) The tendency of a response to weaken with repeated presentation of a stimulus; similar to desensitization (*q.v.*). (2) A condition resulting from repeated use of a drug and characterized by a desire for the drug, little or no tendency to increase the dose, and psychological, but not physical, dependence on the drug. *Cf. addictions.*
hair cell Pressure sensitive cells located in the organ of Corti (*q.v.*) which convert pressure waves to nerve impulses.
hallucination Sensory experience in the absence of stimulation of receptors. Hallucinations are present in certain behavior disorders such as schizophrenia (*q.v.*).
hallucinogen Drugs (*q.v.*) that cause distortions of perception. They rarely cause true hallucinations (*q.v.*), which are sensory experiences without sensory input.
harmonics Components of complex tones that are multiples of the fundamental frequency.
hebephrenic type A variety of schizophrenia (*q.v.*) characterized by childishness and regressive behavior.
Hering theory *See opponent process theory.*
hertz (Hz) One cycle per second; e.g., the alpha rhythm (*q.v.*) has a frequency of XX 8–12 Hz.
higher order conditioning Conditioning of a response to a stimulus by pairing the stimulus with another stimulus to which the response has previously been conditioned.
hindbrain The third of three divisions of the brain. It includes the medulla, cerebellum, and pons. *See also forebrain, midbrain.*
hippocampus An important structure in the limbic system (*q.v.*).
histogram A frequency distribution (*q.v.*) represented by bars whose heights vary with the frequencies of the scores or classes of scores.
homeostasis The tendency of the body to maintain a balance among internal physiological conditions, such as temperature, sugar level, oxygen level, and mineral levels.
homonymous hemianopsia Complete blindness, except for some possible vision in the foveal (*q.v.*) region, in the right or left visual field. Caused by lesions of the visual projections in the central nervous system (*q.v.*).
hormones Secretions of endocrine glands that help or inhibit certain chemical steps in the body.
hostility *See aggression.*
hue The aspect of a color that is largely determined by wavelength and that enables us to discriminate blue from red, red from yellow, and so on, as distinguished from brightness and saturation (*q.v.*).
human engineering In psychological usage, the field of specialization concerned with the design of equipment and of tasks performed in the operation of equipment. *See engineering psychology.*
hunger A drive stemming from a physiological need for food.
hypercomplex unit Cells, or units, of the cortex that respond to complex patterns presented to the retina. *Cf. simple unit, complex unit.*
hyperphagia Eating abnormally large quantities of food; associated with injuries in certain regions of the hypothalamus.
hyperpolarization An increase in the internal negativity of a nerve cell, especially when stimulated. *See inhibitory postsynaptic potential. Cf. depolarization.*

hypnosis A state in which a person is extremely susceptible to the suggestion of the hypnotist.
hypnotherapy The use of hypnosis as an aid in therapy; especially useful in the temporary alleviation of certain symptoms and in the temporary lifting of repression (*q.v.*).
hypochondriasis A neurotic reaction (*q.v.*) in which a person is excessively concerned with his physical welfare or constantly complaining of minor ailments; seen in anxiety reactions.
hypothalamus A region of the forebrain which contains centers for the regulation of sleep, temperature, thirst, sex, hunger, and emotion.
hysteria *Cf. conversion reactions.*
Hz *See hertz.*

iconic imagery Fleeting images that may represent persistent activity in sensory channels after exposure to stimulation. *See image.*
id In psychoanalytic theory, the aspect of personality concerned with instinctual reactions for satisfying motives. The id seeks immediate gratification of motives with little regard for the consequences or for the realities of life. *See also ego, superego.*
identical twins Twins who develop from the same fertilized egg (ovum). They have exactly the same kinds of chromosomes and genes and hence the same hereditary characteristics. Also called monozygotic (MZ) twins. *Cf. fraternal twins.*
identification The tendency of children to model their behavior after that of appropriate adults; a defense mechanism (*q.v.*) in which one thinks himself to be like someone else.
idiographic Emphasis on the study of an individual's characteristics. *Cf. nomothetic.*
illusion A perception that does not agree with other, more trustworthy perceptions.
image A representation in the brain of sensory experience. Images may be involved in some thinking (*q.v.*).
imageless thought Thought occurring without the presence of images. The phrase refers particularly to a theory of the nature of thinking entertained by a group of German psychologists about 1900.
imitation Copying the behavior of another.
immunization The hardening of a person's attitude on a particular subject by giving him a mild exposure to an opposing attitude. This exposure hardens the originally held attitude so that it is resistant to change by further facts or arguments, no matter how strong.
implicit response A minute muscle movement ordinarily detectable only by special electrical or mechanical recording methods. Implicit responses, miniatures of large, observable movements, are acquired in previous learning and may be involved in thinking (*q.v.*).
imprinting The very rapid development of response to a stimulus at some critical period of development (*q.v.*). Particularly characteristic of some species of birds.
impulse (1) Sometimes used in psychoanalysis to refer to motive (*q.v.*). (2) The spike potential—the nerve impulse.
incentive A term approximately synonymous with goal, but implying the manipulation of a goal to motivate the individual. Money, for example, is used as an incentive to motivate people to work.
incidental learning In animal learning, learning without incentive or reinforcement. In human learning, learning without intending to learn. *See latent learning.*
incubation A stage in creative thinking during which the problem is put aside and unconscious factors are permitted to work.
independent variable The variable that may be selected or changed by the experimenter and is responsible for changes in the dependent variable (*q.v.*).
individual psychograph A profile of an individual's traits and abilities. It may be compared with a job

psychograph (*q.v.*) to determine whether the individual is fitted for a particular job.

individual test A test that can be given to only one individual at a time, e.g., the Stanford-Binet intelligence Scale (*q.v.*).

individual therapy The school of psychotherapy, developed by Alfred Adler, which stresses neurotic life styles, or neurotic ways of expressing power motivation.

individuation In social situations, the condition in which individual persons in a group are known personally by name and characteristics. *Cf. deindividuation.*

induced movement Movement of a stationary spot perceived when the background of the spot moves. The moon "racing" through the clouds is an example.

induction The logical process by which principles or rules are derived from observed facts.

industrial psychology A field of specialization concerned with methods of selecting, training, counseling, and supervising personnel in business and industry. It sometimes includes problems of increasing efficiency in work and of redesigning machines to suit better the capacities of the worker. *See also human engineering.*

inferential statistics The statistical methods for inferring population values from obtained sample values. *See statistical decisions.*

inferiority complex A concept put forth by Alfred Adler; an attitude developed out of frustration (*q.v.*) in striving for superiority. *See individual therapy.*

inferotemporal region The lower, or ventral, portion of the temporal lobes (*q.v.*); plays a role in visual form discrimination learning.

informal group A social group having no formal or permanent structure and consisting of people who happen to be assembled together at a particular time. Sometimes, however, the members of a formal group (e.g., the employees of a company) may constitute an informal group that is different from the one prescribed by the formal structure of the organization.

inhibition (1) A decreasing tendency to respond with repetition of a response. (2) Hyperpolarization (*q.v.*) of a nerve cell making it less responsive to stimulation.

inhibitory postsynaptic potential (IPSP) An electrical potential of the nerve cell due to hyperpolarization (*q.v.*); an increase in the internal negativity of a nerve cell, due to impulses arriving over inhibitory fibers, makes the cell less excitable.

innate releasing stimuli *See releasing stimuli.*

inner ear *See cochlea, vestibular sense.*

insight (1) In learning and problem solving, the relatively sudden solution of a problem. (2) In psychotherapy, the understanding of one's own motives and their origins.

insight therapy Treatment of a personality disorder by attempting to uncover the deep causes of the patient's difficulty and to help him rid himself of his defense mechanisms. It represents an attempt to guide the patient in self-understanding of his motives and his resources for satisfying them. Sometimes it is called uncovering therapy. *Cf. supportive therapy.*

instinctive behavior A complex, unlearned, pattern of behavior which persists beyond the duration of the stimulus instigating it.

instrumental behavior Behavior that typically accomplishes a purpose, usually the satisfaction of a need, e.g., working for a living.

instrumental conditioning Learning situations in which the responses of the subject are instrumental in producing reinforcement. Sometimes known as instrumental learning. *See also operant conditioning.*

insulin A hormone secreted by the pancreas and concerned in controlling the amount of sugar in the blood; used in insulin-shock therapy.

insulin shock A method, infrequently used today, for treating severe psychotic reactions; causes convulsions and coma.

integrative organization theory A theory, sometimes called Theory Y, that the development of self-control is the critical element in a working organization. *Cf. classical organization theory.*

intelligence A general term covering a person's abilities on a wide range of tasks involving vocabulary, numbers, problem solving, concepts, and so on. As measured by a standardized intelligence test, it generally involves several specific abilities, with special emphasis on verbal abilities.

intelligence quotient (IQ) Classically, a number obtained by dividing chronological age into mental age and multiplying by 100. Now other methods are used to compute the intelligence quotient. *See deviation IQ.*

intensity A general term referring to the amount of physical energy stimulating a sense organ. It is expressed in physical units appropriate to the kind of energy involved.

interference A factor in learning and forgetting; the incompatibility of two learned associations.

interference theory A theory of extinction which holds that nonreinforced responses decline in strength because other incompatible responses are learned during the extinction period.

internal environment The environment of the bodily organs, including the temperature of the body, oxygen, food supplies, minerals, hormones, and related substances.

interpersonal attraction The study of the reasons why people like (or dislike) each other.

interposition A cue in depth perception (*q.v.*) in which near objects block off portions of faraway objects.

interstimulus interval In a classical conditioning situation, the time between the onset of the CS (*q.v.*) and the onset of the US (*q.v.*).

interval scale A scale in which differences between numbers may be regarded as equal, e.g., $3 - 1 = 4 - 2$. *Cf. nominal scale, ordinal scale, ratio scale.*

intoxication psychosis (alcohol) A psychosis developing as a result of prolonged alcoholism. It is characterized by defects of memory, disorientation, delusions, and other symptoms similar to those seen in senile psychosis (*q.v.*).

introspection A method of psychological experimentation in which a subject is presented with some stimulus, such as a colored light, and asked to give a detailed report of his sensations.

introspectionism A viewpoint held early in the twentieth century by one group of experimental psychologists who employed the method of introspection. It regarded sensation as the important psychological element in consciousness and attempted to analyze mental content.

intuitive thought The third stage in Piaget's characterization of mental development in which the child begins to group objects according to their outstanding perceptual qualities.

inventory A detailed questionnaire that provides specific information about a person's likes, dislikes, habits, preferences, and so on. It usually refers to a personality or interest test.

involutional reaction Agitated depression or paranoid reactions (*q.v.*) in women at menopause and in men at slightly older ages. Perhaps a physical brain disorder is responsible, but the most prevalent idea of causation emphasizes the psychological stress of approaching old age.

iodopsin A photosensitive substance found in the cones of the retina of some animals.

ion A charged particle; it is charged by an excess or deficiency of electrons. If there is an excess of electrons, the charge is negative; if there is a deficiency of electrons, the charge is positive. The potassium ($K+$) and sodium ($Na+$) ions

are the ones most directly involved in the nerve impulse (*q.v.*).
IPSP *See inhibitory postsynaptic potential.*
IQ *See intelligence quotient.*
iris The set of muscles, controlled by the autonomic system, that varies the amount of light admitted to the eye by narrowing or enlarging the pupil. It gives the eye its distinctive color, such as blue or brown.
item analysis Techniques for discriminating between good and bad items on a psychometric scale.

JND *See just noticeable difference.*
Job A set of activities performed by an individual worker.
job analysis The process of finding out what constitutes a particular job. It is carried out with a variety of different methods, according to the type of job being analyzed.
job description A statement of the significant characteristics of a job and of the worker characteristics (*q.v.*) necessary to perform the job satisfactorily.
job evaluation The assessment of the remuneration to be offered or paid for a particular job.
job psychograph A profile of the traits and abilities required in a job or a family of jobs. *Cf. individual psychograph.*
just noticeable difference (JND) *See differential threshold.*

kinesthesis *See kinesthetic receptors.*
kinesthetic receptors Sense organs located in the muscles, tendons, and joints that provide information about the position of the limbs and body in space.
knowledge of results A person's knowledge of how he is progressing in training or in the performance of his job. It is usually necessary for the most rapid learning and for the best performance of the job.
Korsakoff's syndrome A collection of traits, or syndrome (*q.v.*), in chronic brain syndromes, especially in intoxication psychosis (alcohol). Characterized by disorientation, confusion of thought, memory disorders (e.g., confabulation, *q.v.*), and impulsiveness.
kymograph A device which records the amplitude of a response through time.

Landolt ring A test object used in measurements of visual acuity; consists of an incompleted circle.
language A set of symbols used for communication and in thinking.
latency The time between the presentation of a stimulus, or the beginning of a learning trial, and a response.
latency period In psychoanalysis (*q.v.*), the period from approximately age 6 to age 12, the middle childhood years. Characterized by the elaboration of defense mechanisms (*q.v.*).
latent content In dream interpretation, the real meaning of the dream, which is symbolized by the manifest content (*q.v.*).
latent learning Learning that becomes evident only when the occasion arises for using it. *See incidental learning.*
lateral fissure A deep cleft in the cerebral cortex dividing the temporal lobe from the frontal and parietal lobes. *Cf. central fissure.*
law of complementary colors *See complementary colors.*
law of effect *See empirical law of effect and theoretical law of effect.*
learned goal A goal that has been acquired through learning, as distinguished from a physiological goal.
learning A general term referring to a relatively permanent change in behavior that is the result of past experience or practice. It includes classical conditioning, operant conditioning, and perceptual learning.
learning curve Any graphical representation of progress in learning. Usually a curve in which performance is plotted on the ordinate (*q.v.*) and trials or time are plotted on the abscissa (*q.v.*).
learning set A kind of transfer of training (*q.v.*) in which a subject becomes increasingly adept at

learning problems of the same general type.

lens The adjustable refractive element of the eye.

lesion Any damage or change in a tissue due to injury or disease.

level of aspiration The level at which a person sets certain goals.

level of performance The achievement of a person, as distinguished from his level of aspiration.

libido Freud's term for the instinctive drives, or energies, that motivate behavior. *See also id.*

lie detector A popular name for a device designed to detect emotional responses when a person lies. It usually involves measures of breathing, heart rate, blood pressure, and galvanic skin response.

life style In Adlerian personality theory, the way a person handles power motivation and expresses it in his way of living. *See inferiority complex, individual therapy.*

light The visible spectrum (*q.v.*) of electromagnetic radiation. It may be specified by wavelength and intensity.

Likert scale A method for constructing attitude scales based on the intercorrelation of items.

limbic system A series of related structures in the core of the brain concerned with emotion and motivation. The septal area (*q.v.*), hypothalamus (*q.v.*), amygdala (*q.v.*), and cingulate gyrus (*q.v.*) are important limbic system structures.

linear perspective The perception of far-away objects as close together and of nearby objects as far apart. It is an important factor in depth perception.

linguistics The study of languages as systems of rules.

loaded words Words having an emotional tone, used by propagandists and advertisers for creating and maintaining attitudes.

logical thinking Reasoning carried out according to the formal rules of logic; not very common in human thinking.

longitudinal fissure The midline crevice which divides the cerebrum (*q.v.*) into two symmetrical halves.

longitudinal method Study of an individual or process either continuously or at selected points in the course of its development. *Cf. cross-sectional method.*

loudness A psychological attribute of tones, related to intensity but not directly proportional to it. *See also psychophysics.*

luminosity The perceived brightness of a visual stimulus. *See also luminosity curve.*

luminosity curve A curve depicting the visual threshold at different wavelengths. The luminosity curve for daylight vision has its greatest sensitivity at about 555 millimicrons; the comparable curve for night vision has its greatest sensitivity at about 505 millimicrons. *See also cone, rod.*

MA *See mental age.*

Mach bands Perceptual effects due to complex interactions of excitation (*q.v.*) and inhibition (*q.v.*). For instance, in vision, dark and light bands are seen when there are abrupt changes in the physical intensity of the light over an area that we are looking at.

magnitude estimation A method of making sensory measurements in which the observer estimates the magnitude, or some other characteristic, of a single stimulus.

maladjustment A broad term covering not only the psychoneurotic and psychotic but also mild disturbances in which a person is anxious or behaves peculiarly.

manic-depressive psychosis *See affective reactions.*

manifest content In dream interpretation, the actual content of the dream as the dreamer experiences it. *Cf. latent content.*

manipulative drive A tendency to explore and manipulate objects; considered to be a general unlearned drive not clearly distinguishable from curiosity or exploratory drive (*q.v.*). Also called *manipulative motive.*

manipulative motive *See manipulative drive.*

market research Research consisting of surveys conducted in much the same manner as public-opinion polls but with the purpose of measuring attitudes concerning specific products, the effectiveness of advertising, and the relative preferences of consumers for different brands.

masking The deleterious effect of one sound on a person's ability to hear other sounds simultaneously.

maternal behavior Behavior concerned with giving birth to young, nursing them, and caring for them.

maturation The completion of developmental processes in the body. Maturation is governed both by heredity and by environmental conditions. Growth; changes of behavior through growth of the body.

maze A device used in animal and human learning experiments that has blind alleys and a correct path. It presents the subject with the task of taking a path through it without entering any blind alleys.

mean *See arithmetic mean.*

mechanical-ability test A vocational-aptitude test for predicting success in jobs requiring mechanical ability.

median The middle score in a frequency distribution (*q.v.*) when all scores are ranked from highest to lowest (or lowest to highest). It is one measure of central tendency (*q.v.*). *Cf. arithmetic mean, mode.*

mediating process An associative process connecting previously learned processes and responses. *See thinking.*

medical therapy The treatment of an illness by using medicines, drugs, or surgery. *Cf. psychotherapy.*

medulla The lowest division of the brain stem; contains several kinds of nuclei, especially those concerned with the vital functions of breathing and cardiovascular regulation.

Meissner corpuscle A specialized structure in the skin regarded as a sense organ for pressure or touch.

memory *See retention.*

memory drum Apparatus used to present verbal material in studies of verbal learning.

mental age (MA) A type or norm. Gives the relative degree of mental development of a child by stating the age level at which the child is performing. For example, if a five-year-old child does as well on an intelligence test as the average child of seven, his mental age is 7. *See also intelligence quotient.*

mental deficiency Often synonomous with mental retardation (*q.v.*), but more often used for mental retardation caused specifically by injury or disease.

mental disease *See behavior disorder.*

mental disorder *See behavior disorder.*

mental-faculty theory The theory that formal education generally develops mental faculties so that a person is better able to solve all sorts of problems. The theory is sometimes called formal-discipline theory, or the doctrine of formal discipline.

mental health A general term referring to personal adjustments relatively free of psychoneurotic and psychotic symptoms.

mental hygiene A general term, similar in meaning to mental health, which refers to the maintenance of satisfying personal adjustments.

mental illness *See behavior disorder.*

mental retardation A condition marked by a deficiency in general intellectual ability. Usually an IQ below 70. *See also intelligence quotient. See mental deficiency.*

metabolism A general term referring to chemical processes in the cells of the body. It includes the assimilation of food, the storing of energy, the utilization of energy, the repairing of tissues, and the disposition of cellular wastes.

meter A unit of length in the metric system; 39.37 inches.

method of adjustment A method of obtaining sensory thresholds in which the observer adjusts the intensity of a stimulus until he just barely senses it or distinguishes the difference between it and a standard stimulus.

method of constant stimuli Presenting a stimulus of a given intensity to an observer and asking him to indicate whether or not he detects it; numerous trials with several intensities of stimuli are used in determining absolute threshold (*q.v.*).

method of limits A method for determining sensory thresholds in which series of stimuli of ascending and descending order are presented.

method of rating A method that requires a person to assign comparative adjectives or numbers on a scale to indicate preferences, judgments, or opinions. *See also rating.*

method of systematic observation Scientific study of a natural situation or problem, under controlled conditions, without any experimental manipulation of the variables involved. *Cf. experimental method.*

Metrazol A drug which causes convulsions, infrequently used today in the treatment of psychotic reactions.

microelectrode An electrode so small that it can provide a record of electrical activity in a single neuron or sensory cell.

midbrain The middle of three divisions of the brain. It contains reflex centers for hearing and vision, pathways to and from the forebrain, and several other centers. *See also forebrain, hindbrain.*

middle ear A bony cavity containing ossicles which link the eardrum to the cochlea.

mild retardation A degree of mental retardation characterized by an IQ of from 69 to 53.

milieu therapy Therapy that strives to make the environment (often a mental hospital) a stimulating and interesting place in which learning can occur. Also called *environmental therapy.*

millilambert A physical unit of reflected light energy.

millimicron A nanometer (*q.v.*).

mind Conscious experience (*q.v.*) as reported by an individual.

Minnesota Multiphasic Personality Inventory (MMPI) A widely used pencil-and-paper personality questionnaire. An important feature is its empirical validity (*q.v.*).

MMPI *See Minnesota Multiphasic Personality Inventory.*

mode The most frequent score or category in a distribution of measurements. *Cf. arithmetic mean, median.*

mode of adjustment The characteristic way in which an individual attempts to satisfy his motives. *See defense mechanism.*

modeling A behavior modification (*q.v.*) technique which depends upon imitation and perceptual learning (*q.v.*).

moderate retardation A degree of mental retardation characterized by an IQ of from 52 to 36.

Mongolism A mild to moderate form of mental retardation in which the facial features resemble somewhat those of Mongoloid people.

Mongoloid *See Mongolism.*

monocular Pertaining to the use of only one eye. *Cf. binocular.*

monozygotic (MZ) twins *See identical twins.*

mores Customs that enforce social values having ethical or moral significance. Violation brings strong social disapproval.

motivated forgetting Forgetting due to active forces relating to a person's needs. Repression (*q.v.*) and forgetting due to weakening of tension systems are two examples.

motivation A general term referring to behavior instigated by needs and directed toward goals (*q.v.*).

motivational conflict A conflict between two or more motives resulting in the frustration of a motive. Most motivational conflict involves acquired motives. *See approach-approach conflict, avoidance-avoidance conflict, and approach-avoidance conflict.*

motive A term implying a need and the direction of behavior toward a goal; often used synonymously with need or drive (*q.v.*).

motoneuron A nerve cell of the spinal cord that sends its axon (*q.v.*) to muscle fibers. A motor neuron.

motor area An area of the cerebral cortex lying around the central fissure. Movements can be elicited by stimulation of this region. The threshold for movement is least for the portion just in front of the central fissure.

motor learning The learning of a skill such as driving, typewriting, or playing a musical instrument.

multiple personality A dissociative reaction (*q.v.*) in which a person displays two or more relatively distinct personalities, each with its own set of memories. *See also amnesia, dissociative reaction.*

muscle spindle Receptors in muscles that signal stretch of the muscle. *See kinesthetic receptor.*

mutation A change in a gene and, hence, in the characteristic it determines.

myelin sheath A white covering around some fibers of the nervous system.

nanometer (NM) A billionth of a meter; 10^{-9} meters.

narcoanalysis Analysis of a person's memories, usually those involving a traumatic experience, and of his emotional problems under the influence of a sleep-inducing drug, e.g., sodium amytal.

narcosis Sleep or sleepness caused by drugs, e.g., sodium amytal. Sometimes an aid in psychotherapy (*q.v.*).

narcotics (1) Drugs (*q.v.*) which produce sleep as well as lessen pain. (2) In legal usage, illegal drugs.

nationalism A set of attitudes, held by numbers of people; the attitudes are prejudicial to foreigners and other countries. It includes a feeling that one's own country is superior in manners and way of life.

natavist One who argues that behavioral tendencies, especially perceptual organizing tendencies, are inborn, or innate. *Cf. emipiricist.*

natural observation The observation of events as they occur in nature or in the course of human affairs without exercising experimental controls and without using methods of systematic sampling. *Cf. method of systematic observation.*

nature The genetic factors contributing to behavior. *Cf. nurture.*

need Any lack or deficit within the individual, either acquired or physiological (*q.v.*); often used synonymously with drive or motive (*q.v.*). *See also social needs.*

need complementarity The idea that people with different needs like each other because they provide mutual satisfaction of opposed needs.

negative acceleration The characteristic of a curve that is steep at its beginning but becomes increasingly flat as it approaches its end. Learning curves are typically of this shape.

negative reinforcement A reinforcement is a stimulus or event that strengthens a response when it follows the response; *negative* means that reinforcement occurs when the learner escapes from or avoids a noxious, or unpleasant, stimulus. *Cf. positive reinforcement.*

negative transfer The harmful effect on learning in one situation because of previous learning in another situation. It is due to incompatible responses being required in the two situations. *Cf. positive transfer.*

neoanalytic theories of personality Recent varieties of psychoanalytic theory, e.g., the theories of Erikson, Fromm, Horney, and Sullivan.

neocortex The six-layered covering of the cerebrum. *See gray matter, cerebral cortex.*

nerve A bundle of nerve fibers.

nerve deafness Deafness due to an impairment of the sense organs or of the nerves concerned in hearing. It is also called perception deafness or perceptual deafness. *Cf. conduction deftness.*

nerve fiber An axon or a dendrite of a neuron. It conducts nerve impulses.

nerve impulse An electrical change in the membrane of a nerve fiber, propagated along the length of the fiber. It is the basic message unit of the nervous system and obeys an all-or-none law (*q.v.*).

nervous system The brain, spinal cord, and nerves serving the various sense organs, endocrine glands, and muscles of the body.

neurasthenia Type of anxiety reaction (*q.v.*) in which the person complains of general nervousness, fatigue, and insomnia; often accompanied by depression, feelings of inadequacy, and inability to work.

neuron The cell that is the basic unit of the nervous system. It conducts nerve impulses and consists of dendrite(s) (*q.v.*), cell body, and axon (*q.v.*).

neurosis or neurotic reaction *See psychoneurotic reaction.*

neurotic need According to Horney, a learned need for something connected with the alleviation of basic anxiety (*q.v.*).

NM *See nanometer.*

nominal scale A scale in which numbers are assigned to objects or persons only to distinguish those that are alike from those that are different, e.g., postal ZIP numbers. The numbers of a nominal scale may not be used additively.

nomothetic Emphasis on the development of general laws of behavior. *Cf. idiographic.*

noncontinuity theory A theory of learning stressing perceptual reorganization as the important link in learning a response. *Cf. continuity theory; See field theory.*

nondirective therapy Psychotherapy in which the patient is dominant and given the greatest possible opportunity to express himself. The method is based on the principle that the patient must learn how to solve his own problems and cannot have them solved for him by the therapist. *Cf. directive therapy. See client-centered therapy.*

nonreversal shift A change in the cues that are correct in discrimination learning (*q.v.*) so that the cues previously irrelevant become relevant.

nonsense figure A set of lines, marks, or contours having little or no meaning. *See nonsense syllable.*

nonsense syllable A syllable, usually of three letters, constructed so as to resemble meaningful English as little as possible. Nonsense syllables are used in learning experiments as new or unfamiliar material.

nonspecific system The projection from the reticular activating system (*q.v.*) to the cortex.

norepinephrine A chemical substance which is believed to be the transmitter (*q.v.*) in some sympathetic synapses (*q.v.*). (Preferred over noradrenaline.) *See epinephrine.*

norm *See group norm.*

normal curve A bell-shaped frequency distribution, also called the normal-probability curve, which is an ideal approximated by many distributions obtained in psychology and biological sciences. It can be derived mathematically from the laws of chance.

norms An average or standard, or a distribution of measurements, obtained from a large number of people. It permits the comparison of an individual score with the scores of comparable individuals.

nucleus A collection of cell bodies of neurons within the central nervous system; also a structure within cells containing chromosomes. Plural: nuclei.

nurture The learned factors contributing to behavior; the factors that depend upon experience. *Cf. nature.*

obsession A seemingly groundless idea that constantly intrudes into a person's thoughts; seen in obsessive-compulsive reactions. *Cf. compulsion.*

obsessive-compulsive personality A behavior pattern characterized by excessive conformity and adherence to standards of conscience; not as severe as the obsessive-compulsive reaction (*q.v.*).

obsessive-compulsive reaction A psychoneurotic reaction characterized by obsessions and/or compulsions (*q.v.*).

obstruction method A method for measuring the strength of a motive by seeing how much noxious stimulation an organism will tolerate in order to satisfy the motive.

occipital lobe The part of the cerebral cortex lying at the back of the head. It contains the primary sensory areas for vision.

oddity method A method used for various purposes in which three or more stimuli are presented and the subject is asked to indicate which stimulus is different.

Oedipus complex A syndrome (*q.v.*) postulated by Freudian personality theory in which the child directs affectional response toward the parent of the opposite sex. *See phallic stage.*

oldsightedness Farsightedness characteristic of old age and typically increasing beyond the age of forty.

olfaction, olfactory sense Smell.

open-end question The type of question that allows a respondent to answer in his own words.

operant conditioning Learning to make a particular response to secure positive reinforcement (*q.v.*) or to escape or avoid negative reinforcement (*q.v.*). *See instrumental conditioning.*

operational definition A method of defining terms and concepts in terms of the operations performed to measure them.

opinion Acceptance of a statement accompanied by an attitude of pro or con. It contrasts with an attitude (*q.v.*) in being both verbalized and public.

opinion effect Distortion of reasoning due to the emotional connotations (*q.v.*) of the premises of syllogisms (*q.v.*).*Cf. atmosphere effect.*

opponent process theory The theory that human color vision depends on three pairs of opposing processes: white-black, yellow-blue, and red-green.

opsin A breakdown product of rhodospin in rod vision.

optic chiasma In humans, the partial crossing of fibers in the optic nerve (*q.v.*). This crossing makes it possible for the right visual field to be projected on the left hemisphere and vice versa.

optic nerve The nerve formed by axons of the ganglion cells of the retina. It leaves the eye at the blind spot and ends in relay centers of the thalamus.

oral stage The stage, postulated in psychoanalytic theory, during which an infant's satisfactions center around his mouth and sucking. *See pregenital stages.*

ordinal scale A scale in which numbers are assigned to objects or persons so as to rank them in order according to some quality or magnitude, e.g., ranking students 1, 2, 3, etc., according to their grades.

ordinate The vertical axis of a graph; values of the dependent variable (*q.v.*) are usually plotted on this axis.

organ of Corti The organ containing receptors for hearing, located on the basilar membrane which separates the vestibular canal and tympanic ducts of the cochlea.

organic senses Sense organs located in the internal organs of the body, such as receptors for cold and warmth in the stomach.

organization theory Assumptions about human motivation on which the working relationships within an organization are based. *See classical organization theory, integrative organization theory.*

orienting reaction A reaction to a novel stimulus in which muscles are tensed and the position of the body is changed to maximize effectiveness in reacting to the stimulus.

oscilloscope An electronic voltage recording device. In psychology, used especially in studies of audition and neural activity. It typically records changes of voltage over time.

osmoreceptor A type of cell in the hypothalamus which is thought to be sensitive to changes in the osmotic pressure of the blood plasma.

ossicles Three bones in the middle ear through which sound is conducted from the eardrum to the oval window of the cochlea.

otolith organs Sense organs found in chambers near the cochlea. They are sensitive to gravity and to the position of the head; they are part of the vestibular sense (*q.v.*).

oval window The entrance to the cochlea through which sound vibrations pass from the ossicles of the middle ear to the canals of the cochlea.

ovariectomy Operative removal of the female ovaries, used experimentally to study the effect on behavior of a reduction in sex hormones. *Cf. castration.*

overcompensation According to Adler, an overreaction to feelings of inferiority so that a person becomes superior in things in which he otherwise would not be. *See also compensation.*

ovum The cell formed in the ovary of the female which, when fertilized by the sperm of the male, may develop into a new individual. Plural: ova.

pacinian corpuscle A specialized structure serving as a receptor for pressure, located below the skin, in joints, and other deep parts of the body. *See kinesthetic receptor.*

paired-associate learning Learning in which the subject must respond with one word or syllable when presented with another word or syllable.

paired comparisons A method of measurement in which things or people are taken two at a time and a judgment is made as to which is greater than the other, better than the other, etc.

pancreas An endocrine gland, located along the lower wall of the stomach, which secretes the hormone insulin. This hormone controls blood-sugar level.

papillae Bumps on the tongue that are heavily populated with taste buds.

paradoxical sleep A state of sleep in which it is difficult to wake a person, yet his EEG (*q.v.*) pattern is like that in light sleep. It is accompanied by rapid eye movements, and is therefore also known as REM sleep. Most dreaming occurs in this stage of sleep.

paranoid reaction Behavior disorder marked by extreme suspiciousness of the motives of others, often taking the form of elaborate beliefs that they are plotting against the person. In the paranoid reactions the delusions (*q.v.*) of persecution are usually systematized. *See also projection.*

paranoid type A kind of schizophrenia (*q.v.*) characterized by delusions (*q.v.*), often of persecution. Different from the paranoid reaction (*q.v.*) in that the delusions are less systematic in the paranoid type of schizophrenia.

parasympathetic system A subdivision of the autonomic system arising in the cranial and sacral portions of the central nervous system. Tends to be active during quiescent states of organism. *Cf. sympathetic system.*

parataxic distortions Fantasies, or distorted ideas, about important people in our lives, according to Sullivanian personality theory.

parathormone The hormone secreted by the parathyroid glands.

parathyroid glands Two pairs of endocrine glands located on the thyroid glands of the neck. They secrete hormones concerned in the regulation of calcium and phosphorus levels in the body.

parietal lobe The part of the cerebral cortex lying immediately behind the central fissure. It contains areas involved in somesthesis and somesthetic discrimination learning.

part learning Learning, usually in the sense of memorizing, in which the task is divided into smaller units and each unit is separately learned. *Cf. whole learning.*

partial reinforcement Reinforcement of some proportion of unconditioned responses (in classical conditioning), or of some proportion of instrumental responses (in operant learning). *See schedule of reinforcement.*
passive-aggressive personality A person who expresses hostility by excessive aggression, stubborn pouting, or extreme dependence.
passive avoidance conditioning Learning *not* to make a response to a warning stimulus to avoid a noxious stimulus, e.g., not approaching an electrified food dish. *Cf. active avoidance conditioning.*
peer An equal in a given respect; an associate at roughly the same level.
perception A general term referring to the awareness of objects, qualities, or events stimulating the sense organs; also refers to a person's experience of the world. *See experience.*
perception deafness *See nerve deafness.*
perceptual constancy A general term referring to the tendency of objects to be perceived in the same way despite wide variations in the energies impinging upon the receptors. *See also brightness constancy, shape constancy, size constancy.*
perceptual learning Used in two senses. (1) the influence of learning on perceptual organization; (2) learning to associate stimulus events with each other. *Cf. response learning.*
performance (1) Observed behavior; as distinct from hypothetical internal states of an organism. *See latent learning.* (2) Nonlinguistic ability; performance tests are so constructed that they do not handicap a person who speaks no English or who has verbal deficiences.
performance test Tests which measure nonverbal activity or performance.
periodic sound A complex sound consisting of repetitive patterns of waves. *Cf. aperiodic sound, random noise.*
peripheral nervous system The part of the nervous system lying outside the skull and the backbone. *Cf. central nervous system.*
personal motive A learned motive that is characteristic of an individual. *See motivation, social motive.*
personality (1) The traits, modes of adjustment, defense mechanisms, and ways of behaving that characterize the individual and his relation to others in his environment. (2) According to G. Allport: "The dynamic organization within the individual of those psychophysical systems that determine his characteristic behavior and thought."
personality disorders Characterized by developmental defects or pathological trends in the personality structure, with minimal accompanying anxiety.
personality dynamics (1) The interactions among personality characteristics, especially motives; (2) the behavioral expression of personality characteristics in the process of adjusting to the environment.
personality psychology *See personality.*
personality structure In general, the unique organization of traits, motives, and ways of behaving that characterizes a particular person; in psychoanalysis, the conception of the personality in terms of id, ego, and supergo.
personality syndrome *See syndrome.*
personnel psychology Concerns the applications of psychology to the selection, training, and supervision of people in business and industrial settings; also concerned with improving communications, counseling employees, and attempting to solve industrial strife. *See industrial psychology.*
phallic stage The third stage in development, according to psychoanalytic theory, during which the child becomes interested in his sexual organs and forms a romantic attachment to the parent of the opposite sex. *See Oedipus complex, pregenital stages.*
phase difference The difference in

intenstiy (negative or positive) between two energies at any particular instant.

phase sequence A combination of cell assemblies (*q.v.*).

phenomenology The study of the phenomena of human experience and behavior without elaboration or analysis into elements.

phenotype The observable characteristics of an organism. *Cf. genotype.*

phenylketonuria (PKU) A form of mental retardation due to an inherited metabolic disorder.

phenylpyruvic oligophrenia A type of mental retardation that is inherited and that is caused by a lack of an enzyme for utilizing phenylpyruvic acid, a product of brain metabolism. It is recognized by the presence of phenylpyruvic acid in the urine. *See phenylketonuria.*

phi phenomenon Perceived movement between two successive presentations of separate points of light. "Pure" movement. *Cf. stroboscopic movement.*

phobia An intense, irrational fear. *See phobic reaction.*

phobic reaction A psychoneurotic reaction (*q.v.*) characterized by intense irrational fear.

phoneme A speech sound which must be disinguished in the everyday use of language.

phonetics The study of the sounds made in speech.

photochromatic interval The interval of intensities, representing the difference between rod and cone sensitivities, in which light but not color is perceived.

photosensitive substances Chemical substances in the rods and cones of the retina that are decomposed by light and initiate the visual process.

physiological motive A motive (*q.v.*) arising from some lack or deficit, from hormones (*q.v.*), or other conditions within the body.

physiological needs (1) *See physiological motive*; (2) The lowest, or most basic, set of needs in the need hierarchy proposed by Maslow. *See self-actualization, safety needs, belongingness and love needs, esteem needs.*

physiological psychology *See biopsychology.*

pictorial display A display that reproduces with some realism the situation it represents. *Cf. symbolic display.*

pinna The part of the external ear that protrudes from the head; the structure which in common parlance is called simply the ear.

pitch A psychological attribute of tones, related to frequency but not directly proportionai to it. *See psychophysics.*

pitch scale A curve depicting the relationship between physical frequency and perceived pitch.

pituitary gland A gland located beneath the hypothalamus (*q.v.*) that secretes a number of hormones (*q.v.*) which stimulate or inhibit other glands of the body. It also secretes a growth hormone that controls general rate of growth of the body.

PKU *See phenylketonuria.*

place learning Learning the place that some event occurs, e.g., shock or eating, without necessarily making any specific response to it.

place theory A theory of pitch, widely accepted, that assumes different places on the basilar membrane (*q.v.*) are activated by different frequencies of a sound stimulus.

placebo Inactive substance used as a control in drug experiments. *See single- and double-blind technique.*

play therapy A technique for the study of personality and for the treatment of personality problems in children. It permits the child to express his conflicts in play. *See also release therapy.*

pleasure principle In psychoanalytic theory, the tendency to satisfy id (*q.v.*) impulses. *Cf. reality principle.*

point-to-point projection *See topographical arrangement.*

polarized *See polarized membrane.*

polarized membrane The inside of a nerve cell is negatively charged

with respect to the outside. *See depolarization, hyper-polarization.*
polydipsia Drinking abnormally large quantities of water.
pons A region of the brain stem above the medulla (*q.v.*) which contains ascending and descending pathways, fibers connecting the lobes of the cerebellum (*q.v.*), and many nuclei.
population The group of individuals on which measurements are made. The total population consists of all possible individuals on which measurements might be made, e.g., all voters. A sample population is a smaller group drawn from the total population so as to be representative of it. *See sampling.*
positive reinforcement A reinforcement is a stimulus or event that strengthens a response when it follows the response; *positive* means that the reinforcement is something that the learner approaches. *Cf. negative reinforcement.*
positive transfer More rapid learning in one situation because of previous learning in another situation. It is due to a similarity of the stimuli and/or responses required in the two situations. *Cf. negative transfer.*
posthypnotic suggestion Suggestion made by the hypnotist while a person is in a hypnotic state but carried out after the hypnosis has been terminated. *See hypnotherapy.*
postsynaptic membrane The membrane in the synaptic region (*q.v.*) of the neuron to which information is being transmitted.
potential (1) Generally an aptitude (*q.v.*), or a psychological capacity that requires training for its realization; (2) a voltage difference.
power In psychological usage, the ability to control or influence the behavior of others; a social need.
power function The psychophysical (*q.v.*) relation that says the strength of experience equals the magnitude of the physical stimulus raised to some power, times a constant. $\psi = k\Phi^n$, where ψ is the experience and Φ is the magnitude of the physical stimulus, k is a constant, and n is the power.
power test A test not limited in time, or a test having a nominal time limit, designed to measure ability, irrespective of speed of taking the test. *Cf. speed test.*
preconceptual thought The second stage in Piaget's characterization of mental development in which representational thought begins.
predisposition In the study of personal adjustment, a tendency that is inherited and gives a biological basis for the development of certain temperamental (*q.v.*) and personality characteristics.
prefrontal areas *See frontal association area.*
prefrontal lobotomy The surgical interruption of pathways from the frontal association areas, sometimes performed in extreme cases of behavior disorder after other forms of therapy have failed.
pregenital stages The oral (*q.v.*), anal (*q.v.*), and phallic (*q.v.*) stages of psychoanalysis (*q.v.*).
prehension The grasping of objects with the hands, the fingers, or (in the case of some monkeys) the tail.
prejudice Literally, a prejudgment; more generally, an emotionally toned attitude (*q.v.*) for or against an object, person, or group of persons. Typically, it is a hostile attitude that places a person or group at a disadvantage.
prenatal Before birth.
prestige The feeling of being better than other persons with whom one compares oneself. The prestige need is a social need to achieve prestige. The need is frequently exploited with propaganda and social techniques.
presynaptic membrane The membrane in the synaptic region along which the nerve impulse comes to the synapse (*q.v.*); contains transmitter (*q.v.*) substances.
primary goal The unlearned goal of a physiological or general drive, e.g., food or water.
primary group A small group with which a person has frequent infor-

mal contacts, such as family, friends, associates.

primary reinforcement In classical conditioning (*q.v.*), the presentation of the unconditioned stimulus immediately following the conditioned stimulus; in operant conditioning (*q.v.*), the presentation of an incentive immediately following the operant response.

primary sensory area An area of the cerebral cortex to which fibers transmit impulses from the receptors of a particular sense. There are primary sensory areas for each of the senses except pain, the vestibular sense, and smell.

private acceptance A type of conformity (*q.v.*) in which we make the norms and values of a group our own. *Cf. compliance.*

proactive inhibition *See negative transfer.*

probability The relative frequency of occurrence of an event expected over the long run.

probability learning A type of discrimination learning in which one stimulus is rewarded a certain percentage of the time and the other stimulus the remaining percentage. In such a task, it is possible either to *maximize* reward by always choosing the stimulus rewarded on more than 50 percent of the trials or to *match* by choosing each stimulus in proportion to the percentages of reward.

process schizophrenia The type of schizophrenia (*q.v.*) in which there is a slow, insidious onset and in which the person's adjustment before hospitalization was poor. *Cf. reactive schizophrenia.*

product-moment correlation A widely used coefficient of correlation (*q.v.*) devised by the British mathematician Karl Pearson. Used for interval and ratio measurements. Symbol: *r.*

profound retardation A degree of mental retardation characterized by an IQ of 20 or below.

programmed learning Self-instruction by means of carefully designed questions or items which, through immediate reinforcement, motivate and enhance the learning process. *See teaching machine; see computer-assisted instruction.*

projection The disguising of a source of conflict by ascribing one's own motives to someone else; prominent in paranoid (*q.v.*) reactions.

projective methods Methods used in the study of personality, in which a subject is presented with a relatively ambiguous stimulus and asked to describe it in a meaningful way or to tell a story about it. *See Thematic Apperception Test, Rorschach test.*

prolactin A hormone (*q.v.*) secreted by the pituitary gland (*q.v.*). It stimulates the development of the breasts and is concerned in maternal behavior.

prompt In operant conditioning, a cue that elicits the behavior which is to be reinforced (*q.v.*).

propaganda The deliberate attempt to influence attitudes (*q.v.*) and beliefs (*q.v.*).

proprioception See proprioceptive sense.

proprioceptive sense The sensory input arising from the kinesthetic (*q.v.*) and vestibular receptors (*q.v.*) within the body.

pseudo-isochromatic plates Plates consisting of colored dots so arranged that the colorblind person sees either no pattern at all or a different pattern of dots from the normal person. They are used as a test for colorblindness.

psychiatry A branch of medicine specializing in the diagnosis and treatment of behavior disorders.

psychoanalysis Primarily a method of psychotherapy developed by Sigmund Freud, but also a theory of the development and structure of personality. As a psychotherapy, it emphasizes the techniques of free association (*q.v.*) and the phenomenon of transference (*q.v.*).

psychodrama A specialized technique of psychotherapy in which patients act out the roles, situations, and fantasies relevant to their personal problems. Psychodrama is usually conducted in front of a small audience of patients.

psychogenic polydipsia Excessive drinking of water with a psychological cause; often occurs on certain schedules of partial reinforcement (*q.v.*) with food.

psychograph A profile of traits and abilities involved in the performance of a job. *See also individual psychograph, job psychograph.*

psycholinguistics The branch of psychology concerned with the ways in which people generate and comprehend language.

psychological needs *See personal needs.*

psychology The science that studies the behavior of animals and human beings.

psychometric psychology The branch of psychology concerned with the development of tests, research on the usefulness of tests, and, in general, ways of measuring behavior.

psychometrist A psychologist primarily concerned with the giving and scoring of tests (*q.v.*).

psychomotor test A test involving movement and coordination; usually a vocational-aptitude test.

psychoneurosis *See psychoneurotic reaction.*

psychoneurotic reaction A behavior disorder, less severe than a psychotic reaction (*q.v.*), in which a person is unusually anxious, miserable, troubled, or incapacitated in his work and his relations with other people. He often attempts to ward off anxiety by using exaggerated defense mechanisms. Also called a neurosis or psychoneurosis.

psychopathic deviate An individual with a personality disorder characterized by antisocial, amoral conduct.

psychopharmacology The study of the effects of drugs (*q.v.*) on behavior and psychological functions.

psychophysics The study of the relationship between physical energy and reported experience. *See power function.*

psychosis *See psychotic reaction.*

psychosomatic illness A bodily disorder precipitated or aggravated by emotional disturbance.

psychosurgery *See prefrontal lobotomy.*

psychotherapeutic drug A drug having beneficial effects in treating behavior disorders. *See tranquilizer.*

psychotherapy The treatment of behavior disorders and mild adjustment problems by means of psychological techniques. *Cf. medical therapy.*

psychotic reaction A behavior disorder more severe than a psychoneurotic reaction (*q.v.*) and often requiring custodial care. *See affective reactions, paranoid reactions, schizophrenic reactions, involutional reactions.*

psychotomimetic drug A drug that induces some of the symptoms of certain psychotic reactions.

public-opinion poll A method of surveying opinions on certain issues by selecting a sample of the population and interviewing each member of the sample.

punctate sensitivity In the study of the skin senses, greater sensitivity in certain spots of the skin than in others. It is a phenomenon that allows us to distinguish four primary senses among the skin senses.

punishment The application of an unpleasant stimulus for the purpose of eliminating undesirable behavior.

pupil The aperture through which light is admitted to the eye; altered in size by the action of the iris muscles.

pure tone One resulting from simple sine-wave (*q.v.*) energy.

purkinje effect A change in the perception of color as the eye shifts from daylight to twilight, or from cone to rod levels of adaptation.

quota sampling A method of sampling (*q.v.*) in which the polling agency sets quotas for certain categories, such as age, sex, and socioeconomic status, and then permits the interviewer to select the particular individuals who satisfy the quota requirements.

random noise A noise consisting of a random mixture of many different frequencies that are not multiples or harmonics of each other. *Cf. periodic soundness.*

random sampling Selecting samples of individuals, objects, or measurements solely by chance. *See also sampling.*

range The difference between the highest score and the lowest score in a frequency distribution (*q.v.*). It is a crude measure of the variability (*q.v.*) of a distribution.

rank-difference correlation A method of computing correlation when individuals have been separately ranked on two different variables. Symbol: ρ.

RAS *See reticular activating system.*

rating A general term for the method in which a judge or observer rates the amount of aptitude, interest, ability, or other characteristic that an individual is considered to have.

ratio scale A scale in which equal ratios may be regarded as equal, e.g., 4:2 = 10:5.

rationalization The interpretation of one's own behavior so as to conceal the motive it expresses and to assign the behavior to some other motive.

reaction formation The disguising of a motive so completely that it is expressed in a form that is directly opposite to its original intent.

reaction time The time from the onset of a stimulus until the organism responds.

reactive schizophrenia The type of schizophrenia (*q.v.*) in which the person's adjustment before the disorder is fairly good and in which the onset of the disorder is rapid. *Cf. process schizophrenia.*

readiness The point in maturation (*q.v.*) when a behavior can emerge with training; before this point, the behavior is not possible, no matter how intense or sophisticated the training.

reality principle In personal adjustment, the behavior which consists of setting attainable goals and of finding practicable ways of eliminating motivational conflicts and, hence, of satisfying motives; in psychoanalysis, a function served by the ego. *Cf. pleasure principle.*

reasoning Thinking (*q.v.*) in which one attempts to solve a problem by combining two or more elements from past experience.

recall A method of measuring retention (*q.v.*) in which the subject reproduces with a minimum of cues something that he has previously learned.

receptive field The area of a receptor (*q.v.*) surface from which the firing of nerve impulses can either be increased or decreased.

receptor The structures at which transduction (*q.v.*) takes place in the sensory systems. Each receptor is most sensitive to a particular kind of energy; it is through the action of the receptors that we know about events in the world around us. *See adequate stimulus.*

recessive gene A gene whose hereditary characteristics are not expressed when it is paired with a dominant gene (*q.v.*).

reciprocal inhibition (1) The relaxation of a muscle simultaneously with the contraction of its antagonist. (2) A form of behavior modification (*q.v.*) in which classical conditioning (*q.v.*) is used to condition responses incompatible with the response to be eliminated. *See counterconditioning, behavior modification.*

recognition A method of measuring retention in which the subject is required only to recognize the correct answer when it is presented to him along with incorrect answers, e.g., in a true-false or multiple-choice examination.

reflex A relatively rapid and consistent unlearned response to a stimulus. It is ordinarily not conscious or subject to voluntary control. It lasts only so long as the stimulus is present. *Cf. instinctive behavior, taxis.*

refraction The bending of light; in vision, the bending of light by the

cornea (*q.v.*) and lens (*q.v.*) to focus images on the retina (*q.v.*).
refractory period *See absolute refractory period, relative refractory period.*
regression A retreat to earlier or more primitive forms of behavior, frequently encountered in children and adults faced with frustration.
regulatory behavior Behavior that aids in maintaining a homeostatic (*q.v.*) balance by leading to the satisfaction of physiological needs.
reinforcement *See primary reinforcement, secondary reinforcement.*
relational concept Defined in terms of relationships between elements rather than in terms of the absolute properties of the elements. *See concept; cf. conjunctive concept, disjunctive concept.*
relational determinant The idea that perception of an object, person, or event depends upon the context (*q.v.*) in which it appears.
relative refractory period A brief period after the discharge of a nerve impulse when the neuron can only be fired by a stimulus that is much stronger than normal. *Cf. absolute refractory period.*
release therapy Similar to play therapy (*q.v.*); useful with older children and adults. It may consist of finger painting, games, or other unstructured activities. Its general purpose is to permit the expression of deep-seated motivational conflicts.
releasers *See releasing stimuli.*
releasing stimuli Stimuli which are thought to release the fixed action patterns (*q.v.*) from inhibition so that they can be expressed.
reliability The self-consistency of a method of measurement, or the degree to which separate, independent measurements of the same thing agree with each other. Reliability is usually expressed by a coefficient of correlation (*q.v.*) representing the relationship between two sets of measurements of the same thing. *See also validity.*
REM sleep *See paradoxical sleep.*
representative sampling Sampling (*q.v.*) so as to obtain a fair cross section of a population without introducing biases that make the sample unrepresentative.
repression A psychological process in which memories and motives are not permitted to enter consciousness but are operative at an unconscious level. Repression is one of several reactions to frustration and anxiety. It serves as a means of altering conscious motives and goals.
resistance A phenomenon observed in psychotherapy, exhibited as an inability to remember important events in one's past or to talk about certain anxiety-charged subjects. Resistance may be indicated by a blocking of free associations or by a person's steering away from certain subjects during free association (*q.v.*).
resistance to stress The second stage of the general-adaptation syndrome (*q.v.*) in which a person endures stress without showing any observable impairment.
respondent conditioning *See classical conditioning.*
response Generally, any behavior of an organism. *See behavior.*
response learning Learning to make a response in a stimulus situation, as distinguished from learning the relations among stimuli without necessarily making a response. *Cf. perceptual learning.*
response-produced stimuli Stimuli produced by stimulation of receptors (*q.v.*) in muscles and joints. *See chaining.*
resting potential A voltage difference, found in the inactive nerve fiber between the outside and the inside of the polarized membrane (*q.v.*). The inside is negative with respect to the outside.
retention The amount correctly remembered. The principal methods of measuring retention are savings, recognition, and recall.
reticular activating system (RAS) A network of cell bodies and fibers extending through the medulla, midbrain, hypothalamus, and thalamus forming an indirect sensory pathway to the cerebral cortex.

retina The photosensitive layer of the eye on which images of objects are projected. It contains receptors, known as rods (*q.v.*) and cones (*q.v.*), and nerve cells that convey impulses to the brain.
retinal disparity A slight difference in the images of an object projected on the retinas (*q.v.*) of the two eyes. It arises from the fact that the two eyes view the object from slightly different angles.
retinene A breakdown product of the photosensitive substances involved in vision.
retroactive inhibition The harmful effect of learning or activity on the retention of previous learning.
reverberating circuit An endless loop made by the fibers of neurons, permitting nerve impulses to circle back to the point from which they originated.
reversal learning Learning the exact opposite of what one has previously learned. Usually the reversal is of cues in discrimination learning (*q.v.*).
reward (1) Loosely equivalent to reinforcement (*q.v.*). (2) In social psychology, pleasures or satisfactions occurring as a result of behaviors chosen.
rhodopsin A photosensitive substance found in the rods (*q.v.*) of man and many animals.
ribonucleic acid (RNA) Complex molecules found within cells. Essential in the production of proteins.
RNA *See ribonucleic acid.*
rod A photosensitive receptor in the retina, long and cylindrical, like a rod, and most sensitive in nighttime conditions of seeing. *Cf. cone.*
role A pattern of behavior that a person in a particular social status (*q.v.*) is expected to exhibit.
role-playing method A technique used in simulation of real situations, designed to promote understanding of the problems involved. Can be used in management training, for example, or as a psychotherapeutic technique.
Rorschach test A projective method (*q.v.*) using inkblots as stimuli.
rotary pursuitmeter A device used in human learning experiments that requires the subject to keep a stylus on a moving spot while the spot rotates on a circular platform.
rotation nystagmus Movement of the eyes, slowly in one direction and quickly in the other, caused by rotation of the head.

safety needs According to Maslow, needs for security, stability, and order that are less important than physiological needs but take precedence over needs for belonging (*q.v.*), esteem (*q.v.*), and self-actualization (*q.v.*).
sampling The process of selecting a set of individuals or measurements from a large population (*q.v.*) of possible individuals or measurements. Almost all frequency distributions (*q.v.*) in psychology are samples. *See also controlled sampling, quota sampling, random sampling, representative sampling.*
sampling error The error due to chance differences in selecting a sample from a population.
saturation A dimension of color that refers to the amount or richness of a hue, as distinguished from brightness or hue (*q.v.*); e.g., a red that is barely distinguishable from a gray is low in saturation.
savings A method of measuring retention (*q.v.*) in which the subject learns again what he previously learned. Savings are measured by the difference between the number of trials or errors originally required to learn and the number required in relearning.
scale of measurement In general, a set of numbers assigned to some aspect of objects or events according to some rule. The term is also used in a more limited sense to refer to a well-standardized test, such as the Wechsler Intelligence Scale for Children.
scale value In the measurement of attitudes, a number assigned to a statement that indicates the degree to which the statement represents an attitude that is favorable or

unfavorable to an object or issue. *See Thurstone scale.*

scapegoating The displacement of aggression to a convenient group or class.

scatter diagram (scattergram) A plot of the scores made by the same individuals on two different variables providing a visual picture of the degree of correlation between the variables.

schedule of reinforcement Some specified sequence of partial reinforcement (*q.v.*) such as a ratio schedule or an interval schedule. *See also partial reinforcement, fixed-internal schedule, fixed-ratio schedule, variable-internal schedule, variable-ratio schedule.*

schema An important idea in Piaget's theory of thought development. It refers to organized patterns of thought and action that are used to adapt to the world. *See assimilation.*

schizoid personality A personality disorder characterized by withdrawal from other people and eccentric thinking; not psychotic. *Cf. schizophrenic reactions.*

schizophrenia *See schizophrenic reactions.*

schizophrenic reactions One of the psychotic reactions, characterized by fantasy, regression, hallucinations (*q.v.*), delusions (*q.v.*), and general withdrawal from contact with the person's environment. Also called schizophrenia.

schizophrenogenic mother The kind of mother who intensifies psychological stress for an individual, possibly playing a role in fostering schizophrenia in her offspring.

schizotypic syndrome A collection of traits, or a syndrome (*q.v.*), similar to those of schizophrenia (*q.v.*), but much milder. Characterized by confusion of thought, a tendency to withdraw from other people, and inappropriate emotional expression.

scholastic aptitude Ability to succeed in some specified type of formal schooling. For example, college aptitude refers to aptitude for doing college work.

school of psychology *See structuralism, functionalism, behaviorism, or gestalt psychology.*

school psychology Counseling psychology (*q.v.*) in the schools. *See educational psychology.*

science A body of systematized knowledge gathered by carefully observing and measuring events. *See empirical.*

sclera layer The white outermost coat of the eyeball. In the front of the eye, it becomes the transparent cornea. *See choroid and retina.*

S^D The positive stimulus in a discrimination. *See simultaneous discrimination, successive discrimination.*

S^{Δ} The negative stimulus in a discrimination. *See simultaneous discrimination, successive discrimination.*

secondary goal A goal learned through association with a primary goal. *Cf. secondary reinforcement.*

secondary reinforcement The reinforcing effect of a stimulus that has been paired with a primary reinforcement (*q.v.*). *See conditioned reinforcement.*

security The feeling of being safe against loss of status, friends, loved ones, income, etc. The need to feel secure is an important social need.

self The individual's awareness or perception (*q.v.*) of his own personality.

self-actualization According to Maslow, the highest need in man's hierarchy of needs; the name for Maslow's motivational theory of personality. *See physiological needs for a listing of other needs in the hierarchy.*

self-stimulation Central stimulation, usually electrical, of the brain which is administered by the animal's pressing a bar or switch.

semantic differential A method of measuring the connotative meaning (*q.v.*) of a concept (*q.v.*) in which the person rates the concept on several bipolar scales.

semantics The study of the meaning of words and sounds.

semicircular canals Three canals found near the cochlea (*q.v.*) in each ear. They are sensitive to rotation and to changes in the position of the head. *See vestibular sense.*
senile psychosis A psychotic reaction that tends to appear in some individuals with advancing age; characterized by defects of memory, general disorientation, and delusions. *See also intoxication psychosis* (*alcohol*).
sensation A general term for the sensitivity of an organism to external and internal stimulus (*q.v.*) events. *See receptor.*
sensitivity groups *See encounter groups.*
sensitization A phenomenon in which a response is facilitated by an intense or unpleasant stimulus. For example, an animal that has become habituated to a loud sound may again show fright to the sound if the sound is preceded by an electric shock.
sensorimotor operations The first stage in Piaget's characterization of mental development in which the child learns to deal with objects.
sensory area An area of the brain concerned in sensory functions. It is usually an area of the cerebral cortex. *See also primary sensory area.*
sensory deprivation Experimental restriction of sensory input; used in the study of perceptual organization.
sensory neuron A neuron that conveys nerve impulses away from sense organs into the central nervous system. *See also afferent fibers.*
sensory scale A curve or function showing the relationship of perceived magnitude to physical units of stimulation. *See psychophysics.*
septal area One of the structures in the limbic system (*q.v.*) of the forebrain containing complex connections with other parts of the brain; seems involved in emotional expression.
serial anticipation A learning method in which items are arranged in a series and the subject must anticipate the next item in the series. *Cf. paired-associate learning.*
serial learning Learning to make a series of responses in exact order. *Cf. free learning.*
serial-position effect The effect of the position of an item in a series on the rate of learning the item. The middle items in a series are usually the most difficult.
set A readiness to react in a certain way when confronted with a problem or stimulus situation.
severe retardation A degree of mental retardation characterized by an IQ of from 35 to 20.
sex hormones Hormones secreted by the gonads and responsible for the development of secondary sex characteristics such as the male's beard and the female's breasts. They are involved in sexual motivation.
sex-linked characteristic A hereditary characteristic controlled by a gene carried on the chromosomes that determine sex; for example, colorblindness (*q.v.*).
sex typing Learning the roles (*q.v.*) appropriate to the status (*q.v.*) of being a woman or a man. *See socialization.*
sexual deviation Sexual excitement and satisfaction from unusual objects and behavior. *See sociopathic personality.*
shape constancy The tendency to perceive the "true " shape of an object even when the image on the retina is distorted. For example, a circle is seen as a circle even when viewed at an angle.
shaping Teaching a desired response through a series of successive steps which lead the learner to the final response. Each small step leading to the final response is reinforced. *See also successive approximations.*
shock therapy The treatment of behavior disorders by some agent causing convulsion and/or coma. Such agents include insulin, metrazol, and electric shock to the brain. *See electroconvulsive shock therapy* (EST).
sibling A brother or sister.

signal A stimulus used to indicate that the time and place for something to happen is at hand.
significance A probability statement of the likelihood of obtaining a given difference or correlation between two sets of measurements by chance. Often stated by giving P values, e.g., $P < .001$.
simple type A kind of schizophrenia (*q.v.*) characterized by apathy, indifference, and mental deterioration.
simple unit A type of neuron in the visual cortex which fires only when the retina is stimulated by a particular kind of stimulus in a particular place. *Cf. complex unit, hypercomplex unit.*
simultaneous contrast Sensory effects produced at the borders of stimulating areas. Probably due to interactions of excitation (*q.v.*) and inhibition (*q.v.*) in the receptor and central nervous system.
simultaneous discrimination learning Presentation of the positive (S^D) and negative (S^Δ) stimuli at the same time, rather than one after the other. *Cf. successive discrimination learning.*
sine wave A particular type of energy wave. In audition, the simplest kind of sound wave, generated by a vibrating object moving back and forth freely like a pendulum. *See also Fourier analysis.*
single-blind technique An experimental method in drug studies in which the subjects of the experiment do not know whether or not they have received the drug.
situation test A test in which a person is observed in some real-life situation, e.g., in managing a group of men in the building of a small bridge.
situational therapy The treatment of a personality problem by changing the person's situation—his work, his way of life, or his relationships with family and associates.
size constancy The tendency to perceive the size of familiar objects as relatively constant even when viewed at a distance that makes the image of them on the retina very small.
skewness The degree to which a frequency distribution (*q.v.*) departs from a symmetrical shape. The curve of a distribution that has its longer tail toward the high scores is said to be positively skewed; with the longer tail toward the low scores, it is said to be negatively skewed.
skin conductance *See galvanic skin response.*
skin senses The senses of pain, warmth, cold, and pressure located in the skin.
Skinner box A simple box with a device at one end, which, if operated, will produce reinforcement; used to study operant conditioning (*q.v.*). Also called a standard environmental chamber.
sleep center A center in the hypothalamus (*q.v.*) whose destruction is said to result in chronic insomnia. *Cf. waking center.*
sleep spindles Bursts of relative high-voltage 12–14 Hz waves on a relatively low-voltage background. Characteristic of the early stages of falling asleep.
smell prism A three-dimensional diagram representing six primary odors and their mixture.
smooth muscle Muscle that under the microscope exhibits no stripes. It is found in blood vessels, intestines, and certain other organs. *Cf. striped muscle.*
social class A grouping of people on a scale of prestige in a society according to their social status. It is determined by many factors, such as nature of occupation, kind of income, moral standing, family genealogy, social relationships and organizations, and area of residence.
social comparison The tendency of people to use the behaviors of others as a standard for their own behavior; especially pronounced in ambiguous situations, such as conformity (*q.v.*) experiments, in which behavioral standards are not obvious.
social facilitation Increased motiva-

tion and effort arising from the stimulus provided by other people.

social group Any group of people, formal or informal, assembled or dispersed, who are related to each other by some common interest or attachment. When a social group is defined in a more limited sense, as people in a face-to-face relationship, other dispersed groups such as unions are defined as social organizations or institutions.

social inhibition In social groups, the retarding, caused by the presence of other people, of action in certain situations.

social institution A collection of objects, customary methods of behavior, and techniques of enforcing such behavior on individuals, e.g., a union, an army, or a political party.

social maturity The degree of development of social and vocational abilities. It may be measured by the Vineland Social Maturity Scale, from which a social-maturity quotient can be computed in much the same way as an intelligence quotient (*q.v.*) is obtained.

social motives Motives (*q.v.*), usually learned, that require the presence or reaction of other people for their satisfaction. In human motivation, *need* and *motive* are used synonymously. *See also achievement motive, affiliative needs.*

social needs *See social motives.*

social prejudice A hostile attitude toward some social group. *See prejudice.*

social psychology A field of specialization concerned with the effects of group membership upon the behavior, attitudes, and beliefs of an individual.

social structure A general term referring to the fact that each society typically assigns ranks to its members, expects them to do certain kinds of work and to have certain attitudes (*q.v.*) and beliefs (*q.v.*).

social value A learned goal involving one's relationship to society and other people.

social worker A person with advanced training in sociology who investigates the family and social background of persons with personality problems and who assists the psychotherapist by maintaining contact with a patient and his family. The social worker is often a member of a psychiatric team consisting also of psychiatrists and clinical psychologists.

socialization Learning to behave in a manner prescribed by one's family and culture (*q.v.*) and to adjust in relationships with other people.

society A group of individuals, as large as several countries or as small as a portion of a community, that have a distinguishable culture.

sociogram A diagram showing preferences and aversions among members of a group; a way of depicting the structure of an informal group.

sociometry A method of mapping social relationships of attraction and rejection within a group. Each member indicates his choices for and against other members, and a diagram (sociogram) is made of the results.

sociopathic personality A type of behavior disorder characterized by little anxiety. May take several forms: antisocial reaction (*q.v.*), sexual deviation (*q.v.*), or an addiction (*q.v.*).

sodium amytal A drug that, given in light doses, tends to make a person talk more freely. It is sometimes used in psychotherapy as a way of uncovering repressed memories.

somatic system The part of the nervous system serving the sense organs and the skeletal muscles.

somesthesis The senses of the skin and of kinesthesis (*q.v.*)—the body sense.

somnolence A tendency to sleep all the time.

sound-pressure level (SPL) The intensity of a tone expressed in decibels (*q.v.*) above a standard

reference level—0.0002 dyne per square centimeter.
sound wave Alternating increases and decreases in pressure propagated through a medium, usually air. It may be regarded as a vibration having a certain frequency (or wavelength) and a certain intensity.
species-specific behavior Behavior (*q.v.*) characteristic of one species of animal, but not another. *See instinctive behavior.*
specific hunger A hunger for a specific kind of food.
spectral-absorption curve A curve representing the absorption, and hence the sensitivity, of a photochemical substance at different wavelengths; often refers to visual photochemical substances of the rods and cones.
spectral sensitivity Sensitivity of the eye, often measured by the absolute threshold (*q.v.*), at different wavelengths of the spectrum.
speed test A test limited in time and favoring the person who can do tasks quickly. *Cf. power test.*
sperm Male germ cell.
sphincter Smooth muscle whose action controls elimination from such organs as the stomach, bladder, and bowels.
spike *See nerve impulse.*
spinal cord The part of the nervous system encased in the backbone. It is a reflex center and a pathway for impulses to and from the brain (*q.v.*).
SPL *See sound-pressure level.*
spontaneous discrimination A discrimination learned without any specific learning procedure and without any identifiable reinforcement. *See perceptual learning.*
spontaneous recovery An increase in the strength of an extinguished (*q.v.*) conditioned response after the passage of an interval of time.
S-R association *See stimulus-response association.*
S-S association *See stimulus-stimulus association.*
standard deviation A precise measure of the variability of a frequency distribution (*q.v.*), computed by squaring the deviation of each score from the arithmetic mean (*q.v.*), summing the resulting squares, dividing by the number of scores, and finally taking the square root of the resulting quantity. In other words, it is the root-mean-square of the deviations from the mean. Symbol: SD.
standard environmental chamber *See Skinner box.*
standard score In the strict sense, the *z* score (*q.v.*), but often a score obtained by multiplying a *z* score by an arbitrary constant (e.g., 10 or 20) and adding the result to an arbitrary mean (e.g., 50 or 100). It permits a direct comparison with scores made by a standardization group.
standardization The establishment of uniform conditions for administering a test and interpreting test results. A large number of individuals are tested in the same way to provide norms (*q.v.*) with which to compare any particular test score.
standardization group The group of people on which a test is standardized. To interpret individual scores on a test, one should know the characteristics of the standardization group.
Stanford-Binet Intelligence Scale An individual test designed by L. M. Terman, based on the early work of Binet, for children and young adolescents; predicts achievement in grammar and high school.
stapes One of the bones in the middle ear. *See ossicles.*
startle pattern An extremely rapid reaction to a sudden, unexpected stimulus (e.g., a gunshot), relatively consistent from person to person. It consists, in part, of a closing of the eyes, a widening of the mouth, and a thrusting forward of the head and neck.
static senses The part of the vestibular senses responding to gravity and to position of the head. *See otolith organs.*
statistical decisions Ways of deciding whether obtained differences

between experimental groups, or in correlations, are real or due to chance sampling errors. *See inferential statistics, sampling error.*

statistics A collection of techniques used in the quantitative analysis of data, and used to facilitate evaluation of the data. Also, numbers used to describe distributions and to estimate errors of measurement.

status In motivation (*q.v.*), a social motive; in a social structure (*q.v.*), a position representing differences that are important in the exchange of goods and services and in the satisfaction of needs in a society. *Cf. role.*

status needs Needs to achieve a status with respect to other people in a group. They include more specific needs, such as needs for prestige, power, and security.

stereotaxic instrument Apparatus which permits precise placement of electrodes in the brain.

stereotype A fixed set of greatly oversimplified beliefs (*q.v.*) that are held generally by members of a group.

stimulus Any object, energy, or energy change in the physical environment that excites a sense organ. *See sensation.*

stimulus generalization The tendency to react to stimuli that are different from, but somewhat similar to, the stimulus used as a conditioned stimulus.

stimulus-response association Learning in which the association is made between a stimulus and a response; S-R association.

stimulus-stimulus association Stimulus-stimulus, or sensory-sensory, association; a learned association between two stimuli; S-S association.

striped muscle Muscle that, under the microscope, appears to be striped. It is found in the muscles of the skeleton, such as those that move the trunk and limbs. *Cf. smooth muscle.*

stroboscopic movement Apparent motion (*q.v.*) due to successive presentation of visual stimuli. *See phi phenomenon.*

structuralism An early school of psychological thought which held that all mental contents could be analyzed into mental elements through the experimental method of introspection (*q.v.*). *Cf. functionalism, gestalt psychology, behaviorism.*

subcortical centers Centers of the brain below the cerebral cortex.

sublimation The use of a substitute activity to gratify a frustrated motive. Freud believed, for example, that a frustrated sex drive could be partially gratified by channeling it into some aesthetic activity.

subliminal perception Perception of a stimulus or some feature of a stimulus, as measured by a response, without conscious awareness of the perception.

subvocal speech Talking that is inaudible to others, but sufficiently stimulating (kinesthetically) to oneself to permit an internal conversation. It may be one kind of implicit response involved in thinking.

successive approximations Reinforcing components of the final complex response in an effort to lead the learner to this final response. *See also shaping.*

successive discrimination learning Presentation of the positive (S^D) and negative (S^Δ) stimuli one after the other, rather than at the same time. *Cf. simultaneous discrimination learning.*

suggestion The uncritical acceptance of an idea. Suggestion is used in psychotherapy (*q.v.*) to effect temporary relief of neurotic symptoms, particularly hysterical symptoms. It is also used by propagandists and advertisers to change or maintain attitudes and beliefs.

sulcus A relatively shallow crevice in the cerebral cortex. *Cf. fissure.*

superego In psychoanalytic theory, that which restrains the activity of the ego and the id (*q.v.*). The superego corresponds closely to what is commonly called conscience;

it keeps a person working toward ideals acquired in childhood.

superiority According to Adler, a major striving of the person. Failure to achieve superiority may generate an inferiority complex.

superstition A belief concerning natural phenomena that is widely held but is demonstrably false.

supportive therapy Treatment of a personality problem by listening to a person's problems, suggesting courses of action, and reassuring him about what he has done or proposes to do. Such therapy may be effective in mild or temporary disturbances. *Cf. insight therapy.*

survey methods Methods of collecting data by sampling a cross section of people, e.g., questioning a large number of married couples about factors in marital happiness, or conducting a public-opinion poll. Sometimes used as a rough synonym for the method of systematic observation (*q.v.*).

syllogism A logical form containing two premises and a conclusion. *See reasoning.*

symbol A stimulus that represents something else by reason of relationship, association, convention, etc. A symbol may be an external stimulus, e.g., a spoken word, or an internal process, e.g., an image involved in thinking. The latter may also be called a symbolic process (*q.v.*).

symbolic display Any means of presenting information indirectly, as by a dial, pointer, or light. *Cf. pictorial display.*

symbolic process A representative process standing for previous experience; essential in thinking.

sympathetic system A subdivision of the autonomic system (*q.v.*) arising in the thoracic and lumbar portions of the spinal cord. Most active in aroused states of the organism. *Cf. parasympathetic system.*

synapse The gap between two neurons. *See synaptic region.*

synaptic knob *See bouton.*

synaptic region The area at the functional connection of two neurons. Includes the synapse (*q.v.*), the presynaptic membrane (*q.v.*), and the postsynaptic membrane (*q.v.*).

syndrome Generally, a collection of symptoms. In psychology, a pattern of personality characteristics and their underlying causes in the life history of the person.

systematic sampling Sample from alphabetic lists of names, every *n*th house, or any means of taking every *n*th person from the total population. *See population.*

tabes dorsalis The result of one type of syphilitic infection of the central nervous system, principally of the spinal cord, in which pathways of the kinesthetic senses degenerate.

taboos The do's and don't's of a particular society, strongly inculcated into most members of that society.

tachistoscope An apparatus for presenting perceptual materials for a very brief time.

TAT *See Thematic Apperception Test.*

taxis Innate tendencies to orient the body toward certain stimuli.

teaching machine A mechanical or electronic device which presents programmed material. *See also programmed learning, computer-assisted instruction.*

temperament The aspects of personality pertaining to mood, activity, general level of energy, and tempo.

temporal lobe The part of the cerebral cortex lying on the side of the head beneath the lateral fissure.

temporal maze A maze so constructed that the subject keeps returning to the same choice point, but must turn left or right each time according to some sequence established by the experimenter. Such a maze has been used in conjunction with the alternation method, in which a sequence of simple or double alternations (*q.v.*) is required.

test A standardized sample of the performance of a person on a task or set of tasks.

thalamus An area in the forebrain concerned with relaying nerve impulses to the cerebral cortex.

Thematic Apperception Test (TAT) A frequently used projective method (*q.v.*) consisting of pictures about which a person tells stories.

theoretical law of effect Several theories which discuss the hypothetical mechanism through which reinforcement (*q.v.*) may act.

theory In science, a principle or set of principles that explains a number of facts and predicts future events and outcomes of experiments.

Theory X *See classical organization theory.*

Theory Y *See integrative organization theory.*

therapy The treatment of an illness. *See also medical therapy, psychotherapy.*

thermocoagulation Destruction of tissue, especially in the nervous system, by heat. *See lesion.*

theta rhythm One of the named rhythms of the EEG (*q.v.*); has a frequency of about 4–7 Hz and somewhat greater voltage than the alpha rhythm (*q.v.*).

thinking Processes that are representative of previous experience; consisting of images, minute muscle movements, language and other activities in the central nervous system. *See also image, implicit response, cognition.*

thirst A drive stemming from a physiological need for water.

thought experiment A type of experiment employed by early experimental psychologists in an attempt to discover the nature of thought. *See also imageless thought.*

threshold Generally, the level of stimulus energy which must be exceeded before a response occurs. In neuron (*q.v.*) physiology, the amount by which a cell must be depolarized before it fires. In psychophysics (*q.v.*), the amount of energy necessary for detection of a stimulus, or the difference between two stimuli. *See absolute threshold, differential threshold.*

Thurstone scale One method of scaling attitudes; it involves the ranking of items by judges.

thyroid gland An endocrine gland in the neck which produces the hormone thyroxin.

thyroxin The hormone secreted by the thyroid gland. It controls the general rate at which energy is produced in the body; it is a regulator of metabolism.

timbre The tonal quality that enables us to distinguish different musical instruments and voices having the same fundamental frequency. It is determined by the pattern of frequencies comprising a sound, especially the harmonics.

token economy The use of secondary reinforcers (*q.v.*)—money-like tokens—to reinforce behaviors in the quasi-social setting of the hospital ward. By the use of these tokens, desirable behaviors which aid therapy can be shaped (*see shaping*) and maintained. *See behavior modification.*

tonotopic The rough topographic (*q.v.*) projection of the basilar membrane (*q.v.*) onto the cerebral cortex (*q.v.*).

topographic projection (arrangement) An orderly mapping, on the brain, of the sensory, or receptor (*q.v.*), surface. *See point-to-point projection.*

trace conditioning An arrangement of the interstimulus interval (*q.v.*) in classical conditioning (*q.v.*) in which the CS terminates before the onset of the US.

trace process A memory lasting for a brief period and serving as a stimulus-cue.

trace theory A physiological theory of forgetting which states that the memory trace in the brain gradually fades away with time.

trade test An achievement test that measures a person's knowledge of important elements in his trade.

trait An aspect of personality that is reasonably characteristic of a person and distinguishes him in some way from many other people.

tranquilizer Any one of several drugs used to reduce anxiety.

transduction The process of converting one kind of energy into another kind. In sensation (*q.v.*), the conversion of physical energy into nerve impulses. *See generator potential.*

transfer of training More rapid learning in one situation because of previous learning in another situation (positive transfer, *q.v.*), or slower learning in one situation because of previous learning in another situation (negative transfer, *q.v.*). *See also stimulus generalization.*

transference In psychotherapy and especially psychoanalysis, the reenactment of previous relationships with people and principally of the parent-child relationship. In psychoanalysis, the therapist becomes the object of transference; the transference aids in the analysis because it permits the patient to express toward the therapist attitudes and feelings he has held toward other people.

transmitter A substance released from the presynaptic element (*q.v.*) which depolarizes (*q.v.*) or hyperpolarizes (*q.v.*) the postsynaptic element (*q.v.*).

transposition Tendency for responding to be controlled by relationships between perceptions rather than by absolute qualities of perceptions. *See relational determinism.*

triad A three-person group.

trial and error A phrase describing attempts to learn, or to solve a problem, by trying alternative possibilities and eliminating those that prove to be incorrect. Such behavior is characteristic of instrumental learning and is involved in some thinking.

***T* score** A derived standard score, obtained by multiplying the *z* score (*q.v.*) by 10 or 100 and adding 50 or 500 to the result. *See also standard score.*

T (training) groups *See encounter groups.*

two-factor theory A theory which postulates that both classical and instrumental conditioning are involved in avoidance learning (*q.v.*).

tympanic membrance Another name for eardrum (*q.v.*).

type A class of individuals alleged to have a particular trait; but a concept not accepted as valid by psychologists because individuals cannot be grouped together into a few discrete classes.

unconditioned response (UR) The response elicited by the unconditioned stimulus (US) (*q.v.*).

unconditioned stimulus (US) A stimulus which consistently elicits a response. *See also classical conditioning.*

unconscious motivation Motivation that can be inferred from a person's behavior, but the person does not realize the presence of the motive.

unconscious processes Psychological processes or events of which a person is unaware.

unique color A pure color judged not to be tinged with any other hue.

unit A single neuron in the nervous system; especially the activity, or firing, of such a neuron.

UR *See unconditioned response.*

US *See unconditioned stimulus.*

valence A term proposed by Lewin to refer to the attraction or repulsion of a goal. It is indicated by a plus or minus sign. Goals with negative valences are those a person fears or tries to avoid; those with positive valences are those he seeks to attain.

validity The extent to which a method of measurement measures what it is supposed to measure. Validity is expressed in terms of a coefficient of correlation (*q.v.*) representing the relationship of a set of measurements to some criterion.

value A learned goal.

variability The spread of scores in a frequency distribution. *See also standard deviation.*
variable One of the conditions measured or controlled in an experiment. *See aso dependent variable, independent variable.*
variable-interval schedule A program used in instrumental learning experiments in which subjects are reinforced after an interval of time which varies around a specified average.
variable-ratio schedule A program used in instrumental learning experiments in which subjects are reinforced after a number of responses which varies around a specified average.
vector A term proposed by Lewin to mean the resultant of motivational forces when a person is attracted and/or repelled by different goals; in psychology, analogous to "vector" as used in physics.
verbal learning Learning that involves words either as stimuli or as responses.
vestibular sense The sense of balance and movement, consisting of two groups of sense organs: the semicircular canals and the otolith organs (*q.v.*).
vicarious trial and error (VTE) Behavior in which the organism substitutes partial responses, correct or incorrect, for completed, reinforced responses.
visible spectrum Those electromagnetic radiations that are visible, extending from about 380 to 780 nanometers (*q.v.*).
visual acuity Ability to discriminate fine differences in visual detail. It may be measured with the physician's eye chart or by more precise tests, such as the Landoit ring (*q.v.*) or parallel bars.
visual cliff An apparatus for measuring depth perception (*q.v.*) in animals and young children. Consists of two areas, a "deep" area and a "shallow" area, covered by glass. Subjects with depth perception avoid crawling out on the glass over the "deep" area.
visual cycle The cycle of decomposition and regeneration of photosensitive substances in rod and cone vision.
visual purple *See rhodopsin.*
vitamin A substance essential to metabolism but not manufactured in the body. Thus, it must be obtained in food.
vocational aptitude Aptitude for learning a specific vocation. For example, clerical aptitude is the ability to learn a clerical vocation.
VTE *See vicarious trial and error.*

WAIS *See Wechsler Adult Intelligence Scale.*
waking center A center in the hypothalamus whose destruction results in somnolence. *Cf. sleep center.*
warming up The tendency for the work curve to rise at the beginning of a period of work; opposite in effect to the beginning spurt (*q.v.*). It is a factor in the shape of the work curve.
Weber's law A constant ratio exists between the amount of energy that must be added to a stimulus and the original intensity of the stimulus before a differential experience. $\triangle I/I$ is a constant. Holds for the middle range of stimulus intensities.
Wechsler Adult Intelligence Scale An individual intelligence test for adults, with eleven subtests.
Wechsler Intelligence Scale for Children (WISC) An individual intelligence test for children, with several subtests.
white matter Nerve fibers covered with a white myelin sheath. The peripheral part of the spinal cord is white matter; so are several different regions of the brain. Its presence indicates tracts of nerve fibers, as distinguished from cell bodies. *Cf. gray matter.*
whole learning Learning, usually in the sense of memorizing, in which the entire learning material is studied before going through it again. *Cf. part learning.*
WISC *See Wechsler Intelligence Scale for Children.*

wish fulfillment In the psychoanalytic theory of dreams, the actual dream, or the manifest content (*q.v.*), is supposed to be a disguised expression of sexual or aggressive urges, or wishes; for this reason, the dream is sometimes said to be fulfilling the wish, or urge. *Cf. cognitive theory of dreams.*

withdrawal symptoms Physical symptoms when use of an addicting drug is discontinued. *See addictions.*

word association A method of testing or measuring in which a person is given a stimulus word and asked to respond with a word he associates with it.

work curve A graph representing some measure of work for some given period of time.

worker characteristics The physical and psychological characteristics required of a person in a particular job.

work-sample performance test A test consisting of a sample of the work for which a person is being evaluated.

X chromosome Carrier of genes. Females have two X chromosomes; males have an X and a Y chromosome (*q.v.*).

Y chromosome Carrier of genes which determine that the individual will be male. Females have two X chromosomes (*q.v.*); males have an X and a Y chromosome.

Young-Helmholtz theory The theory that human color vision depends on three receptors, a "blue" receptor, a "green" receptor, and a "red" receptor.

z score A score obtained by dividing the standard deviation (*q.v.*) into the deviation of an obtained score from the arithmetic mean (*q.v.*) of the frequency distribution (*q.v.*). It is convenient for the comparison of scores without regard to the units of measurement employed. *See standard score.*

zygote The product of the union of a sperm cell from the father and an egg cell from the mother.